Travel Discount Coupon

W9-COD-312

This coupon entitles you to special discounts when you book your trip through the

GLOBAL TRAVEL NETWORK®
RESERVATION SERVICE

Hotels ♦ Airlines ♦ Car Rentals ♦ Cruises
All Your Travel Needs

Here's what you get: *

♦ A discount of $50 USD on a booking of $1,000** or more for two or more people!

♦ A discount of $25 USD on a booking of $500** or more for one person!

♦ Free membership for three years, and 1,000 free miles on enrollment in the unique Miles-to-Go™ frequent-traveler program. Earn one mile for every dollar spent through the program. Earn free hotel stays starting at 5,000 miles. Earn free roundtrip airline tickets starting at 25,000 miles.

♦ Personal help in planning your own, customized trip.

♦ Fast, confirmed reservations at any property recommended in this guide, subject to availability.***

♦ Special discounts on bookings in the U.S. and around the world.

♦ Low-cost visa and passport service.

♦ Reduced-rate cruise packages.

Visit our website at http://www.travnet.com/Frommer or call us globally at 201-567-8500, ext. 55. In the U.S., call toll-free at 1-888-940-5000, or fax 201-567-1838. In Canada, call toll-free at 1-800-883-9959, or fax 416-922-6053. In Asia, call 60-3-7191044, or fax 60-3-7185415.

* To qualify for these travel discounts, at least a portion of your trip must include destinations covered in this guide. No more than one coupon discount may be used in any 12-month period, for destinations covered in this guide. Cannot be combined with any other discount or program.
**These are U.S. dollars spent on commissionable bookings.
***A $10 USD fee, plus fax and/or phone charges, will be added to the cost of bookings at each hotel not linked to the reservation service. Customers must approve these fees in advance.

Valid until December 31, 1997. Terms and conditions of the Miles-to-Go™ program are available on request by calling 201-567-8500, ext 55.

ITA 123

Frommer's® 97

Italy

by Darwin Porter
and Danforth Prince

Macmillan • USA

ABOUT THE AUTHORS

A native of North Carolina, **Darwin Porter** was a bureau chief for the *Miami Herald* when he was 21, and later worked in television advertising. A veteran travel writer, he wrote Frommer's first-ever guide to Italy, and he has been a frequent traveler in Italy ever since. He is joined by **Danforth Prince,** formerly of the Paris bureau of the *New York Times,* who has lived and traveled in Italy extensively. This team writes a number of best-selling Frommer's guides, notably to England, France, the Caribbean, and Germany.

MACMILLAN TRAVEL

A Simon & Schuster Macmillan Company
1633 Broadway
New York, NY 10019

Find us online at **http://www.mgr.com/travel** or
on America Online at Keyword: **Frommer's.**

ISBN 0–02–861133–0
ISSN 1044–2170

Editors: Suzanne Roe and Reid Bramblett
Production Editors: Denise Hawkins and John Carroll
Design by Michele Laseau
Map Editor: Douglas Stallings
Digital Cartography by Roberta Stockwell and Ortelius Design
Maps copyright © by Simon & Schuster, Inc.

SPECIAL SALES

Bulk purchases (10+ copies) of Frommer's and selected Macmillan travel guides are available to corporations, organizations, mail-order catalogs, institutions, and charities at special discounts, and can be customized to suit individual needs. For more information write to: Special Sales, Macmillan General Reference, 1633 Broadway, New York, NY 10019.

Manufactured in the United States of America

Contents

List of Maps

AN INVITATION TO THE READER

In researching this book, we discovered many wonderful places—hotels, restaurants, shops, and more. We're sure you'll find others. Please tell us about them, so we can share the information with your fellow travelers in upcoming editions. If you were disappointed with a recommendation, we'd love to know that, too. Please write to:

Darwin Porter/Danforth Prince
Frommer's Italy '97
Macmillan Travel
1633 Broadway
New York, NY 10019

AN ADDITIONAL NOTE

Please be advised that travel information is subject to change at any time—and this is especially true of prices. We therefore suggest that you write or call ahead for confirmation when making your travel plans. The authors, editors, and publisher cannot be held responsible for the experiences of readers while traveling. Your safety is important to us, however, so we encourage you to stay alert and be aware of your surroundings. Keep a close eye on cameras, purses, and wallets, all favorite targets of thieves and pickpockets.

WHAT THE SYMBOLS MEAN

✪ Frommer's Favorites

Hotels, restaurants, attractions, and entertainment you should not miss.

Ⓢ Super-Special Values

Hotels and restaurants that offer great value for your money.

The following abbreviations are used for credit cards:

AE	American Express	EURO	Eurocard
CB	Carte Blanche	JCB	Japan Credit Bank
DC	Diners Club	MC	MasterCard
DISC	Discover	OPT	Optima Card
ER	enRoute	V	Visa

The Best of Italy

Our aim is to save you time and money since you've come to Italy to relax—not to exhaust yourself searching for the best deals and the most evocative experiences. Spend your vacation in peace and let us do the work. Italy is one of the most beautiful, diverse, and culturally rich countries in the world, with some of the world's best offerings in everything from monuments to cuisine. Although the selections below represent the best of Italy, they by no means exhaust the list of wonderful things to see and do, as you'll soon find out for yourself. For Italy is a land of enchanting discoveries, and whether this is your first trip to the peninsula or your 50th, you're bound to come away with your own favorites to add to your personal "best of" list.

1 The Best Travel Experiences

Italy is a feast for the senses and the intellect, and some of the country's most thrilling experiences involve the simple act of living in the Italian style. Although the country is literally stuffed with the potential for memorable experiences, here's an abbreviated list of some that are, by anyone's estimate, spectacular:

- **Visiting the Art Cities of Italy:** When Italy consisted of dozens of principalities, its art treasures were concentrated in many small capitals. Each of these cities, blessed with the patronage of a papal representative or ducal family, amassed vast quantities of art. Exquisite paintings, statues, and frescoes are displayed in churches, monasteries, and palaces whose architects are world-acclaimed. Although the best known of these troves reside in Florence, Rome, and Venice, stunning art collections are also found in the smaller-scale and often ravishingly beautiful cities of Assisi, Cremona, Genoa, Mantua, Padua, Parma, Palermo, Pisa, Siena, Taormina, Tivoli, Turin, Verona, and Vicenza.
- **Eating Out:** One of the most cherished pastimes of the Italians is eating out. Regardless of how much lasagne you've had in your life, it's never better than the real thing in Italy. Each region has its own specialties, some handed down for centuries. The cuisine can be addictively delicious; and if the weather is fine, and you're dining outdoors with a view of, perhaps, a medieval church or piazza, it's the closest thing to heaven in Italy. *Buon appetito!*

Italy

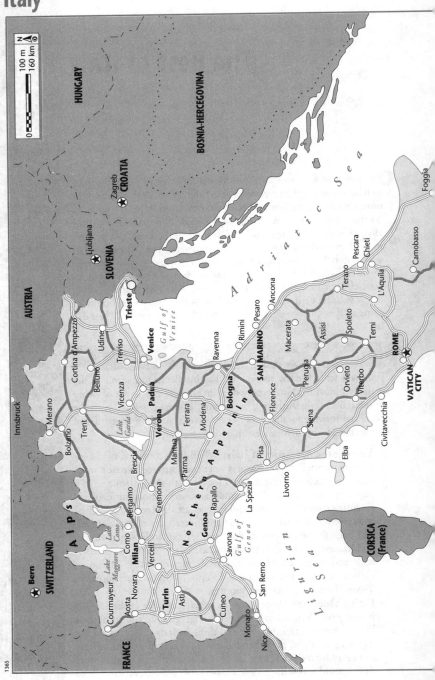

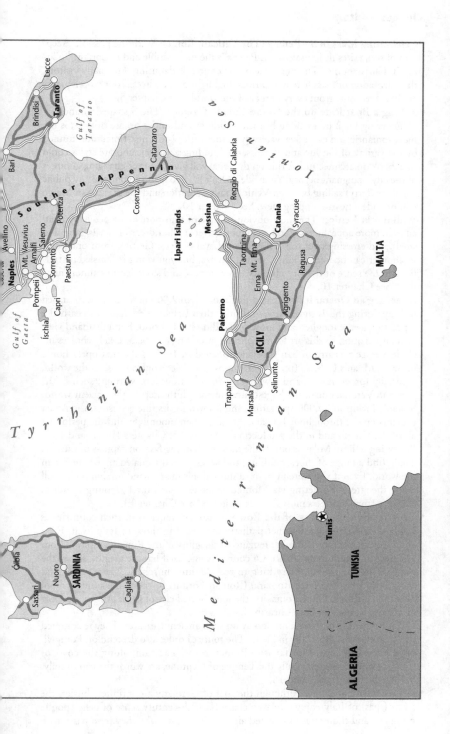

- **Celebrating Mass in St. Peter's (The Vatican, Rome):** With the possible exception of some sites in Jerusalem, St. Peter's is the most visible and important building in Christendom. The huge size of the church is daunting. For many visitors, the celebration of mass here is a spiritual highlight of their lives. Your co-celebrants are likely to come from every corner of the world. See Chapter 5.

- **Taking a Boat Ride on the Grand Canal of Venice:** The S-shaped Grand Canal, curving for 2 miles along historic buildings and under ornate bridges, is the most romantic and evocative waterway in the world. Most first-timers are stunned by the variety of Gothic and Renaissance buildings, whose elaborate styles could fill a book on architecture. A ride on the canal will give you ever-changing glimpses of the city's poignant beauty. Your ride doesn't have to be on a gondola; any public *vaporetto* (ferry) sailing between Venice's railway station and the piazza San Marco will provide a heart-stopping view. See Chapter 10.

- **Walking in Venice:** The most obvious means of transport in Venice is by boat; an even more appealing method is on foot, traversing hundreds of canals, large and small, and crossing over the arches of medieval bridges. Getting from one point to another can be like walking through a maze, but you won't be hassled by traffic, and the sense of the city's beauty, timelessness, and slow decay is almost mystical. See Chapter 10.

- **Attending an Opera:** It's estimated that more than 2,000 new operas were staged in Italy during the 18th century, and since then Italian opera fans have earned a reputation as the toughest and most demanding in the world. For a firsthand view of their devotion to this art form, consider attending an opera. Likely choices include Venice's Teatro di San Cassiano (opened in 1637 as the first opera house in Italy); Milan's La Scala (probably the most prestigious opera house in the world, especially for *bel canto*); and a wide assortment of outdoor settings, such as the Arena in Verona, one of the largest surviving amphitheaters in the ancient world. Suitable for up to 20,000 spectators, and known for its fine acoustics, the Arena presents operas throughout July and August, when moonlight and the perfumed air of the Veneto add to the production's charms. See Chapters 10, 11, and 13.

- **Shopping Milan:** Milan is one of the most enchanting fashion capitals of Europe. You'll find a range of shoes, clothing, and accessories unequaled anywhere else in the world. Even if you weren't born to shop, don't miss a window-shopping stroll along the streets bordering via Montenapoleone, which offer seemingly endless elegance from Europe's most famous designers. See Chapter 13.

- **Experiencing the Glory of the Romans:** Roman remains in such countries as England or Germany are rather pathetic compared to those in Italy itself. Even after centuries of looting, much remains of the glory of the Roman empire—from architectural monuments to art. Of course, Rome itself has the greatest share (the popes didn't tear down everything to recycle into churches). There you'll find everything from the Foro Romano (Roman Forum) to the Colosseum, symbol of Imperial Rome. On the outskirts the long-buried city of Ostia Antica, the port of ancient Rome, has been unearthed.

    But Rome doesn't have a monopoly on such ancient treasures. They're scattered throughout Italy, especially in Sicily. The tourist hordes also descend on Pompeii, once buried by lava. Our favorite Roman ruins? Paestum, along the coast of Campania. Its ruins, especially the Temple of Neptune, are worth the trip to Italy. See Chapters 5, 16, 17, and 18.

- **Rejuvenating at a Spa:** Although the spas of Germany are infinitely busier, the *terme* (spas) of Italy enjoy a relaxed charm, a 19th-century sense of belle époque nostalgia, and thousands of devoted aficionados. Learn why they're so passionate about "the cure" by heading to the Montecatini Terme, Salsomaggiore Terme, Tabiano Terme, Saturnia Terme, Chiusi Terme, Chianchiano Terme, Castrocaro Terme, or the island of Ischia. If you're affluent and exhausted, you can opt for a regime of mud baths and immersion in the sulferous waters bubbling out of geo-thermal springs. Regardless of how deeply you participate in the spa rituals, you're likely to emerge refreshed, more relaxed, and healthier than before you arrived.

- **Reliving the Grand Tour:** During the 18th and 19th centuries, enlightened schoolmasters believed that a tour through Italy was the proper conclusion to a well-rounded education. The sons of prosperous families from France, Britain, and Germany swept southward on grand loops through the Alps; the great art cities of the Veneto, Umbria, and Tuscany; the monuments and churches of Rome; and the ancient ruins of Naples and Sicily. Part of the enchantment of a grand tour of Italy is stumbling upon unexpected charms in the smaller towns as well, as you travel the length of the country.

2 The Best Romantic Getaways

These destinations are known throughout the world as restful, enchanting, secluded places to recuperate from stress and/or rejuvenate a romance.

- **Spoleto** (Umbria): It's as ancient as the Roman Empire and as timeless as the music presented here every summer during its world-renowned arts festival. The architecture of this quintessential Umbrian hill town is centered around a core of religious buildings dating from the 13th century. It's less chic but more romantic during the off-season, when the crowds are less dense. See Chapter 7.

- **Portofino:** It's the most famous small port in the world, largely because of the well-preserved buildings surrounding its small, circular harbor. Located 22 miles southeast of Genoa, in the heart of the Italian Riviera, it's charming, chic, and cos-mopolitan. A cluster of top-notch hotels cater to the very rich and famous. See Chapter 15.

- **Capri:** Floating amid azure seas south of Naples, Capri is called the "Island of Dreams." Roman emperors Augustus and Tiberius both came here for R&R, and since the late 1800s celebrities have flocked here for an escape. A boat ride around the island's rugged coastline is one of our favorite things to do on Capri. See Chapter 17.

- **Ravello** (Campania): It's small, sunny, and loaded with notable buildings (such as its cathedral, founded in 1086). Despite its choice position on the Amalfi coast, it manages to retain the aura of an old-fashioned village. Famous residents have included writer Gore Vidal. See Chapter 17.

- **Taormina** (Sicily): The most charming place in Sicily, this resort is loaded with regional charm, chiseled stonework, and a sense of the ages. Favored by wealthy Europeans and dedicated artists, especially in midwinter when the climate is de-lightful, it's a fertile oasis of olive groves, grapevines, and orchards. Visitors will relish the delights of the sun, the sea, and the medieval setting. See Chapter 18.

3 The Best Offbeat Trips

- **A Motor Trip Around the Gargano Promontory:** Set along the country's south-eastern coast, directly east of Naples, the Gargano Promontory projects like a spur from the "boot" of Italy (across from what used to be known as Yugoslavia). A region of limestone caves and relative poverty, it contains unspoiled scenery and such towns as Peschici, Vieste, Mattinata, and the region's spiritual centerpiece, Testa del Gargano, a rocky promontory at the region's easternmost tip, which juts out into the Adriatic Sea.

- **Short-term Seclusion on the Lipari (Aeolian) Islands:** Set north of Sicily and west of Italy's "toe," these islands were believed to be the home of Aeolus, the god of the winds. The island group is composed of seven members (Alicudi, Filicudi, Lipari, Panarea, Salina, Stromboli, and Vulcano), each of which evokes scenes of North Africa more than of Italy. The the largest, most interesting islands—and the ones most favored by wealthy Italians—are Vulcano and Stromboli; both have been the site of recent investments. See Chapter 18.

- **Sailing the Seas Around Italy:** The four subdivisions of the Mediterranean that surround Italy are the Ionian, the Adriatic, the Ligurian, and the Tyrrhenian. Each area abounds in ports, estuaries, and harbors that have sheltered foreign sailors for thousands of years.

  Words of advice for mariners in Italian waters: Make sure at least one member of your yachting party speaks and understands Italian to translate short-wave radio broadcasts and to negotiate with local harbor authorities. Schedule your visit for anytime other than August, when dock and anchorage space is at a premium. And if you're interested in canoeing or kayaking, look no further than the Veneto, the flat and often humid region of northeastern Italy, where a series of lagoons, rivers, lakes, and saltwater estuaries provides ample sites for practicing your sport. These include the region around Lake Garda, near Verona, and the many lagoons along the Adriatic coast.

  For information on canoeing and kayaking (and schools that teach canoeing), contact the Federazione Italiana Canoe e Kayak, Viale Tiziano 70, 00196 Roma (☎ 06/3685-8525).

- **Hiking along the Cinque Terre:** Set on a 15-mile stretch of rocky coastline along the Ligurian Sea, Cinque Terre is composed of five different fishing villages which, until recently, were accessible only by boat or donkey. Despite its charms, it remains relatively ignored by most vacationers. Its residents make a living by farming and fishing. As such, the region offers unusual insights into an old-fashioned Italian culture. The largest of the villages is Monterosso al Mare (accessible by train and car) and Manarola (accessible by car). Either of these would be a suitable departure point for hikes along the clifftops to the hamlet of Vernazza, the most colorful of the five villages. Lodgings are dull and basic, but there are plenty of places to buy picnic ingredients, and the views of the sea and the terraced hillsides are invigorating. See Chapter 15.

- **Touring the Abruzzi Massif:** A short drive southeast of Rome, amid the highest of the Apennine mountain range, this landlocked district boasts an odd, arid topography riddled with underground caverns, mountains, lakes, gullies, high plateaus, and fertile grazing fields. Looking for scenery and Italian traditions? Devote 2 days to circumnavigating the Abruzzi Massif, incorporating such towns as L'Aquila, Fonte Cerreto, and Castelli, and on a more southerly loop, Scanno, Pescocostanzo, Sulmona, and Castel di Sangro. Other than a peek at local culture, none of the individual towns will be overwhelmingly interesting, but the route passes through the most savage landscapes of the Parco Nazionale d'Abruzzo, with its bizarrely striated rock walls, clannish local families, and 155 square miles of mostly beech and maple forests.

- **Exploring the Campi Flegrei (Phlaegrean Fields):** Bubbling and steaming with geologic emissions, and rich in sites whose architecture was developed by the ancient Greeks and Romans, this is one of the weirdest excursions in Italy. The instability of the region (whose altitude above sea level changes by several inches at regular intervals) can be taken as a metaphor for the sociological turmoil of Naples itself, with its horrendous traffic.

One of the region's highlights is the Greek colony of Cuma (sometimes spelled Cumae), founded in the 8th century B.C. and believed to be the oldest archeological site in Italy. En route from Naples, you'll pass through the town of Pozzuoli, site of a massive ancient Roman amphitheater and hometown of Sophia Loren. Lago d'Averna, another crater lake you'll see en route, was believed by Cicero to be the entrance to the Underworld. See Chapter 16.

4 The Best Castles & Palaces

The dynastic and territorial conflicts of Italy were among the most plentiful in European history. The warlike atmosphere forced people to fortify themselves from attacks by outsiders. As civilization progressed, the thick walls of *castelli* (fortified castles) were replaced by the *palazzi* (palaces) of such Renaissance robber barons as the Medici, the Barberini, the Farnese, and the Borgia families. More or less assured of their status, these families placed less focus on defensive fortifications and more emphasis on comfort and opulence.

- **Castel Sant'Angelo** (Rome): Originating as a mausoleum in A.D. 135 for Hadrian and his family, it was enlarged by Gregory the Great in the 500s, who added a Christian chapel to its uppermost floor. Some 900 years later Pope Nicholas V added a brick upper story and angular towers. Later popes added a bridge across the Tiber (complete with stone angels carved by Bernini) and some of the most luxurious apartments in Christendom. See Chapter 5.
- **Villa d'Este** (Tivoli): The Italian cardinal Hippolyte d'Este decided to retire in the countryside near Tivoli, outside Rome. While building his villa, he created an exquisite garden, where scores of ornate fountains and waterfalls continue to delight visitors to this day. See Chapter 5.
- **Palazzo Vecchio** (Florence): Built over a 15-year period beginning in 1299, the Palazzo Vecchio dominates one of the most memorable piazzas in Italy. Originally intended as an administration building, it was transformed 200 years later into the private residence of Cosimo I of the Medici family. Despite its inner luxury and the airy spaciousness of its courtyard, it has no windows on its ground floor, a reminder of the feudal sense of fortification. See Chapter 6.
- **Palazzo Ducale, the Doge's Palace** (Venice): Built in the 1100s, and radically upgraded between 1400 and 1550, it functioned as the court, prison, seat of government, and the residence of the Venetian doge (ruling prince) during the most glorious years of Venetian history. Designed as a massive block of pink and white geometric patterns poised atop 36 delicately carved columns, it's surpassed in grandeur only by the city's cathedral. See Chapter 10.
- **Palazzo Ducale** (Mantua): One of Mantua's most impressive showcases, this palazzo was created in the 1500s by joining a newly built palace with a Renaissance chapel and a 200-year-old stone fortress. Inside, many of the walls and ceilings are lavishly adorned with *trompe-l'oeil* frescoes and carved and gilded plaster, some of it commissioned by the palace's most legendary occupant, Isabelle d'Este, and some of it executed by Mantegna. See Chapter 13.

5 The Best Museums

Although some fans argue that the entire Italian peninsula is a display of human civilization, the country's museums are incomparable. You're likely to stumble upon many of them in out-of-the-way places, but here's a short list of the country's best:

- **Musei Vaticani (Vatican Museums)** (The Vatican, Rome): Rambling, disjointed, and unbelievably well stocked with the artistic treasures accumulated over the centuries by the popes, this complex contains some of the most famous attractions of Italy. Among them are the Sistine Chapel, such sculptures as *Laocoön and His Sons* and the *Belvedere Apollo,* buildings whose walls were almost completely executed by Raphael, and endless collections of art ranging from (very pagan) Greco-Roman antiquities to Christian art by famous European masters. See Chapter 5.

- **Museo Nazionale di Villa Giulia** (Rome): Mysterious and for the most part undocumented, the Etruscans were the ancestors of the ancient Romans who later conquered most of the known world. They left a legacy of bronze and marble sculpture, sarcophagi, jewelry, and representations of mythical heros, some of which were excavated at Cerveteri, an Etruscan stronghold north of Rome. Most startling about the artifacts is their sophisticated, almost mystical sense of design. The building that houses this collection was a papal villa in the 1500s. See Chapter 5.

- **Galleria degli Uffizi (Uffizi Museum and Gallery)** (Florence): This 16th-century Renaissance palace functioned as the administrative headquarters, or *uffizi* (offices), for the Medici's administration of Florence. It's estimated that up to 90% of Italy's artistic patrimony is stored in this building, the crown jewel of Italy's museums. (The Uffizi was the target of a very destructive car bomb that caused considerable damage in 1993.) See Chapter 6.

- **Bargello Palace and Museum** (Florence): The severely angular 12th-century exterior of the Bargello, located in the heart of Florence, is permeated with the raw power of the governing magistrate who built it. Today its collection of sculpture and decorative accessories is without equal in Italy. See Chapter 6.

- **Pitti Palace** (Florence): The spheres of influence that dominated Florence during its most creative years revolved around the Medicis and the Pittis, two families who ruled the city from their respective banks of the Arno. The Pittis moved into this palazzo in 1560, after it was enlarged with two new wings. Today it houses a museum containing everything from paintings by old masters (such as Raphael and Titian) to works by modern artists and a collection of antique silver. See Chapter 6.

- **Galleria Nazionale dell'Umbria (National Gallery of Umbria)** (Perugia): Italian Renaissance art has roots in Tuscan and Umbrian painting of the 1200s. This collection, set on the uppermost floor of the Palazzo dei Priori (parts of which date from the 1400s), contains a world-class collection of paintings, most executed in Tuscany or Umbria between the 13th and the 18th century. The museum contains works by Perugino, Piero della Francesco, Duccio, Fra Angelico, and Benozzo Gozzoli, among others. See Chapter 7.

- **Gallerie dell'Accademia (Academy of Fine Arts)** (Venice): It's one of the most richly stocked art museums in Italy, boasting hundreds of paintings, many of them Venetian, executed between 1300 and 1790. Among the highlights here are works by Bellini, Giorgione, Carpaccio, and Titian. See Chapter 10.

- **Pinacoteca di Brera** (Milan): Although Milan is usually associated with wealth and corporate power, it contains a worthy assortment of cultural icons as well.

Foremost among these is the Brera Picture Gallery, whose collection—shown in a 17th-century palace—is especially rich in paintings from the schools of Lombardy and Venice. See Chapter 13.

- **Museo Poldi-Pezzoli (Poldi-Pezzoli Museum)** (Milan): In 1881 this museum's namesake donated his extensive art collection to his hometown, thereby creating the base for one of Italy's most influential museums. The collection includes Persian carpets, portraits by Cranach of Martin Luther and his wife, works by Botticelli and Bellini, and massive amounts of decorative art, including furniture. See Chapter 13.
- **Museo Archeologico Nazionale (National Archeological Museum)** (Naples): Naples and the region around it have yielded more sculptural treasures from the ancient Roman Empire than anywhere else in Italy. Many of these riches have been accumulated in a rambling building originally designed as a barracks for the Neapolitan cavalry in the 1500s. Today much of the loot excavated from Pompeii and Herculaneum, as well as the Renaissance collections of the Farnese family, are in this museum, which boasts one of the richest troves of Greco-Roman antiquities in the world. See Chapter 16.

6 The Best Cathedrals

As the home of many of Christianity's most important monuments, Italy has always combined a reverence for churches with a vivid sense of architectural showmanship. The result has been some of the most spectacular cathedrals in the world.

- **Basilica di San Pietro (St. Peter's Basilica)** (The Vatican, Rome): Its roots began with the first Christian emperor, Constantine, in A.D. 324. By 1400 the Roman basilica was in danger of collapsing, prompting the Renaissance popes to commission plans for the largest, most impressive cathedral that the world had ever seen. Amid the rich decor of gilt, marble, and mosaics are countless artworks, including Michelangelo's *Pietà*. Other sights here are a small museum of Vatican treasures and the eerie, underground grottoes containing the tombs of former popes. An elevator ride (or rigorous climb) up the tower to Michelangelo's dome provides breathtaking views of Rome. See Chapter 5.
- **Il Duomo (Santa Maria del Fiore)** (Florence): Begun in the final years of the 1200s, and consecrated 140 years later, the Duomo was a symbol of the prestige and wealth of Florence. With an exterior of pink, green, and white marble, and loaded with world-class art, it's one of the largest and most distinctive religious buildings in Italy. A view of its dome, erected over a 14-year period in what was at the time a radical new design by Brunelleschi, is worth the trip to Florence. Other elements of the Duomo include the Campanile (one of the most charming bell towers in Italy) and the Baptistery (a Romanesque outbuilding with renowned bronze doors and a sheath of green and white marble). See Chapter 6.
- **St. Francis's Basilica** (Assisi): St. Francis, protector of small animals and birds, was long dead when construction began on this double-tiered showcase of the Franciscan brotherhood. Interior decoration, in many cases by Cimabue and Giotto, reached a new kind of figurative realism in Italian art around 1300, long before later masters of the Renaissance carried the technique even further. Consecrated in 1253, the cathedral is one of the highlights of Umbria and the site of many religious pilgrimages. See Chapter 7.
- **Il Duomo** (Orvieto): A well-designed transition between the Romanesque and Gothic styles, this cathedral was begun in 1290 and completed in 1600. It

sheltered an Italian pope (Clement VII) when Rome was sacked by French soldiers in 1527. Part of the building's mystery derives from Orvieto's role as an Etruscan stronghold long before Italy's recorded history. See Chapter 7.

- **Il Duomo** (Milan): Begun in 1386, and finally completed in 1809 on orders of Napoléon, Il Duomo of Milan is an ornate and unusual building. Gathered around a triangular gable bristling with 135 pointed and chiselled spires, it's both massive and airy at the same time. The interior is as severe as its exterior is ornate. One of the most remarkable buildings in Italy, it's often overlooked. See Chapter 13.

7   The Best Ruins

During the 18th century, no self-respecting aristocrat from England or Germany would have dreamed of entering middle age without a tour through the ruins of the ancient world, perhaps picking up a load of ancient Greek or Roman mementoes en route. Here's a list of the ruins they were bound to have visited:

- **Ostia Antica** (Latium): During the height of the Roman Empire, Ostia ("mouth" in Latin) was the harbor town set at the point where the Tiber flowed into the sea. As Rome declined, so did Ostia. By the early Middle Ages, with a population decimated by malaria, the town almost disappeared. In the early 1900s archeologists excavated the ruins of hundreds of ancient buildings, many of which can be viewed. See Chapter 5.
- **Il Foro Romano (Roman Forum)** (Rome): Two thousand years ago most of the known world was directly affected by decisions made in the Roman Forum. Today classicists and archeologists wander among its ruins, conjuring up the glory that was Rome. What you'll see today is a pale, rubble-strewn version of the site's original majesty—it's now surrounded by modern boulevards packed with whizzing cars. See Chapter 5.
- **Il Palatino (The Palatine Hill)** (Rome): According to legend, this hillock was the site where Romulus and Remus (the orphaned infant twins who survived in the wild by suckling a she-wolf) eventually founded the city. Although it's one of the seven hills of ancient Rome, it's hard to distinguish it as such because of the urban congestion that rises all around it. Despite that, scholars come to pay frequent homage. The site is enhanced by the presence of the Farnese Gardens (Orti Farnesiani), laid out in the 1500s on the site of Tiberius's palace. See Chapter 5.
- **Il Coliseo (The Coliseum)** (Rome): Rome boasts only a handful of other ancient monuments that survive in such well-preserved condition. A massive amphitheater set incongruously amid a maze of modern traffic, the Coliseum was once the setting for gladiator combat, lion-feeding frenzies, and public entertainment whose cruelty was a noted characteristic of the Roman Empire. All three of the ancient world's classical styles (Doric, Ionic, and Corinthian) are represented, superimposed in tiers one above the other. See Chapter 5.
- **Villa Adriana (Hadrian's Villa)** (near Tivoli): It slumbered in rural obscurity until the 1500s, when Renaissance popes ordered its excavation. Only then was the scale of this massive and very beautiful villa from A.D. 134 appreciated. Its builder, Hadrian, who had visited almost every part of his empire, wanted to incorporate the widespread wonders of the world into one fantastic building site. See Chapter 5.
- **Ercolano (Herculaneum)** (Near Naples): Legend says that it was founded by Hercules. The historical facts tell us that it was buried under rivers of volcanic mud one fateful day in A.D. 79 after the eruption of Vesuvius. Seeping into the cracks

of virtually every building in town, the scalding mud preserved the timbers of hundreds of structures that would otherwise have rotted in the normal course of time. Devote at least 2 hours to seeing some of the best-preserved houses to survive from the ancient world. See Chapter 16.

- **Pompeii** (Campania): Once it was an opulent resort filled with 25,000 wealthy Romans. In A.D. 79 the same eruption that devastated Herculaneum (see above) buried Pompeii under at least 20 feet of scalding volcanic ash. Beginning around 1750, Charles of Bourbon ordered the systematic excavation of the ruins—the treasures hauled out of Pompeii sparked a wave of interest throughout northern Europe in the classical era. See Chapter 16.

- **Paestum** (Campania): Paestum was discovered by accident around 1750, when local bureaucrats tried to build a road across the heart of what had been a thriving ancient city. Paestum originated as a Greek colony around 600 B.C., fell to the Romans in 273 B.C., and declined into obscurity in the final days of the Empire. Today amateur archeologists can follow a well-marked walking tour through the excavations. See Chapter 17.

- **Valle dei Templi (Valley of the Temples)** (Agrigento, Sicily): Although most of it lies in ruins, this is one of the most beautiful classical sites in Europe, especially in February and March when the almond trees surrounding it burst into pink blossoms. One of the site's five temples dates from as early as 520 B.C.; another—although never completed—ranks as one of the largest temples in the ancient world. See Chapter 18.

- **Segesta** (near Trapani, Sicily): Even its site is impressive: a rocky outcropping surrounded on most sides by a jagged ravine. Built around 430 B.C. by the Greeks, Segesta's Doric colonnade is one of the most graceful in the ancient world. Believed to have been destroyed by the Saracens (Muslim raiders) in the 11th century, Segesta is stark, mysterious, and highly evocative of the ancient world. See Chapter 18.

- **Selinunte** (near Castelvetrano, Sicily): Although its massive columns lie scattered on the ground, as if an earthquake had punished its builders, this is one of our favorite ancient ruins in Italy. Built by immigrants from Syracuse into an important trading port around 600 B.C., and a bitter rival of the neighboring city of Segesta (see above), Selinunte was destroyed around 400 B.C., and again in 250 B.C. by the Carthaginians. See Chapter 18.

8 The Best Wineries

Italy has thousands of vineyards, many of which have been run by families for generations. Here's a guide (listed geographically) to the major wine-growing regions of Italy, with a short list of the best and most interesting vineyards within each region:

- **Alto Adige:** Once part of the Austro-Hungarian province of the South Tyrol, this wine-growing region lies near Bolzano in Italy's extreme north. More Germanic than Italian, it clings to its Austrian traditions and folklore, and grows an Italian version of the gewürtztraminers (a fruity white wine) that would more often be found in Germany, Austria, and Alsace. Venerable wine growers include Alois Lageder (founded in 1855) and Schloss Turmhof, in Entiklar, both near Bolzano. This latter boasts a castle that exudes Teutonic history and some of the highest-altitude vineyards in the South Tyrol. For information, contact Alois Lageder, Tenuta Löwengang, Vicolo dei Conti, Magré, Strada del Vino (☎ 0471/817256), or Schloss Turmhof, Entiklar, Kurtatsch, 39040 (☎ 0471/880122). See Chapter 12.

- **Friuli–Venezia Giulia and Veneto:** Comprised of mostly white wines from adjacent zones in northeastern Italy, these vintages are light, fruity, and very appealing when young. One of the most important vineyards in Friuli-Venezia (near the Slovenian border) is Livio Felluga, near Gorizia. For information, contact Livio Felluga, via Risorgimento 1, Brazzano di Cormons, 34071 Gorizia (☎ 0481/60052). See Chapter 12.

  Important vineyards within the flat, humid borders of the Veneto region include Nino Franco (known for its sparkling prosecco), in the hamlet of Valdobbiadene, via Garibaldi 177, 31049 Treviso (☎ 0423/972051). Also appealing are the vineyards of Masi/Gargagnago di Valpolicella, whose output includes soave whites and valpolicella reds. For information, contact the region's Azienda di Promozione Turistica, via Leoncino 61, 37121 Verona (☎ 045/592828). See Chapter 11.

- **The Piedmont:** Most of the output includes reds with rich and complex flavors fostered by the rolling hills of this rugged region near Italy's border with France. One of the most interesting vineyards is headquartered in a 15th-century abbey near the hamlet of Alba. For information, contact the Antiche Cantine dell' Annunziata, Abbazia dell'Annunziata, La Morra, 12064 Cuneo (☎ 0173/50185). See Chapter 14.

- **Lombardy:** The fertile soil of the Po valley has always been known for its flat vistas, its midsummer humidity, and its excellent wines. The region produces everything from dry flat reds to sparkling whites whose zest resembles that of champagne. Guido Berlucchi, piazza Duranti 4, Borgonato di Cortefranca, 25040 Brescia (☎ 030/984381), one of Italy's largest wineries, is especially willing to receive visitors. See Chapter 13.

- **Tuscany and Umbria:** Some of Italy's most scenic vineyards lie nestled among the verdant and rolling hills of two of its most stately provinces. Virtually any winery in either of the two districts is likely to be permeated with history and local character, but one of the most appealing in Umbria is Azienda Vallesant di Luigi Barberani, Azienda Agricola Vallesant, Loc. Cerreto, Baschi, 05023 Terni (☎ 0763/41820). In Tuscany, one of the province's largest vintners is Villa Banfi, S.p.A Castello Banfi, Sant'Angelo Scalo, Montalcino, 53020 Siena (☎ 0577/840111). See Chapter 7.

- **Campania:** The wines produced in the harsh, hot landscapes of Campania, around Naples in southern Italy, seem stronger, rougher, and in many cases more powerful than those grown in gentler climes. Among the most famous are the lacryma Christi (Tears of Christ), a white that grows in the volcanic soil near Naples, Herculaneum, and Pompeii; a potent red (taurasi); and a pungent white laden with the odors of apricots and apples, the greco di tufo, whose scent is particularly wonderful when consumed with local anchovies and salted cheese. One of the most frequently visited vineyards of Campania is Mastroberardino, 75 via Manfredi, Atripalda, 80342 Avellino (☎ 0825/626123). See Chapter 16.

- **Sicily:** Its hot climate and volcanic soil foster the growth of more vineyards than any other region of Italy. Most of these are devoted to the production of simple table wines that are used to add bulk to blends in Italy's more prosperous north. Of the better vintages, the best-known wines are marsala and, to a lesser extent, muscat dessert wines. Marsala, a heady wine whose alcoholic content is sometimes enhanced with additives, was first discovered by 19th-century British visitors. A vineyard that produces this wine is Corvo Duca di Salaparuta, a 19th-century winery set in the hills above Palermo. For information, contact Casa Vinicola Duca di Salaparuta SpA, via Nazionale, SS113, Casteldaccia, 90014 Palermo (☎ 091/945223). A leading competitor, also near Palermo, is Regaleali, a historic enterprise maintained by the Tasca d'Alerita family. Known mainly for its still and sparkling whites (Nozze d'Oro) and to a lesser extent its reds (Rosso del Conte) and rosés, it welcomes visitors. For information, contact Regaleali, Contrada Regaleali, 93010 Vallelunga, Pratameno Caltanisseta (☎ 0921/542522). See Chapter 18.

9 The Best Luxury Hotels

- **Hassler** (Rome; ☎ 800/223-6800 in the U.S.): At the Hassler, Hollywood mingles easily with old European wealth. The setting (near an obelisk and a baroque Renaissance church) at the top of the Spanish Steps is among the most evocative in Rome. The bar attracts an invigorating mixture of clients. The restaurant offers panoramic views over the city. See Chapter 4.
- **Villa San Michele** (Fiesole, near Florence; ☎ 055/59451): This former 15th-century monastery is set behind a facade reputedly designed by Michelangelo. It lies in a scented garden, in one of the hill towns near Florence. Many visitors consider this charming hotel a worthy escape from the often oppressive midsummer congestion of Florence. With fewer than 45 rooms, and a decor that no set designer could ever duplicate, it evokes an aristocratic private villa. See Chapter 6.
- **Cipriani** (Venice; ☎ 800/992-5055 in the U.S.): Exclusive and elegant, this hotel is in a 3-acre garden on Isola della Giudecca, one of the calmer islands that comprise the ancient city of Venice. This grand hotel was originally built as a cloister in the 15th century and is centered around a very large, modern, and well-maintained swimming pool. See Chapter 9.
- **Gritti Palace** (Venice; ☎ 800/221-2340 in the U.S., 800/955-2442 in Canada): Andrea Gritti, a doge who ruled Venice with an iron hand until his death in 1538, is the namesake for this property, gem of one of the most elegant hotel chains (CIGA) in the world. The exquisite interiors offer a taste of Venice's historic opulence. See Chapter 9.
- **Miramonti Majestic** (Cortina d'Ampezzo; ☎ 0436/4201): Designed like a massive mountain fortress, this hotel is located in the heart of Italy's most glamorous alpine resort. The clientele seems to relish the hotel's Italian panache amid the bracing air of the Dolomites. Despite the modern amenities, there's a 19th-century quality about this place. See Chapter 12.
- **Grand Hotel Villa d'Este** (Cernobbio; ☎ 031/3481): Originally built in 1568, this splendid palace in the Lake District is one of the most famous Renaissance-era hotels in the world. Step inside and you're surrounded by frescoed ceilings, impeccable antiques, and many other exquisite details. Ten magnificently landscaped acres, parts of which have been nurtured since the 1500s, surround the hotel. Cool breezes are provided by nearby Lake Como and the proximity to the Swiss and Italian alps. See Chapter 13.
- **Albergo Splendido** (Portofino; ☎ 800/992-5055 in the U.S.): Originally built as a monastery in the 14th century, and later abandoned because of attacks by North African pirates, this monument was rescued during the 19th century by an Italian baron and converted into a summer home for his family. The posh hillside retreat on the Italian Riviera now accommodates a sophisticated clientele, including many film stars. The scent of mimosas fills the air, and the sea views are blissful. See Chapter 15.
- **Quisisana & Grand Hotel** (Capri; ☎ 081/837-0788): Originally established as a health spa by an English doctor around 1850, in a part of the island sheltered from the sometimes annoying winds of Capri, this hotel is large (165 rooms),

supremely comfortable, and intricately linked to the allure that made Capri popular with the ancient Roman emperors. See Chapter 17.

- **San Pietro** (Positano; ☎ 089/875455): The only marker that identifies this cliffside hotel, located in the Campania region, is a 15th-century chapel set beside the winding road. The hotel doesn't advertise, protects the privacy of its guests, and offers frequent transportation into that hub of midsummer Italian glamour, Positano, less than a mile away. The bedrooms resemble suites and offer views of the sea. Strands of bougainvillea twine around the dramatically terraced, glistening white exterior walls. See Chapter 17.
- **Palazzo San Domenico** (Taormina, Sicily; ☎ 0942/23701): This is one of the great, stylish old hotels of Europe, a 500-year-old Dominican monastery whose severe lines and dignified bulk are softened with antique tapestries, fragrant gardens, and a sense of the eternal that only Sicily can give. Since its transformation into a hotel in 1896 its clients have included movie legends Dietrich, Garbo, and Loren. See Chapter 18.

10 The Best Moderately Priced Hotels

Italy has hundreds of charming inns, *pensiones,* and hotels with reasonable rates. Here's a short list of some of our top choices:

- **Hotel Venezia** (Rome; ☎ 06/445-7101): Set near Rome's main railway terminal, this hotel features such grace notes as Murano glass chandeliers in the bedrooms and public areas, which were recently renovated. Some units have balconies overlooking the street, and everything is clean. See Chapter 4.
- **Romantik Hotel J and J** (Florence; ☎ 055/234005): This charming hotel was built in the 1500s as a monastery and is set on a rarely visited street near the historic Church of Santa Croce. It's named after the initials of its owners' children (James and Jacqueline). The property was renovated in 1990, but still retains much of its Renaissance charm. See Chapter 6.
- **Hotel Palazzo Bocci** (in Spello, near Assisi; ☎ 0742/301021): Built in the late 18th century, and renovated and transformed into a hotel in 1992, this palace is posh, tasteful, and reasonably priced. Many of the public and private rooms have sweeping views of the valley below. See Chapter 7.
- **Hotel Roma** (Modena; ☎ 059/222218): In the 1700s this building was among the real-estate holdings of the duca d'Este. Today it's likely to be the temporary home of whatever opera star happens to be singing in Pavarotti's hometown. Flourishing as a hotel since the 1950s, the Roma, located in the historic heart of town, is comfortable and uncomplicated. See Chapter 8.
- **La Residenza** (Venice; ☎ 041/528-5315): Many of this hotel's clients are art lovers who return to Venice year after year. Originally built in the 14th century, its interior walls have some of the most charming stucco work in Venice. On the medieval piazza outside, older citizens feed pigeons and younger ones play soccer. See Chapter 9.
- **Menardi** (Cortina d'Ampezzo; ☎ 0436/2400): Built a century ago, this alpine inn exudes Austrian *gemütlichkeit* (coziness), with blazing fireplaces and windows that overlook a view of alpine meadows and rugged crags. Best of all, it's a short uphill walk from one of Italy's most glamorous resorts. See Chapter 12.
- **Hotel Asnigo** (Cernobbio; ☎ 031/510062): The Asnigo embodies the Edwardian style of the age in which it was built (1914), and has the atmosphere of a genteel

retreat. Set in a garden, it's clean and run in a friendly, low-key style. Some visitors return year after year. See Chapter 13.

- **Hotel Florence** (Bellagio; ☎ 031/950342): A private villa in the 19th century, this hotel has a dignified facade, an arbor with tumbling wisteria, and stone-sided terraces overlooking a lake. A series of renovations in 1990 brought it tastefully up to date, and Saturday-night jazz concerts and an American-style bar have made it better than ever. Chapter 13.

- **Albergo Nazionale** (Portofino; ☎ 0185/269575): This excellent moderately priced choice is situated right in the heart of the most photographed harbor of Italy, in the most expensive pocket of posh resort on the Italian Riviera. Antique furnishings, coved ceilings, and hand-painted Venetian furniture contribute to an atmosphere of charm and luxury, but nothing equals the view of the harbor from some bedroom windows. See Chapter 15.

11 The Best Restaurants

Italy has always been known for its agricultural bounty—it's a fertile peninsula rich with olive groves and other farmland. The result has been the emergence of one of the world's premier cuisines. Here's a list of Italy's most glamorous and consistently recommended eateries.

- **Relais le Jardin** (Rome; ☎ 06/361-3041): Located in the dignified Lord Byron Hotel, in an upscale residential neighborhood a short drive from the center of Rome, the Relais is always on the short list of the country's best. The menu varies according to what's in season. See Chapter 4.

- **Harry's Bar** (Venice; ☎ 041/528-5777): It's legendary, it's lighthearted, and it's fun. First made famous by writer Ernest Hemingway, Harry's Bar still serves sublime food in the formal dining room upstairs. The Bellini, peach juice with prosecco (Italian sparkling wine), was born here. See Chapter 9.

- **Antico Martini** (Venice; ☎ 041/522-4121): Founded in 1720 as a spot to savor the newly developed rage of coffee drinking, this restaurant is usually cited as one of the very best in Venice. Replete with paneled walls and glittering chandeliers, the Antico Martini specializes in Venetian cuisine. See Chapter 9.

- **Ristorante il Desco** (Verona; ☎ 045/595358): Set in a former palazzo, this restaurant is the best in the Veneto region of northeastern Italy. Its culinary repertoire emphasizes a *nuova cucina* (nouvelle cuisine) that makes use of the freshest ingredients. The wine selections are excellent. See Chapter 11.

- **Ristorante Tivoli** (Cortina d'Ampezzo; ☎ 0436/866400): This charming and friendly restaurant, a cozy chalet on a hillside above the town, serves such dishes as stuffed rabbit in an onion sauce, filet of veal with pine nuts and basil, and a delectable saffron-flavored salmon. See Chapter 12.

- **Ristorante Emiliano** (Stresa; ☎ 0323/31396): Overlooking the soothing waters of Lake Garda, this restaurant attracts many conservative clients from throughout northern Europe who come to the Italian lake district for R&R. Recipes adhere to the traditions of the Emilia-Romagna region, which is known for its pastas, sausages, and cheeses. See Chapter 13.

- **Peck's Restaurant** (Milan; ☎ 02/876774): In the 19th century an entrepreneur from Prague moved to Lombardy and founded the most upscale delicatessen (Peck's) in Milan. His organization also manages this sumptuously elegant restaurant. You're likely to dine surrounded by the business moguls who run Italy. See Chapter 13.

- **Ristorante da Vittorio** (Bergamo; ☎ 035/218060): Set on a busy commercial boulevard in a town known for its feudal fortifications, this restaurant stresses regional cuisine with an array of risottos, pastas, and game dishes. See Chapter 13.
- **L'Aquila Nigra** (Mantua; ☎ 0376/327180): To reach this restaurant, which used to be a Renaissance palace, you'll have to meander through a labyrinth of narrow alleyways in the historic heart of Mantua. Inside, the high-ceilinged rooms offer elegant food, served with dignified panache by a well-trained staff. See Chapter 13.
- **Vecchia Lanterna** (Turin; ☎ 011/537047): Its interior is loaded with ornate 19th-century furniture, belle époque lighting fixtures, and art nouveau accessories that have long added charm to the elegant dinners consumed here. The food is rich and savory. See Chapter 14.
- **Gran Gotto** (Genoa; ☎ 010/564344): Despite the excellence of its cuisine, this eatery manages to remain lighthearted, irreverent, and richly connected to the seafaring life of this ancient Italian port. The zuppa di pesce (a Riviera version of a Marseillaise bouillabaisse) is worth the trip to Genoa. See Chapter 15.

12 The Best Shopping

- **Fashion:** Italian fashion is world renowned. Pucci and Valentino lead the parade to be followed in time by such names as Giorgio Armani, Gianni Versace, Missoni, and, of course, Gucci. Following World War II, Italian design began to compete seriously against the French fashion monopoly. Today Italian designers such as Krizia are among the fashion arbiters of the world. Milan dominates the fashion scene with the largest selection of boutiques, followed by Rome and Florence. Ironically, a lot of "French fashion" is now designed and manufactured in Italy, in spite of what the label says.
- **Glass & Ceramics:** Venetian glass, ranging from the most exquisite and finely designed with delicate colors to the grotesque, is famous the world over. In Venice you'll find literally hundreds of stores peddling Venetian glass in the widest possible price range. Here's the surprise: A great deal of Venetian glass today isn't manufactured on Murano (an island in the Venetian lagoon) but in places as far away as the Czech Republic. That doesn't mean that the glass is unworthy. Many factories outside Italy turn out high-quality glass products that are then shipped to Murano where many so-called glass factories aren't factories at all, but storefronts selling this imported "Venetian" glass.

    The town of Faenza, in the Emilia-Romagna region, has been the center of pottery making, especially *majolica,* ever since the Renaissance. Majolica, also known as *faïence,* is a type of hand-painted, glazed, and heavily ornamented earthenware. Of course, you don't have to go to Faenza to purchase it, as shops throughout the country carry it. The provinces of Umbria and Tuscany are also known for their earthenware pottery, carried by many shops in Rome and Florence.
- **Gold:** The tradition of shaping jewelry out of gold dates from the time of the Etruscans, and this ancient tradition is still going strong in Italy today, where artisans still work in tiny studios and workshops. Many of the designs they follow are based on ancient Roman originals. Of course, many gold jewelers don't follow tradition at all, but design original and often daring pieces in gold. Many shops throughout Italy will even melt down your old gold jewelry and refashion it into something more modern. Italy is the seat of grand international jewelry empires such as Bulgari, but few can afford their offerings. It's better, instead, to seek out those tiny jewelry stores where artisans ply their trade.

- **Lace:** For centuries Italy has been known for its exquisite and delicate lace—fashioned into everything from women's undergarments to heirloom-type tablecloths. Florence long ago distinguished itself for the *punto Firenze* or "Florentine stitch" made by cloistered nuns, although this tradition isn't as plentiful as it used to be. Venetian lace is even more famous, including some of the finest lace products in the world, especially *tombolo* (pillow lace), macramé, and an expensive form of lace known as *chiacchierino*. Of course, the market today is also flooded with cheap machine-made stuff, which a trained eye can quickly spot. Although some pieces of lace, such as a bridal veil, might cost millions of lire, you'll often find lace collars, handkerchiefs, and doilies in the boutiques of Venice and Florence at reasonable prices.
- **Leather:** The Italians—not just Gucci designers—are considered the finest leather craftspeople in the world. From boots to luggage, from leather clothing to purses (or wallets), Italian cities, especially Rome, Florence, Venice, and Milan, abound in leather shops selling quality goods. Leather is one of the best values in Italy, in spite of the substandard work that's now appearing. If you shop carefully, you'll find much of the Italian leather products are still hand-crafted.
- **Prints & Engravings:** Ever since the Renaissance, Italy has been a shopping mecca for engravings and prints, especially in such shopping centers as Rome and Florence. Wood engravings, woodcuts, mezzotints, copper engravings—you name it and you'll find it in Italy. Of course, you have to be a careful shopper when purchasing. Some prints are genuine antiques and works of rare art, whereas others are rushed off the assembly line and into the shops. Since you can no longer go to Italy and take home Roman antiques or a crate of Raphaels, visitors today content themselves with these relatively inexpensive prints and engravings—admittedly reproductions but collectors' items nonetheless.
- **Religious Objects & Vestments:** The religious objects industry—centered mainly at Rome—is big and bustling, mostly in the Greater Vatican area. The greatest concentration of shops in Rome is near the ancient Church of Santa Maria Sopra Minerva. From cardinals' birettas to rosary beads, from religious art to vestments, it's all to be found here.

2 Getting to Know Italy

Conquerors, scholars, artists, and saints as well as curious travelers have been drawn to Italy for centuries. Across turbulent seas and stormy mountains they came, even risking their lives to see Italy. Getting there by plane, sea, rail, or car is considerably easier today, but the age-old attraction remains.

Some have been fascinated by its people, including the novelist E. M. Forster, who wrote that the Italians were "more marvellous than the land." Others have been drawn to its artistic treasures, left by geniuses like Leonardo da Vinci and Michelangelo.

Although ancient, Italy is still a relatively modern country in terms of political unity. As late as the 19th century, the prominent Austrian statesman Prince Metternich dismissed it as no more than a "geographical expression." Unlike the rest of Europe, Italy was late in developing a national identity. It wasn't until 1870 that the country's 20 regions were united under one central government. Although Italy may be a late bloomer among European nations, its culture has flourished since antiquity, and no country in the world has as many reminders of its cultural heritage as does Italy. They range from Rome's Colosseum to Sicily's Greek ruins.

Other visitors come to Italy for the scenery. As any Italian will confide, "Italy is the world's most beautiful country," with cypress-studded landscapes, coastal coves, jagged Dolomite peaks, fishing ports, sandy beaches, and charming little hill towns whose historic cores haven't changed much in hundreds of years.

Many travelers visit Italy just to have fun, and given the country's sense of *la dolce vita,* that goal is almost guaranteed. Other, more serious visitors come here to immerse themselves in its history and culture, and most of them leave thinking that Italy is one of the world's most rewarding travel destinations.

1 The Regions in Brief

Italy is about the size of the state of Arizona. The peninsula's shape, however, gives visitors the impression of a much larger area; the ever-changing seacoast contributes to this feeling, as do the large islands of Sicily and Sardinia. Bordered on the northwest by France, on the north by Switzerland and Austria, and on the east by Slovenia (formerly part of Yugoslavia), Italy is still a land largely surrounded by the sea.

❓ Did You Know?

- The tomato, that quintessentially Italian vegetable, was brought to Europe from North America in the 16th century.
- About 60% of Italy's historical and artistic treasures are not on view, but are kept in storerooms and warehouses.
- Italians made the first super-spectacle, a nine-reel blockbuster, *Quo Vadis,* released in 1912.
- Spaghetti was introduced from China by Marco Polo.
- The wife of slain dictator Benito Mussolini ran a trattoria in northern Italy for many years after the end of World War II; in 1992 her granddaughter, Alessandra Mussolini, won a seat in Parliament as a member of the neo-Fascist party.
- Every 30 or 40 minutes, somewhere in Italy, a historical trophy or work of art disappears.

Two areas within the boundaries of Italy not under the control of the Italian government are the State of Vatican City and the Republic of San Marino. The 109 acres of Vatican City in Rome were established in 1929 by a concordat, or formal agreement, between Pope Pius XI and Benito Mussolini, acting as head of the Italian government; the agreement also gave the Roman Catholic religion special status in the country. The pope is the sovereign of the State of Vatican City, which has its own legal system and its own post office.

Aosta Valley (Valle d'Aosta)   Italy's window on Switzerland and France, the Valle d'Aosta—the smallest region of Italy—often serves as an introduction to the country itself, especially for those journeying from France through the Mont Blanc tunnel into Italy. The introduction is misleading, as the Valle d'Aosta stands apart from the rest of Italy, a semi-autonomous, high-altitude region of towering peaks and valleys in the northwestern corridor of the country. Known for its alpine sunshine and the ancient French-derived dialect of its citizens, it's more closely linked to France (especially the French alpine region of Savoy) than to Italy. An area rich in scenery, dairy products, and wine, its most important city is the ancient Roman city of Aosta—except for some ruins, it's rather dull. More intriguing are two of Italy's major ski resorts, Courmayeur and Breuil-Cervinia, which are rivaled—and topped—only by Cortina d'Ampezzo in the Dolomites. Many of the region's villages are crafted from gray rocks culled from the mountains that rise on all sides. Among these are the legendary Matterhorn and Mont Blanc, parts of which lie across the border in Switzerland and France. The best time to visit is either in the summer or the deep of winter. Late spring and fall get rather sleepy in this part of the world.

The Piedmont   Set at the extreme northwestern edge of Italy, sharing a set of alpine peaks with France (which in some ways it resembles), the Piedmont was the district from which Italy's dreams of unification spread in 1861. Long under the domination of the Austro-Hungarian Empire, the Piedmont enjoys a cuisine laced with alpine cheeses and dairy products. It's proud of its largest city, Turin (Torino in Italian). Called the "Detroit of Italy," Turin is the home of the Fiat empire, as well as vermouth, Asti Spumante, and the Borsalino hat. Although a great cosmopolitan center, it doesn't have the antique charm of its seafront sibling, Genoa, or the sophistication, world-class dining, and chic shopping of its Lombard cousin, Milan. Turin's most controversial sight is the *Sacra Sindone,* or the Holy Shroud, which many

Catholics believe is the exact cloth in which Christ's body was wrapped when removed from the cross.

Lombardy   Flat, fertile, prosperous, and politically conservative, Lombardy is dominated by Milan in the same way that Latium is dominated by Rome. Lombardy is one of the world's leading commercial and cultural centers—it has been immersed in the mercantile ethic ever since Milan developed into Italy's gateway to northern, German-speaking Europe during the early Middle Ages. Although it's fashionable to belittle Milan for its industrial power and its contempt of the poorer regions of Italy's south, its fans compare it to New York. Milan's cathedral is the third largest in Europe, its opera house (La Scala) is the site of some of the finest performances anywhere, and its museums and churches are world class. Nevertheless, in spite of its formidable attractions, which embrace everything from da Vinci's *Last Supper* to one of Europe's greatest cathedrals, Milan is still not in the tourist league of Rome, Florence, and Venice. Work in Milan if you have the time, although you'll find more charm in the neighboring art cities of Bergamo, Brescia, Pavia, Cremona, and Mantua. Also competing for your time will be the lakes of Garda and Maggiore, which lie near Lombardy's eastern edge and are the most preferred vacation destinations of the Milanese themselves.

Trentino–Alto Adige (South Tyrol)   Until this region was annexed by Italy after World War I, it was an integral part of Austria. Despite the changes made almost 80 years ago in the demarcation of the Italian-Austrian border, passions continue to run deep here as family loyalties cling tenaciously to Austrian ways. The region's split personality is enhanced by the mixture of Italian and German spoken on an everyday basis. Also, the architecture dotting the rocky sides of the Dolomites seems mostly influenced by either the chalet or the Austrian Jugendstil style. This region is far richer in culture, artistic treasures, and activities than the Valle d'Aosta (see above), and its ski resort, Cortina d'Ampezzo, is far more fashionable than Courmayer or Breuil-Cervina in the northwestern corridor. Its most interesting bases—especially if you want to see the Austrian version of Italy—are Bolzano (Bozen) and Merano (Meran). Trent, the capital of Trentino, is more historic than either Merano or Bolzano, but lacks their scenic beauty.

Friuli–Venezia Giulia   Set in the extreme northeastern corner of Italy, adjacent to the border of modern-day Slovenia, this is, in its own way, one of the most cosmopolitan and culturally sophisticated regions of Italy. Set at the crossroads of the Balkans and the Teutonic world, it was highly influenced by the Austro-Hungarian Empire. Its capital is the seaport of Trieste, although worthy sites of interest include Udine, Gorizia, and Pordenone. The area is filled with artistic treasures from the Roman, Byzantine, and Romanesque-Gothic eras, and many of the public buildings (especially those of Trieste) might remind you more of Vienna. This area is not a mainstream tourist destination, and that forms its particular appeal. For those on the whirlwind tour, Trieste could be skipped. But those who come to Trieste will be richly rewarded by the unique atmosphere of the largest seaport on the Adriatic. Trieste has enough attractions to fill one busy day, and is an easy drive from Venice.

Veneto   This region, dotted with richly stocked museums and some of the best architecture in Italy, sprawls across the verdant hills and flat and fertile plains of northeastern Italy, between the Adriatic, the Dolomites, Verona, and the edges of Lake Garda. The fortunes of the Veneto revolved, for many generations, in an orbit around Venice. Few travelers need to be sold on the glories of Venice, with its sumptuous

palaces, romantic waterways, its Palazzo Ducale, and Basilica di San Marco. In some ways Venice still looks as if it were waiting for Canaletto in the 18th century to paint it. Aging, decaying, and sinking into the sea, it's such a worthy picture-postcard attraction that we almost want to say visit it if you have to skip Rome and Florence. However, we don't dare, because each of the top three tourist cities of Italy is so special and unique that we hope you can accommodate all three in your itinerary. As special as Venice and its islands in the lagoon are, we also recommended that you tear yourself away and visit at least three fabled art cities in the "Venetian Arc"—Verona of *Romeo and Juliet* fame, Vicenza to see the villas of Andrea Palladio where 16th-century aristocrats lived, and Padua, ennobled by its Giotto frescoes.

Liguria & the Italian Riviera   Comprising most of the Italian Riviera, the unexpected capital of which is the steeply sloping city of Genoa, this region incorporates medieval ports known for their charm (Portofino, Ventimiglia, and San Remo), a massive naval base (La Spezia), and a quintet of coastal communities (Cinque Terra) that cling tenaciously to traditional values. There's also a series of belle époque seaside resorts (Rapallo and Santa Margherita Ligure) whose style and nonchalance are reminiscent of resorts along the nearby French Riviera. As chic as the Italian Riviera is, it's still rivaled and surpassed by the French. But the Italian Riviera has its unique appeal. Although it's overbuilt and overrun with tourists, just as its French counterpart is, it's still a land of great beauty. It's actually two Rivieras—the *Riviera di Ponente,* or western Riviera, which runs from the French border to Genoa, and the *Riviera di Levante* to the east. Faced with a choice, make it the Riviera di Levante as it's more glamorous and cosmopolitan. Italy's largest port, Genoa, also merits a visit to learn of its rich culture and history. The historic harbor was given a face-lift for the celebrations honoring Columbus in 1992.

Tuscany   Tuscany is one of the most culturally and politically influential provinces in Italy—the development of Italy without Tuscany is simply unthinkable. It was the vistas of Tuscany, with their sun-warmed vineyards and towering cypresses fluttering in gentle breezes, that inspired the artists of the Renaissance. Nowhere in the world does the Renaissance live on more than it does in its birthplace, Florence, with its artistic works left by da Vinci and Michelangelo, among others. Since the 19th century travelers have been flocking to Florence to see the Donatello bronzes, the Botticelli smiles, and all the other preeminent treasures. Unfortunately, it's now an invasion, and Florence is overrun like Venice. All the world knows of the city's astounding artistic wealth, including the most reproduced statue on earth (Michelangelo's *David*), but you must risk being trampled underfoot as you, too, come to view the historic heart of Florence. To escape, you can head for nearby attractions in the Tuscan hill towns, former stamping ground of the Guelphs and Ghibellines. The main cities to visit include Lucca, Pisa, and especially Siena, Florence's great historical rival with an inner core that appears to be caught in a time warp. As a final treat for yourself, visit San Gimignano, northwest of Siena, which is celebrated for its medieval "skyscrapers."

Emilia-Romagna   Italians seem to agree on only one thing: The food in Emilia-Romagna is the best in Italy. Its capital, Bologna, boasts a stunning Renaissance core with plenty of majestic churches and arcades, a fine university with roots in the early Middle Ages, and a populace with a reputation for leftist leanings. The region also has one of the highest standards of living in Italy. Should you budget time for a visit? Definitely yes, although the pluckings are richer in Tuscany and Umbria. But Emilia-Romagna has a lot going for it, including tortellini, lasagne, and fettuccine, its greatest contributions to world gastronomy. When not dining in Bologna, you can take time to explore its artistic heritage. The region abounds in other art cities—none more noble than the Byzantine city of Ravenna, still living off its past glory when it was once the capital of the declining Roman Empire.

If you can visit only one more city in the region, make it Parma, to see its city center with its Duomo and Battistero and to view its National Gallery. Parma is also the home of Parmesan cheese and prosciutto. Another noteworthy city is Modena, hometown of opera star Pavarotti—known for its cuisine, its cathedral, and its Este Gallery. The crowded Adriatic resort of Rimini and the medieval stronghold of San Marino are both at the periphery of Emilia-Romagna.

Umbria   Pastoral, hilly, and fertile, it's more similar to Tuscany than any other province, but with fewer tourists. Its once-fortified network of hill towns is among the most charming in Italy. Crafted from millions of tons of gray-brown rocks, each is a testament to the masonry and architectural skills of many generations of Italian craftsmen. Noteworthy examples include Perugia, Gubbio, Assisi, Spoleto (site of the world-renowned annual arts festival), and Orvieto, a mysterious citadel once used as a stronghold by the Etruscans. Called the land of shadows, Umbria is often covered in a bluish haze that evokes an ethereal painted look. Many local artists have tried to capture the province's special glow, with its sun-dappled hills, terraced vineyards, and miles upon miles of olive trees. Visitors arrive today in this birthplace of saints and the *condottieri* to see Giotto's frescoes at Assisi's Basilica di San Francesco, to attend the Festival of Two Worlds at Spoleto, and to see Orvieto's awe-inspiring cathedral. Faced with time limitations, make it Assisi and most definitely Perugia, the largest and richest of the provence's cities.

The Marches   It's the easternmost province of central Italy, with an economy revolving around the beach resorts of its seacoast (the largest of which include Ancona and the relatively modern town of Pesaro) and tourism to its Renaissance gem, Urbino. Located east of Umbria, the Marches—*Marche* in Italian—is filled with turreted castles, scenic valleys, and the ruins of such ancient Roman sites as Urbis Salvia and Macerata. This region of Italy is rarely included on most North American visitors' itineraries. If you can spend only a day in the Marches, make it to Urbino, an ancient town where Raphael was born and spent his boyhood. On a hill 1,500 feet above sea level, Urbino is similar to San Gimignano in Tuscany in that it hasn't changed much since the 15th century. A tour of the beautiful old town, taking in its Palazzo Ducale and its Galleria Nazionale delle Marche, will take at least 3 hours.

Latium   The region of Latium is dominated by Rome, capital of the ancient empire and the modern nation of Italy, and Vatican City, the independent papal state. Containing vast lodes of the world's artistic treasures, Latium is a land of myth, legend, grandeur, and ironies. Much of the civilized world was once ruled from here, going back to the days when Romulus and Remus are said to have founded Rome on April 21, 753 B.C. For generations Rome was justifiably referred to as *caput mundi* (capital of the world). It no longer enjoys such a lofty position, of course, but remains a timeless city, ranking with Paris and London as one of the most visited of Europe. Much of this city's glory is of another day—and the memories live on in all the haunted ruins: Nero fiddled while Rome burned; Mark Antony came to praise Caesar, and Charlemagne to wear an emperor's crown. There's no place else in all the world with more artistic monuments than Rome, not even Venice or Florence. Rome is the country's storehouse of treasures, from the Sistine Chapel to the Roman Forum. It remains the city of *la dolce vita*. How much time should you budget? The Italian writer Silvio Negro said, "A lifetime is not enough."

Abruzzi   Set to the east and southeast of Rome, in central Italy's rugged core, the Abruzzi is one of the poorest and least-visited regions in Italy, even though it lies only 3 hours by train from Rome. Arid and sun-scorched, it's the home of one of the peninsula's largest national forests (Abruzzi National Park), the Gran Sasso mountain range (the highest peak of the Appenines), and such battered resorts as L'Aquila. Prone to frequent earthquakes, the Abruzzi is proud but impoverished and visually stark. Many of its people have emigrated to more prosperous regions of the peninsula. If you visit the region, the best centers are the medieval cities of L'Aquila and Sulmona, directly south of it. Avoid the coast opening onto the Adriatic Sea, especially tacky Pescara. This is beachfront Italy at its worst, with loud music, pizzerias, cheap discos, and some of the country's worst hotels.

Campania   More than any other region of Italy, Campania reverberates with the memories of the ancient Romans, who favored its strong sunlight, fertile soil, and bubbling sulfurous springs. It manages to incorporate the anarchy of Naples with the elegant beauty of Capri and the Amalfi coast. The district also contains many sites specifically identified in ancient mythology (lakes defined as the entrance to the Kingdom of the Dead, etc.), and some of the most prolific ancient ruins (including Pompeii and Herculaneum) in the world. The region is divided into five different provinces: Avellino, Benevento, Caserta, Naples, and Salerno. No longer the treat of artists, kings, and emperors, Campania is overrun, overcrowded, and over everything, but it still lures visitors, the way the Sirens of old entranced Ulysses. If you must go, allow at least a day for Naples, which has amazing museums and the world's worst traffic outside of Cairo. Pompeii and Herculeaneum are for the ruin collectors, and those seeking Italian sun head for Capri, rivaled only by Portofino in the north for chicdom. The best towns along the Amalfi Drive, even though they're no longer unspoiled, are Ravello (not on the sea) and Positano (which is on the sea). Amalfi and Sorrento are much tackier and more overrun.

Apulia   Sun-drenched and poor, and forming the heel of the Italian boot, Apulia is the most frequently visited province of Italy's Deep South. Part of its allure lies in its string of resorts, which line the elongated seacoast. It was the site of some of the most morbid and costliest battles of the Middle Ages. Depending on the dialect you're hearing, the region is referred to as Puglia, Le Puglie, or Apulia. The *trulli* houses of Alberobello are known for their unique cylindrical shapes and conical, flagstone-sheathed roofs. Among the region's largest cities are Bari (the capital), Foggia, and Brindisi (gateway to nearby Greece, with which the town shares many characteristics). Each of these cities is a modern disaster, filled with tawdry buildings, heavy traffic, and a rising crime rate (tourists are often the victims). Visitors mostly pass through Bari in a night—it's a favorite with backpackers—and the only reason to spend a night in Brindisi is while you wait to catch the ferry to Greece the next morning.

Calabria   Welcome to hard-core Italy. The extreme southwestern region of Italy (the toe of Italy's boot) is agrarian, impoverished, cruelly hot in summertime, and, to an alarming extent, almost devoid of younger people, who flee to other regions. A stronghold of the Mafia (referred to locally as the *'ndrangheta*), the region reinforces many of the southern Italian stereotypes the visitor hears about in the industrial north. Life revolves around age-old villages with a somber style of architecture. Cosenza is the district's largest city, and Reggio di Calabria its capital and a port of ferryboat embarkation for nearby Sicily. Local spokespeople hope that a handful of modest beach resorts (Locri, Rossano, Praia a Mare, Cirello, and Pizzo) will lure vacationers to the province. Low-income Italians often flock to these resorts in summer to escape the inland heat. We suggest that you let them sunbathe in peace and head as rapidly as possible for Sicily.

Sardinia   Rugged, arid, and notoriously clannish, Sardinia is the second-largest island in the Mediterranean. Certain regions (especially the Costa Smeralda) are about the chicest places in the world to be during August. Sardinia is populated by a race of people genetically distinct from those inhabiting the Italian peninsula. Its capital is Cagliari. Cone-shaped towers (*nuraghi*) crafted from huge stone slabs and fortified dwellings of the earliest inhabitants dot the island. Encircled by miles of silver-white sandy beaches, rocky coasts, bays, and gulfs, Sardinia is also an island of mountains and hills. D. H. Lawrence called it "unconquered Sardinia"—but that's no longer true. Sardinia has been explored to death, even though it draws only a fraction of the traffic lured to Sicily or the Italian mainland. Yet it's too discovered to qualify as an "offbeat adventure." Outside the summer resorts on the Emerald Coast, the best centers are Cagliari and Alghero, the latter on the northwest coast 142 miles from Cagliari. Alghero was the former Aragonese fishing port, and it's Sardinia's most beautiful town.

Sicily   The largest island of the Mediterranean, Sicily is a land of beauty, mystery, and world-class monuments. Cynical yet passionate, it's endlessly fascinating, a bizarre mixture of bloodlines and architecture from medieval Normandy, Aragonese Spain, Moorish North Africa, ancient Greece, Phoenicia, and Rome. Since the advent of modern times, part of the island's primitiveness has faded, as thousands of newly arrived cars clog the narrow lanes of its biggest city, Palermo. Although poverty remains widespread, the age-old stranglehold of the Mafia seems less certain because of the increasingly vocal protests of an outraged Italian public. On the eastern edge of the island is Mount Etna, the tallest active volcano in Europe. Many of Sicily's larger cities (Trapani, Catania, and Messina) are relatively unattractive, but areas of ravishing beauty and eerie historic interest include Siracusa, Taormina, Agrigento, and Selinunte. Sicily's ancient ruins are rivaled only by those of Rome itself. The Valley of the Temples, for example, is worth the trip here.

2 Italy Today

Modern Italy is a land of contradictions: a Roman Catholic state ruled by the mores and values of a staunchly religious consciousness that nevertheless is the most corrupt country in Western Europe. The nation's politicians claim to fight corruption but often get involved in scandal after scandal themselves. Italy is a land whose sons and daughters emigrated to form large populations throughout the world, especially in America, but its citizens today in large numbers remain viciously opposed to and prejudiced against immigrants arriving on their own shore.

"In the course of a century, we've gone from being a land of emigrants to one that takes in immigrants," said Luigi Manconi, a Milan sociologist. "We're just not equipped."

Widespread unemployment has enhanced racism and prejudice in Italy, primarily directed toward the North African contingent that has descended upon Italy in search of jobs. Most work in the agricultural community as migrant workers. Some are prostitutes in the bustling resorts on the Italian Riviera. These workers are not accepted into the tight-knit Italian communities. Recent violence and retribution by Italians have prompted the government to impose limits on immigration.

Although that government might try to limit immigration, any attempt to clean up its own image seems hopeless. *La politica e una cosa sporca* (politics are dirty) is an expression often heard in Italy. The charge is certainly justified. Corruption, scandal, and political chaos are parts of everyday life on the Italian landscape. The word *politician* is almost always preceded by the word *corrupt*. It's virtually assumed that anyone entering politics is doing so for personal gain.

Italy's precarious modern political system, with 55 governments since World War II, has been compared by many political analysts to the ill-fated First Republic.

Italy's latest and most notorious scandal involving a political figure is the ongoing trial in Palermo of Giulio Andreotti, seven-time Italian prime minister. Andreotti is on trial for alleged Mafia dealings. The trial is expected to last 2 years and cover thousands of pages of allegations. In addition, Andreotti is on trial for his suspected involvement in the assassination of an investigative journalist in Rome.

These proceedings, along with numerous other cases involving high-ranking officals, create a tremendous lack of faith and trust in the political system in Italy. They're at the core of a sweeping aura of discontent, common among Italians. When the subject of politics is breached, Italians today throw up their hands in frustration. They have also learned to live and work outside the government.

Although Italy ranks sixth among world economic powers, the instability of the lira in global markets has forced Italy to retain its position as a second-class participant in global commerce. Its true economy cannot be measured because of the vast underground economy (*economia sommersa*), controlled by the Mafia. Almost every Italian has some unreported income or expenditure. Other global competitors refrain from investing in Italian ventures because of lack of confidence in the government.

Besides soccer (*calcio*), the family, and affairs of the heart, the national obsession of Italy today is *il sorpasso,* a term that describes Italy's surpassing of its archrivals France and Britain in economic indicators. Economists disagree about whether or not *il sorpasso* has happened, and statistics (complicated by the presence of Italy's vast underground economy) vary widely from source to source. All levels of Italian society are actively engaged to some degree in withholding funds from the government. Today Italy's underground economy competes on a monumental scale with the official economy, with participation by all sorts of otherwise respectable businesses and individuals. Complicating Italy's problems for economists, the police, and politicians is the constant interference of the Mafia, whose methods—despite numerous more or less heartfelt crackdowns—continue today even more ruthlessly than ever.

Another complicating factor is the surfeit of laws in Italy and their effect on the citizens. Before they get thrown out of office, Italian politicians pass laws and more laws, adding to the horde already on the books. Italy has more laws on the books than any other nation of Western Europe, and because of those Draconian rules its citizens are forced to live "outside the law" in order to survive.

Michael Mewshaw, author of *Playing Away,* a book about Italy, writes: "In fact, Italy suffers from both a glut of laws, many of them contradictory, and a bloated bureaucracy. Something as simple as cashing a check or paying a bill can devour half a day. To escape the brambles of red tape, Italians have become marvelous improvisers and corner-cutters. Whenever possible they bypass the sclerotic public sector and negotiate private deals *fra amici*—among friends."

Italy can no longer bask in its glorious past, or even utilize its previous shortcomings as a crutch. The country today is a land in transition, struggling to become a stable, viable contender in today's global community.

3 A Look at the Past

THE ETRUSCANS Among the early inhabitants of Italy, the most significant were the Etruscans—but who were they, actually? No one knows, and the many inscriptions they left behind—mostly on graves—are of no help, since the Etruscan language has never been deciphered by modern scholars. It's thought that they arrived on the eastern coast of Umbria several centuries before Rome was built, which was around 800 B.C. Their religious rites and architecture show an obvious contact with Mesopotamia; the Etruscans may have been refugees from Asia Minor who traveled westward about 1200 to 1000 B.C. Within two centuries they had subjugated Tuscany and Campania and the Villanova tribes who lived there.

While the Etruscans built temples at Tarquinia and Caere (present-day Cerveteri), the few nervous Latin tribes who remained outside their sway gravitated to Rome, then little more than a sheepherding village. As its power grew, however, Rome increasingly profited from the strategically important Tiber crossing where the ancient Salt Way (via Salaria) turned northeastward toward the central Apennines.

From their base at Rome, the Latins remained free of the Etruscans until about 600 B.C. But the Etruscan advance was inexorable, and although the tribes concentrated their forces at Rome for a last stand, they were swept away by the sophisticated Mesopotamian conquerors. The new overlords introduced gold tableware and jewelry, bronze urns and terra-cotta statuary, and the best of Greek and Asia Minor art and culture; they also made Rome the governmental seat of all Latium. Roma is an Etruscan name, and the kings of Rome had Etruscan names: Numa, Ancus, Tarquinius, even Romulus.

The Estruscans ruled until the Roman revolt around 510 B.C., and by 250 B.C. the Romans and their Campania allies had vanquished the Etruscans, wiping out their language and religion. However, many of the former rulers' manners and beliefs remained, assimilated into the culture. Even today certain Etruscan customs and bloodlines are believed to exist in Italy, especially in Tuscany.

The best places to see the legacy left by these mysterious people are in Cerveteri and Tarquinia outside Rome. Especially interesting is the Etruscan necropolis, just 4 miles southeast of Tarquinia, where thousands of tombs have been discovered. To learn more about the Etruscans, consider a visit to the

Dateline

- Bronze Age Celts, Teutonic tribes, and others from the Mediterranean and Asia Minor inhabit the peninsula.
- **1000 B.C.** Large colonies of Etruscans settle in Tuscany and Campania, quickly subjugating many of the Latin inhabitants of the Italian peninsula.
- **800 B.C.** Rome begins to take shape, evolving from a strategically located shepherd village into a magnet for Latin tribes fleeing the Etruscans.
- **600 B.C.** Etruscans occupy Rome, designating it the capital of their empire; the city grows rapidly and a major seaport opens at Ostia.
- **510 B.C.** The Latin tribes, still centered in Rome, revolt against the Etruscans; alpine Gauls attack from the north; Greeks living in Sicily destroy the Etruscan navy.
- **250 B.C.** The Romans, allied with the Greeks, Phoenicians, and native Sicilians, defeat the Etruscans; Rome flourishes and begins the accumulation of a vast empire.
- **49 B.C.** Italy (through Rome) controls the entire Mediterranean world.
- **44 B.C.** Julius Caesar assassinated; his successor, Augustus, transforms Rome from a city of brick to a city of marble.
- **3rd century A.D.** Rome declines under a series of incompetent and corrupt emperors.
- **4th century A.D.** Rome is fragmented politically as administrative capitals are established in such cities as Milan and Trier, Germany.

continues

- A.D. **395** The empire splits; Constantine establishes a "New Rome" at Constantinople (Byzantium); Goths successfully invade Rome's northern provinces.
- **410–455** Rome is sacked by barbarians.
- **475** Rome falls, leaving only the primate of the Catholic Church in control; the pope slowly adopts many of the powers once reserved for the Roman emperor.
- **800** Charlemagne is crowned Holy Roman Emperor by Pope Leo III; Italy dissolves into a series of small warring kingdoms.
- **Late 11th century** The popes function like secular princes with private armies.
- **1065** The Holy Land falls to the Muslim Turks; the Crusades are launched.
- **1303–77** Papal schism; the pope and his entourage move from Rome to Avignon.
- **1377** The papacy returns to Rome.
- **1443** Brunelleschi's dome caps the Duomo in Florence as the Renaissance ("rebirth") bursts into full bloom.
- **1469–92** Lorenzo il Magnifico rules in Florence as the Medici patron of Renaissance artists.
- **1499** *The Last Supper* is completed by Leonardo da Vinci in Milan.
- **1508** Michelangelo begins work on the Vatican's Sistine Chapel.
- **1527** Rome is sacked by Charles V of Spain, who is crowned Holy Roman Emperor the following year.
- **1796–97** Napoléon's series of invasions arouses Italian nationalism.
- **1861** Establishment of the Kingdom of Italy.

continues

Museo Nazionale di Villa Giulla, a museum in Rome, housed in a 16th-century papal palace in the Villa Borghese.

THE ROMAN REPUBLIC   This aristocratic republic lasted from 527 to 509 B.C. It was a time of chaos and internal struggles—mainly between the patricians and the lower-class plebeians. Even in the heart of chaos, a Roman code of law was established that would influence civilizations to come in the millennia ahead. The Romans increased their power through conquest of neighboring communities in the highlands and became allied with other Latins of the lowlands. They gave to their Latin allies, and then to conquered peoples, partial or complete Roman citizenship, with the obligation of military service. Citizen colonies were set up as settlements of Roman farmers, and many of the famous cities of Italy today originated as colonies. The colonies were for the most part fortified, and they were linked to Rome by military roads.

The stern Roman republic was characterized by belief in the gods, the necessity of learning from the past, strength of the family, education through books and public service, and—most important—obedience. The all-powerful Senate presided as Rome defeated rival powers one after the other and grew to rule the Mediterranean. The Punic Wars with Carthage in the 3rd century B.C. cleared away a major obstacle to Rome's growth, although people said later that Rome's breaking of its treaty with Carthage (which led to the total destruction of that city) put a curse on the Italian city. No figure was more towering during the republic than Julius Caesar, the charismatic conqueror of Gaul. He was called "the wife of every husband and the husband of every wife," among other honors. Caesar entered Rome in 47 B.C. and for the second time was nominated dictator for a year. After defeating the last resistance of the Pompeians in Spain in 45 B.C., he came to Rome and was made dictator and consul for 10 years. He was at that point almost a king. Conspirators led by Marcus Junius Brutus stabbed him to death in the Senate on March 15, 44 B.C.

THE ROMAN EMPIRE   By 49 B.C., Italy ruled all of the Mediterranean world either directly or indirectly, with all political, commercial, and cultural pathways leading directly to Rome. The possible wealth and glory to be found in Rome lured many there, but drained other Italian communities of human resources. Foreign imports, particularly in the field of agriculture, hurt local farmers and landowners. Municipal governments faltered and civil wars ensued. Public order was restored by the Caesars (planned by Julius but brought to fruition under Augustus). On the eve of the birth of Christ, Rome was a mighty empire whose generals had brought the Western world under the sway of Roman law and civilization.

Augustus, the first Roman emperor, reigned from 27 B.C. to A.D. 14. His reign, called "the golden age of Rome," led to the Pax Romana, or two centuries of peace. Julius Caesar was his great uncle. In Rome today you can still visit the remains of the Forum of Augustus, built before the birth of Christ, and the Domus Augustana, where the imperial family lived on Palatine Hill.

The emperors, whose succession started with Augustus's principate after the death of Julius Caesar, brought Rome to new, almost giddy, heights. Augustus transformed the city from brick to marble—much the way that Napoléon III transformed Paris many centuries later. But success led to corruption. The emperors wielded autocratic power, and the centuries witnessed a steady decay in the ideals and traditions upon which the empire had been founded. The army became a fifth column of barbarian mercenaries, the tax collector became the scourge of the countryside, and for every good emperor (Augustus, Trajan, Vespasian, and Hadrian, to name a few) there were three or four incredibly corrupt and debased heads of state (Caligula, Nero, Domitian, Caracalla, and more).

The Roman citizen in the capital either lived on the public dole and spent his days at gladiatorial games and imperial baths or was a disillusioned patrician at the mercy of emperors who might murder him for his property. The 3rd century A.D. saw so many emperors that it was common to hear in the provinces of the election of an emperor together with a report of his assassination. The 4th-century reforms of Diocletian held the empire together, but at the expense of its inhabitants, who were reduced to tax units. He reinforced imperial power but paradoxically at the same time weakened Roman dominance and prestige by establishing administrative capitals at such outposts as Milan, Trier in Germany, and elsewhere. When the Emperor Constantine built his "New Rome," Constantinople (also known as Byzantium), he moved the administrative functions away from Rome altogether, partly because the menace of possible barbarian attack in the West had increased greatly.

- **1915–18** Italy enters World War I on the side of the Allies.
- **1922** Fascists march on Rome; Benito Mussolini becomes premier.
- **1929** Signing of a concordat between the Vatican and the Italian government delineating the rights and responsibilities of each party.
- **1935** Italian invasion of Abyssinia (Ethiopia).
- **1936** Italy signs "Axis" pact with Germany.
- **1940** Italian invasion of Greece.
- **1943** U.S. Gen. George Patton lands in Sicily and soon controls the island.
- **1945** Mussolini is killed by a mob in Milan.
- **1946** Establishment of the Republic of Italy.
- **1957** The Treaty of Rome, founding the European Community (EC), is signed by six nations.
- **1960s** The country's economy grows under the EC, but the impoverished south lags behind.
- **1970s** Italy is plagued by left-wing terrorism; former Premier Aldo Moro is kidnapped and killed.
- **1980s** Political changes in Eastern Europe induce Italy's strong Communist party to modify its program and even to change its name; the Socialists head their first post-1945 coalition government.
- **1994** A conservative coalition, led by Silvio Berlusconi, wins general elections.
- **1995** Following resignation of Berlusconi, Lamberto Dini, Treasury minister, named prime minister to head transitional government.

continues

■ **1996** Dini steps down as prime minister, as president dissolves both houses of parliament; in general elections, the center-left coalition known as the Olive Tree sweeps both the Senate and the Chamber of Deputies.

Constantine took the best Roman artisans, politicians, and public figures with him to the new capital, creating a city renowned for its splendor, intrigue, jealousies, and passion.

THE EMPIRE FALLS   The eastern and western sections of the Roman Empire split in A.D. 395, leaving Italy without the support it once received from east of the Adriatic. When the Goths moved toward Rome in the early 5th century, citizens in the provinces, who had grown to hate and fear the cruel bureaucracy set up by Diocletian and followed by succeeding emperors, welcomed the invaders. And then the pillage began.

Rome was sacked by Alaric in 410, and after more than 40 troubled years, Attila the Hun laid siege to the once-powerful capital. He was followed in 455 by Gaiseric the Vandal, who engaged in a 2-week spree of looting and destruction. The empire of the West lasted for only another 20 years; it was terminated by Odovacar, a barbarian chief, who opened areas of Italy to Teutonic settlement.

Christianity, a new religion that created a new society, was probably founded in Rome about a decade after Jesus' crucifixion. Gradually gaining strength despite early persecution, it was finally accepted as the official religion of the empire. The best way today to relive the early Christian era is to visit Rome's Appian Way and its Catacombs, along via Appia Antica, built in 312 B.C. According to Christian tradition, it was here that an escaping Peter encountered the vision of Christ. The Catacombs of St. Callixtus form the first cemetery of the Christian community of Rome. By the end of the power of Rome in 476, the Roman popes were under the nominal auspices of an exarch from Byzantium (Constantinople).

THE MIDDLE AGES   After the fall of the Western Empire, the pope took on more and more imperial powers, although there was no political unity in the country. Decades of rule by barbarians and then Goths were followed by takeovers in different parts of the country by various strong warriors, such as the Lombards. Italy was thus divided into several spheres of control. In 731 Pope Gregory II renounced Rome's dependence on Constantinople and thus ended the twilight era of the Greek exarch who had nominally ruled Rome. Papal Rome turned toward Europe, where the papacy found a powerful ally in Charlemagne, a king of the barbarian Franks. In 800 he was crowned emperor by Pope Leo III. The capital that he established at Aachen (in French, Aix-la-Chapelle) lay deep within territory known to the Romans a half millennium ago as the heart of the barbarian world. Although Charlemagne pledged allegiance to the church and looked to Rome and its pope as the final arbiter in most religious and cultural affairs, he launched northwestern Europe on a course toward bitter political opposition to the meddling of the papacy in temporal affairs.

The successor to the empire of Charlemagne was a political entity known as the Holy Roman Empire, which lasted from 962 to 1806. The new empire defined the end of the Dark Ages, but it ushered in a period of long and bloody warfare as well. The Lombard leaders battled Franks. Magyars from Hungary invaded northeastern Lombardy and were in turn defeated by the increasingly powerful Venetians. Eventually Normans gained military control of Sicily in the 11th century, divided it completely from the rest of Italy, and altered forever both the island's racial and ethnic makeup and its architecture.

As Italy dissolved into an increasingly fragmented collection of city-states, the papacy fell under the power of the feudal landowners of Rome. Eventually even the selection process for determining the choice of pope came into the hands of the increasingly Germanic Holy Roman Emperors, although this power balance would very soon shift.

Rome during the Middle Ages was a quaint, rural town. Narrow lanes with over-hanging buildings filled many areas that were originally planned as showcases of an-cient imperial power, including the Campus Martius. Great basilicas were built and embellished with golden-hued mosaics. The forums, mercantile exchanges, temples, and great theaters of the imperial era slowly disintegrated and collapsed. The decay of ancient Rome was assisted by periodic earthquakes, centuries of neglect, and, in particular, the growing need for building materials. Rome receded into a dusty pro-vincialism. The seat of the Roman Catholic Church, it was a state almost completely controlled by priests, with an insatiable need for new churches and convents.

By the end of the 11th century the popes shook off control of the Roman aristoc-racy, rid themselves of what they considered the excessive influence of the emperors at Aachen, and began an aggressive expansion of church influence and acquisitions. The deliberate organization of the church into a format modeled on the hierarchies of the ancient Roman Empire put the church on a collision course with the empire and the other temporal leaders of Europe, resulting in an endless series of not-very-flattering power struggles.

THE RENAISSANCE   The story of Italy from the dawn of the Renaissance to the Age of Enlightenment in the 17th and 18th centuries is as varied and fascinating as that of the rise and fall of the empire. The papacy soon became essentially a feudal state, and the pope was a medieval (later Renaissance) prince engaged in many of the worldly activities that brought criticism upon the church in later centuries. The fall of the Holy Land to the Turks in 1065 catapulted the papacy into the forefront of world politics, primarily because of the Crusades, many of which the popes directly caused or encouraged (but most of which were judged military and economic disas-ters). During the 12th and 13th centuries the bitter rivalries that rocked the secular and spiritual bastions of Europe took their toll on the stability of the Holy Roman Empire, which grew weaker as city-states buttressed by mercantile and trade-related prosperity grew stronger, and as France emerged as a potent nation in its own right. Each investiture of a new bishop to any influential post became a cause of endless jockeying for power among many factions.

These conflicts reached their most visible impasse in 1303 when the papacy was moved to the French city of Avignon. For more than 70 years, until 1377, viciously competing popes (one in Rome, another under the protection of the French kings in Avignon) made simultaneous claims to the legacy of St. Peter, underscoring as never before the degree to which the church was both a victim and a victimizer in the temporal world of European politics.

The seat of the papacy was eventually returned to Rome, where a series of popes were every bit as interesting as the Roman emperors they replaced. The great fami-lies—Barberini, Medici, Borgia—enhanced their status and fortunes impressively when one of their sons was elected pope.

For a look at life in Rome during this tumultuous period, you can visit Castel Sant'Angelo in Rome, which became a papal residence in the 14th century. The mis-tress of Pope Alexander VI bore him two children—Cesare and Lucrezia Borgia, the two names of that era that have captured the public imagination.

Of all the women of the Italian Renaissance, Lucrezia is the only one who com-mands universal recognition in the Western world; her name is a virtual synonym for black deeds such as poisoning. But popular legend is highly unreliable. Many of the charges biographers have made against her (such as incestuous involvements with her brother and father) may have been only successful attempts to blacken her name. In addition to being part of an infamous family, she was a patron of the arts and a devoted charity worker, especially after she moved to Ferrara. Her brother, Cesare, is without defense—he was a Machiavellian figure who is remembered accurately as a symbol of villainy and cruel spite.

Despite the civilizing effects of the Renaissance, and the centuries that had passed since the collapse of the Roman Empire, the age of siege was not yet over. In 1527, Charles V, king of Spain, carried out the worst sack ever. To the horror of Pope Clement VII (a Medici), the entire city was brutally pillaged by the man who was to be crowned Holy Roman Emperor the next year.

During the years of the Renaissance, the Reformation, and the Counter-Reformation, Rome underwent major physical changes. The old centers of culture reverted to pastures and fields, whereas great churches and palaces were built with the stones of ancient Rome. This building boom, in fact, did far more damage to the temples of the Caesars than any barbarian sack had done. Rare marbles were stripped from the imperial baths and used as altarpieces or sent to lime kilns. So enthusiastic was the papal destruction of Imperial Rome that it's a miracle anything is left.

Politics aside, this era is best remembered because of its art. The great ruling families of Italy, especially the Medici in Florence, but also the Gonzaga in Mantua and the d'Este in Ferrara, not only reformed law and commerce, they also sparked a renaissance in art. Out of this period arose such towering figures as Leonardo da Vinci and Michelangelo. Many visitors come to Italy today to view what's left from the art and glory of that era—everything from Michelangelo's Sistine Chapel at the Vatican to his statue of *David* in Florence, from Leonardo da Vinci's *Last Supper* in Milan to the Duomo in Florence graced by Brunelleschi's dome.

UNITED ITALY   The 19th century witnessed the final collapse of the Renaissance city-states, which had existed since the end of the 13th century. These units, eventually coming under the control of a *signore* (lord), were, in effect, regional states, with mercenary soldiers, civil rights, and assistance for their friendly neighbors. Some had attained formidable power under such *signori* as the d'Este family in Ferrara, the Medici in Florence, and the Visconti and the Sforza families in Milan.

During the 17th, 18th, and 19th centuries, decades of turmoil in Italy had lasted through the many years of succession of different European dynasties; Napoléon made a bid for power in Italy beginning in 1796, fueling his war machines with what was considered a relatively easy victory. During the Congress of Vienna (1814–15), which followed Napoléon's defeat, Italy was once again divided among many different factions: Austria was given Lombardy and Venetia, and the Papal States were returned to the pope. Some duchies were put back into the hands of their hereditary rulers, and southern Italy and Sicily went to a Bourbon dynasty. One historic move, which eventually assisted in the unification of Italy, was the assignment of the former republic of Genoa to Sardinia (which at the time was governed by the House of Savoy).

Political unrest became a fact of Italian life, at least some of it encouraged by the rapid industrialization of the north and the almost total lack of industrialization in the Italian south. Despite those barriers, in 1861, thanks to the brilliant efforts of the patriots Camillo Cavour (1810–61) and Giuseppe Garibaldi (1807–82), the Kingdom of Italy was proclaimed and Victor Emmanuel (Vittorio Emanuele) II of the House of Savoy, king of Sardinia, became head of the new monarchy.

Although the hope, pushed by Europe's theocrats and some of its devout Catholics, of attaining one empire ruled by the pope and the church had long ago faded, there was still a fight, followed by generations of hard feelings, when the Papal

States—a strategically and historically important principality under the temporal jurisdiction of the pope—were confiscated by the new Kingdom of Italy.

The establishment of the kingdom, however, did not signal a complete unification of Italy, because the city of Rome was still under papal control and Venetia was still held by Austria. This was partially resolved in 1866, when Venetia joined the rest of Italy after the Seven Weeks' War between Austria and Prussia; in 1871 Rome became the capital of the newly formed country. The Vatican, however, did not yield its territory to the new order, despite guarantees of nonintervention proffered by the Italian government, and relations between the pope and the country of Italy remained rocky until 1929.

In that year, Mussolini—who had acceded to power in a Fascist coup in 1922—defined the divisions between the Italian government and the Vatican by signing a concordat that granted political and fiscal autonomy to Vatican City. It also made Roman Catholicism the official state religion of Italy; that designation was removed in 1978 through a revision of the concordat.

WORLD WAR II & THE AXIS   During the Spanish Civil War (1936–39), Mussolini's support of the Falangists, under Francisco Franco, helped encourage the formation of the "Axis" alliance between Italy and Nazi Germany. Despite its outdated military equipment, Italy added to the general horror of the era by invading Abyssinia (Ethiopia) in 1935, supposedly to protect Italian colonial interests there. In 1940 Italy invaded Greece through Albania, and in 1942 sent thousands of Italian troops to assist Hitler in his disastrous campaign along the Russian front. In 1943 Allied forces, under the command of U.S. Gen. George Patton and British Gen. Bernard Montgomery, landed in Sicily and quickly secured the island as they prepared to move north, toward Rome.

In the face of likely defeat and humiliation, Mussolini was overthrown by his own cabinet (Grand Council). The Allies made a separate deal with Italy's king, Victor Emmanuel III, who had more or less gracefully collaborated with the Fascists during the previous two decades, and who now shifted allegiances without too much visible fuss. A politically divided Italy watched as battalions of fanatical German Nazis released Mussolini from his Italian jail cell to establish the short-lived Republic of Salò, headquartered on the edge of Lake Garda, hoping for a groundswell of popular opinion in favor of Italian Fascism. Events quickly proved this nothing more than a futile dream.

In April 1945, with almost half a million Italians rising in a mass demonstration against him and the German war machine, Mussolini was captured by Italian partisans as he fled to Switzerland. With his mistress, Claretta Petacci, and several others of his intimates, he was shot and strung upside-down from the roof of a gasoline station in Milan.

POSTWAR ITALY   Disaffected with the monarchy and its identification with the fallen Fascist dictatorship, Italian voters in 1946 voted for the establishment of a republic. The major political party that emerged in the aftermath of World War II was the Christian Democratic party, a right-of-center group whose leader, Alcide De Gasperi (1881–1954), served as premier until 1953. The second-largest party was the Communist party, which, however, by the mid-1970s had abandoned its revolutionary program in favor of a democratic form of "Eurocommunism" (in 1991 the Communists even changed their name, to Democratic Party of the Left).

Although after the war Italy was stripped of all its overseas colonies, it quickly succeeded, in part because of U.S. aid under the Marshall Plan (1948–52), in rebuilding its economy, both agriculturally and industrially. By the 1960s, as a member of the European Community (founded in Rome in 1957), Italy had become one of the

The more I see of them the more struck I am with their having no sense of the ridiculous.
                        —Henry James, letter to Ms. Fanny Kemble, March 24, 1881

It is not impossible to govern Italians. It is merely useless.
                        —Benito Mussolini

leading industrialized nations of the world, prominent in the manufacture of automobiles and office equipment.

But the country continued to be plagued by economic inequities between the prosperous, industrialized north and the economically depressed south. It suffered an unprecedented flight of capital (frequently aided by Swiss banks only too willing to accept discreet deposits from wealthy Italians) and an increase in bankruptcies, inflation (almost 20% during much of the 1970s), and unemployment.

During the late 1970s and early 1980s, Italy was rocked by the rise of terrorism, instigated both by neo-Fascists and by left-wing intellectuals from the Socialist-controlled universities of the north. In the early 1990s Italians were stunned as many leading politicians were accused of wholesale corruption. As a result, a newly formed right-wing grouping, led by media magnate Silvio Berlusconi, swept to victory in general elections in 1994. Berlusconi became prime minister at the head of a coalition government.

In December of 1994, Berlusconi resigned as prime minister after the federalist Northern League party defected from his coalition and he lost his parliamentary majority. Treasury Minister Lamberto Dini, a nonpolitical banker with international financial credentials, was named to replace Berlusconi.

Dini signed on merely as a transitional player in Italy's topsy-turvy political game. His austere measures enacted to balance Italy's budget, including cuts in pensions and health care, were not popular among the mostly blue-collar Italian workers or the highly influential labor unions. Pending a predicted defeat in a no-confidence vote, Dini stepped down as prime minister. His resignation in January 1996 left beleaguered Italians shouting "*Basta!*" (enough). This latest shuffling in Italy's political deck prompted President Oscar Scalfaro to dissolve both Italian houses of parliament.

Once again the Italians were faced with forming a new government. The elections in April 1996 proved a shocker, not only for the defeated politicians, but for the victors as well. The center-left coalition known as the Olive Tree, led by Romano Prodi, swept both the Senate and the Chamber of Deputies. The Olive Tree, whose roots stem from the old Communist party, achieved victory by shifting toward the center and focusing their campaign on a strong platform protecting social benefits and supporting Italy's bid to become a solid member of the European Community.

4 Architecture 101: A Guide to What You'll See

Here's a brief chronological run-down of the architectural styles you're most likely to encounter on your tour through Italy.

The art and architecture in the centuries that followed the collapse of Rome became known as early medieval or **Romanesque.** In its many variations, it flourished between A.D. 1000 and 1200, although in isolated pockets away from Europe's commercial mainstreams it continued for several centuries.

Romanesque architecture (the term was unknown during the heyday of this style of building) split into three regional designs, known as the Lombard style, the Tuscan style, and the southern or Sicilian style. In Lombardy, whose center was Milan, the major innovation was the ribbed vault, which consisted of separate stones forming projecting ribs. The stone ceiling rested on these ribs. The best example remaining of this style is Sant'Ambrogio in Milan (A.D. 850, then rebuilt in 1140). The Tuscan style was strongly Byzantine and classic, as best represented by the complex of buildings in the heart of Pisa, including the celebrated Leaning Tower, the baptistery, the bell tower, and the cathedral. The southern style was influenced by the series of different rulers in Sicily, going from the Byzantines and Muslims to the Normans. Churches became very elaborate and colorful, as typified by the Cathedral of Monreale, still standing on a hill outside Palermo. Drawing upon many influences, it was constructed in 1171 when the Normans controlled Sicily.

The best examples of domestic **Gothic** architecture in Italy are found in Florence and Siena. One major example is the Palazzo Vecchio in the heart of Florence, designed by Arnolfo di Cambio in 1298. It was built fortress style with a square and slender watchtower. Another outstanding example of this style was the Palazzo Pubblico constructed in 1289 in the vast shell-shaped piazza in Siena. It's more feminine in style than the Florentine palazzo. Gothic cathedrals burst into "wedding cake" fantasies with the building of the Cathedral of Milan, which was launched in 1385, although it took a century to complete. It, along with the Cathedral of Seville in Spain, is the largest of medieval cathedrals—and the most splendid achievement. Built of white marble, it has a lacy effect with a generous use of flying buttresses.

Venice, of course, followed its own fantasy styles during this period, and remained more under the Byzantine influence than the Roman. One of its greatest achievements of this period was the romantic Palazzo Ducale, constructed, then reconstructed, between 1309 and 1442. This was the most monumental flowering of civic architecture during this period, and it's still standing, still overrun with visitors to this day. In all, however, the Gothic style swept France more than Italy.

The **Renaissance** (rebirth)—generally the period following the dark Middle Ages—flowered in Italy almost two centuries before it reached such countries as England. Rome, Venice, and Florence brought different interpretations to this new style, which was actually born in Florence, the city of the Medici family. An architect during the Renaissance was no longer just a builder, but might be a sculptor, a painter, or even a writer. Humanism and classicism prevailed as ideologies. The Middle Ages were dead and gone, and certainly not lamented.

The towering leader of Florentine architects of this period was the great Brunelleschi. He raised the dome over the Cathedral of Florence, beginning in 1420 and finishing in 1436. He died before the final lantern at the top was added. His towering dome still dominates the city of Florence today, and is a miracle of design. His other major works include the Pitti Palace in Florence, which remains the largest palace in Italy except for the Vatican. This building is bold, monumental, with an invaried repetition of arched windows.

Rome's greatest building achievement in the Renaissance was St. Peter's Basilica, of course, the largest church ever constructed. Its sheer massiveness overwhelms (about five times the area of a football field). Urbino-born Donato Bramante (1444–1514) was only the first of a series of architects who would create this monumental design. Regrettably, very little is left of Bramante's original concept. The decorative excess of this present building was not in Bramante's vision, for example. Even Michelangelo was an architect of St. Peter's, from 1547 to 1564. The artist designed and began the construction of the massive dome.

Glossary of Architectural Terms

Ambone   A pulpit, either serpentine or simple in form, erected in an Italian church.

Apse   The half-rounded extension behind the main altar of a church; Christian tradition dictates that it be placed at the eastern end of an Italian church, the side closest to Jerusalem.

Atrium   A courtyard, open to the sky, in an ancient Roman house; the term also applies to the courtyard nearest the entranceway of an early Christian church.

Baldacchino (also **ciborium**)   A columned stone canopy, usually placed above the altar of a church; spelled in English as baldachin or baldaquin.

Basilica   Any rectangular public building, usually divided into three aisles by rows of columns; in ancient Rome this architectural form was frequently used for places of public assembly and law courts; later, Roman Christians adapted the form for many of their early churches.

Caldarium   The steam room of a Roman bath.

Campanile   A bell tower, often detached, of a church.

Capital   The top of a column, often carved and usually categorized into one of three different orders: Doric, Ionic, or Corinthian.

Castrum   A carefully planned Roman military camp, whose rectangular form, straight streets, and systems of fortified gates quickly became standardized throughout the Roman Empire; modern cities that began as Roman camps and that still more or less maintain their original forms include Chester (England), Barcelona (Spain), and such Italian cities as Lucca, Aosta, Como, Brescia, Florence, and Ancona.

Cavea   The curved row of seats in a classical theater; the most prevalent shape was that of a semicircle.

Cella   The sanctuary, or most sacred interior section, of a Roman pagan temple.

Chancel   Section of a church containing the altar.

Cornice   The decorative flange that defines the uppermost part of a classical or neoclassical facade.

Cortile   Courtyard or cloisters ringed with a gallery of arches or lintels set atop columns.

Crypt   A church's main burial place, usually located below the choir.

Cupola   A dome.

Forum   The main square, and principal gathering place, of any Roman town, usually adorned with the city's most important temples and civic buildings.

Meanwhile, Venice stubbornly clung to Gothic features, which made its buildings of this period "feminine" as opposed to the bold and often severe masculinity of Florentine models. Balconies riddled Venetian facades, whereas in Florence no aristocrat wanted to give his enemies that much a chance to assassinate him. Doorways and capitals of this period were more delicate than anywhere else in the country.

Andrea di Pietro (or Palladio, as he's known to the world) became the towering architect of the High Renaissance, and left many buildings in his native Vicenza. The city outside Venice is still called "Città del Palladio." Although his designs were adopted around the world, especially in England and America, Vicenza remains the best place to view his villas. Palladio arrived in Vicenza in 1523 and worked there until his death in 1580. The **Palladian** style is characterized by its use of pilasters and

Duomo   Cathedral.

Grotesques   Carved and painted faces, deliberately ugly, used by everyone from the Etruscans to the architects of the Renaissance: They're especially amusing when set into fountains.

Hyypogeium   Subterranean burial chambers, usually of pre-Christian origins.

Loggia   Roofed balcony or gallery.

Lozenge   An elongated four-sided figure which, along with stripes, was one of the distinctive signs of the architecture of Pisa.

Narthex   The anteroom, or enclosed porch, of a Christian church.

Nave   The largest and longest section of a church, usually devoted to sheltering and/or seating worshippers, and often divided by aisles.

Pietra Dura   Richly ornate assemblage of semiprecious stones mounted on a flat decorative surface, perfected during the 1600s in Florence.

Pieve   A parish church.

Portico   A porch, usually crafted from wood or stone.

Pulvin   A four-sided stone that serves as a substitute for the capital of a column, often decoratively carved, sometimes into biblical scenes.

Putti   Plaster cherubs whose chubby forms often decorate the interiors of baroque chapels and churches.

Stucco   Colored plaster composed of sand, powdered marble, water, and lime, either molded into statuary or applied in a thin, concretelike layer to the exterior of a building.

Telamone   Structural column carved into a standing male form; female versions are called *caryatids.*

Thermae   Roman baths.

Transenna   Stone (usually marble) screen separating the altar area from the rest of an early Christian church.

Travertine   Known as the stone from which ancient and Renaissance Rome was built; it's noted for its hardness, light coloring, and tendency to be pitted or flecked with black.

Tympanum   The half-rounded space above the portal of a church, whose semi-circular space usually showcases a sculpture.

a composite structure on a gigantic scale. The so-called attic in his design was usually surmounted by statues. His most acclaimed building remains the Villa Rotonda in Vicenza, a cube with a center circular hall topped by a dome.

In the early 17th century and into the 18th century the **baroque** (meaning absurd or irregular) movement swept Europe, including Italy. The development of the baroque movement was linked to the much-needed reforms and restructuring of the Catholic Church that followed the upheavals of the Protestant Reformation. Many great Italian churches and *palazzi* were constructed during this period.

The great name from this period was Giovanni Lorenzo Bernini (1598–1680) whose chief work—which you can see today, of course—is the piazza of Rome's St. Peter's Basilica. The finishing of the basilica itself was the greatest architectural accomplishment of the early baroque period. Along with Bernini, Francesco Borromini (1559–1667) is the second great architect of the age. His Church of Sant'Agnese in Rome reveals his mastery, with curved indentations on its facade. In Venice, the leading exponent of the baroque style was Baldassare Longhena (1598–1682), whose major work remains the Church of Santa Maria della Salute, with its waterside piazza at the head of the Grand Canal.

As is obvious to any visitor, the 19th and 20th centuries did not yield any grand architectural achievements in Italy. The later baroque and flamboyant excesses of their more recent past were dismissed as "gay excesses" by 19th century architects. Italy has produced far more famous painters than architects in the last two centuries.

The United States, and to a degree France, advanced far more in modern architecture than did Italy. A great deal of this had to do with the long and ill-fated reign of Mussolini, who was more intent on producing "pompous" neoclassical buildings than in achieving breakthroughs in modern architectural design. Many of the buildings constructed during his dictatorship have been called "Fascist" and uninspired architecture.

If Italy produced any great modern architect in the 20th century, it was Pier Luigi Nervi, born in 1891 in Milan. He was innovative, creating new buildings in daring styles and shapes best represented by Rome's Palazzo della Sport, designed for the 1960 Olympics. Nervi's buildings are both poetic and practical. For the sports palace he made a bold pattern of concrete thrusts balanced with counterthrusts on the inside. He went on to build a stadium at Florence, an exhibition hall at Turin, and a smaller sports arena in Rome, the Palazzetto, which is still called "the world's most beautiful sports arena."

Italian architects who followed in Nervi's footsteps—Carlo Mollino, Franco Albini, and Riccardo Morandi—helped bring Italy into the modern world, at least architecturally. But where giants of architecture once trod, men and women with visions less grand rule building in Italy today. Since the 1950s the cities of Italy, especially the coastal areas, have been desecrated by a series of functional, ugly buildings that mar the architectural landscape of a country that doesn't even have a Prince Charles to denounce the wreckage.

5 Enjoying Italy's Artistic Treasures

There's an amazing richness of Italian art—there's so much, in fact, that it's often stuck away in dark corners of unlighted churches. In fact, it's a good idea to carry a pocketful of small coins to drop in boxes to turn on the lights in some churches. Italy has so much art that some paintings—world masterpieces—would be the focal point of major museums. But in art-rich Italy these works of art are often tucked away in obscure rooms—small salons, really—of rarely visited museums. There's too much of a good thing and not enough room to display the bounty, much less maintain the art and protect it from thieves.

How did it all begin?

Although not much Etruscan architecture remains, Etruscan art survives in the form of a handful of murals discovered in tombs and more numerous examples of finely sculpted sarcophagi, many of which rest today in Italian museums. Several of the most frequently seen of these tombs can be visited on day trips from Rome. The best collection of sarcophagi is at the National Museum of the Villa Giulia in Rome.

As Rome asserted its own identity and overpowered its Etruscan masters, it borrowed heavily from themes already established by Etruscan artists and architects. In time, however, the Romans discovered Greek art, fell in love with that country's statuary, and looted much of it.

Eventually, as Rome continued to develop its empire, its artisans began to turn out an exact, realistic portrait sculpture, which differed distinctly from the more idealized forms of Greek sculpture. Rome was preoccupied with sculpted images—in fact, sculptors made "bodies" en masse and later fitted a particular head on the sculpture upon the demand of a Roman citizen. Most **Roman** painting that survives is in the form of murals in the fresco technique, and most of these were uncovered when Pompeii and Herculaneum were dug up. Basically, Roman art continued the Hellenistic tradition. Rome's greatest artistic expression was in architecture, not in art such as painting.

The aesthetic and engineering concepts of the Roman Empire eventually evolved into **early Christian** and **Byzantine** art. More concerned with moral and spiritual values than with the physical beauty of the human form or the celebration of political grandeur, early Christian artists turned to the supernatural and spiritual world for their inspiration. Basilicas and churches were lavishly decorated with mosaics and colored marble, whereas painting depicted the earthly suffering (and heavenly rewards) of martyrs and saints.

Supported by monasteries or churches, **Romanesque** art, which flourished between A.D. 1000 and 1200, was almost wholly concerned with ecclesiastical subjects, often with the intention of educating the worshippers who studied it. Biblical parables were carved in stone or painted into frescoes, often useful teaching aids for a church eager to spread its messages.

As the appeal of the Romanesque faded, the **Gothic** or **late-medieval** style encouraged a vast increase in both the quantities and preconceptions of Italian art. The Italians were inspired by 14th-century French art. French art at the time had an affected sentiment—the pose was everything—and this gradually made itself known in Italian works.

Prior to the Renaissance, Italy's greatest sculptor was Nicola Pisano, who lived from 1206 to 1278 and whose major work was the pulpit in the baptistery in Pisa.

With the arrival of Cimabue, the great age of Italian art was about to dawn. Facts about this towering artist aren't well documented, but he worked, mainly in Tuscany, from 1270 to 1300. He painted a number of frescoes for the upper and lower churches of the Sacred Convent of San Francesco at Assisi, but they're in bad condition, his colors obscured over the ages. Cimabue, breaking with the rigidity of Byzantine art, revealed the spirit of his subject. This trail-blazing artist was the harbinger of the greatest art movement in the history of the world: the Italian Renaissance.

He would be followed by Masaccio (1401–28), who also helped usher in the new era in art with his *Expulsion from the Garden* frescoes from the Brancacci Chapel in Florence.

The **Italian Renaissance** was born in Florence during the 15th century, where members of the powerful Medici family emerged as some of the greatest art patrons in history. The Renaissance began with great artistic events, such as Ghiberti defeating Brunelleschi in a contest to design bronze doors for the baptistery of the Cathedral of Florence. (The original doors have been removed to the Duomo Museum for safekeeping and replaced by copies.)

The Renaissance gave birth to artists who excelled in both painting and sculpture. Emerging on the scene was Jacopo della Quercia (1375–1438), who brought vitality and a robust quality to sculpture, as exemplified by his major work, *Fonte Gaia,* in the Duomo Museum at Siena. His sculpture brought in the new quality of emotion, which would be seen to greater effect later in the works of Michelangelo.

Donatello (1386–1466) emerged as the first great name in Renaissance sculpture, and his *David* became the first important free-standing nude done in Europe since the days of the Romans. His most famous equestrian statue, *Gattamelata,* done in 1444, stands in the piazza of the Church of Sant'Antonio in Padua.

The great Michelangelo continued to think of himself as a sculptor, although his greatness was also as an architect and painter. His early triumph came with a *Pietà,* begun at the age of only 23 and now in St. Peter's in Rome.

Working virtually day and night for 2 years, from 1501 to 1503, Michelangelo created the idealized man, his magnificent *David* (now on display in Florence at the Accademia), a statue of titanic power and grace. His other legacies include the Medici tombs, executed between 1521 and 1534 (next door to the Church of San Lorenzo in Florence). The figures of *Night* and *Day* are the best known.

The towering Renaissance painter, of course, was Leonardo da Vinci (1452–1519), the very epitome of a Renaissance man. Naturalist, anatomist, engineer, he even conceived of the practicability of mechanical flight. His *Mona Lisa* (now in the Louvre in Paris) is the most famous painting in the world, and his wall painting *The Last Supper* (now in the process of being restored at the Monastery of Santa Maria delle Grazie in Milan) is his most impressive.

Italy had so many great artists during this period that it's mind-boggling, considering that entire centuries have gone by without the emergence of even one great artist. Chief among the lesser lights was Raphael (1483–1520). He died early, but not before creating lasting works of art, including his masterpiece, *Madonna del Granduca,* in the Pitti Palace in Florence. He painted frescoes in the apartments of Pope Julius II in the Vatican while Michelangelo was painting (very reluctantly) his immortal Sistine Chapel nearby.

The Venetian school was different from the Florentine. In Venice color was crucial, whereas in Florence it was only a decorative note, as most Renaissance artists there were concerned with formal relationships and space through the laws of perspective.

Jacopo Bellini (ca. 1400–70) was the founder of the most celebrated family of artists from the Venetian school. Giovanni Bellini (c. 1430–1516) was the greatest master of Venetian painting in the 1400s. Depicting mankind's spiritual harmony with nature, he created rich, serene landscapes.

Giorgione (1477–1510) surpassed the Bellini family in his achievements, and created works of mystical charm. His *La Tempesta,* for example, was both brooding and tranquil. It's a painting of haunting beauty, defying interpretation. This and other paintings by Giorgione have a hypnotic beauty.

The period known as the **High Renaissance** was said to last for only about 25 years, beginning in the early 16th century. This period in art saw more and more emphasis on rich color and subtle variations within forms. Works of great technical mastery emerged. Despite the subtle differences between the stages of the Renaissance, Italy remained Europe's artistic leader for nearly 200 years.

The transitional period between the Renaissance and the baroque came to be called **Mannerism.** Out of this period emerged such great artists as Tintoretto, whose major work was the cycle of frescoes for the Scuola di San Rocco in Venice (it took 23 years to finish); Verona-born Paolo Veronese; and the most sensitive, and some critics say the finest, of the Mannerists, Parmigianino.

On the trail of Mannerism, the **baroque** movement swept Italy in the early 1600s and lasted until well into the 1700s. Great artists emerged, including Bernini, who became renowned both as a sculptor and as a painter. The two painters who best represented the movement were Carracci, who decorated the Roman palace of Cardinal Farnese, and Caravaggio, one of the pioneers of baroque painting. The even more flamboyant **rococo** grew out of the baroque style.

In the 19th century the great light had gone out of art in Italy. (The beacon was picked up instead by France.) **Neoclassicism**—a return to the aesthetic ideals of ancient Greece and Rome, whose ideals of patriotism were resonant with the growing sense of pan-Italian patriotism—swept through almost every aspect of the Italian arts. Antonio Canova (1757–1822) became the most famous of the neoclassical sculptors. But neoclassicism never attained the grandeur in Italy that it did in France.

The 20th century witnessed the birth of several major Italian artists whose works once again captured the imagination of the world. De Chirico and Modigliani (the latter's greatest contribution lay in a new concept of portraiture) were only two among many. The Bolognese painter of bottles and jugs, Morandi, also became known around the world. The greatest Italian sculptor of the 20th century was Medardo Rosso, who died in 1928.

Since then Italy has been a European leader in sophisticated and witty interpretations of buildings, paintings, fashion, industrial design, and decor. Many modern Italian artists have infused Italian flair into the lines of workaday and utilitarian objects whose quality, humor, and usefulness have become legendary.

6 The Italians

La famiglia still looms large in Italian life, with *mamma mia* at gravity center. That sense of family also extends to distant cousins—even those who left decades ago for Boston or wherever. "They make some money," one old peasant woman in Cefalù said, "then they come back home to show off their fancy clothes and their fancy rented cars. They've got more money than us, but they also buy the sauce for their pasta in jars, and I make my own with vegetables and herbs from my own garden. So, who's got the better life?"

Whether *la famiglia* always stands by you is another matter, but in theory family members are supposed to lend you money when you're about to be made homeless, they're supposed to nurse you back to health when you're sick, and they're supposed to get you a job in the family business should you need one. They're also supposed to provide a roof over your head even if that means allowing you to sleep for months at a time in the living room. After all, Italians don't have a word for privacy.

In truth, although the family remains strong in the Italy of the 1990s, it has also eroded greatly. In spite of the teachings of the Catholic Church and an arch-conservative pope not known for his tolerance of alternative lifestyles, divorce and abortion are commonplace in Italy. That holds true even for some families to which either divorce or abortion only a decade or so ago would have been considered an abomination.

Many old people grew up in a culture that encouraged them to have lots of children who presumably would provide for them in their old age. Many of those elderly now live alone and poor, waiting for the son who went off to Rome to come home for a visit. Often they wait in vain.

The pivotal axis in the Italian family remains mother and son, a virtual cult known as *mammismo*. There is an old joke in Italy that goes: "Jesus Christ—an Italian, of course—was raised at home for 30 or so years. He believed that his mamma was a virgin and he was the son of God." Although incredibly strict with her daughters, that mamma could be overly indulgent with her son. She could even forgive him for his roving eye and philandering, as she once had to forgive papa. Sometimes, when mamma would eventually emerge from that eternal kitchen, she might give her daughter-in-law some advice. Inevitably that would be to overlook the latest sexual indiscretion of her son. "It's just what men do," she'd advise. Eventually, she would assure the daughter-in-law, her husband would come back home to his wife, family, and most definitely his mamma. If for no other reason because mamma cooked better than the wife. Mammas always did and they always will, at least in the view of some Italian men.

In spite of all the talk in the cafe about his sexual exploits, the Italian male often remains a mamma's boy throughout his life. Mamma keeps the family together, regardless of how extended it may be and how unworthy the in-laws are.

In reality, it's almost impossible to provide a national stereotype for the Italians, as they're so widely diverse. Those in the Alto Adige might fit in more comfortably in Germany or Austria. They certainly don't like being ruled from Rome, a city they hold—with lots of justification—in great mistrust. The blue-eyed Sicilians of Norman descent in Palermo call themselves Sicilians, never Italians, as if Sicily were its own separate nation—which perhaps it is. The arrogant Florentine, speaking a perfect Tuscan dialect in this land of Dante, can with some justification appear snobbish and condescending to the wildly gesticulating and semiarticulate countryman in the south. The Roman often has a certain sharpness and abrasiveness in contrast to the more courtly manners of the Venetian. The Piedmontese are sometimes more comfortable speaking French than Italian.

If Italy can be discussed as a single nation (and there are those who say after all these years that it still can't be viewed that way), there's one instinct that stands out above all others—and that is the instinct for survival. Sharpened over the ages, that instinct has gotten the Italians through hordes of foreign invasions and political upheavals. Providing they're not discussing *la famiglia,* Italians are notorious for shifting loyalties. As an old bar owner in Naples once told us: "For me, the war was no problem. When the Germans were here, I displayed the swastika and a portrait of Hitler. About ten minutes before the first Americans arrived, those were down and up went the Stars and Stripes." Could you imagine a German changing political sides as rapidly? Certainly not overnight.

Sometimes the sheer inefficiency of Italians will drive you mad, especially if you make an appointment with someone for 2:30pm and the party shows up at 4 o'clock. Yet there's something to admire in the free spirit of all that. In Italy, we were once told, always invite people an hour or so earlier than when you actually want them to show up.

Italy today has been called a soap opera. Beset with scandal, corruption, and political chaos at every turn, Italy is currently in transition. But it has always been in transition. Some elements are new and different. A feminist movement, for example, is sweeping across the north. We've actually seen Italian women, not necessarily those born and bred in a convent, whistle at men in those tight-fitting Italian pants, instead of the other way around. That would have been unthinkable in Mussolini's day. This Fascist dictator known for his flamboyant braggadocio once raped a woman journalist in his presidential office when he didn't like the question she put to him.

A lot of people believed in Mussolini. Even today portraits of *Il Duce* hang in many an Italian home, especially low-cost slums around Rome and in the south. Few Italians get passionate over their politicians anymore, although traditionally the nation votes in larger turnouts on election day than any other country of Europe. "We must be realistic, however," said one political commentator, "and we must not lose our sense of humor. How could it be otherwise when half of the people you voted for only a year ago are either in jail, under investigation, on trial, or hiding out in Tunisia?"

As one voter said, "When I go into a voting booth, I know both of the leading candidates are already corrupt. Political power will only make them more so. I vote for the candidate I perceive to be less corrupt."

Ever since the days of Machiavelli, there has existed something known as *clientelismo,* a "kickback," so to speak. In other words, "I'll vote you into power where you might be able to turn the office into profit for yourself if you perhaps provide my son with a job, especially a bureaucratic one in government."

This is not to suggest that the old system of graft and corruption that has characterized Italian politics since the postwar era isn't changing. In the 1990s there were just too many government scandals, reaching up to the highest levels. Misappropriation of billions of Italian lire seemed among the least serious of offenses. Murder might top the list. For the first time ever, a party called La Rete, or "the network," organized in the south of Italy to campaign against the political corruption of the Mafia. That would have been unthinkable a few years ago. Or the organizers of La Rete would have ended up dead.

One cynical political observer noted, "These current political upheavals about getting rid of corruption in government will die down. As they are inclined to do, Italians will grow bored with the process. As we approach the millennium, Italians will return to the old way of doing politics Italian style—that is, greed, corruption, bribery, blackmail, and, well, *clientelismo.*"

A visitor to today's Italy might never encounter Italian politics at any level, and might even be unaware of who's running the government. It's the people of Italy, certainly not their government, that are likely to impress the visitor. That passion for sports, especially soccer, is unlikely to be shared by a visitor from America. But the Italian love of cafe life can be infectious.

Exposure to the people of Italy, those same people who gave us Leonardo da Vinci and Michelangelo, will be reason enough to go. If for no other reason, you can share their great style for life and fashion and perhaps some of their spontaneity will rub off.

There's no better place to observe the Italian in action than in the beloved institution of the cafe. It's here that the Italian-style *joie de vivre* is best experienced. Many Italians live in overcrowded apartments, and the cafe is the only place at which to meet and entertain their friends. The cafe becomes like an extended living room of Italian life.

Italians use the cafe as a combination club/tavern/snack bar, and certainly as a rendezvous point. There are spots where you can read your newspaper, magazine, or guidebook; meet a friend or make a new one; do your homework; write your memoirs; order a Cinzano; eat a hard-boiled egg; pick up a stranger; and even drink yourself into oblivion on fine Italian wine, if that's your desire. Above all, cafes are for people-watching.

In Italy, it's always back to the people who make up this country, perhaps the single most fascinating one on earth. Italians will tell you that their country is the most fascinating one without qualification.

CULTURE   No other country of Europe—not even France—has the rich cultural history of Italy. The art of Italy is reason enough to visit. It includes not only what remains from the Etruscan days, but also a smattering of Byzantium, especially in the famous mosaics of Ravenna, which date mainly from the 5th and 6th centuries. All of Italy is a treasure trove of art, none finer than that produced in the *Quattrocento* (15th century). This era gave the world such great names as Brunelleschi, Donatello, and Luca della Robbia, who would be followed by even greater names in the

Cinquecento (16th century), including da Vinci and Michelangelo, along with Raphael and a host of others, ranging from Tintoretto to Veronese.

Italy is not all art and architecture, though. Italians for centuries have firmly established themselves in literature as well. In the days of Rome's glory—shortly before and after the birth of Christ—mighty men of letters included Cicero, Julius Caesar, Virgil, Horace, Ovid, and Livy. When the people's thoughts turned heavenward, which was inevitable when the Christian faith became accepted by the majority of Romans and other Italians, Christian Latin literature became the order of the day. Such writers as St. Augustine, St. Ambrose, and St. Jerome gained repute for their writings and are remembered as among the few voices heard during the Dark Ages.

Arguably the greatest period in Italian literature was ushered in during the 14th century, with world-acclaimed works that made the Tuscan dialect the literary language of Italy. Immortals such as Dante, Petrarch, and Boccaccio flourished in this era. *The Divine Comedy* by Dante is the first masterpiece of the then-modern national language. Petrarch is hailed as the forerunner of humanism, and scholars claim that Boccaccio, best known for the *Decameron,* did for Italian prose what Dante did for its poetry.

Italy has for centuries been known for its music, especially opera. Hearing opera in Italy is another reason to go. Verdi, Puccini, Rossini, Monteverdi, and Vivaldi are still played today in the famous opera houses and concert halls of Italy, including La Scala in Milan. Italy not only gave the world the music but the singers as well—notably Luciano Pavarotti, Renata Tebaldi, Maria Callas, and the great Caruso.

Culturally, Italy has continued to forge ahead as new fields opened. In the 20th century it has made its greatest international artistic contribution in cinema. Great directors to emerge in the 20th century include Fellini, forever immortalized by his 1961 *La Dolce Vita;* Antonioni, who made his debut in 1959 with *L'Avventura;* and Visconti, known for such films as *The Leopard* (1963).

MUSIC   Although the ultimate expression of Italian musicality would not reveal itself until the operatic tradition of the 18th and 19th centuries, music has always been a part of Italian life.

Late in the 900s, a Benedictine monk from Arezzo named Guido Monaco invented a musical scale that was used in monasteries for the notation of single-melody, unharmonized religious chanting known as Gregorian chants.

Many of these medieval traditions were reformed by Palestrina during the 1500s, but a truly idiosyncratic version of Italian music only began to be defined in the late 1600s. At that time Corelli (1653–1713) originated a musical form known as the *concerto grosso* and founded a particular and highly colorful style of violin playing. Scarlatti (1660–1725) refined thematic development of musical scores, popularized the concept of chromatic harmonies, and helped to define the makeup of the operatic orchestra. A few generations later, Boccherini (1743–1805) contributed greatly to sophisticated applications of the chamber orchestra, defining appropriate musical contexts for string quartets at some of the most influential gatherings of Europe.

Especially important was Vivaldi (1678–1741), the Venice-born composer (and ordained priest) who was one of the most influential European composers of his day. An innovator in form and orchestration (and composer of more than 700 musical works), he developed techniques that greatly influenced the compositions of Bach.

As mentioned earlier, however, most musicologists best remember Italy for its opera. Italy and opera are linked by marriage, and, in fact, many visitors to Italy consider it one of the country's prime tourist attractions. (The opera season in Italy begins in early December and continues through mid-April.)

Jacopo Peri's *Dafne* (first performed in 1597, inspired by the recitative style of ancient Greek dramas and commissioned by the Medicis) is now regarded as the world's first opera. Claudio Monteverdi (1567–1643), however, is viewed as the father of modern opera. Developing new styles of operatic oratorios, his masterpiece was *L'Incoronazione di Poppea* (1642). From its origins in Florence, opera moved to Venice before catching on, around 1650, with the audiences of Naples. Even Vivaldi, although best remembered for his orchestral works, composed 43 different operas, the most famous of which is *Armida al campo d'Egitto* (1718).

From this rich musical tradition arose the *bel canto* (beautiful singing) method of the 18th and early 19th centuries. The movement's most famous adherent was Vincenzo Bellini (1801–35), whose masterpiece, *Norma* (composed just 4 years before his early death), is a *tour de force* of the melodic line, and with dozens of famous and challenging arias for coloratura soprano. Opera, particularly its Neapolitan versions, spread around the world. Bellini was followed in the *bel canto* tradition by Gioacchino Rossini (1792–1868). He moved to Paris in 1823 and remained there for most of the rest of his life. His operas retain the Italian-inspired opera buffa comedic tradition (he's the last of the masters of that particular form) as well as a series of brilliant crescendos that express great emotional power. Rossini is best known for his sparkling and witty *The Barber of Seville*.

Romantic opera also flowered, particularly in the works of Donizetti, best known for his *Lucia di Lammermoor,* which many years later brought Joan Sutherland fame at New York's Metropolitan Opera.

It was Giuseppe Verdi (1813–1901) who became the greatest Italian operatic composer, credited (with Richard Wagner) with developing opera into a fully integrated art that combined many different disciplines into a coherent whole. In all, Verdi produced 26 operas, many of which are widely performed today, including *Il Trovatore, La Traviata, Rigoletto, Un Ballo in Maschera,* and *Aïda.*

Verdi's musical heir was Giacomo Puccini (1858–1924), who trained in what had become the operatic headquarters of Italy (Milan). Greatly influenced by Wagner, his music was melodious and romantic, revolving around plots based on tragic love themes. Set in deliberately exotic settings, his most popular operas included *Madama Butterfly, La Bohème, Tosca,* and the incomplete *Turandot* (completed after Puccini's death by his musical disciple, Franco Alfano).

Enrico Caruso (1873–1921), one of the most famous operatic tenors of all time, based his career on his interpretations of Puccini operas, performing some of them for the first time in concert halls from Buenos Aires to San Francisco. Since Verdi and Puccini, however, no Italian composer has entered this exclusive pantheon of the musical greats.

The Italian passion for opera continues. The country remains the supreme place to hear opera, and opera stars from abroad consider an Italian opera-going audience the toughest in the world to win over.

Despite its potency and influence on formal musical compositions around the world, none of the above-mentioned composers or works gives credit to the richness and diversity of Italian popular song. In the early 1900s Italy had one of the wealthiest traditions of folk music in the world, with strongly defined differences among the country's various districts. (Naples, in particular, produced such globally popular songs as "O Sole Mio" and "Funiculè Funiculà.")

The effect of television, radio, and cultural inroads from the rest of the world has obliterated at least some of these musical traditions, although musical output in one form or another is still one of Italy's greatest exports to the world. (You're far more likely to hear someone break into spontaneous song in Italy than in almost any other

---

A Star Is Born

She's young, she's beautiful, and the quality of Cecilia Bartoli's mezzo-soprano voice (which *Newsweek* has referred to as "a rich, dark miracle of expressiveness") has thrilled audiences on at least three continents. Rich with sounds that portray both an ingenue and a sophisticated woman of the world, it is perfectly suited, according to opera directors, for roles by Rossini and Mozart. Scholars call her a "coloratura mezzo"; audiences refer to her as sensational, with a voice that winds its way through a libretto rather than crushing the nuances of the orchestra like a bulldozer.

The great publicity she's earned comes at a time when audiences and impresarios are fed up with the histrionic public behavior of other opera stars. Reared in Rome, she used to sing around her family's apartment ("very loud"), and trained first in flamenco dancing, then in piano and voice. At least part of the credit for her discovery lies with Daniel Barenboim, musical director of the Chicago Symphony Orchestra, and the late Herbert von Karajan.

Today, Ms. Bartoli, after Pavarotti, is the most famous opera star in Italy. (The wizards who manage the train that navigates through the Channel Tunnel recently named one of their locomotives the *Cecilia Bartoli* in her honor.)

Where can you find Italy's newest diva in your musical tour of the peninsula? Probably not at La Scala, and probably not to an excessive degree in Italy at all. In her words, "I don't sing much at La Scala, because it's Verdi, Verdi, Puccini, and Verdi, and I don't do that." (Her coaches say that she doesn't have the vocal projection for those roles.) But to even her own surprise, and despite the fact that her greatest successes have been outside Italy, the Italians are suddenly referring to her with a territorial pride as *la nostra Bartoli*.

---

country in Europe.) In the 1950s and early 1960s, Ornella Vanoni and Gino Paoli, Domenico Modugno (*Volaré*), Mina, and Peppino di Capri provided much of the music for the sybaritic but fleeting moment known ever after as *La Dolce Vita*. Italy seemed carefree, stylish, and romantic as it enjoyed an economic boom and the devoted patronage of the world's most beautiful people. During this era there developed a greater consciousness of what such singers as Frank Sinatra and Peggy Lee were doing musically in America, and an increased awareness of musical trends in both the United States and Britain.

Today, jazz, rock, blues, folk music, and (to a lesser degree) heavy metal flourish in Italy in patterns that frequently parallel similar developments in the United States and the rest of Europe. But Italy, which has always appreciated showmanship, manages to infuse the barrage of outside influences with its own particular expression of style and wit.

LANGUAGE   Italian, of course, is the official language, and it's spoken all over the country, with many regional dialects. The purest form of Italian is spoken in Tuscany. Italian is more directly derived from Latin than many of the other romance languages, which also include French, Spanish, Portuguese, and Romanian.

In the 14th century the dialect of Tuscany became the literary language of Italy. Dante did more than anyone else to promulgate the language, although he was aided by such other Tuscan writers as Petrarch and Boccaccio.

Linguists consider Italian the most "musical" and mellifluous language in the West. In fact, it has always been a puzzle why Casanova chose to write his racy memoirs in French instead of Italian, as he was born in Venice. Some critics have suggested that the memoirs would have had even more of an effect had they been written in Italian.

The Italian language easily lent itself to librettos and operas. Many English-speaking people have to draw on Italian words, especially musical terms, such as *basso profundo,* to describe various items. *Prima donna, la dolce vita* (aided in part by the Fellini film), and *inamorata* are just a few Italian words widely used around the world.

The language is a phonetic one. That means that, unlike many languages, including English, you pronounce a word the way it's written. It has been said that if an Italian sentence sounds "off key," it's because the grammar is incorrect.

The Italian alphabet is not as extensive as the one in English; it doesn't use the letters *J, K, W, X,* and *Y.*

Since the coming of television—mainly in the 1950s—more and more Italians speak the language similarly. Even in World War II many Italian soldiers couldn't understand each other, as some men spoke only in dialect.

A lot of so-called Americanisms have now infiltrated the Italian language, largely because of the success of U.S.–made films in Italy. The films also did much to popularize a Sicilian word now known around the world: *Mafia.* Although it evokes a menacing international crime organization, some linguists claim that it means "I'll beat you so hard you'll dance with pain."

SOCCER   In Italy, a sportsperson is anyone who enjoys watching sports, and not necessarily playing them, and practically no other nation throws itself so wholeheartedly into occasionally fanatical allegiance to favorite *calcio* (soccer) teams. Originally imported from England, soccer first came to Italy in 1898, when about a hundred spectators on a ragged field near Turin came to blows over the much-disputed outcome of the country's first match. Today the sport attracts millions of Italian fans, and is taken so seriously that heart attacks by spectators (both in stadiums and in front of television sets), major riots that have often led to multiple deaths, and endless traffic jams and car accidents have occurred because of it.

At least part of the popularity of soccer was encouraged by Mussolini and the Fascists, who used it to increase the patriotic feelings of Italians, especially by stressing Italy's sports victories over other nations. Today, in a game that seems to renew its modernity with every match, intense competition (and staggeringly large betting pools) accompany matches between Italian villages, Italian cities, and Italian districts. Many famous Italian architects have based their reputations on their designs for sports stadiums. On Sunday afternoon in Italy (the traditional time for the beginning of a match is 2:30pm), all traffic seems to lead in or out of stadium parking lots, all televisions seem to be tuned in to the televised match, and even the most outwardly staid citizens become enmeshed in what has been defined as a regularly scheduled manifestation of national hysteria.

7 Italian Cuisine

Italians are among the world's greatest cooks. Just ask any one of them. Despite the unification of Italy, regional tradition still dominates the various kitchens, ranging from Rome to Lombardy, from the Valle d'Aosta to Sicily. "Italian food" perhaps has little meaning unless it's more clearly defined as Neapolitan, Roman, Sardinian, Sicilian, Venetian, Piedmontese, Tuscan, or whatever. Each region has a flavor and a taste of its own, as well as a detailed repertoire of local dishes.

Whereas in some countries to the north food was consumed as a means of staying alive, the cuisine in Italy has always been a paramount reason to live. This was true from the earliest days. Even the Etruscans—to judge from the lifelike scenes of banquets in their tombs—loved food and took delight in enjoying it. The Romans became famous for their never-ending banquets and for their love of exotic treats such as flamingo tongues.

Although culinary styles vary, Italy abounds in *trattorie* specializing in local dishes—some a delight for carnivores, such as the renowned *bistecca alla fiorentina,* which is cut from flavorful Chianina beef, then charcoal-grilled and served with a fruity olive oil. Other dishes, especially those found at the antipasti buffet, would appeal to every vegetarian's heart: peppers, greens, onions, pastas, beans, tomatoes, and fennel.

Many North American visitors erroneously think of Italian cuisine as limited. Of course, everybody has heard of minestrone, spaghetti, chicken cacciatore, and spumoni. But Italian chefs hardly confine themselves to such a limited repertoire. Incidentally, except in the south, Italians don't use as much garlic in their food as many foreigners seem to believe. Most Italian dishes, especially those in the north, are butter based. Spaghetti and meatballs, by the way, is not an Italian dish, although certain restaurants throughout the country have taken to serving it "for homesick Americans."

THE CUISINE

Rome might be the best place to introduce yourself to Italian cuisine, as it has specialty restaurants that represent all the culinary centers of the country, such as Bologna and Genoa. Throughout your Roman holiday, you'll encounter such savory viands as *zuppa di pesce* (a soup or stew of various fish, cooked in white wine and flavored with herbs), *cannelloni* (tube-shaped pasta baked with any number of stuffings), *riso col gamberi* (rice with shrimp, peas, and mushrooms, flavored with white wine and garlic), *scampi alla griglia* (grilled prawns, one of the best-tasting, albeit expensive, dishes in the city), *quaglie col risotto e tartufi* (quail with rice and truffles), *lepre alla cacciatore* (hare flavored with tomato sauce and herbs), *zabaglione* (a cream made with sugar, egg yolks, and marsala), *gnocchi alla romana* (potato-flour dumplings with a sauce made with meat and covered with grated cheese), *abbacchio* (baby spring lamb, often roasted over an open fire), *saltimbocca alla romana* (literally "jump-in-your-mouth"—thin slices of veal with sage, ham, and cheese), *fritto alla romana* (a mixed fry that's likely to include everything from brains to artichokes), *carciofi alla romana* (tender artichokes cooked with such herbs as mint and garlic, and flavored with white wine), *fettuccine all'uovo* (egg noodles served with butter and cheese), *zuppa di cozze* (a hearty bowl of mussels cooked in broth), *fritto di scampi e calamaretti* (baby squid and prawns, fast-fried), *fragoline* (wild strawberries, in this case from the Alban Hills), and *finocchio* (fennel, a celerylike raw vegetable with the flavor of anisette, often eaten as a dessert or in a salad).

From Rome, it's on to **Florence** and **Siena,** where you'll encounter the hearty, rich cuisine of the Tuscan hills (for comments on that cuisine, refer to the introduction to the dining section of Chapter 6).

The next major city to visit is **Venice,** where the cookery is typical of the Venetia district. It has been called "tasty, straightforward, and homely" by one long-ago food critic, and we concur. One of the most typical dishes is *fegato alla veneziana* (liver and onions), as well as *risi e bisi* (rice and fresh peas). Seafood figures heavily in the Venetian diet, and grilled fish is often served with the bitter red radicchio, a lettuce that comes from Treviso.

In **Lombardy,** of which Milan is the center, the cookery is more refined and tasty, in our opinion. No dish here is more famous than *cotoletta alla milanese* (cutlets of tender veal, dipped in egg and breadcrumbs, and fried in olive oil until they're a golden brown)—the Viennese called it Wiener schnitzel. *Osso buco* is the other great dish of Lombardy; this is cooked with the shinbone of veal in a ragoût sauce and served on a bed of rice and peas. *Risotto alla milanese* is also a classic Lombard dish. This is rice that can be dressed in almost any way, depending on the chef's imagination. It's often flavored with saffron and butter, to which chicken giblets have been added. It's always served, seemingly, with heaps of Parmesan cheese. *Polenta,* a cornmeal mush that's "more than mush," is the staff of life in some parts of northeastern Italy and is eaten in lieu of pasta.

The cooking in the **Piedmont,** of which Turin is the capital, and the Aosta Valley is different from that in the rest of Italy. Its victuals are said to appeal to strong-hearted men returning from a hard day's work in the mountains. You get such dishes as *bagna cauda,* a sauce made with olive oil, garlic, butter, and anchovies in which you dip uncooked fresh vegetables. *Fonduta* is celebrated: It's made with melted Fontina cheese, butter, milk, egg yolks, and, for an elegant touch, white truffles.

In the **Trentino–Alto Adige area,** whose chief towns are Bolzano, Merano, and Trent, the cooking is naturally influenced by the traditions of the Austrian and Germanic kitchens. South Tyrol, of course, used to belong to Austria, and here you get such tasty pastries as strudel.

Liguria, whose chief town is Genoa, turns to the sea for a great deal of its cuisine, as reflected by its version of bouillabaisse, a *buridda* flavored with spices. But its most famous food item is *pesto,* a sauce made with fresh basil, garlic, cheese, and walnuts. It not only dresses pasta or fish, but many dishes such as *gnocchi* (little dumplings).

Emilia-Romagna, with such towns as Modena, Parma, Bologna, Ravenna, and Ferrara, is one of the great gastronomic centers of Italy. Rich in produce, its school of cooking produces many notable pastas that are now common around Italy. They include *tagliatelle, tortellini,* and *cappelletti* (larger than tortellini and made in the form of "little hats"). Tagliatelle, of course, are long strips of macaroni, and tortellini are little squares of dough that have been stuffed with chopped pork, veal, or whatever. Equally popular is *lasagne,* which by now everybody has heard of. In Bologna it's often made by adding finely shredded spinach to the dough. The best-known sausage of the area is *mortadella,* and equally famous is a *cotoletta alla bolognese* (veal cutlet fried with a slice of ham or bacon). The distinctive and famous cheese, *parmigiana,* is a product of Parma and also Reggio Emilia. *Zampone* (stuffed pig's foot) is a specialty of Modena.

Much of the cookery of **Naples**—spaghetti with clam sauce, pizzas, and so forth—is already familiar to North Americans because so many Neapolitans moved to the New World and opened restaurants there. *Mozzarella,* or buffalo cheese, is the classic cheese of this area. Mixed fish fries, done a golden brown, are a staple feature of nearly every table.

Sicily has a distinctive cuisine, with good strong flavors and aromatic sauces. A staple of the diet is *maccheroni con le sarde* (spaghetti with pine seeds, fennel, spices, chopped sardines, and olive oil). Fish is good and fresh in Sicily (try swordfish). Among meat dishes, you'll see *involtini siciliani* on the menu (rolled meat with a stuffing of egg, ham, and cheese cooked in breadcrumbs). A *caponata* is a special way of cooking eggplant in a flavorful tomato sauce. The desserts and homemade pastries are excellent, including *cannoli,* cylindrical pastry cases stuffed with ricotta and candied fruit (or chocolate). Their ice creams, called *gelati,* are among the best in Italy.

ITALIAN WINE

Italy is the largest wine-producing country in the world; as far back as 800 B.C. the Etruscans were vintners. It's said that more soil is used in Italy for the cultivation of grapes than for food. Many Italian farmers produce wine just for their own consumption or for their relatives in "the big city." However, it wasn't until 1965 that laws were enacted to guarantee regular consistency in winemaking. Wines regulated by the government are labeled DOC (*Denominazione di Origine Controllata*). If you see DOCG on a label (the "G" means *garantita*), that means even better quality control.

THE VINEYARDS OF ITALY   Based on traditions and priorities established by the ancient Greeks, Italy produces more wine than any other nation on earth. More than four million acres of Italian soil are cultivated as vineyards, and in recent years there has been an increased emphasis on recognizing vintages from lesser-known growers who may or may not be designated as working within a zone of controlled origin and name. (It's considered an honor, and usually a source of profit, to own vines within a DOC. Vintners who are presently limited to marketing their products as unpretentious table wines—*vino di tavola*—often expend great efforts lobbying for an elevated status as a DOC.)

Italy's wine producers range from among the most automated and technologically sophisticated in Europe to low-tech, labor-intensive family plots turning out just a few hundred bottles of wine a year. You can sometimes save costs by buying direct from a producer (the signs beside the highway of any wine-producing district will advertise VENDITTA DRETTA). Not only will you avoid paying the retailer's markup, but you also might get a glimpse of the vines that produced the vintage you carry home with you.

Useful vocabulary words for such endeavors include *bottiglierie* (a simple wine shop with almost no pretentions) and *enoteca* (a more upscale shop where many different vintages, from several different growers, are displayed and sold like magazines in a bookstore). In some cases you can buy a glass of the product before you buy the bottle, and in some cases platters of cold cuts and/or cheeses are available to offset the tang (and alcoholic effects) of the wine.

REGIONAL WINES   Coming from the volcanic soil of Vesuvius, the wines of **Campania (Naples)** have been extolled for 2,000 years. Homer praised the glory of Falerno, which is straw yellow in color. Neapolitans are fond of ordering a wine known as lacrima Christi, or "tears of Christ," to accompany many seafood dishes. It comes in amber, red, and pink. With meat dishes, try the dark mulberry-colored Gragnano, which has a faint bouquet of faded violets. Also, the red and white wines of Ischia and Capri are justly renowned.

The heel of the Italian boot, **Apulia (Puglia),** produces more wine than any other part of Italy. Try Castel del Monte, which comes in shades of pink, white, and red.

Latium (Rome) is a major wine-producing region of Italy. Many of the local wines come from the Castelli Romani, the hill towns around Rome. Horace and Juvenal sang the praises of Latium wines even in imperial times. These wines, experts agree, are best drunk when young, and they're most often white, mellow, and dry (or else "demi-sec"). There are seven different types, including Falerno (straw yellow in color) and Cecubo (often served with roast meat). Try also Colli Albani (straw yellow with amber tints and served with both fish and meat). The golden-yellow wines of Frascati are famous, produced both in a demi-sec and sweet variety, the latter served with dessert.

The wines of **Tuscany (Florence and Siena)** are also famous, and they rank with some of the finest reds in France. Chianti is the best known, and it comes in several varieties. The most highly regarded is Chianti Classico, a lively ruby-red wine mellow in flavor with a bouquet of violets. A good label is Antinori. A less known but remarkably fine Tuscan wine is Brunello di Montalcino, a brilliant garnet red that's served with roasts and game. The ruby-red, almost-purple Vino Nobile di Montepulciano has a rich, rugged body; it's a noble wine that's aged for 4 years.

The sparkling Lambrusco of **Emilia-Romagna** is by now best known by Americans, but this wine can be of widely varying quality. Most of it is a brilliant ruby red. Be more experimental and try such wines as the dark ruby-red Sanglovese (with a delicate bouquet) and the golden-yellow Albana, which is somewhat sweet. Trebbiano, generally dry, is best served with fish.

From the **Marches** (capital: Ancona) comes one major wine, Verdicchio dei Castelli di Jesi, which is amber-straw in color, clear, and brilliant. Some have said that it's the best wine in Europe "to marry with fish."

From **Venetia (Venice and Verona)** in northeastern Italy, a rich breadbasket of the country, come such world-famous wines as Bardolino (a light ruby-red wine often served with poultry), Valpolicella (produced in "ordinary quality" and "superior dry," and best served with meats), and Soave, so beloved by W. Somerset Maugham, which has a pale amber-yellow color with a light aroma and a velvety flavor. Also try one of the Cabernets, either the ruby-red Cabernet di Treviso (ideal with roasts and game) or the even deeper ruby-red Cabernet Franc, which has a marked herbal bouquet and is also served with roasts.

The **Friuli–Venezia Giulia area,** whose chief towns are Trieste and Udine, attract those who enjoy a "brut" wine with a trace of flint. From classic grapes comes Merlot, deep ruby in color, and several varieties of Pinot, including Pinot Grigio, whose color ranges from straw yellow to gray-pink (good with fish). Also served with fish, the Sauvignon has a straw-yellow color and a delicate bouquet.

The **Trentino–Alto Adige area,** whose chief towns are Bolzano and Trent, produces wine influenced by Austria. Known for its vineyards, the region has some 20 varieties of wine. The straw yellow, slightly pale-green Riesling is served with fish, as is the pale greenish-yellow Terlano. Santa Maddalena, a cross between a garnet and a ruby in color, is served with wild fowl and red meats, and Traminer, straw yellow in color, has a distinctive aroma and is served with fish. A Pinot Bianco, straw yellow with greenish glints, has a light bouquet and a noble history, and is also served with fish.

The wines of **Lombardy (Milan)** are justly renowned, and if you don't believe us, would you then take the advice of Leonardo da Vinci, Pliny, and Virgil? These great men have sung the praise of this wine-rich region bordered by the Alps to the north and the Po River to the south. To go with the tasty, refined cuisine of the Lombard kitchen, add such wines as Frecciarossa (a pale straw yellow in color with a delicate bouquet; order with fish), Sassella (bright ruby red in color; order with game, red meat, and roasts), and the amusingly named Inferno (a deep ruby red in color with a penetrating bouquet; order with meats).

The finest wines in Italy, mostly red, are said to be produced on the vine-clad slopes of the **Piedmont** district (Turin), the word translated literally as "at the foot of the mountain." Of course, Asti Spumante, the color of straw with an abundant champagnelike foam, is the prototype of Italian sparkling wines. While traveling through this area of northwestern Italy, you'll want to sample Barbaresco (brilliant ruby red with a delicate flavor; order with red meats), Barolo (also brilliant ruby red, best when it mellows into a velvety old age), Cortese (pale straw yellow with green glints; order with fish), and Gattinara (an intense ruby-red beauty in youth that changes with age). Piedmont is also the home of vermouth, a white wine to which aromatic herbs and spices, among other ingredients, have been added; it's served as an apéritif.

Liguria, which includes Genoa and the Italian Riviera, doesn't have as many wine-producing regions as other parts of Italy, yet grows dozens of different grapes. These are made into such wines as Dolceacqua (lightish ruby red, served with hearty food) and Vermentino Ligure (a pale yellow in color with a good bouquet; often served with fish).

The wines of **Sicily,** called a "paradise of the grape," were extolled by the ancient poets, including Martial. Caesar himself lavished praise on Mamertine when it was served at a banquet honoring his third consulship. Marsala, of course, an amber-yellow wine served with desserts, is the most famous wine of Sicily; it's velvety and fruity and is sometimes used in cooking, as in veal marsala. The wines made from grapes grown in the volcanic soil of Etna come in both red and white varieties. Also try the Corvo Bianco di Casteldaccia (straw yellow in color, with a distinctive bouquet) and the Corvo Rosso di Casteldaccia (ruby red in color, almost garnet in tone, full-bodied and fruity).

We've only cited a few popular wines. Rest assured that there are hundreds more you may want to discover for yourself.

OTHER DRINKS   Italians drink other libations as well. Perhaps their most famous drink is **Campari,** bright red in color and herb flavored, with a quinine bitterness to it. It's customary to serve it with ice cubes and soda.

Beer is also made in Italy, and in general it's lighter than that served in Germany. If you order beer in a bar or restaurant, chances are it will be an imported beer, for which you'll be charged accordingly unless you specify otherwise. Some famous names in European beer-making now operate plants in Italy where the brew has been "adjusted" to Italian taste.

High-proof **grappa** is made from the "leftovers" after the grapes have been pressed. Many Italians drink this before or after dinner (some put it into their coffee). To an untrained foreign palate, it often appears rough and harsh. Some say it's an acquired taste.

Italy has many **brandies** (according to an agreement with France, Italians are not supposed to use the word "cognac" in labeling them). A popular one is Vecchia Romagna.

Other popular drinks include several **liqueurs,** to which the Italians are addicted. Try herb-flavored Strega, or perhaps an amaretto tasting of almonds. One of the best known is Maraschino, taking its name from a type of cherry used in its preparation. Galliano is also herb flavored, and Sambucca (anisette) is made of aniseed and is often served with a "fly" (coffee bean) in it. On a hot day, an Italian orders a vermouth, Cinzano, with a twist of lemon, ice cubes, and a squirt of soda water.

8   Recommended Books & Films

BOOKS

GENERAL & HISTORY   Luigi Barzini's *The Italians* (Macmillan, 1964) should almost be required reading for anyone contemplating a trip to Italy. The section on Sicily alone is worth the price of the book. Critics have hailed it as the liveliest analysis yet of the Italian character.

Edward Gibbon's 1776 *The History of the Decline and Fall of the Roman Empire* is published in six volumes, but Penguin issues a manageable abridgement. It has been hailed as one of the greatest histories ever written. No one has ever recaptured the saga of the glory that was Rome the way that Gibbon did.

If you like your history short, readable, and condensed, try *A Short History of Italy,* edited by H. Hearder and D. P. Waley (Cambridge University Press, 1963).

One of the best books on the long history of the papacy—detailing its excesses, its triumphs and defeats, and its most vivid characters—is Michael Walsh's *An Illustrated History of the Popes: Saint Peter to John Paul II* (St. Martin's Press, 1980).

The roots of modern Italy are explored in Christopher Hibbert's *Garibaldi and His Enemies: The Clash of Arms and Personalities in the Making of Italy* (Penguin, 1989).

In the 20th century, the most fascinating period in Italian history was the rise and fall of Fascism, as detailed in countless works. One of the best and most recent biographies of Il Duce is Denis M. Smith's *Mussolini: A Biography* (Random House, 1983). Eugen Weber writes of *Varieties of Fascism: Doctrines of Revolution in the Twentieth Century* (Krieger, 1982).

Carlo Levi's *Christ Stopped at Eboli* (Penguin Books, 1982) is a modern classic, an autobiographical account of a Turin doctor's year in exile in southern Italy during World War II. It stands out as a portrait of wartime village life and the southern rural character.

One subject that's always engrossing is the Mafia, and that sinister organization is detailed in Pino Arlacchi's *Mafia Business: The Mafia Ethic and the Spirit of Capitalism* (Routledge, Chapman & Hall, 1987). The Mafia from yet another point of view is described in Norman Lewis's *The Honoured Society: The Sicilian Mafia Observed* (Hippocrene Books, 1985).

William Murray's *The Last Italian: Portrait of a People* (Prentice Hall, 1991) is his second volume of essays on his favorite subject—Italy, its people and civilization. The *New York Times* called it "a lover's keen, observant diary of his affair."

Amzat and His Brothers: Three Italian Tales Remembered, by Floriano Vecchi, retold by Paula Fox (Orchard/Jackson, 1993), is a rare book of folktales told to the author (Fox) by a friend (Vecchi) who grew up near Bologna.

Once Upon a Time in Italy: The Vita Italiana of an American Journalist, by Jack Casserly (Roberts Rinehart, 1995), is the entertaining and affectionate memoir of a former bureau chief in Rome from 1957 to 1964. He captures the spirit of *Italian sparita* (bygone Italy) with cameos by such celebrities as Maria Callas and the American expatriate singer, Bricktop.

ART & ARCHITECTURE   The Renaissance period in Italy seems to capture the public's imagination more than any other art era, and one of the best accounts of this era is Peter Murray's *The Architecture of the Italian Renaissance* (Schocken, 1986). The same subject is covered by Frederick N. Hartt in his *History of Italian Renaissance Painting* (Abrams, 1987).

Giorgio Vasari's *The Lives of the Most Eminent Italian Architects, Painters, and Sculptors* was published in 1550 and, in spite of some fanciful inventions, it remains the definitive work on Renaissance artists—by one who knew many of them personally—from Cimabue to Michelangelo. Penguin Classics issues a paperback abridged version, called *Lives of the Artists* (1985).

Michael Levey has produced two engrossing books: *Early Renaissance* (Penguin, 1967) and *High Renaissance* (Penguin, 1975), both available in paperback.

The Sistine Chapel: A Glorious Restoration, by Michael Hirst et al. (Abrams, 1994), uses nearly 300 color photographs to illustrate the lengthy and painstaking restoration of Michelangelo's 16th-century frescoes in the Vatican.

FICTION & BIOGRAPHY　Both foreign and domestic writers have tried to capture the peculiar nature of Italy—each seen from a completely different angle—in such notable works as Thomas Mann's *Death in Venice* (Random House, 1965) and E. M. Forster's *Room with a View* (Random House, 1923), the subject of a famous movie in the 1980s. Fred M. Stewart's books are so popular they're sold in supermarkets, and he spins a lively tale in his *Century* (NAL, 1981), tracing the saga of several generations of an Italian family.

Umberto Eco is popular worldwide, and his first blockbuster murder mystery *The Name of the Rose* (Harcourt Brace, 1984) can be an entertaining Italy primer—if a bit thick on theological philosophy—on the political and monastic world of medieval Italy. Italo Calvino uses the turbulent times of 18th-century Italy as a backdrop to his delightful fable *The Baron in the Trees* (Harcourt Brace, 1977).

Benvenuto Cellini's *Autobiography,* also available in Penguin Classics, was first printed in Italy in 1728, although Cellini lived from 1500 to 1571. It's a Renaissance romp, filled with gossip and interesting details, so much so that it has been compared to a novel. It launched the tide of the romantic movement.

Giorgio Bassani, born in 1916, provides the bourgeois milieu of a Ferrara Jewish community under Mussolini in *The Garden of the Finzi-Continis* (Harcourt Brace Jovanovich, 1977).

The novels of Alberto Moravia (1907–90) are classified as neo-realism. Moravia is one of the best-known Italian writers read in English. Notable works include *Roman Tales* (Farrar, Straus, and Cudahy, 1957), *The Woman of Rome* (Penguin, 1957), and *The Conformist* (Greenwood Press, 1975).

Maria Meneghini Callas, by Michael Scott (Northeastern University Press, 1992), is written by the same author who published *The Great Caruso.* Here he turns his attention to the controversial diva (1923–77), documenting the prima donna at her prime but also describing the deterioration of her voice.

Donatello, one of the supreme artists of the Western world, was the subject of at least two books in 1994: *Donatello Sculptor,* by John Pope-Hennessy (Abbeville Press, 1994), and *Donatello and His World: Sculpture of the Italian Renaissance,* by Joachim Poeschke (Harry N. Abrams, 1994).

Michelangelo's life was novelized (and later made into a movie) by Irving Stone in the *Agony and the Ecstasy* (Doubleday, 1963), which also offers an insight into Florentine politics at the time. The descriptions of the act of carving itself are powerful, even if his attempts to cast some aspects of the sculptor's life as strictly heterosexual are a bit tenuous.

Verdi: A Biography, by Mary Jane Phillips-Matz (Oxford University Press, 1994), is a towering work by an author who spent more than 30 years in research. Many new details about Verdi are revealed and some myths exploded—namely that Verdi had a poverty-stricken childhood (his father actually had substantial land holdings).

TRAVEL　H. V. Morton's *A Traveler in Italy* (Methuen, 1964) is by one of the world's most widely read travel writers who has a rare sense of history and is at his best in describing great centers of culture such as Florence and Venice.

Many great writers—when faced with the challenge of Italy—decided to become travel writers. These have included Charles Dickens, who wrote *Pictures from Italy* (Ecco Press, 1988), a classic 19th-century account of the Grand Tour, going from Tuscany to Naples via Rome. Wolfgang Goethe's *Italian Journey* (Penguin, 1982) devotes more attention to Roman antiquities, and Henry James's *Italian Hours* (1909) is young James at his best, capturing the special atmosphere of Italy. It's currently issued by Ecco Press.

D. H. Lawrence and Italy (Viking Press, 1972) is three classic Italian travelogs collected in a single volume that includes *Sea and Sardinia* and *Twilight in Italy*. It also includes *Etruscan Places,* which was published posthumously. Lawrence writes of a way of life that was disappearing even as he wrote.

Mary McCarthy gave Italian travel literature two distinguished works, *The Stones of Florence* (Harcourt Brace Jovanovich, 1959) and *Venice Observed* (Penguin, 1972). "The lady of the barbs" pulls no punches in observing these two famed tourist meccas with a sharp eye for detail. These two works were definitely researched on the streets and not in a library.

Kate Simon's *Italy: The Places in Between* (Harper & Row, 1960) explores many of the towns overlooked as one races between Rome, Florence, and Venice, including Ferrara, Gubbio, Spoleto, and Padua.

Within Tuscany: Reflections on a Time and Place, by Matthew Spender (Viking, 1992), is the work of a London-born sculptor who has lived in Tuscany for a quarter of a century. He spins a lively account of the cultural, artistic, and literary soul of the region.

About Florence   The city of the Renaissance is one of the most written about in the world—from many points of view. Peter Burke's *Culture and Society in Renaissance Italy 1420–1540* (London: Batsford, 1972) received acclaim; it's often available in libraries. Florence is a backdrop for much of R. Couglan's *The Life and Times of Michelangelo 1475–1564* (Time-Life International, 1975).

Florence and the Renaissance: The Quattrocento, by Alan J. Lemaître (Stewart, Tabori & Chang, 1995), combines high-quality illustrations and a critical background of the period that gave the world such towering art figures as Fra Angelico and Botticelli. Informed criticism is combined with intriguing details from the lives of the artists. *Florence: The Biography of a City,* by Christopher Hibbert (W. W. Norton, 1993), was hailed as a "lavish celebration" of an extraordinary city.

The City of Florence: Historical Vistas and Personal Sightings, by R. W. B. Lewis (Farrar, Straus & Giroux, 1995), the author of a Pulitzer Prize–winning biography of Edith Wharton, writes of the city where he lived for some half a century. One reviewer called the guide "treasurable."

About Venice   John Ruskin wrote a definitive account of this city in his *The Stones of Venice,* first published in 1853 and in print by Little, Brown (1981). Although Ruskin may have come to Venice to debunk (for example, he found San Giorgio Maggiore "contemptible"), his work has many notable sections, including "The Nature of Gothic."

Peter Lauritzen published *Venice, a Thousand Years of Culture and Civilization* (Atheneum, 1978), and John J. Norwich traces a *History of Venice* (Knopf, 1982). Oliver Logan's *Culture and Society in Venice 1470–1790* (London: Batsford, 1972) is a well-researched work, often available in libraries.

A more recent work is George Bull's *Venice, the Most Triumphant City* (St. Martin's, 1982).

A guide to Venice's sights is *Frommer's Walking Tours: Venice,* by Robert Ullian (Macmillan, 1994).

About Naples   *Naples: A Memoir of Love, Peace and War in Italy,* by Douglas Allanbrook (HoughtonMifflin, 1995), is one of the most memorable books published on Naples in recent years. Allanbrook does for Naples what Hemingway's *A Moveable Feast* did for Paris. Vividly evocative, he relates his experiences there in World War II and in the 1950s. It's particularly rich in detailing daily life among the Neapolitans.

FILMS

Italian films have never regained the glory enjoyed in the postwar era. Roberto Rossellini's *Rome, Open City* (1946) influenced Hollywood's *films noir* of the late 1940s. Set in a poor section of occupied Rome, the film tells the story of a partisan priest and a Communist who aid the resistance.

Vittorio de Sica's *Bicycle Thief* (1948) achieved world renown. Also set in one of Rome's poor districts, it tells of the destruction of a child's illusions and the solitude of a steel worker.

The Leopard (1963), set in Sicily, gained a world audience for Luchino Visconti and was the first major Italian film made in color. Visconti first came to the attention of cinema audiences with his 1942 *Ossessione* (Obsession).

Federico Fellini burst into Italian cinema with his highly individual style, beginning with *La Strada* (1954) and going on to such classics as *Juliet of the Spirits* (1965), *Amarcord* (1974), *Roma,* and *The City of Women* (1980). *La Dolce Vita* (1961) helped to define an era.

Marxist, homosexual, and practicing Catholic Pier Paolo Pasolini was the most controversial of Italian filmmakers until his mysterious murder in 1975. Explicit sex scenes in his *Decameron* (1971) helped make it a world box-office hit.

Bernardo Bertolucci, once an assistant to Pasolini, achieved fame with such films as *The Conformist* (1970), based on the novel by Moravia. His *1900* is an epic spanning 20th-century Italian history and politics. One of his biggest international films was *Last Tango in Paris* (1971), starring Marlon Brando, and the summer of 1996 saw the release of his Tuscan love story, *Stealing Beauty.*

A Neapolitan director, Francesco Rosi became known for semidocumentary films, exploring such subjects as the Mafia in *Salvatore Giuliano* (1962) and the army in *Just Another War* (1970). His *Three Brothers* (1980) examines three different political attitudes, as the brothers have a reunion at their mother's funeral in Apulia.

Current Italian directors include the Taviani brothers, Paolo and Vittorio. Their *Padre Padrone* (1977) takes place in Sardinia and their *Kaos* (1984) is set in Sicily and is an adaptation of a Pirandello story. Their late 1980s film, *Good Morning, Babylon,* brought them worldwide acclaim. The Taviani brothers created a stir in 1994 with the release of their film *Fiorile.* Set in their native Tuscany, this multigenerational saga supposedly was a local folktale passed on by their mother.

Although directors more than stars have dominated Italian cinema, three actors have emerged to gain worldwide fame, including Marcello Mastroianni, star of such hits as *La Dolce Vita* (1961), and Sophia Loren, whose best film is considered *Two Women* (1961). Mastroianni was Fellini's favorite male actor and he starred him once again in *8¹/₂.*

Anna Magnani not only starred in Italian films but made many American films as well, including *The Rose Tattoo* (1955), with Burt Lancaster, and *The Fugitive Kind* (1960), with Marlon Brando.

Several Italian films in the late 1980s and the 1990s have captured an international audience. *Cinema Paradiso,* directed by Giuseppe Tornatore, won the Academy Award for Best Foreign Language Film of 1989. *Fellini's Intervista* (1992) is a film within a film, with the director, who died in 1993, discussing his movies and the actors who starred in them.

Caro Diario (1994), starring and directed by Nanni Moretti, is a three-part traipse through modern-day Italy. Moretti, a cult figure in Italy, began to make an impression in America with this film. The actor-director is noted for his prickly personality, quirky sense of humor, and deadpan tone.

Although directed by an Englishman and about a Cuban poet, the popular *Il Postino / The Postman*, nominated for most major Academy Awards in 1995, is Italian at heart, and most of its charm comes from its Italian island setting and its Italian star, Masimo Troisi, who died just hours after they finished filming.

The Flight of the Innocent (1995) is one of the finest films to come out of Italy in recent times—and one that quickly gained an international audience. The director, Carlo Carlei, takes us inside the world of a 10-year-old boy fleeing for his life. It's one of the best depictions ever of a child alone who must improvise and cope with a world he doesn't understand.

3 Planning a Trip to Italy

This chapter is devoted to the where, when, and how of your trip—the advance-planning issues required to get it together and take it on the road.

After deciding where to go, most people have two fundamental questions: "What will it cost?" and "How do I get there?" This chapter will answer both questions and also resolve other important issues, such as when to go, what pretrip preparations are needed, where to obtain more information about Italy, and much more.

1 Visitor Information & Entry Requirements

VISITOR INFORMATION For information before you go, contact the **Italian National Tourist Office.** In the United States branches are located at 630 Fifth Ave., Suite 1565, **New York,** NY 10111 (☎ **212/245-4822**); 401 N. Michigan Ave., **Chicago,** IL 60611 (☎ **312/644-0990**); and 12400 Wilshire Blvd., Suite 550, **Los Angeles,** CA 90025 (☎ **310/820-0098**). In Canada, contact the Italian National Tourist Office at 1 Place Ville Marie, Suite 1914, **Montreal,** PQ H3B2C3 (☎ **514/866-7667**); and in England at 1 Princes St., **London** W1R 8AY (☎ **0171/408-1254**).

You can also write directly (in English or Italian) to the provincial or local tourist boards of areas you plan to visit. These provincial tourist boards (known as **Ente Provinciale per il Turismo**) operate in the principal towns of the provinces. The local tourist boards (known as **Azienda Autonoma di Soggiorno e Turismo**) operate in all places of tourist interest, and a list can be obtained from the Italian National Tourist Office.

ENTRY REQUIREMENTS United States, Canadian, British, Australian, New Zealand, and Irish citizens with a valid passport do not need a visa to enter Italy if they do not expect to stay more than 90 days and do not expect to work there. Those who, after entering Italy, find that they would like to stay more than 90 days can apply for a permit for an additional stay of 90 days, which as a rule is granted immediately.

2 Money

There are no restrictions as to how much foreign currency you can bring into Italy, although visitors should declare the amount brought

The Italian Lira, the U.S. Dollar & the U.K. Pound

At this writing, $1 U.S. = approximately 1,565 Italian lire (or 100 lire = 6.4¢), and this was the rate of exchange used to calculate the dollar values given throughout this book. The rate fluctuates from day to day, depending on a complicated series of economic and political factors, and might not be the same when you travel to Italy.

Likewise, the ratio of the British pound to the lira fluctuates constantly. At press time, £1 = approximately 2,380 lire (or 100 lire = 4.2p), an exchange rate reflected in the table below.

Lire	U.S.$	U.K.£	Lire	U.S.$	U.K.£
50	0.03	0.02	30,000	19.20	12.60
100	0.06	0.04	40,000	25.60	16.80
250	0.16	0.13	50,000	32.00	21.00
500	0.32	0.21	60,000	38.40	25.20
750	0.48	0.29	70,000	44.80	29.40
1,000	0.64	0.42	80,000	51.20	33.60
1,500	0.96	0.63	90,000	57.60	37.80
2,000	1.28	0.84	100,000	64.00	42.00
2,500	1.60	1.05	125,000	80.00	52.50
3,000	1.92	1.26	150,000	96.00	63.00
4,000	2.56	1.68	175,000	112.00	73.50
5,000	3.20	2.10	200,000	128.00	84.00
7,500	4.80	3.15	250,000	160.00	105.00
10,000	6.40	4.20	300,000	192.00	126.00
15,000	9.60	6.30	400,000	256.00	168.00
20,000	12.80	8.40	500,000	320.00	210.00
25,000	16.00	10.50	750,000	480.00	315.00

in. This proves to the Italian Customs office that the currency came from outside the country and therefore the same amount or less can be taken out. Italian currency taken into or out of Italy may not exceed 200,000 lire in denominations of 50,000 lire or lower.

The basic unit of Italian currency is the **lira** (plural: **lire**). Coins are issued in denominations of 10, 20, 50, 100, 200, and 500 lire, and bills come in denominations of 1,000, 2,000, 5,000, 10,000, 50,000, 100,000, and 500,000 lire. Coins for 50 and 100 lire come in two sizes each, the newer ones both around the size of a dime.

ATM NETWORKS There are more than 13,000 Visa ATMs and more than 2,000 Plus ATMs in Italy. American Express cardholders have access to the ATM machines of Banco Popolare di Milano; the transaction fee is 2% with a minimum charge of $2.50 and a maximum of $20. If your bank card has been programmed with a PIN, it's likely that you can use your card at ATMs abroad to withdraw money from your account or as a cash advance on your credit card. Always determine the frequency limits for withdrawals and cash advances of your credit card. Also, check to see if your PIN code must be reprogrammed for usage in Italy. Discover cards are accepted only in the United States. For ATM locations in Italy, go to your U.S. bank and ask for a brochure of affiliated banks and their location addresses.

What Things Cost in Rome	U.S. $
Taxi (central rail station to piazza di Spagna)	8.80
Subway or public bus (to any destination)	0.95
Local telephone call	0.14
Double room at the Hassler (very expensive)	396.80
Double room at Hotel Columbus (moderate)	172.80
Double room at Hotel Corot (inexpensive)	96.00
Continental breakfast (cappuccino and croissant at most cafes and bars)	3.00
Lunch for one at Ristorante da Pancrazio (moderate)	19.20
Dinner for one, without wine, at Relais Le Jardin (expensive)	75.00
Dinner for one, without wine, at L'Eau Vive (moderate)	32.00
Dinner for one, without wine, at Otello alla Concordi (inexpensive)	23.00
Pint of beer	3.95
Glass of wine	2.00
Coca-Cola	1.50
Cup of coffee	1.30
Roll of color film, 36 exposures	6.50
Admission to the Vatican museums and Sistine Chapel	8.30
Movie ticket	7.95

TRAVELER'S CHECKS   To be on the safe side, you might want to purchase traveler's checks before leaving home and arrange to carry some ready cash (usually about $250, depending on your needs). In the event of theft, the value of your checks will be refunded if properly documented. Most large banks sell traveler's checks, charging fees that average between 1% and 2% of the value of the checks you buy, although some out-of-the-way banks, in rare instances, have charged as much as 7%. If your bank wants more than a 2% commission, it sometimes pays to call the traveler's check issuers directly for the address of outlets where this commission will be less.

Issuers sometimes have agreements with groups to sell checks commission free. For example, Automobile Association of America (AAA) clubs sell American Express checks in several currencies without commission.

American Express (☎ 800/221-7282 in the U.S. and Canada) is one of the largest and most immediately recognized issuers of traveler's checks. No commission is charged to holders of certain types of American Express cards. For questions or problems that arise outside the United States and Canada, contact any of the company's many regional representatives.

There's also **Citicorp** (☎ 800/645-6556 in the U.S. and Canada, or 813/623-1709, collect, from other parts of the world) and **Thomas Cook** (☎ 800/223-7373 in the U.S. and Canada, or 609/987-7300, collect, from other parts of the world), which issues MasterCard traveler's checks. **Interpayment Services** (☎ 800/732-1322 in the U.S. and Canada, or 212/858-8500, collect, from other parts of the world) sells Visa checks that are issued by a consortium of member banks and the Thomas Cook organization.

CURRENCY EXCHANGE   For the best exchange rate, go to a bank, *not* to hotels or shops. Currency and traveler's checks (for which you'll receive a better rate than

What Things Cost in Naples	U.S. $
Taxi from rail station to the port	8.50
Subway (to any destination)	0.90
Local telephone call	0.14
Double room at the Grande Albergo Vesuvio (expensive)	268.80
Double room at the Hotel Britannique (moderate)	172.80
Double room at the Hotel Rex (inexpensive)	108.80
Continental breakfast (cappuccino and croissant)	2.50
Lunch for one at Giuseppone a Mare (moderate)	25.00
Lunch for one at Brandi (historic pizzeria)	15.00
Dinner for one, without wine, at La Sacrestia (moderate)	36.00
Dinner for one, without wine, at Rosolino (inexpensive)	22.00
Dinner for one, without wine, at Dante e Beatrice	18.00
Pint of beer	3.75
Glass of wine	1.60
Coca-Cola	1.50
Cappuccino	1.00
Roll of color film, 36 exposures	5.95
Admission to the Museo Archeologico Nazionale	7.70
Movie ticket	5.50

cash) can be changed at the airport and some travel agencies, such as American Express and Thomas Cook. Note the rates—it can sometimes pay to shop around.

If you need a check drawn upon an Italian bank, for example to pay a deposit on a hotel room, this can be arranged by a large commercial bank or by a currency specialist such as **Ruesch International,** 700 11th St. NW, Washington, DC 20001 (☎ **202/408-1200,** or 800/424-2923), which can perform a wide variety of conversion-related financial transactions for individual travelers. To place an order, call them and tell them the type and amount of the check you need. Ruesch will quote a U.S. dollar equivalent, adding a $2 service fee per check. After receiving your dollar-denominated personal check for the agreed-upon amount, Ruesch will mail you a lire-denominated bank draft, drawn at an Italian bank and payable to whichever party you specified. Ruesch also sells traveler's checks payable in either dollars or any of six foreign currencies—but not in Italian lire. (Most Italian banks and *cambi* prefer traveler's checks denominated in either U.S. dollars or Swiss francs; Ruesch can provide either.)

MONEYGRAM If you find yourself out of money, a new wire service provided by American Express can help you tap willing friends and family for emergency funds. Call **800/926-9400.**

3 When to Go—Climate, Holidays & Events

April to June and September and October are the best months for touring Italy. High season on most airlines' routes to Rome usually stretches from June until the beginning of September. This is the most expensive and most crowded time to travel. Shoulder season is from April to May, early September to October, and December 15 to 24. Low season is November 1 to December 14 and December 25 to March 31.

CLIMATE

It's warm all over Italy in summer. The high temperatures (measured in Italy in degrees Celsius) begin in Rome in May, often lasting until sometime in October. Winters in the north of Italy are cold with rain and snow, but in the south the weather is warm all year, averaging 50°F in winter (summers tend to be very hot, especially inland).

For the most part, it's drier in Italy than in North America. High temperatures, therefore, don't seem as bad since the humidity is lower. In Rome, Naples, and the south, temperatures can stay in the 90s for days, but nights are most often comfortably cooler.

The average high temperatures in Rome during the summer are 82°F in June, 87°F in July, and 86°F in August; the average lows are 63°F in June, and 67°F in July and August. In Venice, the average high temperatures are 76°F in June, 81°F in July, and 80°F in August; the average lows are 63°F in June, 66°F in July, and 65°F in August.

Italy's Average Daily Temperature & Monthly Rainfall

FLORENCE	Jan	Feb	Mar	Apr	May	June	July	Aug	Sept	Oct	Nov	Dec
Temp.(°F)	45	47	50	60	67	75	77	70	64	63	55	46
Rainfall"	3	3.3	3.7	2.7	2.2	1.4	1.4	2.7	3.2	4.9	3.8	2.9

ROME	Jan	Feb	Mar	Apr	May	June	July	Aug	Sept	Oct	Nov	Dec
Temp.(°F)	49	52	57	62	70	77	82	78	73	65	56	47
Rainfall"	2.3	1.5	2.9	3.0	2.8	2.9	1.5	1.9	2.8	2.6	3.0	2.1

VENICE	Jan	Feb	Mar	Apr	May	June	July	Aug	Sept	Oct	Nov	Dec
Temp.(°F)	43	48	53	60	67	72	77	74	68	60	54	44
Rainfall"	2.3	1.5	2.9	3.0	2.8	2.9	1.5	1.9	2.8	2.6	3.0	2.1

HOLIDAYS

Offices and shops in Italy are closed on the following dates: January 1 (New Year's Day), Easter Monday, April 25 (Liberation Day), May 1 (Labor Day), August 15 (Assumption of the Virgin), November 1 (All Saints' Day), December 8 (Feast of the Immaculate Conception), December 25 (Christmas Day), and December 26 (Santo Stefano).

Closings are also observed in the following cities on feast days honoring their patron saints: Venice, April 25 (St. Mark); Florence, Genoa, and Turin, June 24 (St. John the Baptist); Rome, June 29 (Sts. Peter and Paul); Palermo, July 15 (Santa Rosalia); Naples, September 19 (St. Gennaro); Bologna, October 4 (St. Petronio); Cagliari, October 30 (St. Saturnino); Trieste, November 3 (San Giusto); Bari, December 6 (St. Nicola); and Milan, December 7 (St. Ambrose).

In addition, try to avoid traveling to Italy in August, as this is when most Italians take their vacations and many shops and restaurants will be closed.

ITALY CALENDAR OF EVENTS

For more information about these and other events, contact the various tourist offices throughout Italy. Dates often vary from year to year.

January

- **Epiphany Celebrations,** nationwide. All cities, towns, and villages in Italy stage Roman Catholic Epiphany observances. One of the most festive celebrations is the Epiphany Fair at Rome's piazza Navona. Usually January 5–6.
- **Viareggio Carnival,** on the Tuscan coast. Fireworks, pageants, parades, and a flower show. This Carnival is famous for three weekend parades and a Shrove Tuesday parade. Dates vary.
- **Festival of Italian Popular Song,** San Remo (the Italian Riviera). A 3-day festival when major artists perform the latest Italian song releases. Late January.
- **Foire de Saint Ours,** Aosta, Valle d'Aosta. Observing a tradition that has existed for 10 centuries, artisans from the mountain valleys come together to display their wares—often made of wood, lace, wool, or wrought iron—created during the long winter months. Late January.

February

- ✪ **Carnevale in Venice.** Carnevale is a riotous time in Venice. Theatrical presentations and masked balls cap the festivities.

  Where: Throughout Venice and on the islands in the lagoon. **When:** The week before Ash Wednesday, the beginning of Lent. **How:** The balls are by invitation, but the street events and fireworks are open to everyone. More information is available from the Venice Tourist Office, San Marco, Giardinetti Reali, Pal. Selva (☎ 041/522-6356).

March

- **Good Friday Processions,** held nationwide. The most notable one is in Rome. Usually the end of March.

April

- **Easter Week** observances, held nationwide. Processions and age-old ceremonies—some from pagan days, some from the Middle Ages—are staged. The best are in Sicily. Beginning 4 days before Easter Sunday.
- **Scoppio del Carro** (Explosion of the Cart), in Florence. An ancient observance: A cart laden with flowers and fireworks is drawn by three white oxen to the Duomo, where at noon mass a mechanical dove detonates it from the altar. Easter Sunday.

May

- ✪ **Maggio Musicale Fiorentino ("Musical May Florentine").** Italy's oldest and most prestigious festival takes place in Florence, the venue for opera, ballet performances, and concerts.

  Where: Teatro Comunale, via Solferino 16; Teatro della Pergola, via della Pergola 18; and various other venues, including piazza della Signoria and the courtyard of the Pitti Palace. **When:** Late April into July. **How:** Schedule and ticket information are available from Maggio Musicale Fiorentino/Teatro Comunale, via Solferino 16, 50123 Firenze (☎ 055/27791). Tickets cost 25,000 to 180,000 lire ($16 to $115.20).

June

- **L'Infiorata,** Genzano, Lazio. This is a religious procession along streets carpeted with flowers in splendid designs, often copies of famous artworks. Details are available from the Azienda Autonoma di Soggiorno e Turismo dei Laghi e Castelli Romani, via Risorgimento 1, 00041 Albano Laziale (☎ 06/932-4081).
- **San Ranieri,** Pisa. Pisa honors its own saint with candlelit parades, followed the next day by eight-rower teams in 16th-century costumes competing. June 16.

- **Gioco del Ponte,** Pisa. Teams in Renaissance costume take part in a much-contested tug-of-war contest on the Ponte di Mezzo, which spans the Arno River. Last Sunday in June.
- ✪ **Festival dei Due Mondi.** Dating from 1958, this was the creation of Maestro Gian Carlo Menotti. International performers convene for 3 weeks of dance, drama, opera, concerts, and art exhibits.

  Where: Spoleto, an Umbrian hill town north of Rome. **When:** June 26 to July 14. **How:** Tickets and information are available from the Festival dei Due Mondi, via Cesare Beccaria 18, 00196 Roma (☎ 06/321-0288). For information in Spoleto, call the festival's office at either 0743/40700 or 0743/44097. Information is also available from the box office, c/o Teatro Nuovo, piazza Belli, 06049 Spoleto (☎ 0743/220365).

July

- ✪ **Il Palio.** Palio fever grips the Tuscan hill town of Siena for a wild and exciting horse race from the Middle Ages. Pageantry, costumes, and the celebrations of the victorious *contrada* mark the well-attended spectacle. It's a "no rules" event: Even a horse without a rider can win the race.

  Where: Piazza del Campo, in Siena. **When:** July 2 and August 16. **How:** Details are available by contacting the Azienda di Promozione Turistica, piazza del Campo 56, 53100 Siena (☎ 0577/280551).
- **Arena Outdoor Opera Season,** Verona. Brings culture buffs to the 20,000-seat Roman amphitheater. Early July to mid-August.
- **La Festa del Redentore** (Feast of the Redeemer), in Venice. Marks the lifting of the plague in July of 1578, with fireworks, pilgrimages, and boating on the lagoon. Third Saturday and Sunday in July.
- **Festival Internazionale di Musica Antica,** Urbino. A cultural extravaganza, as international performers converge on Raphael's birthplace. It's the most important Renaissance and baroque music festival in Italy. Details are available from the Fondazione Italiana per la Musica Antica, C.P. 6159, I-00195 Roma (☎ 06/827-2447). Ten days in late July.

August

- ✪ **Venice International Film Festival.** Ranking after Cannes, this film festival at Venice brings together stars, directors, producers, and filmmakers from all over the world. Films are shown both day and night to an international jury and to the public.

  Where: Palazzo del Cinema, on the Lido. **When:** Late August to early September. **How:** Contact the Venice Tourist Office (☎ 041/522-6356), for exact dates in 1997.

September

- **Regata Storica,** on the Grand Canal in Venice. A maritime spectacular; many gondolas participate in the canal procession, although gondolas don't race in the regatta itself. First Sunday in September.

October

- **Sagra del Tartufo,** Alba, Piedmont. Honors the expensive truffle in Alba, the truffle capital of Italy, with contests, truffle-hound competitions, and tastings of this ugly but very expensive and delectable fungus. For details, contact the Azienda di Promozione Turistica, piazza Medford, 12051 Alba (☎ 0173/35833).

ROME CALENDAR OF EVENTS

January
- **Carnival,** in piazza Navona. Marks the last day of the children's market and lasts until dawn of the following day. Usually January 5.
- **Festa di Sant'Agnese,** at Sant' Agnese Fuori le Mura. An ancient ceremony in which two lambs are blessed and shorn. Their wool is then used later for palliums. Usually January 17.

March
- **Festa di Santa Francesca Romana,** at piazzale del Colosseo near the Church of Santa Francesca Romana in the Roman Forum. A blessing of cars. Usually March 9.
- **Festa di San Giuseppe,** in the Trionfale Quarter, north of the Vatican. The heavily decorated statue of the saint is brought out at a fair with food stalls, concerts, and sporting events. Usually March 19.

April
- **Festa della Primavera.** The Spanish Steps are decked out with banks of flowers, and later orchestral and choral concerts are presented in Trinità dei Monti. Dates vary.
- **Holy Week.** The most notable procession is led by the pope, passing the Colosseum and the Roman Forum up to Palatine Hill. A torchlit parade caps the observance. Sometimes at the end of March, but often in April.
- **Easter Sunday,** piazza di San Pietro. In an event broadcast around the world, the pope gives his blessing from the balcony of St. Peter's.

May
- **International Horse Show,** at piazza di Siena in the Villa Borghese. Usually May 1 to 10, but the dates can vary.

June
- **Son et Lumière,** at the Roman Forum and Tivoli. These areas are dramatically lit at night. Early June until the end of September.
- **Festa di San Pietro,** St. Peter's Basilica. The most significant Roman religious festival, observed with solemn rites in St. Peter's. Usually around June 29.

July
- ✪ **La Festa di Nolantri.** Trastevere, the most colorful quarter of Old Rome, becomes a gigantic outdoor restaurant, as tons of food and drink are consumed at tables lining the streets. Merrymakers and musicians provide the entertainment.

  Where: Trastevere. **When:** Mid-July. **How:** After reaching the quarter, find the first empty table and try to get a waiter. But guard your valuables. Details are available from Ente Provinciale per il Turismo, via Parigi 11, 00185 Roma (☎ 06/4889-9200).

August
- **Festa delle Catene,** in the Church of San Pietro in Vincoli. The relics of St. Peter's captivity go on display. August 1.

September
- **Sagra dell'Uva,** in the Basilica of Maxentius in the Roman Forum. At this harvest festival, musicians in ancient costumes entertain and grapes are sold at reduced prices. Dates vary, usually early September.

December

- **Christmas Blessing of the Pope,** piazza di San Pietro. Delivered at noon from the balcony of St. Peter's Basilica. It's broadcast around the world. December 25.

4 The Active Vacation Planner

The Italian countryside has always been legendary for its beauty and architectural richness. Several companies specialize in introducing travelers to its wonders, usually through hill treks and mountain climbing.

CYCLING TOURS Cycling tours are a good way to see Italy at your own pace. Some of the best are featured by the **Cyclists' Touring Club,** 69 Meadrow, Godalming, Surrey GU7 3HS, U.K. (☎ 01483/417-217). It charges £25 ($40) a year for adults and £12.50 ($20) for those 17 and under for membership, part of which includes information and suggested cycling routes through most European countries.

HIKING IN THE ALPS For serious trekkers, **Club Alpino Italiano,** via E. Fonseca Pimental 7, Milan 20127 (☎ 02/2614-1378), publishes a guide, *Rifugi Alpini,* listing various huts available to hikers in the Italian Alps. The two-volume guide costs 95,000 lire ($60.80).

HORSEBACK RIDING IN TUSCANY Some travelers prefer to visit Tuscany in a style popularized by everyone from the Etruscans to the soldiers and *condottieri* of the Renaissance: on horseback. One company that can help you combine a trek through the Italian countryside with equestrian panache is **Equitour,** P.O. Box 807, Dubois, WY 82513 (☎ 800/545-0019 in the U.S. and Canada). Established in 1983 from a base in northwestern Wyoming, this company markets highly organized horseback-riding holidays throughout the world. The tours are limited to four to seven participants and last for 8 days, which usually includes 6 days of riding through the region around Siena.

WALKING TOURS IN TUSCANY **Sherpa Expeditions,** 131 A Heston Rd., Hounslow, Middlesex TW5 0RD, U.K. (☎ 0181/577-2717), sponsors tours of Tuscany that offer participants a rare view of the Tuscan countryside, including tours of villages and cities like Siena and Florence.

WILDERNESS/ADVENTURE TRAVEL One of the best adventure travel outfitters is **Mountain Travel–Sobek,** 6420 Fairmount Ave., El Cerrito, CA 94350 (☎ 510/527-8100, or 800/227-2384 in the U.S.). The group offers at least three different hill-climbing itineraries through Italy. The least strenuous (and most historically rewarding) is a 12-day trip through the fields and vineyards of Tuscany and the coastal hills and towns of the Cinque Terre. Traversing most of the width of the district, the tour explores a region dotted with centuries of architectural monuments. There are five departures every year, during spring and fall when the temperature is most comfortable.

The company also offers high-altitude explorations of the rocky (glacier-free) Dolomites. Varying from year to year based on demand and the availability of guides, these usually 12-day treks are designed for experienced mountaineers in excellent physical condition.

Waymark Holidays, 44 Windsor Rd., Slough Berkshire SL1 2EJ, U.K. (☎ 01753/516-477), offers a walking tour along the Alta Via 4, the Italian "highway," which winds its way through the snow-encrusted peaks and lush green valleys of the Gran Paradiso National Park in northern Italy. The route is rigorous, but allows for unparalleled vistas into the mountains of Italy. The tour is 14 nights, with 2 consecutive nights spent in each hut to allow for exploration of individual peaks.

5 Special Interest & Educational Travel

More and more travelers are becoming interested in specialized travel experiences whose goals and objectives are clearly defined.

Note: The inclusion of an organization in this section is in no way to be interpreted as a guarantee. Information about the organization is presented only as a preview to be followed by your own investigations.

OPERA TOURS

Dailey-Thorp, 330 W. 58th St., Suite 610, New York, NY 10019-1817 (☎ **212/307-1515**), in business since 1971, is the best-regarded organizer of music and opera tours operating in the United States. Its focus is on combining guaranteed seats at the finest opera houses in Europe with upscale bus tours and stays in top-notch hotels. Because of its "favored" relations with European box offices, it's often able to purchase blocks of otherwise unavailable tickets to performances in the opera houses of Palermo, Genoa, Milan, Turin, Rome, and Venice. Tours through Italy usually last around 14 days. In 1997, a well-attended tour will include visits to the opera festivals in Verona, Macerata, Pesaro, Montecassiano, Bologna, Rome, and the hill towns of Umbria.

EDUCATIONAL TRAVEL

LEARNING THE LANGUAGE   Courses in Italian language, fine arts, history, literature, and Italian culture for foreign students are available at several centers throughout the Italian peninsula, with the best recommended usually headquartered in what most Italians refer to as their nation's intellectual and cultural capital, Florence. You can write to any of the following addresses for information: The **British Institute of Florence,** Courses on Italian Language and Culture, Palazzo Lanfredini, lungarno Guicciardini 9, 50125 Firenze (☎ **055/284031;** fax 055/289557); the **Centro di Lingua e Cultura Italiana per Stranieri,** piazza Santo Spirito 4, 50134 Firenze (☎ **055/239-6966;** fax 055/280800); and the **Centro Linguistico Italiano Dante Alighieri,** via de' Bardi 12, 50125 Firenze (☎ **055/234-2984;** fax 055/234-2766).

The **Italian Cultural Institute** in New York (☎ **212/879-4242**) may also be able to provide information.

LEARNING TO COOK   Culinary schools abound in Italy. The schools usually combine excellent cooking facilities with evocative settings, where students can absorb Italian culinary tips as well as soak in the culture. **Italian Cuisine in Florence,** via Trieste 1, 50139 Florence (☎ **055/480041**), provides several gourmet classes in both regional and *nouva* cuisine. Most courses last 5 days, but short workshops for larger groups are also available.

The **International Cooking School of Italian Food and Wine,** 201 E. 28th St., New York, NY 10016-8538 (☎ **212/779-1921**), offers courses in Bologna, the "gastronomic capital of Italy." Owner/operator Mary Beth Clark teaches the fine art of *la cucina tradizionale* and *la cucina nuova.* Classes are conducted in English. The course includes excursions into Bologna and the surrounding region, concentrating on the fabulous markets and *ristorantes* found in the Emilia-Romagna region.

JUST FOR SENIORS   One of the most dynamic organizations for senior citizens is **Elderhostel,** 75 Federal St., Boston, MA 02110 (☎ **617/426-8056**), established in 1975. Elderhostel maintains an array of programs throughout Europe, including Italy. Most courses last for around 3 weeks and represent good value, considering that airfare, hotel accommodations in student dormitories or modest inns, all meals, and tuition are included. Courses involve no homework, are ungraded, and are especially focused in the liberal arts. Participants must be 55 or older. Elderhostel's offerings in Italy include a historic and artistic overview of Sicily from headquarters in the fishing village of Mondello (near Palermo), and an introduction to the art and architecture of Umbria and Tuscany. Contact Elderhostel for a free catalog and a list of upcoming courses and destinations. Programs, of course, are subject to change.

6 Health & Insurance

STAYING HEALTHY   You'll encounter few health problems traveling in Italy. The tap water is generally safe to drink, the milk pasteurized, and health services good.

Bring along copies of your prescriptions that are written in the generic—not brand-name—form. If you need a doctor, your hotel can recommend one or you can contact your embassy or consulate. You can also obtain a list of English-speaking doctors before you leave from the **International Association for Medical Assistance to Travelers (IAMAT),** in the United States at 417 Center St., Lewiston, NY 14092 (☎ **716/754-4883**); in Canada, at 40 Regal Rd., Guelph, ON N1K 1B5 (☎ **519/ 836-0102**).

If you suffer from a chronic illness or special medical condition, consider purchasing a Medic Alert identification bracelet or necklace, which will immediately alert any doctor to your condition and will provide Medic Alert's 24-hour hotline phone number so that foreign doctors can obtain medical information on you. The initial membership is $35, and there's a $15 yearly fee. Contact the **Medic Alert Foundation,** 2323 Colorado Ave., Turlock, CA 95381-1009 (☎ **800/432-5378**).

INSURANCE   Before purchasing any additional insurance, check your homeowner's, automobile, and medical insurance policies, as well as the insurance provided by your credit- and charge-card companies and auto and travel clubs. You may have adequate off-premises theft coverage or your credit/charge-card company may even provide cancellation coverage if the ticket is paid for with its card.

Remember, Medicare only covers U.S. citizens traveling in Mexico and Canada.

Also note that to submit any claim you must always have thorough documentation, including all receipts, police reports, medical records, and such.

If you're prepaying for your vacation or are taking a charter or any other flight that has cancellation penalties, look into cancellation insurance.

Some companies offering travel insurance—ranging from trip cancellation, trip interruption, and accident and medical coverage—include **Travel Guard International**, 1145 Clark St., Stevens Point, WI 54481 (☎ **800/826-1300**); **Travel Insured International, Inc.,** P.O. Box 280568, East Hartford, CT 06128-0568 (☎ **800/243-3174** in the U.S., 203/528-7663 outside the U.S. between 7:45am and 7pm EST); **Healthcare Abroad (MEDEX),** c/o Wallach & Co., 107 W. Federal St. (P.O. Box 480), Middleburg, VA 22117-0480 (☎ **540/687-3166,** or 800/ 237-6615); and **Access America,** 6600 W. Broad St., Richmond, VA 23230 (☎ **800/284-8300**).

7 Tips for Travelers with Special Needs

FOR TRAVELERS WITH DISABILITIES   If you're flying around Europe, the airlines and ground staff will help you on and off planes, and reserve seats for you with sufficient leg room, but it's essential to arrange for this assistance in advance by contacting your airline.

Recent laws in Italy have compelled railway stations, airports, hotels, and most restaurants to follow a stricter set of regulations about **wheelchair accessibility** to rest rooms, ticket counters, etc. Even museums and other sightseeing attractions have conformed to the regulations, which mimic many of the regulations presently in effect in the United States. Alitalia, as the most visible airline in Italy, has made special efforts to make its planes, public areas, rest rooms, and access ramps as wheelchair-friendly as possible.

Before you go, there are several agencies that can provide advance-planning information. One is the **Travel Information Service** of Philadelphia's MossRehab Hospital (☎ **215/456-9603,** or 215/456-9602 for TDD), which provides information to telephone callers only.

You may also want to consider joining a tour for visitors with disabilities. Names and addresses of such tour operators and miscellaneous travel information can be obtained by writing to the **Society for the Advancement of Travel for the Handicapped,** 347 Fifth Ave., New York, NY 10016 (☎ **212/447-7248**). Annual membership dues are $45, or $25 for senior citizens and students. Send a stamped, self-addressed envelope.

FEDCAP Rehabilitation Services (formerly known as the Federation of the Handicapped), 154 W. 14th St., New York, NY 10011 (☎ **212/727-4200**), operates summer tours to Europe and elsewhere for its members. Membership costs $4 yearly.

You can also obtain a copy of **"Air Transportation of Handicapped Persons"** from the Distribution Unit, U.S. Department of Transportation, Publications Division, M-4332, Washington, DC 20590. Write for Free Advisory Circular No. AC12032.

For the blind or visually impaired, the best source is the **American Foundation for the Blind,** 11 Penn Plaza, New York, NY 10011 (☎ **212/502-7600,** or 800/232-5463 for ordering information kits and supplies). It offers information on travel and the various requirements for the transport of and border formalities for seeing-eye dogs. It also issues identification cards to those who are legally blind.

The **Information Center for Individuals with Disabilities,** Fort Point Place, 27–43 Wormwood St., Boston, MA 02210 (☎ **617/727-5540** or 800/462-5015), offers lists of travel agents who specialize in tours for persons with disabilities.

Another good organization is **Flying Wheels Travel,** 143 W. Bridge (P.O. Box 382), Owatoona, MN 55060 (☎ **507/451-5005** or 800/535-6790), which offers various escorted tours and cruises internationally.

For a $25 annual fee, **Mobility International USA,** P.O. Box 10767, Eugene, OR 97440 (☎ **541/343-1284** voice and TDD), provides members with information on various destinations and also offers discounts on videos, publications, and programs it sponsors.

FOR GAY & LESBIAN TRAVELERS   Since 1861 Italy has had liberal legislation regarding homosexuality, but that doesn't mean that it has always been looked upon favorably in a Catholic country. Homosexuality is much more accepted in the north than in the south, especially in Sicily, although Taormina has long been a gay mecca. However, all major towns and cities have an active gay life, especially Florence and Rome. Capri is the gay resort of Italy, rivaled only by the gay beaches of Venice. Even more than Rome, where homosexual activity flourishes, Milan considers itself the "gay capital" of Italy, and is the headquarters of ARCI Gay, the country's leading gay organization with branches throughout Italy.

To learn about gay and lesbian travel in Italy, you can secure publications or join data-dispensing organizations before you go. Men can order *Spartacus,* the international gay guide ($32.95), or *Odysseus 1997, The International Gay Travel Planner,* a guide to international gay accommodations ($25). Both lesbians and gay men might want to pick up a copy of *Gay Travel A to Z* ($16), which specializes in general information, as well as listings of bars, hotels, restaurants, and places of interest for gay travelers throughout the world. These books and others are available from **Giovanni's Room,** 1145 Pine St., Philadelphia, PA 19107 (☎ **215/923-2960**).

Our World, 1104 N. Nova Rd., Suite 251, Daytona Beach, FL 32117 (☎ **904/441-5367**), is a magazine devoted to options and bargains for gay and lesbian travel worldwide. It costs $35 for 10 issues. The upscale ***Out and About,*** 8 West 19th St., Suite 401, New York, NY 10011 (☎ **800/929-2268**), has been hailed for its "straight" reporting about gay travel. It profiles the best gay or gay-friendly hotels, gyms, clubs, and other places throughout the world. Its cost is $49 a year for 10 information-packed issues. Both publications are also available at most gay and lesbian bookstores.

The **International Gay Travel Association (IGTA),** P.O. Box 4974, Key West, FL 33041 (☎ **305/292-0217,** or 800/448-8550 for voice mailbox), encourages gay and lesbian travel worldwide. With around 1,200 member travel agencies, it specializes in networking travelers with the appropriate gay-friendly service organization or tour specialist. It offers a quarterly newsletter, marketing mailings, and a membership directory that's updated four times a year.

FOR SENIORS   Many senior discounts are available, but note that some may require membership in a particular association.

For information before you go, obtain the free booklet **"101 Tips for the Mature Traveler,"** from **Grand Circle Travel,** 347 Congress St., Boston, MA 02210 (☎ **617/350-7500** or 800/221-2610).

SAGA International Holidays, 222 Berkeley St., Boston, MA 02116 (☎ **800/343-0273**), runs all-inclusive tours for seniors, preferably for those 50 years old or older. Insurance is included in the net price of their tours.

The **American Association of Retired Persons (AARP),** 601 E St. NW, Washington, DC 20049 (☎ **202/434-AARP**), is the best organization in the United States for seniors. It offers discounts on car rentals and hotels.

Information is also available from the **National Council of Senior Citizens,** 1331 F St. NW, Washington, DC 20005-1171 (☎ **202/347-8800**), which charges $12 per person or per couple, for which you receive a monthly newsletter, part of which is devoted to travel tips. Reduced discounts on hotel and auto rentalsare available.

If you're 45 or older and need a companion to share your travel and leisure with, consider contacting **Golden Companions,** P.O. Box 5249, Reno, NV 89513 (☎ **702/324-2227**). Founded in 1987, this helpful service has found companions for hundreds of mature travelers from all over the United States and Canada. Members meet through a confidential mail network.

Mature Outlook, P.O. Box 10448, Des Moines, IA 50306 (☎ **800/336-6330**), is a travel organization for people over 50. Members are offered discounts at ITC-member hotels and a bimonthly magazine. The $14.95 annual membership fee entitles members to coupons for discounts at Sears, Roebuck & Co., as well as savings on selected auto rentals and restaurants.

FOR STUDENTS   **Council Travel** (a subsidiary of the Council on International Educational Exchange) is America's largest student, youth, and budget travel group, with more than 60 offices worldwide. The main office is at 205 E. 42nd St., New York, NY 10017 (☎ **212/822-2700** or 800/226-8624). International Student

Identity Cards, issued to all bona fide students for $16, entitle holders to generous travel and other discounts. Discounted international and domestic air tickets are available.

Eurail passes, YHA passes, weekend packages, and hostel/hotel accommodations are also bookable. Council Travel sells a number of publications for young people, including *Work, Study, Travel Abroad: The Whole World Handbook; Volunteer: The Comprehensive Guide to Voluntary Service in the U.S. and Abroad;* and *Going Places: The High School Student's Guide to Study, Travel, and Adventure Abroad.*

Real budget travelers should consider joining **Hostelling / International / IYHF** (International Youth Hostel Federation). For information contact Hostelling Information / American Youth Hostels (HI-AYH), 733 15th St. NW, Suite 840, Washington, DC 20005 (☎ **202/783-6161** or 800/444-6111). Membership costs $25 annually, but those under age 18 pay $10 and those over 54 pay $15.

8   Getting to Italy from North America

BY PLANE

Specific upheavals that shook the airline industry during the early 1990s had subsided a bit as of this writing. Despite the relative calm, the industry may still undergo some changes during the life of this edition. For last-minute conditions, including even a run-down on carriers flying into Italy, check with a travel agent or the individual airlines.

THE AIRLINES

THE MAJOR NORTH AMERICAN CARRIERS   American Airlines (☎ **800/ 624-6262**) was among the first North America–based newcomers to fly into Italy. From Chicago's O'Hare airport, American flies nonstop every evening to Milan. Flights from all parts of American's vast network fly regularly into Chicago.

TWA (☎ **800/221-2000**) offers daily nonstop flights from New York's JFK to both Rome and Milan. In summer the airline steps up its service, with two daily flights from New York to Rome. Because of the frequency of flights, it's often convenient and cost-effective to fly into Rome and depart from Milan, or vice versa, depending on your travel plans.

Delta (☎ **800/241-4141**) flies from New York's JFK to both Milan and Rome. Separate flights depart every evening for both destinations, with fine links to the rest of Delta's rapidly growing network of domestic and international destinations. For a few months in midwinter, service to one or both of these destinations might be reduced to six flights a week.

United Airlines (☎ **800/241-6522**) also has service to Italy from the United States.

British Airways (☎ **800/AIRWAYS**), **Air France** (☎ **800/237-2747**), **KLM** (☎ **800/374-7747**), and **Lufthansa** (☎ **800/645-3880**) offer some attractive deals for anyone interested in combining a trip to Italy with a stopover in, say, Britain, Paris, Amsterdam, or Germany along the way.

Canada's second-largest airline, Calgary-based **Canadian Airlines International** (☎ **800/426-7000**), flies every day of the week from Toronto to Rome. Two of the flights are nonstop, whereas the others touch down en route in Montréal, depending on the schedule.

THE MAJOR ITALIAN CARRIER   Alitalia (☎ **800/223-5730**) flies nonstop to both Rome and Milan from different North American cities, including New York (JFK), Newark, Boston, Chicago, Miami, and Los Angeles. Schedules are carefully designed to facilitate easy transfers to all the major cities. Alitalia participates in the frequent-flyer programs of other airlines, including Continental and USAir.

OTHER GOOD-VALUE CHOICES

BUCKET SHOPS   In its purest sense, a bucket shop, also known as a consolidator, acts as a clearinghouse for blocks of tickets that airlines discount and consign during normally slow periods of air travel.

Tickets are sometimes—but not always—priced at up to 35% less than the full fare. Perhaps your reduced fare will be no more than 20% off the regular fare. Terms of payment can vary—say, anywhere from 45 days prior to departure to last-minute sales offered in a final attempt by an airline to fill an empty aircraft.

Since dealing with unknown bucket shops might be a little risky, it's wise to call the Better Business Bureau in your area to see if complaints have been filed against the company from which you plan to purchase a ticket.

One of the biggest U.S. consolidators is **Travac,** 989 Ave. of the Americas, New York, NY 10018 (☎ **212/563-3303** or 800/TRAV-800), which offers discounted seats throughout the United States to most cities in Europe on airlines that include TWA, United, and Delta. Another branch office is at 2601 E. Jefferson St., Orlando, FL 32803 (☎ **407/896-0014**).

CHARTER FLIGHTS   Strictly for reasons of economy (and never for convenience), some travelers are willing to accept the possible uncertainties of a charter flight to Italy.

In a strict sense, a charter flight occurs on an aircraft reserved months in advance for a one-time-only transit to some predetermined point. Before paying for a charter, check the restrictions on your ticket or contract. You may be asked to purchase a tour package and pay far in advance. You'll pay a stiff penalty (or forfeit the ticket entirely) if you cancel. Charters are sometimes canceled when the plane doesn't fill up. In some cases, the charter-ticket seller will offer you an insurance policy for your own legitimate cancellation (hospitalization, death in the family, whatever).

There's no way to predict whether a proposed flight to Rome will cost less on a charter or less through a bucket shop. You'll have to investigate at the time of your trip. Some charter companies have proved unreliable in the past.

One reliable charter-flight operator is **Council Charter,** run by the Council on International Educational Exchange, 205 E. 42nd St., New York, NY 10017 (☎ **212/661-1450** or 800/2-COUNCIL), which arranges charter seats on regularly scheduled aircraft.

One of the biggest New York charter operators is **Travac,** 989 Ave. of the Americas, New York, NY 10018 (☎ **212/563-3303,** or 800/TRAV-800 in the U.S.).

BY PACKAGE TOUR

With a good tour group, you can know ahead of time just what your trip will cost. Perhaps best of all, you won't be bothered with having to arrange your own transportation in places where language might be a problem, looking after your own luggage, coping with reservations and payment at individual hotels, and facing other "nuts and bolts" requirements of travel. Although several of the best-rated tour companies are described below, you should consult a good travel agent for the latest offerings and advice.

There are many different operators eager for a share of your business, but one that meets with consistent approval from participants is **Perillo Tours,** 577 Chestnut Ridge Rd., Woodcliff Lake, NJ 07675-9888 (☎ **201/307-1234,** or 800/431-1515 in the U.S.), family operated for three generations. Since it was established in 1945, it has sent more than a million travelers to Italy. Known and well respected for the value they offer, Perillo tours cost much less than the cost of the assembled elements of each tour if arranged separately. Accommodations are in first-class hotels, and guides tend to be well qualified, well informed, and sensitive to the needs of tour participants.

Perillo operates hundreds of departures year-round. Between April and October, nine different itineraries are offered, ranging from 8 to 15 days each, covering broadly different regions of the peninsula. Between November and April, the "Off-Season Italy" tour covers three of Italy's premier cities during a season when they're likely to be less densely crowded with tourists.

Another contender for the package-tour business in Italy is **Italiatour,** a company of the Alitalia Group (☎ **212/765-2183** or 800/845-3365), which offers a wide variety of tours through all parts of the peninsula. The company appeals to the free-at-heart (clients who don't want any semblance of a tour). It specializes in tours for independent travelers who ride from one destination to another by train or rental car. In most cases the company sells prereserved hotel accommodations, which are usually less expensive than if you had reserved the accommodations yourself. Because of the company's close link with Alitalia, the prices quoted for air passage are sometimes among the most reasonable on the retail market.

Finally, **Abercrombie & Kent,** Sloane Square House, Holbein Place, London SW1W 8NS (☎ **0171/730-9376**), offers a medley of luxurious premium packages. Your overnight stays will be in meticulously restored castles and exquisite Italian villas, most of which are four- and five-star accommodations. Several tours are offered, including tours of the Lake Garda region and the southern territory of Calabria.

9 Getting to Italy from Within Europe

BY TRAIN

If you plan to travel heavily on the European and/or British railroads, you'll do well to secure the latest copy of the *Thomas Cook European Timetable of Railroads.* This comprehensive, 500+-page timetable documents all of Europe's mainline passenger rail services with detail and accuracy. It's available exclusively in North America from **Forsyth Travel Library,** P.O. Box 2975, Shawnee Mission, KS 66201 (☎ **800/FORSYTH**), at a cost of $27.95 (plus $4.50 shipping in U.S. and $5.50 in Canada).

EURAILPASS Many travelers to Europe take advantage of one of its greatest travel bargains, the Eurailpass, which permits unlimited first-class rail travel in any country in Western Europe (except the British Isles) and Hungary in Eastern Europe. Oddly, it does *not* include travel on the rail lines of Sardinia, which are organized independently of the rail lines of the rest of Italy. Passes may be purchased for 15 days to 3 months.

Here's how it works: The pass costs $522 for 15 days, $678 for 21 days, $838 for 1 month, $1,148 for 2 months, and $1,468 for 3 months. Children 3 and under travel free providing they don't occupy a seat (otherwise, they're charged half fare); children under 12 pay half fare.

The advantages are tempting: No tickets; simply show the pass to the ticket collector, then settle back to enjoy the scenery. Seat reservations are required on some trains. Many of the trains have *couchettes* (sleeping cars), for which an additional fee is charged.

Obviously, the 2- or 3-month traveler gets the greatest economic advantages. To obtain full advantage of a 15-day or 1-month pass, you'd have to spend a great deal of time on the train.

Eurailpass holders are entitled to considerable reductions on certain buses and ferries. You'll get a 20% reduction on second-class accommodations from certain companies operating ferries between Naples and Palermo, or for crossings to Sardinia and Malta.

Travel agents in all towns, and railway agents in such major cities as New York, Montréal, and Los Angeles, sell all these tickets. A Eurailpass is available at the North American offices of CIT Travel Service, the French National Railroads, the German Federal Railroads, and the Swiss Federal Railways.

The **Eurail Saverpass** is a money-saving ticket that offers discounted 15-day travel for groups of three or more people traveling together between April and September, or two people traveling together between October and March. The price of a Saverpass, valid all over Europe for first class only, is $452 for 15 days, $578 for 21 days, and $712 for 1 month.

The **Eurail Flexipass** allows passengers to visit Europe with more flexibility. It's valid in first class and offers the same privileges as the Eurailpass. However, it provides a number of individual travel days that can be used over a much longer period of consecutive days. That makes it possible to stay in one city and yet not lose a single day of travel. There are two passes: 10 days of travel within 2 months for $616, and 15 days of travel within 2 months for $812.

If you're under 26, you can purchase a **Eurail Youthpass,** which entitles you to unlimited second-class travel wherever the Eurailpass is honored. The pass costs $418 for 15 consecutive days, $598 for 1 month, or $798 for 2 months. There's also a **Eurail Youth Flexipass** for travelers under 26. Two passes are available: 10 days of travel within 2 months for $438 and 15 days of travel within 2 months for $588.

EUROPASS   The Europass is more limited than the Eurailpass, but may offer better value for visitors traveling over a smaller area. The Europass allows unlimited rail travel within three to five European countries with shared (contiguous) borders. The countries included are Italy, France, Germany, Switzerland, and Spain.

All passes are good for 2 months. For travel in three of the above-mentioned countries (Italy plus two other contiguous countries) the fare for adults in first class is $316 for 5 days of travel, $358 for 6 days of travel, and $400 for 7 days of travel.

For travel in four contiguous countries, the adult fare is $442 for 8 days of travel, $482 for 9 days of travel, and $526 for 10 days of travel. For travel in all five of the above-mentioned countries, the adult fare is $568 for 11 days of travel, $610 for 12 days of travel, and $736 for 15 days of travel.

If two adults travel together, the second adult receives a 50% discount on the above-quoted fares. You can add an "associate country" (Austria, Benelux, Greece, or Portugal) to your Europass by paying a surcharge of between $29 and $90 per country.

For travelers under 26, a Europass Youth is available. The fares are 35% off those quoted above, and the pass is only good for second-class travel. Unlike the adult Europass, there is no companion discount.

Europass can be purchased from any travel agent, or call 800/4-EURAIL.

BY CAR

If you're already on the Continent, particularly in a neighboring country such as France or Austria, you may want to drive to Italy. However, arrangements should be made in advance with your car-rental company.

It's also possible to drive from London to Rome, a distance of 1,124 miles, via Calais/Boulogne/Dunkirk, or 1,085 miles via Oostende/Zeebrugge, not counting Channel crossings either by Hovercraft ferry or the Chunnel. Milan is some 400 miles closer to Britain than is Rome. If you cross over from England and arrive at one of the continental ports, you still face a 24-hour drive. Most drivers play it safe and budget 3 days for the journey.

Most of the roads from Western Europe leading into Italy are toll free, with some notable exceptions. If you use the Swiss superhighway network, you'll have to purchase a special tax sticker at the frontier. You'll also pay to go through the St. Gotthard Tunnel into Italy. Crossings from France can be through the Mont Blanc Tunnel, for which you'll pay, or you can leave the French Riviera at Menton (France) and drive directly into Italy along the Italian Riviera toward San Remo.

If you don't want to drive such distances, ask a travel agent to book you on a Motorail arrangement where the train carries your car. This service, however, is good only to Milan, as there are no car and sleeper expresses running the approximately 400 miles south to Rome.

10 Getting Around

BY PLANE

Italy's domestic air network on **Alitalia** (☎ **800/223-5730**) is one of the largest and most complete in Europe. There are some 40 airports serviced regularly from Rome, and most flights are under an hour. Fares vary, but some discounts are available. Tickets are discounted 50% for passengers 2 to 11 years old; for passengers 12 to 22 years old, there's a youth fare. And anyone can get a 30% reduction by taking domestic flights that depart at night.

BY TRAIN

Trains provide a medium-priced means of transportation, even if you don't buy the Eurailpass or one of the special Italian Railway tickets (see below). As a rule of thumb, second-class travel regardless of the destination usually costs about two-thirds the price of an equivalent trip in first class. A *couchette* (a private fold-down bed in a communal cabin) requires a supplement above the price of first-class travel. In a land where *mamma* and *bambini* are highly valued, children aged 4 to 11 receive a discount of 50% off the adult fare, and children 3 and under travel free with their parents.

Senior citizens get a break, too. Anyone 60 and over can purchase a **Senior Citizen's Silver Card (Carta d'Argento)** by presenting proof of age at any railway station. The card, which can only be purchased in Italy, allows a 20% discount off the price of any ticket between points on the Italian rail network. It's good for 1 year and costs 40,000 lire ($25.60). It's not valid on Friday, Saturday, or Sunday between late June and late August or anytime during Christmas week. The Italian railway system also offers a **Cartaverde,** good for anyone under 26. Valid for 1 year, the card costs 40,000 lire ($25.60) and entitles a passenger to a 20% reduction off any state train fare. This pass can only be purchased in Italy.

An **Italian Railpass** (known within Italy as a BTLC Pass) allows non-Italian citizens to ride as much as they like on the entire rail network of Italy. Buy the pass in the United States or at main train stations in Italy, have it validated the first time you use it at any railway station in Italy, and ride as frequently as you like within the time validity of your pass. An 8-day pass costs $248 in first class and $168 in second class, a 15-day pass is $312 in first class and $208 in second class, a 21-day pass runs $362 in first class and $242 in second class, and a 30-day pass costs $436 in first class and $290 in second class.

With the Italian Railpass and each of the other special passes, a supplement must be paid to ride on certain very rapid trains. These are designated ETR-450 trains (also known as "Pendolino" trains). The rail systems of Sardinia are administered by a separate entity and are not included in the Railpass or any of the other passes mentioned.

Another option is the **Italian Flexirail Card,** which entitles holders to a predetermined number of days of travel on any rail line of Italy within a certain period of time. It's ideal for passengers who plan in advance to spend several days sightseeing before boarding a train for another city. A pass giving 4 possible travel days out of a block of 1 month costs $194 in first class and $132 in second class, a pass for 8 travel days stretched over a 1-month period costs $284 in first class and $184 in second class, and a pass for 12 travel days within 1 month costs $356 in first class and $238 in second class.

In addition, the **Kilometric Ticket** is valid for 2 months' worth of travel on regular trains. (It can also be used on special train rides if you pay a supplement.) The ticket is valid for 20 trips, providing that the total distance covered does not exceed 1,875 miles (3,000 kilometers). The price is $264 in first class, $156 in second class.

In previous years, Italian Railway authorities have required that many of the above-mentioned passes be purchased outside Europe. These rules have relaxed considerably in recent years, and at press time some of the above-mentioned passes could be purchased within Italy. (Check carefully before your departure, as this might change at any time.) The notable exception to this rule is the Italian Flexirail Card, which requires purchase in North America. You can purchase any of these passes from a travel agent or at **CIT Tours,** the official representative of Italian State Railway, with offices at 342 Madison Ave., New York, NY 10173 (☎ **212/697-2100** or 800/223-7987; fax 212/697-1394) and at 6033 W. Century Blvd., Suite 980, Los Angeles, CA 90045 (☎ **310/338-8616** or 800/248-7245; fax 310/670-4269).

A Warning: Many irate readers have complained about train service in Italy—they've found the railroads dirty, overcrowded, unreliable, and with little regard for schedules. As you may have heard, strikes plague the country, and you never know as you board a train when it will reach your hoped-for destination. A sense of humor (and a flexible itinerary) might be your best defense against aggravation and irritating delays.

BY BUS

Italy has an extensive and intricate bus network, covering all regions of the country. However, because rail travel is inexpensive, the bus is not the preferred method of travel.

SITA, viale dei Cadorna 105, Florence (☎ **055/214721**), and **ANAC,** piazza Esquilino 29, Rome (☎ **06/4482-0531**), are two companies that blanket the country with air-conditioned coaches.

Other companies operating buses are **Autostradale,** piazzale Castello, Milan (☎ **02/801161**), which serves a large chunk of northern Italy; and **Lazzi,** via Mercadante 2, Florence (☎ **055/363041**), which goes through Tuscany, including Siena, and much of central Italy.

Where these nationwide services leave off, local bus companies operate in most regions, particularly in the hill sections and in the alpine regions where travel by rail is not possible. For more information about these services, refer to the "By Bus" units under "Getting There" in the various city, town, and village sections.

BY CAR

U.S. and Canadian drivers must carry an International Driver's License when touring Italy or else obtain a declaration from the Automobile Club d'Italia (ACI) that entitles them to drive on Italian roads upon presentation of a valid U.S. or Canadian driver's license (with Italian translation). The declaration is available from any ACI frontier or provincial office. Several organizations, including the AAA, can provide an Italian-language translation of a U.S. or Canadian driver's license. The possession of such a translation is intended to facilitate procedures with Italian police personnel, who don't necessarily understand English text. In practice, however, the translation is often not even looked at. But if you're respecting the letter of the Italian law, it's necessary to have it.

Apply for an International Driver's License at any **American Automobile Association (AAA)** branch. You must be at least 18 years old and have two 2- by 2-inch photographs, a $10 fee, and a photcopy of your U.S. driver's license with an AAA application form. To find the AAA office nearest you, check the local telephone directory or contact AAA's national headquarters at 1000 AAA Dr., Heathrow, FL 32746-5063 (☎ **407/444-4300**). Remember that an International Driver's License is valid only if physically accompanied by your original driver's license. In Canada, you can get the address of the Canadian Automobile Association closest to you by calling its national office (☎ **613/247-0117**).

The **Automobile Club d'Italia (ACI)** is the equivalent of the American Automobile Association. It has offices throughout Italy, including the head office, via Marsala 8, 00185 Rome (☎ **06/4998-2389**), open Monday to Saturday from 8am to 2pm. The 24-hour Information and Assistance Center (CAT) of the ACI is at via Magenta 5, 00185 Roma (☎ **06/4477**). Both offices are located near the main railway station (Stazione Termini) in Rome.

RENTALS   Many of the most charming landscapes lie away from the main cities, far away from the train stations. For that, and for sheer convenience, renting a car is usually the best way to explore the country.

However, the legalities and contractual obligations of renting a car in Italy (where accident and theft rates are very high) are more complicated than in almost any other country in Europe. To rent a car in Italy, a driver must have nerves of steel, a sense of humor, a valid driver's license, a valid passport, and in most cases, be over age 25. In all cases, payment and paperwork are simpler if you present a valid credit or charge card with your completed rental contract. If that isn't possible, you'll almost certainly be required to pay a substantial deposit, sometimes in cash. Insurance on all vehicles is compulsory in Italy, although any reputable car-rental firm will arrange it in advance before you're even given the keys.

The three major car-rental companies in Italy are **Avis** (☎ 800/331-2112), **Budget Rent a Car** (☎ 800/472-3325), **Hertz** (☎ 800/654-3001). Another option is **Kemwel** (☎ 800/678-0678).

In some, but not all, cases, slight discounts are offered to members of the American Automobile Association (AAA) or the American Association of Retired Persons (AARP).

Each company offers a collision-damage waiver (CDW) that costs between $14 and $21 a day (depending on the value of the car). Some companies include CDWs in the prices they quote; others don't. This extra protection will cover all or part of the repair-related costs if there is an accident. (In some cases, even if you purchase the CDW, you'll still pay between $200 and $300 per accident. It pays to ask some questions before you sign the contract.) If you don't have CDW and have an accident, you'll usually pay for all damages, up to the replacement cost of the vehicle. In addition, because of the rising theft rate in Italy, all three of the major U.S.–based companies offer theft and break-in protection policies (Avis and Budget require it). For pickups at most airports in Italy, all three companies must impose a 10%

government tax. To avoid that charge, consider picking your car up at an inner-city location. There's also an unavoidable 19% government tax, although more and more companies are including this in the rates they quote.

GASOLINE   Gasoline (known as *benzina*) is expensive in Italy, as are autostrade tolls. Carry enough cash if you're going to do extensive motoring. Filling the tank of a medium-sized car with "super *benzina*," the octane rating appropriate for most of the cars you'll be able to rent, will usually cost around 65,000 lire ($41.60).

Gas stations on autostrade are open 24 hours a day, but on regular roads gas stations are rarely open on Sunday, many close between noon and 3pm for lunch, and most of them shut down after 7pm. Make sure the pump registers zero before an attendant starts refilling your tank. A popular scam, particularly in the south, is to fill your tank before resetting the meter so that you pay not only your bill but the charges run up by the previous motorist.

DRIVING RULES   The Italian Highway Code follows the Geneva Convention and Italy uses international road signs. Driving is on the right, passing on the left. Violators of the highway code are fined; serious violations may also be punished by imprisonment. In cities and towns, the speed limit is 50 kilometers per hour (kmph) or 31 miles per hour (m.p.h.). For all cars and motor vehicles on main roads and local roads, the limit is 90kmph or 56 m.p.h. For the autostrade (national express highways), the limit is 130kmph or 81 m.p.h. Use of seat belts is compulsory.

ROAD MAPS   The best touring maps are published by the **Automobile Club d'Italia (ACI)** and the **Italian Touring Club,** or you can purchase the maps of the **Carta Automobilistica d'Italia,** covering Italy in two maps on the scale of 1:800,000 (1cm = 8km). These two maps should fulfill the needs of most motorists. If you plan to explore one region of Italy in depth, then consider one of 15 regional maps (1:200,000; 1cm = 2km), published by **Grande Carta Stradale d'Italia.**

All maps mentioned above are sold at certain newsstands and at all major bookstores in Italy, especially those with travel departments. Many travel bookstores in the United States also carry them. If U.S. outlets don't have these maps, they often offer Michelin's red map (no. 988) of Italy, which is on a scale of 1:1,000,000 (1cm = 10km). This map covers all of Italy in some detail.

BREAKDOWNS/ASSISTANCE   In case of car breakdown or for any tourist information, foreign motorists can call **116** (nationwide telephone service). For road information, itineraries, and all sorts of travel assistance, call **06/499-8389** (ACI's information center). Both services operate 24 hours a day.

BY FERRY

Ferries are used primarily in the south. Driving time from Naples to Sicily is cut considerably by taking one of the vessels operated by **Tirrenia Lines,** Molo Angioino, Stazione Marittima, in Naples (☎ **081/761-3688**). Departures are daily at 8pm for the 11-hour trip to Palermo. Frequent ferry services and hydrofoils also depart from Naples for the offshore islands of Capri and Ischia.

SUGGESTED ITINERARIES

If You Have 1 Week: From Rome to Venice

Days 1–3   Fly to Rome and spend most of the day recovering. If it's summer, view the floodlit Roman Forum at sunset from the balcony of the Campidoglio. Have a drink and dinner near the Spanish Steps and turn in early for a big day of sightseeing tomorrow. Your second day, take in the Colosseum and Forum and visit St. Peter's. On the morning of the third day, explore some of the highlights of the Vatican before going outside Rome to see the gardens at Tivoli and Hadrian's Villa.

Days 4–5 Transfer to Florence and soak up as much of the city of the Renaissance as time allows.

Days 6–7 Transfer to Venice, where so many attractions await you that you'll promise yourself a return visit when you have more time.

If You Have Another Week: The Veneto, Lombardy & the Piedmont

Day 1 Leave Venice in the morning and head for the attractions of Padua (Padova) in the west (see Chapter 11). Visit at least the Capella degli Scrovegni and the Basilica di Sant'Antonio. Have lunch at Belle Parti-Toulà and continue northwest to Vicenza for the night. See as many sights in the city of Andrea Palladio as you can before nightfall.

Day 2 In the morning continue west to Verona, city of Romeo and Juliet, which will consume at least a day for only the most superficial of visits. See such attractions as the Arena di Verona, Castelvecchio, Il Duomo, and the Church of San Zeno Maggiore (see Chapter 11).

Day 3 Leave Verona in the morning and stop for a morning in Brescia to visit its piazza della Loggia, piazza del Duomo, and Tosio-Martinengo Civic Picture Gallery. In Brescia you can dine at the excellent La Sosta, via San Martino della Battaglia 20 (☎ 030/25121), in a 17th-century building. It has the finest food in the area but is closed from January 1 to 18 and August 4 to 25. After lunch there, continue for the night to Bergamo (see Chapter 13).

Days 4–5 Milan, Milan, and more Milan (see Chapter 13). In 2 short days you won't be able to see everything you want—much less shop enough.

Day 6 Head west for the city of Turin (see Chapter 14) to visit its Egyptian Museum, Galleria Sabauda, Capella della Santa Sindone, and other attractions.

Day 7 For a final day of sightseeing, go southeast to the ancient seaport of Genoa (see Chapter 15) for an action-packed day. Tour the harbor by boat and dine in a typical seaport restaurant at night.

If You Have 2 Weeks: The Western Coast from the Riviera to Rome

One of the most interesting trips in Italy is along its western coast.

Day 1 Begin at the Italian Riviera near the French border, heading first for an overnight stay in San Remo, capital of the Riviera (see Chapter 15). Visit its old city, its flower market (the most famous in Italy), and drop in at its casino at night.

Day 2 Leave San Remo in the morning and drive along the coast, stopping at random at such towns as Albenga or Savona before reaching Genoa. Spend the night here if you haven't visited it previously (see above).

Day 3 Leave Genoa in the morning and continue in the general direction of Rome, favoring one of three resorts as previewed in Chapter 15—Portofino (the most chic), Rapallo, or Santa Margherita Ligure.

Day 4 Continue along the coast and schedule a luncheon stopover in La Spezia. Your best bet is the elegant Parodi, viale Amendola 212 (☎ 0187/715777). In the afternoon visit the art city of Lucca and see its cathedral, dating from 1060, and its churches of San Michele and San Frediano. For the night, go to Pisa to view its Leaning Tower and other attractions (see Chapter 7).

Days 5–6 Head southeast from Pisa and plan to be in San Gimignano for lunch. Called the "Manhattan of Tuscany" because of its noble brick towers, it's one of the most interesting of the hill towns of Italy. Continue southeast for the night, arriving in Siena. On Day 6, explore history-rich Siena, which is filled with attractions that can hardly be viewed in one day. (See Chapter 7.)

Day 7   From Siena head out in the morning to another hill town, Arezzo, to the east. See at least the frescoes of Piero della Francesca in the Church of St. Francis and perhaps the Romanesque church of Santa Maria della Pieve. Continue southeast to the ancient university city of Perugia for the night. (See Chapter 7.)

Day 8   You'll need most of the following day to see the attractions of Perugia, especially its Galleria Nazionale dell'Umbria, with one of the world's greatest collections of Umbrian art.

Day 9   From Perugia drive through the Umbrian countryside until you reach Assisi (see Chapter 7), hometown of native son, St. Francis. This is one of the most popular destinations in Italy, and you'll want to spend at least a day and a night there.

Day 10   Leave Assisi and head south to Spoleto (see Chapter 7) for a morning visit and lunch. After Spoleto, drive west to Orvieto to see its duomo. After a visit, head south for Rome.

Days 11–14   Explore the riches and architectural treasures of Rome, the former seat of one of the world's greatest empires.

If You Have Another 10 Days

Days 1–2   To save time, take a domestic flight to Naples (see Chapter 16). You can explore once-buried Roman towns and ancient centers of Magna Græcia. You can be in Naples for lunch and afternoon sightseeing. The next morning, catch the hydrofoil to Capri and spend the day there (see Chapter 17), to visit the Blue Grotto and many other attractions, before returning to Naples for the night.

Days 3–4   Leave Naples in the morning and head south to Sorrento or one of the other resorts along the Amalfi Drive, including Amalfi itself or, better yet, Positano (see Chapter 17). Spend the rest of the day enjoying one of these resorts and get to bed early so you'll be prepared for a strenuous day of sightseeing. Either on your own or via an organized tour, make the traditional visits to the two towns that Vesuvius destroyed, Herculaneum and Pompeii (see Chapter 16). If time remains in your day, you can even go up to Mount Vesuvius itself to see the crater from which came the violent eruption. Return to Sorrento or one of the other towns for the night.

Day 5   Head down the coast to Paestum (see Chapter 17) to see its three Doric temples before returning to Naples in the early evening to board a boat for Palermo, the capital of Sicily. If you don't have time for Sicily, you can break the tour here, returning to Rome for your flight back home. If you're going on to Sicily, you'll spend the night aboard the boat in a rented cabin, arriving in Palermo in the early hours of morning.

Day 6   Spend the day in Palermo (see Chapter 18), exploring its monuments and museums, and save time to visit the Church of Monreale in the hills. Overnight in Palermo.

Day 7   Drive west from Palermo and stop over in Erice, Trapani, or Marsala for lunch. However, don't linger too long in any place, as your major goal should be the ruins of Selinunte on the southern coast. Arrive in Agrigento for an overnight stop (see Chapter 18) and drive through the "Valley of the Temples" at night (the ruins are floodlit).

Days 8–9   Spend a leisurely day driving from Agrigento along the southeastern coast of Sicily. Arrive in Siracusa by the late afternoon. Spend 2 nights here, as it will take all of the following day to see its many archeological treasures (see Chapter 18).

Day 10   From Siracusa drive north along the eastern coast, stopping for the night in the resort of Taormina, one of the most idyllic in Italy (see Chapter 18).

11 For British Travelers

CUSTOMS

On January 1, 1993, the borders between Europeam countries were relaxed as the European markets united. When you're traveling within the EU, this will have a big impact on what you can buy and take home with you for personal use.

If you buy your goods in a duty-free shop, then the old rules still apply—you're allowed to bring home 200 cigarettes and 2 liters of table wine, plus 1 liter of spirits or 2 liters of fortified wine. But now you can buy your wine, spirits, or cigarettes in an ordinary shop in Italy, for example, and bring home *almost* as much as you like. (U.K. Customs and Excise does not set theoretical limits.) If you're returning home from a non-EU country, the allowances are the standard ones from duty-free shops. You must declare any goods in excess of these allowances. British Customs tends to be strict and complicated in its requirements. For details, get in touch with **Her Majesty's Customs and Excise Office,** New King's Beam House, 22 Upper Ground, London, SE1 9PJ (☎ **0171/620-1313**), for more information.

TIPS FOR TRAVELERS WITH SPECIAL NEEDS

Before you go, travelers with special needs may want to check with the offerings of the following organizations.

FOR TRAVELERS WITH DISABILITIES   The **Royal Association for Disability and Rehabilitation (RADAR),** Unit 12, City Forum, 250 City Rd., London ECIV 8AF (☎ **0171/250-3222**), publishes three holiday "fact packs" which sell for £2 each or £5 for a set of all three. The first one provides general information, including planning and booking a holiday, insurance, and finances. The second outlines transport and equipment, transportation available when going abroad, and equipment for rent. The third deals with specialized accommodations.

Another good resource is the **Holiday Care Service,** Imperial Building, 2nd Floor, Victoria Road, Horley, Surrey RH6 7PZ (☎ **01293/774-535;** fax 01293/784-647), a national charity that advises on accessible accommodations for the elderly and persons with disabilities. Annual membership costs £25.

FOR FAMILIES   The best deals for families are often package tours put together by some of the giants of the British travel industry. Foremost among these is **Thomsons Tour Operators,** which offers dozens of air/land packages to continental Europe, including Italy, where a designated number of airline seats are reserved for the free use of children 17 and under who accompany their parents. To qualify, parents must book airfare and hotel accommodations lasting 2 weeks or more, and book as far in advance as possible. Savings for families with children can be substantial.

FOR STUDENTS   **Campus Travel,** 52 Grosvenor Gardens, London SW1W OAG (☎ **0171/730-3402**), opposite Victoria Station, open 7 days a week, is Britain's leading specialist in student and youth travel worldwide. Founded to meet the needs of students and young people, it provides a comprehensive travel service specializing in low rail, sea, and airfares, holiday breaks, and travel insurance, plus student discount cards.

The International Student Identity Card (ISIC) is an internationally recognized proof of student status that will entitle you to savings on flights, sightseeing, food, and accommodation. It sells for £5 and is well worth the cost. Always show your ISIC when booking a trip—you may not get a discount without it.

Youth hostels are the place to stay if you're a student or, in some cases, if you're traveling on an ultra-tight budget. You'll need an **International Youth Hostels Association card,** which you can purchase from either of London's youth hostel retail outlets. With locations near Covent Garden at 14 Southampton St., London WC23 7HY (☎ **0171/836-8541**), and in the same building as the previously recommended Campus Travel, 52 Grosvenor Gardens, London SW1W OAG (☎ **0171/823-4739**), they sell rucksacks, hiking boots, maps, and all the paraphernalia a camper, hiker, or shoestring traveler might need. To apply for a membership card, take both your passport and some passport-sized photos of yourself, plus a membership fee of £9.30. For more information contact **Youth Hostels Association of England and Wales (YHA),** 8 St. Stephen's Hill, St. Albans, Hertfordshire AL1 2DY (☎ **01727/855215**).

The Youth Hostel Association puts together a *YHA Budget Accommodations Guide* (Volumes 1 and 2), which lists the address, phone number, and admissions policy for every youth hostel in the world. (Volume 1 covers Europe and the Mediterranean; volume 2 covers the rest of the globe.) They cost £6.99 each and can be purchased at the retail outlets listed above. If ordering by mail, add 61p for postage within the U.K.

Many youth hostels fill up in the summer, so be sure to book ahead.

GETTING THERE

Because getting to Italy from the U.K is often expensive, savvy Brits usually call a travel agent for a "deal." That could be in the form of a charter flight or some special air-travel promotion. These so-called deals—by land or air—are always available because of the great interest in Italy as a tourist destination.

BY PLANE   If a special air-travel promotion is not available or feasible at the time of your anticipated visit, then an APEX ticket might be the way to keep costs trimmed. These tickets must be reserved in advance. However, an APEX ticket offers a discount without the usual booking restrictions. You might also ask the airlines about a "Eurobudget ticket," which imposes restrictions or length-of-stay requirements.

British newspapers are always full of classified advertisements touting "slashed" fares to Italy. One good source is *Time Out,* a magazine published in London. London's *Evening Standard* has a daily travel section, and the Sunday editions of almost any newspaper will run many ads. Although competition is fierce, one well-recommended company that consolidates bulk ticket purchases, and then passes the savings on to its consumers, is **Trailfinders** (☎ **0171/937-5400** in London). It offers access to tickets on such carriers as SAS, British Airways, and KLM.

CEEFAX, a British television information service included on many home and hotel TVs, runs details of package holidays and flights to Italy and beyond. Just switch to your CEEFAX channel and you'll find a menu of listings that includes travel information.

Both **British Airways** (☎ **0181/897-4000**) and **Alitalia** (☎ **0181/745-8200**) have frequent flights from London's Heathrow Airport to Rome, Milan, Venice, Pisa (the gateway to Florence), and Naples. Flying time from London to these cities is anywhere from 2 to 3 hours. BA also has one direct flight a day from Manchester to Rome.

BY TRAIN   Many different rail passes are available in the U.K. for travel in Europe. Stop in at the **International Rail Centre,** Victoria Station, London SW1V 1JZ (☎ **0171/834-6744**). The staff there can help you find the best option for the trip you're planning. Some of the most popular are the **Inter-Rail** and **EuroYouth** passes which entitle pass holders to unlimited second-class travel in 26 European countries.

Eurotrain "Explorer" tickets are another worthwhile option for travelers who can show proof that they're under age 26. They allow passengers to move in a leisurely fashion from London to Rome, with as many stopovers en route as their holders want, using a different route southbound (through Belgium, Luxembourg, and Switzerland) from the return route northbound (exclusively through France). All travel must be completed within 2 months of the date of departure. Such a ticket sells for £195 round-trip.

Wasteels, adjacent to Platform 2 in Victoria Station, London SW1V 1JZ (☎ **071/ 834-7066**), will sell a **Rail Europe Senior Pass** to bona fide residents of the U.K. for £5. With it, a British resident more than 60 years of age can buy discounted rail tickets on many of the rail lines of Europe. To qualify, British residents must present a valid British Senior Citizen rail card, which is available for £16 at any BritRail office if proof of age and British residency is presented.

BY BUS   Eurolines, 52 Grosvenor Gardens (opposite Victoria Rail Station), Victoria, London SW1 (☎ **0171/730-8235,** or 01582/404511 for information and reservations by credit or charge card), is the leading operator of scheduled coach service across Europe. Its comprehensive network of services includes regular departures to destinations throughout Italy, including Turin, Milan, Bologna, Florence, and Rome; plus summer services to Verona, Vicenza, Padua, and Venice.

Eurolines' services to Italy depart from London's Victoria Coach Station and are operated by modern coach, with reclining seats and a choice of smoking or non-smoking areas. Return tickets are valid for up to 6 months, and for added flexibility passengers may also leave their return date open.

A round-trip ticket from London to Rome using as direct a route as possible costs between £129 and £139, and from £87 one-way, depending on the season. Travelers under 26 pay around £10 less each way. Departures in either direction are daily, and the trip takes around 37 hours each way. Passengers can interrupt their journey, pending available space on subsequent legs of their trip, in Paris or Milan en route.

ORGANIZED TOURS   The oldest travel agency in Britain, **Cox & Kings** (☎ **0171/873-5006**) was established in 1758 as the paymasters and transport directors for the British armed forces in India. The company continues to send large numbers of travelers from Britain throughout the rest of the world, specializing in unusual, if pricey, holidays. Their offerings in Italy include organized tours through the country's gardens and sites of historic or aesthetic interest, opera tours, pilgrimage-style visits to sites of religious interest, and food- and wine-tasting tours. The company's staff is noted for their focus on tours of ecological and environmental interest.

If your interests are more varied than those items mentioned in this brief list, call the London headquarters of the **International Association of Travel Agencies (IATA)** (☎ **0181/744-9280**) for the names and addresses of tour operators that specialize in travel relating to your particular interest.

TRAVEL INSURANCE

Most big travel agents offer their own insurance and will try to sell you their package when you book a holiday. Think before you sign. Britain's Consumers' Association recommends that you insist on seeing the policy and reading the fine print before buying travel insurance.

You should also shop around for better deals. You might contact **Columbus Travel Insurance Ltd.** (☎ **0171/375-0011** in London), or, for students, **Campus**

Travel (☎ **0171/730-3402** in London). Columbus Travel will sell travel insurance only to people who have been official residents of Britain for at least a year.

12 Tips on Accommodations

In this guide hotels rated **Very Expensive** generally cost 450,000 lire ($288) and up for a double room. Accommodations judged **Expensive** typically charge 300,000 to 450,000 lire ($192 to $288) for a double room; those in the **Moderate** category usually ask 220,000 to 300,000 lire ($140.80 to $192) for a double. Anything from 80,000 lire ($51.20) all the way up to 220,000 lire ($140.80) is judged **Inexpensive.**

Note that all rooms have **private bath** unless specified otherwise. Most hotels in Italy do not have **parking garages;** in those that do, we have indicated any charges.

Italy controls the prices of its hotels, designating a minimum and a maximum rate. The difference between the two may depend on the season, the location of the room, or even its size. Hotels are classified by stars in Italy, indicating their category of comfort: five stars for deluxe, four stars for first class, three stars for second class, two stars for third class, and one star for fourth class. Government ratings do not depend on the decoration or on frescoed ceilings, but rather on facilities such as elevators and the like. Many of the finest hostelries in Italy are rated second class because they serve only breakfast (a blessing really, for those seeking to escape the board requirements).

Reservations are advised, even in the so-called slow months from November to March. Tourist travel to Italy peaks from May to October, when moderate and budget hotels are full.

ALPINE LIVING The **Club Alpino Italia,** via Silvio Pellico 6, 20121 Milan (☎ **02/2614-1378**), owns and operates hundreds of huts in mountain districts and annually publishes a mini-guide with a map and information on access, equipment, and tariffs. A 1-year membership in the club costs 95,000 lire ($60.80) and includes a copy of this mini-guide plus advice and information about skiing and climbing throughout northern Italy. Write or call for more information.

RELIGIOUS INSTITUTIONS Convents, monasteries, and other religious institutions in Italy offer accommodations, generally of the fourth-class hotel or *pensioni* category. Some are just for men; others are for women only. Many, however, accept married couples. Italian tourist offices generally have abbreviated listings of these accommodations, or you can write directly to the archdiocese (Archidiocesi di Roma, for example) in cities in which you desire such an accommodation.

Accommodations can range from rather luxurious convents to bone-bare monastic cells. It all depends. One of the main reasons to stay in a religious institution is economy, as the accommodations are invariably cheaper than hotels or pensioni.

VILLAS & APARTMENTS For information on renting villas or apartments, you may write directly to the local tourist board or the provincial tourist office in the city or town where you expect to stay. For addresses, refer to "Essentials" in the individual city or town listings. Information on villas and apartments is also available in daily newspapers or through local real-estate agents in Italy. The following organizations deal in the rental of villas or apartments in Italy: Hideaways International, 767 Islington St. (P.O. Box 4433), Portsmouth, NH 03801 (☎ 603/430-4433 or 800/843-4433); At Home Abroad, Inc., 405 E. 56th St., Suite 6H, New York, NY 10022-2466 (☎ 212/421-9165; fax 212/752-1591); Rent a Vacation Everywhere, Inc. (RAVE), 135 Meigs St., Rochester, NY 14607 (☎ 716/256-0760; fax 716/256-2676); Hometours International, Inc., P.O. Box 11503, Knoxville, TN 37939 (☎ 800/367-4668); Grand Luxe International, Inc., 165 Chestnut St., Allendale, NJ

07401 (☎ 201/327-2333); and Rentals in Italy, 1742 Calle Corva, Camarillo, CA 93010 (☎ 805/987-5278 or 800/726-6702; fax 805/482-7976).

FARMHOUSE ACCOMMODATIONS   Another option is to stay in a house, an apartment, or a bedroom on an Italian farm as part of a program known as *agriturismo.* Most of the farms lie in rural areas outside the main tourist centers.

Italy Farm Holidays, 547 Martling Ave., Tarrytown, NY 10591 (☎ **914/ 631-7880;** fax 914/631-8831), represents about 50 working farms scattered for the most part in the Piedmont, Tuscany, Umbria, the Veneto, and Puglia, any of which would be suitable as a base for touring the art cities of the region.

Each farm or cooperative has successfully passed a personal inspection, and some of the most desirable ones lie just a few miles from the heart of Florence and Siena. Most properties require minimum stays of 3 to 7 days, and require payment in full in advance. Many offer meals (usually breakfast) as part of the arrangement; others provide such amenities as free use of bicycles or optional horseback-riding packages. Only a few of the establishments contain more than seven rentable accommodations, most have private bathrooms, and many contain kitchens of their own.

Weekly rates for two people begin at around $400 per week in low season in a modest apartment or B&B, rising to around $3,400 per week in high season for an elegant villa or a historic castle suitable for up to 10 occupants.

House cleaning or maid service is not provided during your occupancy unless it's specifically arranged as a supplement, or when a client stays for more than 1 week in an apartment or house.

YOUTH HOSTELS   The Italian Youth Hostel Association operates more than 50 hostels throughout Italy, and they're likely to be overcrowded in summer, particularly at popular tourist meccas. Reservations can be made by writing directly to the individual youth hostel. Contact the headquarters, **Associazione Italiana Alberghi per la Gioventu,** via Cavour 44, 00184 Roma (☎ **06/487-1152;** fax 06/488-0492), for details. You must be a member. In the United States you can join before you go by contacting **Hostelling International / American Youth Hostels (HI-AYH),** 733 15th St. NW, Suite 840, Washington, DC 20005 (☎ **202/783-6161**). Membership is $25; if you're under 18 the charge is $10, and if you're over 54, it's $15.

13 Tips on Dining

In this guide restaurants rated **Very Expensive** usually charge more than 120,000 lire ($76.80) for the average meal, excluding wine and service; **Expensive** restaurants, 70,000 to 120,000 lire ($44.80 to $76.80); **Moderate** restaurants, 40,000 to 70,000 lire ($25.60 to $44.80); and restaurants charging under 40,000 lire ($25.60) for the average meal, again excluding wine and service, are considered **Inexpensive.**

Some restaurants still offer a tourist menu, or *menu turistico,* at an inclusive price. The tourist menu includes soup (nearly always minestrone) or pasta, followed by a meat dish with vegetables, topped off by dessert (fresh fruit or cheese), as well as a quarter liter of wine or mineral water, along with the bread, cover charge, and service (you'll still be expected to tip something extra). Many restaurants offer this menu only reluctantly, since it's not viewed as a money-maker for the owner.

Some restaurants serve a fixed-price meal called by the less patronizing term *menu a presso fisso,* which rarely includes the cost of your wine. These fixed-price menus include taxes and service, although it's considered proper to tip extra.

Restaurants virtually insist that diners order at least a first and second course. Owners highly disapprove of foreign visitors who come in and order pasta as a main course, perhaps a salad, and then leave. If you want only a plate of spaghetti or something light, you need not reserve a table in a proper restaurant, but can patronize a less formal *trattoria* or any number of fast-food cafeterias, *rosticcerias,* or *tavola caldas.* You don't pay a cover charge, and you can order as much or as little as you wish. Pizzerias are another good option for light meals or snacks. Many bars or cafe-bars also offer both hot and cold food throughout the day. If you're lunching light in the heat, ask for *panini,* rolls stuffed with meat. *Tramezzini* are white-bread sandwiches with the crust trimmed. It's also possible to go into one of hundreds of general food stores throughout the country (called *alimentari*) and have sandwiches prepared on the spot, or purchase the makings for a picnic lunch to be enjoyed in a park.

As a final caveat, phone numbers of restaurants often aren't valid for more than a year or two. For reasons known only to the restaurateurs themselves, opening hours, even days of closing, are changed frequently. So, if possible, always check the specific details with the restaurant before heading there. If the staff doesn't speak English and you need a confirmed reservation (always a good idea), ask someone at your hotel reception desk to make a reservation for you.

FAST FACTS: Italy

American Express   Offices are found in Rome at piazza di Spagna 38 (☎ 06/ 67641), in Florence on via Dante Alighieri (☎ 055/50981), in Venice at San Marco 1471 (☎ 041/520-0844), and in Milan at via Brera 3 (☎ 02/728-5571).

Business Hours   Regular business hours are generally Monday to Friday from 9am (sometimes 9:30am) to 1pm and 3:30 (sometimes 4) to 7 or 7:30pm. In July or August, offices may not open in the afternoon until 4:30 or 5pm. **Banks** in Italy are open Monday to Friday from 8:30am to 1 or 1:30pm, and 2 or 2:30 to 4pm; and are closed all day Saturday, Sunday, and national holidays. This siesta (*riposo*) closing is often observed in Rome, Naples, and most cities of southern Italy; however, in Milan and other northern and central cities the custom has been completely abolished by some merchants. Most shops are closed on Sunday, except for certain barbershops that are open on Sunday morning and tourist-oriented stores in touristy areas that are now permitted to remain open on Sunday during the high season. However, hairdressers are closed on Sunday and Monday. If you're traveling in Italy in summer and the heat is intense, we suggest that you learn the custom of the riposo, too.

Camera/Film   U.S.–brand film is available in Italy but it's expensive. Take in as much as Customs will allow if you plan to take a lot of pictures.

Currency   See "Money," earlier in this chapter.

Customs   Overseas visitors to Italy can bring along most items for personal use duty free, including fishing tackle, a sporting gun and 200 cartridges, a pair of skis, two tennis racquets, a baby carriage, two ordinary hand cameras with 10 rolls of film, and 400 cigarettes (two cartons) or a quantity of cigars or pipe tobacco not exceeding 500 grams (1.1 lb). There are strict limits on importing alcoholic beverages. However, limits are much more liberal for alcohol bought tax-paid in other countries of the European Union.

Upon leaving Italy, citizens of the United States who have been outside the country for 48 hours or more are allowed to bring back to their home country $400 worth of merchandise duty free—that is, if they have claimed no similar exemption within the past 30 days. If you make purchases in Italy, it's important to keep your receipts.

Driving Rules   See "Getting Around," earlier in this chapter.

Drug Laws   Penalties are severe and could lead to either imprisonment or deportation. Selling drugs to minors is dealt with particularly harshly.

Drugstores   At every drugstore (*farmacia*) there's a list of those that are open at night and on Sunday. This list rotates.

Electricity   The electricity in Italy varies considerably. It's usually alternating current (AC), varying from 42 to 50 cycles. The voltage can be anywhere from 115 to 220. It's recommended that any visitor carrying electrical appliances obtain a transformer. Check the exact local current with the hotel where you're staying. Plugs have prongs that are round, not flat; therefore, an adapter plug is also needed.

Embassies/Consulates   In case of an emergency, embassies have a 24-hour referral service.

The Embassy of the **United States** is in Rome at via Vittorio Veneto 121 (☎ 06/45741). Other U.S. consulates are in Florence at Lungarno Amerigo Vespucci 38 (☎ 055/239-8276); and in Milan at Via Principe Amedeo 2/10 (☎ 02/290351). These offices are open Monday to Friday from 8:30am to noon and 2 to 5:30pm. There's also a consulate in Naples on piazza della Repubblica (☎ 081/583-8111), which is open Monday to Friday from 8am to noon. The consulate in Genoa is closed; however, there is an office of the U.S. Foreign Commercial Service, Piazza Portello 6 (☎ 010/543877), which is open Monday to Friday from 8:30am to 12:30pm.

Consulate and passport services for **Canada** are in Rome at via Zara 30 (☎ 06/445981), which is open Monday to Friday from 8:30am to 12:30pm.

The office of the **United Kingdom** is in Rome at via XX Settembre 80A (☎ 06/482-5441), open Monday to Friday from 9:15am to 1:30pm. The Consulate General's office in Naples is located at via Francesco Crispi 122 (☎ 081/663511), open Monday to Friday from 9am to 12:30pm and 2 to 4:30pm. In Milan, contact the office at via San Paolo 7 (☎ 02/723001) Monday to Friday from 9:15am to 12:15pm and 2:30 to 4:30pm.

The Embassy of **Australia** is in Rome at via Alessandria 215 (☎ 06/852721), which is open Monday to Thursday from 8:30am to noon and 2 to 4pm, and on Friday from 8:30am to noon. The consular services for Australia are in Rome at Corso Trieste 25 (☎ 06/852-2721), open Monday to Thursday from 9am to noon and 1:30 to 5pm, and on Friday from 9am to 12:30pm.

For **New Zealand,** the office in Rome is at via Zara 28 (☎ 06/440-2928), open Monday to Friday from 8:30am to 12:45pm and 1:45 to 5pm.

Emergencies   Dial **113** for an ambulance, police, or fire. In case of a breakdown on an Italian road, dial **116** at the nearest telephone box; the nearest Automobile Club of Italy (ACI) will be notified to come to your aid.

Holidays   See "When to Go," earlier in this chapter.

Information   See "Visitor Information & Entry Requirements," earlier in this chapter, and specific cities for local information offices.

Legal Aid   The consulate of your country is the place to turn, although offices cannot interfere in the Italian legal process. They can, however, inform you of your rights and provide a list of attorneys. You'll have to pay for the attorney out of your pocket—there is no free legal assistance. If you're arrested for a drug offense, about all the consulate will do is notify a lawyer about your case and perhaps inform your family.

Liquor Laws   Wine with meals has been considered a normal part of family life for hundreds of years in Italy. Children are exposed to wine at an early age, and consumption of alcohol is not considered anything out of the ordinary. There's no legal drinking age for buying or ordering alcohol. Alcohol is sold day and night throughout the year, as there is almost no restriction on the sale of wine or liquor in Italy.

Mail   At post offices, General Delivery service is available in Italy. Correspondence can be addressed c/o the post office by adding *Fermo Posta* to the name of the locality. Delivery will be made at the local central post office upon identification of the addressee by passport. In addition to all post offices, you can purchase stamps at little *tabacchi* (tobacco) stores throughout the city.

Mail delivery in Italy is notoriously bad. One letter from a soldier, postmarked in 1945, arrived in his home village in 1982. Letters sent from New York, say, in November, are often delivered (if at all) the following year. If you're writing for hotel reservations, it can cause much confusion on both sides. Many visitors arrive in Italy long before their hotel deposits. Fax machines speed up the process tremendously.

Maps   See "Getting Around," earlier in this chapter. Also see certain map recommendations in the city listings for such cities as Rome, Florence, and Venice.

Newspapers/Magazines   In major cities, it's possible to find the *International Herald Tribune* or *USA Today* as well as other English-language newspapers and magazines at hotels and news kiosks, including *Time* and *Newsweek*.

Pets   A veterinarian's certificate of good health is required for dogs and cats and should be obtained by owners before entering Italy. Dogs must be on a leash or muzzled at all times. Other animals must undergo examination at the border or port of entry. Certificates for parrots or other birds subject to psittacosis must state that the country of origin is free of disease. All documents must be certified first by a notary public, then by the nearest Italian consulate.

Police   Dial **113,** the all-purpose number for police emergency assistance in Italy.

Radio/TV   Major radio and television broadcasts are on RAI, the Italian state radio and television network. Occasionally, especially during the tourist season, the network will broadcast special programs in English. Announcements are made in the radio and TV guide sections of local newspapers. Vatican Radio also carries foreign-language religious news programs, often in English. Shortwave transistor radios pick up broadcasts from the BBC (British), Voice of America (United States), and CBC (Canadian). RAI television and private channels broadcast only in Italian. More expensive hotels often have TV sets in the bedrooms with cable subscriptions to the CNN news network. Also, see "Television," below.

Rest Rooms   All airport and railway stations have rest rooms, often with attendants, who expect to be tipped. Bars, nightclubs, restaurants, cafés, and all hotels have facilities as well. Public toilets are also found near many of the major sights.

Usually they are designated as W.C. (water closet) or as DONNE (women) or UOMINI (men). The most confusing designation is SIGNORI (gentlemen) and SIGNORE (ladies), so watch those final *i*'s and *e*'s!

Safety   The most common menace, especially in large cities, particularly Rome, is the plague of pickpockets and roving gangs of gypsy children who virtually surround you, distract you in all the confusion, and steal your purse or wallet. Never leave valuables in a car, and never travel with your car unlocked. A U.S. State

Department travel advisory warns that every car—whether parked, stopped at a traffic light, or even moving—can be a potential target for armed robbery.

Taxes   As a member of the European Union, Italy imposes a tax on most goods and services. It's a "value-added tax," called IVA in Italy. For example, the tax affecting most visitors is that imposed at hotels, which ranges from 9% in first- and second-class hotels and pensions to 19% in deluxe hotels.

If you spend more than 525,000 lire ($336) at any one store, regardless of how many individual items are involved, you're entitled to a refund of the IVA.

At the time of your purchase (of the antique, vase, or garment you couldn't live without), be sure to get a formal receipt from the vendor. When you leave Italy, find an Italian Customs agent at the airport (or at the point of your exit from the country if you're traveling by train, bus, or car). The agent will want to see the item you've bought, confirm that it's physically leaving Italy, and stamp the vendor's receipt.

You should then mail the stamped receipt (keeping a photocopy for your records) back to the original vendor. The vendor will, sooner or later, send you a refund of the tax you paid at the time of your original purchase. Reputable stores view this as a matter of ordinary paperwork and are very businesslike about it. Less honorable stores might lose your dossier. It pays to deal with established vendors on purchases of this size. You can also request that the refund be credited to the credit/charge card with which you made the purchase; this is usually a faster procedure.

Telegrams/Telephone/Telex/Fax   For **telegrams,** ITALCABLE operates services abroad, transmitting messages by cable or satellite. Both internal and foreign telegrams may be dictated over the phone (☎ 186).

A **public telephone** is always near at hand in Italy, especially if you're near a bar. Local calls cost 200 lire. You can use 100-, 200-, or 500-lira coins. Most phones, especially in the cities, accept a multiple-use phone card called *Canta telefonica,* which can be purchased at most *tabacchi* (tobacconists) and bars in increments of 2,000, 5,000, 10,000, or 20,000 lire. To use this card, insert it into the slot in the phone and then dial. A digital display will keep track of how many lire you use up during your call. The card is good until it runs out of lire, so don't forget to take it with you when you hang up.

Thanks to ITALCABLE, **international calls** to the United States and Canada can be dialed directly. Dial 00 (the international code from Italy), then the country code (1 for the United States and Canada), the area code, and the number you're calling. Calls dialed directly are billed on the basis of the call's duration only. A reduced rate is applied from 11pm to 8am Monday to Saturday and all day Sunday.

If you wish to make a **collect call** from a pay phone, simply deposit 200 lire (don't worry—you get it back when you're done), dial 170, and an ITALCABLE operator will come on and will speak English. For **calling card calls,** drop in the refundable 200 lire, then dial the appropriate number for your card's company to be connected with an operator in the United States: for AT&T, 172-1011; for MCI, 172-1022; and for Sprint, 172-1877.

If you make a **long-distance call** from a public telephone, there is no surcharge. *However, hotels have been known to double or triple the cost of the call, so be duly warned.*

To place a call to Italy, the country code is 39.

Chances are your hotel will send or receive a **telex** or **fax** for you.

Television   The RAI is the chief television network broadcasting in Italy, although its format is not as politically oriented as in the past. Every TV in the country receives RAI-1, RAI-2, and RAI-3. In addition, most Italians receive Canale 5, Rete 4, and Italia 1, which are controlled by media-magnate Silvio Berlusconi, as well as several other private stations.

Time   In terms of standard time zones, Italy is 6 hours ahead of eastern standard time in the United States. Daylight saving time goes into effect in Italy each year from the end of March to the end of September.

Tipping   This custom is practiced with flair in Italy—many people depend on tips for their livelihoods. In **hotels,** the service charge of 15% to 19% is already added to a bill. In addition, it's customary to tip the chambermaid 1,000 lire (65¢) per day; the doorman (for calling a cab), 1,000 lire (65¢); and the bellhop or porter 2,000 lire ($1.30) per bag. A concierge expects 3,000 lire ($1.90) per day, as well as tips for extra services performed, which could include help with long-distance calls. In expensive hotels these lire amounts are often doubled.

In **restaurants,** 15% is added to your bill to cover most charges. An additional tip for good service is almost always expected. It's customary in certain fashionable restaurants in Rome, Florence, Venice, and Milan to leave an additional 10%, which, combined with the assessed service charge, is a very high tip indeed. The sommelier expects 10% of the cost of the wine. Checkroom attendants now expect 1,500 lire (95¢), although in simple places Italians still hand washroom attendants 200 to 300 lire (15¢ to 20¢), more in deluxe and first-class establishments. Restaurants are required by law to give customers official receipts.

In **cafes and bars,** tip 15% of the bill, and give a theater usher 1,500 lire (95¢). **Taxi drivers** expect at least 15% of the fare.

Tourist Offices   See "Visitor Information & Entry Requirements," earlier in this chapter, and also specific city chapters.

Visas   See "Visitor Information & Entry Requirements," earlier in this chapter.

Water   It's generally safe to drink. However, if you venture into the south of Italy, particularly the Naples region, it's best to stick to bottled water.

Settling into Rome 4

Rome is a city of images, vivid and unforgettable. One of the most striking may be seen at dawn—ideally from Janiculum Hill—as the city's silhouette, with its bell towers and cupolas, comes gradually into view. Rome is also a city of sounds, beginning early in the morning with the peal of church bells calling the faithful to mass. As the city awakens and comes to life, the sounds multiply and merge into a kind of *sinfonia urbana:* The streets fill with cars, taxis, and motor scooters, blaring their horns as they weave in and out of traffic. The sidewalks become overrun with bleary-eyed office workers rushing off to their desks, but not before stealing into crowded cafes for their first cappuccino of the day. The shops lining the streets open for business by raising their protective metal grilles as loudly as possible, seeming to delight in their contribution to the general din. Even the many fruit-and-vegetable stands are abuzz with activity, as housewives, maids, widowers, cooks, and others arrive to purchase their day's supply of fresh produce, haggling over price and caviling over quality.

By 10am the tourists themselves are on the streets, battling the crowds and traffic as they wend their way from Renaissance palaces and baroque buildings to the famous ruins of antiquity—the Colosseum and the Forum, symbols of a once-great empire whose heart was Rome, the Eternal City. Indeed, Rome often appears to have two populations: one of Romans and one of visitors. During the summer months especially, Rome seems to become one big host for the countless sightseers who converge upon it, guidebook and camera in hand. To all of them—Americans, Europeans, Japanese—Rome extends a warm and friendly welcome, wining them, dining them, and entertaining them in its inimitable fashion. Of course, if you visit in August, you may see only tourists, not Romans—the locals flee at that time. Or as one Roman woman once told us, "Even if we're too poor to go on vacation, we close the shutters and pretend we're away so neighbors won't find out we couldn't afford to leave the city."

The traffic, unfortunately, is worse than ever, restoration programs seem to drag on forever, and, as the capital, Rome remains at the center of the major political scandals and corruption known as *Tangentopoli* ("bribe city") which sends hundreds of government bureaucrats to jail each year (see "Italy Today" in Chapter 2).

But in spite of all this metropolitan and political horror, Romans still experience the good life. After you've done your "duty" to culture, wandering through the Colosseum, being awed that the

Pantheon's still there, after you've traipsed through St. Peter's Basilica and thrown a coin in Trevi Fountain, you can pause in the early evening to experience the charm of Rome as evening comes. Find a cafe at summer twilight and watch the shades of pink turn to gold and copper before the night finally falls. That's when a new Rome comes alive, and when its restaurants and cafes grow more animated and more fun, especially if you've found one on an antique piazza or along a narrow alley deep in Trastevere. After dinner you can stroll by the fountains, or through piazza Navona, have a *gelato* (or *espresso* in winter), and the night is yours.

The big news for Rome is the Holy Year 2000, which will see an array of cultural and artistic events that will draw many thousands more visitors. Everything from major art exhibits to international sporting events is planned. New high-speed lines in and out of Rome are expected to be completed by 2000 (but don't count on it—this is Rome, after all). Since the jubilee year of 1300, Holy Years have been the prime occasions for urban restructuring of Rome. As the city moves toward this year and the millennium, it will be upgrading its urban landscape with better traffic signals, trees planted along the roads, flower beds in traffic islands, small public gardens in various parts of the city, restoration of ancient monuments, and the list goes on.

That's on the horizon. But if you go now, you'll still experience a vast array of activities to delight you, in spite of the traffic, overcrowding, and little gypsy children out to snatch your purse or wallet.

In Chapter 5, "What to See & Do in Rome," we'll take you on fascinating walks through the major historical and architectural sites of Rome. But important though the sites may be to an appreciation of this centuries-old city, they represent only one aspect of Rome—the past. Rome is also a vibrant, exciting *modern* metropolis, pulsing with all kinds of daytime and nighttime activities. As you take part in them, you'll find yourself embracing the city's life with intensity, like a Roman. As the saying goes, "When in Rome. . . ."

1 Orientation

ARRIVING

BY PLANE   Chances are that you'll arrive in Italy at Rome's **Leonardo da Vinci International Airport** (☎ **06/65951,** or 06/6595-3640 for information), popularly known as Fiumicino, 18¹/₂ miles from the center of the capital. (If you're flying by charter, you might arrive at Ciampino Airport; see below.)

After leaving Passport Control, two information desks—one for Rome, one for Italy—come into view. At the Rome desk you can pick up a general (not a detailed) map and some pamphlets Monday to Saturday from 8:30am to 7pm. A *cambio* (money exchange) operates daily from 7:30am to 11pm. Luggage storage, in the main arrivals building and open daily, charges 5,000 lire ($3.20) per bag.

To get into the city, follow the signs marked TRENI for the shuttle service directly to the main rail station, Stazione Termini (arriving on Track 22). It runs between 7am and 10pm for 13,000 lire ($8.30) one-way. A local train, costing 7,000 lire ($4.50), runs between the airport and the Tiburtina Station, from which you can go the rest of the way to the Termini by subway Line B, costing another 1,000 lire (65¢).

Should you arrive on a charter flight at **Ciampino** (☎ **06/79461**), take a COTRAL bus, departing every 30 minutes or so, which will deliver you to the Anagnina stop of Metropolitana Line A. Take Linea A to Stazione Termini where your final connections can be made. Trip time is about 45 minutes, and the cost is 2,000 lire ($1.30).

Taxis from Fiumicino (Da Vinci) are expensive—70,000 lire ($44.80) and up. From Ciampino, the rate is the same (70,000 lire), but the trip is shorter.

BY TRAIN   Trains arrive in the center of old Rome at the **Stazione Termini,** piazza dei Cinquecento (☎ **06/4775**), the train and subway transportation hub for all of Rome, surrounded by many, especially cheaper, hotels.

If you're taking the Metropolitana (Rome's subway network), follow the illuminated red M signs. To catch a bus, go straight through the outer hall of the Termini and enter the sprawling bus lot of piazza dei Cinquecento. You'll also find taxis here (see "Getting Around," later in this chapter, for details on public transportation).

The Termini is filled with services. At a branch of the Banca Nazionale delle Communicazioni (between Tracks 8–11 and Tracks 12–15) you can exchange money. *Informazioni Ferroviarie* (in the outer hall) dispenses information on rail travel to other parts of Italy. There's also a tourist information booth here, along with baggage services, barbershops, gift shops, restaurants, and bars. But beware of pickpockets, perhaps quick-fingered young children. The station is also home to the Albergo Diurno (☎ 06/481-9887), a hotel without beds but with baths, showers, and well-kept toilet facilities open daily from 7am to 8pm.

BY BUS   Arrivals are at the **Stazione Termini** (see "By Train," above).

BY CAR   From the north the main access route is the **Autostrada del Sole (A1),** cutting through Milan and Florence, or you can take the coastal route, SSI Aurelia, from Genoa. If you're driving north from Naples, you take the southern lap of the **Autostrada del Sole (A2).** All these autostrade join with the **Grande Raccordo Anulare,** a ring road that encircles Rome, channeling traffic into the congested city. Long before you reach this ring road, you should study a map carefully to see what part of Rome you plan to enter and mark your route accordingly. Route markings along the ring road tend to be confusing.

VISITOR INFORMATION

Some tourist information is available at the **Ente Provinciale per il Turismo,** via Parigi 5, 00185 Roma (☎ **06/4889-9200**), open Monday to Saturday from 8:15am to 7pm—but the information dispensed here is meager. There's another information bureau at the Stazione Termini (☎ **06/487-1270**), open daily from 8:15am to 7:15pm.

Rome also operates three **Info-Tourism "Boxes,"** kiosks set up in trailers in the historic center. The kiosks offer some brochures and maps, but their main asset is a database with information on attractions, hotels, restaurants, and more. The booths are located on largo Carlo Goldoni (☎ **06/687-5027**), off via del Corso, across from via dei Condotti; on via Nazionale (☎ **06/474-5929**) near the Palazzo delle Esposizioni; and on largo Corrado Ricci (☎ **06/678-0992**), near the Colosseum. All three are open Tuesday to Saturday from 10am to 6pm and on Sunday from 10am to 1pm.

CITY LAYOUT

Inside the still remarkably intact **Great Aurelian Wall** (started in A.D. 271 to calm Rome's barbarian jitters), you'll find a city designed for a population that walked to get where it was going. Parts of Rome actually feel more like an oversize village than the former imperial capital of the Western world.

The Stazione Termini faces a huge plaza, **piazza dei Cinquecento,** named after 500 Italians who died heroically in a 19th-century battle in Africa.

Rome Orientation

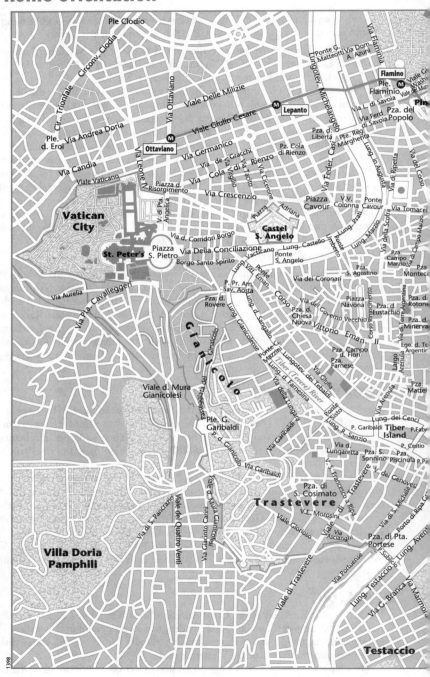

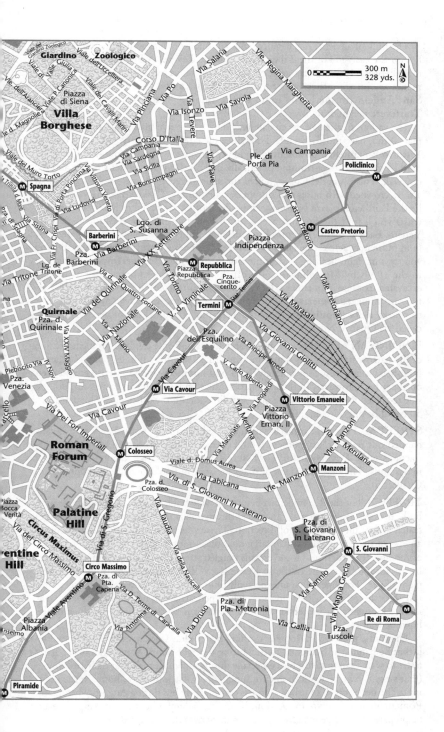

The bulk of ancient, Renaissance, and baroque Rome (as well as the train station) lies on the east side of the **Tiber River (Fiume Tevere),** which meanders through town between 19th-century stone embankments. However, several important monuments are on the other side: **St. Peter's Basilica** and the **Vatican;** the **Castel Sant'Angelo** (formerly the tomb of the emperor Hadrian), and the colorful **Trastevere** neighborhood.

The various quarters of the city are linked by large boulevards (large at least in some places) that have mostly been laid out since the late 19th century. Starting from the **Vittorio Emanuele monument,** a highly controversial pile of snow-white Brescian marble, there's a street running practically due north to **piazza del Popolo** and the city wall. This is **via del Corso,** one of the main streets of Rome—noisy, congested, always crowded with buses and shoppers, called simply "Il Corso." To its left (west) lie the Pantheon, piazza Navona, campo de' Fiori, and the Tiber River. To its right (east) you'll find the Spanish Steps, Trevi Fountain, Borghese Gardens, and via Veneto. Back at the the Vittorio Emanuele monument, the major artery going west (and ultimately across the Tiber to St. Peter's) is **corso Vittorio Emanuele.** Behind you to your right, heading toward the Colosseum, is **via del Fori lmperiali,** laid out in the 1930s by Mussolini to show off the ruins of the imperial forums he had excavated that line it on either side. Yet another central conduit is **via Nazionale,** running from **piazza Venezia** (just in front of the Vittorio Emanuele monument) east to **piazza della Repubblica** (near the Termini). The final lap of via Nazionale is called via Quattro Novembre.

FINDING AN ADDRESS   Finding an address in Rome can be a problem because of the narrow streets of old Rome and the little, sometimes hidden *piazze* (squares). Numbers usually run consecutively, with odd numbers on one side street and even on the other. However, in the old districts the numbers will sometimes run up one side to the end, then back in the opposite direction on the other side. Therefore, no. 50 could be opposite no. 308.

STREET MAPS   Arm yourself with a detailed street map, not the general overview handed out free at tourist offices. You'll need a detailed map even to find such attractions as the Trevi Fountain. The best ones are published by **Falk,** available at most newsstands. The best selections of maps are sold in bookstores (see "Shopping" in Chapter 5).

TRAFFIC   For the $2^1/2$ millennia before the wide boulevards mentioned above were built, the citizens had to make their way through narrow byways and curves that defeated all but the best senses of direction. These streets—among the most charming aspects of the city—still exist in large quantities, mostly unspoiled by the advances of modern construction. However, this tangled street plan has one troublesome element: automobiles. The traffic in Rome is awful! When the claustrophobic street plans of the Dark Ages open unexpectedly onto a vast piazza, every driver accelerates full throttle for the distant horizon, while pedestrians flatten themselves against marble fountains for protection or stride with firm jaws right into the thick of the howling traffic.

The traffic problem in Rome is nothing new. Julius Caesar was so exasperated by it that he banned all vehicular traffic during daylight hours. Sometimes it's actually faster to walk than to take a bus, especially during any of Rome's four daily rush hours (that's right, *four:* to work, home for lunch/*riposo,* back to work, home in the evening). The hectic crush of urban Rome is considerably less during August, when many Romans are out of town on vacation. If you visit at any other time of year, however, be prepared for the general frenzy that characterizes the average Roman street.

NEIGHBORHOODS IN BRIEF

Here are the main districts of interest, spiraling roughly out from the ancient center, through the heart of old Rome, and on to some of the more interesting outlying residential areas. This section will give you some idea of where you may want to stay and where the major attractions are.

Ancient Rome   This is the district that most visitors come to Rome to explore first, taking in the Colosseum, Palatine Hill, the Roman Forum, the Fori Imperiali (Imperial Forums), and Circus Maximus. It forms part of the *centro storico* or historic district (along with campo de' Fiori and piazza Navona and the Pantheon described below), which with its narrow streets and airy piazzas is the accommodations section of choice for many visitors who prefer its antique atmosphere and great location, as opposed to the uglier, duller, and more dangerous districts such as the section around the Termini. If you anchor here—as many do—you can walk to the monuments and not hassle with the inadequate public transportation of Rome. But here's the bad news: Hotel owners are well aware that tourists want to be here, and, for that privilege, room prices are often 30% to 50% higher than in other hotels in less desirable areas. So if you want atmosphere, you must pay for it.

Campo de'Fiori & the Jewish Ghetto   South of corso Vittorio Emanuele, centered around piazza Farnese and the market square of campo de'Fiori, many buildings in this district were constructed in Renaissance times as private homes. Walk on via Giulia—the most fashionable street in Rome in the 16th century—with its antiques stores, interesting hotels, and modern art galleries.

West of via Arenula lies one of the city's most intriguing districts, the old Jewish Ghetto, which has far more opportunities for dining than for lodgings. The Jews, about 8,000 at the time, were ordered here by Pope Paul IV in 1556, and the walls were not torn down until 1849. This is another one of the most desirable places to base yourself in Rome, close to many attractions, although we think Ancient and Medieval Rome have a lot more atmosphere. Nevertheless, hoteliers still sock it to you on prices.

Piazza Navona & the Pantheon   One of the most alluring areas of Rome, this district is a maze of narrow streets and alleys from the Middle Ages and is filled with churches and palaces built during the Renaissance and baroque eras, often with rare marbles and other materials stripped from Ancient Rome. The only way to explore it is on foot. Its nerve center is piazza Navona, built over Emperor Domitian's stadium and bustling with sidewalk cafes, *palazzi* (palaces), street artists, musicians, and pickpockets. There are several hotels in the area and plenty of *trattorie*. Rivaling it— in general activity, the cafe scene, and nightlife—is the area around the Pantheon, which remains from ancient Roman times surrounded by a district built much later (this "pagan" temple was turned into a church and rescued, whereas the buildings that once surrounded it are long gone). If you'd like to anchor in Medieval Rome, you face the same 30% to 50% increase in hotel prices as you do for Ancient Rome.

Piazza di Spagna   Ever since the 17th century these steps—former site of the Spanish ambassador's residence—have been the center of tourist Rome. Keats lived in a house opening onto the steps, and some of Rome's most prestigious shopping streets fan out from it, including via Condotti. The most elegant address here is the Hassler, one of Rome's grandest hotels. If you want to sleep in the hippest part of town, you must be willing to part with a lot of extra lire. This area of Rome joins with Ancient and Medieval Rome in charging some of the capital's highest prices, not only for hotels, but for restaurants, designer silk suits, and leather loafers.

Via Veneto   In the 1950s and early 1960s this was the haunt of the *dolce vita* set, as the likes of King Farouk and Swedish actress Anita Ekberg paraded up and down the boulevard to the delight of the *paparazzi*. The street is still here, still the site of luxury hotels and elegant cafes and restaurants, although it no longer has the allure it did in its heyday. Rome city authorities would like to restore this legendary street to some of its former glory. Frank Sinatra and Elizabeth Taylor may never stroll it again, but Rome is trying to spruce up via Vittorio Veneto by banning vehicular traffic on the top half of the street.

Termini   The main train station adjoins piazza della Repubblica, and for many, this is your introduction to Rome. Much of the area is seedy and filled with gas fumes from all the buses and cars, but there's still much here to see, including the Basilica di Santa Maria Maggiore and the Baths of Diocletian. Although this is one of the least desirable places to stay in Rome—and also one of the most dangerous because of muggings—it's also the cheapest. There are some high-class hotels in the area, including the Grand, but many are long past their heyday. The area directly south of the Termini is traffic-noisy, people-bustling, and seedier than the district to the north. Even though the hotel prices are lower, there's still much overcharging—if innkeepers think they can get away with it. The best *pensioni* and hotels lie north of the Termini, within a 15-minute walk. Many of these hotels are run-down and in dire need of major renovation, although some have recently been improved. There's talk of a "renaissance" for the area.

Appian Way   Via Appia Antica is a 2,300-year-old road that has witnessed much of the history of the ancient world. By 190 B.C. it extended from Rome to Brindisi on the southeast coast, and its most famous sights today are the catacombs, the graveyards of patrician families (despite what it says in *Quo Vadis?*, they were not used as a place for Christians to hide out while fleeing persecution). This is one of the most history-rich areas of Rome to explore—but you don't go there seeking a hotel. There are several restaurants, however.

Testaccio   In A.D. 55, Nero ordered that Rome's thousands of broken amphoras and terra-cotta roof tiles be stacked in a carefully designated pile to the east of the Tiber, just west of Pyramide and today's Ostia Railway Station. Over the centuries, the mound grew to a height of around 200 feet, then compacted to form the centerpiece for one of the city's most unusual neighborhoods. Eventually, houses were built on the terra-cotta mound, and caves were dug into its mass for the storage of wine and foodstuffs (a constant temperature of 50°F was maintained year-round, thanks to the porosity of the terra-cotta). Bordered by the Protestant cemetery, today Testaccio is home to restaurants with *very* Roman cuisine (see "Dining," later in this chapter).

Trastevere   This is the most authentic district of Rome, lying "across the Tiber," and its people are of mixed ancestry, including Jewish, Roman, and Greek, and speak their own dialect. The area centers around the ancient Churches of Santa Cecilia in Trastevere and Santa Maria in Trastevere. Home to many young expatriates, the district after World War II became a gathering place for hedonists and bohemians. It has been called the last of the capital's old *rioni* (neighborhoods). There are those who speak of it as a "city within a city"—or at least a village within a city. It's said that the language is rougher and the cuisine spicier, and although Trastevere doesn't have the glamorous hotels of central Rome, it does have some of the last remaining authentic Roman dining. Trastevere used to be a bastion of the budget traveler, but foreigners from virtually anywhere have been buying real estate en masse here, so change is in the air.

Around Vatican City   Vatican City is a small city-state, but its influence extends around the world. The Vatican museums and St. Peter's take up most of the land area, and the popes have lived here for six centuries. However, you may not prefer to follow their example. Although the neighborhhod contains some good hotels (and several bad ones), it's somewhat removed from the more happening scene of Ancient and Renaissance Rome, and getting to and from it can be time-consuming. Also, the area is rather dull at night and contains few if any of Rome's finest restaurants. Vatican City and its surrounding area is best for exploring during the day.

Prati   Known only to the connoisseurs of Rome, this district is really a 19th-century middle-class suburb north of the Vatican. It's becoming increasingly patronized by budget travelers because of its low-cost *pensioni* (boarding houses). The Trionfale flower-and-food market itself is worth the trip. The area also abounds in shopping streets less expensive than those found in central Rome. If safety is a main concern for you, Prati is a more tranquil district, usually devoid of the pickpockets and thieves who prey on tourists in Ancient Rome and around the Termini.

Parioli   The most elegant residential section of Rome, framed by the green spaces of the Villa Borghese to the south and the Villa Glori and Villa Ada to the north. It's a setting for some of the city's finest restaurants, hotels, and nightclubs. It's not the most central, however, and can be a hassle if you're dependent on public transportation. Parioli lies adjacent to Prati, but across the Tiber to the east, and, like Prati, is one of the safer districts of Rome.

Monte Mario   On the northwestern precincts of Rome, Monte Mario is the site of the deluxe Cavalieri Hilton, where you can stop in for a drink and the panorama of Rome. If you plan to spend a lot of time shopping and sightseeing in the heart of Rome, it's a difficult and often expensive commute. The area lies north of Prati, away from the hustle and bustle of central Rome. Bus 913 runs from piazza Augusto Imperator near the piazza del Popolo to Monte Mario.

2 Getting Around

BY PUBLIC TRANSPORTATION

SUBWAY   The **Metropolitana,** or **Metro** for short, is the fastest means of transportation in Rome. It has two underground lines: Line A goes between via Ottaviano, near St. Peter's, and Anagnina, stopping at piazzale Flaminio (near piazza del Popolo), piazza di Spagna, piazza Vittorio Emmanuele, and piazza San Giovanni in Laterano. Line B connects the Rebibbia district with via Laurentina, stopping at via Cavour, Stazione Termini, the Colosseum, Circus Maximus, the Pyramid, St. Paul's Outside the Walls, and E.U.R. A big red letter M indicates the entrance to the subway.

Tickets are 1,500 lire (95¢), and are available from vending machines at all stations. These machines accept 50-, 100-, and 200-lira coins, and some of them will take 1,000-lira notes. Some stations have managers, but they won't make change. Booklets of tickets (*carnet*) are available at *tabacchi* (tobacco shops) and in some terminals.

Building a subway system for Rome has not been easy, since every time workers start digging they discover an old temple or other archeological treasure and heavy earth-moving has to cease for a while.

BY BUS & TRAM   Roman buses and trams are operated by an organization known as **ATAC (Azienda Tramvie e Autobus del Commune di Roma),** via Volturno 65 (☎ **06/4695-4444** for information).

For only 1,500 lire (95¢) you can ride to most parts of Rome on quite good bus service. The ticket is valid for 1 hour 15 minutes, and you can get on many buses and trams during that time period using the same ticket. At the Stazione Termini, you can purchase a special tourist bus pass, costing 6,000 lire ($3.85) for 1 day or 24,000 lire ($15.35) for a week. This allows you to ride on the ATAC network without bothering to purchase individual tickets. The tourist pass is also valid on the subway—but never ride the trains when the Romans are going to or from work or you'll be mashed flatter than fettuccine. On the first bus you board, you place your ticket in a small machine that prints the day and hour you boarded. And you do the same on the last bus you take during the validity period of the ticket.

Buses and trams stop at areas marked FERMATA. At most of these, a yellow sign will display the numbers of the buses that stop there, and then lists of all the stops along each bus's route in order, so you can easily search out your destination. In general they're in service from 6am to midnight daily. After that and until dawn, you can ride on special night buses (they have an "N" in front of their bus number), which only run on main routes. It's best to take a taxi in the wee hours—if you can find one.

At the bus information booth at piazza dei Cinquecento, in front of the Stazione Termini, you can purchase a directory complete with maps summarizing the particular routes. Ask there about where to purchase bus tickets, or buy them in a *tabacchi* or at a bus terminal. You must have your ticket before boarding the bus, as there are no ticket-issuing machines on the vehicles.

Take extreme caution riding the overcrowded buses of Rome—pickpockets abound! This is particularly true on bus no. 64, a favorite of tourists because of its route through Rome's historic districts, and thus also a favorite of Rome's vast pickpocketing community. Bus no. 64 has earned various nicknames: "The Pickpocket Express" or "The Wallet Eater." Take heed—planned modification of the city bus lines may create a bit of pandemonium throughout 1997 and 1998.

BY TAXI

If you're accustomed to hopping a cab in New York or London, then do so in Rome. If not, take less expensive means of transport. Avoid paying your fare with large bills—invariably, taxi drivers claim they don't have change, hoping for a bigger tip (only give about 10%). Don't count on hailing a taxi on the street or even getting one at a stand. If you're going out, have your hotel call one. At a restaurant, ask the waiter or cashier to dial for you. If you want to phone for yourself, try one of these numbers: 06/6645, 06/3570, or 06/4994.

The meter begins at 6,400 lire ($4.10) for the first 3 kilometers, then increases 300 lire (20¢) per kilometer. Every suitcase is 500 lire (30¢), and on Sunday a 5,000-lira ($3.20) supplement is assessed, plus another 2,000-lira ($1.30) supplement from 10pm to 7am.

BY CAR

For general information, see "Getting Around" in Chapter 3.

Hertz has its main office near the parking lot of the Villa Borghese, at via Vittorio Veneto 156 (☎ **06/321-6831**). The **Budget** headquarters are at via Ludovisi 60 (☎ **06/482-0966**). **Maggiore,** an Italian company, has an office at via di Tor Cervara 225 (☎ **06/229351**).

DRIVING & PARKING   All roads may lead to Rome if you're driving, but don't count on much driving once you get there. Since reception desks of most Roman hotels have at least one English-speaking person, it's wise to call ahead to find out the best route into Rome from wherever you're starting out.

Find out if the hotel has a garage. If not, you're usually allowed to park your car in front of the hotel long enough to unload your luggage. Someone at the hotel—a doorman, if there is one—will direct you to the nearest garage or place to park.

To the neophyte, Roman driving will appear like the chariot race in *Ben-Hur*. When the light turns green, go forth with caution. Many Roman drivers are still going through the light even though it has turned red. Roman drivers in traffic gridlock move bravely on, fighting for every inch of the road until they can free themselves from the tangled mess. To complicate matters, many zones, such as that around piazza di Spagna, are traffic-free, and other traffic-free zones are being tried out in various parts of Rome.

In other words, try to get your car into Rome as safely as possible, park it, and proceed on foot or by public transportation from then on.

BY BICYCLE, MOTORSCOOTER & MOTORCYCLE

St. Peter Moto Renting & Selling, via di Porto Castello 43 (☎ **06/6880-4608**), open Monday to Saturday from 9am to 7pm, rents mopeds. Rates range upward from 40,000 lire ($25.60) per day. Take the Metro to Ottaviano. Another agency that provides mopeds is **Happy Rent,** conveniently located at piazza Esquilino 8H (☎ **06/481-8185**), 300 yards from the Termini. Most mopeds cost 40,000 lire ($25.60) per hour or 60,000 lire ($38.40) for the entire day. Mopeds are delivered to your hotel free. Happy Rent also offers several guided moped tours of Rome and the surrounding area. It's open Monday to Saturday from 9am to 7pm.

Bicycles are rented at many places throughout Rome. Ask at your hotel for the nearest rental location, or go to **I Bike Rome,** via Vittorio Veneto 156 (☎ **06/322-5240**), which rents bicycles from the underground parking garage at the Villa Borghese. Most bikes cost 5,000 lire ($3.20) per hour, or 13,000 lire ($8.30) per day. Mountain bikes rent for 7,000 lire ($4.50) per hour or 18,000 lire ($11.50) per day. It's open daily from 9am to 7pm.

ON FOOT

Much of the inner core of Rome is traffic-free—so you'll need to walk whether you like it or not. Walking is the perfect way to see the ancient narrow cobbled streets of Old Rome. However, in many parts of the city it's hazardous and uncomfortable because of the overcrowded streets, heavy traffic, and very narrow sidewalks. Sometimes sidewalks don't exist at all, and it becomes a sort of free-for-all with pedestrians competing for space against vehicular traffic (the traffic always seems to win). For such a large city, Rome can be covered on foot because so much of what will interest a visitor lies in various clusters.

FAST FACTS: Rome

American Express   The Rome offices of American Express are at piazza di Spagna 38 (☎ 06/67641). The travel service is open Monday to Friday from 9am to 5:30pm and on Saturday from 9am to 12:30pm. Hours for the financial and mail services are Monday to Friday from 9am to 5pm and on Saturday from 9am to noon. The tour desk is open during the same hours as those for travel services and also on Saturday afternoon from 2 to 2:30pm from May to October.

Bookstores   See "Shopping," in Chapter 5.

Business Hours In general, **banks** are open Monday to Friday from 8:30am to 1:30pm and 3 to 4pm. Some banks keep afternoon hours ranging from 2:45 to 3:45pm. Two U.S. banks in Rome are Chase Manhattan Bank, via Michele Mercati 39 (☎ 06/809761), and Citibank, via Bruxelles 61 (☎ 06/478171). **Shopping** hours are governed by the *riposo* (siesta). Most stores are open year-round Monday to Saturday from 9am to 1pm and then from 3:30 or 4pm to 7:30 or 8pm. Most shops are closed Sunday.

Car Rentals See "Getting Around," earlier in this chapter.

Climate See "When to Go," in Chapter 3.

Crime See "Safety," below.

Currency Exchange This is possible at all major rail and airline terminals in Rome, including the Stazione Termini, where the *cambio* (exchange booth) beside the rail information booth is open daily from 8am to 8pm. At some cambi you'll have to pay commissions, often $1^1/_2$%. Banks, likewise, often charge commissions. Many so-called moneychangers will approach you on the street, but often they're pushing counterfeit lire—however, they offer very good rates for their fake money!

Dentist To secure a dentist who speaks English, call the U.S. Embassy in Rome (☎ 06/46741). You may have to call around in order to get an appointment. There's also the 24-hour G. Eastman Dental Hospital, viale Regina Elena 287 (☎ 06/445-3228).

Doctor Call the U.S. Embassy (see "Dentist," above), which will provide a list of doctors who speak English. All big hospitals in Rome have a 24-hour first-aid service (go to the emergency room). You'll find English-speaking doctors at the privately run Salvator Mundi International Hospital, viale delle Mura Gianicolensi (☎ 06/588961). For medical assistance, the International Medical Center is on 24-hour duty at via Giovanni Amendola 7 (☎ 488-2371). You could also contact the Rome American Hospital, via Emilio Longoni 69 (☎ 06/22551), with English-speaking doctors on duty 24 hours a day.

Drugstores A reliable pharmacy is Farmacia Internazionale, piazza Barberini 49 (☎ 06/679-4680), open day and night. Most pharmacies are open from 8:30am to 1pm and 4 to 7:30pm. In general, pharmacies follow a rotation system so that several are always open on Sunday (the rotation schedule is posted outside each).

Embassies/Consulates See "Fast Facts: Italy," in Chapter 3.

Emergencies The police "hotline" number is **21-21-21.** Usually, however, dial **112** for the police, to report a fire, or summon an ambulance.

Eyeglasses Try Vasari, piazza della Repubblica 61 (☎ 06/488-2240), adjacent to the Grand Hotel, a very large shop with lots of choices.

Hospitals See "Doctor," above.

Hotlines Dial **113,** which is a general SOS, to report any kind of danger, such as rape. You can also dial **112,** the police emergency number. For an ambulance call **5100;** for personal crises, call Samaritans, via San Giovanni in Laterano 250 (☎ 06/7045-4444), daily from to 1 to 10pm.

Lost Property Usually lost property is gone forever. But you might try checking at Ogetti Rinvenuti, via Nicolò Bettoni 1 (☎ 06/581-6040), open Monday to Friday from 8:30am to 4pm and on Saturday from 8:30 to 11:30am. A branch at the Stazione Termini off Track 1 (☎ 06/47301) is open daily from 8am to noon and 2 to 8pm.

Luggage Storage/Lockers   These are available at the Stazione Termini along Tracks 1 and 22 daily from 5am to 1am. The charge is 1,500 lire (95¢) per day per piece of luggage.

Mail   Post office boxes in Italy are red and are attached to walls. The left slot is only for letters intended for the city; the right is for all other destinations. Vatican post office boxes are blue, and you can buy special stamps at the Vatican City Post Office. Letters mailed at Vatican City reach North America far more quickly than does mail sent from within Rome for the same cost. The Vatican City Post Office is adjacent to the information office in St. Peter's Square. It's open Monday to Friday from 8:30am to 7pm and on Saturday from 8:30am to 6pm.

The main post office of Rome is at piazza San Silvestro 19, 00186 Roma (☎ 06/6771), between via del Corso and piazza di Spagna, open Monday to Friday from 8:25am to 7:40pm and on Saturday from 8:20am to 11:50pm. Mail addressed to you   this central office, with *fermo posta* written after the name and address of the post office, will be given to you upon identification by passport. Stamps (*francobolli*) can be purchased at *tabacchi* (tobacconists).

Newspapers/Magazines   You can get the *International Herald Tribune* at most newsstands, and the *New York Times* at many, as well as *Time* and *Newsweek* magazines. The expat magazine (in English) *Wanted in Rome* comes out monthly and lists current events and shows. If you want to try your hand at reading Italian, the Thursday edition of the newspaper *La Repubblica* contains *TrovaRoma*, a magazine supplement full of cultural and entertainment listings.

Police   See "Emergencies," above.

Rest Rooms   Facilities are found near many of the major sights, often with attendants, as are those at bars, nightclubs, restaurants, cafes, and hotels, plus the airports and the railway station. You're expected to leave 200 to 500 lire (10¢ to 30¢) for the attendant.

Safety   Pickpocketing is the most common problem. Men—keep your wallets in your front pocket or inside jacket pocket. Women—purse-snatching is also commonplace, with young men on Vespas who will ride past you and grab your purse. To avoid trouble stay away from the curb, keep your purse on the wall side of your body and the strap over both shoulders across your chest. Don't lay anything valuable on tables or chairs where it can be grabbed up easily. Gypsy children are a particular menace. You'll often virtually have to fight them off, if they completely surround you. They'll often approach you with pieces of cardboard hiding their stealing hands.

Taxes   A value-added tax (called IVA in Italy) is added to all consumer products and most services, including restaurants and hotels. The tax is not the same for all goods and services. The tax is 12% on clothing and 19% on most luxury goods.

Taxis   See "Getting Around," earlier in this chapter.

Telegrams/Fax   If your hotel doesn't have a fax, try a tobacconist or photocopy shop. You can send telegrams from all post offices during the day and from the telegraph office at the central post office in San Silvestro, off via della Mercede, at night. See also "Fast Facts: Italy," in Chapter 3.

Transit Information   Leonardo da Vinci International Airport (☎ 06/65951); Ciampino Airport (☎ 06/794941); bus information (☎ 06/4695-4444); rail information (☎ 06/4775).

Water   Rome is famed for its drinking water, which is generally safe, even from the outdoor fountains. If it isn't, there's a sign reading ACQUA NON POTABILE. Nevertheless, Romans traditionally order bottled mineral water in restaurants to accompany the wine with their meals.

3   Accommodations

There have been no exciting breakthroughs on the hotel front in Rome, except for the reopening of the Hotel Eden in central Rome, which is now better than ever, with one of Rome's best restaurants. The cheapest hotels are around the Stazione Termini—but they also tend to be the most run-down and this is the seediest neighborhood. The most central are in the *centro storico* near all the sights and monuments—but you pay for the location. Some wonderful and elegant ones—such as the Cavaliere Hilton—can be found in residential suburb areas. See "Neighborhoods in Brief" under "Orientation," earlier in this chapter, to get an idea of where you may want to base yourself.

Rome is a year-round tourist destination, so you'll need to make reservations no matter what the season. Because of Rome's importance as a religious center, some groups book hundreds of rooms in the winter "low season" because they get better discounts. Many hotels will grant winter discounts—usually no more than 10%—and you may have to negotiate this at the reception desk.

Rome has more than 500 hotels. Decisions on which to recommend were based on whether they offered good value—regardless of their price range—and special considerations, such as charm, comfort, and convenience of location.

All the hotels recommended serve breakfast, and many of them also have good restaurants. Some of the deluxe hotels have among the finest restaurants in Rome. Breakfast is not always included in the room rate, so always determine this when checking in. Breakfast will be of the continental variety—that is, cappuccino and croissants, along with jam and butter.

Most well-recommended hotels in Rome have private baths, but in some of the inexpensive or budget choices you'll have to share with other guests. Nearly all hotels are heated in the cooler months, but not all are air-conditioned in summer, which can be vitally important during July and August. The deluxe and first-class ones are, but after that it's a toss-up.

Nearly all hotels today quote an inclusive rate, including service and value-added taxes—but double-check when checking in. It's rare for Roman hotels to have private garages. Hotel reception desks will advise about nearby garages, where fees usually range from 5,000 to 60,000 lire ($3.20 to $38.40). Of course, the higher price would be for garage space in the heart of Rome, while the lower price would be for an open-air, unguarded space on the outskirts of Rome.

NEAR ANCIENT ROME
INEXPENSIVE

Colosseum Hotel. Via Sforza 10, 00184 Roma. ☎ **06/482-7228.** Fax 06/482-7285. 50 rms. TEL TV. 220,000 lire ($140.80) double. Rates include breakfast. AE, DC, MC, V. Parking 30,000 lire ($19.20). Metro: Cavour. Bus: 11, 27, or 81.

Set two short blocks southwest of the Santa Maria Maggiore Basilica, the Colosseum Hotel offers comfortable, albeit small, cost-conscious accommodations amid public areas that contain vestiges of baronial grandeur. Someone with insight and lira notes designed the public areas and upper hallways as a reflection of the best in Italy's design heritage. The bedrooms are furnished with well-conceived antique reproductions (beds of heavy carved wood, dark-paneled wardrobes, leatherwood chairs)—

and all with monklike white walls and sometimes rather old-fashioned plumbing. Air-conditioning is available on request for 20,000 lire ($12.80). The drawing room, with its long refectory table, white walls, red tiles, and provincial armchairs, invites lingering.

Hotel Duca d'Alba. Via Leonina 14, 00184 Roma. ☎ **06/484471.** Fax 06/488-4840. 27 rms, 11 with shower only. MINIBAR TV TEL. 180,000 lire ($115.20) double with shower only, 240,000 lire ($153.60) double with bath. Rates include breakfast. AE, DC, MC, V. Parking 30,000 lire ($19.20). Metro: Cavour.

A bargain close to the Roman Forum and the Colosseum, this hotel lies in the Suburra *quartier* where the "plebs" of ancient Rome resided. This sector of Rome is being gentrified—it had become seedy—and this hotel is part of that renaissance. Although completely restored, it still retains some of the aura of the 19th century when it was first built. The bedrooms are tasteful, even a bit decorated, with soothing colors and light wood pieces and restored private baths. The most desirable rooms are the four with private balconies.

NEAR CAMPO DE' FIORI
MODERATE

⑤ **Teatro di Pompeo.** Largo del Pallaro 8, 00186 Roma. ☎ **06/6830-0170.** Fax 06/6880-5531. 12 rms. A/C TV TEL. 250,000 lire ($160) double. Rates include breakfast. AE, DC, MC, V. Bus: 46, 62, or 64.

Built on top of the ruins of the Theater of Pompey, which dates from about 55 B.C., this small charmer lies near the spot where Julius Caesar met his end. Intimate and refined, it's on a quiet piazzetta near the Palazzo Farnese and campo de' Fiori. The bedrooms, all doubles, are decorated in an old-fashioned Italian style with hand-painted tiles. The beamed ceilings date from the days of Michelangelo. There's no restaurant, but breakfast is served. Since this is such a historic gem with such a small capacity, reserve as early as possible.

INEXPENSIVE

⑤ **Albergo Campo de' Fiori.** Via del Biscione 6, 00186 Roma. ☎ **06/6880-6865.** Fax 06/687-6003. 27 rms, 9 with bath (tub or shower); 1 honeymoon suite. 120,000 lire ($76.80) double without bath, 140,000 lire ($89.60) double with shower only, 190,000 lire ($121.60) double with bath; 155,000 lire ($99.20) triple without bath, 180,000 lire ($115.20) triple with shower only, 240,000 lire ($153.60) triple with bath. Rates include breakfast. MC, V. Bus: 46, 62, or 64 from the Termini to Museo di Roma; then arm yourself with a good map for the walk.

This seems to be everybody's favorite budget hideaway. Lying in the historic center of Rome in a market area that has existed since the 1500s, this cozy, narrow six-story hotel offers rustic rooms, many quite tiny and sparsely adorned, others with a lot of character. The best, on the first floor, have been restored. Yours might have a ceiling of clouds and blue skies along with mirrored walls. The best accommodation is the honeymoon retreat on the sixth floor, with a canopied king-size bed. Honeymooners beware: There's no elevator. Guests can enjoy the panorama from the terrace overlooking the vegetable-and-flower market below, and, in the distance, St. Peter's.

NEAR PIAZZA NAVONA & THE PANTHEON
EXPENSIVE

◆ **Albergo del Sole al Pantheon.** Piazza della Rotonda 63, 00186 Roma. ☎ **06/678-0441.** Fax 06/6994-0689. 26 rms, 4 suites. A/C MINIBAR TV TEL. 450,000 lire ($288) double; 600,000 lire ($384) suite. Rates include breakfast. AE, DC, MC, V. Parking 35,000 lire ($22.40). Bus: 62, 64, 70, 87, or 119.

🏛 Family-Friendly Hotels

Cavalieri Hilton *(see p. 122)*   This hotel is like a resort at Monte Mario, with a swimming pool, gardens, and plenty of grounds for children to run and play, yet it's only 15 minutes from the center of Rome, reached by the hotel shuttle bus.

Hotel Massimo d'Azeglio *(see p. 114)*   Near the Stazione Termini, this place has long been a family favorite. The rooms are large, well kept, and comfortable, and the well-trained staff is solicitous of children.

Hotel Ranieri *(see p. 117)*   This hotel offers a family-style atmosphere in rooms that are air-conditioned with private bath. Many are large enough to house families of three or four, and baby cots are on hand as well.

Hotel Venezia *(see p. 117)*   At this good, moderately priced family hotel near the Stazione Termini, the rooms have been renovated and most are large enough for extra beds for children.

The Albergo del Sole al Pantheon, overlooking the Pantheon, is an absolute gem. The present-day *albergo* is one of the oldest hotels in the world; the first records of it as a hostelry appear in 1467. Long known as a retreat for emperors and sorcerers, the hotel has hosted such guests as Frederick III of the Habsburg family. Later it drew such distinguished company as Jean-Paul Sartre and his companion, Simone de Beauvoir. Today the rooms are exquisitely furnished and decorated with period pieces and stylized reproductions.

Hotel Raphael. Largo Febo 2, 00186 Roma. ☎ **06/682831.** Fax 06/687-8993. 53 rms, 20 suites. A/C MINIBAR TV TEL. 460,000–600,000 lire ($194.40–$384) double; 580,000–1,000,000 lire ($371.20–$640) suite. AE, DC, MC, V. Parking nearby. Bus: 64, 70, 87, 90, or 492.

In the heart of ancient Rome adjacent to piazza Navona with Bernini's Four Rivers Fountain, this hotel is within easy walking distance of many of Rome's attractions. Its rooftop garden terrace boasts a panorama of the ancient city. The charming ivy-covered facade invites one to enter the lobby decorated with antiques that might rival local museums. Some of the suites have private terraces, and all the well-appointed bedrooms have direct-dial phones and satellite TV. Some of the rooms are quite small, however. The elegant restaurant and bar, Cafe Picasso, serves an international cuisine, and among the services provided are room service, baby-sitting, laundry, and currency exchange. There's also a fitness room.

INEXPENSIVE

Albergo Cesàri. Via di Pietra 89A, 00186 Roma. ☎ **06/679-2386.** Fax 06/679-0882. 50 rms, 40 with bath. A/C TV TEL. 130,000 lire ($83.20) double without bath, 180,000–256,000 lire ($115.20–$163.85) double with bath; 245,000–310,000 lire ($156.80–$198.40) triple with bath; 285,000–355,000 lire ($182.40–$227.20) quad with bath. AE, DC, MC, V. Parking 45,000 lire ($28.15). Bus: 492 from the Termini.

The Albergo Cesàri, on an ancient street in the old quarter of Rome, has occupied its desirable location between the Trevi Fountain and the Pantheon since 1787. Its guests have included Garibaldi and Stendhal, and its well-preserved exterior harmonizes with the Temple of Neptune and many little antiques shops nearby. The bedrooms have mostly functional modern pieces, but there are a few traditional trappings as well to maintain character. In 1996, 16 bedrooms were completely renovated.

Accommodations near Campo de' Fiori & Piazza Navona

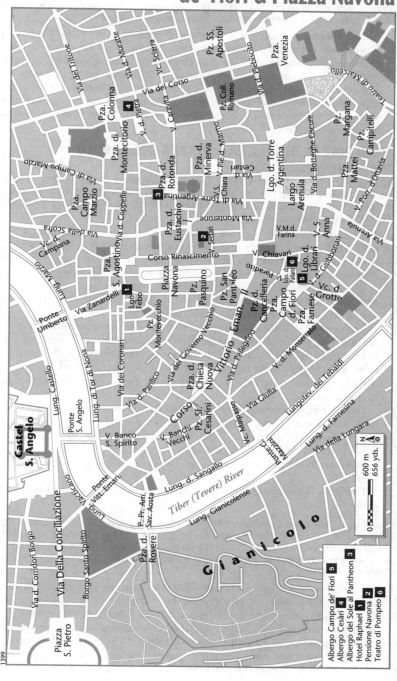

Albergo Campo de' Fiori 5
Albergo Cesàri 4
Albergo del Sole al Pantheon 3
Hotel Raphael 1
Pensione Navona 2
Teatro di Pompeo 6

107

Pensione Navona. Via dei Sediari 8, 00186 Roma. ☎ **06/686-4203.** Fax 06/6880-3802. 22 rms, 17 with bath (shower). 115,000 lire ($73.60) double without bath; 125,000 lire ($80) double with bath. Rates include breakfast. AE. Bus: 64, 70, 75, 87, or 492.

Although the rooms are not as glamorous as the exterior of this palace, the Pensione Navona offers clean and decent accommodations, many of which have been renovated and some of which open to views of the building's central (and quiet) courtyard. Run by an Australian-born family of Italian descent, the place has tiled bathrooms, ceilings high enough to relieve the midsummer heat, and an array of architectural oddities that remain the legacy of the continual construction this palace since 1360. The *pensione* lies on a small street that radiates out from the southeastern tip of piazza Navona.

NEAR PIAZZA DI SPAGNA & PIAZZA DEL POPOLO
VERY EXPENSIVE

Hassler. Piazza Trinità dei Monti 6, 00187 Roma. ☎ **06/699340,** or 800/223-6800 in the U.S. Fax 06/678-9991. 85 rms, 15 suites. A/C MINIBAR TV TEL. 650,000–950,000 lire ($416–$608) double; 1,550,000–2,950,000 lire ($992–$1,888) suite. AE, DC, MC, V. Parking 40,000 lire ($25.60). Metro: Piazza di Spagna.

The Hassler, the only deluxe hotel in this old part of Rome, uses the Spanish Steps as its grand entrance. The original 1885 Hassler was rebuilt in 1944, and while the crown worn by the Hassler is a bit tarnished these days (as is the tiara of the Grand), both hostelries have such a mystique that they continue to prosper and endure in spite of their overpriced rooms. The brightly colored rooms, the lounges with a mixture of modern and traditional furnishings, and the bedrooms with their "Italian Park Avenue" trappings all strike a faded 1930s note.

The bedrooms, some of which tend to be small, have a personalized look—Oriental rugs, tasteful draperies at the French windows, brocade furnishings, comfortable beds, and (the nicest touch of all) bowls of fresh flowers. Some rooms have balconies with views of the city. Each accommodation contains a private bath, usually with two sinks and a bidet. In spite of all this, the Excelsior, for the most part, has better rooms.

Dining/Entertainment: The Hassler Roof Restaurant, on the top floor, is a favorite with visitors and Romans alike for its fine cuisine and view. Its Sunday brunch is a popular rendezvous time in Rome. The Hassler Bar is ideal for an apéritif or a drink; in the evening it has piano music.

Services: Room service, telex and fax, limousine, in-room massages, in-house laundry.

Facilities: Fitness center, tennis court (in summer), free bicycles available; nearby garage.

Hotel de la Ville Inter-Continental Roma. Via Sistina 67–69, 00187 Roma. ☎ **06/67331,** or 800/327-0200 in the U.S. and Canada. Fax 06/678-4213. 192 rms, 23 suites. A/C MINIBAR TV TEL. 510,000–645,000 lire ($326.40–$412.80) double; 800,000–1,525,000 lire ($512–$976) suite. Rates include breakfast. AE, DC, MC, V. Parking 35,000 lire ($22.40). Metro: Piazza di Spagna or Barberini.

The Hotel de la Ville Inter-Continental Roma looks deluxe (it's officially rated first class) from the minute you walk through the revolving door attended by a smartly uniformed doorman. Once inside this palace, built in the 19th century on the site of the ancient Gardens of Lucullus, you'll find Oriental rugs, marble tables, brocade-covered furniture, and a staff who speak English. There are endless corridors leading to what at first seems a maze of ornamental lounges, all elegantly upholstered and hung with their quota of crystal lighting fixtures. Some of the public rooms have

Accommodations near Piazza di Spagna

Carriage **4**
Colosseum Hotel **17**
Grand Hotel Plaza **3**
Hotel Forum **15**
Hotel Duca d'Alba **16**
Hassler **6**
Hotel Cecil **11**
Hotel d'Inghliterra **14**
Hotel de la Ville
   Inter-Continental
   Roma **8**
Hotel Gregoriana **7**
Hotel Internazionale **10**
Hotel Madrid **12**
Hotel Margutta **1**
Hotel Piazza
   di Spagna **13**
Pensione Fiorella **2**
Pensionne Lydia
   Venier **9**
Scalinata di Spagna **5**

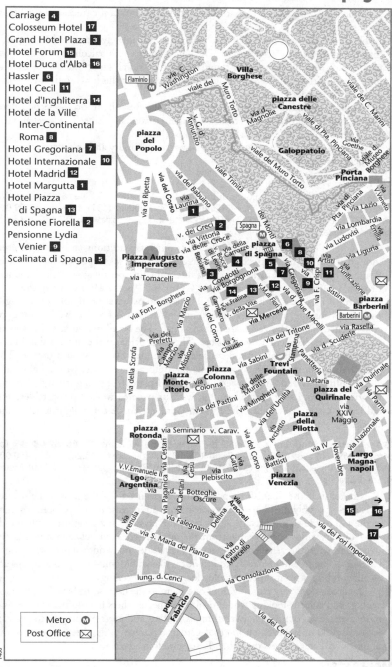

Metro **M**
Post Office ✉

1400

a sort of 1930s elegance, others are strictly baroque, and in the middle of it all is an open courtyard.

The bedrooms and the public areas have been completely renovated in a beautifully classic and yet up-to-date way. The higher rooms with balconies have the most panoramic views of Rome to be found anywhere, and all guests are free to use the roof terrace with the same view. Many savvy guests prefer this hotel to the overpriced glory of the Hassler next door.

Dining/Entertainment: La Piazzetta de la Ville Restaurant, on the second floor overlooking the garden, serves an Italian and international cuisine. The hotel also has an American bar with a pianist during cocktail hours.

Services: Room service (24 hours), baby-sitting, laundry and valet service.

Facilities: Roof terrace.

EXPENSIVE

✪ **Hotel d'Inghliterra.** Via Bocca di Leone 14, 00187 Roma. ☎ **06/69981.** Fax 06/6992-2243. 102 rms, 12 suites. A/C MINIBAR TV TEL. 496,000 lire ($317.45) double; 599,000 lire ($383.35) triple; 840,000 lire ($537.60) suite. Rates include breakfast. AE, DC, MC, V. Metro: Piazza di Spagna.

The Hotel d'Inghliterra nostalgically holds onto its traditions and heritage, even though it has been completely renovated. The most fashionable small hotel in Rome, it has been the favorite of many a discriminating personage—Anatole France, Ernest Hemingway, Franz Liszt, Alec Guinness. (In the 19th century the king of Portugal met here with the pope.) The bedrooms have mostly old pieces—gilt and much marble, mahogany chests, and glittery mirrors—as well as modern conveniences. Some, however, are just too small. The hotel's restaurant, the Roman Garden, serves excellent Roman dishes. The main salon of the hotel is dominated by an impressive gilt mirror and console, surrounded by Victorian furniture. The preferred bedrooms are higher up, opening onto a tile terrace, with a balustrade and a railing covered with flowering vines and plants. The English-style bar is a favorite gathering spot in the evening, with its paneled walls, tip-top tables, and old lamps casting soft light. The Roman Garden Lounge offers light lunches and snacks.

✪ **Scalinata di Spagna.** Piazza Trinità dei Monti 17, 00187 Roma. ☎ **06/679-3006.** Fax 06/6994-0598. 15 rms, 1 suite. A/C MINIBAR TV TEL. 380,000 lire ($243.20) double; 480,000 lire ($307.20) triple; 650,000 lire ($416) suite. AE, MC, V. Parking 35,000 lire ($22.40). Metro: Piazza di Spagna.

This hotel near the Spanish Steps has always been one of the most sought-after in Rome—possibly it will reach four-star status and increase its prices soon. It's right at the top of the steps, directly across from the Hassler, in a delightful little building—only two floors are visible from the outside—nestled between much larger structures, with four relief columns across the facade and window boxes with bright blossoms. The recently redecorated interior is like an old inn—the public rooms are small with bright print slipcovers, old clocks, and low ceilings.

The decorations vary radically from one room to the next; some have low, beamed ceilings and ancient-looking wood furniture, wheras others have loftier ceilings and more average appointments. Everything is spotless and most pleasing to the eye. In season, breakfast is served on the roof-garden terrace with its sweeping view of the dome of St. Peter's across the Tiber. Reserve well in advance.

MODERATE

Carriage. Via della Carrozze 36, 00187 Roma. ☎ **06/699-0124.** Fax 06/678-8279. 24 rms, 2 suites. A/C MINIBAR TV TEL. 295,000 lire ($188.80) double; 380,000 lire ($243.20) triple;

380,000–536,000 lire ($243.20–$343.05) suite. Rates include breakfast. AE, DC, MC, V. Metro: Piazza di Spagna.

The aptly named Carriage caters to the "carriage trade," which in today's sense means staff members of the British and French embassies, plus an occasional movie star or film director. The 18th-century facade covers some charming, although small, accommodations (ask for one of the two rooftop bedrooms). Antiques have been used tastefully, creating a personal aura, even in the bedrooms with their matching bedcovers and draperies. Each bedroom has a radio and other amenities. To meet your fellow guests, head for the Renaissance-style salon that's called an American bar or for the roof garden. There is no dining room.

Hotel Cecil. Via Francesco Crispi 55A, 00187 Roma. ☎ **06/679-7998.** Fax 06/679-7996. 41 rms. TV TEL. 270,000–290,000 lire ($172.80–$185.60) double. Rates include breakfast. AE, MC, V. Parking 25,000–30,000 lire ($16–$19.20). Metro: Piazza Barberini. Bus: 60, 61, 62, or 492.

This hotel in a 17th-century building lies in the heart of Rome near such monuments as piazza di Spagna and the Fontana di Trevi. It has entertained everybody from Casanova to Henrik Ibsen, who wrote *Brandt* and conceived *Peer Gynt* here. Today it's attractively streamlined, with comfortable bedrooms, each with private bath, satellite TV, and radio. Since this is an extremely noisy part of Rome, double windows have been installed in accommodations facing the busy street. There's a panoramic terrace for viewing "monumental Rome."

Hotel Gregoriana. Via Gregoriana 18, 00187 Roma. ☎ **06/679-4269.** Fax 06/678-4258. 19 rms. A/C TV TEL. 300,000 lire ($192) double. Rates include breakfast. No credit cards. Parking 25,000 lire ($16). Metro: Piazza di Spagna.

Although surrounded by much chicer and better neighbors like the Hassler, the small Gregoriana is elite with fans of its own—mainly members of the Italian fashion industry. The ruling matriarch of an aristocratic family left the building to an order of nuns in the 19th century, but they eventually retreated to other quarters. Today there might be a slightly more elevated spirituality in Room C than in the rest of the hotel, as it used to be a chapel. Throughout the establishment the smallish rooms provide comfort and Italian design. The elevator cage is a black-and-gold art deco fantasy, and the door to each room has a reproduction of an Erté print whose fanciful characters indicate the letter designating that room. You'll pay the bill in the tiny, rattan-covered lobby.

Hotel Internazionale. Via Sistina 79, 00187 Roma. ☎ **06/6994-1823.** Fax 06/678-4764. 42 rms, 2 suites. A/C MINIBAR TV TEL. 295,000 lire ($188.80) double; from 600,000 lire ($384) suite. Rates include breakfast. AE, MC, V. Parking 35,000 lire ($22.40). Bus: 60, 61, 62, or 492 from the Termini.

Although this *albergo* sits on the ruins of a series of buildings known as Horti Lucullani from the 1st century B.C., the present structure is rooted in a series of buildings dating from the 1500s. Since 1870 the present hotel has operated, just half a block from the top of the Spanish Steps, on one of the most fashionable shopping streets of Rome. Although lacking the style and grace of the d'Inghilterra, it has antique charm of its own, in spite of the modern intrusions. Accommodations facing the narrow via Sistina have double windows to cut down the noise. Some antique wingback chairs and coffered ceilings charm the bedrooms, contrasting with contemporary built-in pieces.

Hotel Madrid. Via Mario de' Fiori 94–95, 00187 Roma. ☎ **06/699-1511.** Fax 06/679-1653. 26 rms, 7 suites. A/C MINIBAR TV TEL. 260,000 lire ($166.40) double; 360,000 lire ($230.40) suite for four. Rates include breakfast. AE, DC, MC, V. Parking 32,000–34,000 lire ($20.50–$21.75). Metro: Piazza di Spagna.

The Hotel Madrid evokes *fin-de-siècle* Roma on its interior in spite of the modern intrusions in its well-maintained and comfortable, if rather minimalist, bedrooms. The hotel appeals to the individual traveler who wants a good standard of service. Guests often take their breakfast amid ivy and blossoming plants on the roof terrace with a panoramic view of rooftops and the distant dome of St. Peter's. Some of the doubles are large, equipped with small scatter rugs, veneer armoires, and shuttered windows. Others are quite small—so make sure you know what you're getting before you check in. The hotel is an ocher building with a shuttered facade on a narrow street practically in the heart of the boutique area centering around via Frattina, near the Spanish Steps.

Hotel Piazza di Spagna. Via Mario de' Fiori 61, 00187 Roma. ☎ **06/679-6412.** Fax 06/679-0654. 16 rms. A/C MINIBAR TV TEL. 250,000 lire ($160) double. Rates include breakfast. AE, MC, V. Metro: Piazza di Spagna. Bus: 61, 71, 81, or 85.

Set about a block from the downhill side of the Spanish Steps, this hotel was once just an unknown, run-down *pensione* until new owners in the 1990s took it over and substantially upgraded it, as befits its choice location. Originally built in the early 1800s, it has always occupied prime real estate. It's small but classic, with a warm, inviting atmosphere. Some rooms even have a Jacuzzi. The decor of the rooms is functionally streamlined, although hardly inspired. The neighborhood is filled with lots of options for drinking and dining.

INEXPENSIVE

Hotel Margutta. Via Laurina 34, 00187 Roma. ☎ **06/322-3674.** Fax 06/320-0395. 21 rms. 147,000 lire ($94.10) double; 190,000 lire ($121.60) triple. Rates include breakfast. AE, DC, MC, V. Metro: Flaminio. Bus: 95, 119, 490, or 495.

The Hotel Margutta, on a cobblestone street near piazza del Popolo, offers attractively decorated rooms and a helpful staff. The hotel is housed in a two-century-old building that was transformed into a small hotel in 1961. Located off the paneled, black stone-floored lobby is a simple breakfast room with framed lithographs. The best rooms are on the top floor, each with a view. Two of these three rooms (nos. 50 and 51) share a terrace, and the larger bedroom has a private terrace. Management always reserves the right to charge a 20% to 35% supplement for these accommodations. Be alert to the fact that the hotel is not air-conditioned, nor does it have room phones.

Pensione Fiorella. Via del Babuino 196, 00187 Roma. ☎ **06/361-0597.** 7 rms, none with bath. 82,000 lire ($52.50) double. Rates include breakfast. No credit cards. Metro: Flaminio.

A few steps from piazza del Popolo is this utterly basic, unstylish, but comfortable *pensione*. Antonio Albano and his family are one of the best reasons to stay here—they speak little English, but their humor and warm welcome make renting one of their well-scrubbed bedrooms a lot like visiting a lighthearted Italian relative. The bedrooms open onto a high-ceilinged hallway. The doors of the Fiorella shut at 1am. Reservations can only be made a day before you check in.

Pensione Lydia Venier. Via Sistina 42, 00187 Roma. ☎ **06/679-1744.** Fax 06/679-7263. 30 rms, 10 with shower only, 10 with bath. 150,000 lire ($96) double without bath, 180,000 lire ($115.20) double with shower only, 200,000 lire ($128) double with bath. Rates include breakfast. AE, DC, MC, V. Metro: Piazza Barberini or Piazza di Spagna.

This respectable but cost-conscious *pensione* is set on one of the upper floors of a gracefully proportioned apartment building on a street that radiates out from the top of the Spanish Steps. The bedrooms are utterly simple with understated furnishings, a dignified combination of slightly battered modern and antique, and an occasional reminder (such as a ceiling fresco) of an earlier era.

NEAR VIA VENETO
VERY EXPENSIVE

✪ **Excelsior.** Via Vittorio Veneto 125, 00187 Roma. ☎ **06/47081,** or 800/325-3589 in the U.S. and in Canada. Fax 06/482-6205. 327 rms, 45 suites. A/C MINIBAR TV TEL. 530,000–590,000 lire ($339.20–$377.60) double; 1,000,000–1,600,000 lire ($640–$1,024) suite. AE, DC, MC, V. Metro: Piazza Barberini.

This hotel is far livelier and better than its sibling, the Grand. It's also got a lot more *joie de vivre*, even though Elizabeth Taylor checked out a long time ago. She has been replaced by Arab princesses and international financiers. The Excelsior (pronounced Ess-*shell*-see-or) is a limestone palace whose baroque corner tower, which looks right over the U.S. Embassy, is a landmark in Rome. Guests enter a string of cavernous reception rooms with thick rugs, marble floors, gilded garlands and pilasters decorating the walls, and Empire furniture (supported by winged lions and the like). Everything looks just a little bit tarnished today, and competition has drained much of its former patronage, but the Excelsior endures, seemingly as eternal as Rome itself. In no small part that's because of the exceedingly hospitable staff.

The rooms come in two basic varieties: new (the result of a major renovation) and traditional. The doubles are spacious and elegantly furnished, often with antiques and silk curtains. The furnishings in the singles are also of high quality. Most of the bedrooms are different, many with a sumptuous Hollywood-style bath—marble-walled with separate bath and shower, sinks, bidet, and a mountain of fresh towels.

Dining/Entertainment: The Excelsior Bar, open daily from 10:30am to 1am, is the most famous on via Vittorio Veneto, and La Cupola is known for its national and regional cuisine, with dietetic and kosher food prepared on request.

Services: Room service, baby-sitting, laundry and valet service.

Facilities: Beauty salon, barbershop.

✪ **Hotel Eden.** Via Ludovisi 49, 00187 Roma. ☎ **06/478121,** or 800/225-5843 in the U.S. Fax 06/482-1584. 101 rms, 11 suites. A/C MINIBAR TV TEL. 600,000–700,000 lire ($384–$448) double; 1,300,000–2,000,000 lire ($832–$1,280) suite. AE, DC, MC, V. Parking 40,000 lire ($25.60).

For several generations after its inauguration in 1889, this richly ornate five-story hotel reigned over one of the most stylish shopping neighborhoods in the world. Hemingway, Maria Callas, Ingrid Bergman, Fellini—all the big names checked in here during its heyday. In 1994, after its purchase in 1989 by Trusthouse Forte, it reopened after 2 years (and $20 million) of radical renovations that enhanced its original *fin-de-siècle* grandeur and added the modern amenities its five-star status calls for. Set near the top of the Spanish Steps, its hilltop position guarantees a panoramic view over the city from most bedrooms that guests consider worth the rather high expense. The rooms contain marble-sheathed bathrooms, draperies worthy of the pages of *Architectural Digest,* and a plushly configured allegiance to the decor of the late 19th century. Understated elegance is the rule. There's a gym and health club on the premises, a piano bar, and a glamorous restaurant, La Terrazza, that's recommended separately (see "Dining," later in this chapter).

MODERATE

Alexandra. Via Vittorio Veneto 18, 00187 Roma. ☎ **06/488-1943.** Fax 06/487-1804. 39 rms, 6 suites. A/C MINIBAR TV TEL. 260,000 lire ($166.40) double; 360,000 lire ($230.40) suite. Rates include breakfast. AE, DC, MC, V. Parking 35,000 lire ($22.40). Metro: Piazza Barberini. Bus: 52, 53, 56, 58, 95, or 586.

Although guidebooks ignore it, this is one of your few chances to stay on via Veneto without going broke. Set behind the dignified stone facade of what was originally a 19th-century private mansion, this hotel offers clean, comfortable rooms filled with antique furniture and modern conveniences. Rooms facing the front are exposed to the roaring traffic and animated street life of via Veneto; those in back are quieter but with less of a view. No meals are served other than breakfast, although the hall porter or a member of the staff can carry drinks to clients in the reception area. The breakfast room is especially appealing: Inspired by an Italian garden, it was designed by the noted architect Paolo Portoghesi.

Hotel Oxford. Via Boncompagni 89, 00187 Roma. ☎ **06/4282-8952.** Fax 06/4281-5349. 57 rms, 2 suites. A/C MINIBAR TV TEL. 240,000 lire ($153.60) double; 290,000 lire ($185.60) triple; 350,000 lire ($224) suite. Rates include breakfast. 15% reductions Jan–Mar 15. AE, DC, MC, V. Parking 30,000–50,000 lire ($19.20–$32). Bus: 3, 4, 38, 56, 58, or 62.

The centrally located Hotel Oxford is a decent, although not spectacular, choice adjacent to the Borghese Gardens. Recently renovated, the Oxford is now centrally heated and fully carpeted throughout. There's a pleasant lounge and a cozy bar (which serves snacks), plus a dining room offering a good Italian cuisine. The bedrooms, which were recently renovated, are now air-conditioned in summer and centrally heated in winter, with simple modern furnishings and full carpeting. The rooms are a bit sterile and functional in decor, but well maintained.

La Residenza. Via Emilia 22–24, 00187 Roma. ☎ **06/488-0789.** Fax 06/485721. 27 rms, 6 suites. A/C MINIBAR TV TEL. 248,000 lire ($158.70) double; 280,000 lire ($179.20) suite. Rates include buffet breakfast. AE, MC, V. Parking (limited) 5,000 lire ($3.20). Metro: Piazza Barberini. Bus: 52, 53, 56, 58, 95, or 586.

La Residenza successfully combines the intimacy of a generously sized town house with the elegant appointments of a well-decorated hotel. It's a bit old-fashioned and homelike, and doesn't in any way try to pursue chicdom, but is still a favorite among international travelers. The location is superb but noisy. The converted villa has an ivy-covered courtyard and a labyrinthine series of upholstered public rooms with Oriental rugs, Empire divans, oil portraits, and warmly accommodating cushioned rattan chairs. Each bedroom has a radio in addition to other amenities. A series of terraces is scattered strategically throughout the hotel.

NEAR THE TERMINI
VERY EXPENSIVE

Hotel Massimo d'Azeglio. Via Cavour 18, 00184 Roma. ☎ **06/487-0270,** or 800/223-9832 in the U.S. Fax 06/482-7386. 210 rms. A/C MINIBAR TV TEL. 385,000 lire ($246.40) double. Rates include breakfast. AE, DC, MC, V. Parking 35,000–40,000 lire ($22.40–$25.60). Metro: Termini.

This up-to-date hotel near the train station and opera was established as a small restaurant by one of the founders of an Italian hotel dynasty more than a century ago. In World War II it was a refuge for the king of Serbia and also a favorite with Italian generals. Today this centrally located hotel is the "Casa Madre," or Mother House, of the Bettoja chain. Run by Angelo Bettoja and his charming wife, who hails from America's southland, it offers clean, comfortable accommodations, plus a bar and a well-trained staff. Its facade is one of the most elegant neoclassical structures in the area, and its lobby has been renovated, with light paneling.

Le Grand Hotel. Via Vittorio Emanuele Orlando 3, 00185 Roma. ☎ **06/4709,** or 800/ 221-2340 in the U.S., 800/955-2442 in Canada. Fax 06/474-7307. 134 rms, 36 suites. A/C MINIBAR TV TEL. 530,000–580,000 lire ($339.20–$371.20) double; 900,000–1,600,000

Accommodations near Termini & Via Veneto

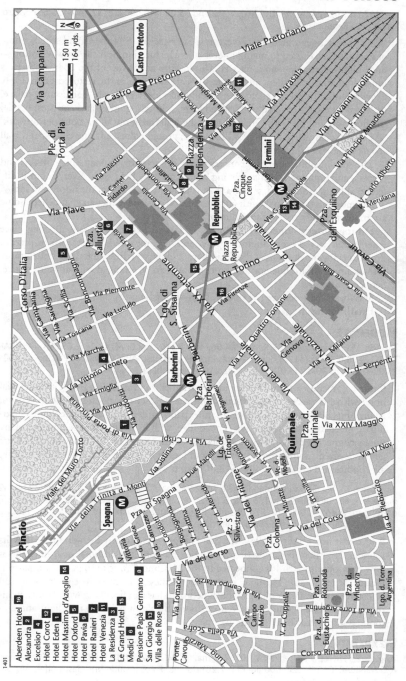

Legend:

- Aberdeen Hotel 16
- Alexandra 2
- Excelsior 4
- Hotel Corot 12
- Hotel Eden 1
- Hotel Massimo d'Azeglio 14
- Hotel Oxford 5
- Hotel Pavia 9
- Hotel Ranieri 7
- Hotel Venezia 11
- La Residenza 3
- Le Grand Hotel 15
- Medici 6
- Pensione Papà Germano 8
- San Giorgio 13
- Villa delle Rose 10

lire ($576–$1,024) suite. AE, DC, MC, V. Parking 35,000–40,000 lire ($22.40–$25.60). Metro: Piazza della Repubblica.

When it was inaugurated by its creator, Cesar Ritz, in 1894, Le Grand struck a note of grandeur it has tried to maintain ever since. Its location near the railway station—once highly desirable—no longer is. The Hassler at the top of the Spanish Steps is more dramatically located, and many VIPs are flocking to the restored Eden. Only a few minutes from via Veneto, the Grand looks like a large late-Renaissance palace, its five-floor facade covered with carved loggias, lintels, quoins, and cornices. Inside, the floors are marble with Oriental rugs, the walls are a riot of baroque plasterwork, and crystal chandeliers, Louis XVI furniture, potted palms, antique clocks, and wall sconces complete the picture.

The spacious bedrooms are conservatively decorated with matching curtains and carpets, and equipped with a dressing room and fully tiled bath. Every room is different, although some are less grand than you might expect from the impressive lobby. While most are traditional, with antique headboards and Venetian chandeliers, some are modern. Every room is soundproof.

Dining/Entertainment: The hotel's Le Grand Bar is an elegant meeting place where tea is served every afternoon in winter, accompanied by a harpist or pianist. You can enjoy quick meals at the Salad Bar, or else try Le Restaurant, the hotel's more formal dining room. Dietetic and kosher foods can be arranged with advance notice. Service is first-rate.

Services: Room service (24 hours), baby-sitting, laundry and valet service.

Facilities: Beauty salon.

MODERATE

Medici. Via Flavia 96, 00187 Roma. ☎ **06/482-7319.** Fax 06/474-0767. 68 rms. MINIBAR TV TEL. 200,000 lire ($128) double. Rates include breakfast. AE, DC, MC, V. Parking 28,000–35,000 lire ($17.90–$22.40). Metro: Piazza della Repubblica.

Quite a comedown from the Grand, the Medici, built in 1906, is still a substantial hotel with easy access to the shops along via XX Settembre and the train station. Many of its better rooms overlook an inner patio garden, with Roman columns holding up greenery and climbing ivy. The lounge, with its white coved ceiling, has many nooks connected by wide white arches. The furnishings in the public areas and the generous-sized rooms are traditional, with lots of antiques. The few rooms that are air-conditioned are 20,000 lire ($12.80) extra.

San Giorgio. Via Giovanni Amendola 61, 00185 Roma. ☎ **06/482-7341,** or 800/223-9832 in the U.S. Fax 06/488-3191. 186 rms, 5 suites. A/C MINIBAR TV TEL. 340,000 lire ($217.60) double; from 465,000 lire ($297.60) suite. Rates include breakfast. AE, DC, MC, V. Parking 35,000–45,000 lire ($22.40–$28.80). Metro: Termini.

A four-star hotel built in 1940, the San Giorgio is constantly being improved by its founders, the Bettoja family (it was the first air-conditioned hotel in Rome, and is now also soundproof). It's connected to the Massimo d'Azeglio so guests can patronize its fine restaurant. The hotel is ideal for families, as many of its corner rooms can be converted into larger quarters. Each bedroom has a radio, along with other amenities that often lie behind wood-veneer doors. Breakfast is served in a light and airy room, and the staff is most helpful.

INEXPENSIVE

Aberdeen Hotel. Via Firenze 48, 00184 Roma. ☎ **06/482-3920.** Fax 06/482-1092. 26 rms. A/C MINIBAR TV TEL. 230,000 lire ($147.20) double. Rates include breakfast buffet. AE, DC, MC, V. Metro: Termini.

In case you want to be welcomed there.

We're here to see that you're always welcomed at establishments everywhere. That's why millions of people carry the American Express® Card — for peace of mind, confidence, and security, around the world or just around the corner.

do more®

Cards

And just in case.

We're here with American Express® Travelers Cheques
and Cheques *for Two.*® They're the safest way to carry
money on your vacation and the surest way to get a
refund, practically anywhere, anytime.

Another way we help you...

do more

**Travelers
Cheques**

This is a completely renovated hotel near the Rome Opera House, central to both landmarks and the train station. It's in a quiet and fairly safe area of Rome—in front of the Ministry of Defense. The rooms are furnished with an uninspired modern styling, and with such amenities as hair dryers and radios. Only a breakfast buffet is served, but many inexpensive *trattorie* lie nearby.

Hotel Corot. Via Marghera 15–17, 00185 Roma. ☎ **06/4470-0900.** Fax 06/4470-0905. 20 rms. A/C MINIBAR TV TEL. 150,000–190,000 lire ($96–$121.60) double; 170,000–205,000 lire ($108.80–$131.20) triple; 190,000–220,000 lire ($121.60–$140.80) quad. Rates include breakfast. 15% weekend discounts for multiple-night stays. AE, DC, MC, V. Parking 25,000–28,000 lire ($16–$17.90). Metro: Termini.

Modernized and comfortable, this hotel occupies the second and third floors of a turn-of-the-century building that contains a handful of private apartments and another, somewhat less well accessorized hotel. The Corot is a safe but lackluster bet north of the Termini, and far better than some of the horrors south of the station. Guests register in a small, paneled area on the building's street level, then take an elevator to their respective floors. The bedrooms are airy, high-ceilinged, and filled with simple but traditional furniture and soothing colors. The bathrooms are modern and contain hair dryers. There's a residents' bar near one of the sun-flooded windows in one of the public rooms.

Hotel Pavia. Via Gaeta 83, 00185 Roma. ☎ **06/483801.** Fax 06/481-9090. 50 rms. A/C MINIBAR TV TEL. 130,000–190,000 lire ($83.20–$121.60) double. Rates include breakfast. AE, DC, MC, V. Parking 12,000–20,000 lire ($7.70–$12.80). Metro: Termini.

The Hotel Pavia is a popular choice on this quiet street near the gardens of the Baths of Diocletian. Established in the 1980s, it occupies a much-renovated century-old private villa. You'll pass through a wisteria-covered passageway that leads to the recently modernized reception area and the public rooms, tastefully covered in light-grained paneling with white lacquer accents and carpeting. The staff is attentive. The front rooms tend to be noisy, but that's the curse of all Termini hotels. Nevertheless, the rooms are comfortable and fairly attractive, with simple, modern wood furnishings and soothing colors. All in all, it's a safe haven in an unsafe area.

Hotel Ranieri. Via XX Settembre 43, 00187 Roma. ☎ **06/481-4467.** Fax 06/481-8834. 40 rms. A/C MINIBAR TV TEL. 180,000–250,000 lire ($115.20–$160) double. Rates include breakfast. Weekend discounts granted except in Oct. AE, MC, V. Parking 20,000–30,000 lire ($12.80–$19.20). Metro: Piazza della Repubblica.

Ranieri is a winning three-star hotel in a very old, freshly restored building. The guest rooms received a substantial renovation in 1995, complete with new furniture, carpets, wall coverings, and even new bathrooms. The location is good; from the hotel you can stroll to the Rome Opera, piazza della Repubblica, and via Vittorio Veneto. The public rooms, the lounge, and the dining room are attractively decorated, in part with contemporary art. You can arrange for a home-cooked meal in the dining room.

⑤ Hotel Venezia. Via Varese 18 (near via Marghera), 00185 Roma. ☎ **06/445-7101.** Fax 06/495-7687. 61 rms. A/C MINIBAR TV TEL. 235,000 lire ($150.40) double; 320,000 lire ($204.80) triple. Rates include breakfast. AE, DC, MC, V. Parking 30,000 lire ($19.20). Metro: Termini.

The Hotel Venezia is the type of place that restores one's faith in moderately priced hotels. The location is good—3 blocks from the railroad station, in a part-business, part-residential area dotted with a few old villas and palm trees. The Venezia had a total renovation in 1991, transforming it into a good-looking and cheerful hostelry with a charming collection of public rooms. The floors are brown marble. The bedrooms are furnished in some cases with furniture in the 17th-century style, although some are beginning to look shop-worn. All units have Murano chandeliers, and some have a balcony for surveying the action on the street below. The housekeeping is superb—the management really cares.

Pensione Papà Germano. Via Calatafimi 14A, 00185 Roma. ☎ **06/486919.** 13 rms, 2 with bath. TEL. 60,000 lire ($38.40) double without bath, 69,000 lire ($44.15) double with bath; 90,000 lire ($57.60) triple without bath, 85,000 lire ($53.15) triple with bath. 10% discounts Nov–Feb. AE, MC, V. Metro: Termini.

It's about as basic and simple as anything in this book. This 1892 belle époque building has undertaken some recent renovations, yet retains its simple, modest ambience. Chances are that your fellow residents will arrive, backpack in tow, directly from the train station 4 blocks to the south. Located on a block-long street immediately east of the Baths of Diocletian, this *pensione* has simple but clean accommodations with plain furniture, well-maintained showers, and a high-turnover clientele of European and North American students. The energetic, English-speaking owner, Gino Germano, offers advice on sightseeing to anyone who asks. The *pensione* doesn't serve breakfast, but there are dozens of cafes nearby that open early.

Villa delle Rose. Via Vicenza 5, 00185 Roma. ☎ **06/445-1788.** Fax 06/445-1639. 38 rms. A/C TV TEL. 240,000–260,000 lire ($153.60–$166.40) double. Rates include breakfast. AE, DC, MC, V. Free parking. Metro: Termini or Castro Pretorio.

Set less than 2 blocks north of the railway station, behind a dignified cut-stone facade inspired by the Renaissance, this hotel was originally built in the late 1800s as a private home. Despite many renovations, the ornate trappings of the wealthy family who built the place are still visible, including a set of Corinthian-capped marble

J. Paul Getty's Former Villa

La Posta Vecchia, in Palo Laziale, just south of Ladispoli (☎ **06/994-9501;** fax 06/994-9507), lies 22 miles northwest of Rome and about 14 miles up the coast from Leonardo da Vinci Airport. Set on foundations of villas possibly built by Tiberius, this palatial villa was owned between 1960 and 1976 by one of the world's richest men, J. Paul Getty. In 1645 it was a guesthouse for the nearby Castello Oldescalchi. Set behind iron gates, the stucco-sided building stands amid formal gardens in a 6-acre park.

The villa retains many antiques collected by Getty, as well as many carefully disguised steel doors, escape routes, and security devices installed to protect him from intruders. Following the tragic kidnapping of his son in the early 1970s, Getty declared that the building's access to the sea was an unacceptable security risk. The house was sold and became a private home until 1990, when it was transformed into an exceptionally elegant hotel. Guests stay in 17 sumptuously decorated suites, which range in price from 640,000 to 2,140,000 lire ($409.60 to $1,369.60) a night. With discretion and politeness, staff members serve traditional Italian and Roman cuisine during lunch and dinner in a richly formal dining room. The villa is closed from January 15 to March 20.

Extensive renovations initiated during Getty's ownership revealed hundreds of ancient Roman artifacts, many of which are on display in a mini-museum. There's an indoor pool, plus a staff (some of whom used to work for Getty) adept at maintaining the illusion that clients have arrived as friends of the long-departed billionaire.

columns in the lobby and a flagstone-covered terrace that fills part of a verdant garden in back. Much of the interior has been redecorated with traditional wall coverings and new carpets. Morning breakfasts in the garden, where the hotel's namesake rows of pink and red roses bloom, do a lot to add country flavor to an otherwise very urban and noisy location. The English-speaking staff is helpful and tactful.

NEAR VATICAN CITY
EXPENSIVE

Hotel Atlante Star. Via Vitelleschi 34, 00193 Roma. ☎ **06/687-3233.** Fax 06/687-2300. 80 rms, 10 suites. A/C MINIBAR TV TEL. 490,000 lire ($313.60) double; 580,000 lire ($371.20) suite. Rates include breakfast. AE, DC, MC, V. Parking 40,000 lire ($25.60). Metro: Ottaviano. Bus: 23, 64, 81, or 492. Tram: 19 or 30.

The Atlante Star is a first-class hotel a short distance from the Vatican, with the most striking views of St. Peter's of any hotel in Rome. The tastefully renovated lobby is covered with dark marble, chrome trim, and lots of exposed wood, whereas the upper floors give the impression of being inside a luxuriously appointed ocean liner. This stems partly from the lavish use of curved and lacquered surfaces, walls upholstered in freshly colored printed fabrics, modern bathrooms, and wall-to-wall carpeting. Even the door handles are art deco–inspired. The rooms are small but posh, outfitted with all the modern comforts. There's also a royal suite with a Jacuzzi. If there's no room at this inn, the owner will try to get you a room at his less desirable Atlante Garden nearby.

Dining/Entertainment: The restaurant, Les Etoiles, is an elegant roof-garden choice at night, with a 360° panoramic view of Rome and an illuminated St. Peter's in the background. The flavorful cuisine is inspired in part by Venice.

Services: Room service (24 hours), laundry/valet, baby-sitting, express checkout.

Facilities: Roof garden, foreign-currency exchange, secretarial services in English, translation services.

MODERATE

✪ **Hotel Atlante Garden.** Via Crescenzio 78, 00193 Roma. ☎ **06/687-2361.** Fax 06/687-2315. 43 rms. A/C MINIBAR TV TEL. 350,000 lire ($224) double. Rates include breakfast. AE, DC, MC, V. Parking 40,000 lire ($25.60). Metro: Ottaviano. Bus: 23, 32, 49, 51, or 492. Tram: 19 or 30.

The Atlante Garden stands on a tree-lined street near the Vatican. Although not as attractive or well appointed as its sibling, the Atlante Star (above), it's much cheaper. The entrance takes you through a garden tunnel lined with potted palms, which eventually leads into a series of handsomely decorated public rooms. More classical in its decor than the Atlante Star, the Garden offers 19th-century–style bedrooms that have been freshly papered and painted and contain tastefully conservative furniture and all the modern accessories. The renovated baths are tiled, and each is equipped with a Jacuzzi.

Hotel Columbus. Via della Conciliazione 33, 00193 Roma. ☎ **06/686-5435.** Fax 06/686-5435. 105 rms, 4 suites. A/C MINIBAR TV TEL. 270,000 lire ($172.80) double; 380,000 lire ($243.20) suite. Rates include breakfast. AE, DC, MC, V. Free parking. Bus: 64.

In an impressive 15th-century palace, built some 12 years before its namesake set off for America, the Hotel Columbus was once the private home of the wealthy cardinal who later became Pope Julius II and tormented Michelangelo into painting the Sistine Chapel. The building looks much as it must have centuries ago—a severe, time-stained facade, small windows, and heavy wooden doors leading from the street to the colonnades and arches of the inner courtyard. The cobbled entranceway leads

Accommodations & Dining in Vatican Area

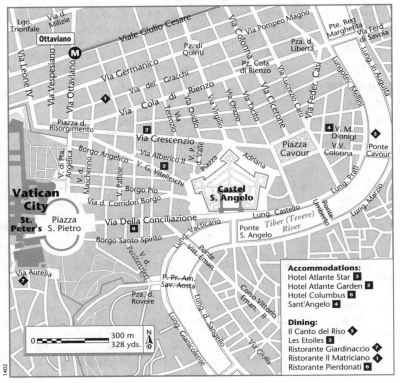

to a reception hall with castlelike furniture, then on to a series of baronial public rooms. Note especially the main salon with its walk-in fireplace, oil portraits, battle scenes, and Oriental rugs.

The bedrooms are considerably simpler than the tiled and tapestried salons, done in soft beiges and furnished with comfortable and serviceable modern pieces. All the accommodations are spacious, but a few are enormous and still have such original details as decorated wood ceilings and frescoed walls. The hotel restaurant serves lunch and dinner.

INEXPENSIVE

Sant'Angelo. Via Mariana Dionigi 16, 00193 Roma. ☎ **06/322-0758.** Fax 06/320-4451. 24 rms. TV TEL. 140,000 lire ($89.60) double. AE, DC, MC, V. Parking 25,000 lire ($16). Bus: 49, 70, 87, 492, or 813.

Right off piazza Cavour (northeast of the Castel Sant'Angelo), this hotel stands in a relatively untouristy area. Maintained and operated by several members of the Torre family, the hotel occupies the second and third floors of an imposing 200-year-old building whose other floors are devoted to offices and private apartments. The bedrooms are simple, modern, clean, and uncomplicated, with wooden furniture and views of either the street or of a rather bleak, but quiet, courtyard in back. Although the hotel serves only breakfast, the neighborhood offers many acceptable dining choices.

IN PARIOLI
VERY EXPENSIVE

✪ **Hotel Lord Byron.** Via G. de Notaris 5, 00197 Roma. ☎ **06/322-0404.** Fax 06/322-0405. 28 rms, 9 suites. A/C MINIBAR TV TEL. Apr–July and Sept–Oct, 430,000–540,000 lire ($275.20–$345.60) double; 800,000–1,200,000 lire ($512–$768) suite. July–Aug and Nov–Mar, 360,000–550,000 lire ($230.40–$352) double; 550,000–1,000,000 lire ($352–$640) suite. Rates include breakfast. AE, DC, MC, V. Metro: Flaminio. Bus: 26 or 52.

The savvy set, fleeing those landmarks of yesterday (the Grand and the Excelsior) are likely to check in here. The Lord Byron exemplifies modern Rome—an art deco villa set on a residential hilltop in Parioli, an area of embassies and exclusive town houses at the edge of the Villa Borghese. From the curving entrance steps off the staffed parking lot in front, you'll notice design accessories that attract the most sophisticated clientele in Italy. An oval Renaissance urn in chiseled marble occupies a niche in the reception area. Flowers are everywhere, the lighting is discreet, and everything is on a cultivated small scale that makes it seem more like a well-staffed (and extremely expensive) private home than a hotel. Each of the guest rooms is different, but most have lots of mirrors, upholstered walls, a spacious bathroom with gray marble accessories, a big dressing room/closet, and all the amenities. Check into room 503, 602, or 603 for the most panoramic views of Rome.

Dining/Entertainment: On the premises is one of Rome's best restaurants, recommended separately (see "Dining," later in this chapter).

Services: Concierge, room service (24 hours), laundry and valet service.

MODERATE

Hotel degli Aranci. Via Barnaba Oriani 9–11, 00197 Roma. ☎ **06/808-5250.** Fax 06/808-5250. 54 rms, 3 suites. A/C MINIBAR TV TEL. 260,000 lire ($166.40) double; 350,000 lire ($224) suite. Rates include breakfast. AE, DC, MC, V. Free parking. Bus: 3 or 53 from the Termini.

The degli Aranci is a long way down the ladder from its Parioli neighbor, the Lord Byron, in style, grace, and amenities, but it's still worthy of serious consideration and it doesn't charge the rarified prices of the Lord Byron. It's a former private villa on a tree-lined residential street in Parioli, surrounded by similar villas now used, in part, as consulates and ambassadorial town houses. Most of the accommodations have tall windows opening onto city views and are filled with provincial furnishings or English-style reproductions. The public rooms have memorabilia of ancient Rome scattered about, including bisque-colored medallions of soldiers in profile, old engravings of ruins, and classical vases highlighted against the light-grained paneling. A marble-topped bar in an alcove off the sitting room adds a relaxed touch. From the glass-walled breakfast room, at the rear of the house, you can see the tops of orange trees.

INEXPENSIVE

✪ **Hotel delle Muse.** Via Tommaso Salvini 18, 00197 Roma. ☎ **06/808-8333.** Fax 06/808-5749. 61 rms. TV TEL. 160,000–180,000 lire ($102.40–$115.20) double; 220,000 lire ($140.80) triple. Rates include buffet breakfast. AE, DC, MC, V. Bus: 4. Tram: 19.

The Hotel delle Muse, a three-star establishment half a mile north of the Villa Borghese, is a winning but unheralded choice. It's run by the efficient, English-speaking Giorgio Lazar. A majority of the rooms have been renewed, but remain rather spartan and minimalist. In the summer Lazar operates a restaurant in the garden. A bar is open 24 hours a day in case you get thirsty at 5am. There's also a TV room, plus a writing room and a dining room.

IN MONTE MARIO

Cavalieri Hilton. Via Cadiolo 101, 00136 Roma. ☎ **06/35091,** or 800/445-8667 in the U.S. and Canada. Fax 06/3509-2241. 376 rms, 17 suites. A/C MINIBAR TV TEL. 450,000–515,000 lire ($288–$329.60) double; from 1,000,000 lire ($640) suite. AE, DC, MC, V. Parking 5,000–30,000 lire ($3.20–$19.20). Free shuttle bus to/from the city center.

The Cavalieri Hilton combines all the advantages of a resort hotel with the convenience of being a 15-minute drive from the center of Rome. Overlooking Rome and the Alban Hills from its perch on top of Monte Mario, it's set in 15 acres of trees, flowering shrubs, and stonework. Its facilities are so complete that many visitors— who have seen the city before—never leave the hotel grounds. The entrance leads into a lavish red-and-gold lobby, whose sculpture and winding staircases are usually flooded with sunlight from the massive windows.

The guest rooms and suites, many with panoramic views, are designed to fit contemporary standards of comfort, quality, and style. Soft furnishings in pastel colors are paired with Italian furniture in warm-toned woods. Each unit has a keyless electronic lock, independent heating and air-conditioning, color TV with in-house movies, radio, and bedside control for all electric apparatus in the room, as well as a spacious balcony. The bathrooms, sheathed in Italian marble, are equipped with large mirrors, a hair dryer, international electric sockets, vanity mirror, piped-in music, and phone.

Dining/Entertainment: The hotel's stellar restaurant, La Pergola, has among the best dining views in Rome. In summer, a garden restaurant, Il Giardino dell'Uliveto, with a pool veranda, is an ideal choice.

Services: Concierge (24 hours), room service, laundry/valet, bus to/from the city center.

Facilities: Tennis courts, jogging paths, fitness center, spa, indoor arcade of shops, indoor and outdoor swimming pool, facilities for the disabled.

4 Dining

Rome is one of the world's great capitals for dining. From elegant, deluxe palaces with lavish trappings to little trattorias opening onto hidden piazzas deep in the heart of Old Rome, the city abounds in good restaurants in all price ranges.

It's difficult to compile a list of the best restaurants in such a city. Everybody— locals, expatriates, even those who have chalked up only one visit—has favorites ("What . . . you don't know about that little trattoria three doors down from piazza Navona?"). What follows is not a list of all the best restaurants of Rome, but simply a running commentary on a number of our personal favorites. For the most part, we've chosen not to document every deluxe spot known to all big spenders. Rather, we've tried to seek out equally fine (or better) establishments often patronized by some of the finest palates in Rome—but not necessarily by the fattest wallets.

Rome's cooking is not subtle, but its kitchen rivals anything the chefs of Florence or Venice can turn out. A feature of Roman restaurants is skill at borrowing—and sometimes improving upon—the cuisine of other regions. Throughout the capital you'll come across Neapolitan (*alla neapolitana*), Bolognese (*alla bolognese*), Florentine (*alla fiorentina*), even Sicilian (*alla siciliana*) specialties. One of the oldest sections of the city, Trastevere, is a gold mine of colorful streets and restaurants with inspired cuisine.

In general, lunch is served from 1 to 3pm and dinner from 8 to around 10:30pm. August is a popular month for Romans to leave on vacation and many restaurants will be closed.

NEAR ANCIENT ROME
MODERATE

Alvaro al Circo Massimo. Via dei Cerchi 53. ☎ **06/678-6112.** Reservations required. Main courses 12,000–20,000 lire ($7.70–$12.80). AE, MC, V. Tues–Sat 1–3pm and 7–11pm, Sun 1–3pm. Closed Aug. Metro: Circo Massimo. Bus: 15, 90, 90b, or 166. ITALIAN.

Alvaro al Circo Massimo, at the edge of the Circus Maximus, is the closest thing in Rome to a genuine provincial inn. Here is all the decor associated with Italian taverns, including corncobs hanging from the ceiling and rolls of fat sausages. Their antipasti and pasta dishes are fine, the meat courses well prepared, and there's an array of fresh fish—never overcooked. Other specialties include tagliolini with mushrooms and truffles, and roasted turbot with potatoes. They're especially well stocked with exotic seasonal mushrooms, including black truffles so good you'd have to go directly to Spoleto to find better. A basket of fresh fruit rounds out the repast. Try to linger longer and make an evening of it—the atmosphere is mellow.

INEXPENSIVE

Ⓢ **Abruzzi.** Via del Vaccaro 1. ☎ **06/679-3897.** Reservations recommended. Main courses 14,000–18,000 lire ($8.95–$11.50). DC, MC, V. Sun–Fri 12:30–3pm and 7:30–10:30pm. Closed 2 weeks in Aug (dates vary). Bus: 57, 64, 70, or 17. ABRUZZESE.

Abruzzi takes its name from a little-explored region east of Rome known for its haunting beauty and curious superstitions. The restaurant is located at one side of piazza SS. Apostoli, just a short walk from piazza Venezia. The good food here at reasonable prices makes it enduringly popular among students. The chef is justly praised for his satisfying assortment of cold antipasti. With your starter, we suggest a liter of garnet-red wine; we once had one whose bouquet was suggestive of the wildflowers of Abruzzi. If you'd like a soup as well, you'll find a good stracciatella (an egg-and-cheese soup). A typical main dish is saltimbocca (literally "jump-in-the-mouth," a veal and prociutto dish flavored with marsala).

NEAR CAMPO DE' FIORI & THE JEWISH GHETTO
EXPENSIVE

Angelino a Tormargana. Piazza Margana 37. ☎ **06/678-3328.** Reservations not necessary. Main courses 50,000–75,000 lire ($32–$48). MC, V. Mon–Sat noon–3:30pm and 7:30–11pm. Bus: 64, 90, 90b, 95, or 710. ROMAN.

Goethe once frequented this tavern 3 blocks from piazza Venezia, as did Anna Magnani, Jean-Paul Sartre, and even Richard Nixon. Back in fashion after a number of years, the tavern has subsequently elevated its prices. Everything else—from the atmosphere to the food—has remained unchanged, and that's why Romans like it so. You can dine alfresco in a setting of old palazzi and cobblestone squares. The food is very much in the typical Roman trattoria style—not exceptionally imaginative, but good. We'd recommend the cold seafood risotto or the peppery penne all'arrabbiata (with a tomato and hot pepper sauce). For a main course, you might select kidneys with mushrooms or veal scaloppine flavored with lemon juice. Other main-dish selections are pollo alla diavola and that staple of Roman cuisine, tripe.

Il Drappo. Vicolo del Malpasso 9. ☎ **06/687-7365.** Reservations required. Main courses 20,000–25,000 lire ($12.80–$16); fixed-price menu (including Sardinian wine) 60,000 lire ($38.40). AE, MC, V. Mon–Sat 8pm–midnight. Closed 2 weeks in Aug. Bus: 46, 62, or 64. SARDINIAN.

Il Drappo, on a narrow street near the Tiber, is operated by a woman known to her habitués only as "Valentina." You'll have your choice of two tastefully decorated dining rooms festooned with yards of patterned cotton draped from supports on the ceiling. Flowers and candles are everywhere. Fixed-price dinners may include a wafer-thin appetizer called carte di musica (sheet-music paper), which is topped with tomatoes, green peppers, parsley, and olive oil, followed by fresh spring lamb in season, a fish stew made with tuna caviar, or a changing selection of strongly flavored regional specialties that are otherwise difficult to find in Rome. Service is first-rate.

MODERATE

La Carbonara. Piazza Campo de' Fiori 23. ☎ **06/686-4783.** Reservations recommended. Main courses 14,000–22,000 lire ($8.95–$14.10). AE, MC, V. Wed–Mon noon–2:30pm and 6:30–10:30pm. Closed 3 weeks in Aug. Bus: 64. ROMAN.

In an antique *palazzetto* at the edge of the market square, this amicable trattoria claims to be the home of the original spaghetti carbonara. According to a much-disputed legend, the forebears of the present owners devised the recipe in the final days of World War II, when American GIs donated their K-rations of powdered eggs and salted bacon to the chef. The result was the egg yolk, cheese, and bacon-enriched pasta dish that's famous throughout the world. The dining room features succulent antipasti, grilled meats, fresh and intelligently prepared seasonal vegetables, and—in addition to the carbonara—several other kinds of pasta, including tagliolini with porcini mushrooms. Another specialty is bucatini al'Amatriciana, with a sauce of tomato, bacon, and hot peppers.

Ristorante da Pancrazio. Piazza del Biscione 92. ☎ **06/686-1246.** Reservations recommended. Main courses 15,000–30,000 lire ($9.60–$19.20); fixed-price menu 45,000 lire ($28.80). AE, DC, MC, V. Thurs–Tues noon–3pm and 7:30–11:15pm. Closed 2 weeks in Aug (dates vary). Bus: 46 or 62. ROMAN.

The Ristorante da Pancrazio is popular as much for its archeological interest as for its culinary allure. One of its two dining rooms is gracefully decorated in the style of an 18th-century tavern; the other occupies the premises of Pompey's ancient theater, and as such is lined with marble columns, carved capitals, and bas-reliefs that would be the envy of many museums. Classified as a national monument, it's probably the only such establishment that feeds your body as well as your sense of history. They serve the full range of traditional Roman dishes, such as risotto alla pescatora (with seafood), several kids of scampi, saltimbocca, and abbacchio al forno (roast lamb with potatoes). You might also order ravioli stuffed with artichoke hearts. No one gets innovative around here—these dishes are prepared according to time-tested recipes. If it was good enough for Caesar, it's good enough for the patrons of da Pancrazio.

Vecchia Roma. Via della Tribuna di Campitelli 18. ☎ **06/686-4604.** Reservations recommended. Main courses 22,000–25,000 lire ($14.10–$16). AE, DC. Thurs–Tues 1–3:30pm and 8–11:30pm. Closed 10 days in Aug. Bus: 64, 90, 90b, 97, or 774. ITALIAN.

Vecchia Roma is a charming, moderately priced trattoria in the heart of the ghetto. Movie stars have frequented the place, sitting at the crowded tables in one of the four small dining rooms (the back room is the most popular). The owners are known for their "fruits of the sea," a selection of fresh seafood. The minestrone of the day is made with fresh vegetables, and an interesting selection of antipasti, including salmon or vegetables, is always available. The pastas and risottos are excellent, including linguine alla marinara with scampi. A "green" risotto with porcini mushrooms is invariably good. The chef prepares excellent cuts of meat, including his specialty, lamb.

INEXPENSIVE

Da Giggetto. Via del Portico d'Ottavia 21–22. ☎ **06/686-1105.** Reservations recommended. Main courses 18,000–24,000 lire ($11.50–$15.35). AE, DC, MC, V. Tues–Sun 12:30–3pm and 7:30–11pm. Closed Aug 1–15. Bus: 62, 64, 75, 90, or 170. ROMAN.

Dining near Campo de' Fiori & Piazza Navona

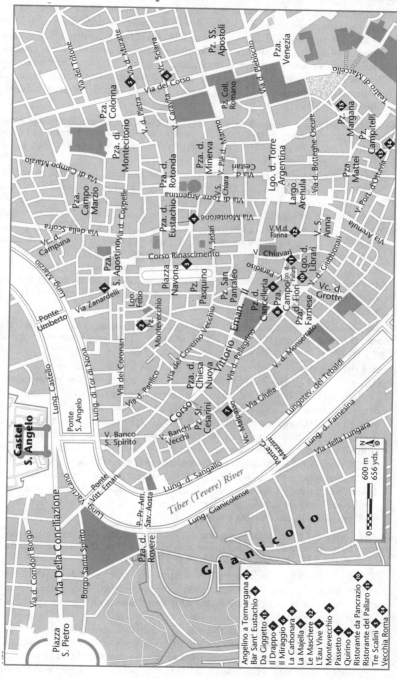

Angelino a Tormargana 6
Bar Sant' Eustachio 4
Da Giggetto 13
Il Drappo 6
Il Miraggio 11
La Carbonara 8
La Majella 3
Le Maschere 12
L'Eau Vive 2
Montevecchio 1
Passetto 7
Quirino 5
Ristorante da Pancrazio 10
Ristorante del Pallaro 9
Tre Scalini 3
Vecchia Roma 14

125

Da Giggetto, in the old ghetto, is right next to the Theater of Marcellus and old Roman columns extend practically to its doorway. Romans flock to this bustling trattoria for their special traditional dishes. None is more typical than carciofi alla giudia, baby-tender fried artichokes—thistles to make you whistle with delight—a true delicacy. The cheese concoction, mozzarella in carrozza, is another delight, as are the zucchini flowers stuffed with mozzarella and anchovies. You could also sample fettuccine al'Amatriciana, shrimp sautéed in garlic and olive oil, a bold tripe dish, or saltimbocca (the eternal favorite).

$ **La Majella.** Piazza del Teatro di Pompeo 18. ☎ **06/686-4174.** Reservations recommended for dinner. Main courses 15,000–20,000 lire ($9.60–$12.80); fixed-price menu 28,000 lire ($17.90). AE, MC, V. Mon–Sat 12:30–3pm and 8pm–midnight. Closed 2 weeks in Aug. Bus: 62 or 64. ABRUZZESE/ITALIAN.

In 1993, because of the encroachment of a nearby museum, La Majella moved out of the small *palazzo* where it had served well-prepared food to the likes of Polish Cardinal Karol Wojtyla (before his elevation to the papal throne). It didn't move very far, and now lies within a trio of old-fashioned dining rooms in an old building a block northeast of campo de' Fiori. The cuisine, fortunately, has changed hardly at all, and includes such Abruzzi mountain food as partridge and venison with polenta, an array of savory pastas (including pappardelle with rabbit), and roast lamb aromatically flavored with herbs. Fish includes grilled or fried versions of sea bass, flounder, lobster, and shrimp. We especially recommend the risotto with zucchini flowers and wild mushrooms—a primavera delight—and the oven-baked pork served with roast potatoes.

Le Maschere. Via Monte della Farina 29. ☎ **06/687-9444.** Reservations recommended. Main courses 18,000–30,000 lire ($11.50–$19.20). AE, DC, MC, V. Tues–Sun 7:30pm–midnight. Bus: 26, 44, 60, 65, or 75. CALABRESE.

Le Maschere, near largo Argentina, specializes in the fragrant, often-fiery cookery of Calabria's Costa Viola—lots of fresh garlic and wake-up-your-mouth red peppers. In a cellar from the 1600s that's decorated with regional artifacts of Calabria but located deep in the heart of Rome, it has recently enlarged its kitchen and added three more dining rooms festooned with fantastic medieval- and Renaissance-inspired murals. Begin with a selection of antipasti calabresi. For *primo* (first course), you can try one of their many different preparations of eggplant or a pasta—perhaps with broccoli or with devilish red peppers, garlic, breadcrumbs, and more than a touch of anchovy. The chef also grills meats and fresh swordfish caught off the Calabrian coast. For dessert, finish with a Calabrian sheep cheese or a fresh fruit salad. If you don't want a full meal, you can just visit for pizza and beer, and in summer you can dine at a small table outside overlooking a tiny piazza.

$ **Ristorante del Pallaro.** Largo del Pallaro 15. ☎ **06/6880-1488.** Reservations recommended for dinner on weekends. Fixed-price menu 30,000 lire ($19.20). No credit cards. Tues–Sun 1–3pm and 7:30–12:30pm. Bus: 46, 62, 64, or 70. ROMAN.

The cheerful and kind-hearted woman in white who emerges with clouds of steam from this establishment's bustling kitchen is the owner, Paola Fazi. She maintains a simple duet of very clean dining rooms where price-conscious Romans go for good food at bargain prices. She also claims—although others dispute it—that Julius Caesar was assassinated on this very site. No à la carte meals are served, but the fixed-price menu has made the place famous. As you sit down, your antipasto, the first of eight courses, will appear. Then comes the pasta of the day, followed by roast veal, white meatballs or (only on Friday) dried cod, along with potatoes and eggplant. For your final courses, you're served mozzarella, cake with custard, and fruit in season. The

⊕ Family-Friendly Restaurants

Césarina *(see p. 134)*   A long-time family favorite, this restaurant with a cuisine from the Emiliana-Romagna region serves the most kid-pleasing pastas in town, each handmade and presented with a different sauce. You can request a selection of three kinds of pasta on one plate for a little taste of each.

Otello alla Concordia *(see p. 130)*   This place is as good as any to introduce your child to the hearty Roman cuisine. If your child doesn't like the spaghetti with clams, then maybe the eggplant parmigiana will tempt. Families can dine in an arbor-covered courtyard.

Tre Scalini *(see p. 128)*   All families visit piazza Navona at some point, and this is the best choice if you'd like a dining table overlooking the square. The cookery is Roman and the menu is wide enough to accommodate most palates—including children's. Even if your child doesn't like the main course, the tartufi (ice cream with a coating of bittersweet chocolate, cherries, and whipped cream) at the end of the meal is a classic bound to please.

meal also includes bread, mineral water, and half a liter of the house wine. This is the type of food you might be served if you were invited to the home of a prosperous Roman family.

NEAR PIAZZA NAVONA & THE PANTHEON
MODERATE

Montevecchio. Piazza Montevecchio 22. ☎ **06/686-1319.** Reservations required. Main courses 24,000–30,000 lire ($15.35–$19.20). AE, MC, V. Tues–Sun 1–3pm and 8–11:30pm. Closed Aug 10–25 and Dec 26–Jan 9. Bus: 70, 81, 90, 90b, or 492. ROMAN/ITALIAN.

To visit, you must negotiate the winding streets of one of Rome's most confusing neighborhoods, near piazza Navona. The heavily curtained restaurant on this Renaissance piazza is where both Raphael and Bramante had studios and where Lucrezia Borgia spun many of her intrigues. The entrance opens onto a high-ceilinged room filled with rural mementos and bottles of wine. Your meal might begin with a strudel of porcini mushrooms followed by the invariably good pasta of the day, perhaps a bombolotti stuffed with prosciutto and spinach. Then select roebuck with polenta, roast Sardinian goat, or one of several veal dishes (on one occasion, served with salmon mousse). Many of these recipes, such as the mushroom strudel and the Sardinian goat, are virtually impossible to find on Roman menus anymore.

Passetto. Via Zanardelli 14. ☎ **06/6880-6569.** Reservations recommended. Main courses 24,000–40,000 lire ($15.35–$25.60). AE, DC, MC, V. Daily noon–3pm and 7pm–midnight. Bus: 70, 87, or 90. ROMAN/ITALIAN.

Passetto, dramatically positioned at the north end of piazza Navona, has drawn patrons with its reputation for excellent Italian food for 142 years. Regrettably, its success has spoiled it somewhat and service is now among the rudest in town. The interior is stylish—three rooms, one containing frosted-glass cylinder chandeliers. In summer, however, sit outside looking out on piazza Sant'Apollinare. The pastas are exceptional, including penne alla Norma. One recommended main dish is orata (sea bass) al cartoccio (baked in a paper bag with tomatoes, mushrooms, capers, and white wine). Another house specialty is rombo passetto (a fish similar to sole) cooked in a cognac and pine nuts. Fresh fish is often priced by its weight, so tabs can soar quickly. Fresh vegetables are abundant in summer, and a favorite dessert is seasonal berries with fresh thick cream.

Tre Scalini. Piazza Navona 30. ☎ **06/687-9148.** Reservations recommended. Main courses 20,000–30,000 lire ($12.80–$19.20). AE, DC, MC, V. Thurs–Tues 12:15–3:30pm and 7:15–11:15pm. Closed Dec–Feb. Bus: 46, 62, 70, 87, or 492. ROMAN.

Established in 1882, this is the most famous and respected restaurant on piazza Navona—a landmark for ice cream as well as more substantial meals. Yes, it's literally crawling with tourists, but its waiters are a lot friendlier and more helpful than those at the nearby Passetto. Although there's a cozy bar on the upper floor, outfitted with simple furniture with a view over the piazza, most visitors opt for a seat either in the ground-floor cafe or restaurant, or, during warm weather, at tables on the piazza.

House specialties include risotto con porcini, spaghetti with clams, roast duck with prosciutto, a carpaccio of sea bass, saltimbocca, and roast lamb in the Roman style. No one will object if you order just a pasta and salad, unlike at other restaurants nearby. Their famous tartufi (ice cream disguised with a coating of bittersweet chocolate, cherries, and whipped cream) and other ice creams cost 10,000 lire ($6.40) each.

INEXPENSIVE

L'Eau Vive. Via Monterone 85. ☎ **06/6880-1095.** Reservations recommended. Main courses 10,000–28,000 lire ($6.40–$17.90); fixed-price menus 15,000, 22,000, and 28,000 lire ($9.60, $14.10, and $17.90). AE, MC, V. Mon–Sat 12:30–2:30pm and 8–10:30pm. Closed Aug 1–20. Bus: 46, 62, 64, 78, or 492. FRENCH/INTERNATIONAL.

Dining at L'Eau Vive qualifies as an offbeat adventure since it's run by lay missionaries who wear the dress or costumes of their native countries. The restaurant fills the cellar and the ground floor of the 17th-century Palazzo Lantante della Rovere, and is filled with monumental paintings under vaulted ceilings. In this formal atmosphere, at 10 o'clock each evening, the waitresses sing religious hymns and *Ave Marias*. Pope John Paul II used to dine here when he was still archbishop of Krakow. Specialties include hors d'oeuvres and frogs' legs, and the cellar is well stocked with French wines. Main dishes range from guinea hen with onions and grapes in a wine sauce to couscous. Other selections include several kinds of homemade pâté, salad niçoise, and beefsteaks in wine sauce. A smooth finish is the chocolate mousse. The tasteful place settings include fresh flowers and good glassware. Some of the most flamboyant members of international society have adopted L'Eau Vive as their favorite spot. Your tip will be turned over for religious purposes.

Il Miraggio. Vicolo Sciarra 59. ☎ **06/678-0226.** Reservations recommended. Main courses 12,000–18,000 lire ($7.70–$11.50). AE, V. Mon–Sat 12:30–3:30pm and 7:30–10:30pm. Bus: 60, 61, 62, or 85. ROMAN/SARDINIAN.

While shopping near piazza Colonna, you may want to escape the roar of traffic along the Corso by dining at this informal, hidden-away "mirage" in a charming location on a crooked street. It's a cozy, neighborhood setting with good simple Roman food—nothing more. The decor includes a wine keg set in the wall. A specialty of the house is tortellini alla papalina. You might want to try filet of beef with truffles, rosetta di vitello modo nostro (veal "our style"), or spiedino alla siciliana (rolls of veal with ham and cheese inside, onions and bay leaves outside, grilled on a skewer). There's also an array of fresh fish.

Quirino. Via delle Muratte 84. ☎ **06/679-4108.** Reservations not necessary. Main courses 15,000–32,000 lire ($9.60–$20.50). AE, MC, V. Mon–Sat 12:30–3:30pm and 7–11pm. Closed 3 weeks in Aug. Metro: Piazza Barberini. ROMAN/SICILIAN.

Quirino is a good place to dine right after you've tossed your coin into the Trevi Fountain. The atmosphere inside is typical Italian, with hanging chianti bottles, a beamed ceiling, and muraled walls. The food is strictly in the "home-cooking" style of Roman *trattorie*. We're fond of a mixed fry of tiny shrimp and squid rings that resemble onion rings. For an opening course, we recommend risotto milanese, spaghetti with clams, or the classic Sicilian pasta dish, pasta alla Norma (tomatoes, eggplant, and salted ricotta). You can also order involtini alla messinese, a roulade of either fish or meat, filled with cheese, grilled, and served with salad greens in the Sicilian style. For dessert, a basket of fresh fruit will be placed on your table.

NEAR PIAZZA DI SPAGNA & PIAZZA DEL POPOLO
EXPENSIVE

☺ El Toulà. Via della Lupa 29B. ☎ **06/687-3498.** Reservations required for dinner. Main courses 50,000 lire ($32); fixed-price menu 100,000 lire ($64). AE, DC, MC, V. Mon 8–11pm, Tues–Sat 1–3pm and 8–11pm. Closed Aug. Bus: 81, 90, 90b, 628, or 913. ROMAN/VENETIAN.

El Toulà ("The Hayloft" in the alpine dialect of Cortina d'Ampezzo) offers the quintessence of Roman haute cuisine with a creative flair, and is the glamorous flagship of an upscale, now international chain. The elegant setting of vaulted ceilings and large archways attracts the international set. Guests stop in the charming bar to order a drink while perusing the impressive, always-changing menu (one section devoted to Venetian specialties, in honor of the restaurant's origins). Items include fegato (liver) alla veneziana, calamari stuffed with vegetables, baccala (codfish mousse served with polenta), and another Venetian classic, broetto, a fish soup made with monkfish and clams. The selection of sherbets changes seasonally—the cantaloupe and fresh strawberry are celestial concoctions—and you can request a mixed plate if you'd like to sample several of them. El Toulà usually isn't crowded at lunchtime.

MODERATE

Babington's Tea Rooms. Piazza di Spagna 23. ☎ **06/678-6027.** Main courses 19,000–37,000 lire ($12.15–$23.70); brunch 45,000 lire ($28.80). AE, MC, DC, V. Wed–Mon 9am–11:30pm. Metro: Piazza di Spagna. ENGLISH/MEDITERRANEAN.

When Victoria was on the English throne in 1893, an Englishwoman named Anne Mary Babington arrived in Rome and couldn't find a place for "a good cuppa." With stubborn determination, she opened her own tea rooms near the foot of the Spanish Steps, and the rooms are still going strong, although because of its heartbeat location prices are too high. You can order everything from Scottish scones and Ceylon tea to a club sandwich and American coffee. Brunch is served at all hours. Pastries cost 4,000 to 13,000 lire ($2.55 to $8.30), while a pot of tea (dozens of varieties available) goes for 12,000 lire ($7.70).

Dal Bolognese. Piazza del Popolo 1–2. ☎ **06/361-1426.** Reservations required. Main courses 20,000–26,000 lire ($12.80–$16.65); fixed-price menu 60,000 lire ($38.40). AE, MC, V. Tues–Sun 12:30–3pm and 8:15–1am. Closed 20 days in Aug. Metro: Flaminio. BOLOGNESE.

If *La Dolce Vita* were being filmed now, this restaurant would probably be used as a backdrop—it's one of those rare dining spots that's not only chic, with patrons in the latest Fendi drag, but noted for its food as well. Young actors, shapely models, artists from nearby via Margutta, even industrialists on an off-the-record evening on the town show up here, quickly booking the limited sidewalk tables. To begin your repast, we suggest a misto de pasta—four pastas, each with a different sauce, arranged on the same plate. A worthy substitute would be thin, savory slices of Parma ham or perhaps the prosciutto and melon (try a little freshly ground pepper on the latter). For your main course, specialties include lasagne verde, tagliatelle alla bolognese, and a most recommendable cotolette alla bolognese. You may want to cap your evening by calling on the Rosati cafe next door (or its competitor, the Canova, across the street), to enjoy one of the tempting pastries.

INEXPENSIVE

Da Mario. Via della Vite 55–56. ☎ **06/678-3818.** Reservations recommended. Main courses 14,000–20,000 lire ($8.95–$12.80); fixed-price menu 38,000–43,000 lire ($24.30–$27.50). AE, DC, MC, V. Mon–Sat 12:30–3pm and 7:30–11pm. Closed Aug. Metro: Piazza di Spagna. ROMAN/FLORENTINE.

Da Mario is noted for its moderately priced game specialties. Mario also does excellent Florentine dishes, although the typical steak is too costly these days for most budgets. You can dine in air-conditioned comfort on the street level or descend to the cellars. A good beginning is the wide-noodle pappardelle, best when served with a game sauce (caccia) or with chunks of rabbit (lepre), available only in winter. Capretto (kid) and beefsteaks are served in the Florentine fashion, although you may prefer roast quail with polenta. We heartily recommend the gelato misto, a selection of mixed ice cream.

Margutta Vegetariano. Via Margutta 119. ☎ **06/3600-1805.** Reservations recommended. Main courses 10,000–16,000 lire ($6.40–$10.25). AE, DC, MC, V. Mon–Sat 1–3pm and 7:30–10:30pm. Closed 2 weeks in Aug. Metro: Piazza di Spagna. VEGETARIAN.

Established in 1980 by Claudio Vannini, an enthusiast of new-wave thinking and Indian philosophy, this place functioned for many years as one of Rome's only vegetarian restaurants. Partly because of the patronage of Signor Vannini's friend and neighbor, the late Federico Fellini, and partly because of its excellent cuisine, the restaurant quickly became a stylish favorite of Italian film stars and TV personalities. Its hundreds of clients ignore the traditional riches of Italian cuisine in favor of the high-fiber specials served in this 18th-century building. You can order from a sophisticated list of risotto and pasta, herb-enriched soups, mixed salads, a melange of fried vegetables, meatless goulash, soyburgers, and a selection of soufflés made with potatoes, spinach, or wild mushrooms. Eggplant parmigiana is a perennial favorite. There's also a large selection of wines and ciders.

Otello alla Concordia. Via della Croce 81. ☎ **06/679-1178.** Main courses 13,000–36,000 lire ($8.30–$23.05); fixed-price menu 36,000 lire ($23.05). AE, DC, MC, V. Mon–Sat 12:30–3pm and 7:30–11pm. Closed 2 weeks in Feb. Metro: Piazza di Spagna. ROMAN.

Set on a side street amid the glamorous boutiques near the northern edge of the Spanish Steps, this is one of the most popular and consistently reliable restaurants of Rome. A stone corridor from the street leads into a dignified building, the Palazzo Povero. Choose a table (space permitting) in either the arbor-covered courtyard or in the cramped but convivial series of inner dining rooms. Displays of Italian bounty decorate an interior well known to many of the shopkeepers from the surrounding fashion district. The spaghetti alle vongole veraci (spaghetti with clams) is excellent, as are Roman-style saltimbocca, abbacchio arrosto (roasted baby lamb), eggplant parmigiana, a selection of grilled or sautéed fish dishes (including swordfish), and several different preparations of veal.

Ristorante Nino. Via Borgognona 11 (off via Condotti). ☎ **06/679-5676.** Reservations recommended. Main courses 20,000–30,000 lire ($12.80–$19.20). AE, DC, MC, V. Mon–Sat 12:30–3pm and 7:30–11pm. Closed Aug. Metro: Piazza di Spagna. TUSCAN.

Ristorante Nino, a short walk from the Spanish Steps, is a tavern mecca for writers, artists, and an occasional model from one of the nearby high-fashion houses. Nino's enjoys deserved acclaim for its Tuscan cooking—hearty and completely

Dining near Piazza di Spagna

Abruzzi **10**
Alvaro al Circo
  Massimo **11**
Babington's Tea
  Rooms **5**
Da Mario **8**
Dal Bolognese **1**
El Toula **9**
Il Ristorante 34
  (Al 34) **7**
Margutta
  Vegetariano **2**
Otello alla
  Concordia **3**
Ristorante Nino **6**
Ristorante Ranieri **4**

Metro **M**
Post Office ✉

Villa
Borghese

plazza delle
Canestre

Galoppatoio

Porta
Pinciana

plazza
del
Popolo

Flaminio M

Vle. C.
Washington
viale del
Muro Torto
V. G. d'Annunzio
viale Trinità
viale del Muro Torto
via d.
Magnolie
viale di Pta. Pinciana
Viale del C. Marini
via
Goethe
Viale d.
Museo
Borghese

via di Ripetta
via del Corso
via del Babuino
via
Laurina
via dei Greci
via Vittoria
via delle Croce
via della
Carrozze
v. Bocca
di Leone
via
Belsiana
via Condotti
via Borgognona
via Frattina
v. della Vite
via M
di Fiori
via d. Due Macelli
via Gregoriana
via F. Crispi
Sistina
via di
Pta. Pinciana
via
V. Veneto
via Lazio
via Lombardia
via Ludovisi
via Liguria
via
Artisti
via
Purificazione
via Emilia

Piazza Augusto
Imperatore
via Tomacelli

Spagna

5
plazza
di Spagna
6
7
8
via Mercede

plazza
Barberini
Barberini M
via Rasella
via d. Scuderie

via Font. Borghese
via Marzio
via del Corso
via Campo Marzio
via Missione
via della Scrofa
via dei
Prefetti
via S.
Claudio
via del Tritone
via Stamperia
via Panetteria
via Rasella

9

plazza
Colonna
via
Colonna
plazza
Monte-
citorio
via Sabini
via delle
Muratte
via dei Pastini
via Minghetti
via dell'Umiltà
Trevi
Fountain
via Dataria
plazza del
Quirinale
via
XXIV
Maggio
via del
Corso
via Nazionale
Largo
Magna-
napoli
via IV
Novembre
via Quirinale
via Parma
via
Parma

plazza
Rotonda
via Seminario
v. Carav.
V.V.Emanuele
Lgo.
Argentina
via
d. Cestari
via
Paganica
via d. Caetani
via
Gesù
via
Plebiscito
via
Botteghe
Oscure
via
Arenula
via
Falegnami
via
Delfina
via
Aracoeli
via S. Maria del Pianto
via
Gatta
via C.
Battisti
plazza
Venezia
10
plazza
della
Pilotta
via
Archetto

lung. d. Cenci
via
Teatro di
Marcello
via Consolazione
via dei Fori Imperiale

ponte
Fabricio
Via dei Cerchi

11

131

unpretentious. The restaurant is particularly known for its steaks shipped in from Florence and charcoal broiled, priced according to weight. However, they're not as succulent or tender as those served at the more famous and expensive Giarrosto Toscano. A plate of cannelloni Nino is one of the chef's specialties. Other good dishes include grilled veal liver, fagioli cotti al fiasco, codfish alla livornese, and zucchini pie.

Ristorante Ranieri. Via Mario de' Fiori 26 (off via Condotti). ☎ **06/679-1592.** Reservations required. Main courses 22,000–32,000 lire ($14.10–$20.50). AE, DC, MC, V. Mon–Sat 12:30–3pm and 7:30–11pm. Metro: Piazza di Spagna. INTERNATIONAL/ITALIAN.

Ristorante Ranieri is well into its second century (it was founded in 1843). Neapolitan-born Giuseppe Ranieri was the chef to Queen Victoria. Long a favorite dining place of the *cognoscenti,* Ranieri still maintains its Victorian trappings. Nothing ever seems to change here. Many of the dishes reflect the restaurant's ties with royalty: veal cutlet l'Impériale, mignonettes of veal à la Regina Victoria, and tournedos Enrico IV. A suitable starter might be crêpes Ranieri, stuffed with eight kinds of cheese. The imperial veal cutlet dish—served with asparagus and mushrooms—was actually created sometime in the 19th century for the queen herself. Most of the dishes are French and Italian, although overall the cookery is international.

Il Ristorante 34 (also Al 34). Via Mario de' Fiori 34. ☎ **06/679-5091.** Reservations required. Main courses 16,000–28,000 lire ($10.25–$17.90); fixed-price menu 55,000 lire ($35.20). AE, DC, MC, V. Tues–Sat 12:30–3pm and 7:30–10:30pm, Sun 12:30–3pm. Closed 1 week at Easter and 3 weeks in Aug. Metro: Piazza di Spagna. ROMAN.

Il Ristorante 34 is a very good and increasingly popular restaurant close to the most famous shopping district of Rome. Its long and narrow interior is sheathed in scarlet wallpaper, ringed with modern paintings, and capped with a vaulted ceiling. In the rear, stop to admire a display of antipasti proudly exhibited near the entrance to the bustling kitchen. The cookery is highly reliable and the chef might whip caviar and salmon into the noodles to enliven the dish, or else cook chunks of lobster into the risotto. He also believes in rib-sticking fare such as pasta lentil soup, or meatballs in a sauce with "fat" mushrooms. One of his most interesting pastas comes with a pumpkin-flavored cream sauce, and his spaghetti with clams is among the best in Rome.

NEAR VIA VENETO
VERY EXPENSIVE

Sans Souci. Via Sicilia 20. ☎ **06/482-1814.** Reservations required. Main courses 36,000–58,000 lire ($23.05–$37.10). AE, DC, MC, V. Tues–Sun 8pm–1am. Closed Aug 10–30. Metro: Piazza Barberini. Bus: 52, 53, 95, 490, or 495. FRENCH.

Sans Souci may no longer be the best restaurant in Rome—at least Michelin no longer awards it stars—but for glitz and glamour, and nostalgia for *la dolce vita,* nothing quite matches the overly decorated Sans Souci. The cuisine is better at Relais Le Jardin or La Terrazza, but Sans Souci does serve good food to those on the see-and-be-seen circuit, and might be your best bet for spotting a movie star, albeit a faded one. You enter a small dimly lit lounge to the right at the bottom of the steps. Here, amid tapestries and glittering mirrors, the maître d' will present you with the menu, which you can peruse while sipping a drink. The menu is ever changing, as "new creations" are devised. You might begin with a terrine of goose liver with truffles, a special creation of the chef. The fish soup is, according to one Rome restaurant critic, "a legend to experience." The soufflés are also popular, including artichoke, asparagus, and spinach, and risottos are prepared for two. One of the most popular pasta dishes is large fettuccine with wild mushrooms and black truffles. Dessert soufflés, also prepared for two, are also a specialty, including chocolate and Grand Marnier.

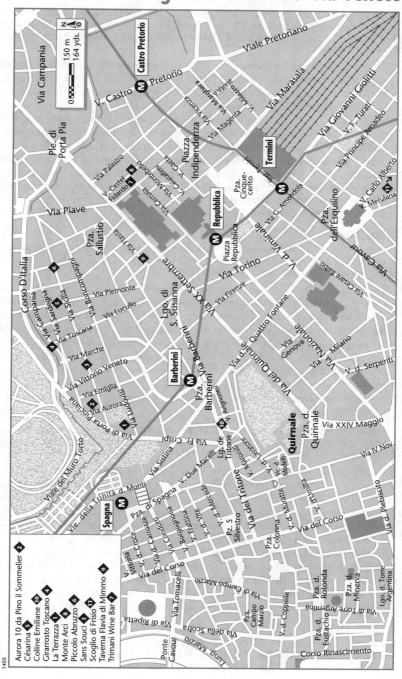

Aurora 10 da Pino il Sommelier 2
Césarina 5
Colline Emiliane 10
Girarrosto Toscano 4
La Terrazza 1
Monte Arci 8
Piccolo Abruzzo 6
Sans Souci 3
Scoglio di Frisio 11
Taverna Flavia di Mimmo 9
Trimani Wine Bar 7

⭘ **La Terrazza.** In the Hotel Eden, via Ludovisi 49. ☎ **06/478121.** Reservations recommended. Main courses 42,000–68,000 lire ($26.90–$43.50); fixed-price menu 120,000 lire ($76.80). AE, DC, MC, V. Daily 12:30–2:30pm and 7:30–10:30pm. Metro: Piazza Barberini. ITALIAN/INTERNATIONAL

This restaurant serves the finest cuisine in the city (a title shared with Relais Le Jardin) along with a sweeping view over St. Peter's from the fifth floor of the Eden Hotel. Service manages to be formal and flawless, yet not at all intimidating at the same time. Chef Enrico Derfligher, the commercial and culinary catalyst behind about a dozen top-notch Italian restaurants throughout Europe, prepares a menu that varies with the season and is among the most urbane and polished in Rome. Examples include a warm salad of grilled vegetables lightly toasted with greens in balsamic vinegar, red tortelli (whose pink coloring comes from a tomato mousse) stuffed with mascarpone cheese and drizzled with lemon, grilled tagliata of beef with eggplant and tomatoes, and a superb "symphony" of seafood. Artfully arranged onto a platter, and prepared only for two or more diners, it includes perfectly seasoned Mediterranean sea bass, turbot, gilthead, and prawns.

MODERATE

Aurora 10 da Pino il Sommelier. Via Aurora 10. ☎ **06/474-2779.** Reservations recommended. Main courses 20,000–30,000 lire ($12.80–$19.20). AE, DC, MC, V. Tues–Sun noon–3pm and 7–11:15pm. Metro: Piazza Barberini. ITALIAN.

Established in 1981 a few paces from the top of via Veneto, this restaurant lies in the vaulted interior of what was originally a Maronite convent. The high-energy direction of its Sicilian manager, Pino Salvatore, and his staff have attracted some of the capital's most influential diplomats and a sprinkling of film stars. The place is noted for its awesome array of more than 250 wines, representing every province of Italy. Unusual for Rome, the restaurant features a large soup menu, along with a tempting array of fresh antipasti. Dishes include linguine with lobster, a Sicilian-style fish fry, swordfish in herb sauce, filet of beef with porcini mushrooms, risotto with asparagus, and beef stew flambé. The cookery is savory and first-rate, using top-quality ingredients.

Girarrosto Toscano. Via Campania 29. ☎ **06/482-3835.** Reservations required. Main courses 20,000–50,000 lire ($12.80–$32). AE, DC, MC, V. Thurs–Tues 12:30–3pm and 7:30–11:30pm. Bus: 90B, 95, 490, or 495. TUSCAN.

Girarrosto Toscano, facing the walls of the Borghese Gardens, draws a coterie of guests from via Veneto haunts, which means that you may have to wait. Under the vaulted ceilings of a cellar it serves some of the finest Tuscan specialties in Rome. Begin by enjoying an enormous selection of antipasti, from succulent little meatballs and melon with prosciutto, to fritatte (omelets) and an especially delicious Tuscan salami. You're then given a choice of pasta, such as fettuccine in a cream sauce. Although expensive, bistecca alla fiorentina—grilled and seasoned with oil, salt, and pepper—is the best item to order. The oysters and fresh fish from the Adriatic are served every day. Order with care if you're on a budget—both meat and fish are all priced according to weight, and can run considerably higher than the prices quoted above. For dessert, we'd recommend the assortment of ice cream called gelato misto.

INEXPENSIVE

Césarina. Via Piemonte 109. ☎ **06/488-0828.** Reservations recommended. Main courses 16,000–25,000 lire ($10.25–$16). AE, DC, MC, V. Mon–Sat 12:30–3pm and 7:30–11pm. Bus: 52, 53, 56, 58, or 95. EMILIANA-ROMAGNOLA/ROMAN.

Specializing in the cuisines of Rome and the region around Bologna, this former hole-in-the-wall has grown since matriarch Césarina Masi established it around 1960 (many Rome veterans fondly remember Ms. Masi's strict supervision of her kitchens, and how she would lecture regulars who didn't finish their tagliatelle). Although Césarina died in the mid-1980s, the restaurant perpetuates her culinary traditions today in three dining rooms. The tactful and polite staff roll an excellent bollito misto (an array of well-seasoned boiled meats) from table to table on a trolley, and often follow with a misto Césarina—three kinds of homemade pasta, each served with a different sauce. Equally appealing is the saltimbocca and the cotoletta alla bolognese, a veal cutlet baked with ham and cheese. A dessert specialty is semifreddo Césarina served with hot chocolate. The food is excellent, and the selection of fresh antipasti is very appealing.

Colline Emiliane. Via Avignonesi 22 (right off piazza Barberini). ☎ **06/481-7538.** Reservations required. Main courses 16,000–25,000 lire ($10.25–$16). MC, V. Sat–Thurs 12:45–2:45pm and 7:45–10:45pm. Closed Aug. Metro: Piazza Barberini. EMILIANA-ROMAGNOLA.

Colline Emiliane, established in 1936, is a small restaurant serving the *classica cucina bolognese*. It's a family-run place—the owner is the cook, and his wife makes the pasta (which, incidentally, is about the best you'll encounter in Rome). The house specialty is an inspired tortellini alla panna (cream sauce) with truffles, but the less expensive pastas are all excellent as well—maccheroncini al funghetto and tagliatelle alla bolognese. As an opener for your meal, we suggest culatello di Zibello, a delicacy from a small town near Parma known for having the finest prosciutto in the world. Main courses include braciola di maiale, boneless rolled pork cutlets that have been stuffed with ham and cheese, breaded, and sautéed. Ciambonnetto (roast veal Emilian style with roast potatoes) is another specialty. To finish your meal, we'd recommend budino al cioccolato, a chocolate pudding that's baked like flan.

Piccolo Abruzzo. Via Sicilia 237. ☎ **06/482-0176.** Reservations recommended. Main courses 15,000–20,000 lire ($9.60–$12.80). AE, DC, MC, V. Mon–Sat 12:30–3pm and 7pm–midnight. Closed 1 week in August. Bus: 95, 490, or 495. ABRUZZESE.

An imaginative array of antipasti and copious portions make Piccolo Abruzzo one of the most popular restaurants in its neighborhood. Many habitués plan a meal either early or late to avoid the jam, as the place is small and popular. Full meals are priced according to what you take from the antipasti buffet groaning with at least 20 offerings. You can follow with a pasta course, which might be samples of three different versions, followed by a meat course, then cheese and dessert. A meat specialty is agnello d'Abruzzi, roast lamb full of flavor and herbally scented. All this lively scene takes place in a brick- and stucco-sheathed room perfumed with hanging cloves of garlic, salt-cured hams, and beribboned bunches of Mediterranean herbs.

NEAR THE TERMINI
MODERATE

Ⓢ **Scoglio di Frisio.** Via Merulana 256. ☎ **06/487-2765.** Reservations recommended. Main courses 16,000–30,000 lire ($10.25–$19.20); fixed-price menu 24,000 lire ($15.35) at lunch, 62,000–90,000 lire ($39.70–$57.60) at dinner. AE, DC, MC, V. Mon–Fri 12:30–3pm and 7:30–11pm, Sat–Sun 7:30–11pm. Bus: 714 from the Termini. NEAPOLITAN.

Scoglio di Frisio is the choice *suprême* to introduce yourself to the Neapolitan kitchen. While here, you should get reacquainted with a genuine, plate-sized Neopolitan pizza (crunchy, oozy, and excellent) with clams and mussels. After a medley of stuffed vegetables and antipasti, you may then settle for chicken cacciatore or veal scaloppine. Scoglio di Frisio also makes for an inexpensive night on the town as all the fun, cornball "O Sole Mio" and Neapolitan *bel canto* elements spring forth from a guitar, mandolin, and strolling tenor (who is like Mario Lanza reincarnate). The nautical decor—in honor of the top-notch fish dishes—is complete with a high-ceilinged grotto with craggy walls, fisher's nets, crustaceans, and a miniature three-masted schooner hanging overhead.

Taverna Flavia di Mimmo. Via Flavia 9. ☎ **06/474-5214.** Reservations recommended. Main courses 16,000–30,000 lire ($10.25–$19.20). AE, DC, MC, V. Mon–Fri 12:30–3pm and 7:30–11pm, Sat 7:30–11pm. Metro: Piazza della Repubblica. ROMAN/INTERNATIONAL.

The Taverna Flavia di Mimmo, just a block from via XX Settembre, is a robustly Roman restaurant where during the heyday of *la dolce vita* movie people used to meet over tasty dishes. The restaurant still serves the same food that used to delight Frank Sinatra and the "Hollywood on the Tiber" crowd. As a chic rendezvous, however, its day is long past. Specialties include a risotto with scampi and spaghetti al whisky. A different regional dish is featured daily, which might be Roman-style tripe prepared in such a savory manner that it tastes far better than it sounds. Exceptional dishes include osso buco with peas, a seafood salad, and fondue with truffles.

INEXPENSIVE

Monte Arci. Via Castelfidardo 33. ☎ **06/494-1220.** Reservations recommended. Main courses 13,000–20,000 lire ($8.30–$12.80). AE, V. Mon–Fri 12:30–3pm and 7–11:30pm, Sat 7–11:30pm. Bus: 36, 75, 310, or 492. ROMAN/SARDINIAN.

Monte Arci, on a cobblestone street near piazza Indipendenza not far from the Termini, is set behind a sienna-colored facade. The restaurant features low-cost Roman and Sardinian specialties (you'll spend even less for pizza). Typical dishes include nialoreddus (a regional form of gnocchetti); pasta with clams or lobster or those delectable porcini mushrooms; green and white spaghetti with bacon, spinach, cream, and cheese; saltimbocca; and lamb sausage flavored with herbs and pecorino cheese. Much of this food is just like mamma would make, with all the strengths and weaknesses that that implies.

Trimani Wine Bar. Via Cernaia 37b. ☎ **06/446-9630.** Fixed-price lunch 26,000 lire ($16.65); salads and platters of light food 12,000–19,000 lire ($7.70–$12.15); glass of wine (depending on the vintage) 4,000–12,000 lire ($2.55–$7.70). AE, DC, MC, V. Mon–Sat 11:30am–3pm and 5:30pm–midnight. Closed several weeks in Aug. Metro: Piazza della Repubblica or Castro Pretorio. CONTINENTAL.

Conceived as a tasting center for French and Italian wines, spumantis, and liqueurs, this elegant wine bar lies at the edge of a historic district. Amid a postmodern, award-winning interior decor inspired by classical Rome, you'll find comfortable seating, occasional live music, and a staff devoted to pressurizing half-full bottles of wine between pours. Menu items are inspired by the stylish bistros of Paris, and might include vegetarian pastas (in summertime only), salades niçoises, herb-laden bean soups (fagiole), slices of quiche, Hungarian goulash, and platters of French and Italian cheeses and pâtés. Trimani, a family of wine brokers whose company was established in 1821, maintains a well-stocked shop about 40 yards from its wine bar, at via Goito 20 (☎ 06/446-9661), where an astonishing array of the oenological bounty of Italy is for sale.

ON THE APPIAN WAY

Hostaria l'Archeologia. Via Appia Antica 139. ☎ **06/788-0494.** Reservations recommended, especially on weekends. Main courses 12,000–24,000 lire ($7.70–$15.35); fixed-price menu 25,000 lire ($16). AE, DC, MC, V. Fri–Wed 12:30–3:30pm and 8–10:30pm. Bus: 660 from San Giovanni. ROMAN/ITALIAN.

The Hostaria l'Archeologia is only a short walk from the catacombs of St. Sebastian. The family-run restaurant is like an 18th-century village tavern with lots of atmosphere, strings of garlic and corn, oddments of copper hanging from the ceiling, earth-brown beams, and sienna-washed walls. In summer guests dine in the garden out back under the wisteria. The Roman victuals are first-rate; you can glimpse the kitchen from behind a partition in the exterior garden parking lot. Many Roman families visit on the weekend, sometimes as many as 30 diners in a group. Of special interest is the wine cellar, excavated in an ancient Roman tomb, with bottles dating back to 1800. You go through an iron gate, down some stairs, and into the underground cavern. Along the way, you can still see the holes once occupied by funeral urns.

IN TESTACCIO

Checchino dal 1887. Via di Monte Testaccio 30. ☎ **06/574-3816.** Reservations recommended. Main courses 13,000–28,000 lire ($8.30–$17.90). AE, DC, MC, V. Tues–Sat 12:30–3pm and 8–11pm, Sun 12:30–3pm. Closed Aug, 1 week around Christmas, and Sun June–Sept. Bus: 27. ROMAN.

During the 1800s a local wine shop flourished by selling drinks to the butchers working in the neighborhood's many slaughterhouses. In 1887 the ancestors of the present owners obtained a license to sell food, thus giving birth to the restaurant you'll find here today. Slaughterhouse workers in those days were paid part of their meager salaries with the *quinto quarto* (fifth quarter) of each day's slaughter (the tail, the feet, the intestines, and the offal), which otherwise had no commercial value. Following many centuries of Roman traditions, Ferminia, the wine shop's cook, somehow transformed these products into the tripe and oxtail dishes that form an integral part of the menu.

Many Italian diners come here to relish these dishes, which might not be to every foreign visitor's taste. They include rigatone con pajata (pasta with small intestines), coda alla vaccinara (oxtail stew), fagiole e cotiche (beans with intestinal fat), and other examples of *la cocina povera* (food of the poor). Less adventurous, and possibly more appealing, are the restaurant's array of well-prepared salads, soups, pastas, steaks, cutlets, grills, and ice creams, which the kitchens produce in abundance. The English-speaking staff is helpful and kind, tactfully proposing well-flavored alternatives to a cuisine which, at least in Rome, is a well-established legend.

IN TRASTEVERE
EXPENSIVE

Alberto Ciarla. Piazza San Cosimato 40. ☎ **06/581-8668.** Reservations required, especially on weekends. Main courses 24,000–45,000 lire ($15.35–$28.80); fixed-price menus 80,000–90,000 lire ($51.20–$57.60). AE, DC, MC, V. Mon–Sat 8:30pm–12:30am. Closed 1 week in Jan and 1 week in Aug. Bus: 44, 75, 170, 280, or 718. SEAFOOD.

Alberto Ciarla is the best and most expensive restaurant in Trastevere. Some critics still consider it one of the finest restaurants in all of Rome, although it's not as chic as it was when discovered by fickle fashion in the late 1980s. In an 1890 building set into an obscure corner of an enormous square, it serves some of the most elegant fish dishes in the city. You'll be greeted at the door with a cordial reception and a lavish display of seafood on ice. A dramatically modern decor plays shades of brilliant light against patches of shadow for a Renaissance chiaroscuro effect. Specialties include a handful of ancient recipes subtly improved by Signor Ciarla (an example is the soup of pasta and beans with seafood). Original dishes include a delectable salmon Marcel Trompier with lobster sauce, a well-flavored sushi, spaghetti with clams, and a full array of shellfish. The filet of sea bass is prepared in at least three different ways, including an award-winning version with almonds.

Dining in Trastevere

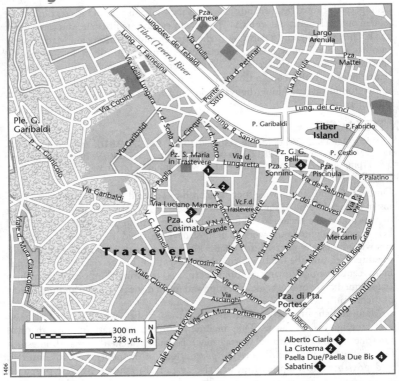

Alberto Ciarla ❸
La Cisterna ❷
Paella Due/Paella Due Bis ❹
Sabatini ❶

MODERATE

La Cisterna. Via della Cisterna 13. ☎ **06/581-2543.** Reservations recommended. Main courses 16,000–30,000 lire ($10.25–$19.20). AE, DC, MC, V. Mon–Sat 7pm–midnight. Bus: 44, 75, 170, 280, or 710. ROMAN.

La Cisterna, named for an ancient well from Imperial times discovered in the cellar, lies deep in the heart of Trastevere. For more than half a century it has been run by the Simmi family, who are genuinely interested in serving only the best as well as providing a good time for all guests. In good weather you can dine outside at sidewalk tables. If it's rainy or cold you'll be in rooms decorated with murals, including the *Rape of the Sabine Women.* Food critics have never awarded any stars to this place—and probably never will—but if you like traditional cookery based on the best of regional produce, then come here. In summer you can inspect the antipasti right out on the street before going in. Specialties of the house include Roman-style suckling lamb (abbacchio), rigatoni a l'amatriciana, pappallini romana (wide noodles flavored with prosciutto, cheese, and eggs), shrimp, and fresh fish—especially sea bass baked with herbs.

Sabatini. Piazza Santa Maria in Trastevere 13. ☎ **06/581-2026.** Reservations recommended. Main courses 20,000–40,000 lire ($12.80–$25.60). AE, DC, MC, V. Daily noon–3pm and 8pm–midnight. Closed 2 weeks in Aug (dates vary). Bus: 44, 75, or 170. ROMAN/SEAFOOD.

This is one of the most popular dining spots in Rome, although *la dolce vita* is over and the glitz and glitter crowd have moved on to more fashionable oases. At night, piazza Santa Maria—one of the settings used in Fellini's *Roma*—is the center of the liveliest action in Trastevere. The place is very tied to the hustle-bustle of the Trastevere landscape. In summer, tables are placed out on this charming piazza and you can look across at the floodlit golden frescoes of the church. If you can't get a table outside, you may be assigned to a room under beamed ceilings, with stenciled walls, lots of paneling, and framed oil paintings. So popular is this place that you may have to wait for a table even if you have a reservation. The spaghetti with seafood is excellent, and fresh fish and shellfish, especially grilled scampi, may tempt you as well (although these aren't as good as at Alberto Ciarla). For a savory treat, try pollo con pepperoni, chicken cooked with red and green peppers. The meal price will rise exorbitantly if you order grilled fish or the Florentine steaks. For wine, try a white Frascati or an Antinori chianti in a hand-painted pitcher.

INEXPENSIVE

Paella Due/Paella Due Bis. Via della Lungarette 173. ☎ **06/588-2876.** Pizzas 7,000–11,000 lire ($4.50–$7.05); main courses 15,000–30,000 lire ($9.60–$19.20); fixed-price meals (paella) 35,000–70,000 lire ($22.40–$44.80) for two diners. No credit cards. Tues–Sun noon–midnight. Bus: 23. SPANISH.

This is one of the best relatively inexpensive restaurants in Trastevere, with references to Spain that derive from a decade the owner/chef spent cooking in a restaurant there. No one will mind if you stop in during the midafternoon for just a cup of coffee, or during lunch or dinner for the array of pizzas and pastas. The antipasti buffet contains focaccio, grilled vegetables, sliced mozzarella, and many of the fruits of the Italian harvest—a mini-meal in itself beginning at 10,000 lire ($6.40). You'll find a trio of dining rooms, paintings of the nearby Tiber, and a sense of Old Trastevere. The cost of a heaping paella platter for two varies widely according to what you want it to contain. Least expensive is the vegetarian version; the most expensive is the authentic paella valenciana with seafood and meat. Most clients are served in Paella Due, although if it's full, the overflow heads next door to additional seating in Paella Due Bis.

NEAR VATICAN CITY

EXPENSIVE

✪ **Les Etoiles.** In the Hotel Atlante Star, via Vitelleschi 34. ☎ **06/689-3434.** Reservations required. Main courses 85,000–125,000 lire ($54.40–$80). AE, DC, MC, V. Daily 12:30–2:30pm and 7:30–11pm. Metro: Ottaviano. Bus: 23, 49, 64, 81, or 492. MEDITERRANEAN.

Les Etoiles, "The Stars," deserves all the stars it receives. The restaurant in this previously recommended hotel has been called "the most beautiful rooftop in Italy." At this garden in the sky you'll have an open window over the rooftops of Rome—a 360° view of landmarks, especially the floodlit dome of St. Peter's. A flower terrace contains a trio of little towers, named Michelangelo, Campidoglio, and Ottavo Colle. In summer everyone wants a table outside, but in winter almost the same view is available from tables near the picture windows. The color and fragrance of a refined Mediterranean cuisine, with perfectly balanced flavors, includes quail cooked either with radicchio or in a casserole with mushrooms and herbs, artichokes stuffed with ricotta and pecorino cheese, Venetian-style risotto with squid ink, and roast suckling lamb with mint. The creative chef is rightly proud of his many regional dishes, and the service is deluxe, with a wine list some Roman food critics have labeled "exciting."

MODERATE

Il Canto del Riso. Moored in the Tiber, in front of lungotevere dei Mellini 7. ☎ **06/324-0128.** Reservations required. Main courses 15,000–28,000 lire ($9.60–$17.90). No credit cards. Daily noon–4pm and 8pm–2am. Closed Sun night and Mon in winter. Metro: Piazza Cavour. Bus: 49, 70, 87, or 492. ITALIAN.

This barge and passenger ship is permanently moored beside one of the quays of the Tiber, a short walk north of ponte (bridge) Cavour. The barge was originally designed as a floating swimming pool in the 1960s, but has functioned since 1990 as a floating restaurant. Below decks you'll find a cozy dining room outfitted with nautical accessories. Many diners prefer to eat here during warm weather, when management expands its premises by setting up tables on the riverside quay. Then, strings of colored lights and potted plants add a festive note, despite the nearby traffic that races along. The menu is based on the classics, but also manages to include many regional favorites. The food is mild, flavorful, and faultlessly prepared. Menu items include veal, lamb, beef, and lots of fish and seafood, especially shrimp, mussels, and clams in tomato-garlic sauce, served as dressings for pastas or as main courses. Also featured are many kinds of vegetarian risotto.

Ristorante Il Matriciano. Via dei Gracchi 55. ☎ **06/321-2327.** Reservations required, especially for dinner. Main courses 14,000–24,000 lire ($8.95–$15.35). AE, DC, MC, V. Daily 12:30–3pm and 8–11:30pm. Closed Aug 5–25, Wed Nov–Apr, and Sat May–Oct. Metro: Lepanto or Ottaviano. ROMAN.

Il Matriciano is a family restaurant with a devoted following. Its location near St. Peter's makes it all the more distinguished. The food is good, but it's mostly country fare—nothing fancy. The decor, likewise, is kept to a minimum. In summer try to get one of the sidewalk tables behind a green hedge and under a shady canopy. For openers you might enjoy a zuppa di verdura or ravioli di ricotta. From many dishes, we recommend scaloppa alla valdostana, abbacchio (suckling lamb) al forno, and trippa (tripe) alla romana. The most obvious specialty of the house, bucatini matriciana, is derived from what some experts say is the favorite sauce in the Roman repertoire: Amatriciana. Here, it's prepared with bucatini pasta, and richly flavored with bacon, tomatoes, and basil. Dining at the homelike convivial tables, you're likely to see an array of Romans, from prelates and cardinals escaping from the confines of the nearby Vatican for a while, to stars of the Italian cinema.

Ristorante Pierdonati. Via della Conciliazione 39. ☎ **06/6880-3557.** Reservations not necessary. Main courses 12,000–28,000 lire ($7.70–$17.90); fixed-price menu 28,000 lire ($17.90). AE, MC, V. Fri–Wed noon–3:30pm and 7–10:30pm. Closed Aug. Bus: 23 or 64 from the Termini. ROMAN.

Ristorante Pierdonati has been serving wayfarers to the Vatican since 1868. In the same building as the previously recommended Hotel Columbus, this restaurant was the former home of Cardinal della Rovere. Today it's the headquarters of the Knights of the Holy Sepulchre of Jerusalem, and the best restaurant in the gastronomic wasteland of the Vatican area. Its severely classical facade is relieved inside by a gargoyle fountain spewing water into a basin. You'll dine beneath a vaulted ceiling. Try the calves' liver Venetian style, the stewed veal with tomato sauce, or ravioli bolognese. To get really Roman, order the tripe. The cuisine isn't refined or pretentious, but robust and heavy. It can get rather crowded here on days that see thousands upon thousands flocking to St. Peter's.

INEXPENSIVE

Ristorante Giardinaccio. Via Aurelia 53. ☎ **06/631367.** Reservations recommended, especially on weekends. Main courses 10,000–15,000 lire ($6.40–$9.60). AE, DC, MC, V. Wed–Mon 12:15–3:30pm and 7:15–11pm. Bus: 46, 62, or 98. ITALIAN/MOLISIAN.

This popular restaurant, operated by Nicolino Mancini, is only 200 yards from St. Peter's. Unusual for Rome, it offers Molisian specialties from southeastern Italy. It's rustically decorated in the country-tavern style with dark wood and exposed stone. Flaming grills provide succulent versions of perfectly done quail, goat, and other dishes, but perhaps the mutton goulash would be more adventurous. You can order many versions of pasta, including taconelle, a homemade pasta with lamb sauce. Vegetarians and others will like the large self-service selection of antipasti. Some snooty diners might dismiss this food as too regional—or "too peasant" if you're being catty—but it's a perfect introduction to the hearty cuisine of an area rarely visited by Americans.

IN PARIOLI
VERY EXPENSIVE

✪ **Relais Le Jardin.** In the Hotel Lord Byron, via G. de Notaris 5. ☎ **06/361-3041.** Reservations required. Main courses 45,000–53,000 lire ($28.80–$33.90). AE, DC, MC, V. Mon–Sat 1–3pm and 8–10:30pm. Closed Aug. Bus: 26 or 52. ITALIAN.

The Relais Le Jardin is one of the best places to go in Rome for both traditional and creative cuisine, and a chichi crowd with demanding palates patronize it nightly. There are places in Rome with greater views, but not with such an elegant setting. Inside one of the most elite small hotels of the capital (see "Accommodations," earlier in this chapter), the aggressively lighthearted decor combines white lattice with bold colors and flowers. Many of the cooks and service personnel were trained at embassies or diplomatic residences abroad. A Relais Gourmands, the establishment serves a seasonally changing array of dishes. The pasta and soups are among the finest in town, as exemplified by the tonnarelli pasta with asparagus and smoked ham served with concassé tomatoes. The chef can take a dish once served only to the plebes in Roman days, bean soup with clams, and make it elegantly refined. For your main course you face such selections as roast loin of lamb with artichoke romana or grilled beef sirloin with hot chicory and sautéed potatoes. The single best risotto served in Rome in our view is the chef's risotto with pheasant sauce, asparagus, and black truffle flakes with a hint of fresh thyme.

MODERATE

Al Ceppo. Via Panama 2. ☎ **06/841-9696.** Reservations recommended. Main courses 18,000–25,000 lire ($11.50–$16). AE, DC, MC, V. Tues–Sun 12:30–3pm and 8–11pm. Closed the last 3 weeks of Aug. Bus: 4, 52, or 53. ROMAN.

Because of its somewhat hidden location (although it's only 2 blocks from the Villa Borghese, near piazza Ungheria), the clientele is likely to be Roman rather than foreign. This is a longtime and enduring favorite that fashion has passed by, although the cuisine is as good as it ever was. "The Log" (its name in English) features an open wood-stoked fireplace on which the chef does lamb chops, liver, and bacon to charcoal perfection. The beefsteak, which hails from Tuscany, is also succulent. Other dishes on the menu include linguine monteconero (made with clams and fresh tomatoes); a savory spaghetti with peppers, fresh basil, and pecorino cheese; a filet of swordfish filled with grapefruit, parmesan cheese, pine nuts, and dry grapes; and a fish carpaccio (raw sea bass) with a green salad, onions, and green pepper. Save room for dessert, especially the apple cobbler, the pear and almond tart, or the chocolate meringue hazelnut cake.

5 | What to See & Do in Rome

Rome is studded with ancient monuments that silently evoke its history as one of the greatest centers of Western civilization. In the millennium of the Eternal City's influence, all roads led to Rome with good reason. It was one of the first cosmopolitan cities in the world, importing slaves, gladiators, great art—even citizens—from the far corners of the Empire. Along with all its carnage and misman-agement, it left a legacy of law and an uncanny lesson in how to con-quer enemies by absorbing their cultures.

But ancient Rome is only part of the spectacle. The Vatican has had a major effect in making the city a center of world tourism. Al-though Vatican architects stripped down much of the glory of the past, they created great Renaissance treasures, occasionally incorpo-rating the old—as Michelangelo did in turning the Baths of Diocletian into a church.

In the years that followed, Bernini adorned the city with the won-ders of the baroque, especially the fountains. The modern sightseer even owes a debt (as reluctant as one may be to acknowledge it) to Mussolini, who did much to dig out the past, particularly at the Imperial Forum. Today, besides being the Italian capital, Rome, in a larger sense, belongs to the world.

SUGGESTED ITINERARIES

These itineraries obviously are designed for the first-time visitor; the more seasoned traveler will want to seek out other treasures. How-ever, such sights as the Vatican Museum can be visited virtually every day of the year, and something new and artistically different will be waiting.

If You Have 1 Day

Far too brief—after all, Rome wasn't built in a day and you aren't likely to see it in a day either, but make the most of your limited time. You'll basically have to decide on the legacy of imperial Rome—mainly the Roman Forum, the Imperial Forum, and the Colosseum—or St. Peter's and the Vatican. Walk along the Spanish Steps at sunset. At night go to piazza del Campidoglio for a fantastic view of the Forum below. Have a nightcap on via Veneto which, although past its prime, is still a lure for the first-time visitor. Toss a coin in the Trevi Fountain and promise a return visit to Rome.

If You Have 2 Days

If you elected to see the Roman Forum and the Colosseum, then spend the second day exploring St. Peter's and the Vatican Museum (or vice versa). Have dinner that night in a restaurant in Trastevere.

If You Have 3 Days

Spend your first 2 days as above. Go in the morning to the Pantheon in the heart of Old Rome; then try to explore two museums after lunch: Castel Sant'Angelo and the Etruscan Museum. Have dinner at a restaurant on piazza Navona.

If You Have 5 Days

Spend your first 3 days as above. On Day 4 head for the environs, notably Tivoli, where you can see the Villa d'Este and Hadrian's Villa. On Day 5 explore the ruins of Ostia Antica, return to Rome for lunch, and visit the Capitoline Museum and Basilica di San Giovanni in Laterano in the afternoon.

1 The Vatican & St. Peter's

On the left side of piazza San Pietro, near the Arco delle Campane, is the **Vatican Tourist Office** (☎ **06/6988-4466**), open Monday to Saturday from 8:30am to 7pm. Here you can buy a map of the Vatican and have your questions answered about St. Peter's or the Vatican museums.

✪ **St. Peter's Basilica (Basilica di San Pietro).** Piazza San Pietro. ☎ **06/6988-4466.** Admission: Basilica (including the sacristy, treasury, and grottoes), free; guided tour of the excavations around St. Peter's tomb, 10,000 lire ($6.40); dome, 5,000 lire ($3.20) adults, 1,000 lire (65¢) students, or 6,000 lire ($3.85) to take the elevator. Basilica (including the sacristy and treasury), Apr–Aug, daily 7am–7pm; Sept–Mar, daily 7am–6pm. Grottoes, Apr–Sept, daily 7am–6pm; Oct–Mar, daily 7am–5pm. Dome, Mar–Sept, daily 8am–6pm; Oct–Feb, daily 8am–4:30pm. Bus: 23, 30, 32, 49, 51, or 64.

As you stand in Bernini's **St. Peter's Square** (piazza San Pietro), you'll be in the arms of an ellipse dominated by St. Peter's Basilica. Like a loving parent, the Doric-pillared colonnade reaches out to embrace the faithful. Holding 300,000 is no problem for this square.

In the center of the square is an Egyptian obelisk, brought from the ancient city of Heliopolis on the Nile Delta, and used to adorn the nearby Nero's Circus. Flanking the obelisk are two 17th-century fountains—the one on the right (facing the basilica) by Carlo Maderno, who designed the facade of St. Peter's, was placed there by Bernini himself; the other is by Carlo Fontana.

Inside, the size of this famous church is awe-inspiring—although its dimensions (about two football fields) are not apparent at first. St. Peter's is said to have been built over the tomb of the crucified saint. Originally it was erected on the order of Constantine, but the present structure is essentially Renaissance and baroque; it showcases the talents of some of Italy's greatest artists: Bramante, Raphael, Michelangelo, and Maderno.

In a church of such grandeur—overwhelming in its detail of gilt, marble, and mosaic—don't expect subtlety. But the basilica is rich in art. In the nave on the right (the first chapel) is the best-known piece of sculpture, the *Pietà* that Michelangelo sculpted while still in his early 20s. In one of the worst acts of vandalism on record, a madman screaming "I am Jesus Christ" attacked the *Pietà* in the 1970s, battering

Rome Attractions

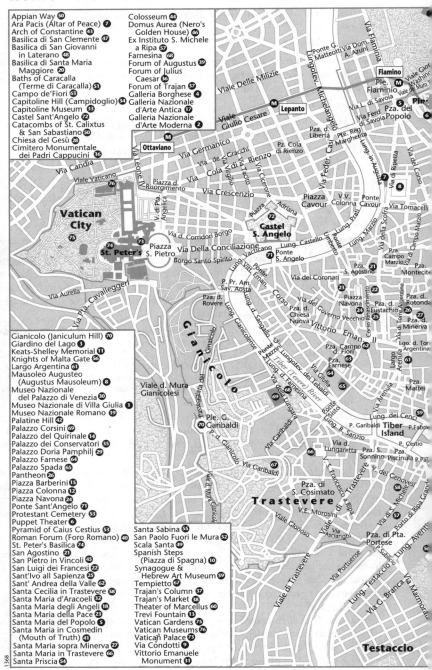

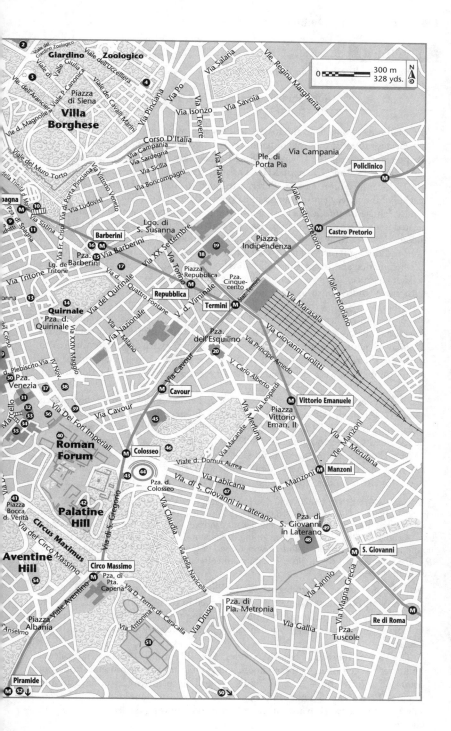

145

Impressions

As a whole St. Peter's is fit for nothing but a ballroom, and it is a little too gaudy even for that.
        —John Ruskin, letter to the Rev. Thomas Dale, December 1840

the Madonna's stone arm, the folded veil, her left eyelid, and nose. Now restored, the *Pietà* is protected by a wall of reinforced glass. Much farther on, in the right wing of the transept near the Chapel of St. Michael, rests Canova's neoclassic sculptural tribute to **Pope Clement XIII.** The truly devout are prone to kiss the feet of the 13th-century bronze of **St. Peter,** attributed to Arnolfo di Cambio (at the far reaches of the nave, against a corner pillar on the right). Under Michelangelo's dome is the celebrated *baldacchino* by Bernini, resting over the papal altar. The canopy was created in the 17th century—in part, so it's said, from bronze stripped from the Pantheon. However, analysis of the bronze seems to contradict that.

In addition, you can visit the **sacristy and treasury,** filled with jewel-studded chalices, reliquaries, and copes. One robe worn by Pius XII strikes a simple note in these halls of elegance. Later you can make a visit underground to the **Vatican grottoes,** with their tombs, both ancient and modern (Pope John XXIII gets the most adulation).

To go even farther down, to the area around St. Peter's tomb, you must apply several days beforehand to the **excavations** office. You can make your applications Monday to Saturday from 9am to noon and 2 to 5pm by passing under the arch to the left of the facade of St. Peter's. For 10,000 lire ($6.40), you'll take a guided tour of the tombs that were excavated in the 1940s, 23 feet beneath the floor of the church.

The grandest sight is yet to come: the climb to Michelangelo's **dome,** which towers about 375 feet high. Although you can walk up the steps, we recommend taking the elevator for as far as it'll carry you. You can also walk along the roof, for which you'll be rewarded with a panoramic view of Rome and the Vatican.

Note: To be admitted to St. Peter's, women must wear longer skirts or pants—anything that covers the knees. Men cannot wear shorts. Sleeveless tops are not allowed for either gender. You *will* be turned away.

✪ **Vatican Museums & the Sistine Chapel.** Vatican City, viale Vaticano. ☎ **06/6982.** Admission 15,000 lire ($9.60) adults, 10,000 lire ($6.40) children, free for everyone the last Sun of each month (be ready for a crowd). June 15–Aug and Nov–Mar, Mon–Sat 8:45am–1pm; Apr–June 14 and Sept–Oct, Mon–Fri 8:45am–4pm, Sat 8:45am–1pm; also open the last Sun of each month. Last admission 1 hour before closing. Closed religious holidays. Metro: Ottaviano. Bus: 19, 23, 32, 34, 49, 51, or 64. *Note:* The museum entrance is a long walk around the Vatican walls from St. Peter's Square.

In 1929 the Lateran Treaty between Pope Pius XI and the Italian government created the world's smallest independent state, located in Rome. Though small, this state contains a gigantic repository of treasures from antiquity and the Renaissance housed in labyrinthine galleries. The Vatican's art collection reaches its apex in the Sistine Chapel.

The Vatican museums comprise a series of lavishly adorned palaces and galleries built over the centuries. You can choose your route through the museum from four color-coded itineraries—A, B, C, or D—according to the time you have at your disposal (from 1½ to 5 hours) and your interests. You determine your choice by consulting large-size panels placed at the entrance and following the letter/color of your choice.

Obviously, 1, 2, or even 20 trips will not be enough to see the wealth of the Vatican, much less digest it. With that in mind, we've previewed only a representative sampling of the masterpieces on display here.

Pinacoteca (Picture Gallery): After climbing the spiral stairway, keep to the right to the Pinacoteca, which houses paintings and tapestries from the 11th to the 19th century. For the break with the Byzantine, see one of the Vatican's finest artworks—the *Stefaneschi Triptych* (six panels) by Giotto and his assistants. You'll also see the works of Fra Angelico, the 15th-century Dominican monk who distinguished himself as a miniaturist (his *Virgin with Child* is justly praised—look for the microscopic eyes of the Madonna).

In the Raphael salon you'll find three paintings by that giant of the Renaissance—the *Coronation of the Virgin,* the *Virgin of Foligno,* and the massive *Transfiguration* (completed by Raphael shortly before his death). There are also eight tapestries made by Flemish weavers from cartoons by Raphael. Seek out Leonardo da Vinci's masterful—but uncompleted—*St. Jerome with the Lion,* as well as Giovanni Bellini's *Pietà* and one of Titian's greatest works, the *Virgin of Frari.* Finally, feast your eyes on one of the masterpieces of the baroque period, Carvaggio's *Deposition from the Cross.*

Egyptian-Gregorian Museum: Review the grandeur of the Pharaohs by studying sarcophagi, mummies, statues of goddesses, vases, jewelry, sculptured pink-granite statues, and hieroglyphics.

Estruscan-Gregorian Museum: With sarcophagi, a chariot, bronzes, urns, jewelry, and terra-cotta vases, this gallery affords remarkable insights into an ancient civilization. One of the most acclaimed exhibits is the Regolini-Galassi tomb, unearthed at Cerveteri (see "Side Trips from Rome," later in this chapter) in the 19th century. It shares top honors with the *Mars of Todi,* a bronze sculpture that probably dates from the 5th century B.C.

Pio Clementino Museum: Here you'll find Greek and Roman sculptures, many of which are immediately recognizable masterpieces. The rippling muscles of the *Belvedere Torso,* a partially preserved Greek statue (1st century B.C.) that was much admired by the artists of the Renaissance, especially Michelangelo, reveal an intricate knowledge of the human body. In the rotunda is a large gilded bronze of Hercules that dates from the late 2nd century A.D. Other major works of sculpture are under porticoes that open onto the Belvedere courtyard. Dating from the 1st century B.C., one sculpture shows Laocoön and his two sons locked in an eternal struggle with the serpents. The incomparable *Apollo of Belvedere* (a late Roman reproduction of an authentic Greek work from the 4th century B.C.) has become the symbol of classic male beauty.

Chiaramonti Museum: You'll find a dazzling array of Roman sculpture and copies of Greek originals in these galleries. In the following section, called Braccio Nuovo, you can admire *The Nile,* a magnificent reproduction of a long-lost Hellenistic original, and one of the most remarkable pieces of sculpture from antiquity. The imposing statue of Augustus of Prima Porta presents him as a regal commander.

Vatican Library: The Library is richly decorated and frescoed, representing the work of a team of Mannerist painters commissioned by Sixtus V.

Stanze of Raphael: While still a young man, Raphael was given one of the greatest assignments of his short life: the decoration of a series of rooms in the apartments of Pope Julius II. The decoration was carried out by Raphael and his workshop between 1508 and 1524. In these works, Raphael achieves the Renaissance aim of blending classic beauty with realism. In the first chamber, the Stanza dell'Incendio, you'll see much of the work of Raphael's pupils but little of the master—except in the fresco across from the window. The figure of the partially draped Aeneas rescuing his father (to the left of the fresco) is sometimes attributed to Raphael, as is the surprised woman with a jug balanced on her head to the right.

Raphael reigns supreme in the next and most important salon, the Stanza della Segnatura, the first room decorated by the artist, where you'll find the majestic *School of Athens,* one of the artist's best-known works, which depicts such philosophers from the ages as Aristotle, Plato, and Socrates. Many of these figures are actually portraits of some of the greatest artists of the Renaissance, including Bramante (on the right as Euclid, bent over and balding as he draws on a chalkboard), Leonardo da Vinci (as Plato, the bearded man in the center pointing heavenward), even Raphael himself (looking out at you from the lower right corner). While he was painting this masterpiece, Raphael stopped work to walk down the hall for the unveiling of Michelangelo's newly finished Sistine Chapel ceiling. He was so impressed that he returned to his *School of Athens* and added to his design a sulking Michelangelo sitting on the steps. Another well-known masterpiece in this room is the *Disputà del Sacramento.*

The Stanza d'Eliodoro, also by the master, manages to flatter Raphael's papal patrons (Julius II and Leo X) without compromising his art (although one rather fanciful fresco depicts the pope driving Attila from Rome). Finally, there's the Sala di Constantino, which was completed by his students after Raphael's death. And the loggia, frescoed with more than 50 scenes from the Bible, was designed by Raphael, although the actual work was done by his loyal students.

Collection of Modern Religious Art: This museum, opened in 1973, represents the American artists' first invasion of the Vatican (the church had limited itself to European art created before the 18th century). But Pope Paul VI's hobby changed all that. Of the 55 rooms in the new museum, at least 12 are devoted to American artists. All the works chosen for the museum were judged the basis of their "spiritual and religious values." Among the American works is Leonard Baskin's 5-foot bronze sculpture of *Isaac.* Modern Italian artists such as de Chirico and Manzù are also displayed, and there's a special room for the paintings of the French artist Georges Rouault.

Borgia Apartments: These apartments, frescoed with biblical scenes by Pinturicchio of Umbria and his assistants, were designed for Pope Alexander VI (the infamous Borgia pope). The rooms, although badly lit, have great splendor and style. At the end of the Stanze of Raphael is the Chapel of Nicholas V, an intimate room frescoed by the Dominican monk Fra Angelico, probably the most saintly of all Italian painters.

Sistine Chapel: Michelangelo considered himself a sculptor, not a painter. While in his 30s, he was commanded by Julius II to stop work on the pope's own tomb and to devote his considerable talents to painting ceiling frescoes—an art form of which the Florentine master was contemptuous.

Michelangelo labored for 4 years (1508–12) over this epic project, which was so physically taxing that it permanently damaged his eyesight. All during the task he had to contend with the pope's incessant urgings to hurry up; at one point Julius threatened to topple Michelangelo from the scaffolding—or so Vasari relates.

It's ironic that a project undertaken against the artist's wishes would form his most enduring legend. Glorifying the human body as only a sculptor could, Michelangelo painted nine panels, taken from the pages Genesis, and surrounded them with prophets and sibyls. The most notable panels detail the expulsion of Adam and Eve from the Garden of Eden, and the creation of man—where God's outstretched hand imbues Adam with spirit.

The Florentine master was in his 60s when he began to paint the masterly *Last Judgment* on the altar wall. Again working against his wishes, Michelangelo presents a more jaundiced view of people and their fate; God sits in judgment, and sinners are plunged into the mouth of hell.

A master of ceremonies under Paul III, Monsignor Biagio da Cesena, protested to the pope against the "shameless nudes" painted by Michelangelo. Michelangelo showed he wasn't above petty revenge by painting the prude with the ears of a jack-ass in hell. When Biagio complained to the pope, Paul III maintained that he had no jurisdiction in hell. However, Daniele de Volterra was summoned to drape cloth-ing over some of the bare figures—thus earning for himself a dubious distinction as a haberdasher.

On the side walls are frescoes by other Renaissance masters such as Botticelli, Perugino, Luca Signorelli, Pinturicchio, Cosimo Roselli, and Ghirlandaio. We'd guess that if these paintings had been displayed by themselves in other chapels, they would be the object of special pilgrimages. But since they have to compete unfairly with the artistry of Michelangelo, they're virtually ignored by the average visitor.

The restoration of the Sistine Chapel in the 1990s touched off a worldwide de-bate among art historians. The Sistine Chapel was on the verge of collapse, both from its age and the weather, and restoration has taken years, as restorers used advanced computer analyses in their painstaking and controversial work. They reattached the fresco and repaired the ceiling. No longer dark and shadowy, Michelangelo's frescoes are now bright and pastel. Critics claim that in addition to removing centuries of dirt and grime—and several of the added "modesty" drapes—a vital second layer of paint was removed as well. Purists argue that many of the restored figures seem flat com-pared to the original which had more shadow and detail. Others in the media have hailed the project for having saved Michelangelo's masterpiece for future generations to appreciate.

History Museum: This museum, founded by Pope Paul VI, was established to tell the history of the Vatican. It exhibits arms, uniforms, and armor, some of which dates back to the early days of the Renaissance. The carriages on display are those used by the popes and cardinals in religious processions. Among the showcases of dress uniforms are the colorful outfits worn by the Pontifical Army Corps, which was dis-continued by Pope Paul VI.

Ethnological Museum: The Ethnological Museum is an assemblage of works of art and objects of cultural significance from all over the world. The principal route is a half-mile walk through 25 geographical sections, which display thousands of ob-jects covering 3,000 years of world history. The section devoted to China is especially interesting and worthwhile.

THE VATICAN GARDENS

Separating the Vatican from the secular world on the north and west are 58 acres of lush, carefully tended gardens filled with winding paths, brilliantly colored flowers, groves of massive oaks, and ancient fountains and pools. In the midst of this pasto-ral setting is a small summer house, the Villa Pia, built for Pope Pius IV in 1560 by Pirro Ligorio. You can visit the gardens only on a guided tour, which must be ar-ranged in advance and is limited to 33 people, so reserve as far in advance as possible during the busy summer period (*note:* you cannot get tickets by phone). Tours run Monday, Tuesday, and Thursday to Saturday (except holidays) from 10am to noon. Tickets are 16,000 lire ($10.25) per person, and are available at the Vatican Tour-ist Office.

PAPAL AUDIENCES

The pope gives public audiences each Wednesday morning except when he is absent from Rome. The audience begins at 11am, but sometimes at 10am in the hot summer. It takes place in the Paul VI Hall of Audiences, although sometimes the Basilica of St. Peter and St. Peter's Square are used to accommodate very large attendances. Anyone is welcome, but you must obtain a free ticket first from the office of the Prefecture of the Papal Household, accessible from St. Peter's Square by the Bronze Door, where the right-hand colonnade (as you face the basilica) begins. The office is open Monday to Saturday from 9am to 1pm. Tickets are readily available on Monday and Tuesday, but sometimes you won't be able to get into the office on Wednesday morning. Occasionally, if there's enough room, you can attend without a ticket.

You can also write ahead of time to the **Prefecture of the Papal Household,** 00120 Città del Vaticano (☎ **06/6982**), indicating your language, the dates of your visit, the number of people in your party, and, if possible, the hotel in Rome to which the cards should be sent the afternoon before the audience. American Catholics, armed with a letter of introduction from their parish priest, should apply to the **North American College,** via dell'Umiltà 30, 00187 Rome (☎ **06/678-9184**).

At noon on Sunday the pope speaks briefly from his study window and gives his blessing to the visitors and pilgrims gathered in St. Peter's Square. From about mid-July to mid-September the Angelus and blessing take place at the summer residence at Castelgandolfo, some 16 miles out of Rome and accessible by Metro and bus.

❓ Did You Know?

- Along with miles of headless statues and acres of paintings, Rome has 913 churches.
- Some Mongol khans and Turkish chieftains pushed westward to conquer the Roman Empire after it had ceased to exist.
- At the time of Julius Caesar and Augustus, Rome's population reached the million mark, the largest city in the Western world. Some historians claim that by the year A.D. 500 only 10,000 inhabitants were left.
- Pope Leo III sneaked up on Charlemagne and set an imperial crown on his head, a surprise coronation that launched a precedent of Holy Roman Emperors being crowned by popes in Rome.
- More than 90% of Romans live in private apartments, some rising 10 floors without elevators.
- The bronze of Marcus Aurelius in the Capitoline Museums, one of the world's greatest equestrian statues, escaped being melted down because the early Christians thought it was of Constantine.
- The Theater of Marcellus incorporated a gory realism in some of its stage plays: condemned prisoners were often butchered before audiences as part of the plot.
- Christians were not fed to the lions at the Colosseum, but in one day 5,000 animals were slaughtered (one about every 10 seconds). North Africa's native lions and elephants were rendered extinct.

2 Other Top Attractions

✪ **Roman Forum (Foro Romano).** Via dei Fori Imperiali. ☎ **06/699-0110.** Admission 12,000 lire ($7.70) adults, free for children 17 and under and for seniors 60 and over. Mon and Wed-Sat 9am to 1 hour before sunset, Tues and Sun 9am–2pm. Last admission 1 hour before closing. Closed Jan 16–Feb 15. Metro: Colosseo. Bus: 27, 81, 85, 87, or 186.

When it came to cremating Caesar, raping Sabine women, purchasing a harlot for the night, or sacrificing a naked victim, the Roman Forum was where the action was hot. Traversed by via Sacra (the Sacred Way), it was built in the marshy land between the Palatine and the Capitoline hills. It flourished as the center of Roman life in the days of the Republic, before it gradually lost prestige to the Imperial Forums.

Be warned: Expect only fragmented monuments, an arch or two, and lots of over-turned boulders. That any semblance of the Forum remains today is miraculous, as it was used for years, like the Colosseum, as a quarry. Eventually it reverted to what the Italians call *campo vaccino* (cow pasture). But excavations in the 19th century began to bring to light one of the world's most historic spots.

By day, the columns of now-vanished temples and the stones from which long-forgotten orators spoke are mere shells. Bits of grass and weed grow where a tri-umphant Caesar was once lionized. But at night, when the Forum is silent in the moonlight, it isn't difficult to imagine that vestal virgins still guard the sacred temple fire. (Historical footnote: The function of the maidens was to keep the temple's sa-cred fire burning—but their own flame under control. Failure to do the latter sent them to an early grave . . . alive!)

You can spend at least a morning wandering alone through the ruins of the Fo-rum. If you're content with just looking at the ruins, you can do so at your leisure. But if you want the stones to have some meaning, you'll have to purchase a detailed plan at the gate, as the temples are hard to locate otherwise. The first half of our walk-ing tour "Rome of the Caesars," later in this chapter, will take you around what remains of the ancient buildings and temples, as well as up the Palatine Hill.

A long walk up from the Roman Forum leads to the **Palatine Hill** (you can visit on the same ticket, and at same hours, as the Forum), one of the seven hills of Rome. The Palatine, tradition tells us, was the spot on which the first settlers built their huts, under the direction of Romulus. In later years the hill became a patrican residential district that attracted such citizens as Cicero. In time, however, the area was gobbled up by imperial palaces, and it drew a famous and infamous roster of tenants, such as Caligula (who was murdered here), Nero, Tiberius, and Domitian.

Only the ruins of its former grandeur remain today, and you really need to be an archeologist to make sense of them, as they're more difficult to understand than those in the Forum. But even if you're not interested in the past, it's worth the climb for the panoramic, sweeping view of both the Roman and Imperial forums, as well as the Capitoline Hill and the Colosseum. To explore, again, see our "Rome of the Caesars" walking tour, later in this chapter.

✪ **Colosseum (Colosseo).** Piazzale del Colosseo, via dei Fori Imperiali. ☎ **06/700-4261.** Admission: Street level, free; upper levels, 8,000 lire ($5.10). Mon–Tues and Thurs–Sat 9am to 1 hour before sunset, Wed and holidays 9am–2pm. Metro: Colosseo.

In spite of the fact that it's a mere shell, the Colosseum remains the greatest archi-tectural inheritance from ancient Rome. Vespasian ordered the construction of the elliptically shaped bowl, called the Amphitheatrum Flavium, in A.D. 72; it was inaugurated by Titus in A.D. 80 with a many-weeks-long bloody combat between gladiators and wild beasts. At its peak, under the cruel Domitian, the Colosseum could seat 50,000 spectators. The vestal virgins from the temple screamed for blood, as more and more exotic animals were shipped in from the far corners of the empire to satisfy jaded tastes (lion vs. bear, two humans vs. hippopotamus, etc.). Not-so-mock naval battles were staged (the canopied Colosseum could be flooded) in which the defeated combatants might have their lives spared if they put up a good fight. Many historians now believe that one of the most enduring legends linked to the Colosseum—that Christians were fed to the lions here—is unfounded.

Long after it ceased to be an arena to amuse sadistic Romans, the Colosseum was struck by an earthquake. Centuries later it was used as a quarry, its rich marble facing stripped away to build palaces and churches.

On one side, part of the original four tiers remains; the first three levels were constructed in Doric, Ionic, and Corinthian styles to lend it variety.

A highly photogenic memorial (next to the Colosseum), the **Arch of Constantine** was erected in honor of Constantine's defeat of the pagan Maxentius (A.D. 306). It's a landmark in every way. Physically, it's beautiful, perhaps marred by the aggravating traffic that zooms around it at all hours, but so intricately carved and well preserved that you almost forget the racket of the cars and buses. Many of the reliefs have nothing whatsoever to do with Constantine or his works, but tell of the victories of earlier Antonine rulers—they were apparently lifted from other, long-forgotten memorials.

Historically, the arch marks a period of great change in the history of Rome and therefore the history of the world. Converted to Christianity by a vision on the battlefield, Constantine officially ended the centuries-long persecution of the Christians during which many devout followers of the new religion had been put to death, oftentimes horribly. While Constantine did not ban paganism (which survived officially until the closing of the temples more than half a century later), he espoused Christianity himself and began the inevitable development that culminated in the conquest of Rome by the Christian religion. The arch, a tribute to the emperor, was erected by the Senate in A.D. 315.

After visiting the Colosseum, it's also convenient to look at the site of the **Domus Aurea,** or the Golden House of Nero, on via Labicana on the Esquiline Hill; it faces the Colosseum and is adjacent to the Forum. The Domus Aurea was one of the most sumptuous palaces of all time, constructed by Nero after disastrous fire swept over Rome in A.D. 64. Not much remains of its former glory, but once the floors were made of mother-of-pearl and the furniture of gold. The area that is the Colosseum today was an ornamental lake, which reflected the grandeur and glitter of the Golden House. The hollow ruins—long stripped of their lavish decorations—lie near the entrance of the Oppius Park.

During the Renaissance, painters such as Raphael chopped holes in the long-buried ceilings of the Domus Aurea to gain admittance. Once there, they were inspired by the frescoes and the small "grotesques" of cornucopia and cherubs. The word *grotto* came from this palace, as it was believed to have been built underground. Remnants of these original, almost-2,000-year-old frescoes and fragments of mosaics remain. All interiors have been closed for years.

Capitoline Hill (Campidoglio). Piazza del Campidoglio. Bus: 46, 89, or 92.

Of the Seven Hills of Rome, the Campidoglio is the most sacred—its origins stretch way back into antiquity (an Etruscan temple to Jupiter once stood on this spot). The approach to the Capitoline Hill is dramatic—climbing the long, sloping steps designed by Michelangelo. At the top is a perfectly proportioned square, piazza del

> ⭐ **Frommer's Favorite Rome Experiences**
>
> **Fountain Hopping**   Rome abounds in Renaissance and baroque fountains—lavish, theatrical, spectacular—none more so than the Trevi Fountain. They're fed by an abundant freshwater supply. A tour of them will lock in your memory. See "The Fountains of Rome," below.
>
> **Seeing the Campidoglio at Night**   Climb steps designed by Michelangelo to the back of the square to see a sound-and-light summer spectacle. Suddenly you hear marching legions, blaring trumpets, rumbling drums—all the sounds needed to convince you that you're back in the days of ancient Rome, with soldiers, soothsayers, and vestal virgins.
>
> **Flea-Market Shopping**   Every Sunday morning (until 1pm) make your way to the flea market of Rome, stretching for 2 miles from Porta Portese to the Trastevere rail station. Barter, bargain, buy, or "window shop"—this array of merchandise, everything from fake antiques to illegally cut tapes, from "oddities" from the attic to portraits of Mussolini, will equal one of the shopping adventures of a lifetime.

Campidoglio, also laid out by the Florentine artist. Michelangelo also positioned the ancient bronze equestrian statue of Marcus Aurelius in the center, but it has now been moved inside to be protected from pollution and you will only occasionally find a replacement copy out on the pedestal.

One side of the piazza is open; the others are bounded by the **Senatorium** (Town Council), the statuary-filled **Palazzo dei Conservatori,** and the **Capitoline Museum** (see "Near Ancient Rome" under "More Attractions," later in this chapter). The Campidoglio is dramatic at night (walk around to the back for a regal view of the floodlit Roman Forum). On your return, head down the small steps on your right. The other steps adjoining Michelangelo's approach will take you to Santa Maria d'Aracoeli.

✪ Pantheon. Piazza della Rotonda. ☎ **06/6830-0230.** Free admission. July–Sept, daily 9am–6pm; Oct–June, Mon–Sat 9am–4pm, Sun 9am–1pm. Bus: 46, 62, 64, 170, or 492 to largo di Torre Argentina; then walk up via di Torre Argentina or via dei Cestari.

Of all the great buildings of ancient Rome, only the Pantheon ("All the Gods") remains intact today. It was built in 27 B.C. by Marcus Agrippa, and later reconstructed by the emperor Hadrian in the first part of the 2nd century A.D. This remarkable building is among the architectural wonders of the world because of its dome and its concept of space.

The Pantheon was once ringed with white marble statues of Roman gods in its niches. Animals were sacrificed and burned in the center, and the smoke escaped through the only means of light, an opening at the top 27 feet in diameter. The Pantheon is 142 feet wide and 142 feet high. Michelangelo came here to study the dome before designing the cupola of St. Peter's (whose dome is 2 feet smaller than the Pantheon's).

Other statistics are equally impressive. The walls are 25 feet thick, and the bronze doors leading into the building weigh 20 tons each. The temple was converted into a church in the early 7th century, which helped save it from destruction.

About 125 years ago the tomb of Raphael was discovered in the Pantheon (fans still bring him flowers). Victor Emmanuel II, king of Italy, and his successor, Umberto I, are interred here.

⚫ **Spanish Steps (Piazza di Spagna).** Metro: Piazza di Spagna.

The Spanish Steps were the last part of the outside world that Keats saw before he died in a house at the foot of the stairs (see the Keats-Shelley Memorial, in "Around the Spanish Steps" under "More Attractions," later in this chapter). The steps—filled in the spring with flower vendors, jewelry dealers, and photographers snapping pictures of tourists—and the square take their names from the Spanish Embassy, which used to have its headquarters here. Designed by Italian architect Francesco de Sanctis between 1723 and 1725, they were funded almost entirely by the French as a preface to the French national church, Trinità dei Monti, at the top. Unfortunately in recent years, even during tourist season, the steps have been vacant because of massive restorations. Work is underway to complete the project by the year 2000.

At the foot of the steps is a boat-shaped fountain designed by Pietro Bernini (not to be confused with his son, Giovanni Lorenzo Bernini, who proved to be a far greater sculptor). About two centuries ago, when the foreign art colony was in its ascendancy, the 136 steps were covered with young men and women who wanted to pose for the painter—men with their shirts unbuttoned to show off what they hoped was a Davidesque physique, and women consistently draped like Madonnas.

THE FOUNTAINS OF ROME

Rome is a city of fountains—a number of which are so exceptionally beautiful that they're worth a special pilgrimage. The two that hold the most enduring interest are the Trevi Fountain and the waterworks at piazza Navona.

Piazza Navona, surely one of the most beautifully baroque sites in all of Rome, is like an ocher-colored gem, unspoiled by new buildings or even by traffic. The shape results from the ruins of the Stadium of Domitian, which lie underneath. Great chariot races were once held here, some rather unusual, such as the one in which the head of the winning horse was lopped off as it crossed the finish line and was carried by runners to be offered as a sacrifice by the vestal virgins on top of the Capitoline Hill. In medieval times the popes used to flood the piazza to stage mock navel encounters. Today the most strenuous activities are performed by occasional fire-eaters, who go through their evening paces before an interested crowd of Romans and visitors.

Beside the twin-towered facade of the Church of Saint Agnes (17th century), the piazza boasts several other baroque masterpieces. The best known, in the center, is Bernini's **Fountain of the Four Rivers,** whose four stone personifications symbolize the world's greatest rivers—the Ganges, Danube, della Plata, and Nile. It's fun to try to figure out which is which. (Hint: The figure with the shroud on its head is the Nile, so represented because the river's source was unknown at the time.) The fountain at the south end, the **Fountain of the Moor,** is also by Bernini and dates from the same period as the church and the Fountain of the Four Rivers. The **Fountain of Neptune,** which balances that of the Moor, is a 19th-century addition. During the summer there are outdoor art shows in the evening, but visit during the day—it's the best time to inspect the fragments of the original stadium under a building on the north side of the piazza. If you're interested, walk out at the northern exit and turn left for a block. It's astonishing how much the level of the ground has risen since ancient times.

As you elbow your way through the summertime crowds around the **Trevi Fountain (Fontana di Trevi)** at piazza di Trevi, you'll find it hard to believe that this little piazza was nearly always deserted before *Three Coins in the Fountain* brought the tour buses. Today it's a must on everybody's itinerary. To do it properly, hold your lira coin in the right hand, turn your back to the fountain, and toss the coin over your shoulder (being careful not to bean anyone behind you). Then the spirit of the fountain will see to it that you return to Rome one day—or that's the tradition, at least. Actually, this is an evolution of an even older tradition of drinking from the fountain. Nathaniel Hawthorne (1804–64), in the novel *The Marble Faun,* wrote that anyone drinking from this fountain's water "has not looked upon Rome for the last time." Because of pollution, no one drank from it for years. Since the fountain has been restored in 1994 and is running again, the water is supposedly pure, owing to an electronic device that keeps the pigeons at bay. We'd still suggest that you skip a "Trevi cocktail" and have a mineral water at a cafe instead.

Supplied by water from the Acqua Vergine aqueduct, and a triumph of the baroque style, it was based on the design of Nicolo Salvi (who is said to have died of illness contracted during his supervision of the project) and completed in 1762. The design centers around the triumphant figure of Neptunus Rex, standing on a shell chariot drawn by winged steeds and led by a pair of tritons. Two allegorical figures in the side niches represent good health and fertility.

On the southwestern corner of the piazza that contains the fountain, you'll see a somber, not particularly spectacular-looking church (Chiesa S.S. Vincenzo e Anastasio) with a strange claim to fame. In it are contained the hearts and intestines of several centuries of popes. According to legend, the church was built on the site of a spring that burst from the earth after the beheading of St. Paul, at one of three sites where his head is said to have bounced off the ground.

Piazza Barberini lies at the foot of several Roman streets, among them via Barberini, via Sistina, and via Vittorio Veneto. It would be a far more more pleasant spot were it not for the heavy traffic swarming around its principal feature, Bernini's **Fountain of the Triton.** For more than three centuries the strange figure sitting in a vast open clam has been blowing water from his triton. Off to one side of the piazza is the clean, aristocratic side facade of the Palazzo Barberini, named for one of Rome's powerful families. The Renaissance Barberini reached their peak when a son was elected pope (Urban VIII). This Barberini pope encouraged Bernini and gave him great patronage.

As you go up via Vittorio Veneto, look for the small fountain on the right-hand corner of piazza Barberini, which is another of Bernini's works, the small **Fountain of the Bees.** At first they look more like flies, but they are the bees of the Barberini, the crest of that powerful family complete with the crossed keys of St. Peter above them (the keys were always added to a family crest when a son was elected pope).

3 More Attractions

NEAR ANCIENT ROME

Basilica di San Clemente. Piazza San Clemente, via Labicana 95. ☎ **06/7045-1018.** Admission: Basilica, free; grottoes, 2,000 lire ($1.30). Mon–Sat 9:30am–12:30pm and 3:30–6pm, Sun 10am–noon and 3:30–6pm. Metro: Colosseo. Bus: 81, 85, 87, or 186. Tram: 13 or 30.

From the Colosseum, head up via di San Giovanni in Laterano to the Basilica of Saint Clement. This isn't just another Roman church—far from it! In this church-upon-a-church, centuries of history peel away. In the 4th century a church was built over a secular house of the 1st century A.D., beside which stood a pagan temple dedicated to Mithras (god of the sun). Down in the eerie grottoes (which you can explore on your own—unlike the catacombs on the Appian Way), you'll discover well-preserved frescoes from the 9th to the 11th century A.D. After the Normans destroyed the lower church, a new one was built in the 12th century. Its chief attraction is the bronze-orange mosaic (from that period) that adorns the apse, as well as a chapel honoring St. Catherine of Alexandria with frescoes by Masolino.

Basilica di San Giovanni in Laterano. Piazza San Giovanni in Laterano 4. ☎ **06/ 6988-6433.** Admission: Basilica, free; cloisters, 2,000 lire ($1.30). Daily 7am–6pm. Metro: San Giovanni.

This church—not St. Peter's—is the cathedral of the diocese of Rome. Originally built in A.D. 314 by Constantine, the cathedral has suffered the vicissitudes of Rome, and was badly sacked and forced to rebuild many times. Only fragmented parts of the baptistery remain from the original structure.

The present building is characterized by its 18th-century facade by Alessandro Galilei (statues of Christ and the Apostles ring the top). A terrorist bomb in 1993 caused severe damage, especially to the facade. Borromini gets the credit (some say blame) for the interior, built for Innocent X. It's said that in the misguided attempt to redecorate, frescoes by Giotto were destroyed (remains believed to have been painted by Giotto were discovered in 1952 and are now on display against a column near the church entrance on the right inner pier). In addition, look for the unusual ceiling and the sumptuous transept, and explore the 13th-century cloisters with their twisted double columns.

The popes used to live next door at the **Lateran Palace** before the move to Avignon in the 14th century. But the most unusual sight is across the street at the "Palace of the Holy Steps," called the **Santuario della Scala Sancta,** piazza San Giovanni in Laterano (☎ **06/7049-4619**). It's alleged that these were the actual steps that Christ climbed when he was brought before Pilate. These steps are supposed to be climbed only on your knees, which you're likely to see the faithful doing throughout the day.

Baths of Caracalla (Terme di Caracalla). Via delle Terme di Caracalla 52. ☎ **06/ 575-8626.** Admission 8,000 lire ($5.10) adults, free for children 11 and under. Apr–Sept, Tues–Sat 9am–6pm, Sun–Mon 9am–1pm; Oct–Mar, Tues–Sat 9am–3pm, Sun–Mon 9am–1pm. Bus: 90 or 118.

Named for the emperor Caracalla, the Terme di Caracalla were completed in the early part of the 3rd century. The richness of decoration has faded and the lushness can only be judged from the shell of brick ruins that remain.

✪ **Museo Capitolino and Palazzo dei Conservatori.** Piazza del Campidoglio. ☎ **06/ 6710-2071.** Admission (to both) 10,000 lire ($6.40). Apr–Sept, Tues 9am–1:45pm and 5–8pm, Wed–Fri and Sun 9am–1:30pm, Sat 9am–1:30pm and 8–11pm; Oct–Mar, Tues and Sat 9am–1:45pm and 5–8pm, Wed–Fri and Sun 9am–1:30pm. Bus: 46, 89, 92, 94, or 716.

These museums house some of the greatest pieces of classical sculpture in the world. The **Capitoline Museum** was built in the 17th century, based on an architectural sketch by Michelangelo. In the first room is *The Dying Gaul,* a work of majestic skill. It's a copy of a Greek original that dates from the 3rd century B.C. In a special gallery all her own is the *Capitoline Venus,* who demurely covers herself. This statue was the symbol of feminine beauty and charm down through the centuries (also a Roman copy of a 3rd century B.C. Greek original). *Amore* (Cupid) and *Psyche* are up to their old tricks near the window.

The famous equestrian statue of Marcus Aurelius, whose years in the middle of the piazza made it a victim of pollution, has recently been restored and is now kept in the museum for protection. This is the only bronze equestrian statue to have survived from ancient Rome, mainly because for centuries it was thought to be a statue of Constantine the Great and Papal Rome respected the memory of the first Christian emperor. It's a beautiful statue even though the perspective is rather odd. The statue is housed in a glassed-in room on the street level called Cortile di Marforio; it's a kind of Renaissance greenhouse, surrounded by windows.

The **Palace of the Conservatori,** across the way, was also based on an architectural plan by Michelangelo and is rich in classical sculpture and paintings. One of the most notable bronzes—a work of incomparable beauty—is *Lo Spinario* (a little boy picking a thorn from his foot), a Greek classic that dates from the 1st century B.C. In addition, you'll find *Lupa Capitolina* (the Capitoline Wolf), a rare Etruscan bronze that may go back to the 5th century B.C. (Romulus and Remus, the legendary twins that the wolf suckled, were added at a later date). The palace also contains a "Pinacoteca"—mostly paintings from the 16th and 17th centuries. Notable canvases include Caravaggio's *Fortune-Teller* and his curious *John the Baptist,* the *Holy Family* by Dosso Dossi, *Romulus and Remus* by Rubens, and Titian's *Baptism of Christ.* The entrance courtyard is lined with the remains—head, hands, foot, and a kneecap—of an ancient colossal statue of Constantine the Great.

Saint Peter in Chains (Chiesa di San Pietro in Vincoli). Piazza San Pietro in Vincoli 4A (off via degli Annibaldi). ☎ **06/488-2865.** Free admission. Mon–Sat 7am–12:30pm and 3:30–6pm, Sun 7–11:45am and 3–7pm. Metro: Via Cavour. Bus: 11, 27, or 81.

From the Colosseum, head up the "spoke" street via degli Annibaldi to this church, founded in the 5th century A.D. to house the chains that bound St. Peter in Palestine. The chains are preserved under glass. But the drawing card is the tomb of Julius II, with one of the world's most famous pieces of sculpture, *Moses* by Michelangelo. As readers of Irving Stone's *The Agony and the Ecstasy* know, Michelangelo was to have carved 44 magnificent figures for Julius's tomb. That didn't happen, of course, but the pope was given one of the greatest consolation prizes—a figure intended to be "minor" that is now numbered among Michelangelo's masterpieces. Of the stern father symbol of Michelangelo's *Moses,* Vasari, in his *Lives of the Artists,* wrote: "No modern work will ever equal it in beauty, no, nor ancient either."

Museo Nazionale del Palazzo di Venezia. Via del Plebiscito 118. ☎ **06/679-8865.** Admission 12,000 lire ($7.70) adults, 8,000 lire ($5.10) children 11 and under. Tues–Sat 9am–2pm, Sun 9am–1pm. Bus: 64, 75, 85, 170, or 492.

The Museum of the Palazzo Venezia, in the geographic heart of Rome, is the building that served until the end of World War I as the seat of the Embassy of Austria. During the Fascist regime (1928–43), it was the seat of the Italian government. The balcony from which Mussolini used to speak to the Italian people was built in the 15th century. You can now visit the rooms and halls containing oil paintings, porcelain, tapestries, ivories, and ceramics. No one particular exhibit stands out—it's the sum total that adds up to a major attraction. The State Rooms are currently only open occasionally to host temporary exhibitions.

Standing outside the museum, you can't help but notice the 20th-century **monument of Victor Emmanuel II,** king of Italy, built on part of the Capitoline Hill and overlooking the piazza, a lush work that has often been compared to a wedding cake. Here you'll find the Tomb of the Unknown Soldier that was created in World War I.

Chiesa di Santa Maria in Cosmedin. Piazza della Bocca della Verità 18. ☎ **06/678-1419.** Free admission. Daily 9am–1pm and 2:30–6pm. Bus: 15, 23, 57, 95, or 716.

This little church was founded in the 6th century, but subsequently rebuilt—and a campanile was added in the 12th century in the Romanesque style. The church is ever popular with pilgrims drawn not by its great art treasures but by its "Mouth of Truth," a large disk under the portico. As Gregory Peck demonstrated to Audrey

Hepburn in *Roman Holiday*, the mouth is supposed to chomp down on the hand of liars who insert their paws. According to local legend, a former priest used to keep a scorpion in back to bite the fingers of anyone he felt was lying. On one of our visits to the church, a little woman, her head draped in black, sat begging a few feet from the medallion. A scene typical enough—except that this woman's right hand was covered with bandages.

Chiesa di Santa Maria d'Aracoeli. Piazza d'Aracoeli. ☎ **06/679-8155.** Free admission. Daily 7am–noon and 3:30–5:30pm. Bus: 46, 89, 92, 94, or 95.

Sharing a spot on Capitoline Hill, this landmark church was built for the Franciscans in the 13th century. According to legend, Augustus once ordered a temple erected on this spot, where a sibyl, with her gift of prophecy, forecast the coming of Christ. In the interior of the present building you'll find a coffered Renaissance ceiling and a mosaic of the Virgin over the altar in the Byzantine style. If you're sleuth enough, you'll also find a tombstone carved by the great Renaissance sculptor Donatello. The church is known for its Bufalini Chapel, a masterpiece of Pinturicchio, who frescoed it with scenes illustrating the life and death of St. Bernardino of Siena. He also depicted St. Francis receiving the stigmata. These frescoes are a highpoint in early Renaissance Roman painting. You have to climb a long flight of steep steps to reach the church, unless you're already on the neighboring piazza del Campidoglio, in which case you can cross the piazza and climb the steps on the far side of the Museo Capitolino.

AROUND CAMPO DE' FIORI & THE JEWISH GHETTO

During the 1500s **campo de' Fiori** was the geographic and cultural center of secular Rome, site of dozens of inns that would almost certainly have been reviewed by this guidebook had it existed at the time. From its center rises a statue of a severe-looking monk (Giordano Bruno) whose presence is a reminder of the occasional burning at the stake in this piazza of religious heretics. Today, ringed with venerable and antique houses, the campo is the site of an open-air food market held Monday to Saturday from early in the morning until around noon, or whenever the food runs out. Take bus no 64 from the Termini to Museo de Roma; then walk from there.

Palazzo Farnese. Piazza Farnese. Closed to the public. Bus: 46, 62, 70, 71, 87, 90, or 186.

Built between 1514 and 1589, this palace designed by Sangallo, Michelangelo, and others was astronomically expensive at the time. Its famous residents have included a 16th-century member of the Farnese family, Pope Paul III, Cardinal Richelieu, and the former Queen Christina of Sweden, who moved to Rome after abdicating her throne. During the 1630s, when the building's heirs could not afford to maintain it, the palace became the site of the French embassy, a function it has served ever since. It's closed to the public. For the best view of the palazzo, cut west from via Giulia along any of the narrow streets—via Mascherone or via dei Farnesi would do nicely.

Palazzo Spada. Capo di Ferro 3. ☎ **06/686-1158.** Admission 4,000 lire ($2.55) adults, free for children 17 and under and seniors 60 and over. Tues–Sat 9am–7pm, Sun 9am–12:30pm. Bus: 46, 62, 70, 71, 87, 90, or 186.

Built around 1550 for Cardinal Gerolamo Capo di Ferro, and later inhabited by the descendants of several other cardinals, this palace was sold to the Italian government in the 1920s. Its richly ornate facade, covered in high-relief stucco decorations in the mannerist style, is the finest of any building from 16th-century Rome. Although the State Rooms are closed to the public, the richly decorated courtyard and a handful of galleries of paintings are open.

AROUND PIAZZA NAVONA & THE PANTHEON

Chiesa del Gesù. Piazza del Gesù. ☎ **06/678-6341.** Free admission. Apr–Sept, daily 6am–12:30pm and 4–7:30pm; Oct–Mar, daily 6am–12:30pm and 4:30–7:15pm. Bus: 44, 46, 56, 60, 62, 64, 65, 70, 81, or 90.

Built between 1568 and 1584 by donations from a Farnese cardinal, this structure functioned for several centuries as the most potent and powerful church in the Jesuit order. Conceived as a bulwark against the perceived menace of the Protestant Reformation, it's sober, monumental, and very important to the history of the Catholic Counter-Reformation. The sheathing of yellow marble that covers part of the interior was added during the 1800s.

Palazzo Doria Pamphilj. Piazza Collegio Romano 2. ☎ **06/679-7323.** Admission: Gallery, 12,000 lire ($7.70) per person; apartments, 9,000 lire ($5.75) adults, 5,000 lire ($3.20) students and senior citizens. Tues and Fri–Mon 10am–1pm. Private visits may be arranged. Bus: 44, 46, 56, 60, 61, 64, 65, 70, or 75.

Located off via del Corso, this museum offers visitors a look at what it's really like to live in an 18th-century palace. Like many Roman palaces of the period, the mansion is partly leased to tenants (on the upper levels), and there are even shops on the street level, but all this is easily overlooked after you enter the grand apartments of the historic princely Doria Pamphilj family, which traces its lines to before the great 15th-century Genoese admiral Andrea Doria. The regal apartments surround the central court and gallery of the palace. The 18th-century decor pervades the magnificent ballroom, drawing rooms, dining rooms, and even the family chapel. Gilded furniture, crystal chandeliers, Renaissance tapestries, and portraits of family members are everywhere. The Green Room is especially rich in treasures, with a 15th-century Tournay tapestry, paintings by Memling and Filippo Lippi, and a semi-nude portrait of Andrea Doria by Sebastiano del Piombo. The Andrea Doria Room is dedicated to the admiral and to the ship of the same name. It contains a glass case with mementos of the great maritime disaster of the 1950s.

Skirting the central court is a picture gallery with a memorable collection of frescoes, paintings, and sculpture. Most important among a number of great works are the portrait of Innocent X by Velázquez, called one of the three or four best portraits ever painted; *Salome* by Titian; and works by Rubens and Caravaggio. Notable also are *The Bay of Naples* by Pieter Brueghel the Elder and a copy of Raphael's portrait of Principessa Giovanna d' Aragona de Colonna (who looks remarkably like Leonardo's *Mona Lisa*). Most of the sculpture came from the Doria country estates. It includes marble busts of Roman emperors, bucolic nymphs, and satyrs. Even without the paintings and sculptures, that gallery would be worth a visit just for its fresco-covered walls and ceilings.

Chiesa di San Agostino. Via della Scrofa 80 ☎ **06/6880-1962.** Free admission. Daily 8am–noon and 4:30–7:30pm. Bus: 81, 90, or 90B.

Built between 1479 and 1483, this was one of the first churches erected during the Roman Renaissance. Originally commissioned by the archbishop of Rouen, France, its interior was altered and redecorated in the 1700s and 1800s. A painting by Caravaggio, *Madonna of the Pilgrims* (1605), hangs in the first altar on the left, as you enter.

Chiesa di San Luigi dei Francesi. Via Santa Giovanna d'Arco. ☎ **06/683-3818.** Fri–Wed 8am–12:30pm and 3:30–7pm, Thurs 8am–12:30pm. Bus: 70, 81, 97, or 186.

This has been the national church of France in Rome since 1589. There's a stone salamander—the symbol of the Renaissance French monarch François I—subtly carved into its facade. Inside, in the last chapel on the left, are a noteworthy series of frescoes by Caravaggio—the celebrated *Calling of St. Matthew* on the left, *St. Matthew and the Angel* in the center, and *The Martyrdom of St. Matthew* on the right.

Piazza Colonna. Off via del Corso. Bus: 81, 90, or 90B.

The centerpiece of this square is one of the most dramatic obelisks in town, the **Column of Marcus Aurelius,** a hollow bronze column rising 83 feet above the piazza. Built between 180 and 196 A.D., and restored (some say "defaced") in 1589 by a pope who replaced the statue of the Roman warrior on top with a statue of St. Paul, it's one of the ancient world's best examples of heroic bas-relief and one of the most memorable sights of Rome. Beside the piazza's northern edge rises the Palazzo Chigi, official residence of the Italian prime minister.

Chiesa di Santa Maria della Pace. Vicolo del Arco della Pace 5, off via piazza della Pace. ☎ **06/686-1156.** Free admission. Tues–Sat 10am–noon and 4–6pm, Sun 9–11am. Bus: 70, 81, 87, 90, 90B, 186, or 492.

According to legend, blood flowed from a statue of the Virgin above the altar after someone threw a pebble at it. This legend motivated Pope Sixtus to rebuild the church in the 1500s on the foundations of an even older sanctuary. For generations after that, its curved porticos, cupola atop an octagonal base, cloisters by Bramante, and frescoes by Raphael helped make it one of the most fashionable churches for aristocrats residing in the surrounding palazzos.

Chiesa di Santa Maria Sopra Minerva. Piazza della Minerva 42. ☎ **06/679-3926.** Free admission. Daily 7am–noon and 4–7pm. Bus: 119.

Beginning in 1280, early Christian leaders ordained that the foundation of an already ancient temple dedicated to Minerva (goddess of wisdom), be reused as the base for Rome's only Gothic church. Architectural changes and redecorations during the 1500s and the 1900s stripped this building of some of its original allure. Despite that, the roster of ornaments inside—including an awe-inspiring collection of medieval and Renaissance tombs—create an atmosphere that's something akin to a religious museum. Inside you'll find a beautiful chapel frescoed by Fillipino Lippi, and, to the left of the apse, a muscular *Risen Christ* carrying a rather small cross carved from marble by Michelangelo himself (the bronze drapery covering Christ's shocking nudity was added later). Under the altar lies the body of St. Catherine of Siena, and in the passage to the left of the choir, surrounded by a small fence, is the floor tomb of the great monastic painter Fra Angelico. The amusing baby elephant carrying a small obelisk in the piazza outside was designed by Bernini.

AROUND PIAZZA DI SPAGNA

Altar of Peace (Ara Pacis). Via di Ripetta. ☎ **06/6710-3569.** Admission 4,000 lire ($2.55). Apr–Sept, Tues–Wed and Fri–Sun 9am–1:30pm, Thurs and Sat 4–7pm; Oct–Mar, Tues–Wed and Fri–Sun 9am–1:30pm. Bus: 81, 90, or 90B.

In an airy glass-and-concrete building beside the eastern banks of the Tiber at ponte Cavour rests a reconstructed treasure from the reign of Augustus. It was built by the Senate as a tribute to that emperor and the peace he had brought to the Roman world. You can see portraits of the imperial family—Augustus, Livia (his wife), Tiberius (Livia's son and the successor to the empire), even Julia (the unfortunate daughter of Augustus, exiled by her father for her sexual excesses) on the marble walls. The altar was reconstructed from literally hundreds of fragments scattered in museums for centuries. A major portion came from the foundations of a Renaissance palace on the Corso. The reconstruction—quite an archeological adventure story in itself—was executed (and sometimes enhanced) by the Fascists during the 1930s.

☼ Galleria Borghese. Piazzale del Museo Borghese, off via Pinciano, in the Villa Borghese. **☎ 06/854-8577.** Admission 4,000 lire ($2.55). Tues–Sat 9am–2pm, Sun 9am–7pm. Bus: 910 from the Termini or 56 from piazza Barberini.

Still under restoration, the handsome villa is home to some of the finest paintings in Rome; there's a representative collection of Renaissance and baroque masters, along with important Bernini sculpture. Among these is the *Conquering Venus* by Antonio Canova, Italy's greatest neoclassic sculptor. Actually, this early 19th-century work created a sensation in its day, because its model was Pauline Bonaparte Borghese, sister of Napoléon (if the French dictator didn't like to see his sister naked, he was even more horrified at Canova's totally nude version of himself). In the rooms that follow are three of Bernini's most widely acclaimed works: *David, Apollo and Daphne* (his finest piece), and finally *The Rape of Persephone.*

The second floor, which normally houses the collection of Renaissance and baroque paintings, is closed for restoration, and may be for a long time. The paintings are more or less on semipermanent display at **San Michele à Ripa,** via di San Michele 22 (**☎ 06/58431**), in the Trastevere district. Admission is included in your Galleria Borghese ticket, and it's open Monday to Friday from 9:30am to 1pm and 4 to 8pm and on Saturday from 9:30am to 1pm.

After visiting the gallery, you many want to join the Italians in their strolls through the Villa Borghese (see below), replete with zoological gardens and small bodies of water. Horse shows are staged at piazza Siena.

Galleria Nazionale d'Arte Moderna. Viale delle Belle Arti 131. **☎ 06/322-4151.** Admission 8,000 lire ($5.10) adults, free for children 17 and under. Tues–Sat 9am–7pm, Sun 9am–1pm. Bus: 19 or 30.

The National Gallery of Modern Art is in the Villa Borghese Gardens, a short walk from the Etruscan Museum. With its neoclassic and romantic paintings and sculpture, it's a dramatic change from the glories of the Renaissance and the Romans. Its 75 rooms also house the largest collection in Italy of 19th- and 20th-century artists. Included are important works of Balla, Boccioni, de Chirico, Morandi, Manzù, Marini, Burri, Capogrossi, and Fontana, and a large collection of Italian optical and pop art.

Look for Modigliani's *La Signora dal Collaretto* and the large *Nudo.* Several important sculptures, including one by Canova, are on display in the museum's gardens. The gallery also houses a large collection of foreign artists, including French impressionists Degas, Cézanne, and Monet, and the post-impressionist van Gogh. Surrealism and expressionism are well represented in works by Klee, Ernst, Braque, Miró, Kandinsky, Mondrian, and Pollock. You'll also find sculpture by Rodin. The collection of graphics, the storage rooms, and the Department of Restoration can be visited by appointment Tuesday to Friday.

Keats-Shelley Memorial. Piazza di Spagna 26. **☎ 06/678-4235.** Admission 5,000 lire ($3.20). May–Sept, Mon–Fri 9am–1pm and 3–6pm; Oct–Apr, Mon–Fri 9am–1pm and 2:30–5:30pm. Metro: Piazza di Spagna.

At the foot of the Spanish Steps is this 18th-century house where Keats died of consumption on February 23, 1821, at the age of 25. "It is like living in a violin," wrote Italian author Alberto Savinio. Since 1909, when it was bought by well-intentioned English and American aficionados of English literature, the building has been a working library established in honor of Keats and Shelley, who drowned off the coast of Viareggio with a copy of Keats in his pocket. Mementoes inside range from the kitsch to the immortal, and are almost relentlessly laden with literary nostalgia. The apartment where Keats spent his last months, carefully tended by his close friend, Joseph Severn, shelters a strange death mask of Keats as well as the "deadly sweat" drawing by Severn.

Augustus Mausoleum (Mausoleo Augusteo). Via di Ripetta and piazza Augusteo Imperatore.

This seemingly indestructible pile of bricks along via di Ripetta has been here for 2,000 years, and will probably remain for another 2,000. Like the larger tomb of Hadrian across the river, this was once a circular, marble-covered affair with tall cypress trees, symmetrical groupings of Egyptian obelisks, and some of the most spectacular ornamentation in Europe. Many of the emperors of the 1st century had their ashes deposited in golden urns inside this building, and it was probably due to the resultant crowding that Hadrian later decided to construct an entirely new tomb (today, the Castel Sant'Angelo) for himself in another part of Rome. The imperial remains stayed intact in this building until the 5th century, when invading barbarians smashed the bronze gates and stole the golden urns, probably emptying the ashes on the ground outside. After periods when it functioned as a Renaissance fortress, a bullfighting ring, and a private garden, the tomb was restored in the 1930s by Mussolini, who might have envisioned it as a burial place for himself. You cannot enter the mausoleum, but you should walk along the four streets that encircle it.

✪ **Museo Nazionale di Villa Giulia (Etruscan).** Piazzale di Villa Giulia 9. ☎ **06/322-6571.** Admission 8,000 lire ($5.10) adults, free for children 18 and under and seniors 60 and over. Tues–Sat 9am–7pm, Sun 9am–1pm. Metro: Flaminio. Bus: 19, 30, 225, or 926.

A 16th-century papal palace in the Villa Borghese Gardens shelters this priceless collection of art and artifacts of the mysterious Etruscans, who predated the Romans. Known for their sophisticated art and design, the Etruscans left a legacy of sarcophagi, bronze sculptures, terra-cotta vases, and jewelry, among other items.

If you have time only for the masterpieces, head for Sala 7, which has a remarkable 6th century B.C. *Apollo* from Veio (clothed, for a change). The other two widely acclaimed pieces of statuary in this gallery are *Dea con Bambino* (a goddess with a baby) and a greatly mutilated, but still powerful, *Hercules* with a stag. In the adjoining room, Sala 8, you'll see the lions' sarcophagus from the mid-6th century B.C. which was excavated at Cerveteri, north of Rome.

Finally, one of the world's most important Etruscan art treasures is the bride and bridegroom coffin from the 6th century B.C., also dug out of the tombs of Cerveteri (in Sala 9). Near the end of your tour, another masterpiece of Etruscan art awaits you in Sala 33: the *Cista Ficoroni,* a bronze urn with paw feet, mounted by three figures, which dates from the 4th century B.C.

Palazzo del Quirinale. Piazza del Quirinale. Free admission (but a passport or similar ID is required for entrance). Sun 9am–1pm. Metro: Barberini.

Until the end of World War II this palace was the home of the king of Italy, and before that it was the residence of the pope. Despite its origins during the Renaissance, when virtually every important architect in Italy worked on some aspect of its sprawling premises, it's rich in associations with ancient emperors and deities. The colossal statues of the *dioscuri* Castor and Pollux, which now form part of the fountain in the piazza, were found in the nearby great baths of Constantine, and in 1793 Pius VI had the ancient Egyptian obelisk moved here from the Mausoleum of

Augustus. The sweeping view of Rome from the piazza, which crowns the highest of the seven ancient hills of Rome, is itself worth the trip.

VILLA BORGHESE

This park in the heart of Rome is 3¹/₂ miles in circumference. One of the most elegant parks in Europe, it was created by Cardinal Scipione Borghese in the 1600s. Umberto I, king of Italy, acquired it in 1902 and presented it to the city of Rome, renaming it Villa Umberto I. However, Romans preferred their old name, which has stuck. A park of landscaped vistas and wide-open "green lungs," the greenbelt is crisscrossed by roads, but you can escape from the traffic and seek a shaded area—usually pine or oak—to enjoy a picnic or simply relax. In the northeast of the park is a small zoo, and the park is also home to the Galleria Borghese (see above), one of the finest museums of Rome, with many masterpieces by Renaissance and baroque artists.

AROUND VIA VENETO

Cimitero Monumentale dei Padri Cappucini. Under the Church of the Immaculate Conception, via Vittorio Veneto 27. ☎**06/487-1185.** Free admission (but a donation expected). Daily 9am–noon and 3–6pm. Metro: Piazza Barberini.

Qualifying as one of the most horrifying sights in all Christendom, this is a cemetery of skulls and crossbones woven into mosaic "works of art" just a short walk from piazza Barberini. To make this allegorical dance of death, the bones of more than 4,000 Capuchin brothers were used. Some of the skeletons are intact, draped with Franciscan habits. The creator of this chamber of horrors? The tradition of the friars is that it was the work of a French Capuchin. Their literature suggests that the cemetery should be visited keeping in mind the historical moment of its origins, when Christians had a rich and creative cult for their dead, when great spiritual masters mediated and preached with a skull in hand. Those who have lived through the days of crematoriums and other such massacres may view the graveyard differently, but to many who pause to think, this macabre sight of death has a message. It's not for the squeamish. The entrance is halfway up the first staircase on the right of the church.

Galleria Nazionale d'Arte Antica. Via delle Quattro Fontane 13. ☎ **06/481-4430.** Admission 8,000 lire ($5.10) adults, free for children 17 and under and for seniors 60 and over. Tues–Sat 9am–2pm, Sun 9am–1pm. Metro: Piazza Barberini.

The Palazzo Barberini, right off piazza Barberini, is one of the most magnificent baroque palaces in Rome. It was begun by Carlo Maderno in 1627 and completed in 1633 by Bernini, whose lavishly decorated rococo apartments, called the Gallery of Decorative Art, are on view.

The bedroom of Princess Cornelia Costanza Barberini and Prince Giulio Cesare Colonna di Sciarra still stands just as it was on their wedding night, and many household objects are displayed in the decorative art gallery. In the chambers, which have frescoes and hand-painted silk linings, you can see porcelain from Japan and Bavaria, canopied beds, and a wooden baby carriage.

On the first floor of the palace, a splendid array of paintings includes works from the 13th to the 16th century, most notably the *Mother and Child* by Simone Martini, and works by Filippo Lippi, Andrea Solario, and Francesco Francia. Il Sodoma has some brilliant pictures here, including *The Rape of the Sabines* and *The Marriage of St. Catherine.* One of the best-known paintings is Raphael's beloved *La Fornarina,* the baker's daughter who was his mistress and who posed for his Madonna portraits. Titian is represented by *Venus and Adonis.* Other artists exhibited include Tintoretto,

El Greco, and Holbein the Younger. Many visitors come here just to see the magnificent Caravaggios, including *Narcissus.*

AROUND THE TERMINI

Basilica di Santa Maria Maggiore. Piazza di Santa Maria Maggiore. ☎ **06/483194.** Free admission. Daily 7am–7pm. Metro: Termini.

This great church, one of the four major basilicas of Rome, was originally founded by Pope Liberius in A.D. 358 but was rebuilt by Pope Sixtus III in 432–440. Its campanile, erected in the 14th century, is the loftiest in the city. Much doctored in the 18th century, the church's facade is not an accurate reflection of the treasures inside. The basilica is especially noted for the 5th-century Roman mosaics in its nave, as well as for its coffered ceiling, said to have been gilded with gold brought from the New World. In the 16th century Domenico Fontana built a now-restored "Sistine Chapel." In the following century Flaminio Ponzo designed the Pauline (Borghese) Chapel in the baroque style. The church contains the tomb of Bernini, Italy's most important sculptor and architect during the the baroque era in the 17th century. Ironically, the man who changed the face of Rome with his elaborate fountains is buried in a tomb so simple it takes a sleuth to track it down (to the right near the altar). Restoration of the 1,600-year-old church has begun and is scheduled for completion in the year 2000.

✪ **National Roman Museum (Museo Nazionale Romano).** Via Enrico de Nicola 79. ☎ **06/488-2298.** Admission 12,000 lire ($7.70). Tues–Sat 9am–2pm, Sun and holidays 9am–1pm. Metro: Piazza della Repubblica.

Located near piazza dei Cinquecento, which fronts the railway station, this museum occupies part of the 3rd-century A.D. Baths of Diocletian and a section of a convent that may have been designed by Michelangelo. It houses one of Europe's finest collections of Greek and Roman sculpture and early Christian sarcophagi.

The Ludovisi Collection is the apex of the museum, particularly the statue of the Gaul slaying himself after he has done in his wife (a brilliant copy of a Greek original from the 3rd century B.C.). Another prize is a one-armed Greek *Apollo.* A galaxy of other sculptured treasures includes *The Discus Thrower of Castel Porziano* (an exquisite copy), *Aphrodite of Cirene* (a Greek original), and the so-called *Hellenistic Ruler,* a Greek original of an athlete with a lance. A masterpiece of Greek sculpture, *The Birth of Venus,* is in the Ludovisi Throne room. *The Sleeping Hermaphrodite* (Ermafrodito Dormiente) is an original Hellenistic statue. You can stroll through the cloister, filled with statuary and fragments of antiquity, including a fantastic mosaic.

Chiesa di Santa Maria degli Angeli. Piazza della Repubblica 12. ☎ **06/488-0812.** Free admission. Daily 7:30am–12:30pm and 4–6pm. Metro: Piazza della Repubblica.

On this site, which adjoins the National Roman Museum near the railway station, once stood the "tepidarium" of the 3rd-century Baths of Diocletian. But in the 16th century Michelangelo—nearing the end of his life—converted the grand hall into one of the most splendid churches in Rome. Surely the artist wasn't responsible for

Impressions

Turn all the pages of history, but Fortune never produced a greater example of her own fickleness than the city of Rome, once the most beautiful and magnificent of all that ever were or will be . . . not a city in truth, but a certain part of heaven.
—Poggio Bracciolini (1380–1459)

"gilding the lily"—that is, putting *trompe-l'oeil* columns in the midst of the genuine pillars. The church is filled with tombs and paintings, but its crowning treasure is the genuine statue of St. Bruno by the great French sculptor Jean-Antoine Houdon. His sculpture is larger than life and about as real.

THE APPIAN WAY & THE CATACOMBS

Of all the roads that led to Rome, **via Appia Antica**—built in 312 B.C.—was the reigning leader. It eventually stretched all the way from Rome to the seaport of Brindisi, through which trade with the colonies in Greece and the East was funneled. According to Christian tradition, it was on the Appian Way that an escaping Peter encountered the vision of Christ, which caused him to go back into the city to face subsequent martyrdom.

Of the Roman monuments on via Appia Antica, the most impressive is the **Tomb of Cecilia Metella,** within walking distance of the catacombs. The cylindrical tomb honors the wife of one of Julius Caesar's military commanders from the Republican era. Why such an elaborate tomb for such an unimportant person in history? Cecilia Metella happened to be singled out for enduring fame because her tomb remained and the others decayed.

Along the Appian Way the patrician Romans built great monuments above the ground and Christians met in the catacombs beneath the earth. The remains of both can be visited today. In some dank, dark grottoes (never stray too far from either your party or one of the exposed lightbulbs), you can still discover the remains of early Christian art. Only someone wanting to write a sequel to *Quo Vadis?* would visit all the catacombs, but of those open to the public, the catacombs of St. Callixtus and St. Sebastian are the most important.

Tomb of St. Sebastian (Catacombe di San Sebastiano). Via Appia Antica 136. ☎ **06/788-7035.** Admission 8,000 lire ($5.10) adults, 4,000 lire ($2.55) children 6–15, free for children 5 and under. Wed–Mon 9am–noon and 2:30–5:30pm. Bus: 118 from near the Colosseo Metro station.

Today the tomb of the martyr is in the basilica (church), but his original tomb was in the catacombs under the basilica. From the reign of the emperor Valerian to the reign of the emperor Constantine, the bodies of Saint Peter and Saint Paul were hidden in the catacombs. The big church was built here in the 4th century. None of the catacombs, incidentally, is a grotto; all are dug from *tufo,* a soft volcanic rock. This is the only Christian catacomb in Rome that's always open. The tunnels here, if stretched out, would reach a length of 7 miles. In the tunnels and mausoleums are mosaics and graffiti, along with many other pagan and Christian objects from centuries even before the time of Constantine.

Catacombe di San Callisto (Callixtus). Via Appia Antica 110. ☎ **06/513-6725.** Admission 8,000 lire ($5.10) adults, 4,000 lire ($2.55) children 6–15, free for children 5 and under. Thurs–Tues 8:30am–noon and 2:30–5pm (to 5:30pm in summer). Bus: 218 from San Giovanni in Laterano to Fosse Ardeatine; ask driver to let you off at "Catacombe di San Callisto."

"The most venerable and most renowned of Rome," said Pope John XXIII of these funerary tunnels. The founder of Christian archeology, Giovanni Battista de Rossi (1822–94), called them "catacombs par excellence." They are the first cemetery of the Christian community of Rome, burial place of 16 popes in the 3rd century. They bear the name of St. Callixtus, the deacon whom Pope St. Zephyrinus put in charge of them and who was later elected pope (217–22) in his own right. The cemeterial complex is made up of a network of galleries stretching for nearly 12 miles, structured in five different levels, and reaching a depth of about 65 feet. There are many sepulchral chambers and almost half a million tombs. Paintings, sculptures, and epigraphs (with such symbols as the fish, the anchor, and the dove) provide invaluable material for the study of the life and customs of the ancient Christians and the story of their persecutions.

Entering the catacombs, you see at once the most important crypt, that of the nine popes. Some of the original marble tablets of their tombs are still preserved. The next crypt is that of St. Cecilia, the patron of sacred music. This early Christian martyr received three ax strokes on her neck, the maximum allowed by Roman law, which failed to kill her outright. Farther on, you'll find the famous Cubicula of the Sacraments with its 3rd-century frescoes. The catacombs were dug in the middle of the 2nd century up until the middle of the 5th century as cemeteries and places of prayers—never private dwellings.

THE TESTACCIO AREA & SOUTH

Protestant Cemetery. Via Caio Cestio 6. ☎ **06/574-1141.** Free admission (but a 1,000-lira/65¢ offering is customary). Apr–Sept, Tues–Sun 9am–6pm; Oct–Mar, Tues–Sun 9am–5pm. Metro: Piramide. Bus: 13, 27, 30b, 57, or 318.

Near Porta San Paola, in the midst of a setting of cypress trees, lies the old cemetery where John Keats is buried. In a grave nearby, Joseph Severn, his "deathbed" companion, was interred beside him six decades later. Dejected, and feeling his reputation as a poet diminished by the rising vehemence of his critics, Keats asked that the following epitaph be written on his tombstone: "Here lies one whose name was writ in water." A great romantic poet Keats certainly was, but a prophet, thankfully not.

Percy Bysshe Shelley, author of *Prometheus Unbound*, drowned off the Italian Riviera in 1822, before his 30th birthday. His ashes rest alongside those of Edward John Trelawny, fellow romantic and man of the sea. Trelawny maintained—but this was not proved—that Shelley may have been murdered, perhaps by petty pirates bent on robbery.

Pyramid of Caius Cestius. Piazzale Ostiense. Bus: 30.

Dating from the 1st century B.C., the Pyramid of Caius Cestius, about 120 feet high, looks as if it belongs to the Egyptian landscape. It was constructed during the "Cleopatra craze" in architecture that swept across Rome. The pyramid can't be entered, but it's fun to circle and photograph. Who was Caius Cestius? A rich magistrate in Imperial Rome whose tomb is more impressive than his achievements. You can visit at any time.

St. Paul Outside the Walls (Basilica di San Paolo Fuori le Mura). Via Ostiense. ☎ **06/541-0341.** Free admission. Basilica, daily 7am–6pm; cloisters, daily 9am–12:45pm and 3–6pm. Metro: San Paolo Basilica. Bus: 4, 11, 23, 170, or 673.

The Basilica of St. Paul, whose origins go back to the time of Constantine, is the fourth great patriarchal church of Rome. It burned in 1823 and was subsequently rebuilt. This basilica is believed to have been erected over the tomb of St. Paul. From the inside, its windows may appear at first to be stained glass, but they're actually translucent alabaster. With its forest of single-file columns and its mosaic medallions (portraits of the various popes), this is one of the most streamlined and elegantly decorated churches in Rome. Its single most important treasure is a 12th-century candelabrum designed by Vassalletto, who is also responsible for the remarkable cloisters—in themselves worth the trip "outside the walls." They contain twisted pairs of columns enclosing a rose garden. The Benedictine monks and students sell a fine collection of souvenirs, rosaries, and bottles of Benedictine every day except Sunday and religious holidays.

IN TRASTEVERE

From many vantage points in the Eternal City the views are panoramic. Scenic gulpers, however, have traditionally preferred the outlook from the **Gianicolo (Janiculum Hill),** across the Tiber, not one of the "Seven Hills" but certainly one of the most visited (and a stopover on many bus tours). The view is at its best at sundown, or at dawn, when the skies are often fringed with mauve. The Janiculum was the site of a battle between Guiseppe Garibaldi and the forces of Pope Pius IX in 1870—an event commemorated today with statuary. To reach the Gianicolo, take bus no. 41 from ponte Sant'Angelo.

Chiesa di Santa Cecilia in Trastevere. Piazza Santa Cecilia. ☎ **06/589-9289.** Admission Church, free; Cavallini frescoes, free (but a donation is requested); excavations, 12,000 lire ($7.70) per person. Main church, daily 10am–noon and 4–6pm; frescoes, Tues and Fri 10–11am. Bus: 56, 60, 75, 170, or 710 to viale Trastevere.

A cloistered and still-functioning convent with a fine garden, Santa Cecilia contains a difficult-to-visit fresco by Cavallini in its inner sanctums, and a late 13th-century baldacchino by Arnalfo di Cambio over the altar. The church is built on the reputed site of Cecilia's long-ago palace, and for a small fee you can descend under the church to inspect the ruins of some Roman houses as well as peer through a gate at the highly stuccoed grotto underneath the altar.

Chiesa di Santa Maria in Trastevere. Piazza Santa Maria in Trastevere. ☎ **06/581-4802.** Free admission. Daily 7:30am–12:30pm and 4–7pm. Bus: 56, 60, 75, 170, or 710 to viale Trastevere.

This Romanesque church at the picturesque center of Trastevere was originally built around 350 A.D., and is considered one of the oldest churches in Rome. The body was added around 1100, and the portico in the early 1700s. The restored mosaics on the apse date from around 1140, and below them are the 1293 mosaic scenes from the life of Mary by Pietro Cavallini. The faded mosaics on the facade are 12th or 13th century, and the octagonal fountain in the piazza is an ancient Roman original restored and added to in the 17th century by Carlo Fontana.

AROUND VATICAN CITY

Castel Sant'Angelo. Lungotevere Castello 50. ☎ **06/687-5036.** Admission 8,000 lire ($5.10) adults, free for children 17 and under and for seniors 60 and over. Daily 9am–1pm; closed second and last Tues of each month. Metro: Ottaviano. Bus: 23, 46, 49, 62, 64, 87, 98, 280, or 910.

This overpowering structure, in a landmark position on the Tiber, was originally built in the 2nd century A.D. as a tomb for the emperor Hadrian; it continued as an imperial mausoleum until the time of Caracalla. If it looks like a fortress, it should—that was its function in the Middle Ages, built over the Roman walls and linked to the Vatican by an underground passageway that was much used by the fleeing papacy, who escaped from unwanted visitors like Charles V during his sack of the city in 1527.

In the 14th century it became a papal residence, enjoying various connections with Boniface IX, Nicholas V, even Julius II, patron of Michelangelo and Raphael. But its legend rests largely on its link with Pope Alexander VI, whose mistress bore him two children—Cesare and Lucrezia Borgia.

Today the highlight of the castle is a trip through the Renaissance apartments with their coffered ceilings and lush decoration. Their walls have witnessed plots and intrigues that make up some of the arch-treachery of the High Renaissance. Later, you can go through the dank cells that once rang with the screams of Cesare's victims of torture. The most famous figure imprisoned here was Benvenuto Cellini, the eminent sculptor and goldsmith, remembered chiefly for his classic, candid *Autobiography.* Now an art museum, the castle halls display the history of the Roman mausoleum, along with a wide-ranging selection of ancient arms and armor. You can climb to the top terrace for another one of those dazzling views of the Eternal City.

PONTE SANT'ANGELO

The trio of arches in the river's center has been basically unchanged since the bridge was built around A.D. 135; the arches that abut the river's embankments were added late in the 19th century as part of a flood-control program. On December 19, 1450, so many pilgrims gathered on this bridge (which at the time was lined with wooden buildings) that about 200 of them were crushed to death. Since the 1960s the bridge has been reserved exclusively for pedestrians who can stroll across and admire the statues designed by Bernini. On the southern end is the site of one of the most famous executions of the Renaissance, **piazza San Angelo.** There, in 1599, Beatrice Cenci and several members of her family were beheaded on orders of Pope Clement VIII. Their crime? Plotting the successful death of their very rich and very brutal father. Their tale later inspired a tragedy by Shelley and a novel by a 19th-century Italian politician named Francesco Guerrazzi.

WALKING TOUR
Rome of the Caesars

Start: Via Sacra in the Roman Forum.
Finish: Circus Maximus.
Time: 5¹/₂ hours.
Best Time: Any sunny day.
Worst Times: After dark, or when the place is overrun with tour groups.

This tour tries to incorporate the most centrally positioned of the monuments that attest to the military and architectural grandeur of Rome. As a whole, they comprise the most famous and evocative ruins in the world, despite such drawbacks as roaring traffic that's the bane of the city's civic planners, and a general dustiness and heat that might test the strength of even the hardiest of amateur archeologists.

After the collapse of Rome and during the Dark Ages, the Forum and many of the other sites on this tour were lost to history, buried beneath layers of debris, until Mussolini set out to restore the grandeur of Rome by reminding his compatriots of their glorious past.

THE ROMAN FORUM   The more westerly of the two-entrances to the Roman Forum is at the corner of via dei Fori Imperiali and via Cavour, adjacent to piazza Santa Maria Nova. The nearest Metro is Colosseo.

As you walk down into the Forum along a masonry ramp you'll be heading for the **Via Sacra,** the ancient Roman road that ran through the Forum connecting the Capitoline Hill, to your right, with the Arch of Titus (1st century A.D.), situated off to your left. The Roman Forum is the more dignified and more austere of the two forums you'll visit on this walking tour. Although it consists mostly of artfully evocative ruins scattered confusingly around a sun-baked terrain, it represents almost 1,000 years of Roman power during the severely disciplined period before the legendary decadence of the later Roman emperors.

During the Middle Ages, when this was the *campo vaccino* (cow pasture) and all these stones were underground, there was a dual column of elm trees connecting the

Arch of Titus, off to your left, with the Arch of Septimius Severus (A.D. 200) to your right.

Arriving at the via Sacra, turn right. The random columns on the right as you head toward the Arch of Septimius Severus belong to the:

1. **Basilica Aemilia,** formerly the site of great meeting halls and shops all maintained for centuries by the noble Roman family who gave it its name. At the corner nearest the Forum entrance are some traces of melted bronze decoration that fused to the marble floor during a great fire set by invading Goths in A.D. 410.

   The next important building is the:

2. **Curia,** or Senate house—it's the large brick building on the right that still has its roof. Romans had been meeting on this site for centuries before the first structure was erected, and that was still centuries before Christ. The present building is the fifth (if one counts all the reconstructions and substantial rehabilitations) to stand on the site. Legend has it that the original building was constructed by an ancient king with the curious name of Tullus Hostilius. The tradition he began was a noble one indeed, and our present legislative system owes much to the Romans who met in this hall. Unfortunately, the high ideals and inviolate morals that characterized the early Republican senators gave way to the bootlicking of imperial times, when the Senate became little more than a rubber stamp. Caligula, who was only the third emperor, had his horse appointed to the Senate (it was a life appointment), and that pretty much sums up where the Senate was by the middle of the 1st century A.D.

   The building was a church until 1937, when the Fascist government tore out the baroque interior and revealed what we see today. The original floor of Egyptian marble and the tiers that held the seats of the senators have miraculously survived. In addition, at the far end of the great chamber we can see the stone on which rested the fabled golden statue of Victory. Originally installed by Augustus, it was disposed of in the 4th century by a fiercely divided Senate, whose Christian members convinced the emperor that it was improper to have a pagan statue in such a revered place.

   Outside, head down the Curia stairs to the:

3. **Lapis Niger,** the remains of black marble that reputedly mark the tomb of Romulus. They bask today under a corrugated roof. Go downstairs for a look at the excavated tomb. There's a stone here with the oldest Latin inscription in existence, which unfortunately is nearly unintelligible. All that can be safely assumed is that it genuinely dates from the Rome of the kings, an era that ended in a revolution in 510 B.C.

   Across from the Curia, the:

4. **Arch of Septimius Severus** was dedicated at the dawn of the troubled 3rd century to the last decent emperor who was to govern Rome for some time. The friezes on the arch depict victories over the Arabs and the Parthians by the cold but upright Severus and his two dissolute sons, Geta and Caracalla. Severus died on a campaign to subdue the unruly natives of Scotland, and at the end of the first decade of the 3rd century Rome unhappily fell into the hands of young Caracalla, chiefly remembered today for the baths he had built.

   Walk around to the back of the Severus arch, face it, and look to your right. There amid the rubble can be discerned a semicircular stair that led to the famous:

5. **Rostra,** the podium from which dictators and caesars addressed the throngs in the Forum below. One can just imagine the emperor, shining in his white toga surrounded by imperial guards and distinguished senators, gesticulating grandly like one of the statues on a Roman roofline. The motley crowd falls silent, the elegant

senators pause and listen, the merchants put down their measures, even the harlots and unruly soldiers lower their voices in such an august presence. Later emperors didn't have much cause to use the Rostra, making their policies known through edict and assassination instead.

Now, facing the colonnade of the Temple of Saturn, once the public treasury, and going to the left, you'll come to the ruins of the:

6. **Basilica Julia,** again little more than a foundation. The basilica gets its name from Julius Caesar, who dedicated the first structure in 46 B.C. Like many buildings in the Forum, the basilica was burned and rebuilt several times, and the last structure dated from those shaky days after the Gothic invasion of A.D. 410. Throughout its history it was used for hearing civil court cases, which were conducted in the pandemonium of the crowded Forum, open to anyone who happened to pass by. The building was also reputed to be particularly hot in the summer, and it was under these sweaty and unpromising circumstances that Roman justice, the standard of the world for a millennium, was meted out.

Walking back down the ruined stairs of the Basilica Julia and into the broad area whose far side is bounded by the Curia, you'll see the:

7. **Column of Phocas.** Probably lifted from an early structure in the near vicinity, this was the last monument to be erected in the Roman Forum, and it commemorates the Byzantine emperor Phoca's generous donation of the Pantheon to the pope of Rome, who almost immediately transformed it into a church.

Now make your way down the middle of the Forum nearly back to the ramp from which you entered. The pile of brick with the semicircular indentation that stands in the middle of things was the:

8. **Temple of Julius Caesar,** erected some time after the dictator was deified. Judging from the reconstruction, it was quite an elegant building. As you stand facing the ruins, with the entrance to the Forum on your left, you'll see on your right three columns that originally belonged to the:

9. **Temple of the Castors.** This temple perpetuated the legend of Castor and Pollux, who appeared out of thin air in the Roman Forum and were observed watering their horses at the fountain of Juturna (still visible today), just as a major battle against the Etruscans turned in favor of Rome. Castor and Pollux, the heavenly twins—and the symbol of the astrological sign Gemini—seem a favorite of Rome.

The next major monument is the circular:

10. **Temple of Vesta,** wherein dwelt the sacred flame of Rome, and the Atrium of the Vestal Virgins. A vestal virgin was usually a girl of good family who signed a contract for 30 years. During that time she lived in the ruin you're standing in right now. Of course, back then it was an unimaginably rich marble building with two floors. There were only six vestal virgins at a time during the imperial period, and even though they had the option of going back out into the world at the end of their 30 years, few did. The cult of Vesta came to an end in 394, when a Christian Rome secularized all its pagan temples. A man standing on this site before then would have been put to death immediately.

Stand in the atrium with your back to the Palatine and look beyond those fragmented statues of former vestals to the:

11. **Temple of Antoninus and Faustina.** It's the building with the freestanding colonnade just to the right of the ramp where you first entered the Forum. Actually, just the colonnade dates from imperial times; the building behind is a much later church dedicated to San Lorenzo.

After you inspect the beautifully proportioned Antoninus and Faustina temple, head up via Sacra away from the entrance ramp toward the Arch of Titus. Pretty soon, on your left you'll see the twin bronze doors of the:

Walking Tour—Rome of the Caesars

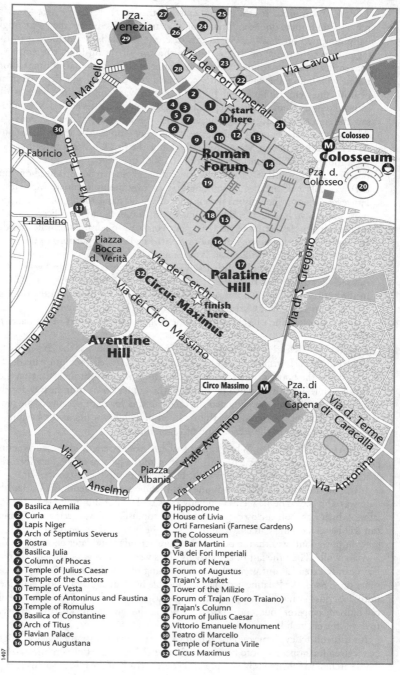

1. Basilica Aemilia
2. Curia
3. Lapis Niger
4. Arch of Septimius Severus
5. Rostra
6. Basilica Julia
7. Column of Phocas
8. Temple of Julius Caesar
9. Temple of the Castors
10. Temple of Vesta
11. Temple of Antoninus and Faustina
12. Temple of Romulus
13. Basilica of Constantine
14. Arch of Titus
15. Flavian Palace
16. Domus Augustana
17. Hippodrome
18. House of Livia
19. Orti Farnesiani (Farnese Gardens)
20. The Colosseum
    Bar Martini
21. Via dei Fori Imperiali
22. Forum of Nerva
23. Forum of Augustus
24. Trajan's Market
25. Tower of the Milizie
26. Forum of Trajan (Foro Traiano)
27. Trajan's Column
28. Forum of Julius Caesar
29. Vittorio Emanuele Monument
30. Teatro di Marcello
31. Temple of Fortuna Virile
32. Circus Maximus

171

12. **Temple of Romulus.** It's the doors themselves that are really of note here—they're the original Roman doors, and swing on the same massive hinges they were originally mounted on in A.D. 306. In this case, the temple is not dedicated to the legendary cofounder of Rome, but to the son of its builder, the emperor Maxentius, who gave Romulus his name in a fit of antiquarian patriotism. Unfortunately for both father and son, they competed with a general who deprived them of both their empire and their lives. That man was Constantine, who, while camped outside Rome during preparations for one of his battles against Maxentius, saw the sign of the Cross in the heavens with the insignia *in hoc signo vinces* (in this sign shall you conquer). Raising the standard of Christianity above his legions, he defeated the emperor Maxentius and became the first Christian emperor.

　　At the time of Constantine's victory (A.D. 306) the great:

13. **Basilica of Constantine** (marked by those three gaping arches up ahead on your left) was only half finished, having been started by the unfortunate Maxentius. However, Constantine finished the job and affixed his name to this, the largest and most impressive building in the Forum. To our taste, the more delicate, Greek-influenced temples are more attractive, but you have to admire the scale and the engineering skill that erected this monument. The fact that portions of the original coffered ceiling are still intact is amazing. The basilica once held a statue of Constantine so large that his little toe was as wide as an average man's waist. You can see a few fragments from this colossus—the remnants were found in 1490—in the courtyard of the Conservatory Museum on the Capitoline Hill. As far as Roman emperors went, Christian or otherwise, ego knew no bounds.

　　From Constantine's basilica, follow the Roman paving stones of via Sacra to the:

14. **Arch of Titus,** clearly visible on a low hill just ahead. Titus was the emperor who sacked the great Jewish temple in Jerusalem, and the bas-relief sculpture inside the arch shows the booty of the Jews being carried in triumph through the streets of Rome, while Titus is crowned by Victory, who comes down from heaven for the occasion. You'll notice in particular the candelabrum, for centuries one of the most famous pieces of the treasure of Rome. In all probability it lies at the bottom of the Busento River in the secret tomb of Alaric the Goth.

THE PALATINE HILL When you've gathered your strength in the shimmering hot sun, head up the Clivus Palatinus, the road to the palaces of the Palatine Hill. With your back to the Arch of Titus, it's the road going up the hill to the left.

　　It was on the Palatine Hill that Rome first became a city. Legend tells us that the date was 753 B.C. The new city originally consisted of nothing more than the Palatine, which was soon enclosed by a surprisingly sophisticated wall, remains of which can still be seen on the Circus Maximus side of the hill. As time went on and Rome grew in power and wealth, the boundaries were extended and later enclosed by the Servian Wall. When the last of the ancient kings was overthrown (510 B.C.), Rome had already extended onto several of the adjoining hills and valleys. As Republican times progressed, the Palatine became a fashionable residential district. So it remained until Tiberius—who, like his predecessor, Augustus, was a bit too modest to really call himself "emperor" out loud—began the first of the monumental palaces that were to cover the entire hill.

　　It's difficult today to make sense out of the Palatine. The first-time viewer might be forgiven for suspecting it to be an entirely artificial structure built on brick arches. Those arches, which are visible on practically every flank of the hill, are actually supports that once held imperial structures. Having run out of building sites, the emperors, in their fever, simply enlarged the hill by building new sides on it.

The road goes on only a short way, through a small sort of valley filled with lush, untrimmed greenery. After about 5 minutes (for slow walkers), you'll see the ruins of a monumental stairway just to the right of the road. The Clivus Palatinus turns sharply to the left here, skirting the monastery of San Bonaventura, but we'll detour to the right and take a look at the remains of the:

15. Flavian Palace. As you walk off the road and into the ruins, you'll be able to discern that there were once three rooms here. But it's impossible for anyone but an archeologist to comprehend quite how splendid these rooms were. The entire Flavian Palace was decorated in the most lavish of colored marbles and gold. Much of the decoration survived as late as the 18th century, when the greedy duke of Parma removed most of what was left. The room closest to the Clivus Palatinus was called the Lararium, and held statues of the divinities that protected the imperial family. The middle room was the grandest of the three. It was the imperial throne room, where sat the ruler of the world, the emperor of Rome. The far room was a basilica, and as such was used for miscellaneous court functions, among them audiences with the emperor. This part of the palace was used entirely for ceremonial functions. Adjoining these three rooms are the remains of a spectacularly luxurious peristyle. You'll recognize it by the hexagonal remains of a fountain in the middle. Try, if you can, to imagine this fountain surrounded by marble arcades, planted with mazes, and equipped with mica-covered walls. On the opposite side of the peristyle from the throne room are several other great reception and entertainment rooms. The banquet hall was here, and beyond it, looking over the Circus Maximus, are a few ruins of former libraries. Although practically nothing remains except the foundations, every now and again you'll catch sight of a fragment of colored marble floor, in a subtle, sophisticated pattern.

The imperial family lived in the:

16. Domus Augustana, the remains of which lie toward the Circus Maximus, and slightly to the left of the Flavian Palace. The new building that stands here—it looks old to us, but in Rome it qualifies as a new building—is a museum (usually closed). It stands in the absolute center of the Domus Augustana. In the field adjacent to the stadium well into the present century stood the Villa Mills, a gingerbread Gothic villa of the 19th century. It was quite a famous place, owned by a rich Englishman who came to Rome from the West Indies. Villa Mills was the scene of many fashionable entertainments in Victorian times, and it's interesting to note, as H. V. Morton pointed out, that the last dinner parties that took place on the Palatine Hill were given by an Englishman. At any of several points along this south-facing belvedere of the Palatine Hill, you'll be able to see the faraway oval-shaped walls of the Circus Maximus. Continue with your exploration of the Palatine Hill by heading across the field parallel to the Clivus Palatinus and you'll come to the north end of the:

17. Hippodrome, or Stadium of Domitian. The field was apparently occupied by parts of the Domus Augustana, which in turn adjoined the enormous stadium. The stadium itself is worth examination, although sometimes it's difficult to get down inside it. The perfectly proportioned area was usually used for private games, staged for the amusement of the imperial family. As you look down the stadium from the north end, you can see, on the left side, the semicircular remains of a structure identified as Domitian's private box. Some archeologists claim that the "stadium" was actually an elaborate sunken garden.

The aqueduct that comes up the wooded hill used to supply water for the Baths of Septimius Severus, whose difficult-to-understand ruins lie in monumental poles of arched brick at the far end of the stadium.

Returning to the Flavian Palace, leave the peristyle on the opposite side from the Domus Augustana and follow the signs to the:

18. **House of Livia.** They take you down a dusty path to your left. Although legend says that this was the house of Augustus's consorts, it actually was Augustus's all along. The place is notable for some rather well-preserved murals showing mythological scenes. But more interesting is the aspect of the house itself—it's smallish, and there never were any great baths or impressive marble arcades. Augustus, even though he was the first emperor, lived simply compared to his successors. His wife, Livia, was a fiercely ambitious aristocrat who divorced her own husband to marry the emperor (the ex-husband was made to attend the wedding, incidentally) and, according to some historians, was the true power behind Roman policy between the death of Julius Caesar and the ascension of Tiberius. She even controlled Tiberius, her son, since she had engineered his rise to power through a long string of intrigues and poisonings.

After you've examined the frescoes in Livia's parlor, head up the steps that lead to the top of the embankment to the north. Once on top, you'll be in the:

19. **Farnese Gardens (Orti Farnesiani),** the 16th-century horticultural fantasy of a Farnese cardinal. They're constructed on top of the Palace of Tiberius, which, you'll remember, was the first of the great imperial palaces to be built on this hill. It's impossible to see any of it, but the gardens are cool and nicely laid out. You might stroll up to the promontory above the Forum and admire the view of the ancient temples and the Capitoline heights off to the left.

You've now seen the best of the Forum and the Palatine. To leave the archeological area, you should now continue walking eastward along the winding road that meanders steeply down from the Palatine Hill to via di San Gregorio. When you reach the roaring traffic of that busy thoroughfare, walk north toward the bulk of what some Romans consider the most potent symbol of their city, the:

20. **Colosseum.** Its crumbling, oval-shaped bulk is the greatest monument of ancient Rome, and visitors are impressed with its size, its majesty, and its ability to conjure up the often cruel entertainments that were devised inside for the pleasure of the Roman masses. Either visit it now or return later.

☕ **TAKE A BREAK** On a hill in back of the landmark Colosseum is the **Bar Martini,** at piazza del Colosseo 3A (☎ **06/700-4431**). Have your coffee or cool drink outside at one of the tables and absorb one of the world's greatest architectural views—the Colosseum itself. A pasta dish costs 8,000 lire ($5.10); a sandwich, 3,000 to 5,000 lire ($1.90 to $3.20). Meal service is daily from 8:30am to midnight.

THE IMPERIAL FORUMS With your back to the Colosseum, walk westward along the:

21. **Via dei Fori Imperiali,** keeping to the right side of the street. It was Mussolini who issued the controversial orders to cut through centuries of debris and junky buildings to carve out this boulevard, thereby linking the Colosseum to the grand 19th-century monuments of piazza Venezia. Excavations under his Fascist regime began at once, and many archeological treasures were revealed. Today the vistas over the ruins of Rome's Imperial Forum, visible from the northern side of the boulevard, makes for one of the most fascinating walks in Rome.

Begun by Julius Caesar as an answer to the overcrowding of Rome's older forums during the days of the Empire, the Imperial forums were at the time of their construction flashier, bolder, and more impressive than the buildings in the Roman Forum we've just visited, and as such represented the unquestioned authority of the Roman emperors at the height of their absolute power. After the collapse of Rome and during the Dark Ages, they, like many other ancient monuments, were lost to history, buried beneath layers of debris until Mussolini, in an egomaniacal attempt to draw comparisons between his Fascist regime and the glory of ancient Rome, helped to restore the grandeur of Rome by reminding his compatriots of their glorious Imperial past.

Some of the rather confusing ruins you'll see from the boulevard include the shattered remnants of the colonnade that once surrounded the Temple of Venus and Roma. Next to it, you'll see the back wall of the Basilica of Constantine. Shortly, on the street's north side, you'll come to a large outdoor restaurant, where via Cavour joins the boulevard. Just beyond the small park across via Cavour are the remains of the:

22. Forum of Nerva, built by the emperor whose 2-year reign (A.D. 96–98) followed that of the paranoid Domitian. The Forum of Nerva is best observed from the railing that skirts it on via dei Fori Imperiali. You'll be struck by just how much the ground level has risen in 19 centuries. The only really recognizable remnant is a wall of the Temple of Minerva with two fine Corinthian columns. This forum was once flanked by that of Vespasian, which is now, however, completely gone. It's possible to enter the Forum of Nerva from the other side, but you can see it just as well from the railing.

The next forum you approach is the:

23. Forum of Augustus, built before the birth of Christ to commemorate the emperor's victory over the assassins Cassius and Brutus in the Battle of Philippi (42 B.C.). Fittingly, the temple that once dominated this forum—and whose remains can still be seen—was that of Mars Ultor, or Mars the Avenger. In the temple once stood a mammoth statue of Augustus, which has unfortunately completely vanished. Like the Forum of Nerva, you can enter the Forum of Augustus from the other side (cut across the wee footbridge).

Continuing along the railing, you'll see next the vast semicircle of:

24. Trajan's Market, via Quattro Novembre 95 (☎ 06/679-0048), whose teeming arcades stocked with merchandise from the far corners of the Roman world long ago collapsed, leaving only a few ubiquitous cats to watch after things. The shops once covered a multitude of levels, and you can still wander around many of them. In front of the perfectly proportioned semicircular facade—designed by Apollodorus of Damascus at the beginning of the 2nd century—are the remains of a great library, and fragments of delicately colored marble floors still shine in the sunlight between stretches of rubble and tall grass.

While the view from the railing is of interest, Trajan's Market is worth the descent below street level. To get there, follow the service road you're on until you reach the monumental Trajan's Column on your left, where you turn right and go up the steep flight of stairs that leads to via Nazionale. At the top of the stairs, about half a block farther on the right, you'll see the entrance to the market. It's open Tuesday to Saturday from 9am to 7pm and on Sunday from 9am to 1pm. Admission is 3,750 lire ($2.40) for adults, 2,500 lire ($1.60) for students, and free for children 17 and under and for seniors 60 and older.

Before you head down through the labyrinthine passageways, you might like to climb the:

25. Tower of the Milizie, a 12th-century structure that was part of the medieval headquarters of the Knights of Rhodes. The view from the top (if it's open) is well worth the climb. From the tower, you can wander where you will through the ruins of the market, admiring the sophistication of the layout and the sad beauty of the bits of decoration that still remain. When you've examined the brick and travertine corridors, head out in front of the semicircle to the site of the former library; from here, scan the retaining wall that supports the modern road and look for the entrance to the tunnel that leads to the:

26. **Forum of Trajan (Foro Traiano),** entered on via Quattro Novembre near the steps of via Magnanapoli. Once through the tunnel, you'll emerge in the newest and most beautiful of the Imperial Forums, designed by the same man who laid out the adjoining market. There are many statue fragments and pedestals that bear still-legible inscriptions, but more interesting is the great Basilica Ulpia, whose gray marble columns rise roofless into the sky. You wouldn't know it to judge from what's left, but the Forum of Trajan was once regarded as one of the architectural wonders of the world. Constructed between 107 and 113, it was designed by the Greek architect Apollodorus of Damascus.

Beyond the Basilica Ulpia is:

27. **Trajan's Column,** which is in magnificent condition, with intricate bas-relief sculpture depicting Trajan's victorious campaign (although from your vantage point you'll only be able to see the earliest stages). The emperor's ashes were kept in a golden urn at the base of the column. If you're fortunate, someone on duty at the stairs next to the column will let you out there. Otherwise, you'll have to walk back the way you came.

The next stop is the:

28. **Forum of Julius Caesar,** the first of the Imperial Forums. It lies on the opposite side of via dei Fori Imperial, the last set of sunken ruins before the Victor Emmanuel Monument. While it's possible to go right down into the ruins, you can see everything just as well from the railing. This was the site of the Roman stock exchange, as well as of the Temple of Venus, a few of whose restored columns stand cinematically in the middle of the excavations.

ON TO THE CIRCUS MAXIMUS   From here, retrace your last steps until you're in front of the white Brescian marble monument around the corner on piazza Venezia, where the:

29. **Vittorio Emanuele Monument** dominates the piazza. The most flamboyant landmark in Italy, it was constructed in the late 1800s to honor the first king of Italy. It has been compared to everything from a frosty wedding cake to a Victorian typewriter. An eternal flame burns at the Tomb of the Unknown Soldier. The interior of the monument has been closed to the public for many years.

Keep close to the monument and walk to your left, in the opposite direction from via dei Fori Imperiali. You might like to pause at the fountain that flanks one of the monument's great white walls and splash some icy water on your face. Stay on the same side of the street, and just keep walking around the monument. You'll be on via del Teatro Marcello, which takes you past the twin lions that guard the sloping stairs and on along the base of the Capitoline Hill.

Keep walking along this boulevard until you come to the:

30. **Teatro di Marcello,** on your right. You'll recognize the two rows of gaping arches, which are said to be the models for the Colosseum. Julius Caesar is credited with starting the construction of this theater, but it was finished many years after his death (in 11 B.C.) by Augustus, who dedicated it to his favorite nephew, Marcellus. A small corner of the 2,000-year-old arcade has been restored to what presumably was the original condition. Here, as everywhere, there are numerous cats stalking around the broken marble.

The bowl of the theater and the stage were adapted many centuries ago as the foundation for the Renaissance palace of the Orsini family. The other ruins belong to old temples. To the right is the Porticus of Octavia, dating from the 2nd century B.C. Note how later cultures used part of the Roman structure without destroying its original character. There's another good example of this on the other side of the theater. There you'll see a church with a wall that completely incorporates part of an ancient colonnade.

Keep walking along via del Teatro Marcello away from piazza Venezia for 2 more long blocks, until you come to piazza della Bocca della Verità. The first item to notice in the attractive piazza is the rectangular:

31. Temple of Fortuna Virile. You'll see it on the right, a little off the road. Built a century before the birth of Christ, it's still in magnificent condition. Behind it is another temple, dedicated to Vesta. Like the one in the forum, it's round, symbolic of the prehistoric huts where continuity of the hearthfire was a matter of survival.

About a block to the south you'll pass the facade of the Church of Santa Maria in Cosmedin, set on piazza della Bocca della Verità. Even more noteworthy, a short walk to the east, is the:

32. Circus Maximus, whose elongated oval proportions and ruined tiers of benches might remind visitors of the setting for *Ben-Hur.* Today a formless ruin, the victim of countless raids upon its stonework by medieval and Renaissance builders, the remains of the once-great arena lie directly behind the church. At one time 250,000 Romans could assemble on the marble seats, while the emperor observed the games from his box high on the Palatine Hill.

The circus lies in a valley formed by the Palatine Hill on the left and the Aventine Hill on the right. Next to the Colosseum, it was the most impressive structure in ancient Rome, located certainly in one of the most exclusive neighborhoods. Emperors lived on the Palatine, while the great palaces of patricians sprawled across the Aventine, which is still a rather nice neighborhood. For centuries the pomp and ceremony of imperial chariot races filled this valley with the cheers of thousands.

When the dark days of the 5th and 6th centuries fell on the city, the Circus Maximus seemed a symbol of the complete ruination of Rome. The last games were held in 549 on the orders of Totilla the Goth, who had seized Rome in 547 and established himself as emperor. He lived in the still-glittering ruins on the Palatine and apparently thought that the chariot races in the Circus Maximus would lend credence to his charade of empire. It must have been a pretty miserable show, since the decimated population numbered something like 500 when Totilla recaptured the city. The Romans of these times were caught between Belisarius, the imperial general from Constantinople, and Totilla the Goth, both of whom fought bloodily for control of Rome. After the travesty of 549, the Circus Maximus was never used again, and the demand for building materials reduced it, like so much of Rome, to a great dusty field.

To return to other parts of town, head for the bus stop adjacent to the Santa Maria in Cosmedin Church, or walk the length of the Circus Maximus to its far end and pick up the Metro to Termini or anywhere else in the city that appeals to you.

4 Especially for Kids

Rome has lots of other amusements for children when they tire of ancient monuments, although they're usually fond of wandering around the **Colosseum** and the **Roman Forum** (see "Other Top Attractions," above). Many children also enjoy the climb to the top of **St. Peter's Basilica.**

The **Fun Fair (Luna Park),** along via delle Tre Fontane (☎ **06/592-5933**), at E.U.R. (a suburban area south of the city; take the Métro B line to E.U.R. stop), is one of the largest in Europe. It's known for its "big wheel" at the entrance, and there are merry-go-rounds, miniature railways, and shooting galleries, among other attractions. Admission is free, but you pay for each ride. Open Monday and Wednesday through Friday from 4pm to midnight, Saturday from 4pm to 1am, and Sunday 10am to 1pm and 3pm to midnight. It's closed Tuesday

The **Teatro delle Marionette degli Accettella,** performing at the Teatro Mongiovino, via Giovanni Genocchi 15 (☎ **06/513-9405**), has performances for children on Saturday and Sunday (except in July and August) at 4:30pm. Tickets are 12,000 lire ($7.20) per person, adult or child.

The **Puppet Theater** on Pincio Square in the Villa Borghese gardens above piazza del Popolo has "Punch and Judy" performances nearly every day. While there, you might also like to take your children through the park to enjoy the fountain displays and the lake, and the many wide spaces in which they can play. You can rent boats at the **Giardino del Lago,** or stop by the **zoo** at viale del Giardino Zoologico 20 (☎ **06/321-6564**). The zoo is open in summer, Monday to Friday from 8:30am to 5pm and on Saturday and Sunday from 8:30am to 6pm; in winter, Monday to Friday from 8:30am to 4pm and on Saturday and Sunday from 8:30am to 5pm. Admission is 10,000 lire ($6.40) for adults, free for small children. Take bus no. 19 or 30.

At 4pm every day there's a military band and a parade as the guard changes at the **Quirinale Palace,** piazza del Quirinale, the residence of the president of Italy.

5 Organized Tours

Because of the sheer volume of artistic riches, some visitors prefer to begin their stay in Rome with an organized tour. While few things can really be covered in any depth on these "overview tours," they're sometimes useful for getting the feel and geography of a complicated city. One of the leading tour operators (among the zillions of possibilities) is **American Express,** piazza di Spagna 38 (☎ **06/67641**), open Monday to Friday from 9am to 5:30pm and on Saturday from 9am to 12:30pm. Its tours are the most closely geared to American visitors, and all tours are conducted strictly in English.

One of the most popular tours is a 4-hour orientation tour of Rome and the Vatican, which departs most mornings at 9:30am and costs 60,000 lire ($38.40) per person. Another 4-hour tour, which focuses on the Rome of antiquity (including visits to the Colosseum, the Roman Forum, the ruins of the Imperial Palace, and the Church of San Pietro in Vincoli), costs 50,000 lire ($32). Of the many excursions offered to sites outside the city limits of Rome, the most popular is a 5-hour bus tour to Tivoli, where visits are conducted to the Villa d'Este and its spectacular gardens and the ruins of the Villa Adriana, all for the price of 63,000 lire ($40.30) per person.

If your time in Italy is rigidly limited, you might opt for 1-day excursions to points farther afield on tours that are marketed (but not conducted) by American Express. Although rushed and far too short to expose the many-layered majesty of these destinations, a series of 1-day tours is offered to Pompeii, Naples, and Sorrento for a price of 132,000 lire ($84.50) per person; to Florence for 162,000 lire ($103.70); and to Capri for 184,000 lire ($117.75). Lunch is included on each of these full-day trips, but to participate you'll need a lot of stamina, as each tour departs from Rome around 7am and returns sometime after 9 or 10pm to your hotel.

Another option is **Scala Reale,** via Varese 46 (☎ **06/4470-0898,** or 800/732-2863 ext. 4052 in the U.S.). Scala Reale is a cultural association founded by the American architect Tom Rankin. He offers small-group tours and excursions focusing on the architectural and artistic significance of Rome. Tours include visits to monuments, museums, and piazzas as well as to neighborhood trattorie. In addition, custom-designed tours are available. Tours begin at 30,000 lire ($19.20). Children 11 and under are admitted free to walking tours.

6 Soccer Matches & Other Outdoor Activities

BIKING   The traffic is murderous and the pollution might make your head spin, but there are quiet times (early mornings and Sunday) when a spin beside the Tiber or through the Borghese Gardens might prove very appealing. It's highly advisable to wear a helmet when bicycling, even if the local Vespa riders don't.

Bike-rental concession stands are found in the following areas: piazza del Popolo, largo San Silvestro, largo Argentina, piazza di Spagna, and viale della Pineto in the Villa Borghese.

BOWLING   One of the city's largest bowling complexes, whose hordes of participants provide a spectacle almost more interesting than the game itself, **Bowling Roma** is at viale Regina Margherita 181 (☎ **06/855-1184**), off via Nomentana.

GOLF   Rome boasts several golf courses that will usually welcome members of other golf clubs. Each, of course, will be under the greatest pressure on Saturday and Sunday, so as a nonmember try to schedule arrival for a weekday.

One of the capital's best courses, with a clubhouse in a villa built during 1600s and fairways designed by Robert Trent Jones, is the **Country Club Castelgandolfo,** via Santo Spirito 13, Castelgandolfo (☎ **06/931-2301**). An older, more entrenched, and more prestigious course is the **Circolo del Golf Roma,** via Appia Nuova 716/A (☎ **06/780-3407**). About 8¹/₂ miles from the center of town lies the **Olgiata Golf Club,** largo Olgiata 15, off via Cassia (☎ **06/3088-9141**).

HORSEBACK RIDING   The most convenient of Rome's several riding clubs is the **Associazione Sportiva Villa Borghese,** via del Galoppatoio 23 (☎ **06/320-0487**). Other stables are in the **Circolo Ippico Olgiata,** largo Olgiata 15 (☎ **06/3088-8792**), near Cassia, and the **Società Ippica Romana,** via del Monti della Farnesina 18 (☎ **06/324-0591**). Tack and equipment are English style.

JOGGING   Jogging provides a moving view of the city's monuments—but beware the city's heat and be alert to speeding traffic. Several possible itineraries include the park of the **Villa Borghese,** where the series of roads and pathways, some of them beside statuary, provide a verdant oasis in the city's congestion. The best places to enter the park are at piazza del Popolo or at the top of via Vittorio Veneto. The **Cavalieri Hilton,** via Cadlolo 101, Monte Mario (☎ **06/35091**), offers a jogging path (measuring a third of a mile) through the trees and flowering shrubs of its landscaping. The grounds that surround the **Villa Pamphilj** contain three running tracks, although they might either be locked or in use by local sports teams. A final possibility, not recommended for jogging after dark, is the rounded premises of the Circus Maximus (about half a mile).

SOCCER   Soccer is one of the three or four all-consuming passions of thousands of Italians, richly intertwined with their image of the country. Rome boasts two intensely competitive teams, Lazio and Roma, which tend to play either against each other or against visiting teams from other parts of the country every Sunday afternoon. Matches are held at the **Stadio Olimpico,** Foro Italico dei Gladiatori

(☎ **06/36851**), originally built by Mussolini as a nationalistic (Fascist) statement. Thousands of tickets are sold during the 2 or 3 hours before each game. The players usually take a break during June, July, and August, beginning the season with something approaching pandemonium in September.

SWIMMING   One of the busiest all-year pools is at the **Roman Sport Center,** via del Galoppatoio 33 (☎ **06/320-1667**), which lies adjacent to the parking lot on the grounds of the Villa Borghese. Open to the public, it contains two large swimming pools, squash courts, a gym, and saunas. In another part of town, the **Piscina della Rose,** viale America (☎ **06/592-6717**), is an Olympic-size pool open to the public (and crowded with teenagers and *bambini*) between June and September. More sedate, set in lushly landscaped gardens, and open to nonresidents, is the pool on the resort-inspired premises of the **Cavalieri Hilton,** via Cadlolo 101 (☎ **06/35091**).

TENNIS   The best tennis courts are at private clubs, many of which are in a handful of suburbs. Players are highly conscious of proper tennis attire, so be prepared to don your most sparkling whites and your best manners. One of the city's best-known clubs is the **Tennis Club Parioli,** largo Umberto de Morpurgo 2, via Salaria (☎ **06/8620-0882**), open daily from 8am to noon only.

7 Shopping

Rome offers temptations of every kind, but this section will try to focus on the urge to shop that sometimes overcomes even the most stalwart of visitors. You might find hidden oases of charm and value in unpublicized streets and districts, but what follows is a listing and description of certain streets known throughout Italy for their shops. The monthly rent on these famous streets is very high, and those costs are passed on to the consumer. Nonetheless, a stroll down some of these streets presents a cross section of the most desirable wares in Italy.

Cramped urban spaces and a well-defined sense of taste have encouraged most Italian stores to elevate the boutique philosophy to its highest levels. The theory is that if you like what you see in a shop window, you'll find it duplicated, in spirit and style, inside. Lack of space, and definition of a merchandising program, usually restrict an establishment's merchandise to one particular style, degree of formality, or mood.

Caveat: We won't pretend that Rome is Italy's finest shopping center (Florence and Venice are), or that its shops are unusually inexpensive—many of them aren't. But even on the most elegant of Rome's thoroughfares, there are values mixed in with the costly boutiques.

Shopping hours are generally Monday from 3:30 to 7:30pm and Tuesday to Saturday from 9:30 or 10am to 1pm and from 3:30 to 7 or 7:30pm. Some shops are open on Monday mornings, however, and some shops don't close for the afternoon break.

THE SHOPPING SCENE

Via Borgognona   Beginning near piazza di Spagna, both the rents and the merchandise are chic and very, very expensive. Like its neighbor, via Condotti, it's a mecca for wealthy, well-dressed women from around the world. Its storefronts have retained their baroque or neoclassical facades.

Via Condotti   Easy to find because it begins at the base of the Spanish Steps, this is the poshest and the most visible upper-bracket shopping street in Rome, and the best example in Europe of avidly elegant consumerism. Even the recent incursion of some less elegant stores hasn't diminished the allure of this street as a consumer's playground for the rich and the very, very rich.

Via del Corso   Not attempting the stratospheric image (or prices) of via Condotti or via Borgognona, the styles here are aimed at younger consumers. There are, however, some gems scattered amid the shops selling jeans and sporting equipment. The most interesting shops are the section nearest the fashionable cafes of piazza del Popolo.

Via Francesco Crispi   Most shoppers reach this street by following via Sistina (see below) 1 long block from the top of the Spanish Steps. Near the intersection of these streets are several shops well suited for unusual and less expensive gifts.

Via Frattina   Running parallel to via Condotti, it begins, like its more famous sibling, at piazza di Spagna. Part of its length is closed to traffic. Here, the concentration of shops is denser, although some aficionados claim that its image—and its prices—are slightly less chic and slightly lower than its counterparts on via Condotti. It's usually thronged with shoppers who appreciate the lack of motor traffic.

Via Nazionale   The layout here recalls 19th-century grandeur and ostentatious beauty, but the traffic is horrendous; crossing via Nazionale requires a good sense of timing and a strong understanding of Italian driving patterns. It begins at piazza della Repubblica and runs down almost to the 19th-century monuments of piazza Venezia. There's an abundance of leather stores—more reasonable in price than those in many other parts of Rome—and a welcome handful of stylish boutiques.

Via Sistina   Beginning at the top of the Spanish Steps, via Sistina runs to piazza Barberini. The shops are small, stylish, and based on the personalities of their owners. The pedestrian traffic is less dense than on other major streets.

Via Vittorio Veneto & via Barberini   Evocative of *La Dolce Vita* fame, via Veneto is filled these days with expensive hotels and cafes and an array of relatively expensive stores selling shoes, gloves, and leather goods.

SHOPPING A TO Z
ANTIQUES

Some visitors to Italy consider the trove of antiques for sale the country's greatest treasure. The value of almost any antique has risen to alarming levels as increasingly wealthy Europeans outbid one another in frenzies of acquisitive lust. You might remember that any antiques dealer who risks the high rents of central Rome is acutely aware of the value of almost everything ever made, and will probably recognize anything of value long before his or her clients. Beware of fakes, remember to insure anything you have shipped home, and for larger purchases—anything more than 525,000 lire ($336) at any one store—keep your paperwork in order to obtain your tax refund. (See "Tips on Shopping" in Chapter 3.)

One street you shouldn't miss is **via dei Coronari.** Buried in a colorful section of the Campus Martius, via dei Coronari is an antiquer's dream, literally lined with magnificent vases, urns, chandeliers, breakfronts, chaises, refectory tables, and candelabra. To find the entrance to the street, turn left out of the north end of piazza Navona, pass the excavated ruins of Domitian's Stadium, and the street will be just ahead of you. There are more than 40 antiques stores in the next 4 blocks. Bring your pocket calculator with you, and keep in mind that stores are frequently closed between 1 and 4pm.

Galleria Coronari. Via dei Coronari 59. ☎ **06/686-9917.**

The Galleria Coronari is a desirable shop that might be used as a starting point. Many of its antiques are nostalgia-laden bric-a-brac small enough to fit into a suitcase, including jewelry, dolls, paintings, and elaborately ornate picture frames from the 19th century. Also represented is furniture from the 18th, 19th, and early 20th centuries, and such oddities as a completely furnished dollhouse, accurate down to the miniature champagne bottles in the miniature pantry.

ART

Alberto di Castro. Via del Babuino 71. ☎ **06/361752.**

Aldo di Castro is one of the largest dealers of antique prints and engravings in Rome. You'll find rack after rack of depictions of everything from the Colosseum to the Pantheon, each evocative of the best architecture in the Mediterranean world, priced between $25 and $1,000 depending on the age and rarity of the engraving.

Galleria d'Arte Schneider. Rampa Mignanelli 10. ☎ **06/678-4019.**

Near the top of the Spanish Steps, this is one of the most enduring art galleries in Rome. Established in 1953 by an American-born professor of languages and art connoisseur, it specializes in lesser-known sculpture and paintings by Italians or foreign residents of Rome. Among the artists promoted early in their careers by this gallery are Dimitre Hadzi, George d'Almeida, Paolo Buggiani, and Mirko Balsedella. The frequently changing inventories here are relatively affordable, ranging in price from 1,000,000 to 10,000,000 lire ($640 to $6,400). The building that contains the gallery, incidentally, was designed in the 19th century by a Danish sculptor with the intention that it serve as a refuge for artists ever after. The day-to-day operations of the gallery are conducted by Mr. Schneider's charming wife, Dolores. The gallery keeps no set hours, and some days it doesn't open at all—so call first. When the gallery is open, it's only in the late afternoon. Always closed in August.

Giovanni B. Panatta Fine Art Shop. Via Francesco Crispi 117. ☎ **06/679-5948.**

You'll find excellent color and black-and-white prints covering a variety of subjects from 18th-century Roman street scenes to astrological charts in this fine art shop up the hill toward the Borghese Gardens. There's also a good selection of reproductions of medieval and Renaissance art that are attractive and reasonably priced.

BOOKSTORES

Economy Book and Video Center. Via Torino 136. ☎ **06/474-6877.**

Catering to the English-speaking communities of Rome, this bookstore sells only English-language books (both new and used, paperback and hardcover), greeting cards, and videos. Staffed by British, Australian, or American workers, it lies about a block from the piazza della Repubblica Metro station, and bus lines no. 64 and 70. In summer, it's open Monday to Friday from 9am to 8pm and on Saturday from 9am to 2pm; in winter, on Monday from 3 to 8pm and Tuesday to Saturday from 9am to 8pm.

The Lion Bookshop. Via del Babuino 181. ☎ **06/322-5837.**

The Lion Bookshop is the oldest English-language bookshop in town, specializing in literature, both American and English. It also sells children's books and photographic volumes on both Rome and Italy. A vast choice of English-language videos is for sale or rent. The store is closed in August.

Rizzoli. Largo Chigi 15. ☎ **06/679-6641.**

Rizzoli's collection of Italian-language books is one of the largest in Rome, but if your native language is French, English, German, or Spanish, the interminable shelves of this very large bookstore have a section to amuse, enlighten, and entertain you. Open Monday to Saturday from 9am to 2pm and 2:30 to 7:30pm and on Sunday from 10:30am to 1:30pm and 4 to 8pm.

DEPARTMENT STORES

La Rinascente. In piazza Colonna, at via del Corso 189. ☎ **06/679-7691.**

This upscale department store offers clothing, hosiery, perfume, cosmetics, housewares, and furniture. It also has its own line of clothing (Ellerre) for men, women, and children. This is the largest of the Italian department-store chains. Open Monday from 2 to 7:30pm and Tuesday to Saturday from 9:30am to 7:30pm.

Standa. Corso Francia 124. ☎ **06/333-8719.**

Rome's six Standa branches could not be considered stylish by any stretch of the imagination, but some visitors find it enlightening to wander—just once—through the racks of department-store staples to see what an average Italian household might accumulate. Other branches are at corso Trieste 200, via Trionfale, via Cola di Rienzo 173, viale Regina Margherita, and viale Trastevere 60.

DISCOUNT SHOPPING

Certain stores that can't move their merchandise at any price often consign these goods to discounters. In Italy, the original labels are usually still inside the garment, and you'll find some very chic ones strewn in with mounds of other garments. Why wouldn't they sell at higher prices in more glamorous shops? Some garments are the wrong size, some have gone out of fashion, and some are a stylistic mistake that the original designer wishes had never been produced.

Discount System. Via del Viminale 35. ☎ **06/482-3917.**

Discount System sells men's and women's wear by many of the big names (Armani, Valentino, Nino Cerruti, Fendi, and Krizia). Even if an item isn't from a famous designer, it often came from a factory that produces some of the best quality of Italian fashion. However, don't give up hope: If you find something you like, know that it will be priced at around 50% of its original price tag, and it just might be a cut-rate gem well worth your effort.

FASHION

For Men

Angelo. Via Bissolati 34. ☎ **06/474-1796.**

This exclusive store is a custom tailor for discerning men. It has been featured in such publications as *Esquire* and *Gentleman's Quarterly.* Angelo employs the best cutters and craftspeople, and his taste in style and design is impeccable. Custom shirts, dinner jackets, even casual wear, can be made on short notice. If you don't have time to wait, Angelo will ship anywhere in the world. The outlet also sells ready-made items such as cardigans, cashmere pullovers, evening shirts, suits, and overcoats.

Emporio Armani. Via del Babuino 119. ☎ **06/322151.**

This store stocks relatively inexpensive men's wear crafted by the couturier who has dressed perhaps more stage and screen stars than any other designer in Italy. The designer's more expensive line—sold at sometimes staggering prices that are nonetheless sometimes 30% less than what you'd pay in the United States—lies a short walk away, at Giorgio Armani, via Condotti 77 (☎ 06/699-1460).

Valentino. Via Condotti 13. ☎ **06/678-3656.**

Behind all the chrome mirrors at via Condotti is this swank emporium where you can become the most fashionable man in town—if you can afford the high prices. Valentino's women's haute couture is sold around the corner, in an even bigger showroom at via Bocca di Leone 15 (☎ 06/679-5862). Open Monday from 3 to 7pm and Tuesday to Saturday from 10am to 7pm.

For Women

Benetton. Via Condotti 18. ☎ **06/679-7982.**

Prices at this branch of the worldwide sportswear distributor are about the same as those at less glamorous addresses. Famous for woolen sweaters, tennis wear, blazers, and the kind of outfits you'd want to wear on a private yacht, this company has suffered (like every other clothier) from inexpensive Asian copies of its designs. The original, however, is still the greatest.

Gianfranco Ferre. Via Borgognona 42B. ☎ **06/679-0050.**

Here you can find the women's line of this famous designer whose clothes have been called "adventurous."

Givenchy. Via Borgognona 21. ☎ **06/678-4058.**

This is the Roman headquarters of one of the great designer names of France, Givenchy, a company known since World War I for its couture. Here the company emphasizes ready-to-wear garments for stylish women with warm Italian weather in mind.

Max Mara. Via Frattina 28, at largo Goldoni. ☎ **06/679-3638.**

Max Mara is one of the best outlets in Rome for women's clothing if you like to look chic. The fabrics are appealing and the alterations are free. Open Monday from 3:30 to 7:30pm and Tuesday to Saturday from 10am to 2pm and 3:30 to 7:30pm.

Renato Balestra. Via Sistina 67. ☎ **06/679-5424.**

Rapidly approaching the stratospheric upper levels of Italian fashion is Renato Balestra, whose women's clothing attains standards of lighthearted elegance at its best when designed and worn in Italy. This branch carries a complete line of the latest Balestra ready-to-wear designs for women. The company's administrative headquarters and the center of its couture department are nearby at via Ludovisi 35 (☎ 06/482-1723), although advance appointments are recommended there. It's advisable to stop into the via Sistina branch for an idea of the designer's style before launching yourself into a dialogue with Balestra's couture department, if only to save costs.

For Children

Baby House. Via Cola di Rienzo 117. ☎ **06/321-4291.**

Baby House offers what might be the most label-conscious collection of children's and young people's clothing in Italy. With an inventory of clothes suitable for children and adolescents to age 15, it sells clothing by Valentino, Bussardi, and Laura Biagiotti, whose threads are usually reserved for adult, rather than juvenile, playtime.

Benetton. Via Condotti 19. ☎ **06/679-7982.**

Despite its elegant address (see above), Benetton isn't as expensive as you might expect. This store is an outlet for children's clothes (from infants to age 12) of the famous sportswear manufacturer. You can find rugby shirts, corduroys and jeans, and accessories in a wide selection of colors and styles. Open Monday from 3:30 to 7:30pm and Tuesday to Saturday from 10am to 7:30pm.

The College. Via Vittoria 52. ☎ **06/678-4073.**

The College has everything you'll need to make adorable children more adorable—and less-adorable children at least presentable. Part of the inventory of this place is reserved for adult men and women, but the majority is intended for the infant and early adolescent offspring of the store's older clients. This establishment maintains another branch at via Condotti 47 (☎ 06/678-4036), which sells only clothes for women.

Sportswear
Oliver. Via del Babuino 61. ☎ **06/3600-1906.**

Specializing exclusively in sportswear for men and for women, Oliver carries the least expensive line of clothing offered by the otherwise chillingly expensive designer Valentino. The clothing is easy to wear and casually stylish, with warm-weather climates in mind.

FOOD
Castroni. Via Cola di Rienzo 196. ☎ **06/687-4383.**

Castroni carries an amazing array of unusual foodstuffs from throughout the Mediterranean. If you want herbs from Apulia, pepperoncino oil, cheese from the Valle d'Aosta, or that strange brand of balsamic vinegar whose name you can never remember, Castroni will have it. Large, old-fashioned, and filled to the rafters with the abundance of agrarian Italy, it also carries certain foods that are exotic in Italy but commonplace in North America, such as taco shells, corn curls, and peanut butter.

GIFTS
A. Grispigni. Via Francesco Crispi 59 (at via Sistina). ☎ **06/679-0290.**

A. Grispigni has a large assortment of leather-covered boxes, women's purses, compacts, desk sets, and cigarette cases. Many items, like Venetian wallets and Florentine boxes, are inlaid with gold. Open Monday from 3:30 to 7pm and Tuesday to Saturday from 9:30am to 1pm and 3:30 to 7pm.

Anatriello del Regalo. Via Frattina 123. ☎ **06/678-9601.**

This store is known for stocking an inventory of new and antique silver, some of it among the most unusual in Italy. All the new items are made by Italian silversmiths, in designs ranging from the whimsical to the severely formal and dignified. Also on display are antique pieces of silver from England, Germany, and Switzerland.

JEWELRY
Bulgari. Via Condotti 10. ☎ **06/679-3876.**

Bulgari has been Rome's most prestigious jeweler for more than a century. The shop window, on a conspicuously affluent stretch of via Condotti, is a visual attraction in its own right. Bulgari designs combine classical Greek aesthetics with Italian taste, changing in style with the years, yet clinging to tradition as well. Prices range from "affordable" to "the sky's the limit."

E. Fiore. Via Ludovisi 31 (near via Veneto). ☎ **06/481-9296.**

At E. Fiore you can choose a jewel and have it set to your specifications. Or you can make your selection from a rich assortment of charms, bracelets, necklaces, rings, brooches, corals, pearls, and cameos. Also featured are elegant watches, silverware, and goldware. Fiore also does expert repair work on jewelry and watches. Open Monday to Saturday from 9am to 7pm (closed in August).

Federico Buccellati. Via Condotti 31. ☎ **06/679-0329.**

Federico Buccellati, one of the best gold- and silversmiths in Italy, sells neo-Renaissance creations that will change your thinking about the way gold and silver are designed. Here you'll discover the tradition and beauty of handmade jewelry and holloware with designs that recall those of the Renaissance goldmaster Benvenuto Cellini. Closed Monday.

LEATHER

Italian leather is among the very best in the world; it can attain butter-soft textures more pliable than cloth. You'll find hundreds of leather stores in Rome, many of them excellent.

Cesare Diomedi Leather Goods. Via Vittorio Emanuele Orlando 96–97. ☎ **06/488-4822.**

You'll find one of the most outstanding collections of leather goods in Rome here, in front of the Grand Hotel. And the leather isn't all. There are many other distinctive gift items—small gold cigarette cases, jeweled umbrellas—that make this a good stopping-off point for that last important item. Upstairs is a wide assortment of elegant leather luggage and accessories. Open Monday to Saturday from 9am to 1pm and 3:30 to 7:30pm.

Fendi. Via Borgognona 36A–39. ☎ **06/679-7641.**

Fendi is mainly known for its avant-garde leather goods, but it also has furs, stylish purses, ready-to-wear clothing, and a new men's line of clothing and accessories. Fendi's also carries gift items, home furnishings, and sports accessories. Closed Saturday afternoon from July to September.

Gucci. Via Condotti 8. ☎ **06/679-0405.**

Gucci, of course, is a legend, an established firm since 1900. Its merchandise consists of high-class leather goods, such as suitcases, handbags, wallets, shoes, and desk accessories. It also has departments of elegant men's and women's wear, including beautiful shirts, blouses, and dresses, as well as ties and neck scarves of numerous designs. *La bella figura* is alive and well at Gucci, and prices have never been higher.

Pappagallo. Via Francesco Crispi 115. ☎ **06/678-3011.**

At Pappagallo ("Parrot"), a suede-and-leather factory, the staff make all manner of leather goods, including bags, wallets, and suede coats. The quality is fine, too, and the prices are reasonable.

LINGERIE

Brighenti. Via Frattina 7–8. ☎ **06/679-1484.**

At Brighenti, amid several famous neighbors on via Frattina, you might run across a "seductive fantasy." It's strictly *lingerie di lusso,* or perhaps better phrased, *haute corseterie.* Closed in August.

Tomassini di Luisa Romagnoli. Via Sistina 119. ☎ **06/488-1909.**

Tomassini di Luisa Romagnoli offers delicately beautiful lingerie and negligees, all original designs of Luisa Romagnoli. Most of the merchandise sold here is of shimmery Italian silk; other items, to a lesser degree, are of fluffy cotton or frothy nylon. Highly revealing garments are sold either ready-to-wear or are custom-made.

LIQUORS

Ai Monasteri. Piazza delle Cinque Lune 76. ☎ **06/6880-2783.**

Offbeat Shopping

Galleria 2 RC, via dei Delfini 16 (☎ **06/6992-2414**), has the best print studio in Rome, a collection of beautifully reproduced works from famous artists. It's almost as good as owning the real thing.

Avignonese, via Margutta 16 (☎ **06/361-4004**), can be counted on to come up with unusual and tasteful objects for the home. Each object, from lamps to terra-cotta boxes, is unique.

Alinari, via d'Albert 16A (☎ **06/679-2923**), takes its name from the famed Florentine photographer of the 19th century. Original prints of Alinari are almost as prized as paintings in national galleries, and you can pick up your own here.

Olivi, via del Babuino 136 (☎ **06/3600-0064**), is called "The Old Curiosity Shop of Rome." Professor Olivi is a whiz when it comes to knowing Roman history and collecting a treasure trove of old prints.

Fava, via del Babuino 180 (☎ **06/361-0807**), recaptures the era when Neapolitans sold 17th- and 18th-century pictures of the eruptions of Vesuvius, once highly sought by collectors. Many of these "volcanic paintings" of yesterday—so eagerly sought by Britishers in particular—can still cause a conflagration today. Really unusual art from the attics of yesterday.

Livio di Simone, via San Giacomo 23 (☎ **06/3600-1732**). Unusual suitcases (in many shapes and sizes) in which hand-painted canvas has been sewn into the bags are sold here. Every one is chic and lovely.

Battistoni, via Condotti 61A (☎ **06/678-6241**), is known for the finest men's shirts in the world. After having said that, as Marlene Dietrich once noted, you don't need to sell the shop anymore. In addition, it also hawks a men's cologne, called Marte (Mars), for the "man who likes to conquer."

Siragusa, via delle Carrozze 64 (☎ **06/679-7085**), is more like a museum than a shop, specializing in unusual jewelry based on ancient carved stones or archeological pieces. Handmade chains, for example, often hold coins and beads discovered in Asia Minor that date from the 3rd to the 4th century B.C.

Ai Monasteri is a treasure trove of liquors (including liqueurs and wines), honey, and herbal teas made in monasteries and convents all over Italy. You can buy excellent chocolates and other candies here as well. You make your selections in a quiet atmosphere reminiscent of a monastery, just two blocks from Bernini's Fountain of the Four Rivers in piazza Navona. The shop will ship some items home for you.

MARKETS

At the sprawling **Porta Portese** open-air flea market of Rome held every Sunday morning, every peddler from Trastevere and the surrounding Castelli Romani sets up a temporary shop. The vendors are likely to sell merchandise ranging from second-hand paintings of Madonnas and termite-eaten Il Duce wooden medallions, to pseudo-Etruscan hairpins, bushels of rosaries, 1947 TV sets, and books printed in 1835. Serious shoppers can often ferret out a good buy. If you've ever been impressed with the bargaining power of the Spaniard, you haven't seen anything till you've viewed an Italian.

Go to this Trastevere flea market, near the end of viale Trastevere (bus no. 75 to Porta Portese, then a short walk to via Portuense), to catch the workday Roman in an unguarded moment. By 10:30am the market is full of people. Some of the vendors arrive there as early as midnight to get their choice space. As at any street market, beware of pickpockets. Open on Sunday from 7am to 1pm.

MOSAICS

Savelli. Via Paolo VI 27. ☎ **06/6830-7017.**

Mosaics are an art form as old as the Roman Empire itself. Many of the objects displayed in this company's gallery were inspired by ancient originals discovered in thousands of excavations throughout the Italian peninsula, including those at Pompeii and Ostia. Others, especially the floral designs, depend on the whim and creativity of the artist. Objects include tabletops, boxes, and vases. The cheapest mosaic objects begin at around $125, and are unsigned products crafted by students at an art school partially funded by the Vatican. Objects made in the Savelli workshops that are signed by the individual artists (and that tend to be larger and more elaborate) range from $500 to as much as $25,000. The outlet also contains a collection of small souvenir items such as keychains and carved statues. Open Monday to Saturday from 9am to 6:30pm and on Sunday from 9:30am to 1:30pm.

RELIGIOUS OBJECTS

Anna Maria Gaudenzi. Piazza delle Minerva 69A. ☎ **06/679-0431.**

Set in a neighborhood loaded with purveyors of religious art and icons, this shop claims to be the oldest of its type in Rome. If you collect depictions of the Madonna, paintings of the saints, exotic rosaries, chalices, small statues, or medals, you can feel secure in knowing that thousands of pilgrims have spent their money here before you. Whether you view its merchandise as a devotional aid or as bizarre kitsch, this shop has it all. Closed August 10–20.

SHOES

Dominici. Via del Corso 14. ☎ **06/361-0591.**

Dominici, located behind an understated facade a few steps from piazza del Popolo, shelters an amusing and lighthearted collection of men's and women's shoes in a pleasing variety of vivid colors. The style is aggressively young at heart and the quality is good.

Ferragamo. Via Condotti 73–74. ☎ **06/679-8402.**

Ferragamo sells elegant and fabled footwear, plus women's clothing and accessories, and ties, in an atmosphere full of Italian style. The name became famous in America when such silent screen vamps as Pola Negri and Greta Garbo began appearing in Ferragamo shoes. The shop is open Monday to Saturday from 10am to 7pm. There are always many customers waiting to enter the shop. Management allows them in in small groups. Figure on a 30-minute wait outside.

Fragiacomo. Via Condotti 35. ☎ **06/679-8780.**

Fragiacomo sells shoes for men and women in a champagne-colored showroom with gilt-painted chairs and big display cases.

Lily of Florence. Via Lombardia 38 (off via Vittorio Veneto). ☎ **06/474-0262.**

This famous Florentine shoemaker now has a shop in Rome, with the same merchandise that made the outlet so well known in the Tuscan capital. The colors come in a wide range, the designs are stylish, and the leather texture is of good quality. Lily sells shoes for both men and women, and features American sizes. Open Monday to Saturday from 9:30am to 7:30pm.

WINE

Buccone. Via Ripetta (near piazza del Popolo). ☎ **06/361-2154.**

At this historic wine shop the selection of wines and gastronomic specialties is among the finest in Rome. Open Monday to Saturday from 9am to 1:30pm and 4 to 8:30pm.

Trimani. Via Goito 20. ☎ **06/446-9661.**

Trimani, established in 1821, sells wines and spirits from Italy, among other offerings. Purchases can be shipped to your home. Trimani collaborates with the Italian wine magazine *Gambero Rosso,* organizing some lectures about wine where devotees can improve their knowledge and educate their tastebuds. Open Monday to Saturday from 8:30am to 1:30pm and 3:30 to 8pm and on Sunday from 10am to 1:30pm and 4 to 7:30pm.

8 Rome After Dark

When the sun goes down across the city, palaces, ruins, fountains, and monuments are bathed in a theatrical white light. There are actually few evening occupations quite as pleasurable as a stroll past the solemn pillars of old temples or the cascading torrents of Renaissance fountains glowing under the blue-black sky. Of the **fountains,** the Naiads (piazza della Repubblica), the Tortoises (piazza Mattei), and, of course, the Trevi are particularly beautiful at night. The **Capitoline Hill** is magnificently lit after dark, with its measured Renaissance facades glowing like jewel boxes. Behind the Senatorial Palace is a fine view of the illuminated **Roman Forum.** If you're staying across the Tiber, **piazza San Pietro** (in front of St. Peter's Basilica) is impressive at night without tour buses and crowds. And a combination of illuminated architecture, Renaissance fountains, and, frequently, sidewalk shows and art expositions enliven **piazza Navona.** If you're ambitious and have a good sense of direction, try exploring the streets to the west of piazza Navona, which look like a stage set when they're lit at night.

There are no inexpensive nightclubs in Rome. *Another important warning:* During the peak of the summer visiting days, usually in August, all nightclub proprietors seem to lock their doors and head for the seashore, where they operate alternate clubs. Some of them close at different times each year, so it's hard to keep up-to-date. Always have your hotel check to see if a club is operating before you make a trek to it. Many of the legitimate nightclubs, besides being expensive, are highlighted by hookers plying their trade. Younger people fare better than some more sedate folk, as the discos open and close with freewheeling abandon.

But remember that for many Romans, a night on the town means dining late at a trattoria. The local denizens like to drink wine and talk after their meal, even when the waiters are putting chairs on top of empty tables.

Even if you don't speak Italian, you can generally follow the listings of special events and evening entertainment featured in *La Repubblica,* one of the leading Italian newspapers. *TrovaRoma,* a special weekly entertainment supplement—good for the coming week—is published in this paper on Thursday.

THE PERFORMING ARTS
CLASSICAL MUSIC

Academy of St. Cecilia. Via della Conciliazione 4. ☎ **06/678-0742.** Tickets 25,000–80,000 lire ($16–$51.20).

Concerts given by the orchestra of the Academy of St. Cecilia usually take place at piazza Villa Giulia, site of the Etruscan Museum, from the end of June to the end of July (take bus no. 30); in winter they're held in the Academy's concert hall on via della Conciliazione. Depending on circumstances, the organization sometimes selects other addresses in Rome for its concerts, including a handful of historic churches, when available. Performance nights are either Saturday, Sunday, Monday, or Tuesday.

Teatro Olimpico. Piazza Gentile da Fabriano. ☎ **06/323-4890.** Tickets 20,000–80,000 lire ($12.80–$51.20).

Large and well publicized, this echoing stage hosts a widely divergent collection of singers, both classical and pop, who perform according to a schedule that sometimes changes at the last minute. Occasionally the space is devoted to chamber orchestras or visiting foreign orchestras.

OPERA

Teatro dell'Opera. Piazza Beniamino Gigli 1. ☎ **06/481601.** Tickets 20,000–260,000 lire ($12.80–$166.40).

If you're in the capital for the opera season, usually from the end of December until June, you may want to attend the historic Rome Opera House, located off via Nazionale. Nothing is presented here in August. In the summer, the venue switches to piazza Siena.

BALLET & DANCE

Performances of the **Rome Opera Ballet** are given at the Teatro dell'Opera (see above). The regular repertoire of classical ballet is supplemented by performances of internationally acclaimed guest artists, and Rome is on the major agenda for troupes from around the world. Watch for announcements in the weekly entertainment guides to Rome about venues outside the Teatro dell'Opera, including Teatro Olimpico or even open-air ballet performances. Both modern (such as the Alvin Ailey dancers) and classical dance troupes appear frequently in Rome.

A MEAL & A SONG

Da Ciceruacchio. On piazza dei Mercanti, at via del Porto 1, in Trastevere. ☎ **06/580-6046.**

This restaurant was once a sunken jail—the ancient vine-covered walls date from the days of the Roman Empire. Folkloric groups appear throughout the evening, especially singers of Neapolitan songs, accompanied by guitars and harmonicas—a rich repertoire of old-time favorites, some with bawdy lyrics. There are charcoal-broiled steaks and chops along with lots of local wine, and bean soup is a specialty. The grilled mushrooms are another good opening, as is the spaghetti with clams. You can dine here Tuesday to Sunday from 8pm to midnight for 35,000 to 60,000 lire ($22.40 to $38.40).

Da Meo Patacca. Piazza dei Mercanti 30, in Trastevere. ☎ **06/5833-1086.**

Da Meo Patacca would have pleased Barnum and Bailey. On a gaslit piazza from the Middle Ages, it serves bountiful self-styled "Roman country" meals to flocks of tourists. The atmosphere is one of extravaganza—primitive, colorful, theatrical in a carnival sense—good fun if you're in the mood. Downstairs is a vast cellar with strolling musicians and singers. Utilizing a tavern theme, the restaurant is decked out with wagon wheels, along with garlands of pepper and garlic. And many offerings are as adventurous as the decor—wild boar, wild hare, and quail. But there are also corn on the cob, pork and beans, thick-cut sirloins, and chicken on a spit. Come here for general fun and entertainment—not refined cuisine. Expect to spend 60,000 lire ($38.40) and up for a meal here. In summer, you can dine at outdoor tables. It's open daily from 8 to 11:30pm.

Fantasie di Trastevere. Via di Santa Dorotea 6, in Trastevere. ☎ **06/588-1671.**

Roman rusticity is combined with theatrical flair at Fantasie di Trastevere, the people's theater where the famous actor Petrolini made his debut. Dressed in regional garb of Italian provinces, the waiters serve with drama. The cuisine isn't subtle, but it's bountiful. Such dishes as the classic saltimbocca (ham with veal) are preceded by tasty pasta, and everything is aided by Castelli Romani wines. Accompanying the main dishes is a big basket of warm, country-coarse herb bread (you'll tear off hunks). Expect to pay 75,000 to 85,000 lire ($48 to $54.40) for a full meal. If you visit for a drink, the first one will cost 35,000 lire ($22.40). Some two dozen folk singers and musicians in regional costumes perform, making it a festive affair. Meals begin daily at 8pm, with piano bar music from 8:30 to 9:30pm, followed by the show, lasting until 10:30pm.

THE CLUB & MUSIC SCENE
NIGHTCLUBS

Arciliuto. Piazza Monte Vecchio 5. ☎ **06/687-9419.** Cover (including the first drink) 35,000 lire ($22.40). Closed July 20–Sept 3.

Arciliuto is one of the most romantic candlelit spots in Rome. It was reputedly the former studio of Raphael. From 10pm to 2am Monday to Saturday guests enjoy a musical salon ambience, listening to both a guitarist and a flutist. The evening's presentation also includes live Neapolitan songs and new Italian madrigals, even current hits from Broadway or London's West End. The setting and atmosphere are intimate. Drinks run 10,000 lire ($6.40). This highly recommended establishment is hard to find, but it's within walking distance of piazza Navona.

La Cabala / The Blue Bar / Hostaria dell'Orso. Via dei Soldiati 25. ☎ **06/686-4221.** No cover, but a one-drink minimum of 15,000–35,000 lire ($9.60–$22.40) in the Blue Bar and La Cabala.

During the heyday of *la dolce vita,* these premises were the most talked-about evening venue of Rome, and although the spotlight has since shifted, many Romans continue to view the place with affection and nostalgia. The setting is a 14th-century palazzo, near piazza Navona, which began its life as a simple inn. Clients who used its dining and/or overnight facilities through the ages have included St. Francis of Assisi, Dante, Rabelais, Montaigne, and Goethe.

Today the establishment contains three separate areas. In the cellar, the **Blue Bar** is a moody but mellow enclave featuring cocktails and the music from two pianists and guitarists. On the street level, the formal **Hostaria dell'Orso** restaurant serves international cuisine. Main courses cost 25,000 to 50,000 lire ($16 to $32), and include spigolo in cartoccio con frutti di mar (sea bass cooked in a paper bag, garnished with shellfish) and spaghetti in cartoccio with lobster and risotto served with scampi and radiccio. One floor above street level is **La Cabala,** a disco that attracts a well-dressed, over-25 crowd who tend to know their way around. Some clients merge time in all three areas during a night on the town. You can visit only the disco or only the bar if you wish. The restaurant serves dinner only, Monday to Saturday from 7:30pm to midnight. The Blue Bar and La Cabala are open Monday to Saturday from 10:30pm to 3 or 4am, depending on business. All three floors are closed on Sunday. If you plan to dine here, reservations are recommended.

Club Picasso. Via Monte di Testaccio 63. ☎ **06/574-2975**. Cover: none Tues–Thurs, 15,000 lire ($9.60) Fri–Sat (including the first drink).

Everything about this place was inspired by the large, gregarious L.A.–style night-clubs, where rhythm and blues, rock 'n' roll, and funk blare out across a crowd that loves to dance, dance, dance. Don't expect only a crowdful of teeny-boppers, as clients here include 20-year-olds, 50-year-olds (who remember some of the music as original to their college years), and lots of high-energy people-watchers in between. A bouncer at the door maintains strict provisions against anyone who looks like troublemaking is part of his or her entertainment. Beer begins at 10,000 lire ($6.40). Open Tuesday to Saturday from 10pm to 4am.

The Gossip Café. Via Romagnosi 11A. ☎ **06/361-1348**. Cover: Mon–Thurs none, but there's a 15,000-lira ($9.60) one-drink minimum; Fri–Sat (including the first drink) 25,000 lire ($16) for men and 15,000 lire ($9.60) for women.

The Gossip Café, formerly Divina (the owners are the same; the look updated), is a chic rendezvous—a relaxing piano bar and a raging disco. The tables are small and clustered around an expanded dance floor. You can still find a romantic evening, but you can also find a trendy spot to dance the night away. It's open Tuesday to Saturday from 11pm to 4 or 5am. *Note:* It's important to call for a reservation, as some nights are by invitation only, when you can't get in unless you're a "friend of the club" (frequent patron).

Folkstudio. Via Frangipane 42. ☎ **06/487-1063**. Tickets 10,000–20,000 lire ($6.40–$12.80), plus a one-time membership fee of 5,000 lire ($3.20).

Very little about this place has changed since it was founded in 1962. It prides itself on a battered and well-used venue that resembles "an old underground cantina" from the earliest days of the hippie era. The sound system and lighting aren't very sophisticated, but the ambience is refreshing and can be fun, and the musical acts manage to draw out some likable performances of old-fashioned soul music, gospel, funk, and folk, as well as traditional music from such countries as Ireland. From time to time a musician might even break into a recital of poetry. Some kind of act is presented Tuesday to Sunday from 9:30 to 11pm. No drinks are served inside, as the place considers itself a concert hall rather than a nightclub, but several bars and cafes in the neighborhood sell bottles of beer and whisky in plastic cups to go, and no one at Folkstudio will object if you carry them in with you. The place is closed from early July until late September.

Yes, Brazil. Via San Francesco a Ripa 103. ☎ **06/581-6267**. No cover.

This is one of Rome's most animated and popular Latin American nightspots. Set in the dimly lit recesses of a 16th-century Trastevere building, it manages to incorporate the mobs of Italians and South Americans who dip and sway to dance steps that are usually some derivation of the samba. There's live music every night of the week, a point of honor at the club. It's open every night from 9:30pm to 2am. Beer ranges in price from 8,000 to 10,000 lire ($5.10 to $6.40); a whiskey and soda goes for 12,000 lire ($7.70).

JAZZ, SOUL & FUNK

Alexanderplatz. Via Ostia 9. ☎ **06/3974-2171**. No cover, but a 3-month membership costs 12,000 lire ($7.70).

At this leading club you can hear jazz (not rock) every night except Sunday from 9pm to 2am, with live music beginning at 10:15pm. A whiskey goes for 10,000 lire ($6.40). There's also a restaurant, with a good kitchen, that serves everything from gnocchi alla romana to Japanese cuisine. Full meals cost 35,000 to 40,000 lire ($22.40 to $25.60).

Big Mama. Vicolo San Francesco a Ripa 18. ☎ **06/581-2551.** Cover 20,000–30,000 lire ($12.80–$19.20) for big acts (free for minor shows), plus 20,000 lire ($12.80) for a one-time membership fee.

Big Mama is a hangout for jazz and blues musicians where you're likely to meet the up-and-coming jazz stars of tomorrow, and sometimes even the big names. The club is open Monday to Saturday from 9pm to 1:30am. Drinks range from 5,000 to 12,000 lire ($3.20 to $7.70). Closed July to September.

Fonclea. Via Crescenzio 82A. ☎ **06/689-6302.** Cover: none Sun–Thurs, 10,000 lire ($6.40) Sat.

Fonclea offers live music every night—Dixieland, rock, rhythm and blues. This is basically a cellar jazz establishment and crowded pub that attracts patrons from all walks of Roman life. The music starts at 9:15pm and usually lasts until 12:30am. The club is open nightly from 7pm to 2am (on Friday and Saturday it stays open until 3:30am). There's also a restaurant that features grilled meats, salads, and crêpes. A meal starts at 35,000 lire ($22.40), but if you want dinner it's best to reserve a table. Drinks run 5,000 to 12,000 lire ($3.20 to $7.70). Closed July and August.

Gilda. Via Mario dei Fiori 97. ☎ **06/678-4838.** Cover (including the first drink) 40,000 lire ($25.60).

Gilda is an adventurous combination of nightclub, disco, and restaurant known for its glamorous acts. In the past it has hosted Diana Ross and splashy, Paris-type revues. The artistic direction assures first-class shows, a well-run restaurant, and disco music played between the live musical acts. The restaurant and pizzeria open at 9:30pm and occasionally present shows. An international cuisine is featured, with meals costing from 35,000 lire ($22.40). The nightclub, opening at midnight, presents music of the 1960s as well as modern recordings. The club stays open until 4am. There's also an attractive piano bar on the premises called Swing, featuring Italian and Latin music.

Music Inn. Largo dei Fiorentini 3. ☎ **06/6880-2220.** Cover 15,000 lire ($9.60).

The Music Inn is considered among the leading jazz clubs of Rome. Some of the biggest names in jazz, both European and American, have performed here. Open Thursday to Sunday from 8pm to 2am. Closed July and August.

Notorious. Via San Nicola de Tolentino 22. ☎ **06/474-6888.** Cover (including the first drink) 40,000 lire ($25.60).

Notorious really isn't. It's one of the most popular discos of Rome, open Tuesday to Saturday from 11pm to 4am. The music is always recorded. Some of the most beautiful people of Rome show up in these crowded confines, often in their best disco finery. Show up late—it's more fashionable.

Saint Louis Music City. Via del Cardello 13A. ☎ **06/474-5076.** Cover 7,000 lire ($4.50), which includes club membership.

The Saint Louis Music City is another leading jazz venue with large, contemporary surroundings, but it doesn't necessarily attract the big names in jazz. What you get instead are young and sometimes very talented groups beginning their careers. Many celebrities patronize the place. Soul and funk are also performed on occasion. You can dine at a restaurant on the premises, where meals cost 35,000 lire ($22.40) and up. Drinks range from 8,000 to 12,000 lire ($5.10 to $7.70). Open Tuesday to Sunday from 9pm to 2am.

GAY CLUBS

L'Alibi. Via Monte Testaccio 44. ☎ **06/574-3448.** Cover 10,000 lire ($6.40) Thurs, 12,000 lire ($7.70) Wed and Fri–Sun. Bus: 20N or 30N from largo Argentina near the Piramide.

L'Alibi, in the Testaccio sector, away from the heart of Rome, is a year-round venue on many a gay man's agenda. The crowd, however, tends to be mixed, both Roman and international, straight and gay, male and female. One room is devoted to dancing. It's open Wednesday to Sunday from 11pm to 5am. Drinks run 10,000 lire ($6.40).

Angelo Azzuro. Via Cardinal Merry del Val 13. ☎ **06/580-0472.** Cover (including the first drink) 10,000 lire ($6.40).

Angelo Azzuro is a gay "hot spot" deep in the heart of Trastevere, open on Friday, Saturday, and Sunday from 11pm to 4am. There's no food or live music—men dance with men to recorded music, and women are also invited to patronize the club. Friday is for women only. Libations cost 10,000 lire ($6.40) each.

The Hangar. Via in Selci 69. ☎ **06/488-1397.** No cover.

Established in 1984 by a Louisiana-born expatriate, John, and his Italian partner, Gianni, this is the premier gay bar in Rome. It's set on one of Rome's oldest streets, adjacent to the Roman Forum, in the house on the site of the palace inhabited by Emperor Claudius's deranged wife, Messalina. (Her ghost is rumored to inhabit the premises.) Each of the establishment's two bars has its own independent sound system. Women are welcome any night except Monday, when the club features videos and entertainment for gay men. The busiest nights are Saturday, Sunday, and Monday, when as many as 500 people cram inside. Beer begins at 6,000 lire ($3.85); whisky, at 10,000 lire ($6.40). It's open Wednesday to Monday from 10:30pm to 2:30am. The Hangar is closed for 3 weeks in August.

Joli Coeur. Via Sirte 5. ☎ **06/8621-5827.** Cover (including the first drink) 10,000 lire ($6.40).

A fixture upon the city's lesbian nighttime scene, Joli Coeur attracts women from around Europe during its very limited hours—it's open only on Saturday and Sunday nights from 10:30pm to 2am. Saturday night is reserved for women only, although Sunday the crowd can be mixed. Information about Joli Coeur is available at the Hangar (see above) because of the difficulties in reaching Joli Coeur directly. Libations cost 10,000 lire ($6.40) and up.

THE BAR & CAFE SCENE

Unless you're dead set on making the Roman nightclub circuit, try what might be a far livelier and less expensive scene—sitting late at night on via Veneto or piazza del Popolo, all for the cost of an espresso.

ON VIA VENETO

Back in the 1950s—a decade that *Time* magazine gave to Rome, in the way it conceded the 1960s to London—via Vittorio Veneto rose in fame and influence as the choicest street in Rome, crowded with aspirant and actual movie stars, their directors, and a fast-rising group composed of card-carrying members of the so-called jet set. Today the *bella gente* (beautiful people), movie stars, and directors wouldn't be caught dead on via Veneto—even with night-owl sunglasses, and the street has moved into the mainstream of world tourism. It's about as "in" and undiscovered today as pretzels, but you may want to spend some time there.

Caffè de Paris. Via Vittorio Veneto 90. ☎ **06/488-5284.**

The Caffè de Paris rises and falls in popularity depending on the decade. In the 1950s it was a haven for the fashionable, and now it's a popular restaurant in summer when the tables spill right out onto the sidewalk and the passing crowd walks through the maze. A cup of coffee costs 6,000 lire ($3.85) if you sit outside but only 1,200 lire (75¢) if you stand at the bar. A whisky and soda costs 12,000 lire ($7.70). Open Thursday to Tuesday from 8am to 1am.

Harry's Bar. Via Vittorio Veneto 50. ☎ **06/484643.**

Harry's Bar is a perennial favorite. Every major Italian city (Florence and Venice, for example) seems to have one, and Rome is no exception, although the one here has no connection with the others. The haunt of the IBF—International Bar Flies—at the top of via Veneto is elegant, chic, and sophisticated. In summer, sidewalk tables are placed outside. For those who wish to dine outdoors, but want to avoid the scorching Roman sun, a new air-conditioned sidewalk cafe is open May to November. Meals oustside cost about double what you'd pay inside. In back is a small dining room, which serves some of the finest food in central Rome; meals go for 90,000 to 100,000 lire ($57.60 to $64). A whisky costs 9,000 to 12,000 lire ($5.75 to $7.70). The restaurant is open Monday to Saturday from 12:30 to 3pm and 7:30pm to 12:30am. The bar is open from 11:30am to 1:30am; closed Sunday and August 1–10.

PIAZZA DEL POPOLO

The piazza is haunted with memories. According to legend, the ashes of Nero were enshrined here, until 11th-century residents began complaining to the pope about his imperial ghost. The Egyptian obelisk seen here today dates from the 13th century B.C., removed from Heliopolis to Rome during the reign of Augustus (it originally stood at the Circus Maximus). The present piazza was designed in the early 19th century by Valadier, Napoléon's architect. Two almost-twin baroque churches stand on the square, overseeing the never-ending traffic.

Café Rosati. Piazza del Popolo 4–5. ☎ **06/322-5859.**

The Café Rosati, which has been around since 1923, attracts guys and dolls of all persuasions who drive up in Maseratis and Porsches. It's really a sidewalk cafe/ice-cream parlor/candy store/confectionery/ristorante that has been swept up in the fickle world of fashion. The later you go, the more interesting the action. Whisky at the table begins at 10,000 lire ($6.40). Open daily from 7:30am to 1am. The restaurant serves lunch only, daily from noon to 4pm.

Canova Café. Piazza del Popolo. ☎ **06/361-2231.**

Although management has filled the interior with boutiques that sell expensive gift items, including luggage and cigarette lighters, many Romans still consider this the place to be on piazza del Popolo. The Canova has a sidewalk terrace for pedestrian-watching, plus a snack bar, a restaurant, and a wine shop inside. In summer you'll have access to a courtyard whose walls are covered with ivy and where flowers grow in terra-cotta planters. Expect to spend 1,300 lire (85¢) for coffee at the stand-up bar, 5,300 lire ($3.40) at a table. A meal costs 18,000 lire ($11.50) and up. Food is served daily from noon to 3:30pm and 7 to 11pm, but the bar is open from 7am to midnight or 1am.

NEAR THE PANTHEON

Many visitors to the Eternal City now view piazza della Rotonda, located across from the Pantheon and reconstructed by the emperor Hadrian in the first part of the 2nd century A.D., as the "living room" of Rome. This is especially true on a summer night.

Caffè Sant'Eustachio. Piazza Sant'Eustachio 82. ☎ **06/686-1309.**

Strongly brewed coffee is one of the elixirs of Italy, and many Romans will walk many blocks for what they consider a superior brew. The Caffè Sant'Eustachio is one of Rome's most celebrated espresso shops, where the water supply is funneled into the city by an aqueduct built in 19 B.C. Rome's most experienced espresso judges claim that the water plays an important part in the coffee's flavor, although steam forced through ground Brazilian coffee roasted on the premises has an important effect as well. Stand-up coffee at this well-known place costs 1,400 lire (90¢); if you sit you'll pay 3,000 lire ($1.90). Purchase a ticket from the cashier for as many cups as you want, and leave a small tip—about 200 lire (15¢)—for the counterperson when you present your receipt. Open Tuesday to Friday and Sunday from 8:30am to 1am, and on Saturday from 8:30am to 1:30am.

Di Rienzo. Piazza della Rotonda 8–9. ☎ **06/686-9097.**

Di Rienzo, the most desirable cafe here, is open daily from 7am to either 1 or 2am. In fair weather you can sit at one of the sidewalk tables (if you can find one free). In cooler weather you can retreat inside, where the walls are inlaid with the type of marble found on the Pantheon's floor. You can order a coffee for 4,000 lire ($2.55) at a table or 1,200 lire (75¢) at the bar. Many types of pastas appear on the menu, as does risotto alla pescatora (fisherman's rice) and several meat courses. You can also order pizzas.

IN TRASTEVERE

Piazza del Popolo lured the chic and sophisticated from via Veneto, and now several cafés in the district of Trastevere, across the Tiber, threaten to attract the same from Popolo. Fans who saw Fellini's *Roma* know what **piazza Santa Maria in Trastevere** looks like at night. The square—filled with milling throngs in summer—is graced with an octagonal fountain and a church that dates from the 12th century. Children run and play on the piazza, and occasional spontaneous guitar fests break out when the weather's good.

Café-Bar di Marzio. Piazza Santa Maria in Trastevere 18B. ☎ **06/581-6095.**

This warmly inviting place, which is strictly a cafe (not a restaurant), has both indoor and outdoor tables at the edge of the square with the best view of its famous fountain. Whisky begins at 9,000 lire ($5.75), and a coffee goes for 3,000 lire ($1.90). Open Tuesday to Saturday from 7am to 2am.

ON THE CORSO

Café Alemagna. Via del Corso 181. ☎ **06/678-9135.**

The monumental Café Alemagna is usually filled with busy shoppers. You'll find just about every kind of dining facility a hurried resident of Rome could want, including a stand-up sandwich bar with dozens of selections from behind a glass case, a cafeteria, and a sit-down area with waiter service. The decor includes high coffered ceilings, baroque wall stencils, crystal chandeliers, and black stone floors. Pastries start at 1,700 lire ($1.10); coffee, at 1,300 to 1,600 lire (85¢ to $1). Open daily from 7am to 10pm.

NEAR THE SPANISH STEPS

Antico Caffè Greco. Via Condotti 86. ☎ **06/679-1700.**

Since 1760 the Antico Caffè Greco has been the poshest and most fashionable coffee bar in Rome—the gathering place of the literati. Previous sippers have included Stendhal, Goethe, even D'Annunzio. Keats would also sit here and write. Today, however, you're more likely to see dowagers on a shopping binge and American tourists, but there's plenty of atmosphere here. In the front is a wooden bar, and beyond that a series of small salons. You sit at marble-topped tables of Napoleonic design, against a backdrop of gold or red damask, romantic paintings, and antique mirrors. Waiters are attired in black tailcoats. A cup of cappuccino costs 8,000 lire ($5.10) if you're seated. The house specialty is paradisi, made with lemon and orange. The cafe is open Monday to Saturday from 8am to 9pm, but closed for 10 days in August.

Enoteca Fratelli Roffi Isabelli. Via della Croce 76B. ☎ **06/679-0896.**

The fermented fruits of the vine have played a prominent role in Roman life since the word *bacchanalian* was first invented (and that was very early indeed), and one of the best places to taste the wines of Italy is at the Enoteca Fratelli Roffi Isabelli. A stand-up drink in its darkly antique confines is the perfect ending to a visit to the nearby Spanish Steps. Set behind an unflashy facade in a chic shopping district, this is the city's best repository for Italian wines, brandies, and grappa. You can opt for a postage-stamp table in back, if you desire, or stay at the bar with its impressive display of wines that lie stacked on shelves in every available corner. Open daily from 11am to midnight. A glass of wine costs 4,000 to 12,000 lire ($2.55 to $7.70), depending on its quality. Grappa costs 6,000 lire ($3.85) and up.

NEAR PIAZZA COLONNA

Giolitti. Via Uffici del Vicario 40. ☎ **06/699-1243.**

For devotees of gelato (addictively tasty ice cream), Giolitti is one of the city's most popular nighttime gathering spots; in the evening it's thronged with strollers with a sweet tooth. To satisfy that craving, try a whipped cream–topped cup of Giolitti gelato. The ice cream costs 3,500 lire ($2.20) and up—8,000 lire ($5.10) if you sit at a table. Some of the sundaes look like Vesuvius about to erupt. Many people take gelato out to eat on the streets; others enjoy it in the post-Empire splendor of the salon inside. You can have your "coppa" Sunday and Tuesday to Friday from 7am to 2am and on Saturday from 7am to 3am. There are many excellent, smaller *gelaterie* throughout Rome, wherever you see the cool concoction advertised as *produzione propria* (homemade).

NEAR PIAZZA NAVONA

Bar della Pace. Via della Pace 3–5. ☎ **06/686-1216.**

The Bar della Pace, located near piazza Navona, has elegant neighbors, such as Santa Maria della Pace. The bar dates from the beginning of this century, with wood, marble, and mirrors forming its decor. Open Tuesday to Sunday from 11am to 2:30am. A whisky begins at 10,000 lire ($6.40).

Hemingway. Piazza delle Coppelle 10. ☎ **06/686-4490.**

Hemingway's discreet door is located off one of the most obscure piazzas in Rome. Inside, the owners have re-created a 19th-century decor beneath soaring vaulted ceilings that shimmer from the reflection of glass chandeliers. Evocations of a Liberty-style salon are strengthened by the sylvan murals and voluptuous portraits of reclining odalisques. Assorted painters, writers, and creative dilettantes occupy the clusters of overstuffed armchairs, listening to conversation or classical music. On Saturday and

Sunday after 5pm there are small musical concerts and shows. It's open during the winter, Monday and Wednesday to Saturday from 9pm to 2am; in summer, daily from 9pm to 2am. Drinks cost 10,000 lire ($6.40) and up.

IRISH PUBS

It's an indication of the diversity of their tastes that young Italians are drawn in large numbers to Irish-style pubs. The two most popular ones are:

Druid's Den. Via San Martino ai Monti 28. ☎ **06/488-0258.**

The popular Druid's Den is open daily from 5pm to 12:30am. Here, while enjoying a pint of beer at 7,000 lire ($4.50), you can listen to recorded Irish music and dream of Eire. A group of young Irishmen one night even did an Irish jig in front of delighted Roman spectators. Live music, Irish style, is usually presented on Wednesday. The "den" is near piazza Santa Maria Maggiore and the train station.

Fiddler's Elbow. Via dell'Olmata 43. ☎ **06/487-2110.**

The Fiddler's Elbow, near piazza Santa Maria Maggiore and the railway station, is reputedly the oldest pub in the capital. It's open daily from 4:30pm to 12:30am; a pint of Guinness is 7,000 lire ($4.50). Sometimes, however, the place is so packed you can't find room to drink it.

CINEMA

Pasquino Cinema. Vicolo del Piede 19 (just off piazza Santa Maria in Trastevere). ☎ **06/580-3622.** Bus: 56 or 60 from via Veneto or 170 from the Termini.

In the Trastevere neighborhood, across the Tiber, just off the corner of piazza Santa Maria in Trastevere, the little Pasquino draws a faithful coterie of English-speaking fans, including Italians and expatriates. The average film—usually of recent vintage or a classic—costs 9,000 lire ($5.75). There are usually four screenings daily between 4 and 11pm.

9 Side Trips from Rome

Most European capitals are ringed with a number of scenic attractions, and as far as sheer variety, Rome tops all of them. Just a few miles away you can go back to the dawn of Italian history and explore the dank tombs the Etruscans left as their legacy or drink the golden wine of the Alban hill towns (Castelli Romani).

You can wander around the ruins of Hadrian's Villa, the "queen of villas of the ancient world," or be lulled by the music of baroque fountains in the Villa d'Este. You can turn yourself bronze on the beaches of Ostia di Lido—or explore the ruins of Ostia Antica, the ancient seaport of Rome.

Unless you're rushed beyond reason, allow at least 3 days to take a look at the attractions in the environs. We've highlighted the best of the lot below:

TIVOLI

The town of Tivoli is 20 miles east of Rome on via Tiburtina—about an hour's drive with traffic. If you don't have a car, take Metro Line B to the end of the line, the Rebibbia station. After exiting the station, take an Acotral bus the rest of the way to Tivoli. Generally, buses depart about every 20 minutes during the day.

EXPLORING THE VILLAS

Tivoli, known as Tibur to the ancient Romans, was the playground of emperors. Today its reputation continues unabated: It's the most popular half-day jaunt from Rome.

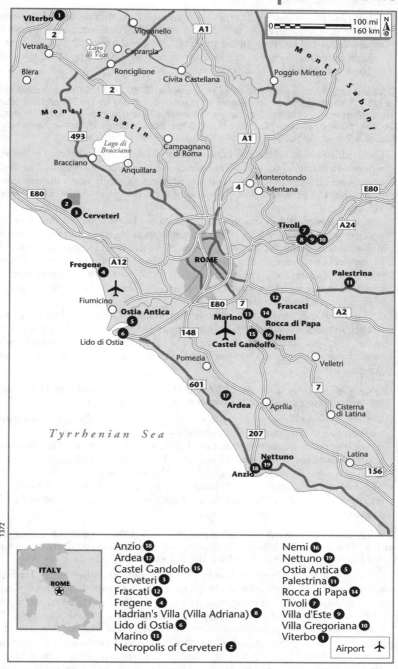

Side Trips from Rome

100 mi
160 km

Viterbo 1
Vetralla
Blera
Vignanello
Caprarola
Roncilione
Cívita Castellana
Poggio Mirteto
Lago di Vico
Monti Sabatin
Lago di Bracciano
Campagnano di Roma
Bracciano
Anquillara
Cerveteri 2 3
Fregene 4
Fiumicino
Ostia Antica 5
Lido di Ostia 6
Monterotondo
Mentana
Monti Sabini
Tivoli 7 8 9 10
Palestrina 11
Frascati 12
Marino 13 14
Rocca di Papa
Castel Gandolfo 15 16 Nemi
Pomezia
Velletri
Ardea 17
Aprília
Cisterna di Latina
Nettuno 18 19
Anzio
Latina

Tyrrhenian Sea

ITALY
ROME

Anzio 18
Ardea 17
Castel Gandolfo 15
Cerveteri 3
Frascati 12
Fregene 4
Hadrian's Villa (Villa Adriana) 8
Lido di Ostia 6
Marino 13
Necropolis of Cerveteri 2

Nemi 16
Nettuno 19
Ostia Antica 5
Palestrina 11
Rocca di Papa 14
Tivoli 7
Villa d'Este 9
Villa Gregoriana 10
Viterbo 1

Airport ✈

The ruins of Hadrian's Villa as well as the Villa d'Este, with their fabulous fountains and gardens, remain the two chief attractions of Tivoli—and both *are* major attractions, even if you must curtail your sightseeing in Rome.

Right inside the town, you can look at two villas before heading to the environs of Tivoli and the ruins of Hadrian's Villa.

✪ **Villa d'Este.** Piazza Trento, viale delle Centro Fontane. ☎ **0774/312070.** Admission 8,000 lire ($5.10) adults when the water jets are set at full power, 5,000 lire ($3.20) adults at other times; always free for children 17 and under and seniors 60 and over. Nov–Jan, daily 9am–4pm; Feb, daily 9am–5pm; Mar and Oct, daily 9am–5:30pm; Apr and Sept, daily 9am–6:30pm; May–Aug, daily 9am–6:45pm. The bus from Rome stops right near the entrance.

Like Hadrian centuries before, Cardinal Ippolito d'Este of Ferrara believed in heaven on earth. In the mid-16th century he ordered this villa built on a hillside. The dank Renaissance structure, with its second-rate paintings, is hardly worth the trek from Rome, but the gardens below—designed by Pirro Ligorio—dim the luster of Versailles.

Visitors descend the cypress-studded slope to the bottom, and on their way are rewarded with everything from lilies to gargoyles spouting water, torrential streams, and waterfalls. The loveliest fountain—on this there is some agreement—is the Fontana del'Ovato, designed by Ligorio. But nearby is the most spectacular achievement—the hydraulic organ fountain, dazzling visitors with its water jets in front of a baroque chapel, with four maidens who look tipsy. The work represents the genius of Frenchman Claude Veanard.

Don't miss the moss-covered, slime-green Fountain of Dragons, also by Ligorio, and the so-called Fountain of Glass by Bernini. The best walk is along the promenade, which has 100 spraying fountains. The garden, filled with rhododendron, is worth hours of exploration but you'll need frequent rest periods after those steep climbs.

Villa Gregoriana. Largo Sant'Angelo. ☎ **0774/334522.** Admission 2,500 lire ($1.60). Daily 9am to an hour before sunset. The bus from Rome stops near the entrance.

Whereas the Villa d'Este dazzles with artificial glamour, the Villa Gregoriana relies more on nature. The gardens were built by Pope Gregory XVI in the 19th century. At one point on the circuitous walk carved along a slope, visitors stand and look out onto the most panoramic waterfall (Aniene) at Tivoli. The trek to the bottom on the banks of the Anio is studded with grottoes and balconies that open onto the chasm. The only problem is that if you do make the full journey, you may need a helicopter to pull you up again (the climb back is fierce). From one of the *belvederes* there's an exciting view of the Temple of Vesta on the hill.

✪ **Hadrian's Villa (Villa Adriana).** Via di Villa Adriana. ☎ **0774/530203.** Admission 8,000 lire ($5.10) adults, free for children 17 and under and seniors 60 and over. Daily 9am–sunset (about 6:30pm in summer, 4pm Nov–Mar). Bus: 2 or 4 from Tivoli.

Of all the Roman emperors dedicated to *la dolce vita,* the globe-trotting Hadrian spent the last 3 years of his life in the grandest style. Less than 4 miles from Tivoli he built one of the greatest estates ever erected in the world, and filled acre after acre with some of the architectural wonders he'd seen on his many travels.

A preview of what he envisioned in store for himself, the emperor even created a representation of hell centuries before Dante got around to recording its horrors in a poem. A patron of the arts, a lover of beauty, and even something of an architect, Hadrian directed the staggering feat of constructing much more than a villa—a self-contained world for a vast royal entourage and the hundreds of servants and guards they required to protect them, feed them, bathe them, and satisfy their libidos.

Hadrian erected theaters, baths, temples, fountains, gardens, and canals bordered with statuary throughout his estate. He filled the palaces and temples with sculpture, some of which now rests in the museums of Rome. In later centuries, barbarians, popes, and cardinals, as well as anyone who needed a slab of marble, carted off much that made the villa so spectacular. But enough of the fragmented ruins remain for us to piece together the story.

For a glimpse of what the villa used to be, see the plastic reconstruction at the entrance. Then, following the arrows around, look in particular for the Marine Theater (ruins of the round structure with Ionic pillars); the Great Baths, with some intact mosaics; and the Canopus, with a group of caryatids whose images are reflected in the pond, as well as a statue of Mars. For a closer look at some of the items excavated, you can visit the museum on the premises and a museum and visitor center near the villa parking area.

STAYING FOR A MEAL

Albergo Ristorante Adriano. Via di Villa Adriana 194. ☎ **0774/535028.** Main courses 20,000–40,000 lire ($12.80–$25.60); fixed-price menu 75,000 lire ($48). AE, DC, MC, V. Mon–Sat 12:30–2:30pm and 8–10pm, Sun 12:30–2:30pm. Bus: 2 or 4 from Tivoli. ITALIAN.

At the bottom of the villa's hill, in a stucco-sided villa a few steps from the ticket office, this is a perfect stopover point either before or after you visit Hadrian's Villa. It offers terrace dining under plane trees or indoor dining in a high-ceilinged room with terra-cotta walls, neoclassical moldings, and white Corinthian pilasters. The food is home-style cooking—nothing fancy. The menu includes roast lamb, saltimbocca, a variety of veal dishes, deviled chicken, a selection of salads and cheeses, and simple desserts—everything homemade. They're especially proud of their homemade pasta dishes.

Le Cinque Statue. Via Quintillio Varo 8. ☎ **0774/335366.** Reservations recommended. Main courses 10,000–20,000 lire ($6.40–$12.80). AE, DC, MC, V. Sat–Thurs 12:30–3pm and 7:30–10pm. Closed Aug 15–Sept 7. The bus from Rome stops nearby. ROMAN.

Established in the 1950s, this restaurant takes its name from the quintet of old carved statues, including Apollo Belvedere and gladiators, that decorate the restaurant. Today this comfortable restaurant is maintained by a hard-working Italian family, who prepare an honest and unpretentious cuisine. Everything is accompanied by the wines of the hill towns of Rome. Begin with a pastiche of mushrooms or brains, or make a selection from the excellent antipasti. Try the rigatoni with fresh herbs, tripe fried Roman style, or a mixed fry of brains and vegetables. All the pasta is freshly made on the premises. They also have a wide array of ice creams and fruits.

OSTIA

Ostia Antica is one of the area's major attractions, particularly interesting to those who can't make it to Pompeii. If you want to see both ancient and modern Rome, get your bikini and take the Metropolitana (subway) Line B from the Stazione Termini to the Magliana stop. Change there for the Lido train to Ostia Antica, about 16 miles from Rome. Departures are about every half hour, and the trip takes only 20 minutes. The Metro lets you off across the highway that connects Rome with the coast. It's just a short walk to the excavations.

Later, board the Metro again to visit the **Lido di Ostia,** the beach. Italy may be a strongly Catholic country, but the Romans don't allow religious conservatism to affect their bathing attire. This is the beach where the denizens of the capital frolic on the seashore and at times create a merry carnival atmosphere, with dance halls, cinemas, and pizzerias. The Lido is set off best at Castelfusano, against a backdrop of pinewoods. This stretch of shoreline is referred to as the Roman Riviera.

Ostia Antica: Rome's Ancient Seaport. Viale dei Romagnoli 717. ☎ **06/565-0022.**
Admission 8,000 lire ($5.10) adults, free for children 17 and under. Apr–Sept, daily 9am–6pm;
Oct–Mar, daily 9am–5pm. Metro: Ostia Antica Line Roma–Ostia–Lido.

Ostia, located at the mouth of the Tiber, was the port of ancient Rome. Through it were funneled the riches from the far corners of the empire. It was founded in the 4th century B.C., and became a major port and naval base primarily under two later emperors, Claudius and Trajan.

A thriving, prosperous city developed, full of temples, baths, theaters, and patrician homes. Ostia Antica flourished for about eight centuries before it began eventually to wither and the wholesale business of carting off its art treasures began. Gradually it became little more than a malaria bed, a buried ghost city that faded into history. Although a papal-sponsored commission launched a series of digs in the 19th century, the major work of unearthing was carried out under Mussolini's orders from 1938 to 1942 (the work had to stop because of the war). The city is only partially dug out today, but it's believed that all the chief monuments have been uncovered.

The principal monuments are clearly labeled. The most important spot in all the ruins is **piazzale delle Corporazioni,** an early version of Wall Street. Near the theater, this square contained nearly 75 corporations, the nature of their businesses identified by the patterns of preserved mosaics.

Greek dramas were performed at the ancient **theater,** built sometime in the early days of the empire. The classics are still aired here in summer (check with the tourist office for specific listings), but the theater as it looks today is the result of much rebuilding. Every town the size of Ostia had a forum, and during the excavations a number of pillars of the ancient **Ostia Forum** were uncovered. At one end is a 2nd-century B.C. temple honoring a trio of gods—Minerva, Jupiter, and Juno (little more than the basic foundation remains). In addition, there's a well-lit museum in the enclave that displays Roman statuary along with some Pompeii-like frescoes. There are perfect picnic spots beside fallen columns or near old temple walls.

CASTELLI ROMANI

For the Roman emperor, and the wealthy cardinal in the heyday of the Renaissance, the Castelli Romani (Roman Castles) exerted a powerful lure, and they still do. Of course, the Castelli are not castles, but hill towns—many of them with an ancient history. The wines from the Alban Hills will add a little *feu de joie* to your life. The ideal way to explore the hill towns is by car. But you can get a limited review by taking one of the buses that leave every 20 minutes from Rome from the Subaugusta stop of the Metro system (A).

CASTELGANDOLFO

Since the early 17th century this resort on Lake Albano, 16 miles from Rome, has been the summer retreat of the popes. As such, it attracts thousands of pilgrims yearly, although the papal residence, Villa Barberini, and its surrounding gardens are private and open only on special occasions. Interestingly, the pope's summer place incorporates part of the notoriously despotic emperor Domitian's palace (but the pastimes have changed).

On days that the pope grants a mass audience, thousands of visitors—many of whom arrive on foot—stream into the audience hall. Pope Pius XII, worried about the thousands of people who waited out in the rain to see him, built this air-conditioned structure to protect the faithful from the elements. On a summer Sunday the pope usually appears on a small balcony in the palace courtyard, reciting with the crowd the noon Angelus prayers.

The seat of the papacy opens onto a little square in the center of the town, where holiday-makers sip their wine—nothing pontifical here. A chair lift transports visitors from the hillside town to the lake, where some of the aquatic competitions were held in the 1960 Olympics. The Church of St. Thomas of Villanova, on the principal square, as well as the fountain, reveal Bernini's hand. If you need to be sold more on visiting Castelgandolfo, remember that it was praised by the eminent guidebook writer Goethe.

NEMI

The Romans flock to Nemi in droves, particularly from April to June for the succulent strawberry of the district—acclaimed by some gourmets as the finest in Europe. In May there's a strawberry festival. Nemi was also known to the ancients. A temple to the huntress Diana was erected on Lake Nemi, which was said to be her "looking glass." In A.D. 37 Caligula built luxurious barges to float on the lake. Mussolini, much later, drained Nemi to find the barges, but it was a dangerous time to excavate them from the lake's bottom. They were senselessly destroyed by the Nazis during the infamous retreat.

Exploring the Town

At the Roman Ship Museum, or **Museo delle Navi,** via di Diana (☎ **06/936-8140**), you can see two scale models of the ships destroyed by the Nazis. The major artifacts on display are mainly copies, as the originals now rest in world-class museums. The museum is open April to September, Monday to Saturday from 9am to 1:30pm and on Sunday from 9am to 1pm; October to March, Monday to Saturday from 9am to 1pm. Admission is 4,000 lire ($2.55) for adults, free for children 17 and under and for seniors 60 and over. To reach the museum, head from the center of Nemi toward the lake.

The 15th-century **Palazzo Ruspoli,** a baronial estate, is the focal point of Nemi, but the hill town itself invites exploration—particularly the alleyways the local denizens call streets and the houses with balconies jutting out over the slopes. While darting like Diana through the Castelli Romani, try to time your schedule to have lunch here in Nemi.

An Excellent Restaurant

La Taverna. Via Nemorense 13. ☎ **06/936-8135.** Reservations required. Main courses 13,000–16,000 lire ($8.30–$10.25). AE, DC, MC, V. Thurs–Tues 12:30–2pm and 8–10pm. INTERNATIONAL.

Offering a large array of regional dishes and a rustic atmosphere, La Taverna is worth the trouble it takes to get here. In April the fragole (wild strawberries) signs go out. Try fettuccine with mushrooms. For a main dish we suggest the chef's specialty, arrosto di abbacchio e maiale (it consists of both a pork chop and grilled lamb) or a fresh fish dish. If you want to have a Roman feast, accompany your main dish with large roasted mushrooms, priced according to size, and a small fennel salad. To top off the galaxy of goodies, it's traditional to order Sambucca, a clear white drink like anisette, "with a fly in it." The "fly" is a coffee bean, which you suck on for added flavor.

FRASCATI

Located about 13 miles from Rome out via Tuscolana, and some 1,073 feet above sea level, Frascati is one of the most beautiful of the hill towns—known for the wine to which it lends its name and its villas—which luckily bounced back from the severe destruction caused by bombers in World War II.

To get there, take one of the Cotral buses leaving from the Subaugusta stop of the Metro system (A). You can also take a small train that leaves from the Ferrovie Laziali section of the central Stazione Termini in Rome. This train runs only to Frascati.

Wine Tasting, Renaissance Gardens & Ancient Ruins

Although bottles of Frascati wine are exported—and served in many of the restaurants and trattorie of Rome—tradition holds that the wine is best near the golden vineyards from which it came. Romans drive up on Sunday just to drink the *vino*. To sample some of the golden white wine yourself, head for **Cantina Comandini,** via E. Filiberto 1 (☎ 06/942-0915), right off piazza Roma. The Comandini family welcomes you to the wine cellar, a regional tavern in which they sell Frascati wine from their own vineyards. You can stop and drink the wine on the spot for 6,000 lire ($3.85) for a liter or 1,500 lire (95¢) for a glass. This is not a restaurant, but they sell sandwiches to go with your wine for 4,500 lire ($2.90). The tavern is open Monday to Saturday from 4 to 8pm.

For your other sightseeing, stand in the heart of Frascati, at piazza Marconi, to see the most important of the estates: **Villa Aldobrandini,** via Massala. The finishing touches to this 16th-century villa were applied by Maderno, who designed the facade of St. Peter's in Rome, but you can only visit the gardens. Still, with its grottoes, yew hedges, statuary, and splashing fountains, it makes for an exciting outing. The gardens are open only in the morning, but you must go to the Azienda di Soggiorno e Turismo, piazza Marconi 1 (☎ 06/942-0331), and ask for a free pass. The office is open Monday to Friday from 8am to 2pm and 3:30 to 6:40pm and on Saturday from 8am to 2pm.

If you have a car, you can continue past the Villa Aldobrandini to **Tuscolo,** about 3 miles beyond the villa. An ancient spot with the ruins of an amphitheater dating from about the 1st century B.C., Tuscolo offers what may be one of Italy's most panoramic views.

You may also want to go to the bombed-out **Villa Torlonia.** Its grounds have been converted into a public park whose chief treasure is the "Theater of the Fountains," also designed by Maderno.

A Meal to Go with Your Wine

Cacciani Restaurant. Via Armando Diaz 13. ☎ **06/942-0378.** Reservations required on weekends. Main courses 15,000–25,000 lire ($9.60–$16). AE, DC, MC, V. Tues–Sun 12:30–3pm and 7:30–10:30pm. Closed Jan 7–19 and Aug 18–27. ROMAN.

Cacciani is the choicest restaurant in Frascati, where the competition has always been tough (Frascati foodstuffs once attracted the epicurean Lucullus). A large, modern restaurant in the center of town, with a terrace commanding a view of the valley, Cacciani has drawn such celebrities as Clark Gable. The kitchen is exposed to the public, and it's fun just to watch the women wash the sand off the spinach. To get you started, we recommend the pasta specialties, such as fettuccine or rigatoni alla vaccinara (oxtail in tomato sauce). For a main course, the baby lamb with a special sauce of white wine and vinegar is always reliable. There is, of course, a large choice of wines, which are kept in a cave under the restaurant. The owners, the Cacciani family, will arrange a combined visit to several of the wine-producing villas of Frascati along with a memorable meal at their elegant restaurant, if you call ahead.

PALESTRINA

If you go out of Rome through the Porta Maggiore and travel on Via Prenestina for about 24 miles, you'll eventually come to Palestrina, a medieval hillside town which overlooks a wide valley.

THE ANCIENT TEMPLE

When U.S. airmen flew over in World War II and bombed part of the town, they scarcely realized their actions would launch Palestrina as an important tourist attraction. After the debris was cleared, a pagan temple—once one of the greatest in the world—emerged: the **Fortuna Primigenia,** rebuilt in the days of the empire but dating from centuries before.

Palestrina antedates the founding of Rome by several hundred years. It resisted conquest by the early Romans, and later took the wrong side in the civil war between Marius and Sulla. When Sulla won, he razed every stone in the city except the Temple of Fortune, and then built a military barracks on the site. Later, as a favorite vacation spot for the emperors and their entourages, it sheltered some of the most luxurious villas of the Roman Empire.

In medieval feuds, the city was repeatedly destroyed. Its most famous child was Pier Luigi da Palestrina, who is recognized as the father of polyphonic harmony.

The **Barberini Palace** (☎ 06/953-8100), high on a hill overlooking the valley, today houses Roman statuary found in the ruins, plus Etruscan artifacts, such as urns the equal of those in the Villa Giulia Museum in Rome. But the most famous work—worth the trip itself—is the "Nile Mosaic," a well-preserved ancient Roman work, the most remarkable one ever uncovered. The mosaic details the flooding of the Nile, a shepherd's hunt, mummies, ibises, and Roman warriors, among other things. The museum is open daily from 9am to an hour before sunset. Admission is 4,000 lire ($2.55) for adults and free for children 17 and under and for seniors 60 and over.

You'll also find a cathedral here that dates from 1100, with a mostly intact bell tower. It rests on the foundation of a much earlier pagan temple.

SPENDING THE NIGHT

Albergo Ristorante Stella (Restaurant Coccia). Piazza della Liberazione 3, Palestrina, 00036 Roma. ☎ **06/953-8172.** Fax 06/957-3360. 27 rms, 2 suites. AC TV TEL. 90,000 lire ($57.60) double; 150,000 lire ($96) suite. AE, DC, V.

The Albergo Ristorante Stella, a buff-colored hotel set in the commercial center of town, is located on a cobblestone square filled with parked cars, trees, and a small fountain. It was renovated in 1995, although the bedrooms remain rather basic, but comfortable. The simple lobby is filled with warm colors, curved leather couches, and autographed photos of local sports heroes. The restaurant is sunny. There's a small bar where you might have an apéritif before lunch. Meals begin at 40,000 lire ($25.60). The restaurant is open daily from noon to 3pm and 7 to 9pm.

FREGENE

The fame of this coastal city north of the Tiber—24 miles from Rome—dates back to the 1600s when the land belonged to the Rospigliosi, a powerful Roman family. Pope Clement IX, a member of that wealthy family, planted a forest of pine that extends along the shoreline for 2 1/2 miles and stands half a mile deep to protect the land from the strong winds of the Mediterranean. Today the wall of pines makes a dramatic backdrop for the golden sands and luxurious villas of the resort. You can take a Civitavecchia-bound train from the Stazione Termini in Rome to Fregene, the first stop.

WHERE TO STAY & DINE

La Conchiglia. Lungomare di Ponente 4, Fregene, 00050 Roma. ☎ **06/668-5385.** Fax 06/668-5385. 36 rms. A/C MINIBAR TV TEL. 160,000 lire ($102.40) double. Rates include breakfast. AE, DC, MC, V. Free parking. The bus from Rome leaves from the Lepanto Metro stop and takes passengers to the center of Fregene.

La Conchiglia means "The Shellfish" in Italian—an appropriate name for this hotel and restaurant right on the beach with views of the water and the pines. Built in 1934, the hotel features a white, circular lounge with built-in curving wall banquettes that face a cylindrical fireplace with a raised hearth—seemingly a setting for a modern Italian film. A resort aura, however, is created by the large green plants. The bar in the cocktail lounge, which faces the terrace, is also circular. The rooms are comfortable and well furnished.

It's also possible to stop by just for a meal, and the food is good. Try, for example, spaghetti with lobster and grilled fish or one of many excellent meat dishes. Meals start at 50,000 lire ($32). The restaurant is in the garden, shaded by bamboo. Oleander flutters in the sea breezes. The restaurant is open daily from 1 to 3pm and 8 to 10pm.

ETRUSCAN HISTORICAL SIGHTS
CERVETERI (CAERE)

As you walk through the Etruscan Museum in Rome (Villa Giulia), you'll often see the word *Caere* written under a figure vase or a sarcophagus. This is a reference to the nearby town known today as Cerveteri, one of the great Etruscan cities of Italy, whose origins may go as far back as the 9th century B.C. Of course, the Etruscan town has long since faded, but not the **Necropolis of Cerveteri** (☎ **06/994-0001**). The effect is eerie; Cerveteri is often called a "city of the dead."

When you go beneath some of the mounds, you'll discover the most striking feature of the necropolis—the tombs are like rooms in Etruscan homes. The main burial ground is called the Necropolis of Banditacca. Of the graves thus far uncovered, none is finer than the Tomba Bella (sometimes called the Reliefs' Tomb), the burial ground of the Matuna family. Articles such as utensils and even house pets were painted in stucco relief. Presumably these paintings were representations of items the dead family would need in the world beyond. The necropolis is open May to September, Tuesday to Sunday from 9am to 7pm; October to April, Tuesday to Sunday from 9am to 3:30pm. Admission is 8,000 lire ($5.10).

Relics from the necropolis are displayed at the **Museo Nazionale Cerite,** piazza Santa Maria Maggiore (☎ **06/994-1354**). The museum is housed within the ancient walls and crenellations of Ruspoldi Castle. It's open May to September, Tuesday to Sunday from 9am to 7pm; October to April, Tuesday to Sunday from 9am to 2pm. Admission is free.

You can reach Cerveteri by bus or car. If you're driving, head out via Aurelia, northwest of Rome, for a distance of 28 miles. By public transportation, take Metro Line A in Rome to the Lepanto stop; from via Lepanto you can take a Cotral bus (☎ 06/324-4724) to Cerveteri; the trip takes about an hour and costs 4,900 lire ($3.15). Once at Cerveteri, it's a 1¼-mile walk to the necropolis. Just follow the signs that point the way.

TARQUINIA

If you wish to see tombs even more striking and more recently excavated than those at Cerveteri, go to Tarquinia. The medieval turrets and fortifications atop the rocky cliffs overlooking the sea seem to contradict the Etruscan name of Tarquinia. Actually, Tarquinia is the adopted name of the old medieval community of Corneto, in honor of the major Etruscan city that once stood nearby. The main attraction in the town is the **Tarquinia National Museum,** piazza Cavour (☎ **0766/856036**), devoted to Etruscan exhibits and sarcophagi excavated from the necropolis a few miles away. The museum is housed in the Palazzo Vitelleschi, a Gothic palace that dates from the mid-15th century. Among the exhibits are gold jewelry, black vases with carved and painted bucolic scenes, and sarcophagi decorated with carvings of animals and relief figures of priests and military leaders. But the biggest attraction is in itself worth the ride from Rome—the almost life-size pair of winged horses from the pediment of a Tarquinian temple. The finish is worn here and there, and the terra-cotta color shows through, but the relief stands as one of the greatest Etruscan masterpieces ever discovered. The museum is open Tuesday to Sunday from 9am to 7pm, and charges 8,000 lire ($5.10) for adults, free admission for children 17 and under and for seniors 60 and over.

The same ticket also admits you to the **Etruscan Necropolis** (☎ **0766/856308**), which covers more than 2¹/₂ miles of rough terrain near where the ancient Etruscan city once stood. Thousands of tombs have been discovered here, some of which have not been explored even today. Others, of course, were discovered by looters, but many treasures remain even though countless pieces were removed to museums and private collections. The paintings on the walls of the tombs have helped historians reconstruct the life of the Etruscans—a heretofore impossible feat without a written history. They depict feasting couples in vivid colors mixed from iron oxide, lapis lazuli dust, and charcoal. One of the oldest tombs (from the 6th century B.C.) depicts young men fishing while dolphins play and colorful birds fly high above. Many of the paintings convey an earthy, vigorous, sex-oriented life among the wealthy Etruscans. The tombs are generally open Tuesday to Sunday from 9am to an hour before sunset (until 2pm November to March). You can reach the grave sites by taking a bus from the Barriera San Giusto to the Cimitero stop. Or try the 20-minute walk from the museum. Inquire at the museum for directions.

To reach Tarquinia by car, take via Aurelia outside Rome and continue on the autostrada toward Civitavecchia. Bypass Civitavecchia and continue another 13 miles north until you see the exit signs for Tarquinia. As for public transportation, going by train is the preferred choice: A *diretto* train from Roma Ostiense station takes 50 minutes. Also, eight buses a day leave from the via Lepanto stop in Rome for the 2-hour trip to the neighboring town, Barriera San Giusto, which is 1¹/₂ miles from Tarquinia. Bus schedules are available at the tourist office in Barriera San Giusto (☎ 0766/856384), which is open Monday to Saturday from 8am to 2pm.

6 | Florence (Firenze)

No other city today in Europe, with the exception of Venice, lives off its past the way Florence does. The city was the birthplace of the Renaissance, and the world has been beating a path here ever since. At first glance, Florence is a bit foreboding and architecturally not the Gothic fantasy of lace that Venice is, for example. Many of its *palazzi* look like severe fortresses, as was the Medici style. They were built, after all, to keep foreign enemies at bay. These facades, though, however uninviting, contain treasures within, as the thousands upon thousands of visitors who overrun the too-narrow streets of the city today know and appreciate.

Ever since the 19th century Florence has been visited by seemingly half the world—wanting to see Michelangelo's *David*, Botticelli's "Venus on the Half Shell," or Brunelleschi's dome. The city has impressed some hard-to-impress people, including Mark Twain, who found that it overwhelms with "tides of color that make all the sharp lines dim and faint and turn the old city to a city of dreams."

Although to some extent Florence appears to be caught in a time warp, the city virtually pulsates with present-day life while jealously guarding its Renaissance treasures. Students racing to and from the university quarter add renewed vibrance and culture to the city, and it's amusing to watch how many local businesspeople avoid the city's impossible traffic today: They whiz by on Vespas while cars are stalled in traffic.

The locals both bemoan the fact that their city is overrun with visitors and at the same time welcome them, because they know that it puts tripe on the table (tripe is a Florentine's favorite dish). The 400,000 people of Florence are almost guaranteed a good living off the tourists, whereas Milan, which gets far fewer visitors, is subjected to various economic depressions that come and go. "It's the price we pay for fame," laments one local merchant. "The visitors have crowded our city and strained our facilities, but they make it possible for me to own a villa in Fiesole and take my children on vacation to San Remo every year."

City fathers or mothers have been wise to keep the inner Renaissance core relatively free of modern architecture and polluting industry. Florence has industry, but it's sent packing to the suburbs. It's a relatively clean city and safe as Italian cities go, with far less crime than Rome, and certainly far less than Naples. You can generally walk the narrow cobblestone streets at night unmolested, although caution is always advised.

Florentines say that they like to present *una bella figura,* or "a good appearance," to the rest of the world, and are incredibly upset when that appearance is attacked, as in the case of the May 1993 bombing of the Uffizi that cost them many treasures. The entire city rallied to reopen this treasure trove of Renaissance and other works of art.

By all means, Florence should be on the itinerary of even the most rushed tours of Europe. There's nothing like it anywhere else in the world. Venice and Rome are too different from Florence to invite sane comparisons. The one myth you must not believe—and it's heard more and more frequently—is that Florence is becoming "the Los Angeles of Italy." How did the rumor get started? Perhaps because Florentines have the highest per capita number of cellular phones in Europe. That's because they're trying to be modern and keep up with the changing world, but they also know that you're coming to pay homage to their glorious past and not to their achievements of today. Even though still a great cultural center of art and fashion, nobody seriously suggests that anything magnificent has been created in Florence in a few centuries at least.

A LOOK AT THE PAST   Florence became a Roman stronghold in the 1st century B.C., but it was not until after A.D. 1200 that it began to come into its own as a commercial and cultural center. During the 13th century, merchants and tradesmen organized the guilds that controlled the city's economy and government for nearly 150 years. These guilds, with their newfound wealth, commissioned works of art to adorn the churches and palaces.

This revival of interest in art and architecture brought about the Italian Renaissance, an amazing outburst of activity between the 14th and the 16th century that completely changed the face of the Tuscan town. During its heyday under the benevolent eye (and purse) of the Medicis, the city became the world's greatest repository of art treasures. The list of geniuses who lived or worked here reads like a "who's who" in the world of art and literature: Dante, Boccaccio, Fra Angelico, Brunelleschi, Donatello, da Vinci, Raphael, Cellini, Michelangelo, Ghiberti, and Giotto.

1 Orientation

ARRIVING

BY PLANE   If you're flying from New York, the best air connection is Rome, where you can board a domestic flight to the **Galileo Galilei Airport** at Pisa (☎ **050/ 500707**), 58 miles west of Florence. You can then take an express train to Florence in an hour.

There's also a small domestic airport, **Amerigo Vespucci,** on via del Termine, near the A11 highway (☎ **055/373498**), which lies 3¹/₂ miles northwest of Florence, a 15-minute ride. This airport not only receives domestic flights from such cities as Rome and Milan, but also planes from international destinations, notably Brussels, Frankfurt, London, Munich, Nice, and Paris. The airport can be reached by city bus service available on the ATAF line (no. 62), departing from the main Santa Maria Novella rail terminal. Domestic air service is provided by **Alitalia,** lungarno degli Acciaiuoli 10–12 in Florence (☎ **055/27881**).

BY TRAIN   Florence lies in the heart of Italy and is a major stopover in Europe for Eurailpass holders. If you're coming north from Rome, count on a 2- to 3-hour trip, depending on your connection. Bologna is just an hour away by train, and Venice, 4 hours. The **Santa Maria Novella rail station,** in piazza della Stazione (☎ **055/288785** for railway information), adjoins piazza Santa Maria Novella, which has one of the great churches of Florence. From here, most of the major hotels are within easy reach, either on foot or by taxi or bus.

Facilities in the train station include a currency exchange open Monday to Saturday from 8:20am to 6:30pm; a day hotel, Albergo Diurno, where you can take a shower after a long train ride and rest up; and luggage storage at the top of Track 16.

Some trains into Florence stop at the **Stazione Campo di Marte,** on the eastern side of Florence. A 24-hour bus service (no. 91) runs between the two rail terminals.

BY BUS   Two long-distance bus lines service Florence: **SITA,** viale Cadorna 103–105 (☎ **055/483651**), and **Lazzi Eurolines,** piazza della Stazione 4–6 (☎ **055/ 215154**). SITA connects Florence with such Tuscan hill towns as Siena, Arezzo, Pisa, and San Gimignano, and Lazzi Eurolines provides service from such cities as Rome and Naples.

BY CAR   Florence, because of its central location, enjoys good autostrada connections with the rest of Italy, especially Rome and Bologna.

Autostrada A1 connects Florence with both the north and south of Italy. Florence lies 172 miles north of Rome, 65 miles west of Bologna, and 185 miles south of Milan. Bologna is about an hour away by car, and Rome is 3 hours away. The Tyrrhenian coast is only an hour from Florence on the A11 heading west.

Use a car only to get to Florence. Don't even comtemplate using it once there, as most of central Florence is closed to all vehicles except those of local residents.

VISITOR INFORMATION

Contact the **Azienda Promozione Turistica,** via A. Manzoni 16 (☎ **055/ 234-6284**), open Monday to Saturday from 8:30am to 1:30pm. Another helpful office handling data about Florence and Tuscany as well is at via Cavour 1R (☎ **055/ 290832**), open Monday to Saturday from 8am to 1:45pm. Yet another helpful information office is near piazza della Signoria, at Chiasso dei Baroncelli 17R (☎ **055/ 230-2124**).

CITY LAYOUT

Florence is a city seemingly designed for walking. It's amazing how nearly all the major sights can be discovered on foot. The only problem is that the sidewalks in summer are so crowded that we only hope you don't suffer from claustrophobia.

MAIN ARTERIES & STREETS   The city is split by the **Arno River,** which usually looks serene and peaceful, but can turn ferocious with flood waters on rare occasions. The major part of Florence, certainly its historic core with most of the monuments, lies on the north or "right" side of the river. But the "left" side is not devoid of attractions. Many long-time visitors frequent the left bank for its tantalizing trattoria meals; they also maintain that the shopping here is less expensive. Even the most hurried visitor will want to cross over to the left bank to see the Pitti Palace with its many art treasures and walk through the Giardini di Boboli, a series of formal gardens, the most impressive in Florence. In addition, you'll also want to cross over to the left bank to check out the panoramic views of the city from piazzale Michelangiolo. To reach it, follow viale Michelangelo up the flank of the hill (one easy way to go is to take bus no. 13 from the train station).

The Arno is spanned by eight bridges, of which the **ponte Vecchio,** with jewelry stores on either side, is the most celebrated and most central. Many of these bridges were ancient structures until the Nazis, in a hopeless and last-ditch effort, senselessly destroyed them in their "defense" of Florence in 1944. With tenacity, Florence rebuilt its bridges, using pieces from the destroyed structures whenever possible. The **ponte Santa Trinità** is the second-most important bridge. After crossing it you can continue along **via dei Tornabuoni,** which is the most important right-bank shopping street (don't look for bargains, however). At the ponte Vecchio you can walk, again on the right bank, along via por Santa Maria, which will become Calimala. This will lead you into **piazza della Repubblica,** a commercial district known for its cafes.

From there, you can take via Roma, which leads directly into **piazza San Giovanni.** There you'll find the baptistery and its neighboring sibling, the larger **piazza del Duomo,** with the world-famous cathedral and bell tower by Giotto. From the far western edge of piazza del Duomo you can take via del Proconsolo south to **piazza della Signoria,** to see the landmark Palazzo Vecchio and its sculpture-filled Loggia della Signoria.

High in the hills overlooking Florence is the ancient town of **Fiesole,** with Etruscan and Roman ruins and a splendid cathedral.

FINDING AN ADDRESS   Florence has two different systems for street numbering—red (*rosso*) or blue or black (*blu* or *nero*). Red numbers identify commercial enterprises such as shops and restaurants. Blue or black numbers indentify office buildings, private homes, apartment houses, or hotels.

Since street numbers are chaotic in Florence, it's better to get a cross street or some landmark if you're looking for an address along a long boulevard.

STREET MAPS   At the very least, arm yourself with a map from the tourist office (see "Visitor Information," above, for the location of the tourist offices). But if you'd like to see Florence in any depth—particularly those little side streets, ask for a **Falk** map (indexes are included), which gives all the streets. These are available at all bookstores and at most newsstands.

NEIGHBORHOODS IN BRIEF

Florence isn't divided into neighborhoods the way many cities are. Most locals refer to either the left bank or the right bank of the Arno—and that's about it, unless they head out of town for the immediate environs, such as Fiesole. The following selection of "neighborhoods"—most of them grouped around a palace, church, or square—is therefore rather arbitrary.

Centro   Called simply that by the Florentines, Centro could, in effect, be all the historic heart of Florence, but mostly the term is used to describe the area southwest of the Duomo. This district is not as important as it used to be, as piazza della Signoria now attracts more visitors. The heyday of Centro was in the 1800s when it was filled with narrow medieval streets that were torn down to make a grander city center. Lost forever were great homes of the Medici and the Sacchetti families, among others. Piazza della Repubblica, although faded, is still lively day and night with its celebrated cafes, such as Giubbe Rosse, founded in 1888, and Caffè Gilli, founded in 1733. The most fashionable street of Centro is via dei Tournabuoni, the most elegant shopping street in Florence. Pause on this street at no. 83 (La Giacosa) for a patisserie before continuing to survey the *palazzi* and the high-quality but lethally priced merchandise.

Piazza del Duomo   Situated in the heart of Florence, this square and its surrounding area are dominated by the Duomo, Santa Maria del Fiore, site of the former local grain and hay markets. One of the largest buildings in the Christian world, this cathedral is exceeded only by St. Peter's in Rome. You come upon it unexpectedly because the surrounding buildings were not torn down to give it breathing room. Capped by Brunelleschi's dome—an amazing architectural feat—the structure now dominates the skyline of Florence. Every visitor flocks to the area, to see not only the Duomo but the neighboring *campanile* (bell tower), one of the most beautiful in all of Italy, and the Baptistry across the way. Now consecrated to St. John the Baptist, the Baptistry was originally a pagan temple honoring Mars. Its doors are among the jewels of Italian Renaissance sculpture. Here, too, in this same neighborhood is the Museum of the Opera del Duomo, a sculpture haven, including some of the most important works of Donatello. A few hotels and trattorie are also found around the Duomo, and they are among the most touristy in the city.

Piazza della Signoria   This section of Florence—and the square in particular—has been the center of many dramatic moments in the city's history, including Savonarola's "bonfire of the vanities," in which Florentines burned precious items such as jewelry and paintings to purify themselves. Today the most visited square in Florence is home to the Loggia dei Lanzi, with Cellini's *Perseus* holding a beheaded Medusa. This is the most photographed statue in Florence still standing outside. Michelangelo's *David* on the square is a copy, the original having been moved inside to protect it from the elements. To the south are the Uffizi Galleries and the Palazzo Vecchio.

Santa Maria Novella   On the northwestern edge of central Florence is the large piazza Santa Maria Novella with its church of the same name. Founded in the 13th century by the Dominicans, the church is one of the most important and most visited in Florence. Completed in 1360, the church is filled with admirable frescoes by Domenico Ghirlandaio and a *Crucifix* by Brunelleschi. Donatello allegedly was so taken with the crucifix that upon seeing it he dropped a basket of eggs he was carrying. This area is not all art and culture, however. Northwest of Santa Maria Novella lies the busiest section of Florence, centered at piazza della Stazione, the main railway terminal of the city. Like all railway stations in Italy, it's surrounded by budget hotels, some of dubious quality. Southwest of Santa Maria Novella, via del Melarancio goes a short distance east to San Lorenzo, the first cathedral of Florence. Beyond San Lorenzo is piazza Madonna degli Aldobrandini, one of the more forgettable squares of Florence were it not the entrance to the Medici Chapels. Because it is, half the world can be seen flocking here to see the famous Medici tombs, the work of Michelangelo whose allegorical figures of *Day* and *Night* are among the most famous sculptures in the world.

Piazza San Marco   Although having none of the grandeur of a square of the same name in Venice, this district is nevertheless one of the most important in Florence—centered around its church, now the Museo di San Marco. Located in a former Dominican monastery, the museum houses a collection of the greatest works of Fra Angelico, who decorated the walls of the monks' cells with edifying scenes. Like the other areas previously previewed, this *quartier* of Florence is also overrun by visitors, most of them rushing to the Galleria dell'Accademia on via Ricasoli to see the monumental figure of *David* (1501–04) sculpted by Michelangelo. A perfect example of the sculptor's humanism, it's the most reproduced statue in the world. Other highlights of the area include piazza della Santissima Annunziata, one of the most beautiful in Florence and dominated by an equestrian statue of Ferdinand I de' Medici by Bologna.

Santa Croce   This section is in the southeastern part of the old town of Florence, near the Arno, and is dominated by the Gothic Santa Croce (or Holy Cross) Church, completed in 1442. Once the scene of jousts and festivals, even *calcio* (a local game of football), the square in time became the headquarters of the Franciscans, who established a firm base here in 1218. Although the square and the area have little of their former prestige, the section remains a much-visited part of Florence, although not as tourist-trodden as the districts previously highlighted. Today the church is the virtual Pantheon of Florence, containing the tombs, among others, of Michelangelo and Machiavelli. A little distance to the north of Santa Croce is Casa Buonarroti, on via Ghibellina, which Michelangelo acquired for his nephew. Today it's a museum with a collection of works by Michelangelo, mainly drawings, gathered by his nephew. From here you can follow via Buonarroti to the piazza dei Ciompi, a lively square unknown to many visitors. It's filled with stalls peddling secondhand goods. Look for old coins, books, and even antique Italian uniforms.

Ponte Vecchio   Southwest of piazza della Signoria is the ponte Vecchio (Old Bridge) area. The oldest of the bridges of Florence, it's flanked by jewelry stores and will carry you across the Arno onto the left bank. This has always been a strategic crossing place in Florence, even when it was an old stone bridge. In the Middle Ages it was the center for leather craftspeople, the fishmongers, and the butchers of Florence, but over the years jewelers' shops have replaced these less glamorous industries. Corridoio Vasariano runs the length of the ponte Vecchio above the shops—built by Vasari in just 5 months. Actually, the ponte Vecchio was almost destroyed on the night of August 4, 1944, when the Nazi heirarchy gave orders to blow up all the bridges along the Arno. Even though mined, the ponte Vecchio was miraculously spared. This area is one of the most congested parts of Florence, but on every visitor's itinerary nevertheless.

The Oltrarno (Across the Arno)   The "left bank" of the Arno River is home to the Pitti Palace, with its picture gallery and Boboli Gardens, Massacio's frescoes in the church of Santa Maria del Carmine, artisans' workshops, some good restaurants, and the postcard panorama of Florence and its dome from piazzale Michelangiolo. Even those visitors who stay glued to the right bank cross the Arno to visit the Palazzo Pitti. It's outranked only by the Uffizi in its treasure troves of art. When the crowds at the Pitti get you down, you can always escape to the lush greenery of the Boboli Gardens. At the top of the gardens is an elegant fortress known as Forte Belvedere, built between 1590 and 1595. It affords one of the most beautiful views of Florence and is well worth the climb.

Fiesole   Although a town in its own right, Fiesole is treated by some as a neighborhood or suburb of Florence. An ancient town on a hill overlooking Florence, it has panoramic views of the city of the Renaissance and of the Arno Valley. It was founded by the Etruscans, perhaps as early as the 7th century B.C. Its center is the large piazza Mino da Fiesole. The fresh, clean air of Fiesole makes it an ideal retreat when the heart of Florence is sultry and overrun with visitors. There are hotels here, as well as trattorie, or you can visit to see the sights, including the Convent of San Fancesco and the Duomo, or to just take in the view.

2 Getting Around

ON FOOT   Because Florence is so compact, walking is the ideal way—and at times the only way, because of numerous pedestrian zones—to get around. In theory at least, pedestrians have the right of way at uncontrolled zebra crossings, but don't count on that should you encounter a speeding Vespa.

BY PUBLIC TRANSPORTATION   The major sights in the small city of Florence are within walking distance of most hotels, but you might prefer to use the public **buses.** You must purchase your ticket before boarding, but for 1,400 lire (90¢), you can ride on any public bus in the city for a total of 70 minutes. A 24-hour pass costs 5,000 lire ($3.20). Bus tickets can be purchased from tobacconists and news vendors. The local **bus station** (which serves as the terminal for ATAF city buses) is at piazza del Duomo 57F (☎ **055/56501**). Bus routes are posted at bus stops, but for a comprehensive map of the Florentine bus network, go to the ATAF booth at the rail station. If you're caught riding a bus without a ticket, you'll be fined 71,400 lire ($45.70).

BY TAXI   Taxis can be found at stands at nearly all the major squares in Florence. If you need a radio taxi, call 055/4390 or 055/4798.

BY CAR   As mentioned, driving a car in Florence is a hopeless undertaking—not only because of the snarled traffic, but because much of the district you've come to see is a pedestrian zone. If your hotel doesn't have a garage, someone on the staff will direct you to the nearest garage after you've unloaded your luggage. Garage fees for the night average 25,000 to 50,000 lire ($16 to $32).

You will, however, need a car to explore the surrounding countryside of Tuscany in any depth. Rental-car agencies in Florence include at **Avis,** borgo Ognissanti 128R (☎ 055/213629); **Budget,** borgo Ognissanti 134R (☎ 055/287161); and **Hertz,** via del Termine 1 (☎ 055/307370).

BY BICYCLE OR MOTORSCOOTER   Bicycles and motorscooters, if you avoid the whizzing traffic, are two other practical ways of getting around. **Alinari,** located near the railway station at via Guelfa 85R (☎ **055/280500**), rents bikes for 2,000 to 5,000 lire ($1.30 to $3.20) per hour, or 15,000 to 30,000 lire ($9.60 to $19.20) per day, depending on the model. Also available are small-engined, rather loud motorscooters. These rent for 9,000 lire ($5.75) per hour, or 38,000 lire ($24.30) per day. Renters must be 18 or over, and must leave either a cash deposit of 200,000 lire ($128) or a passport, driver's license, and the number of a valid credit or charge card. It's open Monday to Saturday from 9am to 1pm and 3 to 7:30pm and on Sunday from 10am to 1pm and 3 to 7:30pm.

FAST FACTS: Florence

American Express   Amex is at via Dante Alighieri 20–22r (☎ 055/50981) and at via Guicciardini 49r (☎ 055/288751). Both offices are open Monday to Friday from 9am to 5:30pm and on Saturday from 9am to 12:30pm.

Baby-sitters   Most hotel desks will make arrangements for you to have a baby-sitter. If you need an English-speaking sitter, try to make arrangements as far in advance as possible.

Bookstores   See "Shopping," later in this chapter.

Business Hours   From mid-June to mid-September most shops and business offices are open Monday to Friday from 9am to 1pm and 4 to 8pm. Off-season hours, in general, are Monday from 3:30 to 7:30pm and Tuesday to Saturday from 9am to 1pm and 3:30 to 7:30pm.

Consulates   The consulate of the **United States** is at lungarno Amerigo Vespucci 46 (☎ 055/239-8276); it's open Monday to Friday from 8am to noon and 2 to

4pm. The consulate of the **United Kingdom** is at lungarno Corsini 2 (☎ 055/ 284133), near piazza Santa Trinità; it's open Monday to Friday from 9:30am to 12:30pm and 2:30 to 4:30pm.

Citizens of other English-speaking countries, including Canada, Australia, and New Zealand, should contact their diplomatic representatives in Rome.

Currency Exchange   Local banks in Florence grant the best rates. Most banks are open Monday to Friday from 8:30am to 1:30pm and 2:45 to 3:45pm. The tourist office (see "Orientation," earlier in this chapter) exchanges money at official rates when banks are closed and on holidays, but a commission is often charged. You can also go to the Ufficio Informazione booth at the rail station, which is open daily from 7:30am to 7:40pm. American Express (see locations above) also exchanges money.

One of the best places to exchange currency is the post office (see below).

Dentist   For a list of English-speaking dentists, consult your consulate, if possible, or contact Tourist Medical Service, via Lorenzo il Magnifico 59 (☎ 055/475411). Visits without an appointment are only possible Monday to Friday from 11am to noon and 5 to 6pm and on Saturday from 11am to noon. After hours, an answering service gives names and phone numbers of dentists and doctors who are on duty.

Doctor   Contact your national consulate for a list of English-speaking physicians. You can also contact Tourist Medical Service, via Lorenzo il Magnifico 59 (☎ 055/ 475411). See also "Dentist," above.

Drugstores   Pharmacy service is available at Farmacia Molteni, via Calzaiuoli 7R (☎ 055/215472), which is open 24 hours a day, including Sunday.

Emergencies   For fire, call **115;** for an ambulance, call **212222;** for the police, **113;** and for road service, **116**.

Eyeglasses   Two well-accessorized and centrally located possibilities are Salmoiraghi, via dei Calzaioli 73R (☎ 055/290869), and the Centro Ottico Optometrico, via Cavour 94R (☎ 055/287210).

Hairdressers/Barbers   Both women and men are fond of Big Art, piazza della Repubblica 3 (☎ 055/212016), located right in the center of Florence. Call for an appointment. It's on the floor above street level.

Hospitals   Call the General Hospital of Santa Maria Nuova, piazza Santa Maria Nuova 1 (☎ 055/27581).

Laundry/Dry Cleaning   The self-service Lavanderia Superlava Splendid, via del Sole 29R (☎ 055/218836), is a good choice because of its central location off piazza Santa Maria Novella. It's open Monday to Friday from 8:30am to 7:30pm. Most hotels can arrange for dry cleaning, although you'll pay extra for the convenience. You can also ask at your hotel reception desk for the nearest dry cleaner in your neighborhood.

Lost Property   The lost-and-found office, Oggetti Smarriti, is at via Circondaria 19 (☎ 055/367943), near the rail terminal.

Luggage Storage   This is available at Santa Maria Novella Stazione, in the center of the city on piazza della Stazione (☎ 055/278785). It's open daily from 4:15am to 1:45am.

Photographic Needs   One of the best places is Bottega della Foto, piazza del Duomo 17 (☎ 055/283006), across from the cathedral in the center of Florence.

Police   Dial **113** in an emergency. English-speaking foreigners who want to see and talk to the police should go to the Ufficio Stranieri station at via Zara 2

(☎ 055/49771), where English-speaking personnel are available daily from 9am to 2pm.

Post Office   The Central Post Office is at via Pellicceria 3, off piazza della Repubblica (☎ 055/212305), open Monday to Friday from 8:15am to 6pm and on Saturday from 8:15am to 12:30pm. You can purchase stamps at Windows 21–22. If you want your mail sent to Italy general delivery (*fermo posta*), have it sent in care of this post office (use the 50100 Firenze postal code). Mail can be picked up at Windows 23–24. A telegram, telex, and fax office on the second floor is open daily from 8:15am to 10pm (you can also send telegrams by phoning 186 during the same hours). A foreign exchange office is open Monday to Friday from 8:15am to 6pm; you can also exchange money at automatic tellers on the second floor daily from 7am to 10pm. If you want to send packages, go to the rear of the building and enter at piazza Davantzi 4; hours are the same as the main post office.

Radio   Although there are some private stations, the air waves are dominated by RAI, the national radio network. In the summer months RAI broadcasts some news in English. Vatican Radio's foreign news broadcasts (in English) also reach Florence. Shortwave radio reception is also possible, and you can pick up American (VOA), British (BBC), and Canadian (CBC) radio broadcasts. The American Southern European Broadcast Network (SEB) from Vicenza can also be heard on regular AM radio (middle or medium wave).

Rest Rooms   Public toilets are found in most galleries, museums, bars and cafés, and restaurants, as well as bus, train, and air terminals. Usually they are designated as W.C. (water closet) or DONNE (women) or UOMINI (men). The most confusing designation is SIGNORI (gentlemen) and SIGNORE (ladies), so watch those final *i*'s and *e*'s!

Safety   Violent crimes are rare in Florence; most crime consists mainly of pickpockets who frequent crowded tourist centers, such as corridors of the Uffizi Galleries. Members of group tours who cluster together are often singled out as victims. Car thefts are relatively common: Don't leave your luggage in an unguarded car, even if it's locked in the trunk. Women should be especially careful in avoiding purse snatchers, some of whom grab a woman's purse while whizzing by on a Vespa, often knocking the woman down. Documents such as passports and extra money are better stored in safes at your hotel if available.

Taxes   A value-added tax (IVA) is added to all consumer products and most services, including those at hotels and restaurants. The tax is refundable if you spend more than 525,000 lire ($336) at any one store.

Taxis   See "Getting Around," earlier in this chapter.

Telegrams/Telex/Fax   Most of these can be sent from your hotel.

Transit Information   For international flights from Galileo Galilei Airport, call 050/500707; for domestic flights at Peretola, call 055/30615; for railway information, dial 055/288785; for long-distance bus information, call 055/215154; and for city buses, dial 055/56501.

Weather   May and September are the ideal times to visit. The worst times to go are the week before and including Easter and from June until the first week of September. Florence is literally overrun with tourists, and the city streets, or anything else, weren't designed for mass tourism. Temperatures in July and August hover in the 70s, dropping to a low of 45° or 46° Fahrenheit in December and January, the coldest months.

3 Accommodations

For sheer charm and luxury, the hotels of Florence are among the finest in Europe. Many of the city's grand old villas and palaces have been converted into hotels. There are not too many tourist cities where you can find a 15th- or 16th-century palace—tastefully decorated and most comfortable—rated as a second-class *pensione* (boarding house). Florence is equipped with hotels in virtually all price ranges and with widely varying standards, comfort, service, and efficiency.

However, during the summer months there simply aren't enough rooms to meet the demand, and if you arrive without a reservation you may not find a place for the night and will have to drive to nearby Montecatini, where you'll always stand a good chance of securing accommodations.

In Florence, the most desirable place to stay in terms of shopping, nightlife, sightseeing attractions, and restaurants is Centro, the historic heart of Florence on the right bank of the Arno.

Yes, it's much too touristy, and in summer the streets are like an international camp, but it's still a lot better than staying on the outskirts, where commuting into Centro is difficult because of inadequate public transportation.

Driving into Centro is almost impossible, because of the heavy traffic and because major districts of Florence are pedestrians-only zones. The drawback to Centro is that it's expensive, since this is where most visitors want to lodge. The cheapest lodgings in Centro are found around the Termini (rail station); these are also the least desirable, of course. This area around the Termini and Santa Maria Novella, although generally safe during the day, is the center of major drug-dealing late at night and should be avoided then for safety reasons.

Also in Centro, but less tourist trodden and a bit more tranquil, is the area around piazza San Marco and the University quarter.

Once you cross the Arno to the left bank, lodgings are much scarcer, although there are places to stay, including some *pensioni*. In general, prices are lower across the Arno, and you'll be located next to one of the major attractions of Florence: the Pitti Palace.

Many luxury hotels exist on the outskirts of Florence, as do cheaper boarding houses. Again, these are acceptable alternatives if you don't mind the commute into the center. As a final option, consider lodging in Fiesole, where it's cooler and much more tranquil. Bus no. 7 runs back and forth between Fiesole and Centro.

If you should arrive without a reservation and don't want to wander around town on your own looking for a room, go in person (instead of calling) to the **Consorizio ITA office** in the rail terminal at piazza della Stazione (☎ **055/282893**), open daily from 9am to 9pm. The Consorizio ITA charges a small fee for the service and collects the first night's room charge.

NEAR PIAZZA OGNISSANTI

One of the most famous squares in Florence, piazza Ognissanti is a car-clogged Renaissance square opening onto the Arno. It's the site of the two most famous hotels of Florence.

VERY EXPENSIVE

Grand Hotel. Piazza Ognissanti 1, 50123 Firenze. ☎ **055/288781**, or 800/325-3589 in the U.S. and Canada. Fax 055/217400. 90 rms, 17 suites. A/C MINIBAR TV TEL. 580,000–650,000 lire ($371.20–$416) double; from 1,000,000 lire ($640) suite. AE, DC, MC, V. Parking from 50,000 lire ($32). Bus: 6 or 17.

Florence Accommodations

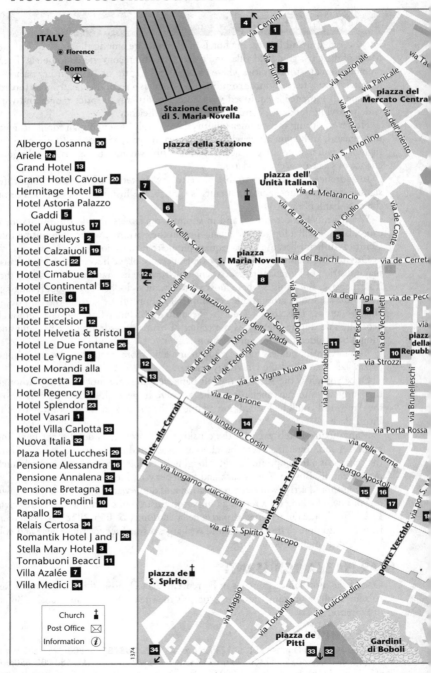

Albergo Losanna **30**
Ariele **12a**
Grand Hotel **13**
Grand Hotel Cavour **20**
Hermitage Hotel **18**
Hotel Astoria Palazzo
   Gaddi **5**
Hotel Augustus **17**
Hotel Berkleys **2**
Hotel Calzaiuoli **19**
Hotel Casci **22**
Hotel Cimabue **24**
Hotel Continental **15**
Hotel Elite **6**
Hotel Europa **21**
Hotel Excelsior **12**
Hotel Helvetia & Bristol **9**
Hotel Le Due Fontane **26**
Hotel Le Vigne **8**
Hotel Morandi alla
   Crocetta **27**
Hotel Regency **31**
Hotel Splendor **23**
Hotel Vasari **1**
Hotel Villa Carlotta **33**
Nuova Italia **32**
Plaza Hotel Lucchesi **29**
Pensione Alessandra **16**
Pensione Annalena **32**
Pensione Bretagna **14**
Pensione Pendini **10**
Rapallo **25**
Relais Certosa **34**
Romantik Hotel J and J **28**
Stella Mary Hotel **3**
Tornabuoni Beacci **11**
Villa Azalée **7**
Villa Medici **34**

Church ✝
Post Office ✉
Information ⓘ

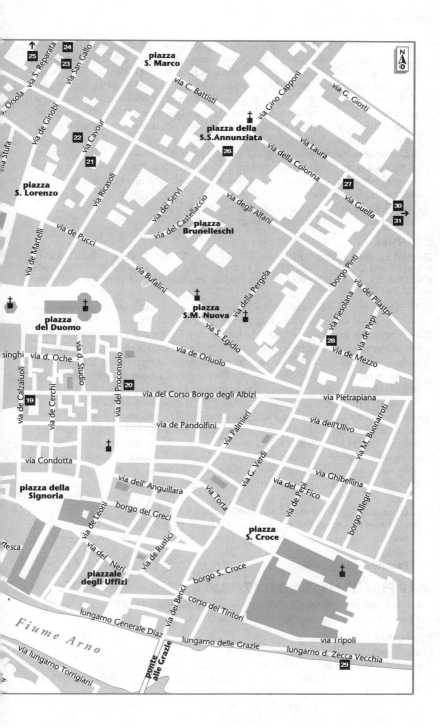

The Grand Hotel is a bastion of luxury. It fronts the piazza and is across from the Hotel Excelsior, which is more luxurious with more facilities. Neither the Grand nor the Excelsior, although among the top three or four hotels of Florence, is as exclusive as the more refined Hotel Regency (see below). A hotel of history and tradition, the Grand is known for its halls and salons. In both the 19th and 20th centuries it has attracted many famous people. Its rooms and suites have a refined elegance, and the most desirable overlook the Arno. Each bedroom contains silks, brocades, and real or reproduction antiques.

Dining/Entertainment: A highlight of the hotel is the restored Winter Garden, an enclosed court lined with arches where regional and seasonal specialties are served along with an array of international dishes. Guests gather at night in the Fiorino Bar to listen to piano music.

Services: Room service, baby-sitting, laundry, valet.

Facilities: Foreign currency exchange.

EXPENSIVE

✪ **Hotel Excelsior.** Piazza Ognissanti 3, 50123 Firenze. ☎ **055/264201**, or 800/325-3535 in the U.S. and Canada. Fax 055/210278. 172 rms, 23 suites. A/C MINIBAR TV TEL. 550,000–620,000 lire ($352–$396.80) double; from 900,000 lire ($576) suite. AE, DC, MC, V. Parking 50,000 lire ($32). Bus: 6 or 17.

The Hotel Excelsior is the ultimate in well-ordered luxury in Florence. Grander than the Grand (see above), the Excelsior for years has reigned as the most famous luxury hotel in Florence. Cosmpolitan and sophisticated, it has the best trained staff in town, but in recent years more tranquil and less commercial establishments, including the Regency and Helvatia e Bristol, have been attracting customers away from it. But if you like glamour and glitz, check into the Excelsior (but be sure to make reservations well in advance). Part of the hotel was once owned by Carolina Bonaparte, sister of Napoléon. The present hotel was formed in 1937. The opulent bedrooms have 19th-century Florentine antiques and sumptuous fabrics. The spacious rooms offer lots of comfortable chairs, and baths with heated racks, thick terrycloth towels, and high ceilings. All the rooms reflect Ciga's heavy-handed style of decorating, and some are much more luxurious than others. In these old palaces, expect accommodations to come in a variety of configurations. Naturally, the rooms on the top floor with balconies overlooking the Arno and the ponte Vecchio are the best and most sought after.

Dining/Entertainment: Il Cestello is the hotel's deluxe restaurant. The Donatello Bar is reviewed later in this chapter (see "Florence After Dark").

Services: Room service, baby-sitting, laundry, valet, express checkout, translation services.

Facilities: Foreign currency exchange.

NEAR PIAZZA MASSIMO D'AZEGLIO

Piazza Massimo d'Azeglio is set northeast of the historic core of Florence, within a 12-minute walk from the streets around the center.

EXPENSIVE

✪ **Hotel Regency.** Piazza Massimo d'Azeglio 3, 50121 Firenze. ☎ **055/245247.** Fax 055/234-6735. 29 rms, 5 suites. A/C MINIBAR TV TEL. 380,000–600,000 lire ($243.20–$384) double; from 800,000 lire ($512) suite. Rates include breakfast. AE, DC, MC, V. Parking 45,000 lire ($28.80). Bus: 6.

Much less overtly commercial than either the Grand or the Excelsior, the Regency is an intimate villa of taste and exclusivity. It's like lodging in a grand private

⊕ Family-Friendly Hotels

Hotel Casci *(see p. 223)*   This hotel is not only inexpensive but it's well located in the historic district. Many of its bedrooms are rented as triples and quads, ideal for families.

Nuova Italia *(see p. 223)*   This 17th-century building near the rail station offers some very large rooms suitable for families, for whom management offers special discounts.

Relais Certosa *(see p. 231)*   For families wanting to escape the congestion of over-crowded Florence, this *relais* hotel—a former monastery—is set on 5 acres of land. Motorists like its wide-open spaces and inviting, family-type atmosphere.

residence, and to many savvy (and well-heeled) travelers it's *the* place to stay in Florence today. It lies a bit apart from the shopping and sightseeing center of Florence, but it's only a 15-minute stroll to the cathedral. And although its location isn't central (a blessing for tranquillity seekers), it's conveniently and quickly reached by taxi or bus. This well-built, old-style villa, a member of Relais & Châteaux, has its own garden across from a park in a residential area of the city. This luxurious hideaway, filled with stained glass, paneled walls, and reproduction antiques, offers exquisitely furnished rooms. There are some special rooms on the top floor with walk-out terraces.

Dining/Entertainment: The attractive dining room, Relais le Jardin, is renowned for its *alta cucina*. You can also take your meals in the well-lit winter garden.

Services: Room service (24 hours), baby-sitting, laundry, valet.

Facilities: Garden.

INEXPENSIVE

Albergo Losanna. Via Vittorio Alfieri 9, 50121 Firenze. ☎ and fax **055/245840.** 10 rms, 4 with bath; 1 suite. TEL. 90,000 lire ($57.60) double without bath, 110,000 lire ($70.40) double with bath; 200,000 lire ($128) suite. Rates include breakfast. MC, V. Parking 30,000–35,000 lire ($19.20–$22.40). Bus: 6.

A good, inexpensive choice, the Albergo Losanna is a tiny, family-run place off viale Antonio Gramsci, between piazzale Donatello and piazza Massimo d'Azeglio. It's quite a come-down from the palaces just recommended, but its prices are much more affordable. It offers utter simplicity and cleanliness. The bus stops a block and a half away. The bedrooms, all doubles, are homey and well kept, but the furnishings are simple and a bit tired.

NEAR THE TERMINI
VERY EXPENSIVE

Villa Medici. Via il Prato 42, 50123 Firenze. ☎ **055/238-1331.** Fax 055/238-1336. 93 rms, 14 suites. A/C MINIBAR TV TEL. 380,000–540,000 lire ($243.20–$345.60) double; 800,000 lire ($512) suite. Parking from 48,000 lire ($30.70). Bus: 3, 6, 11, 31, or 32.

Although showing its age, this old-time favorite—former stamping grounds of kings and princesses—is an 18th-century Medici palace lying 2 blocks southwest of the train station. Turned into a luxury hotel in 1962, it's the most tattered of the five-star choices of Florence, but an enduring favorite nonetheless. In general this hotel appeals more to tradition-oriented Europeans than to Americans who may want more up-to-date facilities. Out back is a private garden (not Florence's finest), with a motel-size swimming pool. The most peaceful rooms front the garden. However, during the day there's noise from the convent school next door. The rooms are traditionally and often handsomely furnished, although rather cramped. Thick towels, hair dryers, and minibars are some of the amenities. We prefer the accommodations on the sixth floor, as they open onto terraces. The staff is one of the best trained in Florence.

Dining/Entertainment: The Lorenzo de' Medici Restaurant offers both international and Florentine cuisine. The restaurant is graced with marble pilasters and illuminated by Murano chandeliers, but the cuisine is only standard fare.

Services: Room service, baby-sitting, laundry, valet.

Facilities: Cleaning and pressing facilities, swimming pool.

EXPENSIVE

Hotel Astoria Palazzo Gaddi. Via del Giglio 9, 50123 Firenze. ☎ **055/239-8095.** Fax 055/214632. 90 rms, 5 suites. A/C MINIBAR TV TEL. 360,000 lire ($230.40) double; 450,000 lire ($288) suite. Rates include buffet breakfast. AE, DC, MC, V. Parking 40,000 lire ($25.60) nearby. Bus: 19, 22, 23, 29, or 30.

In spite of its location in a setting of cheap Termini hotels, this is an impressive and classic Renaissance palace, the finest in the area. The Hotel Astoria at one time housed the office of a now-defunct newspaper. In the 17th century John Milton wrote parts of *Paradise Lost* in one of the bedrooms. This 16th-century palace has been renovated and turned into a serviceable and enduring choice, with a helpful staff and experienced management. From the bedrooms on the upper floors you'll have a view over the terra-cotta rooftops of Florence. The bedrooms have stylish and traditional furnishings for the most part, although some are decorated in a more sterile modern style. The bathrooms are first-rate, with fluffy towels and hair dryers. The front rooms are the noisiest as they overlook a traffic-clogged avenue.

Dining/Entertainment: The garden-style Palazzo Gaddi restaurant serves an international cuisine.

Services: Room service, laundry, baby-sitting.

Facilities: Car-rental desk, shopping boutique, foreign currency exchange.

MODERATE

Villa Azalée. Viale Fratelli Rosselli 44, 50123 Firenze. ☎ **055/214242.** Fax 055/268264. 24 rms. A/C MINIBAR TV TEL. 280,000 lire ($179.20) double; 295,000 lire ($188.80) triple. Rates include buffet breakfast. AE, DC, MC, V. Parking from 30,000 lire ($19.20). Bus: 17.

The Villa Azalée, a handsome structure set on a street corner with a big garden, is a remake of a private home originally built in the 1860s and transformed into a hotel in 1964. The owners have provided a personal touch in both atmosphere and decor. The decorating is tasteful: tall, white-paneled doors with ornate brass fittings, parquet floors, crystal chandeliers, and antiques intermixed with credible reproductions. The lounge is like a private home, and the bedrooms are distinctive (one, in particular, boasts a flouncy canopy bed). The hotel is a 5-minute walk from the rail station. Guests can rent bicycles at the hotel for 5,000 lire ($3.20) per day.

INEXPENSIVE

Hotel Berkleys. Via Fiume 11, 50123 Firenze. ☎ and fax **055/212302.** 9 rms. TV TEL. 130,000 lire ($83.20) double; 170,000 lire ($108.80) triple; 200,000 lire ($128) quad. Rates include breakfast. MC, V.

This pleasant but modest hotel occupies the top floor of a 19th-century apartment building whose lower floors contain two less desirable two-star hotels. It lies about a block east of the railway station. The owners, the Andreoli family, are polite but friendly, and there's an employee on duty throughout the day and night. The simple lobby leads into a breakfast nook and a bar area, where drinks are served on request.

The bedrooms are simple but clean. Of course, you stay here for the prices, not for any grandeur.

⑤ Hotel Casci. Via Cavour 13, 50129 Firenze. ☎ **055/211686.** Fax 055/239-6461. 25 rms. TV TEL. 100,000–150,000 lire ($64–$96) double; 135,000–200,000 lire ($86.40–$128) triple; 170,000–250,000 lire ($108.80–$160) quad. Rates include breakfast. AE, DC, MC, V. Parking 35,000–40,000 lire ($22.40–$25.60). Bus: 1, 6, 7, 11, or 17.

The Casci is a well-run little hotel in the historic district, 200 yards from the main railway station and 100 yards from piazza del Duomo. As one reader wrote, "For *location, location, location,* there's nothing better in Florence." The building dates from the 14th century, and some of the public rooms feature the original frescoes. Gioacchio Rossini, the famous composer of *The Barber of Seville* and *William Tell,* lived in the building between 1851 and 1855. The hotel is both traditional and modern, and the English-speaking reception staff looks after guests very well. The bedrooms are comfortably furnished, and each contains a hair dryer. Each year four or five bedrooms are upgraded and renovated. The few rooms that overlook the busy street are soundproofed against noise.

Hotel Cimabue. Via B. Lupi 7, 50129 Firenze. ☎ **055/475601.** Fax 055/471989. 16 rms. TV TEL. 130,000–160,000 lire ($83.20–$102.40) double. Rates include breakfast. AE, DC, MC, V. Parking 25,000 lire ($16). Bus: 7 or 11.

This building was constructed in 1904 as a private, Tuscan-style *palazzo.* The most charming bedrooms are the five that contain original frescoed ceilings. Four of these lie one floor above street level, the fifth on the ground floor. The hotel was last renovated in 1991, but contains Liberty-style, turn-of-the-century antiques that correspond to the building's age. Its Belgian-Italian management team extends a warm, multicultural welcome.

⑤ Hotel Elite. Via della Scala 12, 50123 Firenze. ☎ **055/215395.** 8 rms, 3 with shower only, 5 with bath (shower). TV TEL. 130,000 lire ($83.20) double with bath. Rates include breakfast. No credit cards. Parking from 25,000 lire ($16). Bus: 7, 31, or 32.

The Elite is a little *pensione* worthy of being better known. It lies two floors above street level in a 19th-century apartment building. Attractive in scale and appointments, it's about a 2-block walk from the main railway station. It's also convenient for exploring most of the major monuments. The owner, Maurizio Maccarini, speaks English and is a helpful, welcoming host. The small hotel rents light and airy bedrooms, divided equally between singles and doubles. Some singles have only a shower (no toilet).

Hotel Vasari. Via B. Cennini 9–11, 50123 Firenze. ☎ **055/212753.** Fax 055/294246. 30 rms. A/C MINIBAR TV TEL. 150,000–210,000 lire ($96–$134.40) double. Rates include breakfast. AE, DC, MC, V. Parking 15,000 lire ($9.60). Bus: 7 or 11.

The Vasari has ties to some of the most prestigious literary associations in Florence, thanks to the fact that it functioned for several years as the home of the 19th-century French poet Alphonse de la Martine. Originally built in the 1840s as a private home, it was a rundown two-star hotel until 1993, when its owners poured money into its renovation and upgraded it to one of the most reasonably priced three-star hotels in town. Its three stories are connected by elevator, and the bedrooms are comfortable, albeit somewhat spartan-looking, and clean. Some of the public areas retain their original elaborate vaulting.

Nuova Italia. Via Faenza 26, 50123 Firenze. ☎ **055/287508.** Fax 055/210941. 20 rms. TEL. 130,000–170,000 lire ($83.20–$108.80) double; 180,000–220,000 lire ($115.20–$140.80) triple. Rates include breakfast. AE, DC, MC, V. Parking 35,000–40,000 lire ($22.40–$25.60) nearby. Bus: 31 or 32.

This little hotel has been welcoming Frommer's readers since 1958. It's situated in a renovated 17th-century building in the center of Florence. All the bedrooms have private bath, direct-dial phones, and soundproof windows, and are pleasantly furnished and decorated with paintings and posters. Some large rooms are suitable for families, to whom the management—the Viti family—grants special discounts. The family helps guests face the problems of getting around Florence, giving them tips on where to shop and what to do. It's located only a block from the railway station, near the San Lorenzo Market and the Medici Chapels.

Stella Mary Hotel. Via Fiume 17, 50123 Firenze. ☎ **055/215694.** Fax 055/264206. 7 rms. TV TEL. 60,000–120,000 lire ($38.40–$76.80) double; 95,000–150,000 lire ($60.80–$96) triple. MC, V. Parking 20,000 lire ($12.80). Bus: 7, 9, 13, 28, or 31.

The Stella Mary Hotel is a small *pensione* lying 12 blocks from the train station and around the corner from a busy bus station. The owners operate a clean and comfortable "home in Firenze." The rooms are cozy and full of light. Breakfast is extra. A sitting room with a TV set is reserved for guests. The English-speaking owners, Mrs. Vittoria and her son, run the hotel personally. Although the hotel only serves breakfast, the staff can recommend several good restaurants nearby. The hotel, in a classic Florentine-style building with an elevator, is only a short walk from the San Lorenzo Church and the San Lorenzo Market.

AT PIAZZA SANTA MARIA NOVELLA
INEXPENSIVE

Hotel Le Vigne. Piazza S. Maria Novella 24, 50123 Firenze. ☎ **055/294449.** Fax 055/230-2263. 19 rms, 16 with bath; 2 suites. A/C TEL. 150,000 lire ($96) double with bath; 200,000 lire ($128) triple with bath; 250,000 lire ($160) suite for four. Rates include buffet breakfast. AE, DC, MC, V. Parking 25,000 lire ($16). Bus: 11, 36, or 37.

The Hotel Le Vigne offers comfortably furnished bedrooms and enjoys a prime location on one of the most central squares of Florence. Its sitting room overlooks the square. An Italian family took over this 15th-century building and restored it in the early 1990s, preserving the old features, including frescoes, whenever possible. This small hotel is on the first floor (second to Americans) of this old-fashioned building. Five of the units are air-conditioned, and a few singles don't have baths. Breakfast is the only meal served, and it's a generous self-service buffet.

ON VIA DEI TORNABUONI
MODERATE

Tornabuoni Beacci. Via dei Tornabuoni 3, 50123 Firenze. ☎ **055/212645.** Fax 055/283594. 29 rms. A/C MINIBAR TV TEL. 230,000–260,000 lire ($147.20–$166.40) double. Rates include breakfast. AE, DC, MC, V. Parking 30,000 lire ($19.20). Bus: 14, 31, 32, 36, or 37.

The Tornabuoni Beacci is located near the Arno and piazza Santa Trinità, on the city's principal shopping street. The *pensione* occupies the three top floors of a 14th-century *palazzo*. All its living rooms have been furnished in a tatty provincial style, with bowls of flowers, parquet floors, a formal fireplace, old paintings, murals, and rugs. The hotel was completely renovated recently, but it still bears an air of old-fashioned gentility. The roof terrace, surrounded by potted plants and flowers, is for late-afternoon drinks or breakfast. Dinner, typically Florentine and Italian dishes, is served here in summer. The view of the nearby churches, towers, and rooftops is worth experiencing. The bedrooms are moderately well furnished.

AT PIAZZA DELLA REPUBBLICA
VERY EXPENSIVE

Savoy Hotel. Piazza della Repubblica 7, 50123 Firenze. ☎ **055/283313.** Fax 055/284840. 97 rms, 4 suites. A/C MINIBAR TV TEL. 390,000–530,000 lire ($249.60–$339.20) double; from 550,000 lire ($352) suite. Rates include breakfast. AE, DC, MC, V. Parking 40,000–50,000 lire ($25.60–$32). Bus: 1, 17, 20, 31, or 32.

Ranking after (a long way after) both the Grand and the Excelsior, the five-star Savoy stands in the clamorous commercial center of Florence (also the historic district), an area filled with fine stores and a 5-minute walk from the railway station. It's a five-story *fin-de-siècle* palace that used to be a more important stopover than it is today. The dignified Savoy Hotel was built at the height of the belle époque era and has a buff-colored facade with neoclassical trim. The predictably upper-class interior includes potted plants, period art, patterned carpeting, and coffered ceilings. The bedrooms have traditional Italian styling. The pink and black marble baths have more style than the rather somber bedrooms.

Dining/Entertainment: Guests can dine in the hotel's elegant Tuscan restaurant, which features both a regional and international cuisine. There's also a bar area with frescoed walls reminiscent of a *trompe l'oeil* view from an 18th-century balcony.

Services: Room service, baby-sitting, laundry, valet.

Facilities: Limited facilities for the disabled.

INEXPENSIVE

Pensione Pendini. Via degli Strozzi 2, 50123. ☎ **055/211170.** Fax 055/281807. 42 rms. TEL. 210,000 lire ($134.40) double. AE, DC, MC, V. Rates include breakfast. Parking 30,000–43,000 lire ($19.20–$27.50). Bus: 4 or 22.

Founded in 1879, the family-owned and -run Pensione Pendini offers an old-fashioned environment in a distinguished but faded setting. Your room may overlook the active piazza or front an inner courtyard (more peaceful). One of the oldest *pensioni* in Florence, it's located on the fourth floor of an arcaded building. The all-purpose lounge is furnished family style with a piano and card tables. The breakfast room, a redecorated large room inside one of the arcades, offers a view of the whole of via degli Strozzi. All the bedrooms are soundproofed, and some have quite a lot of character, with reproduction antiques. The bar/lounge is open 24 hours. The Pendini is not for everyone, but it's one of the long-enduring favorites among *pensione* fans visiting Florence. Only breakfast is served.

NEAR THE DUOMO
VERY EXPENSIVE

✪ **Hotel Helvetia & Bristol.** Via dei Pescioni 2, 50123 Firenze. ☎ **055/287814.** Fax 055/288353. 52 rms, 15 suites. A/C MINIBAR TV TEL. 410,000–510,000 lire ($262.40–$326.40) double; 660,000–1,400,000 lire ($422.40–$896) suite. AE, DC, MC, V. Parking 40,000 lire ($25.60). Bus: 31 or 32.

The Hotel Helvetia & Bristol is located in the most elegant part of Florence, just a few steps from the Duomo between via dei Tornabuoni and via degli Strozzi. Constructed in the late 19th century, and reopened in 1989 after a massive restoration, it was once the most exclusive hotel in Florence. Today it has reclaimed a lot of that old glory and is rivaled only by the Regency. It lacks the Regency's modern flair, however, and is rather somber and heavy, with draped windows, tasseled chairs,

15th-century paintings, and regal period furnishings. Strict attention was paid to preserving its original architectural features. The bedrooms come in about three different sizes, ranging from extremely generous to rather cramped. Some of the better rooms have whirlpool tubs.

Dining/Entertainment: The first-class Giardino d'Inverno (Winter Garden) was a gathering spot for Florentine intellectuals in the 1920s. It's now a cocktail bar serving light food. The main dining room, the Bristol, serves a deluxe cuisine (dinner only).

Services: Room service, baby-sitting, laundry, valet.

Facilities: Car-rental desk.

EXPENSIVE

Romantik Hotel J and J. Via di Mezzo 20, 50121 Firenze. ☎ **055/234005.** Fax 055/240282. 15 rms, 5 suites. A/C MINIBAR TV TEL. 350,000–450,000 lire ($224–$288) double; 500,000–575,000 lire ($320–$368) suite. Rates include breakfast. AE, DC, MC, V. Parking 35,000 lire ($22.40). Bus: 15.

This charming hotel, located within a 5-minute walk of the Church of Santa Croce, was originally built in the 16th century as a monastery. It underwent massive restoration in 1990 and was soon after transformed into the hotel you'll see today. Although acquired by the Romantik Hotel chain in 1994, the hotel has managed to preserve its familial atmosphere. You'll find many sitting areas throughout the property, including a flagstone-covered courtyard with stone columns, and a salon with vaulted ceilings and several preserved frescoes. The bedrooms combine modern furniture, some of it built in, with the monastery's original beamed ceilings. The suites usually contain sleeping lofts, and in some cases rooftop balconies overlooking Florence's historic center. There's a bar on the premises, but breakfast is the only meal served.

MODERATE

Grand Hotel Cavour. Via del Proconsolo 3, 50122 Firenze. ☎ **055/282461.** Fax 055/218955. 89 rms. A/C MINIBAR TV TEL. 243,000 lire ($155.50) double. Rates include breakfast. AE, DC, MC, V. Parking 30,000–55,000 lire ($19.20–$35.20). Bus: 14.

Located opposite the Bargello Museum, between via del Proconsolo and via Dante Alighieri, the Grand Hotel Cavour, originally an elaborate 13th-century palace, stands on one of the busiest and noisiest streets in Florence. The hotel is located on an important corner of the city, near the Badia Church, between the houses of the Cerchi and Pazzi families. It once belonged to the Cerchis, and in the lounge you can see where the old courtyard was laid out. The Hotel Cavour came into being in 1860–65, when Florence was the capital of Italy. It was nicknamed "The Senators' Hotel" because it was frequented by the members of the highest assembly of the new state.

The Cavour maintains its architectural splendor. The coved main lounge, with its frescoed ceiling and crystal chandelier, is of special interest, as is the old chapel, now used as a dining room. The altar and confessional are still there. The ornate ceiling and stained-glass windows reflect superb crafting. The bedrooms are traditionally styled and comfortably furnished. Each unit has a hair dryer.

INEXPENSIVE

Hotel Europa. Via Cavour 14, 50129 Firenze. ☎ **055/210361.** 13 rms. TV TEL. 130,000–140,000 lire ($83.20–$89.60) double. Rates include breakfast. AE, DC, MC, V. Bus: 1, 6, or 17.

Located 2 long blocks north of the Duomo, this 16th-century building has functioned as a family-run hotel since 1925. Despite the antique appearance of the simple exterior, much of the interior has been modernized. Plenty of homey touches remind guests of the hotel's ongoing administration by members of the Cassim family. All but four of the bedrooms overlook the back, usually opening onto a view of the campanile of the Duomo. Those that face the street are noisier, but benefit from double glazing that keeps out at least some of the traffic noise. Breakfast is the only meal served.

NEAR THE OPERA HOUSE
INEXPENSIVE

Ariele. Via Magenta 11, 50123 Firenze. ☎ **055/211509.** Fax 055/268521. 40 rms. AC TV TEL. 200,000 lire ($128) double; 230,000 lire ($147.20) triple. Rates include breakfast. AE, DC, MC, V. Parking 15,000 lire ($9.60). Bus: 1 or 13.

Located just a block from the Arno, the Ariele bills itself as "Your Home in Florence." It's an old corner villa that has been converted into a roomy *pensione.* The building is architecturally impressive, with large salons and lofty ceilings. The furnishings, however, combine antique with functional. The bedrooms are a grab bag of comfort.

Pensione Bretagna. Lungarno Corsini 6, 50123 Firenze. ☎ **055/289618.** Fax 055/289619. 18 rms, 10 with bath. 115,000 lire ($73.60) double without bath, 145,000 lire ($92.80) double with bath. Rates include breakfast. AE, MC, V. Parking 35,000 lire ($22.40). Bus: 13, 14, 15, 23, 31, or 32.

The centrally located Pensione Bretagna is in an early Renaissance palace that was the residence of Louis Napoléon in the 1820s, although it's a rather basic and simply furnished place today. It's a good cost-conscious choice though, and is run by a helpful staff, most of whom speak English. The rates depend on the plumbing, as some rooms don't have private bath. The bedrooms are rather basic, but the public rooms are impressive, with gilded stucco work, painted ceilings, fireplaces, and a balcony overlooking the Arno.

NEAR PIAZZA DELLA SANTISSIMA ANNUNZIATA
MODERATE

Hotel Le Due Fontane. Piazza della SS. Annunziata 14, 50122 Firenze. ☎ **055/210185.** Fax 055/294461. 53 rms, 3 suites. A/C MINIBAR TV TEL. 240,000 lire ($153.60) double; 350,000 lire ($224) suite. Rates include breakfast. AE, DC, MC, V. Parking 20,000 lire ($12.80). Bus: 17.

The Hotel Le Due Fontane is a small palace on the best-known Renaissance square in Florence, right in the heart of the artistic center of the city, within an easy walk of the Duomo. In spite of its antique origins in the 14th century, the hotel has been completely renovated and modernized. Today it offers simply but tastefully furnished bedrooms that are well kept if a bit uninspired. The upper-floor rooms offer the most tranquil night's sleep. Services and facilities include laundry, personal hotel bus service, car-rental facilities, shopping boutiques, a concierge, a business center, babysitting, and a bar.

INEXPENSIVE

Hotel Morandi alla Crocetta. Via Laura 50, 50121 Firenze. ☎ **055/234-4747.** Fax 055/248-0954. 10 rms. A/C MINIBAR TV TEL. 180,000 lire ($115.20) double; 249,000 lire ($159.35) triple. AE, DC, MC, V. Parking 14,000–18,000 lire ($8.95–$11.50). Bus: 1, 7, 10, 11, or 17.

This small, charming hotel is administered by one of the most experienced hoteliers in Florence, a sprightly matriarch, Katherine Doyle, who came to Florence from her native Ireland when she was 12. It contains all the elements needed for a Florence *pensione* and is situated on a little-visited backstreet near a university building. The structure was built in the 1500s as a convent. The bedrooms have been tastefully restored, filled with framed examples of 19th-century needlework, beamed ceilings, and antiques. In the best Tuscan tradition, the tall windows are sheltered from the summer sunlight with heavy draperies. You register in a high-ceilinged and austere salon filled with Persian carpets. The hotel lies right behind the Archeological Museum and 2 blocks from the Accademia (which displays Michelangelo's *David*).

OFF PIAZZA DELL'INDIPENDENZA
MODERATE

Rapallo. Via Santa Caterina d'Alessandria 7, 50129 Firenze. ☎ **055/472412.** Fax 055/470385. 30 rms. MINIBAR TV TEL. 212,000 lire ($135.70) double. Rates include breakfast. AE, DC, MC, V. Parking 25,000 lire ($16). Bus: 12.

Although the Rapallo is not typical of Florence, it is, nevertheless, completely revamped and inviting. The small lounge is brightened by planters, Oriental rugs, and barrel stools set in the corners for drinking and conversation. The bedrooms are furnished mostly with blond-wood suites, quite pleasant, and all have a private safe and, upon request, a TV. The hotel is within walking distance of the railway station.

INEXPENSIVE

Hotel Splendor. Via S. Gallo 30, 50129 Firenze. ☎ **055/483427.** Fax 055/461276. 31 rms, 25 with bath (tub or shower). TV TEL. 135,000 lire ($86.40) double without bath, 195,000 lire ($124.80) double with bath; 240,000 lire ($153.60) triple with bath. Rates include buffet breakfast. AE, MC, V. Parking 30,000 lire ($18.75). Bus: 1, 7, 10, 17, or 25.

Although the Hotel Splendor is within a 10-minute walk of the Duomo, the residential neighborhood it occupies is a world away from the milling hordes of the tourist district. The hotel occupies three high-ceilinged floors of a 19th-century apartment building. Its elegantly faded public rooms evoke the kind of family-run *pensione* that early in the century attracted genteel visitors from northern Europe for prolonged art-related visits, a sort of *Room with a View* crowd that used to descend on Florence from England. This is the domain of the Masoero family, whose homelike rooms contain an eclectic array of semi-antique furniture. All the singles have baths. There is no restaurant, but room service is available.

ON THE ARNO
EXPENSIVE

Plaza Hotel Lucchesi. Lungarno della Zecca Vecchia 38, 50122 Firenze. ☎ **055/26236,** or 800/223-9832 in the U.S. Fax 055/248-0921. 97 rms, 10 suites. A/C MINIBAR TV TEL. 440,000 lire ($281.60) double; 560,000 lire ($358.40) suite. Rates include breakfast. AE, DC, MC, V. Parking 25,000–40,000 lire ($16–$25.60). Bus: 32.

The Plaza Hotel Lucchesi—often a favorite with tour groups—was originally built in 1860 but has been renovated many times since then. It lies along the banks of the Arno, a 10-minute walk from the Duomo and a few paces from the imposing Church of Santa Maria della Croce. It also lies 6 blocks east of the Uffizi. Its interior decor includes lots of glossy mahogany, acres of marble, and masses of fresh flowers. Even though the bedrooms feature up-to-date equipment, they seem dated. Nevertheless, they're comfortable and well maintained, with many conveniences, including as trouser presses and well-stocked bathrooms. About 20 accommodations open onto private terraces or balconies, some with enviable views over the heart of historic Florence.

Dining/Entertainment: A large breakfast buffet and dinner are served in the sunny lobby-level restaurant, La Serra. The food is only average, however; you'll fare better at one of the independently run restaurants nearby. There's also a bar.

Services: Room service (24 hours), baby-sitting, laundry, valet.

Facilities: Car-rental desk.

MODERATE

Hotel Augustus. Vicolo del'Oro 5, 50123 Firenze. ☎ **055/283054.** Fax 055/268557. 62 rms, 8 suites. A/C MINIBAR TV TEL. 215,000–430,000 lire ($137.60–$275.20) double; 260,000–520,000 lire ($166.40–$332.80) suite. Rates include buffet breakfast. AE, DC, MC, V. Parking 30,000–40,000 lire ($19.20–$25.60). Bus: 7, 13, 14, 16, or 23.

The Hotel Augustus is for those who require modern comforts in a historic setting. The ponte Vecchio is just a short stroll away, as is the Uffizi Gallery. The exterior is rather pillbox modern, but the interior seems light, bright, and comfortable. The expansive lounge and drinking area is like an illuminated cave, with a curving ceiling and built-in conversation areas. Some of the bedrooms open onto little private balconies with garden furniture. The decor in the bedrooms consists of relatively simple provincial pieces, and the overall effect is rather lackluster but well maintained. You might find better lodgings at the Continental (see below) instead. Views of the Arno are often blocked by neighboring buildings. Laundry, baby-sitting, and 24-hour room service are provided.

NEAR THE PONTE VECCHIO

EXPENSIVE

Hotel Continental. Lungarno Acciaiuoli 2, 50123 Firenze. ☎ **055/282392.** Fax 055/283139. 48 rms, 1 suite. A/C MINIBAR TV TEL. 330,000–440,000 lire ($211.20–$281.60) double; 510,000 lire ($326.40) suite. Rates include continental breakfast. AE, DC, MC, V. Parking 35,000–40,000 lire ($22.40–$25.60).

Located at the entrance of the ponte Vecchio, the Hotel Continental occupies some select real estate and is a better choice than its sibling, the Augustus. Through the lounge windows and from some of the bedrooms you can see the little jewelry and leather shops that flank the much-painted bridge. Despite its perch in the center of historic Florence, the hotel was created in the 1960s, so its style of accommodation is utilitarian, with functional furniture that's softened by decorative accessories. The hotel was overhauled in 1992. You reach your bedroom by the elevator or by climbing a wrought-iron staircase (note that parts of the old stone structure have been retained). The management likes to put up North Americans, knowing they'll be attracted to the roof terrace, a vantage point for viewing piazzale Michelangiolo, the Pitti Palace, the Duomo, the campanile, and Fiesole. Artists fight to get the penthouse suite up in the tower (Torre Guelfa dei Consorti). Laundry, baby-sitting, and room service are available.

MODERATE

Hermitage Hotel. Vicolo Marzio 1, piazza del Pesce I, 50122 Firenze. ☎ **055/287216.** Fax 055/212208. 22 rms. AC TV TEL. 210,000–280,000 lire ($134.40–$179.20) double. Rates include breakfast. MC, V. Parking 30,000–40,000 lire ($19.20–$25.60).

The offbeat, intimate Hermitage Hotel is a charming place to stay right on the Arno. It has a rooftop sun terrace providing a view of much of Florence, including the nearby Uffizi. It competes effectively with the Continental nearby, but undercuts it with lower rates. You can take your breakfast under a leafy arbor surrounded by potted roses and geraniums. The success of this small hotel has much to do with its English-speaking owner, Vincenzo Scarcelli, who has made the Hermitage an extension of his home, furnishing it in part with antiques and well-chosen reproductions. Best of all is his warmth toward guests, many of whom keep coming back.

The extremmly small bedrooms are pleasantly furnished, many with Tuscan antiques, rich brocades, and good beds. The tiled baths are superb and contain lots of gadgets. Breakfast is served in a dignified, beam-ceilinged dining room. The rooms overlooking the Arno have the most scenic view, and they've been fitted with double-glass windows that reduce the traffic noise by 40%.

INEXPENSIVE

Hotel Calzaiuoli. Via dei Calzaiuoli, 50122 Firenze. ☎ **055/212456.** Fax 055/268310. 45 rms. A/C MINIBAR TV TEL. 210,000 lire ($134.40) double. Rates include breakfast. AE, DC, MC, V. Parking 30,000–45,000 lire ($19.20–$28.80). Bus: 1, 6, or 14.

The Hotel Calzaiuoli has one of the city's most desirable locations in terms of sightseeing, as the major attractions lie virtually on its doorstep. Although the building is old (it was a private home in the 1800s) and the location historic, the interior has been completely modernized in a rather severe contemporary style. The rooms are simple but comfortable, each furnished with functional and efficient pieces.

Pensione Alessandra. Borgo S.S. Apostoli 17, 50123 Firenze. ☎ **055/283438.** Fax 055/210619. 25 rms, 15 with bath. TEL. 110,000 lire ($70.40) double without bath, 160,000 lire ($102.40) double with bath. Rates include breakfast. AE, MC, V. Bus: 6, 11, or 36.

Within a block of the quays of the Arno, near the ponte Vecchio, this is a three-story, two-star, completely unpretentious *pensione*. Although the facade has retained some of its 15th-century severity, the bedrooms inside have been modernized into an efficient, not particularly luxurious format that many visitors find well suited to their needs. Those rooms on the uppermost floor are air-conditioned, and management has announced plans to add air-conditioning to the lower floors sometime during the lifetime of this edition. Some of the rooms contain TV. Breakfast is the only meal served.

ACROSS THE ARNO
MODERATE

Pensione Annalena. Via Romana 34, 50125 Firenze. ☎ **055/222403.** Fax 055/222403. 20 rms. TV TEL. 233,000 lire ($149.10) double. Rates include breakfast. AE, DC, MC, V. Parking 20,000 lire ($12.80). Bus: 36 or 37.

In existence since the 15th century, the Pensione Annalena has had many owners, including the Medici family. Once a convent, in the past three-quarters of a century it has been a haven for artists, poets, sculptors, and writers (Mary McCarthy once wrote of its importance as a cultural center). During a great deal of that period it was the domain of the late sculptor Olinto Calastri. Now it's owned by Claudio Salvestrini, who attracts paying guests sympathetic to the *pensione*'s special qualities. Most of the simply furnished and rather severe accommodations overlook a garden. During the war the Annalena was the center of much of the underground, as many Jews and rebel Italians found safety hidden away in an underground room behind a secret door. The *pensione* is about a 5-minute walk from the Pitti Palace, 10 minutes from the ponte Vecchio.

NEAR PIAZZALE MICHELANGIOLO
EXPENSIVE

Hotel Villa Carlotta. Via Michele di Lando 3, 50125 Firenze. ☎ **055/220530.** Fax 055/233-6147. 32 rms. A/C MINIBAR TV TEL. 240,000–370,000 lire ($153.60–$236.80) double. Rates include breakfast. AE, DC, MC, V. Free parking. Bus: 11, 36, or 37.

The lavish renovations that the owner poured into her distinguished establishment transformed it into one of the most charming smaller hotels in Florence. It was built during the Edwardian age as a private villa and acquired in the 1950s by Carlotta Buchholz, who named it after herself. The aura here is still very much like that of a private villa, and it's located in a residential section of the city. In 1985 all bedrooms were upgraded with the addition of pink or blue silk wallpaper, reproduction antiques, silk bedspreads, private safety-deposit boxes, and crystal chandeliers; each also has a view of the surrounding garden. The hotel is only a 10-minute walk from the ponte Vecchio; by taxi, it's a 5-minute ride.

Dining/Entertainment: The dining room, Il Bobolino, serves meals ranging from fresh salads to full culinary regalias.

Services: Room service, baby-sitting, laundry, valet.

Facilities: Garden, car-rental desk.

AT GALLUZZO
EXPENSIVE

Relais Certosa. Via di Colle Ramole 2, 50124 Firenze. ☎ **055/204-7171,** or 800/223-9832 in the U.S. Fax 055/268575. 69 rms, 6 suites. A/C MINIBAR TV TEL. 340,000 lire ($217.60) double; 495,000 lire ($316.80) suite. Rates include breakfast. AE, DC, MC, V. Free parking. Bus: 37 from the station. Take the Rome–Milan expressway to exit A1, "Firenze/Certosa"; go 300 yards and turn left on a signposted road leading to the hotel.

The four-story Relais Certosa is set on 5 acres of land with tennis courts. It was originally a guesthouse for the nearby monastery, but during the Renaissance it became the villa that stands today. After centuries of use in private hands, it became a hotel in the 1970s, which today could easily become your home in Florence. Convenient for motorists who want to avoid the hysterical city center, it's only 10 minutes from the monumental district and 5 minutes from the Rome–Milan expressway. Its rooms are well furnished, and each has individual climate control. Somehow the owners, the Bettoja family, have managed to blend Renaissance charm and style with modern comfort. All rooms face a park with views of the Tuscan hills and the Certosa monastery. There's parking space for 200 cars.

Dining/Entertainment: The Greenhouse Resaurant offers guests and nonguests alike some of the best Tuscan dining in the area, featuring regional specialties as well as continental dishes. Guests also enjoy a garden and terrace for drinks and snacks and a bar.

Services: Room service, laundry, valet.

Facilities: Tennis courts, parking.

4 Dining

The Florentine table has always been set with the abundance provided by the Tuscan countryside. That means the best of olive oil and wine, such as chianti, succulent fruits and vegetables, fresh fish from the coast, and the best of game in season. Meat-lovers all over Italy sing the praise of *bistecca alla fiorentina,* a thick and juicy steak on the bone often served with white Tuscan beans.

The Tuscan cuisine (except for some of its hair-raising specialties) should please most North Americans, as it's simply flavored, without rich spices, and based on the hearty, bountiful produce brought in from the hills. Florentine restaurants are not generally as acclaimed by gourmets as those of Rome, although good, moderately priced establishments abound. Florentines often assert that the cooking in the other regions of Italy "offends the palate."

The one Italian wine all foreigners recognize, the ruby-red chianti, usually served in a straw bottle, comes from Tuscany. Although shunned by some wine snobs, it's a fit complement to many a local repast.

Florence Dining

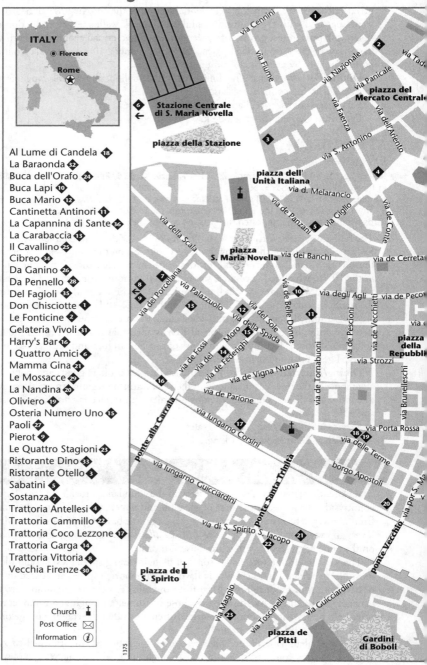

Al Lume di Candela **18**
La Baraonda **32**
Buca dell'Orafo **24**
Buca Lapi **10**
Buca Mario **12**
Cantinetta Antinori **11**
La Capannina di Sante **36**
La Carabaccia **13**
Il Cavallino **25**
Cibreo **34**
Da Ganino **26**
Da Pennello **28**
Del Fagioli **35**
Don Chisciotte **1**
Le Fonticine **2**
Gelateria Vivoli **31**
Harry's Bar **16**
I Quattro Amici **6**
Mamma Gina **21**
Le Mossacce **29**
La Nandina **20**
Oliviero **19**
Osteria Numero Uno **15**
Paoli **27**
Pierot **9**
Le Quattro Stagioni **23**
Ristorante Dino **33**
Ristorante Otello **3**
Sabatini **5**
Sostanza **7**
Trattoria Antellesi **4**
Trattoria Cammillo **22**
Trattoria Coco Lezzone **17**
Trattoria Garga **14**
Trattoria Vittoria **8**
Vecchia Firenze **30**

Church †
Post Office ✉
Information ⓘ

232

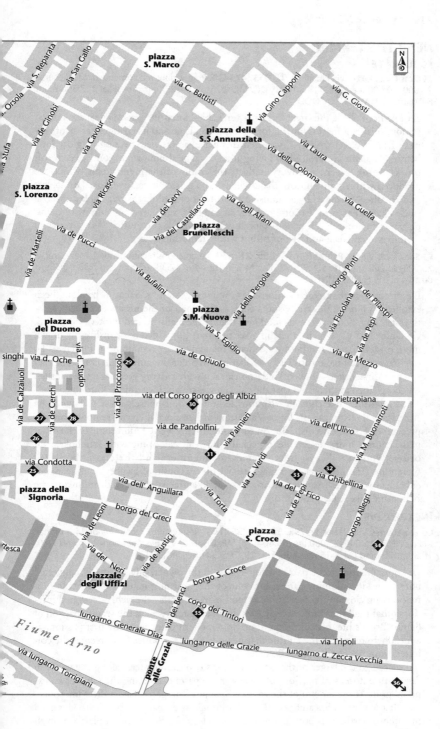

NEAR THE TERMINI
MODERATE

✪ Don Chisciotte. Via Ridolfi 4R. ☎ **055/475430.** Reservations recommended. Main courses 25,000–30,000 lire ($16–$19.20). AE, DC, MC, V. Mon 8–10:30pm, Tues–Sat 1–2:30pm and 8–10:30pm. ITALIAN/SEAFOOD.

Set one floor above the street level in a venerable Florentine *palazzo* near the railway station, this restaurant is known for its creative cuisine and its changing array of very fresh fish. We feel that we discovered this place, as we were touting its glory long before Michelin got around to giving it a star. The dining room, outfitted in soft tones of pink, green, and ivory, reflects the colors of the menu items, which are produced with a flourish from the kitchens. The cuisine is creative, based on flavors that are often enhanced by an unusual assortment of fresh herbs, vegetables, and fish stocks. Examples include risotto of broccoli and baby squid; red taglierini with clams, pesto, and cheese; black ravioli colored with squid ink and stuffed with a purée of shrimp and crayfish; and filet of turbot with a radicchio sauce.

✪ Sabatini. Via de' Panzani 9A. ☎ **055/211559.** Reservations recommended. Main courses 25,000–38,000 lire ($16–$24.30). AE, DC, MC, V. Tues–Sun 12:30–2:30pm and 7:30–10:30pm. Bus: 14 or 19. FLORENTINE.

Despite its less than chic location near the railway station, Sabatini has long been extolled by Florentines and visitors alike as the finest of the restaurants characteristic of the city. You'll get better food here than at the highly touted Enoteca Pinchiorri, via Ghibellina 87, which Michelin gives two stars but which has consistently drawn more reader disapproval (and we concur) than any other restaurant in Florence. To celebrate our annual return visit to Sabatini, we order the same main course we had when we first visited—boiled Valdarno chicken with a savory green sauce. Back then we complained to the waiter that the chicken was tough. He replied, "But, of course!" The Florentines like chicken with muscle, not the hot-house variety so favored by Americans. Having eaten a lot of Valdarno chicken since then, we're now more appreciative of Sabatini's dish. But on subsequent visits we've found some of the other main courses more delectable, especially the veal scaloppine with artichokes. Of course, you can always order a good sole meunière and the classic beefsteak Florentine. Another specialty is spaghetti Sabatini, a cousin of spaghetti carbonara but enhanced with fresh tomatoes. American-style coffee is also served, following the Florentine cake, called zuccotto.

INEXPENSIVE

Le Fonticine. Via Nazionale 79R. ☎ **055/282106.** Reservations recommended for dinner. Main courses 15,000–25,000 lire ($9.60–$16). AE, DC, MC, V. Tues–Sat noon–3pm and 7:30–10:30pm. Closed Jan 1–15 and Aug. Bus: 19. TUSCAN/BOLOGNESE.

Le Fonticine used to be part of a convent until the owner, Silvano Bruci, converted both it and its adjoining garden into one of the most hospitable restaurants in Florence, lying close to the San Lorenzo food market. Today the richly decorated interior contains all the abundance of an Italian harvest, as well as the second passion of Signor Bruci's life, his collection of original modern paintings. The first passion, as a meal here reveals, is the cuisine that he and his wife produce from recipes she collected from her childhood in Bologna.

Proceed to the larger of the establishment's two dining areas; along the way you can admire dozens of portions of freshly made pasta decorating the table of an exposed grill. At the far end of the room a wrought-iron gate shelters the wine collection that Mr. Bruci has amassed, like his paintings, over many years. The food, served in copious portions, is both traditional and delectable. Begin with a platter of fresh antipasti, then follow with samplings of three of the most excellent pasta dishes of the day. This might be followed by fegatina di pollo (chicken), veal scaloppine, or one of the other main dishes.

AT PIAZZA SANTA MARIA NOVELLA
MODERATE

I Quattro Amici. Via degli Orti Oricellari 29. ☎ **055/215413.** Reservations recommended. Main courses 43,000–70,000 lire ($27.50–$44.80). AE, DC, MC, V. Daily noon–3pm and 7–10:30pm. Bus: All buses from the station. SEAFOOD.

Established in 1990 by four Tuscan entrepreneurs who had known one another since childhood, this restaurant occupies the street level of a modern building near the railway station. Inside, amid a vaguely neoclassical decor, the place serves endless quantities of fish to a landlocked clientele eager for memories of the sea. Specialties include pasta with fish sauce and fragments of sausage, fish soup, fried shrimp and squid in the style of Livorno, and grilled, stewed, or baked versions of all the bounty of the Mediterranean. The roast sea bass and roast snapper, flavored with Mediterranean herbs, are among the finest dishes. The vegetables are fresh and flavorful. Every Thursday, Friday, and Saturday evening, guests are treated to live music while they dine.

Osteria Numero Uno. Via del Moro 22. ☎ **055/284897.** Reservations recommended. Main courses 12,000–25,000 lire ($7.70–$16). AE, DC, MC, V. Mon 7:30–11:30pm, Tues–Sat 12:30–3:30pm and 7:30–11:30pm. Closed Aug. Bus: All buses from the station. ITALIAN/INTERNATIONAL.

This restaurant derives its name from its original location, since 1959, at number one (*numero uno*) on a street near its present location on via del Moro. In 1985 the restaurant moved to its new premises in a 15th-century *palazzo* within a 3-minute walk from the railway station. Its cuisine is a well-prepared, well-presented blend of international foods and Italian dishes.

Many diners prefer a seat in the main dining room, with its vaulted ceiling and oversize fireplace, although two adjacent dining rooms contain part of the spillover. Menu choices include taglierini with mushrooms (with or without truffles); ravioli stuffed with either ricotta and basil or fresh artichokes; risotto with asparagus or sweet peppers; carpaccio of beef or salmon; the classic Florentine tripe; chicken with marsala or with parmesan; turbot baked with artichokes, herbs, and potatoes; and Florentine-style beefsteak, which is usually prepared for two diners. Dessert might be succulent torta della nonna.

Ristorante Otello. Via degli Orti Oricellari 36R. ☎ **055/216517.** Reservations recommended. Main courses 12,000–30,000 lire ($7.70–$19.20). AE, DC, MC, V. Daily noon–3pm and 7:30–11pm. Bus: 14, 17, 23, 28, 35, or 62. FLORENTINE.

😊 Family-Friendly Restaurants

Da Pennello (*see p. 238*)   This family-style trattoria near Dante's house offers filling, tasty, and inexpensive dishes.

Gelateria Vivoli (*see p. 243*)   After tasting the ice cream here—in virtually every known flavor—your child might agree that this place was worth the trip to Florence.

La Nandina (*see p. 239*)   Florentine families frequent this place off the Arno, a 4-mile walk from the Uffizi.

Located next to the train station, Ristorante Otello is a long-established Florentine dining room that serves an animated clientele in comfortably renovated surroundings. Its antipasto Toscano is one of the best in town, an array of appetizing hors d'oeuvres that practically becomes a meal in itself. The waiter urges you to "*Mangi, mangi, mangi!*" ("Eat, eat, eat!") and that's what diners do here, as the victuals at Otello have been known to stir the most lethargic of appetites. The true trencherperson goes on to order one of the succulent pasta dishes, such as spaghetti with small baby clams or pappardelle with garlic sauce. The meat and poultry dishes are equally delectable, including sole meunière or veal pizzaiola with lots of garlic.

INEXPENSIVE

La Carabaccia. Via Palazzuolo 190R. ☎ **055/214782.** Main courses 16,000–35,000 lire ($10.25–$22.40). AE, MC, V. Mon 7:30–10:30pm, Tues–Sat 12:30–2:30pm and 7:30–10:30pm. Closed 15 days in Aug. Bus: 19. FLORENTINE.

Two hundred years ago a *carabaccia* was a workaday boat, shaped like a hollowed-out half onion and used on the Arno to dredge silt and sand from the river bottom. The favorite onion soup of the Medici was zuppa carabaccia, which this restaurant still features today. It's a creamy white onion soup served with croutons (and not in the French style, the chef rushes to tell you). You can, of course, eat more than onions here. The menu changes every day and is based on whatever fresh local ingredients are available. There's always one soup, followed by four or five pastas, including crespelle (crêpe) of such fresh vegetables as asparagus or artichokes. The restaurant was established in the 1970s in a building two centuries old.

Ⓢ Le Mossacce. Via del Proconsolo 55R. ☎ **055/294361.** Main courses 9,000–14,000 lire ($5.75–$8.95). AE, MC, V. Mon–Fri noon–2:30pm and 7–9:30pm. Closed Aug. TUSCAN.

Le Mossacce, patronized by a long list of faithful Tuscan fans, is conveniently located midway between two of the city's most famous monuments, the Bargello and the Duomo. This small 35-seat restaurant was established at the turn of the century. Within its 300-year-old walls, a team of hard-working waiters serve excellent meals, offering selections from a wide range of Florentine and Italian specialties, including ribollita (a thick regional vegetable soup), cannelloni, and heavily seasoned baked pork. Bistecca alla fiorentina is also a favorite selection.

Ⓢ Sostanza. Via del Porcellana 25R. ☎ **055/212691.** Reservations recommended. Main courses 14,000–28,000 lire ($8.95–$17.90). No credit cards. Mon–Fri noon–2:10pm and 7:30–9:30pm. Closed Aug and 2 weeks at Christmas. Bus: All buses from the station. FLORENTINE.

Sostanza is the city's oldest and most revered trattoria. It has long been where working people have gone for excellent, moderately priced food. But in recent years, however, it has begun attracting a more sophisticated set as well. Florentines call the place Troia, which means "hog," but also suggests a woman of easy virtue. The small dining room has crowded family tables. When you taste what comes out of that kitchen, you'll know that fancy decor would be superfluous. Specialties include breaded chicken breast and a succulent T-bone steak. You might also want to try tripe in the Florentine way—that is, cut into strips, then baked in a casserole with tomatoes, onions, and parmesan cheese.

Ⓢ Trattoria Antellesi. Via Faenza 9R. ☎ **055/216990.** Reservations recommended. Main courses 15,000–22,000 lire ($9.60–$14.10). AE, DC, MC, V. Mon–Sat noon–3pm and 7–10:30pm. Bus: All buses from the station. TUSCAN.

Set on the ground floor of a 15th-century historic monument, a few steps from the Medici Chapel, this restaurant is devoted almost exclusively to well-prepared versions of time-tested Tuscan recipes. Owned by Enrico Verrecchia and his Arizona-born wife, Janice, the restaurant prepares at least seven *piatti del giorno* (daily specials) that change according to the availability and seasonality of the ingredients. Dishes might include tagliatelle with porcini mushrooms or with braised arugula, crespelle alla fiorentina (cheesy spinach crêpe introduced to France by Catherine de Medici's kitchen staff), pappardelle with wild boar, market-fresh fish (generally on Friday), delicious Valdostana chicken, and properly grilled bistecca alla fiorentina. The array of quality Italian wines (with an emphasis on Tuscany) has for the most part been selected by Janice herself.

NEAR THE DUOMO
MODERATE

Trattoria Coco Lezzone. Via del Parioncino 26R. ☎ **055/287178.** Reservations accepted only for groups of 10 or more. Main courses 15,000–50,000 lire ($9.60–$32). No credit cards. Mon–Sat noon–2:30pm and 7–10pm. Closed the last week of July to Aug and Dec 25–Jan 6. Bus: 27 or 31. FLORENTINE.

In Florentine dialect this establishment's name refers to the sauce-stained apron of the extroverted chef who established this place more than a century ago. Today this is a good place to sample the hearty fare of the Tuscan countryside. During the bustling lunch hour Florentines crowd in for a spot at one of the long tables. Go early before the rush begins if you want a seat. The hearty fare includes generous portions of boiled meats with a green sauce, pasta fagiole (beans), osso buco, tripe, or beefsteak Florentine, which must be ordered by phone in advance.

INEXPENSIVE

⑤ **Vecchia Firenze.** Borgo degli Albizi 18. ☎ **055/234-0361.** Main courses 10,000–20,000 lire ($6.40–$12.80). AE, DC, MC, V. Daily noon–2pm and 7–10pm. FLORENTINE.

Established in the 1950s, Vecchia Firenze combines atmosphere and budget meals. It's housed in an old palace with an elegant entrance through high doors. Some of the tables are in the courtyard; others are inside the vaulted dining rooms. The restaurant is lit by a wrought-iron chandelier. It's not elaborately voguish—in fact, it caters to students and the working people of Florence, who eat here regularly and never seem to tire of its simple but good-tasting offerings. You might begin with a tagliatelle Vecchia Firenze, then follow with a quarter of a roast chicken or sole in butter.

NEAR PIAZZA DELLA SIGNORIA
INEXPENSIVE

⑤ **Il Cavallino.** Via della Farine 6R. ☎ **055/215818.** Reservations recommended. Main courses 12,000–25,000 lire ($7.70–$16); fixed-price menu 30,000 lire ($19.20). AE, DC, MC, V. Thurs–Tues noon–2:30pm and 7–10pm. Bus: 31 or 32. TUSCAN/ITALIAN.

Il Cavallino is the kind of discreetly famous restaurant where Florentines invariably go just to be with one another. The place has been a local favorite since the 1930s. It's on a tiny street (which probably won't even be on your map) that leads off piazza della Signoria at its northern end, not far from the equestrian statue. There's usually a gracious reception at the door, especially if you called ahead for a reservation. Two of the three dining rooms have vaulted ceilings and peach-colored marble floors. The main room looks out over the piazza. Menu items are typical hearty Tuscan fare, including an assortment of boiled meats in green herb sauce, grilled filet of steak, breast of chicken Medici style, and the inevitable Florentine spinach.

Da Ganino. Piazza dei Cimatori 4R. ☎ **055/214125.** Reservations recommended. Main courses 15,000–25,000 lire ($9.60–$16). AE, DC, MC, V. Mon–Sat 1–3pm and 8–11pm. Bus: All buses from the Duomo. FLORENTINE/TUSCAN.

The small and intimate Da Ganino is staffed with the kind of waiters who take the quality of your meal as their personal responsibility. Someone will recite to you the frequently changing specialties of the day, which might include well-seasoned versions of Tuscan beans, spinach risotto, grilled veal liver, grilled veal chops, and Florentine beefsteak on the bone. The tagliatelle con tartufo makes an excellent, if expensive, appetizer. Also worthwhile is filet of chicken with a lemon-cream sauce and a fritto misto of meats, including brains, kidneys, beef filets, lamb chops, and a selection of grilled vegetables.

⑤ Da Pennello. Via Dante Alighieri 4R. ☎ **055/294848.** Main courses 15,000–22,000 lire ($9.60–$14.10); fixed-price menu 25,000 lire ($16). AE, MC, V. Tues–Sat noon–3pm and 7–10pm, Sun noon–3pm. Closed Aug 1–30 and Dec 25–Jan 3. FLORENTINE/ITALIAN.

This informally operated trattoria offers many Florentine specialties on its à la carte menu and is known for its wide selection of antipasti; you can make a meal out of these delectable hors d'oeuvres. The ravioli is homemade and one pasta specialty—beloved of locals—is spaghetti carretiera, made with tomatoes and pepperoni. To follow, you can have deviled roast chicken. The chef posts daily specials, and sometimes it's best to order one of these, as the food offered was bought fresh that day at the market. A Florentine cake, zuccotto, rounds out the meal. The restaurant is on a narrow street, near Dante's house, about a 5-minute walk from the Duomo toward the Uffizi.

Paoli. Via dei Tavolini 12R. ☎ **055/216215.** Reservations required. Main courses 15,000–28,000 lire ($9.60–$17.90); fixed-price menu 38,000 lire ($24.30). AE, DC, MC, V. Wed–Mon noon–2:30pm and 7–10:30pm. Closed 3 weeks in Aug. Bus: 14 or 23. TUSCAN/ITALIAN.

Paoli, located between the Duomo and piazza della Signoria, is one of the finest restaurants in Florence. It was established in 1824 by the Paoli brothers in a building that dated in part from the 13th century. It turns out a host of specialties, but it could be recommended almost solely for its medieval-tavern atmosphere, with arches and ceramics stuck into the walls like medallions. The walls are adorned with frescoes. The pastas are homemade, and the chef also does a superb rognoncino (kidney) trifolato and a sole meunière. A recommendable side dish is piselli (garden peas) alla fiorentina.

ON THE ARNO
EXPENSIVE

La Capannina di Sante. Piazza Ravenna, adjacent to the ponte Giovanni da Verrazzano. ☎ **055/688345.** Reservations recommended. Main courses 20,000–40,000 lire ($12.80–$25.60); fixed-price menu 90,000 lire ($57.60). AE, DC, MC, V. Mon–Sat 7:30pm–1am. Closed 1 week in Aug. Bus: 23. SEAFOOD.

This simple and unpretentious restaurant, featuring a river-view terrace for outdoor dining, has functioned in more or less the same way on and off since 1935. The restaurant serves only the best and freshest seafood, prepared in a simple and healthy manner, usually with olive oil or butter and Mediterranean seasonings. Examples include filets of sea bass or turbot, mixed seafood grills, and an occasional portion of veal or steak for anyone who doesn't care for fish. For an appetizer, we recommend the sampling of hot seafood appetizers—there's none finer in Florence. The wines are simple and straightforward, and the greeting is warm and friendly.

Harry's Bar. Lungarno Vespucci 22R. ☎ **055/239-6700.** Reservations required. Main courses 18,000–33,000 lire ($11.50–$21.10). AE, MC, V. Mon–Sat noon–3pm and 7–11pm. Closed Dec 18–Jan 8 and 1 week in August. Bus: 6. ITALIAN/AMERICAN.

Harry's Bar, located in an 18th-century building in a prime position on the Arno, has been an enclave of expatriate and well-heeled visiting Yankees since 1953. Harry's is the easiest place in Florence to meet fellow Americans. The international menu is small but select, and beautifully prepared. A specialty is either risotto or tagliatelle with ham, onions, and cheese. The gamberetti (crayfish) cocktail is very tempting. Harry has created his own tortellini, but his hamburger and his club sandwich are the most popular items. The chef also prepares about a dozen specialties every day: breast of chicken "our way," grilled giant-size scampi, and a lean broiled sirloin steak. An apple tart with cream nicely finishes off a meal.

NEAR THE PONTE VECCHIO
INEXPENSIVE

Ⓢ Buca dell'Orafo. Via Volta dei Girolami 28R. ☎ 055/213619. Main courses 10,000–30,000 lire ($6.40–$19.20). No credit cards. Tues–Sat 12:30–2:30pm and 7:30–10:30pm. Closed Aug and 2 weeks in Dec. Bus: 3, 6, 22, 31, or 32. FLORENTINE.

Established in the 1940s, Buca dell'Orafo is a little dive (one of the many cellars or *buca*-type establishments beloved by Florentines). An *orafo* is a goldsmith, and it was in this part of Florence that the goldsmith trade grew. The buca, once part of an old goldsmith shop, is reached via a street under a vaulted arcade right off piazza del Pesce. The trattoria is usually stuffed with regulars, so if you want a seat, go early. Over the years the chef has made little concession to the foreign palate, turning out instead genuine Florentine specialties, including tripe and mixed boiled meats with a green sauce and stracotto e fagioli (beef braised in a sauce of chopped vegetables and red wine), served with beans in a tomato sauce. There's a feeling of camaraderie among the diners here.

La Nandina. Borgo SS. Apostoli 64R. ☎ **055/213024.** Reservations recommended. Main courses 20,000–30,000 lire ($12.80–$19.20). AE, DC, MC, V. Mon 7–10:30pm, Tues–Sat noon–3pm; and 7–10:30pm. Closed 2 weeks in Aug. Bus: 3, 11, 14, or 19. TUSCAN/INTERNATIONAL.

This family-run restaurant is located just off the Arno, about a 4-minute walk from the Uffizi (in fact, it's an excellent choice for lunch if you're visiting the galleries). Established in 1924, this elegant restaurant is an old favorite with both Florentines and visitors alike. You can have an apéritif in the intimate and plushly upholstered cocktail lounge. There's also a 14th-century cellar for dining. The cuisine consists of dishes from the provinces and such cities as Rome, Tuscany, and Venice, and might include ravioli with flap mushrooms, spinach crêpes, curried breast of capon, veal piccatina, several kinds of beefsteak, and a changing array of daily specials. All the food is of high quality but not fussy.

NEAR SANTA CROCE
MODERATE

La Baraonda. Via Ghibellina 67R. ☎ **055/234-1171.** Reservations recommended. Main courses all 20,000 lire ($12.80). AE, DC. Mon 8–10:30pm, Tues–Sat 1–2:30pm and 8–10:30pm. Bus: 14. TUSCAN.

Locals make up about 80% of the clientele of this bustling trattoria, many of them merchants and hotel employees. This small, gregarious establishment—with a name that translates as "hubbub" or "disorder"—serves a Tuscan cuisine flavored with seasonally available local ingredients. Some members of the staff speak fluent English, and in many cases will propose carefully assembled fixed-price meals. Examples from the ever-changing menu include an array of sformato di verdure (vegetable soufflés made from, among other ingredients, artichokes or whatever else is in season at the moment), risotto with fresh greens, and a savory meatloaf (polpettone in umido) made with veal and fresh tomatoes. At the end of the meal, complimentary sweets and grappa are served.

$ **Cibreo.** Via dei Macci 118R. ☎ **055/234-1100.** Reservations recommended in the restaurant, not accepted in the trattoria. Main courses all 40,000 lire ($25.60) in the restaurant, all 15,000 lire ($9.60) in the trattoria. AE, DC, MC, V (restaurant only). Tues–Sat 12:30pm and 8–11pm. Closed late July to early Sept. Bus: 6 or 14. MEDITERRANEAN.

The unpretentious Cibreo consists of a restaurant, a less formal tavern-style trattoria, and a cafe-bar across the street. The small and impossibly old-fashioned kitchen is noteworthy for not containing a grill and for not serving pastas. Instead, Cibreo specializes in food cooked in a wood-burning oven and cold marinated dishes (especially vegetables). Menu items include a sformato (a soufflé made from potatoes and ricotta, served with parmesan cheese and tomato sauce), inzimmino (Tuscan-style squid stewed with spinach), and a flan of Parmesan cheese, veal tongue, and artichokes.

Some of the staff are expatriate New Yorkers who excel at explaining the restaurant's culinary themes. The restaurant takes its name from (and serves) an old Tuscan dish (Cibreo) that was allegedly so delectable it nearly killed Catherine de' Medici. (She consumed so much that she was overcome with near-fatal indigestion.)

$ **Del Fagioli.** Corso dei Tintori 47R. ☎ **055/244285.** Reservations recommended. Main courses 18,000–25,000 lire ($11.50–$16). No credit cards. Mon–Fri noon–2:30pm and 7:30–10:30pm. Closed Aug. Bus: 19, 31, or 32. FLORENTINE/TUSCAN.

Devoted to the pleasures of country-style Tuscan cuisine, this restaurant (whose name translates as "beans") was established in 1966 in a pair of dining rooms lined with old engravings of the monuments of Florence. It serves a choice of locally made affettati toscani (sausages, pâtés, and dried or salted meats), a hearty ribollita (cabbage and bread soup), several types of spaghetti and tagliatelle, sliced breast of turkey, Florentine beefsteak, and game dishes in season. Fish might include oven-roasted sea bass or monkfish, its flavor enhanced with herbs. Fagioli, incidentally, was also a traditional name for the buffoons (clowns and humorists) who performed throughout the Renaissance for the political rulers of Florence.

INEXPENSIVE

Ristorante Dino. Via Ghibellina 51. ☎ **055/241452.** Reservations recommended. Main courses 16,000–6,000 lire ($10.25–16.65). AE, DC, MC, V. Tues–Sat noon–3pm and 7:30–10:30pm, Sun noon–3pm. Bus: 14. TUSCAN.

In a 14th-century building near the Casa Buonarroti, this restaurant has vaulted ceilings and a cuisine inspired by members of the Casini family. Specialties include spaghetti alla Dino, flavored with carrots, celery, chile peppers, and aromatic herbs; risotto della Renza, rich with aromatic herbs and fresh tomatoes; and ribollita, the cabbage, bean, and bread soup of Tuscany. Tuscan purists are often jolted with memories of their childhood at the mention of one of the restaurant's ever-present dishes, garetto Ghibellino, a historic recipe made from pork shanks with celery and sage. The excellent wine list features vintages from throughout Italy, especially Tuscany.

NEAR THE STRAW MARKET
MODERATE

Al Lume di Candela. Via delle Terme 23R. ☎ **055/294566.** Reservations required. Main courses 20,000–35,000 lire ($12.80–$22.40). AE, MC, V. Mon–Sat 7:30–11pm. Closed 1 week in Aug. Bus: 6, 11, 17, 19, or 22. TUSCAN/INTERNATIONAL.

Established in 1948, Al Lume di Candela is uniquely located in a 13th-century tower that was partially leveled when its patrician family fell from grace (the prestige of Tuscan families was once reflected in how high their family towers soared). With a tavern decor, the restaurant offers a typically Florentine cuisine. The candelit atmosphere makes for romantic dining, and the place has attracted celebrities in the past.

The food is precise and often inventive, combining rich tastes and unusual flavors. Dishes include taglierini with sage and porcini mushrooms; a very light version of house-smoked salmon; veal chops stuffed with white beans (cannellini) and arugula; entrecôte (sirloin) of beef grilled with pepper, olive oil, and Tuscan herbs; maccheroncini served with thyme; and calamari seared in sherry with pecorino cheese.

Oliviero. Via delle Terme 51R. ☎ 055/287643. Reservations required. All main courses 28,000 lire ($17.90). AE, DC, MC, V. Mon–Sat 7:30–11:30pm. Closed Aug. Bus: 11, 31, or 32. TUSCAN.

This is a small but smart, luxurious dining room. From 8pm on, live music is featured in the piano bar. The finest traditions of Tuscan cookery are maintained here, with highly select, fresh ingredients. The menu is frequently changed to keep abreast of what's in season. You might, for example, savor such appetizers as octopus salad with basil, string beans, and tomatoes; fried mussels and squash blossoms; or Tuscan ham with figs and bread coated with virgin olive oil. Main courses usually include fresh fish; grilled, boned rabbit and young cock with shell beans; or ravioli stuffed with chopped liver and served with a delicate sauce of white onions. For dessert, you might try the green fig mousse with almonds and chocolate.

NEAR PIAZZA GOLDONI
MODERATE

⑤ **Trattoria Garga.** Via del Moro 48–52. ☎ **055/239-8898.** Reservations required. Main courses 24,000–60,000 lire ($15.35–$38.40). AE, DC, MC, V. Tues–Sat 12:30–3pm and 7:30pm–midnight, Sun 7:30pm–midnight. Bus: All buses from the station. TUSCAN.

Some of the most creative cuisine in Florence is served here. The building's thick Renaissance walls contain paintings by both Florentine and American artists, including those painted by the owners themselves, Giuliano Gargani and his Canadian wife, Sharon. Both operatic arias and heavenly odors emerge from a postage-stamp-size kitchen. Many of the Tuscan menu items are so unusual that Sharon's bilingual skills are put to good use. Dishes include octopus with peppers and garlic, boar with juniper berries, grilled marinated quail, and "whatever strikes the mood" of Giuliano. One dish, created in 1992, has earned a lot of publicity—tagliarini magnifico, made with angel-hair pasta, orange and lemon rind, mint-flavored cream, and Parmesan cheese. The location is between the ponte Vecchio and Santa Maria Novella.

AT PIAZZA ANTINORI
MODERATE

Buca Lapi. Via del Trebbio 1R. ☎ **055/213768.** Reservations required for dinner. Main courses 22,000–35,000 lire ($14.10–$22.40). AE, DC, MC, V. Mon 7:30–10:30pm, Tues–Sat 12:30–2:30pm and 7:30–10:30pm. Closed 2 weeks in Aug. Bus: 22. TUSCAN.

Buca Lapi, a cellar restaurant founded in 1880, is big on glamour, good food, and the enthusiasm of fellow diners. Its decor alone—under the Palazzo Antinori—makes it fun: The vaulted ceilings are covered with travel posters from all over the world. There's a long table of interesting fruits, desserts, and vegetables. The cooks know how to turn out the most classic dishes of the Tuscan kitchen with superb finesse. Specialties include scampi giganti alla griglia, a super-size shrimp, and bistecca alla fiorentina (local beefsteak). In season, the fagioli toscani all'olio (Tuscan beans in the native olive oil) are a delicacy to many palates. For dessert, try the international favorite, crêpes Suzette, or the local choice, zuccotto, a Florentine cake that's *delicato*.

INEXPENSIVE

Buca Mario. Piazza Ottaviani 16R. ☎ **055/214179.** Reservations required. Main courses 12,000–25,000 lire ($7.70–$16). AE, DC, MC, V. Thurs 12:15–2:30pm, Fri–Tues 12:15–2:30pm and 7:15–10:30pm. Closed Aug. Bus: All buses from the station. FLORENTINE.

Buca Mario, in business for a century, is one of the most famous cellar restaurants of Florence. It's located right in the historic center in the 1886 Palazzo Niccolini. Tables are placed beneath vaulted ceilings. Some of the waiters have worked in the States; they might suggest an array of Florentine pastas, beefsteak, Dover sole, or beef carpaccio, followed by a tempting selection of desserts. Cookery is in the most robust of the *buca* style. It bursts with flavor and there's a wonderful exuberance about the place, but in the enigmatic words of one longtime habitué: "It's not for the faint-hearted."

Cantinetta Antinori. Piazza Antinori 3. ☎ **055/292234.** Reservations recommended. Main courses 22,000–28,000 lire ($14.10–$17.90). AE, DC, MC, V. Mon–Fri 12:30–2:30pm and 7–10:30pm. Closed Aug and Dec 24–Jan 6. Bus: 1, 14, 23, 31, or 32. ITALIAN/TUSCAN.

Hidden behind the severe stone facade of the 15th-century Palazzo Antinori is the Catinetta Antinori, one of Florence's most popular restaurants and one of the city's few top-notch wine bars. Small wonder that the cellars should be supremely well stocked since the restaurant is one of the city's showplaces for the vintages of the oldest and most distinguished wine company in Tuscany, Umbria, and Piedmont. Vintages can be consumed by the glass at the stand-up bar or by the bottle as an accompaniment to the Italian meals served at wooden tables. The not especially large room is decorated with floor-to-ceiling racks of aged and undusted wine bottles. You can eat a full meal or just snacks. The cookery is standard but satisfying, especially the sausages with white haricot beans and the fresh Tuscan ewe's cheese.

NEAR PIAZZA TADDEO GADDI
MODERATE

Ⓢ Trattoria Vittoria. Via della Fonderia 52R. ☎ **055/225657.** Reservations recommended. Main courses 21,000–60,000 lire ($13.45–$38.40). AE, DC, MC, V. Thurs–Tues noon–3:30pm and 7:30–10:30pm. Bus: 6. SEAFOOD.

This unheralded and untouristy establishment serves some of the finest fish dishes in Florence. It's a big and bustling trattoria, and service is frenetic. Most of the fresh fish dishes of the day are priced according to weight, making a main dish considerably higher than the prices quoted above. Sole is the most expensive, although you can also order equally tempting lower-priced dishes. Two outstanding choices to begin your meal include risotto alla marinara and spaghetti alla vongole (clams). The mixed fish fry gives you a little bit of everything. Desserts are homemade and extremely rich.

INEXPENSIVE

Pierot. Piazza Tadeo Gaddi 25R. ☎ **055/702100.** Reservations recommended. Main courses 12,000–25,000 lire ($7.70–$16). AE, DC, MC, V. Mon–Sat noon–3pm and 7–11:30pm. Closed July 15–31. Bus: 1, 2, 9, 26, or 27. SEAFOOD/TUSCAN.

Pierot is housed in a 19th-century building constructed during the reign of Vittorio Emanuel. Since 1955 Pierot has been a fixture of Florence. Although a few other places—already previewed—also specialize in seafood, this place is considered a bit of an oddity in landlocked Florence. The seasonal menu varies with the availability of ingredients, but might include linguini with frutti di mare (fruits of the sea), pasta with lobster sauce, and an array of traditional Tuscan steaks, soups, and vegetables. Seafood risotto is deservedly a perennial favorite.

ACROSS THE ARNO
INEXPENSIVE

Mamma Gina. Borgo Sant' Jacopo 37R. ☎ **055/239-6009.** Reservations required for dinner. Main courses 17,000–25,000 lire ($10.90–$16). AE, DC, MC, V. Mon–Sat noon–2:30pm and 7–10pm. Closed Aug 7–21. Bus: 6. TUSCAN.

Mamma Gina is a rustic left-bank restaurant that prepares fine foods in the traditional bustling manner. Although it's run by a corporation that operates other restaurants scattered throughout Tuscany, this restaurant is named after its founding matriarch (Mamma Gina), whose legend has continued despite her death in the 1980s. This exceptional trattoria, well worth the trek across the ponte Vecchio, is a center for hearty Tuscan fare. Some of the rich and savory menu items include cannelloni Mamma Gina (stuffed with a purée of minced meats, spices, and vegetables); tagliolini with artichoke hearts or mushrooms, and whatever else is in season at the time; and chicken breast Mamma Gina, baked in the northern Italian style with prosciutto and Emmenthaler cheese. This is an ideal spot for lunch after visiting the Pitti Palace.

Le Quattro Stagioni. Via Maggio 61R. ☎ **055/218906.** Reservations recommended. Main courses 7,000–15,000 lire ($4.50–$9.60). AE, DC, MC, V. Mon–Sat 12:15–2:30pm and 7:30–10:30pm. Closed Aug and Dec 25. Bus: 11, 13, 15, 36, or 37. TUSCAN/SEAFOOD.

Set in a historic building near the Pitti Palace, this charming and old-fashioned restaurant specializes in both seafood and classic Tuscan recipes, and does so exceedingly well. An efficient and professional staff serves such dishes as gnocchi, crostinis, pasta with squid in its own ink, roast lamb with artichokes, sea bass roasted with fennel, a succulent array of fresh vegetables, beefsteak, several different preparations of veal, and homemade desserts. As the establishment's name (The Four Seasons) implies, the menu changes according to the seasonal availability of the ingredients.

Trattoria Cammillo. Borgo Sant' Jacopo 57. ☎ **055/212427.** Reservations required. Main courses 12,000–45,000 lire ($7.70–$28.80). AE, DC, MC, V. Fri–Tues noon–2:30pm and 7:30–10:30pm. Closed mid-Dec to Jan and Aug 1–21. Bus: 1, 3, 6, 11, or 36. TUSCAN.

Housed on the ground floor of a former Medici palace, the Trattoria Cammillo is one of the most popular—and perhaps the finest—of the left-bank dining spots. Its most serious rival is Mamma Gina, which is also good, but not quite as good as this savvy choice. Snobbish boutique owners cross the Arno regularly to feast here. They know they'll get such specialties as tagliatelle flavored with fresh peas and truffles. This sounds like such as simple dish, but when it's prepared right, as it most often is here, it's a celestial treat. You'll also find excellent assortments of fried or grilled vegetables; super-fresh scampi and sole; fried, de-boned pigeon served with artichokes; and breast of chicken with truffles and Parmesan. The trattoria is between the ponte Vecchio and the ponte Santa Trinità. Because of increased business, you're likely to be rushed through a meal.

GELATO

✪ **Gelateria Vivoli.** Via Isola delle Stinche 7R. ☎ **055/292334.** Gelati 2,500–14,000 lire ($1.60–$8.95). No credit cards. Tues–Sun 8am–1am. Closed 3 weeks in Aug (dates vary). Bus: 14 or 23. ICE CREAM.

Established in the 1930s, and today run by the third generation of the Vivoli family, this establishment produces some of the finest ice cream in Italy. Of course, to hear it here, it's *the* finest. They provide the gelati for many of the restaurants of Florence. Buy your ticket first and then select your flavor. Choose from blueberry, fig, melon, and other fruits in season, as well as chocolate mousse, or even coffee ice cream flavored with espresso. A special ice cream is made from rice. The establishment offers a number of semifreddi concoctions—an Italian ice cream using cream as a base instead of milk. The most popular flavors are almond, marengo (a type of meringue), and zabaglione (eggnog). Other flavors include limoncini alla crema (candied lemon peels with vanilla-flavored ice cream) and aranciotti al cioccolate (candied orange peels with chocolate ice cream). The shop is located on a backstreet near the church and cloisters of Santa Croce.

5 What to See & Do

Florence was the fountainhead of the Renaissance, the city of Dante and Boccaccio. Characteristically, it was the city of Machiavelli, and uncharacteristically, of Savonarola. For three centuries it was dominated by the Medici family, patrons of the arts, masters of assassination. But it is chiefly through its artists that we know of the apogee of the Renaissance: Ghiberti, Fra Angelico, Donatello, Brunelleschi, Botticelli, and the incomparable Leonardo da Vinci and Michelangelo.

In Florence we can trace the transition from medievalism to an age of "rebirth." For example, all modern painters owe a debt to an ugly, awkward, unkempt man who died at age 27. His name was Masaccio (Vasari's "Slipshod Tom"). Modern painting began with his frescoes in the Brancacci Chapel in the Church of Santa Maria del Carmine, which you can go see today. Years later Michelangelo painted a more celebrated Adam and Eve in the Sistine Chapel, but even this great artist never realized the raw humanity of Masaccio's Adam and Eve fleeing from the Garden of Eden.

SUGGESTED ITINERARIES

These itineraries were obviously designed for the first-time visitor. Those calling on Florence for the second or third time might want to discover more esoteric treasures in this city of the Renaissance. However, you could wander every day of the year through the Uffizi and always find something new and different to look at. Readers who'll be spending only 2 or 3 days in Florence should try to visit the city toward the middle or end of the week if possible. Most museums close at 12:30 or 1pm on Sunday and are closed all day Monday.

If You Have 1 Day

You'll have to accept the inevitable—you can see only a small fraction of Florence's three-star attractions. Go to the Uffizi Galleries as soon as they open and concentrate only on some of the masterpieces. Before 1:30pm, visit the Accademia to see Michelangelo's *David* . . . at least that.

Have lunch on piazza della Signoria, dominated by the Palazzo Vecchio, and admire the statues in the Loggia della Signoria. After lunch, visit the Duomo and Baptistery, then pay a late-afternoon visit to the open-air straw market, Mercanto San Lorenzo, before crossing the ponte Vecchio at sunset. Finish a very busy day with a hearty Tuscan dinner in one of Florence's many *bucas,* or cellar restaurants.

If You Have 2 Days

Spend your first day in Florence as suggested above.

> ### ❷ Did You Know?
>
> - In 1503 both Michelangelo and Leonardo da Vinci won commissions to fresco the walls of the council chamber of the republic. Neither work has survived.
> - Some 500 sculptures and 1,000 paintings—priceless in the art world—were destroyed in the disastrous flood of 1966.
> - In 1865, Florence—not Rome—became the capital of Italy.
> - The word *renaissance* to describe the historic and artistic period that swept across Florence did not come into vogue until the publication in 1855 of Jules Michelet's *La Renaissance*.
> - Mark Twain, working on *Pudd'nhead Wilson* in the 1890s, claimed that he could write more in 4 months in the Tuscan countryside than he could produce in 2 years at home.
> - No dome since antiquity had been raised more than 180 feet above the ground until Brunelleschi created the dome for the Duomo of Florence.
> - The oldest bridge in Florence, the ponte Vecchio, was the only bridge over the Arno spared in August 1944 by the retreating Nazis.

On Day 2, return to the Uffizi Galleries for a more thorough look at this museum—the most important in Italy. Then in the afternoon visit the Pitti Palace, on the other side of the Arno, and wander through the Galleria Palatina, with its 16th- and 17th-century masterpieces, including 11 works by Raphael alone. After a visit, stroll through the adjoining Boboli Gardens. At sunset, go again to the Duomo and the Baptistery for a much better look.

If You Have 3 Days

Spend your first 2 days as suggested above.

In the morning of Day 3, visit the Palazzo Vecchio on piazza della Signoria, then walk to the nearby Palazzo del Bargello, which contains the most important works of Tuscan and Florentine sculpture from the Renaissance era. After lunch, visit the Museo dell'Opera del Duomo, with its sculptural masterpieces from the Duomo, including Donatello's *Mary Magdalene.*

If You Have 5 Days

Spend Days 1 to 3 as suggested above.

On Day 4, continue your exploration of Renaissance masterpieces by visiting the Medici Chapels, with Michelangelo's tomb for Lorenzo de Medici, including the figures of *Dawn* and *Dusk*. Later in the morning, go to the Museo di San Marco, a small museum that's a monument to the work of Fra Angelico. Before it closes at 6:30pm, call at the Basilica di Santa Croce, with its two restored chapels by Giotto.

On Day 5, leave Florence, as fascinating as it is, and head south to yet another fascinating art city, Siena, the most important of the Tuscan hill towns.

THE TOP ATTRACTIONS

In the heart of Florence, at piazza del Duomo and piazza San Giovanni (named after John the Baptist), is a complex of ecclesiastical buildings that form a triumvirate of top sightseeing attractions.

In addition to the sights listed below, consider visiting **piazza della Signoria.** This square, although never completed, is one of the most beautiful in Italy; it was the

Florence Attractions

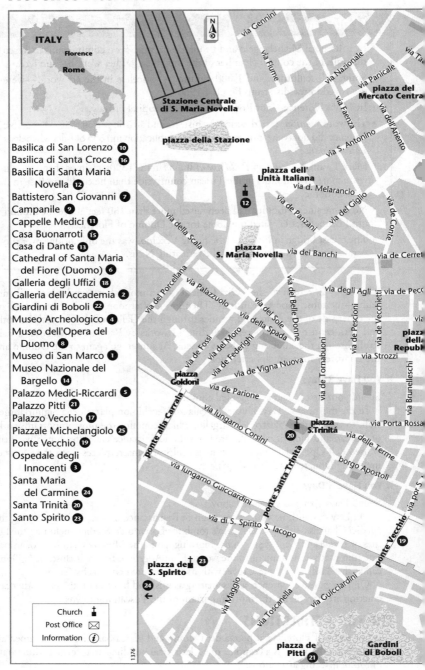

ITALY

Florence

Rome

Basilica di San Lorenzo ⑩
Basilica di Santa Croce ⑯
Basilica di Santa Maria
    Novella ⑫
Battistero San Giovanni ❼
Campanile ❾
Cappelle Medici ⑪
Casa Buonarroti ⑮
Casa di Dante ⑬
Cathedral of Santa Maria
    del Fiore (Duomo) ❻
Galleria degli Uffizi ⑱
Galleria dell'Accademia ❷
Giardini di Boboli ㉒
Museo Archeologico ❹
Museo dell'Opera del
    Duomo ❽
Museo di San Marco ❶
Museo Nazionale del
    Bargello ⑭
Palazzo Medici-Riccardi ❺
Palazzo Pitti ㉑
Palazzo Vecchio ⑰
Piazzale Michelangiolo ㉕
Ponte Vecchio ⑲
Ospedale degli
    Innocenti ❸
Santa Maria
    del Carmine ㉔
Santa Trinità ⑳
Santo Spirito ㉓

Church †
Post Office ✉
Information ⓘ

1376

Stazione Centrale
di S. Maria Novella

piazza della Stazione

via Gennini
via Fiume
via Nazionale
via Panicale
via Ta
via Faenza
via dell'Ariento
via S. Antonino

piazza del
Mercato Centra

piazza dell'
Unità Italiana
via d. Melarancio
via de Panzani
via del Giglio
via de Conte

piazza
S. Maria Novella
via dei Banchi
via de Cerret

via della Scala

via del Porcellana
via Palazzuolo
via del Belle Donne
via degli Agli
via de Pecc
via de Vecchietti
via de Pescioni
via

piazz
della
Republ

via del Sole
via della Spada
via Strozzi
via Tornabuoni
via del Moro
via de Fossi
via de Federighi
via de Vigna Nuova
via de Brunelleschi

piazza
Goldoni
via de Parione

ponte alla Carraia
via lungarno Corsini
piazza
S.Trinità
via Porta Rossa
via delle Terme
borgo Apostoli
via por S

ponte Santa Trinità
via lungarno Guicciardini
via di S. Spirito S. Iacopo
ponte Vecchio

piazza del
S. Spirito

via Maggio
via Toscanella
via Guicciardini

piazza de
Pitti

Gardini
di Boboli

246

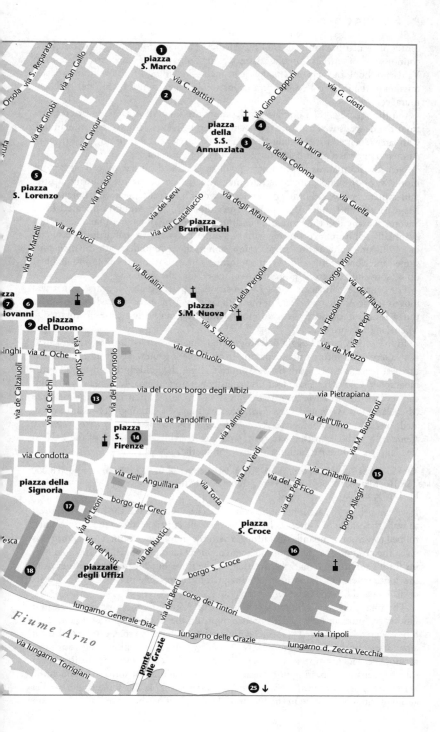

❶ piazza S. Marco

via C. Battisti

❷

via de S. Reparata · via de Ginobi · via San Gallo

via Cavour

via Ricasoli

via Gino Capponi

via G. Giosti

❹ †

piazza della S.S. Annunziata **❸**

via Laura

via della Colonna

❺ piazza S. Lorenzo

via de Martelli

via de Pucci

via dei Servi

via del Castellaccio

via degli Alfani

via Guelfa

piazza Brunelleschi

via Bufalini

via della Pergola

borgo Pinti

via dei Pilastri

zza **❼** **❻** iovanni

❽

† piazza del Duomo **❾**

.inghi via d. Oche

via Calzaiuoli

via de Cerchi

via d. Studio

via del Proconsolo

† ■ piazza S.M. Nuova

via S. Egidio

via de Oriuolo

via Fiesolana

via de Pepi

■ †

via de Mezzo

via del corso borgo degli Albizi

via Pietrapiana

❶❸

via de Pandolfini

via dell'Ulivo

via M. Buonarroti

† ■ piazza S. Firenze **❶❹**

via Palmieri

via Condotta

piazza della Signoria

via dell' Anguillara

❶❼

via de Leoni

borgo del Greci

via G. Verdi

via del Pepi Fico

via Ghibellina

borgo Allegri

❶❺

'esca

❶❽

via del Neri

piazzale degli Uffizi

via de Rustici

via Torta

piazza S. Croce

❶❻

■ †

borgo S. Croce

Fiume Arno

lungarno Generale Diaz

via del Benci

corso dei Tintori

lungarno delle Grazie

via Tripoli

via lungarno Torrigiani

ponte alle Grazie

lungarno d. Zecca Vecchia

㉕ ↓

center of secular life in the days of the Medici. Through it pranced church robbers, connoisseurs of entrails, hired assassins seeking employment, chicken farmers from Valdarno, book burners, and many great men—including Machiavelli, on a secret mission to the Palazzo Vecchio, and Leonardo da Vinci, trailed by his inevitable entourage.

On the square is the Fountain of Neptune, the sea god surrounded by creatures from the deep, as well as frisky satyrs and nymphs. It was designed by Ammannati, who later repented for chiseling Neptune in the nude. But Michelangelo, to whom Ammannati owes a great debt, judged the fountain inferior.

Near the fountain is a spot where Savonarola walked his last mile. This zealous monk was a fire-and-brimstone reformer who rivaled Dante in conjuring up the punishment hell would inflict on sinners. Two of his chief targets were Lorenzo the Magnificent and the Borgia pope, Alexander VI, who excommunicated him. Savonarola whipped the Florentine faithful into an orgy of religious fanaticism, but eventually fell from favor. Along with two other friars, he was hanged in the square in 1498. Afterward, as the crowds threw stones, the pyre underneath the men consumed their bodies. It's said that the reformer's heart was found whole and grabbed up by souvenir collectors. His ashes were tossed into the Arno.

For centuries Michelangelo's *David* stood in piazza della Signoria, but it was moved to the Academy Gallery in the 19th century. The work you see on the square today is an inferior copy, commonly assumed by many first-time visitors to be Michelangelo's original.

In the 14th-century **Loggia della Signoria** (sometimes called the Loggia dei Lanzi) is a gallery of sculpture often depicting fierce, violent scenes. The most famous and the best piece is a rare work by Benvenuto Cellini, the goldsmith and tell-all autobiographer. Critics have said that his exquisite but ungentlemanly *Perseus,* who holds the severed head of Medusa, is the most significant Florentine sculpture since Michelangelo's *Night* and *Day.* Two other well-known, although less skillfully created, pieces are Giambologna's *Rape of the Sabines* and his *Hercules with Nessus the Centaur.* For those on the mad rush, we suggest saving the interior of the Palazzo Vecchio (see "More Attractions," below) for another day.

✪ **Giotto's Bell Tower (Campanile).** Piazza del Duomo. ☎ **055/215380.** Admission 8,000 lire ($5.10). Mid-Mar to Sept, daily 9am–7:30pm; Oct to mid-Mar, daily 9am–5:30pm. Bus: 1, 6, 11, 17, 19, or 23.

If we can believe the accounts of his contemporaries, Giotto was the ugliest man ever to walk the streets of Florence. Ironically, then, he left to posterity the most beautiful bell tower, or campanile, in Europe, rhythmic in line and form. That Giotto was given the position of *capomastro* and grand architect (and pensioned for 100 gold florins for his service) is remarkable in itself, for he is famous for freeing painting from the confinements of Byzantium. He designed the campanile in the last 2 or 3 years of his life, and he died before its completion.

The final work was admirably carried out by Andrea Pisano, one of the greatest Gothic sculptors in Italy (see his bronze doors on the nearby Baptistery). The 274-foot tower, a "Tuscanized" Gothic, with bands of colored marble, can be scaled for a panorama of the sienna-colored city. The view will surely rank among your most memorable—it encompasses the enveloping hills and Medici villas. If a medieval pageant happens to be passing underneath (a likely possibility in spring), so much the better. After Giotto's death, Pisano and Luca della Robbia did some fine bas-relief and sculptural work, now in the Duomo Museum behind the cathedral.

✪ Battistero San Giovanni (Baptistery). Piazza S. Giovanni. ☎ **055/215380.** Admission 3,000 lire ($1.90). Mon–Sat 1:30–6pm, Sun 9am–1:30pm. Bus: 1, 6, 11, 17, 19, or 23.

Named after the city's patron saint, Giovanni (John the Baptist), the present octagonal Battistero dates from the 11th and 12th centuries. The oldest structure in Florence, the baptistery is a highly original interpretation of the Romanesque style, with its bands of pink, white, and green marble. Visitors from all over the world come to gape at its three sets of bronze doors. The east door is a copy; the other two are originals. In his work on two sets of doors, Lorenzo Ghiberti reached the pinnacle of his artistry in *quattrocento* Florence. To win his first commission on the north door, the then-23-year-old sculptor had to compete against such formidable opposition as Donatello, Brunelleschi (architect of the dome crowning the cathedral), and Siena, born Jacopo della Quercia. Upon seeing Ghiberti's work, Donatello and Brunelleschi conceded defeat. By the time he completed the work, Ghiberti was around 44 years old. The gilt-covered panels—representing scenes from the New Testament, including the Annunciation, the Adoration, and Christ debating the elders in the temple—make up a flowing rhythmic narration in bronze.

After his long labor, the Florentines gratefully gave Ghiberti the task of sculpting the east door (directly opposite the entrance to the Duomo). Upon seeing the doors, Michelangelo is said to have exclaimed, "The Gateway to Paradise!" Given carte blanche, Ghiberti designed his masterpiece, choosing as his subject familiar scenes from the Old Testament, including Adam and Eve at the creation. This time Ghiberti labored over the rectangular panels from 1425 to 1452 (he died in 1455).

Shuttled off to adorn the south entrance and to make way for Ghiberti's "gate" to paradise were the oldest doors of the baptistery, by Andrea Pisano, mentioned earlier for his work on Giotto's bell tower. For his subject, the Gothic sculptor represented the "Virtues" as well as scenes from the life of John the Baptist, whom the baptistery honors. The door was completed in 1336. On the interior (just walk through Pisano's door—no charge) the dome is adorned with 13th-century mosaics, dominated by a figure of Christ. Mornings are reserved for worship.

✪ Cathedral of Santa Maria del Fiore (Duomo). Piazza del Duomo. ☎ **055/294514.** Admission: Cathedral, free; excavations, 3,000 lire ($1.90); cupola, 8,000 lire ($5.10). Cathedral, daily 10am–5pm; excavations, Mon–Sat 9:30am–5pm; cupola, Mon–Fri 9am–6pm, Sat 8:30am–5pm.

The Duomo, graced by Brunelleschi's dome, is the crowning glory of Florence. But don't rush inside too quickly, as the view of the exterior, with its bands of white, pink, and green marble—geometrically patterned—is, along with the dome, the best feature. One of the world's largest churches, the Duomo represents the flowering of the "Florentine Gothic" style. Typical of the history of cathedrals, construction stretched over centuries. Begun in 1296, it was finally consecrated in 1436, although finishing touches on the facade were applied as late as the 19th century. The cathedral was designed by Arnolfo di Cambio in the closing years of the 13th century, and the funds were raised in part by a poll tax.

Brunelleschi's efforts to build the dome (1420–36) would make the subject of a film, as did Michelangelo's vexations over the Sistine Chapel. At one time before his plans were eventually accepted, the architect was tossed out on his derrière and denounced as an idiot. He eventually won the commission by a clever "egg trick," as related in Giorgio Vasari's *Lives of the Painters,* written in the 16th century, a book to which we are here indebted (as are all authors of books dealing with Italian Renaissance art). His dome—a "monument for posterity"—was erected without supports. When Michelangelo began to construct a dome over St. Peter's, he paid tribute to Brunelleschi's earlier cupola in Florence: "I am going to make its sister larger, yes, but not lovelier."

Inside, the overall effect of the cathedral is bleak, except when you stand under the cupola, frescoed in part by Vasari. Some of the stained-glass windows in the dome were based on designs by Donatello (Brunelleschi's friend) and Ghiberti (Brunelleschi's rival). If you resisted scaling Giotto's bell tower, you may want to climb Brunelleschi's ribbed dome. The view is well worth the trek.

Also in the cathedral are some terra-cottas by Luca della Robbia. In 1432 Ghiberti, taking time out from his "Gateway to Paradise," designed the tomb of St. Zenobius. Excavations in the depths of the cathedral have brought to light the remains of the ancient Cathedral of Santa Reparata (tombs, columns, and floors), which was probably founded in the 5th century and transformed in the following centuries until it was demolished to make way for the present cathedral.

Incidentally, during some 1972 excavations the tomb of Brunelleschi was discovered, and new discoveries indicate the existence of a second tomb nearby. Giotto's tomb, which has never been found, may be in the right nave of the cathedral, beneath the campanile that bears his name.

✪ **Galleria dell'Accademia.** Via Ricasoll 60. ☎ **055/238-8609.** Admission 12,000 lire ($7.70). Tues–Sat 8:30am–7pm, Sun 8:30am–2pm. Bus: 1, 6, 10, 11, 17, 20, or 25.

After coming out of the entrance to the Duomo, turn right, then head down via Ricasoll to the Academy Gallery. This museum contains paintings and sculpture, but it's completely overshadowed by one work, Michelangelo's colossal *David,* unveiled in 1504. One of the most sensitive accounts we've ever read of how Michelangelo turned the 17-foot "Duccio marble" into *David* is related in Irving Stone's *The Agony and the Ecstasy.* Stone describes a Michelangelo "burning with marble fever" who set out to create a *David* who "would be Apollo, but considerably more; Hercules, but considerably more; Adam, but considerably more; the most fully realized man the world had yet seen, functioning in a rational and humane world." How well he succeeded is much in evidence today.

David once stood in piazza della Signoria but was moved to the Academy in 1873 (a copy was substituted). Apart from containing the masterwork, the sculpture gallery is also graced with Michelangelo's unfinished quartet of slaves, carved around 1520 and intended for the ill-fated tomb of Julius II, and his *St. Matthew,* which he worked on (shortly after completing *David*) for the Duomo. His unfinished *Palestrina Pietà* displayed here is a much later work, dating from 1550.

In the connecting picture gallery is a collection of Tuscan masters, such as Botticelli, and Umbrian works by Perugino (teacher of Raphael).

✪ **Cappelle Medici.** Piazza Madonna degli Aldobrandini 6. ☎ **055/23885.** Admission 10,000 lire ($6.40). Tues–Sat 9am–2pm, Sun 9am–1pm. Bus: 1, 6, 11, 17, 19, or 23.

A mecca for all pilgrims, the Medici tombs are sheltered adjacent to the Basilica of San Lorenzo (see "Churches" in "More Attractions," below). The tombs, housing the "blue-blooded" Medici, are actually entered in back of the church by going around to piazza Madonna degli Aldobrandini. First you'll pass through the octagonal baroque Chapel of the Princes, which has colored marble but a cold decoration. In back of the altar is a collection of Italian reliquaries.

The real reason the chapels are visited en masse, however, is the New Sacristy, designed by Michelangelo. Working from 1521 to 1534, he created the Medici tomb in a style that foreshadowed the coming of the baroque. Lorenzo the Magnificent—a ruler who seemed to embody the qualities of the Renaissance itself, and one of the greatest names

Great Art & High Camp

The world's most reproduced statue—Michelangelo's *David*—has spawned controversy down through the centuries. When it was exposed out in the open at piazza della Signoria, it was the subject of cruel jeers and was frequently targeted for rotten egg attacks. In his grand tour of Italy, a 19th-century visitor, William Hazlitt, recorded his impression and called the masterpiece an "awkward overgrown actor at one of our minor theatres, without his clothes."

In 1873, to protect the statue from the elements, *David* was rolled on logs to the Galleria dell'Accademia, where it stands inside today. The statue on piazza della Signoria is a copy, although many visitors rushing through Florence assume it to be Michelangelo's original.

Many critics consider the sculpture (1501–04) the world's greatest, although some art historians cite other works. The artist's study of the male anatomy has been hailed as "flawless," even though Michelangelo had hardly turned 26 when he began the 4-year project. Michelangelo worked from a towering, columnlike stone that the Tuscans had nicknamed *il Gigante*. Another artist, Agostino di Duccio, had attempted to work on the marble but had abandoned it.

This controversial statue of David brought Michelangelo the recognition he wanted as the leading sculptor of the Renaissance, earning for him sponsors such as the pope, who brought commissions including the Sistine Chapel. The artist's depiction of this biblical figure in the nude caused a scandal in its day, and to some extent it still does. Note all those horrible reproductions of the statue sold all over Florence with and without the fig leaf.

In 1991 a frustrated artist attacked the statue with a hammer, but succeeded only in making a few minor nicks on its toes, which are undetectable.

Over the years *David* has also become a symbol of homosexual camp, its reproductions adorning gay venues such as restaurants, bars, hotels, and certainly apartments all over the world. There's even a restaurant in Las Vegas where the statue's rhinestone-studded figleaf is raised and lowered every 5 minutes.

In spite of all the tawdry reproductions, in spite of all the hype and camp surrounding the figure, it remains in Florence to welcome new generations, an enduring legacy of the ideals of the High Renaissance in art. A true Goliath. Or, as one visitor put it, "So alive!"

in the history of the Medici family—was buried near Michelangelo's uncompleted *Madonna and Child* group, a simple monument that evokes a promise unfulfilled.

Ironically, the finest, world-renowned groups of sculpture were reserved for two Medici "clan" members, who (in the words of Mary McCarthy) "would better have been forgotten." Both are represented by Michelangelo as armored, regal, idealized princes of the Renaissance. In fact, Lorenzo II, duke of Urbino, depicted as "the thinker," was a deranged young man (just out of his teens before he died). Clearly, Michelangelo was not working to glorify these two Medici dukes. Rather, he was chiseling for posterity. The other two figures on Lorenzo's tomb are most often called *Dawn* and *Dusk,* with morning represented as woman and evening as man.

The two best-known figures—Michelangelo at his most powerful—are *Night* and *Day* at the feet of Giuliano, the duke of Nemours. *Night* is chiseled as a woman in troubled sleep; *Day* is a man of strength awakening to a foreboding world. These two figures were not the sculptural works of Michelangelo's innocence.

Discovered in a sepulchral chamber beneath the Medici Chapel was Michelangelo's only group of mural sketches. Access is through a trap door and a winding staircase. The walls apparently had been used by the great artist as a giant doodling sheet. Drawings include a sketch of the legs of Duke Giuliano, Christ risen, and a depiction of the Laocoön, the Hellenistic figure group. Fifty drawings, done in charcoal on plaster walls, were found. The public can sometimes view these sketches in the choir.

✪ **Galleria degli Uffizi.** Piazzale degli Uffizi 6. ☎ **055/2388-6512.** Admission 12,000 lire ($7.70). Tues–Sat 9am–7pm, Sun and holidays 9am–1pm (last entrance 45 minutes before closing). Bus: 14 or 15.

When the last grand duchess of the Medici family died, she bequeathed to the people of Tuscany a wealth of Renaissance, even classical, art. The paintings and sculpture had been accumulated by the powerful grand dukes in three centuries of rule that witnessed the height of the Renaissance. Vasari designed the palace in the 16th century for Cosimo I.

To see and have time to absorb all the Uffizi paintings would take at least 2 weeks. We'll present only the sketchy highlights. The Uffizi is nicely grouped into periods or schools to show the development and progress of Italian and European art.

The first room begins with classical sculpture. You'll then meet up with those rebels from Byzantium, Cimabue and his pupil Giotto, with their Madonnas and Bambini. Since the Virgin and Child seem to be the overriding theme of the earlier of the Uffizi artists, it's enlightening just to follow the different styles over the centuries, from the ugly, almost midget-faced babies of the post-Byzantine works to the chubby, red-cheeked cherubs that glorified the baroque.

Look for Simone Martini's *Annunciation,* a collaborative venture. The halo around the head of the Virgin doesn't conceal her pouty mouth. Fra Angelico of Fiesole, a 15th-century painter, lost in a world peopled with saints and angels, makes his Uffizi debut with (naturally) a *Madonna and Bambino.* A special treasure is a work by Masaccio, who died at an early age, but is credited as being the father of modern painting. In his madonnas and bambini we see the beginnings of the use of perspective in painting. Fra Angelico's *Coronation of the Virgin* is also in this salon.

In another room you'll find Friar Filippo Lippi's far-superior *Coronation,* as well as a galaxy of charming madonnas. He was a rebel among the brethren.

The Botticelli rooms, which contain his finest works, are especially popular with visitors. Many come to contemplate what is commonly referred to as "Venus on the Half-Shell." This supreme conception of life—the *Birth of Venus*—really packs 'em in. But before being captured by Venus, check out *Minerva Subduing the Centaur,* an important painting that brought about a resurgence of interest in mythological subjects. Botticelli's *Allegory of Spring* or *Primavera* is a gem; it's often called a symphony because you can listen to it. Set in a citrus grove, the painting depicts Venus with Cupid hovering over her head. Mercury looks out of the canvas to the left. Before leaving the room, look for Botticelli's *Adoration of the Magi,* in which we find portraits of the Medici (the vain man at the far right is Botticelli). Also here is Botticelli's small, allegorical *Calumny.*

The *Adoration of the Shepherds* is a superbly detailed triptych, commissioned for a once-important Tuscan family and painted by Hugo van der Goes, a 15th-century artist. In another room we come across one of Leonardo da Vinci's unfinished paintings, the brilliant *Adoration of the Magi,* and Verrocchio's *Baptism of Christ,* not a very important painting, but noted because da Vinci painted one of the angels when he was 14 years old. Also in this salon hangs da Vinci's *Annunciation,* which reflects the early years of his genius with its twilight atmosphere and each leaf painstakingly in place. Proof that Leonardo was an architect? The splendid Renaissance palace he designed is part of the background.

The most beautiful room in the gallery with its dome of pearl shells contains the *Venus of the Medici* at center stage; it's one of the most reproduced of all Greek sculptural works.

In the rooms to follow are works by Perugino, Dürer, Mantegna, Giovanni Bellini, Giorgione, and Correggio. Finally, you can view Michelangelo's *Holy Family,* as well as Raphael's *Madonna of the Goldfinch,* plus his portraits of Julius II and Leo X. There is also what might be dubbed the Titian salon, which has two of his interpretations of Venus (one depicted with Cupid). When it came to representing voluptuous females on canvas, Titian had no rival. In other rooms are important Mannerists: Parmigianino, Veronese, and Tintoretto (*Leda and the Swan*). In the rooms nearing the end are works by Rubens, Caravaggio (*Bacchus*), and Rembrandt.

On May 27, 1993, a terrorist bomb—presumably planted by the Mafia—blasted through a section of the gallery. Although paintings were destroyed, many of the Uffizi's masterpieces, including works by Botticelli and Michelangelo, were spared, some because they were protected by shatterproof glass. Today most of what one goes to see at the Uffizi is proudly exhibited, although a lot of important masterpieces may not be in their usual positions. In all, 200 works of art were damaged, but only three of these paintings were completely destroyed.

○ **Palazzo Pitti.** Piazza de' Pitti. ☎ **055/238-8611.** Admission: Palatina, 12,000 lire ($7.70); Modern Art Gallery, 8,000 lire ($5.10); Argenti, 8,000 lire ($5). Tues–Sat 9am–7pm. Bus: 3.

The Palatine Gallery, on the left bank (a 5-minute walk from the ponte Vecchio), houses one of Europe's great art collections, with masterpieces hung one on top of the other, as in the days of the Enlightenment. If for no other reason, it should be visited for its Raphaels alone. The Pitti, built in the mid-15th century (Brunelleschi was the original architect), was once the residence of the powerful Medici family.

There are actually several museums in this complex, the most important of which is the **Galleria Palatine,** a repository of old masters. Other museums include the **Appartamenti Reali,** which the Medici family once called home, and the **Museo degli Argenti,** 16 rooms devoted to displays of the "loot" acquired by the Medici

---

○ Frommer's Favorite Florence Experiences

Standing in Awe in front of Michelangelo's *David*   Some one million visitors a year can't be wrong: In spite of countless copies, there's nothing as majestic as seeing the original statue of "The Giant"—carved from a single block of Carrara marble.

Going on a Shopping Spree   Florence, Italy's most fashionable city, dazzles with merchandise—everything from gold jewelry to leather and fashion. Stroll the ponte Vecchio, via dei Tornabuoni, via della Vigna Nova, and via Roma.

Having a Campari at piazza della Signoria   In the "living room" of Florence, at an open-air café, enjoy a refreshing drink while surrounded by some of the world's most famous statues—everything from Cellini's *Perseus* to Giambologna's *Rape of the Sabines.*

Wandering in the Uffizi Galleries   There are those who come to Florence every year with good reason: to explore gallery after gallery of Italy's most important museum, a treasure trove of Renaissance masterpieces.

dukes. Others are the **Coach and Carriage Museum** and the **Galleria d'Arte Moderna,** as well as the **Museo della Porcellane** (porcelain) and the **Galleria del Costume.**

After passing through the main door, proceed to the Sala di Venere (Room of Venus). In it are Titian's *La Bella,* of rich and illuminating color (entrance wall), and his portrait of Pietro Aretino, one of his most distinguished works. On the opposite wall are Titian's *Concert of Music,* often attributed to Giorgione, and his portrait of Julius II.

In the Sala di Apollo (on the opposite side of the entrance door) are Titian's *Man with Gray Eyes*—an aristocratic, handsome romanticist—and his *Mary Magdalene,* covered only with her long hair. On the opposite wall are Van Dyck portraits of Charles I of England and Henrietta of France.

In the Sala di Marte (entrance wall) is an important *Madonna and Child* by Murillo of Spain, as well as the Pitti's best-known work by Rubens: *The Four Philosophers.* On the left wall is one of Ruben's most tragic and moving paintings, depicting the *Consequences of War*—an early *Guernica.*

In the Sala di Giove (entrance wall) are Andrea del Sarto's idealized John the Baptist in his youth, Fra Bartolomeo's *Descent from the Cross,* and one of Rubens's most exciting paintings (even for those who don't like art), which depicts a romp of nymphs and satyrs. On the third wall (opposite the entrance wall) is the Pitti's second famous Raphael, the woman under the veil, known as *La Fornarina,* his bakery-girl mistress.

In the following gallery, the Sala di Saturno, look to the left on the entrance wall to see Raphael's *Madonna of the Canopy.* On the third wall near the doorway is the greatest Pitti prize, Raphael's *Madonna of the Chair,* his best-known interpretation of the Virgin, and what is in fact probably one of the six most celebrated paintings in all of Europe.

In the Sala dell'Iliade (to your left on the entrance wall) is a work of delicate beauty, Raphael's rendition of a pregnant woman. On the left wall is Titian's *Portrait of a Gentleman,* which he was indeed. (Titian is the second big star in the Palatine Gallery.) Finally, as you're leaving, look to the right of the doorway to see one of Velázquez's representations of the many faces of Philip IV of Spain.

✪ **Museo Nazionale del Bargello.** Via del Proconsolo 4. ☎ **055/238-8606.** Admission 8,000 lire ($5.10). Tues–Sat 9am–2pm; 2nd and 4th Sun of the month 9am–2pm, 1st and 3rd Mon of the month 9am–2pm. Bus: 14.

The National Museum, a short walk from piazza della Signoria, is a 13th-century fortress palace whose dark underground chambers once resounded with the echoing cries of the tortured. Today it's a vast repository of some of the most important sculpture of the Renaissance, including works by Michelangelo and Donatello.

Here you'll see another Michelangelo *David* (referred to in the past as *Apollo*), chiseled perhaps 25 to 30 years after the statuesque figure in the Academy Gallery. The Bargello *David* is totally different—even effete when compared to its stronger brother. The gallery also displays Michelangelo's grape-capped *Bacchus* (one of his earlier works), who is tempted by a satyr. Among the more significant sculptures is Giambologna's *Winged Mercury.*

The Bargello displays two versions of Donatello's John the Baptist—one emaciated, the other a younger and much kinder edition. Donatello, of course, was one of the outstanding and original talents of the early Renaissance. In this gallery you'll learn why. His *St. George* is a work of heroic magnitude. According to an oft-repeated story, Michelangelo, upon seeing it for the first time, commanded it to "March!" Donatello's bronze *David* in this salon is one of the most remarkable figures of all

Renaissance sculpture—it was the first freestanding nude since the Romans stopped chiseling. As depicted, *David* is narcissistic (a stunning contrast to Michelangelo's latter-day virile interpretation). For the last word, however, we'll have to call back our lady of the barbs, Mary McCarthy, who wrote: "His David . . . wearing nothing but a pair of fancy polished boots and a girlish bonnet, is a transvestite's and fetishist's dream of alluring ambiguity."

Look for at least one more notable work, another *David*—this one by Andrea del Verrocchio, one of the finest of the 15th-century sculptors. The Bargello contains a large number of terra-cottas by the della Robbia clan.

Museo di San Marco. Piazza San Marco 1. ☎ **055/238-8608.** Admission 8,000 lire ($5.10). Tues–Sun 9am–2pm. Closed 1st and 3rd Sun of the month, and 2nd and 4th Mon of the month. Bus: 1, 6, 7, 10, 11, 17, or 20.

The Museo di San Marco, a state museum, is a handsome Renaissance palace whose cell walls are decorated with frescoes by the mystical Fra Angelico, one of Europe's greatest 15th-century painters. In the days of Cosimo dei Medici, San Marco was built by Michelozzo as a Dominican convent. It originally contained bleak, bare cells, which Angelico and his students then brightened considerably with some of the most important works of this pious artist of Fiesole, who portrayed recognizable landscapes in strong, vivid colors.

One of his better-known paintings found here is *The Last Judgment,* which depicts people with angels on the left dancing in a circle, and lordly saints towering overhead. Hell, as it's depicted on the right, is naïve—Dante-esque—infested with demons, reptiles, and sinners boiling in a stew. Much of hell was created by his students; Angelico's brush was inspired only by the Crucifixion, madonnas, and bambini—or landscapes, of course. Here, also, are his *Descent from the Cross* and a panel of scenes from the life of Christ, including the *Flight into Egypt.*

In one room are frescoes and panels by Fra Bartolomeo, who lived from 1475 to 1517 and was highly influenced by Raphael. Note his *Madonna and Child with Saints.* In the Capitolo is a powerful *Crucifixion* by Angelico.

Turn right at the next door and you'll enter a refectory devoted to the artistic triumph of Domenico Ghirlandaio, who taught Michelangelo how to fresco. Ghirlandaio's own *Last Supper* in this room is rather realistic; his saints have tragic faces and silently evoke a feeling of impending doom.

Upstairs on the second floor—at the top of the hallway—is Angelico's masterpiece, *The Annunciation.* From here, you can walk down the left corridor to explore the cells of the Dominicans. Most of the frescoes depict scenes from the Crucifixion.

After turning to the right, you may want to skip the remaining frescoes, which appear to be uninspired student exercises. But at the end of the corridor is the cell of Savonarola, which was the scene of his arrest. The cell contains portraits of the reformer by Bartolomeo, who was plunged into acute melancholy by the jailing and torturing of his beloved teacher. Pictures of the reformer on the pyre at piazza della Signoria are on display.

If you retrace your steps to the entrance, then head down still another corridor, you'll see more frescoes, past a library with Ionic columns designed by Michelozzo. Finally, you'll come to the cell of Cosimo dei Medici, with a fresco by Gozzoli, who worked with Angelico.

MORE ATTRACTIONS
PIAZZALE MICHELANGIOLO

For a view of the wonders of Florence below and Fiesole above, climb aboard bus no. 13 from the central station and head for piazzale Michelangiolo, a 19th-century belvedere overlooking a view seen in many a Renaissance painting. It's best at dusk, when the purple-fringed Tuscan hills form a frame for Giotto's bell tower, Brunelleschi's dome, and the towering hunk of stones that stick up from the Palazzo Vecchio. Another copy of Michelangelo's *David* dominates the square.

Warning: At certain times during the day the square is overcrowded with tour buses and peddlers selling trinkets and cheap souvenirs. If you go at these times, often mid-day in summer, you'll find that the view of Florence is still intact—but you may be run down by a Vespa if you try to enjoy it.

PONTE VECCHIO

Spared by the Nazis in their bitter retreat from the Allied advance in 1944, "The Old Bridge" is the last remaining medieval *ponte* spanning the Arno (the Germans blew up the rest). The bridge was again threatened in the flood of 1966 when the waters of the Arno swept over it and washed away a fortune in jewelry from the goldsmiths' shops that flank the bridge.

Today the restored ponte Vecchio is closed to vehicular traffic. The little shops continue to sell everything from the most expensive of Florentine gold to something simple—say, a Lucrezia Borgia poison ring. Florentine hog butchers once peddled their wares on this bridge.

OSPEDALE DEGLI INNOCENTI

At piazza della Santissima Annunziata 12 is the **Hospital of the Innocents** (☎ 055/ **249-1723**), the oldest of its kind in Europe. The building, and the loggia with its Corinthian columns, was conceived by Brunelleschi and marked the first architectural bloom of the Renaissance in Florence. On the facade are terra-cotta medallions done in blues and opaque whites by Andrea della Robbia that depict babes in swaddling clothes.

Still used as an orphanage, the building also contains an art gallery. Notable among its treasures is a terra-cotta *Madonna and Child* by Luca della Robbia, plus works by Andrea del Sarto and Filippo Lippi. One of the gallery's most important paintings is an *Adoration of the Magi* by Domenico Ghirlandaio (the chubby Bambino looks a bit pompously at the Wise Man kissing his foot). The gallery is open Monday, Tuesday, and Thursday to Saturday from 9am to 1pm and on Sunday from 8am to noon. Admission is 4,000 lire ($2.55).

CHURCHES

The wealth of architecture, art, and treasures of Florence's churches is hardly second-ary, but if you want to see even a sampling of the best, you'll have to schedule an extra day or more in the city.

Basilica di Santa Croce. Piazza Santa Croce 16. ☎ **055/244619.** Admission: Church, free; cloisters and church museum, 4,000 lire ($2.55) adults, 1,000 lire (65¢) children. Church, daily 8am–12:30pm and 3–6:30pm. Museum and cloisters, Mar–Sept, Thurs–Tues 10am–12:30pm and 2:30–6:30pm; Oct–Feb, daily 10am–12:30pm and 3–5pm. Bus: 13, 14, or 19.

The Pantheon of Florence, this church shelters the tombs of everyone from Michelangelo to Machiavelli, from Dante (he was actually buried at Ravenna) to an astronomer (Galileo) who—at the hands of the Inquisition—"recanted" his concept that the earth revolves around the sun. Just as Santa Maria Novella was the church of the Dominicans, Santa Croce, said to have been designed by Arnolfo di Cambio, was the church of the Franciscans.

In the right nave (first tomb) is the Vasari-executed monument to Michelangelo, whose body was smuggled back to his native Florence from its original burial place in Rome. Along with a bust of the artist are three allegorical figures who represent the arts. In the next memorial a prune-faced Dante, a poet honored belatedly in the city that exiled him, looks down. Farther on, still on the right, is the tomb of Machiavelli, whose *The Prince* became a virtual textbook in the art of wielding power. Nearby is a lyrical bas-relief, *The Annunciation* by Donatello.

The *Trecento* frescoes are reason enough for visiting Santa Croce—especially those by Giotto to the right of the main chapel. Once whitewashed, the Bardi and Peruzzi chapels were "uncovered" in the mid-19th century in such a clumsy fashion that they had to be drastically restored. Although badly preserved, the frescoes in the Bardi Chapel are most memorable, especially the deathbed scene of St. Francis. The cycles in the Peruzzi Chapel are of John the Baptist and St. John. In the left transept is Donatello's once-controversial wooden *Crucifix*—too gruesome for some Renaissance tastes, including that of Brunelleschi, who is claimed to have said: "You [Donatello] have put a rustic upon the cross." (For Brunelleschi's "answer," go to Santa Maria Novella.) Incidentally, the Pazzi Chapel, entered through the cloisters, was designed by Brunelleschi, with terra-cottas by Luca della Robbia.

Inside the monastery of this church the Franciscan fathers established the **Leather School** at the end of World War II. The purpose of the school was to prepare young boys technically to specialize in Florentine leather work. The school has flourished and produced many fine artisans who continue their careers here. Stop in and see the work when you visit the church.

Basilica di San Lorenzo. Piazza San Lorenzo. ☎ **055/216634.** Free admission. Library, Mon–Sat 9am–1pm; study room, Mon–Sat 8am–2pm. Bus: 1, 6, 11, or 17.

This is Brunelleschi's 15th-century Renaissance church, where the Medici used to attend services from their nearby palace on via Larga, now via Camillo Cavour. Most visitors flock to see Michelangelo's "New Sacristy" with his *Night* and *Day* (see the Medici Chapels under "The Top Attractions," above), but Brunelleschi's handiwork deserves some time, too.

Built in the style of a Latin cross, the church is distinguished by harmonious grays and rows of Corinthian columns. The Old Sacristy (walk up the nave, then turn left) was designed by Brunelleschi and decorated in part by Donatello (see his terra-cotta bust of St. Lawrence).

After exploring the Old Sacristy, go through the first door (unmarked) on your right, then turn right again and climb the steps.

The **Biblioteca Medicea Laurenziana** (☎ **055/210760**) is entered separately at piazza San Lorenzo 9 and was designed by Michelangelo to shelter the expanding library of the Medici. The library is filled with some of Italy's greatest manuscripts—many of which are handsomely illustrated. Visitors are kept at a distance by protective glass, but it's well worth the visit.

Basilica di Santa Maria Novella. Piazza Santa Maria Novella. ☎ **055/215918.** Admission: Church, free; Spanish Chapel and cloisters, 5,000 lire ($3.20). Church, Mon–Fri 7–11:30am and 3:30–6pm, Sat 10–11:30am and 3:30–5pm, Sun 3:30–5pm; Spanish Chapel and cloisters, Mon–Thurs and Sat 9am–2pm, Sun 8am–1pm. Bus: All buses from the station.

Near the railway station is one of Florence's most distinguished churches, begun in 1278 for the Dominicans. Its geometric facade, with bands of white and green marble, was designed in the late 15th century by Leon Battista Alberti, an aristocrat and true Renaissance man (philosopher, painter, architect, poet). The church borrows from and harmonizes the Romanesque, Gothic, and Renaissance styles.

In the left nave as you enter, the third large painting is the great Masaccio's *Trinity,* a curious work that has the architectural form of a Renaissance stage setting, but whose figures—in perfect perspective—are like actors in a Greek tragedy. If you view the church at dusk you'll see the stained-glass windows in the fading light cast kaleidoscope fantasies on the opposite wall.

Head straight up the left nave to the Gondi Chapel for a look at Brunelleschi's wooden *Christ on the Cross,* which is said to have been carved to compete with Donatello's same subject in Santa Croce (see above). According to Vasari, when Donatello saw Brunelleschi's completed Crucifix, he dropped his apron full of eggs intended for their lunch. "You have symbolized the Christ," Donatello is alleged to have said. "Mine is an ordinary man." (Some art historians reject this story.)

In the late 15th century Ghirlandaio contracted with a Tornabuoni banker to adorn the choir with frescoes illustrating scenes from the lives of Mary and John the Baptist. Michelangelo, only a teenager at the time, is known to have studied under Ghirlandaio (perhaps he even worked on this cycle).

If time remains, you may want to visit the cloisters, going first to the "Green Cloister," and then the splendid Spanish Chapel frescoed by Andrea di Bonaiuto in the 14th century (one panel depicts the Dominicans in triumph over heretical wolves).

Santa Maria del Carmine. Piazza Santa Maria del Carmine. ☎ **055/212331.** Admission 5,000 lire ($3.20). Mon and Wed–Sat 10am–4:30pm, Sun 1–4:30pm. Bus: 6.

This baroque church, a result of rebuilding after a fire in the 18th century, is located a long walk from the Pitti Palace on the left bank. Miraculously, the renowned Brancacci Chapel was spared—miraculous because it contains frescoes by Masaccio, who ushered in the great century of *Quattrocento* Renaissance painting. Forsaking the ideal, Masaccio depicted man and woman in their weakness and their glory.

His technique is seen at its most powerful in the expulsion of Adam and Eve from the Garden of Eden. The artist peopled his chapel, a masterpiece of early perspective, with scenes from the life of St. Peter (the work was originally begun by his master, Masolino). Note especially the fresco *Tribute Money,* and the baptism scene with the nude youth freezing in the cold waters.

Masaccio did the upper frescoes, but because of his early death, the lower ones were completed by Filippino Lippi (not to be confused with his father, Filippo Lippi, a greater artist).

La Sinagoga di Firenze. Via Farini 4. ☎ **055/245252.** Admission 6,000 lire ($3.85) adults, 5,000 lire ($3.20) children 15–18, free for children 13 and under. Apr–Sept, Sun–Thurs 10am–1pm and 2–5pm, Fri 10am–1pm; Oct–Mar, Mon–Thurs 11am–1pm and 2–5pm, Fri and Sun 10am–1pm. Closed Jewish holidays. Bus: 6.

The synagogue is in the Moorish style, inspired by Constantine's Byzantine church of Hagia Sophia. Completed in 1882, it was badly damaged by the Nazis in 1944 but has been restored to its original splendor. A museum is upstairs.

PALACES

Palazzo Medici-Riccardi. Via Camillo Cavour 1. ☎ **055/276-0360.** Admission 6,000 lire ($3.85). Mon–Tues and Thurs–Sat 9am–1pm and 3–6pm, Sun 9am–1pm. Bus: 1, 6, 11, 14, or 23.

This palace, a short walk from the Duomo, was the home of Cosimo dei Medici before he took his household to the Palazzo della Signoria. Built by palace architect Michelozzo in the mid-15th century, the brown stone building was also the scene, at times, of the court of Lorenzo the Magnificent. Art lovers visit today chiefly to see the mid–15th-century frescoes by Benozzo Gozzoli in the Medici Chapel.

Gozzoli's frescoes, which depict the *Journey of the Magi,* form his masterpiece—in fact, they're a hallmark in Renaissance painting in that they abandoned ecclesiastical themes to celebrate emerging man.

Another gallery, which has to be entered by a separate stairway, was frescoed by Luca Giordano in the 18th century, but his work seems merely decorative. The apartments, where the prefect lodges, are not open to the public. The gallery, incidentally, may also be viewed free.

Palazzo Vecchio. Piazza della Signoria. ☎ **055/276-8325.** Admission 10,000 lire ($6.40). Mon–Wed and Fri–Sat 9am–7pm, Sun 8am–1pm. Last admission 1 hour before closing. Bus: 13, 14, or 23.

The secular "Old Palace" is without doubt the most famous and imposing palace in Florence. It dates from the closing years of the 13th century. Its remarkable architectural feature is its 308-foot tower, an engineering feat that required supreme skill. Once home to the Medici, the Palazzo Vecchio (also called the Palazzo della Signoria) is occupied today by city employees, but much of it is open to the public.

The 16th-century "Hall of the 500" (Dei Cinquecento), the most outstanding part of the palace, is filled with Vasari & Co. frescoes as well as sculpture. As you enter the hall, look for Michelangelo's *Victory.* It depicts an insipid-looking young man treading on a bearded older man (it has been suggested that Michelangelo put his own face on that of the trampled man).

Later you can stroll through the rest of the palace, through its apartments and main halls. You can also visit the private apartments of Eleanor of Toledo, wife of Cosimo I, and a chapel that was begun in 1540 and frescoed by Bronzino. The palace displays the original of Verrocchio's bronze *putto* (from 1476) from the courtyard fountain. This work is called both *Winged Cherub Clutching a Fish* and *Boy with a Dolphin.* The palace also shelters a 16th-century portrait of Machiavelli that's attributed to Santi di Tito. Donatello's famous bronze group, *Judith Slaying Holofernes,* once stood on piazza della Signoria, but it was brought inside.

The salons, such as a fleur-de-lis apartment, have their own richness and beauty. Following his arrest, Savonarola was taken to the Palazzo Vecchio for more than a dozen torture sessions, including "twists" on the rack. The torturer pronounced him his "best" customer.

MUSEUMS & GALLERIES

Museo Archeologico. Via della Colonna 38. ☎ **055/23575.** Admission 8,000 lire ($5.10). Tues–Sat 9am–2pm, Sun 9am–1pm. Bus: 6, 31, or 32.

The Archeological Museum, a short walk from piazza della Santissima Annunziata, houses one of the most outstanding Egyptian and Etruscan collections in Europe. Its Egyptian mummies and sarcophagi are on the first floor, along with some of the better-known Etruscan works. Pause to look at the lid to the coffin of a fat Etruscan (unlike the blank faces staring back from many of these tombs, this overeater's countenance is quite expressive).

One room is graced with three bronze Etruscan masterpieces, among the rarest objets d'art of these relatively unknown people. They include the *Chimera,* a lion with a goat sticking out of its back. The lion's tail—in the form of a venomous reptile—lunges at the trapped beast. The others are a statue of *Minerva* and one of an *Orator.* These pieces of sculpture range from the 5th to the 1st century B.C. Another rare find is a Roman bronze of a young man, the so-called *Idolino from Pesaro.* The François vase on the ground floor, from the year 570 B.C., is celebrated.

Museo dell'Opera del Duomo. Piazza del Duomo 9. ☎ **055/215380.** Admission 8,000 lire ($5.10). Apr–Oct, Mon–Sat 9am–6:50pm; Nov–Mar, Mon–Sat 9am–5:20pm. Bus: 1, 6, 11, 14, 19, or 23.

The Museo dell'Opera del Duomo, across the street but facing the apse of Santa Maria del Fiore, is beloved by connoisseurs of Renaissance sculpture. It houses the sculpture removed from the campanile and the Duomo—not only to protect the pieces from the weather, but from visitors who want samples. A major attraction here is an unfinished *Pietà* by Michelangelo, which is in the middle of the stairs. It was carved between 1548 and 1555 when the artist was in his 70s. In this vintage work, a figure representing Nicodemus (but said to have Michelangelo's face) is holding Christ. The great Florentine intended it for his own tomb, but he is believed to have grown disenchanted with it and to have attempted to destroy it. The museum has a Brunelleschi bust, as well as della Robbia terra-cottas. The museum's premier attraction is four restored panels of Ghiberti's "Doors to Paradise" removed from the Baptistery.

You'll see bits and pieces from what was the old Gothic-Romanesque fronting of the cathedral, with ornamental statues, as conceived by the original architect, Arnolfo di Cambio. One of Donatello's early works, *St. John the Evangelist,* is here—not his finest hour certainly, but anything by Donatello is worth looking at, including one of his most celebrated works, the *Magdalene,* which is in the room with the *cantorie* (see below). This wooden statue once stood in the Baptistery, and had to be restored after the flood of 1966. Dating from 1454–55, it's stark and penitent.

A good reason for visiting the museum is to see the marble choirs—*cantorie*—of Donatello and Luca della Robbia (the works face each other, and are in the first room you enter after climbing the stairs). The Luca della Robbia choir is more restrained, but it still "Praises the Lord" in marble—with clashing cymbals and sounding brass that constitute a reaffirmation of life. In contrast, all restraint breaks loose in the *cantoria* of dancing cherubs in Donatello's choir. It's a romp of chubby bambini. Of all of Donatello's works, this one is the most lighthearted. But, in total contrast, don't miss Donatello's *Zuccone,* which some consider to be one of his greatest masterpieces; it was done for Giotto's bell tower.

GARDENS

Giardini di Boboli (Boboli Gardens). Piazza de' Pitti 1. ☎ **055/218741.** Admission 4,000 lire ($2.55). Apr–May and Oct, daily 8:30am–6:30pm; June–Sept, daily 8:30am–7:30pm; Nov–Mar, daily 9am–4:30pm. Last admission 1 hour before closing. Bus: 3 or 15.

Behind the Pitti Palace are the Giardini di Boboli, through which the Medici romped. The gardens were originally laid out by Triboli, a great landscape artist, in the 16th century. The Boboli is ever-popular for a promenade or an idyllic interlude in a pleasant setting. The gardens are filled with fountains and statuary, such as a *Venus* by Giambologna in the "Grotto" of Buontalenti. You can climb to the top of the Fortezza di Belvedere for a dazzling view of the city.

SPECIAL-INTEREST SIGHTSEEING

FOR THE LITERARY ENTHUSIAST

Casa di Dante. Via Santa Margherita 1. ☎ **055/219416.** Admission 5,000 lire ($3.20) adults, free for children 9 and under. Mon 10am–4pm, Wed–Sat 10am–4pm, Sun 10am–2pm. Closed approximately 3 weeks during July-Aug (dates vary). Bus: 7, 14, or 17.

For those of us who were spoon-fed hell but spared purgatory, a pilgrimage to this rebuilt medieval house may be of passing interest, although it contains few specific exhibits of note. Dante was exiled from his native Florence in 1302 for his political involvements. He never returned, and thus wrote his *Divine Comedy* in exile, conjuring up fit punishment in the *Inferno* for his Florentine enemies. Dante certainly had the last word. The house is reached by walking down via Dante Alighieri.

FOR THE MICHELANGELO ENTHUSIAST

Casa Buonarroti. Via Ghibellina 70. ☎ **055/241752.** Admission 8,000 lire ($5.10) adults, 6,000 lire ($3.85) children and seniors 60 and over. Wed–Mon 9:30am–1:30pm. Bus: 14

Only a short walk from Santa Croce stands the house that Michelangelo managed to buy for his nephew. Turned into a museum by his descendants, the house was restored in 1964. It contains some fledgling work by the great artist, as well as some models by him. Here you can see his *Madonna of the Stairs*, which he did when he was 16 years old, as well as a bas-relief he did later, depicting the *Battle of the Centaurs*. The casa is enriched by many of Michelangelo's drawings, shown to the public in periodic exhibitions.

FOR VISITING AMERICANS

Florence American Cemetery and Memorial. Via Cassia, 50023 Impruneta. ☎ **055/202-0020.** Free admission. May 15–Sept 15, daily 8am–6pm; Sept 16–May 14, daily 8am–5pm. The SITA city bus stops at the cemetery entrance every 2 hours, except on holidays, when there's usually no bus service; the bus follows via Cassia.

The Florence American Cemetery and Memorial is on a 70-acre site about $7\frac{1}{2}$ miles south of the city on the west side of via Cassia, the main highway connecting Florence with Siena and Rome. One of 14 permanent American World War II military cemetery memorials built on foreign soil by the American Battle Monuments Commission, the memorial is on a site that was liberated on August 3, 1944, and later became part of the zone of the U.S. Fifth Army. It's adjacent to the Greve River and framed by wooded hills. Most of the 4,402 servicemen and women interred here died in the fighting that occurred after the capture of Rome in June 1944.

WALKING TOUR
In the Footsteps of Michelangelo

Start: Piazzale Michelangiolo.
Finish: Church of San Lorenzo.
Time: About $2\frac{1}{2}$ hours, not counting interior visits.
Best Times: Early morning or late afternoon.
Worst Times: During the midafternoon heat. If you plan to visit the museums that dot this tour, avoid Monday, when most of them are closed.

The walking tour actually begins with a bus trip (or cab ride. First head to the city bus station, in the piazza della Stazione. From there, take bus no. 13 (or a cab) to the opposite side of the Arno to the much-visited but nonetheless charming:

1. **Piazzale Michelangiolo.** From its panorama, you'll have a view over the city like the one that fed the creative juices of Michelangelo. Appropriately, the piazzale's crowning feature is yet another copy of Michelangelo's *David*, which overlooks from afar most of the monuments you've already examined close at hand.

   Next, take the nearby ponte alle Grazie across the Arno and head along via dei Benci to piazza Santa Croce. There you will find the elegant marble geometrics that adorn the facade of the:

2. **Church of Santa Croce,** whose confines contain Michelangelo's tomb. After paying your respects, and admiring the design of what might be Florence's second most famous church, head west along borgo de' Greci, which begins at the piazza's southwestern corner. It will eventually narrow to become via de' Gondi before opening onto the piazza whose buildings once housed the administration of some of the most famous rulers of the Renaissance:

3. **Piazza della Signoria.** Notice the elaborate Fountain of Neptune, close to which lies a brass plaque commemorating the site where the religious fanatic Savonarola's body was burned in 1498. (Michelangelo at the time was 23.) The square contains a series of dramatically displayed statues, some of them beneath soaring loggias.

The most instantly recognizable statue is a copy of Michelangelo's *David,* the original of which was removed for safekeeping.

Exit the piazza from its northeastern corner (take via dei Maggazzini) and follow the signs to the once-fortified walls of one of Florence's most famous galleries, the:

4. **Bargello Museum (Palazzo del Bargello).** Originally built during the 13th century, it contains depictions of David by both Donatello and Verrocchio (both of which Michelangelo studied intensely), as well as many of the greatest art treasures of Florence.

Continue north along the clearly marked via del Proconsolo for 4 blocks, passing between the solid stone buildings of one of Florence's oldest neighborhoods, until you arrive at:

5. **Piazza del Duomo.** The architectural ensemble on the piazza has changed little (apart from the roaring traffic) since Michelangelo first saw it. The cupola atop the cathedral, designed by Brunelleschi and completed in 1436 after 16 years of construction, inspired Michelangelo in his design of St. Peter's in Rome. (The soaring square bell tower was designed by Giotto.) Constructed of the same pink, green, and white marble as the cathedral itself is the octagonal:

6. **Baptistery,** whose eastern doors (designed by Ghiberti) are masterpieces of the metalworker's art. (What you'll see on the Baptistery are excellent copies of originals now in the Museo dell'Opera del Duomo.)

After exploring the famous buildings on the piazza, exit from a point near its northwestern corner, via Ricasoli, and walk 2¹/₂ blocks to no. 60, which marks the site of:

7. **The Academy (Galleria dell'Accademia),** home of the original of what might be the most famous statue in the world, Michelangelo's *David.* Less famous but immensely intriguing are the artist's *Four Prisoners,* whose forms struggle to be released from the marble that seems to enslave them. The museum also contains a *Pietà,* and Michelangelo's figures of St. Matthew.

Retrace your path south, walking toward piazza del Duomo, but turn right before you reach it at via dei Pucci. Within a block, at the corner of via Cavour, you'll come to the:

8. **Medici Palace (Palazzo Medici-Riccardi).** Originally constructed by the founder of the legendary dynasty (Cosimo dei Medici) as the ancestral home for his offspring, it was the birthplace of Lorenzo the Magnificent and the home of young Michelangelo during his art studies with Bertoldo.

One block southwest of the palace, along the continuation of via dei Pucci (which changes its name to via Canto de Nelli), you'll arrive at the:

9. **Church of San Lorenzo,** parish church of the Medici family. Within its massive confines lie the Laurentian Library (piazza San Lorenzo 9), which is sometimes more easily accessible via the church's cloisters. Designed by Michelangelo to shelter the Medici family's impressive collection of original manuscripts, it contains the most photographed staircase (also designed by Michelangelo) in Florence. At the rear of the church, accessible from the small and sun-flooded piazza Madonna dei Aldobrandini, lies the:

10. **New Sacristy,** designed by Michelangelo and adorned with some of his most evocative sculptures. These include *Dawn, Dusk, Day,* and *Night.* (In the same church is another chapel known as the Old Sacristy, designed by Brunelleschi and partly decorated by Donatello.)

In the Footsteps of Michelangelo

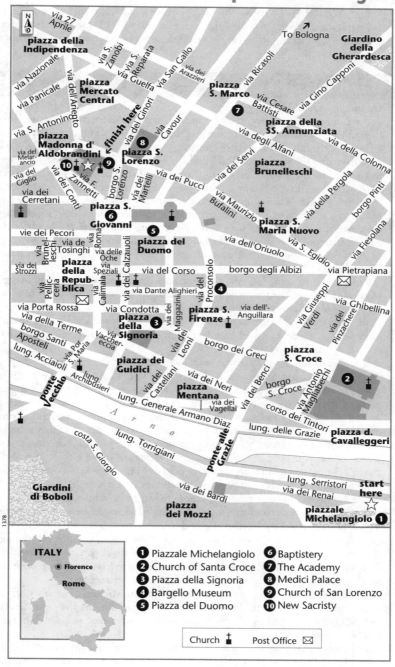

To Bologna

piazza della Indipendenza

Giardino della Gherardesca

via 27 Aprile

via Nazionale

via S. Zanobi

via S. Reparata

via Guelfa

via San Gallo

via dei Arazzieri

via Ricasoli

via Cesare Battisti

via Gino Capponi

piazza S. Marco

via dell'Ariegto

via Panicale

piazza Mercato Central

via S. Antonino

piazza Madonna d' Aldobrandini

via del Melarancio

via del Giglio

via dei Cerretani

via dei Conti

via F. Zannetti

borgo S. Lorenzo

via dei Ginori

via Cavour

7

piazza della SS. Annunziata

via degli Alfani

via dei Servi

piazza Brunelleschi

via della Colonna

8

piazza S. Lorenzo

finish here

10

9

via dei Martelli

via dei Pucci

via Maurizio Buralini

via della Pergola

borgo Pinti

6

piazza S. Giovanni

vie dei Pecori

via Roma

5

piazza del Duomo

piazza S. Maria Nuova

via dell'Oriuolo

via S. Egidio

via Fiesolana

via Brunelleschi

via de Tosinghi

via delle Oche

via dei Calzaiuoli

via del Corso

borgo degli Albizi

via Pietrapiana

via dei Strozzi

via Speziali

piazza della Repubblica

via Calimala

via Pellicceria

via dei Speziali

via Dante Alighieri

via del Proconsolo

4

via dell'-Anguillara

via Giuseppi Verdi

via Ghibellina

via Porta Rossa

via Condotta

piazza S. Firenze

via della Terme

borgo Santi Aposteli

lung. Acciaioli

via Por S. Maria

via Vaccher-eccia

piazza della Signoria

3

via dei Magazzini

via dei Leoni

borgo dei Greci

via dei Pinzachere

piazza S. Croce

Ponte Vecchio

lung. Archibusieri

piazza dei Guidici

via dei Castelani

via dei Neri

via dei Benci

borgo S. Croce

via Antonio Magliabechi

2

piazza Mentana

via dei Vagellai

corso dei Tintori

A r n o

lung. Generale Armano Diaz

lung. delle Grazie

piazza d. Cavalleggeri

costa S. Giorgio

lung. Torrigiani

Ponte alle Grazie

lung. Serristori

start here

Giardini di Boboli

via dei Bardi

via dei Renai

piazza dei Mozzi

piazzale Michelangiolo

1

1378

ITALY

● Florence

Rome

1 Piazzale Michelangiolo   **6** Baptistery
2 Church of Santa Croce   **7** The Academy
3 Piazza della Signoria   **8** Medici Palace
4 Bargello Museum   **9** Church of San Lorenzo
5 Piazza del Duomo   **10** New Sacristy

Church ✝   Post Office ✉

263

🍴 **WINDING DOWN**   An ideal place for a lunch after all that walking, **La Loggia,** overlooking piazzale Michelangiolo (☎ **055/234-2832**), has outdoor tables in summer and serves Florentine classic dishes such as bistecca alla fiorentina. Dress is casual.

6 Festivals & Free Events

Despite the appeal of "everyday Florence," with its rich collections of architecture and art, there are, however, several annual events and celebrations that might—depending on your interests—further heighten your appreciation of the city.

Much of the innate religiosity of Florence is especially visible during **Holy Week.** Two days after the sobriety of Good Friday, Easter is an extroverted religious event highlighted by the Scoppio del Carro (Explosion of the Cart). A two-wheeled cart filled with fireworks and flowers is drawn to the historic piazza in front of the Duomo by six white oxen. Then, during the Easter Sunday High Mass, a small rocket attached to a facsimile of a white dove is lit at the cathedral's high altar, which whizzes down the length of the nave along a taut wire high above the heads of the congregation until it reaches the cart and sets off the fireworks. Simultaneously, displays of flowers—which often continue until June—are shown in the Uffizi and piazza della Signoria.

From late April until July, the city welcomes classical musicians for its **Maggio Musicale** festival of cantatas, madrigals, concertos, operas, and ballets, many of which are presented in Renaissance buildings.

Between June and September, don't overlook the many musical events presented in Florence's hillside suburb of **Fiesole.** Its summer festival draws enthusiastic audiences from throughout Italy.

The feast day of Florence's patron saint, John the Baptist, occurs every year on June 24 during the **Calcio Storico** (also known as the Gioco del Calcio). To celebrate, groups of young Florentine men organized into teams representing the four original parishes of the city compete in a reenactment of a medieval sport that combines elements of both soccer and rugby. Dressed in Renaissance costumes, players face each other at either piazza Santa Croce or piazza della Signoria (and sometimes at both). The contest uses a wooden ball, a minimum of protective padding, and rules that to an observer appear fluid and/or nonexistent. During the evening of the day of the contest, displays of fireworks are shot from piazzale Michelangiolo out over the Arno. The contests are repeated, in somewhat different forms, on June 28.

On **Assumption Day,** August 15, caged crickets are sold throughout the city as part of a modern interpretation of a medieval custom where children ran through the nearby fields catching wild crickets as good-luck charms.

On September 7, on the eve of the Nativity of the Virgin, children run through the city's medieval streets carrying colorful paper lanterns as part of the **Festa delle Rificolone (Lantern Day).** The festival continues the following day in processions leading from the Duomo to the Church of Santissima Annunziata.

Every September 28, the eve of the **Festival of St. Michael,** Tuscany's official hunting season begins. At the Porta Romana, hunting equipment and caged birds of all kinds (parakeets, falcons, bluebirds, and owls) are assembled and sold to hunters and bird lovers alike.

In October, the collections of the **winter fashions** from the couturiers of Italy are assembled and shown to photographers, fashion editors, and buyers in the Pitti Palace. A similar exposition is held in early March, also in the Pitti Palace, for the spring collections.

Also in October, the **winter musical season** for orchestral and chamber music pieces begins at the Teatro Comunale. This is followed in November by the opening of the **opera season.** These musical diversions continue till mid-December and mid-January, respectively.

7 Soccer Matches & Other Outdoor Activities

GOLF   You'll find an 18-hole golf course, **Golf Club Ugolino,** in the nearby suburb of Impruneta, at via Chiantigiana 3 (☎ **055/230-1009**). Impruneta lies about 9 miles south of the center.

JOGGING   One of the city's finest stretches of uninterrupted pedestrian footpaths is in **La Cascine Park,** west of the center on the north bank of the Arno. Its eastern end begins beside the ponte della Vittoria, and it includes tennis courts, a racetrack, a public swimming pool, and miles of pedestrian walkways. (You can jog there by following the river to piazza Vittorio Veneto, although bus no. 17 will carry you there from the cathedral.) Another possibility is to jog amid the ornamental walkways of the **Boboli Gardens,** behind the Pitti Palace, although there you might find greater crowds of art lovers. If none of this appeals to you, you might jog along any of the city's **riverside quays** (the best time is early morning, if you're up to it), although you'll have to pay close attention to breakneck traffic feeding onto the Arno bridges.

SOCCER   Florence's hometown team is Fiorentina, and the city's residents take their games very seriously indeed. To watch them, head for the **Stadio Comunale,** viale Manfredi Fanti 4–6 (☎ **055/26241**), near campo di Marte, about 1½ miles northeast of the town's historic center. Games are usually held on Sunday afternoon between September and May, and tickets go on sale at the stadium 2 or 3 hours before the scheduled beginning. Any hotel receptionist in Florence can give you details for the upcoming week.

If you're interested in practicing your dribble and playing with local enthusiasts, head for the previously mentioned La Cascine Park, beside the river west of town, or to campo di Marte, the soccer headquarters of Florence, where a handful of youths will likely be practicing.

SQUASH   The city's squash headquarters is at the **Centro Squash Firenze,** via Empoli 16 (☎ **055/732-3055**), about 1½ miles due west of the center.

SWIMMING   There's a public pool at the eastern edge of La Cascine, open June to September, the **Piscine Le Pavoniere,** viale degli Olmi (☎ **055/367506**). Another possibility is the **Piscina Bellariva,** lungarno Aldo Moro 6 (☎ **055/333979**). These pools are crowded, however, with lots of *bambini.*

TENNIS   Although technically classified as semiprivate clubs, you'll often find an available court at one of a handful of Florentine tennis venues. Be aware of dress codes which might strongly encourage you to dress in tennis court whites with appropriate shoes. Possibilities include the **Tennis Club Rifredi,** via Facibeni (☎ **055/432552**); **Il Poggetto,** via Michele Mercati 24B (☎ **055/481285**); and the **Circolo Tennis alle Cascine,** viale Visarno 1 (☎ **055/332651**).

8 Shopping

THE SHOPPING SCENE

Skilled craftsmanship and traditional design unchanged since the days of the Medici have made Florence a serious shopping destination. Florence is noted for its hand-tooled **leather goods** and its various **straw merchandise,** as well as superbly crafted

The Art of Marbleizing

The city that prides itself as the literary cradle of Italy has always known how best to present its folios and manuscripts.

The brilliantly colored marbleized end pages that decorate the inside covers of book and photo albums use techniques that were originally developed in Persia and Turkey, and were imported to Italy during the 1400s by Florentine and Venetian merchants. The technique was improved and kept alive in Florence throughout the 19th and 20th centuries.

How do they do it? The "marbleizing" technique takes advantage of the relative densities of water and oil-based pigments to "float" layers of ink above the basins of water. By jiggling sheets of paper through multicolored brew, teams of trained artisans create the peacock-feathered effect that has been so popular throughout the ages. Part of the expense of marbleized paper involves the need to discard large amounts of ink, as the basinful of pigment is usually thrown away after the treatment of each piece of paper.

gold jewelry. Its reputation for fashionable custom-made clothes is no longer what it was, having lost its position to Milan.

The whole city of Florence strikes many visitors as a gigantic department store. Entire neighborhoods on both sides of the Arno offer good shops, although those along the medieval ponte Vecchio (with some exceptions) strike most people as too touristy.

Florence is not a city for bargain shopping. In general the merchandise is rather high priced. Most visitors interested in gold or silver jewelry head for the ponte Vecchio and its tiny shops. It's difficult to tell one from the other, but you really don't need to since the merchandise is similar. If you're looking for a charm or souvenir, these shops are fine. But the heyday of finding gold jewelry bargains on the ponte Vecchio is long gone.

The street for antiques in Florence is **via Maggio;** some of the furnishings and objets d'art here are from the 16th century. Another major area for antiques shopping is **borgo Ognissanti**.

Florence's Fifth Avenue is **via dei Tornabuoni.** This is the place to head for the best-quality leather goods, for the best clothing boutiques, and for stylish but costly shoes. Here you'll find everyone from Giorgio Armani to Salvatore Ferragamo.

The better shops are for the most part along Tornabuoni, but there are many on **via Vigna Nuova, via Porta Rossa,** and **via degli Strozzi.** You might also stroll on the lungarno along the Arno.

For some of the best buys in leather, check out **via del Parione,** a short narrow street that offers some of the best-quality leather items in Florence.

Shopping hours are generally Monday from 4 to 7:30pm and Tuesday to Saturday from 9 or 10am to 1pm and 3:30 or 4 to 7:30pm. During the summer some shops are open Monday morning. However, don't be surprised if some shops are closed for several weeks in August or for the entire month.

SHOPPING A TO Z
ANTIQUES

There are many outlets for antiques in Florence (but those high prices!). If you're in the market for such expensive purchases, or if you just like to browse, try the following:

Bottega San Felice. Via Maggio 39R. ☎ **055/215479.**

The Bottega San Felice offers many intriguing items from the 19th century, sometimes in the style known as "Charles X." The shop also sells more modern pieces. Many art deco items are for sale, as are many Biedermeier pieces.

Gallori Turchi. Via Maggio 10–12–14R. ☎ **055/282279.**

Gallori Turchi is one of the best antiques stores in Florence for the serious collector—that is, the serious well-heeled collector. Some of its rare items date to the 15th century. Each item seems well chosen, ranging from polychrome figures to gilded Tuscan pieces. The shop is closed from July 20 to August 20.

ART

Galleria Masini. Piazza Goldoni 6R. ☎ **055/294000.**

Established in 1870, the oldest art gallery in Florence, the Galleria Masini lies a few minutes' walk from the Hotel Excelsior and other leading hotels. The selection of modern and contemporary paintings by top artists is extensive, representing the work of more than 500 Italian painters. Even if you're not a collector, this is a good place to select a picture that will be a lasting reminder of your visit to Italy—you can take it home duty-free.

BOOKS

Bm Bookshop. Borgo Ognissanti 4R. ☎ **055/294575.**

This is the oldest English bookstore in Florence devoted to American and British books and one of the finest bookstores in Europe. It carries a large and excellent selection of paperbacks, travel guides, art and architecture books, history, Italian interest, fashion, design, and children's books, plus the largest collection of Italian cookbooks in English to be found in the city. Books are chosen by an expert staff and can be shipped anywhere in the world at nominal rates. The bookshop is near the Excelsior Hotel.

Libreria il Viaggio. Borgo degli Albizi 41R. ☎ **055/240489.**

This specialty bookstore in the center of Florence sells maps and guidebooks from all over the world, in a wide variety of languages, including English. It's one of the finest bookstores of its type in Italy, with a tempting variety of titles and merchandise.

DEPARTMENT STORES

Coin. Via de' Calzaiuoli 56r. ☎ **055/280531.**

Most stores in Florence are small mom-and-pop outfits with often quirky and limited selections. A noteworthy exception is a relatively new branch of the nationwide department store Coin. Comparable to Macy's in the United States, Coin is more glamourous and upscale than either Standa or Upim. Open Monday to Saturday from 9:30am to 8pm and on Sunday from 11am to 8pm.

Standa. Via Panzani 31R. ☎ **055/239-8963.**

Here you'll find general merchandise, including moderately priced clothing, household goods, and other items.

Upim. Piazza della Repubblica 1. ☎ **055/239-8544.**

Upim is a nationwide chain of stores similar to Standa. Open June to September, Monday to Friday from 8:45am to 7:45pm and on Saturday from 8:45am to 7pm; October to May, on Monday from 2 to 7:45pm and Tuesday to Saturday from 8:45am to 7:45pm.

FABRIC

Casa di Tessuti. Via de' Pecori 20R. ☎ **055/215961.**

In business for more than half a century, Casa di Tessuti is a shop for connoisseurs, those seeking one of the nation's largest and highest-quality selections of linen, silk, wool, and cotton. The Romoli family, longtime proprietors, are proud of their assortment of fabrics, and rightly so, and are known for their selections of design and colors.

FASHION (MEN & WOMEN)

Mariposa. Lungarno Corsini 18R. ☎ **055/284259.**

Mariposa offers women's fashions from such famous designers as Krizia, Fendi, Rocco Barocco, Missoni, and Mimmina. Foreign customers are often granted a 10% discount.

Romano. Piazza della Repubblica. ☎ **055/239-6890.**

In the commercial center of town near the Duomo is Romano, a glamorous clothing store for both women and men. The owners commissioned a curving stairwell to be constructed under the high ornate ceiling. But even more exciting are leather and suede goods found here, along with an assortment of dresses, shoes, and handbags—prices are high, but so is the quality.

GIFTS

Balatresi Gift Shop. Lungarno Acciaiuoli 22R. ☎ **055/287851.**

Among the many treasures found here are Florentine mosaics created for the shop by Maestro Metello Montelatici, who is arguably one of the greatest mosaicists alive today. The store also sells original ceramic figurines by the sculptor Giannitrapani, and a fine selection of hand-carved alabaster, enamel ware, and Tuscan glass. Many Americans come into this store every year to do their Christmas shopping.

Menegatti. Piazza del Pesce, Ponte Vecchio. ☎ **055/215202.**

The wide inventory here includes pottery from Florence, Faenza, and Deruta. There are also della Robbia reproductions made in red clay like the originals. Items can be sent home if you arrange it at the time of your purchase.

JEWELRY

Buying jewelry is almost an art in itself, so proceed with caution. Florence, of course, is known for its jewelry. You'll find some stunning antique pieces, and if you know how to buy, much good value.

Aurum. Lungarno Corsini 16R. ☎ **055/284259.**

Aurum sells contemporary 18-karat-gold jewelry. Many pieces are modern, based on designs created exclusively for this store. Others are reproductions of Etruscan designs.

Befani E Tai. Via Vacchereccia 13R. ☎ **055/287825.**

Befani E Tai is one of the most unusual jewelry stores in Florence—some of its pieces date back to the 19th century. The store was established right after World War II by expert goldsmiths who were childhood friends. Some of their clients even design their own jewelry for special orders. Artisans are skilled at working in gold and platinum.

Faraone-Settepassi. Via dei Tornabuoni 25R. ☎ **055/215506.**

Faraone-Settepassi, one of the most distinguished jewelers of the Renaissance city, draws a well-heeled patronage.

Mario Buccellati. Via dei Tornabuoni 69–71R. ☎ **055/239-6579.**

Located away from the ponte Vecchio, Mario Buccellati specializes in exquisite handcrafted jewelry and silver. A large selection of intriguing pieces at high prices is offered.

LEATHER

Universally acclaimed, Florentine leather is still the fine product it always was—smooth, well shaped, and vivid in such colors as green and red.

Bojola. Via dei Rondinelli 25R. ☎ **055/211155.**

Bojola is a leading name in leather. Sergio Bojola has distinguished himself in Florence by the variety of his selections, in both synthetic materials and beautiful leathers. Hundreds of customers are always enthusiastic about the items found here, which reflect first-class quality and craftsmanship.

John F. Lungarno Corsini 2. ☎ **055/239-8985.**

John F., located near the Santa Trinità Bridge, is a high-fashion house of leather in a Florentine palace. The leather clothing is of exclusive design, and the salon shows models from the *crème de la crème* of its collection. Although foreign patronage is high, the shop also dresses some of the most chic Florentine women. Accessories, including handbags and leather articles, made here are well crafted and beautifully styled. There's also a vast selection of Missoni sports sweaters.

Leonardo Leather Works. Borgo dei Greci 16A. ☎ **055/292202.**

The Leonardo Leather Works concentrates on two of the oldest major crafts of Florence: leather and jewelry. Leather goods include wallets, bags, shoes, boots, briefcases, clothing, travel bags, belts, and gift items, with products by famous designers. No imitations are permitted here. The jewelry department has a large assortment of gold chains, bracelets, rings, earrings, and charms.

Pollini. Via Calimala 12R. ☎ **055/214738.**

Pollini, one of the leading leathergoods stores of Florence, offers a wide array of stylized merchandise, including shoes, suitcases, clothing, belts, and virtually anything made of leather. It's located in the historic heart of Florence, near the ponte Vecchio.

MARKETS

After checking into their hotels, the most intrepid shoppers head for **piazza del Mercato Nuovo (the Straw Market)**, called "Il Porcellino" by the Italians because of the bronze statue of a reclining wild boar there. (It's a copy of the one in the Uffizi.) Tourists pet its snout (which is well worn) for good luck. The market stands in the monumental heart of Florence, an easy stroll from the Palazzo Vecchio. It sells not only straw items but leather goods as well, along with an array of typically Florentine merchandise—frames, trays, hand-embroidery, table linens, and hand-sprayed and painted boxes in traditional designs. Open Monday to Saturday from 9am to 7pm.

However, even better bargains await those who make their way through pushcarts to the stalls of the open-air **Mercato Centrale** (also called the Mercato San Lorenzo), in and around borgo San Lorenzo, near the railway station. If you don't mind bargaining, which is imperative here, you'll find an array of merchandise that includes raffia bags, Florentine leather purses, salt-and-pepper shakers, straw handbags, and art reproductions.

Offbeat Shopping

Fratelli Favilli, piazza del Duomo 16R (☎ **055/211846**), is the finest engraver in the city, with a specialty in signet rings. Virtually any design you bring to them can be crafted here.

Taddei, via Santa Margherita 11R (☎ **055/239-8960**), is *the* place for exquisitely made leather boxes and desk accessories. This family-owned and -run business has been turning out quality items for three generations.

I Mascherari, via dei Tavo Tavolini 13R (☎ **055/213823**), is the best shop for masks, which after a long sleep have become a fad again. Some of the masks are based on Florentine Renaissance patterns; others are in the Venetian *commedia dell'arte* style.

Alessandro Bizzarri, via della Condotta 32R (☎ **055/211580**), is one of those musty old stores found only in Europe. It's been in business since 1842, dispensing spices and minerals, the only store of its kind in Florence. Some of its extracts and essences are based on formulas in use in the Middle Ages or Renaissance era.

Antica Farmacia del Cinghiale, piazza del Mercato Nuovo 4R (☎ **055/ 282128**), in business for some three centuries, is an erboristeria, dispensing herbal teas and fragrances, along with herbal potpourris. A pharmacy is also situated here.

Cirri, via por Santa Maria (☎ **055/239-6593**), continues to market Florentine embroidery known for its delicacy and design. Although once considered a dying art, Cirri keeps the art of embroidery alive, with literally hundreds of beautiful designs in linen, cotton, or silk.

Mosaics

Arte Musiva. Largo Bargellini 2–4. ☎ **055/241647.**

Florentine mosaics are universally recognized. Bruno Lastrucci, the director of Arte Musiva, located in the old quarter of Santa Croce, is one of the most renowned living exponents of this art form. In the workshop you can see artisans plying their craft; some of the major mosaicists of Italy are here. In addition to traditional Florentine, modern mosaic has developed. A selection of the most significant works is permanently displayed in the gallery. These include decorative panels and tiles.

Paper & Stationery

Giulio Giannini & Figlio. Piazza Pitti 36–37R. ☎ **055/212621.**

Giulio Giannini & Figlio is the leading stationery store in Florence. Much of its merchandise is so exquisite that it's snapped up by foreigners for gift-giving later in the year. The English-speaking staff is helpful. This has been a family business for more than 140 years.

Il Papiro. Via Cavour 55R. ☎ **055/215262.**

Its specialty is party-colored marbelized paper that's skillfully incorporated into objects ranging from bookmarks to photo albums (have a favorite relative who's getting married soon? these make great wedding albums). More unusual are the marbelized wood (such as music boxes) and leather (couture-style purses and bags) objects, as well as the marbelized fabric. The staff is charming, and the prices are reasonable, considering the high quality and charm of virtually everything sold in the store. The flagship store is on via Cavour, but there are well-managed branches at piazza del Duomo 24R (☎ 055/215262) and lugarno Acciaiuoli 42R (☎ 055/215262).

Pineider. Piazza della Signoria 13R. ☎ **055/284-4655.**

Established on this site in 1774, and maintained today by descendents of its original founders, this is the oldest store in Florence specializing in the art of printing and engraving. The most aristocratic-looking greeting cards, business cards, stationery, and formal invitations come from this outfit, which employs a battalion of artisans who custom-make the steel plates for each engraving job. This is the flagship of a discreet, small-scale chain. Because most orders take between 2 and 3 weeks to fill, many clients place their orders at this store, then arrange to have the final product shipped home. Less complicated gift items can be made from the wide stock of merchandise that includes beautifully crafted diaries, stationery, the kinds of desk sets you'd offer your favorite CEO, portfolios, address books, photo albums, and etchings of vistas unique to Florence. A less extensive branch of this store, that doesn't take custom engraving orders, is at via dei Tornbuoni 76 (☎ 055/211605).

A PHARMACY

Officina Profumo Farmaceutica di Santa Maria Novella. Via della Scala 16N. ☎ **055/216276.**

This is the most fascinating pharmacy in Italy. Located northwest of the Church of Santa Maria Novella, it opened its doors to the public in 1612, offering a selection of herbal remedies that were created by friars of the Dominican order. Those closely guarded secrets have been retained, and many of the same elixirs are still sold today. You've heard of papaya as an aid to digestion, but what about elixir of rhubarb? A wide selection of perfumes, scented soaps, shampoos, and of course potpourris, along with creams and lotions, is handsomely presented in these old-fashioned precincts, which qualify as a sightseeing attraction. The shop is closed on Saturday afternoon in July and August.

PRINTS & ENGRAVINGS

Giovanni Baccani. Via della Vigna Nuova 75R. ☎ **055/214467.**

Giovanni Baccani has long been a specialist in this field. Everything it sells is old—there's nothing new here. "The Blue Shop," as it's called, offers a huge array of prints and engravings, often of Florentine scenes. These are found in bins, and you're free to look as long as you want. Tuscan paper goods are also sold.

SHOES

Ferragamo. Via dei Tornabuoni 16R. ☎ **055/292123.**

Salvatore Ferragamo has long been one of the most famous names in shoes. Although he started in Hollywood just before the outbreak of World War I, the headquarters of this famed manufacturer were installed here in the Palazzo Ferroni, on the most fashionable shopping street of Florence, before World War II broke out. Ferragamo sells shoes for both men and women, along with some of the most elegant boutique items in the city, including men's and women's clothing, scarves, handbags, ties, luggage, and other merchandise. But chances are you'll want to visit it for its stunning shoes, known for their durability and style.

If you're really interested, check out the **Ferragamo Museum** at via dei Tornabuoni 2 (☎ **055/336-0456**), open on Monday, Wednesday, and Friday from 9am to 1pm and 2 to 6pm. This free museum, set on the second floor of a block devoted completely to the Ferragamo aesthetic, chronicles the family-run empire from its beginnings, and documents everything from the design to the manufacturing process. There's also a display of exquisite shoes from other eras.

Lily of Florence. Via Guicciardini 2R. ☎ **055/294748.**

Both men and women can buy shoes in American sizes at Lily of Florence. For women, Lily distributes both her own designs and those of other well-known designers. The stylish shoes come in a wide range of colors and are made of high-quality leather.

SILVER

Pampaloni. Borgo Santi Apostoli, 47R. ☎ **055/289094.**

This shop is headed by Gianfranco Pampaloni, the third-generation silversmith in his family. An inspired artist, he often bases designs on past achievements, for example a 1604 drinking goblet by the Roman artist Giovanni Maggi. The business was launched in 1902, and some of the classic designs turned out back then are still being made. Gianfranco doesn't live in the past, however, as his own adverturous designs are carried in such prestigious outlets as the Rome-based jeweler Bulgari and Tiffany & Co.

9 Florence After Dark

Evening entertainment in Florence is not an exciting prospect, unless you simply like to walk through the narrow streets or head up toward Fiesole for a view of the city at night (truly spectacular). The typical Florentine begins an evening early at one of the cafes listed below.

For theatrical and concert listings pick up a free copy of **"Welcome to Florence,"** available at the tourist office. This handy publication contains information on recitals, concerts, theatrical productions, and other cultural offerings.

Many cultural presentations are performed in churches. These might include open-air concerts in the cloisters of the Badia Fiesolana in Fiesole (the hill town above Florence), or at the Ospedale degli Innocenti, the foundling "hospital of the innocents" on summer evenings only.

Orchestral offerings—performed by the Regional Tuscan Orchestra—are often presented at the Church of Santo Stefano al Ponte Vecchio.

THE PERFORMING ARTS

Teatro Comunale di Firenze / Maggio Musicale Fiorentino. Corso Italia 16. ☎ **055/211158.** Tickets 30,000–180,000 lire ($19.20–$115.20) for the opera, 25,000–180,000 lire ($16–$115.20) for concerts.

This is the main theater in Florence, with opera, concert, and ballet seasons presented from September to April. The short Florence opera season usually lasts from mid-December to mid-January only. This theater is also the major venue for the Maggio Musicale, the festival of opera, ballet, concerts, and recitals that lasts from late April until July. The box office is open Tuesday to Friday from 11am to 5:30pm and on Saturday from 9am to 1pm.

Teatro della Pergola. Via della Pergola 18. ☎ **055/247-9651.** Tickets 11,500–70,000 lire ($7.35–$44.80).

This is the major legitimate theater of Florence, but you'll have to understand Italian to appreciate most of its plays, except for opera, which is universal. Plays are performed year-round except during the Maggio Musicale, when the theater becomes the setting for many of the musical presentations of the festival. Performances are Tuesday to Saturday at 8:45pm. The box office is open Tuesday to Saturday from 9:30am to 1pm and 3:45 to 6:45pm and on Sunday from 9:45am to noon.

THE CLUB & MUSIC SCENE
NIGHTCLUBS

Full-Up. Via della Vigna Vecchia 23–25R. ☎ **055/293006.** Cover (including the first drink) 15,000–25,000 lire ($9.60–$16).

Contained in the cellar of an antique building in the historic heart of town, this well-known establishment attracts college students from the city's many universities, who appreciate the establishment's two-in-one format. One section contains a smallish dance floor and recorded dance music; another is devoted to the somewhat more restrained ambience of a piano bar. The place can be fun, and even older clients usually feel at ease here. Drinks cost 10,000 to 15,000 lire ($6.40 to $9.60). Open Wednesday to Monday from 11pm to 4am.

ROCK

The Red Garter. Via de' Benci 33R. ☎ **055/234-4904.** No cover.

Perhaps nothing could be more unexpected in this city of Donatello and Michelangelo than a club called the Red Garter, right off piazza Santa Croce. The American Prohibition era lives on—in fact, it has been exported. Visitors to the Red Garter can hear a variety of music, from rock to bluegrass. The club attracts young people from all over the world. A mug of Heineken lager on tap goes for 7,000 lire ($4.50), and most tall drinks, made from "hijacked hootch," as it's known here, begin at 10,000 lire ($6.40). The club is open Monday to Thursday from 8:30pm to 1am and Friday to Sunday from 9pm to 1:30am. "Happy Hour" is every evening until 9:30pm.

Space Electronic. Via Palazzuolo 37. ☎ **055/293082.** Cover (including the first drink) 25,000 lire ($16).

This club is the only disco in Florence with karaoke. The decor consists of gigantic carnival heads, wall-to-wall mirrors, and an imitation space capsule that goes back and forth across the dance floor. If karaoke doesn't thrill you, however, head to the new ground-floor pub, which stocks an ample supply of imported beers. On the upper level is a large dance floor with a wide choice of music and the best sound-and-light show in town. This place attracts a lot of foreign women who want to hook up with Florentine men on the prowl. The disco opens nightly at 10pm and usually goes until 2:30am or later, depending on business.

THE BAR & CAFE SCENE
BARS & PUBS

Donatello Bar. In the Hotel Excelsior, piazza Ognissanti 3. ☎ **055/264201.**

The Donatello Bar, on the ground floor of this previously recommended deluxe hotel, is the city's most elegant watering hole. Named in honor of the great Renaissance artist, this bar and its adjoining restaurant, Il Cestello, attracts well-heeled international visitors along with the Florentine cultural and business elite. The ambience is enlivened by a marble fountain and works of art. Piano music is featured daily from 7pm to 1am and the bar is open daily from 11am to 1:30am. Drinks begin at 12,000 lire ($7.70).

Fiddler's Elbow. Piazza Santa Maria Novella 7R. ☎ **055/21506.**

After an initial success in Rome, this Irish pub has now invaded the city of Donatello and Michelangelo. It quickly became one of the most popular watering holes in Florence. An authentic pint of Guinness is the most popular item to order. The location is in the vicinity of the rail station. You can order a pint of beer for 7,000 lire ($4.50). The pub is open daily from 3pm to 12:30am.

CAFES

Café Rivoire. Piazza della Signoria 4R. ☎ **055/214412.**

The Café Rivoire offers a classy and amusing old-world ambience with a direct view of the statues of one of our favorite squares in the world. You can sit at one of the metal tables set up on the flagstones outside, or at one of the tables in a choice of inner rooms filled with marble detailing and unusual oil renderings of the piazza outside. If you don't want to sit at all, try the mahogany and green-marble bar, where many of the more colorful characters making the Grand Tour of Europe talk, flirt, or gossip. A member of the staff will serve you an espresso for 4,000 lire ($2.55) at a table or a long drink for 14,000 lire ($8.95). There's also a selection of small sandwiches, omelets, and ice creams. The cafe is noted for its hot chocolate as well. It's open Tuesday to Sunday from 8am to midnight.

Giacosa. Via dei Tornabuoni 83R. ☎ **055/239-6226.**

Giacosa is a deceptively simple-looking cafe whose stand-up bar occupies more space than its limited number of sit-down tables. Set behind three Tuscan arches on a fashionable shopping street in the center of the old city, it has a warmly paneled interior, a lavish display of pastries and sandwiches, and a reputation as the birthplace of the Negroni. That drink, as you probably know, is a combination of gin, Campari, and red vermouth. Other drinks served here include Singapore slings, Italian and American coffee, and a range of apéritifs. A Negroni costs 7,500 lire ($4.80) at a counter or 12,000 lire ($7.70) at a table. Light meals are also served, and the cafe is famous for its ice cream. Open Monday to Saturday from 7:30am to 8:30pm.

Gilli. Piazza della Repubblica 39R. ☎ **055/213896.**

Gilli, the oldest and most beautiful cafe in Florence, occupies a desirable position in the center of the city, a few minutes' walk from the Duomo. It was founded in 1733, when piazza della Repubblica had a different name. You can sit at a small, brightly lit table near the bar, or retreat to an intricately paneled pair of rooms to the side and enjoy the flattering light from the Venetian-glass chandeliers. A cappuccino costs 5,000 lire ($3.20) at a table or 1,700 lire ($1.10) if you stand at the bar. Daily specials, sandwiches, toasts, and hard drinks are sold, along with an array of "tropical" libations. The cafe is open March 16 to November 14, Wednesday to Monday from 7:30am to 1am; November 15 to March 15, Wednesday to Friday from 7:30am to 9pm and Saturday to Monday from 7:30am to 1am.

Giubbe Rosse. Piazza della Repubblica 13R. ☎ **055/212280.**

The waiters of this place still wear the red coats as they did when the establishment was founded in 1888. Originally a beer hall, today it's an elegantly paneled cafe, bar, and restaurant filled with turn-of-the-century chandeliers and polished granite floors. You can enjoy a drink or cup of coffee at one of the small tables near the zinc-top bar. An inner dining room has a soaring vaulted ceiling of reddish brick. Italian meals begin at 39,000 lire ($24.95). Light lunches are a specialty, as are full American breakfasts. Open daily from 7:30am to 2am.

GAY NIGHTLIFE

Crisco. Via S. Egidio 43R. ☎ **055/248-0580.** Cover 12,000–16,000 lire ($7.70–$10.25), depending on the night of the week.

This, Florence's leading gay bar, caters only to men and is located in an 18th-century building that contains both a bar and a dance floor. Drinks start at 8,000 lire ($5.10) each. Classified as a *club privato,* it's open on Wednesday, Thursday, Sunday, and Monday from 10:30pm to 3:30am, and on Friday and Saturday from 10:30pm to 5 or 6am.

Santanassa Bar. Via del Pandolfini 26. ☎ **055/243356.** Cover (including the first drink) 12,000 lire ($7.70) Sun–Thurs, 15,000–20,000 lire ($9.60–$12.80) Fri–Sat.

Specifically tailored to Tuscany's community of gay men, this club is considered a Saturday-night staple by many. In summertime the crowd gets very international, looking like a cross section of all the nations of Europe. There's a crowded bar on the street level, sometimes with a live piano player, where many of the clients seem to have known one another for years. On Friday and Saturday the cellar is transformed into a disco. It's open Sunday to Thursday from 10pm to 4am and on Friday and Saturday from 10pm to 6am. The bar is open year round; the disco is open September through June.

Tabasco. Piazza Santa Cecelia 3. ☎ **055/213000.** Cover 15,000–20,000 lire ($9.60–$12.80) including first drink.

One of the leading gay bars of Florence, Tabasco stands near piazza della Signoria in the heart of the city. Renewed in 1989, it's open Tuesday to Sunday from 10pm to at least 3am or later on weekends. The club offers a bar, along with video games and X-rated male-action movies. Drinks cost 5,000 to 10,000 lire ($3.20 to $6.40). You must be 18 to be admitted.

10 A Side Trip to Fiesole

For more extensive day trips, you can refer to the next chapter. But Fiesole is a virtual suburb of Florence.

When the sun shines too hot on piazza della Signoria and tourists try to prance bare-backed into the Uffizi, Florentines are likely to head for the hills—usually to Fiesole. But they'll encounter more tourists, as this town—once an Etruscan settlement—is the most popular outing from the city. Bus no. 7, which leaves from piazza San Marco, will take you there in 25 minutes and give you a panoramic view along the way. You'll pass fountains, statuary, and gardens strung out over the hills like a scrambled jigsaw puzzle.

EXPLORING THE TOWN

When you arrive at Fiesole, by all means don't sit with the throngs all afternoon in the central square sipping Campari (although that isn't a bad pastime). Explore some of Fiesole's attractions. You won't find anything as dazzling as the Renaissance treasures of Florence, however—the charms of Fiesole are more subtle. Fortunately, all major sights branch out within walking distance of the main piazza, beginning with the **Cattedrale di San Romolo.** At first this cathedral may seem austere, with its concrete-gray Corinthian columns and Romanesque arches. But it has its own beauty. Dating from A.D. 1000, it was much altered during the Renaissance. In the Salutati Chapel are important sculptural works by Mino da Fiesole. It's open daily from 7:30am to noon and 4 to 7pm.

Bandini Museum. Via Dupre. ☎ **055/59477.** Admission 6,000 lire ($3.85) adults, 3,000 lire ($1.90) children 17 and under and seniors 60 and over. Daily 9am–6pm. Bus: 7.

This ecclesiastical museum, around to the side of the Duomo, belongs to the Fiesole Cathedral Chapter, established in 1913. On the ground floor are della Robbia terra-cotta works, as well as art by Michelangelo and Nino Pisano. On the top floors are paintings by the best Giotto students, which reflect ecclesiastical and worldly themes, most of them the work of Tuscan artists of the 14th century.

Museo Missionario Francescano Fiesole. Via San Francesco 13. ☎ **055/59175.** Free admission (but a donation is expected). Mon–Fri 9am–noon and 3–6pm, Sat 3–6pm. Bus: 7.

The hardest task you'll have in Fiesole is to take the steep goat-climb up to the Convent of San Francesco. You can visit the Gothic-style Franciscan church, which was built in the first years of the 1400s. The church was consecrated in 1516. Inside are many paintings by well-known Florentine artists. In the basement of the church is the ethnological museum. Begun in 1906, the collection has a large section of Chinese artifacts, including ancient bronzes. An Etruscan-Roman section contains some 330 archeological pieces, and an Egyptian section also has numerous objects.

Teatro Romano e Museo Civico. Via Portigiani 1. ☎ **055/59477.** Admission 5,000 lire ($3.20) adults, 3,000 lire ($1.90) children 6–16 and seniors 60 and over, free for children 5 and under. Mon–Fri 9am–6pm and Wed–Sun 9am–pm. Bus: 7.

On this site is the major surviving evidence that Fiesole was an Etruscan city six centuries before Christ, and later a Roman town. In the 1st century B.C. a theater was built, the restored remains of which you can see today. Near the theater are the skeletonlike ruins of the baths, which may have been built at the same time. Try to visit the Etruscan-Roman museum, with its many interesting finds that date from the days when Fiesole—not Florence—was supreme (a guide is on hand to show you through).

WHERE TO STAY

Hotel Aurora. Piazza Mino da Fiesole 39, Fiesole, 50014 Firenze. ☎ **055/59100.** Fax 055/59587. 27 rms. A/C MINIBAR TV TEL. 227,000–335,000 lire ($145.30–$214.40) double. Rates include breakfast. AE, DC, MC, V. Free parking. Bus: 7.

Set on the Fiesole's main square, behind a facade of green shutters and ochre-colored stucco, the Aurora occupies a structure built in the 18th century as a private house. In 1890 it became a hotel that catered almost exclusively to arts-conscious English people making their grand tour through the historic cities of Italy. The hotel continues to rent rooms, which have been modernized and simplified to meet today's needs. Views over faraway Florence are visible from the hotel's back bedrooms, which cost more than those overlooking the piazza in front. On the premises is a back terrace with hanging vines, a pergola, and views of the city. Connecting doors can be opened between some rooms to create suites, which cost around 550,000 lire ($352) each.

Pensione Bencista. Via Benedetto de Maiano 4, Fiesole, 50014 Firenze. ☎ **055/59163.** Fax 055/59163. 44 rms, 32 with bath. TEL. 105,000 lire ($67.20) per person without bath, 125,000 lire ($80) per person with bath. Rates include half board. No credit cards. Free parking. Bus: 7.

The Pensione Bencista has been the family villa of the Simoni family for years. One guest found that it was like E. M. Forester's *"A Room with a View* gone to the country." It was built around 1300, with additions made to the existing building about every 100 years after that. In 1925 Paolo Simoni opened the villa to paying guests. Today it's run by his son, Simone Simoni. Its position, high up on the road to Fiesole, is commanding, with an unmarred view of the city and the hillside villas. The driveway to the formal entrance, with its circular fountain, winds through olive trees.

The spread-out villa has many lofty old rooms furnished with family antiques. The bedrooms vary in size and interest; many are without bath and have hot and cold running water only. In chilly weather guests meet each other in the evening in front of a huge fireplace. The Bencista is suitable for parents who might want to leave their children in the country while they take jaunts into the city. It's a 10-minute bus ride from the heart of Florence.

WHERE TO DINE

Trattoria le Cave di Maiano. Via delle Cave 16. ☎ **055/59133.** Reservations required. Main courses 20,000–26,000 lire ($12.80–$16.65). AE, DC, MC, V. Mon 7–11:30pm, Tues–Sun noon–3pm and 7–11:30pm. Closed Aug 10–20. Bus: 7. TUSCAN.

This restaurant, at Maiano, is a 15-minute ride east from the heart of Florence and just a short distance south of Fiesole. It's a family-run establishment, which since the 17th century has been an esoteric address to discerning Florentines. It's imperative, incidentally, that you reserve a table before heading here. The rustically decorated trattoria is a garden restaurant, with stone tables and large sheltering trees. Inside, the restaurant is in the tavern style, with a beamed ceiling. We recommend highly the antipasto and the homemade green tortellini. For a main course, there's a golden grilled chicken or perhaps a savory herb-flavored roast lamb. For side dishes, we suggest fried polenta, Tuscan beans, and fried potatoes. As a final treat, the waiter will bring you homemade ice cream with fresh raspberries.

7

Tuscany & Umbria

The hill towns of Tuscany and Umbria are prized not only for their essential beauty (for example, the unspoiled medieval severity in the heart of Siena and San Gimignano) but for their spectacular art treasures, created by such "hometown boys" as Leonardo da Vinci. From Florence, you can explore numerous nearby cities, including Pisa and Siena, as well as San Gimignano with its medieval towers.

And if you're traveling between Rome and Florence, why not veer off the autostrada and visit a string of other hill towns, such as Spoleto and Perugia, that preserve the past? The joy of Tuscany and Umbria is that almost any corner of its varied and beautiful landscape harbors some natural or man-made treasure.

EXPLORING TUSCANY & UMBRIA BY CAR

Day 1   From Florence take the autostrada west toward Lucca and Pisa, but, if time permits, consider an overnight stopover in the most fashionable spa in Italy, Montecatini Terma, which is signposted right off the autostrada. Here you can get in some R&R after having experienced all the Renaissance glories of Florence.

Day 2   Back on the autostrada west, you can be in Lucca within the hour—enough time for a full day of sightseeing. Situated in the center of a fertile plain, Lucca is also known for its foodstuff, so in addition to seeing its major attractions, especially its Duomo with a green and white marble facade, you can enjoy good eating. After a night in Lucca, the trail heads south.

Day 3   From Lucca, your next destination on the autostrada is Pisa. Although it's too dangerous to climb the Leaning Tower anymore, Pisa is a great art city, known especially for its architecture. In addition to its Duomo, chief attractions include the Baptistery, the Camposanto, and the Museo dell'Opera del Duomo.

Day 4   Travel southeast for a visit to San Gimignano, ringed by three sets of historic walls and known for its medieval towers. No cars are allowed inside the city walls. Most of the sights can be covered in a day, and San Gimignano is one of the most romantic stopovers in the province.

☕ **TAKE A BREAK**   In San Gimignano, **Perucá Center,** via Capassi 16 (☎ **0577/943136**), is your typical Tuscan pizzeria/

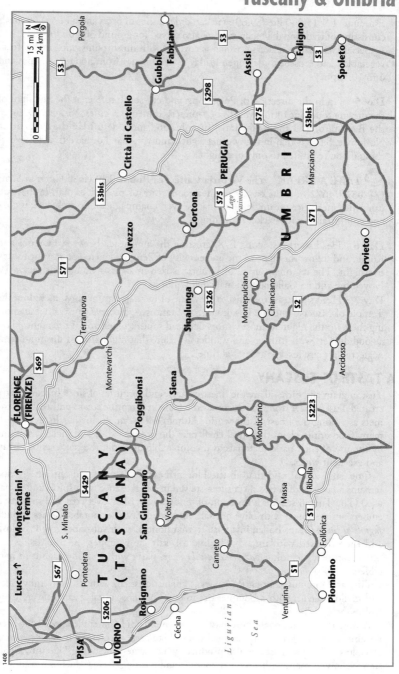

ristorante. For 15,000 lire ($9.60) you can order a slice of pizza and a beer. Full meals consisting of traditional Tuscan fare are also served for around 30,000 lire ($19.20). A specialty is calzone alla casa, which is covered with mushrooms, mozzarella, fresh vegetables, and prosciutto. It's open Friday to Wednesday from noon to 2:30pm and 6 to 10:30pm.

Day 5   Go in the direction of Poggibonsi and cut south to Siena, the highlight of the driving tour, one of the world's best-preserved medieval cities. Visit the Duomo, the Battistero, and the Cathedral Museum, and most definitely the Pinacoteca Nazionale. Siena is rich in many other sights, and you may not have time for everything if you're limited to only one night.

⚫ **TAKE A BREAK**   The **Victoria Caffè Tea Room,** 130 via di Città, in Siena (☎ **0577/46720**), is the city's finest tea room. But it's more than that, in that you can order meals, ice cream, various snacks, even champagne. The ambience is cozy and comfortable, with wicker furnishings.

Day 6   Head southeast along E78, crossing the autostrada between Florence and Rome, and follow the signs to the ancient city of Perugia, where you'll want to stay overnight. The regional capital of Umbria is rich in sights—notably its piazza IV Novembre and its Galleria Nazionale dell'Umbria.

Day 7   Head southeast to Assisi to see some of its major attractions, including the Temple of Minerva and the Basilica di San Francesco. However, instead of anchoring there for the night, as most visitors do, head south to Spoleto for the night. Have a good dinner (with truffles) and wander at leisure that night around this too-often-neglected art city (except at festival time).

A TASTE OF TUSCANY

Tuscan grain and olive oil are the finest in Italy, and centuries of stock breeding have created Tuscan beef from which comes the fabled Florentine steak, praised by gourmets as among the finest in the world. Although Tuscan cuisine has its detractors, many food critics claim that local chefs take the ordinary dish and make it sublime by the use of such basic materials as incomparable olive oil, the tenderest of meat, and excellent wines.

One early visitor said that all the Florentines "eat is tripe and entrails." Tripe remains a favorite dish (it's most often stewed in a meat sauce with spices and tomatoes). The Tuscan steak is a thick cut of tender beef grilled over coal and soft-wood embers and seasoned with olive oil, salt, and pepper. Other notable dishes include *fagioli al fiasco* (beans boiled in a flash so that none of their substance might be lost, and then dressed with uncooked olive oil, salt, and pepper). Game dishes are often featured, including *pappardella alla lepre,* pasta with a strong ragoût of hare giblets.

First and foremost among the wines is chianti classico, with its lively ruby color and mellow flavor, with a bouquet of violets. The most notable chiantis are from Coltibono and Brolio.

A wine that has no rivals with roasts is vino nobile di Montepulciano, so ruby red it's almost purple, with a rich rugged body. Like certain chiantis, it has a perfume of violets as it ages. Tuscany also produces white wines, including Ugolino, a pale straw-yellow in color, with a refined bouquet and pleasing flavor, which is served with fish.

1 Siena

21 miles S of Florence, 143 miles NW of Rome

After visiting Florence, it's altogether fitting, certainly bipartisan, to call on what has been labeled in the past its natural enemy. In Rome we saw classicism and the baroque; in Florence, the Renaissance; but in the walled city of Siena we stand solidly planted back in the Middle Ages. On three sienna-colored hills in the center of Tuscany, Sena Vetus lies in chianti country. Perhaps preserving its original character more markedly than any other city in Italy, it is even today a showplace of the Italian Gothic.

William Dean Howells, the American novelist (*The Rise of Silas Lapham*), called Siena "not a monument but a light." Although it's regrettably too often visited on a quick day's excursion, Siena is a city of contemplation and profound exploration. It's characterized by Gothic palaces, almond-eyed madonnas, aristocratic mansions, letter-writing St. Catherine (patron saint of Italy), narrow streets, and medieval gates, walls, and towers.

Although such a point of view may be heretical, one can almost be grateful that Siena lost its battle with Florence. Had it continued to expand and change after reaching the zenith of its power in the 14th century, chances are it would be markedly different today, influenced by the rising tides of the Renaissance and the baroque (represented here only in a small degree). But Siena retained its uniqueness (certain Sienese painters were still showing the influence of Byzantium in the late 15th century).

ESSENTIALS

GETTING THERE   By Plane   Fly either to Florence's Peretola Airport or Pisa's Galileo Galilei Airport.

By Train   Trains arrive hourly from both Florence and Pisa.

By Bus   Headquartered in Siena, **TRA-IN,** piazza San Domenico 1 (☎ **0577/ 204245**), in Siena, offers bus service to all of Tuscany, with air-conditioned coaches. The one-way fare between Florence and Siena is 10,000 lire ($6.40) per person. The trip takes 1$^1/_4$ hours.

By Car   Head south from Florence along the Firenze–Siena autostrada, a superhighway that links the two cities, going through Poggibonsi.

VISITOR INFORMATION   The **tourist information office** is at piazza del Campo 56 (☎ **0577/280551**). It's open Monday to Saturday from 8:30am to 7:30pm and on Sunday from 8:30am to 2pm.

SPECIAL EVENTS   The best time to visit is usually on July 2 or August 16, the occasions of the **Palio delle Contrade,** a historical pageant and tournament known throughout Europe, which draws thousands annually. In the horse race, each bareback-riding jockey represents a *contrada* (one of the wards into which the city is divided). The race, which requires tremendous skill, takes place on piazza del Campo, the historic heart of Siena. Before the race, much pageantry evoking the 15th century parades by, with colorfully costumed men and banners. The flag-throwing ceremony, depicted in so many travelog films, takes place at this time. And just as enticing is the victory celebration.

Don't buy expensive tickets for the day of the Palio. It's free to stand in the middle—and a lot more fun. Just get there very early, and bring a book and a

Thermos. The square becomes almost impossibly crowded. The temperature can range from rainy and cold to blistering hot. If it's a sunny day, it's a good idea to bring some sort of head covering, since most of the viewing area is not shaded. For a memorable dinner and lots of fun, join one of the 17 *contrade* attending a *cena* (supper) that's held outdoors the night before the race.

EXPLORING THE MEDIEVAL CITY

There's much to see here. Let's start in the heart of Siena, the shell-shaped **piazza del Campo,** described by Montaigne as "the finest of any city in the world." Pause to enjoy the Fonte Gaia, the fountain of joy, with embellishments by Jacopo della Quercia (the present sculptured works are reproductions; the badly beaten original ones are found in the town hall).

Palazzo Pubblico. Piazza del Campo. ☎ **0577/292263.** Admission 6,000 lire ($3.85) adults, 3,000 lire ($1.90) students and seniors 65 and over, free for children. Nov 6–Feb, daily 9:30am–1:30pm; Mar–Nov 5, Mon–Sat 9am–7pm, Sun and holidays 9am–1:30pm.

The Palazzo Pubblico dates from 1288–1309 and is filled with important artworks by some of the leaders in the Sienese school of painting and sculpture. This collection is the Museo Civico. Upstairs in the museum is the Sala della Pace, frescoed from 1337 to 1339 by Ambrogio Lorenzetti; the allegorical frescoes show the idealized effects of good government and bad government. In this depiction, the most notable figure of the Virtues surrounding the king is *La Pace* (Peace). To the right of the king and the Virtues is a representation of Siena in peaceful times.

On the left Lorenzetti showed his opinion of "ward heelers," but some of the sting has been taken out of the frescoes, as the evil-government scene is badly damaged. Actually, these were propaganda frescoes in their day, commissioned by the party in power, but they are now viewed as among the most important of all secular frescoes to come down from the Middle Ages.

In the Sala del Mappomondo is Simone Martini's *Majesty,* the Madonna enthroned with her Child, surrounded by angels and saints. It's his earliest-known documented work (ca. 1315). The other remarkable Martini fresco (on the opposite wall) is the equestrian portrait of Guidoriccio da Fogliano, general of the Sienese Republic, in ceremonial dress.

✪ **Il Duomo.** Piazza del Duomo. ☎ **0577/283048.** Free admission. Nov–Mar 16, daily 7:30am–1:30pm and 2:30pm–sunset; Mar 17–Oct, daily 7:30am–7:30pm.

At piazza del Duomo, directly southwest of piazza del Campo, stands an architectural fantasy. With its colored bands of marble, the Sienese cathedral is an original and exciting building, erected in the Romanesque and Italian Gothic styles and dating from the 12th century. The dramatic facade—designed in part by Giovanni Pisano—dates from the 13th century, as does the Romanesque bell tower.

The zebralike interior, with its black and white stripes, is equally stunning. The floor consists of various embedded works of art, many of which are roped off to preserve the richness in design, which depict both biblical and mythological subjects. Numerous artists worked on the floor, notably Domenico Beccafumi. For most of the year a large part of the cathedral floor is covered to protect it.

The octagonal 13th-century pulpit is by Niccolò Pisano (Giovanni's father), who was one of the most significant Italian sculptors before the dawn of the Renaissance (see his pulpit in the Baptistery at Pisa). The Siena pulpit is his masterpiece; it reveals in relief such scenes as the slaughter of the innocents and the Crucifixion. The elder Pisano finished the pulpit in 1268, aided by his son and other artists. Its pillars are supported by four marble lions, again reminiscent of the Pisano pulpit at Pisa.

Siena

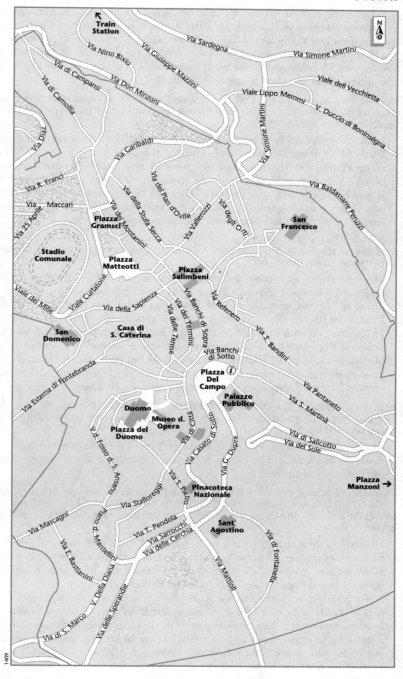

In the chapel of the left transept (near the library) is a glass-enclosed box with an arm that tradition maintains is John the Baptist's, used to baptize Christ, and Donatello's bronze of John the Baptist. To see another Donatello work in bronze— a bishop's gravemarker—look at the floor in the chapel to the left of the pulpit's stairway. Some of the designs for the inlaid wooden stalls in the apse were by Riccio. A representational blue starry sky twinkles overhead.

Libreria Piccolomini. Inside Il Duomo, piazza del Duomo. ☎ **0577/283048.** Admission 2,000 lire ($1.30). Mar 16–Oct, daily 9am–7:30pm; Nov–Mar 15, daily 10am–1pm and 2:30–5pm. Closed Jan 1 and Dec 25.

Founded by Cardinal Francesco Piccolomini (later Pius III) to honor his uncle (Pius II), the library inside Il Duomo is renowned for its cycle of frescoes by the Umbrian master Pinturicchio. His frescoes are well preserved, even though they date from the early 16th century. In Vasari's words, the panels illustrate "the history of Pope Pius II from birth to the minute of his death." Raphael's alleged connection with the frescoes, if any, is undocumented. In the center is an exquisite *Three Graces*, a Roman copy of a 3rd-century B.C. Greek work from the school of Praxiteles.

Museo dell'Opera Metropolitana. Piazza del Duomo 8. ☎ **0577/283048.** Admission 5,000 lire ($3.20). Mar 16–Sept, daily 9am–7:30pm; Oct, daily 9am–6pm; Nov–Mar 15, daily 9am–1:30pm. Closed Dec 25–Jan 1.

This museum houses paintings and sculptures originally created for the cathedral. On the ground floor you'll find much interesting sculpture, including works by Giovanni Pisano and his assistants. But the real draw hangs on the next floor in the Sala di Duccio: his fragmented *La Maestà*, a Madonna enthroned, painted from 1308 to 1311. The panel was originally an altarpiece by Duccio di Buoninsegna for the cathedral, filled with dramatic moments that illustrate the story of Christ and the Madonna. A student of Cimabue's, Duccio was the first great name in the school of Sienese painting. In the rooms upstairs are the collections of the treasury, and on the very top floor is a display of paintings from the early Sienese school.

Battistero. Piazza San Giovanni. ☎ **0577/283048.** Admission 3,000 lire ($1.90). Mar 16–Sept, daily 9am–7:30pm; Oct, daily 9am–6pm; Nov–Mar 15, daily 10am–1pm and 2:30–5pm. Closed Jan 1 and Dec 25.

The facade of the Baptistery dates from the 14th century. In the center of the interior is the baptismal font by Jacopo della Quercia, which contains some bas-reliefs by Donatello and Ghiberti.

Pinacoteca Nazionale (Picture Gallery). In the Palazzo Buonsignori, via San Pietro 29. ☎ **0577/281161.** Admission 8,000 lire ($5.10) adults, free for children 17 and under and for seniors 60 and over. Apr–Oct, Tues–Sat 9am–7pm, Sun 8am–1pm; Nov–Mar, Tues–Sun 8:30am–1:30pm.

Housed in a 14th-century palazzo near piazza del Campo is the national gallery's collection of the Sienese school of painting, which once rivaled that of Florence. Displayed here are some of the giants of the pre-Renaissance. Most of the paintings cover the period from the late 12th century to the mid-16th century.

The principal treasures are on the second floor, where you'll contemplate the artistry of Duccio in the early salons. The gallery is rich in the art of the two Lorenzetti brothers, Ambrogio and Pietro, who painted in the 14th century. Ambrogio is represented by an *Annunciation* and a *Crucifix*, but one of his most celebrated works, carried out with consummate skill, is an almond-eyed *Madonna and Bambino* surrounded by saints and angels. Pietro's most important entry here is an altarpiece— *The Madonna of the Carmine*—made for a church in Siena in 1329. Simone Martini's *Madonna and Child* is damaged but one of the best-known paintings here.

In the salons to follow are works by Giovanni di Paolo (*Presentation at the Temple*), Sano di Pietro, and Giovanni Antonio Bazzi (called "Il Sodoma," allegedly because of his sexual interests).

Santuario e Casa di Santa Caterina (St. Catherine's Sanctuary). Costa di S. Antonio. ☎ **0577/280330.** Free admission (but an offering is expected). Mon–Sat and holidays 9am–12:30pm and 3:30–6:30pm.

Of all the personalities associated with Siena, the most enduring legend surrounds that of St. Catherine, acknowledged by Pius XII in 1939 as the patron saint of Italy. The mystic, who was the daughter of a dyer, was born in 1347 in Siena. She was instrumental in persuading the papacy to return to Rome from Avignon. The house where she lived, between piazza del Campo and San Domenico, has now been turned into a sanctuary—it's really a church and oratory, with many works of art, located where her father had his dyeworks. Nearby at the 13th-century Basilica of St. Domenico is a chapel dedicated to St. Catherine, frescoed by Il Sodoma.

Enoteca Italica Permanente. Fortezza Medicea, viale Maccari. ☎ **0577/288497.** Free admission. Daily noon–1am.

Owned and operated by the Italian government, Enoteca Italica Permanente, which serves as a showcase for the finest wines of Italy, would whet the palate of even the most demanding wine lover. An unusual architectural setting is designed to show bottles to their best advantage. The establishment lies just outside the entrance to an old fortress, at the bottom of an inclined ramp, behind a massive arched doorway. Marble bas-reliefs and wrought-iron sconces, along with regional ceramics, are set into the high brick walls of the labyrinthine corridors, the vaults of which were built by Cosimo dei Medici in 1560. On the premises are several sunny terraces for outdoor wine tasting, an indoor stand-up bar, and voluminous lists of available vintages, which are for sale either by the glass or by the bottle. Count yourself lucky if the bartender will agree to open an iron gate for access to the subterranean wine exposition. There, in the lowest part of the fortress, carpenters have built illuminated display racks containing bottles of recent vintages.

WHERE TO STAY

You'll *definitely* need hotel reservations if you're here in summer for the Palio. Make them far in advance, and secure your room with a deposit.

VERY EXPENSIVE

✪ **Certosa di Maggiano.** Strada di Certosa 82, 53100 Siena. ☎ **0577/288180.** Fax 0577/288189. 5 rms, 12 suites. A/C MINIBAR TV TEL. 600,000 lire ($384) double; 700,000–900,000 lire ($448–$576) suite. Rates include breakfast. AE, DC, MC, V. Parking 50,000 lire ($32) in the garage, free outside. Bus: Pollicino C.

The Certosa di Maggiano had been lying in dusty disrepair until 1975, when Anna Grossi Recordati renovated it and began attracting some of the world's social luminaries into its 700-year-old interior. It lacks the facilities and the formal service of the Park Hotel Siena, but many savvy guests prefer the intimacy of this cozy retreat. The hotel was built as a monastery by Certosinian monks in the early 13th century. The public rooms fill the spaces between what used to be the ambulatory of the central courtyard and include a stylish and plush collection of intimate gathering places. A medieval church with a separate entrance adjoins the hotel and still holds mass on Sunday. The entire hotel contains only 17 accommodations, one of which has a private walled garden. Most of them are spacious and generally filled with antiques mixed with art objects. The hotel is not easy to find; it's set away from the center of town on a narrow road barely wide enough for two cars. You might phone

Spectacle of Violence

Like the Spanish bullfight, Siena's major event of the year, its Palio della Contrade (see "Italy Calendar of Events" in Chapter 3) is coming under increasing fire for its brutality. For the event, the temperature in town rises higher than the blistering Tuscan sun. All the pomp and ritual of the Middle Ages live again, as heralds, child drummers, flag-bearers, and Renaissance costumes evoke the pomp of the festival.

Three days before the big race, trial races are held, the final trial on the morning of the event. Siena is divided into 17 *contrade,* or wards, and each district—identified by its characteristic colors—competes. However, because the site of the event, Il Campo, will hold only 10 *contrade,* wards are chosen by lot. Young partisans, flaunting the colors of their *contrada,* race through the medieval streets of Siena in packs. Food and wine are bountiful on the streets of each *contrada* on the eve of the race.

The event could easily be considered all in good fun, except that some partisans take it too seriously. There have been kidnappings of the most skilled jockeys before the race. Bribery has been reported as commonplace. So fiercely competitive is the race that all that seems to remain taboo is the sabotaging of the horse's reins.

During the race jockeys have been known to unseat the competition, although a horse without a rider is allowed to win. The event has been cited for its cruelty to animals, as horses are sometimes impaled by guardrails along the track. TV cameras move in on the gore, capturing live the spurting blood as a horse collides with the rail. Jockeys have been caught on camera kicking the horses. In theory, riders are supposed to alternate whip strokes between their mounts and their competitors.

The crowd screams with an excitement unheard in Italy since gladiators battled lions in the Roman Colosseum.

One local Siennese who has attended 30 different Palios said, "Winning, not sportsmanship, is the only thing that's important. There are rules, but we Italians never bother to worry about rules. Instead of a horse race, you might call the event a rat race."

for directions before you set out, although the city has made efforts to post signs for general directions.

Dining/Entertainment: The small vaulted dining room contains a marble fireplace and entire walls of modern ceramics. It's open to nonresidents who make a reservation. The cuisine is excellent.

Services: Room service, guide service, massages, baby-sitting.

Facilities: Heliport, tennis courts, swimming pool.

EXPENSIVE

Park Hotel Siena. Via di Marciano 18, 53100 Siena. ☎ **0577/44803.** Fax 0577/49020. 63 rms, 6 suites. A/C MINIBAR TV TEL. 400,000 lire ($256) double; from 600,000 lire ($384) suite. AE, DC, MC, V. Closed Dec 3–Feb. Free parking. Bus: Hotel shuttle bus to center.

This building was originally commissioned in 1530 by one of Siena's most famous Renaissance architects. It was transformed into a luxurious hotel around the turn of the century and has remained the leading hotel in Siena ever since. It doesn't have the antique charm of the Certosa di Maggiano, but it's more professionally run. A difficult access road leads around a series of hairpin turns (watch the signs carefully) to a buff-colored villa set with a view over green trees and suburbanite houses about a 12-minute drive (1¹/₂ miles) southwest of the city center. The landscaped swimming pool, double-glazed windows, upholstered walls, and plush carpeting have set new standards around here. The hotel is well tended, with stylish modern decoration and comfortably furnished public salons.

Dining/Entertainment: Meals in the hotel restaurant might include wild mushroom salad with black truffles, tortellini with spinach and ricotta, and a regularly featured series of regional dishes from Tuscany, Umbria, or Emilia-Romagna.

Services: Room service, laundry, valet.

Facilities: Swimming pool, public salons, two tennis courts.

MODERATE

Garden Hotel. Via Custoza 2, 53100 Siena. ☎ **0577/47056.** Fax 0577/46050. 136 rms. TV TEL. 154,000–264,000 lire ($98.55–$168.95) double. Rates include breakfast. AE, DC, MC, V. Free parking. Bus: 6.

The Garden Hotel is a well-styled country house, built by a Sienese aristocrat in the 16th century. Located on the edge of the city, high up on the ledge of a hill, it commands a view of Siena and the surrounding countryside that has been the subject of many a painting. The hotel stands formal and serene, with an entrance on the garden side and a long avenue of clipped hedges. There's a luxurious sense of space and an aura of freshness. Its outstanding feature is obviously its garden, plus its price, and many prefer it because they can partially escape the noise of Siena here. Some of the rooms are in the old villa, and the others are in adjoining buildings. Some 100 rooms contain a minibar and 60 are air-conditioned. The breakfast room, with its flagstone floor, decorated ceiling, and view of the hills, is a perfect spot for morning coffee. You can take your other meals in an open-air restaurant on the premises. There's also a swimming pool open June to September.

Jolly Hotel Excelsior. Piazza La Lizza, 53100 Siena. ☎ **0577/288448.** Fax 0577/41272. 123 rms, 3 suites. A/C MINIBAR TV TEL. 275,000–400,000 lire ($176–$256) double; 350,000–600,000 lire ($224–$384) suite. Rates include breakfast. AE, DC, MC, V. Parking 45,000 lire ($28.80).

Set in the commercial center of the newer section of Siena, near the sports stadium, this hotel is a distinguished member of a nationwide chain, although it lacks the ambience and beauty of either the Certosa di Maggiano or the Park Hotel Siena. It was originally built as the Excelsior Hotel in the 1880s and was completely renovated about a century later. The high-ceilinged lobby is stylishly Italian, with terra-cotta accents and white columns. The bedrooms have modern but uninspired furniture, a trim monochromatic color scheme, and many conveniences. The hotel's restaurant features both regional and international dishes. Room service, laundry, valet, and baby-sitting are available.

Villa Scacciapensieri. Via di Scacciapensieri 10, 53100 Siena. ☎ **0577/41441.** Fax 0577/270854. 26 rms, 5 suites. A/C MINIBAR TV TEL. 260,000–330,000 lire ($166.40–$211.20) double; 400,000 lire ($256) suite. Rates include breakfast. AE, DC, MC, V. Closed Jan–Feb. Free parking. Bus: 8 or 12 into Siena (an 8-minute ride) every 15 minutes.

This is one of the lovely old villas of Tuscany, where you can stay in a personal, if timeworn, atmosphere. Standing on the crest of a hill about 2 miles from Siena, the villa is approached by a private driveway under shade trees. Although it's not as state-of-the-art as it once was, it's still preferred by many tradition-minded Europeans, who seem to appreciate its antiquated charms more than Americans do. The bedrooms vary widely in style and comfort, and your opinion of this hotel may depend on your room assignment. The hotel also features a handsomely landscaped swimming pool and a tennis court. Services include room service, laundry, valet, and baby-sitting.

A Tuscan and Italian cuisine is served in the informal restaurant, Altri Tempi. You can dine here Thursday to Tuesday; it's advisable to call and make a reservation.

INEXPENSIVE

Albergo Chiusarelli. Via Curtatone 15, 53100 Siena. ☎ **0577/280562.** Fax 0577/271177. 50 rms. TV TEL. 120,000 lire ($76.80) double; 162,000 lire ($103.70) triple. AE, MC, V. Bus: 3.

The Albergo Chiusarelli is housed in an ochre-colored building with Ionic columns and Roman caryatids supporting a second-floor loggia. It looks much older, but the building was constructed in 1870. The interior has been almost completely renovated, and each functional, albeit lackluster, room contains a modern bath and an electric hair dryer. Ask for a room in back to escape the street noise. The hotel is just at the edge of the old city, and is convenient to the parking areas at the sports stadium a 5-minute walk away. A bar and restaurant on the basement level serve standard full meals—often to tour groups.

☺ Castagneto Hotel. Via del Cappuccini 39, 53100 Siena. ☎ **0577/45103.** Fax 0577/283266. 11 rms. TV TEL. 160,000 lire ($102.40) double. No credit cards. Closed Jan 10–Mar 15. Free parking. Bus: 1.

Set on a low hill commanding a view over Siena, about a mile northwest of the center, this modestly proportioned brick villa was built in the 1700s as a farmhouse for a family of local landowners. Today it's a hotel maintained by the Francioni brothers, and is set behind a gravel-covered parking lot near a garden with birds, vines, and trees. It was renovated into a hotel in 1973, and contains simple, unpretentious rooms in clean and functional working order. Only doubles are available, although single travelers are often accepted at the rate quoted above. It's way down the scale from the hostelries previously considered, but an acceptable choice because of its prices.

Villa Belvedere. Belvedere, 53034 Colle di Val d'Elsa Siena. ☎ **0577/920966.** Fax 0577/924128. 15 rms. TEL. 170,000–220,000 lire ($108.80–$104.80) double. Rates include breakfast. AE, DC, MC, V. Free parking. Exit the autostrada from Florence at Colle di Val d'Elsa and follow the signs.

The Villa Belvedere, about 7¹/₂ miles from Siena and halfway to San Gimignano, occupies a structure built in 1795. In 1820 it was the residence of Ferdinand III, archduke of Austria and grand duke of Tuscany, and in 1845 of Grand Duke Leopold II. Surrounded by a large park with a swimming pool, the hotel has bar service, a garden with a panorama, and elegant dining rooms where typical Tuscan and classic Italian dishes are served. The old-fashioned bedrooms, furnished in part with antiques, all have central heating and overlook the park. Each room is a double. There's also a tennis court.

WHERE TO DINE

Even those on a brief excursion sometimes find themselves in Siena for lunch, and that's a happy prospect, as the Sienese are good cooks, in the best of the Tuscan tradition.

MODERATE

Al Mangia. Piazza del Campo 42. ☎ **0577/281121.** Reservations recommended. Main courses 18,000–30,000 lire ($11.50–$19.20); fixed-price menu 35,000–50,000 lire ($22.40–$32). AE, DC, MC, V. Daily noon–3pm and 7–10pm. Closed Mon Nov–Mar. TUSCAN.

Al Mangia, one of the finest restaurants in the heart of the city, dates from 1937 and has outside tables that overlook the town hall. The food is not only well cooked but appetizingly presented. To begin with, the house pasta specialty is cannoli alla Mangia. Craving a savory Tuscan main dish? Try a bollito di manzo con salsa verde (boiled beef with green sauce). Another excellent course is the osso buco with artichokes, and roast boar hunter's style is featured in season. This is also a good place for beefsteak fiorentino. For dessert, it's got to be panforte, made of spicy delights, including almonds and candied fruits. It's known all over Europe.

INEXPENSIVE

Al Marsili (Ristorante Enoteca Gallo Nero). Via del Castoro 3. ☎ **0577/47154.** Reservations recommended. Main courses 14,000–25,000 lire ($8.95–$16). AE, DC, MC, V. Tues–Sun 12:30–2:30pm and 7:30–10:30pm. Bus: 9 or 10. SIENESE/ITALIAN.

This beautiful restaurant, the best in Siena, stands between the Duomo and via di Città in a neighborhood packed with medieval and Renaissance buildings. You dine beneath crisscrossed ceiling vaults whose russet-colored brickwork was designed centuries ago. Specialties of the chef include roast boar with tomatoes and herbs, *ribollita* (a savory vegetable soup in the Sienese style), spaghetti covered with a sauce of seasonal mushrooms, and veal scaloppine with tarragon and tomato sauce. There's also *una cantina* of wines (the *enoteca* part of its name), where glasses begin at 3,000 lire ($1.90) if you'd like to indulge in a little wine tasting.

Da Guido. Vicolo Pier Pettinaio 7. ☎ **0577/280042.** Reservations required. Main courses 12,000–25,000 lire ($7.70–$16). AE, DC, MC, V. Thurs–Tues 12:30–3:30pm and 7:30–10:30pm. Bus: 2, 3, 4, 9, or 10. SIENESE/INTERNATIONAL.

Da Guido is a medieval Tuscan restaurant about 100 feet off the promenade street near piazza del Campo. It's decked out with crusty old beams, time-aged brick walls, arched ceilings, and iron chandeliers. Our approval is backed up by the public testimony of more than 300 prominent people who have left autographed photographs to adorn the walls of the three dining rooms—film stars, diplomats, opera singers, and car-racing champions, even popes and presidents. There's a grill for steaks, chickens, and roasts. The antipasti are most rewarding. For a main dish, you may want to stick to the roasts, or try a pasta, tagliata alla Guido. The signature appetizer is fiocchi di neve alla tartufo, a gnocchi-like object made with wheat flour, filled with ricotta, eggs, basil, and spices—everything topped with a black truffle. The desserts are good, too.

Grotta Santa Caterina–Da Bagoga. Via della Galluzza 26. ☎ **0577/282208.** Reservations recommended. Main courses 11,000–20,000 lire ($7.05–$12.80); fixed-price menu 22,000 lire ($14.10). AE, MC, V. Tues–Sat 12:30–3pm and 7–10pm, Sun 12:30–3pm. Closed July 21–30, Nov, and Sun night and Mon Dec–Mar. TUSCAN/INTERNATIONAL.

Located in the heart of historic Siena, this building dates from the 1400s, although the restaurant wasn't established until 1953. Midway up a narrow, steeply inclined cobblestone street, the restaurant is an unpretentious gathering place popular with local residents. Inside are brick arches, lots of rustic detailing, plants, and wooden chairs. Specialties include eight kinds of scaloppine, beef or gnocchi with truffles, and chicken cooked in beer. Rabbit in champagne is a favorite, and the kitchen will also prepare a wide variety of mixed roast meats, including veal, pork, and lamb. Many dishes are based on 16th-century recipes—which means no tomatoes and no potatoes, since these vegetables were not in use at the time.

Nello la Taverna. Via del Porrione 28–30. ☎ **0577/289043.** Reservations required. Main courses 14,000–25,000 lire ($8.95–$16). AE, DC, MC, V. Tues–Sat noon–3pm and 7–10pm, Sun noon–3pm. Closed Jan. Bus: Pollicino 6. TUSCAN.

Established in the 1930s, Nello la Taverna offers an ambience that's about as typical of the Sienese region as anything you'll find. Situated on a narrow stone-covered street about half a block from piazza del Campo, the restaurant, as its name implies, offers a tavern decor that includes brick walls, hanging lanterns, racks of wine bottles, and sheaves of corn hanging from the ceiling. Best of all, you can view the forgelike kitchen with its crew of uniformed cooks busily preparing your dinner from behind a row of hanging copper utensils. Specialties include a salad of fresh radicchio, green lasagne ragoût style, and lamb cacciatore with beans. The best wines, according to the owner, come from the region. Your waiter will gladly suggest a local vintage for you.

2 San Gimignano

23 miles NW of Siena, 34 miles SW of Florence

A golden lily of the Middle Ages! Called the Manhattan of Tuscany, the town preserves 13 of its noble brick towers, which give it a skyscraper skyline. The approach to the walled town today is dramatic, but once it must have been fantastic, as San Gimignano in the heyday of the Guelph and Ghibelline conflict had as many as 72 towers. Today its fortresslike severity is softened by the subtlety of its quiet, harmonious squares, and many of its palaces and churches are enhanced by Renaissance frescoes, as San Gimignano could afford to patronize major painters.

ESSENTIALS

GETTING THERE   By Bus   TRA-IN buses service San Gimignano (☎ **055/ 483651**) from Florence with a change at Poggibonsi (trip time: 75 minutes); the one-way fare is 9,100 lire ($5.80). The same company also operates service from Siena, with a change at Poggibonsi (trip time: 50 minutes); the one-way fare is 7,600 lire ($4.85).

By Car   From Florence or Siena, take the Firenze–Siena autostrada to Poggibonsi, where you'll need to cut west along a secondary route (no. 324) to San Gimignano.

VISITOR INFORMATION   Information is available from the **Associazione Pro Loco,** piazza del Duomo 1 (☎ **0577/940008**), open daily from 9am to 1pm and 3 to 7pm.

EXPLORING THE MANHATTAN OF TUSCANY

In the center of town is the palazzo-flanked **piazza della Cisterna** (see our hotel recommendations)—so named because of the 13th-century cistern in its heart. Connected with the irregularly shaped square is its satellite, **piazza del Duomo.** The square's medieval architecture—towers and palaces—is almost unchanged, and it's the most beautiful spot in town. One ticket, available at any of the sites listed below, allows admission to all of them. The ticket costs 16,000 lire ($10.25) for adults and 12,000 lire ($7.70) for students and children.

The **Palazzo del Popolo** was designed by Arnolfo di Cambio in the 13th century. Its tower, the Torre Grossa, built a few years later, is believed to have been the tallest "skyscraper" (about 178 feet high) in town. You can scale this tower and be rewarded with a bird's-eye view of this most remarkable town. Hours and admission charges are the same as for the Museo Civico (see below).

Duomo Collegiata o Basilica di Santa Maria Assunta. Piazza del Duomo. No phone. Church, free; chapel, 3,000 lire ($1.90) adults, 2,000 lire ($1.30) students. Daily 9am–noon and 3–6pm.

The present Duomo dates essentially from the 12th century. Inside, the church is richly frescoed. In the right aisle panels trace scenes from the life of Christ—the kiss of Judas, the Last Supper, the flagellation, and the Crucifixion. In the left are frescoes by Bartolo di Fredi; this mid–14th-century cycle represents scenes from the Old Testament, including the massacre of Job's servants.

The chief attraction of the basilica is the Chapel of Santa Fina, designed by Giuliano and da Maiano. It was frescoed in about 1475 by Domenico Ghirlandaio, who depicted scenes from the life of Saint Fina, as in the memorable deathbed panel. Ghirlandaio, you may recall, was Michelangelo's fresco teacher.

Museo Civico. In the Palazzo del Popolo, piazza del Duomo 1. ☎ **0577/940340.** Admission 7,000 lire ($4.50) adults, 5,000 lire ($3.20) students, 3,500 lire ($2.25) children. Apr–Oct, daily 9:30am–7:30pm; Nov–Mar, Tues–Sun 9:30am–1:30pm and 2:30–4:30pm.

Installed upstairs in the Palazzo del Popolo (Comune, or town hall) is the Museo Civico. Most notable here is the Sala di Dante, where the Guelph-supporting poet spoke out for his cause in 1300. Look for one of the masterpieces of San Gimignano—the *Maestà*, or Madonna enthroned, by Lippo Memmi (later "touched up" by Gozzoli).

The first large room you enter upstairs contains the other masterpieces of the museum—a *Madonna in Glory*, with Saints Gregory and Benedict, painted by Pinturicchio when perspective was flowering. On the other side of it are two different depictions of the *Annunciation* by Filippino Lippi. On the opposite wall, note the magnificent primitive *Crucifix* by Coppo di Marcovaldo.

Around to the left of the cathedral on a little square (piazza Luigi Pecori) is the Museum of Sacred Art, an unheralded museum of at least passing interest for its medieval tombstones and wooden sculpture. It also has an illustrated-manuscript section and an Etruscan section.

WHERE TO STAY

Bel Soggiorno. Via San Giovanni 91, 53037 San Gimignano. ☎ **0577/940375.** Fax 0577/943149. 18 rms, 4 suites. A/C TV TEL. 140,000 lire ($89.60) double; from 180,000 lire ($115.20) suite. AE, DC, MC, V. Parking 15,000 lire ($9.60).

Athough no longer the town's best, having bowed to increasing competition—notably from the Relais Santa Chiara and La Cisterna—this hotel is still going strong. The Bel Soggiorno's rear bedrooms and dining room open on the lower pastureland and the bottom of the village, providing a panoramic view of the Val d'Elsa. Although rated only three stars by the government, the lodgings offered are far superior to what you might expect. The rooms are small and pleasantly revamped, and they offer excellent views (some have antiques and terraces). All of them were designed in the High Tuscan style by an architect from Milan; eight contain air-conditioning and four offer minibars.

In summer you'll be asked to have your meals here—which is no great hardship as the cuisine is excellent. Done in the medieval style, the dining room contains murals depicting a wild boar hunt. Nonresidents are welcome to dine here Tuesday to Sunday.

La Cisterna. Piazza della Cisterna 24, 53037 San Gimignano. ☎ **0577/940328.** Fax 0577/942080. 50 rms, 1 suite. TV TEL. 105,000–140,000 lire ($67.20–$89.60) double; 170,000–190,000 lire ($108.80–$121.60) suite. Rates include breakfast. AE, DC, MC, V. Closed Jan 7–Mar 9. Parking 18,000 lire ($11.50).

A second-class hotel, ivy-covered La Cisterna is modernized but still retains its medieval lines (it was built at the base of some 14th-century patrician towers). In its heyday La Cisterna was the palazzo of a Tuscan family of nobility. Today it's the town's leading inn, although the Relais Santa Chiara outside the medieval ramparts is more elegant. Many tourists visit it just for the day and to patronize Le Terrazze restaurant (see "Where to Dine," below). The bedrooms are generally large; some of the best rooms open onto terraces with views of the Val d'Elsa (the hotel rests on a hilltop). It's located just 2 minutes from all the major sightseeing attractions.

Pescille. Località Pescille, 53037 San Gimignano. ☎ **0577/940186.** Fax 0577/940186. 31 rms, 9 suites. TEL. 140,000–150,000 lire ($89.60–$96) double; 200,000–220,000 lire ($128–$140.80) suite. AE, DC, MC, V. Closed Nov 6–Mar 10. Free parking.

This is the most tranquil hotel in the San Gimignano area, set in olive groves and vineyards 2¹/₂ miles outside town. A castle stood on this site as early as A.D. 1000, and later the property was a monastery. Napoléon came this way in 1812 and chased out the monks. Later the building became a winery, and, finally, in 1971 was turned into a hotel. The most desirable of the traditional accommodations is the two-level Tower Room, opening onto a picture-perfect view of San Gimignano. Since it costs the same as the other accommodations, this "room with a view" is naturally every guest's first choice. The Pescille lies north of the center of town heading toward Volterra, and therefore is best for motorists.

Relais Santa Chiara. Via Matteotti 15, 53037 San Gimignano. ☎ **0577/940701.** Fax 0577/942096. 39 rms, 2 suites. A/C MINIBAR TV TEL. 195,000–305,000 lire ($124.80–$195.20) double; 225,000–350,000 lire ($144–$224) suite. Rates include buffet breakfast. AE, DC, MC, V. Parking 25,000 lire ($16).

Originally built in the 1960s as a lingerie factory, this solid and comfortable hotel lies in a residential neighborhood about a 10-minute walk south of the medieval ramparts of San Gimignano. It's the prestige place to stay in town, far superior to either La Cisterna or the Bel Soggiorno. It's surrounded with elegant gardens and a swimming pool, and its spacious public rooms contain Florentine terra-cotta floors and mosaics. The comfortable bedrooms are furnished in precious brierwood and walnut. Although the hotel is relatively new, the furnishings and ambience blend in harmoniously with the Tuscan countryside. The hotel does not have a restaurant, but serves a buffet breakfast, along with snacks at lunch in summer.

WHERE TO DINE

Ristorante le Terrazze. In La Cisterna hotel, piazza della Cisterna 24. ☎ **0577/940328.** Reservations required. Main courses 20,000–40,000 lire ($12.80–$25.60). AE, DC, MC, V. Wed 7:30–10pm, Thurs–Mon 12:30–2:30pm and 7:30–10pm. Closed Nov–Mar 9. TUSCAN.

Set in the center of San Gimignano, one of this restaurant's two dining rooms boasts stones originally laid in the 1300s. The newer dining room, which was added in 1969, has lots of rustic accessories and large windows overlooking the old town and the Val d'Elsa beyond. The setting is one of a country inn, and the food features an assortment of produce from the surrounding Tuscan farms. The soups and pastas make fine beginnings, and specialties of the house include such delectable and unusual items as sliced filet of wild boar prepared with polenta and chianti; breast of goose with walnut sauce and roasted potatoes; vitello (veal) alla Cisterna, served with buttered beans; and breaded lamb cutlets with fried artichokes.

3 Pisa

47 miles W of Florence, 207 miles NW of Rome

One of Katherine Anne Porter's best short stories is called "The Leaning Tower." A memorable scene in that story deals with a German landlady's sentimental attachment to a 5-inch plaster replica of the Leaning Tower of Pisa, a souvenir whose ribs caved in at the touch of a prospective tenant. "'It cannot be replaced,' said the landlady, with a severe, stricken dignity. 'It was a souvenir of the Italian journey.'" Ironically the year (1944) Miss Porter published her "Leaning Tower," a bomb fell near the real campanile, but, fortunately, it wasn't damaged.

Few buildings in the world have captured imaginations as much as the Leaning Tower of Pisa. It's the single most instantly recognizable building in all the Western world. Perhaps visitors are drawn to it as a symbol of the fragility of people, or at least the fragility of their work.

The Leaning Tower is a landmark powerful enough to entice visitors to call, and once there, they usually find other sights to explore as well.

ESSENTIALS

GETTING THERE   By Plane   Both domestic and international flights arrive at Pisa's Galileo Galilei Airport (☎ **050/500707** for information). Trains make the 5-minute trip into the center of Pisa for 1,500 lire (95¢) per person; buses, for 1,100 lire (70¢).

By Train   Trains link Pisa and Florence every 30 minutes. Trip time is 1 hour, and a one-way fare is 7,200 lire ($4.60). Coastal trains also link Pisa and Rome.

By Bus   There is frequent bus service to Florence operated by **APT** (☎ **050/ 505511** in Pisa for more information and schedules).

By Car   From Florence, take the autostrada west (A11) to the intersection (A12) going south to Pisa.

VISITOR INFORMATION   The **tourist information office** is at piazza del Duomo 3 (☎ **050/560464**). It's open daily from 8am to 8pm.

WHAT TO SEE & DO

In the Middle Ages, Pisa reached the apex of its power as a maritime republic before it eventually fell to its rivals, Florence and Genoa. As is true of most cities at their zenith, Pisa turned to the arts, and made contributions in sculpture and architecture. Its greatest legacy remains at **piazza del Duomo,** which D'Annunzio labeled "piazza dei Miracoli" (miracles). Here you'll find an ensemble of the top three attractions, all original "Pisan-Romanesque" buildings—the Duomo, the Baptistery, and the Leaning Tower itself. Nikolaus Pevsner, in his classic *An Outline of European Architecture,* wrote: "Pisa strikes one altogether as of rather an alien character—Oriental more than Tuscan."

Construction of the ✪ **Leaning Tower,** an eight-story campanile, began in 1174 by Bonanno, and a persistent legend is that the architect deliberately intended the bell tower to lean (but that claim is undocumented). Another legend is that Galileo let objects of different weights fall from the tower, then timed their descent to prove his theories on bodies in motion.

Unfortunately, the tower is in serious danger of collapse. The government is taking various measures to keep the tower from falling, including clamping five rings of half-inch steel cable around its lower stones and pouring tons of lead around its base to keep it stabilized. The tower is said to be floating on a sandy base of water-soaked clay; it leans at least 14 feet from perpendicular. If it stood up straight, the tower would measure about 180 feet tall.

In 1990 the government suspended visits inside the tower. In years gone by, one of the major attractions in Europe was to climb the Tower of Pisa—taking all 294 steps. But that's too dangerous today, and visitors must be content to observe the tower from the outside—but at a safe distance, of course.

⭘ **Il Duomo.** Piazza del Duomo 17. ☎ **050/560547.** Free admission. Dec–Feb, 2,000 lire ($1.30) Mar–Nov. May–Oct, Mon–Sat 10am–7:40pm, Sun 1–7:40pm; Nov–Apr, Mon–Sat 10am–12:45pm and 3–4:45pm, Sun 3–4:45pm. Bus: 1.

The cathedral, which dates from 1063, was designed by Buschetto, although Rainaldo in the 13th century erected the unusual facade with its four layers of open-air arches that diminish in size as they ascend. The cathedral is marked by three bronze doors—rhythmic in line—which replaced those destroyed in a disastrous fire in 1596. The south door, the most notable, was designed by Bonanno in 1180.

In the restored interior, the chief art treasure is the pulpit by Giovanni Pisano, which was finished in 1310. The pulpit, damaged in the cathedral fire, was finally rebuilt (with bits and pieces of the original) in 1926. The polygonal pulpit is held up by porphyry pillars and column statues that symbolize the Virtues. The relief panels depict scenes from the Bible. The pulpit is similar to an earlier one by Giovanni's father, Niccolò Pisano, which is in the Baptistery across the way.

There are other treasures, too, including Galileo's lamp (according to unreliable tradition, the Pisa-born astronomer used the chandelier to formulate his laws of the pendulum).

Battistero. Piazza del Duomo. ☎ **050/560547.** Admission (including entry to another monument) 10,000 lire ($6.40). Dec–Feb, daily 9am–4:40pm; Mar–May and Sept–Nov, daily 9am–5:40pm; June–Aug, daily 8am–7:40pm. Closed Dec 31–Jan 1. Bus: 1.

Begun in 1153, the Baptistery is like a Romanesque crown. Although its most beautiful feature is the exterior, with its arches and columns, you should visit the interior to see the hexagonal pulpit made by Niccolò Pisano in 1260. Supported by pillars that rest on the backs of three marble lions, the pulpit contains bas-reliefs of the Crucifixion, the Adoration of the Magi, the presentation of the Christ child at the temple, and the Last Judgment (many angels have lost their heads over the years). Column statues represent the Virtues. At the baptismal font is a contemporary John the Baptist by a local sculptor. The echo inside the Baptistery shell has enthralled visitors for years.

Museo dell'Opera. Piazza Arcivescovado. ☎ **050/560547.** Admission (including entry to another monument) 10,000 lire ($6.40). Dec–Feb, daily 9am–4:20pm; Mar–May and Sept–Nov, daily 9am–5:20pm; June–Aug, daily 8am–7:20pm. Bus: 1, 3, or 4.

Opened in 1986, this museum exhibits works of art removed from the monumental buildings on the piazza. The heart of the collection, on the ground floor, consists of sculptures spanning the 11th to the 13th century. The most famous exhibit is an ivory *Madonna* and the *Crucifix* by Giovanni Pisano. Also exhibited is the work of French goldsmiths, which was presented by Maria de' Medici to Archbishop Bonciani in 1616. Upstairs are paintings from the 16th to the 18th century. Some of the textiles and embroideries date from the 15th century. Another section of the museum is devoted to Egyptian, Etruscan, and Roman works of art.

Camposanto. Campo dei Miracoli. ☎ **050/560547.** Admission 10,000 lire ($6.40). Dec–Feb, daily 9am–4:40pm; Mar–May and Sept–Nov, daily 9am–5:40pm; June–Aug, daily 8am–7:40pm. Bus: 1.

This cemetery was originally designed by Giovanni di Simone in 1278, but a bomb hit it in 1944. Recently it has been partially restored. It's said that earth from Calvary was shipped here by the Crusaders on Pisan ships (the city was a great port before the water receded). The cemetery is of interest because of its sarcophagi, statuary, and frescoes. Notable frescoes, badly damaged, were by Benozzo Gozzoli, who illustrated scenes from the Old Testament; he paid special attention to architectural details. One room contains three of the most famous frescoes from the 14th century: *The Triumph of Death, The Last Judgment,* and *The Inferno,* with the usual assortment of monsters, reptiles, and boiling caldrons. *The Triumph of Death* is the most interesting, with its flying angels and devils. In addition, you'll find lots of white-marble bas-reliefs, including Roman funerary sculpture.

Museo Nazionale di San Matteo. Piazzetta San Matteo 1 (near piazza Mazzini). ☎ **050/ 541865.** Admission 8,000 lire ($5.10) adults, free for children 17 and under and for seniors 60 and over. Tues–Sat 9am–7pm, Sun 9am–1pm. Bus: 5 or 7.

The well-planned Museo Nazionale di San Matteo contains a good assortment of paintings and sculpture, many of which date from the 13th to the 16th century. In the museum are statues by Giovanni Pisano; Simone Martini's *Madonna and Child with Saints,* a polyptych, as well as Nino Pisano's *Madonna de Latte* (milk), a marble sculpture; Masaccio's *St. Paul,* painted in 1426; Domenico Ghirlandaio's two *Madonna and Saints* depictions; works by Strozzi and Alessandro Magnasco; and very old copies of works by Jan and Pieter Brueghel. You enter from piazza San Matteo.

WHERE TO STAY

Grand Hotel Duomo. Via Santa Maria 94, 56126 Pisa. ☎ **050/561894.** Fax 050/560418. 94 rms, 2 suites. A/C MINIBAR TV TEL. 270,000 lire ($172.80) double; 300,000 lire ($192) suite. Rates include breakfast. AE, DC, MC, V. Parking 30,000 lire ($19.20). Bus: 1.

The five-story Grand Hotel Duomo, dating from the 1940s (and showing it), lies in the heart of Pisa, a short walk from the Leaning Tower, which is the most compelling reason to stay here. A buff-colored stucco building, it has a covered roof garden for uninterrupted views. Inside there's a liberal use of marble, crystal chandeliers, even tall murals in the dining room. The restaurant, serving very standard fare, is often filled with tour groups. A garage is on the premises. The bedrooms are furnished haphazardly, with parquet floors, big windows, built-in headrests, and individual lights. Laundry service is provided, as is 24-hour room service. Baby-sitting can be arranged.

Hotel D'Azeglio. Piazza Vittorio Emanuele II 18B, 56125 Pisa. ☎ **050/500310.** Fax 050/ 28017. 29 rms. A/C MINIBAR TV TEL. 190,000 lire ($121.60) double. AE, DC, MC, V. Parking 15,000 lire ($9.60). Bus: 1, 3, or 4.

This is an unremarkable hotel in the vicinity of the railway station and the air terminal, in the historic and commercial center of Pisa. It's viewed as the third best hotel in town, after the Duomo and Cavalieri, but don't expect too much, as competition in innkeeping isn't too keen in Pisa. On the premises is an American bar and roof garden with a view of the city. A garage is adjacent to the hotel. The standard rooms are well maintained and reasonably comfortable.

Jolly Hotel Cavalieri. Piazza della Stazione 2, 56125 Pisa. ☎ **050/43290.** Fax 050/502242. 100 rms. A/C MINIBAR TV TEL. 270,000–380,000 lire ($172.80–$243.20) double. Rates include breakfast. AE, DC, MC, V. Parking 30,000 lire ($19.20). Bus: 1, 3, or 4.

This is supposedly the best hotel in Pisa, which doesn't say a lot for Pisan innkeeping standards. A bland commercial chain-run property, it opens onto a view of the monumental train station and the piazza in front of it. The seven-story hotel was built in 1948, but since then has been practically rebuilt from the inside out. Today the rooms are filled with time-worn furniture, paneling, and large expanses of glass; each one has a radio and a TV. The hotel also hosts dozens of business travelers, who appreciate the quiet bar and restaurant for their meetings. The Restaurant Cavalieri, with an adjacent piano bar, is open daily for lunch and dinner. Parking is often possible in the square in front of the station or in a nearby garage.

Royal Victoria. Lungarno Pacinotti 12, 56126 Pisa. ☎ **050/940111.** Fax 050/940180. 48 rms, 42 with bath (tub or shower). TEL. 80,000 lire ($51.20) double without bath, 130,000 lire ($83.20) double with bath; 141,000 lire ($90.25) triple with bath; 150,000 lire ($96) quad with bath. Rates include breakfast. AE, DC, MC, V. Parking 30,000 lire ($19.20). Bus: 7 from Central Station.

The Royal Victoria is conveniently located on the Arno, within walking distance of most of the jewels in Pisa's crown. The oldest hotel in Pisa, it was launched in 1839 and is still under the same family management today. Although hardly a perfect hotel, its location is second only to the Grand Hotel. Also, it's less sterile in atmosphere than the choices previously recommended. Its tastefully decorated lounge sets the hospitable scene. Most rooms are devoted to the past only through painted ceilings, spaciousness, and the warmth of antiques suitable to contemporary comfort. The decor can also be a functional modern.

WHERE TO DINE

⭘ **Al Ristoro dei Vecchi Macelli.** Via Volturno 49. ☎ **050/20424.** Reservations required. Main courses 15,000–25,000 lire ($9.60–$16); fixed-price menu 40,000–90,000 lire ($25.60–$57.60). AE, DC. Mon–Tues and Thurs–Sat noon–3pm and 8–10:30pm. Closed 2 weeks in Aug. Bus: 1, 3, or 4. INTERNATIONAL/TUSCAN.

This is the best restaurant in Pisa, set in a comfortably rustic 1930s building near piazzetta di Vecchi Macelli. Residents of Pisa claim that the cuisine is prepared with something akin to love, and they prove their devotion by returning frequently. After selecting from a choice of two dozen varieties of seafood antipasti, you can enjoy a homemade pasta with scallops and zucchini or fish-stuffed ravioli in a shrimp sauce. Other dishes include gnocchi with pesto and shrimp and roast veal with a velvety truffle-flavored cream sauce.

Da Bruno. Via Luigi Bianchi 12. ☎ **050/560818.** Reservations recommended for dinner. Main courses 25,000–45,000 lire ($16–$28.80); fixed-price menu 30,000 lire ($19.20). AE, DC, MC, V. Mon noon–2:30pm, Wed–Sun noon–2:30pm and 7:30–10pm. Bus: 2 or 4. PISAN.

For around half a century Da Bruno has survived in its location some 400 yards from the Leaning Tower. One of Pisa's finest restaurants, although charging moderate tabs, the restaurant is decorated like a Tuscan inn under beamed ceilings. Locals are particularly fond of this place, which lies outside Pisa's old walls but still within walking distance of the Duomo. Many in-the-know diners prefer the old-fashioned dishes of the Tuscan kitchen, including hare with pappardelle (a wide noodle), a thick regional vegetable soup (zuppa all pisana), and codfish with leeks (bacalà con porri).

Emilio. Via del Cammeo 44. ☎ **050/562141.** Reservations recommended. Main courses 10,000–30,000 lire ($6.40–$19.20); fixed-price menu 26,000 lire ($16.65). AE, DC, MC, V. noon–3:30pm and 7–10:30pm. Bus: 1, 3, or 4. PISAN/ITALIAN.

Partly because of its well-prepared food, and partly because of its proximity to the piazza dei Miracoli (site of the Leaning Tower), this restaurant attracts more foreign tourists than almost any other restaurant in Pisa. Built in the 1960s, and renovated in 1991 in a style some visitors compare to a South American hacienda, it contains a large, high window similar to what you might expect in a church, which filters light down on the brick-walled interior. The menu features a very fresh assortment of antipasti, spaghetti with clams, risotto with mushrooms, such fish dishes as branzini a l'Isolana oven-baked with tomatoes and vegetables, and Florentine-style beefsteaks.

4 Perugia

50 miles SE of Arezzo, 117 miles N of Rome, 96 miles SE of Florence

Perugia was one of a dozen major cities in the mysterious Etruscan galaxy. In Perugia we can peel away the epochs. For example, one of the town gates is called the **Arco di Augusto,** or Arch of Augustus. The loggia spanning the arch dates from the Renaissance, but the central part is Roman. Builders from both periods used the reliable Etruscan foundation, which was the work of architects who laid stones to last.

Today the city is the uncrowned capital of Umbria; it has retained much of its Gothic and Renaissance charm, although it has been plagued with wars and swept up in disastrous events. The city today is one of universities and art academies, attracting a young, vibrant crowd—some of whom can be seen in one of the zillions of local bars and cafes enjoying the infamous chocolate baci (kisses). To capture the essence of the Umbrian city, you must head for piazza IV Novembre in the heart of Perugia. During the day the square is overrun, so try to go late at night when the old town is sleeping. That's when the ghosts come out to play.

ESSENTIALS

GETTING THERE   By Train   Perugia enjoys excellent rail connections with central Italy. Daily trains arrive from Rome (trip time: 3 hours); a one-way ticket costs 17,200 lire ($11). Daily trains also arrive from Florence ($2^{1}/_{2}$ hours), a one-way ticket costing 13,600 lire ($8.70).

By Bus   Frequent ASP buses arrive from Rome and Florence.

By Car   From either Florence (coming from the north) or Rome (coming from the south) use the A1 autostrada until you reach the junction signposted to Perugia, at which point you head east.

VISITOR INFORMATION   The **tourist information office** is at piazza IV Novembre 3 (☎ **075/573-6458**). It's open April to October, Monday to Saturday from 8:30am to 1:30pm and 4 to 7pm; November to March, Monday to Saturday from 8:30am to 1:30pm and 3:30 to 6:30pm.

EXPLORING THE CITY

As the villages of England compete for the title of most picturesque, so the cities of Italy vie for the honor of having the most beautiful square. As you stand on the central ✪ **piazza IV Novembre,** you'll know that Perugia is among the top contenders for that honor.

In the heart of the piazza is the **Fontana Maggiore** (Grand Fountain), built some time in the late 1270s by a local architect, a monk named Bevignate. The fountain's artistic triumph stems from the sculptural work by Niccolò Pisano and his son, Giovanni. Along the lower basin of the fountain—which is the last major work of the elder Pisano—is statuary that symbolizes the arts and sciences, Aesop's fables, the months of the year, the signs of the zodiac, and scenes from the Old Testament and Roman history. On the upper basin (mostly the work of Giovanni) is allegorical sculpture, such as one figure representing Perugia, as well as saints, biblical characters, even local officials of the city in the 13th century.

After viewing the marvels of the fountain, you'll find that most of the other major attractions either open onto piazza IV Novembre or lie only a short distance away.

The exterior of the **Cathedral of San Lorenzo,** piazza IV Novembre (☎ 075/572-3832), is rather raw-looking, as if the builders were suddenly called away and never returned. The basilica is built in the Gothic style, and dates from the 14th and 15th centuries. Inside, you'll find the *Deposition* of Frederico Barocci. In the museum, Luca Signorelli's *Virgin Enthroned* with saints is displayed. Signorelli was a pupil of della Francesca. It's open daily from 8:30am to noon and 4 to 6:45pm.

On the opposite side of piazza IV Novembre is the **Palazzo dei Priori (Palace of the Priors),** at corso Vannucci 19 (☎ 075/572-0316). The town hall, one of the finest secular buildings in Italy, it dates from the 13th century and shelters the Galleria Nazionale dell'Umbria. Its facade is characterized by a striking row of mullioned windows. Over the main door is a Guelph (member of the papal party) lion and a griffin of Perugia, which hold chains once looted from a defeated Siena. You can walk up the stairway—the Vaccara—to the pulpit. By all means explore the interior, especially the vaulted Hall of the Notaries, frescoed with stories of the Old Testament and from Aesop. It's open Monday to Saturday from 9am to 7pm and on Sunday from 9am to 1pm.

An escalator has been installed to take passengers from the older part of Perugia at the top of the hill and the upper slopes to the lower city. During construction of the escalator the old fortress, **Rocco Paolina,** via Marzia, was rediscovered, along with buried streets. The fortress had been covered over to make the gardens and viewing area at the end of corso Vannucci in the last century. The old streets and street names have been cleaned up, and the area is well lighted, with an old wall exposed and modern sculpture added. The fortress was built in the 1500s by Sangallo. The Etruscan gate, Porta Marzia, is buried in the old city walls and can be viewed from via Bagliona Sotterranea. This street lies within the fortress and is lined with houses, some of which date from the 1400s and were buried at one time when gardens were constructed above them. The escalator to the Rocca operates daily from 6am to 1am; the Rocca is open daily from 8am to 7pm.

✪ **Galleria Nazionale dell'Umbria.** Upstairs in the Palazzo dei Priori (see above), corso Vannucci 19. ☎ **075/572-0316.** Admission 8,000 lire ($5.10) adults, free for children 17 and under and seniors. Mon–Sat 9am–1:45pm and 3–7pm, Sun 9am–1pm. Closed the first Mon of every month. Bus: All buses from the station.

Upstairs in the Palace of the Priors is the National Gallery of Umbria, which houses the most comprehensive collection of Umbrian art from the 13th to the 19th century. Among the earliest paintings of interest is a *Virgin and Child* by Duccio di Buoninsegna, the first important master of the Sienese school. You'll see statuary by the Pisano family, who designed the Grand Fountain out front, and by Arnolfo di Cambio, the architect of the Palazzo Vecchio in Florence.

Tuscan artists are well represented—the pious Fra Angelico's *Virgin and Child* with saints and angels is there, as well as the same subject treated differently by Piero della Francesca and Benozzo Gozzoli.

You'll also see works of native-son Perugino, among them his *Adoration of the Magi.* Perugino, of course, was the master of Raphael. Often accused of sentimentality, Perugino does not enjoy the popularity today that he did at the peak of his career, but he remains a key painter of the Renaissance, who is noted especially for his landscapes.

The gallery also displays art by Pinturicchio, who studied under Perugino, and whose most notable work was the library of the Duomo of Siena.

Collegio del Cambio. Corso Vannucci 25. ☎ **075/572-8599.** Admission 5,000 lire ($3.20) adults, free for children 17 and under. Mar–Oct, Mon–Sat 9am–12:30pm and 2:30–5:30pm, Sun 9am–12:30pm; Nov–Feb, Tues–Sat 8am–2pm. Bus: 26, 27, 29, 32, or 36.

Right off piazza IV Novembre, this medieval exchange building—part of the Palazzo dei Priori—opens onto the main street of Perugia, corso Vannucci (Vannucci was the real name of Perugino). The collegio is visited chiefly by those seeking to view the Hall of the Audience, frescoed by Perugino and his assistants, including a teenage Raphael. On the ceiling Perugino represented the planets allegorically. The Renaissance master peopled his frescoes with the Virtues, sybils, and such biblical figures as Solomon. But his masterpiece is his own countenance. It seems rather ironic that— at least for once—Perugino could be realistic. Another room of interest is the Chapel of S. J. Battista, which contains many frescoes painted by a pupil of Perugino, G. Nicola di Paolo.

WHERE TO STAY

Hotel Brufani. Piazza Italia 12, 06121 Perugia. ☎ **075/573-2541.** Fax 075/572-0210. 21 rms, 3 suites. A/C MINIBAR TV TEL. 300,000–400,000 lire ($192–$256) double; 600,000 lire ($384) suite. AE, DC, MC, V. Parking 25,000 lire ($16). Bus: 26, 27, 28, 29, or 36.

Located at the top of the city, this five-star hotel, the best in town, was built by Giacomo Brufani in 1884 on the ruins of the ancient Rocca Paolina, a site known to the ancient Romans that later served as the home of one of the Renaissance popes. It's placed on a cliff edge, only a few yards from the main street of Perugia, corso Vannucci. Most of accommodations offer a view of the Umbrian landscape so beloved by painters. The hotel was last renovated in 1984 and is a bit tired today. All rooms are equipped with radio and color TV (with news broadcasts from the United States). The hotel has a good cafe-restaurant, Collins, named for the great-grandfather of Mr. Bottelli, who succeeded the original owner, Mr. Brufani, nearly a century ago.

Hotel la Rosetta. Piazza Italia 19, 06121 Perugia. ☎ and fax **075/572-0841.** 95 rms, 1 suite. MINIBAR TV TEL. 195,000–240,000 lire ($124.80–$153.60) double; 275,000 lire ($176) suite. Rates include breakfast. AE, DC. Parking 25,000–35,000 lire ($16–$22.40). Bus: 26, 27, 28, 29, or 36.

Since 1927 when this Perugian landmark was established, it has expanded from a seven-room pensione to a labyrinthine complex. It's one of the leading inns in town, although not quite as desirable as its nearest competitor, the Locanda della Posta. With its frescoed ceiling, Room 55 has been declared a national treasure. (The bullet holes that papal mercenaries shot into the ceiling in 1848 have been artfully preserved.) The other, less grandiose accommodations include decors ranging from slickly contemporary to Victorian to 1960s style. Each unit is peaceful, clean, and comfortable. The in-house restaurant is recommended separately (see "Where to Dine," below).

Locanda della Posta. Corso Vannucci 97, 06121 Perugia. ☎ and fax **075/572-8925.** 40 rms, 1 suite. A/C MINIBAR TV TEL. 200,000–295,000 lire ($128–$188.80) double; 300,000– 350,000 lire ($192–$224) suite. Rates include breakfast. AE, DC, MC, V. Parking 25,000–30,000 lire ($16–$19.20) in nearby garage. Bus: 26, 27, 28, 29, or 36.

Goethe slept here. So did Hans Christian Andersen. The hotel sits on the main street of the oldest part of Perugia, behind an impressive ornate facade that was originally sculpted in the 1700s. We prefer this luxuriously decorated small hotel to the Brufani Hotel, which is five stars only in the eyes of the local government raters. The Della Posta's views may not be as grand, but it's better run and has more comfortable and better kept rooms. The hotel lies in the center of town, 15 yards from piazza Italia. All buses coming to the center stop at piazza Italia, so it's very convenient if you're depending on public transportation. The hotel, which used to be the only hotel in Perugia, is at the beginning of a pedestrian zone.

WHERE TO DINE
MODERATE

✪ **Osteria del Bartolo.** Via Bartolo 30. ☎ **075/573-1561.** Reservations recommended. Main courses 26,000–36,000 lire ($16.65–$23.05); fixed-price all-Umbrian menu 40,000 lire ($25.60); 75,000 lire ($48) *menu degustazione*. AE, DC, MC, V. Mon–Sat 1–2:45pm and 8–10:30pm. Closed Jan 7–25 and July 26–Aug 5. Bus: 33, 36, 52, or 56. UMBRIAN.

Set in the historic center of town in a palazzo whose foundations date from the 14th century, this family-run restaurant is known for its fresh ingredients, culinary flair, and elegant presentations. It's the pacesetter in Perugia. Many dishes are quite traditional. Straight from the cookbooks of the 1600s, botaccio is made with farmer's bread stuffed with sausage, vegetables, and a sharp pecorino cheese that's baked in the oven. Also tempting are fresh tortelli with porcini (flap mushrooms), ricotta de pecora, steamed tomatoes, and olive oil. The restaurant makes its own butter twice a day, its own bread once a day, and its own pasta fresh with every order. The chef also makes his own desserts. There's enough distance between tables to allow discreet conversations.

La Rosetta. In the Hotel La Rosetta, piazza Italia 19. ☎ **075/572-0841.** Reservations recommended, especially in summer. Main courses 18,000–27,000 lire ($11.50–$17.30). AE, DC, MC, V. Tues–Sun 12:30–3pm and 7:30–10pm. Bus: 26, 27, 29, 32, or 36. UMBRIAN.

La Rosetta has gained more fame than the hotel in which it's lodged. Every politician from the region uses the restaurant, and during the Perugia jazz festival (10 days in midsummer), virtually every jazz star always stays and dines here. Food-smart Italian travelers manage to arrive here at mealtime—it's that good and reasonable. You'll find three areas in which to dine: an intimate wood-paneled salon, a main dining area divided by Roman arches and lit by brass chandeliers, and a courtyard enclosed by the walls of the villa-style hotel. Under shady palm trees you can have a leisurely meal that's both simple and reliable. The menu choice is vast, but a few specialties stand out over the rest. To begin, the finest dishes are either spaghetti alla Norcina (with a truffle sauce) or vol-au-vent di tortellini Rosetta. Among the main dishes, the outstanding entry is scaloppine alla Perugina.

Trattoria Ricciotto. Piazza Danti 19. ☎ **075/572-1956.** Reservations recommended. Main courses 20,000–40,000 lire ($12.80–$25.60); fixed-price menu 35,000 lire ($22.40). AE, DC, MC, V. Mon–Sat 12:30–2:30pm and 7:30–9:30pm. Bus: 33 or 36. UMBRIAN.

Since 1888 this rustically elegant restaurant has been owned and operated by members of the Betti family, who cook, serve the food, uncork the wine, and welcome visitors to Perugia. In a building that dates in part from the 14th century, the restaurant offers a variety of well-prepared specialties, including fettuccine with truffles, maccheroni arrabbiata (pasta with tomatoes and red and green peppers), spring lamb chasseur, and fagotti Monte Bianco (turkey with parmigiano, ham, and a cream sauce).

INEXPENSIVE

$ **Il Falchetto.** Via Bartolo 20. ☎ **075/573-1775.** Main courses 12,000–30,000 lire ($7.70–$19.20). AE, DC, MC, V. Tues–Sun 12:30–2:30pm and 7:30–10:30pm. Bus: 27 or 36. UMBRIAN/ITALIAN.

The restaurant has flourished in this 19th-century building since it was established in 1941. Many of the dishes here adhere to traditional themes and have a certain zest that has won critical approval for this medieval-style restaurant. Menu items include tagliatelle with truffles, grilled trout from the Nera River, prosciutto several different ways, pasta with chickpeas, grilled filet of goat, and filet steak with truffles. One special dish, of which the chef is justly proud, is falchetti (gnocchi with ricotta and spinach). The restaurant is a short walk from piazza Piccinino (where you'll be able to park).

La Taverna. Via delle Streghe 8. ☎ **075/572-4128.** Reservations recommended. Main courses 15,000–30,000 lire ($9.60–$19.20). AE, DC, MC, V. Tues–Sun 12:30–2:30pm and 7:30–10:30pm. Bus: 26, 27, 29, 32, or 36. UMBRIAN.

One of the finest and most innovative restaurants in Umbria, La Taverna is in a medieval house originally built around 700 years ago. Its entrance is at the bottom of one of the narrowest alleyways in town, in the heart of Perugia's historic center. (Prominent illustrated signs indicate its position off corso Vannucci at the bottom of a flight of stairs.) Three dining rooms, each filled with exposed masonry, oil paintings, and a polite staff, radiate out from the high-ceilinged vestibule. The cuisine is inspired by Claudio Brugalossi, an Umbrian chef who spent part of his career in Tampa, Florida, working for the Hyatt chain. Your meal might include ravioli filled with rapini and ricotta, a soup of lima beans and artichokes, half-moon-shaped ravioli filled with salmon and saffron, or a creative array (depending on what's in season) of fish, polentas, risottos, and fresh meats.

5 Assisi

110 miles N of Rome, 15 miles SE of Perugia

Ideally placed on the rise to Mount Subasio, watched over by the medieval Rocco Maggiore, this purple-fringed Umbrian hill town retains a mystical air. The site of many a pilgrimage, Assisi is forever linked in legend with its native son, St. Francis. The gentle saint founded the Franciscan order and shares honors with St. Catherine of Siena as the patron saint of Italy. But he is remembered by many, even non-Christians, as a lover of nature (his preaching to an audience of birds is one of the legends of his life). St. Francis obviously put this town on the map, and making a pilgrimage here is one of the highlights of a visit to Umbria, as exemplified by the friars in brown habits and belts of knotted rope wandering about. But even without St. Francis, the hill town merits a visit for its interesting sights and architecture. Sightseers and pilgrims mingling together get a little thick in summer, and at Easter or Christmas you are likely to be tramped underfoot. We've found it best and less crowded in spring or fall.

ESSENTIALS

GETTING THERE   By Train   Assisi lies on the Foligno–Teròntola train line, a 30-minute ride from the terminal at Foligno. The one-way fare from Perugia is 2,700 lire ($1.75). At Teròntola connections are made for Florence and at Foligno for Rome.

By Bus   One bus a day arrives from Rome and two from Florence. Local buses also run back and forth between Assisi and Perugia.

By Car   From Perugia (see Section 3 in this chapter), continue east on Route 3, driving east toward Assisi at the junction of Route 147.

VISITOR INFORMATION   The **tourist information office** is at piazza del Comune 12 (☎ **075/812534**). It's open Monday to Friday from 8am to 2pm and 3:30 to 6:30pm, on Saturday from 9am to 1pm and 3:30 to 6:30pm, and on Sunday from 9am to 1pm.

WHAT TO SEE & DO

In addition to the sights listed below, you might also visit the **Cattedrale di San Rufino** (☎ 075/812285). Built in the mid-12th century at piazza San Rufino, the Duomo of Assisi is graced with a Romanesque facade, greatly enhanced by rose windows. It's one of the finest churches in the hill towns, as important as the one at Spoleto. Adjoining the cathedral is a bell tower, or campanile. Inside, the church has been baroqued, an unfortunate decision that lost the purity that the front suggests. St. Francis and St. Clare were both baptized here. It's open daily from 7am to noon and 2 to 7pm. It costs 2,500 lire ($1.60) to visit the crypt.

The **Basilica of Santa Chiara** (Clare), on piazza Santa Chiara (☎ 075/812282), is dedicated to "the little plant of Blessed Francis," as St. Clare liked to describe herself. Born in 1193 into one of the richest and noblest families of Assisi, Clare was to give all her wealth to the poor and to found, together with St. Francis, the Order of the Poor Clares. She was canonized by Pope Alexander IV in 1255. Pope Pius XII declared her Patroness of Television in 1958. It was decided to entrust to her this new means of social communication on the basis of a vision that she related she had on Christmas Eve in 1252 in which she saw the manger and heard the friars sing in the Basilica of St. Francis while she was bedridden in the Monastery of San Damiano.

Although many of the frescoes that once adorned the basilica have been either completely or partially restored, much remains that's worthy of note. On entering, your attention is caught by the striking *Crucifix* behind the main altar, a painting on wood dating from the time of the church itself (ca. 1260). The work is by "the Master of St. Clare," who is also responsible for the beautiful icons on either side of the transept. An oft-reproduced fresco of the Nativity from the 14th century can be admired in the left transept. The basilica houses the remains of St. Clare as well as the crucifix under which St. Francis received his command from above.

The closest bus stop to the Basilica of Santa Chiara is to be found near Porta Nuova, the eastern gate to the city at the beginning of viale Umberto I. The bus does not have a number; it departs from the depot in piazza Matteotti for its first run to the train station at 5:35am and concludes its final run at 11:59pm. Buses arrive at half-hour intervals. Admittance to the basilica is free; however, the custodian turns away visitors in shorts, miniskirts, plunging necklines, and backless attire. It's open daily from 6:30am to noon and 2 to 6:55pm.

The **Temple of Minerva** opens onto piazza del Comune, the heart of Assisi. The square is a dream for a lover of architecture from the 12th through the 14th century. A pagan structure, with six Corinthian columns, the Temple of Minerva dates from the 1st century B.C. With Minerva-like wisdom, the people of Assisi let it stand, and turned it into a baroque church inside so as not to offend the devout. Adjoining the temple is the 13th-century Tower of the People, built by Ghibelline supporters.

✪ **Basilica di San Francesco.** Piazza San Francesco. ☎ **075/819001.** Free admission. Apr–Oct, daily 8:30am–7pm; Nov–Mar, daily 8:30am–6pm.

This important church, which consists of both an upper and lower church, houses some of the most important cycles of frescoes in Italy, including works by such pre-Renaissance giants as Cimabue and Giotto. Both churches were built in the first part of the 13th century. The basilica and its paintings form the most significant monument to St. Francis.

Upon entering the upper church through the principal doorway, look to your immediate left to see one of Giotto's most celebrated frescoes, that of St. Francis preaching to the birds. In the nave of the upper church you'll find the rest of the cycle of 27 additional frescoes, some of which are by Giotto, although the authorship of the entire cycle is a subject of controversy. Many of the frescoes are almost surrealistic—in architectural frameworks—like a stage setting that strips away the walls and allows us to see the actors inside. In the cycle we see pictorial evidence of the rise of humanism that led to Giotto's and Italy's split from the rigidity of Byzantium.

Proceed up the nave to the transept and turn left to find a masterpiece by Cimabue, his *Crucifixion.* Time has robbed the fresco of its former radiance, but its power and ghostlike drama remain. The cycle of badly damaged frescoes in the transept and apse are other works by Cimabue and his paint-smeared helpers.

From the transept, proceed down the stairs through the two-tiered cloisters to the lower church, which will put you in the south transept. Look for Cimabue's faded but masterly *Virgin and Child* with four angels and St. Francis looking on from the far right. The fresco is often reproduced in detail as one of Cimabue's greatest works. On the other side of the transept is the *Deposition from the Cross,* a masterpiece by the Sienese artist Pietro Lorenzetti, plus a *Madonna and Child* with St. John and St. Francis (stigmata showing). In a chapel honoring St. Martin of Tours, Simone Martini of Siena painted a cycle of frescoes, with great skill and imagination, that depicts the life and times of that saint. Finally, under the lower church is the crypt of St. Francis. Recently placed on display are the relics of St. Francis. In the past, visitors were not allowed access to the vaults containing these highly cherished articles, only scholars and clergymen. Some of the items on display are the saint's tunic and cowl, his shoes, and the chalice and communion plate used by Francis and his followers.

Eremo delle Carceri. Via Eremo delle Carceri. ☎ **075/812301.** Free admission (donations accepted). Daily 8am–sunset.

The Eremo delle Carceri (Prisons' Hermitage), in a setting 2¹⁄₂ miles east of Assisi (out via Eremo delle Carceri), dates from the 14th and 15th centuries. The "prison" is not a penal institution but rather a spiritual retreat. It's believed that St. Francis retired to this spot for meditation and prayer. Out back is a gnarled, moss-covered ilex (or live oak) tree, more than 1,000 years old, where St. Francis is believed to have blessed the birds, after which they are said to have flown in the four major directions of the compass to symbolize that Franciscans, in coming centuries, would spread out from Assisi all over the world. The friary contains some faded frescoes. One of the handful of friars who still inhabit the retreat will show you through. Donations are accepted to defray the cost of maintenance. In keeping with the Franciscan tradition, the friars at Le Carceri are completely dependent on alms for their support.

Rocca Maggiore. Reached by an unmarked stepped street opposite the basilica. Admission 5,000 lire ($3.20). Apr–Oct, daily 10am–dusk; Nov–Mar, daily 10am–4pm.

The Rocca Maggiore (Great Fortress) sits astride a hill overlooking Assisi. It should be visited if for no other reason than for the view of the Umbrian countryside from its ramparts. The present building—now in ruins—dates from the 14th century, and the origins of the structure go back beyond time.

WHERE TO STAY

Space in Assisi tends to be tight—so reservations are vital. Still, for such a small town, Assisi has a good number of accommodations.

Hotel Giotto. Via Fontebella 41, 06082 Assisi. ☎ **075/812209.** Fax 075/816479. 70 rms, 2 suites. MINIBAR TV TEL. 195,000 lire ($124.80) double; 325,000 ($208) suite. Rates include breakfast. AE, DC, MC, V. Parking 15,000 lire ($9.60). Bus: 2.

The five-story Hotel Giotto is an up-to-date and well-run hotel, built at the edge of town on several levels. Although targeted by tour groups, the Giotto is the second-best hotel in Assisi (we find the Subasio, discussed below, more tranquil and better appointed). Located near the Basilica of St. Francis, and opening onto panoramic views, the Giotto offers small formal gardens and terraces for meals or sunbathing. It has spacious modern public rooms, which lead to the well-furnished and comfortable rooms. Bright colors predominate. The hotel is open all year.

Hotel Subasio. Via Frate Elia 2, 06082 Assisi. ☎ **075/812206.** Fax 075/816691. 66 rms. MINIBAR TV TEL. 270,000 lire ($172.80) double. Rates include breakfast. AE, DC, MC, V. Bus: 2.

This is a first-class four-story hotel with a decidedly old-fashioned aura. The Subasio has been the unquestioned choice of many a famous visitor—from movie stars to royalty. But such a chic clientele from yesterday has often given way today to milling groups. Despite that, however, the Subasio still reigns as the finest choice in Assisi in which to lay your head for the night. The hotel is linked to the Church of St. Francis by a covered stone arched colonnade, and its dining terrace (with extremely good food) is the most dramatic in Assisi. Dining is also an event on the vaulted medieval loggia. The bedrooms at the front open onto balconies with a good view.

⑤ St. Anthony's Guest House. Via Galeazzo Alessi 10, 06081 Assisi. ☎ and fax **075/812542.** 20 rms. 54,000–76,000 lire ($34.55–$48.65) double. Rates include breakfast. No credit cards. Closed Nov–Mar. Bus: 2. Parking available (fee left to discretion of client).

This special hotel provides economical and comfortable accommodations in a medieval villa turned guesthouse. Operated by the Franciscan Sisters of the Atonement (an order that originated in Graymoor, New York), the guesthouse offers the pilgrim/traveler hospitality and a peaceful atmosphere. Located on the upper ledges of Assisi, St. Anthony's Guest House contains its own terraced garden and panoramic view. In all, 35 people can be accommodated. For an additional 20,000 lire ($12.80) a midday meal is served at 1pm. Meals and companionship are enjoyed in a restored 12th-century dining room. The sisters and their co-workers welcome you, showing you their library with English-language books.

Umbra. Via degli Archi 6, 06081 Assisi. ☎ **075/812240.** Fax 075/813653. 25 rms, 5 suites. TEL. 130,000–170,000 lire ($83.20–$108.80) double; 140,000–160,000 lire ($89.60–$102.40) suite. AE, DC, MC, V. Closed Jan–Feb. Bus: 2. Parking 10,000 lire ($6.40).

Umbra is the most centrally located accommodation in Assisi, in a position right off piazza del Comune with its Temple of Minerva. The outdoor terraced dining room forms an important part of the hotel's entryway. You enter through old stone walls covered with vines and walk under a leafy pergola. The lobby is compact and functional. The rooms are arranged as small apartments. The bedrooms offer comfortable beds; some have a tiny balcony overlooking the crusty old rooftops and the Umbrian countryside. Five rooms are air-conditioned.

A NEARBY PLACE TO STAY

Hotel Palazzo Bocci. Via Cavour 17, 06038 Spello. ☎ **0742/301021.** Fax 0742/301464. 17 rms, 6 suites. A/C MINIBAR TV TEL. 180,000–220,000 lire ($115.20–$140.80) double; 240,000–320,000 lire ($153.60–$204.80) suite. Rates include breakfast. AE, DC, MC, V. Free parking. Head 6¹/₂ miles southeast of Assisi along S147.

Located in the historical center of Spello, this palace dates from the second half of the 18th century. The owner of the hotel purchased the palace in 1989, renovated it, and opened it as a hotel in 1992. Inside is a courtyard with a view of the valley, a beautiful fountain, and two age-old palms. Taste and restraint went into designing both public and private rooms, some of which open onto panoramic views. The bedrooms have such equipment as hydromassage, a safe, a writing desk with two chairs, a hair dryer, and soundproofing.

Dining/Entertainment: For hotel guests there's a nice bar and a large open garden with a panoramic view where drinks are served. A buffet breakfast is served, and a well-known restaurant, Il Molino, is just in front of the hotel.

Services: Room service, laundry, baby-sitting.

Facilities: Riding school, tennis courts, and swimming pool—nearby.

WHERE TO DINE

Il Medio Evo. Via dell'Arco dei Priori 4B. ☎ **075/813068.** Reservations recommended. Main courses 20,000–30,000 lire ($12.80–$19.20). AE, DC, MC, V. Thurs–Tues noon–2:30pm and 7:30–9:45pm. Closed Jan 7–Feb 7 and July 1–20. UMBRIAN/INTERNATIONAL.

Assisi's best restaurant is Il Medio Evo, one of the architectural oddities of the town's historic center. The foundations on which the restaurant rests are at least 1,000 years old. During the Middle Ages and again in Renaissance times the structure was successively enlarged and modified until today it's an authentic medieval gem of heavy stonework. Fresh ingredients and skill go into the genuine Umbrian cooking served here. Alberto Falsinotti and his family prepare superb versions of Umbrian recipes whose origins are as old as Assisi itself. Specialties include tortelloni stuffed with minced turkey, veal, and beef, served simply but flavorfully with butter and Parmesan; gnocchi stuffed with ricotta and spinach, and sprinkled with Parmesan; roasted rabbit with red-wine sauce and truffles; and roast lamb with rosemary, potatoes, and herbs.

Ristorante Buca di San Francesco. Via Brizi 1. ☎ **075/812204.** Reservations recommended. Main courses 12,000–28,000 lire ($7.70–$17.90). AE, DC, MC, V. Tues–Sun noon–2:30pm and 7:30–9:30pm. Closed Jan 10–30 and July. Bus: 2. UMBRIAN/ITALIAN.

This restaurant is set in a medieval palace, with masonry believed to be as old as St. Francis himself. The menu changes frequently, according to the availability of ingredients. One of the specialties is spaghetti alla buca, as well as onion soup. Grilled meats are always featured, and sometimes they are served with truffles, which are so popular in the Umbrian countryside. In summer, guests can dine outside on a terrace.

Umbra. Via degli Archi 6. ☎ **075/812240.** Reservations recommended. Main courses 14,000–21,000 lire ($8.95–$13.45). AE, DC, MC, V. Tues–Sat noon–2pm, Mon–Sat 7:30–9pm. Closed Jan 10–Mar 15. UMBRIAN.

Although most of the building that contains this venerable restaurant dates from the Middle Ages, the walls of the laundry and the kitchens (which occupy the basement) are from the final days of the Roman Empire. The restaurant was originally established as an inn in either 1926 or 1928 (the owners can't remember exactly which), and its shaded garden is charming enough to have pleased even St. Francis—on a warm day you'll hear birds chirping. Situated in the heart of the old city, not far from the basilica, the establishment is the personal statement of the owner and his staff of capable helpers. The Umbrian menu items range from the fanciful to the classically popular. In any event, ample use is made of truffles. The best cuts of meat are generally used, along with very fresh vegetables. A specialty is roast lamb infused with Umbrian herbs.

6 Spoleto

80 miles N of Rome, 30 miles SE of Assisi

Hannibal couldn't conquer it, but Gian-Carlo Menotti did—and how! Before Maestro Menotti put Spoleto on the tourist map in 1958, it was known mostly to art lovers, teachers, and students. Today the chic and fashionable, artistic and arty flood the Umbrian hill town to attend performances of the world-famous **Festival dei Due Mondi (Festival of Two Worlds),** most often held in June and July. Menotti searched and traveled through many hill towns of Tuscany and Umbria before making a final choice. When he saw Spoleto, he fell in love with it. And quite understandably.

Long before Tennessee Williams arrived to premiere a new play, Thomas Schippers to conduct the opera *Macbeth,* or Shelley Winters to do three one-act plays by Saul Bellow, Spoleto was known to St. Francis and to Lucrezia Borgia (she occupied the 14th-century castle that towers over the town, the Rocca dell'Albornoz). The town is filled with palaces of Spoletan aristocracy, medieval streets, and towers built for protection during the time when visitors weren't as friendly as they are today. There are churches, churches, and more churches—some of which, such as **San Gregorio Maggiore,** were built in the Romanesque style in the 11th century.

But the tourist center is **piazza del Duomo,** with its cathedral and **Teatro Caio Melisso (Chamber Theater).** The cathedral is a hodgepodge of Romanesque and medieval architecture, with a 12th-century campanile. Its facade is of exceptional beauty, renowned especially for its mosaic by Salsterno. The interior should be visited if for no other reason than to see the cycle of frescoes in the chancel by Filippo Lippi. His son, Filippino, also an artist, designed the tomb for his father. The keeper of the apse will be happy to unlock it for you. These frescoes, believed to have been carried out largely by students, were the elder Lippi's last work; he died in Spoleto in 1469. As friars went in those days, Lippi was a bit of a swinger; he ran off with a nun, Lucrezia Buti, who later posed as the Madonna in several of his paintings.

Spoleto should be visited even when the festival isn't taking place, as it's a most interesting town. It has a number of worthwhile sights, including the remains of a **Roman theater** off piazza della Libertà (entrance on via S. Agata). Motorists wanting a view can continue up the hill from Spoleto around a winding road (about 5 miles) to **Monteluco,** an ancient spot 2,500 feet above sea level. Monteluco is peppered with summer villas.

ESSENTIALS

GETTING THERE   By Train   Daily trains arrive from Rome (trip time: 2 hours); the one-way fare is 12,200 lire ($7.80). Ten trains arrive daily from Perugia (1 hour); a one-way ticket is 6,000 lire ($3.85).

By Bus   Spoleto is served by daily buses from Rome. Two buses a day arrive from Perugia and Assisi.

By Car   From Perugia, continue south along Route 3.

VISITOR INFORMATION   The **tourist information office** is at piazza della Libertà 7 (☎ **0743/220311**). It's open Monday to Friday from 9am to 1pm and 4:30 to 7:30pm, on Saturday from 10am to 1pm and 4:30 to 7:30pm, and on Sunday from 10am to 1pm.

SPECIAL EVENTS   Dates, programs, and ticket prices change yearly for the **Festival dei Due Mondi** (discussed above). In Spoleto, the general offices of the festival are at via del Duomo 7 (☎ **06/321-0288**).

WHERE TO STAY

Spoleto offers an attractive range of hotels, but when the "two worlds" crowd in at festival time, the going's rough (one year a group of students bedded down on piazza del Duomo). In an emergency, the **tourist information office,** at piazza della Libertà 7 (☎ **0743/220311**), can arrange for you to stay in a private home—at a moderate price. The office is open only during regular business hours, but it's imperative to telephone in advance for a reservation. Many of the private rooms are often rented well in advance to artists appearing at the festival. Innkeepers are likely to raise all the prices listed below to whatever the market will bear.

Albornoz Palace Hotel. Viale Matteotti, 06049 Spoleto. ☎ **0743/221221.** Fax 0743/221600. 92 rms, 4 suites. A/C MINIBAR TV TEL. 160,000–210,000 lire ($102.40–$134.40) double; from 370,000 lire ($236.80) suite. Rates include breakfast. AE, DC, MC, V. Free parking. Bus: A, B, C, D, or E.

Starkly modern, and perched in a residential neighborhood half a mile south of the town center, this five-story building is the largest and newest (ca. 1990) hotel in Spoleto. It's the most prestigious address in town, with the best facilities, although the tiny Gattapone is more luxurious and much more tranquil. A small garden in back contains a swimming pool. On the premises are two restaurants, a bar, and a marble-trimmed lobby decorated with large modern paintings created by American-born artist Sol Lewitt. The bedrooms are painted in cool tones of blue-gray, and contain modern bathrooms and views over either Spoleto, Monte Luco, or the surrounding hills. The hotel, incidentally, is named after the 14th-century cardinal-soldier (Albornoz) who built parts of Spoleto.

Dei Duchi. Viale Giacomo Matteotti 4, 06049 Spoleto. ☎ **0743/44541.** Fax 0743/44543. 51 rms, 2 suites. MINIBAR TV TEL. 180,000 lire ($115.20) double; 350,000 lire ($224) suite. Rates include breakfast. AE, DC, MC, V. Free parking. Bus: A, B, or C.

This bare-brick, modern hotel is within walking distance of the major sights—yet it perches on a hillside with views and terraces. It lacks the style of the Gattapone and Albornoz Palace and seems more geared to commercial travelers. Near the Roman theater, Dei Duchi is graced with walls of natural brick, open-to-the-view glass, and lounges with modern furnishings and original paintings. Some bedrooms have their own balconies, plus bland bed coverings, wood-grained furniture, and built-in cupboards—in all, a bit drab. In high season half board is required. In summer you have a choice of two dining rooms, each airy, light, and roomy.

☺ Gattapone. Via del Ponte 6, 06049 Spoleto. ☎ **0743/223447.** Fax 0743/223448. 7 rms, 9 junior suites. MINIBAR TV TEL. 230,000 lire ($147.20) double; from 330,000 lire ($211.20) suite. Rates include continental breakfast. AE, DC, MC, V. Free parking. Bus: A, B, or C.

The Gattapone is more a spectacle than a hotel, and we'd rank it as the finest choice for the discriminating traveler visiting Spoleto, with a lot more personality and style than the Albornoz Palace. Probably the only 14-room hotel in Italy to be rated first class, it's among the clouds, high on a twisting road leading to the ancient castle and the 13th-century ponte delle Torri, a bridge 250 feet high. The hotel occupies two side-by-side stone cottages. The buildings cling closely to the road, and each descends the precipice overlooking the gorge. The hotel's view side is equipped with a two-story picture window and an open spiral stairway that leads from the intimate lounge to the bedrooms. Each of the rooms is individually furnished, with comfortable beds, antiques, and plenty of space. Only breakfast is served.

Hotel Charleston. Piazza Collicola 10, 06049 Spoleto. ☎ **0743/220052.** Fax 0743/222010. 18 rms. MINIBAR TV TEL. 155,000 lire ($99.20) double. Rates include breakfast. AE, DC, MC, V. Parking 15,000 lire ($9.60). Bus: A, B, or C.

This tile-roofed, sienna-fronted building was originally built in the 17th century. Today it serves as a pleasantly accessorized hotel, conveniently located in the historic center. Although not as good as the hostelries recommended above, it's a solid and reliable choice. Each of the bedrooms has a ceiling accented with beams of honey-colored planking, and comfortable mattresses. Many of the guest rooms have been updated with new furnishings and bathrooms. On the premises is a sauna, as well as a bar, library, and a sitting room with sofas and a writing table.

⑤ Hotel Clarici. Piazza della Vittoria 32, 06049 Spoleto. ☎ **0743/223311.** Fax 0743/222010. 24 rms. A/C MINIBAR TV TEL. 149,000 lire ($95.35) double. Rates include breakfast. AE, DC, MC, V. Parking 10,000 lire ($6.40). Bus: A, B, C, D, or E.

The Clarici is rated only third class, but it's airy and modern, the best of the budget bets in Spoleto. Each accommodation has a private balcony that opens onto a view. The hotel doesn't emphasize style, but rather the creature comforts: soft low beds, built-in wardrobes, steam heat, an elevator. There's a large terrace for sunbathing or sipping drinks.

WHERE TO DINE

Il Tartufo. Piazza Garibaldi 24. ☎ **0743/40236.** Reservations required. Main courses 15,000–25,000 lire ($9.60–$16); fixed-price menu 28,000–60,000 lire ($17.90–$38.40). AE, DC, MC, V. Thurs–Tues noon–3pm and 7:30–10:30pm. Closed July 15–31. Bus: A, B, or C. UMBRIAN.

At Il Tartufo, outside the heart of town near the amphitheater, you may be introduced to the Umbrian *tartufo* (truffle) if you can afford it. It's served in the most expensive appetizers and main courses. This immaculately kept, excellent tavern serves at least nine regional specialties that use the black tartufo of Spoleto. An ever-popular dish—and a good introduction for neophyte palates who may never have tried truffles—is strengozzi al tartufo, a pasta dish with truffles. Alternatively, you may want to start your meal with an omelet—for instance, frittata al tartufo. Main dishes of veal and beef are also excellently prepared. For such a small restaurant, the menu is large.

7 Other Hill Town Excursions

We've explored the most popular of the Italian hill towns, but, by all means, not the most important. Although the previously discussed towns are more frequently visited by tourists, many other less known gems are scattered throughout the Tuscan and Umbrian hills. **Montecatini Terme,** one of Europe's most renowned spa towns, draws visitors from all over the world for its thermal cures. The ancient town of **Lucca,** once a Roman military stronghold, is now home to some of the finest churches and *palazzi* in Italy. The striking sight of **Orvieto,** precariously perched on a mass of rock, commands one of the greatest views in Italy, and contains one of the masterpieces of the Renaissance, the cathedral of Orvieto. The Tuscan towns of **Arezzo,** birthplace of such luminaries as Petrarch and Vasari, and **Gubbio** offer some of the most remarkably preserved medieval structures in Europe.

MONTECATINI TERME

The best known of all Italian spas, Montecatini Terme has long been frequented for its cures and scenic location. It's a peaceful Tuscan town set among green hills of the valley called Valdinievole. The location is 19 miles northeast from Florence and 26 miles from the Pisa International Airport.

The spa's fame began in the latter part of the 18th century when the grand duke of Tuscany, one Pietro Leopoldo, opened a thermal spa here. But centuries before that it had been discovered by the Romans. The fame of Montecatini spread rapidly, and by 1890 it was a regular stopover for some of the titled aristocrats of Europe. In the 20th century it drew such luminaries as Gary Cooper, Rose Kennedy, and Gabriel D'Annunzio.

Many visitors are just regular tourists who enjoy a restful stopover in a spa town; others come to lose weight, to take the mud baths, and to visit the sauna-cum-grotto.

The mineral waters are said to be the finest in Europe, and the most serious visitors go to the 19th-century Tettuccio spa, with its beautiful gardens, to fill their cups from the curative waters.

The spa is filled with dozens of hotels and *pensiones,* and many would-be visitors to Florence—unable to find a room in that overcrowded city—journey to Montecatini instead. The spa has a season lasting from April to October.

When you tire of all that rest, you can take a cableway up to Montecatini Alto, enjoying its panoramic view. The funicular leaves from viale Diaz. Montecatini Alto was important in the Middle Ages, containing about two dozen towers that were demolished in 1554 on orders of Cosimo Medici I. You can walk along narrow streets to the ruins of a fortress here, paying a short visit to St. Peter's Church. You'll invariably come across the main square, named for the poet Guiseppe Giusti. From the hillside town, you can see Florence on a clear day.

ESSENTIALS

GETTING THERE   From Florence a train leaves every hour during the day for Montecantini. Trip time is 45 minutes, and a one-way passage costs 7,000 lire ($4.50). The **railroad station** at Montecatini is at piazza Italia (☎ **0572/78551**).

VISITOR INFORMATION   The **Montecatini Terme Tourist Office** is on viale Verdi (☎ **0572/772244**), open Monday to Saturday from 9am to noon and 3 to 6pm.

WHERE TO STAY

Grand Hotel Vittoria. Viale della Libertà, 51016 Montecatini Terme. ☎ **0572/79271.** Fax 0572/910520. 84 rms. A/C MINIBAR TV TEL. 160,000 lire ($102.40) double. Rates include breakfast. AE, DC, MC, V. Free parking.

Despite a renovation in 1993, this cost-conscious hotel retains a pleasantly old-fashioned aura that's a holdover from its initial construction in 1905. Set away from the center of town amid a dignified collection of private homes, it's one of the best of the town's many middle-bracket hotels. Semi-antique touches abound, including a double stairway built of travertine and flanked with masses of flowers. Verdi stayed here shortly after the hotel opened, just before it went through other transitions, including a brief stint as a monastery. It served as the town's headquarters for the Nazis, and later, for the Americans during World War II. On the premises are a small swimming pool, a pleasant garden, a tennis court, and a covered terrace. It receives a good number of conventioneers, especially throughout the winter.

Gran Hotel Croce di Malta. Viale IV Novembre 18, 51016 Montecatini Terme. ☎ **0572/ 75871.** Fax 0572/767516. 92 rms, 12 suites. A/C MINIBAR TV TEL. 250,000 lire ($160) double; 320,000 lire ($204.80) suite. Rates include breakfast. Half board 35,000 lire ($22.40) per person extra. AE, DC, MC, V. Free parking.

Located in a residential neighborhood near the spa, the imposing facade of this pleasant, turn-of-the-century hotel rises from behind a screen of shrubbery and an outdoor terrace. It's the most accommodating, and most attractive, of the upper-middle-bracket hotels of Montecatini, with a vaguely modernized interior last renovated in 1995 and touches of polished marble scattered throughout the conservatively modern bedrooms and the public areas. Don't expect the lavish gilt and ornate architecture of the Gran Hotel e la Pace, recommended below, but the genteel staff, and the less lower prices, make up for it.

✪ Gran Hotel e la Pace. Via della Toretta 1, 51016 Montecatini Term. ☎ **0572/75801.** Fax 0572/78451. 142 rms, 8 suites. A/C MINIBAR TV TEL. 490,000 lire ($313.60) double; 700,000 lire ($448) suite. AE, DC, MC, V. Closed Nov–Apr 4. Free parking.

This is the dowager grand empress hotel of Montecatini Terme, a gilded-age bastion that has maintained its white-glove formality since its establishment in 1869. Rivaled only by the Bella Vista, a competing five-star hotel that doesn't have the Gran Hotel's panache, it's outfitted with frescoes, elaborate ceilings, flowered sun terraces, soaring columns, lots of gilt, and all the ornate detailing that characterizes formal 19th-century architecture. A renovation upgraded the premises in 1994.

The bedrooms are less lavish than the public areas, but discreetly comfortable. There's an elegant restaurant (the Michelangelo) and an outdoor swimming pool. Anyone who wants full access to Montecatini Terme's most technical health and beauty treatments must leave the hotel and go into the nearby park. Despite that, the hotel offers a limited array of supervised spa facilities on its premises, one of the few hotels in town that does.

WHERE TO DINE

Gourmet. Via Amendla 6. ☎ **0572/771012.** Reservations recommended. Main courses 30,000–45,000 lire ($19.20–$28.80). AE, DC, MC, V. Wed–Mon noon–2pm and 7:30–10:30pm. ITALIAN.

In a 19th-century building with a Liberty-style interior, this is the best independent restaurant in Montecatini. Established in 1984, it prides itself on formal, elegant service and dishes that are more unusual than the run-of-the-mill pastas and veal dishes of lesser competitors. Menu items change with the seasons and the availability of the ingredients. You'll find a spectacular array of antipasti (the restaurant refers to it as "antipasti fantasia") concocted from seafood and fresh vegetables, ravioli stuffed with pulverized sea bass and herbs, risotto with scampi, and a medley of fruit garnishes (melon slices with lobster and a honey-vinegar sauce, for example). Most items are delicious, impeccably fresh, and beautifully presented by a gracious team of servers. The desserts are made fresh daily, and might include a soufflé flavored with Grand Marnier.

LUCCA

At the time of the collapse of the Roman Empire, Lucca, 46 miles northwest of Florence, was virtually the capital of Tuscany. Periodically in its valiant, ever-bloody history, it functioned as an independent principality, similar to Genoa. This autonomy attests to the fame and prestige Lucca enjoyed. Now, however, it's largely bypassed by time and travelers, rewarding the discriminating few.

Lucca

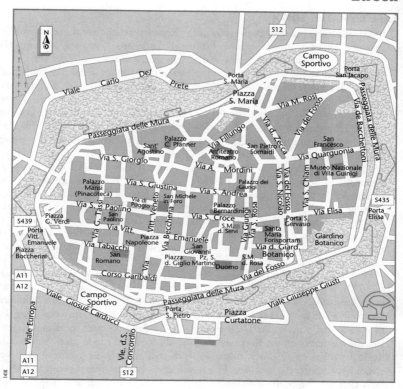

Thriving, cosmopolitan, and perfectly preserved, Lucca today is a sort of Switzerland of the south. Banks have latticed Gothic windows; shops look like well-stocked linen cupboards. Plump children play in landscaped gardens, and geraniums bloom from the roofs of medieval tower houses.

ESSENTIALS

GETTING THERE   By Train   There are about eight trains per day between Florence and Lucca, with three or four in the morning, a slowdown between noon and around 2:30pm, and the remainder in the afternoon and early evening. The trip takes 1¼ hours and costs 7,000 lire ($4.50) each way. The railway station lies south of Lucca's historic core, a short walk from the city's ramparts and medieval fortifications. For railway information in Lucca, call 0583/47013.

By Bus   The **Ladzi** bus company (☎ **0583/1668-45010**) operates half a dozen buses per day between Florence and Lucca. They take less time than the train (about 50 minutes to an hour) and cost the same. Buses pick up passengers in front of the railway station in Florence and drop them off in Lucca at both the railway station and in the historic core of town at piazzale Verdi, near the tourist office.

VISITOR INFORMATION   The **Lucca Tourist Office** is on piazzale Verdi (☎ **0583/419689**), open in summer daily from 9am to 9pm, to 4:30pm October 15 to March 15.

EXPLORING THE TOWN

Its city walls, built largely in the days of the Renaissance, enclose the old town, the zone of the most interest to visitors, of course. For orientation, you may want to walk (even drive your car) along the tree-shaded ramparts, a distance of $2^1/2$ miles.

Afterward, we suggest that you head to piazza San Martino to visit the **Cathedral of San Martino (Duomo)** (☎ 0583/494726), dating back to 1060, although the present structure was mainly rebuilt. The facade is exceptional, evoking the "Pisan-Romanesque" style, but with enough originality to distinguish it from the Duomo at Pisa. Designed mostly by Guidetto da Como in the early years of the 13th century, the west front contains three wide ground-level arches, surmounted by three scalloped galleries with taffy-like twisting columns tapering in size.

The relic of St. Martin is the *Volto Santo,* a crucifix carved by Nicodemus (so tradition has it) from the Cedar of Lebanon. The face of Christ was supposedly chiseled onto the statuary. The main art treasure in the Duomo is Jacopo della Quercia's tomb of Ilaria del Carretto, who died in 1405 (while still young), the wife of Paolo Guinigi. The marble effigy of the young lady, in regal robes, rests atop the sarcophagus—the cathedral's diffused mauve light in the afternoon casts a ghostly glow on her countenance. The tomb in the sacristy is fringed with chubby bambini. Open daily from 9am to 7pm; admission free.

Within the city walls, the **Chiesa San Frediano,** piazza San Frediano (☎ 0583/493627), is one of the most important and famous in Lucca. Romanesque in style, it was erected when Lucca enjoyed its greatest glory, in the 12th and 13th centuries. Its severe white facade is relieved by a 13th-century mosaic of Christ ascending. Its campanile rises majestically. The interior is dark, and visitors often speak in whispers. But the bas-reliefs on the Romanesque font add a note of comic relief. Supposedly depicting the story of Moses, among other themes, it shows Egyptians in medieval armor chasing after the Israelites. Two tombs in the basilica were the work of Jacopo della Quercia, the celebrated Sienese sculptor. They're in the fourth chapel on the left. The church is open Monday to Saturday from 7:30am to noon and 3 to 6pm and on Sunday from 9am to 1pm and 3 to 6pm.

At piazza San Michele, a short walk away, **San Michele in Foro** (☎ 0583/48459) often surprises first-timers to Lucca, who mistake it for the Duomo. A 12th-century church, it's the most memorable example of the style and flair the denizens of Lucca brought to the Pisan-Romanesque school of architecture. Its west front, again employing the scalloped effect, is spanned by seven arches on the ground level, then surmounted by four tiers of galleries, utilizing imaginatively designed columns. Dragon-slaying St. Michael, wings outstretched, rests on the friezelike peak of the final tier. Inside, seek out a Filippo Lippi painting of four saints. Open daily from 7:30am to 12:30pm and 3 to 6pm.

WHERE TO STAY

✪ **Principessa Elisa.** Strada Statale 12, 55050 Massa Pisana (Lucca). ☎ **0583/379737.** Fax 0583/379019. 10 junior suites. A/C MINIBAR TV TEL. 500,000 lire ($320) suite for two. AE, DC, MC, V.

In 1992 this blue-fronted 18th-century villa was reunited with its neighbor (the Hotel Villa La Principessa, see below) across the road. It was a renewal of a pattern that had been established long ago, when the villa housed an army officer who happened to be the favorite gentleman escort of Napoléon's sister, the owner of the larger villa across the road. Following its transformation, after years of neglect, into a posh country-house hotel, the villa immediately replaced its better-established neighbor as the most elegant lodging in Lucca, a fact that Relais & Châteaux recognized by ending its association with the Hotel Villa La Principessa and beginning a wholehearted endorsement of the Principessa Elisa. That didn't really matter to the owners, the Mugnani family, since both lodgings belong to them anyway. The resulting complex that was created is now one of the most charming hotel compounds in Tuscany.

The white-fronted neoclassical villa has verdant gardens, a worthy collection of Italian antiques, discreet and charming service, and bedrooms that are larger and more plushly decorated than those in its elegant but somewhat simpler sibling across the highway. Each accommodation is a skillfully decorated junior suite, with views either of gardens or a park, and furnishings that the Bonapartes themselves might have lived with comfortably. The restaurant, Il Gazebo, is recommended separately (see "Where to Dine," below).

Villa La Principessa. Strada Statale 12 bis, 55050 Massa Pisana (Lucca). ☎ **0583/370037.** Fax 0583/379136. 35 rms, 5 suites. A/C MINIBAR TV TEL. 335,000–375,000 lire ($214.40–$240) double; 410,000 lire ($262.40) suite. AE, DC, MC, V. Closed Nov–Mar.

Associated with the previously recommended Principessa Elisa, which is set across the highway and with which it's frequently confused, this is a well-managed, four-star hotel. It's less luxurious than its sister hotel, but also less expensive. Like its five-star neighbor, it's set less than 2 miles south of Lucca's center, beside a meandering highway with sharp turns and limited visibility. It's sheltered with hedges, flowering trees, and the best kinds of architectural detailings from other eras. It was originally built in 1320 as the private home of one of the dukes of Lucca, Castruccio Castracani, who was later depicted by Machiavelli as "The Ideal Prince." Later, when the hills around Lucca were dotted with the homes of members of the Napoleonic court, the house was rebuilt into a severely dignified stylistic representative of the region around Lucca. The bedrooms are comfortably renovated with everything you'll need. There's a swimming pool set in a garden. Breakfast is the only meal served.

WHERE TO DINE

Buca di Sant'Antonio. Via della Cervia 1. ☎ **0583/55881.** Reservations recommended. Main courses 18,000–25,000 lire ($11.50–$16). AE, DC, MC, V. Tues–Sat noon–3pm and 7:30–10:30pm, Sun noon–3pm. Closed 2 weeks in Jan. TUSCAN.

Set in the historic core of Lucca, on a difficult-to-find alleyway near piazza San Michele, this is one of the finest and least pretentious regional restaurants in town. Steeped in traditions that have made it endlessly popular since the 1950s, it's outfitted with country-rustic implements (such as copper pots and an open fireplace) and has a hearty and hospitable staff. Menu items include grilled dishes, especially in summer; a savory compendium of stews designed to ward off midwinter chill; and such regional specialties as red bean minestrone, a succulent version of codfish, and such pastas as tortellini in meat sauce. If you happen to arrive in Lucca on the days this place is closed, its owners will graciously refer you to nearby restaurants, including Giglio (see below), whose prices and quality are roughly comparable.

Da Giulio in Pelleria. Via della Conce 45. ☎ **0583/55948.** Reservations recommended. Main courses 12,500–17,000 lire ($8–$10.90). AE, DC, MC, V. Tues–Sat and the third Sun of every month, noon–2:30pm and 7:15–10:15pm. Closed Aug. LUCCHESE.

Less expensive than many of its competitors, this restaurant occupies a 200-year-old building near the Porta San Donato, and attracts lots of locals with uncompromising allegiance to local traditions and time-honored recipes. Under its present management since 1991, it presents dishes that might appeal to visiting foreigners, such as succulent minestrones, pastas, veal, hearty soups, and chicken dishes served in generous, robust portions. There are also some regional dishes that might just be a little too ethnic for most North American tastebuds, such as cioncia, which is concocted with veal snout and herbs.

Il Gazebo della Principessa Elisa. In the Hotel Principessa Elisa, strada Statale 12. ☎ **0583/ 379737.** Reservations recommended. Fixed-price menu 75,000–85,000 lire ($48–$54.40). AE, DC, MC, V. Mon–Sat 12:30–2:30pm and 8–10pm. ITALIAN/TUSCAN.

Some diners from the surrounding region chose to dine here as a means of visiting one of Tuscany's most elegant hotels. Set in a previously recommended country house less than 2 miles south of Lucca's center, the restaurant is in a re-creation of an English conservatory. Wraparound windows in an almost circular room offer views out over a garden that was replanted at great expense in the early 1990s. Service, as you'd expect from a five-star hotel with Relais & Châteaux status, is impeccable. Menu items include upscale versions of local Luccan recipes, including, among others, a farro Lucchese, red-bean soup with locally grown greens. Other, less ethnic dishes include steamed scampi with fresh tomato sauce, smoked swordfish with grilled eggplant, and ravioli stuffed with herbed eggplant and served with prawn sauce.

Giglio. Piazza del Giglio 2. ☎ **0583/494058.** Reservations recommended. Main courses 18,000–5,000 lire ($11.50–$16). AE, DC, MC, V. Thurs–Mon noon–3pm and 7–10pm. REGIONAL/TUSCAN.

In earthy regional appeal and popularity this place is rivaled only by the previously recommended Buca di Sant'Antonio. It has flourished in this location in the heart of town since 1957. The secret to its appeal might be its rustic decor (including 15th-century architectural detailing), its attentive and helpful staff, and its succulent interpretations of time-honored Tuscan and regional recipes. You'll find nothing experimental here, a fact that doesn't seem to bother any of its local clients one bit. Chow down on red-bean soup with local greens, all kinds of pasta, including a local version of maccharoni with rabbit meat; well-prepared antipasti; and a wide choice of Tuscan wines.

AREZZO

The most landlocked of all towns or cities of Tuscany, Arezzo lies about 50 miles southeast of Florence. Originally an Etruscan settlement, and later a Roman center, Arezzo flourished in the Middle Ages before its capitulation to Florence.

The walled town grew up on a hill, but large parts of the ancient city, including native son Petrarch's house, were bombed during World War II before the area fell to the Allied advance in the summer of 1944. Apart from Petrarch, famous sons of Arezzo have included Vasari, the painter-architect remembered chiefly for his history of the Renaissance artists, and Guido of Arezzo (sometimes known as Guido Monaco), who gave the world the modern musical scale before his death in the mid-11th century.

ESSENTIALS

GETTING THERE   By Train   There's a train that comes from Florence every 50 minutes throughout the day. The trip takes between 40 and 60 minutes, and a one-way ticket costs 6,500 lire ($4.15). Trains depart and arrive at the **Stazione Centrale,** piazza della Repubblica (☎ **0575/22663**). Because there are no direct train routes from Siena to Arezzo, railway passengers from Siena are required to make hot, prolonged, and tiresome rail transfers in Florence. Therefore, unless it happens to be Sunday (see below) it's better to opt for bus transfers if your point of origin is Siena.

By Bus   Travel by bus from Florence to Arezzo is not a good idea. Bus routes from Siena to Arezzo, however, are preferable to the difficult transfers that are needed via the train through Florence. Monday to Saturday, five buses per day travel from Siena directly to Arezzo. On Sunday, however, the trip isn't feasible, so travelers coming from Siena should take the train, which, as stated, requires a transfer in Florence. For information on bus routes, call the bus station in Siena (☎ **0577/280551**).

VISITOR INFORMATION   The **Arezzo Tourist Information Office,** at piazza della Repubblica 28 (☎ **0575/377678**), is open Monday to Saturday from 9am to 1pm and 3 to 7pm and on Sunday from 9am to 1pm.

EXPLORING THE TOWN

The biggest event on the Arezzo calendar is the "**Giostra** (joust) **del Saraceno**," staged the third Sunday of June and the first Sunday of September on piazza Grande. Horsemen in medieval costumes reenact the lance-charging ritual—with balled whips cracking in the air—as they have since the 13th century. But piazza Grande should be visited at any time of the year for the medieval and Renaissance palaces and towers that flank it, including the 16th-century Loggia Palace by Vasari.

The **Church of Santa Maria della Pieve,** corso Italia (☎ **0575/22629**), is a Romanesque structure, with a front of three open-air loggias (each pillar designed differently). On the front side is a 14th-century bell tower, known as "the hundred holes," as it's riddled with windows. Inside, the church is bleak and austere, but there's a notable polyptych of the *Virgin with Saints* by one of the Sienese Orenzetti brothers (Pietro), painted in 1320. The church is open daily from 8am to 1pm and 3 to 6:30pm.

A short walk away is **Petrarch's House**, via dell'Orto 28A (☎ **0575/24700**), which has been rebuilt after war damage. Born at Arezzo in 1304, Petrarch was, of course, the great Italian lyrical poet and humanist, who immortalized his love, Laura, in his sonnets. His house is open Monday to Saturday from 10am to noon and from 3 to 5pm. Ring the bell for admission.

If you have only an hour for Arezzo, run—don't walk—to the **Basilica di San Francesco,** piazza San Francesco (☎ **0575/20630**), a Gothic church finished in the 14th century for the Franciscans. In the church is a fresco cycle—*Legend* (or Story) *of the True Cross*—by Piero della Francesca, his masterpiece.

His frescoes are remarkable for their grace, clearness, dramatic light effects, well-chosen colors, and ascetic severity. Vasari credited della Francesca as a master of the laws of geometry and perspective. The frescoes depict the burial of Adam, Solomon receiving the queen of Sheba at the court (the most memorable scene in the cycle), the dream of Constantine with the descent of an angel, as well as the triumph of the Holy Cross with Heraclius, among other subjects. The church can be visited daily from 8am to noon and 2 to 6:30pm. Admission is free.

You might also want to check out **Il Duomo,** piazza del Duomo (☎ **0575/23991**), which was built in the so-called pure Gothic style—rare for Tuscany. The cathedral was begun in the 13th century, but the final touches (the facade) weren't applied until the outbreak of World War I. Its art treasures include a *Mary Magdalen* by della Francesca, stained-glass windows by Marcillat, and a main altar in the Gothic style. It's open daily from 8am to noon and 2 to 6:30pm.

WHERE TO STAY

Hotel Continentale. Piazza Guido Monaco 7, 52100 Arezzo. ☎ **0575/20251.** Fax 0575/ 350485. 74 rms. MINIBAR TV TEL. 150,000 lire ($96) double. AE, DC, MC, V. Parking 15,000 lire ($9.60). Bus: D, S, or 9.

This modern, geometric hotel is certainly different from the more antique architecture that characterizes most of the town's historic core. However, located less than 200 yards from the town's railway station, in the town's commercial core, the Continentale offers cost-conscious accommodations in an early 1950s setting. Renovations have kept the place up-to-date. About 70% of the bedrooms—which are scattered over five efficiently decorated floors—have air-conditioning, and since the price is the same for all rooms in the hotel, it pays to request it specifically in advance. The hotel restaurant is open for three meals a day every day except Sunday evening and Monday.

WHERE TO DINE

Buca di San Francesco. Via San Francesco 1. ☎ **0575/23271.** Reservations recommended. Main courses 16,000–36,000 lire ($10.25–$23.05). AE, DC, MC, V. Wed–Sun 12:30–3pm and 7–11pm. ITALIAN.

Located in the historic core of the old city, this admirable restaurant is set in the cellar of a building from the 1300s, and decorated with medieval references and strong Tuscan colors of sienna and blue. Menu items include pollo del Valdarno arrosto (roast chicken from the valley of the Arno) flavored with anise, homemade tagliolini with tomatoes and ricotta, and calves' liver with onions according to a regional recipe. A popular first course is green noodles with a rich meat sauce, oozing with creamy cheese and topped with a hunk of fresh butter. All ingredients are fresh, many of the staples are produced in-house, and even the establishment's olive oil is from special, private sources not shared by other restuarants.

GUBBIO

Gubbio, 25 miles northeast of Perugia, is one of the best-preserved medieval towns in Italy. It has modern apartments and stores on its outskirts, but once you press through that, you're firmly back in the Middle Ages. The best-known streets of its medieval core are via XX Settembre, via dei Consoli, via Galeotti, and via Baldassini. All these streets are found in the old town, or **Città Vecchia,** set against the steep slopes of **Monte Ingino.**

ESSENTIALS

GETTING THERE   By Bus   Because Gubbio doesn't have a rail station, visitors arrive by car or bus. There are eight buses a day from Perugia. Trip time is 1 hour 10 minutes, and a one-way ticket costs 8,000 lire ($5.10). Buses arrive and depart from piazza 40 Martiri (☎ **075/922-0066**).

VISITOR INFORMATION   The **Gubbio Tourist Office,** at piazza Oderisi 6 (☎ **075/922-0693**), is open Monday to Saturday from 8am to 2pm and 3 to 6pm, and on Sunday from 9am to 1pm.

EXPLORING THE OLD TOWN

If the weather is right you can take a cable car up to **Monte Ingino,** at a height of 2,690 feet, for a panoramic view of the area. In July and August service is Monday to Saturday from 8:30am to 7:30pm and on Sunday from 8:30am to 8pm; in June and September, from 9:30am to 1:15pm and 2:30 to 6:30pm; off-season, daily from 2:30 to 5pm. A one-way ticket costs 4,000 lire ($2.55).

Back in Gubbio, you can set about exploring a town that knew its golden age in the 1300s. You might begin at piazza della Signoria, the most important square. Nearby you can visit the **Palazzo dei Consoli,** piazza Grande (☎ **075/927-4298**), a Gothic edifice housing the famed bronze *tavole eugubine,* a series of tablets as old as Christianity, which were discovered in the 15th century. The tablets contain writing in the mysterious Umbrian language. The museum has a display of antiques from the Middle Ages and a collection of not very worthwhile paintings. It's open Tuesday to Saturday from 9am to 12:30pm and 3:30 to 6pm and on Sunday from 9am to 1pm. Admission is 4,000 lire ($2.55) for adults and 3,000 lire ($1.90) for children.

The other major sight is the **Palazzo Ducale,** or ducal palace, via Ducale (☎ 075/927-5872). This palace is associated with the memories (not always good ones) of the ruling dukes of Urbino. It was built by Federico of Montefeltro. It's open daily from 9am to 1pm; admission is 4,000 lire ($2.55).

After visiting the ducal palace, you can go inside **Il Duomo,** via Ducale (☎ 075/927-3980), across the way. The cathedral of Gubbio is a relatively unadorned pink Gothic building with some stained-glass windows from the 12th century. It has a single nave. It's open daily from 9am to 12:30pm and 3:30 to 8:30pm.

Gubbio has some minor attractions as well, including the **Chiesa di San Francesco,** piazza 40 Martiri (☎ 075/927-3460), built in the Gothic style. The interior walls of the north apse are covered with a set of stunning frescos executed in the early 1400s. The name of the local painter, Ottaviano Nelli, is relatively unknown but reproductions of his work often appear in Italian art books.

You can also visit the **Teatro Romano,** via del Teatro Romano—at least from the outside. Dating from the time of Augustus, this former theater is now a ruin and is closed to the public. Special permission is needed to enter (usually granted only for academic research).

Be sure to save time for exploring many of the shops in town that make **ceramics,** some of which are known for their unique iridescent red luster. Gubbio is also known for many famous processions and festivals, including the Procession of the Dead Christ on Good Friday and the Corsa dei Ceri on May 15, when hourglass-shaped wooden towers are hauled through the streets.

WHERE TO STAY

Hotel Gattapone. Via Beni 6, 06024 Gubbio. ☎ **075/927-2489.** Fax 075/927-1269. 15 rms. TV TEL. 90,000 lire ($57.60) double. AE, DC, MC, V. Closed Jan.

This is a pleasant but not particularly plush hotel. What the hotel lacks in luxuries it makes up for in low prices. It's set at the bottom of a narrow alleyway whose flagstone pavement is spanned with soaring medieval buttresses. Guests enter a modernized lobby, in place since the site became a hotel in the 1970s, and head for a sun-flooded breakfast room where large windows offer glimpses of a tiny garden. Although the furniture throughout is modern and relatively uninspired, there are a few handcrafted details, such as timbered ceilings and arches of chiseled stone, here and there. Breakfast is the only meal served. For other meals, the hotel staff usually refers its clients to the Taverna del Lupo (see below).

Palace Hotel Bosone. Via XX Settembre 22, 06024 Gubbio. ☎ **075/922-0698.** Fax 075/922-0552. 25 rms, 5 suites. A/C MINIBAR TV TEL. 140,000 lire ($89.60) double; 240,000–295,000 lire ($153.60–$188.80) suite. Closed 3 weeks in Feb.

This is the most scenically located hotel in town, and also one of the most lavishly historic. Set at the meeting point of an almost endless flight of stone steps and a narrow street in the upper regions of town, it was built in the 1300s and enlarged during the Renaissance. The three-story stone building was converted from a private home into a hotel in 1974, welcoming guests ever since into cozy bedrooms trimmed with stone set into place by masons of earlier centuries. No meals are served other than breakfast, although the hotel usually directs its clients to the Taverna del Lupo, a short walk from the hotel.

San Marco. Via Perugino 5, 06024 Gubbio. ☎ **075/922-0234.** Fax 075/927-3716. 63 rms. TV TEL. 120,000 lire ($76.80) double. AE, DC, MC, V. Parking (in nearby garage) 15,000 lire ($9.60).

Its unpromising location on the busiest street corner in town is the San Marco's only real drawback. Other than that, this is a worthwhile, not particularly expensive, hotel set near the town's municipal parking lot. Built in solid, stone-sided stages between 1300 and the 1700s, it contains an arbor-covered terrace in back and cozy but simple bedrooms. The Restaurant San Marco serves Italian food beneath russet-colored brick vaulting.

WHERE TO DINE

Ristorante Federico de Montefeltro. Via della Repubblica 35. ☎ **075/927-3949.** Reservations recommended. Main courses 15,000–22,000 lire ($9.60–$14.10). AE, DC, MC, V. Fri–Wed 12:30–2:30pm and 7:20–10:30pm. Closed Feb. ITALIAN/REGIONAL.

Named after the feudal lord who built the ducal palace of Gubbio, this restaurant stands beside steeply inclined flagstones in the oldest part of the city, Inside is a pair of tavern-style dining rooms ringed with exposed stone and pinewood planking. Many of the specialties are based on ancient regional recipes, although the selection of tasty, fresh antipasti covers the traditions of most of the Italian peninsula. Menu items include chicken cooked with garlic, rosemary, and wine; roast suckling pig; several preparations of polenta; and broad noodles (pappardelle) with wild hare. You'll also be served a local version of unleavened bread fried in oil as part of the meal.

Taverna del Lupo. Via Giovanni Ansidei 21. ☎ **075/927-4368.** Reservations recommended. Main courses 18,000–23,000 lire ($11.50–$14.70). AE, DC, MC, V. Tues–Sun 12:30–11pm. Closed Jan. ITALIAN/TUSCAN.

This is the most authentically medieval of the many competing restaurants in Gubbio. Originally built in the 1200s, with unusual rows of tiles, it contains ceilings supported by barrel vaults and ribbing of solid stone, from which are suspended iron chandeliers. Menu items include a terrine of duck studded with truffles, suprême of pheasant, rich and steaming minestrones, and many of the pork, veal, and beef dishes that are distinctly Tuscan.

ORVIETO

Built on a pedestal of volcanic rock above vineyards in a green valley, Orvieto is the closest hill town to Rome and, as such, is often visited by those who don't have the time to explore other spots in Umbria.

Lying on the Paglia, a tributary of the Tiber, Orvieto is 75 miles north of Rome and 47 miles southwest of Perugia. This hill town sits on an isolated rock some 1,035 feet above sea level. Crowning the town is its world-famed cathedral. A road runs from below up to piazza del Duomo.

The most spectacularly sited hill town in Umbria (but not the most spectacular town), Orvieto was founded by the Etruscans, who were apparently drawn to it because of its good defensive possibilities. Likewise, long after its days as a Roman colony Orvieto beaome a papal stronghold. It was a natural fortress, as its cliffs rise starkly from the valley below, even though Orvieto, when you finally reach it, is relatively flat. Although the tall, sheer cliffs on which the town stands saved it from the incursion of railroads and superhighways, which are down in the valley, time and traffic vibrations have caused the soft volcanic rock to disintegrate so that work is imminently necessary to shore up the town.

Orvieto is known for its white wine, which, everybody agrees, is best enjoyed at a wine bar on piazza del Duomo as you contemplate the facade of the cathedral. If you're in town on a Saturday morning, be sure to visit the **pottery market** that takes place on piazza del Papolo.

ESSENTIALS

GETTING THERE   Three trains a day arrive from Perugia. Because of frequent stops, the trip takes 1 1/2 hours. A one-way ticket costs 8,800 lire ($5.65). From Florence, the trip time is 2 hours, and a one-way ticket costs 15,000 lire ($9.60). From Rome, the train takes 1 1/2 hours and costs 11,500 lire ($7.35) one-way. The trains arrive in the valley; shuttle buses run back and forth between the train station and piazza del Duomo.

VISITOR INFORMATION   The **Orvieto Tourist Office,** at piazza del Duomo 24 (☎ **0763/341772**), is open Monday to Friday from 8am to 2pm and 4 to 7pm, on Saturday from 10am to 1pm and 4 to 7pm, and on Sunday from 9am to 7pm.

EXPLORING THE TOWN

Erected on the site of two older churches, the ✪ **Duomo,** piazza del Duomo (☎ **0763/41147**), dedicated to the Virgin, was begun in 1288 (maybe even earlier). The cathedral was built to commemorate the Miracle of Bolsena. This alleged miracle came out of the doubts of a priest who questioned the Transubstantiation (that is, the incarnation of Jesus Christ in the Host). However, so the story goes, at the moment of consecration, the Host started to drip blood. The priest doubted no more and the Feast of Corpus Christi was launched.

The cathedral is known for its elaborately adorned facade, rich statuary, marble bas-reliefs, and mosaics. Pope John XXIII once proclaimed that on Judgment Day God would send his angels down to earth to pick up the facade of this cathedral and transport it back to heaven.

There's a rose window over the main door, but the most controversial parts of the cathedral are the modern bronze portals that many art historians journey from around the world to see. The doors, installed in 1970, were the work of Emilio Greco, an eminent sculptor. He took as his theme the Misericordia, the seven acts of corporal charity. One panel depicts Pope John XXIII's famous visit to the prisoners of Rome's Queen of Heaven jail in 1960. Some critics have called the doors "outrageous"; others have praised them as "one of the most original works of modern sculpture." You decide for yourself.

On the west facade the richly sculptured marble was based on designs of Lorenzo Maitani of Siena. It's divided into three gables. Four wall surfaces around the three doors were adorned with sculpture in relief, also based on designs of Maitani. He worked on the cathedral facade until his death in 1330. The bas-reliefs depict scenes from the Bible, including the Last Judgment. After Maitani's death, Andrea Pisano took over, but the actual work carried on until the dawn of the 17th century.

For decades every guidebook writer has suggested that the cathedral facade is best viewed at sunset. However, there's nothing wrong with dawn's early light.

Inside, the nave and aisles were constructed in alternating panels of black and white stone. You'll want to seek out the Cappella del Corporale with its mammoth silver shrine based on the design of the facade of the cathedral. This 1338 masterpiece, richly embellished with precious stones, was the work of Ugolino Vieri of Siena. It was designed to shelter the Holy Corporal from Bolsena (the cloth in which the bleeding Host was wrapped). The most celebrated chapel inside is the Chapel of San Brizio, which contains newly restored frescoes of the Apocalypse by Luca Signorelli and Fra Angelico, who completed the cycle between 1499 and 1504. Michelangelo was said to have been inspired by the frescoes at the time he was contemplating the Sistine Chapel. The church is open April to September, daily from 7am to 1pm and 2:30 to 7:30pm; November to February, daily from 7am to 1pm and 2:30 to 5:30pm; and in March and October, daily from 7am to 1pm and 2:30 to 6:30pm.

The famous **Il Pozzo di San Patrizio** (St. Patrick's Well), viale Sangallo, off piazza Cahen (☎ 0763/43768), is an architectural curiosity. In its day it was an engineering feat. Pope Clement VII ordered the well built when he feared that Orvieto might come under siege and its water supply be cut off. The well was entrusted to the design of Antonio da San Gallo the Younger in 1527. It's some 200 feet deep and about 42 feet in diameter, cut into volcanic rock. Two spiral staircases, with about 250 steps, lead into the wells. These spiral ramps never meet. Admission is 6,000 lire ($3.85). It's open April to October, daily from 9:30am to 7pm; November to March, daily from 10am to 6pm.

Across from the cathedral stands the **Palazzo Faina,** piazza Duomo 29 (☎ 0763/341511), a 17th-century palace. Originally a private collection, the museum here contains many Etruscan artifacts found in and around Orvieto. In addition to the stone sarcophagi, terra-cotta portraits, and vials of colored glass left by the Etruscans, the museum also contains many beautiful Greek vases. It's open Tuesday to Sunday from 10am to 1pm and 3 to 7pm. Admission is 7,000 lire ($4.50).

WHERE TO STAY

Hotel La Badia. S.N.C. Località La Badia 8, 05019 Orvieto Terni. ☎ and fax **0763/92796.** 18 rms, 7 suites. AE, MC, V. 255,000–261,000 lire ($163.20–$167.05) double; 370,000–450,000 lire ($236.80–$288) suite. Half board 67,000 lire ($42.90) per person extra. AE, DC, MC, V. Parking 15,000 lire ($9.60).

This is one of the most memorable of the country inns in this part of Italy. Set 3 miles east of the town center atop a hill that faces the rocky foundations of the old Etruscan fortress of Orvieto, the location was the site of a Benedictine abbey (*Badia,* in local dialect) in the 8th century A.D. It was upgraded to a monastery in the 12th century, when a church was erected nearby with funds donated by a local noblewoman. In the 19th century the buildings were renovated by an aristocratic family called Fiumi, who did what they could to preserve the irreplaceable stonework. Today the hotel is the finest, most historic, and most charming hotel in Orvieto, with tennis courts, a swimming pool, a well-chosen collection of antiques, and luxurious bedrooms with an appealing sense of history. Views extend over the surrounding countryside, and a restaurant provides elegant meals with discreet service.

Hotel Maitani. Via Maitani 5, 05018 Orvieto. ☎ and fax **0763/342011.** 20 rms, 8 suites. A/C TV TEL. 185,000 lire ($118.40) double; 220,000–260,000 lire ($140.80–$166.40) suite. AE, DC, MC, V. Parking 15,000 lire ($9.60) extra.

The stone-sided building that houses this family-run hotel was originally built as a palazzo around 600 years ago. It was transformed into a hotel in 1966. The bedrooms, scattered over four floors of the structure, are mostly modernized but do retain some reminders of their medieval origins. The rooms are small but cozy and comfortable. Other than breakfast, no meals are served on the premises, though several restaurants are nearby. Both the hotel and the street it sits on were named after the architect who designed Orvieto's famous cathedral, a short walk away. If you have a car, it's best to try to check in early, as the hotel has parking space for only eight vehicles.

WHERE TO DINE

La Grotte del Funaro. Via Rip Serancia 41. ☎ **0763/343276.** Main courses 14,000–28,000 lire ($8.95–$17.90). AE, DC, MC, V. Tues–Sun noon–2:30pm and 7pm–1am. UMBRIAN.

The cuisine here is the type of solid, traditional fare that Umbrian grandmothers have served their families for generations—fresh, flavorful, and nutritious, with absolutely no attempt to be creative or newfangled in any way. The setting, however, a surprisingly dry cave below the city center, includes many eerie references to other days and other times. No one seems to have any idea how long the cave has been in everyday use—the staff believes that it was part of the storerooms used by the ancient Etruscans. Menu items include an array of grilled meats, including grilled lamb, grilled pork with potatoes and vegetables, pastas flavored with local mushrooms and truffles, and well-prepared, very fresh vegetables. The steps that lead down to this restaurant are only about a hundred yards from piazza della Repubblica, in the historic town, a bit to the west of center.

8 Bologna & Emilia-Romagna

Lying in the northern reaches of central Italy, Emilia-Romagna is known for gastronomy and for its art cities, Modena and Parma. Once-great families, including the Renaissance dukes of Ferrara, rose in power and influence, creating courts that attracted painters and poets, notably Tasso and Ariosto.

Bologna, the capital, stands at the crossroads between Venice and Florence, and is linked by express highways to Milan and Tuscany. By basing yourself in this ancient university city, you can branch out in all directions: north for 32 miles to Ferrara, southeast for 31 miles to the ceramics-making town of Faenza, northwest for 25 miles to Modena with its Romanesque cathedral, or 34 miles farther northwest to Parma, the legendary capital of the Farnese family duchy in the 16th century. Ravenna, famed for its mosaics, lies 46 miles east of Bologna on the Adriatic Sea.

Most of our sightseeing destinations lie on the ancient Roman road, via Emilia, that began in Rimini and stretched all the way to Piacenza, a Roman colony that often attracted invading barbarians.

This ancient land (known to the Romans as Æmilia, and to the Etruscans before them) is rich in attractions—the cathedral and baptistery of Parma, for instance—and in scenic beauty (the green plains and the slopes of the Apennines). Emilia is one of the most bountiful farming districts in Italy, and sets a table highly praised in Europe—both for its wines and for its imaginatively prepared pasta dishes.

EXPLORING EMILIA-ROMAGNA BY CAR

There's much to see and do in Emilia-Romagna, but those on a tight schedule may want to confine themselves to the following route.

Day 1   Begin in Bologna, sampling its excellent cuisine and viewing its major sights, all in the city center. These include the Basilica di San Petronius and Fontana del Nettuno.

Day 2   Take autostrada A13 northwest to Ferrara, a distance of only 32 miles but a world apart. The former seat of the Este dynasty is filled with many palaces and castles from that era.

☕ **TAKE A BREAK**   The **Osteria Al Brindisi,** via G. degli Adelandi 9B in Ferrara (☎ **0532/209142**), is the oldest *osteria* in

What's Special About Bologna & Emilia-Romagna

Great Towns/Villages
- Bologna, gastronomic capital of Italy, a historic city that reached its artistic peak in the 16th century.
- Parma, home of Correggio, Il Parmigianino, Bodoni (of type fame), Toscanini, and Parmesan cheese.
- Ravenna, a city of faded glory, once the capital of the Roman Empire.

Museums
- Pinacoteca Nazionale, in Bologna, containing major works from the 14th century to the advent of the baroque.
- Galleria Estense, in Modena, with a collection of Emilian works from the 14th through the 18th century.

Religious Shrines
- The Duomo at Modena, one of the glories of the Romanesque in northern Italy.
- St. Petronius Basilica, in Bologna, begun in 1390 but never fully completed.
- Tomb of Galla Placidia, at Ravenna, located in the city's oldest structure and featuring mosaics famous for their range of color.

Ace Attraction
- San Domenico, a restaurant in Imola, outside Bologna, praised by many food critics as the greatest in Italy.

Italy, known to such former habitués as Cellini and Copernicus. It makes the best sandwiches in town, starting at 4,500 lire ($2.90), and it also serves some 600 varieties of wine, beginning at 1,000 lire (65¢) per glass. It's open Tuesday to Friday from 8:30am to 9pm and on Saturday from 8:30am to midnight.

Day 3   From Ferrara, drive south until you link up with the highway to the Adriatic, cutting southeast toward Ravenna. As you near the coast, continue south along Route E55 until you approach Ravenna, a former imperial city, the Byzantium of the West. Consider at least an overnight stopover, more if you have the time—there's much to see here (see below).

Day 4   Connect with the autostrada west going to Bologna, but this time bypass the city and head for Modena for the night. In Modena visit its Duomo and Galleria Estense, two of the major attractions of Emilia-Romagna. At one of the many local restaurants, sample such regional dishes as zampone (stuffed pig's feet), washing it down with a glass of Lambrusco.

🕮 **TAKE A BREAK**   **Forno San Giorgio,** via Taglio 6 in Modena (☎ **059/ 223514**), is the town's leading baker. You can purchase bread for a picnic, or try some of the town's best pizzas and pastries.

Day 5   For a final look at the province, continue northwest along autostrade 9 (A1) to Parma, where you can overnight, visiting at least the Duomo and Baptistery before wandering through the city's National Gallery.

A TASTE OF EMILIA-ROMAGNA

Emilia-Romagna is acclaimed for having the best cuisine in Italy. A land rich in agricultural resources, Emilia-Romagna prepares a bountiful table. In the field of

Emilia-Romagna

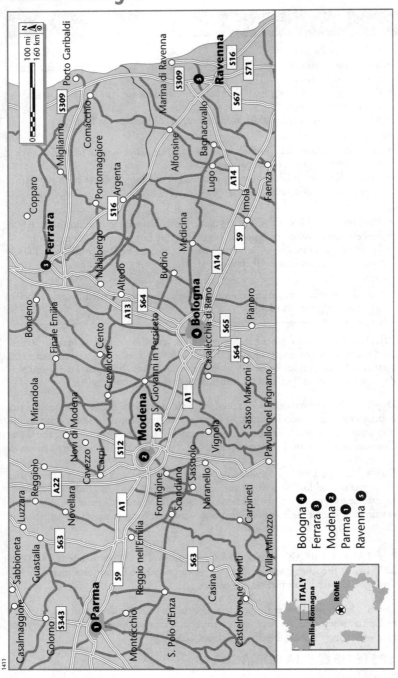

gastronomy "well-fed Bologna" is known for its *tagliatelle*, which exists all over Italy but is at its best in Emilia-Romagna. These long strips of macaroni are boiled and served with a ragoût. *Tortellini* is the second most fabled pasta dish—little squares of dough stuffed with chopped veal, turkey, pork, egg, beef marrow, spices, and cheese and served in consommé or with ragoût. *Cappelletti* is rather larger than tortellini, really "little hats" made of dough and filled with such items as minced turkey and Parmesan cheese. *Zampone* is the specialty of Modena—a pig's foot deboned and stuffed with minced and spicy pork, then boiled for several hours. *Cotechino* is a highly spiced pork sausage renowned locally, and Parmesan cheese from Parma now is sprinkled on dishes around the world. *Ragoût à la bolonaise* is actually a bolognese sauce (meat and tomato sauce), and it has gone on to become the world's most famous spaghetti meat sauce.

The list of foodstuffs in the province is endless, ranging from *involtini* (stuffed veal rolls) to fragrant smoked meats. *Cotoletta alla bolognese* is veal prepared with slices of ham and fondant cheese (often called veal Cordon Bleu around the world). It's the most famous meat dish of the area. *Mortadella* is a large, tasty sausage made with highly spiced pork that's cut into paper-thin slices.

Among wines, the limpid Albana, with its golden-yellow color, has a mellow flavor and an enticing bouquet; the sparkling, incomparable Lambrusco is ruby red in color, with a bouquet of violets and is perfect with tortellini or tagliatelle. Sanglovese is a dark ruby-red "brut" wine with a trace of flint in the flavor and a tartish aftertaste, again evoking the bouquet of violets.

1 Bologna

32 miles S of Ferrara, 94 miles SW of Venice, 227 miles N of Rome

The manager of a hotel in Bologna laments: "The Americans! They spend a week in Florence, a week in Venice. Why not 6 days in Florence, 6 days in Venice, and 2 days in Bologna?" That's a good question. Bologna is one of the most sadly overlooked Italian cities—we've found cavernous accommodation space here in July and August, when the hotels in Venice and Florence were packed as tightly as a can of Progresso clam sauce.

"But what is there to see in Bologna?" is also a common question. True, it boasts no Uffizi or Doge's Palace. However, it does offer a beautiful city that's one of the most architecturally unified in Europe—a panorama of marbled sidewalks and porticos that, if spread out, would surely stretch all the way to the border.

Filled with sienna-colored buildings, Bologna is the leading city of Emilia. Its rise as a commercial power was almost assured by its strategic location as the geographic center between Florence and Venice. Its university, the oldest in Europe, has for years generated a lively interest in art and culture.

Bologna is also the gastronomic capital of Italy. Gourmets flock here just to sample the food—the pasta dishes (tortellini, tagliatelle, lasagne verde), the meat and poultry specialties (zampone, veal cutlet bolognese, tender breasts of turkey in sauce supreme), and, finally, mortadella, the incomparable sausage of Bologna, as distant a cousin to baloney as porterhouse is to the hot dog.

The city seems to take a vacation in August, becoming virtually dead. Everywhere you see signs proclaiming CHIUSO ("closed").

ESSENTIALS

GETTING THERE By Plane The international airport, the **Aeroporto Guglielmo Marconi** (☎ 051/647-9615 for information about flights), is 4 miles north of the center of town and serviced by such domestic carriers as Aermediterranea and ATI. All the main European airlines have connections through this airport. A frequent bus runs from the airport to the air terminal at the rail station in the center of Bologna.

By Train   There is one **railroad station** in Bologna, at piazza delle Medaglie d'Oro (☎ **051/1478-88088**). Trains arrive every hour from Rome (trip time: $3^1/2$ hours) and from Milan (trip time: $1^3/4$ hours).

By Bus   ATC buses serve the area from their terminal at piazza XX Settembre 6 (☎ **051/248374** for information). Buses to and from Florence run once every hour (trip time: $1^1/2$ hours). Buses also arrive every hour from Venice (trip time: 2 hours) and from Milan (trip time: 3 hours).

By Car   From Florence, continue north along autostrada A1 until you reach the outskirts of Bologna where signs direct you to the center of the city. Coming over the Apennines, the Autostrada del Sole (A1) runs northwest to Milan just before reaching the outskirts of Bologna. The A13 superhighway cuts northeast to Ferrara and Venice and the A14 dashes east to Rimini, Ravenna, and the towns along the Adriatic.

VISITOR INFORMATION   The **tourist information office** is at piazza Maggiore 6 (☎ **051/239660**). It's open Monday to Saturday from 9am to 7pm and on Sunday from 9am to 12:30pm.

GETTING AROUND   Bologna is easy to cover on foot; most of the major sights are in and around piazza Maggiore, the heart of the city. However, if you don't want to walk, **city buses** leave for most points from either piazza Nettuno or piazza Maggiore. Free maps are available at the storefront office of the A.T. at piazza Galvani 4, behind the Church of San Petronio. Tickets can be purchased at one of many booths and tobacconists throughout Bologna. Once on board, however, you must have your ticket validated.

  Taxis are on radio call (☎ **051/372727**).

WHAT TO SEE & DO

Basilica di San Petronius. Piazza Maggiore. ☎ **051/231415.** Free admission. Daily 9am–5pm. Bus: Any bus from the Termini.

Sadly, the facade of this enormous Gothic basilica honoring the patron saint of Bologna was never completed. Although the builders went to work in 1390, after three centuries the church was still not finished (even though Charles V was crowned emperor here in 1530). However, Jacopo della Quercia of Siena did grace the central door with a Renaissance sculpture that's a masterpiece. Inside, the church could accommodate the traffic of New York's Grand Central Terminal. The central nave is separated from the aisles by pilasters shooting upward to the flying arches of the ceiling. Of the 22 art-filled chapels, the most interesting is the Bolognini Chapel, the fourth chapel on the left as you enter. It's embellished with frescoes representing heaven and hell. The purity and simplicity of line represent some of the best of the Gothic in Italy.

✪ **Fontana del Nettuno.** Piazza del Nettuno. Bus: 25 or 30.

Characteristic of the pride and independence of Bologna, this fountain has gradually become a symbol of the city, but it was in fact designed in 1566 by a Frenchman named Giambologna by the Italians (his fame rests largely on the work he did in Florence). Viewed as irreverent by some, vulgar by others, and magnificent by those with more liberal tastes, this 16th-century fountain depicts Neptune with rippling muscles,

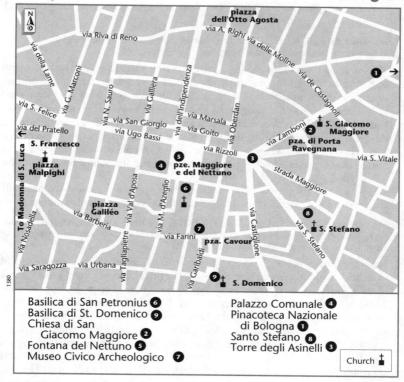

Basilica di San Petronius **6**
Basilica di St. Domenico **9**
Chiesa di San
   Giacomo Maggiore **2**
Fontana del Nettuno **5**
Museo Civico Archeologico **7**

Palazzo Comunale **4**
Pinacoteca Nazionale
   di Bologna **1**
Santo Stefano **8**
Torre degli Asinelli **3**

Church †

a trident in one arm, and a heavy foot on the head of a dolphin. Around his feet are four cherubs, also with dolphins. At the base of the fountain are four very erotic sirens, each spouting five different streams of water from her breasts.

Palazzo Comunale. Piazza Maggiore 6. ☎ **051/203526.** Admission: Each museum separately, 5,000 lire ($3.20) adults, 2,500 lire ($1.60) children 14–18 and seniors 60 and over, free for children 13 and under; combined ticket to both museums, 8,000 lire ($5.10) adults, 4,000 lire ($2.55) children 14–18 and seniors 60 and over, free for children 13 and under. Tues–Sat 10am–6pm, Sun guided tour at 4pm. Closed holidays. Bus: Any bus from the Termini.

Built in the 14th century, this town hall has seen major restorations, but happily retains its splendor. Enter through the courtyard, then proceed up the steps on the right to the **Comunal Collection of Fine Arts,** which includes many paintings from the 14th- and 19th-century Emilian school. Another section comprises the **Museum of Giorgio Morandi,** an entire section devoted to the works of this famed Italian artist.

Basilica di St. Domenico. Piazza San Domenico 13. ☎ **051/640-0411.** Free admission. Daily 7am–7pm. Bus: 30.

The basilica dates from the 13th century, but it has seen many alterations and restorations. The church houses the tomb of St. Domenico, in front of the Capella della Madonna. The sculptured tomb—known as an *area*—is a Renaissance masterpiece, a joint enterprise of Niccolò Pisano, Guglielmo (a friar), Niccolò dell'Arca, Alfonso Lombardi, and the young Michelangelo. The choir stalls, the second major artistic work in the basilica, were carved by Damiano da Bergamo, another friar, in the 16th century.

Torre degli Asinelli. Piazza di Porta Ravegnanna. Admission 3,000 lire ($1.90). May–Sept, daily 9am–6pm; Oct–Apr, daily 9am–5pm. Bus: 25 or 30.

These leaning towers keep defying gravity year after year. The Due Torri were built by patricians in the 12th century. In the Middle Ages Bologna had dozens of these skyscraper towers, anticipating Manhattan by several centuries. They were status symbols: the more powerful the family, the taller the tower. The smaller one, the **Garisenda,** is only 162 feet tall and leans approximately $10^{1}/_{2}$ feet from the perpendicular. The taller one, the **Asinelli** (334 feet tall, a walk up of nearly 500 steps), inclines almost $7^{1}/_{2}$ feet. Those who scale the Asinelli should be awarded a medal, but instead they're presented with a panoramic view of the tile roofs of Bologna and the hills beyond.

After visiting the towers, take a walk up what must be the most architecturally elegant street in Bologna, strada Maggiore, with its colonnades and mansions.

Santo Stefano. Via Santo Stefano. ☎ **051/223256.** Free admission to church and museum. Church, Apr–Sept, daily 7am–noon and 3:30–6pm; Oct–Mar, daily 9am–noon and 3:30–5:30pm. Museum, daily 9:30am–noon. Bus: 25 or 30.

From the leaning towers, head up via Santo Stefano to see a virtual community of churches linked together like Siamese twins. The first church you enter is the Church of the Crucifix, relatively simple with only one nave and a crypt. It dates from the 11th century. To the left is the entrance to the Church of Santo Sepolcro, its present structure dating principally from the 12th century. Under the altar is the tomb of patron saint Petronius. Continuing left, you enter another rebuilt church, this one honoring Saints Vitale and Agricola. The present building, graced with three apses, also dates from the 11th century. Reentering Sepolcro, take the back entrance this time into the Courtyard of Pilate, onto which several more chapels open. Through the courtyard entrance to the right, proceed into the Romanesque cloisters, dating from the 11th and 12th centuries. The names on the wall of the lapidary honor Bolognese war dead.

Chiesa di San Giacomo Maggiore. Piazza Rossini or via Zamboni 15. ☎ **051/225970.** Free admission. Daily 7am–noon and 3:30–6pm. Bus: 14, 25, or 50.

The Church of St. James was originally a Gothic structure in the 13th century. But, like so many others, it has been altered and restored at the expense of its original design. Still, it's one of Bologna's most interesting churches, filled with art treasures. The Bentivoglio Chapel is the most sacred haunt, even though time has dimmed the luster of its frescoes. Near the altar, seek out a *Madonna and Child* enthroned, one of the most outstanding works of the artist Francesco Erancia. The holy pair are surrounded by angels and saints, as well as by a half-naked Sebastian to the right. Nearby is a sepulchre of Antonio Bentivoglio, designed by Jacopo della Quercia, who labored so long over the doors to the Basilica of San Petronio. In the Chapel of Santa Cecilia you'll discover important frescoes by Francia and Lorenzo Costa.

Museo Civico Archeologico. Via dell'Archiginnasio 2. ☎ **051/233849.** Admission 5,000 lire ($3.20) adults, 2,500 lire ($1.60) children 15–18, free for children 14 and under. Tues–Fri 9am–2pm, Sat–Sun 9am–1pm and 3:30–7pm. Bus: Any bus to piazza Maggiore.

This museum houses one of the major Egyptian collections in Italy, as well as important discoveries dug up in Emilia. As you enter, look to the right in the atrium to see a decapitated marble torso, said to be that of Nero. Opened in 1994, on the lower floor, a modern new Egyptian section presents a notable array of mummies and

The World's Greatest China Shop

Faenza lent its name to a form of ceramics known as faïence, which had originated on the Balearic island of Majorca, off the east coast of Spain. The town of Faenza, only 36 miles southeast of Bologna, became the Italian center of this industry. Faenza potters found inspiration in the work coming out of Majorca and began to produce their own designs—characterized by brilliant, rich colors and floral decorations—in the 12th century. The art reached its pinnacle in the 16th century when the "hot-fire" process was perfected, during which ceramics were baked at a temperature of 1,742°F.

The legacy of this fabled industry is preserved today at the **Museo Internazionale delle Ceramiche (International Museum of Ceramics),** via Campidoro 2 (☎ **0546/21240**), called "the world's greatest china shop." Housed here are works not only from the artisans of Faenza, but from throughout the world including pre-Columbian pottery from Peru. Of exceptional interest are Etruscan and Egyptian ceramics, as well as a wide-ranging collection from the Orient, even from the days of the Roman Empire.

Deserving special attention is the section devoted to modern ceramic art, including works by Matisse and Picasso. On display are Picasso vases and a platter with his dove of peace, a platter in rich colors by Chagall, a "surprise" from Matisse, and a framed ceramic plaque of the Crucifixion by Georges Rouault. Another excellent work, the inspiration of a lesser-known artist, is a ceramic woman by Dante Morozzi. Even the great Léger tried his hand at ceramics.

The museum, which attracts not only ceramic makers but interested visitors worldwide, is open June to September, Tuesday to Saturday from 9am to 7pm and on Sunday from 9:30am to 1pm; October to May, Tuesday to Friday from 9am to 1:30pm, on Saturday from 3 to 6pm, and on Sunday from 9:30am to 1pm. Admission is 8,000 lire ($5.10) for adults, 4,000 lire ($2.55) for children 17 and under and for seniors 60 and over.

sarcophagi. The chief attraction in this collection is a cycle of bas-reliefs from Horemheb's tomb. On the ground floor a new wing contains a gallery of casts, displaying copies of famous Greek and Roman sculptures. On the first floor, reached through a gallery of casts, two exceptional burial items from Verucchio (Rimini) are exhibited. Note the wood furnishings, footrests, and the throne of tomb 89, which is decorated with scenes from everyday life and ceremonial parades.

Upstairs are cases of prehistoric objects, tools, and artifacts. The relics of the Etruscans comprise the best part of the museum, especially the highly stylized Askos Benacci, depicting a man on a horse that is perched on yet another animal. Also displayed are terra-cotta urns, a vase depicting fighting Greeks and Amazons, and a bronze Certosa jar dating from the 6th century B.C. The museum's greatest single treasure is Phidias's head of Athena Lemnia, a copy of a Greek work dating from the 5th century B.C.

Pinacoteca Nazionale di Bologna. Via delle Belle Arti 56. ☎ **051/243222.** Admission 8,000 lire ($5.10), free for children 17 and under and for adults 60 and over. Tues–Sat 9am–2pm, Sun 9am–1pm. Closed holidays. Bus: 36, 37, or 50.

The most significant works of the school of painting that flourished in Bologna from the 14th century to the heyday of the baroque have been assembled under one roof in this second-floor *pinacoteca*. The gallery also houses works by other major Italian artists, such as Raphael's *St. Cecilia in Estasi.* Guido Reni (1575–1642) of Bologna steals the scene with his *St. Sebastian* and his *Pietà,* along with his equally penetrating *St. Andrea Corsini, The Slaying of the Innocents,* and his idealized *Samson the Victorious.* Other Reni works at the National include *The Flagellation of Christ, The Crucifixion,* and his masterpiece—*Ritratto della Madre*—a revealing portrait of his mother that must surely have inspired Whistler. Then, don't miss Vitale de Bologna's (1330–61) rendition of St. George slaying the dragon—a theme in European art that parallels Moby Dick in America. Also displayed are works by Francesco Francia, and especially noteworthy is a polyptych attributed to Giotto.

WHERE TO STAY

Bologna has four to six trade fairs a year, during which hotel room rates rise dramatically. Some hotels announce their prices in advance; others prefer to wait until bookings are actually being accepted, perhaps to see what the market will bear. Be duly warned: At trade fair times (dates vary yearly, check with the tourist office) business clients from throughout Europe book the best rooms and you—as a tourist—will be paying a lot of money to visit Bologna.

VERY EXPENSIVE

Grand Hotel Baglioni. Via dell'Indipendenza 8, 40121 Bologna. ☎ **051/225445.** Fax 051/234840. 117 rms, 8 suites. A/C MINIBAR TV TEL. 440,000–615,000 lire ($281.60–$393.60) double; 800,000–1,700,000 lire ($512–$1,088) suite. Rates include breakfast. AE, DC, MC, V.Parking 40,000 lire ($25.60). Bus: 11 or 27.

Far better and more atmospheric than its chief rival, the Royal Hotel Carlton, the Grand Hotel Baglioni boasts a desirable location in the center of Bologna, near the main square and Neptune's fountain. Its four-story facade is crafted of the same reddish brick that distinguishes many of the city's older buildings. The interior is noted for its wall and ceiling frescoes. Each soundproof room contains reproductions of antique furniture as well as all the modern conveniences that one would expect in a grand hotel. The rooms are generally spacious, the fourth-floor units being the largest of all.

Dining/Entertainment: Good-tasting Bolognese cooking is served in the elegant à la carte restaurant, I Carracci (see "Where to Dine," below).

Services: Room service, baby-sitting, laundry, valet.

Facilities: Hairdresser.

EXPENSIVE

Royal Hotel Carlton. Via Montebello 8, 40121 Bologna. ☎ **051/24936.** Fax 051/249724. 251 rms, 22 suites. A/C MINIBAR TV TEL. 395,000 lire ($252.80) double; 570,000–670,000 lire ($364.80–$428.80) suite. Rates include breakfast. AE, DC, MC, V. Parking 30,000 lire ($19.20). Bus: 20, 25, 27, or 30.

The Royal Hotel Carlton, only a few minutes' walk from the railway station and many of the national monuments, is L-shaped, rises six stories high, and has a triangular garden. Some claim it's the best hotel in Bologna, but we happen to think that that honor goes to the Baglioni. The Hilton-style Carlton, 2 blocks south of the station, is a rather austere commercial establishment, catering mainly to business travelers. It's in the modern style, with a balcony and picture window for each bedroom, although the views aren't particularly inspiring.

Dining/Entertainment: One of the most dramatic staircases in Bologna sweeps from the second floor in an elegant crescent to a point near the comfortable American Bar, a grill restaurant that serves decent regional and international food.

Services: Room service, baby-sitting, laundry, valet.
Facilities: Limited facilities for the disabled.

MODERATE

Grand Hotel Elite. Via Aurelio Saffi 36, 40131 Bologna. ☎ **051/649-8222.** Fax 051/649-2426. 153 rms, 20 suites. A/C MINIBAR TV TEL. 175,000 lire ($112) double; 235,000 lire ($150.40) suite. During trade fairs, 350,000 lire ($224) double; 410,000 lire ($262.40) suite. Rates include breakfast. AE, DC, MC, V. Parking 20,000–27,000 lire ($12.80–$17.30). Bus: 13 or 19.

Located on the city's northwestern edge, a 12-minute walk to the center, this eight-story establishment was originally built in the 1970s as a combination of private apartments and hotel rooms. In 1993 the entire structure was transformed into a hotel. The bedrooms are comfortable but lackluster. Even if you're not staying at the hotel, you may want to patronize its restaurant, the Cordon Bleu, which features international food and the classic cuisine of Emilia-Romagna. Also popular is a bar with comfortable banquettes and a good selection of whisky and regional wines.

Hotel Milano Excelsior. Viale Pietramellara 51 (near piazza Medaglie d'Oro), 40121 Bologna. ☎ **051/246178.** Fax 051/249448. 72 rms, 4 suites. A/C MINIBAR TV TEL. 270,000 lire ($172.80) double; 350,000 lire ($224) suite. During trade fairs, 390,000 lire ($249.60) double; 470,000 lire ($300.80). Rates include breakfast. AE, DC, MC, V. Free parking. Bus: 25, 30, 37, 91, or 98.

The Hotel Milano Excelsior, built in the 1950s, is a first-class hotel, and it has all the trappings and fringe benefits associated with its class: a private bath in every soundproof room, an American bar, and a restaurant decorated with crystal chandeliers. The hotel attracts largely a commercial clientele. It has a completely modern decor, although a number of its bedrooms contain more traditional furnishings. The hotel offers excellent service and an attentive staff. The hotel dining room, the Ristorante Felsineo, serves tasty Emilian food.

Tre Vecchi. Via dell'Indipendenza 47, 40121 Bologna. ☎ **051/231991.** Fax 051/224143. 96 rms. A/C MINIBAR TV TEL. 226,000 lire ($144.65) double. During trade fairs, 290,000 lire ($185.60) double. Rates include breakfast. AE, DC, MC, V. Parking 30,000 lire ($19.20); free on street. Bus: 25 or 30.

This hotel was established in the 1970s in a century-old building on a much-traveled street in the center of town. Despite the traffic, the bedrooms are clean, bright, and relatively quiet, thanks to the insulated windows and soundproofing. The gentle humor in the establishment's name ("Three Geriatrics") was conceived by the trio of aging entrepreneurs who originally founded it. The four-story hotel contains two elevators and several lounges where guests can relax and watch TV. The hotel lies a 5-minute walk from the railway station. No meals are served except breakfast.

INEXPENSIVE

Alexander. Viale Pietramellara 47, 40121 Bologna. ☎ **051/247118.** Fax 051/247248. 108 rms. A/C MINIBAR TV TEL. 200,000 lire ($128) double. During trade fairs, 260,000 lire ($166.40) double. Rates include breakfast. AE, DC, MC, V. Parking 10,000 lire ($6.40) outside. Closed Aug. Bus: 25, 30, 37, 91, or 98.

Built in the early 1960s, the Alexander is the best hotel buy near the piazza Medaglie d'Oro, the main hub of car and trail traffic in the city. Perched near the more expensive Hotel Milano Excelsior, the Alexander features desirable bedrooms, with brightly painted foyers, compact furnishings, and neat, tidy baths. The double glass windows help to blot out street noise. The main lounge is crisp and warm, with wood paneling and lounge chairs placed on Turkish rugs.

⑤ **Regina Hotel.** Via dell'Indipendenza 51 (off piazza dell'Otto Agosta), 40121 Bologna. ☎ **051/248878.** Fax 051/224143. 61 rms. A/C MINIBAR TV TEL. 170,000 lire ($108.80) double. During trade fairs (with breakfast), 210,000 lire ($134.40) double. AE, DC, MC, V. Parking 30,000 lire ($19.20). Bus: 25 or 30.

The Regina Hotel was originally built in the 1800s, then modernized in the 1970s. Its functional bedrooms are small and plain, but they're comfortably furnished and a bit of a budget haven in high-priced Bologna. The staff is helpful, and the maids keep everything clean. The hotel has no restaurant, but there's a pleasant bar and a modern lounge dotted with sofas.

WHERE TO DINE
EXPENSIVE

I Carracci. In the Grand Hotel Baglioni, via dell'Indipendenza 8. ☎ **051/225445.** Reservations required. Main courses 25,000–35,000 lire ($16–$22.40); fixed-price menu 90,000 lire ($57.60). AE, DC, MC, V. Mon–Sat 12:30–2:30pm and 7:30–10:30pm. Closed Aug 1–25. Bus: 11 or 27. ITALIAN/INTERNATIONAL.

The most fashionable and *bellissimo* dining spot in Bologna—and arguably the best—this restaurant is named after a family of artists who decorated the premises with frescoes. Its cuisine equals that of the Notai (see below), and the service is impeccable. The elegant dining room, the most harmonious in the city, dates from the 16th century. The frescoes on the ceiling were painted in the 1700s by the Carracci brothers, and their interpretation of the four seasons is richly allegorical and mythical. The seasonally adjusted menu features the freshest produce and the highest-quality meat, poultry, and fish. Some dishes we've enjoyed here include tortellini in brodo, tagliatelle in ragú de Bologna, veal scallop alla bolognese, wild boar cacciatore, and grilled filet of salmon. The wine list is among the finest of any restaurant in the province.

Nuovi Notai. Via de' Pignattari 1. ☎ **051/228694.** Reservations required. Main courses 18,000–25,000 lire ($11.50–$16); fixed-price menu 48,000–60,000 lire ($30.70–$38.40). AE, DC, MC, V. Mon–Sat 12:30–2:30pm and 8–10:30pm. Bus: Any bus from the Termini. ITALIAN.

Hidden behind a lattice- and ivy-covered facade next to the cathedral, within view of one of the most beautiful squares in Italy, this sublime restaurant, often cited as the city's best, draws from a loyal clientele. In summer, sidewalk tables are placed outside. Music lovers and relaxing businesspeople appreciate the piano bar. The decor combines the belle époque with Italian flair and includes artwork, hanging Victorian lamps, and clutches of beautifully arranged flowers on each table.

The fine cooking is based on the best local products Emilia-Romagna has to offer. An attachment to culinary traditions doesn't preclude a modern approach to the cuisine. Menu items include a flan of cheese fondue, gratin of gnocchi with truffles, a filet of beef cooked in *cartoccio* (a paper bag) and garnished with porcini mushrooms, and deboned breast of wild goose. Dessert might be a suprême of almonds served with ricotta cheese and coffee sauce.

MODERATE

Diana. Via dell'Indipendenza 24. ☎ **051/231302.** Reservations recommended. Main courses 18,000–26,000 lire ($11.50–$16.65); fixed-price menu 70,000 lire ($44.80). AE, DC, MC, V. Tues–Sun noon–2:30pm and 7–10:30pm. Closed Jan 1–10 and Aug. Bus: 25 or 27. REGIONAL/INTERNATIONAL.

Set in a late medieval building in the heart of town, this well-recommended restaurant has been a popular fixture in Bologna since around 1920. It offers three gracefully decorated dining rooms and a verdant terrace for outdoor dining. This restaurant was named in honor of the goddess of the hunt, because of the many game and seasonal dishes it served when it was first established. In recent years, although game is still featured in season, it opts for a staple of regional and international cuisine, all of it ompetently prepared. Begin your meal with one of the city's most delicious appetizers—spuma di mortadella, a pâté made of mortadella sausage and served with dainty white toast. You'll never eat baloney again.

Montegrappa da Nello. Via Montegrappa 2. ☎ **051/236331.** Reservations recommended for dinner. Main courses 12,000–40,000 lire ($7.70–$25.60). AE, DC, MC, V. Tues–Sun noon–3pm and 7–11:30pm. Closed Aug. Bus: Any bus from the Termini. BOLOGNESE/ INTERNATIONAL.

The Montegrappa da Nello has a faithful following that swears by its pasta dishes. It's one of the few restaurants that still does the old-fashioned and classic Bolognese cuisine. It's said that if you can't get an invitation to visit a local's house, this is the place to go for tasty Bolognesi specialties. Franco and Ezio Bolini are your hosts, and they insist that all produce be fresh. The restaurant, just a short walk from piazza Maggiore, offers tortellina Montegrappa, a pasta favorite served in a cream-and-meat sauce. Another fine spaghetti pasta dish is graminia, a very fine white spaghetti presented with mushrooms, cream, and pepper. The restaurant is also known for its fresh white truffles and mushrooms. Another sublime salad is made with truffles, mushrooms, Parmesan cheese, and artichokes. For a main course, misto del cuoco is a mixed platter from the chef, featuring a selection of his specialties, including zampone, cotoletta alla bolognese, and scaloppine with fresh mushrooms.

Ristorante al Pappagallo. Piazza della Mercanzia 3C. ☎ **051/232807.** Reservations required. Main courses 36,000–38,000 lire ($23.05–$24.30). AE, DC, MC, V. Mon–Sat 12:30–2:30pm and 8–10:20pm. Bus: Any bus from the Termini. BOLOGNESE.

This restaurant has a faithful following. Long-ago diners have included Einstein, Hitchcock, and Toscanini. It's still going strong, with memories of a glorious past, but it's no longer the finest restaurant in Italy. "The Parrot" is housed on the ground floor of a Gothic mansion, across the street from the landmark 14th-century Merchants' Loggia (a short walk from the leaning towers).

For the best possible introduction, begin your meal with lasagne verde al forno (baked lasagne that gets its green color from minced spinach). And then, for the main course, the specialty of the house: filetti di tacchino, superb turkey breasts baked with white wine, parmigiano cheese, and truffles. Modern low-calorie offerings also appear on today's menu. With your meal, the restaurant serves the amber-colored Albana wine and the sparkling red Lambrusco, two of the best-known wines of Emilia.

INEXPENSIVE

Antica Osteria Romagnola. Via Rialto 13. ☎ **051/263699.** Reservations recommended for dinner. Main courses 15,000–25,000 lire ($9.60–$16). AE, DC, MC, V. Tues 7:30–11pm, Wed–Sat 12:30–2:30pm and 7:30–11pm, Sun 12:30–2:30pm. Closed Jan 1–10 and Aug. Bus: 25, 30, or 50. ITALIAN.

Unlike many of its competitors in Bologna, this establishment offers cuisine from throughout Italy, including the distant south, instead of focusing exclusively on the dishes of Emilia-Romagna. You might begin your meal with one of the unusual and well-flavored risottos, or choose from a savory selection of antipasti. The variety of pastas is also impressive, including ravioli with essence of truffles, garganelli pasta with zucchini, or pasta whipped with asparagus tips. You might also select a terrine of ricotta and arugula; the latter was considered an aphrodisiac by the ancient Romans. For your main course you might try a springtime specialty of capretto (roast goat) with artichokes and potatoes, or filet mignon prepared with aromatic basil.

Grassilli. Via del Luzzo 3. ☎ **051/237938.** Reservations required. Main courses 15,000–25,000 lire ($9.60–$16). AE, DC, MC, V. Thurs–Tues 12:30–2:30pm and 8–10:15pm. Closed July 15–Aug 15, Dec 7–Jan 8, and holidays. Bus: All buses. BOLOGNESE.

Grassilli is a good bet for conservative regional cooking with few deviations from the time-tested formulas that have made Bolognese cuisine famous. It's located in a 1750s building across from an antiques store, on a narrow cobblestone alleyway a short block from the two leaning towers. The restaurant also has a summertime streetside canopy for outdoor dining. At night it can be festive, and your good time will be enhanced if you order such specialties as tortellini in a mushroom-cream sauce, the chef's special tournedos, maccheroni with fresh peas and prosciutto, or from the range of succulent grilled and roasted meats.

⑤ Rosteria da Luciano. Via Nazario Sauro 19. ☎ **051/231249.** Reservations recommended. Main courses 16,000–25,000 lire ($10.25–$16); fixed-price lunch 20,000–35,000 lire ($12.80–$22.40). AE, DC, MC, V. Thurs–Tues noon–2pm and 7:30–10:30pm. Closed Jan 1–8 and Aug. Bus: Any bus from the Termini. BOLOGNESE.

The Rosteria da Luciano is seriously challenging the competition. It serves some of the best food in Bologna. Located on a side street, within walking distance of the city center, it has an art deco style and contains three large rooms with a real Bolognese atmosphere. The front room, opening onto the kitchen, is preferred. As a novelty, there's a see-through window on the street that looks directly into the kitchen.

The chefs not only can't keep any secrets from you, but you get an appetizing preview of what awaits you before you step inside. To begin your gargantuan repast, request the tortellini Petroniani. Well-recommended main dishes include the fritto misto all'Italiana (mixed fry) and the scaloppe con porcini (mushrooms). One savory offering is cotoletta alla bolognese, layered with ham and Parmesan, then baked. A dramatic dessert is crêpes flambés.

A NEARBY PLACE TO DINE

✪ San Domenico. Via Gaspara Sacchi 1, Imola. ☎ **0542/29000.** Reservations recommended. Main courses 45,000–50,000 lire ($28.80–$32); fixed-price lunch (Tues–Sat) 55,000 lire ($35.20); fixed-price Sun lunch or fixed-price dinner (including wine) 80,000 lire ($51.20). AE, DC, MC, V. Tues–Sun 12:30–2:30pm and 8–10:30pm. Closed Jan 1–11 and the first 3 weeks in Aug. ITALIAN.

To an increasing degree, gastronomes from all over Europe and America are traveling to the unlikely village of Imola, which lies 21 miles southeast of Bologna, to savor the offerings of what some food critics consider the best restaurant in Italy. The restaurant can also be easily reached from Ravenna.

The cuisine here is sometimes compared to modern cuisine creations in France. However, owner Gian Luigi Morini claims that his delectable offerings are nothing more than adaptations of festive regional dishes rendered lighter and subtler, then served in more manageable portions. He was born in this rambling stone building whose simple facade faces the courtyard of a neighboring church. For 25 years Signor Morini worked at a local bank, returning home every night to administer his restaurant. Now his establishment is among the primary attractions of Emilia-Romagna.

A tuxedo-clad member of his talented young staff will escort you to a table near the tufted leather banquettes. Meals include heavenly concoctions made with the freshest ingredients. You might select goose-liver pâté studded with white truffles, fresh shrimp in a creamy sweet bell-pepper sauce, roast rack of lamb with fresh rosemary, stuffed suprême of chicken wrapped in lettuce leaves, or fresh handmade spaghetti with shellfish. Signor Morini has collected some of the best vintages in Europe for the past 30 years.

2 Ferrara

259 miles N of Rome, 32 miles N of Bologna, 62 miles SW of Venice

When Papa Borgia, also known as Pope Alexander VI, was shopping around for a third husband for the apple of his eye, darling Lucrezia, his gaze fell on the influential house of Este. From the 13th century, this great Italian family had dominated Ferrara, building up a powerful duchy and a reputation as builders of palaces and patrons of the arts. Alfonse d'Este, son of the shrewd but villainous Ercole I, who was the ruling duke of Ferrara, was an attractive, virile candidate for Lucrezia's much-used hand (her second husband had already been murdered, perhaps by her brother, Cesare, who was the apple of nobody's eye—with the possible exception of Machiavelli).

Although the Este family may have had private reservations (after all, it was common gossip that the pope "knew" his daughter in the biblical sense), they finally consented to the marriage. As the duchess of Ferrara, a position she held until her death, Lucrezia was to have seven children. But one of her grandchildren, Alfonso II, wasn't as prolific as his forebear, although he had a reputation as a roué. He left the family without a male heir. The greedy eye of Pope Clement VIII took quick action on this, gobbling up the city as his fief in the waning months of the 16th century. The great house of Este went down in history, and Ferrara sadly declined under the papacy.

Incidentally, Alfonso II was a dubious patron of Torquato Tasso (1544–95), author of the epic *Jerusalem Delivered*, a work that was to make him the most celebrated poet of the late Renaissance. The legend of Tasso—who is thought to have been insane, paranoid, or at least tormented—has steadily grown over the centuries. It didn't need any more boosting, but Goethe fanned the legend through the Teutonic lands with his late 18th-century drama *Torquato Tasso*. It's said that Alfonso II at one time made Tasso his prisoner.

Ferrara today is still relatively undiscovered, especially by globe-trotting North Americans. The city is richly blessed, with much of its legacy intact. Among the historic treasures remaining are a great cathedral and the Este Castle, along with enough ducal palaces to make for a fast-paced day of sightseeing. Its palaces, for the most part, have long been robbed of their lavish furnishings, but the faded frescoes, the paintings not carted off, and the palatial rooms are reminders of the vicissitudes of power.

ESSENTIALS

GETTING THERE   By Train   Getting there by train is fast and efficient, as Ferrara lies on the main train line between Bologna and Venice. A total of 33 trains a day originating in Bologna pass through here. Trip time is 40 minutes, and the fare is 4,200 lire ($2.70) one-way. Some 24 trains arrive from Venice (trip time: 1 1/2 hours); the one-way fare is 9,800 lire ($6.25).

By Bus   From most destinations the train is best, but if you're in Modena (see below) you'll find 11 bus departures a day for Ferrara. Trip time is between 1 1/2 and 2 hours, and a one-way ticket costs 8,200 lire ($5.25). In Ferrara, bus information for the surrounding area is available by calling 0532/771302.

By Car   From Bologna, take A13 north. From Venice, take A4 southwest to Padua and continue on A13 south to Ferrara.

VISITOR INFORMATION   The **tourist information office** is at corso Giovecca 21 (☎ **0532/209370**). It's open Monday to Saturday from 8:30am to 7pm and on Sunday from 2:30 to 5:30pm.

EXPLORING THE TOWN

Castello Estense. Piazza della Repubblica. ☎ **0532/299279.** Admission 6,000 lire ($3.85) adults, 4,000 lire ($2.55) seniors 65 and over, free for children 9 and under. Tues–Sat 9:30am–5:30pm, Sun 9:30am–4pm. Bus: 1, 2, or 9.

A moated, four-towered castle (lit at night), this proud fortress began as a bricklayer's dream near the end of the 14th century, although its face has been lifted and wrenched around for centuries. It was home to the powerful Este family. Here the dukes went about their daily chores: murdering their wives' lovers, beheading or imprisoning potential enemies, whatever. Today it's used for the provincial and pre-fectural administration offices, and many of its once-lavish rooms may be inspected—notably the Salon of Games, the Room of Games, and the Room of Dawn, as well as a chapel that once belonged to Renata di Francia, daughter of Louis XII.

Il Duomo. Piazza Cattedrale. ☎ **0532/207449.** Free admission. Apr–Sept, daily 7:30am–noon and 3–6:30pm. Oct–Mar, daily 10am–noon and 3–5pm. Bus: 1, 2, or 9.

Located only a short stroll from the Este castle, the Duomo weds the delicate Gothic with the more virile Romanesque. The offspring: an exciting marble facade. Behind the cathedral is a typically Renaissance campanile (bell tower). Inside, the massive structure is heavily baroqued, as the artisans of still another era festooned it with trompe l'oeil. The entrance to the **Museo del Duomo** lies to the left of the atrium as you enter. It's worth a visit just to see works by Ferrara's most outstanding painter of the 15th century, Cosmé Tura. Aesthetically controversial, the big attraction here is Tura's St. George slaying the dragon to save a red-stockinged damsel in distress. Opposite is a work by Jacopo della Quercia depicting a sweet, regal Madonna with a pomegranate in one hand and the Child in the other. This is one of della Quercia's first masterpieces. Also from the Renaissance heyday of Ferrara are some bas-reliefs, notably a *Giano bifronte,* a mythological figure looking at the past and the future, along with some 16th-century *arazzi,* or tapestries, woven by hand.

Palazzo Schifanoia. Via Scandiana 23. ☎ **0532/64178.** Admission 6,000 lire ($3.85) adults, 3,000 lire ($1.90) students and seniors 60 and over, free for children 17 and under. Daily 9am–7pm. Closed major holidays. Bus: 9.

Home to the **Museo Civico d'Arte Antica,** the first part of the Schifanoia Palace was built in 1385 for Albert V d'Este, and later enlarged by Borso d'Este (1450–71). The museum was founded in 1758 and was transferred to its present site in 1898. The first part of the collection then exhibited, which consisted of coins and medals, was enhanced by donations of archeological finds, antique bronzes, small Renaissance plates and pottery, and other collections.

Art lovers are lured to the Salon of the Months to see the astrological cycle. The humanist Pellegrino Prisciani at court conceived the subjects of the cycle, though Cosmé Tura, the official court painter for the Estes, was probably the organizer of the works. Tura was the founder of the Ferrarese School, to which belonged, among others, Ercole de' Roberti and Francesco del Cossa, who painted the March, April, and May scenes. In the wall cycle, which represents the 12 months of the year, each month is subdivided into three horizontal bands: the lower band shows scenes from the daily life of courtiers and people, the middle one the relative sign of the zodiac, and the upper one presents the triumph of the classical divinity for that particular myth. The frescoes form a complex presentation, leading to varying interpretations as to their meaning.

Palazzo dei Diamanti. Corso Ercole d'Este 21. ☎ **0532/20988.** Admission 10,000 lire ($6.40). Tues–Sun 9:30am–1pm and 3:30–7pm. Bus: 9.

The Palazzo dei Diamanti, another jewel of d'Este splendor, is so named because of the diamond-shaped stones on its facade. Of the handful of museums sheltered here, the **National Picture Gallery (Pinacoteca Nazionale)** is the most important. It houses the works of the Ferrarese artists—notably the trio of old masters, Tura, del Cossa, and Roberti. The collection covers the chief period of artistic expression in Ferrara from the 14th to the 18th century. The palace also houses the **Municipal Gallery of Modern Art,** which sponsors the most important modern art exhibitions in town.

Casa Romei. Via Savonarola 30. ☎ **0532/240341.** Admission 4,000 lire ($2.55). Mon–Fri 8:30am–2pm, Sat–Sun 8:30am–7:30pm. Bus: 1 or 9.

This 15th-century palace was the property of John Romei, a friend and confidant of the fleshy Duke Borso d'Este, who made the Este realm a duchy. John (or Giovanni) was later to marry one of the Este princesses, although we don't know if it was for love or power or both. In later years, Lucrezia and her gossipy coterie—the ducal carriage drawn by handsome white horses—used to descend on the Romei house, perhaps to receive Borgia messengers from Rome. The house is near the Este tomb. Its once-elegant furnishings have been carted off, but the chambers—many with terracotta fireplaces—remain, and the casa has been filled with frescoes and sculpture.

WHERE TO STAY

✪ **Duchessa Isabella.** Via Palestro 70, 44100 Ferrara. ☎ **0532/202121.** Fax 0532/202638. 22 rms, 6 suites. A/C MINIBAR TV TEL. 430,000 lire ($275.20) double; 550,000–950,000 lire ($352–$608) suite. Rates include breakfast. AE, DC, MC, V. Free parking. Bus: 1, 2, or 9.

This hotel was the private home of the head of one of the region's most respected Jewish organizations until the late 1980s. In 1990 it reopened as a five-star hotel with a spectacular decor. Today it's a member of the illustrious Relais & Châteaux hotel chain. Named in honor of the d'Este family's most famous ancestor, Isabella, the hotel maintains a lavish garden—which adjoins several other gardens to appear larger than it is—and many of the building's original frescoes. The bedrooms are each decorated in a different color scheme, and are identified by the names of the flowers whose colors they most closely resemble. Each imbues a sense of history, is outfitted with all the electronic amenities a visitor might want, and is very, very comfortable.

Dining/Entertainment: The hotel operates an elegant restaurant that's set beneath lavishly gilded and painted ceilings. (In summer the venue moves outside into the garden.) The cuisine is based on the traditional recipes of Emilia-Romagna, although a wide choice of less esoteric dishes is also available.

Services: A horse-drawn landau will take guests on excursions around Ferrara's historic center. There's also room service, conference facilities, laundry and valet service, and free use of bicycles.

Ripagrande Hotel. Via Ripagrande 21, 44100 Ferrara. ☎ **0532/765250.** Fax 0532/764377. 20 rms, 20 junior suites. A/C MINIBAR TV TEL. 300,000 lire ($192) double; from 350,000 lire ($224) junior suite. Rates include breakfast. AE, DC, MC, V. Parking 20,000 lire ($12.80). Bus: 1 or 9.

The Ripagrande, one of the most unusual hotels in town, occupies one of the city's Renaissance palaces. Rich coffered ceilings, walls in Ferrarese brickwork, 16th-century columns, and a wide stairway with a floral cast-iron handrail characterize the broad entrance hall. Inside the hotel are two Renaissance courtyards decorated with columns and capitals. Half of the hotel's 40 rooms are junior suites with sleeping areas connected to an internal stairway. The furnishings are modern and tasteful. Laundry and room service are provided.

WHERE TO DINE

Grotta Azzurra. Piazza Sacrati 43. ☎ **0532/209152.** Reservations recommended. Main courses 11,000–20,000 lire ($7.05–$12.80). AE, DC, MC, V. Mon–Tues and Thurs–Sat 12:30–2:30pm and 7:30–9:30pm, Sun 12:30–2:30pm. Closed Jan 2–10 and Aug 1–15. Bus: Any bus from the Termini. BOLOGNESE/EMILIANA.

Behind a classic brick facade on a busy square, the Grotta Azzurra seems like a restaurant you might encounter on the sunny isle of Capri, not in Ferrara. It was established back in the *la dolce vita* days of the 1950s. However, the cuisine is firmly entrenched in the northern Italian kitchen. It's best to visit in the autumn when favorite dishes include wild boar and pheasant, usually served with polenta. Many sausages, served as antipasti, are made with game as well. More esoteric dishes include a boiled calf's head and tongue, while a local favorite is boiled stuffed pork leg. The chef is also an expert at grilled meats, especially pork, veal, and beef.

La Provvidenza. Corso Ercole I d'Este 92. ☎ **0532/205187.** Reservations required. Main courses 15,000–30,000 lire ($9.60–$19.20). AE, DC, MC, V. Tues–Sun noon–2:30pm and 8–10pm. Closed Aug 11–17. Bus: 3, 5, or 11. ITALIAN.

La Provvidenza stands on the same street as the Palazzo dei Diamanti. The building itself is from around 1750, and there has been a restaurant here for at least a century, although the present management dates only from the 1970s. It has a farm-style interior, with a little garden where the regulars request tables in fair weather. The antipasti table is the finest we've seen—or sampled—in Ferrara. Really hearty eaters should order a pasta, such as fettuccine with smoked salmon, before tackling the main course, perhaps perfectly grilled and seasoned veal chops. Other specialties include pasticchio alla Ferrarese (macaroni mixed with a mushroom-and-meat sauce laced with a creamy white sauce) and fritto misto di carne, or mixed grill. The dessert choice is wide and luscious. Take a large appetite to this local favorite.

3 Modena

25 miles NW of Bologna, 250 miles NW of Rome, 81 miles N of Florence

After Ferrara fell to Pope Clement VIII, the duchy of the Este family was established at Modena in the closing years of the 16th century. Lying in the Po Valley, the provincial and commercial city possesses many great art treasures that evoke its more glorious past. On the food front, the chefs of Modena enjoy an outstanding reputation in hard-to-please gastronomic circles. Traversed by the ancient Roman road, via Emilia, Modena (pronounced *Mo*-den-ah) is often visited by European art connoisseurs, less frequently by overseas travelers.

Many visitors who care little about antiquities come to Modena just to visit the Ferrari and Maserati car plants. Ask at the tourist office (see below) for details and a map. Those who can veer from northern Italy's mainline attractions for a few hours will find a visit to Modena very rewarding.

ESSENTIALS

GETTING THERE **By Train** There are good connections to and from Bologna (one train every 30 minutes); trip time is 20 minutes, and a one-way fare is 3,400 lire ($2.20). Trains arrive from Parma once per hour (trip time: 40 minutes); the one-way fare is 5,000 lire ($3.20).

By Bus The train is better. However, if you're in Ferrara (see above), one local ATCM bus (no. 7) leaves Ferrara for Modena every hour; trip time is 1 1/2 hours and a one-way fare is 8,200 lire ($5.25). In Modena, call 059/308801 for information.

By Car   From Bologna, take autostrada A1 northeast until you see the turnoff for Modena.

VISITOR INFORMATION   The **tourist information office** is on via Canalgrande (☎ **059/220136**), open Monday, Tuesday, and Thursday to Saturday from 10:30am to 12:30pm and 4 to 7pm.

SEEING THE SIGHTS

✪ **Il Duomo.** Piazza del Duomo. ☎ **059/216078.** Free admission. Mon–Sat 10:30am–noon and 3:30–5:30pm. Bus: 7 or 11.

One of the glories of the Romanesque in northern Italy, the Duomo of Modena was built in a style that will be familiar to those who've been to Lombardy. It was founded in the summer of the closing year of the 11th century, and designed by an architect named Lanfranco, with Viligelmo serving as decorator.

The work was carried out by Campionesi masons from Lake Lugano. The cathedral, consecrated in 1184, was dedicated to St. Geminiano, the patron saint of Modena, a 4th-century Christian and defender of the faith. Towering from the rear is the Ghirlandina, a 12th- to 14th-century campanile, 285 feet tall. Leaning slightly, the bell tower guards the replica of the Secchia Rapita (stolen bucket), which was garnered as booty from a defeated Bolognese.

The facade of the Duomo features a 13th-century rose window by Anselmo da Campione. It also boasts Viligelmo's main entryway, with pillars supported by lions, as well as Viligelmo bas-reliefs depicting scenes from Genesis. But don't confine your look to the front. The south door, the so-called Princes' Door, was designed by Viligelmo in the 12th century and is framed by bas-reliefs that illustrate scenes in the saga of the patron saint. You'll find an outside pulpit from the 15th century, with emblems of Matthew, Mark, Luke, and John.

Inside, there's a vaulted ceiling, and the overall effect is gravely impressive. The Modenese wisely and prudently restored the cathedral during the first part of the 20th century, so that its present look resembles the original design. The gallery above the crypt is an outstanding piece of sculpture, supported by four lions. The pulpit, also intriguing, is held up by two hunchbacks. The crypt, where the body of the patron saint was finally taken, is a forest of columns. In it, you'll find Guido Mazzoni's *Holy Family* group in terra-cotta, which was completed in 1480.

After visiting the crypt, head up the stairs on the left, where the custodian (tip expected) will lead you to the Museum of the Cathedral. In many ways the most intriguing of the Duomo's art displayed here are the metopes, which used to adorn the architecture. Like gargoyles, these profane bas-reliefs are a marvelous change of pace from solemn ecclesiastical art. One, for example, is part bird and part man—with one hoof. But that's not all: He's eating a fish whole.

✪ **Galleria Estense.** Palazzo del Musei, largo Sant'Agostino 48 (off via Emilia). ☎ **059/235004.** Admission: Gallery, 8,000 lire ($5.10) adults, free for children 17 and under and seniors 60 and over; library, free. Gallery, Tues and Fri–Sat 9am–7pm, Wed–Thurs 9am–2pm, Sun 9am–1pm. Library, Apr–Oct, Mon–Sat 9am–2pm; Nov–Mar, Mon–Fri 9am–8pm, Sat 9am–2pm. Bus: 7 or 11.

The Estense Gallery is noted for its paintings from the Emilian or Bolognese school from the 14th to the 18th century. The nucleus of the collection was created by the Este family in Ferrara's, and afterward, Modena's heyday as duchies. Some of the finest work is by Spanish artists, including a miniature triptych by El Greco of Toledo and a portrait of Francesco I d'Este by Velázquez. Other works of art include Bernini's bust of Francesco I, plus paintings by Cosmé Tura, Correggio, Veronese, Tintoretto, Carracci, Reni, and Guercino.

One of the greatest libraries in southern Europe, the **Biblioteca Estense** (☎ 059/222248), contains around 500,000 printed works and 13,000 manuscripts. An assortment of the most interesting volumes is kept under glass for visitors to inspect. Of these, the most celebrated is the 1,200-page *Bible of Borso d'Este,* bordered with stunning miniatures.

WHERE TO STAY

Canalgrande Hotel. Corso Canalgrande 6, 41100 Modena. ☎ **059/217160.** Fax 059/221674. 68 rms, 4 suites. A/C MINIBAR TV TEL. 290,000 lire ($185.60) double; from 450,000 lire ($288) suite. Rates include breakfast. AE, DC, MC, V. Parking 15,000 lire ($9.40). Bus: 7, 12, or 14.

Located in the old town, the Canalgrande Hotel is housed in a 300-year-old stucco palace. It has more atmosphere and charm than the much bigger and more highly rated Hotel Real Fini on via Emilia. The Canalgrande has elaborate mosaic floors, Victorian-era furniture, carved and frescoed ceilings, and chandeliers. There's a garden behind the hotel whose central flowering tree seems filled with every kind of bird in Modena. Some visitors find the monumental oil paintings of the salons like a museum. Under the basement's vaulted ceiling is a tavern, La Secchia Rapita (the Stolen Bucket).

❸ Hotel Roma. Via Farini 44, 41100 Modena. ☎ **059/222218.** Fax 059/223747. 53 rms. MINIBAR TV TEL. 130,000 lire ($83.20) double. Rates include breakfast. AE, DC, MC, V. Parking 15,000 lire ($9.60). Bus: 7 or 11.

The Hotel Roma, which became a hotel around 1950, is a buff-and-white neoclassical building about 2 blocks from the cathedral. The building dates from the 17th century, when it belonged to the duke of Este. It's one of our favorite hotels in its category in Modena. It's also the preferred hotel of many of the opera stars who gravitate to Pavarotti's hometown for concerts and auditions. The windows and doors are soundproof, presumably so anyone can imitate his or her favorite diva while practicing an aria. The guest rooms have high ceilings, tasteful colors, and comfortable and attractive furnishings. The lobby is a long skylit room with an arched ceiling and a bar and a snack bar at the far end.

WHERE TO DINE

❉ Fini. Rue Frati Minori 54. ☎ **059/223314.** Reservations recommended. Main courses 26,000–50,000 lire ($16.65–$32). AE, DC, MC, V. Wed–Sun 12:30–2:30pm and 8–10:30pm. Closed last week in July, all of Aug, and Dec 24–31. Bus: 7 or 11. MODENESE/INTERNATIONAL.

A visit to this restaurant alone is well worth making the trip to Modena. Proudly maintaining the high reputation of the city's kitchens, Fini is one of the best restaurants you're likely to encounter in Emilia-Romagna. It's Pavarotti's favorite restaurant when he's in town. In spite of its modernized art nouveau decor, including Picasso-esque murals and banquettes, the restaurant was founded in 1912.

For an appetizer, try the creamy green lasagne or the tortellini (prepared in six different ways here—for example, with truffles). For a main dish, the gran bollito misto reigns supreme. A king's feast of boiled meats, accompanied by a selection of four different sauces, is wheeled to your table. The meat board includes zampone, a specialty of Modena, here prepared with stuffed pigs' trotters boiled with beef, a calf's head, ox tongue, chicken, and ham. After all this rich fare, you may settle for the fruit salad for dessert. For wines, Lambrusco is the local choice, and it's superb.

Ristorante Da Enzo. Via Coltellini 17 (off piazza Mazzini). ☎ **059/225177.** Reservations recommended. Main courses 15,000–30,000 lire ($9.60–$19.20). AE, DC, MC, V. Tues–Sun noon–3pm and 7–10:30pm. Bus: 7, 9, 12, 14, or 19. MODENESE.

Clean, conservative, and well known in Modena, this restaurant lies one floor above street level in an old building in the historic center's pedestrian zone. Specialties of the house include all the classic dishes of Modena, such as pappardelle (wide noodles) with rabbit meat, lasagne verde, several kinds of tortellini, and an array of grilled meats liberally seasoned with herbs and balsamic vinegar. Zampone (stuffed pigs' trotters) is another specialty.

4 Parma

284 miles NW of Rome, 60 miles NW of Bologna

Parma, which straddles via Emilia, was the home of Correggio, Il Parmigianino, Bodoni (of type fame), Toscanini, and Parmesan cheese. It rose in influence and power in the 16th century as the seat of the Farnese duchy, then in the 18th century came under Bourbon rule. For years Parma has been a favorite of art lovers.

It has also been a mecca for opera lovers such as Verdi, the great Italian composer. Verdi, whose works included *Il Trovatore* and *Aïda,* was born in the small village of Roncole, north of Parma, in 1813. In time his operas echoed through the Teatro Regio, the opera house that was ordered constructed by Queen Marie Louise. Because of Verdi, Parma became a center of music, and even today the opera house is jam-packed in season. It's said that the Teatro Regio is the most "critical Verdi house" in Italy.

ESSENTIALS

GETTING THERE **By Train** Parma is conveniently served by the Milan–Bologna rail line, with 20 trains a day arriving from Milan (trip time: 80 minutes); the one-way fare is 11,700 lire ($7.50). From Bologna, 34 trains per day arrive in Parma (trip time: 1 hour); the one-way fare is 7,200 lire ($4.60). There are also seven connections a day from Florence; a one-way fare is 15,500 lire ($9.90).

By Bus From major towns or cities in Italy, it's best to go by train because of faster connections. The bus comes into play only if you're planning to visit provincial towns in the Parma area. Information and schedules are available at the **bus terminal** at piazzale della Chiesa near the train station (☎ **0521/273251**).

By Car From Bologna, head northwest along autostrada A1.

VISITOR INFORMATION The **tourist information center** is at piazza del Duomo 5 (☎ **0521/234735**), open Monday to Friday from 9am to 12:30pm and 3 to 5pm and on Saturday from 9am to 12:30pm.

WHAT TO SEE & DO
THE TOP ATTRACTIONS

✪ **Il Duomo.** Piazza del Duomo. ☎ **0521/235886.** Free admission. Daily 7am–12:30pm and 3–7pm. Bus: Any bus from the Termini.

Built in the Romanesque style in the 11th century, with 13th-century Lombard lions guarding its main porch, the dusty-pink Duomo stands side by side with a campanile (bell tower) constructed in the Gothic-Romanesque style and completed in 1294. The facade of the cathedral is highlighted by three open-air loggias. Inside, two darkly elegant aisles flank the central nave. The octagonal cupola was frescoed by the "divine" Correggio. Master of light and color, Correggio (1494–1534) was one of Italy's greatest painters of the High Renaissance. His fresco here, *Assumption of the Virgin,* foreshadows the baroque. The frescoes were painted from 1522 to 1534. In the transept to the right of the main altar is a Romanesque bas-relief, *The Deposition from the Cross* by Benedetto Antelami, which is somber, with each face bathed in tragedy. Made in 1178, the bas-relief is the best-known work of the 12th-century artist, who was the most important sculptor of the Romanesque in northern Italy.

❂ Battistero. Piazza del Duomo 7. ☎ **0521/235886.** Admission: 3,000 lire ($1.90). Daily 9am–noon and 3–6pm. Bus: Any bus from the Termini.

Among the greatest Romanesque buildings in northern Italy, the Baptistery was the work of Antelami. The project was begun in 1196, although the date it was actually completed is in doubt. Made of salmon-colored marble, it's spanned by four open tiers (the fifth one is closed off). Inside, the Baptistery is richly frescoed with biblical scenes: a *Madonna Enthroned* and a *Crucifixion*. But it's the sculpture by Antelami that forms the most worthy treasure and provides the basis for that artist's claim to enduring fame.

Abbey of St. John (San Giovanni Evangelista). Piazzale San Giovanni 1. ☎ **0521/235592.** Free admission. Daily 8:30am–noon and 3–6pm. Bus: Any bus from the Termini.

Behind the Duomo is this church of unusual interest. After admiring the baroque front, pass into the interior to see yet another cupola by Correggio. Working from 1520 to 1524, the High Renaissance master depicted the *Vision of San Giovanni.* Vasari liked it so much that he became completely carried away in his praise, suggesting the "impossibility" of an artist's conjuring up such a divine work and marveling that it could actually have been painted "with human hands." Correggio also painted a St. John with pen in hand, in the transept (over the doorway to the left of the main altar). Il Parmigianino, the second Parmesan master, also did some frescoes in the chapel at the left of the entrance.

Casa Natale e Museo di Arturo Toscanini. Via Rodolfo Tanzi 13. ☎ **0521/285499.** Free admission. Tues–Sun 10am–1pm, Tues–Sat 3–6pm. Bus: 1, 7, or 11.

This is the house where the great musician and conductor was born in 1867. Toscanini was unquestionably the greatest orchestral conductor of the first half of the 20th century, and one of the most astonishing musical interpreters of all time. He spent his childhood and youth in this house, which has been turned into a museum with interesting relics and a record library, containing all the recorded works that he conducted.

MORE ATTRACTIONS

After viewing Parma's ecclesiastical buildings, you'll find its second batch of attractions conveniently sheltered under one roof at the **Palazzo della Pilotta,** via della Pilotta 5. This palazzo once housed the Farnese family in Parma's heyday as a duchy in the 16th century. Badly damaged by bombs in World War II, it has been restored and turned into a palace of museums.

❂ Galleria Nazionale. In the Palazzo della Pilotta, piazza della Pace, via della Pilotta 5. ☎ **0521/233309.** Admission 12,000 lire ($7.70) adults, free for children 17 and under and for seniors 60 and over. Daily 9am–1:45pm. Bus: Any bus from the Termini.

The most important component of the Palazzo della Pilotta is the National Gallery. Filled with the works of Parma artists from the late 15th century to the 19th century—notably paintings by Correggio and Parmigianino—the National Gallery offers a limited but well-chosen selection of art. In one room is an unfinished head of a young woman attributed to da Vinci. Correggio's *Madonna della Scala* (of the stairs), the remains of a fresco, is also displayed. But his masterpiece—one of the celebrated paintings of northern Italy—is *St. Jerome with the Madonna and Child.* Imbued with a delicate quality, it represents age, youth, love—a gentle ode to tenderness. In the next room is Correggio's *Madonna della Scodella* (with a bowl), with its agonized faces. You'll also see Correggio's *Coronation*, a golden fresco and a work of great beauty, and his less successful *Annunciation*. One of Parmigianino's best-known paintings is here, *St. Catherine's Marriage*, with its rippling movement and subdued colors.

You can also view **St. Paul's Chamber,** which Correggio frescoed with mythological scenes, including one of Diana. The chamber faces onto via Macedonio Melloni. On the same floor as the National Gallery is the **Farnese Theater,** evocative of Palladio's theater at Vicenza. Originally built in 1618, the structure was bombed in 1944 and has been restored.

Museo Archeologico Nazionale. In the Palazzo della Pilotta, piazza della Pace, via della Pilotta 5. ☎ **0521/233718.** Admission 4,000 lire ($2.55) adults, free for children 17 and under 18 and for seniors 60 and over. Tues–Sun 9am–1:30pm. Bus: Any bus from the Termini.

This most interesting museum houses Egyptian sarcophagi, Etruscan vases, Roman- and Greek-inspired torsos, Bronze Age relics, and its best-known exhibit called *Tabula Alimentaria,* a bronze-engraved tablet dating from the reign of Trajan and excavated at Velleia in the province of Piacenza.

WHERE TO STAY

Farnese International. Via Reggio 51A, 43100 Parma. ☎ **0521/994247.** Fax 0521/992317. 76 rms. A/C MINIBAR TV TEL. 169,000 lire ($108.15) double. Rates include breakfast. AE, DC, MC, V. Free parking outdoors, 12,000 lire ($7.70) indoors. Bus: 11.

This hotel is not up to the standards of the Stendhal (see below) but makes for a good overnight stopover. It's located in a quiet area but convenient to the town center, air-port, and fairs. Parma specialties are served in the hotel restaurant, Il Farnese. The bedrooms are comfortably furnished in Italian marble. Laundry and room service are provided.

❸ Hotel Button. Strada San Vitale 7 (off piazza Garibaldi), 43100 Parma. ☎ **0521/208039.** Fax 0521/238783. 41 rms. TV TEL. 139,000 lire ($88.95) double. Rates include continental breakfast. AE, DC, MC, V. Closed July 8–31. Bus: Any bus from the Termini.

The Hotel Button is a local favorite, one of the best bargains in the town center. This is a family-owned and -run hotel, and you're made to feel welcome. The rooms are simply but comfortably furnished. The hotel doesn't have a restaurant—in Parma this is no problem at all—but will serve you a complimentary continental breakfast.

Palace Hotel Maria Luigia. Viale Mentana 140, 43100 Parma. ☎ **0521/281032.** Fax 0521/ 231126. 101 rms. A/C MINIBAR TV TEL. 325,000 lire ($208) double. Rates include breakfast. AE, DC, MC, V. Parking 20,000 lire ($12.50). Bus: Any bus from the Termini.

This hotel, built of brick in 1974 and located near the station, was and still is a wel-come addition to the Parma hotel scene. It caters especially to business travelers and is still superior to the Stendhal (see below). Bold colors and molded-plastic built-ins set the up-to-date mood, and the comfortable modern bedrooms feature soundproof walls as well as other amenities such as tiled baths with toiletries. There's a very Italian-looking American bar on the premises. The hotel also has one of the best res-taurants in Parma, Maxim's, which serves excellent Italian and international specialties daily (closed in August). Room service is available around the clock.

Park Hotel Stendhal. Piazzetta Bodini 3, 43100 Parma. ☎ **0521/208057.** Fax 0521/ 285655. 60 rms. A/C MINIBAR TV TEL. 290,000 lire ($185.60) double. Rates include breakfast. AE, DC, MC, V. Parking 15,000 lire ($9.40). Bus: 2, 8, 9, or 13.

The Park Hotel Stendhal sits on a square near the opera house, a few minutes' walk from many of the city's important sights and 6 blocks south of the station. The bedrooms are well maintained and furnished with contemporary pieces that are reproductions of various styles, ranging from rococo to provincial. Try for one of the traditional-looking rooms where the furnishings are classic with matching fabrics and patterned carpets. Some of the rooms are more standard and modern. There's a traditional American bar and lounge, with comfortable armchairs for before- and after-dinner drinks. La Pilotta, the hotel restaurant, serves a cuisine typical of Parma, with a medley of international dishes. Laundry service and room service are also provided.

WHERE TO DINE

The chefs of Parma are known throughout Italy for the quality of their cuisine. Of course, Parmesan cheese has added just the right touch to millions of Italian meals, and the word *parmigiana* is quite familiar to American diners.

Croce di Malta. Borgo Palmia 8. ☎ **0521/235643.** Reservations recommended. Main courses 15,000–25,000 lire ($9.60–$16). AE, DC, MC, V. Mon–Sat 12:30–2:30pm and 7:30–10:30pm. Closed 2 weeks in Aug. Bus: Any bus from the Termini. PARMIGIANA.

Local legend has it that angry citizens plotted to assassinate the last duke of Parma while he was drowning in *vino* at this tavern.

All the dishes for which Parma is famous are served here, even some esoteric ones, such as cappellotti, a pasta that turns magenta because it's made with beets, or tortelli, made a golden amber with the addition of pumpkin, although another version is made with potatoes. Tagliatelle is served here almost in any style. Other dishes include roast veal stuffed with cheese and chicken flavored with wine and Gorgonzola cheese.

✪ La Greppia. Strada Garibaldi 39A. ☎ **0521/233686.** Reservations required. Main courses 22,000–40,000 lire ($14.10–$25.60). AE, DC, MC, V. Wed–Sun 12:30–2:30pm and 7:30–10:30pm. Closed July. Bus: 2, 8, or 13. PARMIGIANA.

La Greppia has an unpretentious decor yet it's near the top of every gourmet's list of the finest dining rooms of Parma. The competition is keen in Parma, but its only serious rival is Parizzi, with which it's locked in a neck-to-neck race. Through a plate-glass window at one end of the dining room, you can see the all-woman staff at work in the kitchen. Leading the team is the co-owner, Paola Cavassini, and her good-natured husband, Maurizio Rossi, who presides over the dining room. The chefs adjust their menus depending on the season. Likely dishes include veal kidneys sautéed with fines herbes and a demi-glacé sauce, breast of chicken with orange sauce, pappardella alla Greppia (prepared with cream and dried flap mushrooms), and roast rack of rabbit flavored with thyme. Many dishes are flavored, in season, with fresh thyme or mushrooms, even cherries. All of this good food is served in a building dating from the 17th century. The tarts made with fresh fruit are succulent desserts. Even better, the kitchen is known for its compelling chocolate cake, which one reviewer claimed was much better than the famed Sachertorte served at the Hotel Sacher in Vienna.

✪ Parizzi. Strada della Repubblica 71. ☎ **0521/285952.** Reservations required. Main courses 20,000–35,000 lire ($12.80–$22.40); fixed-price menu 65,000 lire ($41.60). Tues–Sat noon–2:30pm and 7–9:30pm. Closed Dec 24–25. AE, DC, MC, V. Bus: 3, 4, 5, or 8. PARMIGIANA.

Located in the historic core of Palma, the building that houses Parizzi dates to 1551, when it was first established as an inn. Seated under the restaurant's skylit patio, the people of Parma, known for their exacting tastes and demanding palates, here enjoy the rich cuisine for which their town is celebrated. This restaurant is among the two best in Parma, comparable in cuisine to La Greppia. Both richly deserve their

Frommer stars. After you're shown to a table in one of the good-size dining rooms, a trolley cart filled with antipasti is wheeled before you, containing shellfish and salmon among its many delectable offerings. The stuffed vegetables are especially good (try the zucchini). You might begin with the chef's specialty, crêpes alla parmigiana— that is, crêpes stuffed with fontina, Parma ham, and ricotta, or with truffles in September. In May you'll want to try the asparagus fresh from the fields. A good main course is the veal scaloppine with fontina and ham. Desserts include zabaglione laced with marsala.

5 Ravenna

46 miles E of Bologna, 90 miles S of Venice, 227 miles N of Rome

Ravenna is one of the most unusual towns in Emilia-Romagna. It's a sleepy town today, but one with memories of a great past, which is the only reason people show up on its doorstep, which they do today in hordes. It's famous for its Early Christian and Byzantine mosaics, the most splendid outside Istanbul, many of them dating from the 6th century. In turn the capital of the Western Roman Empire (from A.D. 402), the Visigoth Empire (from A.D. 473), and the Byzantine Empire under the emperor Justinian and the empress Theodora (A.D. 540–752), Ravenna became one of the greatest cities on the Mediterranean. Although today it looks much like any other Italian city, the low Byzantine domes of its churches still evoke its Eastern past.

ESSENTIALS

GETTING THERE   By Train   Ravenna can be visited on a day trip from Bologna as there is frequent service; a one-way fare is 7,200 lire ($4.60). There's also frequent service to Ferrara; a one-way fare is 11,700 lire ($7.50). At Ferrara, you can make connections to Venice, for 17,200 lire ($11) each way.

By Bus   Trains are better. Once at Ravenna, however, you'll find both a regional (ATR) system and a municipal (ATM) bus network serving the area. Buses depart from outside the train station. The tourist office (see below) will have bus schedules and more details, depending on where you want to go, or call 0544/35288 for information.

By Car   From Bologna, head east along autostrada A14.

VISITOR INFORMATION   The **tourist information center** is at piazza Mameli 4 (☎ **0544/35404**). Here you can purchase a ticket to visit six monuments for a single cost of 9,000 lire ($5.75). These sights are the Battistero Neoniano, the Archepiscopal Museum and Church of St. Andrea, the Church of San Vitale, the Mausoleum of Galla Placidia, the Adrian Baptistery, and the Basilica of St. Apollinare Nuovo. The office is open Monday to Saturday from 9am to 1pm and 3 to 6pm; in summer it's also open on Sunday from 9am to noon.

EXPLORING THE TOWN

Battistero Neoniano. Piazza del Duomo. ☎ **0544/33696.** Admission (including admission to Museo Arcivescovile) 4,000 lire ($2.55). Daily 9am–7pm; off-season, daily 9:30am–4:30pm. Closed Dec 25 and Jan 1. Bus: All buses.

The octagonal Baptistery was built in the 5th century. In the center of the cupola is a tablet showing John the Baptist baptizing Christ. The circle around the tablet depicts in dramatic mosaics of deep violet-blues and sparkling golds the 12 crown-carrying Apostles. The Baptistery originally serviced a cathedral that no longer stands. (The present-day Duomo of Ravenna was built around the mid-18th century and is of little interest except for some unusual pews.) Beside it is a campanile from the 11th century, perhaps earlier.

Museo Arcivescovile and Church of St. Andrea. Piazza Arcivescovado. ☎ **0544/33696.** Admission 4,000 lire ($2.55). Tues–Sat 9am–7pm (to 4:30pm in winter), Sun 9am–1pm. Bus: Any bus from the Termini.

This twofold attraction is housed in the Archbishop's Palace, which dates from the 6th century. In the museum, the major exhibit is a throne carved out of ivory for Archbishop Maximian, which dates from around the mid-6th century.

In the chapel or oratory dedicated to St. Andrea are brilliant mosaics. Pause a while in the antechamber to look at an intriguing mosaic above the entrance. It's an unusual representation of Christ as a warrior, stepping on the head of a lion and a snake. Although haloed, he wears partial armor, evoking "Onward, Christian Soldiers." The chapel—built in the shape of a cross—contains other mosaics that are "angelic," both figuratively and literally. Busts of saints and apostles stare down at you with the ox-eyed look of Byzantine art.

Basilica di San Vitale. Via San Vitale 17. ☎ **0544/33696.** Admission 5,000 lire ($3.20). Daily 9am–7pm; off-season, daily 9:30am–4:30pm. Bus: Any bus from the Termini.

This octagonal domed church dates from the mid-6th century. The mosaics inside—in brilliant greens and golds, lit by light from translucent panels—are among the most celebrated in the Western world. Covering the apse is a mosaic rendition of a clean-shaven Christ astride the world, flanked by saints and angels. To the right is a mosaic of Empress Theodora and her court, and to the left, the man who married the courtesan-actress, Emperor Justinian, and his entourage. If you can tear yourself away from the mosaics long enough, you might admire the church's marble decoration. Seven large arches span the temple, but the frescoes of the cupola are unimaginative.

۞ Mausoleum of Galla Placidia. Via San Vitale. ☎ **0544/34266.** Entrance included with admission to Basilica di San Vitale (see above). Daily 9am–7pm. Bus: Any bus from the Termini.

This 5th-century chapel is so unpretentious that you'll think you're at the wrong place. But inside it contains some exceptional mosaics—dripping with antiquity, but not looking it. Translucent panels bring the mosaics alive in all their grace and harmony—rich and vivid with peacock-blue, moss-green, Roman gold, eggplant, and burnt orange. The mosaics in the cupola literally glitter with stars. Popular tradition has it that the cross-shaped structure houses the tomb of Galla Placidia, sister of Honorius, but there is evidence that this claim may be false.

Museo Nazionale di Ravenna. Via Fiandrini (adjacent to via San Vitale). ☎ **0544/34424.** Admission 8,000 lire ($5.10) adults, free for children 17 and under and for seniors 60 and over. Tues–Sun 8:30am–7:30pm. Bus: Any bus from the Termini.

This museum contains archeological objects from the early Christian and Byzantine periods—icons, fragments of tapestries, medieval armaments and armory, sarcophagi, ivories, ceramics, and bits of broken pieces from the stained-glass windows of St. Vitale.

Basilica of St. Apollinare in Classe. Località Classe. ☎ **0544/527004.** Free admission. Daily 8:30am–noon and 2–5:50pm (to 6:30pm in summer). Bus: 4 or 44 from the railroad station (every 20 minutes) or piazza Caduti.

Located about 3¹/₂ miles south of the city (it can be visited on the way to Ravenna if you're heading north from Rimini), this church dates from the 6th century, having been consecrated by Archbishop Maximian. Before the waters receded, Classe was a seaport of Rome's Adriatic fleet. Dedicated to St. Apollinare, the bishop of

Ravenna, the early basilica stands side-by-side with a campanile—both symbols of faded glory now resting in a lonely low-lying area. Inside the basilica is a central nave flanked by two aisles, the latter containing tombs of ecclesiastical figures in the Ravenna hierarchy. The floor—once carpeted with mosaics—has been rebuilt. Along the central nave are frescoed tablets. Two dozen marble columns line the approach to the apse, where you'll find the major reason for visiting the basilica. The mosaics are exceptional, rich in gold and turquoise, set against a background of top-heavy birds nesting in shrubbery. St. Apollinare stands in the center, with a row of lambs on either side lined up as in a processional, the 12 lambs symbolizing the Apostles, of course.

WHERE TO STAY

⑤ Bisanzio. Via Salara 30, 48100 Ravenna. ☎ **0544/217111.** Fax 0544/32539. 38 rms. A/C MINIBAR TV TEL. 158,000–198,000 lire ($101.10–$126.70) double. Rates include breakfast. AE, DC, MC, V. Parking 20,000 lire ($12.80).

Bisanzio stands in the heart of town, just a few minutes' walk from many of Ravenna's treasures. It's cheaper and has more personality than the Jolly (see below). This is a pleasantly coordinated and completely renovated modern hotel. The guest rooms have attractive Italian styling, some with mottled batik wall coverings. It's ideal for those who want the comfort of a well-organized hotel, with good bedrooms, offering simplicity and all the other modern conveniences that travelers have come to expect. There's an uncluttered breakfast room with softly draped windows, and guests also have use of a garden.

Hotel Centrale Byron. Via IV Novembre 14, 48100 Ravenna. ☎ **0544/212225.** Fax 0544/34114. 54 rms. A/C TV TEL. 116,000–138,000 lire ($74.25–$88.30) double. Rates include breakfast. AE, DC, MC, V. Bus: 1 or 11.

The Hotel Central Byron is an art deco–inspired hotel located a few steps from piazza del Popolo. The lobby is an elegantly simple combination of white marble and brass detailing. The long, narrow public rooms, arranged "railroad style," include an alcove sitting room, a long hallway, and a combination TV room, bar, and snack and breakfast-room area. The rooms are simply but comfortably furnished, although not as good as those at the Bisanzio.

Jolly Hotel. Piazza Mameli 1, 48100 Ravenna. ☎ **0544/35762.** Fax 0544/216055. 75 rms, 3 suites. A/C MINIBAR TV TEL. 190,000–230,000 lire ($121.60–$147.20) double; from 300,000 lire ($192) suite. Rates include breakfast. AE, DC, MC, V. Parking 20,000–30,000 lire ($12.80–$19.20). Bus: 1 or 11.

This four-story hotel, built in 1950 in the postwar crackerbox style with a bunkerlike facade, contains two elevators and a conservative decor of stone floors and lots of paneling. The Jolly is a favorite of business travelers, but it's too sterile for our tastes. Ravenna, however, suffers from a dearth of first-class accommodations. The hotel lies 50 yards from the railway station. Its La Veranda restaurant serves a standard local and international cuisine. Services include baby-sitting, laundry, and room service from 7am to 11pm.

WHERE TO DINE

Bella Venezia. Via IV Novembre 16. ☎ **0544/212746.** Reservations required. Main courses 13,000–22,000 lire ($8.30–$14.10); fixed-price menu 28,000 lire ($17.90). AE, DC, MC, V. Mon–Sat noon–2:30pm and 7–10pm. Closed Dec 23–Jan 15. Bus: 1 or 11. EMILIA-ROMAGNA.

Bella Venezia, located a few steps from piazza del Popolo and next door to the Hotel Centrale Byron, is the kind of well-known restaurant hotel managers recommend to their clients. Despite this restaurant's name, the only Venetian dish prepared here is fegato (liver) alla veneziana, which is, admittedly, delicious. Other than that, the repertoire is almost exclusively regional, with such dishes as risotto, cappelletti alla romagnola (round, cap-shaped pasta stuffed with a mixture of ricotta, roasted pork loin, chicken breast, and nutmeg, served with a meat sauce), and garganelli pasta served with whatever happens to be in season (baby asparagus, mushrooms, or peas). All pastas are made by hand, and the place is very family-run, very warm, very old Italy.

⑤ **Ristorante La Gardèla.** Via Ponte Marino 3. ☎ **0544/217147.** Reservations recommended. Main courses 10,000–12,000 lire ($6.40–$7.70). AE, DC, MC, V. Fri–Wed noon–1:45pm and 7–10pm. Closed Aug 10–25. Bus: 1 or 11. EMILIA-ROMAGNA.

Ristorante La Gardèla, located a few steps from one of Ravenna's most startling leaning towers, is spread out over two levels with paneled walls lined with racks of wine bottles. The waiters bring out an array of typical but savory dishes. Specialties include tortelloni della casa (made with ricotta, cream, spinach, tomatoes, and herbs) and spezzatino alla contadina (roast veal served with potatoes, tomatoes, and herbs). Considering the quality of the food and the first-rate ingredients, this is Ravenna's best restaurant buy.

Ristorante Tre Spade. Via Faentina 136. ☎ **0544/500522.** Reservations recommended. Main courses 18,000–30,000 lire ($11.50–$19.20); fixed-price menu 55,000 lire ($35.20). AE, DC, MC, V. Tues–Sat 12:30–2:30pm and 7:30–10:30pm, Sun 12:30–2:30pm. Closed the first 3 weeks of Aug. Bus: 1 or 11. INTERNATIONAL/EMILIAN.

This is an appealing spot that has been serving good cuisine since 1980. The town's finest dining choice, Ristorante Tre Spade keeps prices under control while magically combining solid technique and inventiveness. Specialties include an asparagus parfait accompanied by a zesty sauce of bits of green peppers and black olives, and an appetizing assortment of carpaccio (thinly sliced raw meat covered with sliced sheets of Parmesan cheese with raw artichoke hearts in olive oil). This might be followed by taglioni with smoked-salmon sauce, veal cooked with sage, spaghetti with fruits of the sea (which includes clams in their shells), green gnocchi in Gorgonzola sauce, or roast game in season, plus a good collection of wines. The menu changes frequently, and daily specials are offered according to the market.

Settling into Venice 9

One rainy morning as we were leaving our hotel—a converted *palazzo*—a decorative stone fell from the lunette, narrowly missing us. For a second it looked as if we were candidates for a gondola funeral cortège to the island of marble tombs, San Michele. In dismay, we looked back at the owner, a woman straight from a Modigliani portrait. From the doorway, she leaned like the Tower of Pisa, mocking the buildings of her city. Throwing up her hands, she sighed: "Venezia, Venezia," then turned and went inside.

Stoically, she had long ago surrendered to the inevitable decay that embraces Venice like moss at the base of the pilings. Venice is a preposterous monument to both the folly and the obstinacy of humankind. It shouldn't exist . . . but it does, much to the delight of thousands upon thousands of tourists, gondoliers, lacemakers, hoteliers, restaurateurs, and glassblowers.

Centuries ago, in an effort to flee the barbarians, Venetians left drydock and drifted out to a flotilla of "uninhabitable" islands in the lagoon. Survival was difficult enough, but no Venetian has ever settled for mere survival. The remote ancestors of the present inhabitants created the world's most beautiful city.

To your children's children, however, Venice may be nothing more than a legend. It's sinking at a rate of about $2^1/_2$ inches per decade. It's estimated that one-third of the city's art will have deteriorated hopelessly within the next decade or so, if action is not taken to save it. Clearly, Venice is in peril. One headline proclaimed, "The Enemy's at the Gates."

But for however long it lasts, the Venice of today, decaying or not, will be one of be the highlights of your trip through Italy. It lacks the speeding cars and roaring mopeds of Rome; instead, you make your way through Venice either by boat or on foot. The city would be ideal were it not for the hordes upon hordes—far more than any barbarian invasion—that tramp across Venice today, creating a virtual emergency for those who need space to walk and air to breathe. These masses overwhelm the squares, such as piazza San Marco, and make thoroughfares almost impossible to navigate.

In the sultry heat of the Adriatic in summer, the canals of Venice become a smelly stew. Steamy, overcrowded July and August are the worse times to visit. May and June and September and October are much more ideal.

Although it's one of the most—if not *the* most—enchantingly lovely and evocative cities on earth, you do pay a price, literally and figuratively, for all this beauty. The city is virtually selling its past to the world, even more so than Florence, and anybody who's been here leaves complaining of the outrageous prices.

In addition, tourists have virtually eroded what local life and flavor is left in the city. Since the 19th century Venice has thrived off its visitors, everyone from Lord Byron to Thomas Mann, but high prices have forced out many locals who used to live here. They fled across the lagoon to tacky, dreary Mestre, an industrial complex that was launched to help boost the regional economy and make it far less dependent on tourism. Mestre, with its factories, helps keep Venice relatively industry free, although it spews pollution across the city, which is hardly what the art of Venice needs.

Still, Venice endures.

For how long? That is the question.

1 Orientation

ARRIVING

All roads lead not necessarily to Rome but, in this case, to the docks on the mainland of Venice. The arrival scene at the unattractive piazzale Roma is filled with nervous expectation; even the most veteran traveler can become confused. Whether you arrive by train, bus, car, or airport limo—everyone walks to the nearby docks to select a method of transport to his or her hotel. The cheapest way is by *vaporetto* (public motorboat), the more expensive by gondola or motor launch (see "Getting Around," later in this chapter).

If your hotel lies near one of the public vaporetto stops, you can sometimes struggle with your own luggage until you reach the hotel's reception area. In any event, the one time-tested rule for Venice-bound travelers is that excess baggage is bad news, unless you're willing to pay dearly to have it carried for you. Porters cannot accompany you and your baggage on the vaporetto.

BY PLANE   You can now fly from North America to Venice via Rome on Alitalia. You'll land at the **Marco Polo Aeroporto** at Mestre. Boats depart directly from the airport, taking visitors to a terminal near piazza San Marco.

It's less expensive, however, to take a bus from the airport, a trip of less than 5 miles. The bus takes you across the ponte della Libertà to the Stazione Santa Lucia, Venice's train station, at piazzale Roma. From there you can make connections to most parts of Venice, including the Lido.

If you need to find out about flight arrivals or departures at Marco Polo Airport, call 041/541-5491.

BY TRAIN   Trains pull into the **Stazione di Santa Lucia,** at piazzale Roma (☎ **041/715555** for information about rail connections). Travel time from Rome is about $5^1/_4$ hours; from Milan, $3^1/_2$ hours; from Florence, 4 hours; and from Bologna, 2 hours. The best—and least expensive—way to get from the station to the rest of town is to take a vaporetto, which depart near the main entrance to the station.

BY BUS   Buses from mainland Italy arrive at piazzale Roma. For information about schedules, call the **ACTV office** at piazzale Roma (☎ **041/528-7886**). If you're coming from a distant city in Italy, it's better to take the train. But Venice has good bus connections with nearby cities such as Padua. A one-way fare from Padua to Venice

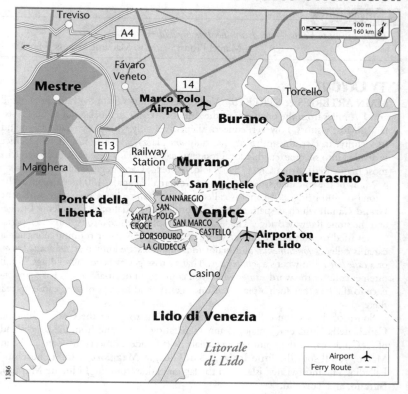

Treviso

A4

Fávaro
Veneto

Mestre

14

Marco Polo
Airport ✈

Torcello

Burano

E13

Railway
Station

Marghera

Murano

11

San Michele

Sant'Erasmo

**Ponte della
Libertà**

CANNAREGIO

SAN
POLO

SANTA
CROCE

SAN MARCO

Venice

DORSODURO

CASTELLO

LA GIUDECCA

✈ **Airport on
the Lido**

Casino

Lido di Venezia

*Litorale
di Lido*

Airport ✈
Ferry Route – – –

0   100 m
     160 km

1386

(or vice versa) is 4,800 lire ($3.05). The cheapest way to reach the heart of Venice from the bus station is by vaporetto.

BY CAR Venice has autostrada links with the rest of Italy, with direct routes from such cities as Trieste (driving time: 1½ hours), Milan (3 hours), and Bologna (2 hours). Bologna is 94 miles southwest of Venice; Milan, 165 miles west of Venice; and Trieste, 97 miles east. Rome is 327 miles to the southwest.

If you arrive by car, there are several multitiered parking areas at the terminus where the roads end and the canals begin. One of the most visible is the **Garage San Marco,** piazzale Roma (☎ 041/523-5101), near the vaporetto, gondola, and motor launch docks. You'll be charged 30,000 to 45,000 lire ($19.20 to $28.80) per day, maybe more, depending on the size of your car. From spring to fall this municipal car park is nearly always filled. You're more likely to find parking on the **Isola del Tronchetto** (☎ 041/520-7555), which costs 34,000 lire ($21.75) for the first 12 hours and 12,000 lire ($7.70) for each additional 12-hour period. From Tronchetto, take vaporetto no. 82 to piazza San Marco. If you have heavy luggage, you'll need a water taxi. Parking is also available at Mestre.

VISITOR INFORMATION

Visitor information is available at the **Azienda di Promozione Turistica,** Palazzetto Selva-Giardinetti Reali (Molo S. Marco) (☎ 041/522-6356). It's open Monday to Saturday from 9:40am to 3:30pm. However, these hours are not always consistent.

Impressions

When I went to Venice—my dream became my address.
                                    —Marcel Proust, letter to Madame Strauss, May 1906

CITY LAYOUT

MAIN ARTERIES & STREETS   Venice lies $2^1/_2$ miles from the Italian mainland
and $1^1/_4$ miles from the open seas of the Adriatic. It's an archipelago of some 117 islands. Most visitors, however, concern themselves only with piazza San Marco and
its vicinity. In fact, the entire city has only *one* piazza, which is San Marco. Venice
is divided into six quarters that local residents call **sestieri.** These are San Marco (the
most frequented), Santa Croce, San Paolo, Castello, Cannaregio, and Dorsoduro.

Many of the so-called streets of Venice are actually **canals,** 150 in all, spanned by
a total of 400 bridges. A canal is called a *rio.* If Venice has a main street, it's the
Grand Canal, which is spanned by three bridges: the Rialto, the Academy Bridge,
and the stone Railway Bridge. The Grand Canal splits Venice into two unequal parts.

Get used to a lot of unfamiliar street designations. A street running alongside a
canal is called a *fondamenta,* and major thoroughfares are known as *salizzada, ruga,*
or a *calle larga.* But what's a *sottoportego?* That's a passageway beneath buildings. You'll
often encounter the word *campo* when you come to an open-air area. That's a reference to the fact that such a place was once grassy, and in days of yore cattle grazed
there.

South of the section called Dorsoduro, which is south of the Grand Canal, is
Canele della Guidecca, a major channel separating Dorsoduro from the large island
of La Guidecca. At the point where Canale della Guidecca meets the Canale di San
Marco, you'll spot the little **Isola di San Giorgio Maggiore,** with a church by
Palladio. The most visited islands in the lagoon, aside from the **Lido,** are **Murano,
Burano,** and **Torcello.**

FINDING AN ADDRESS   A maniac must have numbered the buildings of Venice
at least six centuries ago. The numbering system is completely illogical. Therefore,
before you set out for a specific place, get detailed instructions and have someone
mark the establishment on your map. Instead of depending on street numbers, try
to locate the nearest cross street instead. Once there, look for signs posted outside
rather than trying to find a number, since many have decayed so much over the ages
that they're no longer legible.

But with all the directions in the world and with all the signposts and maps, the
best thing for an explorer in Venice is to get lost, which you'll invariably do anyway.

STREET MAPS   If you really want to tour Venice and find that little hidden
trattoria on a nearly forgotten street, you can forget about using any map that doesn't
detail every street and have an index in the back. The best of the lot is the **Falk** map
of Venice. It details everything, and since it's pocket size, you can open it in the
Adriatic winds without fear of it blowing away as many larger maps do. It's sold at
many news kiosks and at all bookstores. Another good source is *Frommer's Walking
Tours: Venice,* which includes 13 maps of the city and the environs.

THE NEIGHBORHOODS IN BRIEF

San Marco   Everybody goes here: It's the center of Venice. Napoléon called it the
drawing room of Europe, and it's one crowded drawing room today. The heart of
Venetian life for more than a thousand years, it's here that you'll find the major attractions: piazza San Marco, or St. Mark's Square, dominated by St. Mark's Basilica.

Just outside the basilica is the campanile, or bell tower, a reconstruction of the one that collapsed in 1902. Around the corner is the Palazzo Ducale, or Doge's Palace, with its Bridge of Sighs. In spite of these stellar attractions, this is basically a gaudy tourist belt filled with some of the most overpriced coffee shops in the world, including Florian's, founded in 1720, and Quadri, which opened in 1775. The most celebrated watering hole, however, is away from the square—Harry's Bar, founded by Giuseppe Cipriani but made famous by Hemingway. In and around the square are some of the most convenient hotels in Venice (although not necessarily the best) and an array of expensive shops and trattorie catering to the Yankee dollar, the British pound, the German mark, or whatever.

Cannaregio   This is the gateway to Venice. It lies away from the railroad station at the northwest side of Venice and is the first of the six sestieri. It shelters about a third of the population of Venice, some 20,000 residents. At its heart is Santa Lucia Station, dating from 1955. The area also embraces the old Jewish Ghetto, the first one on the continent. Jews began to move here at the beginning of the 16th century, when they were segregated from the rest of the city. From here, the word *ghetto* later became a generic term all over Europe. Attractions in this area include the Ca' d'Oro, the finest example of the Venetian-Gothic style of palatial architecture; the Chiese della Madonna dell'Orto, a 15th-century church known for its Tintorettos, and Church of Santa Maria dei Miracoli, with a Madonna portrait supposedly able to raise the dead. Unless you're coming here to view some church or palace, or even the Ghetto, this area of Venice may not detain you long, as its hotels and restaurants are not the best. Some of the cheapest lodging is found along Lista di Spagna, immediately to the left as you exit the train station.

San Polo   This is the heart of commerical Venice and the smallest of the six sestieri. It's reached by crossing the ponte di Rialto (Rialto Bridge) spanning the Grand Canal. The shopping here is much cheaper than in the boutiques around piazza San Marco. One of the major attractions here is the Erberia, which Casanova wrote about in his 18th-century biography. Both wholesale and retail markets still pepper this ancient site. At its center is the Church of San Giacomo di Rialto, oldest in the city. The district also encloses the Scuola Grande di San Rocco, a repository of the works of Tintoretto, which is the reason most upmarket tourists visit San Polo. Campo San Polo is one of the oldest and widest squares in Venice and is one of the principal venues for Carnival. San Polo is also filled with moderately priced hotels and a large number of trattorie, many of which specialize in seafood. In general, the hotels and restaurants are cheaper here than along San Marco but not as cheap as those around the Termini in Cannaregio.

Castello   The shape of Venice is often likened to a fish. If so, Castello is the tail of the fish. The largest and most varied of the six sestieri, Castello is home to many attractions, such as the Arsensal, and some of the city's plushest hotels, including the Danieli. One of the district's most notable attractions is the Gothic Church of Santa Giovanni e Paolo, or Zanipolo. This was the Pantheon of the doges of Venice. Cutting through the sestiere is campo Santa Maria Formosa, one of the largest open squares of Venice. The district's most elegant and frequented street is riva degli Schiavoni, running along the Grand Canal and the site of some of the finest hotels and restaurants in Venice. It's also one of the city's favorite promenades.

Santa Croce   This district, which takes its name from an old church that was long ago destroyed, generally follows the snakelike curve of the Grand Canal from piazzale Roma to a point just short of the ponte di Rialto. It's split into two rather different neighborhoods. The eastern part is in the typically Venetian style and is one of the least crowded parts of Venice, although it has some of the Grand Canal's loveliest palazzi. The western side is more industrialized and isn't very interesting to explore.

Dorsoduro This district is compared variously to New York's Greenwich Village or London's Chelsea, although in truth it doesn't resemble either section very much. The least populated of the sestieri, it's filled with old homes and half-forgotten churches. It's the southernmost section of the historic district, and its major attraction is the Gallerie dell'Accademia. Its second-most-visited attraction is the Guggenheim Foundation. It's less trampled than the areas around the Rialto Bridge and piazza San Marco. Its most famous church is La Salute, whose first stone was laid in 1631. The Zattere, a broad quay built after 1516, is one of the favorite promenades in Venice. Cafás and pensiones abound in the area, as do trattorie.

The Lido This slim, sandy island cradles the Venetian lagoon, offering protection against the Adriatic Sea. The Lido is Italy's most fashionable bathing resort and site of the fabled Venice Film Festival. It's $7^1/2$ miles long and about half a mile wide, although reaching $2^1/2$ miles at its broadest point. It was the setting for many famous books, including Thomas Mann's *Death in Venice* and Evelyn Waugh's *Brideshead Revisited.* Some of the most fashionable and expensive hotels in Venice are found along the Lido Promenade. The most famous places to stay include the Grand Hotel Excelsior and the Grand Hotel des Bains, but there are cheaper establishments as well. The best way to get around is by bike or tandem, which can be rented at via Zara and Gran Viale.

Torcello Lying $6^1/2$ miles northeast of Venice, Torcello is called "the mother of Venice," having been settled between the 9th and 17th centuries. Once it was the most populous of the islands in the lagoon, but since the 18th century it has been nearly deserted. If you ever hope to find solitude in Venice, you'll find it here, following in the footsteps of Hemingway. It's visited today chiefly by those wishing to see its Cattedrale di Torcello, with its stunning Byzantine mosaics, and to lunch at Locanda Cipriani.

Burano Perched $5^1/2$ miles northeast of Venice, Burano is the most populous of the lagoon islands. In the 16th century it produced the finest lace in Europe. Today lace is still made here, although nothing like the production of centuries ago. Inhabited since Roman times, Burano is different from either Torcello or Murano. Forget lavish palaces. The houses are often simple and small and painted in deep blues, strong reds, and striking yellows. The island is still peopled by fisherfolk, and one of the reasons to visit is to dine in one of its trattorie where, naturally, the specialty is fish.

Murano This island, located three-quarters of a mile northeast of Venice, has been famed for its glassmaking since 1291. Today Murano is the most visited island in the lagoon. Once a closely guarded secret, Murano glassmaking is now clearly visible to any tourist who wants to visit the island and observe the technique on a guided tour. You can also visit a glass museum, the Museo Vetrario di Murano, and see two of the island's notable churches, San Pietro Martire and Santi Maria e Donato. You will likely be on the island for lunch, and there are a number of moderately priced trattorie to be found here as well.

2 Getting Around

Since you can't hail a taxi, at least not on land, get ready to walk and walk and walk. Of course, you can break up your walks with vaporetto or boat rides.

Wonderful city, streets full of water, please advise.

—Robert Benchley

It may seem that excessive attention is devoted in this chapter to porters, water taxis, vaporetti, and gondoliers, but we've seen too many visits to Venice marred by a hassle that dampens the tourist's enthusiasm for the city at the outset. Providing you can overcome the problem of getting yourself and your luggage transported safely—and without fisticuffs—to your hotel, you'll be set to embark on one of life's grand experiences: the exploration of Venice.

BY PUBLIC TRANSPORTATION Much to the chagrin of the once-ubiquitous gondolier, the motorboats, or *vaporetti,* of Venice provide inexpensive and frequent, if not always fast, transportation in this canal-riddled city. An *accelerato* is a vessel that makes every stop and a *diretto* makes only express stops. The average fare is 4,000 lire ($2.55). In summer, the vaporetti are often fiercely crowded. Pick up a map of the system at the tourist office. Rarely will you have to wait more than 15 minutes for the approach of a vaporetto. The vaporetti run daily, with frequent service from 7am to midnight, then hourly between midnight and 7am.

Visitors to Venice can purchase a **biglietto turistico,** or tourist ticket, for 15,000 lire ($9.60) that allows unlimited travel all day long on any of city's boat services. A 3-day ticket costs 30,000 lire ($19.20).

BY WATER TAXI/MOTOR LAUNCH It costs more than the public vaporetto, but you won't be hassled as much when you arrive with your luggage if you hire one of the city's many private motor launches, called **taxi acquei.** You may or may not have the cabin of one of these sleek vessels to yourself, since the captains fill their boats with as many passengers as the law allows before taking off. Your porter's uncanny radar will guide you to one of the inconspicuous piers where a water taxi waits.

The price of a transit by water taxi from piazzale Roma (the road and rail terminus) to piazza San Marco costs 80,000 lire ($51.20) and up for one to six passengers. The sailors seem to follow in the footsteps of the most cunning of doges. To their credit, the captains are usually adroit at depositing you, with your luggage, at the canalside entrance to your hotel or on one of the smaller waterways within a short walking distance of your destination. You can also call for a water taxi—try the **Cooperativa San Marco** (☎ 041/522-2303).

BY GONDOLA When riding in a gondola, two major agreements have to be reached: (1) the price of the ride and (2) the length of the trip. If you even vaguely seem like one of Barnum's suckers, you're likely to be taken on both counts. It's a common sight in Venice to see a gondolier huffing and puffing to take his passengers on a "quickie," often reducing the hour to 15 minutes. The gondolier, with his eye on his watch, is anxious to dump his load and pick up the next batch of passengers. Consequently, his watch almost invariably runs fast.

There *is* an accepted official rate schedule for gondoliers, but we've never known anyone to honor it. The actual fare depends on how effective you are in standing up to the gondolier's attempt to get more money out of you. The official rate is 80,000 lire ($51.20), but virtually no one pays that amount. Prices begin at 100,000 lire ($64) for up to 50 minutes, maybe a lot more. One gondolier confided to us that he settled for that amount in 1972. Today most gondoliers will ask *at least* double the official rate, and will reduce your time aboard to 30 to 40 minutes, or even less. Prices go up after 8pm. In fairness to the gondoliers, it must be said that they have

The Gondola

In *Death in Venice,* Thomas Mann wrote: "Is there anyone but must repress a se-cret thrill, on arriving in Venice for the first time—or returning thither after long absence—and stepping into a Venetian gondola? That singular conveyance, come down unchanged from ballad times, black as nothing else on earth except a cof-fin—what pictures it calls up of lawless, silent adventures in the plashing night; or even more, what visions of death itself, the bier and solemn rites and last soundless voyage!"

In the 12th century the word *gondola* referred to the canal boats with flat bot-toms traversing the canals of Venice. But it wasn't until the latter 18th century that the gondola became "the taxi of Venice." The building of gondolas became a thriv-ing and highly individualized craft, calling forth great artistry.

When gondolas once got too ostentatious, the doge in 1562 thought too much money was being spent on them so he decreed that henceforth all gondolas would be painted black. Gondolas—at least the best of them—became known for their precision at maneuvering through the canals of the city.

It's estimated that in the heyday of the Renaissance, long before the age of the vaporetto, there were some 15,000 gondolas afloat in Venice, and what a sight it must have been, like a giant festive regatta. Nowadays there are only about 350 gondolas, mostly serving tourists wanting a ride for the thrill of it as opposed to using it as a taxi.

There are only about three gondola makers still left in Venice, although at one time there were dozens. In former days, a gondola workshop might turn out 35 gondolas a year. Nowadays a gondola maker makes perhaps only four vessels, sell-ing each craft for some $25,000 apiece, although the price could be much higher depending on elaborate ornamentation.

You can still visit a gondola workshop. Dating from the 17th century, **Squèro di San Trovaso,** Dorsoduro 1097 (☎ **041/523-7762**), is the oldest boatyard in Venice. The kings of Italy used to have gondolas constructed for themselves at this workshop in sleepy Dorsoduro. Once this boatyard was the official one sanctioned by the city to make its gondolas. To show how times have changed, today's official municipal water vehicle is a speedboat.

an awful job, which is romanticized out of perspective by the world. They row boat-loads of tourists across hot, smelly canals with such endearments screamed at them as "No sing! No pay!" And these fellows must make plenty of lire while the sun shines, as their work ends when the first cold winds blow in from the Adriatic.

Two major **gondola stations** at which you can rent gondolas include piazza San Marco (☎ **041/520-0685**) and ponte di Rialto (☎ **041/522-4904**).

ON FOOT   This is the only way to explore Venice unless you plan to see it from a boat on the Grand Canal. Everybody walks in Venice—there's no other way. The streets are too crowded for bicycles or much else. In summer the overcrowding is so severe you'll often have a hard time finding room for your feet on the street.

FAST FACTS: Venice

American Express   AMEX is located at San Marco 1471 (☎ 041/520-0844), in the San Marco area. City tours and mail handling can be obtained here. The office is open May to October, Monday to Saturday from 8am to 8pm for currency exchange and from 9am to 5:30pm for all other transactions; November to April, Monday to Friday from 9am to 5:30pm and on Saturday from 9am to 12:30pm.

Baby-sitters   In lieu of a central booking agency, arrangements have to be made individually at various hotels. Obviously, the more advanced your notice, the better your chances of getting an English-speaking sitter.

Bookstores   One of the best stocked, with titles in both English and Italian, is Serenissima, Salizzada San Julian 739 (☎ 041/520-0919).

Car Rentals   Obviously you won't need a car in Venice. But you may need one upon departure. You can make arrangements at Europcar, piazzale Roma 496H (☎ 041/523-8616), or at Avis, piazzale Roma 496G (☎ 041/522-5825). Both offices are open Monday to Friday from 8:30am to 12:30pm and 2:30 to 6pm and on Saturday from 8:30am to noon.

Consulates   There is no **U.S. Consulate** in Venice; the closest is in Milan, at via Principe Amedeo 2 (☎ 02/290351). The **British Consulate** is at Dorsoduro 1051 (☎ 041/522-7207), open Monday to Friday from 10am to noon and 2 to 3pm.

Currency Exchange   There are many banks in Venice where you can exchange money. You might try the Deutch Bank SPA, San Marco 2216 (☎ 041/520-7024). Many travelers find that Guetta Viaggi, San Marco 1289 (☎ 041/520-8711), offers the best rates in Venice.

Dentist   Your best bet is to have your hotel call and set up an appointment with an English-speaking dentist. The American Express office and the British Consulate also have lists.

Doctors   See "Hospitals," below. The suggestion given for a dentist in Venice (see above) also pertains to English-speaking doctors.

Drugstores   If you need a drugstore in the middle of the night, call **192** for information about which one is open. Pharmacies take turns staying open late. A well-recommended centrally located pharmacy is International Pharmacy, via XXII Marzo 2067 (☎ 041/522-2311).

Emergencies   Call **113** for police, **523-0000** for an ambulance, and **522-2222** to report a fire.

Eyeglasses   This service is available at Querzola, Cannaregio 5902 (☎ 041/522-8366).

Hairdressers/Barbers   A good choice for both women and men is Bruno, Cannaregio 3924 (☎ 041/528-5833). Call first for an appointment.

Holidays   See "When to Go" in Chapter 3.

Hospitals   Get in touch with the Civili Riuniti di Venezia, campo Santi Giovanni e Paolo (☎ 041/260711).

Information   See "Visitor Information" under "Orientation," earlier in this chapter.

Laundry/Dry Cleaning   Go to Lavaget, Cannaregio 1269 (☎ 041/715976), on fondamenta Pescaria off rio Tera San Leonardo. It's open Monday to Friday from 8:15am to 12:30pm and 3 to 7pm. This is the most convenient self-service laundry to the rail station, only a 5-minute walk away. It also does dry cleaning.

Lost Property   The central office for recovering lost property is the Ufficio Oggetti Rinvenuti, an annex to the Municipio (town hall) at San Marco 4134 (☎ 041/

270-8225), on calle Piscopia o Loredan, lying off rive del Carbon on the Grand Canal. It's open on Monday, Wednesday, and Friday from 9:30am to 12:30pm.

Luggage Storage/Lockers   These services are available at the main rail station, Stazione di Santa Lucia, at piazzale Roma (☎ 041/715555).

Newspapers/Magazines   The *International Herald Tribune* and *USA Today* are sold at most newsstands and in many first-class and deluxe hotels, as are the European editions (in English) of *Time* and *Newsweek.*

Police   See "Emergencies," above.

Post Office   The main post office is at Fondaco dei Tedeschi (☎ 041/271-7111), in the vicinity of the Rialto Bridge. It's open Monday to Saturday from 8:15am to 7pm.

Radio   The main station is run by RAI, the Italian state radio and TV network, and broadcasts in Italian only (at least you can listen to the music even if you don't speak the tongue). Vatican Radio is received in Venice and often carries English-language news broadcasts. Throughout the night and for part of the day, short-wave radio reception in Venice is excellent, including British (BBC), American (VOA), and Canadian (CBC). At night, the American Armed Forces Network (AFN) from Munich or Frankfurt can be heard on regular AM radio (middle or medium wave).

Rest Rooms   These are available at piazzale Roma and various other places in Venice, but are not as plentiful as they should be. Often you'll have to rely on the facilities of a cafe, although you should purchase something, perhaps a light coffee, as in theory commercial establishments reserve their toilets for customers only. Most museums and galleries have public toilets. You can also use the public toilets at the Albergo Diurno, on via Ascensione, just behind piazza San Marco. Remember, SIGNORI means men and SIGNORE is for women.

Safety   The curse of Venice is the pickpocket artist. Violent crime is rare. But because of the overcrowding in vaporetti and even on the small narrow streets, it's easy to pick pockets. Purse snatchers are commonplace as well. A purse snatcher can dart out of nowhere, grab a purse, and in seconds have disappeared down some narrow dark alleyway. Keep valuables locked in a safe in your hotel, if one is provided.

Taxes   A 19% value-added tax (called IVA) is added to the price of all consumer goods and products and most services, such as those in hotels and restaurants.

Taxis   See "Getting Around," earlier in this chapter.

Telegrams/Telex/Fax   The post office maintains a telegram and fax service 24 hours a day. You can also call Italcable at 170 if you wish to send an international telegram; otherwise, call 186.

Television   The RAI is the chief television network broadcasting in Italy. Every TV in Venice receives three government-sponsored channels—RAI-1, RAI-2, and RAI-3—as well as numerous independent channels including Rete 4, Canale 5, and Italia 1.

Transit Information   For flight information, call 041/541-5491; for rail information, 041/715555; and for bus schedules, 041/528-7886.

Useful Telephone Numbers   To check on the time, call 161; for the weather, 191.

3 Accommodations

Venice has some of the most expensive hotels in the world, including the Gritti Palace and the Cipriani. But there are also dozens of unheralded and moderately priced places to stay, often on narrow, hard-to-find streets. Venice has never been known, however, as an inexpensive destination.

Because of their age and lack of uniformity, hotels in Venice offer widely varying rooms. For example, it's entirely possible to stay in a hotel generally considered "expensive," while paying only a "moderate" rate—that is, if you'll settle for the less desirable accommodation. Many so-called inexpensive hotels and boarding houses have two or three rooms considered in the "expensive" category. Usually these accommodations are more spacious and open to a view.

The cheapest way to visit Venice is to book in a *locanda,* or small inn, which are rated below the *pensioni* (boarding houses). Standards are highly variable in these places, many of which are dank, damp, and dark. Rooms even in many second- or first-class hotels are often cramped, as space has always been a problem in Venice. It's estimated that in this "City of Light," at least half the bedrooms in any category are dark, so be duly warned. Rooms with lots of light opening onto the Grand Canal carry a hefty price tag.

Often facilities normally associated with first-class and deluxe hotels don't exist in Venetian hotels, many of which have floor plans laid out centuries ago. If an elevator is essential for you, always inquire in advance when booking a room.

The most difficult times to find rooms are during the February Carnevale, Easter, and anytime from June to September. Because of the tight hotel situation, it's advisable to make reservations as far in advance as possible. After those peak times, you can virtually have your pick of rooms, as many travelers avoid the damp, cold, and windy months of winter.

Most hotels, if you ask at the reception desk, will grant you a 10% to 15% discount in winter (that is, from November until March 15). But getting this discount may require a little negotiation at the desk. A few hotels close in January if there's no prospect of business.

Should you arrive without a reservation, go to the one of the **AVA (Hotel Association) reservations booths** located at the train station, at the municipal parking garage at piazzale Roma, at the airport, and at the information point on the mainland where the highway comes to an end. The main office is at piazzale Roma (☎ **041/522-8640**). You're required to post a deposit to secure a room, which is then rebated on your final hotel bill. Depending on the classification of hotel, deposits range from 20,000 to 75,000 lire ($12.80 to $48) per person. All hotel booths are open daily from 9am to 8 or 9pm.

If you want to avoid the crowds, consider staying in San Polo or Dorsoduro, which aren't as touristy and where you stand a chance of experiencing the "real" Venice. Connoisseurs of Venice often prefer the Dorsoduro because the presence of the university means that there are lots of informal cafás and inexpensive trattorie.

Most visitors, however, prefer the hotels in and around piazza San Marco, although these tend to be expensive and the district is virtually overrun with visitors. Hotels around the more commercial ponte de Rialto are often far less expensive, but also less desirable. In the Castello district, hotel prices vary according to the proximity to piazza San Marco. The farther you go into Castello away from piazza San Marco, the lower the prices.

Venice Accommodations

American Hotel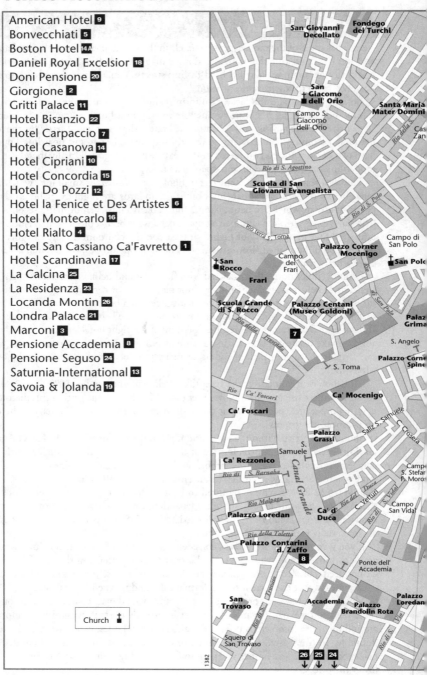
Bonvecchiati
Boston Hotel
Danieli Royal Excelsior
Doni Pensione
Giorgione
Gritti Palace
Hotel Bisanzio
Hotel Carpaccio
Hotel Casanova
Hotel Cipriani
Hotel Concordia
Hotel Do Pozzi
Hotel la Fenice et Des Artistes
Hotel Montecarlo
Hotel Rialto
Hotel San Cassiano Ca'Favretto
Hotel Scandinavia
La Calcina
La Residenza
Locanda Montin
Londra Palace
Marconi
Pensione Accademia
Pensione Seguso
Saturnia-International
Savoia & Jolanda

Church

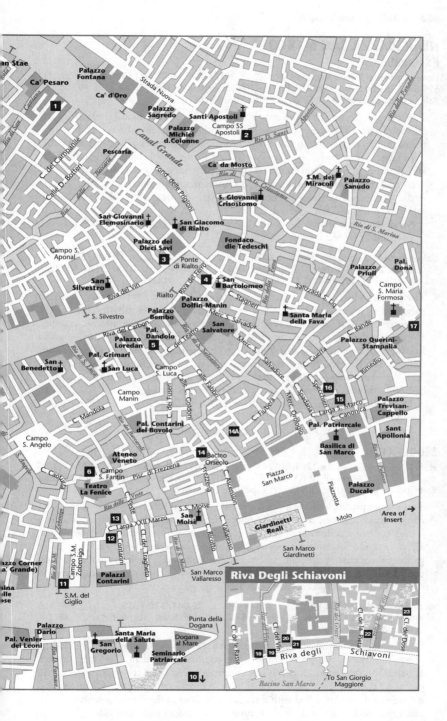

Ca' Pesaro

Palazzo Fontana

Ca' d'Oro

1

an Stae

Strada Nuova

Palazzo Sagredo

Santi Apostoli

Palazzo Michiel d.Colonne

Campo SS Apostoli

2

Rio D. Santi

C. del Campanile

Pescaria

Ca' da Mosto

Canal Grande

Fond. delle Prigioni

Rio di

S.G. Crisostomo

S.M. dei Miracoli

Palazzo Sanudo

Palazzo Priuli

Pal. Donà

Calle D. Botteri

S. Giovanni Crisostomo

San Giovanni Elemosinario

San Giacomo di Rialto

Palazzo dei Dieci Savi

3

Fondaco die Tedeschi

Rio di S. Marina

Campo S. Aponal

Ponte di Rialto

Riva del Vin

San Silvestro

Rialto

4

San Bartolomeo

Salizzada S. Lio

Campo S. Maria Formosa

17

S. Silvestro

Palazzo Dolfin-Manin

Riva del Carbon

Palazzo Bembo

Merc S. Salvador

Santa Maria della Fava

Palazzo Querini-Stampalia

San Salvatore

Pal. Dandolo

5

C. Bande

Pal. Grimani

Palazzo Loredan

San Luca

Campo S. Luca

Merc. S.

Salvatore

Merc S.

Salvatore

C. Guerra

C. Rimedio

San Benedetto

16

15

Palazzo Trevisan-Cappello

Campo Manin

Calle Fabbri

Calle Goldoni

Fiubera

Spadaria

Larga S. Marco

Merc. Orologio

Sant Apollonia

C Mandola

Pal. Contarini del Bovolo

14A

Pal. Patriarcale

Campo S. Angelo

Ateneo Veneto

14

Bacino Orseolo

Basilica di San Marco

6

Campo S. Fantin

Pisc. di Frezzeria

Piazza San Marco

Palazzo Ducale

Teatro La Fenice

Frezzeria

Ascension

Piazzetta

C. Caotorta

Rio delle Veste

S.S. Moise

13

Larga XXII Marzo

San Moise

Molo

Area of Insert

12

Cl. del Traghetto

Cl. Contarini

C Vallaresso

Ricotto

Giardinetti Reali

San Marco Giardinetti

zzo Corner a' Grande)

Campo S.M. Zobenigo

11

Palazzi Contarini

San Marco Vallaresso

Riva Degli Schiavoni

23

22

S.M. del Giglio

Palazzo Dario

Punta della Dogana

Cl. de la Rasse

20

Cl. del Dose

Pal. Venier dei Leoni

San Gregorio

Santa Maria della Salute

Dogana al Mare

Seminario Patriarcale

18 **19**

21

Riva degli

Schiavoni

10

Bacino San Marco

To San Giorgio Maggiore

NEAR PIAZZA SAN MARCO
EXPENSIVE

Hotel Concordia. Calle larga San Marco 367, 30124 Venezia. ☎ **041/520-6866.** Fax 041/ 520-6775. 55 rms. A/C MINIBAR TV TEL. 260,000–510,000 lire ($166.40–$326.40) double. Rates include breakfast. AE, DC, MC, V. Vaporetto: San Marco.

The four-star Concordia is the only hotel in Venice that has rooms overlooking piazza San Marco. The completely renovated, century-old hotel is housed in a five-story russet-colored building with stone-trimmed windows. A series of gold-plated marble steps takes you to the lobby, where you'll find a comfortable bar area, good service, and elevators to whisk you to the labyrinthine corridors upstairs. All bedrooms are decorated in a Venetian antique style and contain, among other amenities, an electronic safe and a hair dryer. Light meals and Italian snacks are available in the bar; otherwise only breakfast is served.

Services: Room service (24 hours), baby-sitting, laundry valet.
Facilities: Business center.

Saturnia-International. Calle larga XXII Marzo 2398, 30124 Venezia. ☎ **041/520-8377.** Fax 041/520-7131. 95 rms. A/C MINIBAR TV TEL. 300,000–520,000 lire ($192–$332.80) double. Rates include breakfast. AE, DC, MC, V. Vaporetto: San Marco.

The Saturnia-International was skillfully created from a 14th-century Venetian palazzo near piazza San Marco. The hotel is not as commercially oriented as the Moncaco & Grand Canal, and is infinitely superior to the highly touted but cramped Flora across the way. You're surrounded by richly embellished beauty here—a grand hallway with a wooden staircase, heavy iron chandeliers, fine paintings, and beamed ceilings. The individually styled bedrooms are spacious and furnished with chandeliers, Venetian antiques, tapestry rugs, gilt mirrors, and ornately carved ceilings. Many bedrooms overlook the hotel's quiet and dignified courtyard.

Dining/Entertainment: Its restaurant, La Caravella, is recommended separately (see "Dining," later in this chapter).
Services: Room service, baby-sitting, laundry, valet.

MODERATE

Hotel Casanova. Frezzeria 1284, 30124 Venezia. ☎ **041/520-6855.** Fax 041/520-6413. 43 rms, 3 suites. A/C MINIBAR TV TEL. 340,000 lire ($217.60) double; 445,000 lire ($284.80) suite. Rates include breakfast. AE, DC, MC, V. Vaporetto: San Marco.

This former private home is located a few steps from piazza San Marco. The hotel's name is more romantic than it is. The hotel doesn't have a lot of character, although it does contain a collection of church art and benches from old monasteries. These sit on flagstone floors near oil portraits. The modernized bedrooms are for the most part devoid of charm, although generally well maintained. The accommodations vary considerably in size—some are quite small. The most intriguing units are found on the top floor, with exposed brick walls and sloping beam ceilings.

Hotel Do Pozzi. Corte do Pozzi 2373, 30124 Venezia. ☎ **041/520-7855.** Fax 041/522-9413. 35 rms. MINIBAR TV TEL. 240,000 lire ($153.60) double. Rates include breakfast. AE, DC, MC, V. Vaporetto: Santa Maria del Griglio.

Small, modernized, and centrally located just a short stroll from the Grand Canal and piazza San Marco, this place is more like a country tavern than a hotel. Its original structure is 200 years old, and it opens onto a paved front courtyard with potted greenery. You can arrive via water taxi, boat, gondola, or vaporetto. The sitting and dining rooms are furnished with antiques (and near antiques), all intermixed with utilitarian modern decor. Baths have been added, and a major refurbishing has given everything a fresh touch. Laundry and baby-sitting are available.

Hotel La Fenice et Des Artistes. Campiello de la Fenice 1936, 30124 Venezia. ☎ **041/ 523-2333.** Fax 041/520-3721. 65 rms, 4 suites. TV TEL. 310,000 lire ($198.40) double; 420,000 lire ($268.80) suite. Rates include breakfast. AE, DC, MC, V. Vaporetto: San Marco.

This hotel offers widely varying accommodations in two connected buildings, each at least 100 years old. One building is rather romantic although a bit timeworn, with an impressive staircase leading to the overly decorated bedrooms (one room was once described as "straight out of the last act of *La Traviata,* enhanced by small gardens and terraces"). Your satin-lined room may have an inlaid desk and a wardrobe painted in the Venetian manner to match a baroque bed frame. The carpets might be thin, however, and the fabrics aging. The bedrooms in the other building are far less glamorous, with modern, rather sterile furniture. All but about three of the rooms are air-conditioned.

Hotel Montecarlo. Calle dei Specchieri 463, 30124 Venezia. ☎ **041/520-7144.** Fax 041/ 520-7789. 48 rms. A/C TV TEL. 180,000–400,000 lire ($115.20–$256) double. Rates include breakfast. AE, DC, MC, V. Vaporetto: San Marco.

Located just a 2-minute walk from piazza San Marco, this hotel was established some years ago in a 17th-century building, but was recently renovated to include modern baths. The upper hallways are lined with paintings by Venetian artists. The double rooms are comfortably proportioned and decorated with Venetian-style furniture and Venetian-glass chandeliers. The hotel's restaurant, Antico Pignolo, serves lunch and dinner and features both Venetian and international dishes.

Hotel Scandinavia. Campo Santa Maria Formosa 5240, 30122 Venezia. ☎ **041/522-3507.** Fax 041/523-5232. 34 rms, 30 with bath. A/C MINIBAR TV TEL. 170,000–250,000 lire ($108.80– $160) double without bath, 250,000–500,000 lire ($160–$320) double with bath. Rates include breakfast. AE, MC, V. Vaporetto: San Zaccaria.

A radical overhaul in 1992 added a third star to this hotel's rating. The entrance to the hotel is set behind a dark-pink facade just off one of the most colorful squares in Venice. The public rooms are filled with copies of 18th-century Italian chairs, Venetian-glass chandeliers, and a re-created rococo decor. The bedrooms are decorated in the Venetian style, but modern comforts have been added. There's also a bar and 24-hour room service (for drinks). A lobby lounge overlooks campo Santa Maria Formosa.

INEXPENSIVE

Boston Hotel. Ponte dei Dai 848, 30124 Venezia. ☎ **041/528-7665.** Fax 041/522-6628. 42 rms. TEL. 110,000–240,000 lire ($70.40–$153.60) double. Rates include buffet breakfast. AE, DC, MC, V. Closed Nov–Feb. Vaporetto: San Marco.

Built in 1962, the Boston Hotel is just a whisper away from St. Mark's. The hotel was named after an uncle who left to seek his fortune in Boston . . . and never returned. The little living rooms combine the old and the new, containing many antiques and Venetian ceilings. For the skinny guest, there's a tiny, self-operated elevator and a postage-stamp-size street entrance. Most of the bedrooms, with parquet floors, have built-in features, snugly designed beds, chests, and wardrobes. Fortunately, several have tiny balconies that open onto canals. Some rooms are air-conditioned, and a TV is available upon request.

ON OR NEAR THE GRAND CANAL
VERY EXPENSIVE

✪ **Gritti Palace.** Campo Santa Maria del Giglio 2467, 30124 Venezia. ☎ **041/794611,** or 800/221-2340 in the U.S., 800/955-2442 in Canada. Fax 041/520-0942. 96 rms, 10 suites. A/C MINIBAR TV TEL. 660,000–760,000 lire ($422.40–$486.40) double; from 1,600,000 lire ($1,024) suite. AE, DC, MC, V. Vaporetto: Santa Maria del Giglio.

The Gritti Palace, in a stately setting on the Grand Canal, is the renovated four-story palazzo of the 15th-century doge Andrea Gritti. It's a bit starchy, but in terms of prestige, only the Cipriani tops it. The place has a bit of a museum aura to it (some of the original furnishings are roped off, for example). "Our home in Venice" to Ernest Hemingway, it has for years drawn a select clientele of some of the world's greatest theatrical, literary, political, and royal figures—Queen Elizabeth and Prince Philip, Greta Garbo, Herbert von Karajan, Winston Churchill. The range and variety of guest rooms seem almost limitless, from elaborate suites to relatively small singles. But in every case, the glamour is evident. For a splurge, ask for Hemingway's old suite or the Doge Suite, once occupied by W. Somerset Maugham.

Dining/Entertainment: The hotel's Ristorante Club del Doge is among the best in Venice, but also egregiously priced.

Services: Room service (24 hours), baby-sitting, laundry, valet.

Facilities: Use of the Hotel Excelsior's facilities on the Lido.

MODERATE

⑤ American Hotel. Campo San Vio 628, 30123 Venezia. ☎ **041/520-4733.** Fax 041/520-4048. 29 rms. A/C MINIBAR TV TEL. 310,000 lire ($198.40) double; 37,000 lire ($236.80) triple. Rates include breakfast. AE, DC, MC, V. Vaporetto: Accademia.

Set on a small waterway, the American Hotel (there's nothing American about it) lies in an ochre building across the Grand Canal from the most heavily touristed areas. It's one of your best budget bets in Venice. The modest lobby is filled with murals, warm colors, and antiques, and the location is perfect for anyone wanting to avoid the crowds that descend on Venice in summer. The bedrooms are comfortably furnished in a Venetian style, but they vary in size; some of the smaller ones are a bit cramped. Many rooms with their own private terrace face the canal. On the second floor is a beautiful terrace where guests relax over drinks. The staff is attentive and helpful.

Hotel Carpaccio. San Tomà 2765, 30125 Venezia. ☎ **041/523-5946.** Fax 041/524-2134. 18 rms. MINIBAR TV TEL. 280,000 lire ($179.20) double. Rates include breakfast. MC, V. Closed mid-Nov to mid-Mar. Vaporetto: San Tomà.

Don't be put off by the narrow, winding alleyways that lead to the wrought-iron entrance of this second-class hotel—the building was meant to be approached by gondola. Once inside, you'll realize that your location in the heart of the oldest part of the city justifies your confusing arrival. This building used to be the Palazzo Barbarigo della Terrazza, and part of it is still reserved for private apartments. The tasteful and spacious bedrooms are filled with serviceable furniture. The salon is decorated with gracious pieces, marble floors, and a big arched window overlooking the Grand Canal. Breakfast is the only meal served.

ON OR NEAR RIVA DEGLI SCHIAVONI

VERY EXPENSIVE

✪ Danieli Royal Excelsior. Riva degli Schiavoni 4196, 30122 Venezia. ☎ **041/522-6480,** or 800/325-3535 in the U.S. and Canada. Fax 041/520-0208. 231 rms, 9 suites. A/C MINIBAR TV TEL. 693,000–825,000 lire ($443.50–$528) double; from 1,221,000 lire ($781.45) suite. Rates include breakfast. AE, DC, MC, V. Vaporetto: San Zaccaria.

The Danieli Royal Excelsior was built as a grand showcase by the doge Dandolo in the 14th century. In 1822 it was transformed into a deluxe "hotel for kings." It's the most ornate hotel in Venice, surpassed only by the Cipriani and the Gritti Palace. Placed in a most spectacular position, right on the Grand Canal, it has sheltered not only kings, but princes, cardinals, ambassadors, and such literary figures as George Sand and Charles Dickens.

You enter into a four-story-high stairwell, with Venetian arches and balustrades. The atmosphere is luxurious throughout—even the balconies opening off the main lounge are illuminated by stained-glass skylights. The bedrooms range widely in price, dimension, decor, and vistas, and those opening onto the lagoon cost more—a lot more. De Musset and Ms. Sand made love in Room 10, the most requested accommodation at the Danieli.

Dining/Entertainment: From the rooftop dining room, Terrazza Danieli, you have an undisturbed view of the canals and "crowns" of Venice. There's also an intimate cocktail lounge and a bar offering piano music.

Services: Room service, baby-sitting, laundry, valet.

Facilities: Hotel launch to the Lido in summer.

EXPENSIVE

✪ Londra Palace. Riva degli Schiavoni 4171, 30122 Venezia. ☎ **041/520-0533.** Fax 041/522-5032. 53 rms, 33 junior suites. A/C MINIBAR TV TEL. 280,000–616,000 lire ($179.20–$394.25) double; 700,000–1,200,000 lire ($448–$768) suite. Rates include breakfast. AE, DC, MC, V. Vaporetto: San Zaccaria.

The Londra Palace is a six-story gabled manor with 100 windows on the Venetian lagoon, a few yards from piazza San Marco. This is the second best hotel along riva degli Schiavoni, not as good as the Danieli but better than the Metropole. The hotel's most famous patron was arguably Tchaikovsky, who wrote his Fourth Symphony in Room 108 in December 1877. He also composed several other works here. The cozy reading room off the main lobby is reminiscent of an English club, with leaded windows and paneled walls with framed blowups of some of Tchaikovsky's sheet music. The bedrooms are luxuriously furnished, often with lacquered Venetian furniture. Romantics ask for one of the two attic rooms decorated in the Regency style with beamed ceilings. The courtyard rooms are quieter and cheaper, opening onto rooftop views of Venice instead of the Grand Canal.

Dining/Entertainment: The hotel has a popular piano bar and an excellent restaurant, Do Leoni.

Services: Room service, baby-sitting, laundry, valet.

Facilities: Conference hall.

Savoia & Jolanda. Riva degli Schiavoni 4187, 30122 Venezia. ☎ **041/520-6644.** Fax 041/520-7494. 80 rms, 3 suites. TEL. 340,000 lire ($217.60) double; 450,000 lire ($288) suite. Rates include breakfast. AE, MC, V. Vaporetto: San Zaccaria.

The Savoia & Jolanda occupies a prize position on Venice's main street, with a lagoon at its front yard. The hotel was established at the turn of the century as one of the most prominent along riva degli Schiavoni, transformed from an old Venetian palazzo. It might not be as spectacular as the Danieli or Londra Palace, but it's a lot more affordable. Most of the bedrooms have a view of the boats and the Lido. Although its exterior reflects much of old Venice, the interior is somewhat spiritless. However, the staff makes life here comfortable and relaxed. The modern bedrooms have plenty of space for daytime living (desk and armchairs). An addition to the hotel contains 20 rooms, each with air-conditioning, minibar, and TV.

MODERATE

Hotel Bisanzio. Calle della Pietà 3651, 30122 Venezia. ☎ **041/520-3100,** or 800/528-1234 in the U.S. Fax 041/520-4114. 40 rms. A/C MINIBAR TV TEL. 290,000 lire ($185.60) double. Rates include buffet breakfast. AE, DC, MC, V. Vaporetto: San Zaccaria.

Lying a few steps from St. Mark's Square, in one of the oldest parts of Venice, this hotel offers hospitality and a good standard of service. Occupying the former home of sculptor Alessandro Vittoria, the hotel has an elevator and terraces, plus a private little bar and a mooring for gondolas and motorboats. The bedrooms are generally quiet, each decorated in a Venetian antique style. Amenities include 24-hour room service, baby-sitting, and laundry. The lounge opens onto a traditional old Venetian courtyard.

INEXPENSIVE

Doni Pensione. Calle de Vino 4656, 30122 Venezia. ☎ **041/522-4267.** Fax 041/522-4267. 12 rms, 2 with bath. 95,000 lire ($60.80) double without bath, 130,000 lire ($83.20) double with bath. Rates include breakfast. No credit cards. Vaporetto: San Zaccaria.

The Doni Pensione sits in a private position, about a 3-minute walk from St. Mark's. Most of its very basic rooms either overlook a little canal, where four or five gondolas are usually tied up, or a garden with a tall fig tree. Simplicity (and cleanliness) prevails, especially in the pristine and down-to-earth bedrooms.

⑤ La Residenza. Campo Bandiera e Moro 3608, 30122 Venezia. ☎ **041/528-5315.** Fax 041/523-8859. 15 rms. MINIBAR TV TEL. 200,000 lire ($128) double. Rates include breakfast. AE, DC, MC, V. Closed Nov and Jan. Vaporetto: Arsenale.

La Residenza is in a pleasingly proportioned 14th-century building that looks a lot like a miniature version of the Doge's Palace. It's on a residential square where children play soccer and older people feed the pigeons. After gaining access (just press the button outside the entrance), you'll pass through a stone vestibule lined with ancient Roman columns before ringing another bell at the bottom of a flight of stairs. First an iron gate and then a door will open into an enormous salon filled with elegant antiques, 300-year-old paintings, and some of the most marvelously preserved walls in Venice.

The bedrooms are far less opulent than the public salons, however, and are furnished with contemporary pieces and functional accessories. The choice ones are usually booked far in advance, especially for carnival season.

NEAR THE PONTE DI RIALTO
EXPENSIVE

Hotel Rialto. Riva del Ferro 5149, 30124 Venezia. ☎ **041/520-9166.** Fax 041/523-8958. 77 rms. A/C MINIBAR TV TEL. 310,000–400,000 lire ($198.40–$256) double. Rates include breakfast. AE, DC, MC, V. Vaporetto: Rialto.

The Hotel Rialto opens right onto the Grand Canal at the foot of the ponte di Rialto, the famous bridge flanked with shops. Its bedrooms are quite satisfactory, combining modern or Venetian furniture with ornate Venetian ceilings and wall decorations. The hotel has been considerably upgraded to second class, and private baths with tub or shower have been installed in each unit. The most desirable and expensive double rooms overlook the Grand Canal, and these go first.

MODERATE

Bonvecchiati. Calle Goldoni 4488, 30124 Venezia. ☎ **041/528-5017.** Fax 041/528-5230. 86 rms. TEL. 230,000–310,000 lire ($147.20–$198.40) double. Rates include breakfast. AE, DC, MC, V. Vaporetto: San Marco or Rialto.

The Bonvecchiati, which looks a lot like a private villa, has seen better days but is still a viable choice because of its location near San Marco. With the closing of its restaurant and terrace, it seems to be running only at half steam and is indifferently staffed. Breakfast is served in a small dining room off the lobby, and maintenance is not always the best. The bedrooms, for the most part, are traditionally appointed with a number of amenities, such as private safes and minibars. Air-conditioning is available upon request. Check carefully before booking in here. Renovations are promised.

Marconi. Riva del Vin 729, 30125 Venezia. ☎ **041/522-2068.** Fax 041/522-9700. 26 rms. A/C MINIBAR TV TEL. 150,000–327,000 lire ($96–$209.30) double. Rates include breakfast. AE, MC, V. Vaporetto: Rialto.

The Marconi was built in 1500 when Venice was at the height of its naval supremacy. The drawing-room furnishings would be appropriate for visiting archbishops. The hotel lies less than 50 feet from the much portraited Rialto Bridge. The Maschietto family operates everything efficiently. Only four of the lovely old bedrooms open onto the Grand Canal, and these, of course, are the most eagerly sought after. Meals are usually taken in an L-shaped room with Gothic chairs. In fair weather, the sidewalk tables facing the Grand Canal are preferred by many.

INEXPENSIVE

Giorgione. SS. Apostoli 4586, 30131 Venezia. ☎ **041/522-5810.** Fax 041/523-9092. 70 rms, 8 suites. A/C MINIBAR TV TEL. 270,000–300,000 lire ($172.80–$192) double; 350,000–390,000 lire ($224–$249.60) suite. Rates include buffet breakfast. AE, DC, MC, V. Vaporetto: Ca' d'Oro.

In spite of modernization, the decor here is traditionally Venetian. The lounges and public rooms are equipped with fine furnishings and decorative accessories. Likewise, the comfortable and stylish bedrooms are designed to coddle guests. The hotel also has a typical Venetian garden. It's rated second class by the government, but the Giorgione maintains higher standards than many of the first-class establishments. Only breakfast is served.

IN SANTA CROCE

MODERATE

Hotel San Cassiano Ca' Favretto. Calle della Rosa 2232, 30135 Venezia. ☎ **041/524-1768.** Fax 041/721033. 36 rms. A/C MINIBAR TV TEL. 170,000–327,000 lire ($108.80–$209.30) double. Rates include breakfast. AE, DC, MC, V. Vaporetto: San Stae.

The Hotel San Cassiano Ca' Favretto used to be the studio of the 19th-century painter Giacomo Favretto. The hotel's gondola pier and the dining room porch both afford views of the lacy facade of the Ca' d'Oro, sometimes considered the most beautiful building in Venice. The building is a former 14th-century palace, and the present owner has worked closely with Venetian authorities to preserve the original details, which include a 20-foot beamed ceiling in the entrance area. Patrons have included George McGovern and guests of the U.S. Embassy. Fifteen of the conservatively decorated rooms overlook one of two canals, and many of them are filled with antiques or high-quality reproductions.

IN DORSODURO

INEXPENSIVE

⑤ La Calcina. Zattere al Gesuati 780, 30123 Venezia. ☎ **041/520-6466.** Fax 041/522-7045. 40 rms, 20 with bath (tub or shower). TEL. 90,000–105,000 lire ($57.60–$67.20) double without bath, 170,000–240,000 lire ($108.80–$153.60) double with bath. Rates include breakfast. AE, MC, V. Closed Jan 9–Feb 4. Vaporetto: Zattere.

Recently renovated (and just in time!), La Calcina lies in a secluded, dignified, and less-trampled district of Venice. This used to be the English enclave before the area developed a broader base of tourism. John Ruskin, who wrote *The Stones of Venice,* stayed here in 1877, and he charted the ground for his latter-day compatriots. This pensione is absolutely clean, and the furnishings are well chosen, but hardly elaborate. The rooms are cozy and comfortable.

⑤ Locanda Montin. Fondamenta di Borgo 1147, 31000 Venezia. ☎ **041/522-7151.** Fax 041/520-0255. 12 rms, 5 with bath (shower). 75,000 lire ($48) double without bath, 85,000 lire ($54.40) double with bath. AE, DC, MC, V. Vaporetto: Accademia.

The well-recommended Locanda Montini is an old-fashioned Venetian inn whose adjoining restaurant is one of the most loved and frequented in the area. The hotel is located in the Dorsoduro section, an area across the Grand Canal from the most popular tourist zones. The establishment is officially listed as a fourth-class hotel, but its accommodations are considerably larger and better than that rating would suggest. Reservations are virtually mandatory, because of the reputation of this locanda. The inn is a little difficult to locate—it's marked only by a small carriage lamp etched with the name of the establishment—but worth the search.

⑤ Pensione Accademia. Fondamenta Bollani 1058, 30123 Venezia. ☎ **041/523-7846.** Fax 041/523-9152. 29 rms. 225,000 lire ($144) double. Rates include breakfast. AE, DC, MC, V. Vaporetto: Accademia.

The Pensione Accademia is the most patrician of the *pensioni*. It's in a villa whose garden extends into the angle created by the junction of two canals. The interior features Gothic-style paneling, Venetian chandeliers, and Victorian-era furniture. The building served as the Russian Embassy before World War II, and as a private house before that. There's an upstairs sitting room flanked by two large windows and a formal rose garden. The bedrooms are spacious and decorated with original furniture from the 19th century. Some of the rooms are air-conditioned and most have been renovated. The Pensione Accademia was the fictional residence of Katharine Hepburn's character in the film *Summertime*. Incidentally, it was when Hepburn was in Venice for the film that she fell into a canal and got a permanent eye infection.

Pensione Seguso. Zattere al Gesuati 779, 30123 Venezia. ☎ **041/528-6858.** Fax 041/522-2340. 40 rms, 30 with bath (tub or shower). TEL. 175,000 lire ($112) double without bath, 190,000 lire ($121.60) double with bath. Rates include breakfast. AE, DC, MC, V. Closed Dec–Feb. Vaporetto: Accademia.

Set at the junction of two canals, this hotel is located on a less-traveled side of Venice across the Grand Canal from piazza San Marco. Its relative isolation made it attractive to such tenants as Ezra Pound and John Julius Norwich and his mother, Lady Diana Cooper. The interior is furnished with the family antiques of the Seguso family, who have maintained the hotel for more than 80 years. Small tables are set up near the hotel entrance, where breakfast is served on sunny days. Half board, obligatory, is served in the elegantly upper-crust dining room, where family heirlooms, and family cats, vie for the attention of the many satisfied guests.

ON ISOLA DELLA GIUDECCA
VERY EXPENSIVE

⊙ Hotel Cipriani. Isola della Giudecca 10, 30133 Venezia. ☎ **041/520-7744,** or 800/992-5055 in the U.S. Fax 041/520-7745. 76 rms, 28 suites. A/C MINIBAR TV TEL. 850,000–1,200,000 lire ($544–$768) double; from 1,850,000 lire ($1,184) suite. Rates include breakfast. AE, DC, MC, V. Closed Nov–Mar. Vaporetto: Zitelle.

With its isolated location, haute service, and exorbitant prices, the Cipriani outclasses every other posh contender in the city, including those traditional favorites, the Danieli and the Gritti Palace. Set in a 16th-century cloister on the residential island of Giudecca, this pleasure palace was established in 1958 by the late Giuseppe Cipriani, the founder of Harry's Bar and the one real-life character in Hemingway's

Venetian novel. Clients in the past have included everyone from Margaret Thatcher to Barbra Streisand. The Cipriani, incidentally, is the only hotel on Giudecca, which otherwise is calm and quiet. Today the hotel is owned and operated by Orient Express Hotels. The guest rooms have different amenities—ranging from tasteful contemporary to an antique design—but all have splendid views.

Dining/Entertainment: Lunch is served at Il Gabbiano, either indoors or on terraces overlooking the water. More formal meals are served at night in the Restaurant.

Services: The best in Venice, with two employees for every room. A private launch service ferries guests, at any hour, to and from the hotel's own pier near piazza San Marco. Room service, baby-sitting, laundry, and valet are available.

Facilities: Olympic-size swimming pool with filtered salt water, tennis courts, sauna, fitness center.

ON THE LIDO
VERY EXPENSIVE

✪ **Excelsior Palace.** Lungomare Marconi 41, 30126. Lido di Venezia. ☎ **041/526-0201,** or 800/325-3535 in the U.S. and Canada. Fax 041/526-7276. 196 rms, 18 suites. A/C MINIBAR TV TEL. 530,000–620,000 lire ($339–$397) double; from 1,460,000 lire ($934) suite. Rates include breakfast. AE, DC, MC, V. Parking 35,000 lire ($22.40). Closed Nov–Mar 15. Vaporetto: Lido; then bus A, B, or C.

When the mammoth Excelsior Palace was built, it was the biggest resort hotel of its kind in the world. The Excelsior is a monument to *la dolce vita* and did much to make the Lido fashionable. Today it offers the most luxury along the Lido, although it doesn't have the antique character of the Hotel des Bains. Its rooms range in style and amenities from cozy singles to suites. Most of the social life here takes place around the angular swimming pool or on the flowered terraces leading up to the cabanas on the sandy beach. All guest rooms—some of them big enough for tennis games—have been modernized, often with vivid, summerlike colors.

Dining/Entertainment: On the premises is one of the most elegant dining rooms of the Adriatic, the Tropicana. The Blue Bar on the ground floor has piano music and views of the beach.

Services: Room service (24 hours), baby-sitting, laundry, valet.

Facilities: Six tennis courts, swimming pool, private pier with boat rental. A private launch makes hourly runs to the other CIGA hotels on the Grand Canal.

EXPENSIVE

✪ **Hotel des Bains.** Lungomare Marconi 17, 30126 Lido di Venezia. ☎ **041/526-5921,** or 800/325-3535 in the U.S. and Canada. Fax 041/526-0113. 191 rms, 19 suites. A/C MINIBAR TV TEL. 320,000–405,000 lire ($204.80–$259.20) double; from 660,000 lire ($422) suite. AE, DC, MC, V. Closed Nov–Mar. Free parking. Vaporetto: Lido; then bus A, B, or C.

The Hotel des Bains was built in the grand era of European resort hotels, but its supremacy on the Lido was long ago lost to the Excelsior. It has its own wooded park and private beach with individual cabanas. Its confectionarylike facade dates from the turn of the century. Thomas Mann stayed here several times before making it the setting for his novella *Death in Venice,* and later it was used as a set for the film of the same name. The renovated interior exudes the flavor of the leisurely life of the belle époque era. The hotel, which overlooks the sea, has well-furnished, fairly large rooms.

Dining/Entertainment: Guests can dine in a large veranda room cooled by Adriatic sea breezes. The food is top-rate and the service is superior.

Services: Room service, baby-sitting, laundry, valet. A motorboat shuttles back and forth between Venice and the Lido.

Facilities: Many resort-type amenities are available at the Golf Club Alberoni (tennis courts, a large swimming pool, a private pier, and a park).

✪ **Quattro Fontane.** Via Quattro Fontane 16, 30126 Lido di Venezia. ☎ **041/526-0227.** Fax 041/526-0726. 57 rms. A/C TV TEL. 350,000–450,000 lire ($224–288) double. Rates include breakfast. AE, DC, MC, V. Closed Nov–Apr 4. Free parking. Vaporetto: Lido; then bus A, B, or C.

In its price bracket, the Quattro Fontane is one of the most charming hotels on the Lido. The trouble is, a lot of people know that, so it's likely to be booked. This former summer home of a 19th-century Venetian family is most popular with British tourists. They seem to appreciate the homelike atmosphere, the garden, the helpful staff, and the rooms with superior amenities, not to mention the good food served at tables set under shade trees. Many of the rooms are furnished with antiques. The hotel has cabanas on the beach and a tennis court.

MODERATE

Hotel Belvedere. Piazzale Santa Maria Elisabetta 4, 30126 Lido di Venezia. ☎ **041/526-5773.** Fax 041/526-1486. 30 rms. A/C TV TEL. 160,000–240,000 lire ($102.40–$153.60) double. Rates include breakfast. AE, DC, MC, V. Free parking. Vaporetto: Lido.

Built in 1857, the Hotel Belvedere is still run by the same family. Restored and modernized, it also offers a popular restaurant (recommended in "Dining," later in this chapter). The hotel is open all year, which is unusual for the Lido. It offers simply furnished double rooms. All have air-conditioning or a view of the St. Mark lagoon. For the Lido, prices are reasonable. The hotel has parking in its garden, and it's located right across from the vaporetto stop. As an added courtesy, the hotel offers guests free entrance to the casino, and in summer guests can use the hotel's bathing huts that have been reserved on the Venetian Lido.

Hotel Helvetia. Gran Viale 4–6, 30126 Lido di Venezia. ☎ **041/526-0105.** Fax 041/526-8903. 56 rms. TEL. 150,000–310,000 lire ($96–$198.40) double. Rates include breakfast. MC, V. Closed Nov–Mar. Parking 10,000 lire ($6.40). Vaporetto: Lido; then bus A, B, or C.

The Hotel Helvetia is a four-story, russet-colored, 19th-century building with stone detailing on a side street near the lagoon side of the island, an easy walk from the vaporetto stop. The quieter rooms face away from the street and rooms in the older wing have belle époque high ceilings and attractively comfortable furniture. The

---

🙂 Family-Friendly Hotels

American Hotel *(see p. 364)*   This secluded hotel is located across the Grand Canal away from the tourist hordes. It's a solid moderately priced choice where many rooms are rented as triples.

Pensione Accademia *(see p. 368)*   The best of the *pensioni* of Venice, this villa has a garden and large rooms. The former Russian Embassy was the fictional home of Katharine Hepburn in the film *Summertime.*

Pensione Seguso *(see p. 368)*   An antique-filled palace dating from the 15th century, this is a relatively secluded family-type place where the half-board rates are good value.

Quattro Fontane *(see p. 370)*   Long a Lido family favorite, this hotel guarantees summertime fun. It's somewhat like staying in the big chalet of a Venetian family. There's a private beach, too. The

Impressions

Venice is like eating an entire box of chocolate liqueurs at one go.

—Truman Capote

newer wing, dating from around 1950, is more streamlined and has been renovated in a more conservative and sterile style. Breakfast is served, weather permitting, in a flagstone-covered wall garden behind the hotel. Baby-sitting, laundry, and 24-hour room service are available.

4 Dining

Although Venice doesn't grow much foodstuff, and is hardly a victory garden, it's bounded by a rich agricultural district and plentiful vineyards in the hinterlands. The city gets the choicest items on its menu from the Adriatic, although the fish dishes, such as scampi, are very expensive. The many rich and varied specialties prepared in the Venetian kitchen will be surveyed in the restaurant recommendations to follow. For Italy, the restaurants of Venice are high priced, although there are many trattorie that cater to moderate budgets.

NEAR PIAZZA SAN MARCO
EXPENSIVE

✪ **Antico Martini.** Campo San Fantin 1983. ☎ **041/522-4121.** Reservations required. Main courses 32,000–50,000 lire ($20.50–$32); fixed-price menu 40,000-55,000 lire ($25.60-$35.20) at lunch, 72,000–98,000 lire ($46.10–$62.70) at dinner. AE, DC, MC, V. Wed 7–11:30pm, Thurs–Mon noon–2:30pm and 7–11:30pm. Vaporetto: San Marco or Santa Maria del Giglio. VENETIAN/INTERNATIONAL.

The Antico Martini, the city's leading restaurant, elevates Venetian cuisine to its highest level. Inside, elaborate chandeliers glitter overhead and gilt-framed oil paintings adorn the paneled walls. Outside, the courtyard is favored in summer.

An excellent beginning is the risotto di frutti di mare ("fruits of the sea"), in a creamy Venetian style with plenty of fresh seafood. For a main dish, try the fegato alla veneziana, tender liver fried with onions and served with a helping of polenta, a yellow cornmeal mush. The chefs are better at regional dishes than they are at international ones. The restaurant has one of the city's best wine lists. The yellow Tocai is an interesting local wine and especially good with fish dishes.

La Caravella. Calle larga XXII Marzo 2398. ☎ **041/520-8901.** Reservations required. Main courses 37,000–52,000 lire ($23.70–$33.30). AE, DC, MC, V. Daily noon–3pm and 7pm–midnight. Vaporetto: San Marco. VENETIAN/INTERNATIONAL.

La Caravella, next door to the Hotel Saturnia International, offers an overblown nautical atmosphere and a leather-bound menu that makes you at first think this might be a tourist trap. Although it's expensive, it's not a trap but a citadel of good food and wine, with a cuisine that's almost as good as at the Antico Martini. The restaurant contains four different dining rooms, and outdoor dining is available in the courtyard during the summer months. The decor is rustically elegant, with frescoed ceilings, bouquets of flowers, and wrought-iron lighting fixtures. Many of the specialties are featured nowhere else in town. You might begin with an antipasti misto de pesce (fish) with olive oil and lemon juice, or perhaps prawns with avocado. Two specialties of the house are granceola (Adriatic sea crab on a bed of carpaccio) and chateaubriand for two. The best item to order, however, is one of the poached-fish

Venice Dining

Alfredo, Alfredo **8**
"Al graspo de ua" **19**
Antico Martini **14**
Arcimboldo **27**
Da Ivo **18**
Do Forni **11**
Do Leoni **29**
Fiachetteria Toscana **23**
Harry's Bar **6**
Harry's Dolci **33**
La Caravella **5**
La Furatola **3**
Le Chat Qui Rit **10**
Locanda Montin **32**
Nuova Rivetta **9**
Osteria da Fiore **2**
Poste Vechie **26**
Quadri **7**
Restaurant da Bruno **22**
Ristorante à la Vecia Cavana **25**
Ristorante al Mondo Novo **21**
Ristorante Belvedere **30**
Ristorante Cipriani **31**
Ristorante Corte Sconta **28**
Ristorante da Raffaele **4**
Ristorante Noemi **12**
Rosticceria San Bartolomeo **20**
Taverna la Fenice **15**
Tiziano Bar **24**
Trattoria Antica Besseta **1**
Trattoria La Colomba **13**
Trattoria Madonna **16**
Vini da Arturo **17**

Church

1383

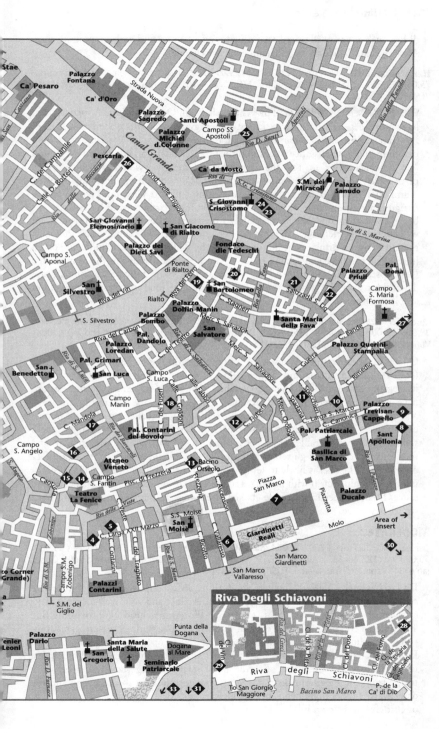

dishes, such as bass—all priced according to weight and served with a tempting sauce. After all that, the ice cream in champagne is welcome.

Harry's Bar. Calle Vallaresso 1323. ☎ **041/528-5777.** Reservations required. Main courses 75,000–85,000 lire ($48–$54.40). AE, DC, MC, V. Daily 10:30am–11pm. Vaporetto: San Marco. VENETIAN.

Harry's Bar serves the best food in Venice, although Quadri and the Antico Martini have more elegant atmospheres. Ernest Hemingway made this place famous. A. E. Hotchner, in his *Papa Hemingway,* quoted the writer as saying, "We can't eat straight hamburger in a Renaissance palazzo on the Grand Canal." So he ordered a 5-pound "tin of beluga cavier" to "take the curse off it." Hemingway would probably skip the place today, and the prices would come as a shock even to him. Harry, by the way, is an Italian named Arrigo, son of the late Commendatore Cipriani. Like his father, Arrigo is an entrepreneur extraordinaire known for the standard of his cuisine. His bar is a watering spot for martini-thirsty Americans—the vodka martini is dry and well chilled, but Hemingway and Hotchner always ordered a Bloody Mary. Actually, the most famous drink of the house is one of the Bellinis (Prosecco and white peach juice). You can have your choice of dining in the bar downstairs or the room with a view upstairs. We recommend the Venetian fish soup, followed by the scampi Thermidor with rice pilaf or the seafood ravioli. The food is relatively simple, but absolutely fresh.

Quadri. Piazza San Marco 120–124. ☎ **041/528-9299.** Reservations required. Main courses 39,000–57,000 lire ($24.95–$36.50). AE, DC, MC, V. Tues–Sun noon–2:30pm and 7–10:30pm. Vaporetto: San Marco. INTERNATIONAL.

One of the most famous restaurants of Europe, Quadri is even better known as a cafe (see "Venice After Dark" in Chapter 10). This deluxe second-floor restaurant, with its elegant decor and clientele, overlooks the "living room" of Venice. Former patrons have included Marcel Proust and Stendhal. Many diners come here just for the view, and are often surprised by the memorable setting, high-quality cuisine, and impeccable service. Harry's Bar and the Antico Martini have better food, although the chef's skills here are considerable. The place is often packed with celebrities during art and film festivals, the world glitterati taking delight in this throwback to the days of *La Serenissima.* The chef is likely to tempt you with such dishes as octopus in fresh tomato sauce, salt codfish with polenta, scallops in a saffron sauce, or sea bass with crab sauce. Dessert specialties include "baked" ice cream and lemon mousse with fresh strawberry sauce.

MODERATE

Da Ivo. Calle dei Fuseri 1809. ☎ **041/528-5004.** Reservations required. Main courses 35,000–50,000 lire ($22.40–$32). AE, DC, MC, V. Mon–Sat noon–2:40pm and 7pm–midnight. Closed Jan 6–31. Vaporetto: San Marco. TUSCAN/VENETIAN.

Da Ivo has such a faithful clientele you'll think at first that you're in a semiprivate club. The rustic atmosphere is both cozy and relaxing, and your well-set table flickers with the glow of candlelight. Homesick Florentines head here for some fine Tuscan cookery, but regional Venetian dishes are also served. In season, game, prepared according to ancient traditions, is cooked over an open charcoal grill. One cold December day our hearts and plates were warmed by an order of a homemade tagliatelli topped with slivers of tartufi bianchi, the unforgettable pungent white truffle from the Piedmont district. Dishes change according to the season and the daily availability of ingredients, but are likely to include anglerfish, a stewpot of fish, or cuttlefish in its own ink.

Do Forni. Calle dei Specchieri 468. ☎ **041/523-2148.** Reservations required. Main courses 20,000–36,000 lire ($12.80–$23.05). AE, DC, MC, V. Daily noon–3pm and 6–11pm. Vaporetto: San Marco. INTERNATIONAL/VENETIAN.

Centuries ago this was the site where bread was baked for some local monasteries, but today it's the busiest restaurant in Venice—even when the rest of the city slumbers under a wintertime Adriatic fog. It's divided into two sections, separated by a narrow alleyway. The Venetian cognoscenti prefer the front part, decorated in *Orient Express* style. The larger section at the back is like a country tavern, with ceiling beams and original paintings. The English menu is entitled "food for the gods" and lists such specialties as spider crab in its own shell, champagne-flavored risotto, calves' kidney in a bitter mustard, and sea bass in papillotte (parchment). The food is international in scope, and dishes appear inspired not only by the cuisine of Venice but the kitchens of the United States, Morocco, England, and Germany as well.

Ristorante Noemi. Calle dei Fabbri 912. ☎ **041/522-5238.** Reservations recommended. Main courses 20,000–35,000 lire ($12.80–$22.40). AE, DC, MC, V. Mon 7–10:30pm, Tues–Sat noon–2:30pm and 7–10:30pm. Closed Dec 15–Jan 15. Vaporetto: San Marco. INTERNATIONAL/VENETIAN.

This simple establishment is on a narrow street just a short walk from piazza San Marco. Its decor features a multicolored marble floor in abstract patterns and swag curtains covering big glass windows. The foundations of the building date from the 14th century and the restaurant itself was established in 1927 and named after the matriarch of the family that continues to own it. House specialties, many of which border on *nuova cucina,* include thin black spaghetti with cuttlefish "in their own sauce" and fresh salmon crêpes with cheese, followed by the special lemon sorbet of the house, made with sparkling wine and fresh mint. More recent dishes include filet of salmon with white raisins, served with a sauce made from white wine and laurel leaves, and a filet of sole "Casanova," concocted with a velouté of white wine, shrimp, and mushrooms.

Taverna La Fenice. Campiello de la Fenice 1938. ☎ **041/522-3856.** Reservations required. Main courses 18,000–28,000 lire ($11.50–$17.90). AE, DC, MC, V. Sept–May, Mon 7–10:30pm, Tues–Sat noon–2:30pm and 7–10:30pm; June–Aug, daily noon–2:30pm and 7–10:30pm. Closed the second week in Jan. Vaporetto: San Marco. ITALIAN/VENETIAN.

Established in 1907, when Venetians were flocking in record numbers to hear the *bel canto* performances in the opera house nearby, this restaurant is one of the most romantic dining spots in Venice. The interior is suitably elegant, but the preferred spot during clement weather is outdoors beneath a canopy, a few steps from the burned Teatro La Fenice. The service is smooth and efficient. The most appetizing beginning is the selection of seafood antipasti. The fish is fresh from the Mediterranean. You might enjoy the risotto con scampi e arugula, the freshly made tagliatelle with cream and exotic mushrooms, John Dory filets with artichokes, turbot roasted with olive oil and broccoli, scampi with tomatoes and rice, or carpaccio alla Fenice.

Trattoria La Colomba. San Marco–Piscina–Frezzeria 1665. ☎ **041/522-1175.** Reservations recommended. Main courses 25,000–60,000 lire ($16–$38.40). AE, DC, MC, V. Daily noon–3pm and 7–11pm. Closed Wed, June 16–Aug, and Nov 16–Apr 14. Vaporetto: San Marco or Rialto. VENETIAN/INTERNATIONAL.

This is one of the most distinctive and popular trattorie in town, with a history going back at least a century and a by-now legendary association with some of the leading painters of Venice. In 1985 a $2-million restoration improved the infrastructure, making it a more attractive foil for the dozens of modern paintings that adorn its walls. These collections change seasonally and are discreetly available for sale.

Menu items are likely to include at least five daily specials based exclusively on the time-honored cuisine of Venice. Otherwise, you can order such specialties as risotto di funghi del Montello (risotto with mushrooms from the local hills of Montello) or baccalà alla vicentina (milk-simmered dry cod seasoned with onions, anchovies, and cinnamon, and served with polenta). Fruits and vegetables used in the dishes are for the most part grown locally on the islands near Venice.

INEXPENSIVE

Alfredo, Alfredo. Campo San Lippo e Giacomo 4294, in Castello. ☎ **041/522-5331.** Main courses 17,000–28,000 lire ($10.90–$17.90); fixed-price menu 19,500–25,000 lire ($12.50–$16). AE, DC, MC, V. Oct– Apr, Thurs–Tues 11am–2am; May–Sept, daily 11am–2am. Vaporetto: San Zaccaria. VENETIAN.

Alfredo, Alfredo might be classified as a coffee shop. Here you can order any number of items, prepared in short order. These include pasta dishes such as spaghetti with a number of sauces, freshly made salads, crêpes, various grilled meats, and omelets. Its long hours make it a convenient spot for a light meal at almost any time of the day. The food is not always first-rate, and the atmosphere is a bit hysterical at times, but it still might come in handy.

Le Chat Qui Rit. San Marco 1131. ☎ **041/522-9086.** Main courses 10,000–14,000 lire ($6.40–$8.95); pizzas 9,000–14,000 lire ($5.75–$8.95). No credit cards. Daily 11am–9:30pm. Closed Sat, Oct–May. Vaporetto: San Marco. VENETIAN/PIZZA.

This is a self-service cafeteria and pizzeria that offers Venetian dishes prepared "just like mama made." It's very popular because of its low prices. Dishes might include cuttlefish simmered in stock and served on a bed of yellow polenta or various fried fish. You can also order a steak grilled very simply, flavored with oil, salt, and pepper, perhaps a little garlic and herbs if you prefer. Main-dish platters are served rather quickly after you order them.

⑤ Nuova Rivetta. Campo San Filippo 4625, in Castello. ☎ **041/528-7302.** Reservations required. Main courses 15,000–35,000 lire ($9.60–$22.40). AE, MC, V. Tues–Sun 10am–10pm. Closed July 23–Aug 20. Vaporetto: San Zaccaria. SEAFOOD.

The Nuova Rivetta is an old-fashioned Venetian trattoria where you get good food at a good price. The restaurant stands in the monumental heart of the old city. Many find it best for lunch during a stroll around Venice. The most representative dish to order is frittura di pesce, a mixed fish fry from the Adriatic, which includes squid or various other "sea creatures" that turned up at the market on that day. Other specialties include gnocchi stuffed with Adriatic spider crab, pasticcho of fish (a main course), and spaghetti flavored with squid ink. The most typical wine of the house is Prosecco, whose bouquet is refreshing and fruity with a slightly sharp flavor. For centuries it has been one of the most celebrated wines of the Veneto region.

Ristorante da Raffaele. Calle larga XXII Marzo 2347 (fondamenta delle Ostreghe). ☎ **041/523-2317.** Reservations recommended. Main courses 22,000–35,000 lire ($14.10–$22.40). AE, DC, MC, V. Fri–Wed noon–3pm and 7–10:30pm. Closed Dec 10 to mid-Feb. Vaporetto: San Marco or Santa Maria del Giglio. ITALIAN/VENETIAN.

The Ristorante da Raffaele, a 5-minute walk from piazza San Marco and a minute from the Grand Canal, has long been a favorite canalside restaurant. The place is often overrun with tourists, but the veteran kitchen staff handles the onslaught well. Dating from 1953, the restaurant offers the kind of charm and special atmosphere that are unique to Venice. However, the inner rooms are popular with Venetians and visitors alike. The huge inner sanctum has a high-beamed ceiling, 17th- to 19th-century pistols and sabers, exposed brick, wrought-iron chandeliers, a massive fireplace, and copper pots (hundreds of them). The food is excellent, beginning with a choice of tasty antipasti or well-prepared pastas. Seafood specialties include scampi, squid, and a platter of deep-fried fish from the Adriatic. The grilled meats are also succulent and can be followed by rich, tempting desserts. The crowded conviviality is part of the experience.

⑤ Trattoria Madonna. Calle de la Madonna 594. ☎ **041/522-3824.** Reservations recommended but not always accepted. Main courses 5,000–20,000 lire ($3.20–$12.80). AE, MC, V. Thurs–Tues noon–3pm and 7:15–10pm. Closed Jan 7–Feb 7 and Aug 1–15. Vaporetto: Rialto. VENETIAN.

Despite the similarity of its name with that of a popular American singer (and many local jokes to that effect), this restaurant was established in 1954 in a 300-year-old building of historical distinction. Named after *another* famous Madonna, it's one of the most popular and characteristic trattorie of Venice, specializing in traditional Venetian recipes and an array of grilled fresh fish. A suitable beginning might be the antipasto frutti di mare (fruits of the sea). Pastas, polentas, risottos, meats (including fegato alla veneziana, liver with onions), and many kinds of irreproachably fresh fish are widely available. Many creatures of the sea are displayed in a refrigerated case near the entrance. The mixed fish fry of the Adriatic is a preferred dish, when available.

Vini da Arturo. Calle degli Assassini 3656. ☎ **041/528-6974.** Reservations recommended. Main courses 25,000–40,000 lire ($16–$25.60). No credit cards. Mon–Sat noon–2:30pm and 7–10:30pm. Closed Aug. Vaporetto: San Marco or Rialto. VENETIAN.

Vini da Arturo attracts many devoted regulars, including artists and writers. Here you get some of the most delectable of the local cooking—and not just the standard Venetian clichés and not seafood, which may be unique for a Venetian restaurant. One local restaurant owner, who likes to dine here occasionally instead of at his own place, explained, "The subtle difference between good and bad food is often nothing more than the amount of butter and cream used." Instead of ordering plain pasta, try the tantalizing spaghetti alla Gorgonzola. The beef is also good, especially when prepared with a cream sauce flavored with mustard and freshly ground pepper. Salads are made with crisp, fresh ingredients, often in unusual combinations. The place is small and contains only seven tables; it's located between the Fenice Opera House and St. Mark's Square.

EAST OF PIAZZA SAN MARCO
MODERATE

Arcimboldo. Calle dei Furiani 3219, in Castello. ☎ **041/528-6569.** Reservations recommended. Main courses 22,000–38,000 lire ($14.10–$24.30); fixed-price menu 40,000 lire ($25.60). AE, DC, MC, V. Wed–Mon 7:30pm–midnight. Vaporetto: Arsenale or San Zaccaria. VENETIAN/ITALIAN.

At the corner where the Scuola di San Giorgio degli Schiavoni (containing Carpaccio's celebrated cycle of paintings) is located, turn into a little street and follow a narrow footpath leading deep into Venice's oldest quarter. At the end of the street, you'll stumble upon Arcimboldo, one of the city's most charming restaurants. It overlooks a canal and is named for Giuseppe Arcimboldo, a famous 16th-century painter who worked at the Habsburg court, making fantastical portraits of fruits and vegetables. Reproductions of his work line the walls.

The intimate and romantic decor is a fitting backdrop for the traditional Venetian fare served here. Both old and modern dishes are prepared with the excellent fruit and vegetables grown on the neighboring islands. Diners can enjoy Venetian-style

---

🧒 Family-Friendly Restaurants

Alfredo, Alfredo *(see p. 376)* This is a great spot for the family on a sightseeing run. Short-order items are served quickly, including spaghetti with a number of sauces and freshly made salads.

Le Chat Qui Rit *(see p. 376)* This is a self-service cafeteria where children are allowed to select what they want. Lots of pasta dishes.

Tiziano Bar *(see p. 381)* You can order hot pasta dishes and sandwiches, consumed standing at the counter or seated on one of the high stools.

---

antipasti, excellent pasta dishes, fish, risotto, and the pick of poultry and meat. Everything is washed down with quality wines. In spring and summer tables are placed outside along the canal.

ON OR NEAR RIVA DEGLI SCHIAVONI
EXPENSIVE

Do Leoni. In the Londra Palace Hotel, riva degli Schiavoni 4171. ☎ **041/520-0533.** Reservations recommended. Main courses 38,000–46,000 lire ($24.30–$29.45); lunch (without drinks) 39,000 lire ($24.95). Residents of the Londra Palace Hotel receive a 20% discount (excludes fixed-price menu). AE, DC, MC, V. Tues 11:30am–3pm, Wed–Mon 11:30am–3pm and 7:30–11pm. Vaporetto: San Zaccaria. VENETIAN/INTERNATIONAL.

For years this restaurant was known by the French version of its name, Les Deux Lions. Set on the street level of an elegant and well-recommended hotel, it offers a panoramic view of a 19th-century equestrian statue ringed with heroic women taming—you guessed it—lions. The restaurant is filled with scarlet and gold, a motif of lions patterned into the carpeting, and reproductions of English furniture.

Lunches are brief, buffet-style affairs, where clients serve themselves from a large choice of hot and cold Italian and international food. The appealing dinners by candlelight are more formal, with emphasis on Venetian cuisine. The chef's undeniable skill is reflected in such dishes as chilled fish terrine, baked salmon with truffles, and baby rooster with green-pepper sauce. At both lunch and dinner, the restaurant, depending on the weather, offers the option of dining outside on the piazza, overlooking the bronze lions and their masters.

NEAR THE ARSENALE
MODERATE

Ristorante Corte Sconta. Calle del Pestrin 3886. ☎ **041/522-7024.** Reservations required. Main courses 20,000–30,000 lire ($12.80–$19.20); fixed-price menu 70,000 lire ($44.80). AE, DC, MC, V. Tues–Sat 12:30–2:30pm and 7:30–9:30pm. Closed Jan 7–Feb 7 and July 15–Aug 15. Vaporetto: Arsenale. SEAFOOD.

The Ristorante Corte Sconta is located behind a narrow storefront that you'd probably ignore if you didn't know about this place. On a narrow alley whose name is shared by at least three other streets in Venice (this particular one is near campo Bandiere e Moro and San Giovanni in Bragora), the modest restaurant whose name in Italian means "hidden courtyard" has a multicolored marble floor, plain wooden tables, and no serious attempt at decoration. It has become well known, however, as a sophisticated gathering place for artists, writers, and filmmakers. As the depiction of the satyr chasing the mermaid above the entrance implies, this is a fish restaurant, serving a variety of grilled creatures (much of the "catch" is largely unknown in North

America). The fresh fish is flawlessly grilled. It's also flawlessly fresh—the gamberi, for example, is placed live on the grill. Begin with marinated salmon with arugula and pomegranate seeds in rich olive oil. If you don't like fish, a tender filet of beef is available. There's a big stand-up bar in an adjoining room that seems to be almost a private fraternity of the locals.

NEAR THE PONTE DI RIALTO
MODERATE

"Al graspo de ua." Calle dei Bombaseri 5093. ☎ **041/520-0150.** Reservations required. Main courses 25,000–35,000 lire ($16–$22.40). AE, DC, MC, V. Wed–Sun noon–3pm and 8–11pm. Closed Jan 2–17. Vaporetto: Rialto. SEAFOOD/VENETIAN.

"Al graspo de ua" is one bunch of grapes you'll want to pluck. For that special meal, it's a winner. Decorated in the old taverna style, it offers several air-conditioned dining rooms. One has a beamed ceiling, hung with garlic and copper bric-a-brac. Among the best fish restaurants in Venice, "al graspo de ua" has been patronized by such celebs as Elizabeth Taylor, Jeanne Moreau, and even Giorgio de Chirico. You can help yourself to all the hors d'oeuvres you want—known on the menu as "self-service mammoth." Next try the gran fritto dell'Adriatico, a mixed treat of deep-fried fish from the Adriatic. The desserts are also good, especially the peach Melba.

Poste Vechie. Pescheria Rialto 1608. ☎ **041/721822.** Reservations recommended. Main courses 20,000–35,000 lire ($12.80–$22.40). AE, DC, MC, V. Wed–Mon noon–3:30pm and 7–10:30pm. Vaporetto: Rialto. SEAFOOD.

This is one of the most charming restaurants in Venice, set near the Rialto fish market and connected to the rest of the city by a small, privately owned bridge. It was established in the early 1500s as the local post office—food was served to the mail carriers to fortify them for their deliveries. Today it's one of the oldest restaurants in Venice, with a pair of intimate dining rooms (both graced with paneling, murals, and 16th-century mantelpieces) and an outdoor courtyard that evokes the countryside northwest of Venice.

Menu items include super-fresh fish from the nearby markets; a salad of shellfish and exotic mushrooms; tagliolini flavored with squid ink, crabmeat, and fish sauce; and the restaurant's *pièce de résistance,* seppie (cuttlefish) à la veneziana with polenta. If you don't like fish, calves' liver or veal shank with ham and cheese are also well prepared. Desserts come rolling to your table on a trolley and are usually delicious.

Ristorante à la Vecia Cavana. Rio Terà SS. Apostoli 4624. ☎ **041/528-7106.** Main courses 20,000–40,000 lire ($12.80–$25.60); fixed-price menu 30,000 lire ($19.20). AE, DC, MC, V. Fri–Wed noon–2:30pm and 7:30–10:30pm. Vaporetto: Ca' d'Oro. SEAFOOD.

The Ristorante à la Vecia Cavana is off the tourist circuit and well worth the trek through the winding streets to find it. A *cavana* is a place where gondolas are parked, a sort of liquid garage, and the site of this restaurant used to be such a place in the Middle Ages. When you enter, you'll be greeted with brick arches, stone columns, terra-cotta floors, framed modern paintings, and a photograph of 19th-century fishermen relaxing after a day's work. It's an appropriate introduction to a menu that specializes in seafood, including a mixed grill from the Adriatic, fried scampi, fresh sole, squid, three different types of risotto (each prepared with seafood), and a spicy zuppa di pesce (fish soup). Another specialty of the house is antipasti di pesce Cavana, which includes an assortment of just about every sea creature. The food is authentic and seems prepared for the Venetian palate—not necessarily for the glitzy foreign tourist.

INEXPENSIVE

Fiaschetteria Toscana. San Giovanni Crisostomo 5719. ☎ **041/528-5281.** Reservations recommended. Main courses 18,000–30,000 lire ($11.50–$19.20). AE, DC, MC, V. Wed–Mon 12:30–2:30pm and 7:30–10:30pm. Closed July. Vaporetto: Rialto. VENETIAN.

A century ago this stone-fronted building stored the wine and olive oil of a Tuscan-born merchant. Today it serves pure Venetian cuisine in a style that has changed very little since the restaurant was established more than 30 years ago. The street-level dining room is spanned by old ceiling beams and contains amusing modern art. A country-style wooden staircase leads past marble columns to an upper room and additional tables. House specialties consist mainly of different varieties of fish, including an octopus-and-celery salad, spider crab in its own shell, grilled razor clams, seafood risotto with champagne, and baked eel. A red-chicory salad from Treviso is the perfect accompaniment.

Restaurant da Bruno. Calle del Paradiso 5731, in Castello. ☎ **041/522-1480.** Main courses 12,000–20,000 lire ($7.70–$12.80); fixed-price menu 23,000 lire ($14.70). AE, DC, MC, V. Wed–Mon noon–3pm and 7–11pm. Closed 1 week in Jan. Vaporetto: San Marco or Rialto. VENETIAN.

The Restaurant de Bruno is like a country taverna in the center of Venice. Located on a narrow street about halfway between the Rialto Bridge and piazza San Marco, the restaurant attracts its crowds by grilling meats on an open-hearth fire. Get your antipasti at the counter and watch your prosciutto order being prepared—paper-thin slices of spicy flavored ham wrapped around breadsticks (grissini). In the right season, da Bruno does some of the finest game specialty dishes in Venice. If featured, try in particular its capriolo (roebuck) and its fagiano (pheasant). A typical Venetian specialty—prepared well here—is the zuppa di pesce (fish soup). Other specialties include filet of beef with pepper sauce, veal scaloppine with wild mushrooms, scampi and calamari, and a local favorite, squid with polenta. After that rich fare, you may settle for a macedonia of mixed fruit for dessert.

Ristorante al Mondo Novo. Salizzada di San Lio 5409, in Castello. ☎ **041/520-0698.** Reservations recommended. Main courses 15,000–24,000 lire ($9.60–$15.35); fixed-price meals 22,000–30,000 lire ($14.10–$19.20). AE, MC, V. Tues–Sun 11am–3pm and 7pm–midnight (last order). Vaporetto: Rialto or San Marco. VENETIAN/SEAFOOD.

In a very old Venetian building originally built during the Renaissance, with a dining room outfitted in a regional style, this well-established restaurant offers professional service and a kindly staff. Plus, it stays open later than many of its nearby competitors. Menu items include a selection of seafood, prepared succulently as frittura misto dell' Adriatico, or charcoal grilled. Other items include maccaroni alla verdura (with fresh vegetables and greens), an antipasti of fresh fish, and filets of beef with pepper sauce and rissole potatoes. Locals who frequent the place always order the fresh fish, knowing that the owner of the restaurant is a wholesaler in the Rialto fish market.

⑤ Rosticceria San Bartolomeo. Calle della Bissa 5424, in San Marco. ☎ **041/522-3569.** Main courses 15,000–22,000 lire ($9.60–$14.10); fixed-price menu 26,000–27,000 lire ($16.65–$17.30). AE, MC, V. Tues–Sun 10am–2:30pm and 5–9pm. Vaporetto: Rialto. VENETIAN.

The Rosticceria San Bartolomeo is the most frequented fast-food eatery in Venice and has long been a haven for budget travelers. Downstairs is a *tavola calda* where you can eat standing up, but upstairs is a budget-level restaurant with waiter service. Typical dishes include baccalà alla vicentina (codfish simmered in herbs and milk), deep-fried mozzarella (which the Italians call *in carrozza*), and seppie con polenta (squid in its own ink sauce, served with a cornmeal mush). Everything is washed down with typical Veneto wine.

Once you leave the vaporetto, take an underpass on your left (that is, with your back facing the bridge). This passageway is labeled sottoportego della Bissa. The restaurant will be at the first corner, off campo San Bartolomeo.

⑤ Tiziano Bar. Salizzada San Giovanni Cristostomo, midway between the Church of San Giovanne Cristostomo and the Teatro Mulibran. ☎ **041/523-5544.** Main dishes 8,000–13,000 lire ($5.75–$8.30). Sun–Fri 8am–10:30pm. Vaporetto: Rialto. SANDWICHES/PASTA/PIZZA.

The Tiziano Bar is a *tavola calda* (literally "hot table"). There's no waiter service— you eat standing at a counter or on one of the high stools. The place is known in Venice for selling pizza by the yard. From noon to 3pm it serves hot pastas such as rigatoni and cannelloni. But throughout the day you can order sandwiches or perhaps a plate of mozzarella.

IN SANTA CROCE
MODERATE

Osteria da Fiore. Calle del Scaleter 2202. ☎ **041/721308.** Reservations required. Main courses 24,000–40,000 lire ($15.35–$25.60). AE, DC, MC, V. Tues–Sat 12:30–2:30pm and 8–9:30pm. Closed Aug and Dec 25–Jan 14. Vaporetto: San Tomà. SEAFOOD.

The breath of the Adriatic seems to blow through this place, although how the wind finds this little restaurant tucked away in a labyrinth is a mystery. The restaurant serves only fish, and has done so since 1910. An imaginative and changing fare is offered, depending on the availability of fresh fish and produce. If you have a love of maritime foods, you'll find them here—everything from scampi (a sweet Adriatic prawn, cooked in as many different ways as there are chefs) to granzeola, a type of spider crab. In days gone by we've sampled everything from fried calamari (cuttlefish) to bottarga (dried mullet roe eaten with olive oil and lemon). Try such dishes as capelunghe alla griglio (razor clams opened on the grill), masenette (tiny green crabs that you eat shell and all), and canoce (mantis shrimp). For your wine, we suggest Prosecco, which has a distinctive golden-yellow color and a bouquet that's refreshing and fruity. The proprietors extend a hearty welcome to match their fare.

INEXPENSIVE

Trattoria Antica Besseta. Calle Savio 1395. ☎ **041/721687.** Reservations required. Main courses 20,000–25,000 lire ($12.80–$16). AE, V. Thurs–Mon 12:30–2:30pm and 7:30–9:30pm. Closed Aug 1–15. Vaporetto: Rive di Biasio. VENETIAN.

If you manage to find this place (go armed with a good map), you'll be rewarded with true Venetian cuisine at its most unpretentious. Head for campo San Giacomo dell'Orio, then negotiate your way across infrequently visited piazzas and winding alleys. Push through saloon doors into a bar area filled with African masks and modern art. The dining room in back is ringed with paintings and illuminated with wagon-wheel chandeliers. Nereo Volpe, his wife, Mariuccia, and one of their sons are the guiding force, the chefs, the buyers, and even the "talking menus." The food depends on what looked good in the market that morning. The menu could include roast chicken, fried scampi, fritto misto, spaghetti in a sardine sauce, various roasts, and a selection from the day's catch. The Volpe family produces two kinds of their own wine, a pinot blanc and a cabernet.

IN DORSODURO
INEXPENSIVE

⑤ La Furatola. Calle lunga San Barnaba 2870A. ☎ **041/520-8594.** Reservations recommended for dinner. Main courses 20,000–30,000 lire ($12.80–$19.20). No credit cards. Fri–Tues noon–2:30pm and 7–9:30pm. Closed July–Aug. Vaporetto: Ca' Rezzonico or Accademia. SEAFOOD.

La Furatola (an old Venetian word meaning "restaurant") is very much a Dorsoduro neighborhood hangout, but it has captured the imagination of local foodies. It's located in a 300-year-old building, along a narrow flagstone-paved street that you'll need a good map and a lot of patience to find. Perhaps you'll have lunch here after a visit to the Church of San Rocco, which is located only a short distance away. You'll push past double glass doors and enter a simple dining room. The specialty is fish brought to your table in a wicker basket so that you can judge its size and freshness by its bright eyes and red gills. A display of seafood antipasti is set out near the entrance. A culinary standout is the baby octopus boiled and eaten with a drop of red-wine vinegar. Eel comes with a medley of mixed fried fish, including baby cuttlefish, prawns, and squid rings.

Locanda Montin. Fondamenta di Borgo 1147. ☎ **041/522-7151.** Reservations recommended. Main courses 12,000–30,000 lire ($7.70–$19.20). AE, DC, MC, V. Tues 12:30–2:30pm, Thurs–Mon 12:30–2:30pm and 7:30–9:30pm. Vaporetto: Accademia. INTERNATIONAL/ITALIAN.

The Locanda Montin is the kind of rapidly disappearing Venetian inn that virtually every literary and artistic figure in Venice has visited. Since it opened just after World War II, famous clients have included Ezra Pound, Jackson Pollock, Mark Rothko, and many of the assorted artist friends of the late Peggy Guggenheim. The inn is owned and run by the Carretins, who have covered the walls with paintings donated by or purchased from their many friends and clients.

Today the arbor-covered garden courtyard of this 17th-century building is filled with regular clients, many of whom allow their favorite waiter to select most of the items for their meal. The frequently changing menu includes a variety of salads, grilled meats, and fish caught in the Adriatic. Dessert might be a semifreddo di fragoline, a tempting chilled liqueur-soaked cake, capped with whipped cream and wild strawberries. The locanda lies in one of the least-trampled sections of Venice, Dorsoduro, across the Grand Canal from piazza San Marco.

ON ISOLA DELLA GIUDECCA
VERY EXPENSIVE

Ristorante Cipriani. In the Hotel Cipriani, Isola della Giudecca 10. ☎ **041/520-7744.** Reservations required. Jacket and tie required for men. Main courses 36,000–59,000 lire ($23.05–$37.75). AE, DC, MC, V. Daily 12:30–3pm and 8–10:30pm. Closed Nov–Mar. Vaporetto: Zitelle. INTERNATIONAL.

The grandest and greatest of the hotel restaurants—better than the cuisine at the Gritti Palace—this restaurant offers dining terraces with extensive views over the lagoon. However, for lunch or dinner (more romantic) the view is not all the attraction. The cuisine is sublime but relatively simple, depending on the freshest of ingredients perfectly prepared by one of the best trained staffs along the Adriatic. This is not a family favorite, and children under 6 aren't allowed.

You can dine in the more formal room with Murano chandeliers and Fortuny curtains when the weather is nippy, or out on the terrace overlooking the lagoon. Freshly made pasta is a specialty, and it's among the finest we've ever sampled in Venice. Try the taglierini verdi with noodles and ham au gratin. Chef's specialties include mixed fried scampi and squid with tender vegetables and sautéed filets of veal with spring artichokes. Come here in October for the last Bellinis of the white peach season and the first white truffles of the season served in a champagne risotto.

EXPENSIVE

Harry's Dolci. Fondamenta San Biago, Isola della Giudecca. ☎ **041/522-4844.** Reservations recommended, especially Sat–Sun. Main courses 30,000–40,000 lire ($19.20–$25.60); fixed-price menu 75,000 lire ($48). AE, MC, V. Wed–Mon noon–3pm and 7–10:30pm. Closed Nov–March 30. Vaporetto: S. Eufemia. INTERNATIONAL/ITALIAN.

The people at the famed Harry's Bar have established their latest enclave far from the maddening crowds of St. Mark's Square on this little-visited island. From the quayside windows of this chic place, you can watch seagoing vessels, including everything from yachts to lagoon-based barges. White napery and uniformed waiters grace a modern room, where no one minds if you order only coffee and ice cream or perhaps a selection from the large pastry menu (the zabaglione cake is divine). Popular items include carpaccio Cipriani, chicken salad, club sandwiches, gnocchi, and house-style cannelloni. Dishes are deliberately kept simple, but each is well prepared.

ON THE LIDO
MODERATE

Ristorante Belvedere. Piazzale Santa Maria Elisabetta 4, Lido di Venezia. ☎ **041/526-5773.** Reservations required. Main courses 10,000–50,000 lire ($6.40–$32); fixed-price menu 26,000 lire ($16.65). AE, DC, MC, V. Tues–Sun noon–2:30pm and 7–9:30pm. Closed Nov 4 to mid-Feb. Vaporetto: Lido. VENETIAN.

Outside the big hotels, the best food on the Lido is served at the Ristorante Belvedere. Don't be put off by its location, across from where the vaporetto from Venice stops. In such a location, you might expect a touristy establishment. Actually, the Belvedere attracts some of the finest people of Venice. They often come here as an excursion, knowing that they can get some of the best fish dishes along the Adriatic. Sidewalk tables are placed outside, and there's a glass-enclosed portion for windy days. The main dining room is attractive, with cane-backed bentwood chairs and big windows. In back, reached through a separate entrance, is a busy cafe. Main dishes include the chef's special sea bass, along with grilled dorade (or sole), fried scampi, and other selections. You might begin with the special fish antipasti or spaghetti en papillote (cooked in parchment).

10 What to See & Do in Venice

Venice appears to have been created specifically to entertain its legions of callers. Ever since the body of St. Mark was smuggled out of Alexandria and entombed in the basilica, Venice has been host to a never-ending stream of visitors—famous, infamous, and otherwise—from all over the world.

Venice has perpetually captured the imagination of poets, artists, and travelers. Wordsworth, Byron, and Shelley addressed poems to the city, and it has been written about or used as a setting by many contemporary writers.

In the pages ahead, we'll explore the city's great art and architecture. But, unlike Florence, Venice would reward its guests with treasures even if they never ducked inside a museum or church. In the city on the islands, the frame eternally competes with the picture it contains.

"For all its vanity and villainy," wrote Lewis Mumford, "life touched some of its highest moments in Venice."

SUGGESTED ITINERARIES

These itineraries are designed for the first-time visitor. Those visiting Venice for the second or third time may want to seek out the city's other mysteries and treasures.

If You Have 1 Day

Get up early in the morning and watch the sun rise over piazza San Marco, as the city wakes up. The pigeons will already be there to greet you. Have an early-morning cappuccino on the square, then visit the Basilica of San Marco and the Palazzo Ducale later. Ride the Grand Canal in a gondola 2 hours before sunset, and spend the rest of the evening wandering the narrow streets of this strangely unreal and fascinating city. Apologize to yourself for such a short visit and promise to return.

If You Have 2 Days

Spend your first day as suggested above. On Day 2 it's time for more concentrated sightseeing. Begin at piazza San Marco (viewing it should be a daily ritual regardless of how many days you have in Venice), then head for the major museum, the Accademia, in the morning. In the afternoon, visit the Collezione Peggy Guggenheim (modern art) and perhaps the Ca' d'Oro and Ca' Rezzonico.

Impressions

A city for beavers.

—Ralph Waldo Emerson, on Venice, in his journal, June 1833

If You Have 3 Days

Spend your first 2 days as suggested above. Begin the morning of Day 3 by having a cappuccino on piazza San Marco, then inspect the Campanile di San Marco. Later in the morning, visit the Museo Correr. In the afternoon, go to the Scuola Grande di San Rocco to see the works of Tintoretto. Spend the rest of the day strolling the streets of Venice and ducking into shops that capture your imagination. Even if you get lost, you'll eventually return to a familiar landmark, and you can't help but see the signs pointing you back to piazza San Marco. Have dinner in one of the most typical of Venetian trattorie, such as Locanda Montin.

If You Have 5 Days

Spend Days 1 to 3 as outlined above. On Day 4, plan to visit the islands of the lagoon, including Murano, Burano, and Torcello. All three can be covered—at least briefly—on one busy day. On Day 5, take an excursion to Verona (see Chapter 11).

1 Piazza San Marco (St. Mark's Square)

Piazza San Marco was the heartbeat of the Serenissima (the Serene Republic) in the heyday of Venice's glory as a seafaring republic, the crystallization of the city's dreams and aspirations. If you have only 1 day for Venice, you need not leave the square, as the city's major attractions, such as the Basilica of St. Mark and the Doge's Palace, are centered here or nearby.

The traffic-free square, frequented by tourists and pigeons, and sometimes by Venetians, is a constant source of bewilderment and interest. If you rise at dawn, you can almost have the piazza to yourself. As you watch the sun come up, the sheen of gold mosaics glisten into a mystic effect of incomparable beauty. At midmorning (9am) the overstuffed pigeons are fed by the city (if you're caught under the whir, you'll think you're witnessing a remake of Hitchcock's *The Birds*). At midafternoon the tourists reign supreme, and it's not surprising in July to witness a display of fisticuffs over a camera angle. At sunset, when the two Moors in the Clock Tower strike the end of another day, lonely sailors begin a usually frustrated search for those hot spots that characterized the Venice of yore but not of today. Deep in the evening the strollers parade by or stop for espresso at the fashionable Florian Caffè and sip while listening to a band concert.

Thanks to Napoléon, the square was unified architecturally. The emperor added the Fabbrica Nuova facing the basilica, thus bridging the Old and New Procuratie on either side. Flanked with medieval-looking palaces, Sansovinos Library, elegant shops, and colonnades, the square is now finished—unlike piazza della Signoria in Florence.

✪ **Basilica di San Marco.** Piazza San Marco. ☎ **041/522-5205.** Admission: Basilica, free; baptistery, free; treasury, 3,000 lire ($1.90); presbytery, 3,000 lire ($1.90); Marciano Museum, 3,000 lire ($1.90). Basilica (including the baptistery and presbytery), Apr–Sept, Mon–Sat 9:30am–5:30pm, Sun 2–5:30pm; Oct–Mar, Mon–Sat 9:30am–5pm, Sun 1:30–4:30pm. Treasury, Mon–Sat 9:30am–5pm, Sun 2–5pm. Marciano Museum, Apr–Sept, Mon–Sat 10am–5:30pm, Sun 2–4:30pm; Oct–Mar, Mon–Sat 10am–4:45pm. *Warning:* Visitors must wear appropriate clothing and remain silent during their visit. Photography is forbidden. Vaporetto: San Marco.

Central Venice Attractions

Church

The so-called Church of Gold dominates piazza San Marco. This is one of the world's greatest and most richly embellished churches. In fact, it looks as if it had been moved intact from Istanbul. The basilica is a conglomeration of styles, although it's particularly indebted to Byzantium. It incorporates other schools of design, such as Romanesque and Gothic, with freewheeling abandon. Like Venice, it's adorned with booty from every corner of the city's once far-flung mercantile empire—capitals from Sicily, columns from Alexandria, porphyry from Syria, sculpture from old Constantinople.

The basilica is capped by a dome that—like a spider plant—sends off shoots, in this case a quartet of smaller-scale cupolas. Spanning the facade is a loggia, surmounted by replicas of the four famous St. Mark's horses—the *Triumphal Quadriga*.

On the facade are rich marble slabs and mosaics that depict scenes from the lives of Christ and St. Mark. One of the mosaics re-creates the entry of the evangelist's body into Venice, transported on a boat. St. Mark's body, hidden in a pork barrel, was smuggled out of Alexandria in 828 and shipped to Venice. The evangelist dethroned Theodore, the Greek saint who up until then had been the patron of the city that had outgrown him.

In the atrium are six cupolas filled with mosaics illustrating scenes from the Old Testament, including the story of the Tower of Babel. The interior of the basilica, once the private chapel and pantheon of the doges, is a stunning wonderland of marbles, alabaster, porphyry, and pillars. Visitors walk in awe across the undulating multicolored ocean floor, which is patterned with mosaics.

To the right is the **baptistery,** dominated by the Sansovino-inspired baptismal font, upon which John the Baptist is ready to pour water. If you look back at the aperture over the entryway, you can see a mosaic of the dance of Salome in front of Herod and his court. Salome is wearing a star-studded russet-red dress and three white fox tails and is dancing under a platter that holds John's head. Her glassy face is that of a Madonna, not an enchantress.

After touring the baptistery, proceed up the right nave to the doorway to the oft-looted **treasury** (*tesoro*). It contains the inevitable skulls and bones under glass, plus goblets, chalices, and Gothic candelabra.

The entrance to the **presbytery** is nearby. In it, on the high altar, the alleged sarcophagus of St. Mark rests under a green marble blanket and is held up by four sculptured, Corinthian-style alabaster columns. The Byzantine-style **Pala d'Oro,** from Constantinople, is the rarest treasure at St. Mark's—made of gold and studded with precious stones.

On leaving the basilica, head up the stairs in the atrium to the **Marciano Museum** and the Loggia dei Cavalli. The star attraction of the museum is the world-famous *Triumphal Quadriga,* four horses looted from Constantinople by Venetian crusaders in the sack of that city in 1204. These horses once surmounted the basilica, but were removed because of damage by pollution. They were subsequently restored. This is the only quadriga (which means a quartet of horses yoked together) to have survived from the classical era. They are believed to have been cast in the 4th century. Napoléon once carted these much-traveled horses off to Paris for the Arc du Carousel, but they were returned to Venice in 1815. The museum, with its mosaics and tapestries, is especially interesting, but also be sure to walk out onto the loggia for a view of piazza San Marco.

✪ **Palazzo Ducale.** Piazzetta San Marco. ☎ **041/522-4951.** Admission 10,000 lire ($6.40). Easter–Oct, daily 9am–6pm; Nov–Easter, daily 9am–4pm. Vaporetto: San Marco.

The Palace of the Doges is entered through the magnificent 15th-century Porta della Carta at the piazzetta. This palace is part of the legend and lore of Venice. It's somewhat like a frosty birthday cake in pinkish-red marble and white Istrian stone. The Venetian-Gothic palazzo—with all the architectural intricacies of a paper doily—gleams in the tremulous Venetian light. The grandest civic structure in Italy, it dates back to 1309, although a fire in 1577 destroyed much of the original building.

If you enter from the piazzetta, past the four porphyry Moors, you'll be right in the middle of the splendid Renaissance courtyard, one of the most recent additions to a palace that has experienced the work of many different architects with widely varying tastes. You can take the "giants' stairway" to the upper loggia—so called because of the two Sansovino statues of mythological figures.

The fire of 1577 made ashes of many of the palace's greatest masterpieces, and almost spelled doom for the building itself, as the new architectural fervor of the post-Renaissance was in the air. However, fortunately, sanity prevailed. Many of the greatest Venetian painters of the 16th century contributed to the restored palace, replacing the canvases or frescoes of the old masters.

After climbing the Sansovino stairway of gold you'll enter some get-acquainted rooms. Proceed to the Anti-Collegio salon, which houses the palace's greatest artworks—notably Veronese's *Rape of Europa,* to the far left on the right-hand wall. One critic called the work delicious. Tintoretto is well represented with his *Three Graces* and his *Bacchus and Ariadne.* Some critics consider the latter his supreme achievement. In the adjoining Sala del Collegio, you'll find allegorical paintings by Veronese on the ceiling. As you proceed to the right, you'll enter the Sala del Senato o Pregadi, with its allegorical painting by Tintoretto in the center of the ceiling.

In the Sala del Consiglio dei Dieci, with its gloomy paintings, the dreaded Council of Ten (often called the Terrible Ten for good reason) used to assemble to decide who was in need of decapitation. In the antechamber, bills of accusation were dropped in the lion's mouth.

Now trek downstairs through the once-private apartments of the doges to the grand Maggior Consiglio, with its allegorical *Triumph of Venice* on the ceiling, painted by Veronese. What makes the room outstanding, however, is Tintoretto's *Paradise,* over the Grand Council chamber—said to be the largest oil painting in the world. Paradise seems to have an overpopulation problem, perhaps a too-optimistic point of view on Tintoretto's part. Tintoretto was in his 70s when he began this monumental work (he died only 6 years later). The second grandiose hall, entered from the grand chamber, is the Sala dello Scrutinio, with paintings that tell of the past glories of Venice.

Reentering the Maggior Consiglio, follow the arrows on their trail across the **Bridge of Sighs,** linking the Doge's Palace with the Palazzo delle Prigioni, where the cell blocks are found, the ones that lodged the prisoners who felt the quick justice of the Terrible Ten. The "sighs" in the bridge's name stemmed from the sad laments of the numerous victims led across it to certain torture and possible death. The cells are just dank remnants of the horror of medieval justice.

Campanile di San Marco. Piazza San Marco. ☎ **041/522-4064.** Admission 6,000 lire ($3.85). May–Oct, daily 9am–8pm; Nov–Apr, daily 9:30am–3:45pm. Vaporetto: San Marco.

One summer night back in 1902, the bell tower of St. Mark's Basilica, which was suffering from years of rheumatism in the damp Venetian climate, gave out a warning sound that sent the elegant and fashionable coffee drinkers in the piazza scurrying for their lives. But the campanile gracefully waited until the next morning—July 14—before it tumbled into the piazza. The Venetians rebuilt their belfry, and it's now safe to ascend. In campanile-crazed Italy, where visitors must often ascend circuitous stairs, it's good to report that the Venetian version has a modern elevator.

You can ride it and get a pigeon's view of the city. It's a particularly good vantage point for viewing the cupolas of the basilica.

Torre dell'Orologio. Piazza San Marco. ☎ **041/523-1879.** Vaporetto: San Marco.

At piazza San Marco is one of the most typical and characteristic of Venetian scenes—the two Moors striking the bell atop the Clock Tower (Torre dell'Orologio). The tower soars over the Old Procuratie. The clock under the winged lion not only tells the time, but is a boon to the astrologer: It matches the signs of the zodiac with the position of the sun. If the movement of the Moors striking the hour seems slow in today's fast, mechanized world, remember how many centuries the poor wretches have been at their task without time off. The "Moors" originally represented two European shepherds. However, after having been reproduced in bronze, they have grown darker with the passing of time. As a consequence, they came to be called Moors by the Venetians.

Sightseers can admire only the exterior, however. Venetian authorities have decided that interior visits are dangerous and have closed the tower indefinitely.

PIAZZETTA SAN MARCO

If piazza San Marco is the drawing room of Europe, then its satellite, piazzetta San Marco, is the antechamber. Hedged in by the Doge's Palace, Sansovinos Library, and a side of St. Mark's, the tiny square faces the Grand Canal. Two tall granite columns grace the square. One is surmounted by a winged lion, which represents St. Mark. The other is topped by a statue of a man taming a dragon, supposedly the dethroned patron saint Theodore. Both columns came from the East in the 12th century.

During the heyday of the Serene Republic, dozens of victims either lost their heads or were strung up here, many of them first being subjected to torture that would have made the Marquis de Sade flinch. One, for example, had his teeth hammered in, his eyes gouged out, and his hands cut off before being strung up. Venetian justice became notorious throughout Europe.

If you stand with your back to the canal, looking toward the south facade of St. Mark's Basilica, you'll see the so-called *Virgin and Child* of the poor baker, a mosaic honoring Pietro Fasiol (also Faziol), a young man unjustly sentenced to death on a charge of murder.

To the left of the entrance to the Doge's Palace are four porphyry figures, which, for want of a better description, the Venetians called "Moors." These puce-colored fellows are huddled close together, as if afraid. Considering the decapitations and torture that have occurred on the piazzetta, we shouldn't wonder.

2 Other Top Attractions

THE LIDO

Along the white sands of the Lido strolled Eleonora Duse and Gabriele d'Annunzio (*Flame of Life*), Goethe in Faustian gloom, a clubfooted Byron trying to decide with whom he was in love that day, de Musset pondering the fickle ways of George Sand, and Thomas Mann's Gustave von Aschenbach with his eye on Tadzio in *Death in Venice*. But gone is the relative isolation of yore. The de Mussets of today aren't mooning over lost loves—they're out chasing bikini-clad new ones.

Near the turn of the century, the Lido began to blossom into a fashionable beachfront resort, complete with deluxe hotels and its Casino Municipale (see "Venice After Dark," later in this chapter). Lido prices are usually stratospheric. It's not a haven for the budget-minded tourist.

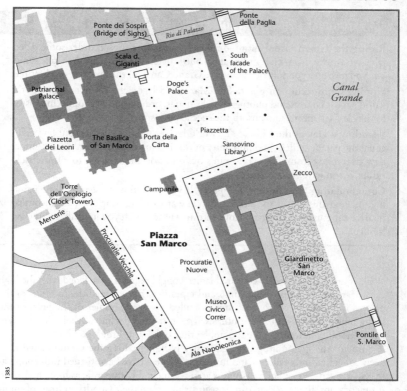

The Lido today is past its heyday. The fashionable and chic of the world still patronize the Excelsior Palace and the Hotel des Bains, but the beach strip is overtouristed and opens onto polluted waters. It's not just the beaches around Venice that are polluted, but reputedly the entire Adriatic. For swimming, guests use the pools of their hotels instead. They can, however, still enjoy the sands along the Lido.

Even if you aren't lodging at the Lido, you may still want to come over for an afternoon. If you don't want to tread on the beachfront property of the rarefied hotel citadels—which have huts lining the beach like those of some tropical paradise—you can try the lungomare G. d'Annunzio Public Bathing Beach at the end of the Gran Viale (piazzale Ettore Sorger), a long stroll from the vaporetto stop. You can book cabins—called *camerini*—and enjoy the sand. Rates change seasonally.

To reach the Lido, take vaporetto no. 6 (the ride takes about 15 minutes). The boat departs from a landing stage near the Doge's Palace.

THE GRAND CANAL

Peoria may have its Main Street, Paris its Champs-Elysées—but Venice, for uniqueness, tops them all with its canale Grande. Lined with palazzi—many in the elegant Venetian-Gothic style—this great road of water is today filled with vaporetti, motorboats, and gondolas. Along the canal the boat moorings are like peppermint sticks. It begins at piazzetta San Marco on one side and Longhena's Salute Church on the opposite bank. At midpoint it's spanned by the Rialto Bridge. Eventually, the canal winds its serpentine course to the railway station. We can guarantee that there's not a dull sight en route.

Frommer's Favorite Venice Experiences

Riding the Grand Canal in a Gondola   Just before sunset, order some delectable sandwiches from Harry's Bar and a bottle of chilled Prosecco, then take someone you love on a gondola ride along the Grand Canal for the boat trip of a lifetime.

Sipping Cappuccino on piazza San Marco   Select a choice spot on one of the world's most famous and photographed squares, order a cup of cappuccino, listen to the classical music, and absorb the special atmosphere of Venice.

Spending a Day at the Lido   The world has seen better beaches, but few sights equal the parade of flesh and humanity of this fashionable beach on a hot summer day. Everybody from Thomas Mann's fictional von Aschenbach to a horseback-riding Byron have romped here.

Contemplating Giorgione's *Tempest*   If you have time to see only one painting, make it this one at the Accademia. The artist's haunting sense of oncoming menace superimposed over a bucolic setting will stay with you long after you leave Venice.

Of course, the gloriously coiffured ladies Longhi painted have faded with the high tide. Many of the lavish furnishings and tapestries that adorned the interiors of the palaces were hauled off to museums or ended up in the homes of the heirs of the rising mercantile class of two centuries ago. In the sad decline of their city, the Venetian nobility didn't become less noble; they only went broke.

Some of the major and most impressive buildings along the Grand Canal have been converted into galleries and museums. Others have been turned into cooperative apartments. Venetian housewives aren't as incurably romantic as foreign visitors. A practical lot, these women can be seen stringing up their laundry in front of thousands upon thousands of tourists.

Along this canal one foggy day came Madame Amandine Lucie Aurore Dudevant, née Dupin (otherwise known as George Sand), with her effete, poetic young lover, Alfred de Musset. John Ruskin came this way to debunk and expose in his *The Stones of Venice*. Robert Browning, burnt out from the loss of his beloved Elizabeth and his later rejection at the hands of Lady Ashburton, came here to settle down in a palazzo where he eventually died. More recently, Eleonora Duse came this way with the young poet to whom she had given her heart, Gabriele d'Annunzio. Even Shakespeare came here in his fantasies. Intrepid guides will point out the "Palazzo de Desdemona."

3 Museums & Galleries

Venice is a city of art. Decorating its palazzi and adorning its canvases were artists such as Giovanni Bellini, Carpaccio, Giorgione, Titian, Lotto, Tintoretto, Veronese, Tiepolo, Guardi, Canaletto, and Longhi, to name just the more important ones. In the museums and galleries to follow, important works by all these artists are exhibited, as well as a number of modern surprises, such as those in the Guggenheim Collection.

Visiting hours are often subject to major variations, so keep this in mind as you go sightseeing. Many visitors who have budgeted only 2 or 3 days for Venice often express disappointment when, for some unknown reason, a major attraction closes abruptly.

⭘ **Accademia.** Campo della Carità, Dorsoduro. ☎ **041/522-2247.** Admission 12,000 lire ($7.70) adults, free for children 17 and under and for seniors 60 and over. Mon–Sat 9am–7pm, Sun 9am–2pm. Vaporetto: Accademia.

The pomp and circumstance, the glory that was Venice, lives on in this remarkable collection of paintings that span the period from the 14th to the 18th century. The hallmark of the Venetian school is color and more color. From Giorgione to Veronese, from Titian to Tintoretto, with a Carpaccio cycle thrown in, the Accademia has samples—often their best work—of its most famous sons. We'll high-light only some of the most-renowned masterpieces for the first-timer in a rush.

You'll first see works by such 14th-century artists as Paolo and Lorenzo Veneziano, who bridged the gap from Byzantine art to Gothic (see the latter's *Annunciation*). Next, you'll view Giovanni Bellini's *Madonna and Saint* (poor Sebastian, not another arrow), and Carpaccio's fascinating, although gruesome, work of mass crucifixion. As you move on, head for the painting on the easel by the window, attributed to the great Venetian artist Giorgione. On this canvas he depicted the *Madonna and Child*, along with the mystic St. Catherine of Siena and John the Baptist (a neat trick for Catherine, who seems to have perfected transmigration to join the cast of characters).

Two of the most important works with secular themes are Mantegna's armored *St. George*, with the slain dragon at his feet, and Hans Memling's 15th-century por-trait of a young man. A most unusual *Madonna and Child* is by Cosmé Tura, the master of Ferrara, who could always be counted on to give a new twist to an old subject.

The madonnas and bambini of Giovanni Bellini, an expert in the harmonious blending of colors, are the focus of another room. None but the major artists could stand the test of a salon filled with the same subjects, but under Bellini's brush each Virgin achieves her individual spirituality. Giorgione's *Tempest*, displayed here, is the single most famous painting at the Accademia. It depicts a baby suckling from the breast of its mother, while a man with a staff looks on. What might have emerged as a simple pastoral scene on the easel of a lesser artist comes forth as a picture of rare and exceptional beauty. Summer lightning pierces the sky, but the tempest seems to be in the background—far away from the figures in the foreground, who are men-aced without knowing it.

The masterpiece of Lorenzo Lorto, a melancholy portrait of a young man, can be seen before you come to a room dominated by Paolo Veronese's *The Banquet in the House of Levi*. This is, in reality, a "Last Supper" that was considered a sacrilege in its day, so Veronese was forced to change its name to indicate a secular work. Imp-ish Veronese caught the hot fire of the Inquisition by including in the mammoth canvas dogs, a cat, midgets, Huns, and drunken revelers. Four large paintings by Tintoretto—noted for their swirling action and powerful drama—depict scenes from the life of St. Mark. Finally, painted in his declining years (some have suggested in his 99th year, before he died from the plague) is Titian's majestic *Pietà*.

After a long and unimpressive walk, you can search out Canaletto's *Porticato*. Yet another room is heightened by Gentile Bellini's stunning portrait of St. Mark's Square, back in the days (1496) when the houses glistened with gold in the sunlight. All the works in this salon are intriguing, especially the re-creation of the *Ponte de Rialto*, and a covered wood bridge, by Carpaccio.

Also displayed is the cycle of narrative paintings that Vittore Carpaccio did of St. Ursula for the Scuola of Santa Orsola. The most famous is no. 578, which shows Ursula asleep on her elongated bed, with a dog nestled on the floor nearby, as the angels come for a visitation. Finally, on the way out, look for Titian's *Presentation of the Virgin*, a fit farewell to this galaxy of great Venetian art.

Museo Civico Correr. In the Procuratie Nuove, piazza San Marco. ☎ **041/552-5625.** Admission 8,000 lire ($5.10) adults, 5,000 lire ($3.20) children 12–18, free for children 10 and under. Sept–May, Thurs–Mon 10am–4pm; June–Aug, Thurs–Mon 10am–5pm. Vaporetto: San Marco.

This museum traces the development of Venetian painting from the 14th to the 16th century. On the second floor are the red and maroon robes once worn by the doges, plus some fabulous street lanterns. There's also an illustrated copy of *Marco Polo in Tartaria.* You can see Cosmé Tura's *La Pietà,* a miniature of renown from the genius in the Ferrara School. This is one of his more gruesome works. It depicts a bony, gnarled Christ sprawled on the lap of the Madonna. Farther on, search out a Schiavone *Madonna and Child* (no. 545), our candidate for ugliest bambino ever depicted on canvas (no wonder the mother looks askance).

One of the most important rooms at the Correr is filled with three masterpieces: *La Pietà* by Antonello da Messina, a *Crucifixion* by the Flemish painter Hugo van der Goes, and a *Madonna and Child* by Dieric Bouts, who depicted the baby suckling his mother in a sensual manner. The star attraction of the Correr is the Bellini salon, which includes works by founding padre Jacopo and his son, Gentile. But the real master of the household was the other son, Giovanni, the major painter of the 15th-century Venetian school (see his *Crucifixion* and compare it with his father's treatment of the same subject).

A small but celebrated portrait of St. Anthony of Padua by Alvise Vivarini is here, plus works by Bartolomeo Montagna. The most important work in the gallery, however, is Vittore Carpaccio's *Two Venetian Ladies,* popularly known as "The Courtesans." A lesser work, *St. Peter,* depicting the saint with the daggers in him, hangs in the same room.

The entrance is under the arcades of Ala Napoleonica at the western end of the square.

Ca' d'Oro. Cannaregio 3931–3932, Ca' d'Oro. ☎ **041/523-8790.** Admission 4,000 lire ($2.55). Daily 9am–1:30pm. Closed Jan 1, May 1, and Dec 25. Vaporetto: Ca' d'Oro.

This is one of the grandest and most handsomely embellished palaces along the Grand Canal. Although it contains the important **Galleria Giorgio Franchetti,** the House of Gold (so named because its facade was once gilded) competes with its own paintings. Built in the first part of the 15th century in the ogival style, it has a lacy Gothic look. Baron Franchetti, who restored the palace and filled it with his own collection of paintings, sculpture, and furniture, presented it to Italy during World War I.

You enter into a stunning courtyard, 50 yards from the vaporetto stop. The courtyard has a multicolored patterned marble floor and is filled with statuary. Then proceed upstairs to the lavishly appointed palazzo. One of the gallery's major paintings is Titian's voluptuous *Venus.* She coyly covers one breast, but what about the other?

In a special niche reserved for the masterpiece of the Franchetti collection is Andrea Mantegna's icy-cold *St. Sebastian,* the central figure of which is riddled with what must be a record number of arrows. You'll also find works by Carpaccio. Don't fail to walk out onto the loggia for a view of the Grand Canal.

Ca' Rezzonico. Fondamenta Rezzonico, Dorsoduro. ☎ **041/241-0100.** Admission 8,000 lire ($5.10) adults, 5,000 lire ($3.20) children 12–18, free for children 11 and under. Sat–Thurs 10am–4pm. Vaporetto: Ca' Rezzonico.

This 17th- and 18th-century palace along the Grand Canal is where Robert Browning set up his bachelor headquarters. Pope Clement XIII also stayed here. It's a virtual treasure house, known for both its baroque paintings and furniture. First you enter the Grand Ballroom with its allegorical ceiling, then proceed through lavishly embellished rooms with Venetian chandeliers, brocaded walls, portraits of patricians, tapestries, gilded furnishings, and touches of chinoiserie. At the end of the first walk is the Throne Room, with its allegorical ceilings by Giovanni Battista Tiepolo.

On the first floor you can walk out onto a balcony for a view of the Grand Canal as the aristocratic tenants of the 18th century saw it. After this, another group of rooms follows, including the library. In these salons, look for a bizarre collection of paintings. One, for example, depicts half-clothed women beating up a defenseless naked man (one Amazon is about to stick a pitchfork into his neck, another to crown him with a violin). In the adjoining room another woman is hammering a spike through a man's skull.

Upstairs you'll find a survey of 18th-century Venetian art. As you enter the main room from downstairs, head for the first salon on your right (facing the canal), which contains the best works of all, paintings from the brush of Pietro Longhi. His most famous work, *The Lady and the Hairdresser,* is the first canvas to the right on the entrance wall. Others depict the life of the idle Venetian rich. On the rest of the floor are bedchambers, a chapel, and salons—some with badly damaged frescoes, including a romp of satyrs.

✪ **Collezione Peggy Guggenheim.** Ca' Venier dei Leoni, Dorsoduro 701, calle San Cristoforo. ☎ **041/520-6288.** Admission 10,000 lire ($6.40) adults, 5,000 lire ($3.20) students and children 16 and under. Wed–Mon 11am–6pm. Vaporetto: Accademia.

This is one of the most comprehensive and brilliant modern-art collections in the Western world, and it reveals both the foresight and critical judgment of its founder. The collection is housed in an unfinished palazzo, the former Venetian home of Peggy Guggenheim, who died in 1979. In the tradition of her family, Peggy Guggenheim was a lifelong patron of contemporary painters and sculptors. Founder of the Art of This Century Gallery in New York in the 1940s, she created one of the most avant-garde galleries for the works of contemporary artists. Critics were impressed not only by the high quality of the artists she sponsored, but by her methods of displaying them.

As her private collection increased, she decided to find a larger showcase and selected Venice, steeped in a long tradition as a haven for artists. While the Solomon Guggenheim Museum was going up in New York according to Frank Lloyd Wright's specifications, she was creating her own gallery in Venice. Guests can wander through and enjoy art in an informal and relaxed way. Max Ernst was one of Peggy Guggenheim's early favorites, as was Jackson Pollock (she provided a farmhouse where he could develop his painting technique). Displayed here are works not only by Pollock and Ernst, but also by Picasso (see his cubist *The Poet* of 1911), Duchamp, Chagall, Mondrian, Brancusi, Delvaux, and Dalí, and a garden of modern sculpture that includes works by Giacometti. Temporary modern-art shows may be presented during the winter months. Since Peggy Guggenheim's death, the collection has been administered by the Solomon R. Guggenheim Foundation, which also operates the Solomon R. Guggenheim Museum in New York. Visitors can also enjoy a museum shop and café in the new wing of the museum, overlooking the sculpture garden.

Museo Storico Navale. Campo San Biasio, Castello 2148. ☎ **041/520-0276.** Admission 2,000 lire ($1.30). Mon–Sat 9am–1pm. Closed holidays. Vaporetto: Arsenale.

The Naval Museum of campo San Biasio is filled with cannons, ships' models, and fragments of old vessels that date back to the days when Venice was supreme in the Adriatic. The prize exhibit is a gilded model of the *Bucintoro,* the great ship of the doge that surely would have made Cleopatra's barge look like an oil tanker in comparison. In addition, you'll find models of historic and modern fighting ships, of local fishing and rowing craft, and a collection of 24 Chinese junks, as well as a number of maritime *ex voto* from churches of Naples.

If you walk along the canal as it branches off from the museum, you come first (about 270 yards from the museum and before the wooden bridge) to the **Ships' Pavilion** where historic vessels are displayed. Proceeding along the canal, you soon reach the **Arsenale,** campo del'Arsenale, guarded by stone lions, Neptune with a trident, and other assorted ferocities. You'll spot it readily enough because of its two towers that flank each side of the canal. In its day the Arsenale turned out galley after galley at speeds usually associated with wartime production.

4 More Attractions

CHURCHES & GUILD HOUSES

Much of the great art of Venice lies in its churches and *scuole* (guild houses or fraternities). Most of the guild members were drawn from the rising bourgeoisie of Venice. The guilds were said to fulfill both the material and spiritual needs of their (male) members, who often engaged in charitable works in honor of the saint for whom their scuola was named. Many of the greatest artists of Venice, including Tintoretto, were commissioned to decorate these guild houses with art. Some of the artists created masterpieces that can still be viewed today. Often the life of the patron saint of the scuola was commemorated. Narrative canvases that depicted the lives of the saints were called *teleri*.

✪ **Scuola di San Rocco.** Campo San Rocco, San Polo. ☎ **041/523-4864.** Admission 8,000 lire ($5.10) adults, 2,500 lire ($1.60) children. Mar 28–Nov 2, daily 9am–5:30pm; Nov 3-Mar 27, Mon–Fri 10am–1pm, Sat–Sun 10am–4pm. Closed Easter and Dec 25–Jan 1. Vaporetto: San Tomà; from the station, walk straight onto Ramo Mondoler, which becomes larga Prima; then take salizzada San Rocco, which opens into campo San Rocco.

Of the scuole of Venice, none is as richly embellished as the Scuola di San Rocco, which is filled with epic canvases by Tintoretto. By a clever trick he won the competition to decorate the darkly illuminated early 16th-century building. He began painting in 1564, and the work stretched on till his powers as an artist waned. The paintings sweep across the upper and lower halls, mesmerizing the viewer with a kind of passion play. In the grand hallway they depict New Testament scenes, devoted largely to episodes in the life of Mary (the *Flight into Egypt* is among the best). In the top gallery are works that illustrate scenes from both the Old and New Testaments, the most renowned being those devoted to the life of Christ. In a separate room is what is considered Tintoretto's masterpiece—his mammoth *Crucifixion,* one of the world's most celebrated paintings. In it he showed his dramatic scope and sense of grandeur as an artist, creating a deeply felt scene that virtually comes alive—filling the viewer with the horror of systematic execution, thus transcending its original subject matter.

Basilica di Santa Maria Gloriosa dei Frari. Campo dei Frari, San Polo. ☎ **041/522-2637.** Admission 2,000 lire ($1.30), free after 3pm. Mon–Sat 7:30–11:45am and 3–7pm, Sun 3–7pm. Vaporetto: San Tomà.

Known simply as the Frari, this Venetian-Gothic church is only a short walk from the Scuola di San Rocco. The church is filled with some great art. The best work is Titian's *Assumption* over the main altar—a masterpiece of soaring beauty that depicts the ascension of the Madonna on a cloud puffed up by floating cherubs. In her robe, but especially in the robe of one of the gaping saints below, "Titian red" dazzles as never before.

On the first altar to the right as you enter is Titian's second major work here—a *Madonna Enthroned*, painted for the Pesaro family in 1526. Although lacking the power and drama of the *Assumption*, it nevertheless is brilliant in its use of color and light effects. But Titian surely would turn redder than his madonna's robes if he could see the latter-day neoclassical tomb built for him on the opposite wall. The kindest word for it: large.

Facing the tomb is a memorial to Canova, the Italian sculptor who led the revival of classicism. To return to more enduring art, head to the sacristy for a Giovanni Bellini triptych on wood, painted in 1488. The Madonna is cool and serene, one of Bellini's finest portraits of the Virgin. Also see the almost primitive-looking wood carving by Donatello of *St. John the Baptist*.

Scuola di San Giorgio degli Schiavoni. Calle Furiani, Castello. ☎ **041/522-8828.** Admission 5,000 lire ($3.20). Apr–Oct, Tues–Sat 9:30am–12:30pm and 3:30–6:30pm, Sun 9:30am–12:30pm; Nov–Mar, Tues–Sat 10am–12:30pm and 3–6pm, Sun 10am–12:30pm. Vaporetto: San Zaccaria.

At the St. Antonino Bridge (fondamenta dei Furlani) is the second important guild house to visit in Venice. Between 1502 and 1509 Vittore Carpaccio painted a pictorial cycle here of exceptional merit and interest. Of enduring fame are his works of St. George and the dragon—these are our favorite art in all of Venice and certainly the most delightful. For example, in one frame St. George charges the dragon on a field littered with half-eaten bodies and skulls. Gruesome? Not at all. Any moment you expect the director to call "Cut!" The pictures relating to St. Jerome are appealing but don't compete with St. George and his ferocious dragon.

Chiesa Madonna dell'Orto. Campo dell'Orto, Cannaregio 3512. ☎ **041/719933.** Admission 2,000 lire ($1.30). May–Oct, daily 9:30am–noon and 3:30–5:30pm; Nov–Apr, daily 9:30am–noon and 3–7pm. Vaporetto: Madonna dell'Orto.

This church provides a good reason to walk to this fairly remote northern district of Venice. At the church on the lagoon you'll be paying your final respects to Tintoretto. The brick structure with a Gothic front is famed not only because of its paintings by that artist, but because the great master is buried in the chapel to the right of the main altar. At the high altar are Tintoretto's *Last Judgment* (on the right) and his *Sacrifice of the Golden Calf* (left)—two monumental paintings that curve at the top like a Gothic arch. Over the doorway to the right of the altar is Tintoretto's superb portrayal of the presentation of Mary as a little girl at the temple. The composition is unusual in that Mary is not the focal point—rather, a pointing woman bystander dominates the scene. The first chapel to the right of the main altar contains a masterly work by Cima de Conegliano, showing the presentation of a sacrificial lamb to the saints (the plasticity of St. John's body evokes Michelangelo). Finally, the first chapel on the left (as you enter) is graced with an exquisite Giovanni Bellini *Madonna and Child*. Note especially the eyes and mouth of both the mother and child. Two other pictures in the apse are *The Presentation of the Cross to St. Peter* and *The Beheading of St. Christopher*.

Chiesa di San Zaccaria. Campo San Zaccaria, Castello. ☎ **041/522-1257.** Free admission. Daily 10am–noon and 4–6pm. Vaporetto: San Zaccaria.

Behind St. Mark's Basilica is this Gothic church with a Renaissance facade. The church is filled with works of art, notably Giovanni Bellini's *Madonna Enthroned*, painted with saints (second altar to the left). Many have found this to be one of Bellini's finest madonnas, and it does have beautifully subdued coloring, although it appears rather static. Apply to the sacristan to see the Sisters' Choir, with works by Tintoretto, Titian, Il Vecchio, Anthony van Dyck, and Bassano. The paintings aren't labeled, but the sacristan will point out the names of the artists. In the Sisters' Choir are five armchairs in which the Venetian doges of yore sat. Also, if you save the best for last, you can see the faded frescoes of Andrea del Castagno in the shrine that honors San Tarasio.

Basilica di San Giorgio Maggiore. San Giorgio Maggiore, across from piazzetta San Marco. ☎ **041/528-9900.** Free admission. June–Sept, daily 9:30am–12:30pm and 2–6pm; Oct–May, daily 10am–12:30pm and 2–4:30pm. Vaporetto: Take the Giudecca-bound vaporetto (no. 82) on riva degli Schiavoni and get off at the first stop, right in the courtyard of the church.

This church sits on the little island of San Giorgio Maggiore. The building was designed by Palladio, the great Renaissance architect of the 16th century—perhaps as a consolation prize since he was not chosen to rebuild the burnt-out Doge's Palace. The logical rhythm of the Vicenza architect is played here on a grand scale. But inside it's almost too stark since Palladio wasn't much on gilded adornment. The chief art hangs on the main altar—two epic paintings by Tintoretto, the *Fall of Manna* to the left and the far more successful *Last Supper* to the right. It's interesting to compare Tintoretto's *Cena* with that of Veronese at the Academy. Afterward you may want to take the elevator—for 3,000 lire ($1.90)—to the top of the belfry for a view of the greenery of the island itself, the lagoon, and the Doge's Palace across the way. In a word, it's unforgettable.

Santa Maria della Salute. Campo della Salute, Dorsoduro. ☎ **041/522-5558.** Free admission (but an offering is expected). Mar–Nov, daily 9am–noon and 3–6:30pm; Dec–Feb, daily 9am–noon and 3–5pm. Vaporetto: Salute.

Like the proud landmark that it is, this church—the pinnacle of the baroque movement in Venice—stands at the mouth of the Grand Canal overlooking piazzetta San Marco. It opens onto campo della Salute, in Dorsoduro. One of the most historic churches in Venice, it was built by Longhena in the 17th century as an offering to the Virgin for delivering the city from the grip of the plague. It was erected on enough pilings to support the Empire State Building (well, almost). Surmounted by a great cupola, the octagonal basilica makes for an interesting visit, as it houses a small art gallery in its sacristy (tip the custodian), which includes a marriage feast of Cana by Tintoretto, allegorical paintings on the ceiling by Titian, a mounted St. Mark, and poor St. Sebastian with his inevitable arrow.

Santi Giovanni e Paolo Basilica. Campo SS. Giovanni e Paolo, Castello 6363. ☎ **041/523-5913.** Free admission. Daily 9am–12:30pm and 3–6pm. Vaporetto: Rialto or Fondamenta Nuove.

This church, also known as Zanipolo, is called the pantheon of Venice since it houses the tombs of many doges. One of the great Gothic churches of Venice, the building was erected during the 13th and 14th centuries. Inside it contains artwork by many of the most noted Venetian painters. As you enter (right aisle), you'll find a retable by Giovanni Bellini (which includes a St. Sebastian filled with arrows). In the Rosary Chapel are ceilings by Veronese depicting New Testament scenes, including *The Assumption of the Madonna*. To the right of the church is one of the world's best-known equestrian statues—that of Bartolomeo Colleoni (paid for by the condottiere), sculpted in the 15th century by Andrea del Verrochio. The bronze has long been acclaimed as his masterpiece, although it was completed by another artist. The horse is far more beautiful than the armored military hero, who looks as if he had just stumbled upon a three-headed crocodile.

To the left of the pantheon is the Scuola di San Marco, with its stunning Renaissance facade (it's now run as a civic hospital).

❓ Did You Know ?

- The Gritti Palace, the most famous hotel of Venice, is named for the notorious womanizer, Doge Andrea Gritti.

- John Ruskin once wrote that nothing could have been more childish in conception, more servile in plagiarism than Palladio's Church of San Giorgio Maggiore.

- Many famous foreigners have asked to be buried on the cemetery island of San Michele: Lord Byron, John Ruskin, and Ezra Pound among them.

- The Lido, the bathing beach of Venice, was the original Lido, lending its name to innumerable bathing spots and cinemas the world over.

- In the 16th century, any master glassblower escaping Murano with the secrets of the trade was tracked down by the Venetian Republic; for punishment, his hands were cut off or he was murdered.

- The idea of encasing a Jewish settlement into a ghetto is of Venetian origin.

- When Paolo Veronese's *The Last Supper*—filled with buffoons, drunkards, Germans, dwarfs, and similar indecencies—brought down the wrath of the Inquisition, he simply retitled it *The Banquet in the House of Levi*.

- The dogeship of Venice was the monopoly of old men because a ruler in his 70s would have fewer chances to abuse his position.

THE GHETTO

The Ghetto of Venice, called the Ghetto Nuovo, was instituted in 1516 by the Venetian Republic in the Cannaregio district. It's considered to be the first ghetto in the world, and also the best kept. The word *geto* comes from the Venetian dialect and means "foundry." Originally there were two iron foundries here where metals were fused. The Ghetto stands in what is now the northwestern corner of Venice. Once Venetian Jews were confined to a walled area and obliged to wear distinctive red or yellow marks sewn onto their clothing and distinctive-looking hats. The walls that once enclosed and confined the Ghetto were torn down long ago, but much remains of the past.

There are **five synagogues** in Venice, each built during the 16th century. The oldest and most beautiful is the Scola Tedesca (German Synagogue), which was restored with funds from Germany. The others are the Spanish (the oldest continuously functioning synagogue in Europe), the Italian, the Levantine-Oriental (also known as the Turkish Synagogue), and the Scola Canton.

The best way to visit the synagogues is to take one of the guided tours that depart from the **Museo Comunità Ebraica,** campo di Ghetto Nuovo 2902B (☎ **041/ 715359;** vaporetto: San Marcuola). The museum itself is open June to September, Sunday to Friday from 10am to 7pm; and October to May, Sunday to Friday from 10am to 4:30pm. Admission to the museum is 4,000 lire ($2.55) adults, 3,000 lire ($1.90) students. Guided tours cost 10,000 lire ($6.40) for adults and 8,000 lire ($5.10) for students. Tours last about an hour each, and depart Sunday to Friday at hourly intervals between 10:30am and 3:30pm from October to May, and at hourly intervals between 10:30am and 5:30pm from June to September. Tours include admission to the museum and visits to whatever three of the five synagogues happen to be open at the time of your visit.

You can also explore the district on your own, wandering among narrow streets where houses huddle together. In all, the district resembles a complex that's unique in the world.

WALKING TOUR
From Piazza San Marco to the Grand Canal

If this walking tour whets your appetite for more strolls through Venice, pick up a copy of *Frommer's Walking Tours: Venice*, which features 10 walking tours as well as detailed maps of the city.

Start: Piazza San Marco.
Finish: Grand Canal at the ponte di Rialto.
Time: 2 hours, not including stops.
Best Times: Any sunny day.
Worst Times: Holidays and festivals (the streets are too crowded).

There are hundreds of byways, alleyways, and canals stretching across the faded splendor of Venice. This 2-hour walking tour will give you at least an exterior view plus a general orientation to the layout of parts of the city, often showing lesser-known sights, which can best be seen from the outside, on foot. Later, you can pick and choose at your leisure the sights you most want to revisit.

Our tour begins, appropriately enough, at the heart of the city:

1. **Piazza San Marco,** or St. Mark's Square, the most famous in Italy. Here and on its satellite square, piazzetta San Marco, you can explore the major attractions of the city. These include the:

2. **Basilica di San Marco,** named for St. Mark, whose body was allegedly stolen from his tomb in Alexandria in 828 and brought to Venice. This basilica was built to enshrine the body of the man who became the city's patron saint. Next door is the:

3. **Palazzo Ducale,** with its adjoining ponte dei Sospiri (Bridge of Sighs), a pink confection that was the home of the doges (dukes) who ruled Venice for years. In front of the palace is the:

4. **Campanile di San Marco,** the bell tower of Venice, which visitors climb for a view of the city and lagoon.

The Renaissance mariners who supplied the lifelines that led to their Adriatic capital realized that the most impressive view of the city was, and perhaps still is, visible only from the water. To better see this unforgettable view, take a brief vaporetto ride across the Grand Canal to the baroque white walls of:

5. **Santa Maria della Salute.** Buy your ticket at either of two vaporetto stops: no 16 (San Zaccaria), just east of St. Mark's Square, or no. 15 (San Marco), which lies just west of the square along the Grand Canal. Enjoy the short water ride and the view before getting off on the opposite side of the canal at the pier marked SALUTE. There you can look back across the Grand Canal at the rows of palazzi, many of which have been turned into glamorous hotels.

Walk to the right side of the church along campo della Salute, past a pair of wooden bridges, and continue until you reach the third bridge, the only one of the three that's made of stone. Cross this bridge and head onto rio Terradei Catecumeni. After 1 block, turn left onto calle Constantina. Now walk toward the water, along a wide flagstone-covered walkway divided by a single row of trees that must struggle to survive in the salt air of Venice. The waterway you'll soon reach separates this section of Venice from the rarely visited:

6. Island of Giudecca, which lies across the broad canale di Giudecca. Although you won't visit it as part of this walking tour, you might decide to return to explore its untrammeled streets later during your visit. From this vantage point, you can also gaze upon the cranes of the industrialized mainland town of Mestre, to the north.

Turn right along the waterfront of a district known to Venetians as Dorsoduro. Much more of a residential neighborhood than the area around piazza San Marco, it has often been compared to New York's Greenwich Village because artists and writers have traditionally been attracted to it. Many, of course, came to avoid the high prices charged on the opposite side of the Grand Canal. With water to your left and a changing panorama of brick and stone buildings to your right, you'll cross over the high arches of several bridges, always continuing along the canalside walkway which, in characteristically Venetian fashion, will change its name at least three times.

At the third and last bridge, the ponte della Calcina, at campiello della Calcina, you'll notice two of the most famous pensiones of Venice—La Calcina, where John Ruskin stayed, and the Pensione Seguso. The name of the pavement that supports you here is Zattere ai Gesuati. You'll notice a pair of wooden platforms, managed by local cafés and separated from one another by drydocked steel-hulled ships. After, perhaps, a coffee, you reach the acanthus-inspired pilasters of the baroque:

7. Chiesa dei Gesuiti. After visiting the church, take the street to its right, which is referred to variously as rio Terrà Antonio Foscarini, the rio Terrà Marco Foscarini, or simply rio Terrà Foscarini, and walk northwest. At the side of the church, admire campo Santa Agnese, where tolling bells call the neighborhood to mass.

Now continue north along rio Foscarini until you reach the Grand Canal and the:

8. Gallerie dell'Accademia. You can either visit this great gallery of art or save it for another day. Cross the bridge, and you may notice the German consulate beside the elegant garden to the left. When you step off the bridge, you'll be on campo San Vidal. At this point, the city of Venice has graciously mapped out one of the most logical walking tours in the city by posting prominent yellow signs with black lettering on dozens of appropriate street corners.

Your walk, if you follow the signs, will take you back to St. Mark's Square through dozens of claustrophobic alleys, which are crumbling from exposure to the Adriatic winds, and into gloriously proportioned squares whose boundaries are often ornamented with exquisite detailing. From this point on, follow the signs that say PER S. MARCO. You can afford to ignore your map and lose yourself in the Renaissance splendor of this most unusual city.

At campo San Vidal, the pavement will funnel you in only one possible direction. After several twists and turns, you'll be in the huge expanse of:

9. Campo San Stefano (whose southern end is referred to on some maps as campo Francesco Morosini). Keep walking across the square, past a wood-and-iron flag-pole capped with the Lion of St. Mark. Midway along the right side of the square, follow the PER S. MARCO sign down a tiny alleyway called calle del Spezier. The alley funnels across a bridge and then changes its name to calle del Piovan. This will open to the wide expanses of:

10. Campo San Maurizio. Walk directly across the square, looking for yet another PER S. MARCO sign, which should direct you over another set of bridges.

This square funnels into the narrow calle Zaguri. Cross another canal's arched bridge and enter campiello de la Feltrina. Keep following the signs to San Marco. Soon you'll come to one of the most famous Venetian squares, which is shaped roughly like a crucifix. One end opens onto the Grand Canal, near the famous hotel in Venice, the Gritti Palace. The full name of the square is campo Santa Maria Zobenigo o del Giglio, a name usually shortened to:

11. Campo del Giglio. The square is dominated by a larger-than-life-size statue, which guards the baroque facade of the Chiesa di Santa Maria del Giglio. Founded in the 9th century, but reconstructed in the 17th, it contains canvases by Tintoretto and Rubens.

As you exit from the church, follow once again the signs to San Marco, going down an alleyway, calle delle Ostreghe. Cross the high arch of a canal-spanning bridge, on the opposite side of which you'll spot a good place to:

☕ **TAKE A BREAK** The **Bar Ducale,** calle delle Ostreghe, offers cocktails and sandwiches. The owner once worked at Harry's Bar and learned the restaurant's culinary secrets. The only difference here is not in taste, but in price—the Bar Ducale charges half the price of Harry's Bar. If not a sandwich, then enjoy a cappuccino.

When you leave the Bar Ducale, follow the street through several twists and turns onto:

12. Calle larga XXII Marzo, whose many shops, cafés, and restaurants make this one of the most-frequented and crowded streets of Venice. In about a block, midway down its length, we recommend a short detour off to the left. Notice the gold, white, and red sign pointing to AL TEATRO LA FENICE. The street this points to is calle del Sartor da Veste. Turn neither to the left nor right, but follow it over two bridges, into what is one of the most intimate summertime "living rooms" of Venice:

13. Campo San Fantin. In fair weather, the enclosed square is dotted with tables set out by the best restaurant in Venice, the Antico Martini, and its lesser rivals. Here you'll find the Teatro La Fenice and the Church of St. Fantin. After visiting the church, retrace your steps along the street you took previously. From the end of the square, its name appears as calle del Cafetier. This walk will take you back over the pair of bridges leading once again to calle larga XXII Marzo.

Head left, toward the San Moisè Church. By now the PER S. MARCO signs will lead you through:

14. Campo San Moisè, whose ornate facade contrasts oddly with the modern bulk of the Hotel Bauer Grünwald & Grand on your right. Take the street to the left of the church, and note the PER S. MARCO sign as you pass by the American Express office while heading straight along the street that, by now, has changed its name once again, this time to calle seconda de l'Ascension. Continue straight under an arched tunnel to the sweeping expanses of piazza San Marco, once again, where you may want to visit the:

15. Museo Correr, in the Procuratie Nuove, opposite the basilica. This museum traces the development of Venetian painting from the 14th to the 16th century.

☕ **TAKE A BREAK** Since **Florian,** piazza San Marco 56–59, was established, it has been the most Venetian of all cafes. Its interior rooms drip with a nostalgic 18th-century decor, but if the weather's sunny most guests prefer to sit outside. The Venetians patronized this cafe during the Austrian occupation, whereas the occupying army's brass went to the rival cafe, the Quadri, across the square.

Walking Tour—From Piazza San Marco to the Grand Canal

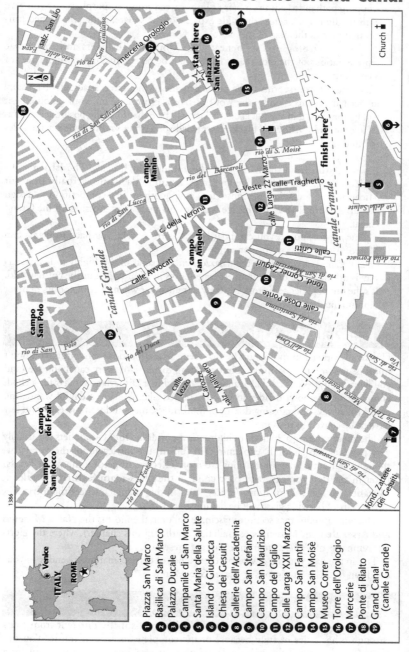

Church ✝

start here

② ③ →

⑯ ④

⑰ mercerie Orologio

① ⑮

piazza San Marco

finish here ⑭ ⑥ →

rio di S. Moisè ⑤

campo Manin

rio del Barcaroli

c.-Veste calle Traghetto

⑬ c. della Verona ⑫ calle Larga 22 Marzo canale Grande

rio di San Salvador

rio di San Salvador

campo San Angelo ⑪ calle Cristi rio della Fornace

calle Avvocati fond. Corner Zaguri rio di San Maurizio

⑩ calle Dose Ponte rio delle Ostreghe

⑨ rio del Santissimo

canale Grande ⑲

rio di San Polo

campo San Polo

rio di Ca' Foscari

campo del Frari

campo San Rocco

calle Lezzo salz. Nell'olio c. Carozze

rio del Duca

rio di San rio Marco Foscarini ⑧ rio de S.

⑦ ✝

fond. Zattere dei Gesuiti

rio di della Fava salz. San Lio rio di San Giuliano

⑱

rio di San

canale Grande

ITALY
● Venice
ROME ★

① Piazza San Marco
② Basilica di San Marco
③ Palazzo Ducale
④ Campanile di San Marco
⑤ Santa Maria della Salute
⑥ Island of Giudecca
⑦ Chiesa dei Gesuiti
⑧ Gallerie dell'Accademia
⑨ Campo San Stefano
⑩ Campo San Maurizio
⑪ Campo del Giglio
⑫ Calle Larga XXII Marzo
⑬ Campo San Fantin
⑭ Campo San Moisè
⑮ Museo Correr
⑯ Torre dell'Orologio
⑰ Mercerie
⑱ Ponte di Rialto
⑲ Grand Canal (canale Grande)

403

Later, walk through the square and pass to the left of the Basilica of St. Mark, stopping perhaps to admire a pair of lions carved from red porphyry. As you gaze with the lions back across the wide expanse of the square, notice the arched tunnel that pierces the base of the:

16. **Torre dell'Orologio.** Pass beneath the Moorish bellringers and the zodiac representations of the clock face. Here you'll be on the major shopping street of Venice, the:

17. **Mercerie.** Of course, this is the popular name of the street. It actually has many longer names, preceded by the word *merceria*. From now on, your guiding light will be the signs that say PER RIALTO. They will be either formally positioned at strategic corners in yellow or black or scrawled sometimes graffiti-style on the sides of buildings.

Soon you'll reach the:

18. **Ponte Rialto,** from the Latin *rivo alto,* meaning high bank. The Istrian-stone bridge dates from 1588. The architect, Antonio da Ponte, actually beat out Michelangelo, Palladio, and Sansovino, among others, in a competition to design this bridge. Until 1854 the bridge was the only pedestrian crossing on the Grand Canal.

Once at this point, you can board a vaporetto to take you back to piazza San Marco. Along the way you can enjoy the:

19. **Grand Canal.** A ride along the palazzo-flanked banks of this highly touted waterway is not only one of the grandest experiences in all of Italy, but the entire world. It's the one experience visitors are likely to remember when their memories of other monuments have gone hazy.

5   Especially for Kids

Unlike any other European city, Venice seems made for kids—providing you don't mind issuing a lot of warnings about avoiding the edge of every canal you see (and you'll see plenty). Venice is like wandering around in a Disneyland fantasy for a child, complete with vaporetto rides to yet-unexplored islands. After a day of wandering endless alleyways and crossing dozens of footbridges, most children tire early and few have to be coaxed to turn in.

The most exciting activity for children is a **gondola ride.** Gondoliers are usually very patient with children, explaining (in Italian) the intricacies of their craft, although their actual demonstrations are more effective in getting the point across. Later in the day you can take your child to the **glass-manufacturing works** at **Murano** (see "Side Trips from Venice," later in this chapter), where the intricacies of the craft of blowing glass will be demonstrated.

The one museum that seems to fascinate children the most is the **Naval Museum and Arsenale** (see "Museums & Galleries," earlier in this chapter), where the glorious remnants of Venice's maritime past are presented.

To cap the day, you can always purchase a bag of corn from a street vendor so your child can feed the fat pigeons at **piazza San Marco.**

6   Organized Tours

Tours through the streets and canals of Venice are distinctly different from tours through other cities of Italy because of the complete absence of traffic. You can always wander at will through the labyrinth of streets, but many visitors opt for a guided tour to at least familiarize themselves with the geography of the city.

American Express, San Marco 1471 (☎ **041/520-0844**), which operates from a historic building a few steps from St. Mark's Square, offers an array of guided city tours. Some of the most popular offerings include the following:

Every morning at 9:10am a 2-hour guided tour of the city departs from in front of the American Express building The tour costs 33,000 lire ($21.10). Sights include St. Mark's Square, the basilica, the Doge's Palace, the prison, the bell tower, and in some cases a demonstration of the art of Venetian glassblowing.

Every afternoon, between 3 and 5pm a 2-hour guided tour incorporates visits to the exteriors of several palaces along campo San Benetto and other sights of the city. The tour eventually crosses the Grand Canal to visit the Church of Santa Maria dei Frari (which contains the *Assumption* by Titian). The tour continues by gondola down the canal to visit the Ca' d'Oro and eventually ends at the Rialto Bridge. The afternoon tour costs 35,000 lire ($22.40). The combined price for both tours is just 60,000 lire ($38.40).

The "Evening Serenade Tour," priced at 50,000 lire ($32) per person, allows a nocturnal view of Venice accompanied by the sound of singing musicians in gondolas. From May to October there are two daily departures, one at 7 and another at 8pm, which leave from campo Santa Maria del Giglio. Five to six occupants fit in each gondola. The experience lasts 50 minutes.

A "Tour of the Islands of the Venetian Lagoon," priced at 25,000 lire ($16), departs twice daily, at 9:30am and again at 2:30pm, and lasts 3 hours. You'll pass— but not land at—the islands of San Giorgio and San Francesco del Deserto, and eventually land at Burano, Murano, and Torcello for brief tours of their churches and landmarks. This trip departs from and returns to the pier at riva degli Schiavoni.

The American Express office is open for tours and travel arrangements Monday to Friday from 9am to 5:30pm and on Saturday from 9am to 5pm.

If you'd like more personalized tours than those offered by American Express, contact the **Venice Travel Advisory Service,** 22 Riverside Dr., New York, NY 10023 (☎ and fax **212/873-1964,** or 041/523-2379 in Venice). Born in New York City, Samantha Durell is a professional photographer, and has lived and worked in Venice as a private tour guide for more than 9 years. Some locals claim that she knows Venice far better than they do.

She arranges tours, conducts orientation sessions, and aids in any advance-planning service, such as securing a hotel during Carnevale or getting opera tickets. She also gives advice on how to search out that little out-of-the-way trattoria, where you can enjoy a typical Venetian cuisine far away from the tourist hordes. In addition, she also has a wealth of information about shopping, sightseeing, art and history, dining, and entertainment. Her private guided tours are individually tailored to your needs. She's known for taking clients through tiny winding back streets and timeless neighborhoods.

Morning and afternoon tours, for a maximum of six people, last about 4 hours and cost $225 for two people, $50 for each additional adult, and $25 for each additional child.

For do-it-yourself walking tours of Venice's major sights, try *Frommer's Walking Tours: Venice.*

7 Special & Free Events

Although cities from New Orleans to Rio celebrate their own respective carnivals with their own kinds of panache, the ✪ **Carnavale of Venice** might be the oldest, most historic, and most eerily evocative. Continuing a tradition established during the

Renaissance, it occupies 10 days in February with sometimes-raucous parties that seem to anticipate the upcoming sobriety of Lent, Good Friday, and Easter. Declared an official holiday by the mayor of Venice in the 1970s, it includes around-the-clock street theater, highly electrified pop concerts, and the presence of thousands of non-Venetians who pour into the city for a series of private and public masked balls. The festival's most famous garb includes three-cornered hats, elaborate wigs, costumes inspired by something out of an opera by Mozart, and blandly enigmatic porcelain masks whose contours and nuances are a well-established art form in their own right.

In springtime, on the first Sunday after Ascension Day, Venetians observe **La Vogalonga** ("The Long Row"). Although it was established rather recently (1975), it's now one of the best-attended events in Venice. More of an oarsman's marathon than a race, it includes all kinds of oar-powered seacraft whose 20-mile course takes them from the base of piazza San Marco around Saint-Elena, to points as far away as San Francesco del Deserto and Burano before returning to Venice via the Cannaregio Canal and the Grand Canal. Boats depart around 9:30am, returning (with very tired oarsmen) anytime from 11am into the early evening. Unlike many other nautical events in Venice's calendar of events, this one is open to any foreigner with a safely outfitted oar-driven craft.

The third weekend in July, during the crush of the tourist season, Venetians celebrate the **Feast of the Redeemer (Festa del Redentore).** Festivities include illuminated gondolas, fireworks above the lagoon, and roaming musicians floating on barges. A bridge of boats is erected across the Guidecca Canal near the base of the Church of the Redentore, commemorating the end of the plague of 1576, and many Venetians spend most of the festival picnicking from the gunnels of their boats. Many end the festival early the next morning, perhaps on the beaches of the Lido.

In September, one of Italy's most famous nautical events is the **Historic Regatta (Regatta Storica),** during which richly decorated gondolas, staffed by boatmen in Renaissance costumes, race one another along the Grand Canal. Floating barges and historically important boats carry the music and parties out into the open lagoon in an event that perhaps better than any other evokes the nautical traditions of imperial Venice.

Late in August and early in September, the **International Film Festival** is hosted on the Lido, during which the stars, starlets, producers, directors, salespeople, artists, charlatans, and wannabees of the film industry congregate. Hundreds of films are shown almost around the clock. Ticket costs spiral as the festival progresses.

During alternate (odd-numbered) years, between June and October, the **International Exposition of Modern Art,** better known as the **Biennale d'Arte,** adds a modern note to the antique charm of Venice with some of the largest imported collections of contemporary paintings and sculptures in the world. These are displayed in a series of approximately 35 different exposition spaces, both indoor and outdoor. Locations are announced as part of each (alternate) year's events. (Most are centered around the vaporetto stop of Giardini.) Originally established in 1895, the Biennale is one of the most famous art events in Europe.

In November, during a wet and rainy season that attracts the fewest numbers of international visitors, the **opera season** at the theater of Malibran begins, continuing till mid-May. On November 21, a **religious procession,** ending within the imperious white walls of Santa Maria della Salute (the most important baroque building in Venice), remembers the end of the plague of 1630. To commemorate the event, a pair of floating bridges are devised, spanning the Grand Canal for the benefit of the faithful and/or nostalgic.

8 Soccer Matches & Other Outdoor Activities

Venice is so full of architectural and artistic riches that few visitors will look for opportunities for sport and conventional recreations. In a city without cars, the labyrinth of pedestrian walkways and steeply inclined bridges offers ample opportunities for walking, with never a dull expanse between landmarks. The densely populated labyrinth of the city itself offers almost no sports facilities in its historic or residential core; if you insist on diversions, you'll have to head out to the flat and sandy expanses of Venice's playground, the Lido.

GOLF   With the salt air whipping in from the Adriatic, a brisk 18 holes of golf might be especially invigorating. At the extreme western end of the Lido you'll find the **Venice Golf Club,** via del Forte (☎ **041/731333**). To reach it, take vaporetto no. 52 from riva degli Schiavoni or the C bus from the Lido's main dock at Santa Maria Elisabetta.

JOGGING   The broad thoroughfares of central Venice's riva degli Schiavoni, just east of piazza San Marco, are usually suitable for jogging, except in midsummer when they tend to be jammed with slowly meandering pedestrians. Another possibility includes the lengthy and often less-crowded expanse of paved-over shoreline beside the Giudecca Canal. More suitable in any season is the beach of the Lido.

SAILING   Sailing boats, with or without skippers, can be rented, and sailing lessons are given, at the **Ciga Yacht Club,** based beside the Excelsior Hotel (☎ **041/526-0201**), the most prominent hotel on the Lido.

SOCCER   The season for spectator soccer (by far the best-attended sports event in Venice) lasts from September to May. The city's soccer team, Venezia, welcomes visiting teams from throughout the rest of Europe for games that are usually held on Sunday afternoon at the **Stadio Comunale P. L. Pezo,** San Elena (☎ **041/523-9999**). Tickets go on sale at the stadium's box office several hours before play begins. If you want to actually play soccer, you'll have to content yourself with joining a scrimmage or spontaneous pickup game in one of the city's residential squares.

SWIMMING   Because the waters of Venice itself are polluted, all swimming should be confined to the tide-scoured beaches of the Lido, and even then it probably isn't such a great idea. Most of the city's public beaches lie along the Lido's northern end, whereas beaches fronting the island's southern and central end tends to be reserved for clients of the various hotels that line its shores. There's a public pool, the **Piscina Gandini,** on the Isola di San Giorgio (☎ **041/528-5430**), where waters might be somewhat healthier.

TENNIS   The **Tennis Club,** lungomare Marconi 41D (☎ **041/526-7194**), offers a handful of courts that, if not being used by members, can be rented by the hour to players appropriately dressed in tennis whites. You can also try the **Tennis Club Lido,** via Sandra Gallo 163 (☎ **041/526-0954**). Because of the frequent winter rainfall, both of these tend to close down in winter.

9 Shopping

THE SHOPPING SCENE

Venetian **glass** and **lace** are known throughout the world. However, selecting quality products in either craft requires a shrewd eye, as there's much that is tawdry and shoddily crafted. Some of the glassware hawked isn't worth the cost of shipping it home. Yet other pieces represent some of the world's finest artistic and ornamental glass. Murano is the island where glass is made, and the women of Burano put in painstaking hours turning out lace. If you're interested in some little glass souvenir of your stay, perhaps an animal or a bird, you'll find such items sold in shops all over Venice.

TIPS ON SHOPPING FOR GLASS   Venice is literally crammed with glass shops. It's estimated that there are at least 1,000 of them in the sestiere of San Marco alone. Unless you go to an absolutely top-quality and reliable dealer, such as those we recommend, you'll often find both shoddy and high-quality glassware for sale at the same shop. Only the most trained eye can sometimes tell the difference. The big secret (which is becoming less a secret all the time) is that much so-called Venetian glass isn't Venetian at all, but comes from former Eastern Bloc countries, including the Czech Republic. Of course, the Czech Republic has some of the finest glassmakers in Europe, so that may not be bad either. It boils down to this: If you like an item, buy it. It may not be high quality, but then again, high-quality glassware can cost thousands of dollars. If you're looking for an heirloom, stick to such award-winning houses as Pauly & Co. or Venini. Even buyers of glassware for distribution outlets in other parts of the world have been fooled by the vast array of glass for sale in Venice, thinking they were purchasing a better quality of glass than they actually got. If even a buyer can be tricked, the layperson has only his or her own good instincts to follow.

TIPS ON SHOPPING FOR LACE   Most of the lace vendors are centered around piazza San Marco. Although high, prices of Venetian lace are still reasonable considering the painstaking work that goes into it. A small handkerchief, for example, with a floral border can sell for as little as 5,000 lire ($3.20), although for large items, such as a heirloom-quality hand-worked tablecloth, the sky's the limit. Much of the lace is shoddy, and some of it—a lot of it, really—isn't Venetian lace but machine made in who knows what country. *The* name in Venetian lace is Jesurum (see below), which has stood for quality since the last century.

Jesurum has its own lacemakers and—to guarantee its future—even has a school to teach apprentices how to make lace. It offers the most expensive, but also the highest quality, lace in Venice. At other places you take your chances. The lace shops are like the glassware outlets. They sell both the shoddy, the machine-made, and the exquisite handmade pieces. Sometimes only the trained eye can tell the difference. Again, the best advice is to buy what you like, if you think the price is reasonable. However, even if a piece is handmade, you can never be sure exactly *where* it was handmade. Maybe China.

SHOPPING STROLLS   All the main shopping streets of Venice, even the side streets, are touristy and overrun. The greatest concentration of shops is around piazza San Marco and around the Rialto. Prices are much higher at San Marco, but the quality of merchandise is also higher. There are two major shopping strolls in Venice. First, from piazza San Marco you can stroll through Venice toward the spacious square of campo Morosini. You just follow one shop-lined street all the way to its end (although the name will change several times along the way). You begin at salizzada San Moisè, which becomes via 22 Marzo, and then calle delle Ostreghe, before it opens onto campo Santa Maria Zobenigo. The street then narrows again and changes its name to calle Zaguri before widening once more into campo San Maurizio, finally becoming calle Piovan before it reaches campo Morosini. The only deviation from this tour is a detour down calle Vallaressa, between San Moisè and the Grand Canal, which is one of the major shopping arteries with some of the biggest designer names in the business.

Venetian Carnival Masks

Venetian masks, now considered collector's items, originated during *carnevale,* which takes place the week before the beginning of Lent. In the old days there was a good reason to wear a mask during the riotous carnival, as wives and husbands did their best to be unfaithful and priests tried to break their vows of chastity. Things got so out of hand that the carnival was banned in the late 18th century. But it came back— and the masks went on again.

Shops selling masks can be found practically on every corner. As with glass and lace, however, quality varies. Many masks are great artistic expressions, while others are shoddy and cheap. The most sought after mask is the *Portafortuna* (luck bringer), with its long nose and birdlike visage. *Orientale* masks evoke the heyday of the Serene Republic and its trade with the Far East. The *Bauta* was worn by men to assert their macho qualities, while the *Neutra* mask blends the facial characteristics of both sexes. The list of masks and their derivations seems endless.

One of the best places to purchase carnival masks is **Laboratorio Artigiano Maschere,** Castello 6657, Barbaria delle Tole (☎ **041/522-3110;** Vaporetto: Rialto), which sells handcrafted masks in papier-mâché or leather. Masks are sold all over Venice, but this well-established store has a particularly good selection, including masks that depict characters of the Commedia dell'Arte. The shop also sells a variety of other handcrafted papier-mâché items, including picture and mirror frames, pots, consoles, and boxes in the shape of pets. The shop is open on Monday from 10 to 11:30am, Tuesday to Friday from 10am to 1pm and 3 to 7pm, and on Saturday from 10am to 1pm and 3 to 5pm.

The other great shopping stroll in Venice wanders from piazza San Marco to the Rialto in a succession of streets collectively known as the Mercerie. It's virtually impossible to get lost because each street name is preceded by the word *merceria,* such as Merceria dell'Orologio, which begins near the clock tower in piazza San Marco. Many commercial establishments—mainly shops—line the Mercerie before it reaches the Rialto, which then explodes into one vast shopping emporium

SHOPPING A TO Z
ANTIQUES
Antichita Santomanco. Frezzeria 1504, San Marco. ☎ **041/523-6643.** Vaporetto: San Marco.

This store is for the specialist only—especially the well-heeled specialist. It specializes in antique furniture, books, prints, and coins. Of course, the merchandise is ever-changing, but you're likely to pick up some little heirloom item in the midst of the clutter. Many of the items date from the Venetian heyday of the 1600s. Open Monday to Saturday from 9am to 12:30pm and 3 to 7pm, and sometimes on Sunday from 9:30am to 12:30pm (call about Sunday openings).

BRASS OBJECTS
Valese Fonditore. Calle Fiubera 793, San Marco. ☎ **041/522-7282.** Vaporetto: San Marco.

Founded in 1913, Valese Fonditore serves as a showcase for one of the most famous of the several foundries that make their headquarters in Venice. Many of the brass copies of 18th-century chandeliers produced by this company grace fine homes in the United States. Many visitors to Venice invest in these brass castings, which eventually become family heirlooms. If you're looking for a brass replica of the sea horses decorating the sides of gondolas, this shop stocks them in five or six different styles and sizes. Open on Monday from 2 to 7:30pm and Tuesday to Saturday from 10:30am to 7:30pm.

FASHION

Belvest Boutique. Calle Vallaresso 1305 (near Harry's Bar), San Marco. ☎ **041/528-7933.** Vaporetto: San Marco.

This is one of the finest boutiques of Venice, specializing in clothing for women and men, both handmade and ready to wear. Fabric from some of the world's leading clothmakers is used in the designs. Linked with Vogini, the famous purveyor of leatherwork, the boutique is a bastion of top-quality craftsmanship and high-fashion style. Open April to October, Monday to Saturday from 9am to 7:30pm; November to March, on Monday from 3 to 7:30pm and Tuesday to Saturday from 9am to 12:30pm and 3 to 7:30pm.

La Bottega di Nino. San Marco 223, Mercerie dell'Orologio. ☎ **041/522-5608.** Vaporetto: San Marco.

In need of some new threads for the film festival? This is the place for elegant male attire. It features the work of many European designers, even some from England, but it shines brightest in its Italian names, such as Nino Cerruti, Valentino, and Zenia. The prices are also better for Italian wear. Open April to October, daily from 9:30am to 7:30pm; November to March, on Monday from 9:30am to 12:30pm and Tuesday to Saturday from 9:30am to 12:30pm and 3:30 to 5:30pm.

La Fenice. Calle larga XXII Marzo 2255, San Marco. ☎ **041/523-1273.** Vaporetto: San Marco.

Despite the similarity of its name with one of Venice's most visible theaters, this is a large and well-stocked outlet for some of the most visible clothing manufacturers of Italy. One of four outlets of a city-wide chain, La Fenice sells clothing for men and women from designers such as Ferré, Dior, Montana, Mügler, and several others. Open on Monday from 4 to 7:30pm and Tuesday to Saturday from 9:30am to 7:30pm.

GIFTS

Il Papiro. Campo San Maurizio 2764. ☎ **041/522-3055.** Vaporetto: Accademia.

Il Papiro is mainly noted for its stationery supplies, but it also carries and sells many different textures and colors of writing paper and cards. In addition to hand-printed paper, it sells any number of easy-to-pack gift items, such as wooden animals and copybooks. It's a good bet for those who want to take back small, inexpensive gifts. Open on Monday from 3:30 to 7:30pm, Tuesday to Saturday from 9:30am to 7:30pm, and on Sunday from 10am to 6pm.

GLASS

Pauly & Co. Ponte Consorzi, San Marco. ☎ **041/520-9899.** Vaporetto: San Zaccaria.

This award-winning house exports its products all over the world. You can wander through its 21 salons, enjoy an exhibition of artistic glassware, and later see a furnace in full action. Pauly's production, which is mainly made to order, consists of continually renewed patterns, subject to change and alteration based on customer desire. Open Easter to October, daily from 10am to 7pm; November to Easter, Monday to Saturday from 10am to 1pm and 3 to 7pm.

Venini. Piazzetta Leoncini 314, San Marco. ☎ **041/522-4045.** Vaporetto: San Zaccaria.

Venini has won collector fans all over the globe for its Venetian art glass, including anything-but-ordinary lamps, bottles, and vases. Many are works of art, representing the best of Venetian craftsmanship in design and manufacture. Along with the previously recommended Pauly & Co. and Salviati, San Gregorio 195 (☎ 041/522-4257), Venini represents the big triumvirate of Venetian glassmakers. Its best-known glass has a distinctive swirl pattern in several colors, which is called a venature. This shop is known for the refined quality of its glass, some of which appears almost transparent. Much of it is very fragile, but they long ago learned how to ship it anywhere safely. Open on Monday from 3:30 to 7:30pm and Tuesday to Saturday from 9am to 7:30pm.

GRAPHICS

Bac Art Studio. Campo San Maurizio 2663, San Marco. ☎ **041/522-8171.** Vaporetto: Santa Maria del Giglio.

This studio sells paper goods, but it's mainly a graphics gallery, noted for its selection of engravings, posters, and lithographs, which represent Venice at carnival time. Many views of Venice parade before you. Items for the most part are reasonably priced as well, and care and selection obviously went into the gallery's choice of its merchandise. Open Monday to Saturday from 10am to 1pm and 3 to 7pm.

Osvaldo Böhm. San Moisè 1349–1350. ☎ **041/522-2255.** Vaporetto: San Marco.

Head here for that just right—and light—souvenir of Venice. Osvaldo Böhm has a rich collection of photographic archives specializing in Venetian art as well as original engravings and maps, lithographs, watercolors, and Venetian masks. You can also see modern serigraphs by local artists and some fine handcrafted bronzes. Open Monday to Saturday from 9am to 7:30pm and sometimes on Sunday from 10am to 5pm.

JEWELRY

Missiaglia. Piazza San Marco 125. ☎ **041/522-4464.** Vaporetto: San Marco.

Since 1864 Missiaglia has been the private supplier to rich Venetians and savvy shoppers from around the world seeking the best in gold and jewelry. Go here for that special, classic piece. However, the family also keeps its antennae trained on the latest developments in jewelry design worldwide.

LACE

Jesurum. Mercerie del Capitello, San Marco N. 4857. ☎ **041/520-6177.** Vaporetto: San Zaccaria.

For serious purchases, Jesurum is the best place. This elegant shop, a center of noted lacemakers and fashion creators, has been located in a 12th-century church since 1868. You'll find Venetian handmade or machine-made lace and embroidery on table, bed, and bath linens; and hand-printed bathing suits. Quality and originality are guaranteed, and special orders are accepted. The exclusive linens created here are expensive, but the inventory is large enough to accommodate any kind of budget. Open Monday to Saturday from 9:30am to 7:30pm and on Sunday from 10am to 1pm and 2 to 7pm.

LEATHER

Bottega Veneta. Calle Vallaresso 1337, San Marco. ☎ **041/522-8489.** Vaporetto: San Marco.

Bottega Veneta is primarily known for its woven leather bags. These bags are sold elsewhere too, but the prices are said to be less at the company's flagship outlet in

Venice. The shop also sells shoes for men and women, suitcases, belts, and everything made of leather. There's also an array of high-fashion accessories. Both men and women will find this store a delight. Men will enjoy the assortment of leather wallets, for example. Open on Monday from 3 to 6:30pm and Tuesday to Saturday from 9:30am to 1pm and 3 to 6:30pm; from March to September and December, also on Sunday from 11am to 1pm and 2 to 6pm.

Furla. Mercerie del Capitello, San Marco 4954. ☎ **041/523-0611.** Vaporetto: Rialto.

Furla is a specialist in women's leather bags. It also sells belts and gloves for women. Many of the bags are stamped with molds, making them appear to be alligator, lizard, or some other exotic creature. These bags come in a varied choice of colors, including what the Austrians call "Maria Theresa ocher." Furla also displays a varied selection of costume jewelry. Open June to September, daily from 9:15am to 7:30pm; October to May, on Monday from 3 to 7:30pm, Tuesday to Saturday from 9:15am to 12:30pm and 3 to 7:30pm, and on Sunday from 10:30am to 1:15pm and 2:15 to 6:30pm.

Marforio. Campo San Salvador 5033, San Marco. ☎ **041/522-5734.** Vaporetto: Rialto.

Marforio is located in the heart of the city. Founded in 1875, it's the oldest and largest leathergoods retail outlet in Italy. The company has been run by the same family for five generations. It's known for the quality of its leather products, and the outlet here has an enormous assortment, including all the famous European labels— Valentino, Giorgio Armani, Cerruti, and Pierre Cardin, among others. Open on Monday from 9am to 12:30pm and Tuesday to Saturday from 9am to 7:30pm.

Vogini. San Marco Ascensione 1291, 1292, and 1301 (near Harry's Bar). ☎ **041/522-2573.** Vaporetto: San Marco.

Every kind of leatherwork is offered at Vogini, especially women's handbags, which are exclusive models. There's also a large assortment of handbags in petit-point, plus men's and women's wear and shoes. The collection of artistic Venetian leather is of the highest quality. The travel-equipment department contains a large assortment of trunks and wardrobe suitcases as well as dressing cases—many of the latest models in luggage. Open April to October, Monday to Saturday from 9am to 7:30pm; November to March, on Monday from 3 to 7:30pm and Tuesday to Saturday from 9am to 12:30pm and 3 to 7:30pm.

MARKETS

If you're looking for some bargain-basement buys, head not for any basement but to one of the little shops that line the **Rialto Bridge.** The shops there branch out to encompass fruit and vegetable markets as well. The Rialto isn't the ponte Vecchio in Florence, but, for what it offers, it isn't bad, particularly if your lire are running short. You'll find a wide assortment of merchandise here, from angora sweaters to leather gloves. Quality is likely to vary widely, so plunge in with the utmost discrimination. Vaporetto: Rialto.

PAPER

Florence is still the major center in Italy for artistic paper—especially marbleized paper. However, craftspeople in Venice still make marble paper by hand—sheet by sheet. The technique of marbling paper originated in Japan as early as 1000, spreading through Persia and finally reaching Europe in the 1400s. Except for France, marbling had largely disappeared with the coming of the Industrial Revolution, but it was revived in Venice in the 1970s. The technique offers unlimited decorative possibilties and the widest range of possible colors (craftspeople are called "color alchemists"). Each sheet of handmade marbleized paper is one of a kind.

Antica Legatoria Piazzesi. Santa Maria del Giglio 2511. ☎ **041/522-1202.** Vaporetto: San Marco.

You'll have fun just browsing among the displays of patterned, hand-painted paper here. Of course, buying is fun, too. The paper-covered objects in bright colors make great souvenirs of Venice. *Legatoria* means bookbindery, and some of this work is still done on special order, but the shop mainly offers such objects as scrapbooks, address books, diaries, Venetian carnival statues, and paperweights. You can also find writing paper and decorative pieces. Open daily from 10am to 1pm and 3:30 to 8pm; closed January 15 to 30.

10 Venice After Dark

For such a fabled city, Venice's nightlife is pretty meager. Who wants to hit the nightclubs when strolling the city at night is more interesting than any spectacle staged inside? Ducking into a cafe or bar for a brief interlude, however, is a nice way to break up your evening walk. Although it offers gambling and a few other diversions, Venice is pretty much an early-to-bed town. Most restaurants close at midnight.

The best guide to what's happening in Venice is **"Un Ospite di Venezia,"** a free pamphlet (part in English, part in Italian) distributed by the tourist office. It lists any music and opera or theatrical presentations, along with art exhibitions and local special events.

In addition, classical concerts are often featured in various churches, such as the Chiesa di Vivaldi. To see if any **church concerts** are being presented at the time of your visit, call **041/520-8722** for information.

THE PERFORMING ARTS

In January 1996 a dramatic fire left the fabled La Fenice at Campo San Fantin, the city's main venue for performing arts, a blackened shell and a smoldering ruin. Opera lovers around the world, including Luciano Pavarotti, mourned its loss. The Italian government has pledged $12.5 million for the reconstruction of the theater, the most beautiful in Italy. The theater's neoclassical facade survived the blaze, and is the subject of sightseeing interest today.

Teatro Goldoni. Calle Goldoni, near campo San Luca. ☎ **041/520-7583.** Tickets 20,000–40,000 lire ($12.80–$25.60).

This theater, close to the ponte di Rialto in the San Marco district, honors Carlo Goldoni (1707–93), the most prolific—critics say the best—Italian playwright. The theater presents a changing repertoire of productions, often plays in Italian, but musical presentations as well. The box office is open Monday to Saturday from 10am to 1pm and 4:30 to 7pm.

A DANCE CLUB

El Souk. Calle Contarini Corfu 1056A. ☎ **041/520-0371.** Cover (including the first drink) 15,000 lire ($9.60) Sun–Tues and Thurs-Fri, 20,000 lire ($12.80) Sat. Vaporetto: Accademia.

This casbahlike nightclub near the Accademia continues year after year to swim in the otherwise shallow sea of Venetian nightlife. It's run somewhat like a private club, but everybody is welcome, provided they're dressed properly. The crowd is often young, and dance music prevails. It's open Thursday to Tuesday from 10pm to 4am, but the action usually doesn't begin until after midnight.

THE BAR SCENE

Want more in the way of nightlife? All right, but be warned: The Venetian bar owners may sock it to you when they present the bill.

Bar ai Speci. In the Hotel Panada, calle dei Specchieri 646. ☎ **041/520-9088.** Vaporetto: San Marco.

The Bar ai Speci is a charming corner bar located only a short walk from St. Mark's Basilica. Its richly grained paneling is offset by dozens of antique mirrors, each different, whose glittering surfaces reflect the rows of champagne and scotch bottles and the clustered groups of Biedermeier chairs. The bar is open to the public Tuesday to Sunday from 5:30pm to midnight; on Monday only hotel guests may use it. Drinks begin at 9,000 lire ($5.75).

Bar Ducale. Calle delle Ostreghe, San Marco 2354. ☎ **041/521-0002.** Vaporetto: San Marco.

The Bar Ducale occupies a tiny corner of a building near a bridge over a narrow canal. Customers stand at the zinc bar facing the carved 19th-century Gothic-reproduction shelves. Mimosas are the specialty here, but tasty sandwiches are also offered. The ebullient owner learned his craft at Harry's Bar before going into business for himself. Today his small establishment is usually mobbed every day of the week. It's ideal for an early-evening apéritif as you stroll about. Open daily from 7am to 11pm (closed Tuesday in winter). Whisky begins at 5,500 lire ($3.50); beer, at 3,000 lire ($1.90).

Do Leoni. In the Londra Palace Hotel, riva degli Schiavoni 4171. ☎ **041/520-0533.** Vaporetto: San Zaccaria.

The hotel's exclusive restaurant has already been recommended (see "Dining" in Chapter 9). Here, the interior is a rich blend of scarlet-and-gold carpeting with a lion motif, English pub–style furniture, and Louis XVI–style chairs, along with plenty of exposed mahogany. While sipping your cocktail, you'll enjoy a view of a 19th-century bronze statue, the lagoon, and the foot traffic along the Grand Canal. Open daily from 11am to 1am. A whisky starts at 12,000 lire ($7.70).

Fiddler's Elbow. Cannaregio 3847. ☎ **041/523-9930.** Vaporetto: Ca' d'Oro.

Five minutes from the Rialto Bridge, this pub—called an Irish pub by the Venetians—is run by the same people who operate the equally popular Fiddler's Elbow in both Florence and Rome. Since its opening late in 1992 it has become one of Venice's most popular watering holes. A half pint of Guinness costs 3,500 lire ($2.25); a full pint goes for 6,500 lire ($4.15). Open Sunday to Tuesday from 5pm to 12:30am.

Guanotto. Ponte del Lovo 4819. ☎ **041/520-8439.** Vaporetto: Rialto.

This is a *gelateria/pasticceria/bar*. It's said to have virtually invented the spritzer, a combination of soda water, bitters, and white wine. Its drinks and cocktails are renowned, although enjoying a cappuccino here can take the chill off a rainy day in Venice as well. A spritzer costs 2,000 lire ($1.30), and gelati range from 1,500 to 5,000 lire (95¢ to $3.20). Open daily from 7:30am to 9:30pm; closed Sunday June to August.

Harry's Bar. Calle Vallaresso 1323. ☎ **041/528-5777.** Vaporetto: San Marco.

The single most famous of all the watering holes of Ernest Hemingway, Harry's Bar is known for inventing its own drinks and exporting them around the world. It's also said that carpaccio, the delicate raw-beef dish, was invented here. Fans say that Harry's makes the best Bellini in the world. A libation costs 16,000 lire ($10.25), although many old-time visitors still prefer a vodka martini at 12,000 lire ($7.70).

Harry's Bar is now found around the world, from Munich to Los Angeles, from Paris to Rome, but this is the original. Except for a restaurant, Harry Cipriani, in New York City, the other bars are unauthorized knockoffs. In Venice the bar is a Venetian tradition and landmark, not quite as famous as the Basilica di San Marco, but almost. Celebrities frequent the place during the various film and art festivals. Open Tuesday to Sunday from 10:30am to 11pm.

Linea d'Ombra. Fondamenta delle Zattere, Dorsoduro 19. ☎ **041/528-5259.** Vaporetto: Salute.

To the surprise of many of its visitors, Venice has few real nightclubs. However, if you're in the mood for a little night music, this place has a good piano bar with a restaurant. On Friday and Saturday a pianist plays and sings international tunes, and if the night is right, it can make for one of the more romantic evenings in Venice. It has a terrace that overlooks the canale della Giudecca. Drinkers and diners are treated to a view of the island of San Giorgio. You should reserve a table if you want to dine. Smokers and nonsmokers are segregated. The restaurant is open Monday, Tuesday, and Thursday to Saturday from 12:30 to 2:30pm and 8 to 10:30pm, and on Sunday from 12:30 to 2:30pm; the bar is open Monday, Tuesday, and Thursday to Saturday from 8am to midnight. Meals run 35,000 to 60,000 lire ($22.40 to $38.40); drinks are 7,000 to 12,000 lire ($4.50 to $7.70).

Martini Scala Club. Campo San Fantin 1980. ☎ **041/522-4121.** Vaporetto: San Marco or Santa Maria del Giglio.

The Martini Scala Club is an elegant restaurant with a piano bar and has functioned as some kind of inn, in one manifestation or another, since 1724. You can enjoy its food and wine until 2am—it's the only kitchen in Venice that stays open late. Dishes include smoked goose breast with grapefruit and arugula, fresh salmon with black butter and olives, or gnocchi (dumplings) with butter and sage. The piano bar gets going after 10pm. It's possible to order drinks without having food. The restaurant is open Wednesday to Monday from 7pm to 2am; meals average 75,000 lire ($48). The bar is open Wednesday to Monday from 10pm to 3am; a whisky and soda costs 12,000 lire ($7.70).

WINE BARS

Cantina do Spade. San Polo 860. ☎ **041/521-0574.** Vaporetto: Rialto.

This historic wine bar beneath an arcade near the main fish and fruit market of Venice dates from 1475. It was once frequented by Casanova. Venetians call it a *bacaro* instead of a wine bar. The place is completely rustic and bare-bones, but devotees come here to order chicchetti, the equivalent of Spanish tapas. Although there's no menu, the kitchen will occasionally turn out typical Venetian fare. Many diners prefer to order one of 250 different sandwiches the kitchen is usually willing to prepare. Often in season, game dishes, including boar, deer, and reindeer, are served, but don't count on this. Venetians delight in the 220 different types of wine, costing 1,000 to 4,000 lire (65¢ to $2.55) per glass. The place is a local favorite, and has been for centuries, but don't come here looking for glamour; head for Harry's Bar if that's what you're after. Meals cost 20,000 lire ($12.80) and up. Open Monday to Wednesday and Friday and Saturday from 9am to 2:30pm and 5 to 11pm, and on Thursday from 9am to 2:30pm.

Mascareta. Calle lunga Santa Maria Formosa 5138, Castello. ☎ **041/523-0744.** Vaporetto: Rialto.

This wine bar was established in 1995. The focus is on dozens of bottles of Italian wines, many from the Veneto region, which sell for 1,500 to 4,000 lire (95¢ to $2.55) a glass, depending on the vintage. There's only room for 20 people seated at cramped tables in an old Venetian building, but if you're hungry you can order simple platters of snack-style food (prosciutto, cheese plates, and other dishes) priced from 6,000 to 10,000 lire ($3.85 to $6.40), depending on what's available that day. Open Monday to Saturday from 5pm to midnight.

Vino Vino. Calle del Cafetier 2007A. ☎ **041/523-7027.** Vaporetto: San Marco.

You can choose from more than 250 Italian and imported wines here. Vino Vino attracts a varied clientele: It wouldn't be unusual to see a Venetian countess sipping Prosecco near a gondolier eating a meal. This place is loved by everyone from snobs to young people to almost-broke tourists. It offers wines by the bottle or glass, including Italian grappas. Popular Venetian dishes are also served, including pastas, beans, baccalà (codfish), and polenta. The two rooms are always jammed like a vaporetto in rush hour, and there's take-away service if you can't find a place. The bar is open daily from 10am to 7pm; glasses of wine cost 2,500 to 12,000 lire ($1.60 to $7.70). Meals are served Tuesday to Sunday from noon to 3pm and 7 to 10:30pm; main courses range from 10,000 to 15,000 lire ($6.40 to $9.60).

CAFES

⭐ **Florian.** Piazza San Marco 56–59. ☎ **041/528-5338.** Vaporetto: San Marco.

This is the most famous cafe in Venice. The Florian was built in 1720, and it remains romantically and elegantly decorated—pure Venetian salons with red plush banquettes, intricate and elaborate murals under glass, and art nouveau lighting and lamps. It's the most fashionable and aristocratic rendezvous in Venice: The Florian roster of customers has included Casanova, Lord Byron, Goethe, Canova, de Musset, and Madame de Staël. Light lunch is served from noon to 3pm, costing 20,000 lire ($12.80) and up, and an English tea from 3 to 6pm, when you can select from a choice of pastries, ice creams, and cakes. Open Thursday to Tuesday from 9am to midnight. An espresso is 6,000 lire ($3.85); long drinks cost 19,000 lire ($12.15), plus 5,000 lire ($3.20) extra if you drink on the square when music is playing (April to October).

Gran Caffè Lavena. Piazza San Marco 133–134. ☎ **041/522-4070.**

The Gran Caffè Lavena is a popular but intimate cafe located under the arcades of piazza San Marco. The establishment was frequented by Richard Wagner during his stay in Venice; he composed some of his greatest operas here. It has one of the most beautifully ornate glass chandeliers in town—the kind you'll love even if you hate Venetian glass. They hang from the ceiling between the iron rails of an upper-level balcony. The most interesting tables are near the plate-glass window in front, although there's plenty of room at the stand-up bar as well. Open May to October, daily from 9am to 12:30am; November to March, Friday to Wednesday from 9am to 12:30am. Coffee costs 1,400 lire (90¢) if you're standing, 5,500 lire ($3.50) if you're sitting at a table. And there's a music surcharge of 4,000 lire ($2.55).

⭐ **Quadri.** Piazza San Marco 120–124. ☎ **041/528-9299.** Vaporetto: San Marco.

Quadri, previously recommended as a restaurant, stands on the opposite side of the square from the Florian. It, too, is elegantly decorated in antique style. It should be, as it was founded in 1638. Wagner used to drop in for a drink when he was working on *Tristan und Isolde.* Its prices are virtually the same as at the Florian, and it, too, imposes a surcharge on drinks ordered during concert periods. The bar was a favorite with the Austrians during their long-ago occupation. Open July to September, daily from 9am to midnight; October to June, Tuesday to Sunday from 9am to midnight. A whisky costs 17,000 lire ($10.90); coffee, 5,500 lire ($3.50). The music surcharge is 4,000 lire ($2.55).

ICE CREAM & PASTRIES

Gelateria Paolin. Campo San Stefano 2962A. ☎ **041/522-5576.**

For many, strolling to the Gelateria Paolin (set in a large colorful square) and ordering some of the tastiest ice cream (gelato) in Venice is nightlife enough. That's the way many a Venetian spends a summer evening. This gelateria has stood on the corner of this busy square since the 1930s, making it the oldest ice-cream parlor in Venice. You can order your ice cream to go or eat it at one of the sidewalk tables. Many interesting flavors are offered, including pistachio. However, you may want to be adventurous and try something known as Malaga. The gelati cost more if consumed at a table. From June to September, the parlor is open daily from 7:30am to 11:30pm; October to May, Tuesday to Sunday from 7:30am to 9:30pm.

Pasticceria Marchini. San Maurizio 2769. ☎ **041/522-9109.** Vaparetto: Accademia.

If you'd like to escape the throngs of visitors that overrun Venice in the early evening, head here, have a pastry and a coffee, and contemplate your evening plans. This is where your Venetian friend (if you have one) would take you for the most delectable pastries served in the city. The small pastries are made according to old recipes—ask for their bigna or cannolo. Open Wednesday to Monday from 8:30am to 8:30pm.

CASINOS

Casino Municipale. Lungomare G. Marconi 4, Lido. ☎ **041/529-7111.** Admission 18,000 lire ($11.50).

If you want to risk your luck and your lire, take a vaporetto ride on the Casino Express, which leaves from stops at the railway station, piazzale Roma, and piazzetta San Marco, and delivers you to the landing dock of the Casino Municipale. The Italian government wisely forbids its nationals to cross the threshold unless they work here, so bring your passport. The building itself is foreboding, almost as if it could have been inspired by Mussolini-era architects. However, the action gets hotter once you step inside. You can try your luck at blackjack, roulette, baccarat, or whatever. You can also dine, drink at the bar, or enjoy a floor show. Open June to September, daily from 4pm to 2:30am.

Vendramin-Calergi Palace. Cannaregio 2040, Strada Nuova. ☎ **041/529-7111.** Admission 18,000 lire ($11.50). Vaporetto: San Marcuola.

From October to May, the casino action moves to the Vendramin-Calergi Palace. Incidentally, in 1883 Wagner died in this house, which opens onto the Grand Canal. Open daily from 3pm to 2:30am.

11 Side Trips from Venice

MURANO

This is the island where for centuries **glassblowers** have turned out those fantastic chandeliers that Victorian ladies used to prize so highly. They also produce heavily ornamented glasses so ruby-red or so indigo-blue you can't tell if you're drinking blackberry juice or pure grain alcohol. Happily, the glassblowers are still plying their trade, although increasing competition—notably from Sweden—has compelled a greater degree of sophistication in design.

Murano remains the chief expedition from Venice, but it's not the most beautiful nearby island. (Burano and Torcello are far more attractive.)

You can combine a tour of Murano with a trip along the lagoon. To reach it, take vaporetto no. 5 at riva degli Schiavoni, a short walk from piazzetta San Marco. The boat docks at the landing platform at Murano where—lo and behold—the first furnace awaits conveniently. It's best to go Monday to Friday from 10am to noon if you want to see some glassblowing action.

TOURING THE GLASS FACTORIES & OTHER SIGHTS

As you stroll through Murano, you'll find that the factory owners are only too glad to let you come in and see their age-old crafts. These managers aren't altogether altruistic, of course. While browsing through the showrooms, you'll need stiff resistance to keep the salespeople at bay. And it's possible to bargain down the initial price quoted. Don't—repeat *don't*—pay the marked price on any item. That's merely the figure at which to open negotiations.

What's not negotiable is the price of made-on-the-spot souvenirs. For example, you might want to purchase a horse streaked with blue. The artisan takes a piece of incandescent glass, huffs, puffs, rolls it, shapes it, snips it, and behold—he has shaped a horse. The showrooms of Murano also contain a fine assortment of Venetian crystal beads, available in every hue of the rainbow. You may find some of the best work to be the experiments of apprentices.

While on the island, you can visit the Renaissance palazzo that houses the **Museo Vetrario di Murano,** fondamenta Giustinian (☎ **041/739586**), which houses a spectacular collection of Venetian glass. It's open April to October, Monday, Tuesday, and Thursday to Saturday from 10am to 5pm; November to March, Monday, Tuesday, and Thursday to Saturday from 10am to 4pm. Admission is 8,000 lire ($5.10) for adults and 5,000 lire ($3.20) for children.

If you're looking for a respite from the glass factories, head to the **Church of San Pietro Martire,** which dates from the 1300s but was rebuilt in 1511 and is richly decorated with paintings by Tintoretto and Veronese. Its proud possession is a *Madonna and Child Enthroned* by Giovanni Bellini, plus two superb altarpieces by the same master. The church lies right before the junction with Murano's Grand Canal, about 250 yards from the vaporetto landing stage. It's open daily from 8am to noon and 4 to 7pm.

Even more notable is **Santi Maria e Donato,** campo San Donato, which is open daily from 8am to noon and 4 to 7pm. This building is a stellar example of the Venetian Byzantine style, in spite of its 19th-century restoration. It dates from the 7th century but was reconstructed in the 1100s. The interior is known for its mosaic floor—a parade of peacocks and eagles, as well as other creatures—and a 15th-century ship's-keel ceiling. Over the apse is an outstanding mosaic of the Virgin against a gold background, which dates from the early 1200s.

WHERE TO DINE

Ai Vetrai. Fondamenta Manin 29. ☎ **041/739293.** Reservations recommended. Main courses 12,000–28,000 lire ($7.70–$17.90). AE, DC, MC, V. Fri–Wed 11am–4pm. Vaporetto: 5 to Murano. VENETIAN.

Ai Vetrai entertains and nourishes its guests in a large room not far from the canale dei Vetrai. If you're looking for fish prepared in the local style, with what might be called the widest selection on Murano, this is it. Most varieties of crustaceans and gilled creatures are available on the spot. However, if you phone ahead and order food for a large party, as the Venetians sometimes do, the owners will prepare what they call "a noble fish." You might begin with spaghetti in a green clam sauce.

Impressions

An overcrowded little island where the women make splendid lace and the men make children.

—Ernest Hemingway, on Burano

Al Corallo. Fondamenta dei Vetrai 73. ☎ **041/739080.** Main courses 8,000–25,000 lire ($5.10–$16); fixed-price menu 18,000 lire ($11.50). AE, DC, MC, V. Wed–Mon noon–3pm and 7–8:30pm. Closed mid-Dec to mid-Jan (dates vary). Vaporetto: 5 to Murano. VENETIAN.

Small and intimate, and somewhat isolated from the bustle and hurry of the larger islands of Venice, this family-run restaurant is one of the best established of the eateries on the island of Murano. Very little English is spoken, but the place is usually filled with a wide variety of clients from all walks of life. Specialties are typically Venetian, and the service is polite. Locals, many of them workers at the nearby glass factories, choose this place for a well-deserved meal after a morning of hard physical labor, and blend with the tourists. The menu changes daily, according to whatever's available in the local markets.

BURANO

Burano became world famous as a center of **lacemaking,** a craft that reached its pinnacle in the 18th century (recall Venetian point?). The visitor who can spare a morning to visit this island will be rewarded with a charming little fishing village far removed in spirit from the grandeur of Venice, but lying only half an hour away by ferry. Boats leave from fondamente Nuove, which overlooks the Venetian graveyard (which is well worth the trip all on its own). To reach fondamente Nuove, take vaporetto no. 5 from riva degli Schiavoni. Get off at fondamente Nuove and catch a separate boat, Line 12, marked Burano.

EXPLORING THE ISLAND

Once at Burano, you'll discover that the houses of the islanders come in varied colors—sienna, robin's-egg or cobalt blue, barn red, butterscotch, grass green. If you need a focal point for your excursion, it should be the **Scuola Merietti,** in the center of the fishing village at piazza Baldassare Galuppi. The Burano School of Lace was founded in 1872 as part of a movement aimed at restoring the age-old craft that had earlier declined, giving way to such other lacemaking centers as Chantilly and Bruges. Go up to the second floor where you can see the lacemakers, mostly young women, at their painstaking work and can purchase hand-embroidered or handmade-lace items.

After visiting the lace school, next walk across the square to the **Duomo** and its leaning campanile (inside, look for the *Crucifixion* by Tiepolo). However, do so at once, because the bell tower is leaning so precariously it looks as if it may topple at any moment.

WHERE TO DINE

Ostaria ai Pescatori. Piazza Baldassare Galuppi 371. ☎ **041/730650.** Reservations recommended. Main courses 18,000–30,000 lire ($11.50–$19.20). AE, MC, V. Thurs–Tues noon–3pm and 6–9:30pm. Closed Jan. Vaporetto: Line 12 from Murano. SEAFOOD.

The family that pools its efforts to run this well-known restaurant maintains strong friendships with the local fishers, who often reserve the best parts of their daily catch for preparation in the kitchen here. The cooking is performed by the matriarch of an extended family. The place has gained a reputation as the preserver of a type of simple and unpretentious restaurant unique to Burano. Locals in dialect call it a *buranello*. Clients often take the vaporetto from other sections of Venice (the restaurant lies close to the boat landing) to eat at the plain wooden tables set up either indoors or on the small square in front. Specialties feature all the staples of the Venetian seaside diet, including fish soup, risotto di pesce, pasta seafarer style, tagliolini in squid ink, and a wide range of crustaceans, plus grilled, fried, and baked fish. Dishes prepared with local game are also available, but you must request them well in advance. Your meal might also include a bottle of fruity wine from the region.

Trattoria de Romano. Via Baldassare Galuppi 223. ☎ **041/730030.** Reservations recommended. Main courses 15,000–24,000 lire ($9.60–$15.35). AE, MC, V. Wed–Mon noon–2:30pm and 7–8:30pm. Closed Dec 15–Feb 15. Vaporetto: Line 12 from Murano. VENETIAN.

If you're on the island at mealtime, you may want to join a long line of people who have patronized the rather simple-looking *caratteristico* Trattoria de Romano, which is around the corner from the lace school. You can enjoy a superb dinner here, which might consist of risotto di pesce (the Italian version of the Valencian paella), followed by fritto misto di pesce, a mixed fish fry from the Adriatic, with savory bits of mullet, squid, and shrimp.

TORCELLO

Of all the islands of the lagoon, Torcello—the so-called Mother of Venice—offers the most charm. If Burano is behind the times, Torcello is positively antediluvian. You can follow in the footsteps of Hemingway and stroll across a grassy meadow, traverse an ancient stone bridge, and step back into that time when the Venetians first fled from invading barbarians to create a city of Neptune in the lagoon.

To reach Torcello, take vaporetto no. 12 from fondamenta Nuova on Murano. The trip takes about 45 minutes.

Warning: If you go on your own, don't listen to the savvy gondoliers who hover at the ferry quay. They'll tell you that both the cathedral and the locanda are miles away. Actually, they're both reached after a leisurely 12- to 15-minute stroll along the canal.

EXPLORING THE ISLAND

Torcello has two major attractions: a church with Byzantine mosaics good enough to make the empress Theodora at Ravenna turn as purple with envy as her robe, and a locanda (inn) that converts day trippers into inebriated angels of praise. First the spiritual nourishment before the alcoholic sustenance.

The **Cattedrale di Torcello,** also called the Church of Santa Maria Assunta Isola di Torcello (☎ **041/730084**), was founded in A.D. 639 and was subsequently rebuilt. It stands in a lonely, grassy meadow beside a campanile that dates from the 11th century. It's visited chiefly because of its Byzantine mosaics. Clutching her child, the weeping Madonna in the apse is a magnificent sight, whereas on the opposite wall is a powerful *Last Judgment*. Byzantine artisans, it seems, were at their best in portraying hell and damnation. At Santa Maria Assunta they don't disappoint. In their Inferno they have re-created a virtual human stew with the fires stirred by wicked demons. Reptiles slide in and out of the skulls of cannibalized sinners. Open April to October, daily from 10am to 12:30pm and 2:30 to 6:30pm; November to March, daily from 10am to 12:30pm and 2:30 to 5pm. Admission is 1,500 lire (95¢).

Tearing yourself away from piazza San Marco in Venice is a task that requires an iron will. However, Venice doesn't have a regional monopoly on art or tourist treasures. Of the cities of interest easily reached from Venice, three tower above the rest: Verona, the home of the eternal lovers, Romeo and Juliet; Padua, the city of Mantegna, with frescoes by Giotto; and Vicenza, the city of Palladio, with streets of Renaissance palazzi and villa-studded hills. The miracle of all these cities is that Venice did not siphon off their creative drive completely, although the Serene Republic dominated them for centuries.

EXPLORING THE VENETO BY CAR

Day 1   Leave Venice (as hard as that is to do) and drive west along autostrada A4 to Padua, a distance of 25 miles. In Padua visit at least the Cappella degli Scrovegni and Basilica di' Sant'Antonio.

☕ **TAKE A BREAK**   The **Caffè Pedrocchi,** piazzetta Pedrocchi 15 in Padua (☎ **049/876-2576**), is the most famous 19th-century monument in Padua. Designed by Giuseppe Jappelli in 1831, it stands in the precincts of the university just off piazza Cavour. This coffeehouse is "the living room" of Padua.

At the end of the afternoon, you can take autostrada A4 northwest to the turnoff north to Vicenza, the city of Palladio. Overnight there.

Day 2   There are a number of attractions to see in Vicenza, including the Teatro Olimpico. A visit will consume most of your day. In the late afternoon you can connect with the autostrada going west to Verona where you'll want to spend at least 2 nights.

Days 3–4   While still based in Verona, set out to explore its rich architectural and artistic legacy, visiting the Arena, Castellvecchio, Teatro Romano, and Giardino Giusti. You might want to skip such artificially created tourist attractions as the "tomb" or "balcony" of Juliet, however.

A TASTE OF THE VENETO

In the northeastern part of the agriculturally rich Po Valley, the Veneto is rich in fruits and vegetables. The cuisine is tasty but straightforward. Three of the region's most famous dishes are *risi e bisi* (rice and peas); *fegato alla veneziana* (liver and onions), and *baccalà alla vicentina* (codfish cooked with milk and flavored with anchovies, garlic, onion, and cinnamon and other spices). Radicchio, dark red with white markings, is the chief salad of the region, in spite of its slightly bitter taste. *Pasta e fagioli* (made with beans and pasta) is the ideal dish for a cold winter's day.

The famous wines of the area include Bardolino, a light ruby-red color, which is generally dry. With a medium alcohol content, it's one of the most popular wines of the area, often served with rabbit, chicken, and young pigeon. Soave, W. Somerset Maugham's favorite, is a pale-amber yellow wine, with a delicate bouquet, a light aroma, and a velvety flavor. Valpolicella is the third famous wine of the region, and is usually served with all meals, especially roasts. It comes in two varieties: ordinary quality and superior dry. The first is ruby red with a delicate and characteristic bouquet, and the second is an even darker ruby in color, with a light bouquet of bitter almonds.

1 Verona

71 miles W of Venice, 312 miles NW of Rome

The home of a pair of star-cross'd lovers, Verona was the setting for the most famous love story in the English language, Shakespeare's *Romeo and Juliet.* A long-forgotten editor of an old volume of the Bard's plays once wrote: "Verona, so rich in the associations of real history, has even a greater charm for those who would live in the poetry of the past." It's not known if a Romeo or a Juliet ever existed, but the remains of Verona's recorded past are much in evidence today. Its Roman antiquities, for example, are unequaled north of Rome.

In the city's medieval golden age under the despotic, cruel Scaligeri princes, Verona reached the pinnacle of its influence and prestige, developing into a town that, even today, is among the great cities of Italy. The best-known member of the ruling Della Scala family, Cangrande I, was a patron of Dante. His sway over Verona has often been compared to that of Lorenzo the Magnificent over Florence.

Verona stands in contrast to Venice, even though both are tourist towns. At least in Verona you can put your feet on solid land—not on water. It overflows with visitors today, and, like Venice, it hustles and often lives off a glorious past. But most of the people walking the streets of Verona are actually residents and not visitors. For a city that hit its peak in the 1st century A.D., Verona is doing admirably well today. However, stick to the inner core and not the newer sections, which are blighted by industry and tacky urban development.

ESSENTIALS

GETTING THERE   By Train   A total of 37 trains a day make the 2-hour run between Venice and Verona, at 9,800 lire ($6.25) one-way. If you're in the west— say, at Milan—there are even more connections, some 40 trains a day, taking 2 hours to reach Verona at a cost of 11,700 lire ($7.50) one-way. Six daily trains arrive from Rome, a 6-hour trip, costing 40,500 lire ($25.90) one-way.

By Bus   APT buses arrive and depart from the **Porta Nuova FS Station** (☎ 045/800-4129) in Verona, serving the province and fanning out to such cities as Brescia, Mantua, and Riva del Garda. From mid-June to mid-September, you can go from Venice to Verona without changing buses (although it's still better to take the train).

By Car   From Venice, take autostrada A4 west to the signposted cutoff for Verona.

VISITOR INFORMATION   The **tourist information office** is on piazza delle Erbe (☎ 045/803-0086). It's open Monday to Saturday from 8am to 8pm.

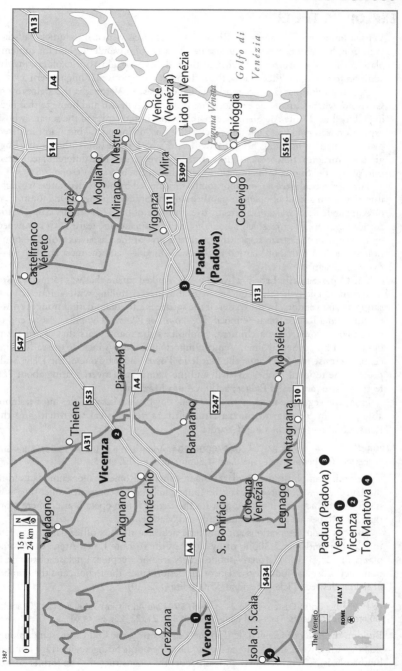

Padua (Padova) ❸
Verona ❶
Vicenza ❷
To Mantova ❹

The Veneto

ITALY

ROME ⊛

1387

EXPLORING THE CITY

Verona lies alongside the Adige River. It's most often visited on a quick half-day excursion, but Verona deserves more time. It's meant for wandering and for contemplation. If you're rushed, head first to the old city to begin your explorations. In addition to the sights listed below, there are other attractions that might merit a visit.

Opening onto piazza dei Signori, the handsomest in Verona, is the **Palazzo del Governo,** where Cangrande extended the shelter of his hearth and home to that fleeing Ghibelline, Dante Alighieri. The marble statue in the center of the square, whose expression is as cold as a Dolomite icicle, is of the "divine poet," but unintimidated pigeons perch on his pious head. Facing Dante's back is the late 15th-century **Loggia del Consiglio,** frescoed and surmounted by five statues. Five different arches lead into **piazza dei Signori,** the innermost chamber of the heart of Verona.

The **Arche Scaligere** are outdoor tombs surrounded by highly decorative wrought iron that form a kind of open-air pantheon of the Scaligeri princes. One tomb, that of Cangrande della Scala, rests directly over the door of the 12th-century Santa Maria Antica Church. The mausoleum contains many Romanesque features. It's crowned by a copy of an equestrian statue (the original is now at the Castelvecchio). The tomb nearest the door is that of Mastino II; the one behind it—and the most lavish of all—that of Cansignorio.

The ✪ **piazza delle Erbe** is a lively, palace-flanked square that was formerly a Roman forum. Today it's the fruit and vegetable market milling with Veronese, both shoppers and vendors. In the center of the square is a fountain dating from the 14th century and a Roman statue dubbed *The Virgin of Verona.* The pillar at one end of the square, crowned by a chimera, symbolizes the many years that Verona was dominated by the Serenissima, Venice. Important buildings include the early 14th-century **House of Merchants;** the **Gardello Tower,** built by one of the Della Scala princes; the restored former city hall and the **Lamberti Tower,** soaring about 260 feet; the baroque **Maffei Palace;** and the **Casa Mazzanti.**

From the vegetable market, you can walk down **via Mazzini,** the most fashionable street in Verona, to **piazza Brà,** with its neoclassical town hall and the Renaissance palazzo, the Gran Guardia.

Arena di Verona. Piazza Brà. ☎ **045/800-3204.** Admission 6,000 lire ($3.85). Tues–Sun 8am–6:30pm (on performance days, 8am–1:30pm). Bus: 11, 12, or 13.

The elliptical amphitheater on piazza Brà, resembling Rome's Colosseum, dates from the 1st century A.D. Four arches of the "outer circle" and a complete "inner ring" still stand. From mid-July to mid-August it's the setting for an opera house, where more than 20,000 people are treated to Verdi and Mascagni.

You can make reservations and purchase tickets at the box office daily from 9am to 12:30pm and 3 to 5:30pm, or by letter: Write to Ente Lirico Arena di Verona, piazza Brà 28, 37100 Verona—phone orders are not accepted. Enclose a bank draft or money order and indicate the date of the performance, the section, and the number of tickets desired. Tickets begin at 35,000 lire ($22.40).

Castelvecchio. Corso Castelvecchio 2. ☎ **045/594734.** Admission 5,000 lire ($3.20) adults, 1,500 lire (95¢) students. Tues–Sun 8am–6:30pm. Bus: 21, 22, 23, 24, or 61.

Built on the order of Cangrar de II in the 14th century, the Old Castle stands alongside the Adige River (head out via Roma) near the ponte Scaligero, a bridge bombed by the Nazis in World War II and subsequently reconstructed. The former seat of the Della Scala family, the restored castle has been turned into an art museum, with important paintings from the Veronese school and other masters of northern Italy. Here, 14th- and 15th-century sculpture are displayed on the ground floor, and on the upper floor you'll see masterpieces of painting from the 15th to the 18th century.

In the Sala Monga is Jacopo Bellini's *St. Jerome,* in the desert with his lion and crucifix. Two sisterlike portraits of Saint Catherina and Veneranda by Vittore Carpaccio grace the Sala Rizzardi Allegri. The Bellini family is also represented by a lyrical *Madonna con Bambino* painted by Giovanni, a master of that subject.

Between the buildings is the most provocative equestrian statue we've ever seen, that of Cangrande I, grinning like a buffoon, with a dragon sticking out of his back. In the Sala Murari dalla Corte Brà is one of the most beguiling portraits in the castle—Giovanni Francesco Caroto's smiling red-haired boy. In the Sala di Canossa are paintings by Tintoretto, a *Madonna Nursing the Child* and a *Nativity,* and by Veronese, a *Deposition from the Cross* and the *Pala Bevilacqua Lazise.*

In the Sala Bolognese Trevenzuoli is a rare self-portrait of Bernardo Strozzi, and in the Sala Avena, among paintings by the most famous Venetian masters such as Gianbattista and Giandomenico Tiepolo and Guardi, hangs an almost satirical portrait of an 18th-century patrician family by Longhi.

Church of San Zeno Maggiore. Piazza San Zeno. ☎ **045/800-6120.** Admission 4,000 lire ($2.55). June–Aug, daily 10am–6pm; Sept–May, daily 10am–5pm. Bus: 32 or 33.

This near-perfect Romanesque church and campanile is graced with a stunning entrance—two pillars supported by puce-colored marble lions and surmounted by a rose window. On either side of the portal are bas-reliefs depicting scenes from the Old and New Testaments, as well as a mythological story portraying Theodoric as a huntsman lured to hell (the king of the Goths defeated Odoacer in Verona). The panels on the bronze doors, nearly 50 in all, are a remarkable achievement of medieval art, sculpted perhaps in the 12th century. They reflect a naïve handling of their subject matter—see John the Baptist's head resting on a platter. The artists express themselves with such candor that they achieve the power of a child's storybook. The interior, somber and severe, contains a major Renaissance work at the main altar, a triptych by Andrea Mantegna, an enthroned Madonna and Child with saints. Although not remarkable in its characterization, it reveals the artist's genius for perspective.

Basilica of Sant'Anastasia. Piazza Sant'Anastasia. ☎ **045/800-4325.** Admission 4,000 lire ($2.55). Apr–Oct, daily 9am–6:30pm; Nov–Mar, daily 10am–4:30pm. Bus: 70.

This church dates from the 13th century. Its facade isn't complete, yet nevertheless it's the finest representation of Gothic design in Verona. Many artists in the 15th and 16th centuries decorated the interior, and few of the works seem worthy of being singled out for special mention. The exception, however, is the Pellegrini Chapel, with terra-cotta reliefs by the Tuscan artist Michele, and the Giusti Chapel, with a fresco by Pisanello representing St. George preparing to face his inevitable dragon. The patterned floor is especially impressive. As you enter, look for two hunchbacks.

Il Duomo. Piazza del Duomo. ☎ **045/595627.** Admission 4,000 lire ($2.55). Apr–Oct, daily 9am–noon and 3–6pm; Nov–Mar, daily 9am–noon and 3–5:30pm. Bus: 70.

The cathedral of Verona is less interesting than San Zeno Maggiore, but it still merits a visit. A blend of the Romanesque and Gothic styles, its facade contains (lower level) 12th-century sculptured reliefs by Nicolaus that depict scenes of Roland and Oliver, two of the legendary dozen knights attending Charlemagne. In the left aisle (first chapel) is an *Assumption* by Titian. The other major work of art is the rood screen in front of the presbytery, with Ionic pillars, designed by Samicheli.

Chiesa di San Fermo. Piazza San Fermo. ☎ **045/800-7287.** Admission 4,000 lire ($2.55). Apr–Oct, Mon–Fri 9am–6pm, Sat noon–6pm; Nov–Mar, Mon–Fri 10am–4pm, Sat noon–5pm. Bus: 11, 12, or 13.

This Romanesque church, which dates from the 11th century, forms the foundation of the 14th-century Gothic building that surmounts it. Through time it has been used by both the Benedictines and the Franciscans. The interior is unusual, with a single nave and a splendid roof constructed of wood and exquisitely paneled. The most important work inside is Pisanello's frescoed *Annunciation,* to the left of the main entrance (at the Brenzoni tomb). Delicate and graceful, the work reveals the artist's keen eye for architectural detail and his bizarre animals.

✪ Teatro Romano (Roman Theater) and Archeological Museum. Via Rigaste Redentore 2A. ☎ **045/800-0360.** Admission (theater and museum) 5,000 lire ($3.20). Theater and museum, Tues–Sun 8:30am–2:30pm. Bus: 72.

The **Teatro Romano,** originally built in the 1st century A.D., now stands in ruins at the foot of St. Peter's Hill. For nearly a quarter of a century a Shakespearean festival has been staged here in July and August, and, of course, a unique theater-going experience is to see *Romeo and Juliet* or *Two Gentlemen of Verona* in this setting. The theater is across the Adige River (take the ponte di Pietra). After seeing the remains of the theater, you can take a rickety elevator to the 10th-century Santa Libera Church towering over it. In the cloister of St. Jerome is the **Roman Archeological Museum** (same phone), which has interesting mosaics and Etruscan bronzes.

Giardino Giusti. Via Giardino Giusti. ☎ **045/803-40029.** Admission 7,000 lire ($4.50) adults, 3,000 lire ($1.90) children. Summer, daily 9am–sunset; winter, daily 9am–6:30pm. Bus: 72.

One of the oldest and most famous gardens in Italy, the Giardino Giusti was created at the end of the 14th century. These well-manicured Italian gardens, studded with cypress trees, form one of the most relaxing and coolest spots in Verona for strolls. You can climb up to the "monster balcony" for an incomparable view of the city.

The layout you see today was given to the gardens by Agostino Giusti. All its 16th-century characteristics—the grottoes, the statues, the fountains, the mascarons, the box-enclosed flower garden, and the maze—have remained intact. In addition to the flower displays, you can admire the statues by Lorenzo Muttoni and Alessandro Vittoria, Roman remains, and the great cypress mentioned by Goethe. The gardens, with their adjacent 16th-century palazzo, form one of Italy's most interesting urban complexes. The maze, constructed with myrtle hedges, faithfully reproduces the 1786 plan of the architect Trezza. Its complicated pattern and small size make it one of the most unusual in Europe. The gardens lie near the Roman Theater, only a few minutes' walk from the heart of the city.

Tomba di Giulietta. Via Luigi da Porto 5. ☎ **045/800361.** Admission 5,000 lire ($3.20). Tues–Sun 8am–6:30pm. Bus: 72.

The so-called Juliet's Tomb is sheltered in a Franciscan monastery entered on via Luigi da Porto, off via del Pontiere. "A grave? O, no, a lantern . . . . For here lies Juliet, and her beauty makes this vault a feasting presence full of light." Don't you believe it! Still, the cloisters, near the Adige River, are graceful. Adjoining the tomb is a museum of frescoes, dedicated to G. B. Cavalcaselle.

Casa Giulietta. Via Cappello 23. ☎ **045/803-4303.** Admission 5,000 lire ($3.20). Tues–Sun 8am–6:30pm. Bus: 11, 12, 70, 71, 72, or 73.

Juliet's house is a small home with a balcony and a courtyard. With a little bit of imagination, it's not difficult to hear Romeo say: "But, soft! what light through yonder window breaks? It is the east, and Juliet is the sun!"

WHERE TO STAY

Hotel rooms tend to be scarce during the County Fair in March and the opera and theater season in July and August.

VERY EXPENSIVE

✪ Due Torri Hotel Baglioni. Piazza Sant'Anastasia 4, 37121 Verona. ☎ **045/595044.** Fax 045/800-4130. 81 rms, 10 suites. A/C MINIBAR TV TEL. 390,000–580,000 lire ($249.60–$371.20) double; from 600,000 lire ($384) suite. Rates include breakfast. AE, DC, MC, V. Parking 40,000 lire ($25.60). Bus: 71.

Owned by a national upscale hotel chain (Cogeta Palace Hotels), this was built in the 1400s as the private home of the Scaligeri dynasty, a family noted for their hospitality. During the 18th and 19th centuries the palace hosted many VIPs, including Mozart, Goethe, and Tsar Alexander I. Set in the monumental heart of Verona, the palace was (and still is) the best address in town, although maintenance is no longer as state-of-the-art as it used to be.

In the 1950s the late, legendary hotelier Enrico Wallner transformed the palace into a hotel, filling it with a stunning collection of antiques. Despite the takeover in 1990 by Cogeta, which richly renovated and restored the entire hotel over 4 years, many of these antiques remain in both the public areas and bedrooms—a splendid range of Directoire, Empire, Louis XVIII, and Biedermeier. There are also many old oil paintings, a very large lobby sited in what was originally conceived as the palace's courtyard, and a series of well-upholstered salons permeated with charm and serviced by a discreet staff.

Dining/Entertainment: The hotel's restaurant, All'Aquila, serves typical local and light cuisine. This is one of the most distinguished restaurants of Verona, and even if you're not a guest, you can visit for a meal daily from 12:30 to 2:30pm and 7:30pm to 10pm. The hotel also contains an elegant bar.

Services: Room service (24 hours), baby-sitting, laundry, valet.

✪ Hotel Gabbia d'Oro. Corso Porta Borsari 4A, 37121 Verona. ☎ **045/800-3060.** Fax 045/590293. 8 rms, 19 suites. A/C MINIBAR TV TEL. 250,000–550,000 lire ($160–$352) double; 410,000–1,200,000 lire ($262.40–$768) suite. Rates include breakfast. AE, DC, MC, V. Parking 50,000 lire ($32) first day, 40,000 lire ($25.60) each additional day. Bus: 11, 12, or 21.

This upscale hotel in a historic 18th-century palazzo in Verona's monumental center was inaugurated in 1990, the first hotel in years to give the Due Torri Baglioni serious competition. It has a more romantic "Romeo and Juliet" atmosphere than the more fabled hostelry. Small, discreet, and devoted to the privacy of its guests, it contains many of the building's original grandiose frescoes, its beamed ceiling, and (in the cozy bar area) much of the original carved paneling. Only hotel guests are allowed into the bar and restaurant, where advance reservations are strictly required. Even the hotel's name, "Golden Cage," seems to enhance its exclusivity. Although there's no garden, the hotel's interior courtyard contains potted plants, flowering shrubs, and tables devoted to drinking and dining facilities during clement weather. The bedrooms contain framed engravings, antique furniture, and—in some cases—narrow balconies with wrought-iron detailing overlooking either the street or the courtyard below.

EXPENSIVE

Hotel Accademia. Via Scala 12, 37121 Verona. ☎ and fax **045/596222.** 92 rms, 5 suites. A/C MINIBAR TV TEL. 230,000–370,000 lire ($147.20–$236.80) double; 320,000–520,000 lire ($204.80–$332.80) suite. Rates include breakfast. AE, DC, MC, V. Parking 25,000 lire ($16). Bus: 71.

This is one of the few older hotels of Verona that was custom-built as a hotel, rather than having been transformed from a monastery or palazzo. Dating from the late 1800s, when it welcomed a goodly percentage of English visitors on their grand tour of Italy, it contains Oriental carpets, a medieval tapestry, and a pair of grandiose marble columns flanking the polished stone stairwell leading to the three floors of bedrooms. The rooms are conservatively traditional and high-ceilinged. There's a paneled, modern bar at the lobby's far end, a parking garage, and a restaurant (the Accademia) that operates under a separate management. Residents of the hotel receive a 10% discount on meals.

MODERATE

Colomba d'Oro. Via C. Cattaneo 10, 37121 Verona. ☎ **045/595300.** Fax 045/594974. 49 rms, 2 suites. A/C MINIBAR TV TEL. 310,000 lire ($198.40) double; 370,000 lire ($236.80) suite. Rates include breakfast. AE, DC, MC, V. Parking 24,000 lire ($15.35). Bus: 11, 12, or 21.

Venerable and historic, the Colomba d'Oro was built as a private villa during the 1600s and later transformed into a monastery. During the 18th and 19th centuries it served as an inn for travelers and employees of the postal services, and eventually grew into the large and much-renovated hotel it is today. Although the Accademia is better, the building is efficiently organized and has an atmosphere somewhere between semitraditional and contemporary. The bedrooms are nicely furnished with matching fabrics and comfortable furniture. Only breakfast is served, but there are many restaurants nearby.

INEXPENSIVE

Hotel de' Capuleti. Via del Pontiere 26, 37122 Verona. ☎ **045/800-0154.** Fax 045/803-2970. 42 rms. A/C MINIBAR TV TEL. 220,000 lire ($140.80) double. AE, DC, MC, V. Rates include breakfast. AE, DC, MC, V. Closed Dec 24–Jan 10. Free parking. Bus: 51 or 70.

The Hotel de' Capuleti is an attractively pristine little hotel, conveniently located a few steps from Juliet's (supposed) Tomb and the chapel where she is said to have been married. The reception area has stone floors and leather-covered couches, along with a tastefully renovated decor that's reflected upstairs in the comfortable bedrooms.

WHERE TO DINE

EXPENSIVE

✪ **Arche.** Via Arche Scaligere 6. ☎ **045/800-7415.** Reservations required. Main courses 32,000–45,000 lire ($20.50–$28.80); fixed-price menu 100,000 lire ($64). AE, DC, MC, V. Mon 7:30–9:30pm, Tues–Sat 12:30–2:30pm and 7:30–9:30pm. Closed Jan. ITALIAN.

Classic and elegant, this restaurant is acclaimed by some critics as the finest in Verona. We'd give that honor to Il Desco (see below), but Arche is a close runner-up. Giancarlo and Paola Gioco, the owners, insist on market-fresh fish from nearby Chioggia. The restaurant was founded in 1879 by Giancarlo's great-grandfather, and the seafood dishes are based on traditional recipes passed down from generation to generation, including some hard-to-find ones discovered in ancient cookbooks. Many locals begin with antipasti, a soup, pasta, or risotto, before going on to the main dish of the day, perhaps sea bass cooked with delectable porcini mushrooms. Sole and scampi are among the eternal favorites here. Baked "sea scorpion" with black olives is one of the chef's finest specialties, as is his ravioli stuffed with sea bass and served with a clam sauce. The furnishings in this 1420 building are in the Liberty style, the setting enhanced by candlelight and fresh flowers.

✪ **Ristorante il Desco.** Via Dietro San Sebastiano 7. ☎ **045/595358.** Reservations recommended. Main courses 35,000–40,000 lire ($22.40–$25.60); *menu dégustation* 120,000 lire

($76.80). AE, DC, MC, V. Mon–Sat 12:30–2pm and 7:30–10pm. Closed Jan 1–7 and Dec 25–26. Bus: 11, 12, or 21. ITALIAN.

The Ristorante il Desco is a handsome restaurant, the tops in Verona. It's located in the city's historic center, inside a tastefully renovated palazzo that's one of the civic prides of the city. The restaurant is ably directed by Elia Rizzo. The menu steers closer to the philosophy of nouvelle cuisine than anything else in town. Specialties make use of the freshest ingredients, including a purée of shrimp, potato pie with mushrooms and black truffles, calamari salad with shallots, tortellini with sea bass, risotto with radicchio and truffles, and tagliolini with fresh mint, lemon, and oranges. The wine cellar is superb, and your sommelier will help you if you're unfamiliar with regional vintages. The cheese selection is wide ranging, featuring choices from France.

MODERATE

Nuovo Marconi. Via Fogge 4. ☎ **045/591910.** Reservations required. Main courses 25,000–32,000 lire ($16–$20.50). AE, DC, MC, V. Mon–Sat 12:30–2:45pm and 8–11:30pm. Bus: Pollicino. ITALIAN.

The Nuovo Marconi is one of the best and most glamorous restaurants in Verona, in an ochre-colored villa on a narrow street just around the corner from piazza dei Signori. The doors are covered with an art nouveau wrought-iron grill, and the interior has stone columns, silk-shaded lamps, and lots of framed paintings. The menu reflects the best of traditional and regional dishes, and changes daily depending on the availability of ingredients at the market. The kitchen uses only fresh products, whether it be pasta, fish, or meat. In season, the chef likes to specialize in game dishes and the fish antipasti is reason enough to visit. The wine list is updated every 6 months, and the service is agreeable.

Ristorante 12 Apostoli. Vicolo Corticella San Marco 3. ☎ **045/596999.** Reservations recommended. Main courses 28,000 lire ($17.90). AE, DC, MC, V. Tues–Sat 12:30–2:30pm and 7:30–10pm, Sun 12:30–2:30pm. Closed Jan 2–8 and June 15–July 5. ITALIAN.

This is the oldest restaurant in Verona, in business for 250 years. It's a festive place, steeped in tradition, with frescoed walls and two dining rooms separated by brick arches. It's operated by the two Gioco brothers. Giorgio, the artist of the kitchen, changes his menu daily in the best tradition of great chefs, while Franco directs the dining room. Just consider some of these delicacies: salmon baked in a pastry shell (the fish is marinated the day before, seasoned with garlic and stuffed with scallops); or chicken stuffed with shredded vegetables and cooked in four layers of paper. To begin, we recommend the tempting antipasti alla Scaligera. For dessert, try the homemade cake.

INEXPENSIVE

Ristorante Re Teodorico. Piazzale di Castel San Pietro 1. ☎ **045/834-9990.** Reservations required. Main courses 25,000–30,000 lire ($16–$19.20). AE, DC, MC, V. Thurs–Tues noon–3pm and 7–10pm. Closed Jan. ITALIAN/INTERNATIONAL.

The Ristorante Re Teodorico is perched high on a hill at the edge of town, with a panoramic view of Verona and the Adige River. From its entrance, you descend a cypress-lined road to the ledge-hanging restaurant suggestive of a lavish villa. Tables are set out on a wide flagstone terrace edged with a row of classical columns and an arbor of red, pink, and yellow vines. Specialties include homemade pasta, which is always delectable; swordfish with tomatoes, capers, and fresh basil; and chateaubriand with a béarnaise sauce. The dessert specialty is crêpes Suzette.

⑤ VeronAntica. Via Sottoriva 10. ☎ **045/800-4124.** Reservations recommended. Main courses 12,000–23,000 lire ($7.70–$14.70); fixed-price menu 24,000 lire ($15.35). AE, DC,

MC, V. Wed–Mon 12:30–2:30pm and 7–10:45pm (July-Aug, 6–10:45pm). Closed Jan 2–14. Bus: 72 or 73. INTERNATIONAL.

VeronAntica is a distinguished local restaurant a short block from the river, across from a cobblestone arcade similar to the ones used in the film *Romeo and Juliet*. This place attracts the locals—not just tourists. It's made even more romantic at night by a hanging lantern that dimly illuminates the street. The chef knows how to prepare all the classic Italian dishes as well as some innovative ones too. Try his seafood risotto or turbot with thyme. He also prepares excellent veal escalopes with wild mushrooms. From June to September you can dine on an open-air terrace.

2 Padova (Padua)

25 miles W of Venice, 50 miles E of Verona, 145 miles E of Milan

Padua no longer looks as it did when Burton tamed shrew Taylor in the Zeffirelli adaptation of *The Taming of the Shrew*. However, it remains a major art center of Venetia. Shakespeare called Padua a "nursery of arts."

Padua is sometimes known as La Città del Santo (City of the Saint), a reference to St. Anthony of Padua, who is buried at a basilica that the city dedicated to him. *Il Santo* was an itinerant Franciscan monk—not to be confused with St. Anthony of Egypt, the hermit who could resist all the temptations of the Devil. Many visitors stay in the cheaper Padua and commute to Venice. Of course, it doesn't have Venice's beauty, and it has been defaced by high-rises and urban blight, but its inner core has a wealth of attractions. Its university, the second oldest in Italy, adds life and vibrancy to Padua, although the likes of Galileo and Dante haven't been seen here in a while.

ESSENTIALS

GETTING THERE   By Train   The train is best if you're coming from Venice, Milan, or Bologna. Trains depart for or arrive from Venice once every 30 minutes (trip time: 30 minutes), at a one-way cost of 3,400 lire ($2.20). Trains from Milan arrive or depart every hour (trip time: $2^{1}/_{2}$ hours), charging 19,000 lire ($12.15) one-way.

By Bus   Buses from Venice arrive every 30 minutes (trip time: 45 minutes); a one-way fare is 4,300 lire ($2.75). There are also connections from Vicenza every 30 minutes (trip time: 30 minutes), charging 4,800 lire ($3.05). The **bus station** is at via Trieste 40 (☎ 045/820-6844), near piazza Boschetti, 5 minutes from the rail station.

By Car   Take autostrada A4 west from Venice.

VISITOR INFORMATION   The **tourist information center** is at the Stazione Ferrovie Stato (☎ 045/875-2077). It's open Tuesday to Sunday from 9am to 7pm. Tickets valid for admission to all museums in Padua are available for 15,000 lire ($9.60) at the tourist office or at any of the city's museums.

SEEING THE SIGHTS

A university that grew to fame throughout Europe was founded here as early as 1222 (Galileo and the poet Tasso attended). Petrarch also lectured here, and the **University of Padua** has remained one of the great centers for learning in Italy. Today its buildings are scattered throughout the city. The historic main building of the university is called **Il Bo,** after an inn that used an ox as its sign, the major font of learning in the heyday of the Venetian Republic. The chief entrance is on via Otto Febbraio. Of particular interest is an anatomy theater, which dates from 1594 and was the first of its kind in Europe. **Guided tours of the university** are conducted on Tuesday from 9 to 11am, on Wednesday and Thursday from 9 to 11am and 3 to 5pm, and on Friday from 3 to 5pm. Tours cost 5,000 lire ($3.20). For information contact the Associazione Guide di Padova (☎ **049/820-9711**).

If you're on a tight schedule when you visit Padua, concentrate on the Cappella degli Scrovegni (Giotto frescoes) and the Basilica di San Antonio.

⚫ **Cappella degli Scrovegni (also Arena Chapel).** In the public gardens off corso Garibaldi. ☎ **049/650845.** Admission (including admission to the Musei Civici di Padova) 10,000 lire ($6.40) adults, 7,000 lire ($4.50) children 6–17, free for children 5 and under. Feb–Oct, daily 9am–7pm; Nov–Jan, daily 9am–6pm. Bus: 3, 8, 12, or 18.

This modest (on the outside) chapel is the best reason for visiting Padua. Sometime around 1305 and 1306 Giotto did a cycle of more than 35 (remarkably well-preserved) frescoes inside, which, along with those at Assisi, form the basis of his claim to fame. Like an illustrated storybook, the frescoes unfold biblical scenes. The third bottom panel (lower level on the right) depicts Judas kissing a most skeptical Christ and is the most reproduced and widely known panel in the cycle. On the entrance wall is Giotto's *Last Judgment*, in which hell wins out in sheer fascination. The master's representation of the *Vices and Virtues* is bizarre; it reveals the depth of his imagination in personifying nebulous evil and elusive good. One of the most dramatic of the panels depicts the raising of Lazarus from the dead. This is a masterfully balanced scene, rhythmically ingenious for its day. The swathed and cadaverous Lazarus, however, looks indecisive as to whether or not he'll rejoin the living.

Chiesa degli Eremitani. Piazza Eremitani 9. ☎ **045/875-6410.** Free admission (donations accepted). Apr–Sept, Mon–Sat 8:15am–noon and 3:30–6:30pm, Sun and religious holidays 9am–noon and 3:30–5:30pm; Oct–Mar, Mon–Sat 8:15am–noon and 3:30–5:30pm, Sun and religious holidays 9am–noon and 3:30–5:30pm. Bus: 3, 8, 12, or 18.

One of the tragedies of Padua is that this church was bombed during World War II. Before that time it housed one of the greatest treasures in Italy, the Ovetari Chapel with the first significant cycle of frescoes by Andrea Mantegna (1431–1506). The church was rebuilt, but, unfortunately, you can't resurrect 15th-century frescoes. Inside, to the right of the main altar, are fragments left after the bombing, a glimpse of what we lost of Mantegna's work. The most interesting fresco saved is a panel depicting the dragging of St. Christopher's body through the streets. Note also the *Assumption of the Virgin.* Mantegna is recommended even to those who don't like "religious painting." Like da Vinci, the artist had a keen eye for architectural detail.

⚫ **Basilica di Sant'Antonio.** Piazza del Santo 11. ☎ **049/663944.** Free admission. Apr–Sept, daily 6:30am–7:45pm; Oct–Mar, daily 6:30am–7pm. Bus: 8, 12, or 18.

This building was constructed in the 13th century and dedicated to St. Anthony of Padua, who's interred within. The basilica is a synthesis of styles, with mainly Romanesque and Gothic features. Campanili and minarets combine to give it an Eastern appearance. Inside it's richly frescoed and decorated, and filled with pilgrims devoutly touching the saint's marble tomb. One of the more unusual relics is in the treasury—the seven-centuries-old, still-uncorrupt tongue of St. Anthony.

The great art treasurers are the Donatello bronzes at the main altar, with a realistic *Crucifix* towering over the rest. Seek out, too, the Donatello relief depicting the removal of Christ from the cross (at the back of the high altar), a unified composition that expresses in simple lines and with an unromantic approach the tragedy of Christ and the sadness of the mourners.

Among his other innovations, Donatello restored the lost art of the equestrian statue with the well-known eaxmple in front of the basilica. Although the man it honors—called Gattamelata—is of little interest to art lovers, the statue is of prime importance. The large horse is realistic, as Donatello was a master of detail. He cleverly directs the eye to the forceful, commanding face of the Venetian military hero. Gattamelata was a dead ringer for the late Lord Laurence Olivier.

Musei Civici di Padova. Piazza Eremitani 8. ☎ **049/875-1153.** Admission included with admission to Cappella degli Scrovegni (see above). Tues–Sun 9am–7pm. Bus: 3, 8, 12, or 18.

This picture gallery is filled with minor works by major Venetian artists, some of which date from the 14th century. Look for a wooden *Crucifix* by Giotto and two miniatures by Giorgione. Other works include Giovanni Bellini's *Portrait of a Young Man* and Jacopo Bellini's miniature *Descent into Limbo*, with its childlike devils. The 15th-century Arras tapestry is also on display. Other works are Veronese's *Martyrdom of St. Primo and St. Feliciano*, plus Tintoretto's *Supper in Simone's House* and his *Crucifixion* (the latter is probably the finest single painting in the gallery).

Palazzo della Ragione. Via VIII Febbraio, between piazza delle Erbe and piazza dell Frutta. ☎ **049/820-5006.** Admission 7,000 lire ($4.40) adults, 4,000 lire ($2.50) children 11 and under. Daily 9am–7pm. Bus: 3, 8, or 18.

This "Palace of Law," which dates from the early 13th century, is among the remarkable buildings of northern Italy. Ringed with loggias, and with a roof shaped like the hull of a sailing vessel, it sits in the marketplace of Padua. Climb the steps and enter the grandiose Salone, a 270-foot assembly hall containing a gigantic, 15th-century wooden horse. The walls are richly frescoed with symbolic paintings that replaced the frescoes by Giotto and his assistants that were destroyed in a fire in 1420.

WHERE TO STAY
MODERATE

Hotel Donatello. Piazza del Santo 102–104, 35123 Padova. ☎ **049/875-0634.** Fax 049/875-0829. 49 rms, 4 suites. A/C MINIBAR TV TEL. 222,000 lire ($142.10) double; from 350,000 lire ($224) suite. AE, DC, MC, V. Closed Dec 15–Jan 15. Parking 28,000 lire ($17.50). Bus: 3, 8, 16, 18, or 22.

The Donatello is a renovated hotel with an ideal location near the Basilica of St. Anthony. Its terraced restaurant is its most alluring feature, although the Plaza has more amenities and is better equipped. Its buff-colored facade is pierced by an arched arcade, and the oversize chandeliers of its lobby combine with the checkerboard marble floor for a hospitable ambience. To prepare you for the eventual sight of Padua's famed wooden horse, the management has placed a big illuminated photo of it in the lobby. The rooms are well maintained and reasonably comfortable, although furnished in a standard and uninspired style.

Hotel Plaza. Corso Milano 40, 35139 Padova. ☎ **049/656822.** Fax 049/661117. 142 rms, 5 suites. A/C MINIBAR TV TEL. 250,000 lire ($160) double; from 360,000 lire ($230.40) suite. Rates include breakfast. AE, DC, MC, V. Parking 20,000 lire ($12.80). Bus: 5, 7, or 10.

The Plaza, the leading hotel in town, is a business hotel with brown ceramic tiles and concrete-trimmed square windows. Constructed in the 1970s, it was last renovated in 1992. The entrance is under a modern concrete arcade, which leads into a contemporary lobby. Its angular lines are softened with an unusual Oriental needlework tapestry, brown leather couches, and a pair of gilded baroque cherubs. The rooms are comfortable and well decorated. The bar, which you reach through a stairwell and an upper balcony dotted with modern paintings, is a relaxing place for a drink. There's also a restaurant on the premises, plus a parking garage.

Majestic Hotel Toscanelli. Piazzetta dell'Arco 2, 35122 Padova. ☎ **049/663244.** Fax 049/ 876-0025. 29 rms, 3 suites. A/C MINIBAR TV TEL. 195,000–220,000 lire ($124.80–$140.80) double; from 280,000 lire ($179.20) suite. Rates include buffet breakfast. AE, DC, MC, V. Parking 25,000 lire ($16). Bus: 5, 7, 8, 16, or 18.

Wrought-iron balconies protect the stone-edged French windows on this pastel-pink building fronting a cobblestone square in the heart of town. There's a Renaissance well and dozens of potted shrubs in front. Inside, you'll find a breakfast room surrounded by a garden of green plants. The lobby has white marble floors, Oriental rugs, an upper balcony, and a mishmash of old and new furniture. There's also a restaurant in the basement. The bedrooms were completely overhauled in 1992. Elegant furniture crafted by Tuscan artisans was added, along with mahogany and white marble. Pastel colors predominate in the bedrooms, with traditional Louis XV or Louis XVI decorating styles.

INEXPENSIVE

⑤ **Europa-Zaramella.** Largo Europa 9, 35137 Padova. ☎ **049/661200.** Fax 049/661508. 59 rms. A/C MINIBAR TV TEL. 180,000 lire ($115.20) double. Rates include breakfast. AE, DC, MC, V. Parking 25,000 lire ($16). Bus: 11, 13, 14, 16, or 22.

The Europa-Zaramella, near the post office, was built in the 1960s and looks its age, but is a recommendable choice because of its modest rates. The tasteful bedrooms are compact and serviceable and have pastel walls and simple built-in furnishings. The rooms open onto small balconies. The public rooms are enhanced by cubist murals, free-form ceramic plaques, and furniture placed in conversational groupings. The American bar is popular, as is the dining room. The Zaramella Restaurant features a good Paduan cuisine, with an emphasis on seafood dishes from the Adriatic.

WHERE TO DINE
EXPENSIVE

Ristorante San Clemente. Corso Vittorio Emanuele II 142. ☎ **049/880-3180.** Reservations recommended. Main courses 25,000–30,000 lire ($16–$19.20); fixed-price menu without wine 35,000 lire ($22.40); fixed-price menu with wine 85,000–130,000 lire ($54.40–$83.20). AE, MC, V. Mon 7:30–10:30pm, Tues–Sat 12:30–2:30pm and 7:30–10:30pm. Bus: 8. ITALIAN.

It's the most charming restaurant in town, thanks partially to its location in a 1646 hunting lodge designed by Palladio, and thanks mainly to its excellent cuisine. You'd have to go all the way to Venice to dine this well. During clement weather you might want to sit on the veranda, facing an elaborate and very old garden. Inside, amid graceful frescoes and antiques, you can order the most succulent cuisine in Padua. Examples change with the season, but might include potato gnocchi with chives and caviar, polenta flavored with foie gras and black truffles, scampi arranged on a bed of artichoke hearts, a heavenly roasted chicken studded with truffles, and such sumptuous desserts as an amaretto soufflé.

MODERATE

✪ **Belle Parti–Toulà.** Via Belle Parti 11. ☎ **049/875-1822.** Reservations required. Main courses 18,000–25,000 lire ($11.50–$16). AE, DC, MC, V. Mon–Sat 12:30–2:30pm and 8– 10:30pm. Closed 3 weeks in Aug. Bus: 2, 4, 10, or 13. INTERNATIONAL/ITALIAN.

The Toulà was established in 1982 under ceiling beams that are at least 500 years old. The age of the physical plant, however, didn't stop a team of designers from creating a sensual decor that showcases Italian style at its best. The ground floor includes a slick black bar, and the main dining area offers the excellent service this most sophisticated of nationwide restaurant chains is eager to provide. The restaurant has lost

---

A Famous Coffeehouse

The ✪ **Caffè Pedrocchi,** piazzetta Pedrocchi 15 (☎ **049/876-2576**), located off piazza Cavour, is a neoclassical landmark. Hailed as the most elegant coffeehouse in Europe when it opened in 1831 under Antonio Pedrocchi, its green, white, and red rooms reflect the national colors of Italy. On sunny days you might want to sit out on one of the two stone porches, and in winter you'll have plenty to distract you inside. The sprawling bathtub-shaped travertine bar has a brass top and brass lion's feet. The velvet banquettes have maroon upholstery, red-veined marble tables, and Egyptian Revival chairs. And if you tire of all this 19th-century outrageousness, you can retreat to a more conservatively decorated English-style pub on the premises, whose entrance is under a covered arcade a few steps away. Coffee costs 1,300 lire (85¢) at the stand-up bar, 2,800 lire ($1.80) at a table. Drinks begin at 5,000 lire ($3.20) at the bar, 8,000 lire ($5.10) at a table. Although drinks cost more than they would in a lesser café, you haven't heard the heartbeat of Padua until you've been at the Pedrocchi. From March to November, it's open Tuesday to Sunday from 7:30am to midnight; during the winter, Tuesday to Sunday from 7:30am to 10:40pm.

---

its supremacy in Padua to the San Clemente, but is still the honored "second choice" in town. The palate-pleasing menu changes monthly, but might include crayfish salad with artichokes; scampi salad with fennel, orange slices, and olives; a salad of radicchio with bacon; a savory salad composed of bottargha fish, beans, and celery; or filet of beef with a sauce of rosemary and balsamic vinegar. The cookery isn't always as refined as that of its sibling in Rome, but is first-rate nevertheless.

INEXPENSIVE

Ristorante Dotto. Via Squarcione 23. ☎ **049/875-1490.** Main courses 18,000–27,000 lire ($11.50–$17.30); fixed-price menu 50,000 lire ($32). AE, DC, MC, V. Tues–Sat noon–2pm and 8–10:15pm, Sun noon–2pm. Closed Aug 8–20. Bus: Any bus from the Termini. PADUAN.

The Ristorante Dotto takes its name from the *dottori* (doctors) of the university for which Padua is famous. The discreet, elegant restaurant is in the heart of the city, suitable not only for an academic or business meal but also for an intimate tête-à-tête dinner. Try the pasta e fagioli, grilled sole, risotto made with fresh asparagus, or the chef's pâté. You could top all this off with a feathery dessert soufflé, the most elaborate of which must be ordered at the beginning of a meal. The cookery is solid and reliable, without ever rising to the sublime.

3 Vicenza

126 miles E of Milan, 32 miles NE of Verona

In the 16th century Vicenza was transformed into a virtual laboratory for the architectural experiments of Andrea Palladio from Padua. One of the greatest architects of the High Renaissance, he was inspired by the classical art and architecture of ancient Greece and Rome. Palladio peppered the city with palazzi and basilicas, and the surrounding hills with villas for patrician families.

The architect was particularly important to England and America. In the 18th century Robert Adam was especially inspired by him, as reflected by many country homes in England today. Then, through the influence of Adam and others even earlier, the spirit of Palladio was imported across the waves to America (examples include

Jefferson's Monticello and plantation homes in the antebellum South). Palladio even lent his name to this architectural style—"Palladianism"—identified by regularity of form, massive, often imposing size, and an adherence to lines established in ancient Greece and Rome. Visitors arrive in Vicenza today virtually for one reason only—to see the works left by Palladio.

ESSENTIALS

GETTING THERE   **By Train**   Most visitors arrive from Venice (trip time: 50 minutes); a one-way ticket costs 5,200 lire ($3.35). Trains also arrive frequently from Padua (trip time: 25 minutes), charging 2,700 lire ($1.75) one-way. There are also frequent connections from Milan (trip time: 2¹/₂ hours), at 15,500 lire ($9.90) one-way.

By Bus   It's best to arrive by train. Once at Vicenza, however, you'll find good bus connections for the province of Vicenza if you'd like to tour the environs. The service is operated by **FTV,** viale Milano 138 (☎ **0444/223111**), to the left as you exit from the rail station.

By Car   From Venice, take autostrada A4 west toward Verona, bypassing Padua.

VISITOR INFORMATION   The **tourist information center** is at piazza Matteotti 12 (☎ **0444/320854**). It's open Monday to Saturday from 9am to 12:30pm and 2:30 to 6pm and on Sunday from 9am to 1pm.

EXPLORING THE WORLD OF PALLADIO

To introduce yourself to the "world of Palladio," head for **piazza dei Signori.** In this classical square stands the **Basilica Palladiana,** partially designed by Palladio. The loggias consist of two levels, the lower tier with Doric pillars, the upper with Ionic. In its heyday this building was much frequented by the aristocrats among the Vicentinos, who lavishly spent their gold on villas in the neighboring hills. They met here in a kind of social fraternity, perhaps to talk about the excessive sums being spent on Palladio-designed or -inspired projects. Originally the basilica was in the Gothic style, and served as the Palazzo della Ragione (justice). The roof collapsed following a 1945 bombing, but has been subsequently rebuilt. To the side is the **Tower of the Piazza,** which dates from the 13th century and soars approximately 270 feet high. Across from the basilica is the **Loggia del Capitanio** (guard), designed by Palladio in his waning years.

✪ **Teatro Olimpico (Olympic Theater).** Piazza Matteotti. ☎ **0444/323781.** Admission 5,000 lire ($3.20) adults, 3,000 lire ($1.90) students, 1,000 lire (65¢) children. Mar 16–Oct 15, Mon–Sat 9:30am–12:20pm and 3–5:30pm, Sun 9:30am–12:30pm; Oct 16–Mar 15, Mon–Sat 9:30am–12:20pm and 2–4:30pm, Sun 9:30am–12:20pm. Bus: 1 or 5.

The masterpiece and last work of Palladio—ideal for performances of classical plays—is one of the world's greatest theaters still in use. It was completed in 1585, 5 years after Palladio's death, by Vincenzo Scamozzi, and the curtain went up on the Vicenza premiere of Sophocles' *Oedipus Rex.* The arena seating area, in the shape of a half moon, is encircled by Corinthian columns and balustrades. The simple proscenium is abutted by the arena. What is ordinarily the curtain in a conventional theater is here a permanent facade, U-shaped, with a large central arch and a pair of smaller ones flanking it. The permanent stage setting represents the ancient streets of Thebes, combining architectural detail with *trompe l'oeil.* Above the arches (to the left and right) are rows of additional classic statuary on pedestals or in niches. Over the area is a dome, with trompe-l'oeil clouds and sky, giving the illusion of an outdoor Roman amphitheater.

Città del Palladio

His name was Andrea di Pietro, but his friends called him "Palladio." In time he would become the most prominent architect of the Italian High Renaissance, living and working in his beloved Vicenza which remains, in spite of the destruction of 14 of his buildings during World War II air raids (luckily, lavishly photographed and documented before their demise), a living museum to his architectural achievements. In time Vicenza would become known as the Città del Palladio. Palladio was actually born in Padua, where he was apprenticed to a stone carver, but fled in 1523 to Vicenza where he would live for most of his life, dying there in 1580.

In his youth Palladio journeyed to Rome where he studied the architecture of the Roman Vitruvius, who was to have a profound influence on him. Returning to Vicenza, Palladio in time perfected the "Palladian style," with its use of pilasters and a composite structure on a gigantic scale. The "attic" in his design was often surmounted by statues. One critic of European architecture wrote, "The noble design, the perfect proportions, the rhythm, and the logically vertical order invites devotion." Palladio's treatise on architecture, published in four volumes, is required reading for aspiring architects.

By no means was Palladio a genius, in the way the Florentine Brunelleschi was. No daring innovator, Palladio was more like an academician who went by the rules. Even though all his buildings are harmonious, there are no surprises in them either.

One of his most acclaimed buildings is the Villa Rotonda in Vicenza, a cube with a center circular hall crowned by a dome. On each external side is a pillared, rectangular portico. The classic features, although dry and masquerading as a temple, captured the public's imagination. This same type of villa was to reappear all over England and America.

The main street of Vicenza, corso Andrea Palladio, honors its most famous hometown boy, who spent much of his life building villas for the wealthy. The street is a textbook illustration of the great architect's work (or that of his pupils), and a walk along the corso is one of the most memorable in Italy.

Museo Civico (City Museum). In Palazzo Chiericati, piazza Matteotti 37–39. ☎ **0444/ 321348.** Admission 3,000 lire ($1.90) adults, 2,000 lire ($1.30) children. Tues–Sat 9am–12:30 and 2:15–5pm, Sun 9am–12:30pm. Bus: 1 or 7.

This museum is housed in one of the most outstanding buildings by Palladio. Begun in the mid-16th century, it was not finished until the late 17th century, during the Baroque period. Visitors today come chiefly to view its excellent collection of Venetian paintings on the second floor. Works by lesser-known artists—Paolo Veneziano, Bartolomeo Montagna, and Jacopo Bassano—hang alongside paintings by such giants as Tintoretto (*Miracle of St. Augustine*), Veronese (*The Cherub of the Balustrade*), and Tiepolo (*Time and Truth*).

Tempio di Santa Corona. Via Santa Corona. ☎ **0444/323644.** Free admission. Daily 8:30am–noon and 2:30–6:30pm. Bus: 1 or 5.

This much-altered Gothic church was founded in the mid-13th century. You should visit if for no other reason than to see Giovanni Bellini's *Baptism of Christ* (fifth altar on the left). In the left transept, a short distance away, is another of Vicenza's well-known works of art—this one by Veronese—depicting the three Wise Men paying tribute to the Christ child. The high altar with its intricate marble work is also worth a look. A visit to Santa Corona is more rewarding than a trek to the Duomo (cathedral), which is only of passing interest.

WHERE TO STAY
EXPENSIVE

Jolly Hotel Europa. Viale San Lorenzo 11, 36100 Vicenza. ☎ **0444/564111,** or 800/ 221-2626 in the U.S. Fax 0444/564382. 120 rms. A/C MINIBAR TV TEL. 330,000 lire ($211.20) double. AE, DC, MC, V. Free parking.

Outside of town, the Jolly quickly became the finest hotel in the area, although it didn't have to face much competition. It's a somewhat sterile but well-run and well-maintained hotel flying the flags of many nations. Frankly, this hotel is geared to the business traveler, as it lies in the Exhibition Center with easy access to the autostrada; however, it can also serve the leisure visitor. The bedrooms are done in a jazzy Italian style, and are medium size with the usual Jolly comforts such as direct-dial phones (and with the inevitable piped music). Some rooms are set aside for nonsmokers. Le Ville restaurant offers both international dishes and regional food of the Veneto.

MODERATE

Hotel Campo Marzio. Viale Roma 21, 36100 Vicenza. ☎ **0444/545700.** Fax 0444/320495. 35 rms. A/C MINIBAR TV TEL. 250,000-300,00 lire ($160–$192) double. Rates include breakfast. AE, DC, MC, V. Free parking. Bus: Any bus from the Termini.

This contemporary hotel is ideally situated in a peaceful part of the historic center of Vicenza, adjacent to a park. The hotel has undergone complete renovation. The sunny lobby has a conservatively comfortable decor that extends into the bedrooms. A cozy restaurant offers regional dining Monday to Friday.

INEXPENSIVE

⑤ Continental. Viale G. G. Trissino 89, 36100 Vicenza. ☎ **0444/505478.** Fax 0444/513319. 55 rms. MINIBAR TV TEL. 110,000–195,000 lire ($70.40–$124.80) double. AE, DC, MC, V. Free parking. Bus: 3.

The Continental is among the best choices for an overnight stopover in a town not known for its hotels. It has been renovated in a modern style and offers comfortably appointed bedrooms, about 70% of which are air-conditioned. The hotel has a good restaurant; however, there's no meal service on Saturday, Sunday, or in August. There's a solarium on the premises.

⑤ Hotel Cristina. Corso San Felice e Fortunato 32, 36100 Vicenza. ☎ **0444/323751.** Fax 0444/543656. 34 rms. A/C MINIBAR TV TEL. 190,000 lire ($121.60) double. Rates include buffet breakfast. AE, DC, MC, V. Parking 10,000 lire ($6.40). Bus: Any bus from the Termini.

The well-maintained, contemporary Hotel Cristina is a cozy place near the city center, with an inside courtyard where visitors can park. The decor consists of large amounts of marble and parquet flooring and lots of exposed paneling, coupled with comfortable furniture in the public rooms. The high-ceilinged bedrooms are also well furnished, although some small. A breakfast buffet is the only meal served.

WHERE TO DINE
MODERATE

✪ Cinzia e Valerio. Piazzetta Porta Padova 65–67. ☎ **0444/505213.** Reservations required. Main courses 18,000–35,000 lire ($11.50–$22.40); fixed-price menu 65,000 lire ($41.60). AE, DC, V. Tues–Sat noon–2:30pm and 7:30–9:30pm. Closed Aug. Bus: 1 or 7. SEAFOOD.

Cinzia is the chef, Valerio the maître d'hôtel, and this is the best and the most elegant restaurant in Vicenza. You'll be greeted by a polite staff and views of masses of seasonal flowers. The house fish specialties are time-tested recipes from the Adriatic coast. Your meal might begin with mollusks and shellfish arranged into an artfully elegant platter. Other dishes include risotto flavored with squid, a collection of crab and lobster that might surprise you by its size and weight, and an endless procession of fish cooked any way you prefer.

INEXPENSIVE

Antica Trattoria Tre Visi. Contrà Porti 6. ☎ **0444/324868.** Reservations required. Main courses 18,000–25,000 lire ($11.50–$16). AE, DC, MC, V. Tues–Sat 12:30–2:30pm and 7:30–10:30pm, Sun 12:30–2:30pm. Closed July. Bus: Any bus from the Termini. VICENTINO/INTERNATIONAL.

This restaurant was established as a simple tavern in the early 1600s. After many variations, it was named "The Three Faces" more than a century ago after the rulers of Austria, Hungary, and Bavaria, whose political influence was very powerful in the Veneto. The decor is rustic, with a fireplace, ceramic wall decorations, baskets of fresh fruit, and tavern chairs. You can see the kitchen from the main dining area. Together with the rich choice of international dishes, you can enjoy a good selection of regional wines. The owner will be pleased to help you with your choice. They might feature baccalà (salt codfish) alla vicentina, roast goat, zuppa di fagiole (bean soup), or spaghetti with duck sauce. Another specialty is capretto alla gambalaro (goat marinated for 4 days in a mixture of wine, vinegar, and spices, then roasted). The best-known dessert is the traditional pincha alla vicentina, made with yellow flour, raisins, and figs.

Ristorante Grandcaffè Garibaldi. Piazza dei Signori 5. ☎ **0444/544147.** Main courses 14,000–22,000 lire ($8.95–$14.10). AE, DC, MC, V. Restaurant, Thurs–Mon 12:30–3pm and 7:30–11pm, Tues 12:30–3pm. Cafe, Thurs–Tues 8am–midnight. Bus: 2, 4, or 5. VICENTINO/INTERNATIONAL.

The most impressive cafe in town has a design worthy of the city of Palladio. In the heartbeat center, it has a wide terrace and an ornate ceiling, marble tables, and a long glass case of sandwiches from which you can make a selection before you sit down (the waitress will bring them to your table). In the cafe, panini (sandwiches) cost 4,000 lire ($2.55), or a cappuccino, 3,000 lire ($1.90). Prices are slightly lower if you stand at the bar. There's also an upstairs restaurant with trays of antipasti and arrangements of fresh fruit set up on a central table. The menu's array of familiar Italian specialties is among the best in town.

Scudo di Francia. Contrà Piancoli 4. ☎ **0444/323322.** Reservations recommended. Main courses 20,000–25,000 lire ($12.80–$16). AE, DC, MC, V. Tues–Sat noon–2pm and 8–10pm, Sun noon–2pm. Closed Aug 1–20. Bus: 1 or 7. VICENTINO.

This 15th-century palace is a short walk from piazza dei Signori. The restaurant has a sunny decor accented with gilt wall sconces, high ceilings, and a garden visible through its rear windows. It doesn't pretend to have the more refined cuisine of Cinzia e Valerio, but it has proven to be a solid and reliable fixture on the local restaurant scene. Menu choices change frequently, but are likely to include pasta fagiole in the Veneto style, ravioli stuffed with pulverized radicchio, spaghetti with squid, and baccalà alla vicentina.

Trieste, the Dolomites & South Tyrol

12

The limestone Dolomites, one of Europe's greatest natural attractions, are a peculiar mountain formation of the northeastern Italian Alps. Some of their peaks soar to a height of 10,500 feet. The Dolomites are a year-round pleasure destination, with two high seasons: in midsummer, and then in winter when the skiers slide in.

At times the Dolomites form fantastic shapes, combining to create a landscape that looks primordial, with chains of mountains that resemble a giant dragon's teeth. Clefts descend precipitously along jagged rocky walls, whereas at other points a vast flat tableland—spared by nature's fury—emerges.

The provinces of Trent and Bolzano (Bozen in German) form the Trentino–Alto Adige region. The area is rich in health resorts, attracting many German-speaking visitors to its alpine lakes and mountains. Many of its waters—some of which are radioactive—are said to have curative powers.

South Tyrol is surrounded by the Dolomite Alps. Until 1919 South Tyrol was part of Austria, and even though today it belongs to Italy, it's still very much Tyrolean in character, both in its language (German) and in its dress.

Today the Trentino–Alto Adige region functions with a great deal of autonomy.

Before we proceed to details, readers with an extra day or so to spare may first want to postpone their Dolomite or Tyrolean adventure for a detour to Trieste.

EXPLORING TRIESTE, THE DOLOMITES & SOUTH TYROL BY CAR

Day 1   After Venice, head 72 miles to the northwest to Trieste on the half moon–shaped Gulf of Trieste, which spills into the Adriatic. Wander around piazza dell'Unità d'Italia and visit the Castello di Miramare and the Grotta Gigante. Overnight in Trieste.

Days 2–3   From Trieste, head northwest into the Dolomites for a 2-day holiday in Cortina d'Ampezzo, taking in its natural attractions. It's both a summer and a winter resort.

Day 4   From Cortina, go along the 68-mile Great Dolomite Road heading west. It's one of the most scenic drives in all of Europe (see below). Overnight in Bolzano.

☕ **TAKE A BREAK** **Birreria Forsterbrau**, via Goethe 6 in Bolzano (☎ **0471/ 977243**), is favored for its rib-sticking food. The kitchen takes special care with its grilled vegetables and is known for its ravioli with purple-red radicchio. At piazza Walther, head up via della Mostra until you reach via Goethe (go right). Open Monday to Saturday from 9am to midnight.

Day 5 From Bolzano, head northwest for only 18 miles to Merano, the old capital of Tyrol before Austria lost the region to Italy at the end of World War I. There are no grand attractions here, other than the site and the spa itself, where visitors flock to take the "grape cure." Overnight in Merano.

Day 6 Return south to other centers in Italy, but budget an overnight stopover if possible in historic Trent, 36 miles southwest of Bolzano. This is where the Council of Trent met from 1545 to 1563.

A TASTE OF TRENTINO & ALTO ADIGE

Trentino and Alto Adige, whose chief towns are Trent and Bolzano, is a land of orchards and vineyards, offering a varied cuisine that's not only pleasing to the taste but colorful on the plate. Austrian and Germanic traditions reign in the kitchen, although in the decades following the Italian takeover of the region, a more Mediterranean flavor became prevalent as well. You get not only strudel and würstel, but also ravioli and gnocchi.

Fish from alpine lakes, including eels from Lake Caldaro, add variety. *Arrosti* (roasts), mainly veal, are a mainstay of the diet. Some dishes are simple, such as *omelette di patate e maiale* (filled with lean pork and diced potatoes), but tasty.

Some 20 varieties of wine exist in the region. Casteller is one of the most popular, although it's almost sweet (it's usually served between meals). Lagrein, ranging from a ruby red to a bright garnet in color, is served with special meals by those who enjoy its nutty, slightly aromatic flavor.

A Rheinish wine like riesling is served with hors d'oeuvres and fish and has a straw yellow color, tending toward pale green, with a nutty, subtle flavor and a characteristic bouquet. Santa Guistina di Bolzano is served with roasts and wild fowl and has a mellow, if a bit sharp, flavor, with a slight undertone of vanilla. Teriano, a pale greenish yellow, has a subtle, persistent bouquet and a dry, harmonious and slightly aromatic flavor, and is served with both soups and hors d'oeuvres and often accompanies alpine fish.

1 Trieste

72 miles NE of Venice, 414 miles NE of Rome, 253 miles E of Milan

The remote city of Trieste, a shimmering, bright city with many neoclassical buildings, is perched on the half-moon Gulf of Trieste, which opens into the Adriatic.

As an Adriatic seaport, Trieste has had a long history, with many changes of ownership. The Habsburg emperor Charles VI declared it a free port in 1719, but by the 20th century it was an ocean outlet for the Austro-Hungarian Empire. Came the war and a secret deal among the Allies, and Trieste was ceded to Italy in 1918. In the late summer of 1943 Trieste again fell to foreign troops—this time the Nazis. The arrival of Tito's army from Yugoslavia in the spring of 1945 changed its destiny once more. A postwar attempt to turn it into a free territory failed. In 1954, after much hassle, the American and British troops withdrew as the Italians marched in, with the stipulation that the much-disputed Trieste would be maintained as a free port. Today that status continues. Politics, as always, dominates the agenda in modern

Trieste, the Dolomites & South Tyrol

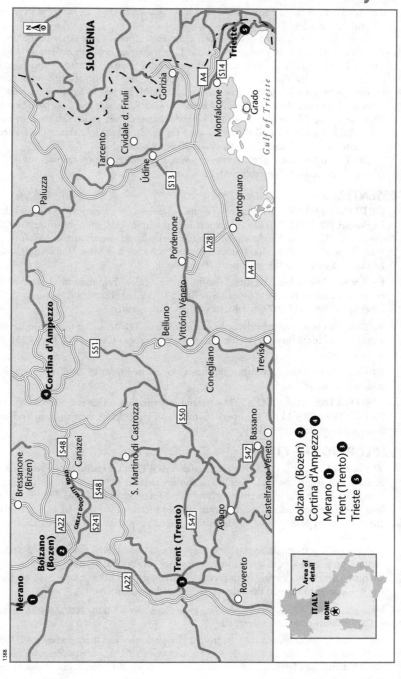

SLOVENIA

Gorizia
Cividale d. Friuli
Tarcento
Paluzza
Udine
S13
Monfalcone
S14
Trieste
Grado
Gulf of Trieste
Portogruaro
A4
A28
Pordenone
Cortina d'Ampezzo
S51
Belluno
Vittório Véneto
Conegliano
Treviso
S50
Bassano
S47
Castelfranco Véneto
Bressanone
(Brizen)
Canazei
S48
S48
GREAT DOLOMITE ROAD
S241
A22
Bolzano
(Bozen)
Merano
S. Martino di Castrozza
Trent (Trento)
S47
Asiago
A22
Rovereto

Bolzano (Bozen) **2**
Cortina d'Ampezzo **4**
Merano **1**
Trent (Trento) **3**
Trieste **5**

ITALY
Area of detail
ROME

Trieste. There is racial tension here, and many Italian fascists are centered here, as are anti-Slav parties.

Trieste has known many glamorous literary associations, particularly in the pre–World War II years. As a stopover on the *Orient Express,* it became a famed destination. Dame Agatha Christie came this way, as did Graham Greene. James Joyce, eloping with Nora Barnacle, arrived in Trieste in 1904. Out of both work and money, Joyce got a job teaching at the Berlitz School. He was to live here for nearly 10 years. He wrote *A Portrait of the Artist as a Young Man* here and may have begun his masterpiece *Ulysses* here as well. The poet Rainer Maria Rilke also lived in the Trieste area. Author Richard Burton, known for his *Arabian Nights* translations, lived in Trieste from 1871 until he died, about 20 years later.

The Teatro Verdi, the opera house, enjoys a deserved reputation throughout Italy, and many compare it favorably with La Scala.

ESSENTIALS

GETTING THERE **By Plane** Trieste is serviced by an airport at **Ronchi dei Legionari** (☎ **0481/773224** for airport information), $21^1/2$ miles northwest of the city. Daily flights on Alitalia connect the airport with Linate airport in Milan (trip time: 50 minutes), Franz Josef Strauss Airport in Munich (1 hour 10 minutes), and Leonardo da Vinci in Rome (1 hour 10 minutes).

By Train Trieste lies on a direct rail link from Venice. Trip time to Venice is $2^1/2$ hours and a one-way ticket costs 13,600 lire ($8.70). The **Termini** is on piazza della Libertà (☎ **040/418207**), northwest of the historic center.

By Bus It's better to fly, drive, or take the train to Trieste. Once there, you'll find a network of **local buses** servicing the region from corso Cavour (☎ **040/425020** for schedules).

By Car From Venice, continue northeast along autostrada A4 until you reach the end of the line at Trieste.

VISITOR INFORMATION The **tourist information office** is at via San Nicolò 20 (☎ **040/679-6111**). It's open Monday to Friday from 9am to 7pm and on Saturday from 8:30am to 1:30pm.

EXPLORING THE CITY

The heart of Trieste is the neoclassic ✪ **piazza dell'Unità d'Italia,** the largest square in Italy that fronts the sea. Opening onto the square is the town hall with a clock tower, the Palace of the Government, and the main office of the Lloyd Triestino ship line. Flanking the square are numerous cafes and restaurants, popular at night with the denizens of Trieste who sip an apéritif, then later promenade along the seafront esplanade.

After visiting the main square, you may want to view Trieste from an even better vantage point. If so, head up the hill for another cluster of attractions. You can take an antiquated tram, leaving from piazza Oberdan, getting off at Obelisco. There, at the **belvedere,** the city of the Adriatic will spread out before you.

Cathedral of San Giusto. Piazza Cattedrale, colle Capitolino. ☎ **040/302874.** Free admission. Daily 8:30am–noon and 4–7pm. Bus: 24.

Dedicated to the patron saint (St. Just) of Trieste, who was martyred in A.D. 303, the basilica atop colle San Giusto was consecrated in 1330, incorporating a pair of churches that had been separate until then. The front is in the Romanesque style, enhanced by a rose window. Inside, the nave is flanked by two pairs of aisles. To the left of the main altar are the best of the Byzantine mosaics in Trieste (note especially the blue-robed Madonna and her Child). The main altar and the chapel to the right contain less interesting mosaics. To the left of the basilica entrance is a small campanile from the 14th century, which you can scale for a view of Trieste and its bay. At its base are preserved the remains of a Roman temple from the 1st century A.D. You may prefer to take a taxi up to the cathedral, then walk back down, allowing a leisurely 15 minutes. From the basilica you can stroll to the nearby Castle of San Giusto.

Castle of San Giusto. Piazza Cattedrale 3. ☎ **040/308300.** Admission: Castle, 1,000 lire (65¢); museum, 2,000 lire ($1.30). Castle, Jan–Mar, daily 9am–2pm; Apr–Sept, daily 9am–7pm; Oct–Dec daily 9am–5pm. Museum, Tues–Sun 9am–12:45pm. Bus: 24.

Constructed in the 15th century by the Venetians on the site of a Roman fort, this fortress maintained a sharp eye on the bay, watching for unfriendly visitors arriving by sea. From its bastions, panoramic views of Trieste unfold. Inside is a **museum** (☎ **040/313636**) with a collection of arms and armor.

In July and August, a film festival is presented within the castle walls at an open-air theater.

✪ **Castello di Miramare.** Viale Miramare, Grignano. ☎ **040/224143.** Admission: Castle, 8,000 lire ($5.10) adults, free for children 18 and under and for seniors 60 and over; grounds, free. Castle, Apr–Sept, daily 9am–6pm; Oct–Mar, daily 9am–2pm. Grounds, Apr–Sept, daily 9am–7pm; Oct–Mar, daily 9am–5pm. Bus: 36 from the center.

Overlooking the Bay of Grignano, this castle was erected by Archduke Maximilian, the brother of Franz Joseph, the Habsburg emperor of Austria. Maximilian, who married Princess Charlotte of Belgium, was the commander of the Austrian navy in 1854. In an ill-conceived move, he and "Carlotta" sailed to Mexico in 1864, where he became the emperor in an unfortunate reign. He was shot in 1867 in Querétaro, Mexico. His wife lived until 1927 in a château outside Brussels, driven insane by the Mexican episode. (You may remember the movie, probably on late at night, about Maximilian and Carlotta, called *Juárez,* starring Bette Davis and Paul Muni.) On the ground floor of the castle, you can visit the bedroom of Maximilian (built like a ship's cabin) and that of Charlotte, as well as an impressive receiving room and more parlors, including a chinoiserie salon.

Enveloping the castle are magnificently designed park grounds (Parco di Miramare), ideal for pleasant strolls. In summer a sound-and-light presentation in the park depicts Maximilian's tragedy in Mexico. Tickets to the presentation, which is staged in July and August, begin at 15,000 lire ($9.60).

GROTTA GIGANTE

In the heart of the limestone plateau called Carso that surrounds the city, you can visit the ✪ **Grotta Gigante** (☎ **040/327312**), an enormous cavern and one of the most interesting phenomena of speleology. First explored in 1840 via the top ceiling entrance, this huge room, some 380 feet deep, was opened to the public in 1908. It's the biggest single-room cave ever opened to tourists and one of the world's largest underground rooms. A visit can be made only with a guide and takes 40 minutes. Near the entrance is the **Man and Caves Museum,** which is unique in Italy.

Tours of the cave are given Tuesday to Sunday; in March and October, they're offered every 30 minutes from 9am to noon and 2 to 5pm; November to February, every hour from 10am to noon and 2:30 to 4:30pm; April to September, every 30 minutes from 9am to noon and 2 to 7pm. Tours cost 10,000 lire ($6.40) for adults, 8,000 lire ($5.10) for children 6 to 12. If you're driving, take strada del Friuli beyond the white marble Victory Lighthouse as far as Prosecco. On the freeway you can take the exit at Prosecco.

WHERE TO STAY

⑤ Hotel al Teatro. Capo di piazza G. Bartoli 1, 31131 Trieste. ☎ **040/366220.** Fax 040/366560. 46 rms, 36 with bath (tub or shower). TEL. 110,000 lire ($70.40) double without bath, 150,000 lire ($96) double with bath. Rates include breakfast. AE, MC, V. Bus: 8, 9, 17, 18, 24, or 30.

The theatrical mask carved into the stone arch above the entrance is an appropriate symbol of this hotel, a favorite with many of Trieste's visiting opera stars. It's located a few steps from the seaside panorama of piazza dell'Unità d'Italia and about a 10-minute walk from the station. The simply furnished and slightly old-fashioned rooms have parquet floors, lots of space, comfortable but minimal furniture, and a tub or shower in the rooms with bath. The hotel was built in 1830 as a private house and later served as headquarters of the British army in the aftermath of World War II.

◐ Hotel Duchi d'Aosta. Piazza dell'Unità d'Italia 2, 34121 Trieste. ☎ **040/760-0011.** Fax 040/366092. 52 rms, 2 suites. A/C MINIBAR TV TEL. 200,000–330,000 lire ($128–$211.20) double; from 600,000 lire ($384) suite. AE, DC, MC, V. Parking 32,000 lire ($20.50). Bus: 8, 9, 17, 18, 24, or 30.

This now-glamorous hotel began about 200 years ago as a restaurant for the dock workers who toiled at the nearby wharves. Today many savvy travelers check in here, preferring it over the Savoia Excelsior, which is not managed or maintained as well as is this choice. In 1873 one of the most beautiful facades in Trieste, a white neo-classical shell with delicate carving, arched windows, and a stone crown of heroic sculptures, was erected to cover the existing building. The design is a lot like that of an 18th-century palace, an effect enhanced by views over the fountains and lamps of the square and the sea beyond it. The hotel was practically rebuilt from the inside in the 1970s. Today the hotel is a favorite with business travelers, who appreciate the food in the ground-floor restaurant (see the recommendation for Ristorante Harry's Grill in "Where to Dine," below) and the 19th-century ambience of the Victorian-style public rooms. Each accommodation has a well-stocked minibar concealed behind panels, antiqued walls, a built-in radio, and tasteful furniture.

Savoia Excelsior Palace. Riva del Mandracchio 4, 34124 Trieste. ☎ **040/77941.** Fax 040/638260. 146 rms, 5 suites. A/C MINIBAR TV TEL. 300,000–350,000 lire ($192–$224) double; 350,000–400,000 lire ($224–$256) suite. Rates include breakfast. AE, DC, MC, V. Parking 40,000 lire ($25.60). Bus: 8, 9, 17, 18, 24, or 30.

This leading choice stands next to the headquarters of the Lloyd Triestino shipping company, right off piazza dell'Unità d'Italia. Fronting the water, the hotel has witnessed much of the pageantry of Trieste. It was originally built by the Austrians in 1912, and still retains many Habsburg-style frills in its ornate decor. The rooms in this first-class hotel are equipped with radios and other amenities, and many are furnished in bold modern designs. There's a tea room, an American bar, and an excellent restaurant.

WHERE TO DINE
MODERATE

Al Bragozzo. Riva Nazario Sauro 22. ☎ **040/303001.** Reservations required. Main courses 12,000–40,000 lire ($7.70–$25.60); fixed-price all-you-can-eat menu 60,000 lire ($38.40). AE, DC, MC, V. Tues–Sat 11am–3pm and 7pm–midnight. Closed June 15–July 1 and 3 weeks in Dec. Bus: 8, 9, or 10. SEAFOOD.

This is the best-known fish restaurant at the port, established in the late 1960s in a Jugenstil building originally constructed as a private house by the Austro-Hungarians a century ago. The outdoor tables, sheltered by a canopy, are popular in summer, although the paneled dining room is better during inclement weather. Specialties include spaghetti al'Giorgio (with tomatoes and herbs), ravioli stuffed with herbs, and many different preparations of salmon and shrimp. The cooks bring considerable experience and talent to turning out their time-tested recipes.

Ristorante Harry's Grill. In the Hotel Duchi d'Aosta, piazza dell'Unità d'Italia 2. ☎ **040/7351.** Reservations required. Main courses 28,000–36,000 lire ($17.90–$23.05). AE, DC, MC, V. Daily 12:15–3pm and 7:15–10:30pm. Bus: 8, 9, 17, 18, 24, or 30. INTERNATIONAL.

Set in Trieste's most upscale hotel, this restaurant manages to be both elegant and relaxed at the same time, a place where a newcomer can have a correctly prepared American-style martini followed by either a simple plate of pasta or a complete, rather sumptuous meal. Despite the similarity of its name with other Harry's Bars, it's not associated with any of those other establishments. The adjoining bar is one of the most popular rendezvous spots in town, particularly for the business community. The big lace-covered curtains complement the paneling, the polished brass, and the blue Murano chandeliers. In summer, tables are set up in the central traffic-free piazza dell'Unità d'Italia. The outdoor terrace, which is sheltered by a canopy, has a separate area for bar clients.

The Mediterranean-inspired cuisine includes fresh shrimp with oil and lemon, pasta and risotto dishes, boiled salmon in sauce, butter-fried calves' liver with onions, and an array of beef and fish dishes. The food is good but not great.

INEXPENSIVE

⑤ **Ai Due Triestini.** Via Cadorna 10. ☎ **040/303759.** Main courses 15,000–28,000 lire ($9.60–$17.90). No credit cards. Mon–Sat noon–2:30pm. Closed Sept. Bus: 8, 9, 10, 11, or 24. ITALIAN/AUSTRIAN.

For one of the best lunch bargains in Trieste, we suggest this tavern behind piazza dell'Unità d'Italia. Run by a husband-and-wife team, this little trattoria covers its tablecloths with plastic and doesn't even bother to print a menu. Some of the cookery is heavily influenced by neighboring Austria. Try, for example, spezzatino, chunks of beef in a goulash ragoût, with fresh peas and potatoes. The Hungarian goulash is quite good, as is a rich strudel in the tradition of Budapest. It's located in the center of town near the sea and the Stazione Marittima.

⑤ **Al Granzo.** Piazza Venezia 7. ☎ **040/306788.** Reservations recommended. Main courses 20,000–25,000 lire ($12.80–$16); fixed-price menu 32,000–50,000 lire ($20.50–$32). AE, DC, MC, V. Mon–Tues and Thurs–Sat 12:30–3pm and 7:30–10pm, Sun 12:30–3pm. Bus: 8, 9, or 10. SEAFOOD.

This restaurant was established in 1923 by the ancestors of the three brothers who run it today. It began life as a simple fish house, serving seafood stews and grilled fish to the mariners who worked in the then-nearby dockyards. Today it's one of the leading seafood restaurants of Trieste, serving flavorful versions of that curious mixture of Italian, Austrian, and Yugoslav cuisines known as Triestino. Menu items include brodetto, a traditional bouillabaisse spiced with saffron and other herbs; vermicelli with black mussels; and risotto with seafood. Fresh fish are displayed on a bed of crushed ice in a wagon, and there's an impressive selection of fresh contorni (vegetables, sold individually) from nearby farms. A suitable wine might be a local Tocai Friulano, aromatic, harmonious, and somewhat tart, and lemon yellow to pale green in color. Dessert might be homemade strudel.

Frommer's Nature Notes: Exploring the Peaks of the Dolomites

The very existence of the high, snowy peaks of the Dolomites comes as a surprise to foreigners who assume that Italy is an exclusively maritime country of rolling hills, steamy flatlands, and sun-flooded harbors. The Dolomites add verticality and alpine charm to Italy, contributing a distinctive high-altitude wealth and Germanic overtones to the peninsula's diversity of cultures. Both the rock of which they're composed (dolomitic limestone) and the peaks themselves are named after an 18th-century French geologist, Déodat Guy Silvani Trancrède Gratet de Domolieu, who spent most of his life analyzing their mineral content.

Part of the eastern Alps, the Dolomites stretch along the northwestern tier of Italy, following the line of the Austrian border between the valleys of the Adige and the Brenta rivers. Although the highest peak is the Marmolada (a few feet shy of 11,000 feet above sea level), the range contains an additional 17 peaks in Italian territory that rise above 10,000 feet. Escaping from the often intense heat of other parts of their country, Italians travel from more low-lying regions to breathe the Dolomites' cool mountain air and to ski and play in such glittering resorts as Cortina.

The mountains' mixture of limestone and porphyry, combined with the angle of the rising and setting sun, contributes to the dramatic coloration of the mountain peaks. Most pronounced in the morning and at dusk, their colors range from soft pinks to brooding tones of russet. When the sun shines directly overhead, the hues fade to a homogenized and rather dull tone of gray. Fortunately for tourists, trekkers, and skiers, the climate isn't as bone-chillingly cold as it is in the alpine regions of western Italy and in the Alps of the Tyrol, farther to the north.

Antica Trattoria Suban. Via Comici 2, at San Giovanni. ☎ **040/54368.** Reservations recommended. Main courses 18,000–30,000 lire ($11.50–$19.20). AE, DC, MC, V. Mon 7:30–10pm, Wed–Sun 12:30–2:30pm and 7:30–10pm. Closed Aug 1–20. Bus: 8, 9, or 35. ITALIAN/AUSTRO-HUNGARIAN.

This country tavern was established in 1865 2 miles north of Trieste in the district of San Giovanni in a spacious terrace opening onto a view of the hills. Today the surrounding landscape contains glimpses of the industrial age, but the brick and stone walls, the terrace, and the country feeling are still intact. The restaurant is still run by descendants of the founding family. The cuisine is both hearty and delicate. In the true Triestino tradition, the cuisine draws its inspiration from northeastern Italy, as well as from the far Slavic, Hungarian, and Germanic recesses of what used to be the Austro-Hungarian empire. The chefs concoct specialties from fresh ingredients gathered from surrounding farmlands. Dishes include a flavorful risotto with herbs, basil-flavored crêpes, beef with garlic sauce, a perfectly prepared chicken Kiev, and veal croquettes with Parmesan and egg yolks. The chef's handling of grilled meats is adept, and the rich pastries are worth the extra calories.

2 Cortina d'Ampezzo

100 miles N of Venice, 82 miles E of Bolzano, 255 miles NE of Milan

This fashionable resort is your best center for exploring the snowy Dolomites. Its reputation as a tourist mecca dates back to before World War I, but its recent growth has been phenomenal. Cortina d'Ampezzo draws throngs of nature lovers in summer and both Olympic-caliber and neophyte skiers in winter. It's a hotel owner's

As you explore the Dolomites, don't expect lush vegetation. When not camouflaged with snow, the slopes tend to be stony and relatively bare of groundcovers. And don't rush out to gather hillside bouquets for your beloved, as many of the wildflowers (including the Austrian national flower, the edelweiss) are endangered species. Picking flowers or destroying vegetation is punishable by stiff fines.

Obviously, the Dolomites are redolent with natural beauty and trekking opportunities. Networks of hiking trails are clearly marked with painted signs, and any local tourist office (as well as most hotel reception staffs) are well versed in the length, duration, and degree of difficulty of most treks in their neighborhood. Maps of hiking trails are broadly distributed, and any local tourist office will refer mail to the nearest branch of whatever Associazione Guide Alpine proliferates in the region.

If you decide to ramble across the Dolomites for a day or two, remember to wear stout shoes, warm clothing, and a waterproof jacket (storms erupt quickly at these altitudes), and never leave the relative safety of a designated hiking path. Chair lifts, cog railways, and alpine gondolas usually operate in both summer and winter, and offer an alternative means of enjoying sweeping views over ferociously beautiful mountain scenery. Networks of hiking trails usually radiate outward from the top and bottom of most mechanical lifts, and rustically charming *refugios* (mountain huts, sometimes with dining and overnight facilities) offer the opportunity for an overnight stay or just a rest.

Shangri-la, charging maximum prices in July and August as well as in the 3 months of winter.

A public relations *signora* once insisted, "Just say Cortina has everything." Such statements of propaganda, even when they come from charming Italian ladies, are suspect—but in this case she's nearly right. "Everything," in the Cortina context, means—first and foremost—people of every shape and hue; New York socialites rub elbows in late-night spots with frumpy Bremen hausfraus. Young Austrian men, clad in Loden jackets and stout leather shorts, walk down the streets with feathers in their caps and gleams in their eyes. French women in red ski pants sample Campari at cafe tables, whereas the tweedy English sit at rival establishments drinking "tea like mother made."

Then, too, "everything" means location. Cortina is in the middle of a valley ringed by enough Dolomite peaks to cause Hannibal's elephants to throw up their trunks and flee in horror. Regardless of which road you choose for a motor trip, you'll find the scenery rewarding. Third, "everything" means good food. Cortina sets an excellent table, inspired by the cuisine of both Venice and Tyrol. Fourth, "everything" means summer and winter sporting facilities—chiefly golf, horseback riding, curling, tennis, fishing, mountain climbing, skiing, skating, and swimming. The resort not only has an Olympic ice stadium, but an Olympic bobsled track and ski jump (the 1956 Olympics were held at Cortina, publicizing the resort all over the world). In addition, it has a skiing school, a large indoor swimming pool, an Olympic downhill track, and a cross-country track.

Finally, "everything" means top-notch hotels, *pensioni,* private homes, and even mountain huts for the rugged. The locations, facilities, types of service, price structures, and decor in these establishments vary considerably, but we've never inspected an accommodation here that wasn't clean. Most of the architecture of Cortina, incidentally, seems more appropriate to Zell am See, Austria, than to an Italian town.

ESSENTIALS

GETTING THERE   By Train   Frequent trains run between Venice and Calalzo di Cadore (trip time: 2 hours 20 minutes), 19 miles south of Cortina. You proceed the rest of the way by bus. For information about schedules, call 0435/32300 in Calalzo.

By Bus   About 14 to 16 buses a day connect Calalzo di Cadore with Cortina. Buses arrive at the **Cortina bus station** on viale Marconi (☎ **0436/2741** for information about schedules).

By Car   Take autostrada A27 from Venice to Pian de Vedoia, continuing north along Route 51 all the way to Cortina d'Ampezzo.

VISITOR INFORMATION   The **tourist information office** is at piazzetta San Francesco 8 (☎ **0436/3231**). The staff can assist you in arranging accommodations (see "Where to Stay," below). The office is open Monday to Saturday from 9am to 12:30pm and 3 to 7pm and on Sunday from 10am to 4pm.

WHAT TO SEE & DO

The Faloria-Cristallo area in the surroundings of Cortina is known for its 18¹/₂ miles of ski slopes and 10 miles of fresh-snow runs.

One of the main attractions in Cortina is to take a cable car "halfway to the stars," as the expression goes. On one of them, at least, you'll be just a yodel away from the pearly gates. It's the **Freccia nel Cielo,** or "Arrow of the Sky" (☎ **0436/5052** for departure information). Beginning at 9am, departures are every 20 minutes, July 12 to September 28 and December 16 to May 1. A round-trip costs 28,000 lire ($17.90). The first station is Col Druscie at 5,752 feet; the second station, Ra Valles, stands at 8,027 feet; and the top station, Tofana di Mezzo, is at 10,543 feet. At Tofana on a clear day, you can see as far as Venice.

WHERE TO STAY

The **tourist information office,** piazzetta San Francesco 8 (☎ **0436/3231**), has a list of all the private homes in Cortina that take in paying guests, lodging them family style for a moderate cost. It's a good opportunity to live with a Dolomite family in comfort and informality. The tourist office, however, will not personally book you into a private home. Those arrangements you must make independently. Even though there are nearly 4,700 hotel beds available, it's best to reserve in advance, especially from August 1 to 20 and December 20 to January 7.

VERY EXPENSIVE

De la Poste. Piazza Roma 14, 32043 Cortina d'Ampezzo. ☎ **0436/4271.** Fax 0436/868435. 77 rms, 3 suites. TV TEL. 400,000–700,000 lire ($256–$448) double; 700,000–1,000,000 lire ($448–$640) suite for two. Rates include half board. AE, DC, MC, V. Closed Apr 12–June 16 and Sept 30–Dec 22. Parking 25,000 lire ($16).

Built like a Tyrolean mountain chalet, this hotel enjoys a central and sunny position in a pedestrian zone and is the finest hotel in the town center, although it's far surpassed by the Miramonti Majestic on the outskirts. It was originally constructed in the 18th century and opened as a hotel shortly after World War II. It has long been a celebrity favorite, attracting such guests as Hemingway and King Hussein of

Jordan. Open wooden balconies and terraces encircle the building, giving bedrooms sun porches. All the bedrooms have double windows and French doors, chintz draperies and bedspreads, and built-in wardrobes. Almost half the rooms have minibars. The get-acquainted, woodsy bar, evoking a country tavern, is the liveliest spot in town. The hotel, once a postal inn, is the most popular place in Cortina for après-ski drinks.

○ Miramonti Majestic Grand Hotel. Via Pezzie 103, 32043 Cortina d'Ampezzo. ☎ **0436/ 4201.** Fax 0436/867019. 106 rms, 11 suites. MINIBAR TV TEL. 240,000–510,000 lire ($153.60– $326.40) per person double; from 800,000 lire ($512) per person suite. Rates include half board. AE, DC, MC, V. Closed Apr–July 6 and Sept–Dec 21. Parking 30,000 lire ($19.20) in garage, free outside. Hotel shuttle bus to/from the town center every 30 minutes.

Built in 1893, this hotel, one of the grandest in the Dolomites, is a short distance from the center of town. It consists of two ochre-colored buildings with alpine hipped roofs. There's a gazebo built in the same style as the hotel on the right as you ascend the curved driveway leading up to the dignified facade. The rustic interior is filled with warm colors, lots of exposed timbers, and the most elegant clientele in Cortina. The well-furnished bedrooms look like those of a private home, complete with matching accessories, built-in closets, and all the modern amenities.

A sports facility is on the premises, with an indoor swimming pool, exercise and massage equipment, a sauna, hydrotherapy, and physical therapy. Other sports facilities for winter and summer exercises are nearby, including golf and tennis.

MODERATE

○ Ancora. Corso Italia 62, 32040 Cortina d'Ampezzo. ☎ **0436/3261.** Fax 0436/3265. 64 rms, 6 suites. TV TEL. 150,000–260,000 lire ($96–$166.40) per person double; 450,000– 780,000 lire ($288–$499.20) suite. Rates include half board. AE, DC, MC, V. Closed after Easter to June and Sept 15–Dec 20. Free parking. Bus: Any bus from the Termini.

This "Romantik Hotel," originally a private home back in 1826, is the domain of that hearty empress of the Dolomites, Flavia Bertozzi, who attracts sporting guests from all over the world and plays hostess to modern art exhibitions and classical concerts. This "hostess with the mostest" believes in her guests' having a good time. The antique sculptures and objets d'art filling the hotel were gathered from Signora Flavia's trips to every province of Italy. Hers is a revamped hotel flanked on two sides by terraces with outdoor tables and umbrellas—the town center for sipping and gossiping. Garlanded wooden balconies encircle the five floors, and most bedrooms open directly onto these sunny porches. The bedrooms are all well furnished, comfortable, and especially pleasant—many with sitting areas. All is kept shiny clean, the service is polite and efficient, and the food is reason enough to check in.

Hotel Corona. Via Val di Sotto 12, 32040 Cortina d'Ampezzo. ☎ **0436/3251.** Fax 0436/ 867339. 44 rms. TV TEL. 220,000–280,000 lire ($140.80–$179.20) per person. Rates include half board. MC, V. Closed Apr 10–June and Sept 15–Dec 20. Free parking. Bus: Any bus from the Termini.

Dating from 1935, the Corona was one of the first hotels built at the resort. Its loyal clients will stay nowhere else during a stopover in Cortina. For anyone interested in modern Italian art, a stopover here is an event. The interior walls are painted a neutral white as a foil for the hundreds of carefully inventoried artworks displayed, all acquired over the past quarter of a century by Luciano Rimoldi, the athletic manager. (He's also a ski instructor, who coached Princess Grace in her downhill technique shortly before her death. He later served as head of the Italian ice-hockey team during the 1988 Winter Olympics at Calgary.)

Many of the most important artists of Italy (and a few from France) from 1948 to 1963 are represented here with paintings, sculptures, and ceramic bas-reliefs. The hotel doesn't overlook sports either. It was chosen for the World Cup competition by a U.S. ski team just before they headed for the Sarajevo Olympics. The hotel prefers guests to take half board.

⑤ Menardi. Via Majon 110, 32043 Cortina d'Ampezzo. ☎ **0436/2400.** Fax 0436/862183. 51 rms. TEL. 110,000–210,000 lire ($70.40–$134.40) per person. Rates include half board. MC, V. Closed Apr 10–June 21 and Sept 15–Dec 20. Free parking. Bus: 1.

This eye-catcher in the upper part of Cortina looks like a great country inn, with its wooden balconies and shutters. Its rear windows open onto a meadow of flowers and a view of the rough Dolomite crags. The inn is 100 years old and is run by the Menardi family, who still know how to speak the old Dolomite tongue, Ladino. Decorated in the Tyrolean fashion, each bedroom has its distinct personality. Considering what you get—the quality of the facilities, the reception, and the food— we'd rate this one of the best values in Cortina. The living rooms and dining rooms have homelike furnishings: lots of knickknacks, pewter, antlers, spinning wheels.

Should this hotel be full, the family will book you into their second accommodation, which contains only eight rooms, each with a private bath and a balcony opening onto the Dolomites.

Parc Hotel Victoria. Corso Italia 1, 32043 Cortina d'Ampezzo. ☎ **0436/3246.** Fax 0436/4734. 42 rms, 4 suites. MINIBAR TV TEL. 110,000–255,000 lire ($70.40–$163.20) per person double; from 500,000 lire ($320) suite for two. Rates include half board. AE, DC, MC, V. Closed Mar 28–July 12 and Sept 10–Dec 22. Free parking. Bus: 1 or 2.

The Parc Hotel Victoria is one of the best hotels in the center of town, a modern structure created in the Tyrolean style, with many good-size balconies opening onto views of the mountaintops. Although not as chic as the Post, it's a successful place, combining the old chalet decor with contemporary, roomy areas and lots of amenities. In the winter, all the well-furnished rooms have plenty of steam heat. The various living and dining rooms are furnished with reproductions of old country furniture (bare-pine tables, peg-legged chairs). The regional fireplace with a raised hearth is the focal point for after-dinner gatherings.

INEXPENSIVE

⑤ Da Beppe Sello. Via Ronco 68, 32043 Cortina d'Ampezzo. ☎ **0436/3236.** Fax 0436/3237. 12 rms. TV TEL. 120,000–180,000 lire ($76.80–$115.20) double. Rates include half board. AE, DC, MC, V. Closed after Easter to May 15 and Sept 20–Oct 27. Bus: Any bus from the Termini.

A recently modernized hotel set at the edge of the resort, Da Beppe Sello is one of the best bargains in the area. It was built in a chalet style in the 1950s, and offers cozily comfortable alpine-style bedrooms, each well maintained and inviting. Its restaurant (see "Where to Dine," below) is recognized as one of the finest at the resort.

Hotel Dolomiti. Via Roma 118, 32043 Cortina d'Ampezzo. ☎ **0436/861400.** Fax 0436/862140. 42 rms. TV TEL. 110,000–210,000 lire ($70.40–$134.40) double. Rates include breakfast. AE, DC, MC, V. Closed Nov. Bus: 1 or 2. Parking 5,000 lire ($3.20).

The Hotel Agip, a member of this popular Italian chain, offers many amenities, although admittedly it's a sterile choice after the atmospheric places previously considered. But if you're watching your lire, this isn't a bad choice. It's also a good bet if you arrive in Cortina in the off-season, when virtually everything else is closed. Its convenient location on the main road just outside the center of town—coupled with its clean, comfortable, contemporary, and no-nonsense format—have gained it increasing favor with visitors. The bedrooms are predictably furnished and fairly quiet, and the management is helpful. The restaurant serves good food, featuring regional specialties.

WHERE TO DINE

Da Beppe Sello. Via Ronco 68. ☎ **0436/3236.** Reservations recommended. Main courses 18,000–32,000 lire ($11.50–$20.50). AE, DC, MC, V. High season, daily 12:30–2pm and 7:30–10pm; low season, Tues–Sun 12:30–2pm and 7:30–10pm. Closed Easter–May 15 and Sept 30–Oct. 31. Bus: 2. ALPINE/INTERNATIONAL/ITALIAN.

When you grow tired of the sometimes oppressive glamour of the more expensive restaurants in town, head for this simple but charming, Tyrolean-style restaurant in a simple hotel at the edge of the village. Named after the double nicknames of the hotel's founder, Joseph (Beppe) Menardi (Sello), and run today by his multilingual niece, Elisa, it's a bastion of superb regional cuisine and has been visited by some of the resort's most elegant clients. Food items include filet of venison from the Dolomites served with pear, polenta, and marmelata di mirtilli (marmalade made from an alpine berry resembling a huckleberry or blueberry); diners get to keep the plate the dish was served on as a souvenir of their visit. Other dishes include pappardelle with rabbit sauce, tagliolini with porcini mushrooms, roast chicken with bay leaves, and filet steak flavored with bacon.

El Toulà. Località Ronco 123. ☎ **0436/3339.** Reservations required. Main courses 28,000–40,000 lire ($17.90–$25.60). AE, DC, MC, V. Tues–Sun 12:30–2:30pm and 8–11pm. Closed Easter to late July and Sept–Christmas. Bus: 2. ITALIAN/VENETIAN.

Located 2 miles east of Cortina, this was the first member of El Toulà chain, which today has around 10 other restaurants scattered throughout Italy and the world. Established in the early 1960s, and dubbed with a name that in the dialect of Cortina translates as "The Hayloft," it's a wood-framed structure with picture windows and an outside terrace. It's perched about a 5-minute drive from the center of town, toward Pocol. You get excellently prepared dishes here, including squab grilled to perfection and served with an expertly seasoned sauce and veal braised with a white truffle sauce. The filet of beef is also recommended. A frittata of sea crabs in the "Saracen" style is served, as are pasta e fagiole (beans and pasta) in the style of Veneto, a pasticcio of eggplant; and Venetian-style calves' liver. In the 1960s this place was terribly chic, tied in almost exclusively with the jet set crowd of Cortina. In the more realistic 1990s the rich and flavorful cuisine is appreciated by more down-to-earth clients.

✪**Ristorante Tivoli.** Località Lacedel. ☎ **0436/866400.** Reservations required. Main courses 22,000–32,000 lire ($14.10–$20.50). AE, DC, MC, V. High season, daily 12:30–2:30pm and 7:30–10pm; off-season, Tues–Sun 12:30–2:30pm and 7:30–10pm. Closed May–June and Oct–Nov. Bus: 1. ITALIAN.

The best restaurant in Cortina, and one of the finest in the area, is this low-slung alpine chalet whose rear seems almost buried in the slope of the hillside. Standing high above the resort, about a mile from the center, it's beside the road leading to the hamlet of Pocol. Vastly popular with an athletic European clientele, it derives its excellence from the hard-working efforts of the gracious Calderoni family, who make this place the most fun and interesting at the resort.

The appetizing aromas emerging from the kitchen whet your appetite for the savory flavors. Only the freshest of ingredients are used. Full meals might include stuffed rabbit in an onion sauce, wild duck with honey and orange, veal filet with basil and pine nuts, or salmon flavored with saffron. The pastas are made fresh in the kitchen daily. For dessert, you might sample an aspic of exotic fruit.

EN ROUTE TO BOLZANO VIA THE GREAT DOLOMITE ROAD

From Cortina d'Ampezzo in the east to Bolzano in the west, the ✪ **Great Dolomite Road** follows a circuitous route of about 68 miles. It ranks among the grandest scenic drives in all of Europe. The first pass you'll cross (Falzarego) is about 11 miles from Cortina. At 6,900 feet above sea level, it offers a panoramic view. The next great pass is called Pordoi, at about 7,350 feet above sea level, the loftiest point along the highway (you can take a cable car to the top). Here you'll find restaurants, hotels, and cafes. In the spring, edelweiss grows in the surrounding fields. After crossing the pass, you'll descend to the little resort of Canazei, then much later pass by sea-blue Carezza Lake.

3 Bolzano

177 miles NE of Milan, 298 miles N of Rome, 95 miles N of Verona

The terminus of the Great Dolomite Road (or the gateway, depending on your approach), Bolzano is a town of mixed blood, reflecting the long rule that Austria enjoyed until 1919. Many names, including that of the town (Bozen), appear in German. As the recipient of considerable Brenner Pass traffic (55 miles north), the city is a melting pot of Italians and both visitors and residents from the Germanic lands. The capital of a province of the same name, Bolzano lies in the center of the Alto Adige region. It's traversed by two rivers, the Isarco and Talvera, one of which splits the town into two sections.

Bolzano is a modern industrial town, yet a worthwhile sightseeing attraction in its own right. It has many esplanades for promenading along the river. The most interesting street is the colonnaded **via dei Portici.** You can begin your stroll down this street of old buildings at either **piazza Municipio** or **piazza delle Erbe,** the latter a fruit market for the orchards of the province.

Bolzano makes a good headquarters for exploring the Dolomites and the scenic surroundings, such as **Renon** (Ritten in German) on the alpine plateau, with its cog train; the village of **San Genesio,** reached by cable north of Bolzano; and **Salten,** 4,355 feet up, an alpine tableland.

ESSENTIALS

GETTING THERE   By Train   Bolzano is a 2¹/₂-hour train ride north of Verona; a one-way fare is 11,700 lire ($7.50). The Austrian city of Innsbruck, which is reached via the Brenner Pass, lies about a 95-minute train ride north of Bolzano.

By Bus   Bolzano can be reached by bus from Cortina d'Ampezzo (see Section 2 in this chapter). Four buses a day make the 3-hour trip. A one-way ticket costs 14,500 lire ($9.30).

By Car   From Trent (see Section 5 in this chapter), continue north to Bolzano on autostrada A22; or head west from Cortina d'Ampezzo along Route 48 until you reach the signposted junction with Route 241, which covers the final circuitous lap into Bolzano.

VISITOR INFORMATION   The **tourist information center** is at piazza Walther 8 (☎ **0471/970660**). It's open Monday to Friday from 8:30am to 6pm and on Saturday from 9am to 12:30pm.

WHERE TO STAY

Hotel Alpi. Via Alto Adige 35, 39100 Bolzano. ☎ **0471/971929.** Fax 0471/971929. 110 rms. A/C MINIBAR TV TEL. 240,000 lire ($153.60) double. Rates include breakfast. AE, DC, MC, V. Parking 15,000 lire ($9.60). Bus: 1.

The exterior of this tastefully contemporary hotel—the second-best choice in town—is dotted with recessed balconies, large aluminum-framed windows, and the flags of many nations. The spacious public rooms are richly covered with paneling, exposed stone, and ceramic wall sculptures, and contain comfortable upholstered seating areas. The hotel is located in the commercial center of town, and has a bar, a restaurant, a well-trained staff, and cozy rooms.

✪ **Park Hotel Laurin.** Via Laurin 4, 39100 Bolzano. ☎ **0471/311000,** or 800/223-5652 in the U.S. Fax 0471/311148. 96 rms, 10 suites. A/C MINIBAR TV TEL. 335,000–395,000 lire ($214.40–$252.80) double; from 440,000 lire ($281.60) suite. Rates include breakfast. AE, DC, MC, V. Parking 19,000 lire ($12.15). Bus: All buses.

The town's best address, the Park Laurin captures the glamour of the past. It's the only superior first-class hotel in the Bolzano, and its rooms and suites have been refurbished, with baths in Italian marble. This has made the Park Hotel among the top first-class hotels in the Dolomites. The private garden is dominated by old shade trees and a flagstone-enclosed swimming pool. The garden terrace is ideal for lunches or dinners. The Laurin Bar offers piano entertainment daily, with jazz performances every Friday.

Scala Hotel Stiegl. Via Brennero 11 (Brennerstrasse 11), 39100 Bolzano. ☎ **0471/976222.** Fax 0471/981141. 60 rms, 5 suites. 200,000 lire ($128) double; 280,000–400,000 lire ($179.20–$256) suite. Rates include breakfast. AE, DC, MC, V. Closed Dec 20–Jan 8. Parking 15,000 lire ($9.60) in garage, free outside. Bus: 8.

The Scala is one of the best of the middle-bracket hotels of Bolzano. Its trilingual staff speaks fluent English, among other languages, and keeps the interior spotless. The neobaroque yellow-and-white facade is well maintained, with plenty of ornamentation scattered symmetrically over its five-story expanse. On the premises is an outdoor pool, plus a summer-garden restaurant specializing in Tyrolean dishes. The hotel affords easy access to the train station and the historic center of town. The rooms are well furnished and most contain minibars and TVs. There's parking for 50 cars.

WHERE TO DINE

Da Abramo. Piazza Gries 16 (Grieserplatz 16). ☎ **0471/280141.** Reservations recommended. Main courses 20,000–25,000 lire ($12.80–$16). AE, DC, MC, V. Mon–Sat noon–2:15pm and 7 –9:45pm. Closed Jan 6–13 and 3 weeks in Aug. Bus: 10A or 10B. MEDITERRANEAN/SEAFOOD.

In a century-old Liberty-style villa, the best and the most elegant restaurant in Bolzano took great pains to introduce a chic modern airiness to its physical decor. Located in a sienna-colored villa across the river from the historic center of town, the restaurant offers a summer garden covered with vine arbors, plus a labyrinthine arrangement of rooms. Full meals range upward from 50,000 lire ($32) and might include, depending on the mood of the chef, veal in a sauce of tuna and capers, roast quail with polenta, fish soup, warm seafood antipasti, codfish Venice style, shellfish with seafood, tagliatelle with prosciutto, and beefsteak flambé with cognac. Flavors are robust, some thanks to the best of herbs and spices.

Zur Kaiserkron. Piazza della Mostra 1 (Mustergasse 1). ☎ **0471/970770.** Reservations recommended. Main courses 23,000–30,000 lire ($14.70–$19.20). AE, DC, MC, V. Mon–Fri noon–2:30pm and 7–9:30pm, Sat noon–2:30pm. Bus: Any bus from the Termini. SOUTH TYROLEAN/FRENCH/INTERNATIONAL.

The food is excellent, the decor appealing, and the multilingual management preserves the bicultural ambience for which Bolzano is known. The restaurant is housed a block from the cathedral in a yellow-and-white baroque building originally built in 1740 as the home of a wealthy Austrian merchant. For warm-weather dining, there's a canopy-covered wooden platform in front surrounded with greenery. You'll be welcomed by a member of the staff and ushered to a table under vaulted ceilings and wrought-iron chandeliers. Favorite dishes include an assortment of alpine-dried charcuterie; pâté of minced pheasant and duck liver; ravioli stuffed with spinach and minced beef; homemade tagliatelle with truffles; a traditional recipe of grüstl made from minced veal fried together with onions, eggs and potatoes; home-smoked salmon; filet of venison with rosemary, pine nuts, and sweet-and-sour sauce; roast lamb or kid; and beef goulash with polenta.

4 Merano

18 miles NW of Bolzano, 202 miles NE of Milan

Once the capital of Tyrol (before Innsbruck), Merano (Meran) was ceded to Italy at the end of World War I, but it retains much of its Austrian heritage today. In days gone by it was one of the most famous resorts in Europe, drawing kings and queens and a vast entourage from many countries, who were attracted to the alpine retreat by the grape cure. (Eating the luscious Merano grapes is supposed to have medicinal value.) After a slump, Merano now enjoys popularity, especially in autumn when the grapes are harvested. Before World War II Merano also became known for its radioactive waters, in which ailing bathers supposedly secured relief for everything from gout to rheumatism.

The Passirio River cuts through the town (and along it are many promenades, evoking the heyday of the resorts of the 19th century). Situated in the Valley of the Adige at the foot of Kuchelberg, Merano makes a good base for excursions in several directions, particularly to Avelengo. A bus from Sandplatz will deliver you to a funicular connection, in which you can ascend 3,500 feet above sea level to Avelengo, with its splendid vista and mountain hotels and pensions.

Merano is rich with tourist facilities and attractions, such as open-air swimming pools at its Lido, tennis courts, and a race track.

ESSENTIALS

GETTING THERE   By Train   Five trains per day make the short run from Bolzano (see Section 3 in this chapter) to Merano. The trip takes 40 minutes and costs 3,400 lire ($2.20) for a one-way ticket.

By Bus   From Bolzano, buses run frequently throughout the day northwest to Merano. The one-way fare is 4,000 lire ($2.55). Buses leave from via Perathoner 4 (☎ 0471/450111) in Bolzano.

By Car   From Bolzano, head northwest along Route 38.

VISITOR INFORMATION   The **tourist information center** is at corso della Libertà 45 (☎ **0473/235223**). It's open Monday to Friday from 8:30am to 6pm and on Saturday from 9am to 12:30pm.

EXPLORING THE TOWN

On the Tappeinerweg promenade, the **Museo Agricolo Brunnenburg,** Ezra Pound Weg 6 (☎ **0473/923533**), is housed in a castle owned by the daughter and grandson of Ezra Pound, who lived in Merano from 1958 to 1964. The museum has displays of Tyrolean country life, including a blacksmith's shop and grain mill. There are also ethnology exhibits, plus a room dedicated to Pound. Open Wednesday to Monday from 9:30 to 5pm. Admission is 4,000 lire ($2.55) for adults, 1,500 lire ($.95) for children. You can reach the castle by taking bus no. 3 from Merano to Dorf Tirol, every hour on the hour, or by climbing the Tappeinerweg. The house is closed November to March.

WHERE TO STAY

Castel Labers (Schloss Labers). Via Labers 25, 39012 Merano. ☎ **0473/234484.** Fax 0473/234146. 30 rms, 1 suite. TEL. 200,000–250,000 lire ($128–$160) double; 400,000 lire ($256) suite. Rates include breakfast. Half board 160,000 lire ($102.40) per person extra. AE, DC, MC, V. Closed Nov to 1 week before Easter. Bus: 2.

Its earliest documentation of this site dates from the 11th century, when the feudal lords of the region, the von Labers, erected a modest fortress here. Since around 1890 the much enlarged and improved site has functioned as a hotel, attracting visitors from around the Italian- and German-speaking world. The establishment is one of the highest hotels in Merano, located on a hillside about 2 miles east of the center of town. Owned and managed by the same family for more than a century, the hotel maintains solid traditions and comfortably rustic bedrooms, usually with panoramas and simple but solid accessories. There's an on-site tennis court, an outdoor swimming pool, and a flowered patio for outside drinking and dining.

Hotel Fragsburg. Via Fragsburg 3 (Fragsburgerstrasse 3) (Postfach 210), 39012 Merano. ☎ **0473/244071.** Fax 0473/244493. 20 rms, 2 suites. TV TEL. 240,000–360,000 lire ($153.60–$230.40) double; 280,000–400,000 lire ($179.20–$256) suite. Rates include half board. No credit cards. Closed Nov–Apr 3.

This hotel is perched midway up the side of a sun-flooded mountain high above Merano, a 15-minute drive from town. As you'd expect, the views from its well-maintained verandas and decks are spectacular. The structure was originally built around 1520 as a hunting lodge and hideaway for the count of Memmingen, but began its role as a hotel in 1904, when an Austrian entrepreneur built (at his own expense) a road leading up to the place from the town center, brought in electricity, and transformed the building into summertime lodgings for guests from throughout the Habsburg empire. Since 1932 the hotel has been restored and improved to the point where it resembles an impeccably maintained historic chalet like what you might find in the Tyrol region of Austria. You'll find pinewood paneling, hunting trophies, art nouveau accessories, and elegantly rustic bedrooms (each with a safe and an outdoor balcony). On the premises is a heated swimming pool, a cocktail lounge, access to nearby tennis courts, and a dining room serving Italian-style meals and one serving Tyrolean meals. What's said to be the highest waterfall in Italy is a 20-minute trek from the hotel.

⑤ Hotel Minerva. Via Cavour 95, 39012 Merano. ☎ **0473/236712.** Fax 0473/230460. 45 rms. TV TEL. 170,000–200,000 lire ($108.80–$128) double. Rates include breakfast. AE, DC, MC, V. Closed Jan 8–Mar and Nov–Dec 25. Bus: 3.

Built in 1909 in the Teutonic style favored by the then-rulers of Merano, this hotel is large, comfortable, and just antique enough to give its clients a sense of tradition. Surrounded by a private garden, near several more expensive hotels, it can be reached after a 10-minute pedestrian trek eastward from the center of town. All but a few of the rooms have balconies with views over the town. On the premises is an outdoor pool and an unpretentious dining room.

◐ Hotel Palace. Via Cavour 2–4 (Cavourstrasse 2), 39012 Merano. ☎ **0473/211300.** Fax 0473/234181. 120 rms, 7 suites. MINIBAR TV TEL. 300,000–450,000 lire ($192–$288) double; 500,000–650,000 lire ($320–$416) suite. Rates include breakfast. Special packages for health and diet available. AE, DC, MC, V. Closed Nov 10–Dec 18. Free parking. Bus: 1 or 3.

This, the most deluxe hotel at the resort, is a turn-of-the-century re-creation of a baroque palace set in the most beautiful formal gardens in town. The gilt- and cream-colored public rooms contain good-quality copies of 18th-century furniture designs and massive crystal chandeliers. From the rear terrace there's a view of the large marble slabs that have been arranged into a chessboard on the lawn. The gardens contain a free-form pool whose waters flow below a tile annex for an indoor extension of the swimming area.

Many of the bedrooms have their own stone or wrought-iron balconies, which overlook the garden. Although it has been in business for decades, the hotel has up-to-date comforts, and most of the units are air-conditioned. Accommodations vary widely, and rates depend on the size, the season, and the view.

Guests gather in the piano bar before going into the Tiffany Grill restaurant, where both regional and international cuisine are served. Lunch and dinner are also served in the hotel dining room. Services include room service, baby-sitting, laundry, valet, and medical supervision for spa, health, and fitness programs. The hotel also features fitness equipment, a sauna, a solarium, a hot whirlpool, thermal treatments, and a beauty farm.

WHERE TO DINE

✪ **Andrea.** Via Galilei 44. ☎ **0473/237400.** Reservations required. Main courses 28,000–34,000 lire ($17.90–$21.75); five-course regional menu 68,000 lire ($43.50); six-course *menu dégustation* 79,000 lire ($50.55). AE, DC, MC, V. Tues–Sun noon–2pm and 7–10pm. Closed Feb. Bus: 3. TYROLEAN.

Well entrenched and charming, the Andrea is known to gastronomes on both sides of the Alps as one of the most respected dining spots in the region, and a sought-after resource for less-experienced chefs who enroll in the cooking classes held here every November and January. The menu is always enticing and satisfying—nothing else in Merano comes close to the cuisine served here. Menu items change with the seasons, but are likely to include a terrine of foie gras served on a fresh brioche, fresh asparagus with a chervil-flavored cream sauce, risotto seasoned with whatever flavorful vegetable is in season at the time, a parfait of smoked trout with fresh horseradish sauce, or black lasagne studded with shrimp and mussels.

Flora. Via Portici 75. ☎ **0473/231484.** Reservations required. Main courses 18,000–35,000 lire ($11.50–$22.40). AE, DC, MC, V. Mon 7pm–midnight, Tues–Sat noon–3pm and 7pm–midnight. Closed Jan 15–Feb 28. Bus: 3. ITALIAN.

The Flora serves a Tyrolean and Italian cuisine of consistently good quality in its conservative, elegant confines. Full meals are likely to include ravioli stuffed with chicken and exotic mushrooms, pasta blackened with squid ink, rack of lamb cooked in a shell of salt, and marinated trout with fines herbes. The menu changes seasonally, and this restaurant is the most solid and dependable choice in town, although not in the same league with Andrea. It's Merano's second-best choice for dining.

5 Trento (Trent)

36 miles S of Bolzano, 144 miles NE of Milan

A northern Italian city that basks in its former glory, this medieval town on the left bank of the Adige is known throughout the world as the host of the Council of Trent (1545–63). Beset with difficulties, such as the rising tide of "heretics," the Ecumenical Council convened at Trent, a step that led to the Counter-Reformation. Trent lies on the main rail line from the Brenner Pass, and many visitors like to stop off here before journeying farther south into Italy.

ESSENTIALS

GETTING THERE   By Train   Trent enjoys excellent rail connections. It lies on the Bologna–Verona–Brenner Pass–Munich rail line, and trains pass through here day and night. The trip from Milan takes 2 hours 40 minutes; from Rome, 7 hours. Trains also connect Trent with Bolzano (see Section 3 in this chapter) once every hour. Seven trains per day make the 3¹/₂-hour run from Venice.

By Bus   It's better to take the train to Trent and then rely on local buses once you get there. The **local bus station** is next to the train station (☎ **0461/821000** for schedules), and has service to such places as Riva del Garda (see Chapter 13). Buses to Riva depart once an hour during the day.

By Car   From Bolzano (see above), head south to Trent along autostrada A22. From Verona, continue north to Trent on A22.

VISITOR INFORMATION   The **tourist information center** is on via Alfieri (☎ **0461/983880**). It's open in July and August, Monday to Saturday from 9am to noon and 3 to 6pm and on Sunday from 10am to noon; the rest of the year, Monday to Friday from 9am to noon and 3 to 6pm and on Saturday from 9am to noon.

EXPLORING THE TOWN

The city has much old charm, offset somewhat by unbridled industrialization. For a quick glimpse of the old town, head for **piazza del Duomo,** dominated by the **Cathedral of Saint Vergilio.** Built in the Romanesque style and much restored over the years, it dates from the 12th century. It's open daily from 8:30am to noon and 2:30 to 8pm. In the center of the square is a mid–18th-century Fountain of Neptune.

The ruling prince-bishops of Trent, who held sway until they were toppled by the French in the early 19th century, resided at the medieval **Castello del Buonconsiglio** (☎ **0461/233770**), reached from via Bernardo Clesio 3. Now the old castle has been turned into a provincial museum, with a collection of paintings and fine art, some quite ancient, including early medieval mosaics. The **Museo del Risorgimento,** also at the castle, is a museum containing mementos related to the period of national unification between 1796 and 1948. The museums are open September to May, Tuesday to Sunday from 9am to noon and 2 to 5pm; June to August, Tuesday to Sunday from 9am to noon and 2 to 5:30pm. Admission is 6,000 lire ($3.85) adults, 2,000 lire ($1.30) for children 12–17 and for seniors 60 and over, free for children 11 and under.

Trent makes a good base for exploring **Monte Bondone,** a sports resort about 22 miles from the city center; **Paganella,** slightly more than 12 miles from Trent (the summit is nearly 7,000 feet high); and the **Brenta Dolomites.** The latter excursion, which will require at least a day for a good look, will reward you with some of the finest mountain scenery in Italy. En route from Trent, you'll pass by **Lake Toblino,** then travel a winding, circuitous road for much of the way, past jagged boulders. A 10-minute detour from the main road is suggested at the turnoff to the Genova valley, with its untamed scenery. Take the detour at least to the thunderous **Nardis waterfall.** A good stopover point is the fast-rising little resort of **Madonna di Campiglio.**

WHERE TO STAY

Albergo Accademia. Vicolo Colico 6, 38100 Trento. ☎ **0461/233600.** Fax 0461/230174. 41 rms, 2 suites. A/C MINIBAR TV TEL. 210,000 lire ($134.40) double; from 310,000 lire ($198.40) suite. Rates include breakfast. AE, DC, MC, V. Free parking on the street. Bus: All buses.

This alpine inn in the center of town is made up of three buildings that have been joined to make a comfortable and attractive hostelry. One of the buildings is believed to be of 11th- or 12th-century origin, based on a brick wall similar to the city walls found during renovation work. According to legend, the older part of the Accademia housed church leaders who attended the Council of Trent in the 16th century. The inn stands behind the Renaissance Church of Santa Maria Maggiore. The rooms are done in light natural wood. A suite at the top of the house has a terrace with a view of the town and the mountains. The alpine influence is carried out in the bar and the restaurant.

Hotel America. Via Torre Verde 50, 38100 Trento. ☎ **0461/983010.** Fax 0461/230603. 50 rms. A/C MINIBAR TV TEL. 160,000 lire ($102.40) double. AE, DC, MC, V. Free parking. Bus: 2, 3, 7, or 11.

This simple, attractive hotel is located in the heart of the historic old town of Trent and is a short walk from the rail station. Iron balconies look out to the Dolomite mountains and a vine-wreathed arbor shelters the main entrance. The newly redecorated rooms are clean and comfortable. The founder of the hotel worked in Wyoming from 1909 to 1923 and named the hotel after the country that afforded him the possibility to build it.

Hotel Buonconsiglio. Via Romagnosi 16–18, 38100 Trento. ☎ **0461/272888.** Fax 0461/272889. 45 rms, 1 suite. A/C MINIBAR TV TEL. 180,000–224,000 lire ($115.20–$143.35) double; 280,000 lire ($179.20) suite. AE, DC, MC, V. Rates include breakfast. Parking 10,000 lire ($6.40). Bus: 2.

Originally built shortly after World War II as the Hotel Alessandro Vittorio, and renamed the Buonconsiglio in 1990 at the time of a massive renovation, this is a clean, well-administered hotel with pleasant bedrooms and an English-speaking staff. It's located on a busy street near the railway station. This place has a slight edge over the Accademia, but both hotels are virtually on a par. In the lobby is a collection of abstract modern paintings. Each bedroom contains a personal safe, satellite TV reception, and soundproofing against traffic noises from outside.

WHERE TO DINE

Orso Grigio. Via degli Orti 19. ☎ **0461/984400.** Reservations recommended. Main courses 15,000–20,000 lire ($9.60–$12.80). AE, DC, MC, V. Mon–Sat 12:30–2:30pm and 7:30–9:30pm. Bus: 2. ITALIAN/TRENTINE.

This elegant and spacious restaurant lies about 30 yards from piazza Fiera, in an old building whose origins may go back to the 1500s. When you see the immaculate table linen, the well-cared-for plants, and the subdued lighting, you know something is going right. Menus are seasonally adjusted to take in the finest fresh produce. The place enjoys local popularity—a good sign, since the Trentino is noted for a refined palate. Rufioli, a green tortellini, is a specialty. Another good regional dish is squazzet con polenta, Trentine-style fried tripe. Finish the feast with a chocolate mousse. Wines of the province are a special feature of the restaurant.

✪ Restaurant Chiesa. Via San Marco 64. ☎ **0461/238766.** Reservations recommended. Main courses 27,000–30,000 lire ($17.30–$19.20); fixed-price "apple menu" 70,000 lire ($44.80). AE, DC, MC, V. Mon–Tues and Thurs–Sat 12:30–2:30pm and 7:30–9:30pm, Wed 12:30–2:30pm. Bus: 2. TRENTINE.

The Restaurant Chiesa offers the largest array of dishes we've ever seen made with apples. Owners Allesandro and Alberto recognized that Eve's favorite fruit, which grows more abundantly around Trent than practically anywhere else, was the base of dozens of traditional recipes. Specialties include risotto with apple, liver pâté with apple, filet of perch with apple, and a range of other well-prepared specialties (a few of which, believe it or not, don't contain apples).

Milan, Lombardy & the Lake District

13

The vicissitudes of Italy's history are reflected in Lombardy as perhaps in no other region. Conquerors from barbarians to Napoléon have marched across its plain. Even Mussolini came to his end here. He and his mistress—both already dead—were strung up in a Milan square as war-weary residents vented their rage upon the two bodies.

Among the most progressive of all the Italians, the Lombards have charted an industrial empire unequaled in Italy. Often the dream of the underfed and jobless worker in the south is to go to Milano for the high wages and the good life, although thousands end up finding neither.

Lombardy isn't all manufacturing. Milan, as we'll soon see, is filled to the brim with important attractions, and nearby are old Lombard art cities—Bergamo, Cremona, and Mantova (Mantua). The Lake District, with its flower-bedecked promenades, lemon trees and villas, parks and gardens, and crystal-clear blue waters, may sound a bit dated, like a penny-farthing bicycle or an aspidistra in the bay window. But the lakes—notably Garda, Como, and Maggiore—continue to form one of the most enchanting splashes of scenery in northern Italy.

Like the lake district in northwestern England, the Italian lakes have attracted poets and writers—everybody from Goethe to Gabriele d'Annunzio. But after World War II the Italian lakes seemed to be largely the domain of matronly English and German types. In our more recent swings through the district, however, we've noticed an increasing *joie de vivre* and a rising influx of the 25 to 40 age group, particularly at such resorts as Limone on Lake Garda. Even if your time is limited, you'll want to have at least a look at Lake Garda.

EXPLORING LOMBARDY & THE LAKE DISTRICT BY CAR

Days 1–2   Milan, 355 miles northwest of Rome, can be your gateway to Lombardy. Take in the panoramic sweep of the city, the industrial and artistic center of the north of Italy, and go on several shopping binges. Visit such major attractions as Il Duomo, Pinacoteca di Brera, Museo Poldi-Pezzoli, and Biblioteca-Pinacoteca Ambrosiana.

Day 3   From Milan, take autostrada A4 (E64) east for a visit to Bergamo, lying 31 miles to the northeast. Explore its Città Alta or Upper Town and visit the Galleria dell'Accademia Carrara.

☕ **TAKE A BREAK**   If you'd like a simple lunch, try the **Trattoria al Castello,** via Castello 14, in Bergamo (☎ **035/259607**), at the foot of the castle. The food is plain and straightforward—the main courses cost from 10,000 lire ($6.40) and up— but the views are among the most panoramic in the area.

Continue east on the autostrada toward Brescia, cutting south on A21 to Cremona for the night.

Day 4   At a point 59 miles southeast of Milan, Cremona is the "city of the violin." In the morning, explore piazza del Comune and the Museo Stradivariano. Enjoy lunch at either Aquila Nera (Black Eagle) or Ceresole. For the night, cut east along SS10 to Mantua (Mantova). If you arrive late, plan a morning visit to its Museo di Palazzo Ducale.

Day 5   Finish with Mantova in the morning. It would take more than a week to explore all the lakes, so we'll just take you around the liveliest of the bunch, Lake Garda. From Mantova, head up autostrada A22 toward Verona, but switch to A4 west toward Brescia, to the southwestern corridor of Lake Garda, largest of all the lakes in Italy, its shores bordering the Veneto, Trentino–Alto Adige regions, and Lombardy. (If you're out of time, you can continue on A4 all the way back to Milan.)

Day 6   Begin your tour at Desenzano del Garda, with its old town and scenic harbor. Most visitors take the road along the western shore (S572) north.

If you're not running late, follow the first turnoff signposted to Salò, 12^1/$_2$ miles north of Desenzano. Mussolini's puppet government, backed by Hitler, was established here in September 1943. Gardone Riviera, with its memories of Gabriele d'Annunzio, who died there in 1938, lies just 3 miles north of Salò. Anchor in at this lakeside resort for an overnight stay.

Day 7   SS45B continues north for 7^1/$_2$ miles north to Gargnano where Mussolini occupied a villa, the Feltrinelli (closed to the public). From here, another 12 miles leads you to one of the most charming spots along the lake, Limone sul Garda, named for its lemon groves, where you may want to stop for lunch and explore the town. In the days when Goethe frequented the place it was accessible only by boat. After Limone, continue on SS45B north to Riva del Garda, as the road passes through tunnel after tunnel blasted out of rock. Overnight at Riva, at the top of the lake.

Day 8   Leave Riva, but this time drive along the less touristy side of the lake, the eastern shore bordering the Veneto. This route is called Gardesana Orientale (S249). It passes through Malcesine, 11 miles south of Riva, a favorite holiday target for Greta Garbo, who called herself Harriet Browne when visiting. At the town of San Vigilio you can stop for lunch at the Locanda San Vigilio, which Churchill chose as a spot to paint and hibernate.

From here drive south for 14 miles to Peschiera del Garda, joining S11 for a 6-mile drive to Colombare where you can follow the signposts heading north on a promontory jutting out into the lake and leading you to the little walled resort town of Sirmione where you'll regret you may be able to spend only 1 night. The next morning, continue on SS11 until it runs into SS572 for the quick jaunt south to A4 headed west toward Milan. If you're out of time, you can return all the way to Milan, or turn north outside the city onto S36 toward Como to explore Lakes Como and Maggiore on your own.

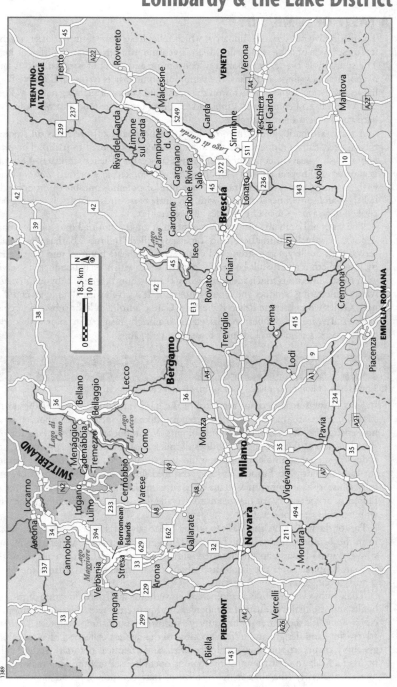

A TASTE OF LOMBARDY

The distinctive cookery of Lombardy, which relies heavily on country butter, reaches its finest levels of achievement in Milan. Even the minestrone tastes different here. The specialty is *risotto,* rice cooked in consommé and flavored with saffron. A land of mountains, valleys, and lakes, the region of Lombardy is fertile, and every village has its own wine, some of which won the praise and poetry of such big names as Pliny and Virgil. Even Leonardo da Vinci and Carducci tasted the food and wine of Lombardy and gave it their blessing.

A tasty, aromatic, and refined cookery, the Lombard cuisine relies on smoked meats, beef, dairy products, and the inevitable rice (as opposed to pasta). The most famous dish is veal cutlet milanese (in Vienna they call it Wiener schnitzel). *Osso buco* is another highly praised dish—shinbone of veal cooked in a ragoût. *Polenta* made with cornmeal always wins praise—"one bite of polenta, one bit of crunchy delight?"—and sometimes it's served with *osei* (little roast birds). *Stufato* is stewing beef cooked in a savory sauce of tomatoes and vegetables.

The vines of Lombardy yield tender grapes that are transformed into such aromatic wines as Barbagallo, Buttafucco, and something called "Inferno." Barbagallo, usually served with poultry, has a strong red color, with a delicate bouquet and fruity quality. Buttafucco is a fairly full-bodied, bright-red wine, with a lively bouquet; it's served with roasts. Inferno is much more appealing than it sounds, a deep ruby red in color, with a penetrating bouquet and a nutty aftertaste. It's served with all lunches and dinners. Other wines include Rosso Riviera del Garda, a brilliant light ruby red in color with a nutty, fruity bouquet, and Sassella, also a bright ruby red in color with a bouquet of roses, served with red-meat roasts and rare game.

1 Milan

355 miles NW of Rome, 87 miles NE of Turin, 88 miles N of Genoa

Italians in the south, perhaps resentful of the hard-earned prosperity of the north, sometimes declare that the Milanese are not unlike their nearby neighbors, the no-nonsense Swiss. With two million inhabitants, Milan doesn't evoke the languor and garrulousness of the rest of Italy, it doesn't muck about with excessive manners, and it doesn't snooze somnolently in the midday heat. It works, it moves, and it bustles. It's Italy's window on Europe, its most advanced showcase, devoid of the dusty and musty history that sometimes seems to paralyze modern developments in Rome or Florence, or the watery rot that seems to pervade the sublimely beautiful Venice with an inevitable sense of decay.

Part of the work ethic that has catapulted Milan toward the 21st century may stem from the Teutonic origins of the Lombards (originally from northwestern Germany), who occupied Milan and intermarried with its population after the collapse of the Roman Empire. Later the Teutonic influence was strengthened during the 18th-century occupation by the Austrians.

Today, however, Milan is a commercial powerhouse and, partly because of the 400 banks and the major industrial companies headquartered here, the most influential city in Italy. It's the center of the country's industries: publishing, silk, television and advertising, and design; and it lies very close to the densest collection of automobile-assembly plants, rubber and textile factories, and chemical plants in Italy. It also boasts La Scala, one of the most prestigious opera houses in Europe, a major commercial university (the alma mater of most of Italy's corporate presidents), and the site of several world-renowned annual trade fairs.

Since its beginning Milan has, with unashamed capitalistic style, purchased more art than it has produced, and lured to its borders the most energetic and hard-working group of creative intellects in all of Italy. To make it in Milan, in either business or the arts, is to have made it to the top of the pecking order in modern Italy. Milan is, in effect, the New York of Italy. If you came to Italy to find sun-flooded piazzas and somnolent afternoons, you won't find them amid the fogs and rains of Milan. You will, however, have placed your finger on the pulse of modern Italy.

Throughout history Milan has had to succeed by its wits. Set on one of the most fertile plains in Europe, with few natural defenses other than the skill of its diplomats and traders, the city has always more or less successfully negotiated through the labyrinth of European politics. Since the A.D. 313 proclamation by Constantine the Great of the Edict of Milan (which declared the Roman Empire officially Christian), Milan has been in the center of events.

In the 14th century the Visconti family, through their wits, wealth, and marriages with the royal families of England and France, made Milan the strongest state in Italy. Realizing its dependence on agriculture early on, Milan initiated a continuing campaign of drainage and irrigation of the Po Valley that helped to make it one of the most fertile regions in the world.

In the 1700s Milan was dominated by the Habsburgs, a legacy that left it with scores of neoclassical buildings in its inner core and an abiding appreciation for music and (perhaps) work. In 1848 Milan was at the heart of the northern Italian revolt against its Austro-Hungarian rulers, encouraged the development of a pan-Italian dialect (through the novelist Manzoni), and, along with neighbor Piedmont, was at the center of the 19th-century nationalistic passion that swept through Italy and culminated in the country's unification. By the turn of the century thousands of workers had immigrated to Milan from the south; they swelled its population and raised its industrial output to envied figures. Milan both elected and then helped destroy Mussolini, who, after being shot repeatedly by Milanese partisans, was hung by his heels on a meat hook, with his mistress, in the town's main square.

Today Milan is the only Italian city other than Rome that receives transatlantic flights. The city is elegant and prosperous; its inhabitants are tuned in to developments in Paris, London, and New York, and are proud of their dynamic and unusual city.

ESSENTIALS

GETTING THERE   By Plane   Milan is serviced by two airports, the **Aeroporto di Linate,** $4^1/2$ miles east of the inner city, and the **Aeroporto della Malpensa,** 31 miles to the northwest. Malpensa is used for most transatlantic flights, whereas Linate is for flights within Italy and Europe. For general flight information about both airports, call 02/74851. Buses for Linate leave from the Porta Garibaldi station every 20 minutes from 5:40am to 7pm and every 30 minutes from 7 to 9pm. Buses for Malpensa leave from the Stazione Centrale every $2^1/2$ hours before international and intercontinental flight departures. (Buses run in both directions, so they're the best bet for new arrivals.) This is much cheaper than taking a taxi.

By Train   Milan is serviced by the finest rail connections in Italy. The main rail station for arrivals is Mussolini's mammoth **Stazione Centrale,** piazza Duca d'Aosta (☎ **02/1478-88088**), where you'll find the National Railways information office open daily from 7:30am to 9:30pm. One train per hour arrives from either Genoa or Turin (trip time: $1^1/2$ to 2 hours from either city); a one-way fare from either point is 13,600 lire ($8.70). Twenty trains arrive daily from Venice (trip time: 3 hours), at a one-way fare of 20,800 lire ($13.30); and one train per hour arrives from Florence (trip time: 3 hours), with a one-way cost of 24,400 lire ($15.60). Trains from Rome arrive every hour, taking 5 hours for the journey and costing 47,700 lire ($30.55) each way.

By Bus   Buses link Milan with Pavia, Bergamo, and other cities of Lombardy. Some of these companies are privately owned and others are under the control of Regione Lombardia. For information about various routings in the province, ask at the **A.T.M. Information Office,** on the departures floor of Stazione Centrale, at piazza Duca d'Aosta (☎ **02/669-7081**).

By Car   The A4 autostrada is the principal east-west route for Milan, with A8 coming in from the northwest, A1 from the southeast, and A7 from the southwest. Autostrada A22 is another major north-south artery, running just east of Lake Garda.

ORIENTATION

VISITOR INFORMATION   You'll find the **Azienda di Promozione Turistica del Milanese,** on piazza del Duomo at via Marconi 1 (☎ **02/809662**), particularly helpful, dispensing free maps and whatever advice they can. There's also a branch at the Stazione Centrale (☎ **02/669-0532**).

CITY LAYOUT   **Piazza del Duomo,** with is spired cathedral, lies at the heart of Milan. Milan is encircled by three "rings," one of which is the **Cerchia dei Navigli,** a road that more or less follows the outline of the former medieval walls. The road runs along what was formerly a series of canals—hence the name *navigli.* The second ring is known both as **Bastioni** or **Viali,** and it follows the outline of the Spanish Walls from the 16th century. It's now a tram route (take no. 29 or 30). A much more recent ring is the **Circonvallazione Esterna,** which connects you with the main roads coming into Milan.

If you're traveling within the Cerchia dei Navigli, which is relatively small, you can do so on foot. We don't recommended that you attempt to drive within this circle unless you're heading for a garage. All the major attractions, including Leonardo's *Last Supper,* La Scala, and the Duomo, lie within this ring.

One of Milan's most important streets, **via Manzoni,** begins near the Teatro alla Scala, and will take you to piazza Cavour, a key point for the traffic arteries of Milan. The **Arch of Porta Nuova,** a remnant of the medieval walls, marks the entrance to via Manzoni. To the northwest of piazza Cavour lie the Giardini Pubblici, and to the northwest of these important gardens is **piazza della Repubblica.** From this square, via Vittorio Pisani leads into **piazza Duca d'Aosta,** site of the cavernous Stazione Centrale.

Back at piazza Cavour, you can head west along via Fatebenefratelli into the **Brera district,** whose major attraction is the Accademia di Brera at via Brera 28. This district in recent years has become a major center in Milan for offbeat shopping and after-dark diversions.

GETTING AROUND

A special 5,000-lira ($3.20) 1-day **travel pass,** good for unlimited use on the city's tram, bus, and subway network, is available at the tourist office, Azienda di Promozione Turistica del Milanese, on piazza del Duomo at via Marconi 1 (☎ **02/809662**). Those planning a longer stay can purchase a weekly pass, costing 11,000 lire ($7.05) and requiring a photo.

The city **bus** system covers most destinations in Milano, at a cost of 1,500 lire (95¢), as does the **subway** at the same fare. Take heed—planned modification of Milan's bus lines may create a bit of pandemonium throughout 1997 and 1998. Wise travelers may wish to find alternative modes of transportation. Some subway tickets are good for continuing trips on city buses at no extra charge, but they must be used within 75 minutes of purchase.

To phone a **taxi,** dial 02/6767, 02/5353, 02/8585, or 02/8388; fares start at 5,000 lire ($3.20), with a nighttime surcharge of 5,000 lire ($3.20).

FAST FACTS: MILAN

American Express   There's an American Express office at via Brera 3 (☎ 02/7200-3693), open Monday to Friday from 9am to 5pm.

Consulates   The Consulate of the **United States,** via Prìncipe Amedeo 2/10 (☎ 02/290351), is open Monday to Friday from 9am to noon and 2 to 4pm. The consulate of **Canada** is at via Vittor Pisani 19 (☎ 02/67581), open Monday to Friday from 9am to 5pm. Citizens of the **United Kingdom** will find their consulate at via San Paolo 7 (☎ 02/723001), open Monday to Friday from 9:15am to 12:15pm and 2:30 to 4:30pm. **Australia** has a consulate at via Borgogna 2 (☎ 02/780569), open Monday to Thursday from 9 m to noon and 2 to 4:30pm and on Friday from 9am to noon. Citizens of **New Zealand** should contact their consulate in Rome.

Emergencies   For the police, call **77271;** for an ambulance, **7733;** for an emergency, **113.**

Hospital   About a 5-minute ride from the Duomo, the Ospedale Maggiore Policlinico, via Francesco Sforza 35 (☎ 02/55031), has English-speaking doctors.

Newspapers   Foreign newspapers can be found at all major newsstands, among them those at the Stazione Centrale and piazza del Duomo. If you read Italian (even just a little bit), you can pick up information about present attractions and coming events, such as cinema and theater schedules, by buying the daily *La Repubblica,* a useful newspaper. If you're seeking secondhand bargains, you can learn about sales in *Secondamano,* which comes out on Monday and Thursday.

Pharmacies   You can find an all-night pharmacy by phoning **192.** The pharmacy (☎ 02/669-0735) at the Stazione Centrale never closes.

Post Offices   Most branches are open from 8:30am to 1:30pm Monday to Saturday. The Central Post Office is at via Cordusio 4 (☎ 02/869-2069), and is open Monday to Friday from 8:30am to 5:30pm and on Saturday from 8:30am to 1pm. Take the subway to the Cordusio stop.

Telephone   If you need to make long-distance calls, try, if possible, to avoid going through your hotel switchboard, which will impose staggering surcharges. The best place is the Central Post Office (see above), where telephone booths and operators maintain a 24-hour service.

WHAT TO SEE & DO
THE TOP ATTRACTIONS

Despite its modern architecture and industry, Milan is a city of great art. The serious sightseer will give the metropolis at least 2 days for exploration. If your schedule is frantic, see the Duomo and the important Brera Picture Gallery. One of the most important galleries of northern Italy, the Biblioteca-Pinacoteca Ambrosiana, is closed for restoration, with no announced date for its reopening. Check with the tourist office about its current status.

✪ **Il Duomo.** Piazza del Duomo. ☎ **02/8646-3456.** Admission: Cathedral, free; roof, 4,000 lire ($2.55) stairs, 7,000 lire ($4.50) elevator. June–Sept, daily 7am–7pm; Oct–May, daily 9am–4:30pm. Subway: Duomo. Tram: 1, 4, or 8.

In the very center of Milan, opening onto the heart of the city's life, is piazza del Duomo. Its impressive lacy Gothic cathedral ranks with St. Peter's in Rome and the cathedral at Seville, Spain, among the largest in the world. It's 479 feet long and 284 feet wide at the transepts. The cathedral, which dates from 1386, has seen numerous architects and builders. The conqueror of Milan, Napoléon, even added his own decorating ideas to the facade in the early years of the 19th century. The imposing structure of marble is the grandest and most flamboyant example of the Gothic style in Italy.

Built in the shape of a Latin cross, the cathedral is divided by soaring pillars into five naves. The overall effect is like a marble-floored Grand Central Terminal—that is, in space—with far greater dramatic intensity. In the crypt rests the tomb of San Carlo Borromeo, the cardinal of Milan. To experience the Duomo at its most majestic, you must ascend to the roof, from which you can walk through a "forest" of pinnacles, turrets, and marble statuary—like a promenade in an early Cocteau film. A gilded Madonna towers over the tallest spire.

Museo del Duomo. In the Palazzo Reale, piazza del Duomo 14. ☎ **02/860358.** Admission 8,000 lire ($5.10) adults, 4,000 lire ($2.55) children and seniors 60 and over. Tues–Sun 9:30am–12:30pm and 3–6pm. Subway: Duomo.

The Museo del Duomo is housed in the Palazzo Reale (Royal Palace). It's like a picture storybook of the cathedral's six centuries of history. The museum has exhibits of statues and decorative sculptures, some of which date from the 14th century. There are also antique art objects, stained-glass windows (some from the 15th century), and ecclesiastical vestments, many as old as the 16th century. The museum also houses the **Museo d'Arte Contemporanea** upstairs, with a permanent exhibition of Italian futurist art, along with some Picasso works.

۞ Chiesa di Santa Maria delle Grazie *(The Last Supper).* Piazza Santa Maria delle Grazie (off corso Magenta). ☎ **02/498-7588.** Admission: Church, free; *The Last Supper,* 12,000 lire ($7.70). Church, Mon–Sat 6:50am–noon and 3–7pm, Sun 3–7pm; *The Last Supper,* Tues–Sun 8:15am–1:45pm. Subway: Cadorna or Conciliazione. Bus: 21 or 24.

This Gothic church was erected by the Dominicans in the mid-15th century. A number of its more outstanding features, such as the cupola, were designed by the great Bramante. But tourists from all over the world flock here to gaze upon a mural in the convent next door. In what was once a refectory, the incomparable Leonardo da Vinci adorned one wall with *The Last Supper.*

Commissioned by Ludovico the Moor, the painting was finished about 1497 and began to disintegrate almost immediately. The 28-by-15-foot mural was totally repainted—once in the 1700s and again in the 1800s. The gradual erosion of the painting makes for one of the most intriguing stories in art. It narrowly escaped being bombed in 1943. The bomb demolished the roof, and—astonishingly—the painting was exposed to the elements for 3 years before a new roof was built at the end of World War II. The current restoration has been controversial, drawing fire from some art critics, as did the Sistine Chapel restoration. The chief restorer of *The Last Supper,* Pinin Brambilla Barcilon, said the Sistine Chapel was a "simple window wash" compared to the da Vinci.

It has been suggested that all that's really left of *The Last Supper* created by da Vinci is a "few isolated streaks of fading color"—everything else is the application and color of artists and restorers who followed in his wake. What remains today, however, is Leonardo's "outline"—and even it is suffering badly. As one Italian newspaper writer put it: "If you want to see *Il Cenacolo,* don't walk—run!" A painting of grandeur, the composition portrays Christ at the moment he announces to his shocked apostles that one of them will betray him. Vasari called the portrait of Judas "a study in perfidy and wickedness."

Viewers admitted 25 at a time, and are required to pass through antechambers designed to remove pollutants from their bodies. After they view the painting—for 10 minutes only—visitors must walk through two additional filtration chambers as they exit.

❂ Pinacoteca di Brera. Via Brera 28. ☎ **02/8646-3501.** Admission 8,000 lire ($5.10). Tues–Sat 9am–5pm, Sun 9am–12:15pm. Subway: Cairoli, Lanza, or Montenapoleone.

The Pinacoteca di Brera, one of Italy's finest art galleries, contains an exceptionally good collection of works by both Lombard and Venetian masters. Like a Roman emperor, Canova's nude Napoléon—a toga draped over his shoulder—stands in the courtyard (fittingly, a similar statue ended up in the duke of Wellington's house in London).

Among the notable artworks, a *Pietà* by Lorenzo Lotto is a work of great beauty, as is Gentile Bellini's *St. Mark Preaching in Alexandria* (it was finished by his brother, Giovanni). Seek out Andrea Mantegna's *Virgin and the Cherubs*, a great work from the Venetian school. Two of the most important prizes at the Brera are Mantegna's *Dead Christ* and Giovanni Bellini's *La Pietà*, as well as Carpaccio's *St. Stephen Debating*.

Other paintings include Titian's *St. Jerome*, as well as such Lombard art as Bernardino Luini's *Virgin of the Rose Bush* and Andrea Solario's *Portrait of a Gentleman*. One of the greatest panels is Piero della Francesca's *Virgin and Child Enthroned with Saints and Angels and the Kneeling Duke of Urbino in Armor*. Seek out, in addition, the *Christ* by Bramante. One wing, devoted to modern art, offers works by such artists as Boccioni, Carrà, and Morandi. One of our favorite paintings in the gallery is Raphael's *Wedding of the Madonna,* with a dancelike quality. *The Last Supper at Emmaus* is another moving work, this one by Caravaggio.

MORE ATTRACTIONS

❂ Museo Poldi-Pezzoli. Via Manzoni 12. ☎ **02/794889.** Admission 10,000 lire ($6.40). Tues–Sat 9:30am–12:30pm and 2:30–6pm, Sun 9:30am–12:30pm and 2:30–7:30pm. Closed Sun afternoon Apr–Sept. Subway: Duomo or Montenapoleone. Tram: 1.

This fabulous museum is done in great taste and is rich with antique furnishings, tapestries, frescoes, and Lombard wood carvings. It also displays a remarkable collection of paintings by many of the old masters of northern and central Italy, including Andrea Mantegna's *Madonna and Child,* Giovanni Bellini's *Cristo Morto,* and Filippo Lippi's *Madonna, Angels, and Saints* (superb composition). One room is devoted entirely to Flemish artists, and there's a collection of ceramics and also one of clocks and watches. The museum grew out of a private collection donated to the city in 1881.

Museo d'Arte Antica. In Castello Sforzesco, piazza Castello. ☎ **02/6208-3191.** Free admission. Tues–Sun 9:30am–5:30pm. Subway: Cairoli.

Castle Sforzesco, the Castle of Milan, is an ancient fortress rebuilt by Francesco Sforza, who launched another governing dynasty. It's believed that both Bramante and Leonardo da Vinci contributed architectural ideas to the fortress. Following extensive World War II bombings, it was painstakingly restored and continued its activity as a Museum of Ancient Art. Displayed on the ground floor are sculpture from the 4th century A.D., medieval art mostly from Lombardy, and armor. The most outstanding exhibit, however, is Michelangelo's *Rondanini Pietà,* on which he was working the week he died. In the rooms upstairs, besides a good collection of ceramics, antiques, and bronzes, is the important picture gallery, rich in paintings from the 14th to the 18th century, including works by Lorenzo Veneziano, Mantegna, Lippi,

Bellini, Crivelli, Foppa, Bergognone, Cesare da Sesto, Lotto, Tintoretto, Cerano, Procaccini, Morazzone, Guardi, and Tiepolo.

Museo Nazionale della Scienza e della Tecnica Leonardo da Vinci. Via San Vittore 21. ☎ **02/485551.** Admission 10,000 lire ($6.40) adults, 6,000 lire ($3.85) children 17 and under and seniors 60 and over. Tues–Fri 9:30am–5pm, Sat–Sun 9:30am–6:30pm. Subway: S. Ambrogio.

If you're a fan of Leonardo da Vinci, as we are, you'll want to visit this vast museum complex where you could practically spend a week devouring the exhibits. For the average visitor the most interesting section is the Leonardo da Vinci Gallery, which displays copies and models from the Renaissance genius. There's a reconstructed pharmacy from a convent, along with a monastic cell, even a sewing-machine collection. You'll also see antique carriages plus exhibits relating to astronomy, telecommunications, watchmaking, goldsmithery, motion pictures, and the subjects of classic physics.

Civica Galleria d'Arte Moderna. Via Palestro 16. ☎ **02/7600-2819.** Free admission. Tues–Sun 9:30am–5:30pm. Subway: Palestro or Turati. Bus: 96 or 97.

The Civica Galleria d'Arte Moderna (Civic Modern Art Gallery) used to be known as the royal villa before its name was changed to the Villa Comunale. Constructed between 1790 and 1793, it was designed by the architect Leopold Pollack. For a short time it was the residence of Napoléon and Eugène de Beauharnais. The gallery has a large collection of works from the Milanese neoclassical period, along with many paintings that show the development of Italian romanticism. It's predictably rich in the works of Lombard artists. Important collections that have been donated are those of Carlo Grassi and the Vismara art accumulation. Also significant is the Marino Marini Museum, which was opened in 1973. Marini, a famous Italian sculptor, has some 200 works displayed, including not only sculpture, but paintings and graphics, all a gift of the artist himself. Many artists are on parade: Picasso, Matisse, Rouault, Renoir, Modigliani, Corot, Millet, Manet, Cézanne, Bonnard, and Gauguin.

Basilica di Sant'Eustorgio. Piazza Sant'Eustorgio 1. ☎ **02/5810-1583.** Admission: Basilica, free; chapel, 2,000 lire ($1.30). Daily 8am–noon and 3–7pm. Subway: Genova. Tram: 3.

The bell tower of the 4th-century Basilica of Sant'Eustorgio dates from the 13th century; it was built in the romantic style by patrician Milanese families. It has the first tower clock in the world, made in 1305. Originally this was the tomb of the Three Kings (4th century A.D.). Inside, its greatest treasure is the Capella Portinari, designed by the Florentine Michelozzo in Renaissance style. The chapel is frescoed and contains a bas-relief of angels at the base of the cupola. In the center is an intricately carved tomb, supported by marble statuary of the 13th century by Balduccio of Pisa. Inside are the remains of St. Peter Martyr. The basement has a Roman crypt.

Basilica di San Ambrogio. Piazza San Ambrogio 15. ☎ **02/8645-0895.** Admission: Basilica, free; museum, 3,000 lire ($1.90). Basilica, Mon–Sat 7am–noon and 2:30–7pm, Sun 7am–1pm and 3–8pm; museum, Mon–Sat 10am–noon and 3–5pm, Sun 3–5pm. Closed Aug. Subway: San Ambrogio. Bus: 50, 54, 58, or 60.

This church was originally erected by St. Ambrose in the later years of the 4th century A.D. The present structure was built in the 12th century in the Romanesque style. The remains of St. Ambrose rest in the crypt. The church, entered after passing through a quadrangle, is rather stark and severe, in the style of its day. The atrium is its most distinguishing architectural feature. In the apse are interesting mosaics from the 12th century. The Lombard tower at the side dates from 1128, and the facade, with its two tiers of arches, is impressive. In the church is the **Museo della Basilica**

Milan

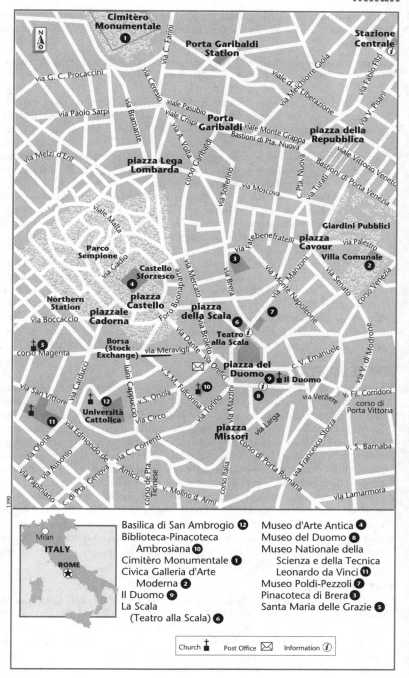

Basilica di San Ambrogio ⑫
Biblioteca-Pinacoteca
    Ambrosiana ⑩
Cimitèro Monumentale ①
Civica Galleria d'Arte
    Moderna ②
Il Duomo ⑨
La Scala
    (Teatro alla Scala) ⑥

Museo d'Arte Antica ④
Museo del Duomo ⑧
Museo Nationale della
    Scienza e della Tecnica
    Leonardo da Vinci ⑪
Museo Poldi-Pezzoli ⑦
Pinacoteca di Brera ③
Santa Maria delle Grazie ⑤

Church ✝   Post Office ✉   Information ⓘ

di S. Ambrogio, containing some frescoes, 15th-century wood paneling, silver and gold objects originally for the altar, paintings, and sculpture, including Flemish tapestries.

Cimitero Monumentale. Piazzale Cimitero Monumentale 1. ☎ **02/659-9938.** Free admission. Apr–Sept, Tues–Sun 8:30am–6pm; Oct–Mar, Tues–Sun 8:30am–4pm. Subway: Garibaldi. Tram: 4, 8, 12, or 14.

The Cimitèro Monumentale (Monumental Cemetery) has catered for more than 100 years to the whims of Milan's elite society. The only requirements for burial in the cemetery are, first, that you are dead, and second, that you can buy your way into a plot. Some families have paid up to 200,000,000 lire ($128,000) just for the privilege of burying their dead here. The graves are marked not only with brass plates or granite markers, but also with Greek temples, elaborate obelisks, or such original works as an abbreviated version of Trajan's Column.

This outdoor museum has become such an attraction that a superintendent has compiled an illustrated guidebook—a sort of "Who *was* who." Among the cemetery's outstanding sights is a sculpted version of *The Last Supper*. Several fine examples of art nouveau sculpture dot the hillside, and there's a tasteful example of Liberty-style architecture (Italy's version of art nouveau) in a tiny chapel designed to hold the remains of Arturo Toscanini's son, who died in 1906. Among the notables buried here are Toscanini himself and novelist Alessandro Manzoni. In the Memorial Chapel is the tomb of Salvatore Quasimodo, who won the 1959 Nobel Prize in literature. Here also rest the ashes of Ermann Einstein, father of the scientist. In the Palanti Chapel is a monument commemorating the 800 Milanese citizens slain in Nazi concentration camps. (A model of this monument is displayed in the Museum of Modern Art in New York.) The location is a few blocks east of Stazione Porta Garibaldi.

WHERE TO STAY

In the city are some deluxe hostelries, as well as a super-abundance of first- and second-class hotels, most of which are big on comfort but short on romance. In the third- and fourth-class bracket and on the *pensione* (boarding house) level there are dozens of choices—many of which rank at the bottom of the totem pole of comparably classed establishments in all of Italy's major cities, with the exception of Naples. Some places are outright dangerous, and others so rock-bottom and unappealing as to hold little interest for the average visitor. In several places, men sit around in the lobby in their bathrobes watching soccer games on the TV.

Our recommendation is—if you can afford it—to stay in a better grade of hotel in Milan, and to leave your serious budgeting to such tourist meccas as Rome, Florence, and Venice, which have clean, comfortable, and often architecturally interesting third- and fourth-class hotels and *pensioni.* However, for the serious economizer we have included the best of the budget lot. We present them as safe and (hopefully) clean shelters, but with no particular enthusiasm.

VERY EXPENSIVE

Four Seasons Hotel Milano. Via Gesù 8, 20121 Milano. ☎ **02/770-8500.** Fax 02/7708-5000. 77 rms, 16 suites. A/C MINIBAR TV TEL. 780,000–920,000 lire ($499–$589) double; from 1,000,000 lire ($640) suite. AE, DC, MC, V. Subway: Montenapoleone or San Babila.

Milan's most exciting five-star hotel opened in 1993 in a location beloved by any shopper—a side street opening onto the most elegant concentration of upscale boutiques in Italy, via Montenapoleone. Housed in what was originally built as a three-story monastery in the 14th century, its acquisition was a real estate coup by

Four Seasons. The building was the residence for the Habsburg-appointed governor of northern Italy in the 1850s, and later housed luxury apartments. The medieval facade, many of the frescoes and columns, and the original monastic details were incorporated into a modern edifice flooded with sunlight and accented with bronze, stone floors, glass, pearwood cabinetry, Murano chandeliers, and acres of Fortuny fabrics. The accommodations are cool, conservative, spacious, and discreetly outfitted in tones of beige and pale green, always with a sense of understated luxury.

Dining/Entertainment: The hotel lounge contains the architectural renderings for stage sets used at the nearby La Scala opera house. Nearby is the hotel's gastronomic showcase, Il Teatro, serving dinner daily from 8pm to midnight. Less formal, La Veranda serves meals continuously every day from 11am to 11pm.

Services: Concierge, room service (24 hours), same-day valet and laundry.

Facilities: A high-tech fitness center and spa. A business center provides virtually any service you'd expect from your own office.

Palace Hotel. Piazza della Repubblica 20, 20124 Milano. ☎ **02/6336,** or 800/221-2340 in the U.S., 800/955-2442 in Canada. Fax 02/654485. 220 rms, 6 suites. A/C MINIBAR TV TEL. 460,000–550,000 lire ($294.40–$352) double; 790,000–1,750,000 lire ($506–$1,120) suite. AE, DC, MC, V. Parking 25,000–60,000 lire ($16–$38.40). Subway: Repubblica. Tram: 1, 4, 11, 29, or 30.

The Palace Hotel, blithely ignoring the noisy pell-mell commercial world around it, stands aloof on a hill near the railway station; it has a formal car entrance and a facade of 14 floors with tiers of balconies. Primarily a business hotel catering to some of Europe's most prominent figures, the Palace also welcomes tourists and occasional entertainers. The Prìncipe di Sovoia, its sibling (another Ciga property) across the street, is superior to the Palace in sheer old-world opulence—and the Four Seasons leaves both properties behind. The bedrooms are furnished with pastel upholstery and carpeting, and reproductions of Italian antiques. Modern conveniences include heated towel racks and minibars concealed behind mahogany chests.

Dining/Entertainment: The hotel bar attracts an international clientele, and the Grill Casanova is acclaimed as one of the finest in Milan, offering both regional and international dishes.

Services: Room service, baby-sitting, laundry, valet.

Facilities: Fitness center.

Prìncipe di Savoia. Piazza della Repubblica 17, 20124 Milano. ☎ **02/6230,** or 800/325-3535 in the U.S. and Canada. Fax 02/659-5838. 252 rms, 47 suites. A/C MINIBAR TV TEL. 510,000–630,000 lire ($326.40–$403.20) double; 950,000–7,500,000 lire ($608–$4,800) suite. AE, DC, MC, V. Parking 50,000 lire ($32) and up. Subway: Repubblica. Tram: 1, 4, 11, 29, or 30.

The Prìncipe was built in 1927 to fill the need for a luxurious hotel near the Stazione Centrale and is still a regal address, although overtaken by the Four Seasons. It was completely restored in 1991. Substantial and luxurious, the six stories offer solid comfort amid crystal, detailed plasterwork, fine carpets, and polished marble. The rooms are spacious and modern, decorated in a 19th-century Lombard style. Many are paneled in hardwoods, and all contain leather chairs, stylish furniture, and modern baths with all the accessories. The front rooms face the hysterical traffic of piazza della Repubblica, whereas the ones in back are more tranquil, opening onto the Alps (which you might see if the wind blows the pollution away).

Dining/Entertainment: The spacious bar area off the main lobby is the hotel's social focal point. The hotel has a notable restaurant, Galleria, serving both regional and international dishes. It also offers the popular Doney cafe (see "Where to Dine," below).

Services: Room service, baby-sitting, laundry, valet.

Facilities: Limited facilities for the disabled, sauna, health club, solarium, indoor pool.

EXPENSIVE

Excelsior Gallia. Piazza Duca d'Aosta 9, 20124 Milano. ☎ **02/6785,** or 800/225-5843 in the U.S. and Canada. Fax 02/6671-3239. 237 rms, 13 suites. A/C MINIBAR TV TEL. 390,000–440,000 lire ($249.60–$281.60) double; from 700,000 lire ($448) suite. AE, DC, MC, V. Parking 40,000 lire ($25.60). Subway: Stazione Centrale. Tram: 33 or 59. Bus: 60, 65, 91, or 92.

This Liberty-style (art nouveau) monument on piazza Duca d'Aosta was built by the Gallia family in 1933. Set near the main railway station, the hotel is one of the most expensive and visible in Milan, and once one of the top hotels of Italy—but today is more of an upmarket rail station hotel. The 1994 renovations combined some of the smaller rooms into larger and more comfortable accommodations. The bedrooms fall into two categories: modern and comfortable in the newer wing and graciously old-fashioned and charming in the original core. All are soundproofed against the roar of traffic in the massive piazza outside. The noted restaurant, Gallia's, serves haute Lombard and international dishes. The Baboon Bar is stylish, and a piano player sometimes performs in the lobby. On the premises are baby-sitting, laundry, valet, and room service, along with a business center, a fitness club with a massage center, a gym, a whirlpool, and a sauna.

Milano Hilton. Via Galvani 12, 20124 Milano. ☎ **02/69831,** or 800/445-8667 in the U.S. and Canada. Fax 02/6671-0810. 303 rms, 18 suites. A/C MINIBAR TV TEL. 370,000–520,000 lire ($236.80–$332.80) double; 520,000–2,240,000 lire ($333–$1,434) suite. Children stay free in parents' room. AE, DC, MC, V. Parking 50,000 lire ($32). Subway: Stazione Centrale.

The 1969 Milano Hilton is a nine-story glass-and-steel cube a few blocks from the main railway station. Its comfortably furnished but very dated bedrooms have long been surpassed by other hotels of Milan, including the Palace. Some rooms need an overhaul. In general, the hotel is more suited to the business traveler (there's a business center) than the leisure visitor, but both mix in the London Bar, with its richly upholstered chairs. The owners spent millions of lire renovating the intimate upstairs restaurant, Da Giuseppe, with warm shades of gilt and brown, belle époque accessories, a grand piano, and portraits of Verdi and his mistress, Giuseppina Strepponi. The specialties are Italian and international dishes. Room service, baby-sitting, laundry, valet, and facilities for the disabled are all available.

MODERATE

Carlton Hotel Senato. Via Senato 5, 20121 Milano. ☎ **02/7601-5535.** Fax 02/783300. 79 rms. A/C MINIBAR TV TEL. 320,000 lire ($204.80) double. AE, DC, MC, V. Closed Aug. Parking 40,000–60,000 lire ($25.60–$38.40). Subway: San Babila.

The facade of this hotel appears like a collection of private ochre-fronted villas joined into a single unit behind an iron fence. The modernized interior is set up to receive dozens of businesspeople from other sections of Europe and from America. Each of the well-furnished bedrooms contains wall-to-wall carpeting and a high ceiling. There's a bar on the premises, and a parking garage. Laundry service, baby-sitting, and room service are also provided.

Casa Svizzera. Via San Raffaele 3, 20121 Milano. ☎ **02/869-2246.** Fax 02/7200-4690. 45 rms. A/C MINIBAR TV TEL. 260,000 lire ($166.40) double. Rates include breakfast. AE, DC, MC, V. Parking 30,000 lire ($19.20). Subway: Duomo.

The Casa Svizzera, right off piazza del Duomo, is one of the most serviceable hotels in the city, following a reconstruction in 1970. Two elevators service five floors of rooms. Features include paneled double windows and soundproofing to keep out the noise. The homelike bedrooms have air-conditioning that can be independently regulated.

Hotel Galles-Milano. Via Ozanam 1 (corso Buenos Aires), Milano 20129. ☎ **02/204841,** or 800/528-1234 in the U.S. and Canada. Fax 02/204-8422. 100 rms, 5 suites. A/C MINIBAR TV TEL. 280,000–480,000 lire ($179.20–$307.20) double; from 400,000 lire ($256) suite. Rates include breakfast. AE, DC, MC, V. Parking: 35,000 lire ($22.40). Subway: Lima.

This hotel was built in 1901 as one of the then-most-glamorous hotels in Milan. In 1990 a consortium of Italian investors poured millions of lire into an elegant reha-bilitation, producing an aggressively marketed hotel that's much favored by businesspeople, conventioneers, and visitors looking for safe, comfortable, and un-pretentious lodgings. The interior lacks the art nouveau glamour of many of its com-petitors, but this doesn't seem to bother the many clients who approve of the building's functional lines and conservatively modern bedrooms. The hotel contains a big-windowed rooftop restaurant (La Terrazza) with additional seating on a canopy-covered terrace, and a cocktail bar with a drink for virtually everyone's taste. In use in spring or summer is a roof garden with a solarium and Jacuzzi.

INEXPENSIVE

Ⓢ **Antica Locanda Solferino.** Via Castelfidardo 2, 20121 Milano. ☎ **02/657-0129.** Fax 02/657-1361. 11 rms. TV TEL. 160,000 lire ($102.40) double. Rates include breakfast. AE, DC, MC, V. Parking 25,000–30,000 lire ($16–$19.20) nearby. Subway: Moscova or Repubblica.

When this country-style hotel opened in 1976, the neighborhood was a depressed backwater of downtown Milan. Today it's an avant-garde community of actors, writ-ers, and poets, and this inn deserves some of the credit for the transformation. The hotel got off to a fortuitous start soon after it opened when editors from *Gentleman's Quarterly* stayed here while working on a fashion feature. Since then Lindsay Kemp and Marcello Mastroianni have become clients, either staying in one of the old-fashioned bedrooms or dining at the ground-floor restaurant (see "Where to Dine," below). Each bedroom is different, reflecting the 19th-century floor plan of the build-ing; there are no singles. The furnishings include Daumier engravings and art nouveau or late 19th-century bourgeois pieces. But the baths are modern. Since the hotel is small and often fully booked, reserve as far in advance as possible.

Ⓢ **Hotel Gran Duca di York.** Via Moneta 1A (piazza Cordusio), 20123 Milano. ☎ **02/874863.** Fax 02/869-0344. 33 rms. TV TEL. 220,000 lire ($140.80) double; 280,000 lire ($179.20) triple. Rates include breakfast. AE, V. Closed Aug. Parking 35,000 lire ($22.40). Sub-way: Cordusio.

When it was built by the Catholic church in the 1890s, this Liberty-style palace housed dozens of priests from the nearby Duomo. Among them was the cardinal of Milan, who later became Pope Pius XI. Today anyone can rent one of the pleasantly furnished and well-kept bedrooms, each with a private bath sheathed with patterned tiles. Behind the ochre-and-stone facade, you'll find a bar in an alcove of the severely elegant lobby, where a suit of armor and leather-covered armchairs contribute to the restrained tone.

Ⓢ **Hotel Manzoni.** Via Santo Spirito 20, 20121 Milano. ☎ **02/7600-5700.** Fax 02/784212. 52 rms. TEL. 220,000 lire ($150) double. AE, DC, MC, V. Parking 22,000–50,000 lire ($14.10–$32). Subway: Montenapoleone or San Babila.

The Hotel Manzoni charges reasonable prices considering its location near the most fashionable shopping streets of Milan. It lies behind a facade of stone slabs on a fairly quiet one-way street. Each of its bedrooms is outfitted with color-coordinated, comfortable functional furniture and carpeting. Many of the rooms have TVs. A brass-trimmed winding staircase leads from the lobby into a bar and TV lounge. The cooperative English-speaking staff will point the way to the hotel's garage.

Hotel Star. Via dei Bossi, 20121 Milano. ☎ **02/801501.** Fax 02/861787. 30 rms. A/C TV TEL. 215,000 lire ($137.60) double. Rates include buffet breakfast. AE, MC, V. Closed Aug. Subway: Cordusio or Duomo.

The Ceretti family welcome guests to their well-run little hotel on a narrow street a few blocks from La Scala and the Duomo. The lobby has been refurbished, making it brighter than before, and the bedrooms are comfortably furnished. Amenities such as hair dryers have been installed in the bathrooms. Double glass windows cut down on the noise from the street. They serve a rich buffet breakfast, including jams, pâté, yogurts, cheese, eggs, ham, and fruit salad, along with cereal, croissants, and various teas, juices, and coffee.

WHERE TO DINE

The wide economic levels of the population—from textile manufacturer to factory worker—are reflected in the prices in the restaurants, which range from haute cuisine to the pizza parlor.

EXPENSIVE

✪ **Giannino.** Via Amatore Sciesa 8. ☎ **02/5519-5582.** Reservations required. Main courses 28,000–70,000 lire ($17.90–$44.80). AE, DC, MC, V. Mon–Sat 12:30–3pm and 7:30pm–midnight. Tram: 12 or 30. Bus: 60. MILANESE/SEAFOOD/TUSCAN.

Giannino continues to enchant its loyal patrons and win new adherents every year. It's one of the top restaurants in all of Lombardy, and has been since 1899. The chef approaches every day as if he must make his reputation anew. Diners have a choice of several attractive rooms, but eyes rivet on the tempting underglass offerings of the *specialità gastronomiche milanesi*. The choice is excellent, including such characteristic Lombard dishes as tender, breaded veal cutlet and risotto simmered in broth and coated with Parmesan cheese. It's difficult to recommend any one dish, as everything we've ordered, or even seen going by, piqued our taste. However, we have special affection for the tagliolini con scampi al verde, fresh homemade noodles with prawn tails in green herb sauce. Also superb are the cold fish and seafood salad and the beautifully seasoned orata al cartoccio (fish baked in a brown paper bag with shrimp butter and fresh herbs).

St. Andrews. Via Sant'Andrea 23. ☎ **02/798236.** Reservations required. Main courses 32,000–60,000 lire ($20.50–$38.40). AE, DC, MC, V. Mon–Sat 12:30–3:30pm and 8pm–1am. Closed Aug. Subway: Montenapoleone or San Babila. INTERNATIONAL.

This restaurant has given much pleasure to many people for many years. It offers one of the finest kitchens in Lombardy, preparing both international and regional food. The cuisine is superior. The menu includes an unusual appetizer of steak tartare mixed with caviar and seasonings, John Dory in a salt crust, and rack of lamb in the Provençal style. The dessert specialty is a tartatelli, composed of pastry with a honey-and-strawberry sauce. At lunch it has somewhat the atmosphere of a private club and is apt to be filled with businesspeople. The armchairs are covered in black leather, the paneling is dark wood, and the lighting is discreet from hooded lamps. Formally attired waiters give superb service to regular guests and to such celebrities as famous Italian fashion stylists, including Gianfranco Ferré, Armani, Versace, and Missoni Fendi.

Il Teatro. In the Four Seasons Hotel Milano, via Gesù 8. ☎ **02/7708-1435.** Reservations recommended. Main courses 32,000–38,000 lire ($20.50–$24.30). Fixed-price dinner 80,000 lire ($51.20). AE, DC, MC, V. Mon–Sat 7:30pm–midnight. Closed Aug. MEDITERRANEAN.

This is the culinary showcase of the shopping district's newest and most glamorous hotel. Favored since its opening in 1993 by such luminaries as Versace, Calvin Klein, and members of the Agnelli family, the restaurant lies one floor below the lobby level of a Milanese palazzo built in the 1400s as a cloister. Although the restaurant seats only 50, the outdoor patio overlooks a garden, and the dining room is sheathed in burnished paneling and nut-colored leather under a tented ceiling of champagne-colored silk. Prices are lower than you might think. The menu changes at least four times a year, but might include a tantalizing involtini of eggplant with ricotta and mint, crispy crayfish with a purée of tomatoes, potato gnocchi stuffed with caviar and fresh dill, and a filet of red mullet with essence of tomato and black truffles. Everything tastes as fresh as the day it was picked, harvested, or caught. Dessert might be a mille-feuille croquante layered with walnuts, chocolate mousse, and raspberries.

MODERATE

Al Chico di Uva. Via Sirtori 24, ☎ **02/2940-6883.** Reservations recommended. Main courses 16,000–35,000 lire ($10.25–$22.40). AE, DC, MC, V. Mon–Sat noon–2:30pm and 7–10:30pm. Closed Aug 3–27. Subway: Porta Venezia. TUSCAN/ITALIAN.

Al Chico, a good neighborhood restaurant specializing in such fare as onion soup and fondue bourguignonne, was established in the 1970s in a much-renovated, century-old building. Tuscan specialties such as Florentine beefsteak are also featured, and portions are tasty and satisfying. The chef is rightly proud of his pappardelle with porcini mushrooms, branzini (sea bass) cooked in a salt crust, and spaghetti with mushrooms and spring onions. The place is usually crowded, but it's worth the wait for a table. The service is good, and the ingredients are fresh and well selected at the market. They stock good house wines from Tuscany, including the classic chianti. In summer you can eat on the veranda.

Alfio-Cavour. Via Senato 31. ☎ **02/7600-0633.** Reservations recommended. Main courses 25,000–45,000 lire ($16–$28.80). AE, DC, MC, V. Mon–Fri 12:30–3pm and 7:30–11pm, Sun 7:30–11pm. Closed Aug. Subway: Montenapoleone or San Babila. ITALIAN/INTERNATIONAL.

There's a luminous quality to the lavish displays of antipasti served with relish at this family-run restaurant. It stems partly from the Tahitian-style decor, where trees grow through the glass panels of a greenhouselike roof and vines entwine themselves among bamboo lattices. The restaurant is best known for its serve-yourself display of antipasti, where the polite but sharp-eyed staff bills you for what you select. A pasta specialty is the flavorful spaghetti pescatore, with bits of seafood. You might follow with large grilled shrimp or a gran misto fish fry, or else one of the many excellent beef or veal dishes.

Al Porto. Piazzale Generale Cantore. ☎ **02/832-1481.** Reservations required. Main courses 25,000–40,000 lire ($16–$25.60). AE, DC, MC, V. Mon 7:30–10:30pm, Tues–Sat 12:30–2:30pm and 7:30–10:30pm. Closed Dec 24–Jan 3 and Aug. Subway: Porta Genova or S. Agostino. Bus: 8 or 19. SEAFOOD.

Established in 1907, this is among the most popular seafood restaurants in Milan. As you enter, you pass by tanks of "demons of the deep" (which might later end up on your plate). The glassed-in garden room is the most sought after by loyal habitués. It's especially popular among business patrons; you may need to reserve several days in adavance. Menu items include orata (dorado) with pink peppercorns and branzini (sea bass) with white Lugurian wine and olives. Many come here just for risotto ai fruitti di mare, the classic Lombard dish served with an assortment of sea creatures. One of the staff confided that the "best patrons" begin with a warm antipasto, then follow with a risotto, and, finally, order the traditional fritto misto—almost anything that swims is likely to turn up on the plate—although some find this far too much food. Everything tastes better with a Friuli wine.

A Santa Lucia. Via San Pietro all'Orto 3. ☎ **02/7602-3155.** Reservations recommended. Main courses 22,000–35,000 lire ($14.10–$22.40). V. Tues–Sun noon–2:30pm and 3:30pm–3am. Closed Aug. Subway: San Babila. ITALIAN/SEAFOOD.

A Santa Lucia pulls out hook, line, and sinker to lure you with some of the best fish dinners in Milan. A festive place, the restaurant is decked out with photographs of pleased celebs, who attest to the skill of its kitchen. You can order such specialties as a savory fish soup, which is a meal in itself; fried baby squid; or good-tasting sole. Spaghetti alle vongole evokes the tang of the sea with its succulent clam sauce. Pizza also reigns supreme. Try either the calzone of Naples or the pizza napoletana.

Bistrot di Gualtiero Marchesi. Via San Raffaele 2. ☎ **02/877120.** Reservations required. Main courses 20,000–30,000 lire ($12.80–$19.20); fixed-price menu 52,000–63,000 lire ($33.30–$40.30). AE, DC, MC, V. Mon 7:30–10:30pm, Tues–Sat 12:30–2:30pm and 7:30–10:30pm. Closed 2 weeks in Aug. Subway: Duomo. LOMBARD/ITALIAN.

Near the Duomo, this bistro was created by Signor Gualtiero Marchesi, the patron saint of *cucina nuova* in Italy. Once hailed by *Time* magazine as among the 10 top chefs in the world, he operated a very expensive restaurant in another part of town which was moved to the town of Erbusco, near Brescia; but this bistro was left as a love token to Milan. It boasts one of the best views of the cathedral in the city. Set on the top floor of the Rinascente Center, which rises seven stories across a narrow street from the cathedral ("almost within touching distance"), the bistro has big walls of glass to better admire the view. The menu depends on the inspiration of the chef, but in the past we've enjoyed an unusual form of half-opened ravioli, or crayfish cooked very al dente with cucumbers. You're almost certain to find a perfect veal cutlet milanese.

Boeucc Antico Ristorante. Piazza Belgioioso 2. ☎ **02/7602-0224.** Reservations required. Main courses 25,000–32,000 lire ($16–$20.50). AE. Mon–Fri 12:40–2:30pm and 7:40–10:40pm, Sun 7:40–10:40pm. Closed Aug, Easter, and Christmas. Subway: Duomo, Montenapoleone, or San Babila. INTERNATIONAL/MILANESE.

This restaurant, established in 1696, is a trio of rooms in a severely elegant old palace, within walking distance of the Duomo and the major shopping streets. Throughout you'll find soaring stone columns and modern art. In summer guests gravitate to a terrace for open-air dining. The hearty specialties, the standard of the kitchen, come from regions of Italy. You might enjoy a spaghetti in clam sauce, a salad of shrimp with arugula and artichokes, or grilled liver, veal, or beef with aromatic herbs. In season sautéed zucchini flowers accompany some dishes.

Doney. In the Prìncipe di Savoia Hotel, piazza della Repubblica 17. ☎ **02/6230.** Main courses 16,000–29,000 lire ($10.25–$18.55); fixed-price menu 70,000–110,000 lire ($44.80–$70.40); afternoon tea 23,000 lire ($14.70). AE, DC, MC, V. Daily noon–12:30am (afternoon tea 4–7pm). Subway: Repubblica. Tram: 1, 4, 11, 29, or 30. LIGHT INTERNATIONAL / AFTERNOON TEA / LOMBARD / VEGETARIAN.

Its burnished paneling, plush upholstery, and soaring frescoed ceiling are some of the high points of one of Milan's most recent (and most expensive) hotel restorations. Doney borrowed its name from a historic cafe in Rome, and much of its decorative allure from the turn-of-the-century "Liberty" style of Italy's gilded age. Its menu features elegant but simple preparations of salads (lobster, artichokes, and pear), sandwiches (smoked salmon on brown bread), and steaks. During teatime you can select from nine kinds of tea, and pastries and finger sandwiches from a trolley. At any hour the place functions gracefully as a popular meeting point.

☼ Peck's Restaurant. Via Victor Hugo 4. ☎ **02/876774.** Main courses 30,000–36,000 lire ($19.20–$23.05); fixed-price menu 60,000–80,000 lire ($38.40–$51.20). AE, DC, MC. V. Mon–Sat 12:15–2:30pm and 7:15–10:30pm. Closed 10 days in Jan and Sun July 1–21. Subway: Duomo. MILANESE/ITALIAN.

Peck's is owned by the famous delicatessen of Milan, which gastronomes view as the Milanese equivalent of Fauchon's in Paris. It was established by Francesco Peck, who came to Milan from Prague in the 19th century. His small restaurant eventually became a food empire. In an environment filled with shimmering marble and modern Italian paintings, an alert staff will serve you an elegant cuisine. The fresh specialties include a classic version of risotto milanese, rack of lamb with fresh rosemary, ravioli alla fonduata, and lombo di vitello (veal) with artichokes, followed by chocolate meringue for dessert. Its cured meats are said to be the richest in Italy.

☼ Savini. Galleria Vittorio Emanuele II. ☎ **02/7200-3433.** Reservations required. Main courses 35,000–45,000 lire ($22.40–$28.80); fixed-price lunch (with wine) 65,000 lire ($41.60); fixed-price dinner (without wine) 80,000 lire ($51.20). AE, DC, MC, V. Mon–Fri noon–3pm and 7:30–11pm, Sat 7:30–11pm. Closed Dec 23–Jan 6 and Aug 10–21. Subway: Duomo. LOMBARD/INTERNATIONAL.

Savini provides a heavenly introduction to the aromatic cookery of Lombardy and has attracted everybody from Puccini to Pavarotti. Perched in the heart of the great glass-enclosed arcade opposite the Duomo, the *classico* restaurant, which dates from 1867, draws both the out-of-towner and the discriminating local. Guests sit on the terrace outside, or dine in the old-world room with its crystal chandeliers and glittering silverware. Waiters in black jackets hover over you to see that you enjoy every mouthful. Many of the most memorable dishes are unassuming, including the Lombardy specialty costoletta alla milanese, tender veal coated with egg batter and breadcrumbs, then fried a rich brown. The *pièce de résistance* of Milan, most often ordered before the main course, is risotto alla milanese—rice simmered in a broth and dressed with whatever the artiste in the kitchen selects that night. Savini is excellently stocked with a wide range of wine (the staff will gladly assist you).

La Scaletta. Piazza Stazione Genova 3. ☎ **02/5810-0290.** Reservations required. Main courses 30,000–35,000 lire ($19.20–$22.40). AE. Mon 8–9:30pm, Tues–Sat noon–1:15pm and 8–9:30pm. Closed 1 week at Easter, Aug, and Dec 24–Jan 6. Subway: Stazione Genova. ITALIAN.

La Scaletta emerges near the top in the highly competitive world of Milanese restaurants, housed in a Liberty-style building from the turn of the century. The chefs practice modern Italian cuisine with a certain flair. Some have likened the elegant setting to a small and exclusive London club. Because this place is so popular with the Milan business community, reserve as far in advance as possible. The quality of the ingredients is superb—the chefs demand that every item be fresh. The veal dishes are heavenly. You might begin with a tripe terrine in gelatin or a scampi salad, before giving serious attention to your main course. A specialty is a risotto made with green peas and wild mushrooms. Other special dishes include a carpaccio with herbs, tagliatelle with clams and broccoli, and a pâté of snails. The signature dessert is freshly made gelato with rosemary and sage.

☉ Trattoria Bagutta. Via Bagutta 14. ☎ **02/7600-2767.** Reservations required. Main courses 22,000–50,000 lire ($14.10–$32.00). AE, DC, MC, V. Mon–Sat 12:30–2:30pm and 7:30–10:30pm. Closed Sun July–Aug. Subway: San Babila. INTERNATIONAL.

Patronized by artists, this restaurant is the most celebrated trattoria in Milan. A venerable-looking establishment from 1927, the Bagutta is known for the carica-tures—framed and frescoed—that cover its walls. Of the many large and bustling dining rooms, the rear one with its picture windows is most enticing. The tempting food draws on the kitchens of Lombardy, Tuscany, and Bologna for inspiration. On offer are assorted antipasti, and main-dish specialties include fried squid and scampi, lingua e purë (tongue with mashed potatoes), linguine with shrimp in a tomato-cream sauce, and scaloppine alla Bagutta. The Bagutta enjoys a vogue among out-of-towners, who consider it chic to patronize the sophisticated little trattoria, as opposed to the more deluxe restaurants.

INEXPENSIVE

Al Tempio d'Oro. Via delle Leghe 23. ☎ **02/2614-5709.** Main courses 10,000–19,000 lire ($6.40–$12.15). No credit cards. Mon–Sat 8pm–2am. Closed 2 weeks in mid-Aug. Subway: Pasteur. ITALIAN/INTERNATIONAL.

This restaurant, near the central railway station, offers inexpensive and well-prepared meals in an ambience similar to what you might have found if an ancient Greek temple had decided to serve beer on tap along with international food specialties. The chef is justifiably proud of his fish soup, Spanish paella, and North African couscous. The crowd scattered among the ceiling columns is relaxed, and they contribute to an atmosphere somewhat like that of a beer hall. No one will mind if you stop by just for a drink.

⑤ La Magolfa. Via Magolfa 15. ☎ **02/832-1696.** Reservations required. Main courses 18,000 lire ($11.50); fixed-price meal 60,000 lire ($38.40). AE, DC, MC, V. Mon–Sat 8pm–midnight. Closed Sat July–Aug. Subway: Porta Genova. MILANESE/LOMBARD.

La Magolfa, one of the city's dining bargains, offers a gargantuan fixed-price meal. The building is a country farmhouse whose origins go back to the 1500s, although the restaurant opened only in 1960. It's likely to be crowded, as is every other res-taurant in Milan that offers such value. If you don't mind its location away from the center of town, in Zona Ticinese in the southern part of the city, you'll be treated to some very good regional cookery that emerges fresh from battered pots and pans. A general air of conviviality reigns, and there's music of local origin nightly.

⑤ Peck. Via Victor Hugo 4. ☎ **02/876774.** Reservations required. Main courses 18,000–22,000 lire ($11.50–$14.10). AE, DC, MC, V. Mon–Sat 7:30am–9pm. Closed 10 days in Jan and July 1–21. Subway: Duomo. MILANESE/LOMBARD.

Peck offers one of the best values in Milan—food served in a glamorous cafeteria as-sociated with the most famous delicatessen in Italy (the high-priced restaurant in the basement is listed under "Moderate," above). Only a short walk from the Duomo, Peck has a stand-up bar in front, and, in the rear, well-stocked display cases of spe-cialties fresh from their treasure trove of produce. Armed with a plastic tray, you can sample such temptations as artichoke-and-Parmesan salad, marinated carpaccio, slabs of tender veal in a herb sauce, risotto marinara, and selections from a carving table laden with a juicy display of roast meats.

Ristorante Solferino. Via Castelfidaro 2. ☎ **02/659-9886.** Reservations recommended. Main courses 20,000–30,000 lire ($12.80–$19.20). AE, DC, MC, V. Mon–Fri noon–2pm and 7–11pm, Sat 7–11pm. Subway: Moscova. MILANESE.

This country-style inn, built 150 years ago, has all the accoutrements you'd expect to find in a farming community rather than in the center of a busy city. A restau-rant was founded here in 1950. Below a beamed ceiling, next to racks of wine bottles and among the fashion stars, you can dine on such specialties as risotto Grande

Milano, Milanese veal with potatoes, gnocchi with salmon, carpaccio, or tagliatelle with grilled vegetables; and follow with a dessert known as "Milanese Custard." The establishment maintains a less formal and much less expensive buffet-style restaurant just around the corner.

⑤ Taverna del Gran Sasso. Piazza Principessa Clotilde 10. ☎ **02/659-7578.** All-you-can-eat meal 58,000 lire ($37.10). MC, V. Mon–Fri 12:30–2pm and 7:30–10:30pm, Sat 7:30–10:30pm. Closed Jan 1 and Aug. Subway: Repubblica. Tram: 29 or 30. ABRUZZI.

This tavern, dating from 1962, provides regional meals. Filled with lots of sentimental baubles, its walls are crowded ceiling to floor with copper molds, ears of corn, strings of pepper and garlic, and cart wheels. A tall, open hearth burns with a charcoal fire, and a Sicilian cart is laden with baskets of bread, dried figs, nuts, and kegs of wine. As you enter, you'll find a mellowed wooden keg of wine with a brass faucet (you're supposed to help yourself, using glass mugs). The cuisine features a number of specialties from the Abruzzi—regional dishes such as maccheroni alla chitarra, a distinctively shaped macaroni with a savory meat sauce. Meals are an all-you-can-eat feast.

SHOPPING

London has Harrods, Paris has all the big-name boutiques you can think of, and Rome and Florence instill an acquisitional fever in the eyes of anyone who even window-gazes. Milan, however, is blessed with one of the most unusual concentrations of shopping possibilities in Europe. Most of the boutiques are infused with the style, humor, and sophistication that has made Milan the dynamo of the Italian fashion industry, a place where the sidewalks sizzle with the hard-driving entrepreneurial spirit that has been part of the northern Italian textile industry for centuries.

One well-heeled shopper from Florida recently spent the better part of her vacation in Italy shopping for what she called "the most unbelievable variety of shoes, clothes, and accessories in the world." A walk on the fashion subculture's focal point, **via Montenapoleone,** will quickly confirm that impression. It's one of Italy's three great shopping streets, a mile-long strip that has become a showcase for famous (and high-priced) makers of clothes and shoes.

Note carefully that beauty does not come cheaply in the garment industry, and the attention you receive will often be based directly on the salesperson's impression of how much money you plan to spend. But as a handful of American models, along with design imitators from around the world, know, there are indeed riches to be discovered.

Early-morning risers will be welcomed only by silent streets and closed gates. Most shops are closed all day Sunday and Monday (although some open on Monday afternoon). Some stores open at 9am unless they're very chic, and then they're not likely to open until 10:30am. They remain open, for the most part, until 1pm, reopening again between 3:30 and 7:30pm.

BOOKS

American Bookstore. Via Camperio 16. ☎ **02/878920.**

There are bigger and flashier bookstores in Rome, but this one will probably stock that paperback novel you're looking for, or the scholarly exegesis of Milanese artwork you should have reviewed before your trip and never did. Only English-language books are stocked, as well as an assortment of periodicals.

DEPARTMENT STORES

La Rinascente. Piazza del Duomo. ☎ **02/88521.**

Shopping Secrets of Milan

Prada, via della Spiga 1 (☎ 02/7600-2019), has the best leather goods and other stylish accessories for women in Milan. *Travel & Leisure* called it "a fashion industry phenomenon." The black nylon backpack is the most popular item.

Salmoiraghi Vigano, corso Matteotti 22 (☎ 02/7600-0100), is known for having the best-looking sunglasses in Italy, attracting all trendoids. It's for those who want to look like Marcello Mastroianni in *La Dolce Vita.*

Sebastian, via Borgospesso 18 (☎ 02/780532), has been called the most "eccentric" shoe store for women and men in Milan. More than 150 styles and a wide range of materials, from fabric to leather and suede, await discriminating shoppers who'd like their shoes custom-made.

G. Lorenzi, via Montenapoleone 9 (☎ 02/7602-2848). In this tiny store, you'll find everything you were looking for in the way of small gifts—and a lot of stuff you've never seen before. Many are one-of-a-kind items.

Dom, corso Matteotti 3 (☎ 02/7602-3410), offers the finest selection of silver, crystal, and porcelain in Milan.

Primavera, via Torino 47 (☎ 02/874565). When the high prices of Milano fashion are beyond your means, go here for stylish clothing (both women and men) at bargain-basement prices.

Giuseppe Falzone, corso Cristoforo Colombo 5, (☎ 02/5810-3673), offers stacks of designer clothing for women. Discounts are about 70% of regular boutique prices.

La Rinascente bills itself with accuracy as Italy's largest fashion department store. In addition to clothing, the basement carries a wide variety of giftware for the home, including handwork from all regions of Italy. There's an information desk on the ground floor, and on the seventh, a bank, a travel agency, Rolando hairdresser, Estée Lauder Skincare Center, a coffee-bar, and the Brunch and Bistro restaurants.

Incidentally, the name of the store was suggested by the poet Gabriele d'Annunzio, for which he received a compensation of 5,000 lire. The store was officially opened right before Christmas in the closing year of World War I, but it burned down on Christmas Eve. Rebuilt, it later met total destruction in an Allied bombing raid in 1943. But it has always rallied from disaster and now is better than ever. Open Monday from 1 to 7:30pm and Tuesday to Saturday from 9:30am to 7:30pm.

FASHION

For Men

Giorgio Armani. Via San Andrea 9. ☎ **02/7600-3234.**

Giorgio Armani houses the style we've come to expect in a large showroom vaguely reminiscent of a very upscale aircraft hangar. Armani's trademark look incorporates loose-fitting, unstructured, and unpadded clothing draped loosely over firm bodies. Although there's a bit more structure to the clothes since Richard Gere made the look popular in *American Gigolo,* Armani still creates elegant upholstery for elegant people.

Galtrucco. Via Montenapoleone 27. ☎ **02/7600-2978.**

This store is a two-floor collection of elegant men's suits, shirts, and knitwear. The ready-to-wear clothes are well made and attractively conservative. There's also a battalion of tailors prepared to create a custom-made suit, laden with details that a discerning eye will pick up immediately, complete with a label by Brioni.

Gemelli. Corso Vercelli 16. ☎ **02/433404.**

This store sells well-made clothes for men, women, babies, and teenagers, which, while stylish and serviceable, are neither as glamorous nor as chillingly expensive as some of the city's more famous clothiers. Everything here is off the rack; there's no custom-tailoring service.

Mila Schön. Via Montenapoleone 2. ☎ **02/781190.**

The sophisticated look is casually chic, hip, and expensive. If you're male, thin, and relatively muscular, you'll look terrific in Mila Schön. Mila's women's line is on the ground floor. Even the somewhat flippant accessories are stratospherically expensive.

Ermenegildo Zenga. Via Pietro Verri 3. ☎ **02/7600-6437.**

This shop, which opened in 1985, offers a complete range of menswear, beginning with the Sartorial line, the Zenga *haute couture* offering of suits, jackets, trousers, and accessories. The "soft line" is dedicated to a younger customer, and the sportswear collection and yachting line allow you to wander the globe with the right apparel. The shop also offers a "made-to-measure" service with a selection of 300 fabrics per season. They can make an outfit in about 4 weeks, then ship it to any destination in the world.

For Women

Gianfranco Ferré. Via della Spiga 11–13. ☎ **02/7600-0385.**

This is the only outlet in Milan for a famous designer whose women's fashions are worn by some of the world's most elegant dressers. The range is wide—perfect tailleurs and soft knitwear, organza shirts, or sensual evening dresses, along with refined leather accessories, bijoux, and foulards. Next door to the women's shop is an outlet for the designer's men's clothing. Closed in August.

Spiga 31 di R. Bilancioni. Via della Spiga 31. ☎ **02/7602-3502.**

The inventory here includes an unusual look that the casually elegant night owl might like. Clothing ranges somewhere between sportswear and formal evening wear, without really fitting into either category. If you choose to show off a purchase from the sometimes flamboyant, sometimes discreet inventory at the country club, you won't need to worry that another woman will be wearing the same dress.

JEWELRY

Mario Buccellati. Via Montenapoleone 4. ☎ **02/7600-2153.**

Mario Buccellati offers the best-known—and the most expensive—silver and jewels in Italy. The designs of the cast-silver bowls, tureens, and christening cups are nothing short of rhapsodic, and the quality is among the finest in the world.

Meru. Via Solferino 3. ☎ **02/8646-0700.**

Meru sells consciously avant-garde jewelry, rumored to have been worn and privately publicized by young and beautiful European film stars. Many of the pieces are set into enameled backgrounds and often include unusual types of gemstones such as rose quartz, coral, and amber. All pieces are made by Meru craftspeople. Closed July 30 to September 10.

LACE

Jesurum. Via Verri 4. ☎ **02/7601-5045.**

This is the Milanese outlet of a Venice-based lace company that has been famous since 1870. Set on a very short street where none of the buildings has an obvious street number, it sells all-lace or lace-edged tablecloths, lace doilies, and all the handmade textiles that a bride might like to add to her trousseau. It also sells lace blouses, even a swimming suit (which might be better suited to a photo session than to a game of water polo) and lace by the meter for trimming curtains or whatever.

LEATHER GOODS & SHOES

Beltrami. Via Montenapoleone 16. ☎ **02/7602-3422.**

Prices are chillingly high here, but the leather goods for men and women are among the best you'll find anywhere. The showroom is appropriately glamorous, the merchandise appropriately chic. Beltrami has another shop, open the same hours, at piazza San Babila 4A (☎ 02/7600-0546).

Salvatore Ferragamo. Via Montenapoleone 3. ☎ **02/7600-6660.**

The label is instantly recognizable and the quality high at this shop that has created and designed shoes since the 1930s for the fashion goddesses and gods of Europe and Hollywood. Rigidly controlled by a large and extended second generation of the original founders, it's still a leader in style and allure. The store contains inventories of shoes, luggage, and accessories for women and men. Also for sale are Ferragamo leather jackets, pants, and a small selection of clothing.

Alfonso Garlando. Via Madonnina 2. ☎ **02/8646-3733.**

The prices on the merchandise here range up to the very expensive, but the shop's size and lack of concern for a stylish showroom almost guarantees a reasonable choice of merchandise at a reasonable price. They sell shoes for men and women, but not children.

Gucci. Via Montenapoleone 5. ☎ **02/7601-3050.**

Gucci is the Milanese headquarters for the most famous leather-goods distributor in Italy. Its shoes, luggage, and wallets for men and women, handbags, and leatherware accessories usually have the colors of the Italian flag (olive and crimson) stitched in the form of a more-or-less discreet ribbon across the front of most of the company's merchandise.

Sebastian. Via Borgospesso 18. ☎ **02/780-532.**

Sebastian sells excellent shoes for men and women from a ready-made stockpile of fashionable models, which Sebastian makes in its own factories. For almost the same price (if you don't mind waiting 2 months or more) you can order custom-made shoes, shipped anywhere. Custom-made shoes are usually available only in women's styles. This is a boon for clients with wide, narrow, large, or small feet, who consider Sebastian something of a sartorial and orthopedic blessing.

Tanino Crisci. Via Montenapoleone 3. ☎ **02/7602-1264.**

Its showroom evokes the interior of a private club in London because of its oiled paneling and conservative leather chairs. Its inventory includes elegantly conservative footwear for men and women, but its most famous products are the leather boots that will make you look like an ace equestrian, polo player, or stalker of big game—even if they haven't been your lifelong hobbies.

LINGERIE

B. Finzi. Galleria Vittorio Emanuele. ☎ **02/8646-0920.**

Styles of underwear have changed since this shop was established in 1859, but the Milanese demand for both practical and frivolous "unmentionables" has continued unabated. (The polite Italian word for these is *biancheria intima.*) Most of the stock here is for all kinds and types of women (look especially for the satin-trimmed silk camisoles), but there's also a selection of underwear for men (most of which is bought for them by their wives or companions).

A MALL

Caffè Moda. Via Durini 14. ☎ **02/7602-1188.**

Despite the implications of its name, this is actually a shopping complex filled with the deliberately informal offshoots of some of the most renowned clothing designers in Italy. Its focal point is a ground-floor cafe and bar around which all the gossip of the neighborhood seems to ebb and flow. Radiating outward, and stretching over three different levels, are at least 20 different shops. These include jeans outlets of both Valentino and Gianfranco Ferré, and informal (but still expensive) outlets for Missoni, Valentino Uomo, and Krizia Poi. Each boutique maintains its own hours, but most of them are open nonstop Monday to Saturday from 10am to 7pm. A few of the smaller shops might close briefly for lunch. The complex is located about a block behind the Palazzo Reale.

PAPER

I Giorni di Carta. Corso Garibaldi 81. ☎ **02/655-2514.**

This is one of the city's most unusual outlets for writing paper and stationery, with dozens of different colors, textures, and weights. Much of the inventory is made from recycled paper. The establishment also sells briefcases to carry your letters, pens and ink, and ornamental paperweights.

PERFUMES

Profumo. Via Brera 6. ☎ **02/7202-3334.**

Profumo sells some of Italy's most exotic perfumes for women, plus cologne and aftershave lotions for men. Some Italian scents are exclusively distributed here near the American Express office.

PORCELAIN & CRYSTAL

Richard-Ginori. Corso Buenos Aires 1. ☎ **02/2951-6611.**

Since 1735 this company has manufactured and sold porcelain to dukes, duchesses, and ordinary bourgeois consumers. A household word in Italy, Ginori sells ovenproof porcelain in both modern and traditional themes, as well as crystal and silverware that they either make themselves or inventory from other manufacturers such as Baccarat or Wedgwood.

PRINTS & ENGRAVINGS

Raimondi di Pettinaroli. Corso Venezia 6. ☎ **02/7600-2412.**

This is considered the finest shop in Milan for antique prints and engravings, plus reprints of old engravings made from the original copper plates. It was originally established in 1776. Of particular interest are the engravings of Italian cityscapes during the 19th century, and the many treasures worth framing after you return home.

MILAN AFTER DARK

As in Rome, many of the top nightclubs in Milan shut down for the summer, when the cabaret talent and the bartenders pack their bags and head for the hills or the seashore. However, Milan is a big city, and there's always plenty of after-dark diversions. This sprawling metropolis is also one of the cultural centers of Europe.

THE PERFORMING ARTS

The most complete list of cultural events appears in the large Milan newspaper, the left-wing *Repubblica*. If you're in town, try for a Thursday edition, usually with the most complete listings.

✪ Teatro alla Scala. Piazza della Scala. ☎ **02/88791,** or 02/861772 or 02/861781 for tickets Tues–Sun noon–3pm. Tickets 35,000–270,000 lire ($22.40–$172.80). Subway: Duomo.

If you have only a night for Milan and are here between mid-December and May, try to attend a performance at the world-famous Teatro alla Scala. Built to the designs of Piermarini, the neoclassic opera house was restored after World War II bomb damage. The greatest opera stars appear here, and the Milanese first-night audience is the hardest to please in the world. Tickets are also extremely hard to come by and are sold out weeks in advance. However, you do stand a chance of getting gallery tickets, seats so far up they should be called celestial. The box office is open Tuesday to Sunday from noon to 7pm. You may also reserve by phone.

Opera lovers will also want to visit the **Museo Teatrale alla Scala** (☎ **02/805-3418**) in the same building. Established in 1913, it contains a rich collection of historical mementos and records of the heady world of opera. Among them are busts and portraits of such artists as Beethoven, Chopin, Donizetti, Verdi, and Puccini. Two halls are devoted to Verdi alone, with objects including scores written in his own hand and the spinet on which he learned to play. Rossini's eyeglasses and his pianoforte tuning key are in a vitrine, and there are many other such treasures, including a death-cast of Chopin's left hand. A small gallery honors Toscanini, with his batons, medals, and pince-nez on display. One of the greatest thrills for opera lovers who may not be in Milan at the time of a performance at La Scala—or may not be able to get tickets—will be the view from the third floor. From here, you can look down on the theater's ornate auditorium with its velvet draperies. Charging 5,000 lire ($3.20) for admission, the museum is open May to September, Monday to Saturday from 9am to noon and 2 to 6pm and on Sunday from 9:30am to 12:30pm and 2 to 6pm; October to April, Monday to Saturday from 9am to noon and 2 to 6pm.

Conservatorio. Via del Conservatorio 12. ☎ **02/7600-1755.** Tickets 25,000–60,000 lire ($16–$38.40). Subway: San Babila.

The Conservatorio, in the San Babila sector, features the finest in classical music. Year round, a cultured Milanese audience enjoys high-quality programs of widely varied classical concerts.

Piccolo Teatro. Via Rovello 2 (near via Dante). ☎ **02/7233-3222.** Tickets 50,000 lire ($32). Subway: Cordusio or Cairoli.

The Piccolo Teatro became a socialist theater in the years after World War II, but now the city of Milan is the landlord. Programs are varied today, and performances are in Italian. Its director, Giorgio Strehler, is acclaimed as one of the most avant garde and talented in the world. The theater lies between the Duomo and the Castle of the Sforzas. It's sometimes hard to obtain seats here. No shows are presented on Monday; closed in August.

THE CLUB & MUSIC SCENE

Ca' Bianca Club. Via Lodovico il Moro 117. ☎ **02/8912-5777.** Cover 25,000 lire ($16) including show and one drink, 90,000–100,000 lire ($57.60–$64) with dinner.

Ca' Bianca has a changing offering of live music, which ranges—depending on the availability of musicians—from folk music to cabaret to Dixieland jazz on Wednesday night. Technically this is a private club, but no one at the door will prevent nonmembers from entering. The show—whatever it may be—begins at 11pm. The club is open daily from 8:30pm to 1am; closed in August.

Club Astoria. Piazza Santa Maria Beltrade 2. ☎ **02/8646-3710.** No cover.

This popular nightclub is one of the most frequented in town, especially by the expense-account-junket crowd. When there's a floor show, a drink might cost around 50,000 lire ($32), which takes the place of a cover charge. Otherwise, drinks begin at 30,000 lire ($19.20). Open Monday to Saturday from 10:30pm to 4am; closed in August.

Facsimile. Via Tallone 11. ☎ **02/738-0635.** No cover, but a one-drink minimum.

This *birreria* is a popular rendezvous point where Milanese rockers can commune with their favorite video stars in living color. The decor is almost entirely gray and red, and there are outdoor tables for star-gazing. Drinks range upward from 9,000 lire ($5.75). The bar is open Tuesday to Sunday from 6:30pm to 2am.

Rolling Stone. Corso XXII Marzo 32. ☎ **02/733172.** Cover 20,000–25,000 lire ($12.80–$16), depending on the event.

This club was originally established for the Beat Generation of the 1950s, later attracting *la dolce vita* people in the 1960s. In 1984 it adopted its present rock 'n' roll preoccupation, featuring heavy-metal and an ocean of aggressively energetic groups in their 20s. Its open every night, usually from 10:30pm to 4am, but don't even consider showing up here until at least midnight (otherwise you'll have the place to yourself). On some selected concerts the place doesn't open until 1am. Drinks cost 8,000 to 10,000 lire ($5.10 to $6.40). Closed in July and August.

Gay Clubs

Nuova Idea International. Via de Castillia 30. ☎ **02/6900-7859.** Cover (including the first drink) 15,000 lire ($9.60) Thurs–Fri and Sun, 25,000 lire ($16) Sat.

This is the largest, oldest, most active, and most fun gay disco in Italy, very much tied in to the urban bustle of modern Milan. Its sense of freedom would be unthinkable in smaller towns in the provinces. It prides itself on mimicking the examples of the large, all-gay discos of northern Europe. It draws a patronage of young and not-so-young men, many of whom are film or theater actors. There's a large video screen and occasional live entertainment. Drinks begin at 9,000 lire ($5.75). It's open Thursday to Sunday from 9:30pm to 2:30am.

Zip. Corso Sempione 76 (at via Salvioni). ☎ **02/331-4904.** Cover (including the first drink) 30,000–40,000 lire ($19.20–$25.60). Tram: 1, 9, or 33.

One of the most deliberately raunchy gay clubs in southern Europe, Zip is a *club privato* although non-Italian newcomers can enter upon presentation of a passport. This dive contains a labyrinth of inner rooms devoted to a disco with a clientele of gay males, a late-night cafeteria, a screen showing gay porno, and a "dark room" where the action is uninhibited. The disco opens nightly at midnight, but no one arrives before 2:30 or 3am. It shuts down for a much-needed rest at 6am (on Saturday, not until 8am). The establishment lies in back of Castello Sforzesco. If you attend, be alert to the neighborhood at this late hour, and exercise caution once you're inside. Drinks cost 10,000 lire ($6.40).

THE BAR SCENE

Al Teatro. Corso Garibaldi 16. ☎ **02/864222.**

Decorated a bit like a bohemian parlor of the last century, this is a popular bar across the street from the Teatro Fossati. It opens for morning coffee Tuesday to Sunday at 7am, and closes (after several changes of ambience) at 2am. At night there's some-times musical entertainment, but most of the time clients seem perfectly happy to drink their drinks, gossip, and flirt. Cocktails cost 8,000 to 10,000 lire ($5.10 to $6.40). In addition to coffee and drinks, the establishment serves toasts and tortes. In fine weather tables are set outside on corso Garibaldi.

Bar Giamaica. Via Brera 32. ☎ **02/876723.**

The place is loud and bustling, and seats its customers with a no-nonsense kind of gruff humor. That, however, is part of the allure of a bar that has attracted writers and artists for many years, and is one of the mainstays of the Milanese night scene. The personalities who work here haven't changed in many years. If you want only a drink, you'll have lots of company among the office workers who jostle around the tiny tables, often standing rather than sitting because of the lack of room. It's open as a restaurant Monday to Saturday from noon to 2:30pm and 7:30 to 10pm. Meals range from 20,000 lire ($12.80) (for a salad and a beer) to as much as 45,000 lire ($28.80) (for a full Italian regalia). Reservations are not accepted, but you won't lack company while waiting at the bar for a table. The bar opens at 9am Monday to Saturday and remains open until around 12:30am or later.

Grand Hotel Pub. Via Ascanio Sforza 75. ☎ **02/8951-1586.**

Despite its name, this establishment does not rent rooms, or even pretend to be grand. Instead, it's a large, animated restaurant and pub with frequent live music or cabaret. In summer the crowds can move quickly from the smoky interior out into a sheltered garden. The evening's entertainment might consist of either vocal or in-strumental music, or Italian-language cabaret/comedy. Most visitors come here only for a drink, at 8,000 to 10,000 lire ($5.10 to $6.40), but if you're hungry, the res-taurant charges around 50,000 lire ($32) for a full meal. The place is open Tuesday to Sunday from 8pm to 11:30pm. Entrance is usually free.

THE CAFE SCENE

Every city in Italy seems to have a cafe filled with 19th-century detailing and memo-ries of Verdi or some such famous person. It usually offers a wide variety of pastries and a particular kind of clientele who gossip, sip espresso, munch in-between-meals snacks, and compare notes on shopping. In Milan the establishments listed below are popular for this kind of activity.

Berlin Café. Via Gian Giacomo Mora 9. ☎ **02/839-2605.**

As its name implies, the decor emulates a cafe in turn-of-the-century Berlin; the am-bience is enhanced with etched glass and marble-topped tables. It's a great spot for coffee or a drink. A beer costs 6,000 lire ($3.85) and drinks begin at 8,500 lire ($5.45). A variety of simple snack food is available, primarily during the day. Snacks cost 5,000 to 18,000 lire ($3.20 to $11.50). One drawback is the surly staff. It's open Tuesday to Sunday from 10am to 2am.

Café Cova. Via Montenapoleone 8. ☎ **02/7600-0578.**

Amid a chic assemblage of garment-district personnel, along with the shoppers who support them, this cafe follows a routine it established in 1817. This involves con-cocting gallons of heady espresso and dispensing staggering amounts of pralines, chocolates, brioches, and sandwiches from behind a glass display case. The more elegant sandwiches contain smoked salmon and truffles. Clients drink their espresso from fragile gold-rimmed cups at one of the small tables in an elegant inner room or while standing at the prominent bar. Most of the action takes place at the bar, so you don't really need a table unless you're exhausted from too much shopping. Coffee at the bar costs 1,500 lire (95¢), or 5,000 lire ($3.20) at a table. Hot and cold food costs anywhere from 500 to 30,000 lire (30¢ to $19.20). Open Monday to Saturday from 8am to 8pm; closed in August.

Caffè Milano. Via Montebello 7. ☎ **02/2900-3300.**

Most visitors consider it a pleasant mixing spot and rendezvous point, with relaxing music and flattering lighting. In summer the crowd sometimes spills outside onto the small piazza. Drinks cost 6,000 to 12,000 lire ($3.85 to $7.70). There's also a restaurant that serves classic Milanese cuisine, such as risotto, fresh pasta, and veal dishes. Full meals start at 50,000 lire ($32), including wine, and are served Monday to Friday from noon to 2:30pm and 7:45pm to 1am, and on Saturday from 7:45pm to 1am. The bar is open from 10:30am to 3pm and 5pm to 2am. Both are closed on Sunday.

Pasticceria Taveggia. Via Visconti di Modrone 2. ☎ **02/7602-1257.**

Established in 1910, this is one of the oldest and most historic cafes of Milan. Behind ornate glass doors set into the 19th-century facade, Taveggia makes the best cappuccino and espresso in town. To match this quality, a variety of brioches, pastries, candies, and tortes is offered. Freshly made on the premises, they can be enjoyed while standing at the bar or seated in the Victorian tea room. All service at the tables is more expensive, as is the rule in Europe. A cappuccino costs 1,800 lire ($1.15) at the bar, 5,500 lire ($3.50) at a table. Food items range from 7,000 to 15,000 lire ($4.50 to $9.60). Taveggia is open Tuesday to Sunday from 7:30am to 8:30pm; closed in August.

SIDE TRIPS FROM MILAN

The ✪ **Certosa (Charter House)** of Pavia, via Monumento 4 (☎ **0382/925613**), marks the pinnacle of the Renaissance statement in Lombardy. The Carthusian monastery is 5 miles north of the town of Pavia and 19 miles south of Milan. It was founded in 1396, but not completed until years afterward, and is one of the most harmonious structures in Italy. The facade, studded with medallions and adorned with colored marble and sculptural work, was designed in part by Amadeo, who worked on the building in the late 15th century. Inside, much of its rich decoration is achieved by frescoes reminiscent of an illustrated storybook. You'll find works by Perugino (*The Everlasting Father*) and Bernardino Luini (*Madonna and Child*). Gian Galeazzo Visconti, the founder of the Certosa, is buried in the south transept.

Through an elegantly decorated portal you enter the cloister, noted for its exceptional terra-cotta decorations. In the cloister is a continuous chain of elaborate "cells," attached villas with their own private gardens and loggia. Admission is free, but donations are requested. It's open May to August, daily from 9 to 11:30am and 2:30 to 6pm; in March, April, September, and October, Tuesday to Sunday from 9 to 11:30am and 2:30 to 5pm; November to February, Tuesday to Sunday from 9 to 11:30am and 2:30 to 4:30pm.

Buses run between Milan and Pavia every hour from 5am to 10pm daily, taking 50 minutes and costing 4,500 lire ($2.90) one-way. Trains leave Milan bound for Pavia once every hour, at a one-way fare of 3,600 lire ($2.30). Motorists can take Route 35 south from Milan or take A7 to Binasco and continue on Route 35 to Pavia and its Certosa.

2 Bergamo

31 miles NE of Milan, 373 miles NW of Rome

Known for its defenses and wealth since the Middle Ages, Bergamo is one of the most characteristic Lombard hill towns. Many of the town's stone fortifications were built on Roman foundations by the medieval Venetians, who looked upon Bergamo one of the gems of their trading network during several centuries of occupation. Set on a hilltop between the Seriana and the Brembana valleys, Bergamo lies in the alpine foothills, in a setting similar to what you might expect in the hills of Umbria or Tuscany. The Old Town (Città Alta), set 900 feet above sea level, is buttressed by and terraced upon the original Venetian fortifications. About half a mile downhill is the New Town (usually identified by residents simply as "Bergamo"), with many 19th- and early 20th-century buildings. A settlement of wide streets and northern Italian bourgeois prosperity, it contains the bus and railway stations, most hotels, and the town's commercial and administrative center. The two-in-one aspect of Bergamo, as well as its role in the mercantile history of Lombardy, was analyzed and praised by one of its strongest champions, the 19th-century French novelist Stendhal.

ESSENTIALS

GETTING THERE   By Train   Trains arrive from Milan once every hour. The trip takes an hour, and a one-way ticket costs 5,000 lire ($3.20). For information about rail connections in Bergamo, call 035/247624.

By Bus   The bus station in Bergamo is across from the train station. For information or schedules, call 035/248150. Buses arrive from Milan once every 30 minutes; a one-way ticket costs 7,000 lire ($4.50).

By Car   From Milan, head east on autostrada A4.

VISITOR INFORMATION   The **tourist information office** is on piazzale Marconi (☎ **035/242226**), open Monday to Friday from 9am to 12:30pm and 3 to 6:30pm.

WHAT TO SEE & DO
THE UPPER TOWN

For the sightseer, the higher the climb the more rewarding the view. The ✪ **Città Alta** is replete with narrow circuitous streets, old squares, splendid monuments, and imposing and austere medieval architecture that prompted d'Annunzio to call it "a city of muteness." To reach the Upper Town, take bus no. 1 or 3, then a 10-minute walk up viale Vittorio Emanuele.

The heart of the Upper Town is **piazza Vecchia,** which has witnessed most of the town's upheavals and a parade of conquerors ranging from Attila to the Nazis. On the square is the Palazzo della Ragione (the town hall), an 18th-century fountain, and the Palazzo Nuovo of Scamozzi (the town library).

A vaulted arcade connects piazza Vecchia with piazza del Duomo. Opening onto the latter is the cathedral of Bergamo, which has a baroque overlay. D'Annunzio said of the **Basilica di Santa Maria Maggiore** that it seemed "to blossom in a rose-filtered light." Built in the R manesque style, the church was founded in the 12th century. Much later it was baroqued on its interior and given a disturbingly busy ceiling. There are exquisite Flemish and Tuscan tapestries displayed that incorporate such themes as the Annunciation and the Crucifixion. The choir, designed by Lotto, dates from the 16th century. In front of the main altar is a series of inlaid panels depicting such themes as Noah's Ark and David and Goliath. The basilica is open Monday to Saturday from 8am to noon and 3 to 6pm and on Sunday from 9am to 12:45pm and 3 to 6pm.

Also opening onto piazza del Duomo is the ✪ **Colleoni Chapel,** which honors the already-inflated ego of the Venetian military hero. The Renaissance chapel, with an inlaid marble facade reminiscent of Florence, was designed by Giovanni Antonio Amadeo, who is chiefly known for his creation of the Certosa in Pavia. For the *condottiere,* Amadeo built an elaborate tomb, surmounted by a gilded equestrian statue (Colleoni, of course, was the subject of one of the world's most famous equestrian statues, which now stands on a square in Venice). The tomb sculpted for the soldier's daughter, Medea, is much less elaborate. Giovanni Battista Tiepolo painted most of the frescoes on the ceiling. It's open Tuesday to Sunday from 9am to 12:30pm and 2 to 6pm. Admission is free.

Facing the cathedral is the baptistery, which dates from the mid-14th century and was rebuilt at the end of the 19th century. The original architect of the octagonal building was Giovanni da Campione.

NEW TOWN

✪ **Galleria dell'Accademia Carrara.** Piazza Giacomo Carrara 82A. ☎ **035/399643.** Admission 3,000 lire ($1.90) adults, free for children 17 and under. Wed–Mon 9:30am–12:30pm and 2:30–5:30pm. Bus: 2, 9, 12, or 14.

Filled with a wide-ranging collection of the works of home-grown artists, as well as Venetian and Tuscan masters, the academy draws art lovers from all over the world. The most important works are on the top floor—head there first if your time is limited. The Botticelli portrait of Giuliano di Medici is well known, and another room contains three different versions of Giovanni Bellini's favorite subject, the *Madonna and Child.* It's interesting to compare his work with that of his brother-in-law, Andrea Mantegna, whose *Madonna and Child* is also displayed, as is Vittore Carpaccio's *Nativity of Maria,* which was seemingly inspired by Flemish painters.

Farther along you encounter a most original treatment of the old theme of the "Madonna and Child"—this one the work of Cosmé Tura of Ferrara. Also displayed are three tables of a predella by Lotto and his *Holy Family with St. Catherine* (wonderful composition), and Raphael's *St. Sebastian.* The entire wall space of another room is taken up with paintings by Moroni (1523–78), a local artist who seemingly did portraits of everybody who could afford it. In the salons to follow, foreign masters, such as Rubens, van der Meer, and Jan Brueghel, are represented, along with Guardi's architectural renderings of Venice and Longhi's continuing parade of Venetian high society.

WHERE TO STAY

Agnello d'Oro. Via Gombito 22, 24100 Bergamo. ☎ **035/249883.** Fax 035/235612. 20 rms. TV TEL. 115,000 lire ($73.60) double. AE, DC, MC, V. Bus: 1 or 3.

Agnello d'Oro is an intimate, old-style country inn right in the heart of Città Alta, facing a handkerchief square with a splashing fountain. It's an atmospheric background for good food or an adequate bedroom, all refurbished in 1995. When you enter the cozy reception lounge, ring an old bell to bring the owner away from the kitchen. You dine at wooden tables and sit on carved ladderback chairs. Among the à la carte offerings are three worthy regional specialties. Try casoncelli alla bergamasca, a succulent ravioli dish, or quaglie farcite (quail stuffed and accompanied by slices of polenta). The room becomes a tavern lounge between meals. The restaurant is closed Sunday night and Monday.

Hotel Cappello d'Oro. Viale Papa Giovanni XXIII 12, 24100 Bergamo. ☎ **035/232503.** Fax 035/242946. 124 rms. MINIBAR TV TEL. 201,000 lire ($128.65) double. Rates include breakfast. AE, DC, MC, V. Parking 30,000 lire ($19.20). Bus: All buses.

The Hotel Cappello d'Oro is a renovated 150-year-old corner building on a busy street in the center of New Town, at Porta Nuova near the railway station. The 19th-century facade has been stuccoed, and the public rooms and the bedrooms are functional, high-ceilinged, and clean. The rooms are adequately but rather plainly furnished, and 80 of them are air-conditioned. If you need a parking space, reserve it along with your room.

Hotel Excelsior San Marco. Piazza della Repubblica 6, 24122 Bergamo. ☎ **035/366111.** Fax 035/223201. 163 rms, 3 suites. A/C MINIBAR TV TEL. 300,001 lire ($192.65) double; 424,000 lire ($271.35) suite. Rates include breakfast. AE, DC, MC, V. Parking 30,000 lire ($19.20) indoors, 20,000 lire ($12.80) outdoors. Bus: 7, 8, 12, or 15.

This 33-year-old establishment at the edge of a city park is about midway between the old and new towns, both of which might be visible from the balcony of your room. The lobby contains a small bar, reddish stone accents, and low-slung leather chairs. The most prominent theme of the ceiling frescoes is the lion of St. Mark. The bedrooms are attractively furnished and comfortable.

WHERE TO DINE

○ Ristorante da Vittorio. Viale Papa Giovanni XXIII 21. ☎ **035/218060.** Reservations required. Main courses 25,000–40,000 lire ($16–$25.60); fixed-priced menu 60,000–130,000 lire ($38.40–$83). AE, DC, MC, V. Thurs–Tues noon–2:30pm and 7:30–9:30pm. Closed 3 weeks in Aug. Bus: All buses. INTERNATIONAL.

This restaurant on the main boulevard in New Town serves a cuisine almost better than anything found in Milan. Set on a corner, the establishment lights its entrance with lanterns. You enter a long and narrow hallway richly paneled with striped pearwood and, in summer, lined with tables laden with all the fruits of the Italian harvest. The menu offers more than a dozen risottos, more than 20 pastas, and around 30 meat dishes, as well as just about every kind of fish that swims in Italy's waters. Examples include grilled "fantasy of the sea" with fresh seasonal vegetables, a breast of goose with a tapenade of black olives, and a tartare of salmon with avocado. The service is efficient, all of it directed by members of the Cerea family, who by now are among the best-known citizens of Bergamo.

Taverna del Colleoni dell'Angelo. Piazza Vecchia 7. ☎ **035/232596.** Reservations required. Main courses 30,000–40,000 lire ($19.20–$25.60); fixed-price lunch (including wine) 50,000 lire ($32). AE, DC, MC, V. Tues–Sat noon–2:30pm and 7:45–10:30pm, Sun noon–2:30pm. Closed Aug 12–25. Bus: 1 or 3. INTERNATIONAL/LOMBARDO.

In the heart of the Città Alta, this restaurant is known to many a gourmet who journeys here to try regional dishes of exceptional merit. The building dates from the 14th century, and is the most historic restaurant in Bergamo. The sidewalk tables are popular in summer, and the view is part of the reward of dining here. Inside, the decor suggests medievalism, but with a fresh approach. The ceiling is vaulted, the chairs are leather, and there's a low-floor dining room with a wood-burning fireplace. Known for its creative interpretations of Lombard cuisines, the establishment features such dishes as a casserole of jumbo shrimp with polenta, homemade flat pasta with a delicate ragoût of wild duck, and Adriatic turbot on a bed of crispy potatoes.

3 Cremona

59 miles SE of Milan, 61 miles S of Bergamo

This city of the violin is found on the Po River plain. Music lovers from all over the world flock to the birthplace of Monteverdi (the father of modern opera) and of Stradivari (latinized to Stradivarius), who made violin making an art. Born in Cremona in 1644, Antonio Stradivari became the most famous name in the world of violin making, far exceeding the skill of his teacher, Nicolò Amati. The third great family name associated with the craft, Guarneri, was also of Cremona.

ESSENTIALS

GETTING THERE   By Train   At least nine trains per day run between Milan and Cremona (trip time: 1¹/₂ hours), at a one-way fare of 7,200 lire ($4.60). Call the **rail station** in Cremona, at via Dante 68 (☎ 0372/22237), for information.

By Bus   One bus a day makes the run from Milan to Cremona, at a one-way fare of 9,300 lire ($5.95). The **bus station** is on via Dante (☎ 0372/29212 for schedules and information).

By Car   From Milan, take Route 415 southeast.

VISITOR INFORMATION   The **tourist information office** is at piazza del Comune 5 (☎ 0372/23233), open Monday to Saturday from 9:30am to 12:30pm and 3 to 6pm and on Sunday from 10am to noon.

WHAT TO SEE & DO

Most of the attractions of the city are centered on the harmonious **piazza del Comune.** The Romanesque **cathedral** dates from 1107, although over the centuries, Gothic, Renaissance, even baroque elements were incorporated. In the typical Lombard style, the pillars of the main portal rest on lions, an architectural detail matched in the nearby octagonal 13th-century baptistery. Surmounting the portal are some marble statues in the vestibule, with a Madonna and Bambino in the center. The rose window over it, from the 13th century, is inserted in the facade like a medallion.

Inside, the pillars are draped with Flemish tapestries. Five arches on each side of the nave are admirably frescoed by such artists as Boccaccio Boccaccino (see his *Annunciation* and other scenes from the life of the Madonna, painted in the early 16th century). Other artists who worked on the frescoes were Gian Francesco Bembo (*Adoration of the Wise Men* and *Presentation at the Temple*), Gerolamo Romanino (scenes from the life of Christ), and Altobello Melone (a *Last Supper*). It's open Monday to Saturday from 7am to noon and 3 to 7pm and on Sunday from 7am to 1pm and 4 to 7pm. Admission is free.

Beside the cathedral is the **Torrazzo,** which dates from the late 13th century and enjoys a reputation as the tallest campanile (bell tower) in Italy, soaring to a height of 353 feet. It's open Monday to Saturday from 10:30am to noon and 3 to 6pm and on Sunday from 10:30am to 12:30pm and 3 to 7pm; from November to Easter, however, it's open only on Sunday and holidays. Admission is 5,000 lire ($3.20) for adults and 3,000 lire ($1.90) for children.

From the same period, and also opening onto the piazza, are the **Loggia dei Militi** and the **Palazzo Comunale** in the typical Lombardy Gothic style.

Museo Stradivariano. Via Palestro 17. ☎ **0372/461886.** Admission 5,000 lire ($3.20) adults, 3,000 lire ($1.90) children. Tues–Sat 9:30am–12:15pm and 3–5:45pm, Sun 9:30am–12:15pm. Bus: 1.

At this museum you can see a collection of models, designs, and shapes and tools of Stradivari (1644–1737). This Italian violin maker produced more than 1,000 strong instruments, many of which are among the best ever made. He learned his craft from Nicolò Amati.

WHERE TO STAY

Hotel Agip. Località San Felice, 26100 Cremona. ☎ **0372/450490.** Fax 0372/451097. 77 rms. A/C MINIBAR TV TEL. 180,000 lire ($115.20) double. Rates include breakfast. AE, DC, MC, V. Free parking. Motorists exit autostrada A21 at Casello and drive 1¹/₂ miles.

This motel, part of a nationwide chain, is at the San Felice exit of the superhighway between Piacenza and Brescia. It's a modern establishment with comfortable bedrooms outfitted with hair dryers and soundproofed against the noise of the nearby highway. A good restaurant on the premises serves copious amounts of food, with a fixed-price menu as well as a self-service area. Parking is easy.

Hotel Continental. Piazza della Libertà 26, 26100 Cremona. ☎ **0372/434141.** Fax 0372/454873. 57 rms, 7 suites. A/C MINIBAR TV TEL. 180,000 lire ($115.20) double; from 230,000 lire ($147.20) suite. Rates include breakfast. AE, DC, MC, V. Parking 15,000–20,000 lire ($9.60–$12.80). Bus: All buses.

Roads from many parts of northern Italy converge on the busy piazza where the comfortable 1980s Hotel Continental stands. It's the best choice in the town, having more atmosphere and personality than the Agip. The staff show an obvious pride in the musical history of Cremona as they eagerly point out their collection of early 20th-century copies of violins by Amati and Stradivari housed in illuminated glass cases. There are also instruments made by master luthiers of Cremona, some of whom seem to be on a first-name basis with the management. A bronze bust of Claudio Monteverdi, the 17th-century composer, looks out over the lobby, and there's a restaurant that can seat 500 people. Each of the hotel's comfortably furnished bedrooms has sound-insulated windows.

WHERE TO DINE

✪ Ceresole. Via Ceresole 4. ☎ **0372/30990.** Reservations required. Main courses 25,000–30,000 lire ($16–$19.20). DC, MC, V. Tues–Sat noon–2:30pm and 8–10:30pm. Closed Jan 22–30 and Aug 6–28. Bus: All buses. ITALIAN.

Near the Duomo, Ceresole is an elegant and well-known culinary institution, lying in a century-old building in the historic heart of Cremona. It's the finest restaurant in the entire surrounding area, and is richly deserving of its star. Behind a masonry facade on a narrow street, it has windows covered with elaborate wrought-iron grills. Specialties include rice with rhubarb, a wide array of delicately seasoned fish (some of them served with fresh seasonal mushrooms and truffles), and the most delectable grilled baby piglet this side of Segovia, Spain. Some of the dishes are based on time-honored regional recipes, including spaghetti alla marinara, straccotto di manza (a regional form of beef stew), and grilled filets of eel.

4 Mantova (Mantua)

25 miles S of Verona, 95 miles SE of Milan, 291 miles NW of Rome

Once a duchy, Mantova had a flowering of art and architecture under the Gonzaga dynasty that held sway over the town for nearly four centuries. Originally an Etruscan settlement, later a Roman colony, it has known many conquerors, including the French and Austrians in the 18th and 19th centuries. Virgil, the great Latin poet, has remained its most famous son (he was born outside the city in a place called Andes). Verdi set *Rigoletto* here, Romeo (Shakespeare's creation, that is) took refuge here, and writer Aldous Huxley called Mantova "the most romantic city in the world."

Mantova is an imposing, at times even austere city, despite its situation near three lakes, Superior, di Mezzo, and Inferiore. It's very much a city of the past and is within easy reach of a number of cities in northern Italy. The historic center is traffic free, but there are buses outside the rail station. Take bus no. 3 to the center.

ESSENTIALS

GETTING THERE   By Train   Mantova has excellent rail connections, lying on direct lines to Milan, Cremona, Modena, and Verona. Six trains a day arrive from Milan, taking $2^1/_4$ hours; a one-way ticket costs 13,600 lire ($8.70). From Cremona, trains arrive every hour (trip time: 1 hour), a one-way ticket costing 5,700 lire ($3.65). The **train station** is on piazza Don Leoni (☎ **0376/321646**).

By Bus   Most visitors arrive by train, but Mantova has good bus connections with Brescia; 17 buses a day make 1-hour and 40 minute journey at a cost of 9,000 lire ($5.75) for a one-way ticket. The **bus station** is on piazza Mondadori (☎ **0376/ 327237**).

By Car   From Cremona (see Section 3 in this chapter), continue east along Route 10.

VISITOR INFORMATION   The **tourist information center** is at piazza Andrea Mantegna 6 (☎ **0376/328253**), open Monday to Saturday from 9am to noon and 3 to 6pm and on Sunday from 9am to noon.

EXPLORING THE PALACES & THE BASILICA

✪ **Museo di Palazzo Ducale.** Piazza Sordello 40. ☎ **0376/320283.** Admission 12,000 lire ($7.70) adults, free for children 17 and under and for seniors 60 and over. Mar–Sept, Sun–Mon 9am–1pm, Tues–Sat 9am–1pm and 2:30–4pm; Oct–Feb, Tues–Sat 9am–1pm and 2:30–3:30pm. Bus: 3.

The ducal apartments of the Gonzagas, with more than 500 rooms and 15 court-yards, are the most remarkable in Italy—certainly when judged from the standpoint of size. Like Rome, the compound wasn't built in a day, or even in a century. The earlier buildings, erected to the specifications of the Bonacolsi family, date from the 13th century. The later 14th and early 15th centuries saw the rise of the Castle of St. George, designed by Bartolino da Novara. The Gonzagas also added the Palatine Basilica of St. Barbara by Bertani.

Over the years the historic monument of Renaissance splendor has lost many of the art treasures collected by Isabella d'Este during the 15th and 16th centuries in her efforts to turn Mantova into "La Città dell'Arte." Her descendants, the Gonzagas, sold their most precious objects to Charles I of England in 1628, and 2 years later most of the remaining rich collection was looted during the sack of Mantova. Even Napoléon did his bit by carting off some of the objects still there.

What remains of the painting collection is still superb, including works by Tintoretto and Sustermans, and a "cut-up" Rubens. The display of classical statuary is impressive, gathered mostly from the various Gonzaga villas at the time of Maria Theresa of Austria. Among the more inspired sights are the Zodiac Room, the Hall of Mirrors (with a vaulted ceiling constructed at the beginning of the 17th century), the River Chamber, the Apartment of Paradise, the Apartment of Troia (with fres-coes by Giulio Romano), and a scale reproduction of the Holy Staircase in Rome.

The most interesting and best-known room in the castle is the Camera degli Sposi (bridal chamber), frescoed by Andrea Mantegna. Winged cherubs appear over a balcony at the top of the ceiling. Look for a curious dwarf and a mauve-hatted portrait of Christian I of Denmark. There are many paintings by Domenico Fetti, along with a splendid series of nine tapestries woven in Brussels and based on cartoons by Raphael. A cycle of frescoes on the age of chivalry by Pisanello has recently been discovered. A guardian takes visitors on a tour to point out the many highlights.

Basilica di Sant'Andrea. Piazza Mantegna. ☎ **0376/328504.** Free admission. Daily 7am–7pm. Bus: 3.

Built to the specifications of Leon Battista Alberti, this church opens onto piazza Mantegna, just off piazza delle Erbe, where you'll find fruit vendors. The actual work on the basilica was carried out by a pupil of Alberti's, Luca Fancelli. However, before Alberti died in 1472, it's said that, architecturally speaking, he knew he had "buried the Middle Ages." The church wasn't completed until 1782, when Juvara crowned it with a dome. As you enter, the first chapel to your left contains the tomb of the great Mantegna (the paintings are by his son, except for the *Holy Family* by the old master himself). The sacristan will light it for you. In the crypt you'll encounter a representation of one of the more fanciful legends in the history of church relics: St. Andrew's claim to possess the blood of Christ, "the gift" of St. Longinus, the Roman soldier who is said to have pierced his side. Beside the basilica is a 1414 campanile (bell tower).

Palazzo Te. Viale Te 13. ☎ **0376/323266.** Admission 10,000 lire ($6.40) adults, 4,000 lire ($2.55) children and seniors 60 and over. Tues–Sun 9am–5:30pm. Bus: 4.

This Renaissance palace, built in the 16th century, is known for its frescoes by Giulio Romano and his pupils. Federigo II, one of the Gonzagas, had the villa built as a place where he could slip away to see his mistress. The name is said to have been derived from the word *tejeto*, which in the local dialect means "a cut to let the waters flow out." This was once marshland drained by the Gonzagas for their horse farm. The frescoes in the various rooms, dedicated to everything from horses to Psyche, rely on mythology for subject matter. The Room of the Giants, the best known, has a scene that depicts heaven venting its rage on the giants who had moved threateningly against it.

WHERE TO STAY

۞ Hotel Dante. Via Corrado 54, 46100 Mantova. ☎ **0376/326425.** Fax 0376/221141. 40 rms. TV TEL. 130,000–135,000 lire ($83.20–$86.40) double. AE, DC, MC, V. Parking 20,000 lire ($12.80). Bus: 3.

Built in 1968, this boxy, modern hotel has a parking area under the recessed entrance area and a marble-accented interior, parts of which look out over a flagstone-covered courtyard. On a narrow street in the busy commercial center, some of the simply furnished but clean rooms have air-conditioning and a minibar.

Mantegna Hotel. Via Fabio Filzi 10B, 46100 Mantova. ☎ **0376/328019.** Fax 0376/368564. 34 rms, 3 suites. A/C TV TEL. 140,000 lire ($89.60) double; 200,000 lire ($128) suite. Rates include breakfast. AE, DC, MC, V. Closed Dec 24–Jan 5. Free parking. Bus: Any bus from the Termini.

Mantegna is in a commercial section of town, a few blocks from one of the entrances to the old city. This six-story hotel has bandbox lines and a facade of light-gray tiles. The lobby is accented with gray and red marble slabs, along with enlargements of details of paintings by (as you probably guessed) Mantegna. About half the units look out over a sunny rear courtyard, although the rooms facing the street are fairly quiet as well. The hotel is a good value for the rates charged.

Rechigi Hotel. Via P. F. Calvi 30, 46100 Mantova. ☎ **0376/320781.** Fax 0376/220291. 60 rms, 5 suites. A/C TV TEL. 230,000 lire ($147.20) double; 280,000 lire ($179.20) suite. AE, DC, MC, V. Parking 25,000 lire ($16). Bus: Any bus from the Termini.

Near the center of the old city stands the Rechigi, a comfortable modern hotel, the best in Mantova, rivaled only by the San Lorenzo at piazza Concordia 14. It's a comfortable, cozy nest, but short on style. Its lobby is warmly decorated with modern paintings, with an alcove bar. The owners maintain the property well, and they have decorated the attractively furnished rooms in good taste. There's a parking garage. Only breakfast is served.

WHERE TO DINE

✪ **L'Aquila Nigra (The Black Eagle).** Vicolo Bonacolsi 4. ☎ **0376/327180.** Reservations recommended. Main courses 20,000–22,000 lire ($12.80–$14.10). AE, DC, MC, V. June–Aug and Nov–Mar, Tues–Sat noon–2pm and 8–10pm; Apr–May, daily noon–2pm and 8–10pm; Sept–Oct, Tues–Sat noon–2pm and 8–10pm, Sun noon–2pm. Closed Jan 1–15 and Aug 8–28. Bus: 3. MANTOVANO/ITALIAN.

This restaurant is in a Renaissance mansion on a narrow passageway by the Bonacolsi Palace. The building's foundations were laid in the 1200s, but the restaurant dates from 1984. Among the excellent food served in the elegant rooms, you can choose from such dishes as pike from the Mincio River, called luccio, served with salsa verde (green sauce) and polenta, as well as other specialties of the region. You also might order a pasta, gnocchi alle ortiche (potato dumplings tinged with puréed nettles), eel marinated in vinegar (one of the most distinctive specialties of Mantova), or tortelli di zucca (with a pumpkin base).

✪ **Il Cigno Trattoria dei Martini.** Piazza Carlo d'Arco 1. ☎ **0376/327101.** Reservations recommended. Main courses 18,000–22,000 lire ($11.50–$14.10). DC, MC, V. Wed–Sun 12:30–1:45pm and 8–9:45pm. Closed Jan 7–14 and Aug 1–22. Bus: 3. MANTOVANO.

This trattoria overlooks a cobblestone square in the old part of Mantova. The exterior is a faded ochre, with wrought-iron cross-hatched window bars within sight of the easy parking on the piazza outside. After passing through a large entrance hall studded with frescoes, you'll come upon the bustling dining rooms. Both freshwater and saltwater fish are featured, as are such dishes as agnoli (a form of pasta) in a light sauce or risotto. Bollito misto (a medley of boiled meats) is served with various sauces, including one made of mustard. One excellent pasta, tortelli di zucca, is stuffed with pumpkin.

Ristorante Pavesi. Piazza delle Erbe 13. ☎ **0376/323627.** Reservations recommended. Main courses 8,000–22,000 lire ($5.10–$14.10). AE, DC, MC, V. Fri–Wed 12:30–2:30pm and 7:30–9:30pm. MANTOVANO.

The Ristorante Pavesi has the advantage of being located under an ancient arcade on the most beautiful square in Mantova. The walls partially date from the 1200s, although the restaurant itself dates from before World War II. It's an intimate family-run establishment with hundreds of antique copper pots hanging randomly from the single barrel vault of the plaster ceiling. There's an antipasti table near the door loaded with delicacies, and in summer, tables spill out into the square. Specialties include agnolotti (a form of tortellini) with meat, cheese, sage, and butter, as well as risotto alla mantovana (with pesto). Also try the roast filet of veal (deboned and rolled), and a well-made blend of fagioli (white beans) with onions.

5 Lake Garda

The easternmost of the northern Italian lakes, Garda is also the largest, 32 miles long and 11$^1/_2$ miles wide at its fattest point. Sheltered by mountains, its scenery, especially the part on the western shore that reaches from Limone to Salo, has been compared to that of the Mediterranean; you'll see olive, orange, and lemon trees, even palms. The almost-transparent lake is ringed with four art cities: Trent to the northeast, Brescia to the west, Mantova (Mantua) to the south, and Verona to the east.

The eastern side of the lake is more rugged, less trampled, but the resort-studded western strip is far more glamorous to the first-timer. On the western side, a circuitous road skirts the lake through one molelike tunnel after another. You can park your car at several secluded belvederes for a panoramic lakeside view. In spring the scenery is splashed with color, everything from wild poppy beds to oleander. Garda is well served by buses, or you can traverse the lake on steamers or motorboats.

ESSENTIALS

GETTING THERE **By Bus and by Train**   Eight buses a day make the one-hour trip from Trent to Riva del Garde. A one-way fare is 5,000 lire ($3.20). The nearest train station is at Roverto, a 20-minute ride from Riva. Frequent buses make the 20-minute trip from the train station to Riva; the one-way bus fare is 3,000 lire ($1.98). For getting around Lake Garda, you'll need a car.

By Car   From Milan or Brescia, autostrada A4 east runs to the southwestern corner of the lake. From Montova, take A22 north to A4 west. From Verona and points east, take A4 west.

GETTING AROUND **By Car**   Most visitors take the road along the western shore, Route S572, north to Riva di Garda. For a less-touristed jaunt, try heading back down the lake along its eastern shore on the Gardesana Orientale (S249). Route S11 runs along the south shore.

A Warning to Motorists: The twisting roads that follow the shores of Lake Garda would be enough to rattle even the most experienced driver. Couple the frightening turns, dimly lit tunnels, and emotional local drivers with convoys of tour buses and trucks that rarely stay in their lane, and you have one of the more frightening drives in Italy. Use your horn around blind curves, and be warned that Sunday is especially risky, since everyone on the lake and from the nearby cities seems to take to the roads after a long lunch with lots of heady wine.

By Boat and by Hydrofoil   Both boats and hydrofoils operate on the lake from Easter through September. For schedules and information, contact Navigazione Lago di Garda (☎ **030/914-1321**).

RIVA DEL GARDA

Some 195 feet above sea level, Riva is the oldest and most traditional resort along the lake. It consists of both an expanding new district and an old town, the latter centered at piazza III Novembre. On the harbor are the Tower of Apponale, dating from the 13th century, and the Rocca, built in 1124 and once owned by the ruling Scaligeri princes of Verona (it has been turned into a museum).

On the northern banks of the lake, between the Benacense plains and towering mountains, Riva offers the advantages of the Riviera and the Dolomites. Its climate is classically Mediterranean—mild in winter and moderate in summer. Vast areas of rich vegetation combine with the deep blue of the lake. Many people come for health cures; others for business conferences, meetings, and fairs. Riva is popular with tour groups from the Germanic lands and from England.

Riva del Garda is linked to the Brenner–Modena motorway (Rovereto Sud / Garda Nord exit) and to the railway (Rovereto station), and is near Verona's Airport.

VISITOR INFORMATION   Tourist information is available at the **Palazzo dei Congressi,** Parco Lido (☎ **0464/554444**), Monday to Saturday from 9am to noon and 3:15 to 7pm and on Sunday from 10am to noon and 4 to 7pm.

WHERE TO STAY

✪ **Hotel du Lac et du Parc.** Viale Rovereto 44, 38066 Riva del Garda. ☎ **0464/551500.** Fax 0464/555200. 172 rms, 6 suites. MINIBAR TV TEL. 310,000–490,000 lire ($198.40–$313.60) double; from 570,000 lire ($364.80) suite for two. Rates include half board. AE, DC, MC, V. Closed Oct 20–Mar 26. Free parking. Bus: Atesina.

This deluxe Spanish-style hotel, the best in town, is set back from the busy road behind a shrub-filled parking lot dotted with stone cherubs. The interior of the main building is freshly decorated, with arched windows and lots of spacious comfort; an enclosed and manicured lawn is visible from the lobby. There's a huge dining room, two additional restaurants, an attractive bar, unusual accessories, and a comfortably sprawling format, each corner of which gives the impression of being part of a large private home. The well-trained staff speaks a variety of languages and seems genuinely concerned with the well-being of their guests. A garden stretches behind the hotel, containing two pools, a lakeside beach, and two tennis courts. Other amenities include a sauna, fitness room, and beauty salon. The bedrooms are well furnished, each with private bath (tub or shower), and 54 are air-conditioned.

Hotel Sole. Piazza III Novembre 35, 38066 Riva del Garda. ☎ **0464/552686.** Fax 0464/ 552811. 52 rms, 3 suites. MINIBAR TV TEL. 95,000–115,000 lire ($60.80–$73.60) double; from 130,000 lire ($83.20) suite. AE, DC, MC, V. Closed Jan 8–Mar and Nov–Dec 25. Parking 10,000 lire ($6.40). Bus: Atesina.

The medium-priced Hotel Sole had far-sighted founders who snared the best position on the waterfront. Although it lags far behind the more resorty du Lac et du Parc, the hotel has amenities worthy of a first-class rating, even though it charges second-class prices. It's an overgrown villa with arched windows and surrounding colonnades, and the interior has time-clinging traditional rooms. The lounge has a beamed ceiling and centers around a cone-shaped hooded fireplace; clusters of antique chairs sit on islands of Oriental carpets. The character and quality of the bedrooms vary considerably according to their position (most of them have views of the lake). Some are almost suites, with living-room areas; the smaller ones are less desirable. Nevertheless, all rooms are comfortable and spotless. You can dine in the formal interior room or on the flagstone lakeside terrace.

⑤ **Hotel Venezia.** Viale Rovereto 62, 38066 Riva del Garda. ☎ **0464/552216.** Fax 0464/ 556031. 24 rms. TV TEL. 138,000–172,000 lire ($88.30–$110.10) double. Rates include breakfast. DC, MC, V. Closed Nov–Easter. Free parking. Bus: Atesina.

The is one of the most attractive budget-category hotels in town. The main section of the Venezia's angular modern building is raised on stilts above a private parking lot set back from the lakefront promenade. The hotel was designed as a villa in 1968, but in the early 1990s it was renovated to become a small, personalized, and unpretentious hotel. The complex is surrounded by trees on a quiet street bordered with flowers and private homes. The reception area is at the top of a flight of red marble steps. There's a private pool surrounded by palmettos, and a clean and sunny dining room with Victorian reproduction chairs. The rooms are pleasantly furnished.

WHERE TO DINE

Most guests in Riva del Garda dine at their hotels. However, there's a good independent eatery.

Ristorante San Marco. Viale Roma 20. ☎ **0464/554477.** Reservations recommended. Main courses 20,000–25,000 lire ($12.80–$16). AE, DC, MC, V. Tues–Sun noon–2:30pm and 7–10pm. Closed Feb. Bus: 1 or 2. ITALIAN/SEAFOOD.

Set back from the lake on one of the main shopping streets of the resort, the San Marco was built in the 19th century as a hotel and converted into a restaurant in 1979. If you arrive early for your reserved table, you can enjoy an apéritif at the bar. The superb food is classically Italian and the service is excellent. You might begin with pasta, such as spaghetti with clams or tortellini with prosciutto. They serve many good fish dishes, including sole and grilled scampi. Among the meat selections, try the tournedos opera or the veal cutlet bolognese. During the summer you may dine in the open-air garden. The owners speak English.

LIMONE SUL GARDA

Limone sul Garda lies 6 miles south of Riva on the western shore of Lake Garda. Taking its name from the fruit of the abundant local lemon tree, Limone is one of the liveliest resorts on the lake, once praised by Goethe and D. H. Lawrence.

Snuggling close to the lake at the bottom of a narrow, steep road, Limone's shopkeepers, faced with no building room on their narrow strip of land, dug right into the rock. There are $2^{1}/_{2}$ miles of beach from which you can bathe, sail, or surf. The only way to get about is on foot, but at Limone you can enjoy playing fields, tennis courts, soccer, and other sports activities, as well as discos.

If you're bypassing Limone, you may still want to make a detour south of the village to the turnoff to Tignale, in the hills. You can climb a modern highway to the town for a sweeping vista of Garda, one of the most scenic spots on the entire lake.

VISITOR INFORMATION From April to September, a **tourist information center** is operated at via Comboni 15 (☎ **0365/954265**). It's open Monday to Friday 9am to 12:30pm and 4 to 6pm.

WHERE TO STAY & DINE

Hotel Capo Reamol. Via IV Novembre 92, 25010 Limone sul Garda. ☎ **0365/954040.** Fax 0365/954262. 60 rms. MINIBAR TV TEL. 316,000–360,000 lire ($202.25–$230.40) double. Rates include half board. MC, V. Closed Nov–Mar. Free parking.

You won't even get a glimpse of this 1960s hotel from the main highway because it nestles on the side of the lake well below road level. Be alert to traffic as you pull into a roadside area indicated by a sign $1^{1}/_{4}$ miles north of Limone, and then follow the driveway down a steep and narrow hill. Since the hotel is built on a series of terraces stretching down to the edge of the lake, you'll go down, not up, to your well-furnished and freshly decorated bedroom after registering at the reception desk. The bar, restaurant, and sports facilities are on the lowest level, sheltered from the lakeside breezes by windbreaks. Many of the public rooms are painted in pastel shades. Clients can swim in the lake or in the pool, and rent windsurfers on the graveled beach. The restaurant serves an Italian cuisine as well as many fine Italian wines. Live music is offered on weekends. A tavern profits, like everything else in the hotel, from views of the water.

⑤ Hotel le Palme. Via Porto 36, 25010 Limone sul Garda. ☎ **0365/954681.** Fax 0365/954120. 28 rms. TEL. 140,000–200,000 lire ($89.60–$128) double. Rates include breakfast. MC, V. Closed Nov–Mar 15. Free parking.

Yesterday's Hero

It's sad and a bit melancholy to visit the former private villa of Gabriele d'Annunzio (1863–1938) at Gardone Riviera and reflect on fleeting fame and the legends of yesterday. Perhaps the young Italians of modern Italy don't even know who this poet and military adventurer was, but in d'Annunzio's heyday he was a legend of towering interest throughout the country.

The writer was notorious in his time, both for his lavish living and particularly for his liaison with Eleonora Duse, the greatest actress of her day, the Sarah Bernhardt of Italy. D'Annunzio broke her heart, along with many other hearts.

As a journalist on the staff of the *Tribuna* in Rome, and a deputy in parliament from 1897 to 1900, d'Annunzio became famous, although the years from 1910 to 1915 saw him living in France to escape his debts. D'Annunzio dominated Italian poetry at the turn of the century and became a leader of the cult of aestheticism. He made no distinction between his poetry and his life. One critic wrote, "He made poetry out of life and life out of poetry." He had an amazing gift for the use of the Italian language, as reflected in the passionate strength of the drama, *Francesca da Rimini* (1902) or the charm of *La Figlia di Iorio* (1904). His writings made him the most popular poet in all of Italy for three decades. He had great influence on young Italian writers of his time. But, sadly, he declined. One long-ago critic put it this way, "Patriotism degenerated into politics, politics into violent dilettantism; national sovereignty became imperialism; love a lascivious sensuality; words became ornamentation."

He ardently advocated Italian entry into World War I, and served in the army, navy, and finally air force (he was to lose an eye in aerial combat). Sensational exploits, including a 1918 reconnaissance flight over Vienna, won him world headlines. In the controversy between Italy and Yugoslavia over the status of Fiume, he led a band of Italian soldiers and occupied the city in September 1919—without the consent of the Italian government. Proclaiming Fiume an "Italian regency of the Carnaro," d'Annunzio ruled as a virtual dictator until the Italian government booted him out in December 1920.

It was rumored that Mussolini would eventually purchase Vittoriale for d'Annunzio to shut up his "poetic mouth." The poet filled the villa with mementos and souvenirs of his conquests in love and war, even dry-docking the prow of the battleship, *Puglia,* in the grounds.

Until his death d'Annunzio continued to collect souvenirs and bizarre objects, often expensive ones, for which he went into excessive debt. In his Sala del Lebbroso, he would lie in a coffin contemplating his own upcoming death. After the war when his "souvenirs" were first inspected by the American press, one reviewer called them "a fascist rummage-sale."

Completely renovated although less desirable than the Capo Reamol, this well-known antique Venetian-style villa with period furniture stands in the shade of two centuries-old palm trees in the historic center of Limone, opening directly onto the shores of Lake Garda. Although extensively remodeled with more private baths, this four-star hotel retains many of its original architectural features. The hotel offers well-furnished bedrooms, each individually decorated, containing a radio. The second floor has a comfortable reading room with a TV set, and the third floor has a wide terrace. The ground floor contains a large dining room with decorative sculpture, opening onto a wide terrace where in fair weather you can order meals and drinks. The cuisine, backed up by a good wine list, is excellent. Because of the popularity of the hotel, it's best to make reservations.

GARDONE RIVIERA

On Garda's western shore 60 miles east of Milan, Gardone Riviera is well equipped with a number of good hotels and sporting facilities. Its lakeside promenade attracts a wide range of predominantly European tourists for most of the year. When it used to be chic for patrician Italian families to spend their holidays by the lake, many of the more prosperous built elaborate villas not only in Gardone Riviera, but in neighboring Fasano (some have been converted to receive guests). The town also has the major attraction along the lake, which you may want to visit even if you're not lodging for the night.

GETTING THERE   The resort lies 26 miles south of Riva on the west coast. Three buses per day arrive from Riva. The trip takes 1 1/4 hours, and a one-way ticket costs 4,600 lire ($2.95). Two buses make the 3-hour trip from Milan; a one-way ticket is 14,300 lire ($9.15). For schedule information call **0365/21061.**

VISITOR INFORMATION   The **tourist information office** is at corso della Repubblica 35 (☎ **0365/20347**). It's open April to October, Monday to Saturday from 9am to 12:30pm and 4 to 7pm; November to March, Monday to Friday from 9am to 12:30pm and 3 to 6pm and on Saturday from 9am to 12:30pm.

VISITING D'ANNUNZIO'S VILLA

Vittoriale, via Vittoriale 12 (☎ **0365/20130**), was once the private home of Gabriele d'Annunzio (1863–1938), the poet and military adventurer, another Italian who believed in *la dolce vita,* even when he couldn't afford it. Most of the celebrated events in d'Annunzio's life occurred before 1925, including his love affair with Eleonora Duse and his bravura takeover as a self-styled commander of a territory being ceded to Yugoslavia. In the later years of his life, until he died in the winter before World War II, the national hero lived the grand life at his private estate on Garda.

North of the town, Vittoriale is open year round; in the winter, Tuesday to Sunday from 9am to 12:30pm and 2 to 4pm (to 5pm in spring and autumn); in summer, Tuesday to Sunday from 8:30am to 8pm. Admission to the grounds only is 7,000 lire ($4.50), or 15,000 lire ($9.60) to the house and grounds. The furnishings and decor passed for avant garde in their day, but now evoke the Radio City Music Hall of the 1930s. D'Annunzio's death mask is of morbid interest, and his bed with a "Big Brother" eye adds a curious touch of Orwell's *1984* (over the poet's bed is a faun casting a nasty sneer). The marble bust of Duse seems sadly out of place, but the manuscripts and old uniforms perpetuate the legend. In July and August d'Annunzio plays are presented at the amphitheater on the premises. It's a bizarre monument to a hero of yesteryear. To reach it, head out via Roma, connecting with via Colli.

WHERE TO STAY

Ⓢ **Bellevue Hotel.** Via Zanardelli 81, 25083 Gardone Riviera. ☎ **0365/290088.** Fax 0365/290088. 33 rms. TEL. 135,000 lire ($86.40) per person. Rates include breakfast. V. Closed Oct 10 to 1 week before Easter. Free parking. Bus: Casino.

This villa perched up from the main road has many terraces surrounded by trees and flowers—and an unforgettable view. You can stay here even on a budget, enjoying the advantages of lakeside villa life complete with swimming pool. The lounges are comfortable, and the dining room affords a view through the arched windows and excellent meals (no skimpy helpings here). In fair weather you can dine in a large garden.

✪ **Grand Hotel.** Via Zanardelli 74, 25083 Gardone Riviera. ☎ **0365/20261.** Fax 0365/ 22695. 180 rms, 14 suites. MINIBAR TV TEL. 270,000–320,000 lire ($172.80–$204.80) double; 350,000–400,000 lire ($224–$256) suite. Rates include breakfast. Half board 35,000 lire ($22.40) per person extra. AE, DC, MC, V. Closed Oct 18–Mar 26. Parking 20,000 lire ($12.80). Bus: SIA.

When it was built in 1881, this was the most fashionable hotel on the lake and one of the biggest resort hotels of its kind in Europe. Its massive tower is visible for miles around. The hotel's reputation as a glamorous resting place convinced Churchill to stay for an extended period in 1948, where he fished, wrote letters, and recovered from his frantic lifestyle. The establishment still boasts a distinguished clientele that returns year after year. It isn't difficult to get lost in the almost-endless high-ceilinged corridors. The main salon's sculpted ceilings, parquet floors, and elegantly comfortable chairs make it an ideal spot for reading or watching the lake. The dining room offers the good food and old-time splendor you would expect from such a place. All the rooms face the lake, avoiding the roadside noise. A series of garden terraces, a private beach, and a swimming pool are scattered throughout the extensive gardens.

A NEARBY PLACE TO STAY

Fasano del Garda is a satellite resort of Gardone Riviera, 1 1/4 miles to the north. Many prefer it to Gardone.

✪ **Hotel Villa del Sogno (Villa of the Dream).** Via Zanardelli 107, Fasano del Garda, 25080 Gardone Riviera. ☎ **0365/290181.** Fax 0365/290230. 33 rms, 5 suites. TV TEL. 320,000– 460,000 lire ($204.80–$294.40) double; 460,000–600,000 lire ($294.40–$384) suite. Rates include breakfast. AE, DC, MC, V. Closed Oct 20–Apr 1. Free parking. Bus: Casino.

This 1920s re-creation of a Renaissance villa offers sweeping views of the lake and spaciously comfortable, old-fashioned bedrooms. This resort hotel is far superior to anything in the area, having long ago surpassed the Grand (see above). Set a few hundred yards above the water, with easy access to its private beach, the hotel also has a pool and is ringed with terraces filled with cafe tables and pots of petunias and geraniums, which combine with bougainvillea and jasmine to brighten the surroundings. The baronial stairway of the interior, as well as many of the ceilings and architectural details, were crafted from wood. The bedrooms are well furnished, each with private bath (tub or shower). Nine rooms are air-conditioned.

WHERE TO DINE

Most visitors to this resort take their meals at their hotels. However, there are some good independent dining selections.

Ristorante la Stalla. Strade per il Vittoriale. ☎ **0365/21038.** Reservations recommended. Main courses 12,000–26,000 lire ($7.70–$16.65); fixed-price menu 25,000 lire ($16). AE, DC, MC, V. Wed–Mon 12:30–2:30pm and 7:30–9:30pm. Closed Jan 8–20. Bus: SIA. INTERNATIONAL.

This charming restaurant is frequented by local families for miles around. In a handcrafted stone building with a brick-columned porch, outdoor tables, and an indoor ambience loaded with rustic artifacts and crowded tables, the restaurant is set in a garden ringed with cypresses on a hill above the lake. To get there, follow the signs toward il Vittoriale (the building was commissioned by d'Annunzio as a horse stable) to a quiet street with singing birds and residential houses. Depending on the shopping that day, the specialties might include a selection of freshly prepared antipasti, risotto with cuttlefish, or crêpes fondue. Polenta is served with Gorgonzola and walnuts, or you may prefer filet of beef in a beer sauce. Sunday afternoon can be crowded.

✪ **Villa Fiordaliso.** Via Zanardelli 132. ☎ **0365/20158.** Reservations required. Main courses 24,000–55,000 lire ($15.35–$35.20); fixed-price menu 75,000 lire ($48) for five courses, 120,000 lire ($76.80) for seven courses. AE, DC, MC, V. Tues–Sun 12:30–2:30pm and 7:30–10:30pm. Closed Jan 10–Feb. Bus: SIA. ITALIAN.

This deluxe establishment is a Liberty-style (art nouveau) villa from 1924 with gardens stretching down to the edge of the lake. The restaurant is not only the most scenic and beautiful on Lake Garda, it also serves the finest cuisine, personalized by the chef, and likely to include a terrine of eel and salmon in a herb-and-onion sauce, a timbale of rice and shellfish with curry, and several succulent fish and meats grilled over a fire. Other specialties include ravioli with Bergoss (a salty regional cheese), sardines from a nearby lake baked in a herb crust, and scampi in a sauce of tomatoes and wild onions. This little bastion of fine food has impeccable service to match.

SIRMIONE

Perched at the tip of a narrowing strip on the southern end of the Lake, Sirmione juts out 2^1/2 miles into Lake Garda. Noted for its thermal baths (used to treat deafness), the town is a major resort, just north of the autostrada connecting Milan and Verona, that blooms in spring and wilts in late autumn.

The resort was a favorite of Giosuè Carducci, the Italian poet who won the Nobel Prize for literature in 1906. In Roman days it was frequented by still another poet, Catullus. Today the **Grotto di Catullo,** on via Catullo (☎ **030/916157**), is the chief sight, an unbeatable combination of Roman ruins and a panoramic view of the lake. You can wander at leisure through the remains of this once-great villa from April to September, Tuesday to Sunday from 9am to 6pm; October to March, Tuesday to Sunday from 9am to 4pm. Admission is 8,000 lire ($5.10) for adults, free for children 17 and under and for seniors 60 and over.

At the entrance to the town stands the moated 13th-century **Rocca Scaligera** castle, piazza Castello (☎ **030/916468**), which once belonged to the powerful Scaligeri princes of Verona. You can climb to the top and walk the ramparts April to September, daily from 9am to 6pm; October to March, Tuesday to Sunday from 9am to 12:30pm. Admission is 8,000 lire ($5.10).

GETTING THERE   Sirmione lies 3^1/2 miles from the A4 autostrada exit and 5 miles from the town of Desanzano. Buses run from Brescia and from Verona to Sirmione every hour. The trip time for either trip (depending on traffic) is 1 hour. A one-way ticket from Brescia costs 5,400 lire ($3.45), and a one-way ticket from Verona is 4,600 lire ($2.95). There is no rail service. The nearest train terminal is at Desenzano. From there, there is frequent bus service to Sirmione; the bus trip takes 30 minutes and a one-way fare is 2,100 lire ($1.35).

VISITOR INFORMATION   The **tourist information center** is at viale Marconi 2 (☎ **030/916245**). It's open April to October, daily from 9am to 12:30pm and 3 to 6pm; November to March, Monday to Friday from 9am to 12:30pm and 3 to 6pm and on Saturday from 9am to 12:30pm.

WHERE TO STAY

During the peak summer season motorists need a hotel reservation to take their vehicles into the crowded confines of the town. However, there's a large parking area at the entrance to the town. Accommodations are plentiful. The only way to visit Sirmione is on foot. All the hotels below are in the center of town.

⑤ Flaminia Hotel. Piazza Flaminia 8, 25019 Sirmione. ☎ **030/916078.** Fax 030/916193. 45 rms. A/C TV TEL. 150,000–180,000 lire ($96–$115.20) double. Rates include breakfast. AE, DC, MC, V. Free parking. Bus: SIA.

This is one of the best little hotels in Sirmione, with a number of facilities and amenities. Recent renovations put air-conditioning in all the rooms. One of the more modern accommodations, it lies near the town center right on the lakefront, with a terrace extending out into the water. The bedrooms are made attractive by French doors opening onto private balconies. The lounges are furnished in a functional modern style. Breakfast is the only meal served.

Grand Hotel Terme. Viale Marconi 1, 25019 Sirmione. ☎ **030/916261.** Fax 030/916568. 58 rms, 15 junior suites, 1 suite. A/C MINIBAR TV TEL. 380,000 lire ($243.20) double; 430,000 lire ($275.20) junior suite; from 750,000 lire ($480) suite. Rates include breakfast. AE, DC, MC, V. Closed Oct 27–Apr 5. Free parking. Bus: SIA.

This rambling, three-story hotel at the entrance of the old town is on the lake next to the Scaligeri Castle. Way down the scale from the resort hotel of Villa Cortine (see below), it's the second-best choice in town, known especially for its lake-bordering garden. The wide marble halls and stairs lead to well-furnished, balconied bedrooms. Constructed in 1948, the hotel has contemporary furnishings, plus a number of spa and physical-therapy facilities and a swimming pool. The food served in the indoor-outdoor dining room is excellent, with such offerings as prosciutto and melon, risotto with snails, fettuccine with fresh porcini, and a wide choice of salads and fruits.

⑤ Olivi. Via San Pietro 5, 25019 Sirmione. ☎ **030/990-5365.** Fax 030/916472. 60 rms. A/C TV TEL. 165,000–200,000 lire ($105.60–$128) double. Rates include breakfast. AE, DC, MC, V. Closed Jan 3–Mar 31 and Nov 15–Dec 27. Free parking. Bus: SIA.

A creation of the sun-loving owner Cerini Franco, this hotel has an excellent location, on the rise of a hill in a grove of olive trees at the edge of town. The all-glass walls of the major rooms never let you forget you're in a garden spot of Italy. Even the compact and streamlined bedrooms have walls of glass leading out onto open balconies. The hotel serves typically Italian meals. Sometimes live music is featured, even country music when the hotel stages a barbecue. The hotel offers an outdoor swimming pool, a solarium, and laundry and room service.

◑ Villa Cortine Palace. Via Grotte 12, 25019 Sirmione. ☎ **030/990-5890.** Fax 030/916390. 43 rms, 6 suites. A/C TV TEL. 500,000–720,000 lire ($320–$460.80) double; 800,000–1,150,000 lire ($512–$736) suite. Rates include breakfast. AE, DC, MC, V. Closed Oct 22–Apr 1. Free parking. Bus: SIA.

This first-class choice is luxuriously set apart from the town center, surrounded by imposing, sumptuous gardens. For serenity, atmosphere, professional service, and even good food, there's nothing to equal it in Sirmione. The hotel was originally built in 1905, although in 1957 a new wing greatly increased its amenities and capacities. Today all but a handful of its bedrooms are in this new wing, with the bar and reception area in the original building. The century-old landscaping in the hotel's park contains a formal entrance through a colonnade, and winding lanes lined with cypress trees, wide-spreading magnolias, and flower-bordered marble fountains with classic sculpture. Each room has a private bath or shower, and some offer a minibar. The interior has one formal drawing room, with much gilt and marble—it's positively palatial.

WHERE TO DINE

Ristorante Grifone da Luciano. Via delle Bisse 5. ☎ **030/916097.** Main courses 12,000–20,000 lire ($7.70–$12.80). AE, DC, MC, V. Thurs–Tues noon–2:30pm and 7–10:30pm. Closed Nov–Easter. Bus: SIA. INTERNATIONAL.

One of the most attractive restaurants in town is separated from the castle by a row of shrubbery, a low stone wall, and a moat. From your seat on the flagstone terrace, you'll have a view of the crashing waves and the plants that ring the dining area. The headquarters of this establishment is an old stone house surrounded with olive trees, but many diners gravitate toward the low glass-and-metal extension stretching toward the lake. The tables inside are covered with candles and flowers. The food includes many varieties of fish and many standard Italian dishes. The place doesn't necessarily rate a rave, but traditionalists like it, and the chef is talented, keeping the quality high and the prices moderate.

La Rucola. Vicolo Strentelle 5. ☎ **030/916326.** Reservations recommended. Main courses 23,000–30,000 lire ($14.70–$19.20); fixed-price menu 80,000 lire ($51.20). AE, MC, V. Fri–Wed 12:30–2:30pm and 7:30–10:30pm. Closed Jan–Feb 9. Bus: SIA. ITALIAN.

In the heart of town, this restaurant lies on a small alley a few steps from the main gate leading into Sirmione. The building looks like a vine-laden, sienna-colored country house and was originally a stable 150 years ago. Full meals, served in a modernized interior, could include fresh salmon, langoustines, mixed grilled fish, and a more limited meat selection. Meats are most often grilled or flambéed, including Florentine beefsteak. Newer items on the menu include gnocchetti de riso with baby squid and squid ink and filet of turbot with potatoes and a zabaglione of spinach. Good pasta dishes include spaghetti with clams and several local specialties. Many of the desserts are made for two, including crêpes Suzette and banana flambé.

6 Lake Como

Everything noble, everything evoking love—that was how Stendhal characterized fork-tongued Lake Como. Others have called it "the looking glass of Venus," and Virgil pronounced it "our greatest lake." More than 30 miles north of Milan, it's a shimmering deep blue spanning $2^1/2$ miles at its widest point. With its flower-studded gardens, villas built for the wealthy of the 17th and 18th centuries, and mild climate, Larius (as it was known to the Romans) is among the most scenic spots in all of Italy.

ESSENTIALS

GETTING THERE AND GETTING AROUND   By Train and by Bus   Trains arrive daily from Milan every hour. The trip takes 40 minutes, and a one-way fare is 7,700 lire ($4.95). Once you arrive by train, you can take buses to explore the rest of the lake. SPT, Piazza Matteotti (☎**031/304744**) offers bus service to the most important centers on the lake. A one-way fare to the most popular resort at Bellagio costs 4,100 lire ($2.60). Travel time depends on the traffic.

By Car   The city of Como is 25 miles north of Milan and is reached via the autostrada A9. Once at the Como, a small road (S583) leads to the popular resort of Bellagio.

By Boat and by Hydrofoil   From Como, there are seven boat trips daily exploring the lake, each lasting two hours. There are also seven 45-minute hydrofoil trips offered daily. Both the boats and the hydrofoils dock at lungo Lario in front of the piazza Cavour in Como. For information or schedules, call **031/304060,** or stop at the dockside ticket office.

COMO

At the southern tip of the lake, 25 miles north of Milan, Como is known for its silk industry. Most visitors will pass through here to take a boat tour of the lake. If you do so, you'll cross piazza Cavour, the lakeside square and the center of local life.

Because Como is also an industrial city, we have generally shunned it for overnighting, preferring to anchor into one of the more attractive resorts along the lake, like Bellagio. However, train passengers who don't plan to rent a car may prefer Como (the city, that is) for convenience.

For centuries the destiny of the town has been linked to that of Milan. Como is called the world capital of silk, the silkmakers of the city joining communal hands with the fashion designers of Milan. Como has been making silk since Marco Polo first returned with silkworms from China (since the end of World War II Como has left the cultivating of silk to the Chinese and just imported the thread to weave into fabrics). Designers such as Giorgio Armani and Bill Blass come here to discuss the patterns they want with silk manufacturers.

VISITOR INFORMATION   The **tourist information center** is at piazza Cavour 17 (☎ **031/269712**), open Monday to Saturday from 9am to 12:30pm and 2:30 to 6pm.

What to See & Do

Before rushing off on a boat for a tour of the lake, you may want to look at the **Cattedrale di Como,** piazza del Duomo (☎ **031/304429**). Construction began in the 14th century in the Lombard-Gothic style, and labored on through the Renaissance until the 1700s, when the Duomo was officially "crowned." The exterior of the cathedral, frankly, is more interesting than the interior. Dating from 1487, it's lavishly decorated with statues, including Pliny the Elder (A.D. 23–79) and the Younger (A.D. 62–113), whom one writer once called "the beautiful people of ancient Rome." Inside, look for the 16th-century tapestries depicting scenes from the Bible.

Where to Stay

Hotel Barchetta Excelsior. Piazza Cavour 1, 22100 Como. ☎ **031/261817.** Fax 031/302622. 82 rms, 3 suites. A/C MINIBAR TV TEL. 250,000 lire ($160) double; 320,000 lire ($204.80) suite. Rates include breakfast. AE, DC, MC, V. Parking 35,000 lire ($22.40). Bus: Any bus from the Termini.

This first-class hotel is set at the edge of the main square in the commercial section of town. Its original construction was a century ago, but it was demolished and reconstructed in a more modern format in 1957. Major additions have been made to the hotel, including the alteration of its restaurant and an upgrading of the bedrooms, which are comfortably furnished, often with a balcony overlooking this heartbeat square and the lake. All accommodations have radios, among other amenities, and most have lake views. There's a parking lot behind the hotel, plus a covered garage just over 50 yards away.

Metropole & Suisse. Piazza Cavour 19, 22100 Como. ☎ **031/269444.** Fax 031/300808. 71 rms, 3 suites. A/C MINIBAR TV TEL. 240,000 lire ($153.60) double; 270,000 lire ($172.80) suite. AE, DC, MC, V. Closed Dec 20–Jan 7. Parking 20,000 lire ($12.80). Bus: Any bus from the Termini.

This hotel offers good value in clean, convenient accommodations. Near the cathedral on a major lake-fronting square, it's composed of three lower floors dating from around 1700 with upper floors added about 60 years ago. The hotel began life as a waterfront store at the edge of the lake (the square you see today is a landfill dating from 1850). A photograph of the Swiss creator of the hotel with his staff in 1892 hangs behind the reception desk. Each of the bedrooms is different, rich with character for the most part. Many repeat clients have staked out their favorite rooms. A parking garage and the city marina are nearby. A popular restaurant, Imbarcadero, under separate management, fills most of the ground floor of the hotel.

WHERE TO DINE

Ristorante Imbarcadero. In the Hotel Metropole & Suisse, Piazza Cavour 20. ☎ **031/270166.** Reservations recommended. Main courses 22,000–32,000 lire ($14.10–$20.50); fixed-price menu 38,000 lire ($24.30). AE, DC, MC, V. Daily 12:30–2:30pm and 7:30–10pm. Closed Jan 1–8. Bus: All buses. INTERNATIONAL.

Established more than a decade ago in a 300-year-old building near the edge of the lake, this restaurant is filled with a pleasing blend of carved Victorian chairs, panoramic windows with marina views, and potted palms. The outdoor terrace set up on the square in summer is ringed with shrubbery and illuminated with evening candlelight. The restaurant attracts clients with demanding tastes who take pleasure in the first-class ingredients deftly handled by the kitchen. The chef makes his own tagliatelle, or you may want to order spaghetti with garlic, oil, and red pepper. Main courses include beef alla Rossini, veal cutlet milanese, sea bass with olives and wine, and whitefish direct from the lake. Desserts are often lavish productions, including banana flambé and crêpes Suzette.

CERNOBBIO

Cernobbio, 3 miles northwest of Como and 33 miles north of Milan, is a small, fashionable resort frequented by the wealthy of Europe because of its deluxe hotel, the 16th-century Villa d'Este. But its idyllic anchor on the lake has also attracted a less affluent tourist, who'll find a number of third- and even fourth-class accommodations as well.

VISITOR INFORMATION   The **tourist information center** is at via Regina 33B (☎ **031/510198**) and is open Monday to Saturday from 9:30am to 12:30pm and 3 to 6pm; closed January.

WHERE TO STAY

✪ **Grand Hotel Villa d'Este.** 22010 Cernobbio. ☎ **031/3481.** Fax 031/34844. 108 rms, 48 suites. A/C MINIBAR TV TEL. 650,000–895,000 lire ($416–$572.80) double; 1,575,000–1,675,000 lire ($1,008–$1,072) suite. Rates include breakfast. AE, DC, MC, V. Closed from the end of Oct to Mar 1. Free parking. Bus: 6.

One of Italy's most legendary hotels, the Villa d'Este was originally built in 1568 as a lakeside home and pleasure pavilion for Cardinal Tolomeo Gallio. One of the most famous Renaissance-era hotels in the world, designed in the neoclassical style by Pellegrino Pellegrini di Valsolda, it passed from owner to illustrious owner for 300 years until it was transformed into a hotel in 1873.

Today the hotel remains a kingdom in itself, a historic and splendid palace surrounded by 10 acres of some of the finest hotel gardens in Italy. The interior lives up to the almost enthralling beauty of the grounds. Noteworthy public areas include the Salon Napoleone, whose silken wall coverings were embroidered especially for the emperor's visit; the Canova room, centered around a statue of Venus by the room's namesake; a Grand Ballroom suitable for some of the most festive banquets in Europe; and a bar outfitted in shades of gold and white. Throughout, frescoed ceilings, impeccable antiques, and attentive service create one of the world's most envied hotels. Each bedroom has a decor of its own, and a roster of historically famous former occupants. Some 34 of the hotel's 156 accommodations are in the Queen's Pavilion, an elegant annex built in 1856.

Dining/Entertainment: The hotel contains two restaurants (the Grill Room and the Verandah), both of culinary merit. Both serve formal à la carte dinners. The cookery is sublime. Lunches are less expensive, especially in summer when light buffets are set on long tables within view of the gardens. Throughout the year there's always at least a live pianist on most nights, and in midsummer a small orchestra plays dance music three evenings a week.

Services: Concierge, room service, baby-sitting, laundry, valet, hairdresser, massage.

Facilities: A swimming pool whose filtered waters float atop Lake Como; access to the world-class golf course at nearby Montofano; red-clay tennis courts; gym, sauna, Turkish bath; squash court; waterskiing and other sports.

Hotel Asnigo. Via Noseda 2, 22012 Cernobbio. ☎ **031/510062.** Fax 031/510249. 30 rms, 3 suites. MINIBAR TV TEL. 180,000 lire ($115.20) double; 230,000 lire ($147.20) suite for three. Rates include breakfast. AE, DC, MC, V. Free parking. Bus: 6.

The Asnigo, 1 mile northeast of the center of Cernobbio, calls itself *un piccolo Grand Hotel.* Commanding a view of Como from its hillside perch at piazza Santo Stefano, this is a good little first-class hotel set in its own garden. Its special and subtle charms have been known to a lake-loving set of British visitors since 1914.

An Englishwoman writes: "Last summer I did something not recommendable to your readers: I went on a trip to Italy with my nephew and his wife from America, who quite frankly patronize a higher type of establishment than I do. Naturally, they were lured to the Villa d'Este on Como. I, fortunately, was able to find a splendid little hotel in the hills, the Asnigo. The proprietor was most helpful, the meals flawless and beautifully served, the room spotlessly clean and comfortable. After being a dinner guest one night at the Villa d'Este, I returned the hospitality the following evening by inviting my relatives for a most enjoyable meal at my hotel. At least they learned that good food and comfort are not the sole domain of a deluxe hotel." We echo her sentiments.

BELLAGIO

Sitting on a promontory at the point where Lake Como forks, 48 miles north of Milan and 18 miles northeast of Como, Bellagio is with much justification given the label of "The Pearl of Larius." It has also been called "the prettiest town in Europe." A sleepy veil hangs over the arcaded streets and little shops. Bellagio is rich in memories, having attracted fashionable, even royal visitors such as Leopold I of Belgium, who used to own the 18th-century Villa Giulia. Still going strong, although no longer the aristocratic address today that it was, Bellagio is a 45-minute drive north of Como.

VISITOR INFORMATION   The **tourist information center** is at piazza della Chiesa 14 (☎ **031/950204**). It's open May to September, daily from 9am to noon and 3 to 6pm; October to April, Monday and Wednesday to Saturday from 8:30am to 12:15pm and 2:30 to 6pm.

WHAT TO SEE & DO

To reach many of the places in Bellagio, you must climb streets that are really stairways. Its lakeside promenade blossoms with flowering shrubbery. From the town, you can take tours of Lake Como and enjoy several sports such as rowing and tennis, or just lounge at Bellagio Lido.

The most important attraction of Bellagio is the garden of the **Villa Melzi** museum and chapel, on lungolario Marconi (☎ **031/950318**). The villa was built in 1808 for Duke Francesco Melzi d'Eril, vice-president of the Italian republic founded by Napoléon. Franz Liszt and Stendhal are among the illustrious guests who have stayed here. The park has many well-known sculptures, and if you're here in the spring you can enjoy the azaleas. Today it's the property of Count Gallarti Scotti, who opens it from April to the end of October, daily from 9am to 6pm. Admission is 6,000 lire ($3.85).

If time allows, try to explore the gardens of the **Villa Serbelloni,** piazza della Chiesa (☎ **031/950204**), the Bellagio Study and Conference Center of the Rockefeller Foundation (not to be confused with the Grand Hotel Villa Serbelloni by the waterside in the village). The villa is not open to the public, but you can visit the park on 1¹/₂-hour guided tours starting at 10:30am and 4pm. Tours are conducted Tuesday to Sunday from mid-April to mid-October at a cost of 10,000 lire ($6.40) per person; the proceeds go to local charities.

A NEARBY VILLA

From Como, car-ferries sail back and forth across the lake to Cadenabbia on the western shore, another lakeside resort, with hotels and villas. Directly south of Cadenabbia on the run to Tremezzo, the **Villa Carlotta** (☎ **0344/40405**) is the most-visited attraction of Lake Como—and with good reason. In a serene setting, the villa is graced with gardens of exotic flowers and blossoming shrubbery, especially rhododendrons and azaleas. Its beauty is tame, cultivated, much like a fairy tale that recaptures the halcyon life available only to the very rich of the 19th century. Dating from 1847, the estate was named after a Prussian princess, Carlotta, who married the duke of Sachsen-Meiningen. Inside the villa are a number of art treasures, including Canova's *Cupid and Psyche,* and neoclassical statues by Bertel Thorvaldsen, a Danish sculptor who died in 1844. There are also neoclassical paintings, furniture, and a stone-and-bronze table ornament that belonged to Viceroy Eugene Beauharnais on display. From March 15 to 31 and in October, it's open daily from 9am to noon and 2 to 4:30pm; April to September, daily from 9am to 6pm. Admission is 10,000 lire ($6.40) for adults, 6,000 lire ($3.85) for seniors 60 and over, and 5,000 lire ($3.20) for children 7 to 14.

WHERE TO STAY & DINE

✪ Grand Hotel Villa Serbelloni. Via Roma 1, 22021 Bellagio. ☎ **031/950216,** or 800/223-6620 in the U.S. Fax 031/951529. 95 rms, 5 suites. MINIBAR TV TEL. 419,000–620,000 lire ($268.15–$396.80) double; 800,000–995,000 lire ($512–$636.80) suite. Rates include breakfast. AE, DC, MC, V. Closed Nov–Mar. Free parking. Bus: Bellagio bus from Como.

This lavish old hotel is for those born to the grand style of life. On the lake, its surpassed only by the Villa d'Este. It stands proud and serene at the edge of town against a backdrop of hills, surrounded by beautiful gardens of flowers and semitropical plants. It's perched on the lakefront, and guests sunbathe on the waterside terrace or doze under a willow tree. Inside, the public rooms rekindle the spirit of the baroque: the grand drawing room with painted ceiling, marble columns, a glittering chandelier, and ornate gilt furnishings and the mirrored neoclassical dining room. The bedrooms are wide-ranging, from elaborate suites with a recessed tile bath, baroque furnishings, and lake-view balconies to more chaste quarters. The most desirable rooms open onto the lake; 13 are air-conditioned. In 1993 it opened a fitness and beauty center.

Hotel du Lac. Piazza Mazzini 32, 22021 Bellagio. ☎ **031/950320.** Fax 031/951624. 48 rms. A/C MINIBAR TV TEL. 180,000 lire ($115.20) double. Rates include breakfast. MC, V. Closed Nov–Mar 25. Parking 12,000 lire ($7.70). Bus: Bellagio bus from Como.

The Hotel du Lac was built 150 years ago, when the waters of the lake came directly up to the front door of the ochre facade. Landfill has since created piazza Mazzini, and today there's a generous terraced expanse of flagstones in front, on which are café tables and an arched arcade. The bedrooms are comfortably furnished, containing such amenities as satellite TV, minibar, hair dryers, and air-conditioning. On the second floor is a glassed-in terrace restaurant, and guests can also bask in the sun or relax in the shade on the rooftop garden, opening onto panoramic views of the lake.

⑤ **Hotel Florence.** Piazza Mazzini 45, 22021 Bellagio. ☎ **031/950342.** Fax 031/951722. 36 rms. TV TEL. 195,000–205,000 lire ($124.40–$131.20) double; 280,000 lire ($179.20) suite. Rates include breakfast. AE, MC, V. Closed Oct 25–Apr 1. Bus: Bellagio bus from Como.

The entrance to this green-shuttered villa, one of the most charming middle-bracket choices in the resort, is under a vaulted arcade near the ferryboat landing. Wisteria climbs over the iron balustrades of the lake-view terraces. The entrance hall's vaulted ceilings are supported by massive timbers and granite Doric columns; there's even a Tuscan fireplace. The main section of the hotel was built around 1720, although most of what you see today was added around 1880. For 150 years the hotel has been run by the Ketzlar family, who originally acquired it as a private villa. You'll probably be welcomed by the charming Roberta Ketzlar, her brother Ronald, and their mother, Friedl. The bedrooms are scattered amid spacious upstairs sitting and dining areas, and often have high ceilings, antiques, and lake views. In the 1990s the hotel was vastly improved, with the addition of a gourmet restaurant and an America Bar, which becomes a kind of jazz club on Sunday evenings.

TREMEZZO

Reached by frequent ferries from Bellagio, Tremezzo, 48 miles north of Milan and 18 miles north of Como, is another popular west-shore resort that opens onto a panoramic view of Lake Como. Around the town is a district known as Tremezzina, with luxuriant vegetation that includes citrus trees, palms, cypresses, and magnolias. Tremezzo is the starting point for many excursions. Its accommodations are much more limited than those in Bellagio.

VISITOR INFORMATION   There's a **tourist information center** at via Regina 3 (☎ **0344/40493**). It's open May to October, Monday to Wednesday and on Friday and Saturday from 9am to noon and 3:30 to 6:30pm.

WHERE TO STAY

Grand Hotel Tremezzo Palace. Via Regina 8, 22019 Tremezzo. ☎ **0344/40446.** Fax 0344/40201. 98 rms, 2 suites. MINIBAR TV TEL. 230,000–280,000 lire ($147.20–$179.20) double; from 350,000 lire ($224) suite. Rates include breakfast. AE, DC, MC, V. Closed Nov–Mar 1. Free parking. Transportation: Ferry or bus from Bellagio or hydrofoil from Como.

Built in 1910 on a terrace several feet above the traffic of the lakeside road, this hotel is one of the region's best examples of the Italian Liberty style, and the unquestioned leading choice at this resort. In 1990 most of the pale-yellow hotel was discreetly modernized, and the bedrooms on two of the hotel's four floors were garnished with air-conditioning. (This allows guests a choice. Many reject the air-conditioning in favor of open-windowed access to lakefront breezes.) The bedrooms are comfortable, traditionally furnished, and high-ceilinged, and priced according to views of either the lake or the park and garden extending from the back of the hotel. Rooms that face the lake are more expensive, and usually have private balconies.

Dining/Entertainment: The hotel contains three restaurants as well as an outdoor dining terrace that closes during inclement weather. All serve regional and international cuisines. On a platform beside the lake is the Club l'Escale, a bar that's popular with hotel guests and residents of surrounding communities. There's also a billiard room, heliport, and conference facilities.

Services: Room service, baby-sitting, laundry, valet.

Facilities: A very large park, a large and elegant pool in back of the hotel (and a slightly less desirable one in front), a tennis court, a lido beside the lake, and a jogging track.

Hotel Bazzoni & du Lac. Via Regina 26, 22019 Tremezzo. ☎ **0344/40403.** Fax 0344/41651. 123 rms. TEL. 132,000–157,000 lire ($84.50–$100.50) double. Rates include breakfast.

AE, DC, MC, V. Closed Oct 15–Apr 12. Free parking. Ferry from Ballagio or hydrofoil from Como.

There was an older hotel on this spot during Napoléon's era, bombed by the British 5 days after the official end of World War II. Today the reconstructed hotel is a collection of glass-and-concrete walls, with prominent balconies at the edge of the lake. It's one of the best choices in a resort town filled with hotels of grander format but much less desirable accommodations. The main restaurant on the ground floor has a baronial but unused fireplace, contemporary wall frescoes of the boats on the lake, and scattered carvings. The pleasantly furnished sitting rooms include antique architectural elements from older buildings. A summer restaurant near the hotel's entrance is constructed like a small island of glass walls.

A NEARBY PLACE TO STAY

✪ **Grand Hotel Victoria.** Via lungolago Castelli 7–11, 22017 Menaggio. ☎ **0344/32003.** Fax 0344/32992. 49 rms, 4 junior suites. A/C MINIBAR TV TEL. 300,000–350,000 lire ($192–$224) double; from 430,000 lire ($275.20) suite. Rates include breakfast. Half board 55,000 lire ($35.20) per person extra. AE, DC, MC, V. Free parking. Ferry from Bellagio or hydrofoil from Como.

This is one of the best hotels on the lake, built in 1806 along a lakeside road bordered with chestnut trees. It was luxuriously renovated in 1983, with attention paid to the preservation of the ornate plasterwork whose tendrils and curlicues entwine the ceiling vaults. There is a lavish use of marble, big windows, and carving on the white facade that resembles the heads of water sprites. Some sections have been purchased for private use by vacationing individuals, but the majority of the rooms are available to rent. The modern furniture and amenities in the bedrooms include a radio, plus a private bath with wall tiles designed by Valentino. The beach in front of the hotel is one of the best spots on Lake Como for windsurfing, especially between 3 and 7pm.

Dining/Entertainment: Guests enjoy drinks on the outdoor terrace near the stone columns of the tree-shaded portico, or in the antique-filled public rooms. The restaurant has well-prepared food, art nouveau chandeliers, and an embellished ceiling showing all the fruits of an Italian harvest scattered amid representations of lyres and mythical beasts.

Services: Room service, baby-sitting, laundry, valet.

Facilities: Swimming pool, beach, tennis court, private boats.

WHERE TO DINE

Al Veluu. Via Rogaro 11, Rogaro di Tremezzo. ☎ **0344/40510.** Reservations recommended. Main courses 18,000–35,000 lire ($11.50–$22.40). AE, MC, V. Wed–Mon noon–2pm and 7:30–9:30pm. Closed Nov–Mar 1. LOMBARD/INTERNATIONAL.

Al Veluu, 1 mile north of the resort in the hills, is an excellent regional restaurant with plenty of relaxed charm and lots of personalized attention from owner Carlo Antonini and his son, Luca. The terrace's well-prepared tables offer a panoramic sweep of the lake, and the rustic dining room with its fireplace and big windows is a welcome refuge in inclement weather. Most of the produce comes freshly picked from the garden; even the butter is homemade. The best cheeses come from a local farmer whose home is visible among the rocks and trees of a nearby mountain. The menu is based on the fresh, light, and flavorful cuisine of northern Italy. Examples include missoltini (dried fish from the lake, marinated, and grilled with olive oil and vinegar), penne al Veluu (made with spicy tomato sauce), risotto al Veluu (made with champagne sauce and fresh green peppers), and an unusual lamb pâté.

7 Lake Maggiore

The waters of this lake wash up on the banks of Piedmont and Lombardy in Italy, but its more austere northern basin (Locarno, for example) lies in the mountainous region of Switzerland. It stretches a distance of more than 40 miles, and it's 6 1/2 miles at its widest stretch. A wealth of natural beauty awaits you: mellowed lakeside villas, dozens of lush gardens, sparkling waters, panoramic views. A veil of mist seems to hover at times, especially in early spring and late autumn.

Maggiore is a most rewarding lake to visit from Milan, especially because of the Borromean Islands in its center (most easily reached from Stresa). If you have time, drive around the entire basin; on a more limited schedule, you may find the western, resort-studded shore the most scenic.

ESSENTIALS

GETTING THERE   By Train   The major resort of the lake, Stresa, is just 1 hour by train from Milan on the Milan-Domodossola line. Service is every hour, and a one-way ticket costs from 7,000 lire to 12,000 lire ($4.50 to $7.70), depending on the train. There is no bus service to the lake.

By Car   From Milan, a 51-mile drive northwest along autostrada A8 (staying on E62 out of Gallarate until it joins Route SS33 up the western shore of the lake) will take you to Stresa, the major resort.

GETTING AROUND   By Car   Route S33 goes up the west side of the lake to Verbania, where it becomes S34 on its way to the Swiss town of Locarno, a distance of about 25 miles. If you want to encircle the lake you'll have to clear Swiss Customs before passing through such famed tourist resorts as Ascona and eventually Locarno. From Locarno you can head south again along the eastern, less touristy shore, which becomes Route SS493 on the Italy side. At Luino, you can cut off on SS233 then A8 to return to Milan, or continue along the lake shore (the road becomes SS629) to the southern point again where you can get E62 back toward Milan.

By Boat   Boats that explore the lake depart from the piazza Marconi along corso Umberto I in Stresa. For boat schedules, contact Navigazione Sul Lago Maggiore, viale F. Baracca 1 (☎ **0322/46651**) in the lakeside town of Arona.

STRESA

On the western shore, 407 miles northwest of Rome and 51 miles northwest of Milan, Stresa has skyrocketed from a simple village of fisherfolk to a first-class international resort. Its vantage on the lake is almost unparalleled, and its level of hotel accommodations is superior to that of other Maggiore resorts in Italy. Scene of sporting activities and an international **Festival of Musical Weeks** (beginning in late August), it swings into action in April, then dwindles in popularity at the end of October. Depending on traffic, Stresa is reached in an hour from Milan on the Simplon Railway. There are no buses for getting about town, but Stresa is small and can easily be walked.

VISITOR INFORMATION   The **tourist information center** is at via Prìncipe Tomaso 70–72 (☎ **0323/30150**). It's open May to September, Monday to Saturday from 8:30am to 12:30pm and 3 to 6:15pm and on Sunday from 9am to noon; October to April, Monday to Friday from 8:30am to 12:30pm and 3 to 6:15pm and on Saturday from 8:30am to 12:30pm.

WHERE TO STAY

⊝ Albergo Ariston. Corso Italia 60, 28049 Stresa. ☎ **0323/31195.** Fax 0323/31195. 11 rms. 130,000 lire ($83.20) double. Rates include breakfast. Half board 90,000 lire ($57.60) per person extra. AE, DC, MC, V. Closed Dec–Apr 1. Free parking.

Here is a good bargain. The hotel is listed as third class, but its comfort is superior. The rooms are well kept and attractively furnished. Nonresidents can stop in for a meal, ordering a lunch or dinner on the terrace, which has a panoramic view of the lake and gardens. Your hosts are the Balconi family.

❖ Grand Hotel des Iles Borromées. Corso Umberto I 67, 28049 Stresa. ☎ **0323/30431.** Fax 0323/32405. 172 rms, 13 suites. A/C MINIBAR TV TEL. 510,000–575,000 lire ($326.40–368) double; 733,000–1,700,000 lire ($469.1–$1,088) suite. AE, DC, MC, V. Free parking.

Set on the edge of the lake in a flowering garden, this hotel is Stresa's leading resort hotel—far superior to such runners-up as the Astoria. You can see the Borromean Islands from many of the bedrooms, all of which are furnished in an Italian/French Empire style, including rich ormolu, burnished hardwoods, plush carpets, and pastel color schemes. Each room has a private bath (tub or shower), which look as if every quarry in Italy had been scoured for matched marble. The hotel opened its doors for the first time in 1863, attracting titled notables. But it wasn't until the opening of the Simplon Tunnel in 1906 that the hotel (and Stresa) could profit from mass tourism. Famous guests have included J. P. Morgan, and Hemingway ordained that the hero of *A Farewell to Arms* should stay here to escape from World War I. The public rooms, elegantly capped with two-tone ornate plasterwork and crystal chandeliers, were even the scene of a top-level meeting among the heads of state of Italy, Great Britain, and France in an attempt to stave off World War II. Today all this splendor can be part of your vacation, but it won't come cheap.

In addition, the hotel also operates the Residenza, with 27 rooms in a building separate from the main hotel. Prices here are 20% less, and each room is decorated in a modern style, with air-conditioning, TV, minibar, and private bath.

Dining/Entertainment: The hotel restaurant serves a cuisine based on specialties of Lombardy and the Piedmont. Special dishes include filet of perch with sage and tenderloin cooked on a black stone.

Services: Room service, laundry, baby-sitting.

Facilities: A medically supervised health and exercise program in the Centro Benessere, two outdoor swimming pools, a tennis court, and a sauna.

Hotel Astoria. Corso Umberto I 31, 28049 Stresa. ☎ **0323/32566.** Fax 0323/933785. 95 rms, 4 suites. MINIBAR TV TEL. 270,000 lire ($172.80) double; 330,000 lire ($211.20) suite. Rates include breakfast. AE, DC, MC, V. Closed from the end of Oct to Easter. Free parking.

A 5-minute walk from either the railway station or the center of Stresa, this hotel fronting the lake was partially rebuilt in 1993, giving an even more modern gloss to an already contemporary hotel. A medium-priced establishment, it's expressly for sunseekers who want a heated swimming pool, Turkish bath, small gym, roof garden, and Jacuzzi. It features triangular balconies—one to each bedroom—jutting out for the view. The bedrooms are streamlined and spacious. The public lounges have walls of glass opening toward the lake view and the garden. The portion of the dining room favored by most guests is the wide-paved, open-air front terrace, where under shelter you dine on good Italian and international cuisine while enjoying a view of Maggiore.

Hotel Moderno. Via Cavour 33, 28049 Stresa. ☎ **0323/30468.** Fax 0323/933775. 59 rms. MINIBAR TV TEL. 160,000–200,000 lire ($102.40–$128) double. Rates include breakfast. AE, DC, MC, V. Closed Nov–Mar. Free parking.

A block from the lake and boat-landing stage, the Moderno lies in the center of Stresa. The hotel dates from the turn of the century, but subsequent modernization, including the most recent one in 1989, has rendered the building's original lines unrecognizable. The bedrooms each have a personalized decor, with good beds and phones for direct dialing and automatic wakeup calls. The Moderno has three restaurants, which is unusual for such a small hotel: the hotel dining room (reserved for hotel guests only), the Gazebo, and Damigiana.

Regina Palace. Corso Umberto I 33, 28049 Stresa. ☎ **0323/933777.** Fax 0323/933776. 167 rms, 7 suites. MINIBAR TV TEL. 360,000 lire ($230.40) double; 420,000–650,000 lire ($268.80–$416) suite. Rates include breakfast. AE, DC, MC, V. Closed Oct–Easter. Parking 15,000 lire ($9.60) in garage, free outside.

The Regina Palace was built in 1908 in a boomerang shape whose central curve faces the lakefront. The art deco illuminated-glass columns (lit from within) inside are capped with gilded Corinthian capitals, and a wide marble stairwell is flanked with carved oak lions. There's a swimming pool in the rear, and a guest roster that has included George Bernard Shaw, Ernest Hemingway, Umberto I of Italy, and Princess Margaret. Lately, about half the guests are American, many of them with the tour groups that stream through Stresa. The bedrooms are equipped with all the modern comforts, and many have views of the Borromean Islands. Facilities include tennis and squash courts, a Jacuzzi, saunas, a health club, and a Turkish bath. The hotel also has two dining rooms, one reserved only for residents. The other dining choice is the Charleston, an à la carte restaurant.

WHERE TO DINE

✪ **Ristorante Emiliano.** Corso Italia 50. ☎ **0323/31396.** Reservations required. Main courses 20,000–38,000 lire ($12.80–$24.30); fixed-price menu 55,000 lire ($35.20). AE, DC, MC, V. Wed–Mon 12:30–2:30pm and 7:30–10pm. Closed Dec 8–Jan 20. EMILIANA.

As its name suggests, the cuisine comes from the Emilia-Romagna region of Italy, and the decor makes it the most elegant non-hotel restaurant in Stresa. It also serves the best food on Lake Maggiore. The entrance is sheltered by a wrought-iron and glass canopy, which extends partially over the outdoor tables with their view of the lake. Changing menu specialties might include slices of fresh goose liver served with a fondant of onions, pink cannelloni stuffed with a purée of fish, braised Piedmont pigeon in wine and herb sauce, or roulades of filet of lakefish prepared with saffron. Desserts include several kinds of crêpes and cassatas.

⊛ Taverna del Pappagallo. Via Principessa Margherita 46. ☎ **0323/30411.** Reservations not accepted. Main courses 15,000–20,000 lire ($9.60–$12.80); pizzas 8,000–16,000 lire ($5.10–$10.25). No credit cards. Thurs–Mon 11:30am–2:30pm and 6:30pm–midnight. ITALIAN.

This formal little garden restaurant and tavern is operated by the Ghiringhelli brothers, who turn out some of the least expensive meals in Stresa. Specialties include gnocchi, many types of scaloppine, scalamino allo spiedoe fagioli (grilled sausage with beans), and saltimbocca alla romana (a veal-and-prociutto dish). At night pizza is king (try the pizza Regina). The service has a personal touch.

THE BORROMEAN ISLANDS

The heart of Lake Maggiore is occupied by this chain of tiny islands, which were turned into sites of lavish villas and gardens by the Borromeo clan. Boats leave about every 30 minutes in summer, and the trip takes 3 hours. The **navigation offices** at Stresa's center port (☎ **0323/30393**) are open daily from 8am to 8pm. The best deal is to purchase an excursion ticket for 13,000 lire ($8.30) from the harbor at Stresa entitling you to go back and forth to all three islands during the day.

EXPLORING THE ISLANDS

The major stopover is on the **Isola Bella** (Beautiful Island), a must if you have time for only one sight. Dominating the island is the 17th-century **Borromeo Palazzo** (☎ 0323/30556). From the front the figurines in the garden evoke the appearance of a wedding cake. On conducted tours, you are shown through the light and airy palace, from which the views are remarkable. Napoléon slept here. A special feature is the six grotto rooms, built piece by piece like a mosaic. In addition, there's a collection of quite good tapestries, with gory cannibalistic animal scenes. Outside, the white peacocks in the garden enchant year after year. The palace and its grounds are open March to October, daily from 9am to noon and 1:30 to 5:30pm; the annual closing is October 25 to March 26. To visit the palace and its gardens costs 12,000 lire ($7.70) for adults and 6,000 lire ($3.85) for children 6 to 15, free for children 5 and under.

The largest of the chain, **Isola Madre** (Mother Island) is visited chiefly for its botanical gardens. You wander through a setting ripe with pomegranates, camellias, wisteria, rhododendrons, bougainvillea, hibiscus, hydrangea, magnolias, even a cypress tree from the Himalayas. You can also visit the 17th-century **palace** (☎ 0323/31261), which contains a rich collection of 17th- and 18th-century furnishings. Of particular interest is a collection of 19th-century French and German dolls belonging to Countess Borromeo and the livery of the House of Borromeo. The unique 18th-century marionette theater, complete with scripts, stage scenery, and devices for sound, light, and other special effects, is on display. Peacocks, pheasants, and other birds live and roam freely on the grounds. Visiting hours are 9am to noon and 1:30 to 5:30pm daily from March 27 to October 24. Admission to both palace and grounds is 12,000 lire ($7.70) for adults, 6,000 lire ($3.85) for children 6 to 15, and free for children 5 and under.

Isola del Pescatori (Fisher's Island) is without major sights or lavish villas, but in many ways it's the most colorful. Less a stage setting than its two neighbors, it's inhabited by fisherfolk who live in cottages. Good walks are possible in many directions.

VILLA TARANTO

Back on the mainland near the resort of Pallanza, north of Stresa, the **Giardini Botanici** at Villa Taranto, via Vittorio Veneto 111, Verbania-Pallanza (☎ 0323/556667), are spread over more than 50 acres of the Castagnola Promontory jutting out into Lake Maggiore. In this dramatic setting between the mountains and the lake, more than 20,000 species of plants from all over the world thrive in a well-tended and cultivated institution, begun in 1931 by a Scotsman, Capt. Neil McEacharn. Plants range from rhododendrons and azaleas to specimens from such faraway places as Louisiana. Seasonal exhibits include fields of Dutch tulips (80,000 of them), Japanese magnolias, giant water lilies, cotton plants, and rare varieties of hydrangeas. The formal gardens are carefully laid out with ornamental fountains, statues, and reflection pools. Among the more ambitious creations is the elaborate irrigation system that pumps water from the lake to all parts of the gardens, and the Terrace Gardens, complete with waterfalls and swimming pool.

The gardens are open April to October, daily from 8:30am to 6:30pm. To arrange a **guided tour,** contact the Palazzo dei Congressi di Stresa (☎ 0323/30389). Guides will take you on tours, which last more than an hour. You may also take a round-trip boat ride from Stresa, which docks at the Villa Taranto pier adjoining the entrance to the gardens. You pay an admission of 12,000 lire ($7.70) for adults, 10,000 lire ($6.40) for children 6 to 14.

Piedmont & Valle d'Aosta

Towering, snow-capped alpine peaks; oleander, poplar, and birch trees; sky-blue lakes; river valleys and flower-studded meadows; the chamois and the wild boar; medieval castles; Roman ruins and folklore; the taste of vermouth on home ground; Fiats and fashion—northwestern Italy is a fascinating area to explore.

Piedmont is largely agricultural, although its capital, Torino (Turin), is one of Italy's front-ranking industrial cities (with more mechanics per square foot than any other location in Europe). The influence of France is strongly felt, both in the dialect and in the kitchen.

Valle d'Aosta (really a series of valleys) has traditionally been associated with Piedmont, but in 1948 it was given wide-ranging autonomy. Most of the residents (in this least-populated district in Italy) speak French. Closing in Valle d'Aosta to the north on the French and Swiss frontiers are the tallest mountains in Europe, including Mont Blanc (15,780 ft.), the Matterhorn (14,690 ft.), and Monte Rosa (15,200 ft.). The road tunnels of Great St. Bernard and Mont Blanc (opened in 1965) connect France and Italy.

EXPLORING PIEDMONT & VALLE D'AOSTA BY CAR

Day 1   Turin, 140 miles southwest of Milan, is the gateway to the region. The autostrada network of Italy links Piedmont and the Valle d'Aosta with the rest of the country and with neighboring France. Travelers from France can go through the Mont Blanc Tunnel outside Chamonix. From the south of Italy, the A21 autostrada cuts northwest into Turin. Once in Turin, visit the Egyptian Museum and the Capella della Santa Sindone, the latter housing the Holy Shroud. If possible, see the Royal Palace—all too much for one day, but perhaps that's all the time you have.

☕   **TAKE A BREAK   Porto Di Savona,** piazza Vittorio Veneto 2 in Turin (☎ **011/817-3500**), is one of the city's oldest restaurants, opening onto a view of the Po valley. Turin has far finer restaurants than this, but if you're a first-time visitor, you can order some of the most typical dishes of Piedmont here, including bagna cauda and bollito misto, the latter a mixed medley of boiled meats with an excellent sauce.

Day 2   From Turin take the A5 autostrada to Aosta to acquaint yourself with its surrounding scenic valley. The old town is still contained within its Roman walls. Visit its major Roman monuments and dine in a typical tavern that night.

Day 3   For a final look at the region, continue on the route west (SS26) to the resort of Courmayeur, 22 miles northwest of Aosta. Although primarily a ski resort, it's visited chiefly for those wanting to take the cable-car lift across Mont Blanc all the way to Chamonix, France. This is one of the most thrilling aerial experiences in northern Italy and will occupy your day. You can return to Courmayeur for the night—or, perhaps better yet—anchor in the satellite resort of Entrèves where you can visit La Maison de Filippo, or "Chalet of Gluttony," and fill up on all the specialties of the region.

A TASTE OF PIEDMONT & VALLE D'AOSTA

The Piedmont kitchen is a fragrant delight, differing in many respects from the Milanese, especially in its liberal use of garlic. What it lacks in subtlety is often made up in large portions of hearty fare.

In the upper Po Valley, an arc of the central and western Alps, the Piedmont and Aosta Valley are industrial in part but have a rich agricultural bounty. Orchards, vineyards, and fields of grass for cattle raising abound.

In such a setting the cookery is often hearty, suitable for the cold, bracing alpine air. First-rate roasts and plenty of stews (heavily flavored with garlic) are featured. *Agnoletti* is the most popular pasta dish, a small ravioli stuffed with minced meat. The most savory fare is a *bagna cauda,* a sauce made with olive oil, butter, garlic, and anchovies, into which vegetables such as chard or celery sticks are dipped. Chamois meat, often served with a wine sauce flavored with herbs and anchovies, is the choicest dish on the table.

A *fonduta* is a sauce of melted Fontina cheese, flavored with white truffles, often from Alba. Although frighteningly expensive, these truffles are sprinkled over many an elegant dish in the region, including risotto and sliced turkey breasts.

The best-known wines of the region are Asti Spumante, a brilliant straw color with a delicate bouquet and abundant foam, the prototype of Italian sparkling wines and served with desserts. Barolo often accompanies the red-meat roasts so popular in the area. It's aged for about seven years, emerging the color of an orange-yellow brick, with a delicate bouquet of violets. Ranked along with Barbera and chianti, it's considered one of the finest wines in Italy.

Barbera, served with game and spicy dishes, is a dark ruby red in color, with the tonic taste of the vine, its bouquet evocative of both the cherry and the violet. The region's fabled apéritif is Vermouth di Torino, often served iced. It's made from the base of a neutral white wine flavored with Moscato d'Asti, herbs, and spices, along with spirits, bitters, sugar, and tonic. Its color ranges from tawny to dark yellow.

1 Torino (Turin)

140 miles SW of Milan, 108 miles NW of Genoa, 414 miles NW of Rome

In Turin, the capital of Piedmont, the Italian Risorgimento (unification) was born. During the years when the United States was fighting its Civil War, Turin became the first capital of a unified Italy, a position it later lost to Florence. Turin was once the capital of Sardinia. Much of the city's history is associated with the House of Savoy, a dynasty that reigned for nine centuries, even presiding over the kingdom of Italy when Victor Emmanuel II was proclaimed king of Italy in 1861. The family ruled, at times in name only, until the monarchy was abolished in 1946.

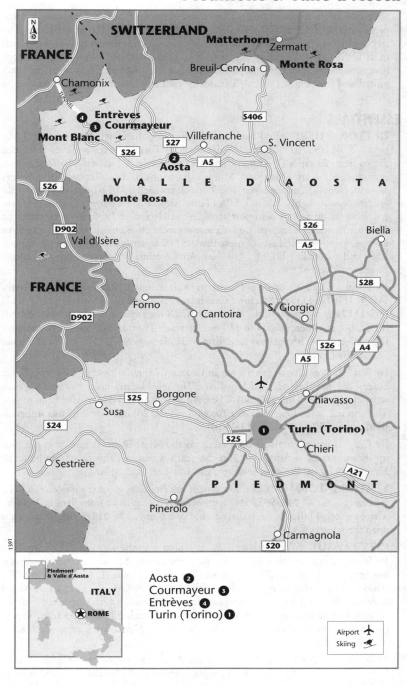

FRANCE

SWITZERLAND

Matterhorn ○ Zermatt

Monte Rosa

Breuil-Cervina ○

Chamonix

S406

Entrèves

④ ③ Courmayeur

Mont Blanc

S26 S27 Villefranche ○ S. Vincent ○

② Aosta A5

V A L L E   D '   A O S T A

S26 Monte Rosa

S26

D902

Val d'Isère ○

S26

A5

Biella ○

FRANCE

S28

Forno ○ Cantoira ○ S. Giorgio

D902

S26 A4

A5

✈

S25 Borgone ○ Chiavasso ○

Susa ○

S24 ① Turin (Torino)

Sestrière ○ S25 Chieri ○

A21

P I E D M O N T

Pinerolo ○

Carmagnola ○

S20

Piedmont
& Valle d'Aosta

ITALY

★ ROME

Aosta ②
Courmayeur ③
Entrèves ④
Turin (Torino) ①

Airport ✈
Skiing ✍

1391

517

In spite of having been subject to extensive bombings, Turin found renewed prosperity after World War II, largely because of the Fiat manufacturers based here. The city has been called the Detroit of Italy. Many buildings were destroyed, but much of its 17th- and 18th-century look remains. Turin is well laid out, with wide streets, historic squares, churches, and parks. For years it has had a reputation as the least-visited and least-known of Italy's major cities. Easily reached, Turin is on the Po River.

ESSENTIALS

GETTING THERE   **By Plane**   Alitalia flies into the **Caselle International Airport** (☎ **011/567611**), about 9 miles north of Turin. It receives direct scheduled flights from 22 cities (7 domestic and 15 international, including London, Paris, Frankfurt, Stuttgart, Düsseldorf, Munich, Barcelona, Lisbon, Amsterdam, Brussels, Madrid, Geneva, Coppenhagen, and Zurich); it's used by 13 scheduled carriers that operate regular flights. SAGAT SPA (Turin Airport Management Company) is responsible for all aspects of airport activities. In December 1993, it inaugurated the New Air Passenger Terminal, one of the most technologically advanced structures in Europe, covering a total area of more than 43,000 square yards, with five operational levels and six loading bridges. The New Air Terminal handles up to three million passengers a year.

By Train   Turin is a major rail terminus, with arrivals at **Stazione di Porta Nuova** (☎ **011/561-3333**) or **Stazione Centrale,** corso Vittorio Emanuele II (☎ **011/665-1111**), in the heart of the city. It takes 1¼ hours to reach Turin by train from Milan, but anywhere from 9 to 11 hours to reach Turin from Rome, depending on the connection. The one-way fare from Milan is 13,600 lire ($8.70); from Rome, 51,000 lire ($32.65).

By Bus   It's possible to catch a bus in Chamonix (France) and go to Turin. Three buses a day run through the Mont Blanc Tunnel. The trip takes 3½ hours; a one-way ticket is 40,000 lire ($25.60). There are also 15 buses a day arriving from Milan. This trip is 2 hours long and costs 16,000 lire ($10.25) one-way. For **bus information,** call SATEM (☎ **011/311-1616**).

By Car   If you're coming from France via the Mont Blanc Tunnel, you can pick up the autostrada at Aosta. You can also reach Turin by autostrada from both the French and Italian Rivieras, and there's an easy link from Milan.

VISITOR INFORMATION   For tourist information, go to the office of **A.P.T.,** via Roma 226 (☎ **011/535901**), open Monday to Saturday from 9am to 7:30pm. There's another office at the train station, Porta Nuova (☎ **011/531327**), which is open the same hours.

CITY LAYOUT   The Stazione di Porta Nuova is in the very center of town. The **Po River,** which runs through Turin, lies to the east of the station. One of the Po main arteries running through Turin is **corso Vittorio Emanuele II,** directly north of the station. Turin is also a city of fashion, with excellent merchandise in its shops. You'll want to walk along the major shopping street, **via Roma,** which begins north of the station, leading eventually to two squares that join each other, piazza Castello and piazza Reale. In the middle of via Roma, however, is **piazza San Carlo,** which is the heartbeat of Turin.

SPECIAL EVENTS   Turin stages two major cultural *fêtes* every year, including the **Sere d'Estate** festival in July, with programs devoted to dance, music, and theater. Classical music reigns supreme in September at the month-long **Settembre Musica,**

with performances at various parts of the city. For details about these festivals, contact **Assesorato per la Cultura,** piazza San Carlo 161 (☎ **011/576-5573**).

FAST FACTS: TURIN

American Express   The representative of American Express in Turin, Malan Viaggi, is at via Accademia delle Scienze 1 (☎ 011/562-4288). It's closed Saturday afternoon and all day Sunday. Some services are not available on Saturday.

Drugstore   If you need an all-night drugstore, try Pharmacie, corso Vittorio Emanuele II 66 (☎ 011/541271).

Emergencies   In a life-threatening emergency, dial **113.** To seek first aid or to call an ambulance, phone **5747.** A major **police station** is at corso Vinzaglio 10 (☎ **011/55881**).

Medical Care   For a medical problem, call Mauriziano Umberto. The hospital is located at largo Turati 62 (☎ 011/50801).

Post Office   The main post office is at via Alfieri 10 (☎ 011/535894); closed on Sunday.

Taxis   To summon a taxi, phone 011/5737.

Telephone   Public telephones are at via Roma 18 bis, via Arsenale 13, and the Stazione di Porta Nuova.

EXPLORING THE CITY

Begin your explorations at ✪ **piazza San Carlo.** Although heavily bombed during World War II, it's still the loveliest and most unified square in the city. It was designed by Carlo di Castellamonte in the 17th century, and covers about $3^1/2$ acres. The two churches are those of Santa Cristina and San Carlo. Some of the most prestigious figures in Italy once sat on this square, sipping coffee and plotting the unification of Italy.

✪ **Egyptian Museum.** In the Palazzo dell'Accademia delle Scienze, via Accademia delle Scienze 6. ☎ **011/561-7776.** Admission 12,000 lire ($7.70) adults, free for children 17 and under and for seniors 60 and over. June–Sept, Tues and Thurs 9am–7pm, Wed and Fri–Sun 9am–2pm; Oct–May, Tues–Sat 9am–7pm, Sun 9am–2pm. Closed Jan 1, May 1, and Dec 25. Bus: 56 or 61.

You'll find the most interesting museums housed in the Guarini-designed, 17th-century Science Academy Building. The Egyptian Museum's collection is so vast that it's rated second only to the one at Cairo. Of the statuary, that of Ramses II is the best known, but there's one of Amenhotep II as well. A room nearby contains a rock temple consecrated by Thutmose III in Nubia. In the crowded wings upstairs, the world of the pharaohs lives on (one of the prize exhibits is the "Royal Papyrus," with its valuable chronicle of the Egyptian monarchs from the 1st through the 17th Dynasties). The funerary art is exceptionally rare and valuable, especially the chapel built for Maia and his young wife, and an entirely reassembled tomb (that of Kha and Merit, 18th Dynasty), discovered in good condition at the turn of the century.

Galleria Sabauda. In the Palazzo dell'Accademia delle Scienze, via Accademia delle Scienze 6. ☎ **011/547440.** Admission 8,000 lire ($5.10) adults, free for children 17 and under and for seniors 60 and over. Guided tours Tues–Sat 9am–2pm, Sun 9am–2pm. Bus: 1 or 4.

In the same building as the Egyptian Museum, you can see one of the richest art collections in Italy, acquired over a period of centuries by the House of Savoy. The gallery's largest exhibition is of the Piedmontese masters, but it has many fine examples of Flemish art as well. Of the latter, the best-known painting is Sir Anthony van Dyck's *Three Children of Charles I.* Other important works include Botticelli's *Venus,* Memling's *Passion of Christ,* Rembrandt's *Sleeping Old Man,* Duccio's *Virgin and Child,* Mantegna's *Holy Conversation,* Jan van Eyck's *The Stigmata of Francis of Assisi,* Veronese's *Dinner in the House of the Pharisee,* Bellotto's *Views of Turin,* intriguing paintings by Brueghel, and a section of the royal collections between 1730 and 1832.

✪ Cathedral of San Giovanni. Piazza San Giovanni. ☎ **011/436-1540.** Free admission. Daily 9am–noon and 3–5pm.

The Renaissance Cathedral of San Giovanni, dedicated to John the Baptist, evokes more passion than virtually any other monument in Turin, thanks to its role as permanent seat of the most controversial relic in the Christian world, the Holy Shroud. The shroud is purported to be the one that Joseph of Arimathea wrapped around the body of Christ after it was removed from the cross.

Despite the church's acceptance of the shroud as authentic to the death and suffering of Christ, preliminary scientific tests have dated the shroud from sometime in the 12th century. Recent findings, however, have convinced some scientists that the shroud is very roughly 1,800 years old—a date that could realistically make it the shroud of Christ.

The usual home of the shroud is in Guarini's Chapel of the Holy Shroud, in the much larger Cathedral of San Giovanni. At press time, however, since the chapel was closed for renovations, the silver box containing the shroud is displayed (behind bulletproof glass) in the main body of the cathedral. There's a replica of the shroud, complete with diagrams and a run-down on the events surrounding its acquisition, on display near the silver box.

The authorities supervising the administration of the shroud maintain a small, rather dusty library and research center near the cathedral, which is open to ecclesiastics and qualified scholars only upon special request. It's the **Museo della Sindone** (Holy Shroud Museum), via San Domenico 28 (☎ **011/436-5832**).

Palazzo Reale (Royal Palace). Piazza Castello. ☎ **011/436-1455.** Admission 8,000 lire ($5.10) adults, free for children 17 and under and for seniors 60 and over. Tues–Sun 9am–5pm. Bus: 1, 4, 57, or 63.

The palace that the Savoys called home was begun in 1645. The halls, the columned ballroom by Palagi, the tea salon, and the "Queen's Chapel" are richly baroque in style. The original architect was Amedeo de Castellamonte, but numerous builders supplied ideas and effort before the palazzo was finally completed. As in nearly all ducal residences of that period, the most bizarre room is the one bedecked with flowering chinoiserie. The Throne Room is of interest, as is the tapestry-draped Banqueting Hall. Le Nôtre, the famous Frenchman, mapped out the gardens, which may also be visited. In the building, you can also visit the Royal Armory (Armeria Reale), with its large collection of arms and armor and many military mementos.

WHERE TO STAY

Like Milan, Turin is an industrial city first and a tourist center second. Most of its hotels were built after 1945 with an eye toward modern comfort but not necessarily style. The hotels generally lack distinction, except those in the expensive range.

EXPENSIVE

Hotel Concord. Via Lagrange 47, 10123 Torino. ☎ **011/517-6756.** Fax 011/517-6305. 139 rms, 4 suites. A/C MINIBAR TV TEL. Mon–Thurs, 350,000 lire ($224) double; 450,000 lire ($288) suite. Fri–Sun, 199,500 lire ($127.70) double; 299,500 lire ($191.70) suite. Rates include breakfast. AE, DC, MC, V. Parking 40,000 lire ($25.60). Bus: 1, 4, 9, 12, or 15.

The Concord is across from the hysterical traffic of a street that runs alongside the Porta Nuova train station. The entire hotel was modernized in 1982, and many of

The Mystery of the Holy Shroud

Listed as one of the world's greatest mysteries, the Santissima Sindone (Holy Shroud) is the most famous and controversial religious artifact on earth. It's housed in the Cathedral of San Giovanni in the Piedmont city of Torino (Turin). The shroud is said to be the one that Joseph of Arimathea wrapped around the body of Christ when he was removed from the cross.

The shroud—really a sheet—reveals the agonized features of a man who suffered crucifixion in almost photographic detail. The face of the bearded man is complete with a crown of thorns, and the marks of a thonged whip and bruises are compatible with the torment of carrying a cross. The shroud is a four-yard length of linen. No one has successfully put forth a scientific explanation as to why the imprint of the man on the cloth exists, or even how its image became impregnated in the threads of the cloth. Photography, of course, was centuries from being invented.

Turin did not always possess this relic. First mentioned in the Gospel of Matthew, the cloth disappeared in history until it mysteriously "turned up" in Cyprus, centuries after the death of Christ. From Cyprus, it was taken to France, where it was first exhibited in 1354, and was immediately denounced as a fraud by a French bishop at the time. In 1578, it was acquired by Duke Emanuele Filiberto, of the House of Savoy, who took the shroud to Turin in 1578.

For centuries the church did not allow scientists to conduct dating tests of the shroud. The first scientific testing of the shroud suggested that it was a fraud, probably dating from the 12th century. In 1988, three teams of scientists—from the United States, Britain, and Italy—each announced that the shroud was a clever forgery, except that they estimated the time frame of its fabrication as between 1260 and 1390. Recent findings, however, propose a much earlier dating. Using calculations based on the fact that the shroud was involved in a fire in the 16th century, scientists now purport that the shroud is roughly 1,800 years old—a date that could realistically make it the shroud of Christ.

The archbishop of Turin has presented the shroud to the Holy See, and the fact that the Vatican accepted it as a holy relic has increased some world belief in the shroud's validity. However, the Vatican has refrained from pronouncing it as "the true shroud." The shroud remains encased in a silver casket. Only two keys can unlock the casket, one held by the archbishop of Turin, another by the Palatine cardinals, church seniors based permanently in the Vatican. The key unlocks only the casket—not the mystery of the shroud.

its guests are business travelers. The lobby is covered in marble, and the comfortable rooms feature individually controlled air-conditioning and double-glazed, soundproof windows. A bank of elevators leads to a stylish bar and restaurant one floor above street level. Additional hotel amenities include room service, baby-sitting, laundry, valet, and facilities for people with disabilities.

✪ **Jolly Hotel Prìncipi di Piemonte.** Via Gobetti 15, 10123 Torino. ☎ **011/562-9693,** or 212/685-3700 in New York City. Fax 011/562-0270. 107 rms, 8 suites. A/C MINIBAR TV TEL. 430,000 lire ($275.20) double; from 690,000 lire ($441.60) suite. Rates include breakfast. AE, DC, MC, V. Parking 25,000–30,000 lire ($16–$19.20). Bus: 1, 4, or 18.

A favorite choice of Fiat executives, this 10-story hotel is in the center of the city, near the railway station. Today it's the finest address in town, having surpassed the Turin Palace. The building itself is from 1939. Owned by the country's Jolly chain, it employed some of Italy's finest architects and designers in its wholesale revamping. The public rooms are grand in style and furnishings, with bas-relief ceilings, gold wall panels, silk draperies, Louis XVI–style chairs, and baroque marble sideboards.

Dining/Entertainment: There are several dining rooms, both formal and informal, as well as a fashionable drinking lounge. A Piedmont-based menu is featured.

Services: Room service, baby-sitting, laundry, valet.

✪ **Turin Palace Hotel.** Via Sacchi 8, 10128 Torino. ☎ **011/562-5511.** Fax 011/561-2187. 123 rms, 2 suites. A/C MINIBAR TV TEL. 310,000 lire ($198.40) double; from 550,000 lire ($352) suite. Rates include breakfast. AE, DC, MC, V. Parking 32,000 lire ($20.50). Bus: 9, 14, or 60.

This aging hotel, with glass doors and a white marble facade, now shows its wear and tear in spite of its five-star rating from the Italian government. A classic six-story building, it still has its admirers who favor it over the Jolly. The location opposite the train station is decidedly unglamorous and seedy, but is convenient to the center of town; its entrance is across from Porta Nuova. The clientele is likely to include top-level General Motors executives from Detroit on business trips to Turin. The faded public rooms contain a scattering of full-size oil portraits as well as opulent but worn chairs and massive carved and gilded console tables. These have been supplemented with an assortment of tasteful contemporary furniture as well. The bedrooms and baths are soundproof.

Dining/Entertainment: Guests, mostly businesspeople, gather in the American Bar for drinks before heading to the Piedmont restaurant for international cuisine. The restaurant is closed in August.

Services: Room service, baby-sitting, laundry, valet.

Facilities: A garage is on the premises, as are facilities for persons with disabilities.

✪ **Villa Sassi.** Via Traforo del Pino 47, 10132 Torino. ☎ **011/898-0556.** Fax 011/898-0095. 15 rms, 2 suites. MINIBAR TV TEL. 340,000 lire ($217.60) double; 500,000 lire ($320) suite. Rates include breakfast. AE, DC, MC, V. Free parking. Bus: 15 or 61.

This classic 17th-century-style estate lies 4 miles east of the town center and is surrounded by park grounds and approached by a winding driveway. If you want tranquillity, head here. It was converted long ago into a top-grade hotel and restaurant. The impressive original architectural details are still intact, including the wooden staircase in the entrance hall. The drawing room features an overscale mural and life-size sculpted baroque figures holding bronze torchiers. Each bedroom has been individually decorated (the furniture is a combination of antiques and reproductions). The accommodations here are equal to those at the Jolly. The manager sees that the hotel is run in a personal way, with "custom-made" service.

Dining/Entertainment: The intimate drinking salon features draped red-velvet walls, a bronze chandelier, black dado, and low seat cushions. See "Where to Dine," below, for a recommendation of the hotel restaurant.

MODERATE

Hotel Victoria. Via Nino Costa 4, 10123 Torino. ☎ **011/561-1909.** Fax 011/561-1806. 90 rms. MINIBAR TV TEL. 220,000–250,000 lire ($140.80–$160) double. Rates include breakfast. AE, DC, MC, V. Parking 25,000 lire ($16). Bus: 18 or 61.

This small but substantial hotel has better accommodations than its second-class designation would lead one to expect. The bedrooms are well designed, and each one has a different monochromatic color scheme. Rooms come in two different categories: standard and deluxe. Graceful furniture and large stained-glass windows contribute to a feeling of luxury in the public rooms. Breakfast is the only meal served.

INEXPENSIVE

Hotel Genio. Corso Vittorio Emanuele II 47, 10125 Torino. ☎ **011/650-5771.** Fax 011/
650-8264. 90 rms. MINIBAR TV TEL. 200,000 lire ($128) double Mon–Thurs, 130,000 lire
($83.20) Fri–Sun. Rates include breakfast. AE, DC, MC, V. Parking 20,000 lire ($12.80). Bus: 1,
9, 15, 52, or 67.

Originally built at the end of the 19th century, this four-story hotel in the center of
town was renovated into a streamlined, modern format in 1990. Set close to the railway station, its accommodations contain a comfortable blend of contemporary and
early 20th-century furniture, and have double-paned windows for soundproofing.
About 40 of the bedrooms are air-conditioned, and rent for a daily supplement of
10,000 lire ($6.40). Only breakfast is served.

Hotel Goya. Via Prìncipe Amedeo 41 bis, 10123 Torino. ☎ **011/817-4951.** Fax 011/
817-4953. 30 rms. A/C MINIBAR TV TEL. 140,000–160,000 lire ($89.60–$102.40) double. Rates
include breakfast. AE, DC, MC, V. Parking: 25,000 lire ($16). Bus: 1 or 4.

This hotel, like many others in the Turin chain that owns it, is named after a famous
artist. Located on a fairly quiet street in the historic core of the city center, this
century-old hotel was renovated in 1993. Breakfast is the only meal served, but the
lobby contains a small bar area just behind the reception desk.

Hotel Piemontese. Via Berthollet 21, 10125 Torino. ☎ **011/669-8101.** Fax 011/669-0571.
35 rms, 5 suites. A/C MINIBAR TV TEL. Mon–Thurs, 200,000 lire ($128) double; 240,000 lire
($153.60) suite. Fri–Sun, 120,000 lire ($76.80) double; 150,000 lire ($96) suite. Rates include
breakfast. AE, DC, MC, V. Parking 15,000 lire ($9.60). Bus: 1, 18, 34, 35, 61, or 67.

The Hotel Piemontese is in a 19th-century building near the historic center and the
Stazione Centrale. The facade is covered with iron balconies and ornate stone trim.
The restructured interior is well maintained, and the comfortable bedrooms and public places have undergone a complete restoration. Breakfast, taken in an airy, sunny
room, is the only meal served at the hotel, but nearby restaurants are willing to offer ample fixed-price menus to guests of the Piemontese. Laundry and 24-hour room
service are available. Guests can patronize a nearby sports center with a swimming
pool.

WHERE TO DINE

EXPENSIVE

Del Cambio. Piazza Carignano 2. ☎ **011/546690.** Reservations required. Main courses
28,000–35,000 lire ($17.90–$22.40); fixed-price menu 90,000 lire ($57.60). AE, DC, MC, V.
Mon–Sat noon–2:30pm and 7:45–10:30pm. Bus: 4, 58, or 63. PIEMONTESE/MEDITERRANEAN.

The Del Cambio is a classic restaurant of old Turin. You dine here amid a grand old-
world setting of white-and-gilt walls, crystal chandeliers, and gilt mirrors. The
restaurant was founded in 1757—it's the oldest restaurant in Turin, possibly in all
of Italy. The statesman Camillo Cavour was one of its loyal patrons, and his much-
frequented corner is immortalized with a bronze medallion.

The white truffle of Piedmont is featured in many specialties of the chef, who has
received many culinary honors. To begin, the assorted fresh antipasti are excellent;
the best pasta dish is the regional agnolotti piemontesi. Among the main dishes, the
fondue with truffles from Alba and the beef braised in Barolo wine deserve special
praise. Some trademark specialties derive from very old recipes of the southwestern
Alps: artichokes stewed with bone marrow and truffles; girello aromatizzato all
piemontese (flank steak marinated for several days in a mixture of sugar, salt, and aromatic herbs, sliced paper-thin, and served with Parmesan and seasonal vegetables);
and tonno di coniglio à la manière antica (rabbit cooked according to ancient
traditions).

✪ Due Lampioni da Carlo. Via Carlo Alberto 45. ☎ **011/817-9380.** Reservations required. Jacket and tie required for men. Main courses 20,000–30,000 lire ($12.80–$19.20); fixed-price menu 45,000 lire ($28.80). AE, V. Mon–Sat 12:30–3pm and 7:30–11pm. Closed Aug. Bus: 61. PIEMONTESE/INTERNATIONAL.

Giovanni Agnelli, the head of Fiat, has a gift for finding the best restaurants in Turin, which is why he has been known to patronize this elegant 17th-century palace in the heart of the city, run by chef Carlo Bagatin. Specialties are from the Piedmont district, and only the finest of ingredients go into the tasty dishes. The antipasto selection is among the very best in Turin, and you can follow with a choice of agnolotti, stuffed with duck and cooked with local white truffles, or perhaps tournedos with olive purée. Other favorite dishes include tripe soup, ravioli stuffed with ricotta and pesto, brains fried in an herb liqueur, a mosaic of fish served as a beautiful antipasto, and a bollito misto (medley of boiled meats) in the "style of the stockbrokers."

✪ El Toulà–Villa Sassi. In the Villa Sassi, via Traforo del Pino 47. ☎ **011/898-0556.** Reservations required. Main courses 25,000–38,000 lire ($16–$24.30). AE, DC, MC, V. Mon–Sat noon–2pm and 8–10:30pm. Closed Aug. Bus: 15 or 61. PIEMONTESE/INTERNATIONAL.

This spacious 17th-century villa is on the rise of a hill 4 miles east of the town center on the road to Chieri. The stylish, antique-decorated establishment has seen the addition of a modern dining room, with glass walls extending toward the gardens (most of the tables have an excellent view). Some of the basic foodstuff is brought in from the villa's own farm—not only the vegetables, fruit, and butter, but the beef as well. For an appetizer, try the frogs' legs cooked with broth-simmered rice, or fonduta, a Piedmont fondue, made with fontina cheese and local white truffles. If it's featured, you may want to try the prized specialty of the house: camoscio in salmi— that is, chamois (a goatlike antelope) prepared in a sauce of olive oil, anchovies, and garlic, laced with wine and served with polenta.

✪ Vecchia Lanterna. Corso Re Umberto 21. ☎ **011/537047.** Reservations required. Main courses 30,000–45,000 lire ($19.20–$28.80); fixed-price menu 70,000–100,000 lire ($44.80–$64). DC, MC, V. Mon–Fri noon–3pm and 8pm–midnight, Sat 8pm–midnight. Closed Aug 10–20. Bus: 1, 9, or 14. PIEMONTESE/INTERNATIONAL.

This is one of Turin's most popular upper-bracket restaurants, and it usually proves to be a rewarding gastronomic experience. It's housed in a building dating from 1740. The bar area near the entrance has belle époque lighting fixtures, heavy gilt mirrors, ornate 19th-century furniture, and Oriental rugs over carpeting. The dining room may remind you of old Venice.

The antipasti selection is a treat—king crab Venetian style, asparagus flan, pâté de foie gras, grilled snails on a skewer, and marinated trout. This could be followed by ravioli stuffed with duck and served with a truffle sauce, your choice of risotto, or snail soup. Main courses change seasonally, but often include goose-liver piccata on a bed of fresh mushrooms, sea bass Venetian style, or garnished frogs' legs. The seafood grill is especially delectable; each element is prepared individually and then assembled afterward.

MODERATE

Ⓢ Ristorante C'Era una Volta. Corso Vittorio Emanuele II 41. ☎ **011/655498.** Reservations required. Fixed-price dinner 35,000–45,000 lire ($22.40–$28.80). AE, DC, MC, V. Mon–Sat 8:30pm–midnight. Closed Aug. Bus: 1, 9, 18, 52, or 67. PIEMONTESE.

Located near the Porta Nuova train station, this restaurant is entered from the busy street through carved doors; you take an elevator one floor above ground level. Because the restaurant adheres to the classic dishes of the Piedmontese cuisine, it's a good introduction to the food of the Italian alpine regions. Many clients are faithful fans. The decor is in the typical Piedmontese style, with hanging copper pots and thick walls of stippled plaster. Fixed-price meals feature an apéritif, a choice of seven or eight antipasti, and two first and two main courses, with vegetables, dessert, and coffee. Typical regional fare includes polenta, crêpes, rabbit, and guinea fowl. The translation of the restaurant's name is "Once upon a time."

INEXPENSIVE

Caffè Torino. Piazza San Carlo 204. ☎ **011/545118.** Main courses 16,000–22,000 lire ($10.25–$14.10). AE, DC, MC, V. Daily 7am–1am. Bus: 4, 10, 15, 58, or 72 to piazza Castello. ITALIAN.

Established in 1903, this famous coffeehouse is the best re-creation in Turin of the days of Vittorio Emanuele. It's decorated with faded frescoes, brass and marble in-lays, and a somewhat battered 19th-century formality. Set on one of the most elegant squares in northern Italy, it has a staff that adheres to a confusing series of rules about where and when clients can and should be seated. There's a stand-up bar near the entrance, a rather formal dining room off to the side, display cases filled with snack food, and a cafe area with tiny tables and unhurried service.

Ⓢ **Da Mauro.** Via Maria Vittoria 21. ☎ **011/817-0604.** Reservations not accepted. Main courses 8,000–20,000 lire ($5.10–$12.80). No credit cards. Tues–Sun noon–2:30pm and 7:30–10pm. Closed July. Bus: 18. ITALIAN/TUSCAN.

Located within walking distance of piazza San Carlo, this place, the best of the town's low-cost trattorie, is generally packed (everybody loves a bargain). The food is con-ventional, but it does have character; the chef borrows freely from most of the gastronomic centers of Italy, although the cuisine is mainly Tuscan. An excellent pasta specialty is the cannelloni. Most main dishes consist of well-prepared fish, veal, and poultry. The desserts are consistently enjoyable.

TURIN AFTER DARK

This city of Fiat is also the cultural center of northwestern Italy. Turin is a major stop-over for concert artists performing between Genoa and Milan. The daily newspaper of Piedmont, *La Stampa,* will list complete details of any cultural events occurring during your stay.

Classical music concerts are presented at the **Auditorium della RAI,** via Rossini 15 (☎ **011/810-4653**), throughout the year, although mainly in the winter months. Tickets range from 30,000 to 200,000 lire ($19.20 to $128), depending on the pro-duction.

Turin is also home to one of the country's leading opera houses, **Teatro Regio,** piazza Castello 215 (☎ **011/88151**). Concerts and leading ballets are also presented here. The box office is open Tuesday to Sunday from 1 to 6:30pm; closed in August. Tickets cost 20,000 to 200,000 lire ($12.80 to $128).

Opera and other classical productions are presented in summer outside the gardens of the **Palazzo Reale.** The last remaining government-subsidized (RAI) orchestra performs at via Nizza 262. The **orchestra hall** (☎ **011/664-4111**) is part of the extensive Lingotto exhibition and conference center that grew out of Fiat's first large-scale automobile assembly plant. Ticket prices vary for each performance.

2 Aosta

114 miles NW of Milan, 78 miles N of Turin, 463 miles NW of Rome

In the capital of Valle d'Aosta are a number of **Roman ruins,** including the Arch of Augustus, built in 24 B.C., the date of the Roman founding of the town. Via

Sant'Anselmo, part of the old city from the Middle Ages, leads to the arch. Even more impressive are the ruins of a Roman theater, reached by the Porta Pretoria, a major gateway built of huge blocks that dates from the 1st century B.C. A Roman forum is today a small park with a crypt, lying off piazza San Giovanni near the cathedral. The ruins of the theater are open year round Monday to Friday from 9am to 6:30pm and on Saturday and Sunday from 9am to noon and 2 to 5pm. The forum is open May to September, daily from 9am to 6:30pm; October to April, daily from 9am to noon and 2 to 5pm.

The town is also enriched by its medieval relics. The Gothic **Church of Sant'Orso,** founded in the 12th century, is characterized by its landmark steeple designed in the Romanesque style. You can explore the crypt, but the cloisters, with capitals of some three dozen pillars depicting biblical scenes, are more interesting. The church lies directly off via Sant'Anselmo and is open daily from 9am to 5pm. Admission is free.

Lying as it does on a major artery, Aosta makes for an important stopover point, either for overnighting or as a base for exploring Valle d'Aosta or taking the cable car to the Conca di Pila, the mountain that towers over the town.

ESSENTIALS

GETTING THERE   By Train   Eleven trains per day run directly from Turin to Aosta (trip time: 2 hours); a one-way ticket costs 11,700 lire ($7.50). From Milan, the trip takes 4^1/2 hours and costs 17,200 lire ($11) one-way; you must change trains at Chivasso.

By Bus   Twelve buses a day travel between Turin and Aosta (trip time: 2^1/2 hours), and four to six buses a day arrive from Milan (4 hours).

By Car   From Turin, continue north along autostrada A5. The autostrada comes to an end just east of Aosta.

VISITOR INFORMATION   The **tourist information center** is at piazza Chanoux 8 (☎ **0165/236627**). It's open Monday to Saturday from 9am to 1pm and 3 to 8pm and on Sunday from 9am to 1pm.

WHERE TO STAY

Hotel Roma. Via Torino 7, 11100 Aosta. ☎ **0165/41000.** Fax 0165/32404. 33 rms. TEL. 98,000–120,000 lire ($62.70–$76.80) double. AE, DC, MC, V. Parking 10,000 lire ($6.40). Bus: 2.

Silvio Lepri and Graziella Nicoli are the owners of this hotel, which is on a peaceful alleyway behind a cubist-style white stucco building; it's surrounded by the balconies and windows of what appear to be private apartments. The entrance is at the top of an exterior concrete stairwell. The public rooms include a warmly paneled bar area, big windows, and a homelike decor filled with bright colors and rustic accessories. There's a garage on the premises, plus public parking nearby.

Hotel Valle d'Aosta. Corso Ivrea 146, 11100 Aosta. ☎ **0165/41845.** Fax 0165/236660. 104 rms. MINIBAR TV TEL. 160,000–220,000 lire ($102.40–$140.80) double. Rates include breakfast. AE, DC, MC, V. Closed Dec 1–27. Bus: 2. Parking 10,000 lire ($6.40).

This modern hotel with its zigzag concrete facade is one of the leading choices in Aosta. Located on a busy road leading from the old town to the entrance of the autostrada, it's a prominent stopover for motorists using the Great Saint Bernard and Mont Blanc tunnels into Italy. The sunny lobby has beige stone floors, paneled walls, and deep leather chairs. All bedrooms have double windows and views angled toward the mountains. A restaurant is on the premises, under a different management (see "Ristorante Le Foyer" in "Where to Dine," below). The lobby contains an oversize bar area. The hotel also offers room service, baby-sitting, laundry, and a garage.

Ⓢ **Le Pageot.** Via Giorgio Carrel 31, 11100 Aosta. ☎ **0165/32433.** Fax 0165/33217. 18 rms. TV TEL. 118,000 lire ($75.50) double. Rates include breakfast. AE, DC, MC, V. Parking 10,000 lire ($6.40). Bus: 2.

Built in 1985, this is one of the best-value hotels in town. It has a modern, angular facade of brown brick with big windows and floors crafted from carefully polished slabs of mountain granite. The bedrooms are clean and functional, and the well-lit public areas include a breakfast room and a TV room. The hotel's name translates from an antiquated local dialect into the word for bed. There's no restaurant.

WHERE TO DINE

Ristorante Le Foyer. Corso Ivrea 146. ☎ **0165/32136.** Reservations recommended. Main courses 20,000–40,000 lire ($12.80–$25.60). AE, DC, MC, V. Mon 12:15–1:50pm, Wed–Sun 12:15–1:50pm and 7:30–9:30pm. Closed Jan 8–25 and July 5–20. Bus: 2. VALDOSTAN/ INTERNATIONAL.

This restaurant sits beside a traffic artery on the outskirts of town. The full Valdostan meals you get here are both flavorful and cost-conscious. In a wood-paneled dining room that's illuminated by a wall of oversize windows, you can dine on specialties such as salmon trout, beef tagliata with balsamic vinegar, vegetable flan with fondue, or fresh noodles with smoked salmon and asparagus. There's also a good selection of French and Italian wines.

Ⓢ **Ristorante Piemonte.** Via Porta Pretoria 13. ☎ **0165/40111.** Main courses 15,000– 25,000 lire ($9.60–$16); fixed-price menu 30,000 lire ($19.20). AE, MC, V. Sat–Thurs noon–3pm and 7–10pm. Closed Nov. Bus: 2. VALDOSTAN/INTERNATIONAL.

On a relatively traffic-free street lined with shops, this family-run place is one of the best of the low-cost trattorie inside the walls of the old town. Established in 1910, it has been popular and unpretentious ever since. In a setting of vaulted ceilings and tile floors, you can savor bagna cauda, cannelloni of the chef, risotto with roast pork, sautéed octopus with ginger, and an array of refreshing desserts, which could include fresh strawberries with lemon.

Ⓢ **Vecchia Aosta.** Piazza Porta Pretoria 4. ☎ **0165/361186.** Reservations recommended. Main courses 18,000–24,000 lire ($11.50–$15.35); fixed-price menu 28,000–35,000 lire ($17.90–$22.40). AE, DC, MC, V. Thurs–Tues noon–3pm and 7:30–10pm. Closed June 15–30 and Nov 15–30. Bus: 2. VALDOSTAN/INTERNATIONAL.

The most unusual restaurant in Aosta lies in the narrow niche between the inner and outer Roman walls of the Porta Pretoria. It's in an old building which, although modernized, still bears evidence of the superb building techniques of the Romans, whose chiseled stones are sometimes visible between patches of modern wood and plaster. Full meals are served on at least two different levels in a labyrinth of nooks and isolated crannies, and might include homemade ravioli, filet of beef with mush-rooms, pepperoni flan, eggs with cheese fondue and truffles, and a cheese-laden ver-sion of Valdostan fondue.

3 Courmayeur & Entrèves

COURMAYEUR

Courmayeur, a 22-mile drive northwest of Aosta, is Italy's best all-around ski resort, with two "high seasons," attracting the alpine excursionist in summer, the ski enthu-siast in winter. Its popularity was given a considerable boost with the opening of the Mont Blanc road tunnel, feeding traffic from France into Italy (estimated trip time: 20 minutes). The cost for an average car is 40,000 lire ($25.60) one-way.

With Europe's highest mountain in the background, Courmayeur sits snugly in a valley. Directly to the north of the resort is the alpine village of Entrèves, sprinkled with a number of chalets (some of which take in paying guests).

In the vicinity, you can take a cable-car lift—one of the most unusual in Europe—across Mont Blanc all the way to Chamonix, France. It's a ride across glaciers that's altogether frightening, altogether thrilling—for steel-nerved adventure seekers only. This is a spectacular achievement in engineering. Departures on the Funivie Monte Bianco are from La Palud, near Entrèves. The three-stage cable car heads for the intermediate stations, Pavillon and Rifugio Torino, before reaching its peak at Punta Helbronner at 11,254 feet. At the latter, you'll be on the doorstep of the glacier and the celebrated 11 1/2-mile Vallée Blanche ski run to Chamonix, France, which is usually opened at the beginning of February every year. The round-trip price for the cable ride is 45,000 lire ($28.80) per person. Departures are every 20 minutes, and service is daily from 8am to 1pm and 2 to 5pm. At the top is a terrace for sunbathing, a bar, and a snack bar. Bookings are possible at **Esercizio Funivie,** Frazione La Palud 22 (☎ **0165/89925**).

ESSENTIALS

GETTING THERE   Proceed to Aosta by rail. In Aosta, you can take any of 11 buses leaving daily for Courmayeur from the bus terminal, piazza Narbonne (☎ **0165/362027**), adjacent to the train station. Trip time is 1 hour, and a one-way ticket costs 3,600 lire ($2.30). Motorists should continue west from Aosta on Route 26 heading for Mont Blanc; Courmayeur lies on the way there.

VISITOR INFORMATION   The **tourist information center** for Courmayeur is on piazzale Monte Bianco (☎ **0165/842060**). It's open Monday to Friday from 9am to 12:30pm and 3 to 6:30pm and on Saturday and Sunday from 9am to 7:30pm.

GETTING AROUND   Once you arrive in the center of Courmayeur, you can easily get around on foot, as the resort is rather compact. However, if you're going somewhere in the environs, such as Entrèves or La Palud (to catch the cable car for Mont Blanc), you'll need to take one of the local buses. Each bus is labeled by destination. The tourist office (see above) has a complete schedule, and buses depart from just outside the office.

WHERE TO STAY

Courmayeur has a number of attractive hotels, many of which are open seasonally. Always reserve ahead in high season, either summer or winter.

Expensive

Grand Hotel Royal e Golf. Via Roma 87, 11013 Courmayeur. ☎ **0165/846787.** Fax 0165/842093. 87 rms, 4 suites. A/C MINIBAR TV TEL. 380,000–450,000 lire ($243.20–$288) double; 500,000–1,000,000 lire ($320–$640) suite. Rates include breakfast. AE, DC, MC, V. Closed Easter–June 20 and Sept 15–Nov. Parking 20,000 lire ($12.80) inside, free outside.

Built in 1950, this hotel is in a dramatic location above the heart of the resort between the most fashionable pedestrian walkway and a thermally heated outdoor swimming pool. As a hotel, it's tops except for the more tranquil and elegant Pavillon (see below). Much of its angular facade is covered with rocks, so it fits in neatly with the surrounding mountainous landscape. The rooms are generally large, with built-in furnishings and streamlined bathrooms.

Dining/Entertainment: The hotel's social center is a large and comfortable lounge, flanked on one side by a bar and on another by a dais where a pianist provides nightly entertainment in season. The hotel's deluxe dining room, La Grill dell'Hotel Royal e Golf, is reviewed in "Where to Dine," below. There's also a regular dining room open daily.

Services: Room service, baby-sitting, laundry, valet, hydromassage.

Facilities: Swimming pool, sauna, Jacuzzi.

Hotel Pavillon. Strada Regionale 60, 110113 Courmayeur. ☎ **0165/846120.** Fax 0165/846122. 50 rms, 10 suites. MINIBAR TV TEL. 190,000–390,000 lire ($121.60–$249.60) double; 360,000–660,000 lire ($230.40–$422.40) suite. Mandatory half board in winter 180,000–390,000 lire ($115.20–$249.60) per person. AE, DC, MC, V. Closed May–June 15 and Oct 2–Dec 2. Parking 10,000 lire ($6.40).

This is easily the swankiest and most important hotel at the resort, in spite of its small size. Many of the clients warming themselves around the stone fireplace are from England, Germany, and France, which adds a continental allure. Built in 1965, renovated in 1990, and designed like a chalet, the hotel is located a 4-minute walk south of Courmayeur's inner-city pedestrian zone. The bedrooms, which are entered through leather-covered doors, feature built-in furniture and a comfortable conservative decor; all but two have private balconies. The hotel is only a short walk from the funicular that goes to Plan Checrouit.

Room service, baby-sitting, laundry, and valet are available. In the basement is a full array of hydrotherapy facilities; there's also a solarium and a covered swimming pool that's visible from the entrance vestibule.

Moderate

✪ **Palace Bron.** Località Plan Gorret 41, 11013 Courmayeur. ☎ **0165/846742.** Fax 0165/844015. 26 rms, 1 suite. TV TEL. 240,000–350,000 lire ($153.60–$224) double; 540,000–690,000 lire ($345.60–$441.60) suite. AE, DC, MC, V. Closed May–June and Oct–Nov. Free parking. Bus: Plan Gorret.

Located about $1^1/_4$ miles from the heart of the resort, this tranquil oasis is one of the plushest addresses in town, although not as good as the Pavillon. The white-walled chalet is the most noteworthy building on the pine-studded hill, and it has a commanding view over all of Courmayeur and the mountains beyond. Guests are often made to feel like members of a baronial private household rather than patrons of a hotel.

The bedrooms are handsomely furnished and well maintained. Winter visitors appreciate its proximity to the many ski lifts in the area. Walking from the chalet to the center of town is a good way to exercise after dining on the kitchen's filling cuisine. There's a nearby parking lot for motorists who prefer to drive the long, steep distance up from town.

The hotel's piano bar is especially lively in winter, hosting skiers from all over Europe and America. The restaurant has a refined international cuisine, with formal service. Other hotel services include room service, baby-sitting, laundry, and valet.

Inexpensive

Bouton d'Or. Strada Traforo del Monte Bianco 10 (off piazzale Monte Bianco), 11013 Courmayeur. ☎ **0165/846729.** Fax 0165/842152. 35 rms. TV TEL. 140,000–180,000 lire ($89.60–$115.20) double. AE, DC, MC, V. Rates include breakfast. Closed June and Nov. Free parking.

Named after the buttercups that cover the surrounding hills in summer, this hotel is owned by the Casale family, who built it in 1970 and renovated it in 1990. It features an exterior painted yellow and gray, stone trim, and a flagstone roof. French windows lead from the clean, comfortable bedrooms onto small balconies. The hotel is about 100 yards (toward the Mont Blanc Tunnel to France) from the most popular restaurant in Courmayeur, Le Vieux Pommier, which is owned by the same family. The hotel also has a garage, sauna, solarium, and garden.

🅢 **Hotel Courmayeur.** Via Roma 158, 11013 Courmayeur. ☎ **0165/846732.** Fax 0165/845125. 26 rms. TV TEL. 90,000–130,000 lire ($57.60–$83.20) per person double. Rates include half board. AE, DC, V. Closed from the end of Apr to June 18 and Oct–Nov.

The Hotel Courmayeur, located right in the center of the resort, was constructed so that most of its rooms would have unobstructed views of the nearby mountains. A number of the bedrooms, furnished in the mountain chalet style, also have wooden balconies. Nonresidents can visit the hotel restaurant, where regional food is served.

Hotel Del Viale. Viale Monte Bianco 74, 11013 Courmayeur. ☎ **0165/846712.** Fax 0165/844513. 23 rms. MINIBAR TV TEL. 120,000–160,000 lire ($76.80–$102.40) double. Rates include breakfast. AE, DC, MC, V. Closed May and Nov. Parking 10,000 lire ($6.40) inside, free outside.

This old-style mountain chalet at the edge of town is a good place to enjoy the indoor-outdoor life. There's a front terrace with tables set out under trees in fair weather, and the rooms inside are cozy and pleasant in the chillier months. In the winter, guests can gather in the taproom to enjoy *après-ski* life, drinking at pine tables and warming their feet before the open fire. The clean and comfortable bedrooms, with natural wood, have a rustic air about them.

WHERE TO DINE

Expensive

✪ **La Grill dell'Hotel Royal e Golf.** In the Grand Hotel Royal e Golf, via Roma 87. ☎ **0165/846787.** Reservations required in winter. Main courses 30,000–35,000 lire ($19.20–$22.40). AE, DC, MC, V. Tues–Sun 7:30–10pm. Closed Apr 15–June 20 and Sept 20–Dec 1. VALDOSTAN.

On the lobby level of this previously recommended hotel is the most fashionable—and certainly the most expensive—restaurant in town. It has only 30 places for diners interested in the cultivated cuisine inspired by the legacy of Harry Cipriani, of Harry's Bar fame. It's sparsely decorated, with a carved Gothic screen from an English church standing against one wall. The relatively simple but fresh and well-prepared dishes include pasta e fagioli, carpaccio, risotto with radicchio, and rosettes of veal Cipriani style. The hotel's foie gras—served on a brioche—is said to be the "best anywhere." The menu changes daily.

Inexpensive

✪ **Cadran Solaire.** Via Roma 122. ☎ **0165/844609.** Reservations required. Main courses 20,000–30,000 lire ($12.80–$19.20); fixed-price menu 30,000 lire ($19.20). AE, DC, MC, V. Wed–Sun 12:30–3pm and 7:30–11pm. Closed May and Oct. VALDOSTAN.

In the center of town is the most interesting restaurant in Courmayeur. It's named after the sundial (*cadran solaire*) that embellishes the upper floor of its chalet facade, and is owned by Leo Garin, whose also-recommended La Maison de Filippo (see under Entrèves, below) is the most popular restaurant in the Valle d'Aosta. Try to come for a before-dinner drink in the vaulted bar; its massive stones were crafted into almost alarmingly long spans in the 16th century using construction techniques that the Romans perfected. A few steps away, the rustically elegant dining room has its own stone fireplace, a beamed ceiling, and wide plank floors.

Specialties change with the season but are likely to include warm goat cheese blended with a salad, noodles with seasonal vegetables, a baked cheese and spinach casserole, and duck breast with plums. The desserts are sumptuous.

Leone Rosso. Via Roma 73. ☎ **0165/846726.** Reservations recommended. Main courses 18,000–30,000 lire ($11.50–$19.20); fixed-price menu 32,000–58,000 lire ($20.50–$37.10).

MC, V. Dec–Mar, daily noon–2:30pm and 7–10pm; Apr and July–Sept, Fri–Sun and Tues–Wed noon–2:30pm and 7–10pm; Nov, Fri–Sun noon–2:30pm and 7–10pm. Closed May–June and Oct. VALDOSTAN.

The Leone Rosso is in a stone- and timber-fronted house in a slightly isolated court-yard, a few paces from the busy pedestrian traffic of via Roma. It serves well-prepared and seasoned Valdostan specialties, including fondues, a thick and steaming regional version of minestrone, tagliatelle with mushrooms and en papillote, and a selection of rich, creamy desserts. Some meats you grill yourself at your table. This place is not to be confused with the Red Lion pub.

⑤ Le Vieux Pommier. Piazzale Monte Bianco 25. ☎ **0165/842281.** Reservations recommended. Main courses 18,000–26,000 lire ($11.50–$16.65). AE, DC, MC, V. Tues–Sun noon–2pm and 7–9:30pm. Closed Oct and 10–15 days in May. VALDOSTAN.

The apple tree that was cut down so that construction of this restaurant could begin is now the focal point of this establishment, which is located on the main square of town. One of its guests was filmmaker Ingmar Bergman, who, like everyone else, appreciated the exposed stone, the copper-covered bar, and the thick pine tables arranged in an octagon around the heavily ornamented tree.

Today Alessandro Casale, the son of the woman who established the restaurant, directs the kitchen, assisted by his wife, Lydia. They have toured Europe teaching the technique of their regional cuisine. Your meal might consist of three kinds of dried alpine beef, followed by noodles in a ham-studded cream sauce, and an arrangement of three kinds of pasta or four types of fondue, including a regional variety with fontina, milk, and egg yolks. Then it's on to chicken suprême en papillote (parchment) or four or five unusual meat dishes that are cooked mountain style, right at your table. Six kinds of grilled meats, flavored with aromatic herbs, are also offered.

COURMAYEUR AFTER DARK

The life expectancy of the average dance club in an alpine resort such as Courmayeur is about that of a snow crystal in July. The local clubs can be fun, however, and might offer a chance to meet someone. As of this writing, the *après-ski* crowd is attracted to the electronic rhythms at the following establishments:

American Bar. Via Roma 43. ☎ **0165/846707.**

Not to be confused with a less desirable bar with the same name at the end of the same street, this is one of the most popular bars on the *après-ski* circuit. It's rowdy and sometimes outrageous, but most often a lot of fun. Most guests end up in one of the two rooms, beside either an open fireplace or a long, crowded bar. The place is open in winter daily from 9am to 1am; it's sometimes closed on Tuesday, but never in ski season.

Café della Posta. Via Roma 51. ☎ **0165/842272.**

The Café della Posta, the oldest, most venerable cafe in Courmayeur, is as sedate as its neighbor, the American Bar, is unruly. Many guests prefer to remain in the warmly decorated bar area, never venturing into the large and comfortable salon with a glowing fireplace in an adjacent room. The place changes its stripes throughout the day, opening as a morning cafe at 8:30am.

Le Clochard. Route de Frazione Dolonne. ☎ **0165/846766.** Cover (including the first drink) 20,000 lire ($12.80).

"The Drunkard" is one of the most popular clubs in town, catering to an over-25 crowd of skiers, hikers, and sports enthusiasts. It lies at the edge of the resort. Near the busy bar and a blazing wintertime fireplace you'll find a warm and comfortable spot to watch the international goings-on. It's open every evening in winter from 9:30pm to 1:30am. In summer its schedule varies with business at the resort.

ENTRÈVES

Even older than Courmayeur, Entrèves is an ancient community that's small and compact, really a mountain village of wood houses. Many discriminating clients prefer its alpine charm to the more bustling resort of Courmayeur. It's reached by a steep and narrow road. Many gourmets book in here just to enjoy the regional fare, for which the village is known.

Just outside Entrèves on the main highway lies the **Val Veny cable car,** which skiers take in winter to reach the Courmayeur lift system.

Entrèves is located 2 miles north of Courmayeur (signposted off Route 26). Buses from the center of Courmayeur run daily to Entrèves.

There is no local tourist office (ask at the tourist office in Courmayeur; see above).

WHERE TO STAY

Note that La Brenva, listed under "Where to Dine," below, also offers accommodations.

⑤ La Grange. 11013 Courmayeur-Entrèves. ☎ **0165/869733.** Fax 0165/869744. 21 rms, 2 suites. MINIBAR TV TEL. 200,000 lire ($128) double; from 400,000 lire ($256) suite. Rates include breakfast. AE, DC, MC, V. Closed May–June and Oct–Nov. Free parking.

This will be one of the first buildings you'll see as you enter this rustic alpine village, a short distance from Courmayeur, toward the Mont Blanc Tunnel. A few stones of the foundation date from as early as the 1300s, when the building was used as a barn for the cows that grazed on the neighboring slopes. What you'll see today is a stone building whose balconies and gables are outlined against the steep hillside into which it's built. The Berthod family transformed a dilapidated property into a rustic and comfortable hotel in 1979, surrounding the establishment with summer flowerbeds. Today it's managed by Bruna Berthod Perri and her nephew, Stefano Pellin, whose enthusiasm is evident. The unusual decor includes a collection of antique tools and a series of thick timbers, stucco, and exposed stone walls. Music is played in the bar, which is open only to residents of the hotel. There's also an exercise room and a sauna. A rich breakfast is the only meal served, but you can choose your menu in different restaurants cooperating with Le Grange. Facilities include a solarium, sauna, and gym.

WHERE TO DINE

⑤ La Brenva. Frazione Entrèves di Courmayeur, 11013 Courmayeur-Entrèves. ☎ **0165/ 869780.** Fax 0165/869726. Reservations required. Main courses 24,000–36,000 lire ($15.35–$23.05). AE, DC, MC, V. Daily 12:30–1:30pm and 7:30–10:30pm. VALDOSTAN/FRENCH.

Many skiers from Courmayeur make a special trek to Entrèves just to have a drink at the old-fashioned bar area of this hotel and restaurant. The copper espresso machine topped by a brass eagle and many of the other decorative accessories here are at least a century old. The core of the building was constructed in 1884 as a rustic hunting lodge for Victor Emmanuel. In 1897 it became a hotel, the closest one to the base of Mont Blanc, and in 1980 the owners enlarged its stone foundations with the addition of extra bedrooms and a larger eating area.

The restaurant consists of three rooms, each with exposed stone walls, wide flooring planks, hunting trophies, copper pots, and straw-bottomed chairs. Fires burn almost all the time in winter, and many diners prefer an apéritif in the unusual salon, within view of the well-chosen paintings. On any given day the menu could include prosciutto, fonduta for two, carbonada with polenta, scaloppine with fresh mushrooms, Valle d'Aostan beefsteak, and zabaglione for dessert.

Each of the 12 simple and comfortable bedrooms has a private bath, TV, phone, and lots of peace and quiet. Many of them have covered loggias. With half board included, they rent for 95,000 to 175,000 lire ($60.80 to $112) per person daily. The inn takes a vacation in either May or June (dates vary, so call first).

⑤ La Maison de Filippo. Frazione Entrèves di Courmayeur. ☎ **0165/869797.** Reservations required. Fixed-price menu 55,000 lire ($35.20). MC, V. Wed–Mon 12:30–2:30pm and 7:30–10:30pm. Closed June and Nov 5–Dec 20. VALDOSTAN.

This colorful tavern, the creation of Leo Garin, is for those who enjoy a festive atmosphere and bountiful regional food. Inside, the three-story open hallway seems like a rustic barn, with an open worn wooden staircase leading to the various dining nooks. You pass casks of nuts, baskets of fresh fruits, window ledges with bowls of salad, fruit tarts, and loaves of freshly baked bread. It's one of the most charming inns in all the valley.

The fare is served either in the mellowed rooms inside, or in the beer garden in summer, which has a full view of Mont Blanc. Mr. Garin features local specialties on an all-you-can-eat basis. Some call his mansion the "Chalet of Gluttony." A typical meal might begin with a selection of antipasti, followed by a 2-foot-long platter of about 60 varieties of sausage. Next comes a parade of pasta dishes. For a main course, you can pick everything from fondue to camoscio (chamois meat) to trout with an almond-and-butter sauce. Accompanying are huge hunks of coarse country bread served from a wicker basket the size of a laundry bin.

15 Genova & the Italian Riviera

For years the retreat of the wintering wealthy, the Italian Riviera now enjoys a broad base of tourism. Even in winter (the average temperature in January hovers around the 50° Fahrenheit mark) the Riviera is popular, although not for swimming. The protection provided by the Ligurian Apennines that loom in the background makes the balmy weather possible.

The winding coastline of the Rivieras, particularly the one that stretches from the French border to San Remo, is especially familiar to moviegoers as the background for countless flicks about sports-car racing, jewel thieves, and spies. Over the years the northwestern coast of Italy has seen the famous and the infamous, especially literary figures: the poet Shelley (who drowned off the shore), d'Annunzio, Byron, Katherine Mansfield, George Sand, and D. H. Lawrence.

The Mediterranean vegetation is characterized by pines, olives, citrus trees, and cypresses. The Western Riviera—the **Riviera di Ponente,** from the border to Genova (Genoa)—is sometimes known as the Riviera of Flowers because of its profusion of blossoms. Starting at the French border, Ventimiglia is the gateway city to Italy. Along the way you'll encounter the first big resort, Bardighera, followed by San Remo, the major center of Riviera tourism.

Genova, which divides the Riviera into two parts, is the capital of the Ligurian region. It's a big, bustling port city that has charm for those willing to take the time to seek out its treasures.

On the **Riviera di Levante** (eastern) are three small, dramatically situated resorts—Rapallo, Santa Margherita, and Portofino (the favorite of the yachting set).

EXPLORING THE ITALIAN RIVIERA BY CAR

Day 1   Let San Remo, lying east of Monaco and the French resort of Menton, be your gateway to the Italian Riviera. The capital of the Riviera di Fiori (Riviera of Flowers), San Remo evokes an Edwardian aura and has been fashionable since the turn of the century, when it attracted German and Russian aristocrats. Visit its Mercato dei Fiori (Flower Market), test your luck at its Municipal Casino, and explore the old town. For a panoramic view of the coast (sometimes you can see as far as Cannes), take the funicular to Monte Bignone. Overnight in San Remo.

Italian Riviera

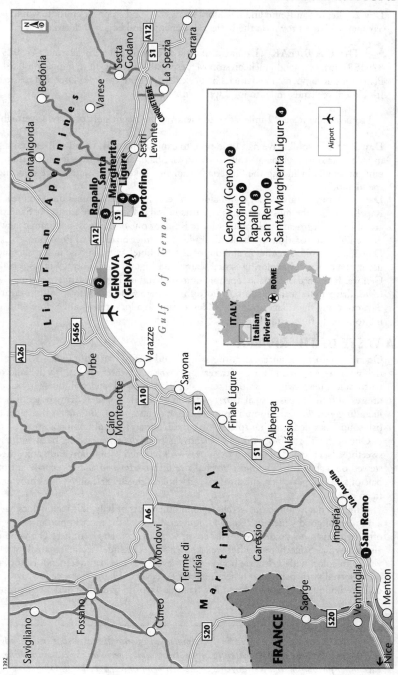

Day 2   Leave San Remo and head for Genova. A good stopover en route would be Savona, the largest town on the Riviera di Ponente, and largely industrial.

☕ **TAKE A BREAK   La Farinata,** via Montesisto 15, in Savona (☎ 019/826458), makes a good luncheon stopover, especially if you want to sample fresh fish. Platters are accompanied by farinata, flat cakes made from chickpea flour and roasted. It's closed weekends and also for 2 weeks in August.

From Savona it's a 29-mile drive to Genova, the major port of Italy. Overnight there.

Day 3   Since you'll have had little time to explore the port, spend this day taking in its attractions; include a stroll down via Garibaldi and a visit to its most important museums, including the Galleria Nazionale. Take a boat tour of the port and spend another night.

Day 4   From Genova, drive south along the cost for about 17 miles until you reach Rapallo, one of the most fashionable resorts in Italy. Take a cable car to the Sanctuary of Montallegro and walk along Monte Rosa for one of the most panoramic views of the Ligurian coastline available. Consider a summer boat trip to Portofino.

Day 5   To avoid checking in and out of another hotel, you can base in Rapallo and use it as a center for exploring Santa Margherita Ligure, lying only 19 miles east of Genova. It's a rival of Rapallo, opening onto the Gulf of Tigullio. After exploring the town, drive about 4 miles south to Portofino, where you'll want to spend the entire day, exploring the village and its hillsides, dining in a local restaurant before returning to Rapallo for the night.

A TASTE OF THE RIVIERA

Opening onto the Ligurian Sea, the area around Genova and the Italian Riviera is rich with vegetation and filled with seaside towns and winter resorts. It's the land of pesto sauce, made with fresh basil, cheese, garlic, olive oil, and walnuts. This sauce dresses all forms of pasta, such as *trenette* (thin noodles), as well as many other dishes, including *gnocchi* (little dumplings of dough or potato flour). *Buridda* is the regional fish soup (seasoned with hot spices)—it's the Ligurian form of bouillabaisse.

One of the most famous dishes of Genova is *cima alla genovese,* beef filled with fat, sweetbreads, chopped pork, and fresh peas—all flavored with onion and garlic, then stewed on a slow fire. The most favored rice dish is *riso arrosto alla genovese,* a timbale of sausage, peas, rice, mushrooms, artichokes, cheese, and onion—all browned in an oven.

Although not as numerous as the wines in other parts of Italy, this region does have a number of good wines, including Cinqueterre, one of the most important. Served often with fish, it's golden yellow in color, with an aromatic bouquet. The wine is also known as Sciacchetra. Other well-known wines include Coronata, a pale straw yellow in color, with a delicate bouquet (however, it verges on sweetness). It, too, is often served with fish. Two others include Polcevera, a light straw yellow, with a delicate bouquet and somewhat nutty flavor, a favorite with fish; and Vermentino

Impressions

The Genoese manner . . . is exceedingly animated and pantomimic; so that two friends of the lower class conversing pleasantly in the street, always seem on the eve of stabbing each other forthwith, and a stranger is immensely astonished at their not doing it.
                                                        —Charles Dickens, letter to John Forster, July 20, 1844

Ligure, also a pale yellow in color, with a good bouquet and refreshing flavor. Served with fish and last courses, this wine is sometimes semi-sparkling.

1 San Remo

10 miles E of the French border, 85 miles SW of Genova, 397 miles NW of Rome

San Remo's reputation has grown ever since Emperor Frederick William wintered in a villa here. It initially attracted the turn-of-the-century wealthy, including the French, the English, and later, the Americans. The flower-filled resort today has been considerably updated, and its casino, race track, 18-hole golf course, and deluxe Royal Hotel still attract the fashionable on occasion. Its climate is the mildest on the entire western Riviera.

ESSENTIALS

GETTING THERE **By Train** Since San Remo lies on the coast between Ventimiglia and Imperia—6 miles from each—it's a major stop for many trains. A train leaves Genova heading for the French border once per hour, stopping in San Remo. Rome is 8 hours by train from San Remo. For train information and schedules, call 0184/284081 in Genova from 7am to 11pm.

By Bus If you've arrived in Italy from France in the gateway town of Ventimiglia, you'll find a bus leaving for San Remo about every 15 minutes. The trip takes 30 minutes, and a one-way ticket costs 3,000 lire ($1.90). It's also possible to take one of three buses per day from Monaco (trip time: 1 1/2 hours). On Saturday a bus departs Milan for San Remo at 8am, arriving at 1:45pm. For information call 0184/502030.

By Car Autostrada A10, which runs east-west along the Riviera, is the fastest way for motorists to reach San Remo from either the French border or Genova.

VISITOR INFORMATION The **tourist information center** is on corso Nuvoloni (☎ **0184/571571**). It's open Monday to Saturday from 8am to 7pm and on Sunday from 9am to 1pm.

SEEING THE TOP ATTRACTIONS

Even if you're just passing through, you might want to stop off and visit **La Città Vecchia** (also known as La Pigna), the Old City on the top of the hill. Far removed in spirit from the burgeoning, sterile-looking town near the water, old San Remo blithely ignores the present, and its tiny houses on narrow, steep lanes seem to capture the past. In the new town, the palm-flanked **passeggiata dell'Imperatrice** attracts promenaders. For a scenic view, drive to the top of **San Romolo** and **Monte Bignone** (4,265 feet).

From October to June you can visit the most famous flower market in Italy, the **Mercato di Fiori,** open daily from 6 to 8am. It's held in the market hall between corso Garibaldi and piazza Colombo. In this market you'll see some 20,000 tons of roses, mimosa, and carnations, which are grown in the balmy climate of the Riviera in winter before shipment to all parts of Europe.

WHERE TO STAY

EXPENSIVE

✪ **Royal Hotel.** Corso dell'Imperatrice 80, 18038 San Remo. ☎ **0184/5391.** Fax 0184/661445. 132 rms, 14 suites. A/C MINIBAR TV TEL. 296,000–548,000 lire ($189.45–$350.70) double; 520,000–980,000 lire ($332.80–$627.20) suite. Rates include breakfast. AE, DC, MC, V. Closed Oct 6–Dec 21. Parking 14,000–25,000 lire ($8.95–$16). Bus: 20.

Although long past its heyday, this resort is still a formidable challenger to all other competition because of its sheer size and facilities. It's complete with terraces and gardens, a heated free-form saltwater swimming pool, a forest of palm trees, bright flowers, and hideaway nooks for shade. The activity centers around the garden terrace, since little emphasis is put on the public lounges (which are decked out in the grand old dowager style). The bedrooms vary considerably—some are tennis-court size with private balconies, many have sea views, and others face the hills. The furnishings range from traditional to modern. Rooms on the fifth floor—all doubles— are more expensive because they have the best views and are more luxuriously appointed.

Dining/Entertainment: There's an American bar with piano music nightly. Lunch is served in fair weather on the veranda. The more formal restaurant features both regional and international cuisine.

Services: Room service, baby-sitting, laundry, valet.

Facilities: Heated pool, sauna, solarium, minigolf, gym, tennis court, facilities for children, hairdresser, covered and open-air parking areas, garage (with a mechanic, a car wash, and a gas pump); 18-hole golf course and horseback riding nearby.

MODERATE

☉ Grand Hotel Londra. Corso Matuzia 2, 18038 San Remo. ☎ **0184/668000.** Fax 0184/668073. 149 rms, 7 suites. MINIBAR TV TEL. 247,000 lire ($158.10) double; 450,000–500,000 lire ($288–$320) suite. Rates include breakfast. AE, DC, MC, V. Closed Oct–Dec 20. Free parking. Bus: U.

Built around 1900 as a two-story hotel, this place was later expanded into the imposing structure you see today. Located within a 10-minute walk of the commercial district, it's set in a park with a view of the sea. The Michelin inspectors no longer come to call, but like the Royal it continues to coast on its past glory. However, standards are much higher at the Royal, in both housekeeping and general maintenance. The well-furnished interior is filled with framed engravings, porcelain in illuminated cases, gilt mirrors, and brass detailing. Many of the bedrooms have wrought-iron balconies. Some rooms are air-conditioned. There's also a bar and an outdoor swimming pool.

Hotel Méditerranée. Corso Cavallotti 76, 18038 San Remo. ☎ **0184/571000.** Fax 0184/541106. 62 rms, 3 suites. A/C MINIBAR TV TEL. 250,000 lire ($160) double; 350,000 lire ($224) suite. Rates include breakfast. Children staying in parents' room receive a 30% discount. AE, DC, MC, V. Parking 30,000 lire ($19.20) in garage, free outside. Bus: U.

The traffic in front of this steel-and-glass structure can be profuse, especially in peak season, but once you're inside, or in the rear garden with its Olympic-size pool, you'll scarcely be aware of it. Originally built about a century ago, the hotel received its present appearance in 1974 during a tasteful modernization. Today it competes effectively with the Grand Hotel Londra. Some of the public rooms retain signs of their turn-of-the-century grandeur and are filled with potted plants, polished floors, and modern sculptures. The bedrooms are modernized and well furnished.

Hotel Miramare Continental Palace. Corso Matuzia 9, 18038 San Remo. ☎ **0184/667601.** Fax 0184/667655. 60 rms, 6 suites. TEL. 250,000–310,000 lire ($160–$198.40) double; 430,000–600,000 lire ($275.20–$384) suite. Full board 100,000 lire ($64) per person extra. AE, DC, MC, V. Free parking. Bus: Any bus from the Termini.

A curved driveway leads past palmettos to this well-maintained traditional building set behind semitropical gardens bordering a busy thoroughfare. After passing through the well-appointed public rooms, you'll discover a seaside garden with sculptures and plenty of verdant hideaways. The bedrooms are clean and comfortable; some are in a neighboring annex with views of the garden. The hotel has a good restaurant. A covered saltwater swimming pool is in one of the outbuildings. There's also a sauna, solarium, and gym.

Suite Hotel Nyala. Strada Solaro 134, 18038 San Remo. ☎ **0184/667668.** Fax 0184/666059. 44 rms, 36 suites. A/C MINIBAR TV TEL. 160,000–300,000 lire ($102.40–$192) double or suite. Rates include breakfast. Half board 45,000 lire ($28.80) per person extra. AE, DC, MC, V.

Built in 1984, and doubled in size in 1993, this well-designed, comfortable, and modern hotel lies among the venerable trees of what was a century ago the English-style park of a since-demolished private villa. Although set in a residential neighborhood containing some impressive antique villas, this is the most modern hotel in San Remo. It's a good choice for those who prefer a more up-to-date atmosphere than that offered at the previous selections.

Most rooms have a view over the sea and a sun-filled terrace. About half of the accommodations are junior suites, with a separate sitting area and a larger balcony. (Suites and double rooms, incidentally, cost the same.) On the premises is a dining room, a palm-fringed outdoor swimming pool, a bar, and a hard-working staff.

INEXPENSIVE

Hotel Belsoggiorno Juana. Corso Matuzia 41, 18038 San Remo. ☎ **0184/667631.** Fax 0184/667471. 43 rms. TV TEL. 120,000 lire ($75) double. Rates include breakfast. Half board 105,000 lire ($67.20) per person extra. DC, MC, V. Closed Oct–Nov. Free parking. Bus: U.

This centrally located hotel is near Imperatrice, the main sea promenade, and the beaches. Attractively furnished and inviting, it contains a large reception area, plenty of living rooms for lounging, and TV rooms. Manager Luciana Maurizi De Benedetti has also provided a nice garden in which to sit and enjoy the sun and plants. Because the food is good, you may prefer to order the fixed-price menu if you're not staying here on half board. Facilities include a garage.

⑤ Hotel Eletto. Corso Matteotti 44, 18038 San Remo. ☎ **0184/531548.** 29 rms. TV TEL. 130,000 lire ($83.20) double. Half board 110,000 lire ($70.40) per person extra. AE, MC, V. Free parking. Bus: U.

This hotel is on the main artery of town, near more expensive hotels. It has a 19th-century facade with cast-iron balconies and ornate detailing. The rear of the hotel is set in a small garden with perhaps the biggest tree in San Remo casting a welcome shade over the flowerbeds. This pleasant stopover point has public rooms filled with carved panels, old mirrors, and antique furniture. The bedrooms are old-fashioned and comfortable. The sunny and well-maintained dining room serves inexpensive meals. The hotel also provides a cabana on the beach.

Hotel Mariluce. Corso Matuzia 3, 16038 San Remo. ☎ **0184/667805.** Fax 0184/667655. 23 rms, 19 with bath (tub or shower). 60,000–80,000 lire ($38.40–$51.20) double without bath, 90,000–105,000 lire ($57.60–$67.20) double with bath. Rates include breakfast. MC, V. Closed Nov–Dec 20. Free parking. Bus: U.

As you're walking along the flowered promenade away from the commercial center of town, you'll notice a flowering garden that's enclosed on one side by the neighboring walls of a Polish Catholic church; one of the walls is emblazoned with a gilded coat-of-arms. Behind the garden is the building that until 1945 housed a refugee center that Poles throughout Europe used as a base for finding friends and relatives. Today it's one of the most reasonably priced hotels in the resort, a bargain for San Remo, offering simply furnished but comfortable bedrooms and sunny public rooms. The Mariluce lies 300 yards from the main rail station. A passage under the street leads from the garden to the beach.

WHERE TO DINE

In San Remo you'll be introduced to the Ligurian cuisine, a table characterized by the Genovese style of cooking, with a reliance on seafood dishes. If it's featured on the menu, try the *buridda,* which is the Ligurian version of Mediterranean bouillabaisse. The white wines from the five villages (the Cinque Terre) are highly valued.

Il Bagatto. Via Matteotti 145. ☎ **0184/531925.** Reservations required. Main courses 25,000–35,000 lire ($16–$22.40); fixed-price menu 40,000–60,000 lire ($25.60–$38.40). AE, DC, MC, V. Mon–Sat noon–3pm and 7:30–10pm. Closed June 15–July 15. Bus: U. LIGURIAN.

Il Bagatto provides good meals in the 16th-century home of an Italian duke, with dark beams, provincial chairs, and even oversize pepper grinders brought to the tables. It's located in the shopping district of the town, about 2 blocks from the sea. Our most recent dinner began with a choice of creamy lasagne or savory hors d'oeuvres. The scaloppine with artichokes and asparagus was especially pleasing, as was (on another occasion) a mixed grill of Mediterranean fish. All orders were accompanied by potatoes and a choice of vegetables, then followed by crème caramel for dessert. Many kinds of Ligurian fish are served here, including filet of sea bass in a sauce made with fresh peppers, and a gallinella, the quintessential white-flesh Ligurian fish, roasted with potatoes and olives.

۞ Da Giannino. Lungomare Trento e Trieste 23. ☎ **0184/504014.** Reservations recommended. Main courses 30,000–45,000 lire ($19.20–$28.80); fixed-price menu 45,000–100,000 lire ($28.80–$64). AE, DC, MC, V. Tues–Sat 12:30–2:30pm and 7:30–10pm, Sun 12:30–2:30pm. Bus: U. ITALIAN/SEAFOOD.

In spite of increasing competition, this is still acclaimed as the finest restaurant in San Remo, although Paolo e Barbara is closing in fast. In a conservatively comfortable and elegant setting, you can enjoy such specialties as a warm seafood antipasti, a flavorful risotto laced with cheese and a pungently aromatic green sauce, and a selection of main courses that change with the availability of ingredients. Some of the more exotic selections are likely to include marinated cuttlefish gratinée. The wine list includes many of the better vintages of both France and Italy.

La Lanterna. Via Molo di Ponente al Porto 16. ☎ **0184/506855.** Reservations required Sat–Sun. Main courses 15,000–31,000 lire ($9.60–$19.85); fixed-price menu 46,000 lire ($29.45). AE, DC, MC, V. Fri–Wed 12:30–2:30pm and 7:30–10pm. Closed Nov 15–Jan 15. Bus: U. SEAFOOD.

Many local residents recommend this place, a nautically decorated enclave of good seafood located in a building near the harbor. Established around 1917, it's one of the few restaurants that has survived in San Remo from the heady days of its Edwardian grandeur. The clientele can get very fashionable here, especially in summer, when outdoor tables are set within view of the harbor. Meals might include an excellent version of fish soup (brodetto di pesce con crostini), a Ligurian fish fry, or a meat dish such as scaloppine in marsala wine sauce. Sea bass and red snapper are both readily available and might be grilled; fried with olive oil, herbs, and lemon; or baked with artichokes, olives, and white-wine sauce.

۞ Paolo e Barbara. Via Roma 47. ☎ **0184/531653.** Reservations recommended. Main courses 35,000–45,000 lire ($22.40–$28.80); *menu degustazione* (without wine) 100,000 lire ($64). AE, DC, MC, V. Thurs–Tues 12:30–2:15pm and 8–10pm. Closed Thurs lunch in summer. Bus: U. LIGURIAN/ITALIAN.

Named after the husband-and-wife team who owns it (the Masieri family), this restaurant near the casino has caught the imagination of San Remo since it was established in 1987. It specializes in traditional regional recipes, as well as in a handful of innovative dishes created by its staff. Meals here tend to be drawn-out affairs, so allow adequate time. Depending on the season, the menu might feature a tartare of raw marinated mackerel served with a garlic mousse and a potato-tomato and basil-flavored garnish, trenette (a regional pasta) with freshly pulverized pesto, or grilled crayfish served on a bed of onion purée with fresh herbs, olive oil, and pine nuts.

SAN REMO AFTER DARK

The high life holds forth at the **San Remo Casino,** corso Inglesi 18 (☎ **0184/5951**), located in the very center of town. For decades fashionable visitors have dined in high style in the elegant restaurant, reserved tables at the roof garden's cabaret, or tested their luck at the gaming tables. Like a white-walled palace, the pristine-looking casino stands at the top of a steep flight of stone steps above the main artery of town.

Visitors today can attend a variety of shows, fashion parades, concerts, and theatrical presentations staged throughout the year. The entrance fee is 15,000 lire ($9.40) for the French and American gaming rooms, which are open daily from 2:30pm to 3am. Presentation of a passport is required, and a jacket and tie are requested as proper attire for men. For the slot machines section, entrance is free and there's no particular dress code; it's open daily from 10am to 3am. The casino's restaurant is open nightly from 8:30pm to 1:30am, charging 60,000 to 100,000 lire ($38.40 to $64) per person for dinner. The restaurant has an orchestra playing everything from waltzes to rock music. A roof-garden cabaret is open only on Friday and Saturday nights, with shows beginning at 10pm. If you visit for drinks only (not dinner), the cost is 35,000 lire ($22.40) per drink.

2 Genova (Genoa)

88 miles SW of Milan, 311 miles NW of Rome, 120 NE of Nice (France)

It was altogether fitting that "Genoa the Proud" (Repubblica Superba) gave birth to Christopher Columbus. Its link with the sea dates back to ancient times. However, Columbus did his hometown a disservice. By blazing the trail to the New World, he dealt a devastating blow to Mediterranean ports in general, as the balance of trade shifted to newly developing centers on the Atlantic.

Even so, Genoa today is Italy's premier port, and ranks with Marseilles in European importance. In its heyday (the 13th century), its empire, extending from colonies on the Barbary Coast to citadels on the Euphrates, rivaled that of Venice. Apart from Columbus, its most famous son was Andrea Doria (the ill-fated oceanliner was named after him), who wrested his city from the yoke of French domination in the early 16th century.

Like a half moon, the port encircles the Gulf of Genoa. Its hills slope right down to the water, so walking is likely to be an up- and downhill affair. Because of the terrain, the Christopher Columbus Airport opened quite late in Genova's development.

The center of the city's maritime life, the **harbor of Genoa** makes for an interesting stroll, particularly in the part of the old town bordering the water. Sailors from many lands search for adventure and women in the little bars and cabarets that occupy the back alleyways. Often the streets are merely medieval lanes, with foreboding buildings closing in.

A Word of Warning: The harbor, particularly after dark, is not for the squeamish. It can be dangerous. If you go wandering, don't go alone and don't carry valuables. Genoa is rougher than Barcelona, more comparable to Marseilles. Not only in the harbor area, but on any side street that runs downhill, a woman is likely to lose her purse.

The present harbor is the result of extensive rebuilding, following massive World War II bombardments that crippled its seaside installations. The best way to view the overall skyline is from a **harbor cruise.** Tours depart from the Stazione Marittima daily at 10am and 2pm and cost 10,000 lire ($6.40) for adults and 7,000 lire ($4.50) for children 9 and under and seniors 60 and over.

ESSENTIALS

GETTING THERE   By Plane   Alitalia and other carriers fly into the **Aeroporto Internazionale de Genova Cristoforo Colombo,** 4 miles west of the city center in Sestri Ponente (☎ **010/60151** for information about flights).

By Train   Genoa has good rail connections with the rest of Italy; it lies only 1 1/2 hours from Milan, 3 hours from Florence, and 1 1/2 hours from the French border. Genoa has two major rail stations, the **Stazione Prìncipe** and the **Stazione Brignole.** Chances are you'll arrive at the Prìncipe, which is nearest to the harbor and the old part of the city. However, both trains and municipally operated buses run between the two stations. You can phone for **train information** (☎ **010/284081**).

By Bus   It's best to arrive in Genoa by car, plane, or rail, then rely on the bus to take you up or down the coast. **SITA buses** (☎ **010/313851**), originating in Genoa, service the full length of the Ligurian coast in both directions.

By Car   Motorists will find Genoa right along the main autostrada (A10) that begins at the French border and continues along the Ligurian coastline.

By Ferry   It's highly likely that you'll find yourself in Genoa waiting for the ferryboat to take you to such offshore destinations as Sardinia or Sicily. If so, the number to call for information is the **Stazione Marittima** (☎ **010/261466**). You can also arrive in Genoa by ferry. There's a 22-hour service to Genoa originating in Palermo (Sicily); a one-way ticket costs 97,300 lire ($62.25) per person. Ferries also leave Porto Torres (Sardinia) for Genoa; the one-way fare is 66,000 lire ($42.25).

VISITOR INFORMATION   Visitors can get information at the major office of **Azienda di Promozione Turistica,** via al Porto Antico-Palazzino S. Maria (☎ **010/24871**). It's open daily from 9am to 4:30pm. Information booths dispensing tourist literature can also be found at the rail stations, at Porta Prìncipe, and at the airport. The rail station office is open Monday to Saturday from 8am to 8pm and Sunday from 9am to noon; the airport office, Monday to Saturday from 8am to 8pm.

CITY LAYOUT   Genoa opens onto the Porto di Genova, and most of the section of interest to visitors lies between the two main rail stations, **Stazione Prìncipe,** on the western fringe of the town, near the port, and **Stazione Brignole,** to the northeast, which opens onto piazza Verdi. A major artery is **via XX Settembre,** which runs between piazza Ferrari in the west and piazza della Vittoria in the east. **Via Balbi** is another major artery, beginning its run east of the Stazione Prìncipe, off piazza Acquaverde. Via Balbi ends at piazza Nunziata. From there, a short walk along via Cairola leads to the most important tourist street in Genoa, the palazzo-flanked **via Garibaldi** (but more about that later).

FAST FACTS: GENOA

American Express   The AMEX representative in Genoa is Viatur, piazza Fontane Marose 3 (☎ 010/561241). But you should be a client—that is, carry an American Express card or use the company's traveler's checks—before you have your mail sent there. The office is open Monday to Friday from 9am to 1pm and 3 to 7pm.

Genova

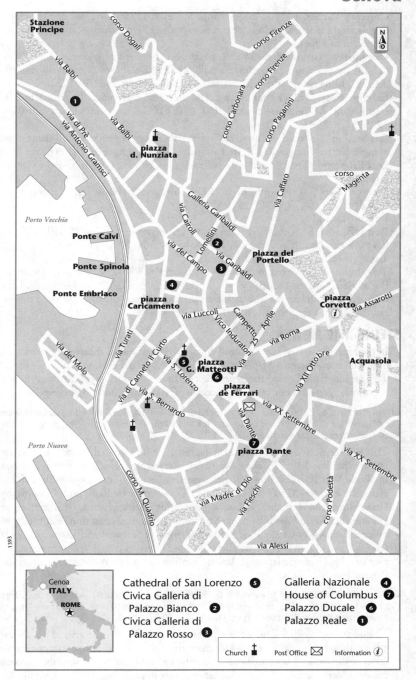

Stazione Principe

corso Dogali

corso Firenze

corso Firenze

via Balbi

via Balbi

via di Prè

via Antonio Gramsci

corso Carbonara

corso Paganini

1 Palazzo Reale

piazza d. Nunziata

corso Magenta

via Caffaro

Porto Vecchio

Galleria Garibaldi

Ponte Calvi

via Cairoli

Lomellini

via del Campo

2

3 via Garibaldi

piazza del Portello

Ponte Spinola

Ponte Embriaco

4

piazza Caricamento

via Luccoli

Vico Indoratori

Campetto

Aprile

25

via Roma

piazza Corvetto
i

via Assarotti

Acquasola

via Turati

via del Molo

via di Canneto il Curto

via S. Lorenzo

5

piazza G. Matteotti

6

piazza de Ferrari

via Dante

via XX Settembre

via XII Ottobre

via S. Bernardo

Porto Nuovo

7 **piazza Dante**

via XX Settembre

corso M. Quadrio

via Madre di Dio

via Fieschi

corso Podestà

via Alessi

1393

Genoa
ITALY

ROME
★

Cathedral of San Lorenzo **5**

Civica Galleria di
Palazzo Bianco **2**

Civica Galleria di
Palazzo Rosso **3**

Galleria Nazionale **4**

House of Columbus **7**

Palazzo Ducale **6**

Palazzo Reale **1**

Church ■   Post Office ✉   Information *i*

Currency Exchange   You can exchange money at Delfino, via Balbi 161R. However, both the Brignole and Prìncipe railway stations have exchange offices open daily from 7am to 10pm.

Drugstores   Genoa has no 24-hour pharmacies, but for a supplement of 5,000 lire ($3.20) after midnight, Pescetto, via Balbi 185R (☎ 010/56921), will fill your order. For the names of other pharmacies operating at night, call 010/192.

Emergencies   Dial **113** for assistance in a general emergency. If it's automobile trouble, call AI, Soccorso Stradale (☎ **010/116**). For an ambulance, call **010/5705951**.

Gas Station   If you don't mind self-service, there's an Agip gas station that's open at night located along viale Brigate Partigiane. You must have the right change.

Lost Property   The lost-and-found office is the Comune, via Garibaldi 9 (☎ 010/20981).

Medical Care   If you're in need of a doctor, try Ospedale San Martino, viale Benedetto XV 10 (☎ 010/35351).

Police   Dial **113**.

Post Office   The post office, at via Dante and piazza de Ferrari (☎ 010/593811), has a telex and fax. It's open Monday to Saturday from 8:15am to 7:40pm.

Taxi   To call a radio taxi, dial **5966**.

Telephone   If you need to make a long-distance call, it's cheapest to go to the office at via XX Settembre 139, which is open 24 hours a day (your hotel is likely to impose heavy surcharges). You can also place calls at both the Brignole and Prìncipe railroad stations until 9pm.

SEEING THE SIGHTS

In the heart of the city, you can stroll down ✪ **via Garibaldi,** the street of patricians, on which noble Genovese families erected splendid palazzi in late Renaissance times. The guiding hand behind the general appearance and most of the architecture was Alessi, who grew to fame in the 16th century (he studied under Michelangelo).

Civica Galleria di Palazzo Rosso. Via Garibaldi 18. ☎ **010/282641.** Admission 6,000 lire ($3.85), free for children 17 and under and for seniors 60 and over. Tues, Thurs-Fri, and Sun 9am–1pm; Wed and Sat 9am–7pm. Bus: 18, 19, 20, 35, 39, or 40.

This 17th-century palace was once the home of the Brignole-Sale, a local aristocratic family who founded a Genovese dynasty. It was restored after having been bombed in World War II, and it now contains a good collection of paintings, with such exceptional works as *Giuditta* by Veronese, *St. Sebastian* by Reni, and *Cleopatra* by Guercino. Perhaps the best-known exhibit is Sir Anthony van Dyck's portrait of Pauline and Anton Giulio Brignole-Sale from the original collection, and the magnificent frescoes by Gregorio de Ferrari (*Spring* and *Summer*) and Domenico Piola (*Autumn* and *Winter*). There are also collections of ceramics and sculpture and a display of gilded baroque statuary. Across from this red palace is the white palace, the Palazzo Bianco Gallery.

Civica Galleria di Palazzo Bianco. Via Garibaldi 11. ☎ **010/291803.** Admission 6,000 lire ($3.75) adults, free for children 17 and under and for seniors 60 and over. Tues, Thurs–Fri, and Sun 9am–1pm; Wed and Sat 9am–7pm. Bus: 18, 19, 20, 35, 39, or 40.

The duchess of Gallier donated this palace, along with her collection of art, to the city. Although the palace originally dates from the 16th century, its appearance today is the work of later architects. Gravely damaged during the war, the restored palace reflects the most recent advances in museum planning. The most significant paintings—from the Dutch and Flemish schools—include Gerard David's *Polittico della Cervara* and Memling's *Jesus Blessing the Faithful,* as well as works by Sir

Anthony van Dyck and Peter Paul Rubens. A wide-ranging survey of European and local artists is presented—with paintings by Caravaggio, Zurbarán, and Murillo, and works by Bernardo Strozzi (a whole room) and Alessandro Magnasco (an excellent painting of a scene in a Genovese garden).

Galleria Nazionale (National Gallery). In the Palazzo Spinola, piazza della Pellicceria 1. ☎ **010/294661.** Admission 8,000 lire ($5.10) adults, free for children 18 and under and for seniors 60 and over. Monday 9am–1pm, Tues–Sat 9am–7pm, Sun 2–7pm. Bus: 1, 8, 18, 19, or 20.

The National Gallery houses a major painting collection. (This palace was designed for the Grimaldi family in the 16th century as a private residence, although the Spinolas took it over eventually.) Its notable works include Joos van Cleve's *Madonna in Prayer,* Antonello da Messina's *Ecce Homo,* and Giovanni Pisano's *Guistizia.* The gallery is also known for its decorative arts collection (furniture, silver, and ceramics, among other items).

Galleria di Palazzo Reale (Royal Palace Gallery). Via Balbi 10. ☎ **010/27101.** Admission 8,000 lire ($5.10) adults, free for children 18 and under and for seniors 60 and over. Sun–Tues 9am–1:30pm, Wed–Sat 9am–7pm. Bus: 18, 19, or 20.

Located a 5-minute walk from Stazione Prìncipe, the Royal Palace was started about 1650, and work continued until the early years of the 18th century. It was built for the Balbi family, then sold to the Durazzos. It later became one of the royal palaces of the Savoias in 1824. King Charles Albert modified many of the rooms around 1840. As in all Genovese palazzi, some of these subsequent alterations marred the original designs. Its Galleria is filled with paintings and sculpture, works of art by van Dyck, Tintoretto, G. F. Romanelli, and L. Giordano. Frescoes and antiques from the 17th to the 19th century are displayed. Seek out, in particular, the Hall of Mirrors and the Throne Room.

Cathedral of San Lorenzo (Lawrence). Piazza San Lorenzo, via Tommaso Reggio 17. ☎ **010/296695.** Free admission. Tues–Sat 9–11:30am and 3–5:30pm. Bus: 18, 19, or 39.

Although Genoa is noted for its medieval churches, this one towers over them all. The cathedral is distinguished by its bands of black and white marble adorning the facade in the Pisan style. In its present form it dates from the 13th century, although it was erected upon the foundation of a much earlier structure. Alessi, referred to earlier, designed the dome, and the campanile (bell tower) dates from the 16th century. The Chapel of John the Baptist, with interesting Renaissance sculpture, is said to contain the remains of the saint for whom it's named.

WHERE TO STAY

Generally, hotels in Genoa are second rate, but some good finds await those who search diligently.

Warning: Some of the cheap hotels and pensions in and around the waterfront are to be avoided. Our recommendations, however, are suitable even for women traveling alone.

EXPENSIVE

Bristol-Palace. Via XX Settembre 35, 16121 Genova. ☎ **010/592541.** Fax 010/561756. 128 rms, 5 suites. A/C MINIBAR TV TEL. 380,000 lire ($243.20) double; 490,000 lire ($313.60) suite. Rates include breakfast. AE, DC, MC, V. Parking 40,000 lire ($25.60). Bus: 18, 19, 20, 33, or 34.

The Bristol-Palace, dating from the late 19th century, has a number of features that will make your stay in Genoa special, even though it's in the grimy heart of town. Its obscure entrance behind colonnades on a commercial street is misleading; the salons and drawing rooms inside are furnished nicely with traditional pieces, although both fabrics and furnishings are beginning to show their age. The larger of the bedrooms have an old-fashioned elegance, are spacious and comfortable, and are tastefully furnished, often with chandeliers, Queen Anne desks, and padded headboards. The hotel's stairway is one of the most stunning in Genoa. The English bar is a favorite rendezvous point, and a small but elegant restaurant, Il Caffè de Bristol, offers daily lunches and dinners.

Hotel Savoia Majestic. Via Arsenale di Terra 5, 16126 Genova. ☎ **010/261641.** Fax 010/261883. 123 rms, 5 suites. MINIBAR TV TEL. 290,000–340,000 lire ($185.60–$217.60) double; from 410,000 lire ($262.40) suite. Rates include breakfast. AE, DC, MC, V. Parking 30,000 lire ($19.20). Bus: 18, 35, 37, 46, or 47.

Located across from piazza Prìncipe, the 1887 Hotel Savoia Majestic still contains some of its original accessories, although its heyday when it entertained dukes and their duchesses has long since past. These days clients tend to be European business travelers. The decor of the high-ceilinged bedrooms ranges from modern to conservatively old-fashioned. Try for a room on the sixth floor for the best views of the harbor. All but 20 of the rooms are air-conditioned. Some of the bathrooms are unusually large with pink marble surfaces, whereas others are extremely cramped. Because the rooms vary so widely from good to bad, your evaluation of this hotel will depend entirely on where you're stashed for the night. The lobby and reception area of this hotel is shared with another establishment, the Hotel Londra & Continentale. The restaurant here is so routine you'll want to seek better fare at one of the nearby trattorie.

Jolly Hotel Plaza. Via Martin Piaggio 11, 16122 Genova. ☎ **010/839-3641,** or 800/221-2626 in the U.S., 800/237-0319 in Canada. Fax 010/839-1850. 146 rms, 1 suite. A/C MINIBAR TV TEL. 310,000–390,000 lire ($198.40–$249.60) double; 520,000–720,000 lire ($332.80–$460.80) suite. Rates include breakfast. AE, DC, MC, V. Parking 30,000 lire ($19.20). Bus: 18, 37, 46, or 47.

A four-star member of the Jolly chain, this hotel is newer than its modified classic facade would suggest. Centrally located near piazza Corvetto, it was built in 1950 to replace an older hotel destroyed during an air raid in World War II. In 1992 the hotel was renovated, upgraded, and enlarged. The Jolly links two former hotels, the Baglioni Eliseo and the Plaza. The rooms in the old Eliseo are generally more spacious than those in the former Plaza. Elegant touches include mother-of-pearl inlay in the doors and marble baths. The rooms in the old Plaza are more cramped and decorated with a dull brown decor. On the premises are an American-style bar and a grill room, La Villetta di Negro. When business is slow, the management sometimes opts not to open the restaurant on weekends.

MODERATE

City Hotel. Via San Sebastiano 6, 16123 Genova. ☎ **010/5545.** Fax 010/586301. 66 rms, 3 suites. A/C MINIBAR TV TEL. 260,000 lire ($166.40) double; 300,000 lire ($192) suite. Rates include breakfast. AE, DC, MC, V. Parking 30,000 lire ($18.75). Bus: 18, 19, 20, 21, 31, or 41.

One of the best hotels in its category is located in a starkly angular stucco and travertine postwar building, surrounded by a crumbling series of town houses. The hotel itself was last renovated in 1990. The convenient location, near piazza Corvetto and via Garibaldi, is one of the hotel's best features. Other pluses include a welcoming staff, a comfortable wood-and-granite lobby, and modernized rooms. The bedrooms contain parquet floors, specially designed furniture, and up-to-date amenities. The hotel also has a cocktail bar serving snacks and a first-class restaurant that serves many regional specialties. A short list of cold and hot foods are served room service–style throughout the day and early evening.

INEXPENSIVE

✪ **Albergo Viale Sauli.** Viale Sauli 5, 16121 Genova. ☎ **010/561397.** Fax 010/590092. 56 rms. A/C MINIBAR TV TEL. 160,000 lire ($102.40) double. Rates include breakfast. AE, DC, MC, V. Bus: 17, 18, 19, or 20.

This hotel is located on the second floor of a modern concrete office building, just off a busy shopping street in the center of town. It's scattered over three floors, each of them reachable by elevator from the building's lobby. The high-ceilinged public rooms include a bar, a breakfast room, and a reception area, all with big windows and lots of comfort. Enore Sceresini is the opera-loving owner, and his clients usually include businesspeople who appreciate cleanliness and comfort. Each of the units has marble floors and a spacious bath.

⑤ **Hotel Agnello d'Oro.** Vico delle Monachette 6, 16126 Genova. ☎ **010/246-2084.** Fax 010/246-2327. 38 rms. TV TEL. 140,000 lire ($89.60) double. AE, DC, MC, V. Bus: 18, 20, 35, 37, or 41.

When the Doria family owned this structure and everything around it in the 1600s, they carved their family crest on the walls of the building near the top of the alley so that all of Genoa would know the point at which their property began. The symbol was a golden lamb, and you can still see one at the point where the narrow street joins the busy boulevard leading to the Stazione Prìncipe. The hotel, which was named after the animal on the crest, is a 17th-century building that includes vaulted ceilings and paneling in the lobby. About half the units are in a newer wing, but if you want the oldest accommodations, ask for Room 6, 7, or 8. Today the hotel is maintained by a family who have installed a small bar and restaurant off the lobby.

Hotel Astoria. Piazza Brignole 4, 16122 Genova. ☎ **010/873316.** Fax 010/831-7236. 73 rms. TV TEL. 208,000 lire ($133.10) double. Rates include breakfast. AE, DC, MC, V. Bus: 18.

Originally built in the 1920s but opened as a hotel only in 1978, this establishment has lots of polished paneling, wrought-iron accents, beige marble floors, and a baronial carved fireplace in one of the public rooms. The rooms are comfortably furnished and well maintained. The hotel sits on an uninspiring square that contains a filling station, and its view encompasses a traffic hub and many square blocks of apartment buildings. There's a bar on the premises, but no restaurant. There's no garage—street parking only.

Hotel Vittoria Orlandi. Via Balbi 33–45, 16126 Genova. ☎ **010/261923.** Fax 010/246-2656. 56 rms. TV TEL. 90,000–140,000 lire ($57.60–$89.60) double. AE, DC, MC, V. Parking 30,000 lire ($19.20). Bus: 18 or 37.

Since this hotel is constructed on one of the hillsides for which Genoa is famous, its entrance is under a tunnel that opens at a point about a block from the Stazione Prìncipe. An elevator will take you up to the reception area. The establishment, built in 1926, welcomes a wide variety of guests to its simple but clean rooms. Many of the rooms have balconies, and about half are air-conditioned and contain a minibar. Best of all, the hotel is quiet because of the way it's sheltered from the busy boulevards by other buildings.

WHERE TO DINE

Genoa, which has been praised for its cuisine, has lots of restaurants and trattorie, many of which are strung along the harbor. The following recommendations will give you several opportunities to judge it for yourself.

Il Cucciolo. Viale Sauli 33. ☎ **010/561321.** Reservations recommended. Main courses 28,000–30,000 lire ($17.90–$19.20). AE, DC, MC, V. Mon–Sat noon–3pm and 7:30–10:30pm. Bus: 17, 18, 20, 36, 37, or 45. TUSCAN.

If you're headed for this place, go armed with a good map, as Il Cucciolo lies on one of those "hidden" squares in the center of the city. (However, parking is available in the restaurant's private lot.) Should you be in the area at night, you'll find lanterns placed festively outside, adorning this ground-floor restaurant in a 19th-century building. The restaurant was established here in 1934. You not only get good Ligurian food, but well-chosen wines as well. Specialties include seafood antipasti, both warm and cold; ravioli with veal and a butter-sage sauce; fish baked in cartoccio (in a paper bag); and calves' liver prepared in the style of Venice. The service is efficient and the reception is gracious.

☼ Da Giacomo. Corso Italia 1R. ☎ **010/362-9647.** Reservations required. Main courses 25,000–45,000 lire ($16–$28.80); fixed-price menu 75,000 lire ($48). AE, DC, MC, V. Tues–Sat 12:30–2:30pm and 7:30–10pm. Closed 1 week in Aug. Bus: 17, 18, or 37. LIGURIAN.

Many food critics regard Da Giacomo as the premier restaurant of Genoa. The service is deluxe, as is the ambiance, decorated in an elegant modern style and graced with plants. Eating has been called "an art" at this refined restaurant, established in 1965. Ligurian cooking is dominated by the sea and so is the menu here, beginning with superb seafood antipasti, some of which is raw but cut and carved with the exquisite care you find in Tokyo. Meat, fish, and poultry dishes are prepared with unusual flair. Pesto sauce accompanies many dishes, especially the pasta. This sauce in Ligure is made of pine nuts (sometimes walnuts), olive oil, basil, and cheese. During the Crusades it was reported that the Genovese contingent could always be identified by the aroma of pesto surrounding them. Some of the finest regional wines in Italy are offered, and desserts are made fresh daily on the premises.

☼ Gran Gotto. Viale Brigate Bisagno 69R. ☎ **010/564344.** Reservations recommended. Main courses 30,000–37,000 lire ($19.20–$23.70); fixed-price menu 85,000 lire ($54.40). AE, MC, V. Mon–Fri 12:30–2:30pm and 7:30–10pm, Sat 7:30–10pm. Closed Aug 12–31. Bus: 17, 18, 31, or 37. SEAFOOD.

Although it was established in 1937, and has been in the same family ever since, this restaurant moved to new quarters in 1995. Today, amid a setting of modern art and vaguely Austrian accessories, it ranks as the top restaurant in Genoa in our view, although some critics still cite Da Giacomo for that honor. Its name translates from Genovese dialect as "large glass" (as in a glass of wine). The emphasis is on seafood, but the meat and pasta dishes aren't neglected. In fact, the most typical offering, trenette al pesto, is quite famous, a pasta of paper-thin noodles (depending on the artistry of the chef) that's served with the characteristic pesto. The delicately simmered risotto is also tempting. The main dishes are reasonably priced and of high standard, including the mixed fish fry and the French baby squid. The zuppa di pesce, like a Mediterranean bouillabaisse, has made many a luncheon for many a gourmet. The rognone al cognac is another superb choice—tender calves' kidneys that have been cooked and delicately flavored in cognac.

Ristorante Saint Cyr. Piazza Marsala 4. ☎ **010/886897.** Reservations required. Main courses 30,000–35,000 lire ($19.20–$22.40). AE, DC, MC, V. Mon–Fri noon–2:30pm and 7:30–10pm, Sat 7:30–10pm. Closed Dec 23–Jan 7 and 1 week in Aug. Bus: 18, 20, 35, 37, or 41. LIGURIAN/PIEMONTESE.

Our favorite time to come to this restaurant is at night, when some of the most discriminating palates in Genoa might be seen enjoying dishes generously adapted from regional recipes. The location is near piazza Corvetto in a 1900 printing factory. The restaurant was established here in 1971. The food items change daily, although a recent menu featured rice with truffles and cheese, a timpale of fresh spinach, a charlotte of fish, and a variety of braised meats, each delicately seasoned and perfectly prepared. Specialties include scamone (a certain cut of beef) cooked in Barolo wine and ravioli al sugo do carne (ravioli with sauce made from meat juices). The restaurant is also open for lunch, when the clientele is likely to be conservatively dressed businesspeople discussing shipping contracts.

Ristorante Zeffirino. Via XX Settembre 20. ☎ **010/591990.** Reservations recommended. Main courses 30,000–60,000 lire ($19.20–$38.40); fixed-price menu 60,000 lire ($38.40). AE, DC, MC, V. Thurs–Tues noon–3pm and 7pm–midnight. Bus: 17, 18, 20, 29, 31, or 36. LIGURIAN.

Located in a cul-de-sac just off one of the busiest boulevards of Genoa, this place has hosted everyone from Frank Sinatra to Luciano Pavarotti, from Pope John Paul II to Liza Minnelli. Established in the 1930s, it moved to its present location in the 1950s. At least 14 members of the Zeffirino family prepare the best pasta in the city, from recipes collected from all over Italy. These include lesser-known varieties such as quadrucci, pettinati, and cappelletti, as well as the more familiar taglietelle and lasagne. Next, you can select from a vast array of meat and fish, along with 1,000 kinds of wine. Ligurian specialties, including risotto alla pescatore and beef stew with artichokes, are featured. Try a wide array of shellfish—either baked or steamed—and served with seasonal vegetables.

3 Rapallo

296 miles NW of Rome, 17 miles SE of Genoa, 100 miles S of Milan

A top seaside resort—known for years to the chic and wealthy crowd who live in the villas studding the hillside—Rapallo occupies a remarkable site overlooking the Gulf of Tigullio. In summer the crowded heart of Rapallo takes on a carnival air, as hordes of bathers occupy the rocky sands along the beach. In the area is an 18-hole golf course, as well as an indoor swimming pool, a riding club, and a modern harbor. You can also take a cable car to the **Sanctuary di Montallegro,** then walk to **Monte Rosa** for one of the finest views of the Ligurian coast. There are many opportunities for summer **boat trips,** not only to Portofino but to the Cinque Terre.

Rapallo's long history is often likened to Genoa's. It became part of the Repubblica Superba in 1229, but Rapallo had existed long before that. Its **cathedral** dates from the 6th century when it was founded by the bishops of Milan. Walls once enclosed the medieval town, but now only the **Saline Gate** remains. Rapallo has also been the scene of many an international meeting, the most notable of which was the 1917 conference of wartime allies.

ESSENTIALS

GETTING THERE   By Train   Three trains from Genoa stop off here each hour. A one-way fare is 2,700 lire ($1.75). Service is daily from 4:30am to midnight.

By Bus   Buses operated by **SITA** (☎ **010/588162** in Genoa for information and schedules) link Rapallo with Genoa.

By Car   From Genoa, continue southeast along the A12 autostrada.

VISITOR INFORMATION   The **tourist information center** is at via Diaz 9 (☎ **0185/51282**). It's open Monday to Saturday from 9am to 12:30pm and 3 to 7pm and on Sunday from 9am to 12:30pm.

GETTING AROUND   Once you arrive in Rapallo by public or private transportation, you can walk around to the following hotels and restaurants.

WHERE TO STAY

EXPENSIVE

✪ Grand Hotel Bristol. Via Aurelia Orientale 369, 16035 Rapallo. ☎ **0185/273313.** Fax 0185/55800. 85 rms, 6 suites. A/C MINIBAR TV TEL. 280,000–360,000 lire ($179.20–$230.40) double; from 800,000 lire ($512) suite. Rates include breakfast. AE, MC, V. Parking 15,000 lire ($9.60) in the garage, free outdoors.

This hotel, one of the Riviera's grand old buildings and Rapallo's finest resort, is still a viable choice in spite of falling standards. Originally built in 1908, it was reopened in 1984 as the personal brainchild of a multimillionaire who died shortly after its transformation. The turn-of-the-century pink-and-white facade, with surrounding shrubbery and iron gates, was spruced up but basically unchanged during the 5-year rebuilding program. The interior, however, was mostly gutted. The inviting waters of a pool are visible from many of the bedrooms. The kitchens are about the most modern anywhere, and the polite staff is dressed in formal morning suits.

Some of the bedrooms have private terraces, and all contain electronic window blinds, lots of mirrors, and oversize beds.

Dining/Entertainment: The hotel, in theory, has several restaurants, including an exposed rooftop restaurant that's often closed when it's too hot. If the house count is low, only one restaurant might be open.

Services: Room service, baby-sitting, laundry, valet, hairdresser, beautician, massage salon.

Facilities: The hotel's free-form swimming pool is one of the biggest in the region. There's also a series of conference rooms.

MODERATE

Eurotel. Via Aurelia di Ponente 22, 16035 Rapallo. ☎ **0185/60981.** Fax 0185/50635. 65 rms. A/C MINIBAR TV TEL. 190,000–220,000 lire ($121.60–$140.80) double. Rates include breakfast. AE, DC, MC, V. Parking 18,000 lire ($11.50) in the garage, free outdoors.

With seven floors and three elevators, this vivid sienna-colored structure is one of the tallest hotels in town, set above the port at the top of a winding road where you'll have to negotiate the oncoming traffic with care. In addition to its room accommodations, the hotel contains about 35 privately owned condominiums that are usually occupied during part of each year by their owners. The lobby has marble floors and a helpful staff. All units contain built-in cabinets, arched loggias with views over the gulf of Rapallo, and beds that fold, Murphy style, into the walls. A bar and a second-floor panoramic restaurant, Antica Aurelia, are on the premises, as is a small rectangular swimming pool set in a verdant garden.

INEXPENSIVE

⑤ Hotel Giulio Cesare. Corso Cristoforo Colombo 52, 16035 Rapallo. ☎ **0185/50685.** Fax 0185/60896. 53 rms. TV TEL. 130,000 lire ($83.20) double; 95,000 lire ($60.80) per person double with half board. AE, MC, V. Closed Nov–Dec 20. Free parking in low season, 10,000–15,000 lire ($6.40–$9.60) in high season.

This modernized, four-story villa is a bargain for the Italian Riviera. When the genial owner skillfully renovated the establishment, he kept expenses down to keep room rates lower. The hotel, which lies on the coast road about 90 feet from the sea, offers bedrooms with a homelike atmosphere, which feature good views of the Gulf of Tigullio and are furnished with tasteful reproductions (most of the rooms have sunny balconies). Ask for the rooms on the top floor if you want a better view and quieter surroundings. The meals are prepared with fine ingredients (the fresh fish dishes are superb).

Hotel Miramare. Lungomare Vittorio Veneto 27, 16035 Rapallo. ☎ **0185/230261.** Fax 0185/273570. 22 rms, 6 suites. MINIBAR TV TEL. 100,000–150,000 lire ($64–$96) double; 150,000–170,000 lire ($96–$108.80) suite. Half board 110,000–150,000 lire ($70.40–$96) per person. AE, DC, MC, V. Closed Nov. Parking 15,000 lire ($9.60).

Located on the water near a stone gazebo is this jazz age (1929) re-creation of a Renaissance villa, with exterior frescoes that have faded in the salt air. The gardens in front have been replaced by a glass extension that contains a clean and contemporary restaurant (see "Where to Dine," below). The accommodations inside are clean and simple, comfortable, and high-ceilinged. Many on them have iron balconies that stretch toward the harbor.

WHERE TO DINE

Ristorante da Monique. Lungomare Vittorio Veneto 6. ☎ **0185/50541.** Reservations required. Main courses 15,000–25,000 lire ($9.60–$16). AE, DC, MC, V. Wed–Mon 12:30–2:30pm and 7:30–10pm. Closed Jan 10–Feb 8. SEAFOOD.

This is one of the most popular seafood restaurants along the harbor, especially in summer when the tavern chairs are almost completely filled. It has been a local favorite since the 1930s. It features nautical decor and big windows that overlook the boats in the marina. As you'd expect, fish is the specialty, including seafood salad, fish soup, risotto with shrimp, spaghetti with clams or mussels, grilled fish, and both tagliatelle and scampi "Monique." Some of these dishes may not always hit the mark, but you'll rarely go wrong ordering the grilled fish.

Ristorante Elite. Via Milite Ignoto 19. ☎ **0185/50551.** Main courses 14,000–27,000 lire ($8.95–$17.30); fixed-price menu 35,000 lire ($22.40). AE, DC, MC, V. Fri–Wed noon–2:30pm and 7:30–10pm. Closed several days in Nov. SEAFOOD.

This restaurant is set back from the water on a busy commercial street in the center of town. It was established in the 1960s in a building from the 1930s. Mainly fish is served; the offering depends on the catch of the day. Your dinner might consist of mussels marinara, minestrone Genovese style, risotto marinara, trenette al pesto, scampi, zuppa di pesci, sole meunière, turbot, or a mixed fish fry from the Ligurian coast. A limited selection of the standard meat dishes is available, too. At the peak of the midsummer tourist invasion, the restaurant is likely to remain open every day.

Ristorante Miramare. In the Hotel Miramare, lungomare Vittorio Veneto 27. ☎ **0185/230261.** Reservations recommended. Main courses 15,000–35,000 lire ($9.60–$22.40). AE, DC, MC, V. Daily 12:30–2pm and 7:30–9:30pm. SEAFOOD/LIGURIAN.

Set in a previously recommended hotel, a building originally conceived as a private villa, this restaurant serves well-prepared and unpretentious food in a modern dining room overlooking the sea. Your meal might include fried calamari, spaghetti with clams, sea bass or turbot baked with potatoes and artichokes, veal in marsala sauce, or flavorful versions of fish soup.

4 Santa Margherita Ligure

19 miles E of Genoa, 3 miles S of Portofino, 296 miles NW of Rome

A resort rival to Rapallo, Santa Margherita Ligure also occupies a beautiful position on the Gulf of Tigullio. Its attractive harbor is usually thronged with fun seekers, and the resort offers the widest range of accommodations in all price levels on the eastern Riviera. It has a festive appearance, with a promenade, flower beds, and palm trees swaying in the wind. As is typical of the Riviera, its beach combines rock and sand. Santa Margherita Ligure is linked to Portofino by a narrow road. It's on the

Rome–Genoa rail line. The climate of Santa Margherita Ligure is mild, even in the winter months, when many elderly clients visit the resort.

The town dates back to A.D. 262. The official name of Santa Margherita Ligure was given to the town by Victor Emmanuel II in 1863. Before that it had many other names, including Porto Napoleone, an 1812 designation from Napoléon.

You can visit the richly embellished **Sanctuary of Santa Maria della Rosa,** piazza Caprera, with its Italian and Flemish paintings, along with relics of the saint for whom the town was named.

ESSENTIALS

GETTING THERE   By Train   Three trains per hour arrive from Genoa daily from 4:30am to midnight. The one-way fare is 2,700 lire ($1.75). The **train station** is at piazza Federico Raoul Nobili (☎ **0185/286630** for rail information).

By Bus   Buses run frequently between Portofino and Santa Margherita Ligure daily. A one-way ticket costs 1,700 lire ($1.10). You can also catch a bus in Rapallo for the 10-minute ride to Santa Margherita; during the day one leaves Rapallo every 20 minutes. For information call 0185/51306.

By Car   Take Route 227 southeast from Genoa.

VISITOR INFORMATION   The **tourist information center** is at via 25 Aprile 2B (☎ **0185/287485**). It's open Monday to Saturday from 9am to 12:30pm and 3 to 7pm and on Sunday from 9am to 12:30pm.

GETTING AROUND   Santa Margherita Ligure is relatively compact, and once you reach the place—by either public or private transportation—you can walk to the following recommendations.

WHERE TO STAY
VERY EXPENSIVE

Imperiale Palace Hotel. Via Pagana 19, 16038 Santa Margherita Ligure. ☎ **0185/288991.** Fax 0185/284223. 102 rms, 13 junior suites. A/C MINIBAR TV TEL. 360,000–540,000 lire ($230.40–$345.60) double; from 650,000 lire ($416) suite. Rates include breakfast. AE, DC, MC, V. Closed Dec–Mar. Parking 20,000 lire ($12.80).

The Imperial looks like an ornate gilded palace, and many guests, attracted to its faded grandeur, choose to spend their "season on the Riviera" here. Although still regal, it's fading a bit, and the Grand Hotel Miramare (see below) has overtaken it for supremacy. Located at the edge of the resort, it's built against a hillside and surrounded by semitropical gardens. The time-worn public rooms of the Imperial live up to the hotel's name—old courtly splendor dominates, with vaulted ceilings, satin-covered antiques, ornate mirrors, and inlaid marble floors.

The bedrooms vary widely, from royal suites to simple singles away from the sea. Many of the rooms have elaborate ceilings, balconies, brass beds, chandeliers, and white antique furniture. Others are rather bare, so your opinion of this hotel will likely depend on the room you get.

Dining/Entertainment: The formal dining room serves Ligurian and international meals. There's also a two-decker open-air restaurant. The music room, with its grand piano and satin chairs, is still enjoyed at teatime. In summer, live music is presented on the terrace.

Service: Room service, baby-sitting, laundry, valet.

Facilities: All along the water's edge, a festive recreation center has been created, with an oval flagstone swimming pool on a terrace, an extended stone wharf for sunbathing, and cabanas.

EXPENSIVE

⚙ **Grand Hotel Miramare.** Via Milite Ignoto 30, 16038 Santa Margherita Ligure. ☎ **0185/ 287013,** or 800/223-6800 in the U.S. Fax 0185/284651. 75 rms, 9 suites. A/C MINIBAR TV TEL. 370,000–450,000 lire ($236.80–$288) double; 580,000–800,000 lire ($371.20–$512) suite. Rates include breakfast. Reduced rates available for children under 12 in parents' room. AE, DC, MC, V. Parking 30,000 lire ($19.20).

Now the prestige address of the resort, this old-world choice, a palatial 1929 six-story building, has kept more up with the times than has the Imperial. It was on the terrace of this hotel in 1933 that Marconi succeeded in transmitting for the first time, by means of microwaves, telegraphic and telephonic signals to a distance of more than 90 miles. Today the building has a festive confectionery look that's enhanced by the blue shutters and dazzling white facade. Separated from a stony beach by a busy boulevard, it's a 3-minute walk from the center of town. The hotel is surrounded by meticulously maintained gardens. To one side is a curved outdoor swimming pool with heated sea water. This adjoins a raised sun terrace dotted with parasols and iron tables. The bedrooms are classically furnished, and many of the bathrooms are spacious and packed with amenities, everything from hair dryers to makeup mirrors. Even some of the standard rooms have large terraces with sea views.

Dining/Entertainment: The hotel restaurant has many Victorian touches, including fragile chairs and blue-and-white porcelain set into the plaster walls.

Services: Room service, baby-sitting, laundry, valet.

Facilities: Heated saltwater outdoor pool, private beach, Miramare Skywater School.

MODERATE

Hotel Continental. Via Pagana 8, 16038 Santa Margherita Ligure. ☎ **0185/286512.** Fax 0185/284463. 76 rms. A/C MINIBAR TV TEL. 290,000 lire ($185.60) double, including breakfast; 160,000–205,000 lire ($102.40–$131.20) per person double with half board. AE, DC, MC, V. Parking 15,000–25,000 lire ($9.60–$16).

You'll see this hotel's grandiose facade from the winding road leading into town. After you enter the high-ceilinged and airy public rooms, however, you'll note the terraced gardens that stretch down to a private beach. The Continental is the only hotel that's directly on the water. In fair weather the hotel operates a snack bar there, where guests enjoy light lunches while admiring a view of Santa Margherita bay. The bedrooms are filled with comfortable, conservative, if somewhat fading furnishings, and often have tall French windows that lead onto wrought-iron balconies. Try for a room on the top floor. A nearby annex contains additional but very lackluster lodgings. The view from the restaurant encompasses the curved harbor in the center of town, a few miles away. Since the turn of the century the Ciana family has managed this year-round property. They also operate the Regina Elena (see below), Metropole, and Laurin. With such a command of rooms, they can almost always accommodate you in any season.

Hotel Regina Elena. Lungomare Milite Ignoto 44, 16038 Santa Margherita Ligure. ☎ **0185/ 287003.** Fax 0185/284473. 103 rms. A/C MINIBAR TV TEL. 236,000–280,000 lire ($151.05–$179.20) double, including breakfast; 166,000–210,000 lire ($106.25–$134.40) per person double with half board. AE, DC, MC, V. Free parking.

This pastel-painted hotel is situated by the sea, along the scenic thoroughfare leading to Portofino. The well-maintained bedrooms are furnished with modern styling, and most of them open onto a balcony with a view of the sea. An annex in the garden contains additional rooms. The hotel was built in 1908 and many turn-of-the-century details remain, including a marble staircase. The hotel is operated by the

The Cinque Terre

North of La Spezia you'll find the Cinque Terre, or Five Lands—five little cliffside-hugging towns that originated as fishing villages in the Middle Ages. They were built at the locations of natural harbors along the Riviera di Levante, between Genoa and La Spezia where the Apuane Alps send high ridges right to the sea. The alpine ridges and rugged country inland from the harbors caused the five towns to be inaccessible by land for centuries. The towns are Riomaggiore, Manarola, Corniglia, Vernazza, and Monterosso al Mare, this last town a favorite with sandy-beach fans.

Today you can take the train or drive (except to Corniglia and Vernazza) to the Cinque Terre. To drive, take autostrada A12, going from Genoa to Livorno, then exit at Brugnato, some 20 miles from Monterosso al Mare, going via Pignone. At Monterosso is a large parking area. A local highway leads from La Spezia to Riomaggiore and Manarola, but cars are not allowed to enter the village and must park outside. Trains stop hourly at all five towns, taking 4 minutes to go from one to the other. Purchase your ticket at the local station.

Many adventurous visitors to the Cinque Terre prefer to hike from town to town. The trail in part goes around coastal ledges and cliff overhangs. A leaflet about the safe walking paths in the area is available form the **tourist information center** at via Fegina in Monterosso al Mare (☎ **0187/817506**). This office is open only from Easter to October.

Among sights along the way are a 1622 Capuchin convent, a crenellated fortress, ancient buildings, and the fishing boats in the harbor at **Monterosso. Vernazza** has a plaza on the harbor. Labyrinthine steps lead through the ancient town, and you can see an elegant Renaissance campanile with an octagonal balustrade. Unlike the other four towns, **Corniglia** is not at the water's edge. Instead, it's on a promontory that juts out, with a long stairway leading down to the quay where fishing boats tie up. In the town stands a Renaissance chapel built in layers of black basalt and white travertine, giving it a striped effect seen mainly in Tuscany. Corniglia was built in a ravine and has houses climbing both sides of the declivity, with fishing boats lining the one street of the town.

Manarola welcomes visitors to its sidewalk cafes, where you can take a rest. The path leading from it to Riomaggiore is called via dell'Amore. **Riomaggiore** rests in the natural valleys, with both an old and a new town. Instead of cars, fishing boats are parked on the street. A weekly market is held every Thursday. All five towns are known for their wines.

Ciana family, which has been receiving guests since the turn of the century. They also operate the Continental (see above) and the Metropole and Laurin.

The dining room is the most interesting part of the hotel. It's in a 12-sided structure with walls made almost entirely of glass. The half-board plan features an excellent cuisine. The hotel offers room service, baby-sitting, laundry, and valet. There's also a conference center and a roof garden pool with a Jacuzzi.

Park Hotel Suisse. Via Favale 31, 16038 Santa Margherita Ligure. ☎ **0185/289571.** Fax 0185/281469. 85 rms. TV TEL. 120,000–360,000 lire ($76.80–$230.40) double. Rates include breakfast. No credit cards. Parking 10,000 lire ($6.40).

Set in a garden above the town center, the Park Hotel Suisse features a panoramic view of the sea and harbor. It has seven floors, all modern in design, with deep private balconies that are like alfresco living rooms for some of the bedrooms. On the lower terrace is a large, free-form, saltwater swimming pool surrounded by semitropical vegetation. A modernistic water chute, diving boards, and a cafe with parasol tables for refreshments all give one the advantages of seaside life and then some. The comfortable bedrooms that open onto the rear gardens, without sea view, cost slightly less. The hotel, although built in 1957, has been renovated many times since. The hotel lies 800 yards from the rail station above a small harbor about 100 yards from the sea. You have to cross a small street to reach the water, or you can use the outdoor pool.

INEXPENSIVE

⑤ Albergo Conte Verde. Via Zara 1, 16038 Santa Margherita Ligure. ☎ **0185/287139.** Fax 0185/284211. 35 rms, 30 with shower. 100,000 lire ($64) double without shower, 125,000–140,000 lire ($80–$89.60) double with shower. Rates include breakfast. AE, DC, MC, V. Closed Mar 1–15 and Dec 1–25. Parking 15,000 lire ($9.60).

This place offers one of the warmest welcomes in town to the budget traveler. Located only 2 blocks from the sea, this third-class hotel has been revamped, and its rooms are simple but adequate. The terrace out front has swing gliders, and the lounge has period furnishings, including rockers. All is consistent with the villa exterior of shuttered windows, flower boxes, and a small front garden and lawn where tables are set out for refreshments. Open year-round, the hotel also has a good and inexpensive restaurant.

⑤ Albergo Fasce. Via Bozzo 3, 16038 Santa Margherita Ligure. ☎ **0185/286435.** Fax 0185/283580. 16 rms. MINIBAR TV TEL. 65,000 lire ($41.60) per person double. Rates include breakfast. AE, DC, MC, V. Parking 15,000 lire ($9.40).

A family-run hotel, the Fasce is functional yet welcoming. Each of its streamlined modern rooms has a private bath, color TV, safety deposit box, and phone. On the roof is a panoramic solarium. English-born Jane McGuffie Fasce runs the hotel along with her husband, Aristide; everything functions in a homelike way. Extra amenities include 4-hour laundry service. The hotel also provides free bicycles and a 3-day bus pass for touring the area.

Hotel Jolanda. Via Luisito Costa 6, 16038 Santa Margherita Ligure. ☎ **0185/287513.** Fax 0185/284763. 40 rms. TV TEL. 126,000–152,000 lire ($80.65–$97.30) double, including breakfast; 85,000–110,000 lire ($54.40–$70.40) per person double with half board. AE, MC, V. Free parking.

Since the 1940s the Pastine family has been welcoming visitors to their little hotel, a short walk from the sea. A patio serves as a kind of open-air living room. The pensione lies on a peaceful little street, away from traffic noise. The rooms are comfortably furnished, with private bath, TV, and phone. Guests often gather in the bar before proceeding to the restaurant, where an excellent Ligurian cuisine is served.

WHERE TO DINE

Ristorante la Ghiaia. In the Lido Palace Hotel, via Andrea Doria 5. ☎ **0185/283708.** Reservations recommended. Main courses 15,000–30,000 lire ($9.60–$19.20); fixed-price menu 40,000 lire ($25.60). AE, DC, MC, V. Thurs–Tues 12:30–2pm and 8–10pm. Closed Nov. SEAFOOD.

This establishment's name in translation means "sea rocks," and that's precisely what you'll see from the windows that overlook the water. It's set on the ground floor of one of the town's most centrally located hotels, and the modern decor includes clear colors and paintings throughout the sunny dining rooms. Outdoor tables are shielded from the pedestrian traffic by rows of shrubbery. Your meal might begin with antipasti di mare, tagliolini al pesto, zuppa di pesce (fish soup), risotto di mare (rice with seafood), or spaghetti with lobster sauce. Fresh fish, including turbot, scampi, gamberini, and sea bass, is priced by the gram. This restaurant, although not particularly distinguished, is still one of the best in town.

Trattoria Cesarina. Via Mameli 2C. ☎ **0185/286059.** Reservations recommended, especially in midsummer. Main courses 25,000–35,000 lire ($16–$22.40). AE, DC, MC, V. Thurs–Tues 12:30–2:30pm and 7:30–10pm. SEAFOOD.

This is the best of the trattorie in town. It lies beneath the arcade of a short but monumental street that runs into piazza Fratelli Bandiere. In an atmosphere of bentwood chairs and discreet lighting, you can enjoy a variety of Ligurian dishes. Specialties include meat, vegetables, and seafood antipasti, along with such classic Italian dishes as taglierini with seafood and pappardella in a fragrant sausage sauce, plus seasonal fish such as red snapper or dorado, best when grilled, that has been caught off the nearby coast.

5 Portofino

22 miles SE of Genoa, 106 miles S of Milan, 301 miles NW of Rome

Portofino is located about 4 miles south of Santa Margherita Ligure, along one of the most beautiful coastal roads in all of Italy.

Favored by the yachting set, the resort is in an idyllic location on a harbor, where the water reflects all the pastel-washed little houses that run along it. In the 1930s it enjoyed a reputation with artists; later, a chic crowd moved in—and they're still here, occupying villas in the hills and refusing to surrender completely to the tourists who pour in during the day.

The thing to do in Portofino: During the day—but preferably before sunset—**take a walk** that leads toward the tip of the peninsula. You'll pass the entrance to an old castle (where a German baron once lived), old private villas, towering trees, and much vegetation, before you reach the lighthouse. Allow an hour at least. When you return to the main piazza, proceed to one of the two little drinking bars on the left side of the harbor that rise and fall in popularity.

Before beginning that walk to the lighthouse, however, you can climb the steps from the port leading to the little parish **Church of St. George.** From here you'll get a panoramic view of the port and bay. In summer you can also take **boat rides** around the coast to such points as San Fruttuoso.

ESSENTIALS

GETTING THERE   By Train   Go first to Santa Margherita Ligure (see above), then continue the rest of the way by bus.

By Bus   Tigullio buses leave Santa Margherita Ligure once every 30 minutes bound for Portofino. The one-way ticket is 1,700 lire ($1.10), and you can purchase tickets aboard the bus.

By Car   From Santa Margherita Ligure, continue south along the only road, which hugs the promontory, until you reach Portofino. In summer, traffic is likely to be heavy.

VISITOR INFORMATION   The **tourist information center** is at via Roma 35 (☎ **0185/269024**). It's open in summer, daily from 9:30am to 1pm and 1:30 to 6:30pm; off-season, daily from 9:30am to 12:30pm and 3 to 6pm.

GETTING AROUND   Portofino is tiny; you can walk wherever you want to go.

WHERE TO STAY

Portofino is severely limited in hotels. Therefore, in July and August you may be forced to book a room in nearby Santa Margherita Ligure or Rapallo.

Albergo Nazionale. 16034 Portofino. ☎ **0185/269575.** Fax 0185/269578. 2 rms, 10 suites. MINIBAR TV TEL. 255,000 lire ($163.20) double; 400,000–500,000 lire ($256–$320) suite. MC, V. Closed Nov 20–Mar 20.

At stage center, right on the harbor, this old villa is modest, yet well laid out. The suites here are tastefully decorated, and the little lounge has a brick fireplace, coved ceiling, antique furnishings, and good reproductions. Most of the bedrooms, furnished in a mixture of styles (hand-painted Venetian in some of the rooms), have a view of the harbor.

✪ **Albergo Splendido.** Viale Baratta 13, 16034 Portofino. ☎ **0185/269551,** or 800/237-1236 in the U.S. Fax 0185/269614. 43 rms, 21 suites. A/C MINIBAR TV TEL. 1,050,000–1,320,000 lire ($672–$845) double; 1,700,000–2,200,000 lire ($1,088–$1,408) suite for two. Rates include half board. AE, DC, MC, V. Closed Jan 3–Mar 16.

This Relais & Châteaux property is reached by a steep and winding road from the port. It provides a luxury base for those who moor their yacht in the harbor below, or have closed down their Palm Beach residences for the summer. In other words, its prices are outrageous. The four-story structure was originally built as a monastery during the Middle Ages, but pirates attacked so frequently that the monks abandoned it. Later it became a family summer home. The building opened as a hotel in 1901, set on 4 acres of semitropical gardens.

The rambling villa offers several levels of public rooms, terraces, and "oh, that view" bedrooms. Each private room is furnished in a personal way—no two alike.

Dining/Entertainment: The bilevel dining room is divided by a row of arches and furnished with Biedermeier chairs, flower bouquets, and a fine old tapestry. The restaurant terrace enjoys a fine view and serves traditional typical Ligurian dishes as well as international specialties.

Services: Room service, baby-sitting, laundry, valet, massage.

Facilities: Hotel speedboat, heated saltwater swimming pool, beauty center, solarium, sauna.

⑤ **Hotel Eden.** Vico Dritto 18, 16034 Portofino. ☎ **0185/269091.** Fax 0185/269047, 9 rms. MINIBAR TV TEL. 180,000–280,000 lire ($115.20–$179.20) double. Rates include breakfast. AE, DC, MC, V. Closed Dec 1–20. Public parking 30,500 lire ($19.50).

Located just 150 feet away from the harbor in the heart of the village, this little albergo is a budget holdout in an otherwise high-fashion resort. Set in a garden (hence its name), it's a good choice in this pricey town. Although the inn doesn't have a view of the harbor, there's a winning vista from the front veranda, where breakfast is served. The hotel is run by Mr. Ferruccio, and life here is decidedly casual.

WHERE TO DINE

Da U'Batti. Vico Nuovo 17. ☎ **0185/269379.** Reservations recommended. Main courses 40,000–45,000 lire ($25.60–$28.80). AE, DC, MC, V. Tues–Sun noon–3pm and 8–11pm. Closed Dec–Jan. SEAFOOD.

Informal, chic, and colorful, this place is on a narrow cobblestone-covered piazza a few steps above the port. Founded in 1963, it still perpetuates some of the *la dolce vita* aura of that heady time. A pair of barnacle-encrusted anchors hanging above the arched entrance hint at the seafaring specialties that have become this establishment's trademark. Owner and sommelier Giancarlo Foppiano serves delectable dishes, which

The Pearl of the Italian Riviera

Even though today overrun by day-trippers eating ice cream, Portofino has gone down in the annals of world chicdom as a haven for the elite who arrive by yacht and occupy villas in the hills. They only appear at the portside bars and piazzetta of Portofino when the day-trippers have mercifully departed. The resident locals call the visitors "barbarians," although most working people in Portofino live exclusively off them.

No one seems to know for sure who launched this tiny fishing village into fashion, making it known worldwide as "the Pearl of the Italian Riviera." Perhaps it was Guy de Maupassant, who arrived in 1889 aboard his sailboat *Bel-Ami,* named after the French author's frivolous but successful novel.

However, it was the British—not the French—who have been enraptured with Portofino, at least since the 19th century. Their connection with the resort goes back even earlier, as Richard the Lion-Hearted sailed from here in 1190 on the Third Crusade. In more modern times—at least the 1960s—the British actor Rex Harrison, famed for *My Fair Lady,* once invited the world's most notorious lovers (at the time), Elizabeth Taylor and Richard Burton, to visit him at Portofino. The three were recovering from the debacle called *Cleopatra* in which they had starred. Taylor's visit is long remembered here. Villagers crowded around her as she emerged from various boutiques. They held up their babies for her to admire, often aggressively thrusting them in her face. It soon became apparent that they were actually trying to sell their babies to the fabled star, and were quoting amounts in lire. Taylor didn't purchase any babies that night, but did spend more than $5,000 in one boutique alone.

Such are the happenings and events likely to occur at the harbor of Portofino and in the Splendido on the hill, one of the most famous and expensive hotels in all of Italy. The hotel, too, would have its stories to tell, especially after such illustrious guests as the duke and duchess of Windsor, Ernest Hemingway, Greta Garbo, Ingrid Bergman, Aristotle Onassis, Clark Gable, John Wayne, and even Larry Hagman had come to call.

Today a lot of villas in the hills around Portofino remain unoccupied. Continuing corruption scandals in Italy have meant that some of the powerful elite are laying low and avoiding such high-profile, *paparazzi*-packed resorts as Portofino.

might include a soup of "hen clams," rice with shrimp or crayfish, or fish alla Battista. It has a good selection of grappa, as well as French and Italian wines.

Delfino. Piazza Martiri delli Olivetta 40. ☎ **0185/269081.** Reservations recommended Sat. Main courses 27,000–45,000 lire ($17.30–$28.80). AE, DC, MC, V. Tues–Sun noon–3pm and 7–11pm. Closed Nov. SEAFOOD.

Delfino is located right on the village square that fronts the harbor. This is Portofino's most fashionable dining spot (along with Il Pitosforo; see below). It's located in a sienna-colored harborside building with forest-green shutters. It's both nautically rustic and informally chic. Less expensive than Il Pitosforo, it offers virtually the same type of food, such as lasagne al pesto. Again, the fish dishes are the best bets: zuppa di pesce (a soup made of freshly caught fish with a secret spice blend) and risotto with shrimp, sole, squid, and other sea creatures. If you can't stand fish, the chef also prides himself on his sage-seasoned vitello all'uccelletto, roast veal with a gamey taste. Try to get a table near the front so you can enjoy (or at least be amused by) the parade of visitors and villagers.

Il Pitosforo. Molo Umberto I 9. ☎ **0185/269020.** Reservations required. Jackets required for men. Main courses 35,000–78,000 lire ($22.40–$49.90). AE, DC, MC, V. Wed–Mon noon–2:30pm and 7:30–11pm. Closed from the end of Nov to Feb and for lunch July–Aug. LIGURIAN/ITALIAN.

You have to climb some steps to reach this place, which draws raves when the meal is served and, most likely, wails when the tab is presented. While not blessed with an especially distinguished decor, its position right on the harbor gives it all the native chic it needs, and has ever since Bogey and Bacall and Taylor and Burton came this way long ago. Zuppa di pesce is a delectable Ligurian fish soup, or you may prefer the bouillabaisse, which is always reliable here. The pastas are especially tasty, and include lasagne al pesto, wide noodles prepared in the typical Genovese sauce. Fish dishes include mussels alla marinara and paella valenciana for two, saffron-flavored rice studded with sea fruit and chicken. Some meat and fish dishes are grilled over hot stones, others over charcoal.

Ristorante da Puny. Piazza Martiri delli Olivetta. ☎ **0185/269037.** Reservations required. Main courses 27,000–35,000 lire ($17.30–$22.40). No credit cards. Fri–Wed noon–3pm and 7–11pm. Closed Dec 15–Feb 8. SEAFOOD.

Da Puny is set up on the stone square that opens onto the harbor. Because of its location, it's practically in the living room of Portofino, within sight of the evening activities of the oh-so-chic and oh-so-tan yachting set. Green-painted tables are set under trees at night on a slate-covered outdoor terrace. The menu includes pappardelle Portofino, antipasto of the house, spaghetti with clams, baked fish with potatoes and olives, fried zucchini flowers, and an array of freshly caught fish.

PORTOFINO AFTER DARK

La Gritta American Bar. Calata Marconi 20. ☎ **0185/269126.**

La Gritta vies for business with its rival a few storefronts away. Between the two of them, they have attracted the biggest names in show business and elsewhere: from Onassis to Frank Sinatra to John Wayne. It's said that Rex Harrison, while drinking in this bar with the duke of Windsor, excused himself to go and purchase a package of cigarettes. He never came back. On the way for the cigarettes, he ran into actress Kay Kendal and the two eloped. These celebrities have intermingled with dozens of tourists and a collection of U.S. Navy personnel in this small, well-appointed restaurant. As James Jones, author of *From Here to Eternity,* noted: "This is the nicest waterfront bar this side of Hong Kong." That's true, but it's always wise to check your bar tab carefully before you stagger out looking for a new adventure. The drinks don't come cheap: Long drinks cost 13,500 to 19,000 lire ($8.65 to $12.15) apiece. Open Friday to Wednesday from 8:30pm to 3am.

Scafandro American Bar. Calata Marconi 10. ☎ **0185/269105.**

This is one of the village's chic rendezvous points, a place that has attracted a slew of yachting guests. The three-quarter-round banquettes inside contribute to the general feeling of well-being. The members of your party will be illuminated by hanging dome lights. If some international celebrity doesn't happen to come in while you're here, you can always study one of the series of unusual nautical engravings adorning the walls. Most drinks cost a steep 13,500 to 19,000 lire ($8.65 to $12.15). Open Wednesday to Monday from 8:30 to 3am.

16 Naples & Pompeii

Campania is in many ways the most eerie, memorable, and beautiful region of Italy, sociologically different from anything else in Europe—haunting, confusing, and satisfying, all at the same time. Campania forms a fertile crescent around the bays of Naples and Sorrento, and stretches inland into a landscape of limestone rocks dotted with patches of fertile soil. It was off the shores of Campania that Ulysses ordered his crew to tie him, ears unstopped, to the mast of his ship, so that he alone would hear the songs of the sirens without throwing himself overboard to sample their pleasures. Today the siren song of Campania still lures, with a chemistry that some visitors insist is an aphrodisiac.

The geological oddities of Campania include a smoldering and dangerous volcano (already famous for having destroyed Pompeii and Herculaneum), sulfurous springs that belch steam and smelly gases, and lakes that ancient myths refer to as the gateway to Hades. Its seaside highway is the most beautiful in the world (and probably the most treacherous); it combines danger at every hairpin turn with some of Italy's most reckless drivers. Despite such dark images, Campania is one of the most captivating regions of Italy, sought out by native Italians and visitors alike for its combination of earth, sea, and sky. Coupled with this are what might well be the densest collection of ancient ruins in Europe, each celebrated by classical scholars as among the very best of its kind.

The ancient Romans dubbed the land Campania Felix, which may reflect their satisfaction with the district that inspired the construction of hundreds of private villas for their rulers. In some ways the beauty of Campania contributed to the decay of the Roman Empire, as Caesars, their senators, and their courtiers spent more and more time pursuing its pleasures and abandoning the cares of Rome's administrative problems.

Even today seafront land in Campania is so desirable that hoteliers have poured their life savings into foundations of buildings that are sometimes bizarrely cantilevered above rock-studded cliffs. Despite their numbers, these hotels tend to be profitably overbooked in summer.

Although residents of Campania sometimes stridently extol the virtues of its cuisine, it's not the most renowned in Italy. Its produce, however, is superb, its wine heady, and its pizzas highly memorable.

Impressions

[Naples] is a country of fiddlers and poets, whores and scoundrels.
    —Horatio Lord Nelson, dispatch to Lord St. Vincent, September 20, 1798

Today Campania typifies the conditions that northern Italians label "the problem of the south." Although the inequities are the most pronounced in Naples, the entire region, outside the resorts along the coast, has a lower standard of living and education, and higher crime rates, plus less developed standards of health care, than the more affluent north.

Television has contributed to leveling regional differences. Nevertheless, Campania is still rife with superstitious myths, vendettas, and restrictive problems. It's also home to a people who can sometimes overwhelm you with kindnesses and spontaneity. Despite, or perhaps because of, these tendencies, it's worth investing your vacation time in Campania. In some way, it captures the soul and soulfulness of southern Italy.

EXPLORING CAMPANIA BY CAR

Day 1   Naples is the traditional gateway to Campania. From Rome, the quickest route is the Rome–Naples A2 autostrada, which passes Caserta 18 miles north of Naples, or the Naples–Reggio di Calabria A3, which goes by Salerno, 33 miles south of Naples. Arrive in Naples for a late lunch and visit the Museo Archeologico Nazionale. At sunset stroll along the waterfront, dining in a sea-bordering tavern there at night.

☕ **TAKE A BREAK**   One of the best places for pizza—the most celebrated culinary offering of Naples—is the **Pizzeria Trianon da Ciro,** via Pietro Collette 44–46 in Naples (☎ **081/553-9426**), where pies cost 6,000 to 12,000 lire ($3.85 to $7.70). The staff is rude but the pizza is savory and tasty. You can select from nearly 20 different concoctions emerging from the fiery ovens. It's open Monday to Saturday from 10am to 3:30pm and 6:30 to 11pm and on Sunday from 6:30 to 11pm.

Day 2   See some more sights of Naples, especially the Museo e Gallerie Nazionali di Capodimonte. In the late morning begin your tour of the Phlaegrean Fields, land of myth and legend. These sights lie west of Naples, beginning at the ancient volcano Solfatara, 7$1/2$ miles away. Other sights include Pozzuoli, where you can visit the ruins of Anfiteatro Flavio and the Temple of Serapis; Baia, a former imperial retreat; Lago d'Averno, a lake occupying an extinct volcano crater; and ancient Cuma, site of one of the first outposts of Greek colonization in Italy, with the cave of the legendary Cumaean Sibyl. Return to Naples for the night.

Day 3   You can continue to be based at Naples or else move south to a hotel at Pompeii (although the choices are very limited). Visit Herculaneum in the morning—destroyed when Vesuvius erupted in August of A.D. 79—and later in the day explore Pompeii and Vesuvius itself.

Day 4   The ancient city of Pompeii, also destroyed by Vesuvius, is so rich in attractions that many visitors plan to spend an extra day here exploring the ruins.

A TASTE OF CAMPANIA

This is the land of spaghetti and pizza, two dishes that have gained popularity around the world. Many Neapolitans prefer their food simple—spaghetti *al pomodoro,* cooked al dente and served with a light sauce of fresh tomatoes cooked in oil and spiced with basil. Spaghetti *alle vongole* (with baby clams) always has that tang of the sea. The classic pizza *alla napoletana* is the most famous dish of Naples. It's usually covered with mozarrella, olive oil, anchovies, marjoram, and tomato sauce before being popped into a fiery oven.

The chief stew of the region is *zuppa alla marinara,* varieties of fish flavored with pepper, salt, parsley, tomatoes, and garlic. *Fritto misto* is a golden-brown fry of fish, cheese, cauliflower, sweetbreads, and potatoes, but even more popular is *melanzane alla parmigiana*—thinly sliced eggplant cooked with mozzarella, tomato sauce, olive oil, spices, and Parmesan cheese. Beefsteak or veal is often served *alla pizzaiola*—with tomato, olive oil, garlic, and marjoram.

The wines of Campania were the most highly placed in ancient days. Pliny put Falerno at the top of his list, and even Horace acclaimed the wine as generous, robust, and fiery. Martial pronounced it "immortal." Virgil and others sang the praise of this vivid ruby-red wine, with a distinctive bouquet, evocative of flowers, and with a dry but fruity flavor. As it ages, it gets better. It's the preferred wine with roasts, poultry, red meat, and game.

Other wines include Biancolella d'Ischia, one of the finest wines produced on that island, and often served with fish. It has a mellow, harmonious flavor, with a delicate bouquet. Gragnana, served with all meats, is a dark mulberry in color, with a purplish foam and a bouquet evocative of faded violets. Nutty and generally mellow, it's the wine that has played a role in the literature and legend of Naples.

1 Naples (Napoli)

136 miles SE of Rome, 162 miles W of Bari

Its city government is reportedly corrupt; many of its businesses are dominated by the Camorra, the Neapolitan Mafia; it indisputably has the worst air pollution and traffic in Italy; and its hordes of street children make it the juvenile delinquency capital of Europe. Naples is Italy's most controversial city: You'll either love it or hate it. It's louder, more intense, more unnerving, but perhaps ultimately more satisfying for the traveler than almost anywhere else in Italy.

Naples has changed a lot since the cholera outbreak of 1973, when the world discovered that the city had no sewers and was basking on the edge of a picturesque but poisoned bay. New civic centers have been planned, and some of the city's baroque palaces have been restored. But to the foreigner unfamiliar with the complexities of the multifarious "Italys" and their regional types, the Neapolitan is still the quintessence of the country—easy to caricature ("O Sole Mio," "Mamma Mia," bel canto). If Sophia Loren (a native who moved elsewhere) evokes the Italian woman for you, you'll find more of her look-alikes here than in any other city. Perhaps more visible are the city's children. In one of the most memorable novels to come out of World War II, *The Gallery* by John Horne Burns, there is this passage: "But I remember best of all the children of Naples, the *scugnizzi*. Naples is the greatest baby plant in the world. Once they come off the assembly line, they lose no time in getting onto the streets. They learn to walk and talk in the gutters. Many of them seem to live there." If Burns were writing this novel today, he might also have warned you that these scugnizzi specialize in *lo scippo* (local dialect for petty thievery). Of course, if it's your purse or wallet that has been stolen, it may be no petty crime to you. Guard your person and your valuables carefully as you explore the tangled, often dangerous streets of Naples.

A LOOK AT THE PAST   Neapolitan legends claim that the city was founded after the body of Parthenope (a nymph who committed suicide after being spurned by Ulysses) washed ashore in the nearby bay. Archeological evidence suggests that it was founded by Greek colonists late in the 5th century B.C.

During the height of the Roman Empire, Naples was only one of dozens of important cities that surrounded the famous bay. Roman emperors, especially Nero, perhaps in order to show that they appreciated the finer (Greek-inspired) things in life, treated Naples as a resort, away from the pressure of imperial Rome. They also used it as a departure point for their nearby villas on Capri. It was visited by poets (Virgil wrote the *Georgics* here) and sybarites alike. Under the Byzantine administration of the remnants of the Roman Empire, Naples actually grew and prospered—unlike many of its Italian neighbors. This was in part because of its excellent harbor and in part because many of its competitors (Pompeii and Herculaneum, for example) were destroyed by economic stagnation or by cascades of molten lava and ash.

Over the centuries Naples has known many conquerors, and lived in constant fear of the potential for a volcanic eruption that might annihilate the city. These facts might help to explain its "live for today" philosophy. Among its conquerors and leaders have been everyone from the Normans in 1139, Charles of Anjou in 1266, the Aragonese of Spain under Alfonso V in 1435, Archduke Charles of Austria in 1707, French Bourbons in 1734, the pan-Italian nationalist armies of Garibaldi in 1861, and, after the fiasco of Mussolini's brand of fascism during World War II, the Americans.

During the 18th and 19th centuries, French, English, and German tourists visited the Bay of Naples as an essential part (perhaps the highlight) of their grand European tour. They flooded the northern European consciousness with legends and images of Naples as the most beautiful and carefree city in the world. "See Naples and die," the popular wisdom claimed. Some historians write that the unabashed sexual permissiveness of 18th- and 19th-century Naples was more of a lure to northern Europeans than the region's archeology.

AND ON TO THE PRESENT   Today the only "dying" you're likely to experience is being run over by a car. Each of the city's 2.2 million inhabitants seems to have a beat-up Fiat, battalions of which speed erratically and incessantly over hopelessly narrow roads laid out more than 2,000 years ago. To add to the confusion, hordes of Neapolitan children will blithely throw lit firecrackers into moving traffic, stop traffic to beg or smear your windshield with a soiled towel, or (sometimes more or less endearingly) try to pick your pocket.

Surely, the Neapolitans are the most spontaneous people on earth, wearing their emotions on the surface of their skin. No Neapolitan housewife gets overheated running up and down steps to convey a message to someone on the street—she handles the situation by screaming out the window.

The Neapolitan dialect is one of the most distinctive and difficult in all of Italy, with an almost alarming number and diversity of words (a source of pride) for describing intimate body parts and functions. Naples even bears the dubious honor of having introduced syphilis to the world in 1495 (history's first recorded version), the outbreak of which was immediately blamed on a group of French soldiers quartered there at the time.

Today Naples is a city to be savored in bits and pieces. It comes at you like a runaway car, with tour-ticket sellers, car thieves, hotel hawkers, and pimps and hustlers, and a series of human encounters that seesaw between extraordinary warmth and kindness and a kind of surrealistic nightmare.

With its almost total absence of parks, its lack of space (it has the highest population density of any city in Europe), and the constant and unrelieved perception that it will disintegrate into total anarchy at any moment, it's not a destination for queasy palates and weak hearts. Add to this the 35% unemployment rate, the unending prevalence of both major and minor larceny, the highest infant-mortality rate in Italy, the heat, and the pollution, and you have a destination many visitors rush through quickly on their way to somewhere else.

Still, the tattered splendor of baroque palaces (whose charm is enhanced by shrubs and bushes growing from cracks in their cornices), the sense of history, and the unalloyed spectacle of humanity struggling, with humor and perseverance, to survive, makes Naples one of the most memorable places you'll visit in Italy. Only one thing, *don't show up on Monday*—most attractions will be closed.

Naples is a fantastic adventure. It's also a bubbling, infectious stew. The best approach, from its bay, is idyllic—a port set against the backdrop of a crystal-blue sky and volcanic mountains. The rich attractions inside the city and in the environs (Pompeii, Ischia, Capri, Vesuvius, the Phlaegrean Fields, Herculaneum) make Naples one of the five top tourist meccas of Italy. The inexperienced may have difficulty coping with it. The seasoned explorer will find it worthy ground, and might even try venturing down side streets, some of which teem with prostitutes and a major source of their upkeep: the ubiquitous sailor.

ESSENTIALS

GETTING THERE   By Plane   The quickest way to get to Naples from Rome and other major Italian cities, including Milan, is to fly there on a domestic flight, which will put you into Aeroporto Capodichino, via Umberto Maddalena (☎ 084/1478-65643), 4 miles north of the city. A city ATAN bus (no. 14) makes the 15-minute run between the airport and Naples's piazza Garibaldi in front of the main rail terminus. The bus fare is 1,200 lire (75¢); a taxi will run about 20,000 lire ($12.50). Domestic flights are available on Alitalia, Alisarda, and Ati. Flying time from Milan is 1 hour 20 minutes; from Palermo, 1 hour 15 minutes; from Rome, 50 minutes; and from Venice, 1 hour 15 minutes.

By Train   Frequent trains connect Naples with the rest of Italy. One or two trains per hour arrive from Rome, taking 2 1/2 hours and costing 17,200 lire ($11) for a one-way passage. It's also possible to reach Naples from Milan in about 7 hours, costing 61,800 lire ($39.55) for a one-way ticket. Trains also run back and forth to the port city of Brindisi on the Rome–Lecce line (used by visitors taking ferries from Greece), taking 6 1/2 hours and costing 33,400 lire ($21.40) for a one-way ticket.

The city has two main rail terminals, **Stazione Centrale,** at piazza Garibaldi, and **Stazione Mergellina,** at piazza Amadeo. If you want rail information, call 081/567111.

Alitalia, in collaboration with FS, the Italian State Railways, links Naples with Rome's Leonardo da Vinci International Airport without intermediate stops. Twice a day, 7 days a week, the "Alitalia Airport Train by FS" departs from Stazione Margellina, heading north to Rome and the airport. To travel on the airport train, you must have an Alitalia airline ticket.

By Car   In the old days the custom was to sail into the Bay of Naples, but today's traveler is more likely to drive there, heading down the autostrada from Rome. The Rome–Naples autostrada (A2) passes Caserta 18 miles north of Naples and the Naples–Reggio di Calabria autostrada (A3) runs by Salerno, 33 miles north of Naples.

By Ferry   If you're already in Sicily, you can go on a ferry to Naples from Palermo on **Tirrenia Lines,** Molo Angionio, Stazione Marritima (☎ **081/761-3688**), in the port area of Palermo. A one-way ticket costs 79,000 lire ($50.55) per person for the 10$^{1}/_{2}$-hour boat trip to Naples.

ORIENTATION

VISITOR INFORMATION   Visitors can ask for information at the **Ente Provinciale per il Turismo** at the Stazione Centrale (☎ **081/268779**). There's another office at piazza del Gesù Nuovo 7 (☎ **081/552-3328**). They're open Monday to Saturday from 9am to 2pm and 3 to 7pm and on Sunday from 9am to 3pm.

CITY LAYOUT   If you arrive by train at the Stazione Centrale, in front of piazza Garibaldi, you'll want to escape from that horror by taking one of the major arteries of Naples, **corso Umberto,** in the direction of the Santa Lucia district. Along the water, many boats, such as those heading for Capri and Ischia, leave from **Porto Beverello.**

Many visitors to Naples confine their visit to the bayside **Santa Lucia** area, and perhaps venture into another section to see an important museum. Most of the major hotels lie along **via Partenope,** which looks out not only to the Gulf of Naples but to the Castel dell'Ovo. To the west is the **Mergellina** district, site of many restaurants and dozens of apartment houses. The far western section of the city is known as **Posillipo.**

One of the most important squares of Naples is **piazza del Plebiscito,** north of Santa Lucia. The Palazzo Reale opens onto this square. On a satellite square, you can visit **piazza Trento y Trieste,** with its Teatro San Carlo and entrance to the famed Galleria Umberto I. To the east is the third most important square, **piazza Municipio.** From piazza Trento y Trieste, you encounter the main shopping street of Naples, **via Toledo/via Roma,** on which you can walk as far as piazza Dante. From that square, take via Enrico Pessina to the most important museum in Naples, located on piazza Museo Nazionale.

GETTING AROUND   By Subway   The Metropolitana line will deliver you from the Stazione Centrale in the west, all the way to the Stazione Mergellina. Get off at piazza Amadeo if you wish to take the funicular to Vómero. Tickets are 1,200 lire (75¢).

By Bus or Tram   It's dangerous to ride buses at rush hours. Never have we seen such pushing, shoving, and jockeying for position. On one recent trip we saw a middle-aged woman fall from a too-crowded bus, injuring her leg. We were later told that this was a routine occurrence. If you're a linebacker, take your chances. Many people prefer to leave the buses to the battle-hardened Neapolitans and take the subway or tram no. 1 or 4, which run from the Stazione Centrale to the Mergellina station. (It will also let you off at the quayside points where the boats depart for Ischia and Capri.)

By Taxi   If you survive the reckless driving (someone once wrote that all Neapolitans drive like the anarchists they are), you'll only have to do battle over the bill. You will inevitably be overcharged. Many cab drivers claim that the meter is broken, and they then proceed to assess the cost of the ride, always to your disadvantage. Some legitimate surcharges are imposed, including night drives and extra luggage. However, many taxi drivers deliberately take you "the long way there" to run up your costs. In repeated visits to Naples, we've never yet been quoted an honest fare. We no longer bother with the meter; instead, we estimate what the fare would be worth, negotiate with the driver, and take off into the night. If you want to take a chance, you can call a radio taxi at 081/556-4444, 081/556-0202, or 081/570-7070.

By Car Getting around Naples is a nightmare! Motorists should pay particular attention, as Neapolitans are fond of driving the wrong way on one-way streets and speeding hysterically along lanes reserved for public transportation, sometimes cutting into your lane without warning. Red lights, if they're turned on at all, seem to hold no terror for a Neapolitan driver. In fact, you may want simply to park your car and walk. There are two dangers in that. One is that your car can be stolen, as ours once was, even though apparently "guarded" by an attendant in front of a deluxe hotel. The other danger is that you're likely to get mugged (nearly a third of the city is unemployed, and people have to live somehow).

By Funicular Funiculars take passengers up and down the steep hills of Naples. The **Funicolare Centrale** (☎ **081/714-5583**), for example, connects the lower part of the city to Vómero. Departures are from piazzetta Duca d'Aosta, just off via Roma. The cable cars run daily, from 7am to 10pm. Watch that you don't get stranded by missing the last car back.

FAST FACTS: NAPLES

Consulates You'll find the consulate of the **United States** on piazza della Repubblica (☎ **081/583-8111**), where the staff has long since grown weary of hearing about another stolen passport. Its consular services are open July to mid-September, Monday to Friday from 8am to 1:30pm; mid-September to June, Monday to Friday from 9am to 12:30pm and 3 to 5:30pm. The consulate of the **United Kingdom** is at via Francesco Crispi 122 (☎ **081/663511**), open in summer, Monday to Friday from 7 to 11am and 1 to 4pm; and off-season, Monday to Friday from 9am to 12:30pm and 3 to 5:30pm.

Citizens of Canada, Australia, and New Zealand will need to go to the embassies or consulates of their home countries in Rome (see "Fast Facts: Rome," in Chapter 4).

Drugstores Try Farmacia Helvethia, piazza Garibaldi 11, near Stazione Centrale (☎ 081/554-8894).

Emergencies If you have an emergency, dial **113**. To reach the police or carabinieri, call **112**. For an ambulance, call **113** or **752-0696**.

Medical Care Try the Guarda Medica Permanente, piazza del Municipio (☎ 081/751-3177) or call 113.

Post Office The main post office is on piazza G. Matteotti (☎ 081/552-0067). Look for the POSTA TELEGRAFO sign outside. It's open Monday to Friday from 8:15am to 1:30pm and on Saturday from 8:15am to 12:10pm.

Telephone If you need to make a long-distance call, you can do so at the Stazione Centrale, where an office is open 24 hours; if you make calls from your hotel, you'll likely be hit with an excessive surcharge.

WHAT TO SEE & DO

Before striking out for Pompeii (see Section 3 in this chapter) or Capri (see Chapter 17), you should try to see some of the sights inside Naples. If you're hard-pressed for time, then settle for the first three museums of renown.

THE TOP ATTRACTIONS

Reconfirm any museum hours before going there. A book issued annually can't keep up with the changes—they've been known to change from month to month, depending on how much or how little money is in the city treasury. Even the posted opening hours seem more ornamental than reliable.

Naples

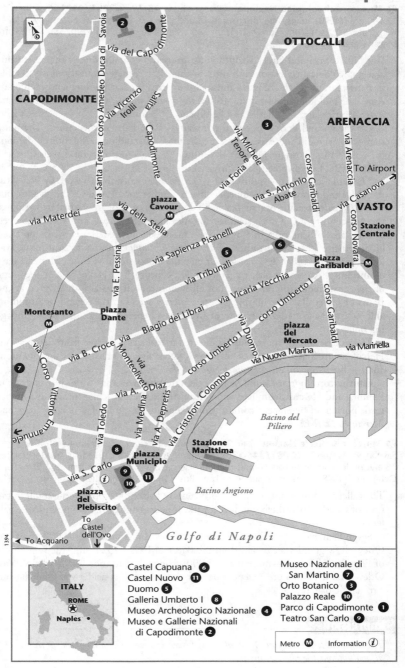

OTTOCALLI

CAPODIMONTE

ARENACCIA

To Airport

VASTO

Stazione Centrale

piazza Cavour

piazza Garibaldi

Montesanto

piazza Dante

piazza del Mercato

Stazione Marittima

piazza Municipio

piazza del Plebiscito

To Castel dell'Ovo

To Acquario

To Castel dell'Ovo

Bacino del Piliero

Bacino Angiono

Golfo di Napoli

ITALY

ROME

Naples

Castel Capuana ⑥
Castel Nuovo ⑪
Duomo ⑤
Galleria Umberto I ⑧
Museo Archeologico Nazionale ④
Museo e Gallerie Nazionali
   di Capodimonte ②

Museo Nazionale di
   San Martino ⑦
Orto Botanico ③
Palazzo Reale ⑩
Parco di Capodimonte ①
Teatro San Carlo ⑨

Metro Ⓜ   Information ⓘ

567

⊕ **Museo Archeologico Nazionale.** Piazza Museo 18–19. ☎ **081/440166.** Admission 12,000 lire ($7.70) adults, free for children 18 and under and for seniors 60 and over. June–Aug, Tues–Sat 9am–7pm, Sun 9am–1pm; Sept–May, Tues–Sat 9am–2pm, Sun 9am–1pm. Metro: Piazza Cavour.

With its Roman and Greek sculpture, this museum contains one of the most valuable archeological collections in Europe—the select Farnese acquisitions are notable in particular, as are the mosaics and sculpture excavated at Pompeii and Herculaneum. The building dates from the 16th century, and was turned into a museum some two centuries later by Charles and Ferdinand IV Bourbon.

On the ground floor is one of the treasures of the Farnese collections: The nude statues of Armodio and Aristogitone are the most outstanding in the room. A famous bas-relief (from an original of the 5th century B.C.) in a nearby salon depicts Orpheus and his wife, Eurydice, with Mercury.

The nude statue of the spear-bearing *Doryphorus,* copied from a work by Polyclitus the Elder and excavated at Pompeii, enlivens another room. Also see the gigantic but weary *Hercules,* a statue of remarkable boldness; it's a copy of an original by Lysippus, the 4th-century B.C. Greek sculptor for Alexander the Great, and was discovered in the Baths of Caracalla in Rome. On a more delicate pedestal is the decapitated but exquisite *Venus* (Aphrodite). The *Psyche of Capua* shows why Aphrodite was jealous. The *Group of the Farnese Bull* presents a pageant of violence from the days of antiquity. A copy of either a 2nd- or 3rd-century B.C. Hellenistic statue—one of the most frequently reproduced of all sculptures—it was also discovered at the Baths of Caracalla. The marble group depicts a scene in the legend of Amphion and Zethus, who tied Dirce, wife of Lycus of Thebes, to the horns of a rampaging bull.

The galleries on the mezzanine are devoted to mosaics excavated from Pompeii and Herculaneum. These include scenes of cock fights, dragon-tailed satyrs, an aquarium, and the finest one of all, *Alexander Fighting the Persians.*

On the top floor are some of the celebrated bronzes that were dug out of the Pompeii and Herculaneum lava and volcanic mud. Of particular interest is a Hellenistic portrait of Berenice, a comically drunken satyr, a statue of a *Sleeping Satyr,* and *Mercury on a Rock.*

⊕ **Museo e Gallerie Nazionali di Capodimonte.** Parco di Capodimonte (off Amedeo di Savoia), via Milano 1. ☎ **081/744-1307.** Admission 8,000 lire ($5.10) adults, free for children 18 and under and for seniors 60 and over. July–Sept, Tues–Sat 9am–7:30pm, Sun 9am–1pm; Oct–June, Tues–Sat 9am–2pm, Sun 9am–1pm. Bus: 110 or 127 from the rail station.

The gallery and museum are in the 18th-century Palace of Capodimonte (built in the time of Charles III), which stands in a park. It houses one of Italy's finest picture galleries.

Seven Flemish tapestries, which were made according to the designs of Bernart van Orley, show grand-scale scenes from the Battle of Pavia (1525), in which the forces of Francis I of France—more than 25,000 strong—lost to those of Charles V. Van Orley, who lived in a pre-*Guernica* day, obviously didn't consider war a horror, but a romantic ballet.

Impressions

The museum is full, as you know, of lovely Greek bronzes. The only bother is that they all walk about the town at night.
   —Oscar Wilde, letter to Ernest Dowson, October 11, 1897

One of the pinacoteca's greatest possessions is Simone Martini's *Coronation* scene, which depicts the brother of Robert of Anjou being crowned king of Naples by the bishop of Toulouse. You'll want to linger over the great Masaccio's *Crucifixion,* a bold expression of grief. The most important room is literally filled with the works of Renaissance masters, notably an *Adoration of the Child* by Luca Signorelli, a *Madonna and Child* by Perugino, a panel by Raphael, a *Madonna and Child with Angels* by Botticelli, and—the most beautiful of all—Fillipino Lippi's *Annunciation and Saints.*

Look for Andrea Mantegna's *St. Eufemia* and his portrait of Francesco Gonzaga, his brother-in-law Giovanni Bellini's *Transfiguration,* and Lotto's *Portrait of Bernardo de Rossi* and his *Madonna and Child with St. Peter.*

In one room is Raphael's *Holy Family and St. John* and a copy of his celebrated portrait of Pope Leo X. Two choice sketches include Raphael's *Moses* and Michelangelo's *Three Soldiers.* Displayed farther on are the Titians, with Danae taking the spotlight from Pope Paul III.

Another room is devoted to Flemish art: Pieter Brueghel's *Blind Men* is an outstanding work, and his *Misanthope* is devilishly powerful. Other foreign works include Joos van Cleve's *Adoration of the Magi.* You can climb the stairs for a panoramic view of Naples and the bay, a finer landscape than any you'll see inside.

The State Apartments downstairs deserve inspection. Room after room is devoted to gilded mermaids, Venetian sedan chairs, ivory carvings, a porcelain chinoiserie salon (the best of all), tapestries, the Farnese armory, and a large glass and china collection.

Museo Nazionale di San Martino. Largo San Martino 5 (in the Vómero residential district). ☎ **081/578-1769.** Admission 8,000 lire ($5.10) adults, free for children 17 and under and for seniors 60 and over. Tues–Sat 9am–2pm, Sun 9am–1pm. Funicular: Centrale from via Toledo.

Magnificently situated on the grounds of the Castel Sant'Elmo, this museum was founded in the 14th century as a Carthusian monastery, but fell into decay until the 17th century, when it was reconstructed by architects in the Neapolitan baroque style. Now a museum for the city of Naples, it displays stately carriages, historic documents, ship replicas, china and porcelain, silver, Campagna paintings of the 19th century, military costumes and armor, and the lavishly adorned crib by Cuciniello. A balcony opens onto a panoramic view of Naples and the bay, as well as Vesuvius and Capri. Many people come to the museum just to drink in the view. The colonnaded cloisters have curious skull sculptures on the inner balustrade.

MORE ATTRACTIONS

Royal Palace (Palazzo Reale). Piazza del Plebiscito 1. ☎ **081/413888.** Admission 6,000 lire ($3.85) adults, free for children 17 and under and for seniors 60 and over. Tues–Fri 9am–1:30pm, Sat 9am–1:30pm and 4–7pm, Sun 9am–1pm. Tram: 1 or 4. Bus: 106 or 150.

This palace was designed by Domenico Fontana in the 17th century. The eight statues on the facade are of Neapolitan kings. Located in the heart of the city, the square is one of the most architecturally interesting in Naples, with a long colonnade and a church, San Francesco di Paolo, that evokes the style of the Pantheon in Rome. Inside the Palazzo Reale you can visit the royal apartments, lavishly and ornately adorned in the baroque style with colored marble floors, paintings, tapestries, frescoes, antiques, and porcelain. Charles de Bourbon, son of Philip IV of Spain, became king of Naples in 1734. A great patron of the arts, he installed a library in the Royal Palace, one of the greatest of the south, with more than 1,250,000 volumes.

New Castle (Castel Nuovo). Piazza del Municipio. ☎ **081/795-2612.** Admission 5,000 lire ($3.20). Mon–Fri 9am–2pm, Sat 9am–1pm. Tram: 1 or 4. Bus: 106 or 150.

The New Castle, which houses municipal offices, was built in the late 13th century on orders from Charles I, king of Naples, as a royal residence for the House of Anjou. It was badly ruined, and virtually rebuilt in the mid-15th century by the House of Aragon. The castle is distinguished by a trio of three round imposing battle towers at its front. Between two of the towers, and guarding the entrance, is an arch of triumph designed by Francesco Laurana to commemorate the expulsion of the Angevins by the forces of Alphonso I in 1442. It has been described by art historians as a masterpiece of the Renaissance. The Palatine Chapel in the center dates from the 14th century, and the city commission of Naples meets in the Barons' Hall, designed by Segreta of Catalonia. You'll find some frescoes and sculptures (of minor interest) from the 14th and 15th centuries inside the castle.

Castle of the Egg (Castel dell'Ovo). ☎ **081/764-5688.** Follow via Console along the seafront from piazza del Plebiscito to the port of Santa Lucia; Castel dell'Ovo is at the end of the promontory. Tram: 1 or 4. Bus: 106 or 150.

This 2,000-year-old fortress overlooks the Gulf of Naples. The site of the castle was important centuries before the birth of Christ, and was fortified by early settlers. In time a major stronghold to guard the bay was erected and duly celebrated by Virgil. In one epoch of its long history it served as a state prison. The view from here is panoramic. It's not open to the public except for special exhibits.

Acquario. Villa Comunale 1, via Caracciolo. ☎ **081/583-3111.** Admission 3,000 lire ($1.90) adults, 1,500 lire (95¢) children. Mar–Oct, Tues–Sat 9am–7pm, Sun 9am–6pm; Nov–Feb, Tues–Sun 9am–5pm. Tram: 1 or 4.

The Aquarium is in a municipal park, Villa Comunale, between via Caracciolo and the Riviera di Chiaia. Established by a German naturalist in the 1800s, the Aquarium is the oldest in Europe. It displays about 200 species of marine plants and fish, all found in the Bay of Naples (they must be a hardy lot).

Catacombs of San Gennaro (St. Januarius). In the Chiesa del Buon Consiglio, via di Capodimonte 16. ☎ **081/741-1071.** Admission 5,000 lire ($3.20). Tours Mon–Fri at 9:30, 10:15, 11, and 11:45am; Sat–Sun 9:30am–6pm (varied intervals). Tram: 1 or 4.

A guide will show visitors through this two-story underground cemetery, which dates back to the 2nd century and has many interesting frescoes and mosaics. You enter the catacombs on via di Capodimonte (head down an alley going alongside the Madre del Buon Consiglio Church).

THE CHURCHES OF NAPLES

Church of Santa Chiara. Via Santa Chiara 49. ☎ **081/552-6209.** Free admission. Apr–Oct, Mon–Sat 8:30am–noon and 4:30–6:30pm, Sun 8:30am–noon; Nov–Mar, Mon–Sat 8:30am–noon and 4–5pm, Sun 8:30am–noon. Tram: 1 or 4.

On a palazzo-flanked street, this church was built on orders from Robert the Wise, king of Naples, in the early 14th century. It became the church for the House of Anjou. Although World War II bombers heavily blasted it, it has been restored somewhat to its original look, a Gothic style as practiced by Provençal architects. The altarpiece by Simone Martini is displayed at the Capodimonte Galleries (see above), which leave the Angevin royal sarcophagi as the principal art treasures, especially the tomb of King Robert in back of the main altar. The Cloister of the Order of the Clares was restored by Vaccaro in the 18th century and is marked by ornate adornment, particularly in the tiles.

Il Duomo. Via del Duomo 147. ☎ **081/449097.** Free admission. Daily 7:30am–12:30pm and 4:30–7:30pm. Metro: Piazza Cavour.

Whoever it was who said (I believe it was Nelson), "See Naples and die," perpetrated one of the greatest hoaxes in history. Or perhaps I am unlucky when I go there.
—Geoffrey Harmsworth, *Abyssinian Adventure,* 1935

The Duomo of Naples may not be as impressive as some in other Italian cities, but it merits a visit nevertheless. Consecrated in 1315, it was Gothic in style, but the centuries have witnessed many changes. The facade, for example, is from the 1800s. A curiosity of the Duomo is that it has access to the Basilica of St. Restituta, which was the earliest Christian basilica erected in Naples and goes back to the 4th century. But an even greater treasure is the chapel dedicated to St. Januarius (San Gennaro), which you enter from the south aisle. In a rich 17th-century baroque style, it contains ampullae with the saint's blood.

ESPECIALLY FOR KIDS

Children can enjoy the **Aquarium** (see above) and the **Giardino Zoologico** (☎ 081/239-5943), which is in the Mostra d'Oltremare at the entrance to viale Kennedy. The zoo, established by a German naturalist in 1873, is open March to October, Tuesday to Saturday from 9am to 5pm and on Sunday from 10am to 6pm; November to February, Tuesday to Saturday from 9am to 5pm and on Sunday from 9am to 2pm. Admission is 5,000 lire ($3.20) for adults and 3,000 lire ($1.90) for children, free for children 3 and under. And to cap it off, take them to the **Edenlandia Amusement Park** (☎ 081/239-1182), also in the area of Mostra d'Oltremare (entrance on viale Kennedy). It's open all year.

In the Naples area, children delight in wandering through the ruins of **Pompeii** as much as their parents do.

WHERE TO STAY

With some exceptions, the accommodations in Naples are a sad lot. Most of the large hotels are in the popular (also dangerous) district of Santa Lucia. Many of the so-called first-class establishments line via Partenope along the water. In and around the central railway station are other clusters, many built in the late 1950s (and some that seemingly haven't been changed since).

Regardless of the price range in which you travel, there's a bed waiting for you in Naples. Regrettably, that bed often isn't clean or comfortable. We'll present a selection of what are generally conceded to be the "best" hotels in Naples, but know that with an exception or two, none of the other candidates leaves us with much enthusiasm. Many of the innkeepers we've encountered seem an indifferent lot.

EXPENSIVE

Grande Albergo Vesuvio. Via Partenope 45, 80121 Napoli. ☎ **081/764-0044,** or 800/223-6800 in the U.S. Fax 081/764-0044. 167 rms, 16 suites. A/C MINIBAR TV TEL. 470,000 lire ($300.80) double; from 700,000 lire ($448) suite. Rates include breakfast. AE, DC, MC, V. Parking 30,000 lire ($19.20). Bus: 102, 112, 128, or 140.

Originally built in 1882, the Vesuvio was restored about 50 years later and features a marble- and stucco-sheathed facade evocative of art deco with curved balconies extending toward the Castel dell'Ovo. When it was constructed, it was the first and foremost hotel along the fabled bay—many aristocratic members of English society flocked here, to be followed later by the likes of Bogie and Errol Flynn—and, with the decline of the Excelsior, is again today. Each of its 1930s-style rooms has a lofty ceiling, rich cove moldings, parquet floors, a renovated tiled bathroom with lots of space, and large closets. Only the bedrooms at the Grand Hotel Parker's are as good. Traditionalists should request rooms on the second floor, as they've been decorated in a 1700s style. You'll also find a scattering of antiques throughout the echoing hallways. The hotel also has a first-class restaurant, Caruso; a roof garden; and a comfortable bar that evokes the most stylish decor of the 1950s.

Hotel Excelsior. Via Partenope 48, 80121 Napoli. ☎ **081/764-0111,** or 800/325-3535 in the U.S. Fax 081/764-9743. 124 rms, 12 suites. A/C MINIBAR TV TEL. 395,000 lire ($252.80) double; 650,000–1,050,000 lire ($416–$672) suite. AE, DC, MC, V. Parking 40,000 lire ($25.60).

The Excelsior is situated in a most dramatic position right on the waterfront, with views of Santa Lucia and Vesuvius. Standards are slipping here and it has lost its number one position to the Vesuvio. Nevertheless, there are many elegant details, such as Venetian chandeliers, Doric columns, wall-size murals, and bronze torchiers. Most of the accommodations are, in reality, bed/sitting rooms, furnished for the most part in a heavy Empire style. Others are much less grand.

Dining/Entertainment: The cuisine at the Excelsior is both Neapolitan and international, served in a windowless room. Breakfast can be ordered on a covered roof terrace.

Services: Room service, baby-sitting, laundry, valet.

MODERATE

Grand Hotel Parker's. Corso Vittorio Emanuele 135, 80121 Napoli. ☎ **081/761-2474.** Fax 081/663527. 73 rms, 10 suites. A/C TV TEL. 290,000–330,000 lire ($185.60–$211.20) double; from 750,000 lire ($480) suite. Rates include breakfast. AE, DC, MC, V. Parking 20,000 lire ($12.80). Metro: Piazza Amedeo. Bus: 118, 120, or 128.

This 1870 hotel sits up and away from the harbor commotion on one of the better hillside avenues of Naples, and many guests check in just to enjoy the view of Naples. It has now been fully restored, and once again has reclaimed its position as one of the finest hotels in Naples. It's topped only by the Vesuvio, and is much better managed than the Excelsior. It was created when architects cared about the beauty of their work—neoclassic walls, fluted pilasters, and ornate ceilings. The bedrooms are traditionally furnished, some quite formal. Each room is in a different style, including Louis XVI, Directoire, Empire, and Charles X. Naturally, all guests try for a "room with a view." The roof garden restaurant offers a fine view along with an international Mediterranean cuisine. The hotel provides laundry, valet, baby-sitting, and room service, and operates a currency exchange and business center.

Hotel Majestic. Largo Vasto a Chiaia 68, 80121 Napoli. ☎ **081/416500.** Fax 081/416500. 129 rms, 6 junior suites. MINIBAR TV TEL. 270,000 lire ($172.80) double; 300,000–400,000 lire ($192–$256) suite. Rates include breakfast. AE, DC, MC, V. Parking 22,000 lire ($14.10). Metro: Piazza Amedeo.

This four-star hotels was built in 1959 on 10 floors. It's now one of the most up-to-date hostelries in a city too often filled with decaying mansions. A favorite with the conference crowd, it lies in the antiques district of Naples—at your doorstep will be dozens of fashionable boutiques. Reservations are important, as this hotel is often fully booked. There's a cozy American bar and a restaurant, the Magic Grill, which serves both Neapolitan dishes and international specialties Monday to Saturday. The garage is small, so reserve parking space with your room.

Hotel Miramare. Via Nazario Saura 24, 80132 Napoli. ☎ **081/764-7589.** Fax 081/764-0775. 31 rms. A/C MINIBAR TV TEL. 250,000–380,000 lire ($160–$243.20) double. Rates include breakfast. AE, DC, MC, V. Parking: 25,000–35,000 lire ($16–$22.40). Bus: 106, 140, or 150.

In a superb location, seemingly thrust out toward the harbor on a dockside boulevard, the Miramare is central and sunny. Originally the hotel was an aristocratic villa, but in 1944 it was transformed into a hotel after serving for a short period as the American consulate. Its lobby evokes a little Caribbean hotel with a semitropical look. The bedrooms have been renovated and now are pleasantly furnished and decently maintained by the management. They have soundproof windows to protect against the traffic noise outside. An American bar and a roof garden are on the premises.

Hotel Paradiso. Via Catullo 11, 80122 Napoli. ☎ **081/761-4161,** or 800/528-1234 in the U.S. Fax 081/761-3449. 71 rms, 2 suites. A/C MINIBAR TV TEL. 240,000 lire ($153.60) double; from 400,000 lire ($256) suite. Rates include breakfast. AE, DC, MC, V. Parking 24,000 lire ($15.35). Bus: 23, 106, or 140. Funicular: C21.

This hotel might be paradise, but only after you reach it. It's only 3$^1/_2$ miles from the central station, but one irate driver claimed that it also takes about 3$^1/_2$ hours to get there. Once you arrive, however, your nerves are soothed by the view, one of the most panoramic of any hotel in Italy. The Bay of Naples unfolds before you, and in the distance Mount Vesuvius looms menacingly. The hotel is one of the best in Naples, with well-furnished and comfortably equipped bedrooms. When you take your breakfast, you may want to linger here before facing the traffic of Naples again. Should you elect not to go out at night, you can patronize the fine restaurant at the Paradiso, which serves both Neapolitan and Italian specialties

Hotel Royal. Via Partenope 38, 80121 Napoli. ☎ **081/764-4800.** Fax 081/764-5707. 273 rms, 14 suites. A/C MINIBAR TV TEL. 230,000–340,000 lire ($147.20–$217.60) double; 560,000 lire ($358.40) suite. Rates include breakfast. AE, DC, MC, V. Parking 26,000 lire ($16.65). Tram: 1. Bus: 106 or 140.

The 10-story Hotel Royal, built in 1955, is in a desirable location on this busy but dangerous street beside the bay in Santa Lucia. A very commercial aura prevails, and the hotel is often filled with groups. You enter a greenery-filled vestibule, where the stairs that lead to the modern lobby are flanked by a pair of stone lions. Each of the bedrooms has a balcony and aging modern furniture. Some, but not all, offer a water view. A seawater pool with an adjacent flower-dotted sun terrace is on the hotel's roof—swimming here is vastly preferred over the polluted bay. The hotel's restaurant has panoramic views but only mediocre food.

Hotel Santa Lucia. Via Partenope 46, 80121 Napoli. ☎ **081/764-0666.** Fax 081/764-8580. 95 rms, 12 suites. A/C MINIBAR TV TEL. 380,000 lire ($243.20) double; from 450,000 lire ($288) suite. Rates include breakfast. AE, DC, MC, V. Parking 35,000 lire ($22.40).

The Santa Lucia's imposing neoclassical facade overlooks a sheltered marina on the bay. It competes effectively with the nearby Royal and is better maintained. From the windows of about half the bedrooms you can watch motorboats and yachts bobbing at anchor, fishermen repairing nets, and all the waterside life that Naples is famous for. But beware of muggers if you do go wandering around the area at night. The interior has undergone extensive renovations, and is decorated in a family-conscious Neapolitan style, with terrazzo floors and lots of upholstered chairs scattered throughout the lobby. The bedrooms are large and high-ceilinged, with French doors that open onto tiny verandas. The noisier rooms overlook the traffic of via Santa Lucia. There's an American-inspired bar on the premises, plus the Restaurant Jardin, serving a superb Mediterranean cuisine.

INEXPENSIVE

Albergo San Germano. Via Beccadelli 41, 80125 Napoli. ☎ **081/570-5422,** or 800/528-1234 in the U.S. Fax 081/570-1546. 104 rms. A/C MINIBAR TV TEL. 240,000 lire ($153.60) double. Rates include breakfast. AE, DC, MC, V. Free parking. Bus: C52.

Designed like an Italian version of a Chinese pagoda, this brick-and-concrete hotel is ideal for late-arriving motorists who are reluctant to negotiate the traffic of Naples. A terraced swimming pool and garden are welcome respites after a day in Naples. The hotel's bedrooms are clean but simple, and each has a tile bath. There's a lobby bar, along with a modern restaurant.

From the autostrada, follow the signs to Tangenziale Napoli; exit 8 miles later at Agnano Terme. After paying the toll, the hotel is on your right in less than a mile. You can park your car here and take bus no. C52 the 4 miles into the center of Naples.

Hotel Rex. Via Palepoli 12, 80132 Napoli. ☎ **081/764-9389.** Fax 081/764-9227. 40 rms. A/C TV TEL. 170,000 lire ($108.80) double. Rates include breakfast. AE, DC, V. Parking 30,000 lire ($18.75). Bus: 104.

The most famous budget hotel in Santa Lucia, the Hotel Rex has played host to lira-watchers around the world since its opening in 1938. Some like it and others don't, but proof of its popularity is that its bedrooms are often fully booked when other hotels have vacancies. The building itself is lavishly ornate architecturally, but the bedrooms are simple and some are very cramped. Breakfast is the only meal served.

Hotel Serius. Viale Augusto 74, 80125 Napoli. ☎ **081/239-4844.** Fax 081/239-4844. 69 rms. A/C MINIBAR TV TEL. 175,000 lire ($112) double. Rates include breakfast. AE, MC, V. Free parking. Metro: Piazza Leopardi. Tram: 1 or 4. Bus: 144, 150, or 152.

Built in 1974 to provide well-organized comfort, this hotel is on a palm-lined street of a relatively calm neighborhood known as Fuorigrotto, a short bus ride north of the center. The paneled split-level lobby contains an intimate bar and several metal sculptures of horses and birds. The bedrooms are simply furnished with boldly patterned fabrics and painted furniture. In addition to the bar, there's a pleasant, contemporary dining room.

WHERE TO DINE

A mixed reaction. Naples is the home of pizza and spaghetti. If you're mad for either of those items, then you'll delight in sampling the authentic versions. However, if you like subtle cooking and have an aversion to olive oil or garlic, you won't fare as well.

One of the major problems is overcharging. It's not uncommon for four foreign visitors to have a dinner in a Naples restaurant, particularly those once-famous ones in Santa Lucia, and be billed for five dinners. Service in many restaurants tends to be poor. Again, as in the hotels, we'll attempt to pick out the best of the lot.

EXPENSIVE

✪ **La Cantinella.** Via Cuma 42. ☎ **081/764-8684.** Reservations required. Main courses 18,000–25,000 lire ($11.50–$16). AE, DC, MC, V. Mon–Sat 12:30–3pm and 7:30pm–midnight. Closed 2 weeks in Aug. Tram: 1 or 4. Bus: 106 or 140. SEAFOOD.

You get the impression of 1920s Chicago as you approach this place, where speak-easy-style doors open after you ring. The restaurant is on a busy street that skirts the bay in Santa Lucia, with a terrace overlooking the sea. Inside, you'll find a well-stocked antipasto table and—get this—a phone on each table. We consistently find the highest-quality meals in Naples served here. The chefs have a deft way of handling the region's fresh produce and they turn out both Neapolitan classics and more imaginative dishes. The menu includes four different preparations of risotto (including one with champagne), many kinds of pasta (including penne with vodka, and linguine with scampi and seafood), and most of the classic beef and veal dishes of Italy. Best known for its fish, Cantinella serves grilled seafood at its finest.

⭕ **Giuseppone a Mare.** Via Ferdinando Russo 13. ☎ **081/575-6002.** Reservations required. Main courses 12,000–30,000 lire ($7.70–$19.20). AE, DC, MC, V. Tues–Sun 12:30–3:30pm and 8pm–midnight. Closed Aug 14–24 and Dec 23–31. Bus: 140. SEAFOOD.

Here you can dine in Neapolitan sunshine on an open-air terrace with a view of the bay. The only better restaurant in Naples is La Cantinella (see above). The restaurant at Capo Posillipo is known for serving the best and the freshest seafood in Campania. Diners make their selections from a trolley in the center of the dining room, which is likely to include everything from crabs to eels. You might precede your fish dinner with some fritters (a batter whipped up with seaweed and fresh squash blossoms). Naturally, they serve linguine with clams—the chef here adds squid and mussels. Much of the day's catch is deep-fried a golden brown. The *pièce de résistance* is an octopus casserole. If the oven's going, you can also order a pizza. They stock some fine southern Italian wines, too, especially from Ischia and Vesuvio.

MODERATE

Don Salvatore. Strada Mergellina 4A. ☎ **081/681817.** Reservations recommended. Main courses 15,000–27,500 lire ($9.60–$17.60); fixed-price menu 35,000 lire ($22.40). AE, DC, MC, V. Thurs–Tues 1–4pm and 8pm–1am. Metro: Mergellina. SEAFOOD.

Don Salvatore is the creative statement of a serious restaurateur, who directs his waterfront establishment with passion and dedication. Antonio Aversano takes his wine as seriously as his food. The latter is likely to include linguine with shrimp or with squid, an array of fish, and a marvelous assortment of fresh Neapolitan vegetables grown in the surrounding countryside. Fish dishes are priced according to weight based on daily market quotations. The fish comes right out of the Bay of Naples, which may, but possibly may not, be a plus. Rice comes flavored in a delicate fish broth, and you can get a reasonably priced bottle from the wine cellar, said to be the finest in Campania. The location is on the seafront near the departure point of hydrofoils for Capri.

Il Gallo Nero. Via Torquato Tasso 466. ☎ **081/643012.** Reservations recommended. Main courses 23,000–30,000 lire ($14.70–$19.20); fixed-price menu 35,000 lire ($22.40). AE, DC, MC, V. Tues–Sat 7pm–midnight, Sun 12:30–3pm. Closed Aug. Metro: Mergellina. PASTA/NEAPOLITAN.

Dinner here is almost like a throwback to the mid–19th century. Gian Paolo Quagliata, with a capable staff, maintains this hillside villa with its period furniture and accessories. In summer the enthusiastic clientele is served on an elegant outdoor terrace. Many of the dishes are based on 100-year-old recipes from the classical Neapolitan repertoire, although a few are more recent inventions of the chef. You might enjoy the Neapolitan linguine with pesto, rigatoni with fresh vegetables, tagliatelle primavera, or macaroni with peas and artichokes. The fish dishes are usually well prepared, whether grilled, broiled, or sautéed. The meat dishes include slightly more exotic creations, such as prosciutto with orange slices, veal cutlets with artichokes, and a savory array of beef dishes.

Rosolino. Via Nazario Sauro 5–7. ☎ **081/764-0547.** Reservations required. Main courses 15,000–25,000 lire ($9.60–$16); fixed-price menu 50,000 lire ($32). AE, DC, MC, V. Mon–Sat 12:30–3:30pm and 8pm–midnight. Tram: 1 or 4. Bus: 128, 140, or 150. INTERNATIONAL/ITALIAN/SEAFOOD.

This stylish place is not defined as a nightclub by its owners, but rather as a restaurant with dancing. Set on the waterfront, it's divided into two distinct areas; there's a piano bar near the entrance, where you might have a drink before passing into a much larger dining room. There, in interiors ringed with stained glass set into striking patterns, you can dine within sight of a bandstand reminiscent of the Big Band era.

Live music is only on Saturday night. The food is traditional—not very imaginative—but well prepared with fresh vegetables. Dishes include rigatoni with zucchini and meat sauce, an impressive array of fresh shellfish, and such beef dishes as tournedos and veal scaloppine. Most fresh fish is priced according to weight. There are three different wine lists, including one for French wines and champagne.

La Sacrestia. Via Orazio 116. ☎ **081/761-1051.** Reservations required. Main courses 18,000–32,000 lire ($11.50–$20.50). AE, DC, MC, V. Tues–Sat 12:30–4:30pm and 7:40–11:30pm. Closed 2 weeks in Aug; open Mon and closed Sun July–Aug. Funicular: From Mergellina. PASTA/SEAFOOD.

The trompe-l'oeil frescoes on the two-story interior and the name La Sacrestia vaguely suggest the ecclesiastical, but that's not the case here. One of the best restaurants in Naples, this bustling place is sometimes called "the greatest show in town." It's perched near the top of one of the belvederes of Naples, at the end of a seemingly endless labyrinth of streets winding up from the port (take a taxi). In summer an outdoor terrace with its flowering arbor provides a view over the lights of the harbor. Meals emphasize well-prepared dishes with strong doses of Neapolitan drama. You might, for example, try what's said to be the most luxurious macaroni dish in Italy ("Prince of Naples"), concocted with truffles and mild cheeses. The fettuccine alla Gran Caruso is made from fresh peas, mushrooms, prosciutto, and tongue. Less ornate selections include a full array of pastas and dishes composed of octopus, squid, and shellfish. Food is served "until the last diner finishes."

INEXPENSIVE

Dante e Beatrice. Piazza Dante 44–45. ☎ **081/549-9438.** Reservations recommended. Main courses 10,000–20,000 lire ($6.40–$12.80). No credit cards. Tues–Sun 12:30–3:30pm and 7:30–11pm. Closed Aug 15–30. Tram: 1 or 4. Bus: 109, 121, 137, 160, or 161. NEAPOLITAN.

Gregarious and unpretentious, and named after the players in one of the great romantic tragedies of the Renaissance, Dante e Beatrice was established in 1956 and remains one of the best restaurants in its neighborhood. Specializing in all the staples of the Neapolitan cuisine, it serves simple, flavorful, and filling portions of lasagne, minestrone, spaghetti with clams, tagliatelle, pasta e fagiole, and grilled fish to the many workday clients who seek this place out.

Ristorante la Fazenda. Via Marechiaro 58A. ☎ **081/575-7420.** Reservations required. Main courses 22,000–24,000 lire ($14.10–$15.35). AE, V. Mon 7:30pm–12:30am, Tues–Sat 1–4pm and 7:30pm–12:30am. Closed Aug 12–18. Bus: 140. SEAFOOD.

It would be hard to find a more typically Neapolitan restaurant than this one, offering a panoramic view that on a clear day can include the island of Capri. The decor is rustic, loaded with agrarian touches and filled with an assortment of Neapolitan families, lovers, and visitors who have made it one of their preferred dining locales since it opened in 1973. In summer the overflow from the dining room spills onto the terrace. Menu specialties include linguine with scampi, an array of fresh grilled fish, sautéed clams, a mixed Italian grill, several savory stews, and many chicken dishes, along with lobster with fresh grilled tomatoes.

Ⓢ Umberto. Via Alabardieri 30. ☎ **081/418555.** Reservations required. Main courses 10,000–22,000 lire ($6.40–$14.10). AE, DC, V. Thurs–Tues 12:30–3:30pm and 7:30–10:30pm. Closed Aug. Bus: 102, 106, 140, or 150. NEAPOLITAN.

Located off piazza dei Martiri, Umberto is one of the most atmospheric places to dine in all of Naples. The tasteful dining room has been directed for many a year by the same interconnected family. There's likely to be an evening dance band playing. The excellent Italian specialties served here include pizzas, gnocchi with potatoes, and grilled meats and fishes, as well as savory stews and a host of pasta dishes. The bel canto era lives on here.

🅢 **Vini e Cucina.** Corso Vittorio Emanuele 761. ☎ **081/660302.** Reservations not accepted. Main courses 5,000–10,000 lire ($3.20–$6.40). No credit cards. Mon–Sat noon–4:30pm and 7pm–midnight. Closed Aug 10–26. Metro: Mergellina. NEAPOLITAN.

The best ragù sauce in all of Naples is said to be made at this trattoria, which has only 10 tables and is known for its home-cookery. You can get a really satisfying meal here, but we must warn you—it's almost impossible to get in. Dedicated diners might do as we do: Arrive early and wait for a table. The cooking is the best home-style version of Neapolitan cuisine we've been able to find in this tricky city. The spaghetti, along with that fabulous sauce, is served al dente. The restaurant is in front of the Mergellina station.

A HISTORIC PIZZERIA

🅢 **Brandi.** Via Miano 27–29. ☎ **081/741-0455.** Reservations required. Main courses 9,000–20,000 lire ($5.75–$12.80). No credit cards. Tues–Sun noon–3pm and 6:30pm–midnight. Bus: 22, 110, or 127. NEAPOLITAN.

The most historic pizzeria in Italy, Brandi was established by Pietro Colicchio in the 19th century. His successor, Raffaele Esposito, who enjoyed the reputation that his hard work had earned, was requested one day to prepare a banquet for Margherita di Savoia, the queen of Italy. So successful was the reception of the pizza made with tomato, basil, olive oil, and mozzarella (the colors of the newly united Italy's flag) that the queen accepted the honor of having it named after her. Thus was pizza Margherita born from the kitchens of Naples's Restaurant Brandi. Today you can order the pizza that pleased a queen, as well as such other specialties as linguine with scampi, fettuccine "Regina d'Italia," and a full array of seafood dishes.

NAPLES AFTER DARK

A sunset **walk through Santa Lucia** and along the waterfront never seems to dim in pleasure, even if you've lived in Naples for 40 years. Visitors are also fond of riding around town in one of the **carrozzelle** (horse-drawn wagons).

Or you can stroll by the glass-enclosed **Galleria Umberto,** off via Roma in the vicinity of the Teatro San Carlo. The 19th-century gallery, which evokes many a memory for aging former GIs, is still standing today, although a little the worse for wear. It's a kind of social center for Naples. John Horne Burns used it for the title of his novel *The Gallery,* in which he wrote: "In August 1944, everyone in Naples sooner or later found his way into this place and became like a picture on the wall of the museum."

On its nightclub and cabaret circuit, Naples offers more sucker joints than any other port along the Mediterranean. If you're starved for action, you'll find plenty of it—and you're likely to end up paying for it dearly.

OPERA

Teatro San Carlo. Via San Carlo (across from the Galleria Umberto). ☎ **081/797-2331.** Tickets, 20,000–175,000 lire ($12.80–$112).

This is one of the largest opera houses in Italy, with some of the best acoustics. Built in only 6 months time for King Charles's birthday in November 1737, it was restored in a gilded neoclassical style. Grand-scale productions are presented here on the main stage. The box office is open December to June, Tuesday to Sunday from 10am to 1pm and 4:30 to 6:30pm.

A Sweet Shop & a Grand Cafe

Giovanni Scaturchio, at piazza San Domenico Maggiore 19 (☎ **081/551-6944**), offers the most caloric collection of pastries in Naples, and is famous for both satisfying and fattening local residents since around 1900. Representative pastries include the entire selection of Neapolitan sweets, cakes, and candies, including brioches soaked in liqueur, cassate (pound cake) filled with layered ricotta, Moor's heads, and cheesy-ricotta pastries known as sfogliatelle, dear to the heart of most Neapolitans since childhood. Another specialty is ministeriale, a chocolate cake filled with liqueur and chocolate cream. Pastries start at 1,600 lire ($1) if consumed standing up, or at 3,500 lire ($2.25) if enjoyed at a table. It's open Monday and Wednesday to Sunday from 7:30am to 8:30pm; closed 2 weeks in August.

The decor of the **Gran Caffè Gambrinus,** via Chiaia 1, near the Galleria Umberto (☎ **081/417582**), the oldest cafe in Naples, dating from 1860, would fit easily into a grand Bourbon palace. Along the vaulted ceiling of an inner room, Empire-style caryatids spread their togas in high relief above frescoes of mythological playmates. The cafe is known for its espresso and cappuccino, as well as pastries and cakes whose variety dazzles the eye. These pastries are the most famous in Naples. You can also order potato and rice croquettes and fried pizzas for a light lunch. Tea costs 3,500 lire ($2.25); cappuccino goes for 4,000 lire ($2.55) at a table. The cafe is open Wednesday to Monday from 7am to 11pm, although it remains open on Saturday until 1am; closed 2 weeks in Aug.

A CLUB & A DISCO

Chez Moi. Via dei Parco Margherita 13. ☎ **081/407526.** Cover 20,000 lire ($12.80).

This is one of the city's best-managed nightclubs, strictly refusing entrance to anyone who looks like a troublemaker. This is appreciated by the designers, government ministers, and visiting socialites who seem to enjoy the place. Clients tend to be over 25, and have included the mayor of Naples. You'll be ushered to a table in an interior with a decor of soft blues and greens, where you'll order your first drink. The place is open Thursday and Friday from midnight to 4am. Occasionally the management will present a cabaret act or a live pianist at the bar, but more frequently the music is highly danceable disco.

Kiss Kiss. Via Sgambati 47. ☎ **081/546-6566.** Cover 20,000 lire ($12.80) Fri and Sun, 25,000 lire ($16) Sat.

Kiss Kiss is huge—the largest disco in Naples. The youngish crowd, usually between 18 and 25, mingle and dance and generally have an uninhibited good time. If you tire of the human melee going on at the several bars or on the dance floor, you can watch video movies or videotaped rock concerts on one of several different screens. There's a restaurant and piano bar on the premises, called the Kiss Kiss Café, set up in a separate (and quieter) room. The place is open only on Friday and Saturday from 10pm to 3am and on Sunday from 8pm to 2am. The Friday-night crowd tends to be older and slightly more sedate.

2 The Environs of Naples

PHLAEGREAN FIELDS

One of the bizarre attractions of southern Italy, the Phlaegrean Fields (Campi Flegrei) form a backdrop for a day's adventure of exploring west of Naples and along its bay.

An explosive land of myth and legend, the fiery fields contain a dormant volcano (Solfatara), the cave of the Cumaean Sibyl, Virgil's gateway to the "Infernal Regions," the ruins of thermal baths and amphitheaters built by the Romans, deserted colonies left by the Greeks, and lots more.

If you're depending on public transportation, the best center for exploring the area is **Pozzuoli,** which is reached by Metropolitana (subway) from the Stazione Centrale in Naples. The fare is 1,500 lire (95¢). Once in Pozzuoli, you can take one of the SEPSA buses at any bus stop, which will take you to places such as Baia in 20 minutes. You can also go to Cumae on one of these buses, or to Solfatara or Lago d'Averno.

۞ SOLFATARA About 7¹/₂ miles west of Naples, near Pozzuoli, is the ancient **Vulcano Solfatara,** via Solfatara 161 (☎ **081/526-7413**). It hasn't erupted since the final year of the 12th century, but it has been threatening ever since. It gives off sulfurous gases and releases scalding vapors through cracks in the earth's surface. In fact, the activity—or inactivity—of Solfatara has been observed for such a long time that the crater's name is used by Webster's dictionary to define any "dormant volcano" emitting vapors.

The crater may be visited daily from 8:30am to sunset, at a cost of 6,500 lire ($4.15) for adults, 3,500 lire ($2.25) for children. Take bus no. 152 from Naples or the Metropolitana line from the Stazione Centrale to Solfatara. Once you get off at the train station, you can board one of the city buses that go up the hill, or you can walk to the crater in about 20 minutes.

POZZUOLI Just 1¹/₂ miles away from Solfatara, the seaport of Pozzuoli opens onto a gulf screened from the Bay of Naples by a promontory. The ruins of the **Anfiteatro Flavio,** via Nicola Terracciano (☎ **081/526-6007**), built in the last part of the 1st century A.D., testify to past greatness. One of the finest surviving examples of the arenas of antiquity, it's particularly distinguished by its "wings"—which, considering their age, are in good condition. You can see the remains where exotic beasts from Africa were caged before being turned loose in the ring to test their jungle skill against a gladiator. The amphitheater, which may be visited daily from 9am to 1pm, is said to have entertained 40,000 spectators at the height of its glory. Admission is 4,000 lire ($2.55).

In another part of town, the **Tempio di Serapide** was really the "Macellum," or market square, and some of its ruined pillars still project upward today. It was erected during the reign of the Flavian emperors.

You can reach Pozzuoli by subway from the Stazione Centrale in Naples.

BAIA In the days of Imperial Rome, the emperors—everybody from Julius Caesar to Hadrian—came here to frolic in the sun while enjoying the comforts of their luxurious villas and Roman baths. Nero is said to have murdered his mother, Agrippina, at nearby Bacoli, with its Pool of Mirabilis. (The ancient "Baiae" was named for Baios, helmsman for Ulysses.) Parts of its illustrious past have been dug out, including both the **Temple of Baiae** and the **Thermal Baths,** said to have been among the greatest erected in Italy.

You can explore this archeological district daily from 9am to 2 hours before sunset. Admission is 6,000 lire ($3.85). The town is 15 minutes by rail from Naples. Ferrovia Cumana trains depart from Stazione Centiale at Piazza Garibaldi in the center of Naples.

LAGO D'AVERNO About 10 miles west of Naples, a bit to the north of Baia, is a lake occupying an extinct volcanic crater. Known to the ancients as the Gateway to Hades, it was for centuries shrouded in superstition. Its vapors were said to

Treading Lightly on Mount Vesuvius

Stand at the bottom of the great market-place of Pompeii, and look up at the silent streets . . . over the broken houses with their inmost sanctuaries open to the day, away to Mount Vesuvius, bright and snowy in the peaceful distance; and lose all count of time, and heed of other things, in the strange and melancholy sensation of seeing the Destroyed and the Destroyer making this quiet picture in the sun.

—Charles Dickens, *Pictures from Italy*

A volcano that has struck terror in Campania, the towering, pitch-black Vesuvius looms menacingly over the Bay of Naples. August 24, A.D. 79, is the infamous date when Vesuvius burst forth and buried Pompeii, Herculaneum, and Stabiae under its mass of lava and volcanic mud. What many fail to realize is that Vesuvius has erupted periodically ever since (thousands were killed in 1631): The last major spouting of lava occurred in this century (it blew off the ring of its crater in 1906). The last spectacular eruption was on March 31, 1944. The approach to Vesuvius is dramatic, with the terrain growing forlorn and foreboding as you near the top. Along the way you'll see villas rising on its slopes and vineyards (the grapes produce an amber-colored wine known as lacrimae Christi; the citizens of Pompeii enjoyed wine from this mountainside, as excavations revealed). Closer to the summit the soil becomes colored puce and an occasional wildflower appears.

Although it may sound like a dubious invitation to some (Vesuvius, after all, is an active volcano), it's possible to visit the rim—or lips, so to speak—of the crater's mouth. As you look down into its smoldering core, you may recall that Spartacus, in a century before the eruption that buried Pompeii, hid in the hollow of the crater, which was then covered with vines.

To reach Vesuvius from Naples, you can take the Circumvesuviana Railway, or (in summer only) a motorcoach service from piazza Vittoria, which hooks up with bus connections at Pugliano. You get off the train at the Ercolano station, the 10th stop. Six SITA buses per day go from Herculaneum to the crater of Vesuvius, costing 4,000 lire ($2.55) round-trip. Once at the top you must be accompanied by a guide, which costs another 5,000 lire ($3.20).

produce illness and even death, and Averno could well have been the source of the expression "still waters run deep." Facing the lake are the ruins of what has been known as the **Temple of Apollo** from the 1st century A.D., and what was once thought to be the Cave of the Cumaean Sibyl (see Cuma, below). According to legend, the Sibyl is said to have ferried Aeneas, son of Aphrodite, across the lake, where he traced a mysterious spring to its source, the River Styx. In the 1st century B.C. Agrippa turned it into a harbor for Roman ships by digging out a canal.

Take the Napoli–Torre Gaveta bus from Baia to reach the site.

CUMA   Ancient Cumae was one of the first outposts of Greek colonization in what is now Italy. Located 12 miles west of Naples, it's of interest chiefly because it's said to have contained the cave of the legendary Cumaean Sibyl. The **cave of the oracle,** really a gallery, was dug by the Greeks in the 5th century B.C. and was a sacred spot to them. Beloved by Apollo, the Sibyl is said to have written the *Sibylline Oracles,* a group of books of prophecy purchased, according to tradition, by Tarquin the Proud. You may visit not only the caves, but also the ruins of temples dedicated to Jupiter and Apollo (later converted into Christian churches), daily from 9am to 2 hours

Herculaneum

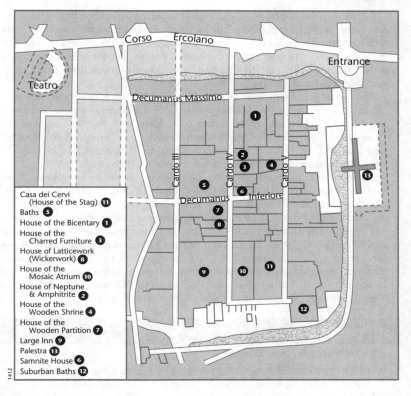

Corso Ercolano

Entrance

Teatro

Decumanus Massimo

Cardo III

Cardo IV

Cardo V

Decumanus Inferiore

1 House of the Bicentary
2 House of Neptune & Amphitrite
3 House of the Charred Furniture
4 House of the Wooden Shrine
5 Baths
6 Samnite House
7 House of the Wooden Partition
8 House of Latticework (Wickerwork)
9 Large Inn
10 House of the Mosaic Atrium
11 Casa dei Cervi (House of the Stag)
12 Suburban Baths
13 Palestra

Casa dei Cervi (House of the Stag) **11**
Baths **5**
House of the Bicentary **1**
House of the Charred Furniture **3**
House of Latticework (Wickerwork) **8**
House of the Mosaic Atrium **10**
House of Neptune & Amphitrite **2**
House of the Wooden Shrine **4**
House of the Wooden Partition **7**
Large Inn **9**
Palestra **13**
Samnite House **6**
Suburban Baths **12**

before sunset, for 4,000 lire ($2.55). On via Domitiana, to the east of Cuma, you'll pass the **Arco Felice,** an arch about 64 feet high, built by the emperor Domitian in the 1st century A.D.

Ferrovia Cumana trains run here. They depart from Stazione Central at piazza Garibaldi in the center of Naples.

✪ HERCULANEUM

The builders of Herculaneum (Ercolano in Italian) were still working to repair the damage caused by an A.D. 62 earthquake when Vesuvius erupted on that fateful August day in A.D. 79. Herculaneum, a much smaller town (about one-fourth the size of Pompeii), didn't start to come to light again until 1709, when Prince Elbeuf launched the unfortunate fashion of tunneling through it for treasures, more intent on profiting from the sale of objets d'art than in uncovering a dead Roman town.

Subsequent excavations at the site, **Ufficio Scavi di Ercolano,** corso Resina, Ercolano (☎ **081/739-0963**), have been slow and sporadic. In fact, Herculaneum is not completely dug out today. One of the obstacles has been that the town was buried under lava, which was much heavier than the ash and pumice stone that piled onto Pompeii. Of course, this formed a greater protection for the buildings buried underneath—many of which were more elaborately constructed than those at Pompeii, as Herculaneum was a seaside resort for patrician families. The complication of having the slum of Resina resting over the yet-to-be-excavated district has further impeded progress and urban renewal.

Although all the streets and buildings of Herculaneum hold interest, some ruins merit more attention than others. The baths (*terme*) are divided between those at the forum and the Terme Suburbane on the outskirts, near the more elegant villas. The municipal baths, which segregated the sexes, are larger, but the ones at the edge of town are more lavishly adorned. The Palestra was a kind of sports arena, where games were staged to satisfy the spectacle-hungry denizens.

The typical plan for the average town house was to erect it around an uncovered atrium. In some areas, Herculaneum possessed the forerunner of the modern apartment house. Important private homes to seek out include the "House of the Bicentenary," the "House of the Wooden Cabinet," the "House of the Wooden Partition," and the "House of Poseidon (Neptune) and Amphitrite," the last containing what is perhaps the best-known mosaic discovered in the ruins.

The finest example of how the aristocracy lived is provided by a visit to the "Casa dei Cervi," named the "House of the Stags" because of the sculpture found inside. Guides are fond of showing their male clients a statue of a drunken Hercules urinating. Some of the best of the houses are locked and can be seen only by permission.

The ruins may be visited daily from 9am to 1 hour before sunset. Admission is 12,000 lire ($7.70) for adults, free for children 17 and under and for seniors 60 and over. To reach the archeological zone, take the regular train service from Naples on the Circumvesuviana Railway, a 20-minute ride leaving about every half hour from corso Garibaldi 387; or take bus no. 255 from piazza Municipio. Otherwise, it's a 4¹/₂-mile drive on the autostrada to Salerno (turn off at Ercolano).

3 Pompeii

15 miles S of Naples, 147 miles SE of Rome

When Vesuvius erupted in A.D. 79, Pliny the Younger, who later recorded the event, thought the end of the world had come. The ruined Roman city of Pompeii (Pompei in Italian), now dug out from the inundation of volcanic ash and pumice stone rained on it by Vesuvius in the year A.D. 79, vividly brings to light the life of 19 centuries ago, and has sparked the imagination of the world.

Numerous myths have surrounded Pompeii, one of which is that a completely intact city was rediscovered. Actually the Pompeiians—that is, those who escaped—returned to their city when the ashes had cooled and removed some of the most precious treasures from the thriving resort. But they left plenty behind to be uncovered at a later date and carted off to museums throughout Europe and America.

After a long medieval sleep, Pompeii was again brought to life in the late 16th century, quite by accident, by the architect Domenico Fontana. However, it was in the mid-18th century that large-scale excavations were launched. Somebody once remarked that Pompeii's second tragedy was its rediscovery, that it really should have been left to slumber for another century or two, when it might have been better excavated and maintained.

ESSENTIALS

GETTING THERE **By Train** The Circumvesuviana Railway departs Naples every half hour from piazza Garibaldi. A round-trip fare is 2,700 lire ($1.75); trip time is 45 minutes each way.

By Bus At the railway station in Pompeii, bus connections take you to the entrance to the excavations. There's an entrance about 50 yards from the railway station at Villa Misteri.

Pompeii

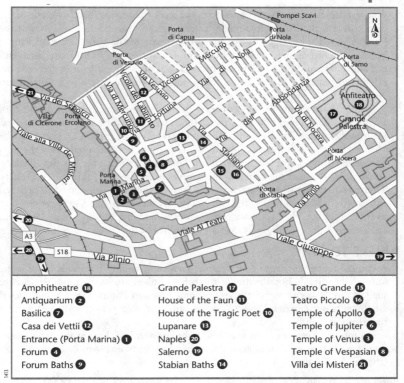

Amphitheatre ⑱	Grande Palestra ⑰	Teatro Grande ⑮
Antiquarium ❷	House of the Faun ⑪	Teatro Piccolo ⑯
Basilica ❼	House of the Tragic Poet ⑩	Temple of Apollo ❺
Casa dei Vettii ⑫	Lupanare ⑬	Temple of Jupiter ❻
Entrance (Porta Marina) ❶	Naples ⑳	Temple of Venus ❸
Forum ❹	Salerno ⑲	Temple of Vespasian ❽
Forum Baths ❾	Stabian Baths ⑭	Villa dei Misteri ㉑

By Car   To reach Pompeii from Naples, take the 13^1/2-mile drive on the autostrada to Salerno.

VISITOR INFORMATION   The **tourist information center** is at via Sacra 1 (☎ 081/850-7255), open Monday to Friday from 8:30am to 3:30pm and on Saturday from 8am to noon.

EXPLORING THE RUINS

The best preserved 2,000-year-old ruins in Europe, **Ufficio Scavi di Pompei,** piazza Esedra (☎ 081/861-1051), is most often visited on a day trip from Naples (allow at least 4 hours for even a superficial look at the archeological site). The most elegant of the patrician villas, the **House of Vettii** has a courtyard, statuary (such as a two-faced Janus), paintings, and a black-and-red Pompeiian dining room frescoed with cupids. The house was occupied by two brothers named Vettii, both of whom were wealthy merchants. As you enter the vestibule, you'll see a painting of Priapus resting his gargantuan phallus on a pair of scales. The guard will reveal other erotic fertility drawings and statuary, although most such material has been removed from Pompeii to the Archeological Museum in Naples. This house is the best example of a villa and garden to be restored, and is also known for its frescoes of delicate miniature cupids.

The second important villa, the **House of Mysteries** (Villa dei Misteri), near the Porto Ercolano, lies outside the walls (go out along viale alla Villa dei Misteri). What makes the villa exceptional, aside from its architectural features, are its remarkable frescoes, depicting scenes associated with the sect of Dionysus (Bacchus), one of the cults that was flourishing in Roman times. Note in some of the backgrounds the Pompeiian red. The largest house, called the **House of the Faun** (Casa del Fauno) because of a bronze statue of a dancing faun found there, takes up a city block and has four different dining rooms and two spacious peristyle gardens. It sheltered the celebrated Battle of Alexander the Great mosaic, which is now in a museum in Naples.

In the center of town is the **Forum**—although rather small, it was the heart of Pompeiian life, known to bakers, merchants, and the wealthy aristocrats who lived luxuriously in the villas. Parts of the Forum were severely damaged in an earthquake 16 years before the eruption of Vesuvius and had not been repaired when the final destruction came. Three buildings that surround the Forum are the **basilica** (the largest single structure in the city) and the temples of Apollo and Jupiter. The **Stabian Thermae** (baths)—where both men and women lounged and relaxed in between games of knucklebones—are in good condition, among the finest to come down to us from antiquity. Here you'll see some skeletons, and in a building called Lupanare, some erotic paintings (these frescoes are the source of the fattest tips to the guides).

WHERE TO STAY

Accommodations appear to be for earnest archeologists only. The Villa Laura is the only really suitable hotel in town; the other choices are barely passable and are suggested only as emergency stopovers. Some hotels in Pompeii are not considered safe because of robberies. Protect your valuables and your person and don't wander the streets at night.

Because the hotel situation here is so poor, most visitors look at the excavations, then seek better accommodations at either Naples (see above) or Sorrento (see Chapter 17) for the night.

Hotel del Santuario. Piazza Bartolo Longo 2–6, 80045 Pompei. ☎ **081/850-6165.** Fax 081/850-2822. 52 rms. TEL. 90,000 lire ($57.60) double. Rates include breakfast. AE, MC, V.

This hotel is in the very center of Pompeii, and opens onto the major square across from the major basilica. The hotel rents simply furnished bedrooms, very basic, and also offers a ristorante, pizzeria, gelateria, and tea room. The restaurant serves reasonably priced meals. You can enjoy such dishes as beefsteak pizzaiola or a mixed fry of shrimp and squid. There's limited parking.

Hotel Villa dei Misteri. Via Villa dei Misteri 11, 80045 Pompei-Scavi. ☎ **081/861-3593.** Fax 081/862-2983. 41 rms. 70,000 lire ($44.80) double. No credit cards. Free parking. From the Pompeii rail station, take the Sorrento train and get off at the Villa dei Misteri stop.

Located 250 yards from the Scavi Station, this 1930s hotel is suitable for motorists. About $1^1/_2$ miles south of the center of town, it features a swimming pool, a little garden, and a place to park your car. The family-style welcome may compensate for a certain lack of facilities and amenities. The place could stand a face-lift, but many readers have expressed their fondness for it. The only rooms are bare-bone doubles.

Villa Laura. Via della Salle 13, 80045 Pompei. ☎ **081/863-1024.** Fax 081/850-4893. 24 rms. A/C TV TEL. 120,000 lire ($76.80) double. AE, DC, MC, V.

The Villa Laura is the best hotel in town, which isn't saying a lot. Located on a somewhat hidden street, it escapes a lot of the street noise that plagues many Pompeii hotels. The hotel is mercifully air-conditioned, and the bedrooms are comfortably but not spectacularly furnished. Try for a room with a balcony. There's a breakfast room with a bar in the basement. The breakfasts are a bit dull, but for lunch and dinner you can escape to many trattorie nearby—or better yet, patronize one of the restaurants recommended below. The hotel also has a garden.

WHERE TO DINE

✪ **Il Prìncipe.** Piazza Bartolo Longo 8. ☎ **081/850-5566.** Reservations required. Main courses 20,000–30,000 lire ($12.80–$19.20); fixed-price menu 50,000 lire ($32). AE, DC, MC, V. Summer, daily 12:30–3pm and 7:30–11:30pm; off-season, Tues–Sun 12:30–3pm and 7:30–11:30pm. CAMPANIAN/MEDITERRANEAN.

The leading restaurant of Pompeii, Il Prìncipe is also acclaimed as one of the best restaurants in Campania. The decor incorporates the best decorative features of ancient Pompeii, including an intelligent scattering of brightly colored frescoes and mosaics. Guests can dine in its beautiful interior or select a sidewalk table at the corner of the most important square in Pompeii, with views of the basilica. For your first course, you might start with carpaccio or a salad of porcini (mushrooms); then follow with one of the pasta dishes, perhaps spaghetti vongole (with baby clams). You can also order superb fish dishes, such as sea bass and turbot, saltimbocca (sage-flavored veal with ham), or steak Diane.

Zi Caterina. Via Roma 20. ☎ **081/850-7447.** Reservations recommended. Main courses 10,000–22,000 lire ($6.40–$14.10). AE, DC, MC, V. Wed–Mon noon–11pm. Closed 2 weeks in July. SEAFOOD/NEAPOLITAN.

This good choice is conveniently located in the center of town near the basilica, with two spacious dining rooms. The antipasto table might tempt you with its seafood, but don't rule out the pasta e fagiole (pasta and beans) with mussels. The chef's special rigatoni, with tomatoes and prosciutto, is tempting, as is the array of fish or one of the live lobsters fresh from the tank.

17 The Amalfi Coast & Capri

When the English say "see Naples and die," they mean the city and the bay, with majestic Mt. Vesuvius in the background. When the Germans use the expression, they mean the Amalfi Drive. And, indeed, several motorists do die each year on the dangerous coastal road, too narrow to accommodate the heavy stream of summer traffic, especially the large tour buses that almost sideswipe each other as they try to pass. Moreover, in driving along the coast you sometimes find it difficult to concentrate on the road because of the view. The drive, remarked André Gide, "is so beautiful that nothing more beautiful can be seen on this earth."

Capri and Sorrento have long been known to international travelers. But the popularity of the resort-studded Amalfi Drive is a more recent phenomenon. It was discovered by German officers in World War II, then later by American and English servicemen (Positano was a British rest camp in the last months of the war). Later, when the war was over, many returned, often bringing their families. The little fishing villages in time became major tourism centers, with hotels and restaurants in all catagories. Sorrento and Amalfi are in the vanguard, with the widest range of facilities; Positano has more snob appeal and remains popular with artists; Ravello is still the choice of the discriminating few, such as Gore Vidal, who desire relative seclusion. To cap off an Amalfi Coast adventure, you can take a boat from Sorrento to Capri, which needs no advance billing. Three sightseeing attractions in this chapter—in addition to the towns and villages—are worthy of a special pilgrimage: The Emerald Grotto between Amalfi and Positano, the Blue Grotto of Capri, and the Greek temples of the ancient Sybarite-founded city of Paestum, south of Salerno.

EXPLORING THE AMALFI COAST BY CAR

Day 1   Begin your tour of the Amalfi Drive in Sorrento, 31 miles south of Naples. Subject of song and legend as the home of the Sirens, the town stands on a cliff overlooking the Bay of Naples. Its shopping is also the best along the coast so you can easily spend a day here (more if you have time).

☕ **TAKE A BREAK**   The **Taverna dell'800,** via dell'Accademia 29, in Sorrento (☎ **081/878-5970**), is a pub/restaurant operated by a friendly chap everybody calls "Tony." Mercifully air-conditioned, it offers such lunchtime fare as sausage with broccoli and pasta with Parmesan cheese, although you can order more substantial fare in the evening. It's also a good place to visit for a beer on a hot day.

Day 2   A narrow, curvy, and twisting highway stretches for 11 miles around the Amalfi peninsula to the enchanting little resort of Positano. Although the scenery is panoramic, this drive may be too scary for most. In that case you can reach Positano another way: From Sorrento head back toward Naples on Route S145. At Meta you can get on Route S163 which cuts across mountainous terrain until you're delivered to the Costa Amalfitana on the south side of the peninsula. Route S163 will continue its hellish way all the way to Salerno. Follow this treacherous drive until you come to Positano, which hopefully will be worth the effort of reaching it. This holiday town deserves an overnight, or a lot more time if your schedule permits. At least stop for lunch:

☕ TAKE A BREAK   At **O Caporale,** via del Saraceno 12 in Positano (☎ **089/ 875374**), you get a wide assortment of seafood and pasta dishes. A specialty is La Caporalesa, pasta whipped up with capers and eggplant. You eat under a vine-covered canopy opening onto the water. It's closed November to February.

Day 3   Figure on an hour to make the twisting 10-mile drive to Amalfi. Pause to take in the views from the villages of Vettica Maggiore and Praiano. The cliffside corniche takes you through the gorges of the Valley of the Furies (Vallone di Furore). Along the way, and only if time permits, visit the Emerald Grotto (Grotta di Smeraldo), the major attraction along the coast. Reach Amalfi for a late-afternoon stroll of exploration and dine in a trattoria along the water.

Day 4   In the morning drive up to Ravello, a distance of 4 miles, and spend the morning exploring this hilltop village where "poets go to die," taking in the panoramic vistas. In the afternoon you can return to the Amalfi Drive and continue along the coast toward Salerno where you can hook up with autostrada E45 going south. Take it until the turnoff onto Route SS18 leading directly south to Paestum, 25 miles south of Salerno. Here you can explore the ancient Sybarite city of Poseidonia, dating back to 600 B.C. These ruins, including a Doric temple (the basilica) and the Temple of Neptune, are among the most evocative in Italy.

1 Sorrento

31 miles S of Naples, 159 miles SE of Rome, 31 miles W of Salerno

Borrowing from Greek mythology, the Romans placed the legendary abode of the Sirens—those wicked mermaids who lured seamen to their deaths with their sweet songs—at Surrentum (Sorrento). Ulysses resisted their call by stuffing the ears of his crew with wax and having himself bound to the mast of his ship. Perched on high cliffs, overlooking the Bays of Naples and Salerno, Sorrento has been sending out its siren call for centuries—luring everybody from Homer to Lord and Lady Astor. It's the birthplace of Torquato Tasso, author of *Jerusalem Delivered.*

The streets in summer tend to be as noisy as a carnival. The hotels on the "racing strip," corso Italia, need to pass out earplug kits when they tuck you in for the night. Perhaps you'll have a hotel on a cliffside in Sorrento with a view of the "sea of the sirens." If you want to swim in that sea, you'll find both paths and private elevators that take guests down.

To enjoy the beauty of the Amalfi Drive, whose perils are noted above, don't drive it yourself. Take a blue SITA bus which runs between Sorrento and Salerno or Amalfi. In Sorrento, bus stations with timetables are outside the railway station and in the central piazza.

An interesting stop for shoppers is **A Gargiulo & Jannuzzi,** piazza Tasso (☎ **081/ 878-1041**), the best-known maker of marquetry furniture in the region. They demonstrate the centuries-old technique in the basement, where an employee will combine multihued pieces of wood veneer to create patterns of arabesques and flowers. The sprawling showrooms, right in the heart of town, feature an array of card tables, clocks, and partners' desks, each inlaid with patterns of elmwood, rosewood, bird's-eye maple, and mahogany. Upstairs is a collection of embroidered napery and table linen. The outlet also has its own ceramic factory, making mugs, plates, vases, cups, tile pictures, plant holders, soup or salad bowls, pizza plates, and wrought-iron tables with tile tops, among other offerings. The pottery can be packed and shipped anywhere in the world. It's open daily from 8am to 10pm.

ESSENTIALS

GETTING THERE **By Train** Sorrento is served by frequent express trains from Naples (trip time: 1 hour). The high-speed train, called Ferrovia Circumvesuviana, leaves from one floor underground at the Stazione Centrale. For information about schedules to Sorrento, call 081/779-2444 in Naples.

By Car From Naples, head south on Route 18, cutting west at the junction with Route 145.

VISITOR INFORMATION The **tourist information office** is at via de Maio 35 (☎ **081/807-4033**), which winds down to the port where ships to Capri and Naples anchor. It's open April to September, Monday to Saturday from 8:30am to 2pm and 4 to 7pm; October to March, Monday to Saturday 8:30am to 2pm and 3:45 to 6:15pm.

WHERE TO STAY

In its first- and second-class hostelries, Sorrento is superior to almost any resort in the south, and offers accommodations in all price ranges.

EXPENSIVE

Grand Hotel Ambasciatori. Via Califano 18, 80067 Sorrento. ☎ **081/878-2025.** Fax 081/ 807-1021. 103 rms, 6 suites. A/C TV TEL. 330,000 lire ($211.20) double; 435,000 lire ($278.40) suite. Rates include breakfast. AE, MC, V. Free parking. Bus: SITA.

The heavily buttressed foundation that prevents this cliffside hotel from plunging into the sea looks like something from a medieval monastery. Built in a style reminiscent of a private villa, it was landscaped to include several rambling gardens along the precipice. A set of steps and a private elevator lead to the wooden deck of a bathing wharf. Inside, a substantial collection of Oriental carpets, marble floors, and well-upholstered armchairs provide plush enclaves of comfort.

Dining/Entertainment: The main restaurant offers both regional and international specialties. There's a snack bar by the pool. Twice a week there's a live-music program of Neapolitan songs.

Services: Room service, baby-sitting, laundry, valet.

Facilities: A garage provides much-needed parking; heart-shaped swimming pool; elevator down the cliff to the beach and barbecue.

Bay of Naples & the Amalfi Coast

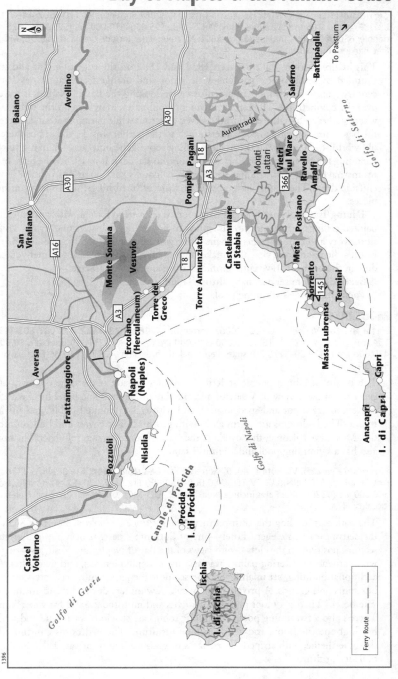

Ferry Route

Grand Hotel Excelsior Vittoria. Piazza Tasso 34, 80067 Sorrento. ☎ **081/807-4488.** Fax 081/877-1206. 106 rms, 12 suites. MINIBAR TV TEL. 395,000–510,000 lire ($252.80–$326.40) double; 650,000–1,080,000 lire ($416–$691.20) suite. Rates include breakfast. AE, DC, MC, V. Free parking. Bus: SITA.

This luxury bastion, built between 1834 and 1882 on the edge of a cliff and surrounded by semitropical gardens with lemon and orange trees, combines 19th-century glamour with modern amenities. Overlooking the Bay of Naples, it towers over the competition. The terrace theme predominates, especially on the water side where you can enjoy the cold drinks served at sunset while gazing at Vesuvius across the bay. Three elevators take bathers down to the harbor. Inside, the atmosphere is old worldish, especially in the mellow dining room. The hotel has 12 luxury suites, including the one named for Enrico Caruso, who stayed in it in 1921. The huge bedrooms have their own drama, some with balconies that open onto the perilous cliffside drop. The rooms have a wide mixture of furnishings, with many antique pieces.

Dining/Entertainment: The dining room is festive and formal, with ornate, hand-painted ceilings that depict clouds, sprays of flowers, and clusters of cherubs. You'll sit in ivory and cane provincial chairs while you enjoy a top-notch Sorrento cuisine. But it's the panoramic view that makes dining here memorable. In summer you can dine in the open air. Live entertainment is presented twice a week.

Services: Room service, baby-sitting, laundry, valet.

Facilities: Large swimming pool.

MODERATE

Hotel Bristol. Via del Capo 22, 80067 Sorrento. ☎ **081/878-4522.** Fax 081/807-1910. 134 rms, 5 suites. A/C TV TEL. 210,000–330,000 lire ($134.40–$211.20) double; 280,000–430,000 lire ($179.20–$275.20) suite. Rates include breakfast. AE, DC, MC, V. Free parking. Bus: SITA.

The Bristol was built pueblo style in 1958 on a hillside at the edge of town, and every room has a view of Vesuvius and the Bay of Naples. The hotel lures with its contemporary decor and spaciousness, and with well-appointed public and private rooms. The bedrooms are warm and inviting, with bright covers and built-in niceties. Most have balconies that overlook the sea, and some contain minibars. The hotel also has a swimming pool and a Finnish sauna.

Parco dei Principi. Via Rota 1, 80067 Sorrento. ☎ **081/878-4644.** Fax 081/878-3786. 93 rms, 3 suites. A/C MINIBAR TV TEL. 280,000–350,000 lire ($179.20–$224) double; from 500,000 lire ($320) suite. Rates include breakfast. AE, DC, MC, V. Closed Nov–Mar. Free parking. Bus: SITA.

The park surrounding the 18th-century villa of Prince Leopold of Bourbon Sicily is the setting for this elegent hotel—one of Sorrento's best. It occupies a desirable seafront position on the cliffs—with views of the Bay of Naples and Vesuvius—ringed with gardens of towering palms, acacias, olives, scented lemons, and magnolias. An additional building, set inland from the sea near the park's entrance, caters only to bus tours and groups. A private elevator takes swimmers down the cliff to the private beach. There's a mooring pier for yachts and motorboats, and for waterskiing. There's also a swimming pool. The public rooms are spacious, with blue-and-white herringbone tile floors and cerulean-blue furniture. The bedrooms continue the sky-blue theme, with striped floors, walls of glass leading to private balconies, and built-in furniture.

INEXPENSIVE

⑤ **Hotel Désirée.** Via del Capo 31 bis, 80067 Sorrento. ☎ and fax **081/878-1563.** 22 rms. TEL. 110,000–120,000 lire ($70.40–$76.80) double. No credit cards. Closed Nov–Mar. Free parking. Bus: SITA.

The Désirée is half a mile from the center of town at the beginning of the Amalfi Drive. This tranquil hotel, directed by the Gargiulo family, is ringed with terraces whose flowered masonry overlooks the Bay of Naples and nearby trees. This used to be an upper-class private home before it was transformed into the good-value hotel it is today. Many attractive personal touches remain in the decor. You'll recognize the hotel by its green glass lanterns in front and the welcoming awning stretched over the entrance. An elevator leads to the private beach.

⑤ **Hotel Regina.** Via Marina Grande 10, 80067 Sorrento. ☎ **081/878-2722.** Fax 081/878-2721. 36 rms. A/C TEL. 150,000 lire ($96) double. Rates include breakfast. AE, V. Closed Nov–Easter. Parking 8,000 lire ($5.10). Bus: SITA.

Evenly spaced rows of balconies jut out over the Regina's well-tended garden. On its uppermost floor, a glassed-in dining room and an outdoor terrace encompass views of the Mediterranean extending as far as Naples and Vesuvius. The clean, functional bedrooms have tile floors and private terraces.

Villa di Sorrento. Via Fuorimura 4, 80067 Sorrento. ☎ **081/878-1068.** Fax 081/807-2679. 20 rms. TEL. 180,000 lire ($115.20) double. Rates include breakfast. AE, DC, MC, V. Bus: SITA.

This is a pleasant villa right in the center of town. Architecturally romantic, it attracts travelers with its petite wrought-iron balconies, tall shutters, and vines climbing the facade. The rooms have such small niceties as bedside tables and lamps, and some accommodations have terraces. There's an elevator as well.

WHERE TO DINE

L'Antica Trattoria. Via P. R. Giuliani 33. ☎ **081/807-1082.** Reservations recommended. Main courses 13,000–28,000 lire ($8.30–$17.90); fixed-price menu 16,000–55,000 lire ($10.25–$35.20). No credit cards. Tues–Sun noon–12:30am. Closed Jan 10–Feb 10. CAMPANESE/INTERNATIONAL.

Set inside the weatherbeaten walls of what was built 300 years ago as a stable, this restaurant is warm, charming, polite, and one of the best recommended in Sorrento. Although all of its food is well prepared, and faithful to the tenets of the Italian repertoire, its real virtue lies in its antipasti. Each is homemade, and features fish and a daunting array of pastas from lasagne to ravioli, which in its best version is stuffed with seafood. A particularly delicious specialty of the house is seafood pezzogna, made with pulverized cherry tomatoes, olive oil, garlic, parsley, crushed red pepper, and shellfish. The assortment of ice creams is especially tempting, some of the best in town.

La Favorita–O'Parrucchiano. Corso Italia 71. ☎ **081/878-1321.** Reservations required. Main courses 12,000–18,000 lire ($7.70–$11.50). MC, V. Daily noon–4pm and 7pm–midnight. Closed Wed Oct 30–June. Bus: SITA. NEAPOLITAN.

This is a good choice on the busiest street in Sorrento. The building is like an old tavern, with an arched ceiling in the main dining room. On the terrace in the rear you can dine in a garden of trees, rubber plants, and statuary. Among the à la carte dishes, classic Italian fare is offered, including ravioli Caprese (filled with fresh cheese and covered with a tomato sauce), cannelloni, a mixed fish fry from the Bay of Naples, and a veal cutlet Milanese. The chef will also prepare a pizza for you.

2 Positano

35 miles SE of Naples, 10 miles E of Sorrento, 165 miles SE of Rome

A hillside, Moorish-style village on the southern strip of the Amalfi Drive, Positano opens onto the Tyrrhenian Sea with its legendary Sirenuse Islands, Homer's siren islands in the *Odyssey,* which form the mini-archipelago of Li Galli. Still privately owned, these islands were once purchased by Leonid Massine, the Russian-born choreographer. It's said that the town was "discovered" after World War II when Gen. Mark Clark stationed troops in nearby Salerno. It has jackrabbited along the classic postwar route of many a European resort: a sleeping fishing village that was visited by painters and writers (Paul Klee, Tennessee Williams), and then was taken over by bohemia-sampling visitors.

Once Positano was part of the powerful Republic of the Amalfis, a rival of Venice as a sea power in the 10th century. Today smart boutiques dot the village, and bikinis add vibrant colors to the mud-gray beach where you're likely to get pebbles in your sand castle. Prices have been rising sharply over the past few years. The 500-lire-a-night rooms popular with sunset-painting artists have gone the way of your baby teeth.

The topography of the village, you'll soon discover, is impossible. If you learn to climb the landscape with relative ease, you'll be qualified to hire out as a "scab" during the next donkey sit-down strike. John Steinbeck once wrote: "Positano bites deep. It is a dream place that isn't quite real when you are there and becomes beckoningly real after you have gone."

ESSENTIALS

GETTING THERE   By Bus   SITA buses leave from Sorrento frequently throughout the day, more often in summer than in winter, for the rather thrilling ride to Positano; a one-way fare is 2,000 lire ($1.30). For information, call SITA at 089/871-009.

By Car   Positano lies along the Amalfi Drive (Route 145, which becomes Route 163 at the approach to the resort).

VISITOR INFORMATION   The telephone area code is 089. The **tourist information center** is at via del Saracino 4 (☎ 089/875067), open Monday to Friday from 8:30am to 2pm and on Saturday from 8:30am to noon.

WHERE TO STAY

VERY EXPENSIVE

✪ **San Pietro.** Via Laurito 2, 84017 Positano. ☎ **089/875455.** Fax 089/811449. 43 rms, 16 suites. A/C MINIBAR TV TEL. 620,000–700,000 lire ($396.80–$448) double; 800,000–1,700,000 lire ($512–$1,088) suite. Rates include breakfast. AE, DC, MC, V. Closed Nov–Mar. Free parking. Bus: SITA.

A mile from Positano toward Amalfi, the San Pietro has only a miniature 15th-century chapel, which projects out on a high cliff, by which to be identified. A behind-the-scenes elevator takes you down to the cliff ledges of what is the chicest resort along the Amalfi Coast and one of the grandest resort hotels in Europe. By changing elevators at the reception lounge, you can descend even farther to the swimming and boating cove. The suitelike bedrooms are super-glamorous, and many have a picture window beside the bathtub (there's even a huge sunken Roman bath in one suite). Bougainvillea from the terraces reaches into the ceilings of many of the living rooms. A collection of antiques and reproductions fills the living room. The San Pietro neither advertises nor posts signs, and the privacy of guests is zealously guarded.

Some of the more distinguished have included Lord Laurence Olivier, Rudolf Nureyev, and Gregory Peck.

Dining/Entertainment: Guests gather at sunset in the piano bar. A dining room has been cut into the cliff and features picture windows the length of the room. A refined international cuisine is served.

Services: Room service, baby-sitting, laundry, valet.

Facilities: Swimming pool, private beach, tennis court.

Le Sirenuse. Via Colombo 30, 84017 Positano. ☎ **089/875066.** Fax 089/811798. 58 rms, 2 suites. A/C MINIBAR TV TEL. 400,000–640,000 lire ($256–$409.60) double; 650,000–1,900,000 lire ($416–$1,216) suite. Rates include breakfast. AE, DC, MC, V. Free parking. Bus: 3.

Good taste reigns supreme at Le Sirenuse, even if it isn't as grand as the San Pietro. Everything exists for its sophisticated clientele, which includes numerous artists and writers. The hotel, an old villa only a few minutes' walk up from the bay, is owned by the aristocratic Sersale family and was their private family residence until 1951. The marchesa personally selects all the furnishings, which include fine carved chests, 19th-century paintings and old prints, a spinet piano, upholstered pieces in bold colors, and a Victorian cabinet from an old jewelry shop. The bedrooms, all with private bath and many with Jacuzzi, are varied, and all have terraces that overlook the village. Your room may have an iron bed, high and ornate and painted red, as well as a carved chest and refectory tables.

Dining/Entertainment: Meals are well served on one of the three terraces, and the chef caters to the international palate with a regional cuisine.

Services: Room service, baby-sitting, laundry, valet.

Facilities: Swimming pool, sauna, gym.

EXPENSIVE

✪ **Hotel Poseidon.** Via Pasitea 148, 84017 Positano. ☎ **089/811111.** Fax 089/875833. 46 rms, 2 suites. A/C MINIBAR TV TEL. 280,000–380,000 lire ($179.20–$243.20) double; 450,000–550,000 lire ($288–$352) suite. Rates include breakfast. AE, DC, MC, V. Closed Nov 4–Mar 29. Parking 30,000 lire ($19.20). Bus: 3.

This hotel, among the very finest in Positano, was built in 1950 by the Aonzo family as their summer residence. In 1955 it was enlarged and transformed into a hotel. Today this first-class, four-star hotel is still owned and managed by the Aonzos, who provide one of the most hospitable welcomes at the resort. Centrally located, it's charming, discreet, and elegant, with tastefully selected antique furniture and objects. The bedrooms are traditionally furnished and beautifully maintained.

Dining/Entertainment: Along with its terraces and garden, the hotel offers both indoor and outdoor dining; its chefs feature both a regional and continental cuisine in La Terrazza del Poseidon, with its antique terra-cotta floors, walnut fixtures, and wrought-iron window frames. From May until the end of September meals are served on the panoramic terrace, covered with a portico of bougainvillea and ivy.

Services: Room service, baby-sitting, laundry, massages, facials.

Facilities: Freshwater swimming pool; health club (the first and only one in Positano), with a sauna, hydromassage spa, and gym with a professional trainer.

MODERATE

⑤ **Albergo L'Ancora.** Via Colombo 36, 84017 Positano. ☎ **089/875318.** Fax 089/811784. 18 rms. MINIBAR TV TEL. 190,000–230,000 lire ($121.60–$147.20) double. AE, DC, MC, V. Closed Nov–Apr 1. Free parking. Bus: SITA.

This is a stand-out choice, a hillside villa turned hotel with the atmosphere of a private club. It's fresh and sunny here—each room, 11 of them air-conditioned, is like a bird's nest on a cliff. Designed to accommodate the maximum of sun terraces and sheltered loggias for shade, the hotel is a 5-minute climb from the beach. Its main lounge has clusters of club chairs, tile floors, and teardrop chandeliers. But the bedrooms—which cater to couples only—are the stars, with their individualized treatments. Well-chosen antiques, such as fine inlaid desks, are intermixed with more contemporary pieces. The bathrooms are tiled and contain a bidet, and each room opens onto a private terrace. Only guests can dine on the informal outdoor terrace under a vine-covered sun shelter.

⑤ Albergo Miramare. Via Trara Genoino 31, 84017 Positano. ☎ **089/875002.** Fax 089/875219. 18 rms, 4 suites. A/C TEL. 210,000–325,000 lire ($134.40–$208) double; 265,000–370,000 lire ($169.60–$236.80) triple; 280,000 lire ($179.20) suite. Rates include breakfast. AE, MC, V. Closed Nov 15–Mar 15. Free parking. Bus: SITA.

This is one of the most charming accommodations in Positano, suited for those who like the personalized touch that only a small inn can provide. Located in the heart of town on a cliff, the hotel attracts a discriminating clientele who appreciate the terraces, both public and private, where one can sip Campari and soda and contemplate the sea. Guests stay in one of two tastefully furnished buildings in a setting of citrus trees and flamboyant bougainvillea. Your bed will most likely rest under a vaulted ceiling, and the white walls will be thick. Even the bathrooms are romantic. The conversation piece of the hotel is a glass bathtub on a flowery terrace. What might seem like questionable taste in Los Angeles—a pink porcelain clamshell serving as a wash basin—becomes charming at the Miramare, even when the water rushes from a sea-green ceramic fish with coral-pink gills. The 3-minute walk from the beach is via a series of stairs.

Albergo Ristorante Covo dei Saraceni. 84017 Positano. ☎ **089/875400.** Fax 089/875878. 58 rms. A/C MINIBAR TV TEL. 220,000–360,000 lire ($140.80–$230.40) double. Rates include buffet breakfast. Half board 50,000 lire ($32) per person extra. AE, DC, MC, V. Closed Nov–Mar. Parking 25,000–30,000 lire ($16–$19.20). Bus: SITA.

You'll find this rambling yellow-ochre building a few steps above the port. It's a desirable choice for those who want to be in the swim of the summer action. The side closest to the water culminates in a rounded tower of rough-hewn stone, inside of which is an appealing restaurant open to the breezes and a firsthand view of the crashing waves. The bedrooms are comfortably furnished.

Buca di Bacco. Via Rampa Teglia 8, 84017 Positano. ☎ **089/875699.** Fax 089/875731. 54 rms. A/C MINIBAR TV TEL. 230,000–280,000 lire ($147.20–$179.20) double. Rates include breakfast. AE, DC, MC, V. Closed Oct 31–Mar. Parking 30,000–35,000 lire ($19.20–$22.40). Bus: SITA.

This is one of the best moderately priced hotels at the resort, also housing one of the best restaurants in the area (see "Where to Dine," below). On the main beach of Positano, it often draws guests who patronize only its bar, one of the best-known rendezvous points along the Amalfi Drive. A large terrace opens onto the beach, and you can enjoy a Campari and soda while still in your bathing suit. The oldest and most expensive part, the Buca Residence, was an old seaside mansion constructed at the dawn of the 19th century. The rooms are well furnished, with many facilities, including balconies that face the sea.

INEXPENSIVE

Casa Albertina. Via Tavolozza 4, 84017 Positano. ☎ **089/875143.** Fax 089/811540. 20 rms. A/C MINIBAR TV TEL. 170,000–220,000 lire ($108.80–$140.80) double with breakfast; 300,000–320,000 lire ($192–$204.80) double with half board. Half board compulsory Apr–Oct. AE, DC, MC, V. Parking 20,000–35,000 lire ($12.80–$22.40). Bus: SITA.

This villa guesthouse, up a steep and winding road, offers a view of the coastline from its hillside perch. Each bedroom is a gem, color coordinated in either mauve or blue. The rooms are furnished with well-selected pieces, such as gilt mirrors, fruitwood end tables, and bronze bed lamps. Each accommodation has wide French doors that lead out to a private balcony, and a few have Jacuzzis. You can have breakfast on the terra-cotta–tile terrace. The hotel also has a good restaurant that specializes in fresh grilled fish. Laundry service and a baby-sitter are available on request, and the hotel has both a bar and a solarium.

✪ **Palazzo Murat.** Via dei Mulini 23, 84017 Positano. ☎ **089/875177.** Fax 089/811419. 28 rms. MINIBAR TV TEL. 225,000–295,000 lire ($144–$188.80) double. Rates include breakfast. AE, DC, MC, V. Closed Nov–Easter. Parking 30,000–40,000 lire ($19.20–$25.60). Bus: 3.

For nostalgic atmosphere and baroque style, this place has no equal in all of Positano. The jasmine and bougainvillea are so profuse in its garden that they spill over their enclosing wall onto the arbors of the narrow street outside. Once this was the sumptuous retreat of Napoléon I's brother-in-law, the king of Naples. Shell designs cap the villa windows, which look out over a cluster of orange trees and the wrought-iron tendrils of the gate that leads into the garden. To enlarge the property, a previous owner erected a comfortable annex in a style compatible with the original villa. Only breakfast is served. Nineteen rooms are air-conditioned.

WHERE TO DINE

Buca di Bacco. Via Rampa Teglia 8. ☎ **089/875699.** Reservations required. Main courses 18,000–40,000 lire ($11.50–$25.60). AE, DC, MC, V. Daily 12:30–3:30pm and 8–11pm. Closed Oct 31–Mar. Bus: SITA. CAMPANIA/ITALIAN.

Right on the beach you'll find one of Positano's top restaurants. Guests often stop for a before-dinner drink in the bar downstairs and then head for the dining room on a big covered terrace that faces the sea. The tone of the *buca* is apparent as you enter. On display are various fresh fish, special salads, and fruit, including luscious black figs and freshly peeled oranges soaked in caramel. An exciting opener is a salad made with fruits of the sea, or you may prefer the zuppa di cozze (mussels), prepared with flair in a tangy sauce. The pasta dishes are homemade, and the meats are well prepared with fresh ingredients.

Chez Black. Via del Brigantino. ☎ **089/875036.** Reservations required in summer. Main courses 15,000–30,000 lire ($9.60–$19.20). AE, DC, MC, V. Apr–Oct, daily 12:30–3pm and 7:30–11pm; Nov–Mar, daily 12:30–3pm. Closed Jan 8–Feb 8. Bus: 3. SEAFOOD.

The owner is Salvatore Russo, but for his restaurant he uses the suntan-inspired name that his friends gave him in college. Founded after World War II, the restaurant occupies a desirable position near the beach. In summer it's in the "eye of the hurricane" of action. Its varnished ribbing, glowing sheath of softwood and brass, and yacht-inspired semaphore symbols make it one of the most beautiful restaurants in town. A stone-edged aquarium holds fresh lobsters, and rack upon rack of local wines give diners a choice. Seafood is the specialty, as well as a wide selection of pizzas fresh from a circular oven. The best-known dish is the spaghetti with crayfish, but you might also be tempted by linguine with fresh pesto, grilled swordfish, sole, or shrimp, along with an array of veal, liver, chicken, and beef dishes.

3 Amalfi

38 miles SE of Naples, 21 miles W of Salerno, 169 miles SE of Rome

From the 9th to the 11th century the seafaring Republic of Amalfi rivaled those great maritime powers, Genoa and Venice. Its maritime code, the Tavole Amalfitane, was used in the Mediterranean for centuries. But raids by Saracens and a flood in the 14th century devastated the city. Its power and influence weakened, until it rose again in modern times as the major resort on the Amalfi Drive.

From its position at the slope of the steep Lattari hills, it overlooks the Bay of Salerno. The approach to Amalfi is very dramatic, whether you come from Positano or from Salerno. Today Amalfi depends on tourist traffic, and the hotels and pensioni in dead center are right in the milling throng of holiday makers. The finest and most highly rated accommodations are on the outskirts.

ESSENTIALS

GETTING THERE   By Bus   SITA buses run every 2 hours during the day from Sorrento, for a one-way fare of 3,400 lire ($2.20). There are also SITA bus connections from Positano, a one-way ticket costing 2,000 lire ($1.30). Information about schedules is available in Amalfi by calling the **bus terminal** at the waterfront on piazza Flavio Gioia (☎ **089/871009**).

VISITOR INFORMATION   The **tourist information center** is at corso delle Repubbliche Marinare 19–21 (☎ **089/871107**), open Monday to Saturday from 8am to 1:30pm.

EXPLORING THE CATHEDRAL & THE EMERALD GROTTO

The **Duomo,** piazza del Duomo—named in honor of St. Andrew (Sant'Andrea), whose remains are said to be buried inside the crypt—evokes Amalfi's rich past. Reached by climbing steep steps, the cathedral is characterized by its black-and-white facade and its mosaics. Inside, the one nave and two aisles are all richly baroqued. The cathedral dates back to the 11th century, although the present structure has been rebuilt. Its bronze doors were made in Constantinople and its campanile (bell tower) is from the 13th century, erected partially in the Romanesque style. The Duomo is open daily from 7am to 1:30pm and 3 to 8pm.

You can also visit the **"Cloister of Paradise" (Chiostro Paradiso),** to the left of the Duomo, originally a necropolis for members of the Amalfitan "establishment." This graveyard dates from the 1200s and contains the broken columns and statues, as well as sarcophagi, of a long-gone civilization. The cloister is open daily from 8am to 1pm and 3:30 to 7pm and charges 3,000 lire ($1.90) for admission.

For your most scenic walk in Amalfi, start at piazza del Duomo and head up via Genova. The classic stroll will take you to the **Valle dei Mulini** (the Valley of the Mills), so called because of the paper mills along its rocky reaches (the seafaring republic is said to have acquainted Italy with the use of paper). You'll pass by fragrant gardens and scented citrus groves.

And for the biggest attraction of all, head west to the ✪ **Emerald Grotto (Grotta di Smeraldo).** This ancient cavern, known for its light effects, is a millennia-old chamber of stalagmites and stalactites. Three miles west of Amalfi, the grotto is reached from the coastal road via a descent by elevator, which costs 5,000 lire ($3.20), including the boat ride. Then you board a boat that traverses the eerie world of the grotto. The stalagmites are unique in that some are underwater. You can visit daily: from 9am to 5pm in March and April, from 8:30am to 6pm May to September, and from 10am to 4pm October to February. Take the SITA bus in Amalfi going toward Sorrento.

WHERE TO STAY

EXPENSIVE

Hotel Luna Convento. Via Pantaleone Comite 33, 84011 Amalfi. ☎ **089/871002.** Fax 089/871333. 45 rms. TV TEL. 210,000 lire ($134.40) double including breakfast; half board (compulsory in summer) 190,000 lire ($121.60) per person. AE, DC, MC, V. Parking 20,000 lire ($12.80). Bus: SITA.

This hotel—the best in Amalfi except for the Santa Caterina—boasts a 13th-century cloister said to have been founded by St. Francis of Assisi. Most of the building you see today was constructed in 1975. The long corridors, where monks of old used to tread, are lined with sitting areas used by the most unmonastic guests seeking a tan. The bedrooms have sea views, terraces, and modern furnishings.

Dining/Entertainment: The rather formal dining room has a coved ceiling, high-backed chairs, arched windows that open toward the water, and good food (Italian and international) efficiently served. The hotel also has a nightclub that projects toward the sea. In summer dancing is offered in the piano bar.

Services: Room service, baby-sitting, laundry, valet.

Facilities: A free-form swimming pool is nestled on the rocks, near the sound of the surf and sea gulls.

✪ **Santa Caterina.** Strada Amalfitana, 84011 Amalfi. ☎ **089/871012.** Fax 089/871351. 70 rms, 11 suites. A/C MINIBAR TV TEL. 430,000–520,000 lire ($275.20–$332.80) double; from 700,000 lire ($448) suite. Rates include breakfast. Half board 75,000 lire ($48) per person extra. AE, DC, MC, V. Parking 25,000 lire ($16) in the garage, free outside. Bus: SITA.

Perched on top of a cliff, the six-story Santa Caterina has an elevator that will take you down to a private beach. This "saint" is one of the most scenic accommodations around, dating from 1902. You're housed in the main structure or in one of the small "villas" in the citrus groves along the slopes of the hill. The rooms are furnished in good taste, with an eye toward comfort. Most have private balconies that face the sea. The furniture respects the tradition of the house, and in every room there's an antique piece. The bathrooms are spacious, with luxurious fittings, and each has a hair dryer.

Dining/Entertainment: The food here is among the best at the resort, so the boarding arrangement is no hardship. Many of the vegetables are grown in the hotel's own garden, and the fish tastes so fresh that we suspect the chef has an agreement with local fishers to bring in the "catch of the day" earmarked for the pampered guests of the Santa Caterina. Also, once or twice a week there's a special evening buffet accompanied by music.

Services: Room service, baby-sitting, laundry, valet.

Facilities: Saltwater pool.

MODERATE

Excelsior Grand Hotel. Via Pogerola, 84011 Amalfi. ☎ **089/830015.** Fax 089/830255. 97 rms. TEL. 125,000–175,000 lire ($80–$112) per person. Rates include full board. AE, DC, MC, V. Free parking. Bus: SITA.

Two miles north of Amalfi at Pogerola, the Excelsior is a modern first-class hotel on a high mountain perch. All its rooms are angled toward the view so you get the first glimmer of sunrise and the last rays of sunlight. The social center is the terrazzo-edged swimming pool filled with filtered mountain spring water. The hotel structure is unconventional—a high octagonal glass tower that rises above the central lobby, with exposed mezzanine lounges and an open staircase. The bedrooms are individually designed, with plenty of room, and the many good reproductions, some antiques, king-size beds, and tile floors all contrast with the white walls. The private balconies, complete with garden furniture, are the most important feature. The dignified dining room serves Italian cuisine with Gallic overtones. At the Bar del Night, musicians play for dancing on weekends. Transportation to and from the private beach is provided by boat and bus for 15,000 lire ($9.60).

INEXPENSIVE

Hotel Belvedere. Via Smeraldo, Conca dei Marini, 84011 Amalfi. ☎ **089/831282.** Fax 089/831439. 36 rms. TEL. 150,000–200,000 lire ($96–$128) double. AE, DC, MC, V. Closed Oct 15–Easter. Free parking. Bus: SITA.

Lodged below the coastal road outside Amalfi on the drive to Positano, the aptly named Belvedere has one of the best pools in the area. It's in a prime location, hidden from the view and noise of the heavily traveled road, and thrust out toward the sea. The rooms have terraces that overlook the water. Signor Lucibello, who owns the hotel, sees to it that guests are content, and provides, among other things, parking space for your car (a bus takes you into Amalfi). You can dine on well-prepared Italian meals either inside (where walls of windows allow for views of the coast) or on the front terrace. There's also a cocktail bar.

⑤ Hotel Lidomare. Largo Piccolomini 9, 84011 Amalfi. ☎ **089/871394.** Fax 089/871394. 13 rms. TV TEL. 80,000 lire ($51.20) double. AE, DC, MC, V. Parking 15,000 lire ($9.60). Bus: SITA.

This pleasant, small hotel is just a few steps from the sea, and its building dates from the 13th century. The high-ceilinged bedrooms are airy and clean, and contain a scattering of modern furniture mixed with Victorian-era antiques. The Camera family extends a warm welcome to their never-ending stream of foreign visitors. They offer 12 double bedrooms (and one single), 7 of which have air-conditioning. Breakfast is the only meal served, but you can order it until 11:30am. This hotel is one of the best bargains in Amalfi.

Hotel MirAmalfi. Via Quasimodo 3, 84011 Amalfi. ☎ **089/871287.** Fax 089/871588. 43 rms, 3 suites. MINIBAR TV TEL. 170,000–210,000 lire ($108.80–$134.40) double; 270,000–310,000 lire ($172.80–$198.40) suite. Rates include breakfast. Half board 120,000–160,000 lire ($76.80–$102.40) per person extra. Air-conditioning 10,000 lire ($6.40) extra per room. AE, DC, MC, V. Free parking. Bus: SITA.

On the western edge of Amalfi, the MirAmalfi lies below the coastal road and beneath a rocky ledge on its own beach. The rooms are wrapped around the curving contour of the coastline and have unobstructed views of the sea. The stone swimming pier—used for sunbathing, diving, and boarding motor launches for waterskiing—is down a winding cliffside path, past terraces of grapevines. The dining room has glass windows and some semitropical plants; the food is good and served in abundant portions. Breakfast is served on one of the main terraces or on your own balcony. Each bedroom is well equipped, with built-in headboards, fine beds, cool tile floors, and efficient maintenance. There's a swimming pool and an elevator to the beach.

Marina Riviera. Via Comite 9, 84011 Amalfi. ☎ **089/871024.** Fax 089/871024. 35 rms. A/C MINIBAR TV TEL. 100,000–130,000 lire ($64–$83.20) double. Rates include breakfast. AE, DC, MC, V. Closed Oct 31–Mar. Parking 10,000 lire ($6.40). Bus: SITA.

Just 50 yards from the beach, this hotel offers rooms with terraces that overlook the sea. Directly on the coastal road, it rises against the foot of the hills, with side verandas and balconies. Two adjoining public lounges are traditionally furnished, and a small bar provides drinks whenever you want them. The newly refurbished rooms are comfortable, with a balcony and such amenities as a hair dryer. There's a gracious dining room with high-backed provincial chairs, but we suggest that you dine alfresco. A restaurant called Eolo opened in the spring of 1995 right below the hotel and is under the same management.

WHERE TO DINE

La Caravella-Amalfi. Via Matteo Camera 12. ☎ **089/871029.** Reservations required. Main courses 16,000–38,000 lire ($10.25–$24.30). AE, V. Daily 12:30–2:30pm and 7:30–11pm. Closed Nov and Tues Sept 15–June 15. Bus: SITA. CAMPANIA.

La Caravella is a leading restaurant and, happily, it's inexpensive. A grottolike, air-conditioned place, it's off the main street next to the road tunnel, only a minute from the beach. You get well-cooked, authentic Italian specialties, such as spaghetti Caravella with a seafood sauce, or fresh fish with lemon. Scaloppine alla Caravella is served with a tangy clam sauce, and a healthy portion of zuppa di pesce (fish soup) is also ladled out. You can have a platter of the mixed fish fry, with crisp, tasty bits of shrimp and squid, followed by an order of fresh fruit served at your table in big bowls.

Da G/emma. Via Frà Gerardo Sassi 9. ☎ **089/871345.** Reservations required. Main courses 20,000–32,000 lire ($12.80–$20.50). AE, DC, MC, V. Daily 1–3pm and 8pm–midnight. Closed Jan and Wed Sept–June. Bus: SITA. SEAFOOD/MEDITERRANEAN.

One of the best restaurants in town, Da Gemma takes inspired liberties with the regional cuisine and gives diners a strong sense of the family unity that makes this place popular. The kitchen sends out plateful after plateful of savory spaghetti, sautéed mixed shellfish, fish casserole, and a full range of other "sea creature" dishes. In summer the intimate dining room more than doubles with the addition of an outdoor terrace.

4 Ravello

171 miles SE of Rome, 41 miles SE of Naples, 18 miles W of Salerno

Known to long-ago personages ranging from Richard Wagner to Greta Garbo—even D. H. Lawrence, who wrote *Lady Chatterley's Lover* here—Ravello is the choice spot along the Amalfi Drive. Its reigning celebrity at the moment is Gore Vidal, who purchased a villa as a writing retreat. The village seems to hang 1,100 feet up, between the Tyrrhenian Sea and some celestial orbit. You approach this sleepy (except for summer tour buses) village from Amalfi, 4 miles to the southwest, by a wickedly curving road that cuts through the villa- and vine-draped hills that hem in the Valley of the Dragone. Celebrated in poetry, song, and literature are Ravello's major attractions, two villas.

ESSENTIALS

GETTING THERE   By Bus   Buses from Amalfi leave for Ravello from the terminal at the waterfront at piazza Flavio Gioia (☎ **089/871009** for schedules and information) every hour from 7am to 10pm. The one-way fare to Ravello is 1,500 lire (95¢).

By Car   From Amalfi, take a circuitous mountain road north of the town (the road is signposted to Ravello).

VISITOR INFORMATION   The **tourist information center** is at piazza del Duomo 10 (☎ **089/857096**). It's open May to September, Monday to Saturday from 8am to 8pm; October to April, Monday to Saturday from 8am to 7pm.

TWO FABULOUS VILLAS

Villa Cimbrone. Via Santa Chiara 26. ☎ **089/857459.** Admission 5,000 lire ($3.20) adults, 3,000 lire ($1.90) children. Daily 9am–sunset.

A long walk past grape arbors and private villas takes you to the Villa Cimbrone. After ringing the bell for admission, you'll be shown into the vaulted cloisters (on the left as you enter); note the grotesque bas-relief. Later you can stroll (everybody "strolls" in Ravello) through the gardens, past a bronze copy of Donatello's *David*. Along the rose-arbored walkway is a tiny, but roofless, chapel. At the far end of the garden is a cliffside view of the Bay of Salerno, a scene that the devout might claim was the spot where Satan took Christ to tempt him with the world.

Villa Rufolo. Piazza Vescovado. ☎ **089/857866.** Admission 4,000 lire ($2.55) adults, 2,000 lire ($1.30) children. Apr–Oct, daily 9am–1pm and 2:30–6:30pm; Nov–Mar, daily 9am–1pm and 2–5pm. Bus: SITA.

The Villa Rufolo was named for the patrician family who founded it in the 11th century. Once the residence of kings and popes, such as Hadrian IV, it's now remembered chiefly for its connection with Richard Wagner. He composed an act of *Parsifal* here in a setting he dubbed the "Garden of Klingsor." Boccaccio was so moved by the spot that he included it as background in one of his tales. The Moorish-influenced architecture evokes the Alhambra at Granada. The large tower was built in what is known as the "Norman-Sicilian" style. You can walk through the flower gardens that lead to lookout points over the memorable coastline.

WHERE TO STAY

The choice of accommodations at Ravello is limited in number, but large on charm.

VERY EXPENSIVE

✪ **Hotel Palumbo/Palumbo Residence.** Via San Giovanni del Toro 28, 84010 Ravello. ☎ **089/857244.** Fax 089/858133. 27 rms, 3 suites. A/C MINIBAR TV TEL. Hotel, 380,000–580,000 lire ($243.20–$371.20) double; 630,000–830,000 lire ($403.20–$531.20) suite. Residence, 240,000–290,000 lire ($153.60–$185.60) double. Rates include breakfast. AE, DC, MC, V. Parking 25,000 lire ($16). Bus: SITA.

This elite retreat on the Amalfi Coast, a 12th-century palace, has been favored by the famous ever since Richard Wagner (who did a lot of composing here) persuaded the Swiss owners, the Vuilleumier family, to take in paying guests. If you stay here you'll understand why Max Reinhardt, Humphrey Bogart, Henry Wadsworth Longfellow, Ingrid Bergman, Zsa Zsa Gabor, Tennessee Williams, Richard Chamberlain, and a young John and Jacqueline Kennedy found its situation in the village ideal. D. H. Lawrence even wrote part of *Lady Chatterley's Lover* while staying here.

The hotel offers gracious living in its series of drawing rooms, furnished with English and Italian antiques. Most of the snug but elegantly decorated bedrooms have a tile bath and their own terrace. Although the original Hotel Palumbo contains by far the more glamorous and better-accessorized accommodations, about seven of the hotel's rooms are in a modern annex in the garden. Built in the 1950s, and modernized in the 1970s, the annex rooms contain TV, telephone, minibar, and functional furniture; a few offer views of the sea.

Dining/Entertainment: Meals are served in a 17th-century dining room with baroque accents and a dining terrace opening to the panoramic outdoors. "Fill-in" bookings are accepted. The cuisine, the finest in Ravello, shows the influence of the Swiss-Italian ownership. It would be worth it to come here just to enjoy the hotel's lemon and chocolate soufflés. The Palumbo also produces its own Episcopio wine, served on the premises. The wine originated in 1860 and is stored in 50,000-liter casks in a vaulted cellar.

Services: Room service, baby-sitting, laundry, valet.

Facilities: Solarium overlooking the Gulf of Salerno.

EXPENSIVE

Hotel Caruso Belvedere. Via San Giovanni del Toro, 84010 Ravello. ☎ **089/857111.** Fax 089/857372. 24 rms. TEL. 170,000–220,000 lire ($108.80–$140.80) double. AE, DC, MC, V. Parking 10,000 lire ($6.40) in the garage, free outside. Bus: SITA.

This spacious clifftop hotel, built into the remains of an 11th-century palace, is operated by the Caruso family, descended from the great Enrico himself. Some of the most famous people of the 20th century, including Greta Garbo, have stayed here—but we ask why here and not at the far superior Palumbo? Much of this property is undistinguished. It does have semitropical gardens and a belvedere that overlooks the Bay of Salerno. From here, you can look down the terraced mountain slopes and see the rows of grapes used to make the "Grand Caruso" wine on the premises. Although antiques appear here and there, many bedrooms are rather plain, about on the same level as some of the town's economy-minded inns. The best rooms have sunrooms for breakfast and open onto "oh, that view" terraces.

Dining/Entertainment: The indoor dining room has the original coved ceiling, plus tile floors. It opens onto a wide terrace where meals are also served under a canopy. Naturally, the locally produced wines are touted.

Services: Room service, baby-sitting, laundry, valet.

MODERATE

Hotel Giordano e Villa Maria. Piazza del Duomo, via S. Chiara 2, 84010 Ravello. ☎ **089/857255.** Fax 089/857071. 46 rms, 2 suites. A/C TV TEL. 210,000–240,000 lire ($134.40–$153.60) double; 320,000–460,000 lire ($204.80–$294.40) suite. Rates include breakfast. AE, DC, MC, V. Ample free parking. Bus: SITA.

The older, but more obviously modernized, of these two hotels is the Giordano, built in the late 1700s as a private manor house of the family who continues to run it today. In the 1970s the owners bought the neighboring 19th-century Villa Maria. The two operate as quasi-independent hotels whose facilities are open to residents of either establishment. Accommodations in the Villa Maria are more glamorous than those in the Hotel Giordano, and usually contain high ceilings, a scattering of antiques, and sea views. The rooms in the Hotel Giordano have garden views and conservative reproductions of traditional furniture. You'll find a large heated pool near the Giordano, at least two bars, and a pair of restaurants. (Unlike its twin, the restaurant in the Villa Maria remains open throughout the winter and has a panoramic view of the sea.) The beach is a 15-minute walk along ancient pathways (you can also take a public bus from Ravello's central square every hour).

⑤ Hotel Parsifal. Via G. D'Anna 5, 84010 Ravello. ☎ **089/857144.** Fax 089/857972. 19 rms. TV TEL. 115,000 lire ($73.60) per person double. Rates include half board. AE, DC, MC, V. Closed Oct 15–Easter. Free parking on the street. Bus: SITA.

This little hotel incorporates portions of a convent founded in 1288 by Augustinian monks, who had an uncanny instinct for picking spots with inspiring views in which to build their retreats. The cloister, with stone arches and a tile walk, has a multitude of potted flowers and vines, and the garden spots, especially the one with a circular reflection pool, are the favorites of all. There are chairs placed for watching the setting sun that illuminates the twisting shoreline in firey lights. Dining is on the trellis-covered terrace where bougainvillea and wisteria scents mix with that of lemon blossoms. The living rooms have bright and comfortable furnishings, set against pure white walls. The bedrooms, although small, are tastefully arranged, and a few have terraces.

Hotel Rufolo. Via San Francesco 3, 84010 Ravello. ☎ **089/857133.** Fax 089/857935. 30 rms, 2 suites. MINIBAR TV TEL. 220,000–280,000 lire ($140.80–$179.20) double; 340,000–390,000 lire ($217.60–$249.60) suite. Rates include breakfast. AE, DC, MC, V. Free parking. Bus: SITA.

This little gem, run by the hospitable Schiavo family, housed D. H. Lawrence for a long while in 1926. The view from the sun decks is superb, and chairs are placed on a wide terrace and around the pool. The bedrooms are cozy and immaculate, some with air-conditioning. Recently enlarged and modernized, the hotel lies in the center between cloisters of pine trees of the Villa Rufolo, from which the hotel takes its name, and the road that leads to the Villa Cimbrone. Mr. Schiavo and his family take good care of their guests. The restaurant is quite good, and the service is efficient.

INEXPENSIVE

Ⓢ **Albergo Toro.** Viale Wagner 3, 84010 Ravello. ☎ **089/857211.** Fax 089/857211. 9 rms. TEL. 85,000–190,000 lire ($54.40–121.60) double. Rates include half-board. AE, DC, MC, V. Closed Nov 6–Mar. Bus: SITA.

This place is a real bargain. It's a small, charming villa that has been converted to receive paying guests. The Toro—entered through a garden—lies just off the village square with its catheral. It has semimonastic architecture, with deeply set arches, long colonnades, and a tranquil character. The rooms are decent, and the owner is especially proud of the meals he serves.

WHERE TO DINE

Most guests take meals at their hotels. But try to escape the board requirement at least once to sample the goods at the following establishments.

Ⓢ **Cumpa' Cosimo.** Via Roma. ☎ **089/857156.** Reservations recommended. Main courses 10,000–35,000 lire ($6.40–$22.40); fixed-price menu 18,000–22,000 lire ($11.50–$14.10). AE, DC, V. Daily 12:30–3pm and 7:30–10pm. Closed Mon Nov–Mar. Bus: SITA. CAMPANIA.

You're likely to find here everyone from the electrician down the street to a well-known movie star searching for the best home-cooking in town. It was established as an offshoot to a nearby butcher shop in 1929 by a town patriarch known affectionately as Cumpa' (godfather) Cosima and his wife, Cumma' (godmother) Chiara. Today their daughter, the kindly Netta Bottone, runs the place, turning out well-flavored regional food in generous portions. Menu items include homemade versions of seven different pastas, served with your choice of seven different sauces. Any of these might be followed by a mixed grill of fish, giant prawns, or roasted lamb well seasoned with herbs. The seasonal availability of vegetables is respected, as the restaurant offers artichokes, asparagus, or mushrooms. Certain fish dishes are priced according to weight based on daily market quotations.

Ristorante Garden. Via Boccacio 4. ☎ **089/857226.** Main courses 13,000–22,000 lire ($8.30–$14.10). AE, DC, MC, V. Apr–Sept, daily noon–2:30pm and 7:30–10pm; Nov–Mar, Wed–Mon noon–2:30pm and 7:30–10pm. Bus: SITA. CAMPANIA.

This pleasant restaurant's greatest claim to fame occurred in 1962 when Jacqueline Onassis, then the wife of President Kennedy, came from a villa where she was staying to dine here with the owner of Fiat. Today some of that old glamour is still visible on the verdant terrace, which was designed to cantilever over the cliff below. The Mansi family offers well-prepared meals, which might include one of four kinds of spaghetti, cheese crêpes, and an array of soups, a well-presented antipasto table, brochettes of grilled shrimp, a mixed fish fry, and sole prepared in several ways. One of the local wines will be recommended.

From April to September they also rent 10 well-scrubbed double rooms, each with its own bath and terrace, for 95,000 lire ($60.80), including breakfast.

5 Paestum

25 miles S of Salerno, 62 miles SE of Naples, 189 miles SE of Rome

The ancient Sybarite city of Paestum (Poseidonia) dates back to 600 B.C. It was abandoned for centuries and fell to ruins. But the remnants of its past, excavated in the mid-18th century, are glorious—the finest heritage left from the Greek colonies that settled in Italy. The roses of Paestum, praised by the ancients, bloom two times yearly, splashing the landscape of the city with a scarlet red, a good foil for the salmon-colored temples that still stand in the archeological garden.

ESSENTIALS

GETTING THERE   By Train   Paestum is within easy reach of Salerno, an hour away. Both buses and trains service the route. You can catch a southbound train, which departs Salerno with a stop at Paestum about every 2 hours. For schedules, call 089/252-200 in Salerno. A one-way fare is 4,200 lire ($2.70).

By Bus   The bus from Salerno leaves from piazza Concordia (near the rail station) about every 30 minutes. Call 089/487111 for information. A one-way fare is 4,200 lire ($2.70).

By Car   From Salerno, take Route 18 south.

VISITOR INFORMATION   The **tourist information center** is at via Magna Grecia 151–156 (☎ **0828/811016**), in the archeological zone. It's open Monday to Saturday from 8am to 2pm.

EXPLORING THE TEMPLES

The ✪ **basilica** is a Doric temple that dates from the 6th century B.C., the oldest temple from the ruins of the Hellenic world in Italy. The basilica is characterized by 9 columns in front and 18 on the sides. The Doric pillars are approximately five feet in diameter. The walls and ceiling, however, long ago gave way to decay. Animals were sacrificed to the gods on the altar.

The **Temple of Neptune** is the most impressive of the Greek ruins at Paestum. It and the Temple of Haphaistos ("Theseum") in Athens remain the best-preserved Greek temples in the world, both dating from around 450 to 420 B.C. Six columns in front are crowned by an entablature, and there are 14 columns on each side. The **Temple of Caeres,** from the 6th century B.C., has 34 columns still standing and a large altar for sacrifices to the gods.

The temple zone may be visited daily from 9am to sunset for 8,000 lire ($5.10). Using the same ticket, you can visit the **Museo Archeologico Nazionale di Paestum,** via Magna Grecia 169 (☎ **0828/811023**), across the road from the Caeres Temple. It displays the metopes removed from the treasury of the Temple of Hera (Juno) and some of southern Italy's finest tomb paintings from the 4th century B.C. *The Diver's Tomb* is an extraordinary example of painting from the first half of the 5th century B.C. The museum is open from 9am to 7pm daily (closed the first and third Monday of every month).

New discoveries have revealed hundreds of Greek tombs, which have yielded many Greek paintings. Archeologists have called the finds astonishing. In addition, other excavated tombs were found to contain clay figures in a strongly impressionistic vein.

WHERE TO STAY

Strand Hotel Schuhmann. Via Laura Mare, 84063 Paestum. ☎ **0828/851151.** Fax 0828/851183. 36 rms. A/C MINIBAR TV TEL. 170,000–190,000 lire ($108.80–$121.60) double. Rates include half board. AE, DC, MC, V. Free parking. Bus: Paestum bus from Salerno.

If you'd like to combine serious looks at Italy's archeological past with the first-class amenities of a beachside resort, try the Strand Hotel Schuhmann, a delightful choice for a holiday. Set in a pine grove removed from traffic noises, the hotel has a large terrace with a view of the sea and a subtropical garden that overlooks the Gulf of Salerno and the Amalfi Coast to Capri. Its bedrooms are well furnished and maintained, and each has a balcony or terrace. Guests get use of the beach facilities and deck chairs. The hotel also has a restaurant.

WHERE TO DINE

Nettuno Ristorante. Zona Archeologica. ☎ **0828/811028.** Main courses 15,000–25,000 lire ($9.60–$16). AE, DC, MC, V. July–Aug, daily 7:30–10pm; May–June and Sept–Oct, daily 12:30–3pm; Nov–Feb, Tues–Sat 12:30–3pm. Bus: Paestum bus from Salerno. CAMPANESE.

If you're looking for lunch, try this special place standing in a meadow just at the edge of the ruins, like a country inn or villa. The interior dining room has vines growing over its arched windows, and from the tables there's a good view of the ruins. The ceilings are beamed, the room divided by three Roman stone arches. Outside is a dining terrace that faces the temples—like a stage for a Greek drama. Under pine trees, hedged in by pink oleander, you can order such a typical selection as beefsteak or roast chicken, a vegetable or salad, plus dessert. Menu suggestions include spaghetti with filets in tomato sauce, veal cutlet, and crème caramel.

6 Capri

3 miles off the tip of the Sorrentine peninsula

The broiling dog-day July and August sun that beats down on Capri illuminates a circus of humanity. The parade of visitors would give Ripley's "Believe It or Not" material for months. In the upper town, a vast snakelike chain of gaudily attired tourists promenades through the narrow quarters (many of the lanes evoke the casbahs of North Africa).

The Greeks called Capri (pronounced *Cap*-ry, not Ca-*pree*) "the island of the wild boars." Before the big season rush, which lasts from Easter to the end of October, Capri is an island of lush Mediterranean vegetation (olives, vineyards, flowers) encircled by emerald waters, an oasis in the sun even before the emperor Tiberius moved the seat of the empire here. Writers such as D. H. Lawrence have in previous decades found Capri a haven. Some have written of it, including Axel Munthe (*The Story of San Michele*) and Norman Douglas (*Siren Land*). The latter title is a reference to Capri's reputation as the "island of the sirens" that tempted Ulysses. Other distinguished visitors have included Mendelssohn, Dumas, and Hans Christian Andersen.

Don't visit Capri, incidentally, for great beaches. The mountainous landscape doesn't make for long sandy beaches. There are some spots for bathing, but many of these have been turned into clubs called *stabilimenti balneari,* which you must pay to visit.

Touring the island is relatively simple. You dock at unremarkable **Marina Grande,** the port area. From there, you can take the funicular to the town of **Capri** above, site of the major hotels, restaurants, cafes, and shops. From Capri, a short bus ride will deliver you to **Anacapri,** at the top of the island near Monte Solaro. The only other settlement you might want to visit is **Marina Piccola,** on the south side of the island with the major beach. There are also beaches at Punta Carnea and Bagni di Tiberio. The tourist office will pinpoint these on a map for you.

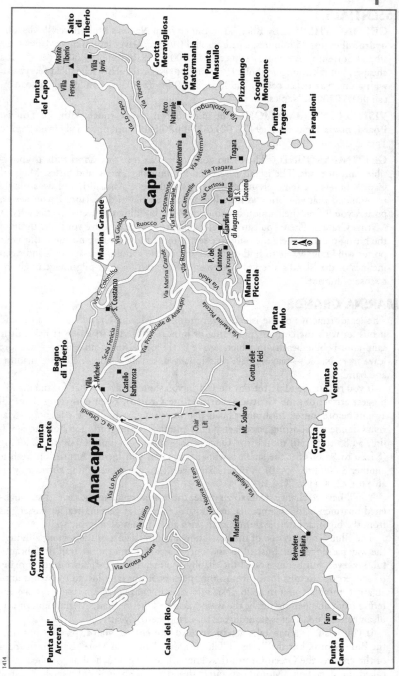

ESSENTIALS

GETTING THERE   By Boat   You can go from Naples's Molo Beverello dock by **hydrofoil** in just 45 minutes. The hydrofoil (*aliscafo*) leaves several times daily (some stop at Sorrento). A one-way trip costs 14,500 to 15,200 lire ($9.30 to $9.75). It's cheaper, but takes longer (about 1 1/2 hours), to go by regularly scheduled **ferryboat,** with a one-way ticket costing 7,900 to 8,800 lire ($5.05 to $5.65). For schedules, call 081/70700 in Naples.

VISITOR INFORMATION   For information, get in touch with the **Tourist Board,** piazza Umberto I 19 (☎ **081/837-0686**), at Capri, open daily from 9am to 1pm and 3:30 to 6:45pm.

GETTING AROUND   There's no need to have a car in tiny Capri with its impossible hairpin roads. The island is serviced by funiculars, taxis, and buses. Many of Capri's hotels are remotely located, especially those at Anacapri, and we strongly recommend that you bring as little luggage as possible to the island. If you need a porter, you'll find their union headquarters in a building connected to the jetty at Marina Grande. There you can cajole, coddle, coerce, or connive your way through the hiring process where the only rule seems to be that there are no rules. But your porter will know where to find the hotel among the winding passageways and steep inclines of the island's arteries. Your best defense during your pilgrimage might be a sense of humor.

MARINA GRANDE

The least attractive of the island's communities, Marina Grande is the port, and it bustles with the coming and going of hundreds of visitors daily. It has a little sand-cum-pebble beach, on which you're likely to see American sailors—on shore leave from Naples—playing ball, occasionally upsetting a Coca-Cola over mamma and bambino.

If you're just spending the day on Capri, you should leave at once for the island's biggest attraction, the **Grotta Azzurra (Blue Grotto),** open daily from 9am till 1 hour before sunset. In summer boats that leave frequently from the harbor at Marina Grande transporting passengers to the entrance of the grotto for 7,600 to 8,300 lire ($4.85 to $5.30) round trip. Once at the grotto, you'll pay 6,600 to 7,200 lire ($4.20 to $4.60) for the small rowboat that takes you inside. Admission itself is another 8,000 lire ($5.10). A ticket that covers the cost of everything above is available for 22,000 lire ($14.10).

You'll have to change boats to go under the low entrance to the cave. The toughened boatmen of the Campania are unusually skilled at getting heavier passengers from the big boat into the skimpy craft with a minimum of volcanic spills.

The Blue Grotto is one of the best-known natural sights of the region, although the way passengers are hustled in and out of it makes it a tourist trap. It *is* beautiful, however, but because of all the shabby commercialism that surrounds it, many passengers opt to miss it. Known to the ancients, it was later lost to the world until an artist stumbled on it in 1826. Inside the cavern, light refraction (the sun's rays entering from an opening under the water) achieves the dramatic Mediterranean cerulean color. The effect is stunning, as thousands testify yearly.

If you wish, you can take a **trip around the entire island,** passing not only the Blue Grotto, but the Baths of Tiberius, the "Palazzo al Mare" built in the days of the empire, the Green Grotto (less known), and the much-photographed rocks called the Faraglioni. Motorboats circle the island in about 1 1/2 hours at a cost of 18,000 lire ($11.50) per person.

Connecting Marina Grande with Capri (the town) is a frequently running **funicular** that charges 1,500 lire (95¢) one-way. However, the funicular, really a cog railway, doesn't operate off-season. Instead, you take a bus from Marina Grande to Capri at a one-way cost of 1,500 lire (95¢).

CAPRI

The main town is the center of most of the hotels, restaurants, and elegant shops— and the milling throngs. The heart of the resort, piazza Umberto I, is like a grand living room.

A PARK, A PLEASURE PALACE & A MONASTARY

One of the most popular walks from the main square is down via Vittorio Emanuele, past the deluxe Quisisana, to the **Giardini di Augusto.** The park is the choice spot on Capri for views and relaxation. From this perch, you can see the legendary Faraglioni, the rocks, once inhabited by the "blue lizard." At the top of the park is a belvedere that overlooks emerald waters and Marina Piccola. Nearby you can visit the **Certosa,** a Carthusian monastery erected in the 14th century in honor of St. James. The monastery is open Tuesday to Sunday from 9am to 2pm and charges no admission.

Back at piazza Umberto I, head up via Longano, then via Tiberio, all the way to Monte Tiberio. Here is the **Villa Jovis,** the splendid ruin of the estate from which Tiberius ruled the empire from A.D. 27 to 37. Actually, the Jovis was one of a dozen villas that the depraved emperor erected on the island. Apparently Tiberius couldn't sleep, so he wandered from bed to bed. From the ruins there's a view of both the Bay of Salerno and the Bay of Naples, as well as of the island. The ruins of the imperial palace may be visited daily from 9am to 1 hour before sunset for 4,000 lire ($2.55) admission.

SHOPPING

Carthusia-Profumi di Capri. Via Camerelle 10. ☎ **081/837-0368.**

This little shop on Capri's luxury shopping street specializes in perfume made on the island from local herbs and flowers. Since 1947 this shop has attracted such clients as Elizabeth Taylor, before she started touting her own perfume. The scents are unique, and many women consider Carthusia perfumes collector's items. Open daily from 9:30am to 9pm.

Carthusia also has a **perfume laboratory,** at via Matteotti 2 (☎ **081/837-0368**), which you can visit daily from 9am to 7pm. There's another Carthusia shop in Anacapri, at via Capodimonte 26 (☎ **081/837-3668**), next to the Villa Axel Munthe. The shops close January to March and on Sunday in April, October, November, and December.

CAFE SITTING

One of the major pastimes in Capri is to occupy an outdoor table at one of the cafes on piazza Umberto I. Each arriving visitor picks his or her own favorite, although they're all about the same. Even some permanent residents (and this is a good sign) patronize **Bar Tiberio,** piazza Umberto I (☎ **081/837-0268**), which is open daily from 7am to 2am, sometimes until 3 or 4am if business merits it. Larger and a little more comfortable than some of its competitors, this cafe has tables both inside and outside that overlook the busy life of the square where virtually every visitor to Capri shows up at one time or another. A cappuccino costs 5,000 lire ($3.20) if you're sitting, but you can order many other types of drinks as well. Whiskey begins at 12,000 lire ($7.70).

WHERE TO STAY

Finding your own bed for the night can be a real problem if you arrive in July or August without a reservation when the demand far exceeds the supply. Capri is also an exclusive enclave of the wealthy, and even the lesser accommodations are able to charge high prices. Many serious economizers find that they have to return to the mainland for the night.

Very Expensive

✪ **Quisisana & Grand Hotel.** Via Camerelle 2, 80073 Capri. ☎ **081/837-0788.** Fax 081/837-6080. 150 rms, 15 suites. A/C MINIBAR TV TEL. 380,000–650,000 lire ($243.20–$416) double; 850,000–1,000,000 lire ($544–$640) suite. Rates include breakfast. AE, DC, MC, V. Closed Nov 15 to mid-March. Take the Capri funicular.

The deluxe choice on the island, this is the favorite nesting place for a regular international clientele. Opened as a small hotel around the turn of the century, the Quisisana was enlarged and became the island's foremost resort hotel after World War II. More spacious than its central location would indicate, its private garden is shut off from the passing tourists. A large, rather sprawling, but imposing structure, it has bedrooms ranging from cozy singles to spacious suites—all of which open onto wide arcades with a view of the seacoast. They vary greatly in decor, with both traditional and conservatively modern furnishings. In the main lounge the furnishings are in antique gold. Capri's social center, the terrace of the hotel, is where everybody who is "anybody" goes for cocktails before dinner.

Dining/Entertainment: The hotel has two restaurants, both under the famed chef Gualtiero Marchesi. Colombaia, ideal for lunch, is proud of its fresh-tasting and attractively displayed fish dishes, as well as its lush fruits and vegetables. In the evening, the Quisi Restaurant is alluring with candlelight, serving a creative Mediterranean and local cuisine. The American bar (which seems appropriate to Berkeley Square, London) overlooks the swimming pool on the lower terrace.

Services: Room service, baby-sitting, laundry, valet.

Facilities: Sauna, Turkish bath and massage facilities, indoor and outdoor swimming pools, beauty shop, gymnasium, tennis courts. The recreational facilities are not as complete as those of Europa Palace (see below).

La Scalinatella (Little Steps). Via Tragara 8, 80073 Capri. ☎ **081/837-0633.** Fax 081/837-8291. 30 junior suites. A/C MINIBAR TV TEL. 630,000 lire ($403.20) suite. Rates include breakfast. AE, MC, V. Closed Nov 15–Mar 15. Take the Capri funicular.

One of the most delightful hotels in Capri is constructed like a private villa above terraces that offer a panoramic view of the water and a nearby monastery. Many former Quisisana guests have deserted to this more intimate and exclusive pair of 200-year-old houses, with a vaguely Moorish design, run by the Morgano family. The ambience is one of unadulterated luxury; the suites include a phone beside the bathtub, beds set into alcoves, elaborate wrought-iron accents that ring both the inner stairwell and the ornate balconies, and a sweeping view over the gardens and pool. The hotel contains a restaurant, open only at lunchtime, where simple but flavorful dishes are served on a terrace beside the pool.

Expensive

Hotel Flora. Via Federico Serena 26, 80073 Capri. ☎ **081/837-0211.** Fax 081/837-8949. 24 rms. A/C MINIBAR TV TEL. 250,000–350,000 lire ($160–$224) double. Rates include breakfast. AE, DC, MC, V. Closed Jan 9–Mar 1 and Oct–Dec 15. Take the Capri funicular.

The terraces—edged with oleander, bougainvillea, and geraniums—overlook the monastery of St. James and the sea. The Flora is not in the same class as the Quisisana

Swinging in Siren Land

Over the centuries, artists and writers have been drawn to the Isle of Capri that the emperor Augustus called Capri Apragopolis ("city of sweet idleness"). The island's first bigtime "swinger" was another emperor, Tiberius, who spent the last decade of his licentious life at his Villa Jovis in Capri, wandering from bed to bed in search of erotic amusement. He is said to have inspired a long line of hedonists over the centuries, ranging from munitions king Baron Von Krupp to the acerbic Oscar Wilde, who appreciated the golden Mediterranean youth of the island.

There's definitely a live-and-let-live attitude on Capri—perhaps that's why even Maxim Gorky settled here from 1907 to 1913, running a school for revolutionaries that is said to have been attended by Lenin and Stalin.

English writers, especially, have been fond of the island. Noel Coward pronounced it "the most beautiful operetta stage in the world." His visits to the island were noted by the playwright Tennessee Williams, who notoriously satirized him in the play *The Milk Train Doesn't Stop Here Any More*, in which the "witch of Capri" was played by Mildred Dunnock. Rather ironically, when the play was rewritten as a movie, *Boom,* starring Richard Burton and Elizabeth Taylor, the part of the "witch of Capri" was recast as a man and Coward played himself. Another, very different writer, Graham Greene found Capri an island of inspiration for his writing, and returned to his villa here frequently.

The English writer most identified with the island was Norman Douglas (1868–1952). Capri provided the inspiration for his best-known novel, *South Wind,* published in 1917. He later told friends he'd fallen in love with Capri when he first saw it in full bloom in the spring of 1888. At the age of only 28, Douglas had been forced into retirement from the Foreign Office in London because of an impending scandal. With what money he had, he purchased a villa along the Posillipo peninsula overlooking the Bay of Naples. Calling it Villa Maya, he lived there for four years in a disastrous marriage to his cousin, Elsa Fitzgibbon, finally divorcing her in 1904.

It was then that he moved to Capri, purchasing Villa Daphne. In about three years he'd spent all his money and told friends that he'd been forced into writing because of "sheer poverty." His first book, *Siren Land* (1911), was followed by *Fountains in the Sand* (1912) and *Old Calabria* (1915). Critics hailed these almost-forgotten books as among the best travel books ever penned, but the public wasn't buying until the publication of the novel *South Wind,* with Capri as a setting.

Other works were to follow: *They Went* (1920), *Alone* (1921), *Together* (1923), *Paneros* (1931), *Looking Back* (1933), and finally, *Late Harvest* (1946). Douglas died in 1952 after writing *Footnote on Capri*. He spent the postwar years of his life at the Villa Tuoro on Capri (owned by a friend), and you can visit his tomb in the Capri cemetery.

or Scalinatella, but it's kinder to purses. There are several tile courtyards with garden furniture, pots of tropical flowers, and spots where you can either sunbathe or be cooled by the sea breezes. The public and private rooms are a wise blend of the old and new. The bedrooms are well furnished. There's a less desirable but comfortable annex across the street. The first-class, reasonably priced restaurant, La Certosa di San Giacomo, offers an impressive cuisine and many excellent regional wines.

Hotel Luna. Viale Matteotti 3, 80073 Capri. ☎ **081/837-0433.** Fax 081/837-7459. 54 rms. A/C MINIBAR TV TEL. 240,000–460,000 lire ($153.60–$294.40) double including breakfast; 170,000–285,000 lire ($108.80–$182.40) per person with half board. AE, DC, MC, V. Closed Oct 10 to Maundy Thurs (the Thurs before Easter). Take the Capri funicular.

This first-class hotel stands on a cliff overlooking the sea and the rocks of Faraglioni. Even more tranquil and inviting than the Flora, it's set almost between the Gardens of Augustus and the Carthusian monastery of St. James. The building is nondescript, the furnishings reproductions of antiques. The bedrooms, a mixture of contemporary Italian pieces and a Victorian decor, incorporate wood and padded headboards and gilt mirrors over the desk, all consistently in good style. Some of the bedrooms have arched, recessed private terraces that overlook the garden of flowers and semitropical plants. There's a clubby drinking lounge, and the dining room lures with good cuisine.

Hotel Punta Tragara. Via Tragara 57, 80073 Capri. ☎ **081/837-0844.** Fax 081/837-7790. 17 rms, 30 suites. A/C MINIBAR TV TEL. 240,000–500,000 lire ($153.60–$320) double; 380,000–520,000 lire ($243.20–$332.80) suite. Rates include breakfast. AE, DC, MC, V. Closed Nov–Easter. Take the Capri funicular.

This former private villa—designed by Le Corbusier—stands above rocky cliffs at the tip of the most desirable panorama on Capri. Its sienna-colored walls and Andalusian-style accents are designed so that each of the apartment accommodations is subtly different. It ranks just under the Quisisana and Scalinatella, but far grander than either the Luna or the Flora. Outfitted with mottled carpeting, big windows, substantial furniture, and all the modern comforts, each unit opens onto a private terrace or a balcony studded with flowers and vines, plus a sweeping view. The premises include two pools (one heated), quiet retreats near a baronial fireplace, and a grotto disco. An often-debated point on Capri involves this hotel's isolation from the other activities of the island, although many clients consider this a virtue, especially in high season when other sections of the island can be very crowded.

La Palma. Via Vittorio Emanuele 39, 80073 Capri. ☎ **081/837-0133.** Fax 081/837-6966. 70 rms. A/C MINIBAR TV TEL. 200,000–420,000 lire ($128–$268.80) double. Rates include breakfast. AE, DC, MC, V. Take the Capri funicular.

On par with the Flora, this hotel was established a century ago as one of the first symbols of modern tourism on the island. Right in the center of Capri town, it caters to guests who seek first-class amenities and comforts—and who are willing to pay the piper for the privilege. Restored and renovated in an appealing style that blends modern and traditional styles, the hotel has a white-walled exterior, and a forecourt with palms and potted shrubs, which is hardly the equal of the Flora's flowery terrace and sea views. Each bedroom is handsomely furnished. Its restaurant, Relais la Palma, is one of the finest on Capri (but it operates only from Easter to late September).

Moderate

Regina Cristina. Via Serena 20, 80073 Capri. ☎ **081/837-0744.** Fax 081/837-0550. 50 rms, 5 suites. A/C MINIBAR TV TEL. 380,000 lire ($243.20) double; from 450,000 lire ($288) suite. Rates include breakfast. Midwinter discounts up to 45%. AE, DC, MC, V. Take the Capri funicular.

The white facade of the Regina Cristina rises four stories above one of the most imaginatively landscaped gardens on Capri. It was built in 1959 and renovated in 1993 in a sun-flooded design of open spaces, sunken lounges, cool tiles, and *la dolce vita* armchairs. Each accommodation has its own balcony and is very restful. Most of the rooms have Jacuzzi bathtubs. In general, for what you get this hotel appears overpriced. But on Capri in July and August you're sometimes lucky to find a room at any price.

La Vega. Via Occhio Marino 10, 80073 Capri. ☎ **081/837-0481.** Fax 081/837-0342. 24 rms. A/C MINIBAR TV TEL. 200,000–350,000 lire ($128–$224) double. Rates include breakfast. AE, DC, MC, V. Closed Nov–Easter. Take the Capri funicular.

This hotel originated as the private home of the family that continues to run it today. Originally built in the 1930s, and renovated in 1993, it has a clear view of the sea and is nestled amid trees against a sunny hillside. Each of the oversize rooms of this four-level building has a shower and a private balcony that overlooks the water. Below the rooms is a garden of flowering bushes, and on the lower edge is a free-form swimming pool with a grassy border for sunbathing and a little bar for refreshments. The rooms have decoratively tiled floors and some of the beds have wrought-iron headboards. Some rooms contain a TV; all units have a Jacuzzi. Breakfast is served on a terrace surrounded by trees and large potted flowers or on your private balcony.

Villa Brunella. Via Tragara 24, 80073 Capri. ☎ **081/837-0122.** Fax 081/837-0430. 10 rms, 10 suites. A/C MINIBAR TV TEL. 345,000 lire ($220.80) double; 435,000 lire ($278.40) suite. Rates include breakfast. AE, DC, MC, V. Closed Nov 6–Mar 20.

Located a 10-minute walk from many of Capri's largest hotels, this hotel was originally built in the late 1940s as a private villa. In 1963 it was transformed into a well-appointed and comfortable hotel by its present owner, Vincenzo Ruggiero, who named it after his hard-working wife, Brunella. The hotel has been completely renovated. Although lacking the ambience of the Flora, it competes with that hotel in its sea views and its flowery terrace. All the doubles have balconies or terraces and views of the sea. There's also a carefully landscaped pool, a bar, and a cozy restaurant.

Inexpensive

Ⓢ **Villa Krupp.** Via Matteotti 12, 80073 Capri. ☎ **081/837-0362.** Fax 081/837-6489. 15 rms. TEL. 170,000–230,000 lire ($108.80–$147.20) double. Rates include breakfast. MC, V. Take the Capri funicular.

During the early years of the 20th century the Russian revolutionaries Gorky and Lenin called this villa home. Surrounded by shady trees, it offers panoramic views of the sea and the Gardens of Augustus from its lofty terraces. At this intimate, family-run place, the front parlor is all glass with views of the seaside and semitropical plants set near Hong Kong chairs, all intermixed with painted Venetian-style pieces. Your bedroom may be large, with a fairly good bathroom. Many of the rooms have a terrace. Breakfast is the only meal offered.

Villa Sarah. Via Tiberio 3A, 80073 Capri. ☎ **081/837-7817.** Fax 081/837-7215. 20 rms. TV TEL. 200,000–270,000 lire ($128–$172.80) double. Rates include breakfast. AE, MC, V. Closed late Oct to Mar 19. Take the Capri funicular.

The Villa Sarah, although far removed from the day-trippers from Naples, is still very central. A steep walk from the main square, it seems part of another world with its Capri garden and good views. All it lacks is a pool. One of the bargains of the island, it's often fully booked, so reserve ahead in summer. The sea is visible only from the upper floors. An old private house stands on the grounds, but is no longer in use as a hotel—the hotel section of bedrooms is in a modern building. Some bedrooms have terraces. Breakfast is the only meal served.

WHERE TO DINE

Moderate

La Capannina. Via Le Botteghe 14. ☎ **081/837-0732.** Reservations required for dinner. Main courses 18,000–38,000 lire ($11.50–$24.30). AE, DC, MC, V. Aug, daily noon–3pm and 7:30–10:30pm; Mar–July and Sept–Oct, Thurs–Tues noon–3pm and 7:30–10:30pm. Closed Nov–Feb. Take the Capri funicular. CAMPANA/ITALIAN.

This restaurant is not pretentious, although it's patronized by a host of famous people from actresses to dress designers to royalty. It's your best bet for nonhotel dining on the island. A trio of inside rooms is decorated in a tavern manner, although the main draw in summer is the inner courtyard, with its ferns and hanging vines. At a table covered with a colored cloth, you can select from baby shrimp au gratin, pollo (chicken) alla Capannina, or scaloppine Capannina. If featured, a fine opener is Sicilian macaroni. The most savory skillet of goodies is the zuppa di pesce, a soup made with fish from the bay. Some of the dishes were obviously inspired by the nouvelle cuisine school. Wine is from vineyards owned by the restaurant.

I Faraglioni. Via Camerelle 75. ☎ **081/873-0320.** Reservations required. Main courses 22,000–36,000 lire ($14.10–$23.05). AE, DC, V. Apr–Sept, daily 12:30–3pm and 7:30pm–midnight; Apr–June and Oct, Tues–Sun 12:30–3pm and 7:30pm–midnight. Closed Nov–Mar. Take the Capri funicular. SEAFOOD/CONTINENTAL.

Some locals say that the food is only a secondary consideration to the social ferment of this popular restaurant. In any event, the kitchen turns out a well-prepared collection of European specialties, usually based on seafood from the surrounding waters. Examples might include linguine with lobster, seafood crêpes, rice Créole, fisherman's risotto, grilled or baked fish of many different varieties, and a wide assortment of meat dishes such as pappardelle with rabbit. For dessert, try one of the regional pastries mixed with fresh fruit.

⑤ La Pigna. Via Roma 30. ☎ **081/837-0280.** Reservations recommended. Main courses 16,000–30,000 lire ($10.25–$19.20). AE, DC, MC, V. Aug, daily noon–3pm and 8pm–2am, July and Sept, Tues 8pm–2am, Wed–Mon noon–3pm and 8pm–2am; Apr–June and Oct, Wed–Mon noon–3pm and 8pm–2am; Nov–Mar, daily noon–3pm. Take the Capri funicular. NEAPOLITAN.

A short walk from the bus station, La Pigna serves the finest meals for the money on the entire island. Dining here is like attending a garden party on Capri, and this has been true since 1875. This restaurant isn't as chic as it once was, but the food is as good as ever. The owner loves flowers almost as much as good food, and the greenhouse ambience includes purple petunias, red geraniums, bougainvillea, and lemon trees. Much of the produce comes from the restaurant's gardens in Anacapri. All the food is excellent, but try in particular the penne tossed in an eggplant sauce, and the chicken suprême with mushrooms, the house specialty. Another recommended dish is the herb-stuffed rabbit, which was raised on the farm. The dessert specialty is an almond-and-chocolate torte. Another feature of the restaurant is homemade liquors, one of which is distilled from local lemons. The waiters are courteous and efficient, and the atmosphere is nostalgic, as guitarists stroll by singing sentimental Neapolitan ballads.

Inexpensive

Al Geranio. In the Giardini Augusto, viale Matteotti 8. ☎ **081/837-0616.** Reservations required Fri–Sat. Main courses 18,000–32,000 lire ($11.50–$20.50). AE, DC, MC, V. Wed–Mon noon–3:30pm and 7:30–10:30pm (to 1am in high season). Closed Oct 30–Easter. Take the Capri funicular. FRENCH/MEDITERRANEAN.

One of the most scenically located restaurants on Capri, Al Geranio stands in the Gardens of Augustus en route to the Villa Krupp, within easy reach of the Quisisana and Luna hotels. Arrive early to enjoy an apéritif in the piano bar. The earlier you arrive in the summer, the better chance you have of getting an outdoor table. The kitchen turns out a good Mediterranean cuisine, which is likely to include such dishes as fish soup, fried shrimp, swordfish, crêpes with cheese, and cannelloni. A savory dish to order is zuppa di cozze (mussel soup). You might also try Capri-style ravioli. Look for the daily specials.

⑤ Casanova. Via Le Botteghe 46. ☎ **081/837-7642.** Reservations required at dinner in summer. Main courses 11,000–30,000 lire ($7.05–$19.20). AE, DC, MC, V. July–Aug, daily noon–3pm and 7–11pm; Apr–June and Sept–Jan 9, Fri–Wed noon–3pm and 7–11pm. Closed Jan 10–Mar. Take the Capri funicular. NEAPOLITAN/CAPRESE.

Run by the D'Alessio family, and only a short walk from piazza Umberto I, this is one of the finest dining rooms on Capri. Its cellar offers a big choice of Italian wines, with most of the favorites of the Campania, and its cooks turn out a savory blend of Neapolitan and Italian specialties. You might begin with a cheese-filled ravioli, then go on to veal Sorrento or even red snapper "crazy waters" (with baby tomatoes). The seafood is always fresh and well prepared. A large and tempting buffet of antipasti is at hand. In a small wine cellar you can enjoy a good selection of Italian and foreign wines with a variety of cheeses. Most meals are inexpensive, but some exotic dishes and specialties that appear infrequently can soar to prices as high as 100,000 lire ($64).

⑤ La Cisterna. Via Madre Serafina 5. ☎ **081/837-5620.** Reservations required. Main courses 14,000–25,000 lire ($8.95–$16). AE, DC, MC, V. Tues–Sun 11:45am–3:30pm and 7pm–midnight. Closed mid-Nov to mid-Mar. Take the Capri funicular. SEAFOOD.

This excellent small restaurant is run by two brothers, Francesco and Salvatore Trama, who extend to guests a warm welcome. Ask what the evening specials are. They might be mamma's green lasagne, or whatever fish was freshest at the dock that afternoon, marinated in wine, garlic, and ginger and broiled. You could also try the lightly breaded and deep-fried baby squid and octopus, a mouth-watering saltimbocca, spaghetti with clams, and a filling zuppa di pesce (fish soup). Pizza begins at 7,000 lire ($4.50). La Cisterna lies only a short walk from piazza Umberto I via a labyrinth of covered "tunnels."

Da Gemma. Via Madre Serafina 6. ☎ **081/837-7113.** Reservations required. Main courses 19,000–20,000 lire ($12.15–$12.80). AE, DC, MC, V. Tues–Sun 12:30–3pm and 7:30pm–midnight. Closed Nov–Dec 15. Take the Capri funicular. REGIONAL/SEAFOOD.

You'll find this place, long a favorite with painters and writers, by going up an arch-covered walkway, reminiscent of Tangier, from piazza Umberto I. Some tables are arranged for the view. Everything's cozy and atmospheric. The cuisine is provincial, with a reliance on fish dishes. The best beginning is the mussel soup, and the finest main dish is the boiled fish of the day with creamy butter, priced according to weight. You can get pizza in the evening, and the desserts are mouth-watering. It has an annex across the street that has a covered terrace offering sea views.

⑤ Ristorante al Grottino. Via Longano 27. ☎ **081/837-0584.** Main courses 15,000–25,000 lire ($9.60–$16). AE, MC, V. Daily noon–3pm and 7pm–midnight. Closed Nov 3–Mar 30. Take the Capri funicular. SEAFOOD/NEAPOLITAN.

Founded in 1937, this was the retreat of the rich and famous during its *la dolce vita* heyday. Ted Kennedy, the late Ginger Rogers, the Gabor sisters, and Princess Soraya of Iran once dined here, and the place remains popular among ordinary folk. To reach it you must walk down a narrow alleyway that branches off from piazza Umberto I. It's not unlike a bistro in North Africa. The chef knows how to rattle his pots and pans. Bowing to the influence of the nearby Neapolitan cuisine, he offers four different dishes of fried mozzarella cheese, any one highly recommended. Try a big plate of the mixed fish fry from the seas of the Campania. The zuppa di cozze (mussel soup) is a savory opener, as is the ravioli alla caprese. The linguine with scampi is truly succulent.

ANACAPRI

Capri is the upper town of Marina Grande. To see the upper town of Capri, you have to get lost in the clouds of Anacapri—more remote, secluded, and idyllic than the main resort, and reached by a daring 3,000-lira ($1.90) round-trip bus ride more thrilling than any roller coaster. One visitor once remarked that all bus drivers to Anacapri "were either good or dead." At one point in island history, Anacapri and Capri were connected only by the Scala Fenicia, the Phoenician Stairs.

When you disembark at piazza della Victoria, you'll find a Caprian Shangri-la, a village of charming dimensions.

To continue your ascent to the top, you then hop aboard a chair lift to **Monte Solaro,** the loftiest citadel on the island at 1,950 feet. The ride takes about 12 minutes, operates winter, spring, and fall daily from 9:30am to sunset, and charges 7,000 lire ($4.50) for a round-trip ticket. During the summer, the chair lift operates Wednesday to Monday from 9:30am to sunset. At the top, the panorama of the Bay of Naples is spread before you.

You can head out on viale Axel Munthe to **Villa San Michele,** to Capodimonte 34 (☎ **081/837-1401**). This was the home of Axel Munthe, the Swedish author (*The Story of San Michele*), physician, and friend of Gustav V, king of Sweden, who visited him several times on the island. The villa is as Munthe (who died in 1949) furnished it, in a harmonious and tasteful way. From the rubble and ruins of an imperial villa built underneath by Tiberius, Munthe purchased several marbles, which are displayed inside. You can walk through the gardens for another in a series of endless panoramas of the island. Tiberius used to sleep out there alfresco on hot nights. You can visit the villa daily: from 9am to 6pm May to September, from 9:30am to 5pm in April and October, from 9:30am to 4:30pm in March, and from 10:30am to 3:30pm November to February. Admission is 6,000 lire ($3.85) for adults, free for children 9 and under. The Villa San Michele is a 5-minute walk from piazza Monumento in Anacapri.

WHERE TO STAY

Expensive

Europa Palace. Via Capodimonte 2, 80071 Anacapri. ☎ **081/837-3800.** Fax 081/837-3191. 92 rms, 20 junior suites, 4 suites. A/C MINIBAR TV TEL. 300,000–480,000 lire ($192–$307.20) double; from 680,000 lire ($435.20) suite. Rates include breakfast. AE, DC, MC, V. Closed Oct 31–Easter. Bus: Anacapri bus.

On the slopes of Monte Solaro, the first-class Europa sparkles with *moderne* and turns its back on the past to embrace the semiluxury of today. Its designer, who had bold ideas, obviously loved wide open spaces, heroic proportions, and vivid colors. The landscaped gardens with palm trees and plenty of bougainvillea have a large swimming pool, which most guests use as their outdoor living room. This is the only major hotel at Anacapri. Although lacking the intimate charms of the Scalinatella, it is nevertheless alluring because of its setting and its so-called Beauty Farm, offering spa treatments. Each of the bedrooms is attractively and comfortably furnished, and from some on a clear day you can see smoking Vesuvius in the background. Each of the four special suites has a private pool.

Dining/Entertainment: The hotel's restaurant, L'Olivo, is known for its fine cuisine with Neapolitan and other Mediterranean specialties, even with some nouvelle cuisine. A snack bar with light lunches is in the pool area.

Services: Room service, baby-sitting, laundry, valet.

Facilities: Swimming pool, beauty spa for medical and beauty treatments.

Hotel San Michele di Anacapri. Via Orlandi 1–3, 80071 Anacapri. ☎ **081/837-1427.**
Fax 081/837-1420. 56 rms. TV TEL. 180,000–220,000 lire ($115.20–$140.80) per person
double. Rates include half board. AE, DC, MC, V. Closed Nov 5–Mar 27. Bus: Anacapri bus.

This well-appointed contemporary hotel, quite a comedown from the Europa Palace, has spacious cliffside gardens and unmarred views as well as enough shady or
sunny nooks to please everybody. It also has the largest swimming pool on Capri.
Guests linger long and peacefully in its private and well-manicured gardens, where
the green trees are softened by splashes of color from hydrangea and geraniums. The
view for diners includes the Bay of Naples and Vesuvius. The bedrooms carry out the
same theme, with a respect for the past, but also with sufficient examples of today's
amenities, such as a tile bath in most rooms, good beds, and plenty of space.

Moderate

Ⓢ **Bellavista.** Via Orlandi 10, 80071 Anacapri. ☎ **081/837-1821.** Fax 081/837-0957.
15 rms. TEL. 140,000–160,000 lire ($89.60–$102.40) double. Rates include breakfast. Half board
100,000–120,000 lire ($64–$76.80) per person extra. AE, MC, V. Closed Nov 30–Easter. Bus:
Anacapri bus.

Only a 2-minute walk from the main piazza, this is a modern holiday retreat with a
panoramic view. Lodged into a mountainside, the hotel is decorated with primary
colors and has large living and dining rooms, and terraces with a view of the sea. The
breakfast and lunch terrace has garden furniture and a rattan-roofed sun shelter, and
the cozy lounge has an elaborate tile floor and a hooded fireplace, ideal for nippy
nights. The bedrooms are pleasingly contemporary (a few have a bed mezzanine, a sitting area on the lower level, and a private entrance). The restaurant is closed Monday.

Inexpensive

Caesar Augustus. Via Orlandi 4, 80071 Anacapri. ☎ **081/837-1444.** Fax 081/556-0119.
50 rms. TEL. 100,000–200,000 lire ($64–$128) double. Rates include breakfast. AE, DC,
MC, V. Closed Oct 15 to late Mar. Bus: Anacapri bus.

Isolated from the island's main population centers, and set beside the road leading
from Capri to Anacapri, this unpretentious modern hotel has pleased other readers
of this guidebook. The rooms are adequately furnished with simple contemporary
furniture, and come with a wide array of views, over either the sea or a pleasant garden. Many of the guests here seem to return over the years. There are also a restaurant and a bar on the premises.

Hotel Loreley. Via Orlandi 12, 80071 Anacapri. ☎ **081/837-1440.** Fax 081/837-1399
18 rms. TEL. 90,000–140,000 lire ($57.60–$89.80) double. Rates include breakfast. AE, MC, V.
Closed Nov 30–Mar 15. Bus: Anacapri bus.

The Loreley has more to offer than economy: It's a cozy, immaculately kept accommodation, with a genial homelike atmosphere. Opened in 1963, it features an
open-air veranda with a bamboo canopy, rattan chairs, and of course, a good view.
The rooms overlook lemon-bearing trees that have (depending on the season) either
scented blossoms or fruit. The bedrooms are quite large, with unified colors and
enough furniture to make for a sitting room. Each room has a balcony. You approach
the hotel through a white iron gate, past a stone wall. It lies off the road toward the
sea, and is surrounded by fig trees and geraniums.

MARINA PICCOLA

You can reach the little south-shore fishing village and beach of Marina Piccola by
bus (later you can take a bus back up the steep hill to Capri). The village opens onto
emerald-and-cerulean waters, with the Faraglioni rocks of the sirens jutting out at the
far end of the bay. Treat yourself to a meal at **La Canzone del Mare,** Marina Piccola
(☎ **081/837-0104**), from Easter to October.

18 Sicily

Sicily is an ancient land of myth and legend. It is also, according to many Italians, a land unto itself, different from the rest of Italy in customs and traditions—and proudly so. On the map, the toe of the Italian boot seems poised to kick Sicily away from the mainland, as if it did not belong to the rest of Italy. The largest of the Mediterranean islands, it's located some 80 miles from the coast of Africa and is swept by winds that dry its fertile fields every summer, crisping the harvest into a sun-blasted palette of browns. Like its landscape, Sicily is a hypnotic place of dramatic turbulence, as absurdly emotional and intense as a play by native son Luigi Pirandello.

For centuries Sicily's beauty and charm have attracted the greedy eye of foreigners: Greeks (before the island was conquered by Rome), Vandals, Arabs, Normans, Swabians, the fanatically religious House of Aragon, and the French Bourbons.

Homer, in the *Odyssey*, recorded ancient myths about cannibalistic tribes (the Laestrygones) living near the site of modern Catania. Centuries later legends grew about Sicily's patron saint, Agatha, martyred by having her breasts cut off. The island still teems with all kinds of tales shrouded in primeval lore and legend, as well as with stories, many fervently believed, about the curative powers of water from certain caves and the harmful powers of the evil eye. That the Sicilians should have created and held on to such phantasmagoric tales and legends is not surprising, in view of their island's history of natural and political disasters.

Through the centuries, a series of plagues, ferocious family vendettas, volcanic eruptions, earthquakes, and economic hardships have threatened many times to destroy the interwoven cultures of Sicily. Always, the island has persevered. Its archeology and richly complex architecture are endlessly fascinating, and the masses of almond and cherry trees in bloom in February make it one of the most beautiful places in Italy.

Too long neglected by travelers wooed by the art cities of the north, Sicily is today attracting greater numbers of foreign visitors. This land of volcanic islands is full of sensual sights and experiences: a sirocco whirling out of the nearby Libyan deserts, horses with plumes and bells pulling gaily painted carts, vineyards and fragrant citrus groves, Greek temples and classical dramas performed in ancient theaters, and the aromatic fragrance of a glass of marsala.

The Sicilians are an intriguing and fiercely proud racial mix, less Latin than the Italians, spiritually akin in many ways to North Africa and the wild wastelands of the Sahara. Luigi Barzini, in *The Italians,* wrote: "Sicily is the schoolroom model of Italy for beginners, with every Italian quality and defect magnified, exasperated, and brightly colored. . . . Everywhere in Italy, life is more or less slowed down by the exuberant intelligence of the inhabitants: In Sicily it is practically paralyzed by it."

There are far too many cars in Palermo, a sometimes-unpleasant reflection of the new (sometimes drug-related) prosperity that seems to have encouraged everyone on the island to buy a car. Parts of the island are heavily polluted by industrialization, but the age-old poverty still remains in the streets, home to thousands of children who seemingly grow up there.

Geologically, Sicily broke away from the mainland of Africa (not Europe) millions of years ago. Even today, the $2^1/_2$-mile channel separating it from the tip of the Italian peninsula is still a dangerously unstable earthquake zone, making hopes for the eventual construction of a bridge unfeasible. The ancient Greeks claimed that the busy strait was the lair of deadly sea monsters, Scylla and Charybdis, who, according to legend, delighted in wrecking Greek ships and devouring the flesh of the sailors aboard.

Today Sicily has a relatively stable population of around five million inhabitants. Its resorts, ancient temples, and distinctive cuisine are bringing it increasingly into the world's consciousness. Even Goethe, who traveled widely here, commented on the sometimes bizarre, always captivating, symbols he saw, but concluded, "To have seen Italy without having seen Sicily is not to have seen Italy at all, for Sicily is the clue to everything."

EXPLORING SICILY BY CAR

Day 1   Arrive in tacky Messina, often by car ferry from the mainland. The third-largest city of Sicily, and the setting of Shakespeare's *Much Ado About Nothing,* it does not invite lingering. Take autostrada A18 down the eastern coast of Italy, about 30 miles to Taormina, where 1 night will be all too brief. Set on Monte Tauro overlooking the Ionian Sea, this is the most majestic resort in Sicily.

Day 2   Autostrada A18 continues south to Catania, Sicily's second-largest city and a busy seaport, where you might want to have lunch.

TAKE A BREAK   **La Siciliana,** viale Marco Polo 52A in Catania (☎ **095/ 370003**), offers both folkloric inner rooms and garden setting for eating. Fresh fish is displayed in a glass case, and the choice of regional Sicilian dishes is wide. One of the most typical Catanese dishes, and recommended to all first-time visitors, is rigatoni alla Norma, made with fresh basil, fried eggplant, and tomatoes. It's closed Sunday evening, Monday, and 2 weeks in August.

Continue south from Catania for 36 miles to Syracuse, where you'll want to overnight.

Day 3   Plan on a full day exploring the ruins and monuments of this town, opening onto the Ionian Sea in southeastern Italy. In ancient times it was the capital of Magna Graecia and was one of the greatest cities on earth. Hours can be spent exploring its archeological zone and such attractions as a steep-walled quarry known as the Latomie del Paradise. Spend yet another night in Syracuse.

Day 4   Driving south from Syracuse, the autostrada soon ends and Route SS115 takes over, leading you to Noto, filled with Sicilian baroque architecture and worth some of your time. Most of the city's monuments are on the main street, corso Vittorio Emanuele. Get back on SS115 which will take you to Ragusa, which is encircled by large chemical plants. Hurry on from here, passing Gela, until you reach your goal for the night: Agrigento.

Day 5   While still based in Agrigento, explore the Valley of the Temples, which will be one of the highlights of your tour in Italy. See them at dawn, when they're hauntingly beautiful, and again at twilight when illuminations by floodlights make for a spectacle.

Day 6   The route west (SS115) leads to Sciacca, 39 miles from Agrigento. Sciacca, which deserves a brief stopover, is known for its ceramics and its thermal baths. Continue along SS115 for 25 miles to Selinunte. This ancient town, founded in 682 B.C., was one of the most prosperous Greek colonies in Italy. After exploring the incredible ruins, continue on Route SS115 north to Castelvetrano, then head west to Marsala for 22 miles. Marsala is known for its fortified wine, often compared to sherry. This is the site where Garibaldi landed with 1,000 men to launch his campaign to liberate Sicily from Bourbon rule.

☕ **TAKE A BREAK**   **Delfino,** lungomare Mediterraneo in Marsala (☎ **0923/ 998188**), makes the best luncheon stopover. This sea-bordering restaurant features alfresco dining. Its specialties are both fish soup and fish salad. The fresh catch of the day is grilled and perfectly seasoned. The chef is also known for his seafood couscous, inspired by North Africa across the way. The location is 3¹/₂ miles south of the town.

From Marsala take SS115 north to Trapani for the night, a distance of 19 miles.

Day 7   In the morning explore Trapani, the westernmost of the towns of Sicily. After passing through its dreary suburbs you head for the narrowing promontory which is the most interesting part of this colorful port to explore. From Trapani continue to Erice, 9 miles to the northeast. This was the ancient Eryx, founded by the Elymnians and mentioned in Virgil's *Aeneid.* With its fortified castles, it owes much of its present look to its Norman conquerors. Take S113 directly out of Erice east for 12 miles to Segesta. A rival of Selinunte, Segesta was founded in the 12th century B.C. It contains one of the world's great Doric temples.

From Segesta follow the autostrada signs (A29) heading for Palermo for the night.

Days 8–9   In Sicily's capital, you'll be kept busy both day and night with its many attractions. You need the 9th day to explore the sights in the environs, including Cefalù and Monreale. Try to work in some time at the beach at Mondello Lido, 7¹/₂ miles to the east of Palermo.

A TASTE OF SICILY

The sauces and stews are complicated and aromatic, as befits this rugged, highly individualistic island. Good vineyards, rich vegetation (in part), and fertile soil have led to the creation of a "perfumed" cuisine on land, but many Sicilians turn to the sea, not only for their livelihood but for their food.

Local specialties include *maccheroni* with shelled prawns mixed into the tomatoes, or else *maccheroni con le sarde,* spaghetti with a spicy sauce of pine nuts, fennel, spices, olive oil, and chopped sardines. *Cannoli* are cylindrical pastry cases stuffed with cottage cheese, candied fruit, or chocolate, and a *cassata* is an ice-cream cake, often with almonds and custard.

Cuscusu is one of the most nourishing items on the Sicilian menu, a fish soup with pasta (every chef makes it differently). *Bottarga di tonno* is tunny roe sometimes

Sicily

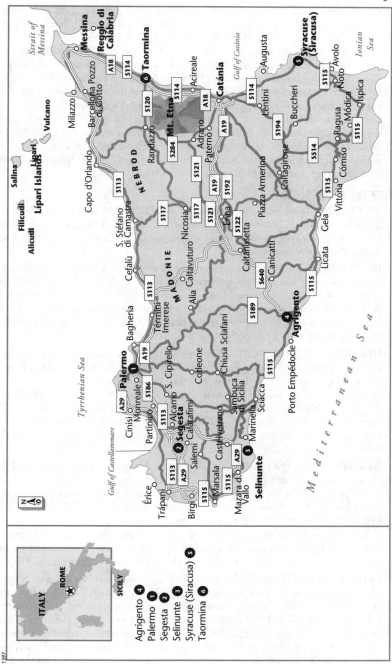

grilled, sometimes boiled, and always served with fresh lemon and oil. *Farsumagru* is a breast of beef or veal stuffed with hard-boiled eggs and spices. Sicilians are known for their *gelati* or ices, the best in Italy, often made with fresh fruits.

The wines are an equal of the cuisine. One of its best known wines, Mamertino, was praised by the ancient poet Martial, and was served to Caesar at the banquet honoring his third consulship. It has a keen bouquet and is a golden yellow in color. It often accompanies fish dishes. Other famous wines of the region include Faro, ruby red in color with a fine bouquet and nutty flavor, served with meats and roasts; and Corco blanco di Casteldaccia, a straw-yellow, intense and brilliant wine with a distinctive bouquet, often served with antipasti. The most celebrated and best known Sicilian wine is marsala, amber yellow in color with orange depths to it. With its pleasing fragrance and special bouquet, marsala is velvety and fruity, and is served with desserts or drunk as a pick-me-up between meals.

GETTING TO SICILY

BY PLANE   There are daily **Alitalia** (☎ **800/223-5730** in the U.S.) flights to Palermo from Milan, Naples, Venice, Pisa, Genoa, Bologna, Turin, and Rome. There are around six flights a day from Rome. Flights go to Catania at least once a day from Milan, Pisa, Rome, and Turin.

BY TRAIN   From Rome, the express train takes 13 hours; the intercity train, 11 hours. A one-way ticket on the express costs 68,900 lire ($44.10), and 92,600 lire ($59.25) on the intercity train. Most visitors, however, take the train from Naples, an 11-hour journey on an express train or a 9-hour journey on an intercity. From Naples, a one-way ticket on the express train costs 54,700 lire ($35), and 74,900 lire ($47.95) on the intercity train.

HEADING SOUTH BY CAR   You won't have the transportation headache that plagued Goethe. The Autostrada del Sole stretches all the way from Milan to Reggio di Calabria, sticking out on the "big toe," the gateway to Sicily.

Until they build a bridge, you must take a ferryboat from Villa San Giovanni or Reggio di Calabria to Messina, costing 1,500 lire (95¢) per passenger. Vessels of the state railway ferry leave daily from 3:20am to 10:05pm, and it takes less than an hour to cross. The cost for ferrying your car along with you depends on the size of the vehicle.

BY HYDROFOIL (NO CAR)   Much quicker, shaving at least 22 minutes off the crossing time, is an *aliscafo* (hydrofoil) leaving from Reggio di Calabria. You'll pay 4,000 lire ($2.55) one-way, and the higher price usually means fewer passengers— hence, less crowding. You cannot take your vehicle on a hydrofoil. Call 0965/898123, 0965/894003, or 0965/29568 for various connections.

Near Reggio di Calabria, incidentally, is a much smaller community, Scilla, famous in Homeric legend. Mariners of old, including Ulysses, crossed the Strait of Messina from here, and faced the double menace of the two monsters, Charybdis and Scylla.

FROM NAPLES TO SICILY BY SEA   The night ferry from Naples leaves at 8pm, arriving in Palermo the next morning at 7am. On Friday there's another departure at 10pm. The service is run by **Tirrenia S.A.** For information, call the company's office in Naples (☎ **081/761-3688**). If you're already in Palermo and want to take the ferry to Naples, dial 091/333300; unfortunately, you won't always find someone who speaks English. Sleeping compartments are often booked days in advance, and there may be space available only on deck. The cost for an average car on the ferry is 110,000 lire ($70.40). First-class passage costs 91,000 lire ($58.25) per person for a one-way ticket, 71,000 lire ($45.45) in second class.

1 Palermo

145 miles W of Messina

As the ferryboat docks in the Bay of Palermo, and you start spotting blond, blue-eyed *bambini* all over the place, don't be surprised. If fair-haired children don't fit your conception of what a Sicilian should look like, remember that the Normans landed here in 1060, six years before William the Conqueror put in at Hastings, and launched a campaign to wrest control of the island from the Arabs. Both elements were to cross cultures, a manifestation still seen today in Palermo's architecture—a unique style, Norman-Arabic.

The city is the largest port of Sicily, its capital, and the meeting place of a regional parliament granted numerous autonomous powers in postwar Italy. Against a backdrop of the citrus-studded Conca d'Oro plain and Monte Pellegrino, it's a city of wide boulevards, old quarters in the legendary Sicilian style (laundry lapping against the wind, smudge-faced kids playing in the street), town houses, architecturally harmonious squares, baroque palaces, and modern buildings (many erected as a result of Allied bombings in 1943). It also has the worst traffic jams in Sicily.

Palermo was founded by the Phoenicians, but it has known many conquerors, some of whom established courts of great splendor (Frederick II), others of whom brought decay (the Angevins).

ESSENTIALS

GETTING THERE   By Plane   If you fly from Rome or Naples, you'll land at **Cinisi-Punta Raisi** (☎ **091/591414**), 19 miles west of Palermo. It's best to catch a local airport bus from the airport to piazza Castelnuovo; the fare is 4,500 lire ($2.90). For the same trip a taxi is likely to charge at least 60,000 lire ($38.40)—more if the driver thinks he can get away with it.

By Train   The **train station** in Palermo is on piazza G. Cesare (☎ **091/616-1806** for information), on the eastern side of town.

By Bus   Palermo has bus connections with other major cities in Italy, operated by **SAIS** (☎ **091/616-6028**). Some 16 buses a day make the $2^1/_2$-hour trip from Catania, at a one-way cost of 16,000 lire ($10.25). One bus a day (except Sunday) arrives from Syracuse; the trip lasts 4 hours and costs 20,000 lire ($12.80) one-way.

By Car   After your arrival from mainland Italy at Messina, head west on autostrada A20, which becomes Route 113, then A20 again, and finally A19 before its final approach to Palermo.

VISITOR INFORMATION   There are tourist information offices at strategic points, including the Palermo airport. The principal office, however, is the **Azienda Autonoma Turismo,** piazza Castelnuovo 34 (☎ **091/583847**), open Monday to Friday from 8am to 8pm and on Saturday from 8am to 2pm.

GETTING AROUND   Most municipally operated buses in Palermo charge 1,500 lire (95¢) for a ticket. Most passengers purchase their tickets at tobacco shops (*tabacchi*) before getting on. Otherwise, you'll need some 100-lira coins handy.

FAST FACTS: PALERMO

American Express   The agent for American Express is Giovanni Ruggieri e Figli, via Emerico Amari 40 (☎ 091/587144), which is open Monday to Friday from 9am to 1pm and 4 to 7pm and on Saturday from 9am to 1pm.

Consulate   You'll find the **U.S. Consular Agency** at via Re Federico 18 bis, 90141 Palermo (☎ **091/611-0020**), open Monday to Friday from 9am to 1pm.

Crime   Be especially alert. Some citizens here are the most skilled pickpockets on the continent. Keep your gems locked away (in other words, don't flaunt any sign of wealth). Women who carry handbags are especially vulnerable to purse-snatchers on Vespas (wear the strap over both shoulders with the purse hanging on the wall side of the sidewalk). Don't leave valuables in your car. In fact, we almost want to say don't leave your car alone, even knowing how impossible that is unless you put it in a garage (highly recommendable). Police squads operate mobile centers through the town to help combat street crime.

Emergencies   To call police, report a fire, or summon an ambulance, dial **113.**

Post Office   The major post office is at via Roma 322 (☎ 091/589737) and is open Monday to Saturday from 8:15am to 7pm.

THE TOP SIGHTS

"The four corners" of the city, the **Quattro Canti di Città,** is in the heart of the old town, at the junction of corso Vittorio Emanuele and via Maqueda. The ruling Spanish of the 17th century influenced the design of this grandiose baroque square, replete with fountains and statues. From here you can walk to **piazza Bellini,** the most attractive plaza of the old city. In an atmosphere reminiscent of the setting for an operetta, you're likely to hear strolling singers with guitars entertaining pizza eaters. Opening onto it is the **Church of Santa Maria dell'Ammiraglio** (also known as "La Martorana"), piazza Bellini 3 (☎ **091/616-1692**), erected in 1143 with a Byzantine cupola by an admiral to Roger II. Its decaying but magnificent bell tower was built from 1146 to 1185. It's open Monday to Saturday from 9:30am to 1pm and 3:30 to 5:30pm and on Sunday from 9:30am to 1pm. Admission is free.

Also fronting the square are the **Church of San Cataldo,** erected in 1160 in the Arab-Byzantine style with a trio of faded pink cupolas, and the Church of Santa Caterina, from the 16th century.

Adjoining the square is **piazza Pretoria,** dominated by a fountain designed in Florence in 1554 for a villa, but acquired by Palermo about 20 years later. A short walk will take you to the cathedral of Palermo.

Cathedral of Palermo. Corso Vittorio Emanuele. ☎ **091/334376.** Free admission. Apr–Oct, daily 7am–noon and 4–7pm; Nov–Mar, daily 7am–noon and 4–6pm. Bus: 3, 24, 101, 102, or 104.

This cathedral is a curious spectacle where East meets West. It was built in the 12th century on the foundation of an earlier basilica that had been converted by the Arabs into a mosque. The cathedral—much altered over the centuries—was founded by an English archbishop known as Walter of the Mill. The impressive "porch" was built in the 15th century on the southern front in the Gothic style. But the cupola, added in the late 18th century, detracts from the overall appearance, and the interior was revamped unsuccessfully at the same time, resulting in a glaring incongruity in styles. The "pantheon" of royal tombs includes that of the emperor Frederick II, in red porphyry under a canopy of marble.

San Giovanni degli Eremiti. Via dei Benedettini Bianchi 3. ☎ **091/651-5019.** Free admission. Mon–Sat 9am–1pm, Sun 9am–12:30pm. Bus: 104, 105, 108, or 109.

The other church worthy of note is Saint John of the Hermits. Perhaps in an atmosphere appropriate for the recluse it honors, this little church with its twin-columned cloister is one of the most idyllic spots in all of Palermo. A medieval veil hangs heavy in the gardens, with their citrus blossoms and flowers, especially on a hot summer day as you wander around in its cloister. Ordered built by Roger II in 1132, the church adheres to its Arabic influence, surmounted by pinkish cupolas, while showing the Norman style as well.

✪ **Palazzo di Normanni.** Piazza del Parlamento. ☎ **091/656-1879.** Free admission. Tours of the palace given by advance reservation only. Chapel, Mon–Fri 9am–noon and 3–5pm, Sat–Sun 9am–noon. Bus: 104, 105, 108, or 109.

This Palace of the Normans contains one of the greatest art treasures in Sicily, the Cappella Palatina (Palatine Chapel). Erected at the request of Roger II in the 1130s, it's the finest example of the Arabic-Norman style of design and building. The effect of the mosaics inside is awe-inspiring. Almond-eyed biblical characters from the Byzantine art world in lush colors create a panorama of epic pageantry, illustrating such Gospel scenes as the Nativity. The overall picture is further enhanced by inlaid marble and mosaics and pillars made of granite shipped from the East. For a look at still more mosaics, this time in a more secular vein depicting scenes of the hunt, you can visit the Hall of Roger II upstairs, the seat of the Sicilian Parliament, where security is likely to be tight. Visitors are taken through on guided tours.

Galleria Regionale della Sicilia. Via Alloro 4. ☎ **091/616-4317.** Admission 2,000 lire ($1.30) adults, free for children 17 and under and for seniors 60 and over. Mon, Wed, Fri, and Sat 9am–1:30pm; Tues and Thurs 9am–1:30pm and 3–5:30pm; Sun 9am–12:30pm. Bus: 101, 102, 104, 105, or 107.

The Palazzo Abatellis was built in the Gothic and Renaissance styles. Today it houses the Regional Gallery, which shows the evolution of art in Sicily from the 13th to the 18th century. On the ground floor is a most famous work, a 15th-century fresco *Triumph of Death,* in all its gory magnificence. A horseback-riding skeleton, representing death, tramples his victims under hoof. Worthy of mention are three majolica plates, valuable specimens of Loza dorada manufactured in the workshops of Manises, and the Giara manufactured in the workshops of Málaga at the end of the 13th century.

Francesco Laurana's slanty-eyed *Eleonora d'Aragona* is worth seeking out, as are seven grotesque D'Roleries painted on wood. Of the paintings on the second floor, *L'Annunziata* by Antonello da Messina, a portrait of the Madonna with depth and originality, is one of the most celebrated paintings in Italy. The 13th room contains a very good series of Flemish paintings from the 15th and 16th centuries, among which the best is the *Trittico Malvagna* by Jean Gossaert, called Mabuse.

✪ **Museo Regionale Archeologico.** Piazza Olivella 4. ☎ **091/662-0220.** Admission 2,000 lire ($1.30). Mon, Wed–Thurs, and Sat 9am–1:30pm; Tues and Fri 9am–1:30pm and 3–6pm; Sun 9am–1pm. Bus: 101, 102, 107, or 122.

Located in a former convent, this is one of the greatest archeological collections in southern Italy, where the competition's stiff. Many works displayed here were excavated at Selinunte, once one of the major towns in Magna Graecia (Greater Greece). See, in particular, the Sala di Selinunte, displaying the celebrated metopes that adorned the classical temples, as well as slabs of bas-relief. The gallery also owns important sculpture from the Temple of Himera. The collection of bronzes is exceptional, including the athlete and the stag discovered in the ruins of Pompeii (a Roman copy of a Greek original) and a bronze ram that came from Syracuse, dating from the 3rd century B.C. Among the Greek sculpture is *The Pouring Satyr,* excavated at Pompeii (a Roman copy of a Greek original by Praxiteles).

✪ **Catacombe Cappuccini.** Piazza Cappuccini 1. ☎ **091/212117.** Free admission (donations accepted). Tours, Mon–Sat 9am–noon and 3–5pm, Sun and holidays 9am–noon. Bus: 327 from piazza Castelnuovo or 105 from Stazione Centrale.

The final attraction, on the outskirts of the city, is the most bizarre of all. The fresco you might have seen in the Galleria Regionale della Sicilia, *Triumph of Death,* dims by comparison to the real thing. The catacombs, it was discovered, contained a preservative that helped to mummify dead people. Sicilians, everyone from nobles to maids, were buried here in the 19th century, and it was the custom on Sunday to go and visit Uncle Luigi to see how he was holding together. If he fell apart, he was wired together again or wrapped in burlap sacking. The last person buried in the catacombs was placed to rest in 1920—a little girl almost lifelike in death. But many Sicilians of the 19th century are in fine shape, considering—with eyes, hair, and even clothing fairly intact (the convent could easily be turned into a museum of costume). Some of the expressions on the faces of the skeletons take the fun out of Halloween—a grotesque ballet. The catacombs may be visited on guided tours.

WHERE TO STAY

Generally you'll find a poor lot of hostelries, aided by only a few fine choices. Hunt and pick carefully.

EXPENSIVE

Villa Igiea Grand Hotel. Via Belmonte 43, 90142 Palermo. ☎ **091/543744.** Fax 091/547654. 117 rms, 6 suites. A/C MINIBAR TV TEL. 350,000 lire ($224) double; from 600,000 lire ($384) suite. Rates include breakfast. AE, DC, MC, V. Free parking. Bus: 139, 603, or 731.

This deluxe hotel was originally built at the turn of the century as one of Sicily's great aristocratic estates, and today it's one of the top two luxury hotels on the island (it lags behind the San Domenico in Taormina). The exterior resembles a medieval Sicilian fortress whose carefully chiseled walls include crenellated battlements and forbidding watchtowers. It was constructed of the same buff-colored stone that Greek colonists used during the Punic Wars when they erected a circular temple which, although heavily buttressed with modern scaffolding, still stands in the garden. Nearby, nestled amid a grove of pines and palms, is an art nouveau statue of Igiea, goddess of flowers. Everywhere are clusters of antiques. The accommodations vary from sumptuous suites with private terraces to rooms of lesser size and glamour. The hotel, reached by passing through an industrial portside north of Palermo, sits on a cliff with a view of the open sea.

Dining/Entertainment: The hotel's bar is baronial, with a soaring stone vault. You dine on Sicilian and classic Italian meals in a grand and glittering room against a backdrop of paneled walls, ornate ceilings, and chandeliers.

Services: Room service, baby-sitting, laundry, valet.

Facilities: Terrace overlooking the water, swimming pool, tennis court.

MODERATE

Albergo Cavour. Via Alessandro Manzoni 11, 90133 Palermo. ☎ **091/616-2759.** 9 rms, 4 with bath (tub or shower). 45,000 lire ($28.80) double without bath, 55,000 lire ($35.20) double with bath. No credit cards. Parking 10,000 lire ($6.40). Bus: Any bus to the Termini.

The Albergo Cavour is on the fifth floor of a 1920s building conveniently located in front of the central station. The rooms are suitable for overnight stopovers, and the manager sees to it that they're well kept and decently furnished, with comfortable mattresses on the beds. No meals are served, but many cafes are nearby.

Grande Albergo Sole. Corso Vittorio Emanuele 291, 90133 Palermo. ☎ **091/581811.** Fax 091/611-0182. 150 rms. A/C MINIBAR TV TEL. 200,000 lire ($128) double. Rates include breakfast. AE, DC, MC, V. Parking 10,000 lire ($6.40). Bus: 101, 104, or 107.

This pleasant, second-class hotel lies in the busy historic center of Palermo. A 1960s remake of a century-old building, it houses a helpful staff and simple and uncomplicated bedrooms, each with radio and modern furniture. There's a residents' lounge, a bar, a restaurant, and a roof garden terrace for sunbathing.

⑤ Hotel Sausele. Via Vincenzo Errante 12, 90127 Palermo. ☎ **091/616-1308.** Fax 091/616-7525. 36 rms. TEL. 135,000 lire ($86.40) double. Rates include breakfast. AE, DC, MC, V. Parking 15,000 lire ($9.60). Bus: Any bus to the Termini.

This hotel near the railway station is the best in a run-down area. It's owned and managed efficiently by Swiss-born Signora Sausele, who has created a clean establishment. It's a modest but quite pleasant albergo, with bedrooms just adequate for a good night's rest. The hotel has an elevator, garage, bar, and TV room. The lounges are air-conditioned.

Jolly Hotel del Foro Italico. Foro Italico 22, 90133 Palermo. ☎ **091/616-5090,** or 800/221-2626 in the U.S., 800/247-1277 in Canada. Fax 091/616-1441. 268 rms, 5 suites. A/C MINIBAR TV. 195,000–225,000 lire ($124.80–$144) double; 225,000 lire ($144) suite. Rates include breakfast. Half board 43,000 lire ($27.50) per person extra. AE, DC, MC, V. Free parking. Bus: 3 or 24.

Off a busy boulevard (the Foro Italico, facing the Gulf of Palermo), this aging 1960s six-story hotel invites with shafts of pale blue supporting triangular balconies. Try for the quieter bedrooms on the upper floors or at the rear. One of the best hotels in town (popular for Sicilian wedding receptions), it offers a contemporary atmosphere and good accommodations. The public rooms have bright colors and serviceable furnishings. The well-organized bedrooms have lots of built-in pieces and comfortable beds. The bedrooms on the top floors provide you with at least a glimpse of the Mediterranean. The Jolly also has a garden, a pool, a restaurant, and an American bar. The food is both Sicilian and Italian.

President Hotel. Via Francesco Crispi 230, 90139 Palermo. ☎ **091/580733.** Fax 091/611-1588. 129 rms. A/C TV TEL. 160,000 ($102.40) double. Rates include breakfast. AE, DC, MC, V. Parking 6,000 lire ($3.85). Bus: 139.

Its eight-story concrete-and-glass facade rising above the harborfront quays, this is one of the better and more up-to-date of the middle-bracket hotels in town, superior to the Grande Albergo Sole. Built in 1978, it was renovated in the early 1990s. You'll pass beneath the facade's soaring arcade before entering the informal stone-trimmed lobby. One of the most appealing coffee shop/bars in town lies at the top of a short flight of stairs next to the reception area. There's a panoramic restaurant on the uppermost floor, plus a guarded parking garage in the basement. The bedrooms are comfortably furnished, each with a radio and TV, although short on style.

WHERE TO DINE
MODERATE

◑ L'Approdo da Renato. Via Messina Marine 224. ☎ **091/630-2881.** Reservations required Fri–Sat. Main courses 18,000–25,000 lire ($11.50–$16). AE, MC, V. Mon–Sat 12:30–3pm and 8–11pm. Closed Aug 10–25. Bus: 101 or 107. SICILIAN.

This restaurant lies in an elegant villa originally built in 1880. From its dining room, or from its flowering outdoor terrace, you'll have a view over the Gulf of Palermo. Run by a husband-and-wife team, it's infused with gaiety. Some visitors are invited to explore the wine cellar, whose contents are said to rival the best in all of Italy. The kitchen adheres to time-tested Sicilian recipes, and the menu depends on the season and the finest of available ingredients at any given time. Nearly all diners begin with a selection of authentic Sicilian antipasti, both vegetarian and seafood, with tuna factored in somehow. You never know what dishes will be offered, but memorable past meals have included fresh fish marinated in refined olive oil and flavored with herbs, crêpes filled with seafood, swordfish in a mandarin orange sauce, and roast goat flavored with Sicilian herbs.

Charleston. Piazzale Ungheria 30. ☎ **091/321366.** Reservations required. Main courses 28,000–30,000 lire ($17.90–$19.20). AE, DC, MC, V. Mon–Sat 1–3 or 4pm and 8–11:30pm. Closed June–Sept. Bus: 101 or 107. SICILIAN/INTERNATIONAL.

For years Charleston was regarded as the finest restaurant in Sicily, although today there's far more competition for that title. Nevertheless, it remains a national culinary monument of Sicilian hospitality and old-fashioned virtues, an appealing choice in Palermo. The owners create a refined and perfect milieu for their presentation of Sicilian dishes, which naturally concentrate on fresh fish. The kitchen prepares a number of international dishes as well.

Gourmand's. Via della Libertà. ☎ **091/323431.** Reservations recommended. Main courses 14,000–18,000 lire ($8.95–$11.50). AE, DC, MC, V. Mon–Sat 1–3pm and 8–11pm. Closed Aug 5–25. SICILIAN.

Gourmand's is among the best restaurants in Palermo for an introduction to the rich, aromatic cookery of Sicily. The cuisine is on par with that of Charleston, although the atmophere is less elegant. A corner restaurant in the commercial district of town, it's a light and airy room filled with original paintings and Chinese-red ceiling lattices. You'll admire the richly laden antipasto table before you're ushered to your table. For a first course, try spaghetti Gourmand's or an involtino of eggplant. Fresh fish is always available—try it grilled. The chef does many Italian dishes well, including veal escalope in the Valdostan style and pepper steak or, if available, roast quail. Risotto with salmon is often featured on the menu, as is rigatoni Henry IV.

La Scuderia. Viale del Fante 9. ☎ **091/520323.** Reservations recommended. Main courses 18,000–40,000 lire ($11.50–$25.60). AE, DC, MC, V. Mon–Sat 12:30–3pm and 8:30pm–midnight. Closed 2 weeks in Aug. Bus: 101 or 107. INTERNATIONAL/ITALIAN.

Dedicated professionals direct this appealing restaurant surrounded by trees at the foot of Monte Pellegrino, north of the city center and directly south of Parco della Favorita. It's the only restaurant in Palermo to equal the cuisine of Gourmand's and Charleston. The inside is augmented in summer with one of the prettiest flowering terraces in town, sought after by everyone from erstwhile lovers to extended families to glamour queens in for a holiday. The sound of falling water, followed by the tunes of a piano player, greet you as you enter. The imaginative cuisine includes a mixed grill of fresh vegetables with a healthy dose of a Sicilian cheese called caciocavallo, along with stuffed turkey cutlet, a wide array of beef and veal dishes, involtini of eggplant, risotto with seafood, veal spiedino, and many tempting desserts, including one known as pernice all'erotica.

INEXPENSIVE

Ⓢ **Al Vicolo.** Cortile Scimecaz. ☎ **091/651-2464.** Reservations recommended. Main courses 10,000–13,000 lire ($6.40–$8.30); fixed-price menu 24,000 lire ($15.35). No credit cards. Mon–Sat 12:30–3pm and 7–11:30pm. Closed Aug 10–25. SICILIAN.

Located off piazza San Francesco Saverio, this is one of the most characteristic trattorie of the city, and deserves more acclaim than it receives. The dining rooms were converted from a former produce warehouse. For antipasti, you might prefer panelle (chickpea or garbanzo fritters) and arancini (rice croquettes) or potato croquettes. As the friendly waiters will point out, if you order too much of these tasty but starchy appetizers you won't have room for the main course. That's all too true, especially if you also select sardines à beccafico (stuffed and flavored with laurel) or squid in a savory sauce as part of your antipasti. They serve many of the most typical dishes of Sicily, including pasta mixed with sardines and wild fennel—for some, an acquired taste, for the devotee of Sicilian cuisine, reason enough to visit the restaurant. Any pasta labeled "alla Norma" comes with vine-ripened tomatoes and eggplant. The local fish is fresh and abundant, and local meats including lamb and kid are always offered. You can wash down the meal—Sicilians say "irrigate"—with a selection of regional wines.

Ⓢ **Friend's Bar.** Via Brunelleschi 138, Borgo Nuovo. ☎ **091/201401.** Reservations required. Main courses 19,000–24,000 lire ($12.15–$15.35). AE, DC, MC, V. Tues–Sun 1–3pm and 8– 10pm. Closed Aug 16–31. Bus: 513 or 540. SICILIAN.

This is one of the finest restaurants in Palermo, located in a suburb called Borgo Nuovo. A meal here is an event to many Sicilians. Friend's Bar has become one of the sought-after places on the island, and a reservation for one of the garden seats is almost essential to get past the bar. First, you might enjoy a few of the many delicacies from the antipasto table, followed by one of the many regional specialties such as subtly flavored pastas, and an array of steamed or grilled fish dishes or one of the meat dishes that have made this place so well known locally. The house wine (red) is a good accompaniment for most any meal.

PALERMO AFTER DARK

We always like to begin our evening by heading to the century-old **Caffè Mazzara,** via Generale Magliocco 15 (☎ **091/321443**), where you can sample Sicilian ice cream—among the best in the world—and order the richest coffee in all the country. Or perhaps you'll prefer to sit quietly, sipping the heady Sicilian wines in the corner where Giuseppe di Lampedusa in the late 1950s wrote a great many chapters of his novel *The Leopard.* Besides an espresso bar and pastry shop on the first floor, there's a so-called American grill on the second floor as well as the prestigious Restaurant Charleston. If you can't find a place to eat in Palermo on a Sunday, when virtually everything is shut, the Mazzara is a good bet. It's open daily from 7:30am to 10pm. Cappuccino costs 2,200 lire ($1.40) at the bar.

SIDE TRIPS FROM PALERMO
MONREALE

The town of Monreale is 6 miles from Palermo, up Monte Caputo and on the edge of the Conca d'Oro plain. If you don't have a car, you can reach it by taking bus no. 389 from piazza Indipendenza in Palermo. The Normans under William II founded a Benedictine monastery at Monreale some time in the 1170s. Near the ruins of that monastery a great cathedral was erected.

As with the Alhambra in Granada, Spain, the ✪ **Church of Monreale** has a relatively drab facade, giving little indication of the riches inside. The interior is virtually covered throughout with shimmering mosaics, illustrating scenes from the Bible, such as the story of Adam and Eve and Noah and the Ark. The artwork provides a distinctly original interpretation of the old, rigid Byzantine form of decoration. The mosaics make for an Eastern look despite the Western-style robed Christ reigning over his kingdom. The ceiling is ornate, even gaudy. On the north and west facade of the church are two bronze doors in relief depicting biblical stories. The cloisters are also of interest. Built in 1166, they consist of twin mosaic columns, every other pair an original design (the lava inlay was hauled from the active volcano, Mount Etna). The church and cloisters are open April to September, Monday to Saturday from 9am to 7pm and on Sunday from 9am to 1pm; October to March, Monday to Saturday from 9am to 1pm and on Sunday from 9am to 2:30pm. Admission is 2,000 lire ($1.30).

You can also visit the treasury and the terraces, each charging another 2,000 lire ($1.30) for admission. They're open from 8:30am to 12:30pm and 3 to 6:30pm. The terraces are actually the rooftop of the church, from which you'll be rewarded with a view of the cloisters.

Where to Stay

Ⓢ **Park Hotel Carrubella.** Corso Umberto 1, 90046 Monreale. ☎ **091/640-2188.** Fax 091/640-2189. 30 rms. A/C TEL. 104,000 lire ($66.55) double. AE, DC, MC, V. Free parking.

The aging Park Hotel is one of the tallest buildings in town, its terraces providing a sweeping view over the famous church, the surrounding valleys, and the azure coastline of faraway Palermo. To reach it, follow a one-lane road from the piazza near the church along a serpentine series of terraces; the hotel is 800 yards from the cathedral. The spacious but tattered interior is filled with luxurious mirrors and deep and comfortable armchairs, along with scattered pieces of sculpture. In the public rooms, as well as in the bedrooms, the floors are covered with rows of Sicilian tiles hand-painted into flowery designs. The hotel offers comfortably furnished accommodations, each with its own balcony. Well-prepared meals are served in the conservatively elegant dining room.

Where to Dine

La Botte. Contrada Lenzitti 416 (SS186). ☎ **091/414051.** Reservations required. Main courses 16,000–22,000 lire ($10.25–$14.10). AE, DC, MC, V. Daily 8–10:45pm, Sat–Sun 1–2:45pm and 8–10:45pm. Closed June 20–Sept 20. Bus: 309 or 389 from Palermo. SICILIAN/ITALIAN.

Most of the dishes are derived from ancient recipes of Palermo, whose origins have long been forgotten. Perhaps you'll begin with an aromatic antipasto of such local ingredients as artichokes, tuna, or shrimp. Pasta specialties are always smooth choices, followed by creative Sicilian meat dishes. This is the best restaurant in the area—everything else is a simple tavern.

MONDELLO LIDO

When the summer sun burns hot and old men on the square seek a place in the shade and *bambini* tire of their toys, it's beach weather. For the denizen of Palermo, that means Mondello, $7^1/_2$ miles to the east. Originally, before this beachfront started attracting the wealthy class of Palermo, it was a fishing village (it still is), and you can see rainbow-colored fishing boats bobbing up in the harbor. A sandy beach, a good one, stretches for about a mile and a half, and it's filled to capacity on a July or August day. You might call it a Palermitan seaside experience. Some women traveling alone have found Mondello more inviting and less intimidating than downtown Palermo. In summer an express bus (no. 6, "Beallo") leaves for Mondello from the central train station in Palermo.

Where to Stay

✪ **Mondello Palace Hotel.** Viale Prìncipe di Scalea 2, 90151 Mondello. ☎ **091/450001.** Fax 091/450657. 83 rms, 10 suites. A/C MINIBAR TV TEL. 250,000 lire ($160) double; from 360,000 lire ($230.40) suite. Rates include breakfast. AE, DC, MC, V. Free parking. Bus: 614 or 615 from Palermo.

Set in a garden of palms and semitropical shrubs across the coastal road from the beach, this is the most visible, the best, and most famous hotel in Mondello. Originally built in 1950, and renovated several times since then, it offers four stories of airy and comfortable bedrooms outfitted in tones of blue, red, and white. All double rooms have balconies and sea views. Clients of yesteryear have included Sophia Loren and Luchino Visconti; today the place might house families vacationing en masse from the hinterlands of Sicily or northern Europe. There's a large swimming pool set into the garden, a bar, and a sea-view indoor/outdoor restaurant serving full meals.

Splendid Hotel la Torre. Via Piano di Gallo 11, 90151 Mondello. ☎ **091/450222.** Fax 091/450033. 170 rms. A/C TV TEL. 189,000 lire ($120.95) double; 255,000 lire ($163.20) triple. Rates include breakfast. AE, DC, MC, V. Free parking. Bus: 614 or 615 from Palermo.

Built in 1962 and renovated in 1984, this four-story hotel beside the beach lies half a mile north of Mondello's center. From your comfortable bed you can get up and walk out onto a private terrace overlooking the sea. Like any Mediterranean resort hotel, La Torre is crowded during the peak summer months, so reservations are important. Some of the well-furnished chambers are quite spacious. All are well maintained (at least the 14 units we recently inspected with a maid who wanted to show us everything, including the linen closet). During the day there are many sports and recreational activities to occupy your time, including swimming pools, a tennis court, a garden, and plenty of games for children. La Torre is very much a family resort, not a romantic retreat. It attracts some heavy drinkers as well—the bar opens at 9am, staying open until 1am. The place is not a gourmet haven, but we've enjoyed our meals here, especially the pasta and fish dishes. The cookery is quite good, the choice is ample, and the staff takes good care of you.

Where to Dine

○ **Charleston le Terrazze.** Viale Regina Elena. ☎ **091/450171.** Reservations required. Main courses 28,000–30,000 lire ($17.90–$19.20). AE, DC, MC, V. Daily 1–3pm and 8–11pm. Closed Oct–May. Bus: 614 or 615 from Palermo. SICILIAN/INTERNATIONAL.

The best food in Mondello is served at this buff-colored seaside fantasy of art nouveau, with spires and gingerbread detailing. The kitchen, fortunately, matches the delights of the eye. The Sicilian staff add to the sense of luxury and refinement—but bring lots of money. The chef specializes in many dishes, including such favorites as melanzana (eggplant) Charleston (in our modest opinion, the Sicilians do the best eggplant dishes in the world). Try also the pesce spada (swordfish) al gratin and scaloppe Conca d'Oro. For dessert, you can have a smooth finish by ordering a parfait di caffè. For a wine, we recommend a Corvo, which comes both bianco and rosso. Of course, with a name like Le Terrazze it's got to deliver the mandatory terrace with a view.

CEFALÙ

For another day's excursion, we recommend a trek east from Palermo for 43 miles to this fishing village, which is known all over Europe for its Romanesque cathedral, an outstanding achievement of the Arab-Norman architectural style. Two SAIS buses a day connect Palermo to Cefalù.

What to See & Do

Il Duomo. Piazza de Duomo, off corso Ruggero. ☎ **0921/922021.** Free admission. Daily 9am–noon and 3:30–7pm.

Resembling a military fortress, the Duomo was built by Roger II to fulfill a vow he made when faced with a possible shipwreck. Construction began in 1131, and in time two square towers dotted the landscape of Cefalù, curiously placed between the sea and a rocky promontory. The architectural line of the cathedral has a severe elegance, and inside are some outstanding Byzantine-inspired mosaics. Seek out especially Christ the Pantocrator in the dome of the apse.

Museo Mandralisca. Via Mandralisca. ☎ **0921/21547.** Admission 5,000 lire ($3.20). Summer, daily 9am–12:30pm and 3:30–7pm; winter, daily 9am–12:30pm and 3:30–6pm.

Before leaving town, try to visit this museum opposite the cathedral, with its outstanding collection of art, none more notable than the 1470 portrait of an unknown by Antennal Messina. Some art critics have journeyed all the way down from Rome just to stare at this handsome work.

Where to Dine

Al Gabbiano da Saro. Viale Lungomare 17. ☎ **0921/21495.** Reservations recommended Sat–Sun. Main courses 10,000–30,000 lire ($6.40–$19.20). AE, DC, MC, V. June 15–Sept 15, daily noon–3pm and 7pm–midnight; Sept 16–June 14, Thurs–Tues noon–3pm and 7pm–midnight. Closed mid-Dec to mid-Jan. SEAFOOD/SICILIAN.

In a century-old building, this rustic seaside trattoria is typical of the area, attracting both locals and visitors in almost equal measure. Fresh fish is the item to order, making your way through a list of unpronounceable sea creatures. You might begin with zuppa di cozze, a savory mussel soup. The vegetables and pastas are good, too, especially pennette alla Norma (with eggplant). Involtini of swordfish is another specialty. The cookery is consistent, as is the service. If you speak a little Italian, it helps.

Da Nino al Lungomare. Viale Lungomare 11. ☎ **0921/22582.** Reservations required. Main courses 13,000–22,000 lire ($8.30–$14.10); fixed-price menu 21,000 lire ($13.45). AE, DC, MC, V. June–Sept, daily noon–3pm and 7–11pm; Oct–May, Wed–Mon noon–3pm and 7–11pm. Closed Nov. SOUTHERN ITALIAN/SICILIAN.

In a century-old building, this is a reasonably good choice for southern Italian and Sicilian cuisine. That means that the kitchen is in no way influenced by trends or food fads. Time-tested recipes are served here, including a delectable risotto marinara (fisher's rice) and an involtini of meat. Fresh fish, however, is the featured item.

2 Segesta

41 miles SW of Palermo, 91 miles NW of Agrigento

Segesta was the ancient city of the Elymi, a people of mysterious origin, although they've been linked by some to the Trojans. As the major city in western Sicily, it was brought into a series of conflicts with the rival power nearby, Selinus (Selinunte). From the 6th through the 5th century B.C. there were near-constant hostilities. The Athenians came from the east to aid the Segestans in 415 B.C., but the expedition ended in disaster, forcing the city to turn eventually for help to Hannibal of Carthage.

Twice in the 4th century B.C. it was besieged and conquered, once by Dionysius and again by Agathocles, the latter a particularly brutal victor who tortured, mutilated, or made slaves of most of the citizenry. Recovering eventually, Segesta in time turned on its old (but dubious) ally, Carthage. Like all Greek cities of Sicily, it ultimately fell to the Romans.

ESSENTIALS

GETTING THERE   By Train   Trains leave Palermo, bound for Segesta, at 6:50am. They make the return trip at 1pm. For information, call 091/617-3456.

By Bus   If you're going to see one of the classical plays (see below), you can take a bus from piazza Politeama in Palermo approximately 2 hours before the show is presented. For information, call 091/616-7919.

By Car   Drive west from Palermo along autostrada A29.

VISITOR INFORMATION   Consult the tourist information office in Palermo (see Section 1 of this chapter).

EXPLORING ANCIENT RUINS & ATTENDING CLASSICAL PLAYS

Visit Segesta for its remarkable ✪ **Doric temple,** dating from the 5th century B.C. Although never completed, it's in an excellent state of preservation (the entablature still remains). The temple was far enough away from the ancient town to have escaped leveling during the "scorched earth" days of the Vandals and Arabs.

From its position on a lonely hill, the Doric temple commands a majestic setting. Although you can scale the hill on foot, you're likely to encounter Sicilian boys trying to hustle you for a donkey ride. From mid-July until the first of August, **classical plays** are performed at the temple. Ask at the tourist information office in Palermo for details. Local travel agents in Palermo sell tickets for 15,000 to 25,000 lire ($9.60 to $16).

In another spot on Mount Barbaro, a theater, built in the Greek style into the rise of the hill, has been excavated. It was erected in the 3rd century B.C.

There's a cafe in the parking area leading to the temple; otherwise, Segesta is bereft of dining or accommodation selections.

3 Selinunte

76 miles SW of Palermo, 70 miles W of Agrigento

One of the lost cities of ancient Sicily, ✪ **Selinunte** traces its history to the 7th century B.C. when immigrants from Megara Hyblaea (Syracuse) set out to build a new colony. They succeeded, erecting a city of power and prestige adorned with many temples. But that was like calling attention to a good thing. As earlier mentioned, much of Selinunte's fate was tied up with seemingly endless conflicts with the Elymi people of Segesta. Siding with Selinunte's rival, Hannibal virtually leveled the city in 409 B.C. The city never recovered its former glory, and fell into ultimate decay.

ESSENTIALS

GETTING THERE   By Train   From Palermo, Trapani, or Marsala, you can make rail connections to Castelvetrano. Once at Castelvetrano, you must board a bus for Selinunte. Most passengers reach Selinunte from Palermo (call 091/616-1806 or 091/617-3456 in Palermo for information).

By Bus   Buses (about five per day) depart from in front of the rail terminal at Castelvetrano. A one-way fare is 2,000 lire ($1.30). For information, call 091/617-5411.

By Car   Selinunte is on the southern coast of Sicily and is best explored by car, as public transportation is awkward. From Segesta, continue south on autostrada A29 until Castelvetrano. From there, follow the signposted secondary road marked SELINUNTE which leads south to the sea.

VISITOR INFORMATION   There are no tourist offices in the area.

AN ARCHEOLOGICAL GARDEN

Today Selinute's temples lie in scattered ruins, the mellowed stone, the color of honey, littering the ground as if an earthquake had struck (as one did in ancient times). From 9am to dusk daily you can walk through the monument zone, exploring such relics as the remains of the Acropolis, the heart of old Selinunte. Parts of it have been partially excavated and reconstructed, as much as is possible with the bits and fragments remaining. Admission is 2,000 lire ($1.30).

The temples, in varying states of preservation, are designated by letters. The Doric **Temple E** contains fragments of an inner temple. Standing on its ruins before the sun goes down, you can look across the water that washes up again on the shores of Africa, from which the Carthaginian fleet emerged to destroy the city. The temples are dedicated to such mythological figures as Apollo and Hera (Juno). Most of them date from the 6th and 5th centuries B.C. **Temple G,** in scattered ruins, was one of the largest erected in Sicily, and was also built in the Doric style.

WHERE TO STAY & DINE IN NEARBY MARINELLA

The site of the ruins of Selinunte contains virtually no hotels, restaurants, or watering holes of note. Most visitors stop at the temple for a daylight visit, heading on to other locales at night. There are a handful of overnight accommodations, however, in the little seafront village of Marinella, which lies about a mile east of Selinunte. To reach Marinella, you'll travel along a narrow country road lined in part with stone walls.

Hotel Alceste. Via Alceste 23, 91020 Marinella di Selinunte. ☎ **0924/46184.** Fax 0924/46143. 26 rms. A/C TV TEL. 65,000–90,000 lire ($41.60–$57.60) double. Rates include half board. AE, DC, MC, V. Closed Nov–Feb. Free parking on street.

After they erected the concrete walls of this hotel, the builders painted it a shade of sienna and filled its three-sided courtyard with dining tables and plants. This seasonal hotel is about a 15-minute walk from the ruins. The simple bedrooms each have private bath and phone. Most visitors, however, stop only for a meal, enjoying a regional dinner for 35,000 lire ($22.40) and up.

4 Agrigento

80 miles S of Palermo, 109 miles SE of Trapani

Greek colonists from Gela (Caltanissetta) named it Akragas when they established a beachhead here in the 6th century B.C. In time their settlement grew to become one of the most prosperous cities in Magna Graecia. A great deal of that growth is attributed to the despot Phalaris, who ruled from 571 to 555 B.C. and is said to have roasted his victims inside a brazen bull, eventually meeting the same fate himself.

Empedocles, the Greek philosopher and politician (also credited by some as the founder of medicine in Italy), was the most famous son of Akragas, born around 490 B.C. He formulated the four-elements theory (earth, fire, water, and air), modified by the agents love and strife. In modern times the town produced Luigi Pirandello, the playwright (*Six Characters in Search of an Author*) who won the Nobel Prize in literature in 1934.

Like nearby Selinunte, the city was attacked by war-waging Carthaginians, the first assault in 406 B.C. In the 3rd century B.C. the Carthaginians and Romans played Russian roulette with the city until it finally succumbed to Roman domination by 210 B.C. The city was then known as Agrigentium.

The modern part of the present town (in 1927 the name was changed from Girgenti to Agrigento) occupies a hill site. The narrow streets—casbahlike—date back to the influence of the conquering Saracens. Heavy Allied bombing in World War II necessitated much rebuilding.

Below the town stretch the long reaches of La Valle dei Templi, containing some of the greatest Greek ruins in the world.

ESSENTIALS

GETTING THERE   By Train   Eleven trains per day arrive from Palermo, taking 2 hours; a one-way ticket costs 11,700 lire ($7.50). For information about schedules, call 091/616-1806 in Palermo. If you're already on the east coast of

Sicily, the best connections are through Catania, with 10 trains per day arriving at Agrigento. Trip time is 3³/₄ hours, and a one-way ticket costs 20,800 lire ($13.30). In Catania, call 095/531625 for information.

By Bus   From Selinunte (see above), take the bus to Castelvetrano, at a one-way cost of 1,500 lire (95¢); then transfer to another bus bound for Agrigento. There are four daily buses from Castelvetrano to Agrigento. The trip takes ¹/₄ hours, and a one-way ticket costs 9,600 lire ($6.15). For information call 0922/20414.

By Car   From Palermo, cut southeast along Route 121, which becomes 188 and 189 before it finally reaches Agrigento and the Mediterranean.

VISITOR INFORMATION   The **tourist information center** is at via Cesare Battisti, 15 (☎ **0922/20454**), open Monday to Saturday from 9am to 1:45pm and 4 to 7pm.

WHAT TO SEE & DO

THE VALLEY OF THE TEMPLES   Many writers are fond of suggesting that Greek ruins be viewed at either dawn or sunset. Indeed, their mysterious aura is heightened then. But for details you can search them out under the bright cobalt-blue Sicilian sky. The backdrop for the temples is idyllic, especially in spring when the striking almond trees blossom into pink.

Riding out the strada Panoramica, you'll first approach (on your left), the ✪ **Temple of Juno (Giunone).** With many of its Doric columns now restored, this temple was erected sometime in the mid-5th century B.C., at the peak of a construction boom that skipped across the celestial globe honoring the deities. As you climb the blocks, note the remains of a cistern as well as a sacrificial altar in front. There are good views of the entire valley from the perch here.

The ✪ **Temple of Concord,** next, ranks along with the Temple of Hephaistos (the "Theseum") in Athens as the best-preserved Greek temple in the world. Flanked by 13 columns on its side, along with 6 in front and 6 in back, the temple was built in the peripteral hexastyle. You'll see the clearest example in Sicily of what an inner temple was like. In the late 6th century A.D. the pagan structure was transformed into a Christian church, which may have saved it for posterity, although today it has been stripped down to its classical purity.

The **Temple of Hercules** is the most ancient, dating from the 6th century B.C. Badly ruined (only eight pillars are standing), it once ranked in size with the Temple of Zeus. At one time the temple sheltered a celebrated statue of Hercules. The infamous Gaius Verres, the Roman magistrate who became an especially bad governor of Sicily, attempted to steal the image as part of his temple-looting tear on the island.

The ✪ **Temple of Jupiter (Zeus)** was the largest in the valley, similar in some respects to the Temple of Apollo at Selinunte. In front of the structure was a large altar. The giant on the ground was one of several telamones (atlases) used to support the edifice.

The so-called **Temple of Dioscuri,** with four Doric columns intact, is a *pasticcio*—that is, it's composed of fragments from different buildings. At various times it has been designated as a temple honoring Castor and Pollux, the twin sons of Leda, and deities of seafarers; and Demeter (Ceres), the goddess of marriage and of the fertile earth; and Persephone, the daughter of Zeus who became the symbol of spring.

The temples can usually be visited daily from 9am till 1 hour before sunset. City buses nos. 8, 9, 10, and 11 leave from the train station in Agrigento, taking you to the site of the temples.

IN TOWN The **Museo Regionale Archeologico** stands near the Church of Saint Nicholas (Chiesa di San Nicola), on contrada San Nicola (☎ 0922/29008), and is open Monday to Friday from 9am to 1pm and on Saturday from 9am to 5pm, admission free. Its single most important exhibit is a head of the god Telamon from the Temple of Jupiter. The collection of Greek vases is also impressive. Many of the artifacts on display were dug up when Agrigento was excavated. Bus: 8, 9, 10, or 11.

WHERE TO STAY

Hotel Tre Torri. Strada Statale 115 no. 7, Viallagio Mosè, 92100 Agrigento. ☎ **0922/606733.** Fax 0922/607-839. 118 rms. A/C TV TEL. 160,000 lire ($102.40) double. Rates include breakfast. AE, MC, V. Free parking. Bus: 3.

Some 4¹/₂ miles south of Agrigento in the village of Villaggio Mosè, this selection lies near the better-known Jolly Hotel in an unattractive commercial district, yet some consider it among the best hotels in town. Sheltered behind a mock-medieval facade of white stucco, chiseled stone blocks, false crenellations, and crisscrossed iron balconies, the hotel, which opened in 1982, is a favorite with the Italian business traveler. A swimming pool in the small, terraced garden is visible from a restaurant. There's also an indoor swimming pool, sauna, and fitness center. For entertainment, the hotel contains a bar, sometimes with live piano music, and a disco. The bedrooms are comfortable, with modern furnishings.

Hotel Villa Athena. Via dei Templi 33, 92100 Agrigento. ☎ **0922/596288.** Fax 0922/402180. 40 rms. A/C MINIBAR TV TEL. 300,000 lire ($192) double. Rates include breakfast. AE, DC, MC, V. Free parking outdoors. Bus: 8, 9, 10, or 11.

This 18th-century former private villa rises from the Sicilian landscape in the Valley of the Temples, less than 2 miles from town. It's the best place to stay in the area. Its grounds have been planted with fruit trees that bloom in January. During the day guests sit in the paved courtyard, enjoying a drink and the fresh breezes. At night you have a view of the floodlit temples, a string of Doric ruins, from one of the windows. There's a pool in a setting of gardenia bushes and flowers. The dining room is in a separate building, serving both regional specialties and international dishes. In summer, make a reservation about two weeks in advance. The rooms are modern, with Italian styling. Room 205 frames a perfect view of the Temple of Concord.

WHERE TO DINE

Le Caprice. Strada Panoramica dei Templi 51. ☎ **0922/26469.** Reservations required. Main courses 13,000–32,000 lire ($8.30–$20.50). AE, DC, MC. V. Sat–Thurs 12:30–3pm and 7:30–11pm. Closed July 1–15. SEAFOOD/ITALIAN.

A loyal clientele return to this well-directed restaurant for special celebrations as well as for everyday fun. Le Caprice is the only restaurant of any consequence in Agrigento; the rest are only simple trattorie. Specialties of the house include an antipasto buffet and a mixed fish fry from the gulf, along with rolled pieces of veal in a savory sauce. The cookery here is filling and satisfying—nothing else.

Trattoria del Vigneto. Via Cavalleri Magazzeni 11. ☎ **0922/414319.** Main courses 18,000–22,000 lire ($11.50–$14.10); fixed-price menu 20,000–25,000 lire ($12.80–$16). V. Wed–Mon 12:30–3pm and 8–10pm. Closed Nov. SICILIAN.

This is a simple place to go for a Sicilian meal after a visit to the Valley of the Temples, just a short distance away. Menu items include a mixed Sicilian grill loaded with many kinds of meat, along with lamb cutlets and a flavor-packed beefsteak laced with cheese and local herbs. The welcome is sincere, and the food is perfectly acceptable and often quite flavorful.

5 Syracuse (Siracusa)

35 miles SE of Catania

Of all the Greek cities of antiquity that flourished on the coast of Sicily, Siracusa was the most important, a formidable competitor of Athens in the West. In the heyday of its power, it dared take on Carthage, even Rome. At one time its wealth and size were unmatched by any other city in Europe.

On a site on the Ionian Sea, colonizers from Corinth founded the city in about 735 B.C. Much of its history was linked to despots, beginning in 485 B.C. with Gelon, the "tyrant" of Gela who subdued the Carthaginians at Himera. Siracusa came under attack from Athens in 415 B.C., but the main Athenian fleet was destroyed and the soldiers on the mainland captured. They were herded into the Latoma di Cappuccini at piazza Cappuccini, a stone quarry. The "jail," from which there was no escape, was particularly horrid, as the defeated soldiers weren't given food and were packed together like cattle and allowed to die slowly.

Dionysius I was one of the greatest despots, reigning over the city during its particular glory in the 4th century B.C., when it extended its influence as a sea power. But in 212 B.C. the city fell to the Romans who, under Marcellus, sacked its riches and art. Incidentally, in this rape Siracusa lost its most famous son, the Greek physicist and mathematician Archimedes, who was slain in his study by a Roman soldier.

Before you go, you might want to read Mary Renault's novel *The Mask of Apollo*, set in Syracuse of the 5th century B.C. As one critic put it, "It brings the stones to life."

Today the city's harborfront is lined with a distinguished collection of 18th- and 19th-century town houses, each brightly painted in a spectrum of colors, whose ensemble provides one of the most charming vistas in Sicily.

ESSENTIALS

GETTING THERE   By Train   From other major cities in Sicily, you'll find Syracuse best reached by train: $1^1/_2$ hours from Catania, 2 hours from Taormina, and 5 hours from Palermo.

By Bus   If you're in Catania, you can continue south by SAIS bus to Syracuse. Eight buses make the $1^1/_2$-hour trip per day, costing 6,100 lire ($3.90) one-way. Phone SAIS (☎ 0931/66710 in Syracuse) for information and schedules.

By Car   From Catania, continue south along Route 114.

VISITOR INFORMATION   The **tourist information center** is at via della Maestranza 33 (☎ 0931/464298), facing the Church of San Giovanni, with a branch office at the entrance to the archeological park, on largo Anfiteatro Romano (☎ 0931/60510). It's open Monday to Saturday from 9am to 1pm and 3 to 6:30pm.

THE TOP SIGHTS

The major attraction is the **Zona Archeologica** (☎ 0931/66206), which you reach by following corso Gelone to its intersection with viale Teocrito (the entrance is down via Augusto to the left). The park is open April to October, daily from 9am to 6pm; November to March, daily from 9am to 3pm. There's a blanket admission of 2,000 lire ($1.30). The park contains the town's most important attractions: the Greek theater (Teatro Greco), the Roman Amphitheater (Anfiteatro Romano), and the Latomia del Paradiso.

On the Temenite Hill, the ✪ **Teatro Greco** was one of the great theaters of the classical period. Hewn from rocks during the reign of Hieron I in the 5th century B.C., the ancient seats have been largely eaten away by time. You can, however, still stand on the remnants of the stone stage that once hosted plays by Euripedes. The theater was much restored in the time of Hieron II in the 3rd century B.C. In the spring the Italian Institute of Ancient Drama presents classical plays by Euripedes, Aeschylus, and Sophocles. In other words, the show hasn't changed much in 2,000 years!

Outside the entrance to the Greek theater is the most famous of the ancient quarries, the **Latomia del Paradiso,** one of four or five latomies from which stones were hauled to erect the great monuments of Siracusa in its glory days. On seeing the cave in the wall, Caravaggio is reputed to have dubbed it "The Ear of Dionysius," because of its unusual shape. But what an ear! It's nearly 200 feet long. You can enter the inner chamber of the grotto where the tearing of paper sounds like a gunshot. Although dismissed by some scholars as fanciful, the story goes that the despot Dionysius used to force prisoners into the "ear" at night, where he was able to hear every word they said. Nearby is the **Grotta dei Cordari,** where ropemakers plied their ancient craft.

The ✪ **Anfiteatro Romano** was created at the time of Augustus. It ranks among the top five amphitheaters left by the Romans in Italy. Like the Greek theater, part of it was carved from rock. Unlike the Greek theater and its classical plays, the Roman amphitheater tended toward more gutsy fare. Gladiators—prisoners of war and "exotic" blacks from Africa—faced each other with tridents and daggers, or naked slaves would be whipped into the center of a to-the-death battle between wild beasts. Either way the victim lost. If his combatant, man or beast, didn't do him in, the crowd would often scream for the ringmaster to slit his throat. The amphitheater is near the entrance to the park, but you can also view it in its entirety from a belvedere on the panoramic road.

OTHER SIGHTS

✪ **Museo Paolo Orsi.** Viale Teocrito 66. ☎ **0931/464022.** Admission 2,000 lire ($1.30) adults, free for children 17 and under and for seniors 60 and over. Tues, Thurs, and Sat–Sun 9am–1pm; Wed and Fri 9am–1pm and 3:30–6:30pm. Bus: Any bus from the Termini.

One of the most important archeological museums in southern Italy, the Museo Paolo Orsi made its debut in 1988, replacing an earlier archeological museum. In these modern quarters you can survey the Greek, Roman, and early Christian epochs in sculpture and fragments of archeological remains. The museum also has a rich coin collection. Of the statues here (and there are several excellent ones), the best known is the headless *Venus Anadyomene* (arising from the sea), dating from the Hellenistic period in the 2nd century B.C. One of the earliest-known works is of an earth mother suckling two babes, from the 6th century B.C. The pre-Greek vases have great style and elegance. The museum stands in the gardens of the Villa Landolina in Akradina.

✪ **Catacombe di San Giovanni (St. John).** At the end of viale San Giovanni. ☎ **0931/67955.** Admission 2,000 lire ($1.30) adults, free for children 17 and under and for seniors 60 and over. Mar 15–Nov 4, Thurs–Tues 9am–1pm and 3–6pm; Nov 5–Mar 14, Thurs–Tues 10am–noon. Bus: 1.

These honeycombed tunnels of empty coffins evoke the catacombs along the Appian Way in Rome. You enter the world down below from the Chiesa di San Giovanni, from the 3rd century A.D.; the present building is of a much later date. Included in the early Christian burial grounds is the crypt of St. Marcianus, which lies under what was reportedly the first cathedral erected in Sicily. *Warning:* Make sure you exit in plenty of time before closing. Two women readers who entered the catacombs after

5pm were accidentally locked in for the night, and managed to escape only after a harrowing and dangerous ordeal of wandering around in the dark.

ORTYGLA ISLAND

Ortygla, inhabited for many thousands of years, is also named Città Vecchia, and contains the town's cathedral, many rows of houses spanning 500 years of building styles, most of the city's medieval and baroque monuments, and some of the most charming vistas in Sicily. Its beauties praised by Pindar, the island, reached by crossing the ponte Nuova, was the heart of Siracusa, having been founded by the Greek colonists from Corinth. In Greek mythology, it's said to have been ruled by Calypso, daughter of Atlas, the sea nymph who detained Ulysses (Odysseus) for 7 years on the island. The island is about a mile long and half again as wide.

Heading out the Foro Italico, you'll come to the **Fountain of Arethusa,** also famous in mythology. Alpheius, the river god, son of Oceanus, is said to have fallen in love with the sea nymph Arethusa. The nymph turned into this spring or fountain, but Alpheius became a river and "mingled" with his love. According to legend, the spring ran red when bulls were sacrificed at Olympus.

At piazza del Duomo, the **cathedral** of Syracuse, with a baroque facade, was built over the ruins of the Temple of Minerva, and employs the same Doric columns. The temple was erected after Gelon the Tyrant defeated the Carthaginians at Himera in the 5th century B.C. The Christians converted it into a basilica in the 7th century A.D.

The **Palazzo Bellomo,** fronting via Capodieci, off Foro Vittorio Emanuele II, dates from the 13th century, with many alterations, and is today the home of the Galleria Regionale, via Capodieci 14 (☎ **0931/69511**). Not only is the palace fascinating, with its many arches, doors, and stairs, but it also has a fine collection of paintings. The most notable is an *Annunciation* by Antennal da Messina from 1474. There's also a noteworthy collection of antiques and porcelain. It's open Monday to Saturday from 9am to 2pm and on Sunday from 9am to 1pm, charging an admission of 2,000 lire ($1.30).

WHERE TO STAY
MODERATE

Jolly. Corso Gelone 46, 96100 Siracusa. ☎ **0931/461111,** or 800/221-2626 in the U.S., 800/237-0319 in Canada. Fax 0931/461126. 100 rms. A/C MINIBAR TV TEL. 230,000 lire ($147.20) double. Rates include breakfast. AE, DC, MC, V. Free parking. Bus: 1-32.

A major group stop, the six-story Jolly is part of the chain that's the Holiday Inn of Italy. You get no surprises here—just clean, modern, tropical-style rooms, short on soul but good on comfort, though a bit worn. The hotel restaurant offers a standard lunch or dinner in its restaurant, Il Giardinetto. At least the view of Mt. Etna and the sea is panoramic.

INEXPENSIVE

Hotel Bellavista. Via Diodoro Siculo 4, 96100 Siracusa. ☎ **0931/411355.** Fax 0931/37927. 45 rms. TV TEL. 138,000 lire ($88.30) double. Rates include breakfast. AE, DC, MC, V. Free parking. Bus: 1, 3, 4, or 7.

Family owned and run, this four story hotel was built in 1960, then renovated several times. It lies in the commercial center, close to the archeological zone. There's an annex in the garden for overflow guests. The main lounge has a sense of space, with leather chairs and semitropical plants. The bedrooms are informal and comfortable, often furnished with traditional pieces. Most rooms feature a sea-view balcony.

Hotel Forte Agip. Viale Teracati 30–32, 96100 Siracusa. ☎ **0931/463232.** Fax 0931/67115. 87 rms. A/C MINIBAR TV TEL. 189,000–209,000 lire ($120.95–$133.75) double. Rates include breakfast. AE, DC, MC, V. Free parking. Bus: All buses.

Located a short drive inland from the medieval Città Vecchia, near the ancient Greek theater and most of the city's classical monuments, this member of a national hotel chain is designed for ease of access and convenience to motorists. Each of the monochromatic bedrooms is simple, streamlined, and similar to other chain-motel rooms throughout Europe. The in-house restaurant is often visited by residents of Syracuse who consider the generous portions, unpretentious service, and flavorful specialties worth the trip. Menu items include pastas, stuffed veal, American-style tournedos, salads, and a changing array of fresh fish.

⑤ Panorama. Via Necropoli Grotticalle 33, 98100 Siracusa. ☎ and fax **0931/412188.** 51 rms. TV TEL. 95,000 lire ($60.80) double. AE, MC, V. Free parking. Bus: 1, 5, 6, or 11.

Near the entrance to the city, on a rise of Temenite Hill, is this bandbox-modern hotel, built on a busy street about five minutes from the Greek theater and Roman amphitheater. It's not a motel, but it does provide parking space. Inside, a contemporary accommodation awaits you. The bedrooms are pleasant and up-to-date, with comfortable but utilitarian pieces. There's a dining room serving only a continental breakfast (not included in the room prices).

WHERE TO DINE

Arlecchino. Via dei Tolomei 5. ☎ **0931/66386.** Reservations recommended. Main courses 14,000–24,000 lire ($8.95–$15.35). AE, DC, MC, V. Daily 12:30–3:30pm and 7:30pm–midnight. Closed Mon Apr–Sept. SEAFOOD.

This restaurant, founded in 1967, occupies the street level of a 250-year-old palace in the heart of the Città Vecchia, a short walk from the cathedral. Despite its understated decor, Arlecchino is the best restaurant in town. Many specialties emerge from this fragrant kitchen. These include a wide array of homemade pastas, a cheese-laden crespelline of the house, pasta with sardines, spiedini with shrimp, and a selection of pungent beef, fish, and veal dishes.

⑤ Darsena da Ianuzo. Riva Garibaldi 6. ☎ **0931/66104.** Reservations required. Main courses 12,000–20,000 lire ($7.70–$12.80). AE, DC, MC, V. Thurs–Tues 12:30–3pm and 8–10pm. Bus: All buses. SEAFOOD.

This might not differ all that much from dozens of other seafood restaurants in the Città Vecchia, except that the food here seems to be exceptionally good and the welcome warm. Specialties include fresh shellfish, spaghetti with clams, a wide collection of fresh grilled and baked fish, and the ever-present fish soup.

Gambero Rosso. Via Eritrea 2. ☎ **0931/68546.** Reservations recommended. Main courses 12,000–24,000 lire ($7.70–$15.35). AE, MC, V. Fri–Wed 12:30–3pm and 8–10pm. Bus: All buses. SICILIAN/MEDITERRANEAN/SEAFOOD.

Ideal for those who want to dine at an old tavern, this restaurant is near the entrance to the bridge leading to the Città Vecchia. It's a mellow building, close to the fishing boats, with a certain charm, and a cuisine dedicated to the best of Sicilian dishes. A reliable dish is the zuppa di pesce (fish soup). An alternative choice is the zuppa di cozze, a plate brimming with fresh mussels in a savory marinade. Among the asciutte, the Sicilian cannelloni are good. The meat dishes feature a number of choices from the kitchens of Latium, Tuscany, and Emilia-Romagna.

Ristorante Jonico E Rutta E Ciauli. Riviera Dionisio il Grande 194. ☎ **0931/65540.** Reservations recommended. Main courses 18,000–25,000 lire ($11.50–$16). AE, DC, MC, V. Wed–Mon 12:30–3pm and 8–10pm. Bus: 1. SICILIAN.

This is one of the best restaurants on the island serving the typical cuisine and local wines of Sicily. The restaurant offers a veranda and garden setting right on the sea, with a panoramic view about 100 yards from the Latomia dei Cappuccini. The decoration is typically Sicilian. The antipasto array alone is dazzling, and the homemade pasta dishes are superb (ask one of the English-speaking waiters to explain some of the many variations or settle for spaghetti with caviar). One of the most interesting fish dishes we recently sampled was spada a pizzaiola (swordfish in a savory, garlic-flavored sauce). Meat specialties include polpettone (rolled meat) alla siracusana, and a delectable stew made of various fish. The dessert specialty is a cassatine siciliana.

⑤ **Ristorante Rossini.** Via Savoia 6. ☎ **0931/24317.** Reservations recommended. Main courses 18,000–22,000 lire ($11.50–$14.10). AE, DC, MC, V. Wed–Mon 12:30–3:30pm and 8–10pm. Bus: 1. MEDITERRANEAN.

The Ristorante Rossini is a homelike and comfortable enclave of regional gastronomy, offering meals to 50 fortunate diners a night. You might begin with an assortment from the amply stocked buffet table of antipasti, then select one of many main dishes, including a mousse of fish with fresh shrimp, perhaps a shellfish risotto with roast peppers and tomato purée. A twice-roasted swordfish is also a specialty.

6 Taormina

33 miles N of Catania, 33 miles S of Messina, 155 miles E of Palermo

Runaway bougainvillea, silvery olive branches, a cerulean sky, cactuses adorning the hills like modern sculpture, pastel-plastered walls, garden terraces of geraniums, trees laden with oranges and lemons, ancient ruins—all that and more is Taormina, Sicily's most desirable oasis.

Dating from the 4th century B.C., Taormina hugs the edge of a cliff overlooking the Ionian Sea. Writers for English Sunday supplements rave of its unspoiled charms and enchantment. The sea, even the railroad track, lie down below, connected by bus routes. Looming in the background is Mount Etna, the active volcano. Noted for its mild climate, the town enjoys a year-round season.

A lot of people contributed to putting Taormina on the tourist map. Since it was first inhabited by a tribe known as the Siculi, it has known many conquerors, including Greeks, Carthaginians, Romans, Saracens, French, and Spanish. Its first tourist was said to have been Goethe, who arrived in 1787. He recorded his impressions in his *Journey to Italy.* Other Germans were to follow over the centuries, including a red-haired Prussian, Otto Geleng. Arriving at the age of 20 in Taormina, he recorded its beauties in his painted landscapes. These were exhibited in Paris and caused much excitement—people had to go themselves to find out if Taormina was all that beautiful.

Another German, Wilhelm von Gloeden, arrived to photograph not only the town, but also nude boys crowned with laurel wreaths. These pictures sent European high society flocking to Taormina. Von Gloeden's photographs, some of which are even printed in official tourist literature to this day, form one of the most enduring legends of Taormina. Souvenir shops still sell his pictures, which, although considered scandalous in their day, would be tame, even innocent, by today's X-rated standards.

Following in the footsteps of von Gloeden came a host of long-faded international celebrities hoping to see what all the excitement was about: Truman Capote, Tennessee Williams, Marlene Dietrich, Joan Crawford, Rita Hayworth, and Greta Garbo. Always in disguise, sometimes as Harriet Brown, Ms. Garbo used Taormina as a vacation retreat from 1950 until her last mysterious arrival in 1979. Many of these stars, including Garbo, stayed at a villa on the road to Castel Mola owned by Gayelord Hauser, the celebrated dietitian to Hollywood stars back in the golden age. In time another wave of stars were to arrive: Taylor and Burton, Cary Grant, and the woman who turned him down, Sophia Loren.

The rich and famous still come here, along with a lot of middle-class visitors as well. Taormina remains chic.

ESSENTIALS

GETTING THERE   By Train   You can make rail connections on the Messina line from Syracuse. Telephone **0942/51511** in Taormina for schedules. The train station at Taormina is a mile from the heart of the resort; buses will take you up a hill every 15 to 45 minutes (schedules vary throughout the year), daily from 9am to 9pm; a one-way ticket costs 2,500 lire ($1.60).

By Bus   Most visitors arrive in Messina, the gateway to Sicily. There you can board a Taormina-bound bus; 13 leave per day, taking 1½ hours. More details are available in Messina by calling **SAIS,** the bus company (☎ **090/771914**).

By Car   From Messina, head south along autostrada A18. From Catania, continue north along A18.

VISITOR INFORMATION   A **tourist information center** is in the Palazzo Corvaja, largo Santa Caterina (☎ **0942/23243**). It's open Monday to Saturday from 8am to 2pm and 4 to 7pm.

WHAT TO SEE & DO

The ✪ **Greek and Roman Theater,** via Teatro Greco (☎ **0942/23220**), is the most visited monument, offering a view of rare beauty of Mount Etna and the seacoast. At an unrecorded time the Greeks hewed the theater out of rock on the slope of Mount Tauro, but the Romans remodeled and modified it greatly for their amusement. The conquering Arabs, who seemed intent on devastating the town in the 10th century, slashed away at it. On the premises is an antiquarium, containing not only artifacts from the classical period but early Christian ones as well. The theater is open Tuesday to Sunday from 9am to 2 hours before sunset. Admission is 2,000 lire ($1.30) for adults; children 17 and under and seniors 60 and over are admitted free.

The other thing to do in Taormina is to walk through the **Giardino Pubblico,** via Bagnoli Croce, a flower-filled garden overlooking the sea, a choice spot for views as well as a place to relax. At a bar in the park you can order drinks. Take bus no. 1 or 2 to reach these attractions.

WHERE TO STAY

The hotels in Taormina are the best in Sicily—in fact, the finest in Italy south of Amalfi. All price levels and accommodations are available, from sumptuous suites to army cots.

VERY EXPENSIVE

✪ **Palazzo San Domenico.** Piazza San Domenico 5, 98039 Taormina. ☎ **0942/23701.** Fax 0942/625506. 101 rms, 8 suites. A/C MINIBAR TV TEL. 685,000 lire ($438.40) double; 1,185,000 lire ($758.40) suite. AE, DC, MC, V. Parking 30,000 lire ($19.20).

This is one of the great old hotels of Europe, converted from a 14th-century Domini-can monastery complete with cloisters. For sheer luxury there's no other hotel in Sicily to equal it. Overhauled, it almost begrudgingly boasts air-conditioning and a flower-edged swimming pool. Its position is legend to discriminating travelers—high up from the sea coast, on several different levels surrounded by terraced gardens of al-mond, orange, and lemon trees. In the 19th century it blossomed as a hotel, with no expense spared, and was a favorite of the elite: kings, artists, writers, statesmen.

The large medieval courtyard is planted with semitropical trees and flowers. The encircling enclosed loggia, the old vaulted-ceilinged cloister, is decorated with potted palms and ecclesiastical furnishings (high-backed carved choir stalls, wooden angels and cherubs, religious paintings in oil). Off the loggia are great refectory halls turned into sumptuously furnished lounges. While antiques are everywhere, the at-mosphere is not museumlike but gracious, with traditional upholstered chairs and sofas. Ornate ceilings climb high and arched windows look out onto the view.

The bedrooms, opening off the cloister, would surely impress a cardinal. One-of-a-kind furniture has been utilized, including elaborate carved beds, gilt, Chinese red, provincial pieces, Turkish rugs, and Venetian chairs and dressers.

Dining/Entertainment: The cuisine, supervised by a masterful chef and a com-bination of Sicilian and Italian dishes, is the most refined in Taormina. Dining in the main hall is an event. Meals are served around the pool in summer.

Services: Room service, baby-sitting, laundry, valet.

Facilities: Swimming pool.

MODERATE

Bristol Park Hotel. Via Bagnoli Croce 92, 98039 Taormina. ☎ **0942/23006.** Fax 0942/24519. 50 rms, 2 suites. A/C MINIBAR TV TEL. 200,000–250,000 lire ($128–$160) double; 250,000–310,000 lire ($160–$198.40) suite. Rates include breakfast. Half board 110,000–170,000 lire ($70.40–$108.80) per person extra. AE, DC, MC, V. Closed mid-Nov to Feb. Parking 15,000 lire ($9.60).

This is one of the all-out comfort hotels, built high on the cliffside at the edge of Taormina. Close to the public gardens of Duca di Cesaro, it offers a panoramic view of the coastline and Mount Etna from most of its private sun balconies. The inte-rior decor is amusing with tufted satin, plush and ornate. In contrast, the bedrooms are traditional, with private baths. The dining room, with arched windows framing the view, offers international meals with an occasional Sicilian dish. There's a private beach with free deck chairs and parasols, plus bus service to the beach (June to Sep-tember). The hotel has a pool, and there's a garage.

Excelsior Palace. Via Toselli 8, 98039 Taormina. ☎ **0942/23975.** Fax 0942/23978. 89 rms. A/C TV TEL. 260,000 lire ($166.40) double with breakfast; 180,000 lire ($115.20) per person double with half board. AE, DC, MC, V. Free parking.

The Excelsior seems like a Moorish palace, lost on the end ridge of the mountain fringe of Taormina. It's the number two hotel in town, topped only by the San Domenico Palace. It's as foreboding as a fortress on two sides, but the severity dis-solves inside into style and comfort. The gardens at the back have terraces of scented semitropical flowers, date palms, yucca, and geraniums. The view of Etna and the seacoast below is of a rare enchantment. Renovated successfully, the hotel is managed so that superior facilities and service await all guests. The bedrooms have plenty of space and are decorated in a traditional manner. You can swim at the hotel's seaside annex, and the kitchen staff will pack you a picnic lunch.

Hotel Monte Tauro. Via Madonna delle Grazi 3, 98039 Taormina. ☎ **0942/24402.** Fax 0942/24403. 30 rms, 40 junior suites. A/C MINIBAR TV TEL. 240,000 lire ($153.60) double; from

290,000 lire ($185.60) suite. Rates include breakfast. AE, DC, MC, V. Closed Jan 15–Mar. Free parking.

Engineering skills and tons of poured concrete went into this dramatic hotel built into the side of a scrub-covered hill rising high above the sea, within view of the coastline. Although not as good as the hotels previously recommended, it does compete successfully against the Jolly Diodoro. Each bedroom has a circular balcony, often festooned with flowers, and a private bath or shower. The social center is the many-angled swimming pool, whose cantilevered platform is ringed with a poolside bar and dozens of plants. The velvet-covered chairs of the modern, tile-floored interior are upholstered in the same blues, grays, and violets of the sunny bedrooms where Mondrian-style rectangles and stripes decorate the bedspreads and accessories.

Jolly Hotel Diodoro. Via Bagnoli Croce 75, 98039 Taormina. ☎ **0942/23312,** or 800/221-2626 in the U.S., 800/237-0319 in Canada. Fax 0942/23391. 102 rms. A/C MINIBAR TV TEL. 250,000 lire ($160) double with breakfast; 163,000 lire ($104.30) per person double with half board. AE, DC, MC, V. Free parking.

The Jolly is one of the most luxurious of the first-class hotels, built and designed privately, then taken over by the Jolly chain. The design of everything—the public lounges, the bedrooms—is well coordinated, on a high taste level. The dining room, with tall windows on three sides, is projected toward the sea and Mount Etna. The outdoor swimming pool is a sun trap; you can sunbathe, swim, and enjoy the view of mountains, trees, and flowers. The bedrooms are tasteful and comfortable, with well-designed furniture and the latest gadgets. Each has a private bath or shower. Many of the rooms are angled toward the sea, with wide-open windows.

INEXPENSIVE

⑤ Ariston. Via Bagnoli Croce 128, 98039 Taormina. ☎ **0942/23838.** Fax 0942/21137. 176 rms. A/C MINIBAR TEL. 70,000–140,000 lire ($44.80–$89.60) per person. Rates include half board. AE, MC, V. Free parking.

Substantial and cost-conscious, and favored by families from Italy and the rest of Europe, this modern hotel was built in 1975 with four stories rising above a verdant park about 400 yards from the center of Taormina. About 36 of its rooms are in a low-rise garden annex nearby. Although the hotel is located inland, a short walk from the sea, there's a pool on the premises, a piano bar, and a restaurant with efficient service and both Sicilian and international specialties.

La Campanella. Via Circonvallazione 3, 98039 Taormina. ☎ **0942/23381.** Fax 0942/625248. 12 rms. TEL. 120,000 lire ($76.80) double. Rates include breakfast. No credit cards.

This hotel is rich in the aesthetics of gardening, painting, and hospitality. It sits at the top of a seemingly endless flight of stairs, which begin at a sharp curve of the main road leading into town. You climb past terra-cotta pots and dangling tendrils of a terraced garden, eventually arriving at the house. The owners maintain clean and uncluttered bedrooms, each with its own bath.

Pensione Svizzera. Via Pirandello 26, 98039 Taormina. ☎ **0942/23790.** Fax 0942/625906. 20 rms. TEL. 90,000 lire ($57.60) double. Rates include breakfast. AE, DC, MC, V. Closed Jan–Feb. Free parking.

This is a pleasant place to stay, about an eighth of a mile from the center of town. Constructed in 1926, this hotel has been run by the same family for three generations, currently Antonino Vinciguerra and his German-born wife, both of whom speak English. Try to get a room that overlooks the sea and Isola Bella. All bedrooms have a shower and toilet, and 12 open onto sea views. There's also a garden with shady palm trees where breakfast is served in summer. The funicular going down to the beach at Mazzarò is a little over 100 yards from the pensione, as is the bus terminal.

Villa Belvedere. Via Bagnoli Croci 79, 98039 Taormina. ☎ **0942/23791.** Fax 0942/625830. 50 rms. TEL. 150,000–239,500 lire ($96–$153.30) double. Rates include breakfast. MC, V. Closed Nov 6–Dec 25. Parking 8,000 lire ($5.10). Bus: 1 or 2.

This is a gracious old villa bathed in Roman gold near the Giardino Pubblico. In its garden is a heated swimming pool. From the cliffside terrace in the rear—a social center for guests—is that view: the clear blue sky, the gentle Ionian Sea, the cypress-studded hillside, and menacing Mount Etna. It's the same view, incidentally, enjoyed by clients at the more expensive first-class hotels nearby. The formal entrance is enhanced by potted plants and wall-covering vines, and the interior is captivating. The bedrooms have been restored, and 25 of them are air-conditioned. Breakfast is served, and there are two bars. Lunch is at a snack bar by the pool.

⑤ Villa Fiorita. Via Pirandello 39, 98039 Taormina. ☎ **0942/24122.** Fax 0942/625967. 24 rms, 2 suites. A/C MINIBAR TV TEL. 160,000 lire ($102.40) double; from 193,000 lire ($123.50) suite. Rates include breakfast. AE, MC, V. Parking 15,000 lire ($9.60). Bus: 1 or 2.

One of the most charming hotels in its category, the Villa Fiorita stretches toward the town's Greek theater from its position beside the road leading up to the top. Designed in 1976, its imaginative decor includes a handful of ceramic stoves, which the owner delights in collecting. A well-maintained garden is bordered by an empty but ancient Greek tomb whose stone walls have been classified as a national treasure. The bedrooms are arranged in a steplike labyrinth of corridors and stairwells, some of which bend to correspond to the rocky slope on which the hotel was built. Each unit contains some kind of antique, as well as a tile bath, radio, and usually a flowery private terrace.

⑤ Villa Nettuno. Via Pirandello 33, 98039 Taormina. ☎ **0942/23797.** Fax 0942/626035. 13 rms. 95,000 lire ($60.80) double. MC, V. Closed Jan 10–Feb and Nov 17–Dec 19. Parking 7,000 lire ($4.50). Bus: 1 or 2.

Our favorite budget accommodation in town is this geranium-colored villa with Renaissance-style stone trim. It lies near the city center, opposite a cableway that transports passengers down to the sea. Visitors must climb several flights of steps after leaving the traffic of the main street, passing beneath an archway whose keystone is carved with a grotesque stone face. The villa was acquired by the Sciglio family in 1887 and converted into a pensione by the warm-hearted but highly discerning Maria Sciglio in 1953. Guests enjoy breakfast in a garden with hibiscus and night-blooming jasmine. The dining room is like the rococo living quarters of an elegant Sicilian family. Each of the attractive, well-scrubbed bedrooms contains its own modernized bath and panoramic terrace (all but two of the terraces look out to sea).

⑤ Villa Paradiso. Via Roma 2, 98039 Taormina. ☎ **0942/23922.** Fax 0942/625800. 35 rms. A/C TV TEL. 140,000–300,000 lire ($89.60–$192) double. Rates include breakfast. AE, DC, MC, V. Closed Nov 4–Dec 20. Parking 20,000 lire ($12.80).

This charming five-story hotel is at one end of the main street of town, near the Greek theater and overlooking the public gardens and tennis courts. The creation of Signor Salvatore Martorana, it's a reasonably priced choice for those who want to live well. He loves his establishment, and that attitude is reflected in the personal manner in which the living room is furnished, with antiques and reproductions. Each of the bedrooms is individually decorated, containing a balcony. Guests spend many sunny hours in the rooftop solarium, the TV room, or the informal drinking bar and lounge. Prices include transportation to and from the private Paradise Beach Club in

Letojanni, use of sun umbrellas, deck chairs, and showers, plus changing cabins, swimming pool, hydromassage, and garden. Guests can also play 45 minutes of tennis free per day.

Villa Schuler. Piazzetta Bastione, via Roma, 98039 Taormina. ☎ **0942/23481.** Fax 0942/23522. 27 rms. TEL. 137,000 lire ($87.70) double. Rates include breakfast. AE, MC, V. Parking 12,000 lire ($7.70) in the garage, free outside.

Family owned and run, this hotel was converted from a Sicilian villa in 1905. High above the Ionian Sea, it offers views of snow-capped Mount Etna and the Bay of Naxos. The hotel lies only a 2-minute stroll from the central corso Umberto, and about a 15-minute walk from the cable car to the beach below. It's also near the ancient theater of Taormina. Surrounded by its own gardens and filled with the fragrance of bougainvillea and jasmine, the hotel is an ideal retreat. The bedrooms are comfortably furnished and many have a small balcony or terrace opening onto a view of the sea. Breakfast can be served in your room or taken on a panoramic palm terrace overlooking the coastline. Facilities and services include a roof terrace solarium, small library, 24-hour bar and room service, and laundry.

PLACES TO STAY IN NEARBY MAZZARÒ

If you arrive in Taormina in summer, you may prefer to stay at Mazzarò, which is about 3 miles from the heart of the more famous resort (same telephone area code). This is the major beach of Taormina, and has some fine hotels. A bus for Mazzarò leaves from the center of Taormina every 30 minutes daily from 8am to 9pm, charging 1,500 lire (95¢).

Grande Albergo Capotaormina. Via Nazionale 105, 98039 Taorminà. ☎ **0942/24000.** Fax 0942/625467. 200 rms, 3 suites. A/C MINIBAR TV TEL. 320,000 lire ($204.80) double; from 380,000 lire ($243.20) suite. Rates include breakfast. AE, DC, MC. V. Closed Dec–Mar. Parking 15,000 lire ($9.60).

The Grande Albergo is a world unto itself, nestled atop a rugged cape projecting into the Ionian Sea. It was designed by one of Italy's most famous architects, Minoletti. There are five floors on five wide sun terraces, plus a saltwater swimming pool at the edge of the cape. Elevators take you through 150 feet of solid rock to the beach below. The bedrooms are handsomely furnished and well proportioned, with wide glass doors opening onto private sun terraces. There are two bars—one intimate, the other more expansive with an orchestra for dancing. The lobby blends the cultures of Rome, Carthage, and Greece, and an open atrium reaches skyward through the center. The food is lavishly presented, and is effectively enhanced by Sicilian wines.

✪ **Mazzarò Sea Palace.** Via Nazionale 147, 98030 Mazzarò. ☎ **0942/24004.** Fax 0942/626237. 84 rms, 3 suites. A/C MINIBAR TV TEL. 320,000–550,000 lire ($204.80–$352) double; 420,000–700,000 lire ($268.80–$448) suite. Rates include half board. AE, DC, MC, V. Parking 22,000 lire ($14.10).

The Sea Palace is a leading four-star hotel in this little satellite resort of Taormina. It opens onto the most beautiful bay in Sicily. Its modern design was completed in the early 1970s, and it's graced with big windows to let in cascades of light and offer views of the coastline. The food in the restaurant terrace is served on fine china and crystal, and guests are pampered by the staff. The piano bar is a popular nighttime spot. There's also a private beach for guests. The rooms are well furnished, most opening onto panoramic views. It's customary to stay here on the half-board plan.

Villa Sant'Andrea. Via Nazionale 137, 98030 Mazzarò. ☎ **0942/23125.** Fax 0942/24838. 67 rms. A/C TV TEL. 290,000–500,000 lire ($185.60–$320) double. Rates include breakfast. AE, DC, MC, V. Parking 20,000 lire ($12.80).

Converted from a villa, this first-class hotel stands at the base of the mountain, directly on the sea with a private beach. You'll feel like part of a house party. The rooms are informal, with a homelike prettiness, and there's a winning dining terrace where you can enjoy good food. Even if you're not a guest, you might want to try the hotel restaurant, Oliviero, which is one of the finest on the island, having won many awards. A cable car, just outside the front gates of the hotel, will whisk you to the heart of Taormina.

WHERE TO DINE

MODERATE

Giova Rosy di Turi Salsa. Corso Umberto 38. ☎ **0942/24411.** Reservations recommended. Main courses 18,000–35,000 lire ($11.50–$22.40). AE, DC, V. July–Sept, daily 12:30–3pm and 8–10:30pm; off-season, Fri–Wed 12:30–3pm and 8–10:30pm. Closed Jan 6–Feb 15. SICILIAN.

This rustically old-fashioned place serves a variety of local specialties, including, for example, an array of linguine, risotto dishes, and a spiedini with shrimp and lobster dosed with a generous shot of cognac. You might also enjoy Sicilian antipasti or eggplant with ricotta. You'll have a view of the ancient theater.

Ristorante da Lorenzo. Via Michele Amari 4. ☎ **0942/23480.** Reservations required. Main courses 16,000–38,000 lire ($10.25–$24.30). AE, DC, MC, V. Thurs–Tues noon–3pm and 6:30–11pm. Closed Nov 15–Dec 15. SICILIAN/ITALIAN.

This is a clean and bright restaurant on a quiet street near the landmark San Domenico Hotel, in front of the town hall. The restaurant has a terrace shaded by an 850-year-old tree—the botanical pride of the town—and oil paintings decorating its white walls. You can enjoy meals that might include a fresh selection of antipasti, spaghetti with sea urchins, scaloppine mozzarella, grilled swordfish, filet of beef with Gorgonzola, and bean soup.

INEXPENSIVE

⑤ Il Ciclope. Corso Umberto. ☎ **0942/23263.** Reservations not accepted. Main courses 15,000–25,000 lire ($9.60–$16). AE, MC, V. Thurs–Tues 12:30–3pm and 7:30–10pm. Closed Jan 10–31. Bus: 1 or 2. SICILIAN/ITALIAN.

This is one of the best of the low-priced trattorie of Taormina. Set back from the main street, it opens onto the pint-sized piazzetta Salvatore Leone. In summer, try for an outside table if you'd like both your food and yourself inspected by the passing parade. Meals are fairly simple but the ingredients are fresh, the dishes well prepared. Try, for example, the fish soup or Sicilian squid. If those don't interest you, then go for the entrecôte Ciclope, or perhaps the grilled shrimp. Most diners begin their meal with a selection from the antipasti di mare, a savory collection of seafood hors d'oeuvres.

Ristorante La Griglia. Corso Umberto 54. ☎ **0942/23980.** Reservations recommended. Main courses 16,000–28,000 lire ($10.25–$17.90). AE, DC, MC, V. Wed–Mon 12:30–2:30pm and 7:30–11:30pm. Closed Nov 20–Dec 20. SICILIAN/INTERNATIONAL.

Opened in 1974, this restaurant is still one of the best in town. The vestibule that funnels visitors from the main street of the old city into the interior contains a bubbling aquarium and a menagerie of carved stone lions. The masses of plants inside almost conceal the terra-cotta floors and big-windowed views over the feathery trees of a garden. Your meal might include a selection from the antipasto display, a fresh fish carpaccio, and an involtino of spaghetti and eggplant.

Ristorante Luraleo. Via Bagnoli Croce 27. ☎ **0942/24279.** Reservations recommended. Main courses 12,000–20,000 lire ($7.70–$12.80). AE, DC, MC, V. Summer, daily noon–3pm and 7–11pm. Closed Wed off-season. SICILIAN/INTERNATIONAL.

The Aeolian Islands

The Greeks who came this way in the 6th century B.C. believed that the Aeolian, or Lipari, Islands were the home of Aeolus, god of the winds. Volcanic activity on these islands has been reported since ancient times. In Messina province, the islands cluster into a Y shape, the northern tip formed by **Stromboli,** with **Vulcano** at the southern tip. Both these islands have volcanic activity, the crater at Stromboli being the most spectacular. The largest island in the archipelago is **Lipari,** which produces a malmsey-type wine.

For the reader willing to make the journey, the islands form one of the most exciting itineraries in southern Italy. After the peak of the summer season is over, you'll have the Aeolians almost to yourself, except for the locals.

The best way to reach these islands is by a surface-skimming hydrofoil departing from Milazzo, about 20 miles west of Messina. There is also regular ferry service to the islands. Ferry schedules change rapidly, depending on the season, so you must check locally. By ferry, Vulcano is only 1 1/2 hours away, and Lipari, 2 hours. To get to Stromboli, you must first go to Lipari and get a ferry from there. It's also possible to take hydrofoil (*aliscafi*) service from Naples. The hydrofoil is more expensive than the ferry, but much quicker.

Lipari is the chief town of the chain, with an important Aeolian archeological museum, **Museo Archeologico Eoliano,** housed in the former bishop's palace. The museum is open Monday to Saturday from 9am to 2pm and on Sunday from 9am to 1pm. Formed of volcanic rock, the town is framed by two beaches, the port Marina Lunga and Marina Corta. The town is dominated by the castle on the site that was the seat of prehistoric settlements from the Neolithic to the Bronze Age and the acropolis of the Greek and Roman towns. The encircling wall of the castle is of the Spanish period (16th century), but it encloses the ruins of the Greek and Norman fortifications.

According to mythology, Vulcano was the actual home of the god of the winds, Aeolus. The island is wild and desolate, attracting only the most adventurous to its rugged, rocky shores to soak in mud baths and lie on black sand beaches. Vulcano is the crater of a volcano that last saw action in 1890. Prehistoric sites have been discovered on the island, but the major interest is in looking at the volcanic formations, the sulfur vapors, and the hot mud flows. Instead of potentially dangerous climbing, we suggest that you negotiate with one of the local fishermen, arranging for a tour around Vulcano by boat. It's much easier that way.

Acclaimed by a handful of city residents as the best place in town, the Ristorante Luraleo is eager to offer excellent value for an attractive price. Many diners prefer the flowering terrace, where pastel tablecloths are shaded by the vine-covered arbor overhead. Of course, if you prefer to dine indoors, there's a country-rustic dining room with tile accents, flowers, evening candlelight, racks of wine bottles, and a richly laden antipasto table. The grilled fish is good here, as are the pastas, regional dishes, and herb-flavored steak. Risotto with salmon and pistachio nuts is a specialty, as is the house tortellini and involtini siciliana.

⑤ Ristorante U'Bossu. Via Bagnoli Croce 50. ☎ **0942/23311.** Reservations required. Main courses 12,000–18,000 lire ($7.70–$11.50); fixed-price menu 20,000 lire ($12.80). MC, V. Tues–Sun 12:30–3pm and 7:30–10pm. Closed Jan 14–Feb 20. Bus: 1 or 2. SICILIAN/MEDITERRANEAN.

Stromboli is the most distant of the Aeolian Islands, about 50 miles north of the coastal town of Milazzo. If you've heard of it, you probably only associate it with the Ingrid Bergman movie made there in 1949 during that so-called scandalous period in her life which put Stromboli on the tourist map. Throughout the year hydrofoils run daily from Milazzo to the major islands in the Aeolians, turning around at Stromboli.

Your first impression as you approach the island is that it's simply a huge black rock jutting out into the sea. The 3,000-foot cone silhouetted against the sky is the only active volcano in the Aeolians, but its activity is more like that of a wheezing old codger than an explosive juvenile. In the late-afternoon sun the volcanic rock reflects its orange-and-red highlights, giving the approaching visitor an exciting, almost Fourth of July display.

As you near the "lee" side—the part of the island away from the volcano activity—you'll see the tiny houses standing out in glaring whiteness against the hillside. The volcanic soil is rich, and bougainvillea, geraniums, petunias, roses, and fig trees grow in profusion.

The real experience on Stromboli is outside. Activities on the island are limited to hiking, swimming, fishing, boating—and eating. You can dine, perhaps on the terrace of a hotel, overlooking the deep blue of the Tyrrhenian Sea with the black backdrop of the Stromboli volcano behind you. The food is always good and plentiful—freshly caught fish and local vegetables make up a great part of the diet.

If you want to get a closer look at the volcano, you can take a motorlaunch—the hotels usually have boats available (for a fee to be negotiated)—around the island. Fortunately, Stromboli pours its molten rock down the side opposite the inhabited portion, and it's exciting to watch the lava as it hisses into the sea. The more energetic may prefer to hike up the hillside. Guides are available for the 3-hour trek, about 3,000 feet over rock and volcanic ash. Swimming off Stromboli is a rare pleasure. Scuba diving is especially popular, since the waters are uncommonly calm and crystal clear. Fishing is an alternative sport, and spearfishing in scuba gear can be a rewarding experience—especially if you take your catch back to your hotel for dinner.

No cars are allowed on Stromboli—only bicycles, mopeds, and three-wheel vehicles, used by locals for transporting goods and guests.

Vines entwine around the facade of this small and crowded restaurant in a quiet part of town. Amid a pleasing decor of fresh flowers, wagon-wheel chandeliers, prominently displayed wine bottles, and burnished wooden panels, you can enjoy a meal pungent with all the aromas of a herb garden. Meals begin with complimentary bruschetta, roasted bread with oil and garlic or tomato. Specialties include pasta con la sarde (pasta with fish), maccheroni alla siciliana (noodles with the Sicilian staple, eggplant), and involtini di pesce spada (a swordfish stew).

A RESTAURANT IN NEARBY MAZZARÓ

Ristorante Angelo a Mare–Il Delfino. Via Nazionale, Mazzarò. ☎ **0942/23004.** Main courses 15,000–28,000 lire ($9.60–$17.90). AE, DC, MC, V. Daily noon–3pm and 7pm–midnight. Closed Nov–Mar. Transportation: Cable car. MEDITERRANEAN/ITALIAN.

Located in Mazzarò, about 3 miles from Taormina, this restaurant offers a flowering terrace with a view over the bay. Both the decor and the menu items are inspired by the sea, and carefully supervised by the chef and owner. Mussels are a specialty, as well as a house-style steak, along with involtini of fish, cannelloni, and risotto marinara (fisherman's rice).

TAORMINA AFTER DARK

Caffè Wunderbar. Piazza IX Aprile 7, corso Umberto. ☎ **0942/625302.**

This popular spot was once a favorite watering hole of Tennessee Williams and his companion, Frank Merlo. It's in two areas of the most delightful square in town. Beneath a vine-covered arbor, the outdoor section is perched as close as is safely possible to the edge of the cliff. We prefer one of the Victorian armchairs in the elegant interior, where an impressionistic pair of sculpted figures fill symmetrical wall niches beneath chandeliers. There's also a well-stocked bar, as well as a piano bar. An espresso costs 3,900 lire ($2.50), and a cappuccino, 4,800 lire ($3.05) if you sit. Open daily from 8:30am to 2:30am; closed Tuesday in December and January.

Tiffany. Van San Pancrazio 5 (Porto Messina). ☎ **0942/625430.**

A gridwork of illuminated lattices stretches above the glossy dance floor of this underground air-conditioned disco/karaoke bar in the historic center of Taormina. Open daily from 10pm to 3:30 or 4am. The disco stands at the entrance to town.

A SIDE TRIP TO MOUNT ETNA

Looming menacingly over the coast of eastern Sicily, **Mount Etna** is the highest and largest active volcano in Europe—and we do mean active! The peak changes in size over the years, but is currently somewhere in the neighborhood of 10,800 feet. Etna has been active in modern times (in 1928 the little village of Mascali was burned under its lava), and eruptions in 1971 and 1992 have rekindled the fears of Sicilians.

Etna has figured in history and in Greek mythology. Empedocles, the 5th-century B.C. Greek philosopher, is said to have jumped into its crater as a sign that he was being delivered directly to Mount Olympus to take his seat among the gods. It was under Etna that Zeus crushed the multiheaded, viper-riddled dragon Typhoeus, thereby securing domination over Olympus. Hephaestus, the god of fire and blacksmiths, was believed to have made his headquarters in Etna, aided by the single-eyed Cyclops.

The Greeks warned that whenever Typhoeus tried to break out of his prison, lava erupted and earthquakes cracked the land. Granted that, the monster must have nearly escaped on March 11, 1669, the date of one of the most violent eruptions ever recorded—it destroyed Catania, about 17 miles away.

Always get the latest report from local tourist offices before contemplating a trip to Mount Etna.

For a good view of the ferocious, lava-spewing mountain, take one of the trains operated by **Ferrovia Circumetnea,** which circumnavigate the base of the mighty volcano. Board at the Stazione Borgo, via Caronda 350 (☎ **095/531402**), in Catania, off viale Leonardo da Vinci. A 5-hour circular tour from Catania costs 12,000 lire ($7.70).

If you'd prefer not to attempt this rather cumbersome do-it-yourself means of seeing Etna, you should consider a package-tour deal from Taormina. **Campagnia Siciliana Turismo,** corso Umberto 101 (☎ **0942/23301**), headquartered at Taormina, offers package deals. For a minimum of 15 people, for 35,000 lire ($22.40) they'll escort you all the way to the top of this heaving beast.

Appendix

English	Italian	Pronunciation
Thank you	**Grazie**	*graht*-tzee-yey
Please	**Per favore**	*pehr* fah-*vohr*-eh
Yes	**Sì**	see
No	**No**	noh
Good morning or Good day	**Buongiorno**	bwohn-*djor*-noh
Good evening	**Buona sera**	*Bwohn*-ah *say*-rah
Good night	**Buona notte**	*Bwohn*-ah *noht*-tay
How are you?	**Come sta?**	koh-may *stah*
Very well	**Molto bene**	*mohl*-toh *behn*-ney
Goodbye	**Arrivederci**	ahr-ree-vah-*dehr*-chee
Excuse me (to get attention)	**Scusi**	*skoo*-zee
Excuse me (to get past someone on the bus)	**Permesso**	pehr-*mehs*-soh
Where is . . . ?	**Dov'è . . . ?**	doh-*vey*
the station	**la stazione**	lah stat-tzee-*oh*-neh
a hotel	**un albergo**	oon ahl-*behr*-goh
a restaurant	**un ristorante**	oon reest-ohr-*ahnt*-eh
the bathroom	**il bagno**	eel *bahn*-nyoh
To the right	**A destra**	ah *dehy*-stra
To the left	**A sinistra**	ah see-*nees*-tra
straight ahead	**Avanti**	ahv-*vahn*-tee
	(or **sempre diritto**)	(*sehm*-pray dee-*reet*-toh)
How much is it?	**Quanto costa?**	*kwan*-toh *coh*-sta?
The check, please	**Il conto, per favore**	eel kon-toh *pehr* fah-*vohr*-eh
When?	**Quando?**	*kwan*-doh
Yesterday	**Ieri**	ee-*yehr*-ree
Today	**Oggi**	*oh*-jee
Tomorrow	**Domani**	doh-*mah*-nee
Breakfast	**Prima colazione**	*pree*-mah coh-laht-tzee-*ohn*-ay
Lunch	**Pranzo**	*prahn*-zoh
Dinner	**Cena**	*chay*-nah

English	Italian	Pronunciation
What time is it?	**Che ore sono?**	kay *or*-ay *soh*-noh
Monday	**Lunedì**	loo-nay-*dee*
Tuesday	**Martedì**	mart-ay-*dee*
Wednesday	**Mercoledì**	mehr-cohl-ay-*dee*
Thursday	**Giovedì**	joh-vay-*dee*
Friday	**Venerdì**	ven-nehr-*dee*
Saturday	**Sabato**	*sah*-bah-toh
Sunday	**Domenica**	doh-*mehn*-nee-kah

NUMBERS

1	**uno** (*oo*-noh)		30	**trenta** (*trayn*-tah)
2	**due** (*doo*-ay)		40	**quaranta** (kwah-*rahn*-tah)
3	**tre** (tray)			
4	**quattro** (*kwah*-troh)		50	**cinquanta** (cheen-*kwan*tah)
5	**cinque** (*cheen*-kway)			
6	**sei** (say)		60	**sessanta** (sehs-*sahn*-tah)
7	**sette** (*set*-tay)		70	**settanta** (seht-*tahn*-tah)
8	**otto** (*oh*-toh)		80	**ottanta** (oht-*tahn*-tah)
9	**nove** (*noh*-vay)		90	**novanta** (noh-*vahnt*-tah)
10	**dieci** (dee-*ay*-chee)		100	**cento** (*chen*-toh)
11	**undici** (*oon*-dee-chee)		1,000	**mille** (*mee*-lay)
20	**venti** (*vehn*-tee)		5,000	**cinque milla** (*cheen*-kway *mee*-lah)
21	**ventuno** (vehn-*toon*-oh)			
22	**venti due** (*vehn*-tee *doo*-ay)		10,000	**dieci milla** (dee-*ay*-chee *mee*-lah)

B Italian Menu Savvy

Abbacchio   Roast haunch or shoulder of lamb baked and served in a casserole and sometimes flavored with anchovies.

Agnolotti   A crescent-shaped pasta shell stuffed with a mixture of chopped meat, spices, vegetables, and cheese; when prepared in rectangular versions, the same combination of ingredients is identified as ravioli.

Amaretti   Crunchy, very sweet, almond-flavored macaroons.

Anguilla alla veneziana   Eel cooked in sauce made from tuna and lemon.

Antipasti   Succulent tidbits served at the beginning of a meal (before the pasta), whose ingredients might include slices of cured meats, seafood (especially shellfish), and cooked and seasoned vegetables.

Aragosta   Lobster.

Arrosto   Roasted meat.

Baccalà   Dried and salted codfish.

Bagna cauda   Hot and well-seasoned sauce, heavily flavored with anchovies, designed for dipping raw vegetables; literally translated as "hot bath."

Bistecca alla fiorentina   Florentine-style steaks, coated before grilling with olive oil, pepper, lemon juice, salt and parsley.

Bocconcini   Veal layered with ham and cheese, and fried.

Bollito misto   Assorted boiled meats served on a single platter.

Braciola   Pork chop.

Bresaola   Air-dried spiced beef.

Bruschetta   Toasted bread, heavily slathered with olive oil and garlic and often topped with tomatoes.
Bucatini   Hollow, coarsely textured spaghetti.
Busecca alla milanese   Tripe (beef intestines) flavored with herbs and vegetables.
Cacciucco ali livornese   Seafood stew.
Calzone   Pizza dough rolled with the chef's choice of sausage, tomatoes, cheese, etc., then baked into a kind of savory turnover.
Cannelloni   Tubular dough stuffed with meat, cheese, or vegetables, then baked in a creamy white sauce.
Cappellacci alla ferrarese   Pasta stuffed with pumpkin.
Cappelletti   Small ravioli ("little hats") stuffed with meat or cheese.
Carciofi   Artichokes.
Carpaccio   Thin slices of raw cured beef, sometimes in a piquant sauce.
Cassatta alla siciliana   A richly caloric dessert combining layers of sponge cake, sweetened ricotta cheese, and candied fruit, bound together with an icing of chocolate buttercream.
Cervello al burro nero   Brains in black-butter sauce.
Cima alla genovese   Baked filet of veal rolled into a tube-shaped package containing eggs, mushrooms, and sausage.
Coppa   Cured morsels of pork filet encased in sausage skins, served in slices.
Costoletta alla milanese   Veal cutlet dredged in bread crumbs, fried, and sometimes flavored with cheese.
Cozze   Mussels.
Fagioli   White beans.
Fave   Fava beans.
Fegato alla veneziana   Thinly sliced calves' liver fried with salt, pepper, and onions.
Foccacia   Ideally, concocted from potato-based dough left to rise slowly for several hours, then garnished with tomato sauce, garlic, basil, salt, and pepper drizzled with olive oil; similar to a high-pan, deep-dish pizza most popular in the deep south, especially Bari.
Fontina   Rich cow's-milk cheese.
Frittata   Italian omelet.
Fritto misto   A deep-fried medley of whatever small fish, shellfish, and squid are available in the marketplace that day.
Fusilli   Spiral-shaped pasta.
Gelato (produzione propria)   Ice cream (homemade).
Gorgonzola   One of the most famous blue-veined cheeses of Europe; strong, creamy, and aromatic.
Gnocchi   Dumplings usually made from potatoes (*gnocchi alla patate*) or from semolina (*gnocchi alla Romana*), often stuffed with combinations of cheese, spinach, vegetables, or whatever combinations strike the chef's fancy.
Granita   Flavored ice, usually with lemon or coffee.
Insalata di frutti di mare   Seafood salad (usually including shrimp and squid) garnished with pickles, lemon, olives, and spices.
Involtini   Thinly sliced beef, veal, or pork, rolled, stuffed, and fried.
Minestrone   A rich and savory vegetable soup usually sprinkled with grated Parmesan cheese and studded with noodles.
Mortadella   Mild pork sausage, fashioned into large cylinders and served sliced; the original lunchmeat baloney (because its most famous center of production is Bologna).

Mozzarella   A nonfermented cheese, made from the fresh milk of a buffalo (or, if unavailable, from a cow), boiled and then kneaded into a rounded ball, served fresh.

Mozzarella con pomodori (also **"caprese"**)   Fresh tomatoes with fresh mozzarella, basil, pepper, and olive oil.

Nervetti   A northern Italian antipasto concocted from chewy pieces of calves' foot or shin.

Osso buco   Beef or veal knuckle slowly braised until the cartilage is tender, and then served with a highly flavored sauce.

Pappardelle alle lepre   Pasta with rabbit sauce.

Pancetta   Herb-flavored pork belly, rolled into a cylinder and sliced—the Italian bacon.

Panettone   Sweet, yellow-colored bread baked in the form of a brioche.

Panna   Heavy cream.

Pansotti   Pasta stuffed with greens, herbs, and cheeses, usually served with a walnut sauce.

Parmigiano   Parmesan, a hard and salty yellow cheese usually grated over pastas and soups but also eaten alone; also known as *granna*.

Peperoni   Green, yellow, or red sweet peppers.

Pesci al cartoccio   Fish baked in a parchment envelope with onions, parsley, and herbs.

Pesto   A flavorful green sauce concocted from basil leaves, cheese, garlic, marjoram, and (if available) pine kernels.

Piccata al marsala   Thin escalope of veal braised in a pungent sauce flavored with marsala wine.

Piselli al prosciutto   Peas with strips of ham.

Pizza   Specific varieties include: *capricciosa* (its ingredients depend on the whim of the chef and can vary widely depending on his or her culinary vision and the ingredients at hand), *margherita* (incorporates tomato sauce, cheese, fresh basil, and memories of the first queen of Italy, Marguerite di Savoia, in whose honor it was first concocted by a Neapolitan chef), *napoletana* (includes ham, capers, tomatoes, oregano, cheese, and the distinctive taste of anchovies), *quatro stagione* (translated as "four seasons" because of the array of fresh vegetables in it and it also contains ham and bacon), and *siciliana* (contains black olives, capers, and cheese).

Pizzaiola   A process whereby something (usually a beefsteak) is covered in a tomato-and-oregano sauce.

Polenta   Thick porridge or mush made from cornmeal flour.

Polenta de uccelli   Assorted small birds roasted on a spit and served with polenta.

Polenta e coniglio   Rabbit stew served with polenta.

Polla alla cacciatore   Chicken with tomatoes and mushrooms cooked in wine.

Pollo all diavola   Highly spiced grilled chicken.

Ragu   Meat sauce.

Ricotta   A soft and bland cheese made from cow's or sheep's milk.

Risotto   Italian rice.

Risotto alla milanese   Rice with saffron and wine.

Salsa verde   "Green sauce," made from capers, anchovies, lemon juice and/or vinegar, and parsley.

Saltimbocca   Veal scallop layered with prosciutto and sage; its name literally translates as "jump in your mouth," a reference to its tart and savory flavor.

Salvia   Sage.

Scaloppina alla Valdostana   Escalope of veal stuffed with cheese and ham.

Scaloppine   Thin slices of veal coated in flour and sautéed in butter.

Semifreddo   A frozen dessert; usually ice cream with sponge cake.

Seppia   Cuttlefish (a kind of squid); its black ink is used for flavoring in certain sauces for pasta, and also in risotto dishes.

Sogliola   Sole.

Spaghetti   A long, round, thin pasta, variously served: *alla Bolognese* (with ground meat, mushrooms, peppers, etc.), *alla carbonara* (with bacon, black pepper, and eggs), *al pomodoro* (with tomato sauce), *al sugo/ragù* (with meat sauce), and *alle vongole* (with clam sauce).

Spiedini   Pieces of meat grilled on a skewer over an open flame.

Strangolaprete   Small nuggets of pasta, usually served with sauce; the name is literally translated as "priest-choker."

Stufato   Beef braised in white wine with vegetables.

Tagliatelle   Flat egg noodles.

Tiramisu   Richly caloric dessert containing layers of triple-crème cheeses and rum-soaked sponge cake.

Tonno   Tuna.

Tortelli   Pasta dumplings stuffed with ricotta and greens.

Tortellini   Rings of dough stuffed with minced and seasoned meat and served either in soups or as a full-fledged pasta covered with sauce.

Trenette   Thin noodles served with pesto sauce and potatoes.

Trippa alla fiorentina   Beef tripe (intestines).

Vermicelli   Very thin spaghetti.

Vitello tonnato   Cold sliced veal covered with tuna-fish sauce.

Zabaglione/zabaione   Egg yolks whipped into the consistency of a custard, flavored with marsala, and served warm as a dessert.

Zampone   Pig's trotter stuffed with spicy seasoned port, boiled and sliced.

Zuccotto   A liqueur-soaked sponge cake, molded into a dome and layered with chocolate, nuts, and whipped cream.

Zuppa inglese   Sponge cake soaked in custard sauce and rum.

Index

FROMMER'S COMPLETE TRAVEL GUIDES

(Comprehensive guides to destinations around the world, with selections in all price ranges—from deluxe to budget)

Acapulco/Ixtapa/Zihuatenjo
Alaska
Amsterdam
Arizona
Atlanta
Australia
Austria
Bahamas
Bangkok
Barcelona, Madrid & Seville
Belgium, Holland & Luxembourg
Berlin
Bermuda
Boston
Budapest & the Best of Hungary
California
Canada
Cancún, Cozumel & the Yucatán
Caribbean
Caribbean Cruises & Ports of Call
Caribbean Ports of Call
Carolinas & Georgia
Chicago
Colorado
Costa Rica
Denver, Boulder & Colorado Springs
Dublin
England

Florida
France
Germany
Greece
Hawaii
Hong Kong
Honolulu/Waikiki/Oahu
Ireland
Italy
Jamaica & Barbados
Japan
Las Vegas
London
Los Angeles
Maryland & Delaware
Maui
Mexico
Mexico City
Miami & the Keys
Montana & Wyoming
Montréal & Québec City
Munich & the Bavarian Alps
Nashville & Memphis
Nepal
New England
New Mexico
New Orleans
New York City
Northern New England
Nova Scotia, New Brunswick & Prince Edward Island

Paris
Philadelphia & the Amish Country
Portugal
Prague & the Best of the Czech Republic
Puerto Rico
Puerto Vallarta, Manzanillo & Guadalajara
Rome
San Antonio & Austin
San Diego
San Francisco
Santa Fe, Taos & Albuquerque
Scandinavia
Scotland
Seattle & Portland
South Pacific
Spain
Switzerland
Thailand
Tokyo
Toronto
U.S.A.
Utah
Vancouver & Victoria
Vienna
Virgin Islands
Virginia
Walt Disney World & Orlando
Washington, D.C.
Washington & Oregon

FROMMER'S FRUGAL TRAVELER'S GUIDES

(The grown-up guides to budget travel, offering dream vacations at down-to-earth prices)

Australia from $45 a Day
Berlin from $50 a Day
California from $60 a Day
Caribbean from $60 a Day
Costa Rica & Belize from $35 a Day
Eastern Europe from $30 a Day

England from $50 a Day
Europe from $50 a Day
Florida from $50 a Day
Greece from $45 a Day
Hawaii from $60 a Day
India from $40 a Day
Ireland from $45 a Day
Italy from $50 a Day

Israel from $45 a Day
London from $60 a Day
Mexico from $35 a Day
New York from $70 a Day
New Zealand from $45 a Day
Paris from $60 a Day
Washington, D.C. from $50 a Day

FROMMER'S PORTABLE GUIDES
(Pocket-size guides for travelers who want everything in a nutshell)

Charleston & Savannah   Las Vegas   Washington, D.C.   New Orleans   San Francisco

FROMMER'S FAMILY GUIDES
(The complete guides for successful family vacations)

California with Kids	New England with Kids	San Francisco with Kids
Los Angeles with Kids	New York City with Kids	Washington, D.C. with Kids

FROMMER'S AMERICA ON WHEELS
(Everything you need for a successful road trip, including full-color road maps and ratings for every hotel)

California & Nevada	Midwest & the Great	Northwest & the	Southwest
Florida	Lake States	Great Plains States	Texas & the South-
Mid-Atlantic	New York & the New	Southeast	Central States
	England States		

FROMMER'S WALKING TOURS
(Memorable neighborhood strolls through the world's great cities)

Berlin	Montréal & Québec City	Spain's Favorite Cities
Chicago	New York	Tokyo
England's Favorite Cities	Paris	Venice
London	San Francisco	Washington, D.C.

SPECIAL-INTEREST TITLES

Arthur Frommer's Branson!	Frommer's National Park Guide
Arthur Frommer's New World of Travel	Outside Magazine's Adventure Guide to New
The Civil War Trust's Official Guide to the	England
Civil War Discovery Trail	Outside Magazine's Adventure Guide to
Frommer's America's 100 Best-Loved State	Northern California
Parks	Places Rated Almanac
Frommer's Caribbean Hideaways	Retirement Places Rated
Frommer's Complete Hostel Vacation Guide to	USA Sports Traveler's and TV Viewer's
England, Scotland & Wales	Golf Tournament Guide
Frommer's Food Lover's Companion to France	USA Sports Minor League Baseball Book
Frommer's Food Lover's Companion to Italy	USA Today Golf Atlas
Frommer's Great European Driving Tours	Wonderful Weekends from NYC

FROMMER'S IRREVERENT GUIDES
(Wickedly honest guides for sophisticated travelers)

Amsterdam	Manhattan	Paris	U.S. Virgin Islands
Chicago	Miami	San Francisco	Walt Disney World
London	New Orleans	Santa Fe	Washington, D.C.

UNOFFICIAL GUIDES
(Get the unbiased truth from these candid, value-conscious guides)

Atlanta	Euro Disneyland	Mini-Mickey
Branson, Missouri	The Great Smoky & Blue	Skiing in the West
Chicago	Ridge Mountains	Walt Disney World
Cruises	Las Vegas	Walt Disney World Companion
Disneyland	Miami & the Keys	Washington, D.C.

BAEDEKER

(With four-color photographs and a free pull-out map)

Amsterdam	Florence	London	Scotland
Athens	Florida	Mexico	Singapore
Austria	Germany	New York	South Africa
Bali	Great Britain	Paris	Spain
Belgium	Greece	Portugal	Switzerland
Budapest	Greek Islands	Prague	Thailand
California	Hawaii	Provence	Tokyo
Canada	Hong Kong	Rome	Turkish Coast
Caribbean	Ireland	San Francisco	Tuscany
China	Israel	St. Petersburg	Venice
Copenhagen	Italy	Scandinavia	Vienna
Crete	Lisbon		

FROMMER'S BY NIGHT GUIDES

(The series for those who know that life begins after dark)

Amsterdam	London	Miami	Paris
Chicago	Los Angeles	New Orleans	San Francisco
Las Vegas	Manhattan		

FROMMER'S BEST BEACH VACATIONS

(The top places to sun, stroll, shop, stay, play, party, and swim, with ratings for each beach)

California	Hawaii	New England
Carolinas & Georgia	Mid-Atlantic (from New	
Florida	York to Washington, D.C.)	

FROMMER'S BED & BREAKFAST GUIDES

(Selective guides with four-color photos and full descriptions of the best inns in each region)

California	Great American Cities	New England	The Rockies
Caribbean	Hawaii	Pacific Northwest	Southwest

FROMMER'S DRIVING TOURS

(Four-color photos and detailed maps outlining spectacular scenic driving routes)

Australia	France	Italy	Spain
Austria	Germany	Scandinavia	Switzerland
Britain	Ireland	Scotland	U.S.A.
Florida			

FROMMER'S BORN TO SHOP

(The ultimate guides for travelers who love to shop)

France	Hong Kong	Mexico
Great Britain	London	New York

TRAVEL & LEISURE GUIDES

(Sophisticated pocket-size guides for discriminating travelers)

Amsterdam	Hong Kong	New York	San Francisco
Boston	London	Paris	Washington, D.C.

WHEREVER YOU TRAVEL, $\mathcal{H}$ELP IS NEVER FAR AWAY.

From planning your trip to providing travel assistance along the way, American Express® Travel Service Offices are always there to help.

Italy

Bigtours Travel Service (R)
Via Indipendenza 12
Bologna
51/224-923

American Express Company S.P.A.
Via Guicciardini 49/R
Florence
55/288-751

American Express Travel Service
Via Dante Alighieri 22R
Florence
55/509-81

Viatur SRL (R)
Piazza Fontane Marose 3
Genoa
10/561-241

American Express Travel Service
Via Brera 3
Milan
2/720-03-693

American Express Travel Service
Piazza Di Spagna 38
Rome
6/676-41

American Express Travel Service
1471 San Marco, San Moise
Venice
41/520-0844

Fabretto Viaggi E Turismo (R)
Corso Porta Nuova 11
Verona
45/800-9040

Travel

http://www.americanexpress.com/travel

American Express Travel Service Offices are found in central locations throughout Italy.